The Challenge of
DEMOCRACY
American Government in Global Politics

Thirteenth Edition

Kenneth Janda
Northwestern University

Jeffrey M. Berry
Tufts University

Jerry Goldman
Chicago-Kent College of Law

Deborah J. Schildkraut
Tufts University

CENGAGE Learning

Australia • Brazil • Mexico • Singapore • United Kingdom • United States

CENGAGE Learning®

The Challenge of Democracy: American Government in Global Politics,
Thirteenth Edition

**Kenneth Janda, Jeffrey M. Berry,
Jerry Goldman, Deborah J. Schildkraut**

Product Team Manager: Carolyn Merrill

Associate Product Manager: Scott Greenan

Content Developer: Betty Slack

Managing Developer: Joanne Dauksewicz

Associate Content Developer: Jessica Wang

Product Assistant: Abigail Hess

Media Developer: Laura Hildebrand

Marketing Manager: Valerie Hartman

Content Project Manager: Cathy Brooks

Art Director: Linda May

Manufacturing Planner: Fola Orekoya

IP Analyst: Alexandra Ricciardi

IP Project Manager: Brittani Morgan

Production Service and Compositor: Cenveo

Text and Cover Designer: Rokusek Design

Cover Images: Building: © IR Stone/
Shutterstock.com; Flag: ©
STILLFX/Shutterstock.com

For product information and technology assistance, contact us at
Cengage Learning Customer & Sales Support, 1-800-354-9706

For permission to use material from this text or product, submit all requests online at **www.cengage.com/permissions**.
Further permissions questions can be emailed to
permissionrequest@cengage.com.

Library of Congress Control Number: 2014954320

Package ISBN:
978-1-285-85297-3
Text-only student edition ISBN:
978-1-285-85846-3

Cengage Learning
20 Channel Center Street
Boston, MA 02210
USA

Cengage Learning is a leading provider of customized learning solutions with office locations around the globe, including Singapore, the United Kingdom, Australia, Mexico, Brazil, and Japan. Locate your local office at **www.cengage.com/global**.

Cengage Learning products are represented in Canada by Nelson Education, Ltd.

To learn more about Cengage Learning Solutions, visit **www.cengage.com**.

Purchase any of our products at your local college store or at our preferred online store **www.cengagebrain.com**.

Printed in the United States of America
Print Number: 02   Print Year: 2015

Brief Contents

Contents

PART V   Civil Liberties and Civil Rights

CHAPTER 15: Order and Civil Liberties 418

CHAPTER 16: Equality and Civil Rights 454

PART VI   Making Public Policy

CHAPTER 17: Economic Policy 490

Letter to Instructors

Dear American Politics Instructor:

Teaching an introductory American Politics course is both a challenging and a rewarding endeavor. Our goal in writing this book is to help you achieve the rewards and overcome the challenges that come with teaching a large introductory course.

The Challenge of Democracy is not a book centered on current events. Rather, we use the recent past to illustrate enduring features of American government. Our text centers on three themes. The first is the clash among the values of **freedom, order, and equality**. These value conflicts are prominent in contemporary American society, and they help explain political controversy and consensus in earlier eras. The second theme focuses on the tensions between **pluralist and majoritarian visions of democracy**. We use these models to illustrate the dynamics of the American political system, including rising partisanship in Congress, the role of interest groups in policymaking, the ways in which public opinion does (or does not) shape public policy, and the influence of money on a range of political processes. Our third theme is **globalization**. More than ever before, Americans are becoming citizens of the world. We cannot escape the deepening interrelationships with the rest of the world. Thus, *The Challenge of Democracy* examines some of the ramifications of a smaller world on the large landscape of American politics.

Our book includes several elements aimed at engaging your students with these enduring themes, including the vignettes at the start of each chapter; features that highlight tensions among freedom, order, and equality; features that situate American government in the context of global politics; critical thinking questions; and updated examples across the text. We do not believe it is our role to tell students our own answers to the broad questions we pose. Instead, we want our readers to learn firsthand that a democracy requires thoughtful and difficult choices. That is why we titled our book *The Challenge of Democracy*.

New to this Edition

The changes and new elements in this edition are all devised to help you make your course a rewarding experience for you and your students.

- We have added a new feature in each chapter entitled "Freedom, Order, or Equality?" to highlight the conflicts among these values through an intriguing case study.

- We have added a second new feature in each chapter called "_____ in Global Politics" to draw greater attention to the impact of globalization on American politics and to encourage reflection on some aspect of American politics in comparison to politics in other countries.

- We have increased the emphasis on chapter learning outcomes by (1) highlighting the list of learning outcomes at the beginning of the chapter, (2) repeating the relevant learning outcome associated with each major topic in the chapter, (3) organizing the chapter summary by learning outcome, and (4) structuring the end-of-chapter quiz by learning outcome.

- We have eliminated a separate chapter on global politics and instead incorporated discussion of the impact of globalization on American governance into all chapters.

- We discuss recent political developments, including the 2014 midterm elections, the Affordable Care Act, gun control, gay marriage, marijuana legalization, government surveillance, income inequality, immigration politics, education policy, net neutrality, campaign finance, and more, focusing our discussion around our three themes.

MindTap

Of great benefit to instructors, MindTap is here to simplify your workload, help you organize and immediately grade your students' assignments, and allow you to customize your course as you see fit. Through deep-seated integration with your learning management system, grades are easily exported and analytics are pulled with just the click of a button. MindTap provides you with a platform to add in current events videos and RSS feeds from national or local news sources. Looking to include more currency in the course? Add in our KnowNow American Government Blog link for weekly updated news coverage and pedagogy.

We are thrilled that you are using *The Challenge of Democracy* in your course. We are honored to play a role as you help your students develop the skills they need to be effective democratic citizens.

Sincerely,

Kenneth Janda, Jeffrey M. Berry, Jerry Goldman, and Deborah J. Schildkraut

Letter to Students

Dear Student:

The title of our book says it all: democracy is a challenge. *The Challenge of Democracy*, however, is designed to help you succeed in your study of American politics. Our goal is to provide perspectives and insights that will connect you to the important and provocative political questions of our time. How can states legalize marijuana if using the drug still violates federal law? Why is it constitutional for the federal government to require you to purchase health insurance? Does rising income inequality affect the quality of our democracy? Our aim is to help you explore contemporary questions like these in a deep and meaningful way.

Finding the right balance among **freedom, order, and equality** is one of the biggest challenges that democracies face, and it is the first theme of our book. In the interest of public order and safety, should we allow police to stop and question suspicious people on the street, or is that an infringement on personal freedom? In the interest of political equality, should we restrict spending on election campaigns, or is that an infringement on freedom of speech? Questions such as these constitute the daily struggles of modern democratic life.

When developing answers to these questions, should policymakers follow the will of the majority, or should they pay more attention to the individuals, groups, and organizations that have the most expertise and experience with the topic? In other words, should they follow **majoritarian or pluralist** principles? Most Americans support universal background checks for the sale of firearms, but certain organized groups in American society do not. Which one should prevail? The trade-off among these models of democracy is the second theme of the book. Both models are on display throughout the American political system. Our goal is to help you identify them and consider the benefits and drawbacks of each.

The place of **globalization** in American politics is our third and final theme. The aims of this theme are to help you think about how various aspect of globalization affect politics at home and to consider the similarities and differences between the American political system and politics in other countries.

Several features of the book are designed to help you succeed in your studies:

- **Chapter-opening vignettes:** Each chapter starts with a story selected to spark your interest and encourage your exploration of the book's themes as they relate to that chapter. For example, Chapter 10 ("Interest Groups") begins with the topic of mass shootings and considers the role that interest groups have played in promoting, and thwarting, new gun control regulations.

- **"Freedom, Order, or Equality?":** Each chapter has a feature that highlights the tensions among these values and connects those values to the specific content of that chapter. For example, the feature in Chapter 5 ("Public Opinion and Political Socialization") examines how self-identified tea party supporters weigh freedom against order on the issue of immigration.

- **"_____ in Global Politics":** Each chapter has a feature that puts political issues in their global context.

- **Learning Outcomes:** Each chapter begins with a set of clearly defined learning outcomes, which are restated throughout the chapter. They are summarized at the end of the chapter, and each chapter ends with a set of study questions tied to each outcome.

MindTap

For students, the benefits of using MindTap with this book are endless. With automatically graded practice quizzes and activities, automatic detailed revision plans on your essay assignments offered through Write Experience, an easily navigated learning path, and an interactive eBook, you will be able to test yourself in and outside of the classroom with ease. The accessibility of current events coupled with interactive media makes the content fun and engaging. On your computer, phone, or tablet, MindTap is there when you need it, giving you easy access to flashcards, quizzes, readings, and assignments.

We are thrilled that you will you be using *The Challenge of Democracy* in your course, and we are honored to play a role as you develop the skills you need to be a thoughtful, engaged, and effective democratic citizen.

Sincerely,

Kenneth Janda, Jeffrey M. Berry, Jerry Goldman, and Deborah J. Schildkraut

MindTap™ QUICK START GUIDE

1. To get started, navigate to: www.cengagebrain.com and select "Register a Product".

A new screen will appear prompting you to add a Course Key. A Course Key is a code given to you by your instructor - this is the first of two codes you will need to access MindTap. Every student in your course section should have the same Course Key.

2. Enter the Course Key and click "Register".

If you are accessing MindTap through your school's Learning Management System such as BlackBoard or Desire2Learn, you may be redirected to use your Course Key/Access Code there. Follow the prompts you are given and feel free to contact support if you need assistance.

3. Confirm your course information above, and proceed to the log in portion below.

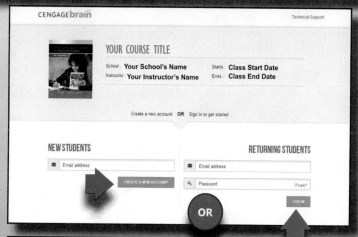

If you have a CengageBrain username and password, enter it under "Returning Students" and click "Login". If this is your first time, register under "New Students" and click "Create a New Account".

4. Now that you are logged in, you can access the course for free by selecting "Start Free Trial" for 20 days, or enter in your Access Code.

Your Access Code is unique to you and acts as payment for MindTap. You may have received it with your book or purchased separately in the bookstore or at CengageBrain.com. Enter it and click "Register".

NEED HELP?

Resources for Students and Instructors

Students...

Access your *The Challenge of Democracy* resources by visiting **www.cengagebrain.com/shop/isbn/9781285852973**

If you purchased MindTap or CourseReader access with your book, enter your access code and click "**Register.**" You can also purchase the book's resources here separately through the "**Study Tools**" tab or access the free companion website through the "**Free Materials**" tab.

Instructors...

Access your *The Challenge of Democracy* resources via **www.cengage.com/login.**

Log in using your Cengage Learning single sign-on user name and password, or create a new instructor account by clicking on "**New Faculty User**" and following the instructions.

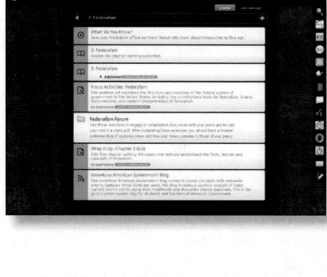

The Challenge of Democracy, 13e – Text Only Edition

ISBN: 9781285858463
This copy of the book does not come bundled with MindTap.

MindTap for Janda

Printed Access Card ISBN: 9781285858449
Instant Access Code ISBN: 9781305074736
MindTap for Janda is a highly personalized, fully online learning experience built upon Cengage Learning content and correlating to a core set of learning outcomes. MindTap guides students through the course curriculum via an innovative Learning Path Navigator where they will complete reading assignments, challenge themselves with focus activities, and engage with interactive quizzes. Through a variety of gradable activities, MindTap provides students with opportunities to check themselves for where they need extra help, as well as allowing faculty to measure and assess student

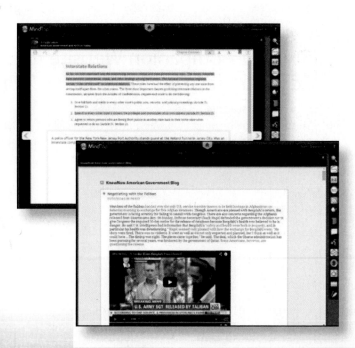

progress. Integration with programs like YouTube, Evernote, and Google Drive allows instructors to add and remove content of their choosing with ease, keeping their course current while tracking local and global events through RSS feeds. The product can be used fully online with its interactive eBook for *The Challenge of Democracy*, 13e, or in conjunction with the printed text.

Instructor Companion Website for Janda/Berry/Goldman/Schildkraut's *The Challenge of Democracy*, 13e

ISBN: 9781285865614

This Instructor Companion Website is an all-in-one multimedia online resource for class preparation, presentation, and testing. Accessible through Cengage.com/login with your faculty account, you will find available for download: book-specific Microsoft® PowerPoint® presentations; a Test Bank compatible with multiple learning management systems; an Instructor's Manual; Microsoft® PowerPoint® Image Slides; and a JPEG Image Library.

The Test Bank, offered in Blackboard, Moodle, Desire2Learn, Canvas, and Angel formats, contains learning objective-specific multiple-choice and essay questions for each chapter. Import the test bank into your LMS to edit and manage questions and to create tests.

The Instructor's Manual contains chapter-specific learning objectives, an outline, key terms with definitions, and a chapter summary. Additionally, the Instructor's Manual features a critical thinking question, a lecture launching suggestion, and an in-class activity for each learning objective.

The Microsoft® PowerPoint® presentations are ready-to-use, visual outlines of each chapter. These presentations are easily customized for your lectures and offered along with chapter-specific Microsoft® PowerPoint® Image Slides and JPEG Image Libraries. Access the Instructor Companion Website at www.cengage.com/login.

Cognero for Janda/Berry/Goldman/Schildkraut's *The Challenge of Democracy*, 13e

ISBN: 9781285874012

Cengage Learning Testing Powered by Cognero is a flexible, online system that allows you to author, edit, and manage test bank content from multiple Cengage Learning solutions, create multiple test versions in an instant, and deliver tests from your LMS, your classroom, or wherever you want. The test bank for *The Challenge of Democracy*, 13e contains learning objective-specific multiple-choice and essay questions for each chapter.

Student Companion Website for Janda/Berry/Goldman/Schildkraut's *The Challenge of Democracy*, 13e

ISBN: 9781285865584

This free student companion website for *The Challenge of Democracy*, 13e is accessible through cengagebrain.com and allows students access to chapter-specific interactive learning tools including flashcards, glossaries, and more.

CourseReader 0-30: American Government

Printed Access Card ISBN: 9781111479954
Instant Access Code ISBN: 9781111479978

CourseReader: American Government allows you to create your reader, your way, in just minutes. This affordable, fully customizable online reader provides access to thousands of permissions-cleared readings, articles, primary sources, and audio and video selections from the regularly updated Gale research library database. This easy-to-use solution allows you to search for and select just the material you want for your courses. Each selection opens with a descriptive introduction to provide context and concludes with critical thinking and multiple-choice questions to reinforce key points. CourseReader is loaded with convenient tools like highlighting, printing, note-taking, and downloadable PDFs and MP3 audio files for each reading. CourseReader is the perfect complement to any political science course. It can be bundled with your current textbook, sold alone, or integrated into your learning management system. CourseReader 0-30 allows access to up to thirty selections in the reader. Please contact your Cengage sales representative for details.

Election 2014 Supplement

ISBN: 9781305500181

Written by John Clark and Brian Schaffner, this booklet addresses the 2014 congressional and gubernatorial elections, with real-time analysis and references.

IDEAlog

IDEAlog, two-time winner of instructional software awards from the American Political Science Association, asks students to rate themselves on the two-dimensional trade-off of freedom versus order and freedom versus equality. It then presents them with twenty recent poll questions, and their responses are classified according to libertarian, conservative, liberal, or communitarian ideological tendencies. IDEAlog is directly accessible to anyone at http://IDEAlog.org, but instructors who choose to register their classes receive a special login link for each class. Instructors then can obtain summary statistics about their students' scores on the ideology quiz.

USPolitics.org

USPolitics.org, Kenneth Janda's personal website for *The Challenge of Democracy*, offers a variety of teaching aids to instructors who adopt any version of the book. The student side is open to all users, but the instructor side is limited to teachers who register online at uspolitics.org as textbook adopters.

Acknowledgments

All authors are indebted to others for inspiration and assistance in various forms; textbook authors are notoriously so. We again want to single out Professor Paul Manna of the College of William and Mary, who assisted us in revising Chapters 4 and 15 for this edition. Timely information technology suggestions and assistance came from Jeff Parsons of The Oyez Project, Professor James Ferolo of Bradley University, and Dr. Francesco Stagno d'Alcontres of Centro Linguistico d'Ateneo Messinese. We also wish to express our gratitude to Professor Julieta Suárez Cao of the Instituto de Ciencia Politica of Pontificia Universidad Catolica de Chile, Shira Rascoe of Tufts University, Professor Jennifer Cyr in the School of Government and Public Policy at the University of Arizona, Andrew Gruen of Cambridge University, and Tom Gaylord, Reference Librarian, and Matt Gruhn, Assistant Director, The Oyez Project, at IIT Chicago-Kent College of Law for their helpful research assistance. We extend thanks as well to Joseph B. Maher, Esq., Deputy General Counsel, DHS; Brad Kieserman, Esq., Chief Counsel, FEMA; and Professor Timothy R. Johnson, University of Minnesota. We would also like to thank Don D. Mirjanian of the College of Southern Nevada for his work on the Instructor's Manual, and Patrick Moore of Richland College for his work on the Test Bank.

We also want to thank the many people at Cengage Learning who helped make this edition a reality. There's not enough room to list all of the individuals who worked on previous editions, so we say a collective "thank you" for your work. Political Science Manager Carolyn Merrill has long been a champion of our text. We've been lucky to have her steady leadership through transformations in the publishing industry. Associate Product Manager Scott Greenan could not have been more enthusiastic and encouraging. We are particularly grateful for his thoughtful attention to our suggestions for product development. Betty Slack, our developmental editor, remained a delight to work with. Our direct production contacts were efficient and helpful throughout the process. Thank you to Jean Findley, Cathy Brooks, and Corey Smith. Finally, we thank the sales representatives who do a terrific job bringing each new edition of *The Challenge of Democracy* to the attention of those who might use it.

Dedication

We dedicate this edition to the generations who came before us, who left their ancestral homes so that we might one day be citizens and scholars of the United States:

To the Jandas from Bohemia and the Mozoláks from Slovakia, K. J.
To the Burnetts from Poland (via England) and the Golds who emigrated from Ukraine, J. B.
To Goldman forbears from the Pale of Settlement, in what is now Ukraine, J. G.
To the Schildkrauts, Hollands, Finks, and Weinbergs, who came to New York from Eastern Europe, D. S.

Reviewers

We would also like to thank the instructors who have contributed their valuable feedback through reviews of this text:

Leslie Baker, *Mississippi State University*

Elsa Dias, *Pikes Peak Community College*

Don D. Mirjanian, *College of Southern Nevada*

Patrick Moore, *Richland College*

Richard J. Powell, *University of Maine*

Alton Slane, *Muhlenberg College*

We would also like to thank the following instructors who reviewed prior editions:

Ruth Ann Alsobrook, *Paris Junior College*

James Anderson, *Texas A&M University*

Elizabeth Bergman, *California State Polytechnic University, Pomona*

Thomas Bowen, *Gloucester County College*

James Chalmers, *Wayne State University*

Gary Copeland, *University of Oklahoma*

Van Davis, *National Park Community College*

Christine L. Day, *University of New Orleans*

Monte Freidig, *Santa Rosa Junior College*

Marilyn Gaar, *Johnson County Community College*

Dorith Grant-Wisdom, *Howard University*

Richard Heil, *Fort Hays State University*

Kema Irogbe, *Claflin College*

Richard Kiefer, *Waubonsee Community College*

Melinda Kovacs, *Sam Houston State University*

Jack Lampe, *Southwest Texas Junior College*

Thomas R. Marshall, *University of Texas at Arlington*

Melissa Michelson, *California State University, East Bay*

Farzeen Nasri, *Ventura College*

Laura Katz Olson, *Lehigh University*

Sara Parker, *Chabot College*

James Perkins, *San Antonio College*

Barbara Salmore, *Drew University*

Todd M. Schaefer, *Central Washington University*

Denise Scheberle, *University of Wisconsin–Green Bay*

James Sheffield, *University of Oklahoma*

Christine Sixta, *Francis Marion University*

Beatrice Talpos, *Wayne County Community College District*

Katrina Taylor, *Northern Arizona University*

Ronnie Tucker, *Shippensburg University*

Sondra Venable, *University of New Orleans*

Shirley Ann Warshaw, *Gettysburg College*

Graham Wilson, *Boston University*

Jerry L. Yeric, *University of North Texas*

About the Authors

Kenneth Janda is the Payson S. Wild Professor Emeritus of Political Science at Northwestern University. Dr. Janda has published extensively in comparative party politics, research methodology, and early use of computer technology in political science, for which he received awards from EDUCOM and support from Apple Computer. His APSA awards include the Samuel Eldersveld Lifetime Achievement Award (2000) and the Frank J. Goodnow Award for distinguished service to the profession and the association (2009). Dr. Janda and fellow author Jerry Goldman shared APSA technology awards in 1992 for IDEAlog, the computer program, and in 2005 for IDEAlog, the website.

Jeffrey M. Berry is the John Richard Skuse Professor of Political Science at Tufts University. He was an undergraduate at the University of California, Berkeley, and received his doctorate from Johns Hopkins University. Dr. Berry is a recipient of the APSA's Samuel Eldersveld Lifetime Achievement Award (2009) and numerous "best book" awards—from the APSA for *The Rebirth of Urban Democracy* (1994), from the Policy Studies Organization for *The New Liberalism* (1999), from the APSA for *A Voice for Nonprofits* (2004), and from the APSA for *Lobbying and Political Change* (2009). His most recent book is *The Outrage Industry: Political Opinion Media and the New Incivility* (with Sarah Sobieraj).

Jerry Goldman is Professor Emeritus of Political Science at Northwestern University and currently Research Professor of Law at IIT Chicago-Kent College of Law where he directs the Oyez Project. Dr. Goldman is the 2010 recipient of the first APSA/CQ Press Award for Teaching Innovation in Political Science. He has received many other awards, including the American Bar Association's Silver Gavel for increasing the public's understanding of the law, the EDUCOM Medal, and the Roman & Littlefield Prize for Teaching Innovation. In 2012, Dr. Goldman made the Fastcase 50: "the fifty most interesting, provocative, and courageous leaders in the world of law, scholarship, and legal technology." Through the Oyez Project, which uses images, audio, and video to bring the Supreme Court alive, he has brought the U.S. Supreme Court closer to everyone.

Deborah J. Schildkraut is Professor of Political Science at Tufts University. She is the author of *Americanism in the Twenty-First Century: Public Opinion in the Age of Immigration* (2011), *Press "One" for English: Language Policy, Public Opinion, and American Identity* (2005), and several other research articles. Her research focuses on the implications of the changing ethnic composition of the United States on public opinion in a variety of domains. Professor Schildkraut has received awards from the American Political Science Association for the best book published in the field of political psychology (2012) and for the best paper presented in the field of elections, public opinion, and voting behavior (2009). She has served on the Board of Overseers for the American National Election Study and as a reviewer for the National Science Foundation.

Career Opportunities: Political Science

Introduction

It is no secret that college graduates are facing one of the toughest job markets in the past fifty years. Despite this challenge, those with a college degree have done much better than those without since the 2008 recession. One of the most important decisions a student has to make is the choice of a major; many consider future job possibilities when making that call. A political science degree is incredibly useful for a successful career in many different fields, from lawyer to policy advocate, pollster to humanitarian worker. Employer surveys reveal that the skills that most employers value in successful employees – critical thinking, analytical reasoning, and clarity of verbal and written communication – are precisely the tools that political science courses should be helping you develop. This brief guide is intended to help spark ideas for what kinds of careers you might pursue with a political science degree and the types of activities you can engage in now to help you secure one of those positions after graduation.

Careers in Political Science

LAW AND CRIMINAL JUSTICE

Do you find that your favorite parts of your political science classes are those that deal with the Constitution, the legal system and the courts? Then a career in law and criminal justice might be right for you. Traditional jobs in the field range from lawyer or judge to police or parole officer. Since 9/11, there has also been tremendous growth in the area of homeland security, which includes jobs in mission support, immigration, travel security, as well as prevention and response.

PUBLIC ADMINISTRATION

The many offices of the federal government combined represent one of the largest employers in the United States. Flip to the bureaucracy chapter of this textbook and consider that each federal department, agency, and bureau you see looks to political science majors for future employees. A partial list of such agencies would include the Department of Education, the Department of Health and Human Services, and the Federal Trade Commission. There are also thousands of staffers who work for members of Congress or the Congressional Budget Office, many of whom were political science majors in college. This does not even begin to account for the multitude of similar jobs in state and local governments that you might consider as well.

CAMPAIGNS, ELECTIONS, AND POLLING

Are campaigns and elections the most exciting part of political science for you? Then you might consider a career in the growing industry based around political campaigns. From volunteering and interning to consulting, marketing and fundraising, there are many opportunities for those who enjoy the competitive and high-stakes electoral arena. For those looking for careers that combine political knowledge with statistical skills, there are careers in public opinion polling. Pollsters work for independent national organizations such as Gallup and YouGov, or as part of news operations and campaigns. For those who are interested in survey methodology there are also a wide variety of non-political career opportunities in marketing and survey design.

INTEREST GROUPS, INTERNATIONAL AND NONGOVERNMENTAL ORGANIZATIONS

Is there a cause that you are especially passionate about? If so, there is a good chance that there are interest groups out there that are working hard to see some progress made on similar issues. Many of the positions that one might find in for-profit companies also exist in their non-profit interest group and nongovernmental organization counterparts, including lobbying and high-level strategizing. Do not forget that there are also quite a few major international organizations - such as the United Nations, the World Health Organization, and the International Monetary Fund, where a degree in political science could be put to good use. While competition for those jobs tends to be fierce, your interest and knowledge about politics and policy will give you an advantage.

FOREIGN SERVICE

Does a career in diplomacy and foreign affairs, complete with the opportunity to live and work abroad, sound exciting for you? Tens of thousands of people work for the State Department, both in Washington D.C. and in consulates throughout the world. They represent the diplomatic interests of the United States abroad. Entrance into the Foreign Service follows a very specific process, starting with the Foreign Service Officers Test – an exam given three times a year that includes sections on American government, history, economics, and world affairs. Being a political science major is a significant help in taking the FSOT.

GRADUATE SCHOOL

While not a career, graduate school may be the appropriate next step for you after completing your undergraduate degree. Following the academic route, being awarded a Ph.D. or Master's degree in political science could open additional doors to a career in academia, as well as many of the professions mentioned earlier. If a career as a researcher in political science interests you, you should speak with your advisors about continuing your education.

Preparing While Still on Campus

INTERNSHIPS

One of the most useful steps you can take while still on campus is to visit your college's career center in regards to an internship in your field of interest. Not only does it give you a chance to experience life in the political science realm, it can lead to job opportunities later down the road and add experience to your resume.

SKILLS

In addition to your political science classes, there are a few skills any number of which will prove useful as a complement to your degree:

Writing: Like anything else, writing improves with practice. Writing is one of those skills that is applicable regardless of where your career might take you. Virtually every occupation relies on an ability to write cleanly, concisely, and persuasively.

Public Speaking: An oft-quoted 1977 survey showed that public speaking was the most commonly cited fear among respondents. And yet oral communication is a vital tool in the modern economy. You can practice this skill in a formal class setting or through extracurricular activities that get you in front of a group.

Quantitative Analysis: As the internet aids in the collection of massive amounts of information, the nation is facing a drastic shortage of people with basic statistical skills to interpret and use this data. A political science degree can go hand-in-hand with courses in introductory statistics.

Foreign Language: One skill that often helps a student or future employee stand out in a crowded job market is the ability to communicate in a language other than English. Solidify or set the foundation for your verbal and written foreign language communication skills while in school.

STUDENT LEADERSHIP

One attribute that many employers look for is "leadership potential" which can be quite tricky to indicate on a resume or cover letter. What can help is a demonstrated record of involvement in clubs and organizations, preferably in a leadership role. While many people think immediately of student government, most student clubs allow you the opportunity to demonstrate your leadership skills.

Conclusion

Hopefully reading this has sparked some ideas on potential future careers. As a next step, visit your college's career placement office, which is a great place to further explore what you have read here. You might also visit your college's alumni office to connect with graduates who are working in your field of interest. Political science opens the door to a lot of exciting careers, have fun exploring the possibilities!

The Challenge of
DEMOCRACY
American Government in Global Politics

Thirteenth Edition

1 Freedom, Order, or Equality?

Learning Outcomes

LO1 Define globalization and explain how globalization affects American politics and government.

LO2 Identify the purposes that government serves and trace their historical roots.

LO3 Describe how political scientists use concepts to structure events and promote understanding.

LO4 Define freedom, order, and equality and discuss the various interpretations of each value.

LO5 Analyze the inherent conflicts between freedom versus order and freedom versus equality.

LO6 Distinguish among these terms: totalitarianism, socialism, capitalism, libertarianism, and anarchism.

LO7 Explain how liberals, conservatives, libertarians, and communitarians view the role of government.

 WATCH & LEARN MindTap for American Government

Watch a brief "What Do You Know?" video about Freedom, Order, and Equality.

SAUL LOEB/AFP/Getty Images

Would you describe your family as poor, wealthy, or average in household income? What has government done, if anything, to help such families?

Let's consider the poor first. In 1964, a government economist calculated that a non-farm family with two children needed an income of $2,621 to provide food and non-food essentials.[1] About 15 percent of families fell below that income, called the "poverty level."[2] Democratic President Lyndon Johnson declared a "war on poverty," and Congress enacted various programs—Head Start educational services for children, Medicare health benefits for seniors, insurance and food stamps for the unemployed—to help the young, old, and poor. Nevertheless, these programs did not reduce the percentage of families in poverty over time. In 2012, about 15 percent still had income below the revised poverty level, boosted by inflation to $23,550.[3] Critics charged that Johnson's programs had failed. Defenders replied that they were not aimed at increasing poor people's income but at alleviating poverty's effects by providing non-cash benefits in the form of education, health care, food, and shelter.

Turning to the wealthy, how did government help them? Here, government policies enacted under Re-publican presidents *did* aim at increasing incomes. In the 1980s, Ronald Reagan engineered a reduction of the top income tax rate from 70 percent to 50 percent. Later that decade, George H. W. Bush lowered the top rate to 28 percent. Raised to 40 percent in the 1990s by Democratic President Bill Clinton, the rate was again reduced to 35 percent in the 2000s by George W. Bush. Drops in the top income tax rate, along with other tax policies that favored the wealthy, had real effects. In 1967, the 5 percent of families with incomes over $114,000 in 2012 dollars captured 15.5 percent of all income, versus 5.1 percent for the bottom 20 percent, who made $18,000 or less.[4] By 2012, the income distribution was even more unequal: the top 5 percent made over $191,000 and gobbled up 21.3 percent of the income, compared with only 3.8 percent for the bottom fifth, who made $20,500 or less. Over the last half-century of government policies, the wealthy prospered more than the poor.

What has the government done for families in the middle of the income distribution? Virtually nothing. In 1967, the median family income was equivalent to $42,934 in 2012 dollars.[5] Although the median income did rise to $51,017 in 2012, the inflation adjusted median income had been $56,681 in 1999. Therefore, middle-income families actually lost income between 1999 and 2012. Data over the last half-century are fairly clear: only wealthy families substantially increased their income. In his 2014 State of the Union speech, President Obama said, "Today, after four years of economic growth, corporate profits and stock prices have rarely been higher, and those at the top have never done better. But average wages have barely budged. Inequality has deepened."

Is income inequality a proper issue for government to address, or should government not be concerned with the gap between the rich and the poor?

LISTEN & LEARN

MindTap for American Government

Access Read Speaker to listen to Chapter 1.

Our textbook inquires into what the U.S. government can do constitutionally, politically, and practically to serve its citizens. Should government even try to reduce economic inequalities? What if that required wealthy citizens to pay more taxes? Wouldn't that infringe on their freedom to spend their money on themselves? What if government tried to reduce social discrimination? Wouldn't that impinge on people's freedom to keep company with their own kind, upsetting the social order? This trade-off among the values of freedom, order, and equality lies at the heart of our discussion. We examine the relationship between individual freedom and social equality as reflected in government policies, which often confront underlying dilemmas such as these:

Which is better: to let all citizens keep the same share of their income or to tax wealthier people at a higher rate to fund programs for poorer people?

Which is better: to live under a government that fiercely protects individual freedom or under one that infringes on freedom while fiercely guarding against threats to physical security and the social order?

These questions reflect dilemmas tied to opposing political philosophies that place different values on freedom, order, and equality.

This book explains American government and politics in the light of these dilemmas. It does more than explain the workings of our government; it encourages you to think about what government should—and should not—do. And it judges the American government against democratic ideals, encouraging you to think about how government should make its decisions. As the title of this book implies, *The Challenge of Democracy* argues that good government often poses difficult choices.

College students often say that American government and politics are hard to understand. In fact, many other people voice the same complaint. About two-thirds of people interviewed in 2012 agreed with the statement "Politics and government seem so complicated that a person like me can't understand what's going on."[6] We hope to improve your understanding of "what's going on" by analyzing the norms, or values, that people use to judge political events. Our purpose is not to preach what people ought to favor in making policy decisions; it is to teach what values are at stake.

Teaching without preaching is not easy; no one can completely exclude personal values from political analysis. But our approach minimizes the problem by concentrating on the dilemmas that confront governments when they are forced to choose between important policies that threaten equally cherished values, such as freedom of speech and personal security.

Politics is sometimes defined as "the authoritative allocation of values for a society." Every government policy reflects a choice between conflicting values. All government policies reinforce certain values (norms) at the expense of others. We want you to interpret policy issues (for example, should assisted suicide go unpunished?) with an understanding of the fundamental values in question (freedom of action versus order and protection of life) and the broader political context (liberal or conservative politics).

By looking beyond the specifics to the underlying normative principles, you should be able to make more sense out of politics. Our framework for analysis does not encompass all the complexities of American government, but it should help your knowledge grow by improving your comprehension of political information. We begin by considering the basic purposes of government. In short, why do we need it? Our main interest in this text is the purpose, value, and function of government as practiced in the United States. However, we live in an era of **globalization**—a term for the increasing interdependence of citizens and nations across the world.[7] So we must consider how politics at home and abroad interrelate, which is increasingly important to understanding our government.[8]

globalization
The increasing interdependence of citizens and nations across the world.

The Globalization of American Government

LO1 ★ Define globalization and explain how globalization affects American politics and government.

Most people do not like being told what to do. Fewer still like being coerced into acting a certain way. Yet billions of people in countries across the world willingly submit to the coercive power of government. They accept laws that state on which side of the road to drive, how many wives (or husbands) they can have, what constitutes a contract, how to dispose of human waste—and how much they must pay to support the government that makes these coercive laws. In the first half of the twentieth century, people thought of government mainly in territorial terms. Indeed, a standard definition of **government** is the legitimate use of force—including firearms, imprisonment, and execution—within specified geographical boundaries to control human behavior. International relations and diplomacy have been based on the principle of national sovereignty, defined as "a political entity's externally recognized right to exercise final authority over its affairs."[9] Simply put, **national sovereignty** means that each national government has the right to govern its people as it wishes, without interference from other nations.

government
The legitimate use of force to control human behavior; also, the organization or agency authorized to exercise that force.

national sovereignty
A political entity's externally recognized right to exercise final authority over its affairs.

Some scholars argued strongly early in the twentieth century that a body of international law controlled the actions of supposedly sovereign nations, but their argument was essentially theoretical. In the practice of international relations, there was no sovereign power over nations. Each enjoyed complete independence to govern its territory without interference from other nations. Although the League of Nations and later the United Nations were supposed to introduce supranational order into the world, even these international organizations explicitly respected national sovereignty as the guiding principle of international relations. The U.N. Charter, Article 2.1, states, "The Organization is based on the principle of the sovereign equality of all its Members."

National sovereignty, however, is threatened under globalization. For example, international treaties ban use of chemical weapons. Concerned that Syrian President Bashar al-Assad might use chemical weapons against rebels, the United Nations forced him to surrender his stockpile to a joint mission of the United Nations and the Organization for the Prohibition of Chemical Weapons. The chemicals were loaded on ships and removed from Syria in 2014, while the civil war continued.

Global forces also generate pressures for international law. Our government, you might be surprised to learn, is worried about this trend of holding nations

Income Equality in Global Politics

Income Ratios

Country	Ratio
Denmark	2.8
Czech Republic	2.9
Norway	3
Slovenia	3
Slovak Republic	3.1
Hungary	3.1
Finland	3.2
Sweden	3.2
Austria	3.2
Iceland	3.2
Belgium	3.3
Netherlands	3.3
Luxemberg	3.4
France	3.4
Germany	3.5
Switzerland	3.7
Ireland	3.7
Poland	4
Greece	4
New Zealand	4.2
Canada	4.2
Estonia	4.3
Italy	4.3
Australia	4.5
Spain	4.6
United Kingdom	4.6
Korea	4.8
Portugal	4.9
Japan	5
UNITED STATES	5.9
Turkey	6.2
Israel	6.2
Chile	8.5
Mexico	9.7

Source: OECD Factbook 2013: Economic, Environmental and Social Statistics, at http://www.oecd-ilibrary.org/sites/factbook-2013-en/03/02/01/index.html?itemId=/content/chapter/factbook-2013-25-en.

Americans like to think of the United States as having an egalitarian society. In many respects it is egalitarian, but not concerning the distribution of income. Compared with thirty-three other democracies, the United States ranks near the bottom in the ratio of income received by the top 10 percent of the population versus the other 90 percent.

The top 10 percent alone takes in 5.9 times as much as all the rest of society. Only four other countries had a more unequal income distribution.

Critical Thinking No single explanation is likely to account for the unequal distribution of income in the United States. What explanations can you come up with?

accountable to international law. In fact, in 2002, the United States "annulled" its signature to the 1998 treaty (no country had ever unsigned a treaty) to create an International Criminal Court that would define and try crimes against humanity.[10] Why would the United States oppose such an international court? One reason is its concern that U.S. soldiers stationed abroad might be arrested and tried in that court. Another reason is the death penalty, practiced in the United States but abolished by more than half the countries in the world and all countries in the European Union. Indeed, in 1996, the International Commission of Jurists condemned the U.S. death penalty as "arbitrarily and racially discriminatory," and there is a concerted campaign across Europe to force the sovereign United States to terminate capital punishment.[11]

The United States is the world's most powerful nation, but as proved by the events of September 11, 2001, it is not invulnerable to foreign attack. Moreover, it is vulnerable to erosion of its sovereignty. As the world's superpower, should the United States be above international law if its sovereignty is compromised?

Although this text is about American national government, it recognizes the growing impact of international politics and world opinion on U.S. politics. The Cold War era of conflict with the Soviet Union, of course, had a profound effect on domestic politics because the nation spent heavily on the military and restricted trading with communist countries. Now we are closely tied through trade to former enemies (we import more goods from China—still communist—than from France and Britain combined), and we are thoroughly embedded in a worldwide economic, social, and political network. (See "Income Equality in Global Politics.") More than ever before, we must discuss American politics while casting an eye abroad to see how foreign affairs affect our government and how American politics affects government in other nations.

★ The Purposes of Government

LO2 ★ Identify the purposes that government serves and trace their historical roots.

Governments at any level require citizens to surrender some freedom as part of being governed. Although some governments minimize their infringements on personal freedom, no government has as a goal the maximization of personal freedom. Governments exist to control; to *govern* means "to control." Why do people surrender their freedom to this control? To obtain the benefits of government. Throughout history, government has served two major purposes: maintaining order (preserving life and protecting property) and providing public goods. More recently, some governments have pursued a third purpose, promoting equality, which is more controversial.

Maintaining Order

Maintaining order is the oldest objective of government. **Order** in this context is rich with meaning. Let's start with "law and order." Maintaining order in this sense means establishing the rule of law to preserve life and protect property. To the seventeenth-century English philosopher Thomas Hobbes (1588–1679), preserving life was the most important function of government. In his classic philosophical treatise, *Leviathan* (1651), Hobbes described life without government as life in a "state of nature."

Without rules, people would live as predators do, stealing and killing for their personal benefit. In Hobbes's classic phrase, life in a state of nature would be "solitary,

order
Established ways of social behavior. Maintaining order is the oldest purpose of government.

CONNECT WITH YOUR CLASSMATES
MindTap for American Government

Access the The Democratic Republic Forum: Discussion Board—Rule of Law and the Constitution.

Leviathan, Hobbes's All-Powerful Sovereign

This engraving is from the 1651 edition of *Leviathan* by Thomas Hobbes. It shows Hobbes's sovereign brandishing a sword in one hand and the scepter of justice in the other. He watches over an orderly town, made peaceful by his absolute authority. But note that the sovereign's body is composed of tiny images of his subjects. He exists only through them. Hobbes explains that such government power can be created only if people "confer all their power and strength upon one man, or upon one assembly of men, that may reduce all their wills, by plurality of voices, unto one will."

Mary Evans Picture Library/Alamy

poor, nasty, brutish, and short." He believed that a single ruler, or sovereign, must possess unquestioned authority to guarantee the safety of the weak and protect them from the attacks of the strong. Hobbes named his all-powerful government "Leviathan," after a biblical sea monster. He believed that complete obedience to Leviathan's strict laws was a small price to pay for the security of living in a civil society.

Most of us can only imagine what a state of nature would be like. But in some parts of the world, whole nations have experienced lawlessness. That has been the situation in Somalia since 1991, when the government was toppled and warlords feuded over territory. Until 2011, the government controlled only a portion of the capital, Mogadishu. Somali pirates seized ships off its shore with impunity. Throughout history, authoritarian rulers have used people's fear of civil disorder to justify taking power. Ironically, the ruling group itself—whether monarchy, aristocracy, or political party—then became known as the *established order*.

Hobbes's conception of life in the cruel state of nature led him to view government primarily as a means of guaranteeing people's survival. Other theorists, taking survival for granted, believed that government protects order by preserving private property (goods and land owned by individuals). Foremost among them was the English philosopher, John Locke (1632–1704). In *Two Treatises on Government* (1690), he wrote that the protection of life, liberty, and property was the basic objective of government. His thinking strongly influenced the Declaration of Independence; it is reflected in the Declaration's famous phrase identifying "Life, Liberty, and the Pursuit of Happiness" as "unalienable Rights" of citizens under government. Locke's defense of property rights became linked with safeguards for individual liberties in the doctrine of **liberalism**, which holds that the state should leave citizens free to further their individual pursuits.[12]

Not everyone believes that the protection of private property is a valid objective of government. The German philosopher Karl Marx (1818–1883) rejected the private ownership of property used in the production of goods or services. Marx's ideas form the basis of **communism**, a philosophy that gives ownership of all land and productive facilities to the people—in effect, to the government. In line with communist theory, the 1977 constitution of the former Soviet Union declared that the nation's land, minerals, waters, and forests "are the exclusive property of the state." Years after the Soviet Union collapsed, Russia remains deeply split over abandoning the old communist-era policies to permit the private ownership of land. Even today's market-oriented China still clings to the principle that all land belongs to the state, and not until 2007 did it pass a law that protected private homes and businesses.

liberalism
The belief that states should leave individuals free to follow their individual pursuits. Note that this differs from the definition of liberal later in this chapter.

communism
A political system in which, in theory, ownership of all land and productive facilities is in the hands of the people, and all goods are equally shared. The production and distribution of goods are controlled by an authoritarian government.

Providing Public Goods

After governments have established basic order, they can pursue other ends. Using their coercive powers, governments can tax citizens to raise money to spend on **public goods**, which are benefits and services available to everyone, such as education, sanitation, and parks. Public goods benefit all citizens but are not likely to be produced by the voluntary acts of individuals. The government of ancient Rome, for example, built aqueducts to carry fresh water from the mountains to the city. Road building was another public good provided by the Roman government, which also used the roads to move its legions and protect the established order.

Government action to provide public goods can be controversial. During President James Monroe's administration (1817–1825), many people thought that building the Cumberland Road (between Cumberland, Maryland, and Wheeling, West Virginia) was not a proper function of the national government, the Romans notwithstanding. Over time, the scope of government functions in the United States has expanded. During President Dwight Eisenhower's administration in the 1950s, the federal government outdid the Romans' noble road building. Although a Republican opposed to big government, Eisenhower launched the massive interstate highway system at a cost of $27 billion (in 1950s dollars). Yet some government enterprises that have been common in other countries—running railroads, operating coal mines, and generating electric power—are politically controversial or even unacceptable in the United States. People disagree about how far the government ought to go in using its power to tax to provide public goods and services and how much of that realm should be handled by private business for profit.

public goods
Benefits and services, such as parks and sanitation, that benefit all citizens but are not likely to be produced voluntarily by individuals.

Promoting Equality

The promotion of equality has not always been a major objective of government. It gained prominence only in the twentieth century, in the aftermath of industrialization and urbanization. Confronted by the paradox of poverty amid plenty, some political leaders in European nations pioneered extensive government programs to improve life for the poor. Under the emerging concept of the welfare state, government's role expanded to provide individuals with medical care, education, and a guaranteed income "from cradle to grave." Sweden, Britain, and other nations adopted welfare programs aimed at reducing social inequalities. This relatively new purpose of government has been by far the most controversial. People often oppose taxation for public goods (building roads and schools, for example) because of cost alone. They oppose more strongly taxation for government programs to promote economic and social equality on principle.

AP Images/Gene Herrick

Rosa Parks: She Sat for Equality

Rosa Parks had just finished a day's work as a seamstress and was sitting in the front of a bus in Montgomery, Alabama, going home. A white man claimed her seat, which he could do according to the law in December 1955. When she refused to move and was arrested, outraged blacks, led by Dr. Martin Luther King, Jr., began a boycott of the Montgomery bus company. Rosa Parks died in 2005 at age ninety-two and was accorded the honor of lying in state in the Capitol rotunda, the first woman to receive that tribute.

Redistributing Income. The key issue here is government's role in redistributing income, that is, taking from the wealthy to give to the poor. Charity (voluntary giving to the poor) has a strong basis in Western religious traditions; using the power of the state to support the poor does not. (In his 1838 novel, *Oliver Twist*, Charles Dickens dramatized how government power was used to imprison the poor, not to support them.) Using the state to redistribute income was originally a radical idea, set forth by Karl Marx as the ultimate principle of developed communism: "from each according to his ability, to each according to his needs."[13] This extreme has never been realized in any government, not even in communist states. But over time, taking from the rich to help the needy has become a legitimate function of most governments.

That function is not without controversy. Especially since the Great Depression of the 1930s, the government's role in redistributing income to promote economic equality has been a major source of policy debate in the United States. Despite inflation, the minimum wage had been frozen at $5.15 per hour from 1997 to 2007, when it was increased to $5.85. In 2009, Congress increased the minimum wage to $7.25 but resisted attempts to raise it further. In his 2014 State of the Union Address, President Obama urged raising the minimum wage to $10.10, but Congress did not comply.

COMPARE WITH YOUR PEERS
MindTap for American Government

Access the The Democratic Republic Forum: Polling Activity—Defining Marriage in California.

Other Policies. Government can also promote social equality through policies that do not redistribute income. For example, in 2000, Vermont passed a law allowing persons of the same sex to enter a "civil union" granting access to similar benefits enjoyed by persons of different sexes through marriage. By 2014, legislatures or courts in twenty-six states put similar laws into effect. Laws advancing social equality may clash with different social values held by other citizens. Indeed, twenty-two states banned same-sex marriages by constitutional referenda and two by statutes.[14]

A Conceptual Framework for Analyzing Government

LO3 ★ Describe how political scientists use concepts to structure events and promote understanding.

Citizens have very different views of how vigorously they want government to maintain order, provide public goods, and promote equality. Of the three objectives, providing for public goods usually is less controversial than maintaining order or promoting equality. After all, government spending for highways, schools, and parks carries benefits for nearly every citizen. Moreover, services merely cost money. The cost of maintaining order and promoting equality is greater than money; it usually means a trade-off in basic values.

To understand government and the political process, you must be able to recognize these trade-offs and identify the basic values they entail. Just as people sit back from a wide-screen motion picture to gain perspective, to understand American government you need to take a broad view—a view much broader than that offered by examining specific political events. You need to use political concepts.

A concept is a generalized idea of a set of items or thoughts. It groups various events, objects, or qualities under a common classification or label. The framework that guides this book consists of five concepts that figure prominently in political analysis. We regard the five concepts as especially important to a broad understanding of

American politics, and we use them repeatedly throughout this book. This framework will help you evaluate political events long after you have read this text.

The five concepts that we emphasize deal with the fundamental issues of what government tries to do and how it decides to do it. The concepts that relate to what government tries to do are *order, freedom,* and *equality.* All governments by definition value order; maintaining order is part of the meaning of government. Most governments at least claim to preserve individual freedom while they maintain order, although they vary widely in the extent to which they succeed. Few governments even profess to guarantee equality, and governments differ greatly in policies that pit equality against freedom. Our conceptual framework should help you evaluate the extent to which the United States pursues all three values through its government.

How government chooses the proper mix of order, freedom, and equality in its policymaking has to do with the process of choice. We evaluate the American governmental process using two models of democratic government: *majoritarian* and *pluralist.* Many governments profess to be democracies. Whether they are or are not depends on their (and our) meaning of the term. Even countries that Americans agree are democracies—for example, the United States and Britain—differ substantially in the type of democracy they practice. We can use our conceptual models of democratic government both to classify the type of democracy practiced in the United States and to evaluate the government's success in fulfilling that model.

The five concepts can be organized into two groups:

- Concepts that identify the values pursued by government:
  Freedom
  Order
  Equality
- Concepts that describe models of democratic government:
  Majoritarian democracy
  Pluralist democracy

The rest of this chapter examines freedom, order, and equality as conflicting values pursued by government. Chapter 2 discusses majoritarian democracy and pluralist democracy as alternative institutional models for implementing democratic government.

 ## The Concepts of Freedom, Order, and Equality

LO4 ★ Define freedom, order, and equality and discuss the various interpretations of each value.

These three terms—*freedom, order,* and *equality*—have a range of connotations in American politics. Both freedom and equality are positive terms that politicians have learned to use to their own advantage. Consequently, *freedom* and *equality* mean different things to different people at different times, depending on the political context in which they are used. *Order,* in contrast, has negative connotations for many people because it symbolizes government intrusion into private lives. Except during periods of social strife or external threat (for example, after September 11, 2001, when terrorists crashed airplanes into the Twin Tower skyscrapers in New York), few politicians in Western democracies openly call for more order. Because all governments infringe on freedom, we examine that concept first.

Freedom

Freedom can be used in two major senses: freedom of and freedom from. President Franklin Delano Roosevelt used the word in both senses in a speech he made shortly before the United States entered World War II. He described four freedoms: freedom of religion, freedom of speech, freedom from fear, and freedom from want. The noted illustrator Norman Rockwell gave Americans a vision of these freedoms in a classic set of paintings published in the *Saturday Evening Post* and subsequently issued as posters to sell war bonds (see "Freedom, Order, or Equality and 'The Four Freedoms' Posters").

Freedom of is the absence of constraints on behavior; it means freedom to do something. In this sense, *freedom* is synonymous with *liberty*.[15] Two of Rockwell's paintings, *Freedom of Worship* and *Freedom of Speech*, exemplify this type of

freedom of
An absence of constraints on behavior, as in *freedom of speech* or *freedom of religion*.

★ ## Freedom, Order, or Equality and "The Four Freedoms" Posters

Posters by Norman Rockwell

Norman Rockwell became famous in the 1940s for the humorous, homespun covers he painted for the *Saturday Evening Post*, a weekly magazine. Inspired by an address to Congress in which President Roosevelt outlined his goals for world civilization, Rockwell painted The Four Freedoms, which were reproduced in the *Post* during February and March 1943. Their immense popularity led the government to print posters of the illustrations for the Treasury Department's war bond drive.

The Office of War Information also reproduced The Four Freedoms and circulated the posters in schools, clubhouses, railroad stations, post offices, and

The Protected Art Archive/Alamy

Nawrocki Stock Photo/Custom Medical Stock Photo CMSP Education/Newscom

freedom. Freedom of religion, speech, press, and assembly (collectively called "civil liberties") is discussed in Chapter 15.

Freedom from is the message of the other paintings, *Freedom from Fear* and *Freedom from Want*.[16] Here freedom suggests immunity from fear and want. In the modern political context, freedom from often symbolizes the fight against exploitation and oppression. The cry of the civil rights movement in the 1960s—"Freedom Now!"—conveyed this meaning. This sense of freedom corresponds to the "civil rights" discussed in Chapter 16. If you recognize that freedom in this sense means immunity from discrimination, you can see that it comes close to the concept of equality.[17] In this book, we avoid using freedom to mean "freedom from"; for this sense, we simply use *equality*. When we use *freedom*, we mean "freedom of."

freedom from
Immunity, as in *freedom from want.*

other public buildings. Officials even had copies circulated on the European front to remind soldiers of the liberties for which they were fighting. Winning the war would safeguard American culture and preserve order, while equality was implied as an outcome of the other freedoms. It is said that no other paintings in the world have ever been reproduced or circulated in such vast numbers as The Four Freedoms.

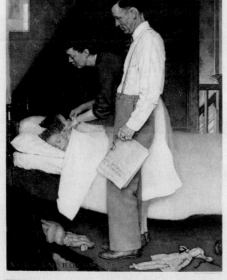

Norman Rockwell/Fine Art/CORBIS

Norman Rockwell/Fine Art/CORBIS

Critical Thinking Times have changed since the 1940s. Which of these four freedoms would resonate best today with the American public? Which the least? Why? What has changed over the decades?

Order

When *order* is viewed in the narrow sense of preserving life and protecting property, most citizens concede the importance of maintaining order and thereby grant the need for government. For example, "domestic Tranquility" (order) is cited in the preamble to the Constitution. However, when order is viewed in the broader sense of preserving the social order, some people argue that maintaining order is not a legitimate function of government. Social order refers to established patterns of authority in society and traditional modes of behavior. It is the accepted way of doing things. The prevailing social order prescribes behavior in many different areas: how students should dress in school (neatly, no purple hair) and behave toward their teachers (respectfully), who is allowed to marry (only adults, preferably of opposite sexes), what the press should not publish (sexually explicit photographs), and what the proper attitude toward religion and country should be (reverential). It is important to remember that the social order can change. Today, perfectly respectable men and women wear bathing suits that would have caused a scandal a century ago.

police power
The authority of a government to maintain order and safeguard citizens' health, morals, safety, and welfare.

A state government can protect the established order by using its **police power**—its authority to safeguard residents' safety, health, welfare, and morals. Under legal tradition and constitutional provisions, state governments can act directly on residents under their police power. The national government only has powers granted by the Constitution and lacks a general police power. That explains why states can require automobile drivers and passengers to wear seat belts and the national government cannot. However, the national government can act on individuals if the action can be traced to a constitutionally delegated power. For example, in 1932, Congress passed the Federal Kidnapping Act, allowing the Federal Bureau of Investigation (FBI) to apprehend kidnappers. The law was based on the constitutional power to regulate interstate commerce, given that kidnappers usually demand ransom by mail or telephone (instrumentalities of interstate commerce) and might cross state boundaries. The extent to which governments at any level should use their police powers is a topic of ongoing debate in the United States and is constantly being redefined by the courts. In the 1980s, many states used their authority to pass legislation that banned smoking in public places. In the 1990s, a hot issue was whether the national government should control the dissemination of pornography on the Internet. Excepting child pornography, courts have tended to strike down such bans. After September 11, 2001, Congress passed new laws increasing government's power to investigate suspicious activities by foreign nationals in order to deter terrorism.

One result was increased use of electronic surveillance of telephone conversations. As revealed in government documents leaked in 2013 by former employee Edward Snowden, the National Security Agency did not restrict its surveillance to "suspicious activities by foreign nationals" but also collected data on domestic phone conversations of ordinary Americans. So despite the desire to be safe from further attacks, issues such as these have caused some citizens to fear the erosion of their civil liberties. Living in a police state—a government that uses its power to regulate nearly all aspects of behavior—might maximize safety, but at a considerable loss of personal freedom. Most governments are inherently conservative; they tend to resist social change. But some governments aim to restructure the social order. Social change is most dramatic when a government is overthrown through force and replaced. This can occur through an internal revolution or a "regime change" effected externally. Societies can also work to change social patterns more gradually through the legal process. Our use of the term order in this book encompasses all three aspects: preserving life, protecting property, and maintaining traditional patterns of social relationships.

Equality

As with *freedom* and *order*, *equality* is used in different senses to support different causes. **Political equality** in elections is easy to define: each citizen has one and only one vote. This basic concept is central to democratic theory, a subject explored at length in Chapter 2. But when some people advocate political equality, they mean more than one person, one vote. These people contend that an urban ghetto dweller and the head of the Bank of America are not politically equal despite the fact that each has one vote. Through occupation or wealth, some citizens are more able than others to influence political decisions. For example, wealthy citizens can exert influence by advertising in the mass media or by contacting friends in high places. Lacking great wealth and political connections, most citizens do not have such influence. Thus, some analysts argue that equality in wealth, education, and status—that is, **social equality**—is necessary for true political equality.

There are two routes to promoting social equality: providing equal opportunities and ensuring equal outcomes. **Equality of opportunity** means that each person has the same chance to succeed in life. This idea is deeply ingrained in American culture. The U.S. Constitution prohibits titles of nobility and does not make owning property a requirement for holding public office. Public schools and libraries are open to all. For many people, the concept of social equality is satisfied by offering equal opportunities for advancement; it is not essential that people actually end up being equal. For others, true social equality means nothing less than **equality of outcome**.[18] President Lyndon B. Johnson expressed this view in 1965: "It is not enough just to open the gates of opportunity.... We seek ... not just equality as a right and a theory but equality as a fact and equality as a result."[19] According to this outlook, it is not enough that governments provide people with equal opportunities; they must also design policies that redistribute wealth and status so that economic and social equality are actually achieved. In education, equality of outcome has led to federal laws that require comparable funding for men's and women's college sports. In business, equality of outcome has led to affirmative action programs to increase minority hiring and to the active recruitment of women, blacks, and Latinos to fill jobs. Equality of outcome has also produced federal laws that require employers to pay men and women equally for equal work. In recent years, the very concept of affirmative action has come under scrutiny.

Some link equality of outcome with the concept of government-supported **rights**—the idea that every citizen is entitled to certain benefits of government— that government should guarantee its citizens adequate (if not equal) housing, employment, medical care, and income as a matter of right. If citizens are entitled to government benefits as a matter of right, government efforts to promote equality of outcome become legitimized.

Clearly, the concept of equality of outcome is quite different from that of equality of opportunity, and it requires a much greater degree of government activity. It also clashes more directly with the concept of freedom. By taking from one to give to another, which is necessary for the redistribution of income and status, the government creates winners and losers. The winners may believe that justice has been served by the redistribution. The losers often feel strongly that their freedom to enjoy their income and status has suffered.

political equality
Equality in political decision making: one vote per person, with all votes counted equally.

social equality
Equality in wealth, education, and status.

equality of opportunity
The idea that each person is guaranteed the same chance to succeed in life.

equality of outcome
The concept that society must ensure that people are equal, and governments must design policies to redistribute wealth and status so that economic and social equality is actually achieved.

rights
The benefits of government to which every citizen is entitled.

Courtesy Photo http://www.dvidshub.net/

Equality in the Military

Marines are tough, but Marine Drill Instructors are tougher. Meet Sgt. Maj. Stephanie Murphy, sergeant major of Officer Candidates School at Marine Corps Base Quantico, Va.

Two Dilemmas of Government

LO5 ★ Analyze the inherent conflicts between freedom versus order and freedom versus equality.

The two major dilemmas facing American government early in the twenty-first century stem from the oldest and the newest objectives of government: maintaining order and promoting equality. Both order and equality are important social values, but government cannot pursue either without sacrificing a third important value: individual freedom. The clash between freedom and order forms the original dilemma of government; the clash between freedom and equality forms the modern dilemma of government. Although the dilemmas are different, each involves trading some amount of freedom for another value.

The Original Dilemma: Freedom versus Order

The conflict between freedom and order originates in the very meaning of government as the legitimate use of force to control human behavior. How much freedom must citizens surrender to government? The dilemma has occupied philosophers for hundreds of years. In the eighteenth century, the French philosopher Jean-Jacques Rousseau (1712–1778) wrote that the problem of devising a proper government "is to find a form of association which will defend and protect with the whole common force the person and goods of each associate, and in which each, while uniting himself with all, may still obey himself alone, and remain free as before."[20]

The original purpose of government was to protect life and property and to make citizens safe from violence. How well is the American government doing today in providing law and order to its citizens? More than a third of the respondents in a 2013 national survey said that they were "afraid to walk alone at night" in areas within a mile of their home.[21] Simply put, Americans view violent crime (which actually has decreased in recent years[22]) as a critical issue and do not believe that their government adequately protects them.

Contrast the fear of crime in urban America with the sense of personal safety while walking in Moscow, Warsaw, or Prague during the 1980s when the old communist governments still ruled in Eastern Europe. It was common to see old and young strolling late at night along the streets and in the parks of these cities. The old communist regimes gave their police great powers to control guns, monitor citizens' movements, and arrest and imprison suspicious people, which enabled them to do a better job of maintaining order. Police and party agents routinely kept their citizens under surveillance—eavesdropping on phone conversations and opening mail from abroad—to ensure that they were not communicating privately with the capitalist world outside official channels. Communist governments deliberately chose order over freedom. With the collapse of communism came the end of strict social order.

The conflict between the values of freedom and order represents the original dilemma of government. In the abstract, people value both freedom and order; in real life, the two values inherently conflict. By definition, any policy that strengthens one value takes away from the other. The balance of freedom and order is an issue in enduring debates (whether to allow capital punishment) and contemporary challenges (whether to prohibit controversial YouTube videos). And in a democracy, policy choices hinge on how much citizens value freedom and how much they value order.

The Modern Dilemma: Freedom versus Equality

Popular opinion has it that freedom and equality go hand in hand. In reality, the two values usually clash when governments enact policies to promote social equality. Because social equality is a relatively recent government objective, deciding between policies that promote equality at the expense of freedom, and vice versa, is the modern dilemma of politics. Consider these examples:

During the 1960s, Congress (through the Equal Pay Act) required employers to pay women and men the same rate for equal work. This legislation means that some employers are forced to pay women more than they would if their compensation policies were based on the employers' free choice.

During the 1970s, the courts ordered the busing of schoolchildren to achieve a fair distribution of blacks and whites in public schools. This action was motivated by concern for educational equality, but it also impaired freedom of choice.

During the 1980s, some states passed legislation that went beyond the idea of equal pay for equal work to the more radical notion of pay equity—that is, equal pay for comparable work. Women had to be paid at a rate equal to men's even if they had different jobs, providing the women's jobs were of "comparable worth." For example, if the skills and responsibilities of a female nurse were found to be comparable to those of a male laboratory technician in the same hospital, the woman's salary and the man's salary would have to be the same.

During the 1990s, Congress prohibited discrimination in employment, public services, and public accommodations on the basis of physical or mental disabilities. Under the 1990 Americans with Disabilities Act, businesses with twenty-five or more employees cannot pass over an otherwise qualified disabled person in employment or promotion, and new buses and trains have to be made accessible to them.

During the first decade of the 2000s, Congress passed the Genetic Information Nondiscrimination Act (GINA). Signed by President Bush in 2008, it prohibited companies from discriminating in hiring based on an individual's genetic tests, genetic tests of a family member, or family medical history.

These examples illustrate the challenge of using government power to promote equality. The clash between freedom and order is obvious, but the clash between freedom and equality is less clear. Americans, who think of freedom and equality as complementary rather than conflicting values, often do not notice the clash. When forced to choose between the two, however, Americans are far more likely to choose freedom over equality than are people in other countries.

The conflicts among freedom, order, and equality explain a great deal of the political conflict in the United States. These conflicts also underlie the ideologies that people use to structure their understanding of politics.

Ideology and the Scope of Government

LO6 ★ Distinguish among these terms: totalitarianism, socialism, capitalism, libertarianism, and anarchism.

People hold different opinions about the merits of government policies. Sometimes their views are based on self-interest. For example, older citizens are more likely than younger taxpayers to support senior discounts when riding public transportation.

political ideology
A consistent set of values and beliefs about the proper purpose and scope of government.

Policies also are judged according to individual values and beliefs. Some people hold assorted values and beliefs that produce contradictory opinions on government policies. Others organize their opinions into a **political ideology**—a consistent set of values and beliefs about the proper purpose and scope of government.

How far should government go to maintain order, provide public goods, and promote equality? In the United States (as in every other nation), citizens, scholars, and politicians have different answers. We can analyze their positions by referring to philosophies about the proper scope of government—that is, the range of its permissible activities. Imagine a continuum. At one end is the belief that government should do everything; at the other is the belief that government should not exist. These extreme ideologies, from the most government to the least government, and those that fall in between are shown in Figure 1.1.

Totalitarianism

totalitarianism
A political philosophy that advocates unlimited power for the government to enable it to control all sectors of society.

Totalitarianism is the belief that government should have unlimited power. A totalitarian government controls all sectors of society: business, labor, education, religion, sports, and the arts. A true totalitarian favors a network of laws, rules, and regulations that guides every aspect of individual behavior. The object is to produce a perfect society serving some master plan for "the common good." Totalitarianism has reached its terrifying full potential only in literature and films (for example, in George Orwell's *1984*, a novel about "Big Brother" watching everyone), but several societies have come perilously close to "perfection." Think of Germany under Hitler and the Soviet Union under Stalin. Not many people openly profess totalitarianism today, but the concept is useful because it anchors one side of our continuum.

FIGURE 1.1 Ideology and the Scope of Government

We can classify political ideologies according to the scope of action that people are willing to allow government in dealing with social and economic problems. In this chart, the three rows map out various philosophical positions along an underlying continuum ranging from least to most government. Notice that conventional politics in the United States spans only a narrow portion of the theoretical possibilities for government action. In popular usage, liberals favor a greater scope of government, and conservatives want a narrower scope. But over time, the traditional distinction has eroded and now oversimplifies the differences between liberals and conservatives. Figure 1.2 (p. 23) offers a more discriminating classification of liberals and conservatives.

Source: © Cengage Learning.

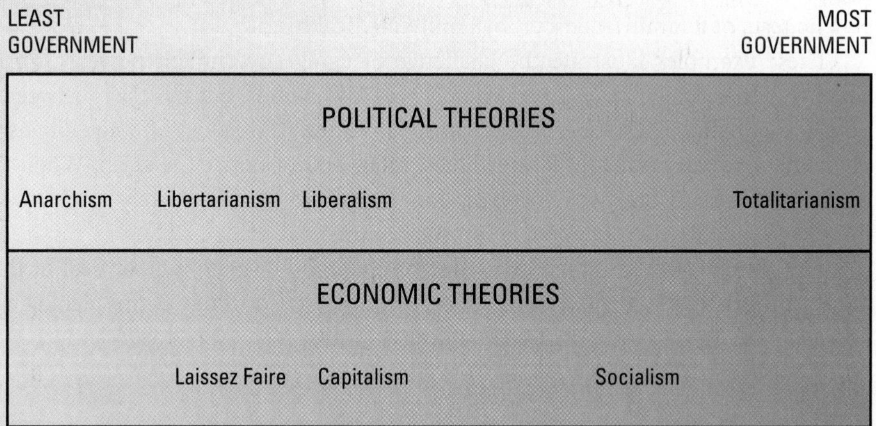

LEAST GOVERNMENT			MOST GOVERNMENT
POLITICAL THEORIES			
Anarchism	Libertarianism	Liberalism	Totalitarianism
ECONOMIC THEORIES			
	Laissez Faire	Capitalism	Socialism
POPULAR POLITICAL LABELS IN THE UNITED STATES			
	Conservative	Liberal	

Socialism

Whereas totalitarianism refers to government in general, **socialism** pertains to government's role in the economy. Like communism, socialism is an economic system based on Marxist theory. Under socialism (and communism), the scope of government extends to ownership or control of the basic industries that produce goods and services. These include communications, mining, heavy industry, transportation, and energy. Although socialism favors a strong role for government in regulating private industry and directing the economy, it allows more room than communism does for private ownership of productive capacity. Many Americans equate socialism with the communism practiced in the old closed societies of the Soviet Union and Eastern Europe. But there is a difference. Although communism in theory was supposed to result in what Marx referred to as a "withering away" of the state, communist governments in practice tended toward totalitarianism, controlling not just economic life but also both political and social life through a dominant party organization. Some socialist governments, however, practice **democratic socialism**. They guarantee civil liberties (such as freedom of speech and freedom of religion) and allow their citizens to determine the extent of the government's activity through free elections and competitive political parties. Outside the United States, socialism is not universally viewed as inherently bad. In fact, the governments of Britain, Sweden, Germany, and France, among other democracies, have at times since World War II been avowedly socialist. More recently, the formerly communist regimes of Eastern Europe have abandoned the controlling role of government in their economies for strong doses of capitalism.

> **socialism**
> A form of rule in which the central government plays a strong role in regulating existing private industry and directing the economy, although it does allow some private ownership of productive capacity.

> **democratic socialism**
> A socialist form of government that guarantees civil liberties such as freedom of speech and religion. Citizens determine the extent of government activity through free elections and competitive political parties.

Capitalism

Capitalism also relates to the government's role in the economy. In contrast to both socialism and communism, **capitalism** supports free enterprise—private businesses operating without government regulation. Some theorists, most notably the late Nobel Prize–winning economist Milton Friedman, argue that free enterprise is necessary for free politics.[23] This argument, that the economic system of capitalism is essential to democracy, contradicts the tenets of democratic socialism. Whether it is valid depends in part on our understanding of democracy, a subject discussed in Chapter 2. The United States is decidedly a capitalist country, more so than most other Western nations. Despite the U.S. government's enormous budget, it owns or operates relatively few public enterprises. For example, railroads, airlines, and television stations, which are frequently owned by the government in other countries, are privately owned in the United States. But our government does extend its authority into the economic sphere, regulating private businesses and directing the overall economy. Both American liberals and conservatives embrace capitalism, but they differ on the nature and amount of government intervention in the economy they deem necessary or desirable.

> **capitalism**
> The system of government that favors free enterprise (privately owned businesses operating without government regulation).

Libertarianism

Libertarianism opposes all government action except what is necessary to protect life and property. **Libertarians** grudgingly recognize the necessity of government but believe that it should be as limited as possible and should not promote either order or equality. For example, libertarians grant the need for traffic laws to ensure safe and efficient automobile travel. But they oppose laws requiring motorcycle riders to wear helmets, and the libertarian ethos in New Hampshire makes it the only state not

> **libertarianism**
> A political ideology that is opposed to all government action except as necessary to protect life and property.

> **libertarians**
> Those who are opposed to using government to promote either order or equality.

requiring seat belts. Libertarians believe that social programs that provide food, clothing, and shelter are outside the proper scope of government. Helping the needy, they insist, should be a matter of individual choice. Libertarians also oppose government ownership of basic industries; in fact, they oppose any government intervention in the economy. This kind of economic policy is called **laissez faire**, a French phrase that means "let (people) do (as they please)." Such an extreme policy extends beyond the free enterprise that most capitalists advocate.

Libertarians are vocal advocates of hands-off government in both the social and the economic spheres. Whereas Americans who favor a broad scope of government action shun the description *socialist*, libertarians make no secret of their identity. The Libertarian Party ran candidates in every presidential election from 1972 through 2012, winning over a million votes in 2012, still under one percent of all votes cast.

Do not confuse libertarians with liberals—or with liberalism, the John Locke– inspired doctrine mentioned earlier. The words are similar, but their meanings are quite different. *Libertarianism* draws on *liberty* as its root (following Locke) and means "absence of governmental constraint." While both liberalism and libertarianism leave citizens free to pursue their private goals, libertarianism treats freedom as a pure goal; it's liberalism on steroids. In American political usage, *liberalism* evolved from the root word *liberal* in the sense of "freely," like a liberal serving of butter. Liberals see a positive role for government in helping the disadvantaged. Over time, *liberal* has come to mean something closer to generous, in the sense that liberals (but not libertarians) support government spending on social programs. Libertarians find little benefit in any government social program.

laissez faire
An economic doctrine that opposes any form of government intervention in business.

Anarchism

anarchism
A political philosophy that opposes government in any form.

Anarchism stands opposite totalitarianism on the political continuum. Anarchists oppose all government in any form. As a political philosophy, anarchism values absolute freedom. Because all government involves some restriction on personal freedom (for example, forcing people to drive on one side of the road), a pure anarchist would object even to traffic laws. Like totalitarianism, anarchism is not a popular philosophy, but it does have adherents on the political fringes.

Anarchists sparked street fights that disrupted meetings of the World Trade Organization (WTO) from Seattle (1999) to Geneva (2009). Labor unions had also protested meetings of the WTO, which writes rules that govern international trade, for failing to include labor rights on its agenda; environmental groups protested its promotion of economic development at the expense of the environment. But anarchists were against the WTO on *principle*—for concentrating the power of multinational corporations in a shadowy "world government." Discussing old and new forms of anarchy, journalist Joseph Kahn said, "Nothing has revived anarchism like globalization."[24] Although anarchism is not a popular philosophy, it is not merely a theoretical category.

Kevin Downs/Corbis News/Corbis

Anarchists Against Globalization

Anarchism as a philosophy views government as an unnecessary evil. Anarchists operate several websites that oppose capitalism and government in general. Their symbol is a circle and bar surrounding the letter "A." Here is their view of NATO and the world's eight leading economies, called G-8.

Liberals and Conservatives: The Narrow Middle

As shown in Figure 1.1, practical politics in the United States ranges over only the central portion of the continuum. The extreme positions—totalitarianism and anarchism—are rarely argued in public debates. And in this era of distrust of "big government," few American politicians would openly advocate socialism. However, more than 120 people ran for Congress in 2014 as candidates of the Libertarian Party. Although none won, American libertarians are sufficiently vocal to be heard in the debate over the role of government.

Still, most of that debate is limited to a narrow range of political thought. On one side are people commonly called *liberals*; on the other are *conservatives*. In popular usage, liberals favor more government, conservatives less. This distinction is clear when the issue is government spending to provide public goods. Liberals favor generous government support for education, wildlife protection, public transportation, and a whole range of social programs. Conservatives want smaller government budgets and fewer government programs. They support free enterprise and argue against government job programs, regulation of business, and legislation of working conditions and wage rates.

But on other topics, liberals and conservatives reverse their positions. In theory, liberals favor government activism, yet they oppose government regulation of abortion. In theory, conservatives oppose government activism, yet they support government surveillance of telephone conversations to fight terrorism. What's going on? Are American political attitudes hopelessly contradictory, or is something missing in our analysis of these ideologies today? Actually something is missing. To understand the liberal and conservative stances on political issues, we must look not only at the scope of government action but also at the purpose of government action. That is, to understand a political ideology, it is necessary to understand how it incorporates the values of freedom, order, and equality.

★ American Political Ideologies and the Purpose of Government

LO7 ★ Explain how liberals, conservatives, libertarians, and communitarians view the role of government.

Much of American politics revolves around the two dilemmas just described: freedom versus order and freedom versus equality. The two dilemmas do not account for all political conflict, but they help us gain insight into the workings of politics and organize the seemingly chaotic world of political events, actors, and issues.

Liberals versus Conservatives: The New Differences

Liberals and conservatives are different, but their differences no longer hinge on the narrow question of the government's role in providing public goods. Liberals do favor more spending for public goods and conservatives less, but this is no longer the critical difference between them. Today that difference stems from their attitudes toward the purpose of government. **Conservatives** support the original purpose of government: maintaining social order. They are willing to use the coercive power of the state to force citizens to be orderly. They favor firm police action, swift and severe punishment for criminals, and more laws regulating behavior. Conservatives would not stop with defining, preventing, and punishing crime, however. They tend to want to preserve traditional patterns of social relations—the domestic role of women and business owners' authority to hire whom they wish, for example. For this reason, they do not think government should impose equality.

conservatives
Those who are willing to use government to promote order but not equality.

liberals
Those who are willing to use government to promote equality but not order.

Liberals are less likely than conservatives to want to use government power to maintain order. In general, liberals are more tolerant of alternative lifestyles—for example, homosexual behavior. Liberals do not shy away from using government coercion, but they use it for a different purpose: to promote equality. They support laws that ensure equal treatment of gays in employment, housing, and education; laws that force private businesses to hire and promote women and members of minority groups; laws that require public transportation to provide equal access to people with disabilities; and laws that order cities and states to reapportion election districts so that minority voters can elect minority candidates to public office. Conservatives do not oppose equality, but they do not value it to the extent of using the government's power to enforce equality. For liberals, the use of that power to promote equality is both valid and necessary.

A Two-Dimensional Classification of Ideologies

To classify liberal and conservative ideologies more accurately, we have to incorporate the values of freedom, order, and equality into the classification.[25] We can do this using the model in Figure 1.2. It depicts the conflicting values along two separate dimensions, each anchored in maximum freedom at the lower left. One dimension extends horizontally from maximum freedom on the left to maximum order on the right. The other extends vertically from maximum freedom at the bottom to maximum equality at the top. Each box represents a different ideological type: libertarians, liberals, conservatives, and communitarians.[26]

Libertarians value freedom more than order or equality. (We will use *libertarians* for people who have libertarian tendencies but may not accept the whole philosophy.) In practical terms, libertarians want minimal government intervention in both the economic and the social spheres. For example, they oppose affirmative action and laws that restrict transmission of sexually explicit material.

Liberals value freedom more than order but not more than equality. They oppose laws that ban sexually explicit publications but support affirmative action. Conservatives value freedom more than equality but would restrict freedom to preserve social order. Conservatives oppose affirmative action but favor laws that restrict pornography. Finally, we arrive at the ideological type positioned at the upper right in Figure 1.2. This group values both equality and order more than freedom. Its members support both affirmative action and laws that restrict pornography. We will call this new group **communitarians**.[27] The term is used narrowly in contemporary politics to reflect the philosophy of the Communitarian Network, a political movement founded by sociologist Amitai Etzioni.[28] This movement rejects both the liberal–conservative classification and the libertarian argument that "individuals should be left on their own to pursue their choices, rights, and self-interests."[29] Like liberals, Etzioni's communitarians believe that there is a role for government in helping the disadvantaged. Like conservatives, they believe that government should be used to promote moral values—preserving the family through more stringent divorce laws, protecting against AIDS through testing programs, and limiting the dissemination of pornography, for example.[30]

By analyzing political ideologies on two dimensions rather than one, we can explain why people can seem to be liberal on one issue (favoring a broader scope of government action) and conservative on another (favoring less government action). The answer hinges on the purpose of a given government action: Which value does it promote: order or equality?[31] According to our typology, only libertarians and communitarians are consistent in their attitude toward the scope of government activity, whatever its purpose. Libertarians value freedom so highly that they oppose most

communitarians
Those who are willing to use government to promote both order and equality.

THE MODERN DILEMMA

Equality ↑

Liberals

Favor: Government activities that promote equality, such as affirmative action programs to employ minorities and increased spending on public housing.

Oppose: Government actions that restrict individual liberties, such as banning sexually explicit movies or mandatory testing for AIDS.

Communitarians

Favor: Government activities that promote equality, such as affirmative action programs to employ minorities and increased spending on public housing.

Favor: Government actions that impose social order, such as banning sexually explicit movies or mandatory testing for AIDS.

Libertarians

Oppose: Government activities that interfere with the market, such as affirmative action programs to employ minorities and increased spending on public housing.

Oppose: Government actions that restrict individual liberties, such as banning sexually explicit movies or mandatory testing for AIDS.

Conservatives

Oppose: Government activities that interfere with the market, such as affirmative action programs to employ minorities and increased spending on public housing.

Favor: Government actions that impose social order, such as banning sexually explicit movies or mandatory testing for AIDS.

Freedom ↓

Freedom ←————————————→ Order

THE ORIGINAL DILEMMA

FIGURE 1.2 Ideologies: A Two-Dimensional Framework

The four ideological types are defined by the values they favor in resolving the two major dilemmas of government: How much freedom should be sacrificed in pursuit of order and equality, respectively? Test yourself by thinking about the values that are most important to you. Which box in the figure best represents your combination of values?

Source: © Cengage Learning.

government efforts to enforce either order or equality. Communitarians (in our usage) are inclined to trade freedom for both order and equality. Liberals and conservatives, on the other hand, favor or oppose government activity depending on its purpose. As you will learn in Chapter 5, large groups of Americans fall into each of the four ideological categories. Because Americans increasingly choose four different resolutions to the original and modern dilemmas of government, the simple labels of *liberal* and *conservative* no longer describe contemporary political ideologies as well as they did in the 1930s, 1940s, and 1950s.

Master the Topic of The Democratic Republic with MindTap™ for American Government

REVIEW MindTap™ for American Government
Access Key Term Flashcards for Chapter 1.

TEST YOURSELF MindTap™ for American Government
Take the Wrap It Up Quiz for Chapter 1.

STAY CURRENT MindTap™ for American Government
Access the KnowNow blog and customized RSS for updates on current events.

STAY FOCUSED MindTap™ for American Government
Complete the Focus Activities for The Democratic Republic.

Summary

The challenge of democracy lies in making difficult choices—choices that inevitably bring important values into conflict. This chapter has outlined a normative framework for analyzing the policy choices that arise in the pursuit of the purposes of government in an era of globalization.

LO1 Define globalization and explain how globalization affects American politics and government.

- We live in an era of globalization—a term for the increasing interdependence of citizens and nations across the world. Globalization infringes on national sovereignty, the right of governments to govern their people as they wish. Global forces generate pressures for economic trade, observance of human rights, and governance by international law. More than ever before, foreign affairs affect American government, and American politics affects government in other nations.

LO2 Identify the purposes that government serves and trace their historical roots.

- Government requires citizens to surrender some freedom as part of being governed. People do so to obtain the benefits of government: maintaining order, providing public goods, and—more controversially—promoting equality.

LO3 Describe how political scientists use concepts to structure events and promote understanding.

- Political concepts are generalized ideas about government and politics. They provide broader views than those offered by examining specific political events. Our conceptual framework consists of five concepts organized into two groups: concepts that identify values pursued by government: freedom, order, and equality; and concepts that describe models of democratic government: majoritarian and pluralist democracy.

LO4 Define freedom, order, and equality and discuss the various interpretations of each value.

- The terms freedom, order, and equality have varied connotations in American politics. Freedom and equality are positive terms that mean different things to different people at different times. Order has negative connotations for many because it symbolizes government intrusion into private lives. *Freedom* can be used in two major senses: freedom of and freedom from. We use it in the "freedom of" sense. Freedom of speech means freedom to speak. *Order* in politics means more than preserving life and property; it also means established patterns of authority in society and traditional modes of behavior. *Equality* in politics can be viewed narrowly as political equality (each person having one vote) or as social equality (equality in wealth, education, and status). It can also be viewed as equality of opportunity or of outcome.

LO5 Analyze the inherent conflicts between freedom versus order and freedom versus equality.

- The conflict between the values of freedom and order represents the original dilemma of government. The modern dilemma of politics is the conflict between the values of freedom and equality.

LO6 Distinguish among these terms: totalitarianism, socialism, capitalism, libertarianism, and anarchism.

- Political ideology is defined as a consistent set of values and beliefs about the proper purpose and scope of government. Ideologies differ about the proper range of permissible activities. Totalitarianism is the belief that government should have unlimited power. Socialism extends the scope of government to ownership or control of the basic industries that produce goods and services. Capitalism is committed to free enterprise—private businesses operating without government regulation. Libertarianism opposes all government action except what is necessary to protect life and property. Anarchists oppose all government in any form. In the United States, most political debate is limited to a narrow range of political thought. On one side are liberals; on the other are conservatives.

LO7 Explain how liberals, conservatives, libertarians, and communitarians view the role of government.

- In popular usage, liberals favor more government, and conservatives less. That is, liberals support a broader role for

government than do conservatives. Liberals and conservatives mainly quarrel over the purpose of government action. Conservatives may want less government, but they are willing to use the government's coercive power to impose social order. Liberals too are willing to use the coercive power of government, but for the purpose of promoting equality. Liberals value freedom more than order and equality more than freedom. Conservatives value order more than freedom and freedom more than equality. Libertarians choose freedom over both order and equality. Communitarians are willing to sacrifice freedom for both order and equality.

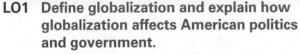

Chapter Quiz

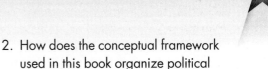

LO1 Define globalization and explain how globalization affects American politics and government.

1. Define globalization and give an example of globalization's effect on American politics.
2. Give an example of the American government's effects on foreign politics.

LO2 Identify the purposes that government serves and trace their historical roots.

1. What are the major purposes of government?
2. Which of these purposes is most controversial?

LO3 Describe how political scientists use concepts to structure events and promote understanding.

1. How does the use of political concepts promote understanding?

2. How does the conceptual framework used in this book organize political concepts?

LO4 Define freedom, order, and equality and discuss the various interpretations of each value.

1. Which of these concepts is linked most closely to the police power of a state?
2. Which is most closely linked to the concept of rights, and why?

LO5 Analyze the inherent conflicts between freedom versus order and freedom versus equality.

1. What are the two dilemmas of government, and which came first?
2. Which dilemma underlies the 1960 law requiring paying men and women the same rate for equal work? Why is it a dilemma?

LO6 **Distinguish among these terms: totalitarianism, socialism, capitalism, libertarianism, and anarchism.**

1. How do the terms libertarianism, liberalism, and liberals differ? In what ways are these terms similar?
2. Give an example of anarchism in contemporary American politics.

LO7 **Explain how liberals, conservatives, libertarians, and communitarians view the role of government.**

1. How can both liberals and conservatives favor greater scope of government?
2. What contemporary politicians exemplify the typological categories of liberal, conservative, libertarian, and communitarian?

2 Majoritarian or Pluralist Democracy?

Learning Outcomes

LO1 Distinguish between the two theories of democratic government used in political science: procedural and substantive.

LO2 Compare and contrast the majoritarian and pluralist models of democracy.

LO3 Evaluate the challenges facing countries trying to move toward a democratic form of government.

 WATCH & LEARN MindTap® for American Government

Watch a brief "What Do You Know?" video summarizing Majoritarian or Pluralist Democracy.

Rob Crandall/Alamy

"These deportations are ripping our families apart; this has got to stop."

These are the words of Christina Jiménez, a leader of United We Dream, a network of young immigrants.[1] Few problems today are as vexing as immigration. There are 11 million people living in the United States who are undocumented, meaning that they came across the border illegally or came into the country on some sort of tourist visa, student visa, or work permit and then remained after the expiration date on their entry papers.

Each year thousands of the undocumented are deported by the government—369,000 in 2013 alone.[2] Often this happens when investigators learn that a factory is employing undocumented workers (sometimes exploiting them) and then raid the company. The young immigrants who belong to United We Dream were likely brought here as very small children, then grew up in this country with little connection to the home nation of their parents. They may be enrolled in high school or college but have no confidence that they can become gainfully employed without documentation that allows them to live in the United States.

But what to do? We typically think that a problem comes before Congress and the majority in that body decides. In this case, one has to ask "what majority would that be?" In Congress there is no majority. In 2013 congressional Republicans controlled the House, and they rejected an immigration proposal developed by their own leadership that would have allowed the undocumented to stay in this country as legal residents (but not as citizens). Conservatives believe that there is an important principle involved: all should follow the law, and permitting the undocumented to stay ignores the laws in force. The Senate, controlled by the Democrats, passed a bill that not only allowed the undocumented to stay in the country as legal residents but also included a path to full citizenship (albeit with a rather long and difficult road to citizenship). Those who favor legislation creating a legal basis for the undocumented to stay cite both compassion and the reality of 11 million people here who, practically speaking, can't all be deported.

In many ways Congress reflects the lack of consensus across the country. A bare majority of Americans back an immigration plan with a path to citizenship. However, there are sharp divisions among partisans: only a third of Republican identifiers are in favor of such a plan while most want to deport those here illegally. In contrast, close to 70 percent of Democrats approve of a plan to give the undocumented the right to stay here and pursue citizenship (see Figure 2.1).[3]

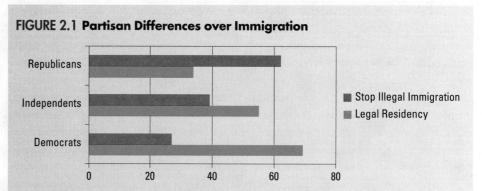

FIGURE 2.1 Partisan Differences over Immigration

Few issues are as divisive in America as what to do with the nation's more than 11 million undocumented immigrants. Republicans, Democrats, and independents view the solution differently.

Question: What should be the main focus of the U.S. government in dealing with the issue of illegal immigration—developing a plan that would allow illegal immigrants who have jobs to become legal U.S. residents, or developing a plan for stopping the flow of illegal immigrants into the United States and for deporting those already here?

Source: CNN/ORC Poll, January 31–February 2, 2014.

Not all Americans feel strongly about this issue, and one can wonder if a better system of determining an appropriate response would give more weight to those who are most intensely concerned about the issue. Such a system would privilege interest groups, organizations representing various constituencies who try to influence government on an issue. There are organizations like United We Dream that are working on behalf of immigration reform. Many business organizations, such as the U.S. Chamber of Commerce, also favor allowing the undocumented to stay in the country because they fill an important role in the nation's economy by their willingness to take low-paying, low-skilled jobs. On the other hand, there are conservative organizations, such as the Heritage Foundation and the Tea Party, that strenuously oppose loosening the restrictions on the undocumented.

Determining who is in the majority and what that majority wants are not simple tasks. Does this country really operate as a majoritarian democracy? Or is there an alternative way of understanding American democracy?

LISTEN & LEARN

MindTap for American Government

Access Read Speaker to listen to Chapter 2.

The Theory of Democratic Government

LO1 ★ Distinguish between the two theories of democratic government used in political science: procedural and substantive.

The origins of democratic theory lie in ancient Greek political thought. Greek philosophers classified governments according to the number of citizens involved in the process. Imagine a continuum running from rule by one person, through rule by a few, to rule by many.

At one extreme is an **autocracy**, in which one individual has the power to make all important decisions. The concentration of power in the hands of one person (usually a

autocracy
A system of government in which the power to govern is concentrated in the hands of one individual.

monarch) was a more common form of government in earlier historical periods, although some countries are still ruled autocratically.

Oligarchy puts government power in the hands of an elite. At one time, the nobility or the major landowners commonly ruled as an aristocracy. Today, military leaders are often the rulers in countries governed by an oligarchy.

At the other extreme of the continuum is **democracy**, which means "rule by the people." Most scholars believe that the United States, Britain, France, and other countries in Western Europe are genuine democracies. Critics contend that these countries only appear to be democracies: although they hold free elections, they are actually run by wealthy business elites, out for their own benefit.

oligarchy
A system of government in which power is concentrated in the hands of a few people.

democracy
A system of government in which, in theory, the people rule, either directly or indirectly.

The Meaning and Symbolism of Democracy

Americans have a simple answer to the question "Who should govern?" It is "The people." Unfortunately, this answer is too simple. It fails to define who *the people* are. Should we include young children? Recent immigrants? Illegal aliens? This answer also fails to tell us how the people should do the governing. Should they be assembled in a stadium? Vote by mail? Choose others to govern for them? We need to take a closer look at what "government by the people" really means.

The word *democracy* originated in Greek writings around the fifth century B.C. Demos referred to the common people, the masses; kratos meant "power." The ancient Greeks were afraid of democracy—rule by rank-and-file citizens. That fear is evident in the term *demagogue*. We use that term today to refer to a politician who appeals to and often deceives the masses by manipulating their emotions and prejudices.

Many centuries after the Greeks defined democracy, the idea still carried the connotation of mob rule. When George Washington was president, opponents of a new political party disparagingly called it a democratic party. No one would do that in politics today. In fact, the term has become so popular that the names of more than 20 percent of the world's political parties contain some variation of the word democracy.[4] Americans reflexively support democracy as the best form of government but are less certain of what democracy entails or of alternative models of democracy.

There are two major schools of thought about what constitutes democracy. The first believes democracy is a form of government. It emphasizes the procedures that enable the people to govern: meeting to discuss issues, voting in elections, running for public office. The second sees democracy in the substance of government policies, in freedom of religion and the provision for human needs. The procedural approach focuses on how decisions are made; the substantive approach is concerned with what government does.

Dennis Brack/Newscom

Time to Vote

However majorities may be formed, they must be expressed in our legislative system through the roll call of members. In the House of Representatives, the scoreboard lists who has or has not participated during the open period for casting votes. The act of voting is done electronically and must be done on the floor of the House.

The Procedural View of Democracy

procedural democratic theory
A view of democracy as being embodied in a decision-making process that involves universal participation, political equality, majority rule, and responsiveness.

Procedural democratic theory sets forth principles that describe how government should make decisions. The principles address three distinct questions:

1. *Who* should participate in decision making?
2. *How much* should each participant's vote count?
3. *How many* votes are needed to reach a decision?

According to procedural democratic theory, all adults should participate in government decision making; everyone within the boundaries of the political community should be allowed to vote. If some people, such as recent immigrants, are prohibited from participating, they are excluded only for practical or political reasons (principally, that they're not yet citizens). The theory of democracy itself does not exclude any adults from participation. We refer to this principle as **universal participation**.

universal participation
The concept that everyone in a democracy should participate in governmental decision making.

How much should each participant's vote count? According to procedural theory, all votes should be counted *equally*. This is the principle of **political equality**.

political equality
Equality in political decision making: one vote per person, with all votes counted equally.

Note that universal participation and political equality are two distinct principles. It is not enough for everyone to participate in a decision; all votes must carry equal weight. President Abraham Lincoln reportedly once took a vote among his cabinet members and found that they all opposed his position on an issue. He summarized the vote and the decision this way: "Seven noes, one aye—the ayes have it."[5] Everyone participated, but Lincoln's vote counted more than all the others combined. (No one ever said that presidents have to run their cabinets democratically.)

Finally, how many votes are needed to reach a decision? Procedural theory prescribes that a group should decide to do what the majority of its participants (a minimum of 50 percent plus one person) wants to do. This principle is called **majority rule**. (If participants divide over more than two alternatives and none receives a simple majority, the principle usually defaults to *plurality rule*, under which the group does what most participants want.)

majority rule
The principle—basic to procedural democratic theory—that the decision of a group must reflect the preference of more than half of those participating; a simple majority.

A Complication: Direct versus Indirect Democracy

participatory democracy
A system of government where rank-and-file citizens rule themselves rather than electing representatives to govern on their behalf.

The three principles of universal participation, political equality, and majority rule are widely recognized as necessary for democratic decision making. Small, simple societies can meet these principles with a direct or **participatory democracy**, in which all members of the group, rather than representatives they elect to govern on their behalf, meet to make decisions, observing political equality and majority rule.[6] The origins of participatory democracy go back to the Greek city-state, where the important decisions of government were made by the adult citizens meeting in an assembly. The people ruled themselves rather than having a small number of notables rule on their behalf. (In Athens, the people who were permitted to attend the assemblies did not include women, slaves, and those whose families had not lived there for generations. Thus, participation was not universal. Still, the Greek city-state represented a dramatic transformation in the theory of government.)[7]

Something close to participatory democracy is practiced in some New England towns, where rank-and-file citizens gather in a town meeting, often just once a year, to make key community decisions together. A town meeting is impractical in large cities, although some cities have incorporated participatory democracy in their decision-making processes by instituting forms of neighborhood government. Portland, Oregon, for example, has a vibrant and effective set of neighborhood associations that can be found in each area of the city. Each is recognized as the official representative of the neighborhood and is involved in decisions that affect that particular area of Portland, such as the issuance of liquor licenses.[8]

Citizens warmly embrace the concept of participatory democracy.[9] Yet in the United States and virtually all other democracies, participatory democracy is rare. Few cities have decentralized their governments and turned power over to their neighborhoods. Participatory democracy is commonly rejected on the grounds that in large, complex societies, we need professional, full-time government officials to study problems, formulate solutions, and administer programs. It is also subject to criticism because only a small proportion of the population engages in such programs.[10]

New technologies have raised hopes that e-government might facilitate greater public involvement. **E-government** refers to the online communications channels that enable rank-and-file citizens to acquire information and documents as well as to register opinions and complaints to government officials. E-government has made it much easier for citizens to find out about various government programs and services and to report problems to city hall. The city of Boston has an Office of the New Urban Mechanics that has established some innovative approaches to e-government. One of them is an app, Street Bump, that people download to their phone. When individuals with that app get in their cars, they just place their phone in a cup holder and the app electronically senses when the car hits a pothole and sends a message to the appropriate office at Boston City Hall that is responsible for filling potholes. The driver never has to lift a finger.[11]

e-government
Online communication channels that enable citizens to easily obtain information from government and facilitate the expression of opinions to government officials.

E-government is a long way from e-democracy. So far it has not facilitated greater public deliberation and has expanded public involvement in only marginal ways.[12] Still, it does make it easier to write your congressman (or state representative, or mayor, or whomever), so it does offer people a quick and convenient way to voice their opinions. Governments at all levels are experimenting with new forms of e-government in the hope that, over time, it will engage citizens more directly in the governmental process.

www.newurbanmechanics.org

The framers of the U.S. Constitution had their own conception of democracy. They instituted **representative democracy**, a system in which citizens participate in government by electing public officials to make decisions on their behalf. Elected officials are expected to represent the voters' views and interests—that is, to serve as the agents of the citizenry and act for them.

representative democracy
A system of government where citizens elect public officials to govern on their behalf.

Within the context of representative democracy, we adhere to the principles of universal participation, political equality, and majority rule to guarantee that elections are democratic. But what happens after the election? The elected representatives might not make the decisions the people would have made had they gathered for the same purpose. To account for this possibility in representative government, procedural theory provides a fourth decision-making principle: **responsiveness**. Elected representatives should respond to public opinion—what the majority of people wants. This does not mean that legislators simply cast their ballots on the basis of whether the people back home want alternative A or alternative B. Issues are not usually so straightforward.

responsiveness
A decision-making principle, necessitated by representative government, that implies that elected representatives should do what the majority of people wants.

Rather, responsiveness means following the general contours of public opinion in formulating complex pieces of legislation.[13] By adding responsiveness to deal with the case of indirect democracy, we have four principles of procedural democracy:

- Universal participation
- Political equality
- Majority rule
- Government responsiveness to public opinion

The Substantive View of Democracy

According to procedural theory, the principle of responsiveness is absolute. The government should do what the majority wants, regardless of what that is. At first, this seems to be a reasonable way to protect the rights of citizens in a representative democracy. But some claim that majority rule should not be permitted to deny rights to citizens. Consider gay marriage in this light. Voters in many states have gone to the polls and enacted laws or amendments to their state constitution that forbids gay marriage. Some argue, however, that marriage among consenting adults is a basic human right. In their view, the majority should not have the power to deny the right of marriage to gays and lesbians. Yet from a strictly procedural view, the anti-gay marriage laws and amendments are democratic. On the other hand, what about the rights of the minority of gays in those states? To limit the government's responsiveness to public opinion, we must look outside procedural democratic theory to substantive democratic theory.

substantive democratic theory
The view that democracy is embodied in the substance of government policies rather than in the policymaking procedure.

Substantive democratic theory focuses on the *substance* of government policies, not on the procedures followed in making those policies. It argues that in a democratic government, certain principles must be incorporated into government policies. Substantive theorists would reject a law that requires Bible reading in schools because it would violate a substantive principle, freedom of religion. The core of our substantive principles of democracy is embedded in the Bill of Rights and other amendments to the Constitution.

In defining the principles that underlie democratic government—and the policies of that government—most substantive theorists agree on a basic criterion: government policies should guarantee civil liberties (freedom of behavior, such as freedom of religion and freedom of expression) and civil rights (powers or privileges that government may not arbitrarily deny to individuals, such as protection against discrimination in employment and housing). According to this standard, the claim that the United States is a democracy rests on its record of ensuring its citizens these liberties and rights. (We look at how good this record is in Chapters 15 and 16.)

Agreement among substantive theorists breaks down when the discussion moves from civil rights to social rights (adequate health care, quality education, decent housing) and economic rights (private property, steady employment). Ordinary citizens divide on these matters too and can change their minds over time (see Figure 2.2). Theorists disagree most sharply on whether a government must promote social equality to qualify as a democracy. For example, must a state guarantee unemployment benefits and adequate public housing to be called democratic? Some insist that policies that promote social equality are essential to democratic government. Others restrict the requirements of substantive democracy to policies that safeguard civil liberties and civil rights. Americans differ considerably from the citizens of most other Western democracies in their view of the government's responsibility to provide

FIGURE 2.2 Health Care: Government's Responsibility?

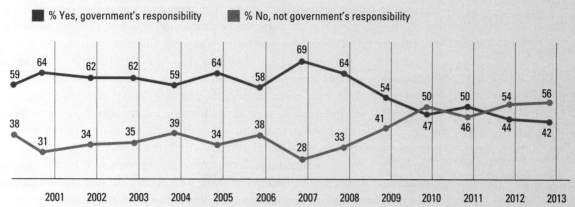

Is health care a right in a democracy like ours? Opinions change over time and, interestingly, support for the position that health care is government's responsibility began to drop before Barack Obama took office. There's a sharp partisan split, with Republicans more antagonistic toward a government role in health care and Democrats more supportive.

social policies. In most other Western democracies, there is much more support for the view that jobs and incomes for the unemployed are a right.[14]

A theorist's political ideology tends to explain his or her position on what democracy really requires in substantive policies. Conservative theorists have a narrow view of the scope of democratic government and a narrow view of the social and economic rights guaranteed by that government. Liberal theorists believe that a democratic government should guarantee its citizens a much broader spectrum of social and economic rights.

Procedural Democracy versus Substantive Democracy

The problem with the substantive view of democracy is that it does not provide clear, precise criteria that allow us to determine whether a government is democratic. It is, in fact, open to unending arguments over which government policies are truly democratic. Substantive theorists are free to promote their pet values—separation of church and state, guaranteed employment, equal rights for women—under the guise of substantive democracy. When Americans are asked to define democracy in their own terms, roughly two-thirds mention freedoms, rights, or liberties. Relatively few describe democracy in terms of the political process or social benefits.[15]

The procedural viewpoint also has a problem. Although it presents specific criteria for democratic government, those criteria can produce undesirable social policies, such as those that harm minorities. This clashes with **minority rights**, the idea that all citizens are entitled to certain things that cannot be denied by the majority. Opinions proliferate on what those "certain things" are, but nearly everyone in the United States would agree, for example, on freedom of religion. One way to protect minority rights is to limit the principle of majority rule—by requiring a two-thirds majority or some other extraordinary majority for decisions on certain subjects, for example. Another way is to put the issue in the Constitution, beyond the reach of majority rule.

minority rights
The benefits of government that cannot be denied to any citizen by majority decisions.

The issue of prayer in school is a good example of the limits on majority rule. No matter how large, majorities in Congress cannot pass a law to permit organized prayer in public schools because the U.S. Supreme Court has determined that the Constitution forbids such a law. The Constitution could be changed so that it would no longer protect religious minorities, but amending the Constitution is a cumbersome process that involves extraordinary majorities. When limits such as these are put on the principle of majority rule, the minority often rules instead.

Clearly, then, procedural democracy and substantive democracy are not always compatible. In choosing one instead of the other, we are also choosing to focus on either procedures or policies. As authors of this text, we favor a compromise. On the whole, we favor the procedural conception of democracy because it more closely approaches the classical definition of democracy: "government by the people." And procedural democracy is founded on clear, well-established rules for decision making. But the theory has a serious drawback: it allows a democratic government to enact policies that can violate the substantive principles of democracy. Thus, pure procedural democracy should be diluted so that minority rights and civil liberties are guaranteed as part of the structure of government. If the compromise seems familiar, it is: the approach has been used in the course of American history to balance legitimate minority and majority interests.

 # Institutional Models of Democracy

LO2 ★ Compare and contrast the majoritarian and pluralist models of democracy.

A small group can agree to make democratic decisions directly by using the principles of universal participation, political equality, and majority rule. But even the smallest nations have too many citizens to permit participatory democracy at the national level. If nations want democracy, they must achieve it through some form of representative government, electing officials to make decisions. Even then, democratic government is not guaranteed. Governments must have a way to determine what the people want, as well as some way to translate those wants into decisions. In other words, democratic government requires institutional mechanisms—established procedures and organizations—to translate public opinion into government policy (and thus be responsive). Elections, political parties, legislatures, and interest groups (which we discuss in later chapters) are all examples of institutional mechanisms in politics.

Some democratic theorists favor institutions that closely tie government decisions to the desires of the majority of citizens. If most citizens want laws banning the sale of pornography, the government should outlaw pornography. If citizens want more money spent on defense and less on social welfare (or vice versa), the government should act accordingly. For these theorists, the essence of democratic government is majority rule and responsiveness.

Other theorists place less importance on the principles of majority rule and responsiveness. They do not believe in relying heavily on mass opinion; instead, they favor institutions that allow groups of citizens to defend their interests in the public policymaking process. Global warming is a good example. Everyone cares about it, but it is a complex problem with many competing issues at stake. What is critical here is to allow differing interests to participate so that all sides have the opportunity to influence policies as they are developed.

Both schools hold a procedural view of democracy, but they differ in how they interpret "government by the people." We can summarize the theoretical positions by using two alternative models of democracy. As a model, each is a hypothetical plan, a blueprint for achieving democratic government through institutional mechanisms. The majoritarian model values participation by the people in general; the pluralist model values participation by the people in groups.

The Majoritarian Model of Democracy

The **majoritarian model of democracy** relies on our intuitive, elemental notion of what is fair. It interprets "government by the people" to mean government by the majority of the people. The majoritarian model tries to approximate the people's role in a direct democracy within the limitations of representative government. To force the government to respond to public opinion, the majoritarian model depends on several mechanisms that allow the people to participate directly.

The popular election of government officials is the primary mechanism for democratic government in the majoritarian model. Citizens are expected to control their representatives' behavior by choosing wisely in the first place and by reelecting or voting out public officials according to their performance. Elections fulfill the first three principles of procedural democratic theory: universal participation, political equality, and majority rule. The prospect of reelection and the threat of defeat at the polls are expected to motivate public officials to meet the fourth criterion: responsiveness.

Usually we think of elections only as mechanisms for choosing among candidates for public office. Majoritarian theorists also see them as a means for deciding government policies. An election on a policy issue is called a referendum. Twenty-four states allow their legislatures to place a policy question on the ballot and allow citizens to vote on it. When citizens circulate petitions and gather a required minimum number of signatures to put a policy question on a ballot, it is called an initiative. Twenty-four states (mostly the same ones) allow for initiatives. Eighteen states also allow the recall of state officials, a means of forcing a special election for an up-or-down vote on a sitting governor or state judge. Like initiatives, a specified percentage of registered voters must sign a petition asking that a vote be held.[16]

Arnd Wiegmann/Reuters

Now That's a Town Meeting

For almost 700 years, citizens of Appenzell Inner-Rhodes, the smallest canton (like a township) in Switzerland, have gathered in the town square on the last Sunday in April to make political decisions by raised hands. At a recent meeting, Appenzellers adopted a leash law for dogs, approved updating property files on a computer, chose a new building commissioner, and acted on other public business before adjourning until the next year.

majoritarian model of democracy
The classical theory of democracy in which government by the people is interpreted as government by the majority of the people.

For New Jersey Fast-Food Workers, Low Wages = Reliance on Government Support

42% of families of NJ low-wage fast-food workers rely on at least one safety net program

The annual cost?
$117 million

www.njpp.org

Source: The University of California's Institute for Research on Labor and Employment

NEW JERSEY POLICY PERSPECTIVE

In 2013, after the governor vetoed a bill to increase the state's minimum wage, New Jersey voters took matters into their own hands and approved a referendum to raise the minimum wage to $8.25 an hour. Annual cost of living increases were also mandated by the referendum.

Statewide initiatives and referenda have been used to decide a wide variety of important questions, many with national implications. Although they are instruments of majoritarian democracy, initiatives are often sponsored by interest groups trying to mobilize broad-based support for a particular policy. In the spring of 2011, the Republican-controlled legislature in Ohio passed a law designed to restrict unions representing municipal workers like police or school teachers. This angered many there, and an initiative placed the issue on the ballot for a statewide election in November of the same year. A clear majority (61 percent) voted to overturn the law.[17]

In the United States, no provisions exist for referenda at the federal level. Some other countries do allow policy questions to be put before the public. In a national vote in 2014, voters in Switzerland passed an initiative limiting the number of immigrants permitted to come into the country. Voters there were concerned about immigrants taking jobs away from Swiss citizens. The government opposed the initiative as it creates problems for Switzerland with other countries in Europe. Unlike most other countries of Europe, Switzerland is not a member of the European Union, which allows for free movement of citizens across the borders of member countries.[18] The majoritarian model contends that citizens can control their government if they have adequate mechanisms for popular participation. It also assumes that citizens are knowledgeable about government and politics, that they want to participate in the political process, and that they make rational decisions in voting for their elected representatives.

Critics contend that Americans are not knowledgeable enough for majoritarian democracy to work. They point to research that shows that only 36 percent of a national sample of voters said that they follow news about politics "very closely."[19] Thus, the average American doesn't pay much attention to the news, and this calls into question how informed public opinion is. In this light, should our policymakers place much credence in polls on policy questions?

Defenders of majoritarian democracy respond that although individual Americans may have only limited knowledge of or interest in government, the American public as a whole still has coherent and stable opinions on major policy questions. Public opinion does not fluctuate sharply or erratically, and change in the nation's views usually emerges incrementally. Change can emerge as different generations with different experiences and backgrounds come into the electorate (see "Freedom, Order, Equality, and Millennials"). People can hold broad if imprecise values that are manifested in the way they vote and in the opinions they express on particular issues.

An Alternative Model: Pluralist Democracy

For years, political scientists struggled valiantly to reconcile the majoritarian model of democracy with polls that showed widespread ignorance of politics among the American people. When 40 percent of the adult population doesn't even bother to vote in presidential elections, our form of democracy seems to be "government by *some* of the people."

The 1950s saw the evolution of an alternative interpretation of democracy, one tailored to the limited knowledge and participation of the real electorate, not an ideal one. It was based on the concept of pluralism—that modern society consists of innumerable groups that share economic, religious, ethnic, or cultural interests. Often people with similar interests organize formal groups—the Future Farmers of America, chambers of commerce, and animal protection groups are examples. Many social groups have little contact with government, but occasionally they find themselves backing or opposing government policies. An organized group that seeks to influence government policy is called an **interest group**. Many interest groups regularly spend much time and money

interest group
An organized group of individuals that seeks to influence public policy; also called a lobby.

Freedom, Order, Equality, and Millennials

Generations differ in their views on values involving freedom, order, and equality. Recent survey research shows stark differences between age cohorts on many important political issues and general attitudinal predispositions. So-called millennials, the youngest political age cohort (ages 18–33 at the time of the survey in 2014), are the most liberal of all age cohorts. In comparison, middle-aged Americans (ages 34–49) are more conservative and baby boomers (ages 50–68) are more conservative still. Are millennials forming a new majority in terms of public opinion? Will they swing America toward larger government and more liberal policies on such issues as immigration and gay marriage? There is no way of knowing for sure at this point, as there may be life cycle effects that will later moderate millennials' liberal views. "Life cycle" effects hypothesizes that young people become a little more conservative as they take on more responsibilities and pay more taxes as they grow older. We also don't know what generations that follow will believe. They could be even more liberal. Finally, what we do know is that millennials are characterized by a much larger proportion of minorities than older generations. As we'll discuss in later chapters, race and ethnicity are critical factors in the development of political opinions.

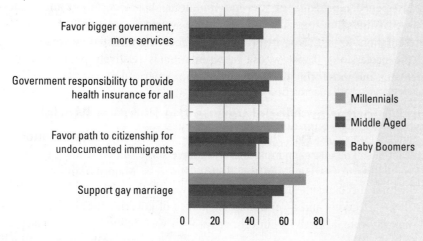

Source: *Millennials in Adulthood*, Pew Research Center, 7 March 2014.

Critical Thinking What might explain why millennials are different from older age cohorts in their political values and views? How might this generation change American politics?

trying to influence government policy (see Chapter 10). Among them are the International Brotherhood of Electrical Workers, the American Hospital Association, the National Association of Manufacturers, and the National Organization for Women.

The **pluralist model of democracy** interprets "government by the people" to mean government by people operating through competing interest groups. According to this model, democracy exists when many (plural) organizations operate separately from the government, press their interests on the government, and even challenge the government. Compared with majoritarian thinking, pluralist theory shifts the focus of democratic government from the mass electorate to organized groups. The criterion for democratic government changes from responsiveness to mass public opinion to responsiveness to organized groups of citizens.

pluralist model of democracy
An interpretation of democracy in which government by the people is taken to mean government by people operating through competing interest groups.

The two major mechanisms in a pluralist democracy are interest groups and a decentralized structure of government that provides ready access to public officials and is open to hearing the groups' arguments for or against government policies. In a centralized structure, decisions are made at one point: the top of the hierarchy. The few decision makers at the top are too busy to hear the claims of competing interest groups or consider those claims in making their decisions. But a decentralized, complex government structure offers the access and openness necessary for pluralist democracy. For pluralists, the ideal system is one that divides government authority among numerous institutions with overlapping authority. Under such a system, competing interest groups have alternative points of access for presenting and arguing their claims.

Although many scholars have contributed to the model, pluralist democracy is most closely identified with political scientist Robert Dahl. According to Dahl, the fundamental axiom of pluralist democracy is that "instead of a single center of sovereign power there must be multiple centers of power, none of which is or can be wholly sovereign."[20] Some watchwords of pluralist democracy, therefore, are divided authority, decentralization, and open access.

On one level, pluralism is alive and well. As will be demonstrated in Chapter 10, interest groups in Washington are thriving, and the rise of many citizen groups has broadened representation beyond traditional business, labor, and professional groups. At the same time, the interest group system is not one that provides equal representation for all. Not surprisingly, the best represented sectors are business and the professions. Those whose representation is relatively poor are low-income Americans and those who are most marginal in American society.[21]

The Majoritarian Model versus the Pluralist Model

In majoritarian democracy, the mass public—not interest groups—controls government actions. The citizenry must therefore have some understanding of government and be willing to participate in the electoral process. Majoritarian democracy relies on electoral mechanisms that harness the power of the majority to make decisions. Conclusive elections and a centralized structure of government are mechanisms that aid majority rule. Cohesive political parties with well-defined programs also contribute to majoritarian democracy because they offer voters a clear way to distinguish alternative sets of policies. In terms of Congress, American parties are becoming more majoritarian as there is more unity among both Republicans and Democrats.

Pluralism does not demand much knowledge from citizens in general. It requires specialized knowledge only from groups of citizens, in particular their leaders. In contrast to majoritarian democracy, pluralist democracy seeks to limit majority action so that interest groups can be heard. It relies on strong interest groups and a decentralized government structure—mechanisms that interfere with majority rule, thereby protecting minority interests. We could even say that pluralism allows minorities to rule.

An Undemocratic Model: Elite Theory

elite theory
The view that a small group of people actually makes most of the important government decisions.

If pluralist democracy allows minorities to rule, how does it differ from **elite theory**—the view that a small group (a minority) makes most important government decisions? According to elite theory, important government decisions are made by an identifiable and stable minority that shares certain characteristics, particularly vast wealth and business connections.[22]

Elite theory argues that these few individuals wield power in America because they control its key financial, communications, industrial, and government institutions.

Their power derives from the vast wealth of America's largest corporations and the perceived importance of the continuing success of those corporations to the growth of the economy. According to elite theory, the United States is not a democracy but an oligarchy.[23] Although the voters appear to control the government through elections, elite theorists argue that the powerful few in society manage to define the issues and constrain the outcomes of government decision making to suit their own interests. Clearly, elite theory describes a government that operates in an undemocratic fashion.

Elite theory appeals to many people, especially those who believe that wealth dominates politics. In the past few years, we have heard a lot about the "1 percent"—the top income stratum of this country whose vast wealth has sharply increased (see Chapter 10 for discussion of the Occupy Movement). The idea of a super wealthy group of political activists working their will in the political system has a great deal of resonance in the contemporary debate over public policy. This top stratum is highly active in politics, and some rich activists contribute vast sums to political campaigns.[24] Elite theory also provides plausible explanations for specific political decisions. Why, over the years, has the tax code included so many loopholes that favor the wealthy? The answer, claim adherents of elite theory, is that the policymakers never really change; they are all cut from the same cloth. Even when a liberal Democrat like Barack Obama is in the White House, many of the president's top economic policymakers are typically drawn from Wall Street or other financial institutions.

Political scientists have conducted numerous studies designed to test the validity of elite theory, but it has proven to be an exceptionally difficult idea to confirm in any conclusive manner. Perhaps the strongest evidence is the documentation of a correspondence between the preferences of the wealthy and policy outcomes. If the wealthy and the rest of the population are divided on a course of action by government, the wealthy are more likely to prevail (though not assured of doing so).[25] Another form of great influence is the elite's alleged power to keep issues off the political agenda. That is, its power derives from its ability to keep people from questioning fundamental assumptions about American capitalism.[26]

A contrary view of the notion of a power elite responds with skepticism. Although it's easy to assume that the super wealthy lean in a conservative direction with strong preferences for a small government that stays out of business markets and taxes them at low rates, the reality is that the top stratum includes people of all political points of view. There are many liberals who donate to progressive candidates and causes. Prior to the 2014 congressional elections, billionaire Tom Steyer said he would spend $100 million to help liberals get elected.[27] Moreover our government and society are enormous and enormously complex. If there were an elite that controlled American politics, what would be the coordinating mechanism that facilitated control by such a large number of individuals (the top 1 percent of earners is in the hundreds of thousands)? And if such an elite exerted such influence, why wouldn't it be clearly evident?

Consequently, elite theory remains part of the debate about the nature of American government. Social scientists continue to do research to try to determine whether we are truly ruled by a ruling class. Americans themselves are divided over whether American society is dominated by those who are wealthy (see Figure 2.3).

Rob Crandall/The Image Works

On Tonight's Menu, Lots of Green

Elitist critics of American government point to the advantages that the wealthy have in our political system. The campaign finance system contributes to this belief. This Washington fundraiser gives lobbyists and wealthy donors a chance to mingle with policymakers and remind them who supports them financially.

FIGURE 2.3 Americans Divided over Whether America Is Divided

Are we a nation of "haves" and "have nots"? In 1989, most Americans believed that the country was not divided. Over time, the proportion of those indicating that the country is divided into haves and have nots increased. The most recent poll (2011) to ask this question found a modest majority believing we are not divided into two camps.

Source: Lymari Morales, "Fewer Americans See U.S. Divided into 'Haves,' 'Have Nots,'" Gallup Poll, 15 December 2011. Copyright © 2011 Gallup, Inc. All rights reserved. The content is used with permission; however, Gallup retains all right of republication.

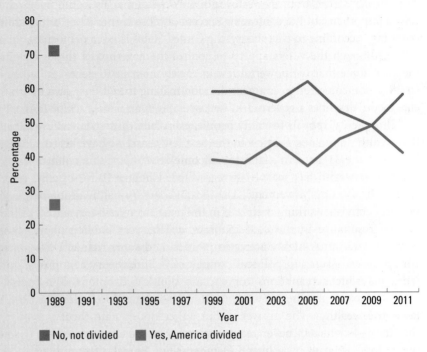

■ No, not divided   ■ Yes, America divided

Some people think of American society as divided into two groups—the "haves" and "have nots"—while others think it's incorrect to think of America that way. Do you, yourself, think of America as divided into haves and have nots, or don't you think of America that way? Note that the Gallup Poll did not ask this question between 1990 and 1998.

Elite Theory versus Pluralist Theory

The key difference between elite and pluralist theory lies in the durability of the ruling minority. In contrast to elite theory, pluralist theory does not define government conflict in terms of a minority versus the majority; instead, it sees many different interests vying with one another in each policy area. In the management of national forests, for example, many interest groups—logging companies, recreational campers, and environmentalists, for example—have joined the political competition. They press their various viewpoints on government through representatives who are well informed about how relevant issues affect group members. According to elite theory, the financial resources of big logging companies ought to win out over the arguments of campers and environmentalists, but this does not always happen.

Pluralist democracy makes a virtue of the struggle between competing interests. It argues for government that accommodates the struggle and channels the result into government action. According to pluralist democracy, the public is best served if the government structure provides access for different groups to press their claims in competition with one another. Note that pluralist democracy does not insist that all groups have equal influence on government decisions. In the political struggle, wealthy, well-organized groups have an inherent advantage over poorer, inadequately organized groups. In fact, unorganized segments of the population may not even get their concerns placed on the agenda for government consideration, which means that what government does not discuss (its "nondecisions") may be as significant as what it does discuss and decide. Indeed, studies of the congressional agenda demonstrate that it is characterized by little in the way of legislation concerned with poor or low-income Americans, while business-related bills are plentiful.[28] This is a critical weakness of pluralism, and critics relentlessly attack the theory because it appears to justify great disparities in levels of political organization and resources among different segments of society.[29]

The Global Challenge of Democratization

LO3 ★ Evaluate the challenges facing countries trying to move toward a democratic form of government.

We have proposed two models of democratic government. The majoritarian model conforms with classical democratic theory for a representative government. According to this model, democracy should be a form of government that features responsiveness to majority opinion. According to the pluralist model, a government is democratic if it allows minority interests to organize and press their claims on government freely.

No government actually achieves the high degree of responsiveness demanded by the majoritarian model. No government offers complete and equal access to the claims of all competing groups, as is required by an optimally democratic pluralist model. Still, some nations approach these ideals closely enough to be considered practicing democracies. There is no consensus among democracies as to what is preferable, majoritarian or pluralist government (see "Majoritarianism and Pluralism in Global Politics").

Establishing Democracies

Whether a political system is "democratic" is not a simple yes-or-no question.[30] Governments can meet some criteria for a procedural democracy (universal participation, political equality, majority rule, and government responsiveness to public opinion) and fail to meet others. They can also differ in the extent to which they support freedom of speech and freedom of association, which create the necessary conditions for the practice of democracy. Various scholars and organizations have developed complicated databases that rate countries on a long list of indicators, providing a means of comparing countries along all criteria.[31] Although the fall of communism in Eastern Europe and developments in other previously authoritarian countries led to an increase in democracies in the not-too-distant past, these past few years have seen a slight decline in the number of democracies around the world.[32] The reality is that **democratization** is a difficult process, and many countries fail completely or succeed only in the short run and lapse into a form of authoritarianism.[33] The "Arab Spring"—revolutions in Egypt, Tunisia, and Libya, and protest movements in other Arab countries—raised the hope that democracy would spread across the Middle East, but this has not been the case. Authoritarian regimes, some of them quite brutal, have maintained power in the Middle East, or in some cases, such as Egypt, democracy was stillborn as the military stepped in after the revolution and replaced a popularly elected government.

One reason that democratization can be so difficult is that ethnic and religious conflict is epidemic. Such conflict complicates efforts to democratize because antagonisms can run so deep that opposing groups do not want to grant political legitimacy to each other. A bitter irony of the United States' 2003 military overthrow of dictator Saddam Hussein's

COMPARE WITH YOUR PEERS
MindTap for American Government

Access the Majoritarian or Pluralistic Democracy Forum: Polling Activity—Choosing Democracy.

democratization
A process of transition as a country attempts to move from an authoritarian form of government to a democratic one.

Majoritarianism and Pluralism in Global Politics

As new democracies have emerged across the world, constitution writers have made decisions as to how to structure elections. One alternative is to design the electoral system to promote majoritarianism. Simply put, such systems use winner-take-all rules—the candidate or party that has the most votes wins. The United States has such a system for its legislative elections. The structure in the United States discourages minor parties, as a third party that receives 20 percent of the vote in every single congressional district will surely receive no seats in Congress. Instead, one of the major parties, the Republicans or the Democrats, will likely win each seat with more than 20 percent.

An alternative approach is proportional representation (PR). Under a PR system, each party running will receive seats in the legislature roughly proportional to the votes it gets. Thus, if there are 100 seats available in a legislature and a party wins 20 percent of the vote, it should receive about 20 seats (see Chapter 8). In a country using a PR system, there is more of an incentive for multiple parties to enter into the electoral systems. And not surprisingly, countries with PR systems do have more parties. Multiparty systems might include religious parties, environmental parties, anti-immigrant parties, and ethnic parties in addition to conventional conservative, moderate, and liberal parties. We can't equate PR systems with pluralist government per se because too many interests are not directly incorporated into parties, but PR systems are certainly more pluralistic than majoritarian systems.

Finally, electoral systems can combine the two. Mixed systems incorporate some proportional representation with majoritarian structures. They do this through voting at two or more levels of government or by allocating votes so as to elect some legislators by majority and some by PR.

As the figure on the following page illustrates, the trend across the world is toward PR and mixed systems and away from majoritarianism. It may be that new democracies prefer multiparty systems in the hope that a broader share of their population will see themselves as truly represented in the political system and will have more trust in the government.

regime in Iraq is that religious conflict between Sunnis and Shiites immediately came to the fore. These two branches of Islam reflect theological differences that have manifested themselves in the form of ethnic hatred. Iraq's steps toward democracy allowed enough freedom for open protest, and religious violence has continued to plague the country.

The political and economic instability that typically accompanies transitions to democracy makes new democratic governments vulnerable to attack by their opponents. The military will often revolt and take over the government on the ground that progress cannot occur until order is restored. As we noted in Chapter 1, all societies wrestle with the dilemma of choosing between freedom and order. The open political conflict that emerges in a new democracy may not be easily harnessed into a well-functioning government that tolerates opposition.[34] Still, a strong incentive toward democratization is that nations find it difficult to succeed economically in today's world without establishing a market economy, and market economies (that is, capitalism) give people substantial freedoms. There is a strong relationship between economic prosperity and democracy; countries that have free markets tend to protect political freedoms as well.[35] Thus, authoritarian rulers may see economic reforms that could make their countries more prosperous as a threat to their regime.

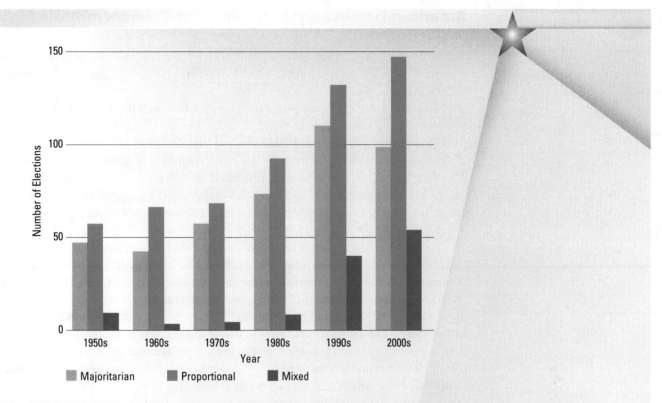

Source: Nils-Christian Bormann and Matt Golder, "Democratic Electoral Systems Around the World, 1946–2011," *Electoral Systems* 32 (2013): 360–369.

Critical Thinking For a newly emerging democracy, should constitution writers create a government facilitating majoritarian rule, or design an electoral system using proportional representation? Would the U.S. government work better if we had multiple parties instead of just two?

The United States has always faced a difficult foreign policy problem determining the degree to which it wants to invest in promoting democracy abroad. It is a noble goal, to be sure, but it may be difficult to impose democracy on a population that cannot accept the tolerance and freedoms allowed to all groups in society that democracy requires. Even as he wound down America's involvement in Iraq, President Obama found limited support for U.S. military intervention in Afghanistan.

Established democracies are also not free of the destabilizing effects of religious and ethnic conflict. Such countries usually try to cope with such pressures with some form of pluralism so that different groups feel they are being treated fairly by their government.[36] Indeed, majoritarian democracy can be risky where ethnic and religious rivalries endure because a majority faction can use its votes to suppress minorities. India, the world's largest democracy and a burgeoning economic power, is still plagued by periodic religious violence. In 2013 in a rural area of Uttar Pradesh, a state in the north of the country, Hindus rioted over an allegation that a Muslim man harassed a Hindu woman. The Hindus chased the Muslims out of their villages and even months later many Muslims were still too afraid to return to their homes.[37]

CONNECT WITH YOUR CLASSMATES
MindTap™ for American Government

Access the Majoritarian or Pluralist Democracy Forum: Discussion— Citizen Participation in a Majoritarian Democracy.

American Democracy: More Pluralist Than Majoritarian

It is not idle speculation to ask what kind of democracy is practiced in the United States. The answer can help us understand why our government can be called democratic despite a low level of citizen participation in politics and despite government actions that sometimes run contrary to public opinion.

Throughout this book, we probe to determine how well the United States fits the two alternative models of democracy: we judge that across all levels of government, the United States adheres more closely to the pluralist than the majoritarian model. Yet the pluralist model is far from a perfect representation of democracy. Its principal drawback is that it favors the well organized, and the poor are the least likely to be members of interest groups. Those who are affluent, have professional skills, and are active in the political system have significant advantages in our governmental process.[38]

In recent years, the parties have become more sharply divided along conservative and liberal dimensions, thus making our system a bit more majoritarian than has traditionally been the case. In particular, the two parties in Congress have become more ideologically homogeneous, thus giving voters a clearer opportunity to select a party more cohesive in its programmatic intent.[39] Yet this step toward majoritarianism has led to widespread criticism that our system of government is becoming too bitterly partisan. That is, as the members of Congress have become more ideological, they seem to have become less inclined to work together to achieve moderate, compromise solutions to the nation's problems. Some critics have also charged that ideological activists, who have mobilized more than moderates, have hijacked the parties and pulled them more sharply toward conservative and liberal extremes.[40] For those uncomfortable with more ideological parties, the continuing strong counterbalance of pluralism is welcome.

Given the survey data that show that the people's trust in American government has fallen over the years, it may seem that pluralist democracy is not serving us very well. Indeed, many Americans describe government and politicians in the harshest terms. Radio talk show hosts like Rush Limbaugh and politicians themselves pile invective on top of insult when they talk about what's wrong with Washington.[41] Compared with citizens in other developed nations, Americans fall in the middle concerning their satisfaction with democracy in the United States. But it's not at all clear that Americans would be more satisfied with another type of democracy.

This evaluation of the pluralist nature of American democracy may not mean much to you now. But you will learn that the pluralist model makes the United States look far more democratic than the majoritarian model would. Eventually, you will have to decide the answers to three questions:

1. Is the pluralist model truly an adequate expression of democracy, or is it a perversion of classical ideals, designed to portray America as democratic when it is not?
2. Does the majoritarian model result in a "better" type of democracy?
3. If it does, could new mechanisms of government be devised to produce a desirable mix of majority rule and minority rights?

Let these questions play in the back of your mind as you read more about the workings of American government in meeting the challenge of democracy.

Master the Topic of Majoritarian or Pluralistic Democracy? with MindTap™ for American Government

REVIEW MindTap™ for American Government
Access Key Term Flashcards for Chapter 2.

TEST YOURSELF MindTap™ for American Government
Take the Wrap It Up Quiz for Chapter 2.

STAY CURRENT MindTap™ for American Government
Access the KnowNow blog and customized RSS for updates on current events.

STAY FOCUSED MindTap™ for American Government
Complete the Focus Activities for Majoritarian or Pluralistic Democracy?

Summary

There are different forms of government around the world, one of which is democracy. But there is no one conception of democracy, and this chapter explores these differing beliefs about how a democracy ought to be constituted.

LO1 Distinguish between the two theories of democratic government used in political science: procedural and substantive.

- The procedural view of democracy emphasizes democratic processes. Four procedural elements seem paramount: universal participation, political equality, majority rule, and government responsiveness to public opinion. Substantive democratic theory focuses on the substance of policies rather than procedures. It holds that there are some rights that are so important that they should not be subject to being overturned by majority decision. Not surprisingly, procedural democracy can come into conflict with substantive democracy. What substantive policies should be beyond the control of popular opinion?

LO2 Compare and contrast the majoritarian and pluralist models of democracy.

- The majoritarian model of democracy is built around majority rule as evidenced by elections. Pluralist democracy conceives of democracy as a competition between opposing groups in society. Elite theorists believe that American government is dominated by a small set of wealthy individuals and large businesses.

LO3 Evaluate the challenges facing countries trying to move toward a democratic form of government.

- Although the number of democracies in the world increased for a time, this trend has leveled off. The process of democratization is difficult, and many democratizing countries fail and return to some form of authoritarianism. We compare the validity of majoritarian and pluralist models of democracy and conclude that the United States is a mix of both, but closer to pluralism. Majoritarian elements (such as more party-line voting in Congress) are on the rise, though.

Chapter Quiz

LO1 Distinguish between the two theories of democratic government used in political science: procedural and substantive.

1. How do procedural democracy and substantive democracy differ?
2. What is direct democracy? What is indirect democracy?

LO2 Compare and contrast the majoritarian and pluralist models of democracy.

1. What are the basic concepts of majoritarian democracy and of pluralist democracy?
2. What criticisms lie at the heart of elite theory?

LO3 Evaluate the challenges facing countries trying to move toward a democratic form of government.

1. How do political and economic instability affect the process of democratization?
2. What trends support the argument that the American system of democracy is becoming more majoritarian?

3 The Constitution

Learning Outcomes

LO1 Explain the reasons for the colonies' declaration of independence from British rule.

LO2 Identify the factors that led to the failure of the Confederation.

LO3 Explain the major points of contention in the writing of the Constitution.

LO4 Explain the contribution of the Constitution to the American political tradition and the principles it establishes.

LO5 Describe the actions taken to ensure the ratification of the Constitution.

LO6 Explain the procedures required to amend the Constitution.

LO7 Evaluate the extent to which the Constitution reflects and embodies the principles of majoritarian or pluralist democracy.

 WATCH & LEARN MindTap™ for American Government

Watch a brief "What Do You Know?" video summarizing The Constitution.

Michael Ventura/Alamy

Over two hundred years ago, former revolutionaries built the United States of America from British colonies by creating a "fundamental law," a Constitution, to guide its government. Today, European leaders are struggling to build a European Union under their own concept of fundamental law.

"You are the 'conventionists' of Europe. You therefore have the power vested in any political body: to succeed or to fail," claimed Chairman Valéry Giscard d'Estaing in his introductory speech on February 26, 2002, to the members of the Convention on the Future of Europe. The purpose of the convention, according to Giscard d'Estaing, was for the members to "agree to propose a concept of the European Union which matches our continental dimension and the requirements of the twenty-first century, a concept which can bring unity to our continent and respect for its diversity." If the members succeeded, he reassured them, no doubt they would in essence write "a new chapter in the history of Europe."[1] Integrating and governing twenty-eight nation-states with a total population

of 500 million are, to say the least, daunting tasks, especially considering that many of those nation-states at one time or another were bitter enemies.

The path to a European constitution has been strewn with pitfalls paralleling the American experience. Ratification required unanimity, which failed when presented to voters in several countries. The European Union (EU) finally took a step toward unity in 2009 with the adoption of the Reform Treaty. Although the process in 1787 on one side of the Atlantic may have differed from that on the other side in 2002, the political passions that these efforts spawned were equally intense and highlight the fragility inherent in designing a constitution. And no wonder. The questions that challenged America's founders and that confronted the women and men charged with setting a future course for Europe do not have easy or obvious answers. A thoughtful European observer asked the same kinds of questions that confronted the delegates at Philadelphia: "How can a balance be achieved in the representation of large and small states? How much

SAUL LOEB/AFP/Getty Images

Leader of the Pack

In 2012, French President François Hollande (left) deferred to German Chancellor Angela Merkel (right) at a meeting in Chicago. Germany remains the EU's economic powerhouse, and Merkel continues to call the shots in addressing the festering economic issues that have roiled the EU economy with ramifications worldwide. Operating with a single currency (the Euro), member states have largely bowed to Germany's economic might.

power should be conferred upon the federal level and what should be the jurisdiction of the EU today? What fundamental set of values underpins political unity? Is there a European equivalent to 'life, liberty and the pursuit of happiness'?"[2]

Economic forces continue to nag the EU as creditors question whether the debt-ridden nations of Greece, Ireland, Italy, Portugal, and Spain will be able to pay or refinance their bonds. To pay their debts, these nations have been forced to adopt painful policies, drastically reducing their spending and increasing their revenue through greater taxation. Complicating matters still further, constitutional courts in these debtor nations, relying on provisions of their own national constitutions, have invalidated several unpopular policies imposed by EU officials.[3]

To stave off collapse of the monetary union, EU leaders (with the exception of Great Britain) have agreed in principle to greater central authority over their respective economies. The EU's political union now hinges on three critical steps: the willingness of individual states to cede more political and economic control to a central government, the relaxation of the unanimity rule that gives any of the twenty-eight member nations a veto, and the assurance that EU law is superior to the laws of the member states.[4] These issues parallel similar choices Americans faced as their initial attempt at government proved unworkable.

The American experience is sure to shed light on the future of a single Europe. In fact, the American experience parallels the European story, since Americans' first step toward unity resulted in failure and then an effort at redesign that ultimately proved successful. This chapter poses questions about the U.S. Constitution. How did it evolve? What form did it take? What values does it reflect? How can it be altered? Which model of democracy—majoritarian or pluralist—does it fit better? In these answers may lie hints of the formidable tasks facing the EU as it moves toward greater political and economic unity.

The Revolutionary Roots of the Constitution

LO1 ★ Explain the reasons for the colonies' declaration of independence from British rule.

LISTEN & LEARN
MindTap® for American Government

Access Read Speaker to listen to Chapter 3.

The U.S. Constitution contains just 4,300 words. But those 4,300 words define the basic structure of our national government. (In contrast, the failed European constitution was more than 60,000 words long. The Reform Treaty is still longer at 68,500 words.) A comprehensive document, the Constitution divides the national government into three branches, describes the powers of those branches and their connections, outlines the interaction between the government and the governed, and describes the relationship between the national government and the states. The Constitution makes itself the supreme law of the land and binds every government official to support it.

Most Americans revere the Constitution as political scripture. To charge that a political action is unconstitutional is akin to claiming that it is unholy. So the Constitution has taken on symbolic value that strengthens its authority as the basis of American government.

The U.S. Constitution, written in 1787 for an agricultural society huddled along the coast of a wild new land, now guides the political life of a massive urban society in the postnuclear age. The stability of the Constitution—and of the political system it created—is all the more remarkable because the Constitution itself was rooted in revolution. How long on average do constitutions last? (See "Constitutions Come of Age in Global Politics," pp. 54–55.)

The U.S. Constitution was designed to prevent anarchy by forging a union of states. To understand the values embedded in the Constitution, we must understand its historical roots. They lie in colonial America, the revolt against British rule, and the failure of the Articles of Confederation that governed the new nation after the Revolution.

Freedom in Colonial America

Although they were British subjects, American colonists in the eighteenth century enjoyed a degree of freedom denied most other people in the world. In Europe, ancient customs and the relics of feudalism restricted private property, compelled support for established religions, and limited access to trades and professions. In America, landowners could control and transfer their property at will. In America, there were no compulsory payments to support an established church. In America, there was no ceiling on wages, as there was in most European countries, and no guilds of exclusive professional associations. In America, colonists enjoyed almost complete freedom of speech, press, and assembly.[5]

By 1763, Britain and the colonies had reached a compromise between imperial control and colonial self-government. America's foreign affairs and overseas trade were controlled by the king and Parliament, the British legislature; the rest was left to colonial rule. But the cost of administering the colonies was substantial. The colonists needed protection from the French and their American Indian allies during the Seven Years' War (1756–1763), an expensive undertaking. Because Americans benefited the most from that protection, their English countrymen argued, Americans should bear the cost.

The Road to Revolution

The British believed that taxing the colonies was the obvious way to meet the costs of administering the colonies. The colonists did not agree. They especially did not want to be taxed by a distant government in which they had no representation. Nevertheless, the Crown imposed a series of taxes (including a tax on all printed matter) on the colonies. In each instance, public opposition was widespread and immediate.

A group of citizens—merchants, lawyers, and prosperous traders—created an intercolonial association called the Sons of Liberty. This group destroyed taxed items (identified by special stamps) and forced the official stamp distributors to resign. In October 1765, residents of Charleston, South Carolina, celebrated the forced

Constitutions Come of Age in Global Politics

Compared with other constitutions across the world, the U.S. Constitution is an antique. Ratified in 1788, it is the world's second oldest constitution. (The tiny landlocked microstate of San Marino boasts the oldest constitution, dating to 1600.) But few 225-year-old antiques still work more or less as their designers intended. Other countries have constitutions, but they tend to come and go.

A national constitution is the fundamental law of a land. It must give voice to a set of inviolable principles that limit the powers of government by setting up governmental institutions and defining their relationships and patterns of authority. Even dictatorships require institutions through which to govern.

Some stable democracies lack a single document as a written constitution. Perhaps the most notable example is Britain, whose fundamental law inheres in other documents, such as the Magna Carta. Other democracies, like Brazil, have gone in the opposite direction by adopting "hyperconstitutions." Brazil tries to pack into its 1988 charter just about every facet of public life, making it one of the longest constitutions ever drafted, nearly six times the length of the U.S. Constitution.

How long do constitutions last? Constitutions have lasted only about seventeen years on average worldwide since 1789. The figure here illustrates many short life spans compared to long life spans, which vary by region and time. African constitutions survive on average ten years. Latin American constitutions last little more than twelve years. For example, the Dominican Republic and Haiti have changed their constitutions every three years. Constitutions in Western Europe last thirty-two years, while constitutions in Asia survive about nineteen years. From 1789 through World War I, the average life span of a constitution was twenty-one years. It has dropped to twelve years since the end of World War I. And whereas the life expectancy of individuals worldwide is increasing, the life expectancy of constitutions is not.

resignation of the colony's stamp distributor by displaying a British flag with the word *Liberty* sewn across it. (They were horrified when a few months later local slaves paraded through the streets calling for "Liberty!")[6]

Women resisted the hated taxes by joining together in symbolic and practical displays of patriotism. A group of young women calling themselves the Daughters of Liberty met in public to spin homespun cloth and encourage the elimination of British cloth from colonial markets. They consumed American food and drank local herbal tea as symbols of their opposition.[7] But their quiet pleas for a vote in a new government fell on deaf ears.[8]

On the night of December 16, 1773, a group of colonists in Massachusetts reacted to a British duty on tea by organizing the Boston Tea Party. A mob boarded three ships and emptied 342 chests of that valuable substance into Boston Harbor. The act of defiance and destruction could not be ignored. "The die is now cast," wrote George III. "The Colonies must either submit or triumph."[9] In an attempt to reassert British control over its recalcitrant colonists, Parliament in 1774 passed the Coercive (or "Intolerable") Acts. One act imposed a blockade on Boston until the tea was paid

Three reasons may explain constitutional durability: (1) they tend to derive from an open, participatory process; (2) they tend to be specific; and (3) they tend to be flexible through amendment and interpretation.

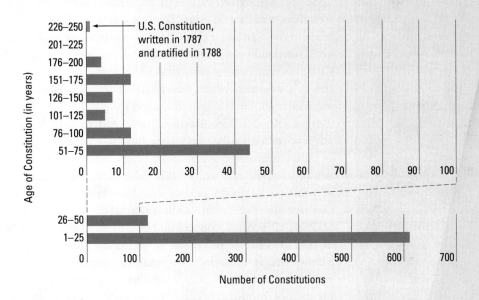

Source: Tom Ginsburg, Zack Elkins, and James Melton, "The Lifespan of Written Constitutions" (Paper No. 3, Law and Economics Workshop, University of California at Berkeley, 21 January 2008, available at http://repositories.cdlib.org/cgi/viewcontent.cgi?article=1212&context=berkeley_law_econ and http://www.loc.gov/law/help/guide/nations/sanmarino.html, accessed 12 February 2008). Thanks to Prof. Tom Ginsburg who graciously shared his data for the figure.

Critical Thinking What might be some of the advantages and disadvantages of having a durable constitution?

for; another gave royal governors the power to quarter British soldiers in private American homes. The taxation issue became secondary; more important was the conflict between British demands for order and American demands for liberty. The Virginia and Massachusetts assemblies summoned a continental congress, an assembly that would speak and act for the people of all the colonies.

All the colonies except Georgia sent representatives to the First Continental Congress, which met in Philadelphia in September 1774. The objective was to restore harmony between Great Britain and the American colonies. In an effort at unity, all colonies were given the same voting power—one vote each. A leader, called the president, was elected. (The terms *president* and *congress* in American government trace their origins to the First Continental Congress.) In October, the delegates adopted a statement of rights and principles; many of these later found their way into the Declaration of Independence and the Constitution. For example, the congress claimed a right "to life, liberty, and property" and a right "peaceably to assemble, consider of their grievances, and petition the king." Then the congress adjourned, planning to reconvene in May 1775.

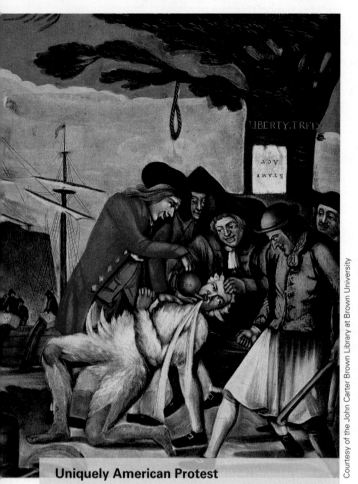

Courtesy of the John Carter Brown Library at Brown University

Uniquely American Protest

Americans protested the Tea Act (1773) by holding the Boston Tea Party (background, left) and by using a unique form of painful punishment, tarring and feathering, on the tax collector (see "STAMP ACT" upside-down on the Liberty Tree). An early treatise on the subject offered the following instructions: "First, strip a person naked, then heat the tar until it is thin, and pour upon the naked flesh, or rub it over with a tar brush. After which, sprinkle decently upon the tar, whilst it is yet warm, as many feathers as will stick to it." In an act of spite, Loyalists felled the tree for firewood during the siege of Boston (1775–1776).

Declaration of Independence
Drafted by Thomas Jefferson, the document that proclaimed the right of the colonies to separate from Great Britain.

social contract theory
The belief that the people agree to set up rulers for certain purposes and thus have the right to resist or remove rulers who act against those purposes.

Revolutionary Action

By early 1775, however, a movement that the colonists themselves were calling a revolution had already begun. Colonists in Massachusetts were fighting the British at Concord and Lexington. Delegates to the Second Continental Congress, meeting in May, faced a dilemma: Should they prepare for war, or should they try to reconcile with Britain? As conditions deteriorated, the Second Continental Congress remained in session to serve as the government of the colony-states while George III assembled a massive force to crush the rebellion once and for all.[10]

On June 7, 1776, owing in large part to the powerful advocacy of John Adams of Massachusetts, a strong supporter of independence, the Virginia delegation called on the Continental Congress to resolve "that these United Colonies are, and of right ought to be, free and Independent States, that they are absolved from all allegiance to the British Crown, and that all political connection between them and the State of Great Britain is, and ought to be, totally dissolved." This was a difficult decision. Independence meant disloyalty to Britain and war, death, and devastation. The congress debated but did not immediately adopt the resolution. A committee of five men was appointed to prepare a proclamation expressing the colonies' reasons for declaring independence.

The Declaration of Independence

Thomas Jefferson, a young farmer and lawyer from Virginia who was a member of the committee, became the "pen" to John Adams's "voice."[11] Because Jefferson was erudite, a Virginian, and an extremely skilled writer, he drafted the proclamation. Jefferson's document, the **Declaration of Independence**, was modestly revised by the committee and then further edited by the congress. It remains a cherished statement of our heritage, expressing simply, clearly, and rationally the many arguments for separation from Great Britain.

The principles underlying the Declaration were rooted in the writings of the English philosopher John Locke and had been expressed many times by speakers in the congress and the colonial assemblies. Locke argued that people have God-given, or natural, rights that are inalienable—that is, they cannot be taken away by any government. According to Locke, all legitimate political authority exists to preserve these natural rights and is based on the consent of those who are governed. The idea of consent is derived from **social contract theory**, which states that the people agree to establish rulers for certain purposes, but they have the right to resist or remove rulers who violate those purposes.[12]

Jefferson used similar arguments in the Declaration of Independence. Taking his cue from a draft of the Virginia Declaration of Rights,[13] Jefferson wrote,

We hold these truths to be self-evident, that all men are created equal, that they are endowed by their Creator with certain unalienable rights, that among these are life, liberty, and the pursuit of happiness. That to secure these rights, governments are instituted among men, deriving their just powers from the consent of the governed. That whenever any form of government becomes destructive of these ends, it is the right of the people to alter or to abolish it, and to institute new government, laying its foundation on such principles, and organizing its power in such form, as to them shall seem most likely to effect their safety and happiness.

Historian Jack Rakove maintains that Jefferson was not proposing equality for individuals. Rather, he was asserting the equality of peoples to enjoy the same rights of self-government that other peoples enjoyed. "It was the collective right of revolution and self-government that the Declaration was written to justify—not a visionary or even utopian notion of equality within American society itself."[14]

Jefferson went on to list the many deliberate acts of the king that had exceeded the legitimate role of government. The last and lengthiest item on Jefferson's original draft of the Declaration was the king's support of the slave trade. Although Jefferson did not condemn slavery, he denounced the king for enslaving a people, engaging in the slave trade, and proposing that if the slaves were freed, they would attack their masters. When South Carolina and Georgia, two states with an interest in continuing the wretched practice, objected, Jefferson and the committee dropped the offending paragraph. Finally, Jefferson declared that the colonies were "Free and Independent States," with no political connection to Great Britain.

To restate the argument in its simplest terms: (1) the people have a right to revolt if they determine that their government is denying them their legitimate rights; and (2) the long list of the king's actions was evidence of such denial; therefore (3) the people had the right to rebel, to form a new government.

On July 2, 1776, the Second Continental Congress finally voted for independence. The vote was by state, and the motion carried 11–0. (Rhode Island was not present, and the New York delegation, lacking instructions, did not cast its yea vote until July 15.) Two days later, on July 4, the Declaration of Independence was approved, with few changes. Several representatives insisted on removing language they thought would incite the colonists. In the end, even though Jefferson's compelling words were left almost exactly as he had written them, the adjustments tugged at the Virginian's personal insecurities. According to historian Joseph Ellis, while the congress debated various changes to the document, "Jefferson sat silently and sullenly, regarding each proposed revision as another defacement."[15]

By August, fifty-five revolutionaries had signed the Declaration of Independence, pledging "our lives, our fortunes and our sacred honor" in support of their rebellion against the world's most powerful nation. This was no empty pledge: an act of rebellion was treason. Had they lost the Revolutionary War, the signers would have faced a gruesome fate.

Lafayette College Art Collection

MOHAMED ABD EL GHANY/Reuters/Corbis

Stomping Out Tyrants: Then and Now

A gilded equestrian statue of George III once stood at the tip of Manhattan. On July 9, 1776, citizens responded to the news of the Declaration of Independence by toppling the statue. It was melted down and converted into musket balls. In 2011, Egyptians aided by the military removed their long-time dictator, Hosni Mubarak, and elected Mohammed Morsi as president. But Morsi quickly lost legitimacy and he too was removed, again by a military coup in 2013. These protestors display their opposition to Morsi by showing the soles of their shoes, a powerful symbol of disrespect in Arab culture.

H. Armstrong Roberts/ClassicStock/Alamy

Voting for Independence

The Second Continental Congress voted for independence on July 2, 1776. John Adams of Massachusetts viewed the day "as the most memorable epocha [significant event] in the history of America." In this painting by John Trumbull, the drafting committee presents the Declaration of Independence to the patriots who would later sign it. The committee, grouped in front of the desk, consisted of (*from left to right*) Adams, Roger Sherman (Connecticut), Robert Livingston (New York), Thomas Jefferson (Virginia), and Benjamin Franklin (Pennsylvania).

Trumbull painted the scene years after the event. Relying on Jefferson's faulty memory and his own artistic license, Trumbull created a scene that bears little resemblance to reality. First, there was no ceremonial moment when the committee presented its draft to the congress. Second, the room's elegance belied its actual appearance. Third, the doors are in the wrong place. Fourth, the heavy drapes substitute for actual venetian blinds. And, fifth, the mahogany armchairs replaced the plain Windsor design used by the delegates. Nevertheless, the painting remains an icon of American political history.

The punishment for treason was hanging and drawing and quartering—the victim was hanged until half-dead from strangulation, then disemboweled, and finally cut into four pieces while still alive. We celebrate the Fourth of July with fireworks and flag waving, parades, and picnics. We sometimes forget that the Revolution was a matter of life and death. The term *revolution* belies a fundamental feature of this conflict: it was a civil war "polarizing communities, destroying friendships, [and] dividing families."[16] As one noteworthy example, Benjamin Franklin's only son William was a loyalist.

The war imposed an agonizing choice on colonial Catholics, who were treated with intolerance by the overwhelmingly Protestant population. No other religious group found the choice so difficult. Catholics could either join the revolutionaries, who were opposed to Catholicism, or remain loyal to England and risk new hostility and persecution. But Catholics were few in number, perhaps 25,000 at the time of independence (or 1 percent of the population). Anti-Catholic revolutionaries recognized that if Catholics opposed independence in Maryland and Pennsylvania, where their numbers were greatest, victory might be jeopardized. Furthermore, enlisting the support of Catholic France for the cause of independence would be difficult in the face of strong opposition from colonial Catholics. So the revolutionaries wooed Catholics to their cause.[17]

The War of Independence lasted far longer than anyone expected. It began in a moment of confusion, when a shot rang out as British soldiers approached the town of Lexington, Massachusetts, on April 19, 1775. The end came six and a half years later with Lord Cornwallis's surrender of his army of 6,000 at Yorktown, Virginia, on October 19, 1781. It was a costly war: a greater percentage of the population died or was wounded during the Revolution than in any other U.S. conflict except the Civil War. And, until the Vietnam War, it was the longest conflict.[18]

Still, one in five colonists remained loyal to the British Crown. In New York, several hundred signed their own declaration of dependence. Prominent family names were easy to spot. But most signers were ordinary people: carpenters and blacksmiths, farmers, bakers, and perfumers. The document lacked Jefferson's rhetorical force, however. After the war, the loyalists were stripped of their rights, property, and dignity. As many as 80,000 abandoned the new United States for other parts of the British Empire. About half headed north to Canada, including 3,000 blacks, former slaves who secured their freedom by fighting for the British. In another migration, 1,200 of these former slaves relocated in 1792 to Sierra Leone, where they formed an experimental free black colony.[19]

With hindsight, of course, we can see that the British were engaged in an arduous and perhaps hopeless conflict. America was simply too vast to subdue without imposing total military rule. Britain also had to transport men and supplies over the enormous distance of the Atlantic Ocean. Also, the Americans' courtship of Britain's rivals, owing in large part to the indefatigable advocacy and diplomacy of John Adams,[20] resulted in support from the French navy and several million dollars in Dutch loans that helped to bolster General Washington's revolutionary forces. Finally, although the Americans had neither paid troops nor professional soldiers, they were fighting for a cause: the defense of their liberty. The British never understood the power of this fighting faith or, given the international support for the American cause, the totality of the forces arrayed against them.

From Revolution to Confederation

LO2 ★ Identify the factors that led to the failure of the Confederation.

By declaring their independence from England, the colonists left themselves without any real central government. So the revolutionaries proclaimed the creation of a **republic**. Strictly speaking, a republic is a government without a monarch, but the term had come to mean a government based on the consent of the governed, whose power is exercised by representatives who are responsible to them. A republic need not be a democracy, and this was fine with the founders; at that time, democracy was associated with mob rule and instability (see Chapter 2). The revolutionaries were less concerned with determining who would control their new government than with limiting its powers. They had revolted in the name of liberty, and now they wanted a government with strictly defined powers. To make sure they got one, they meant to define its structure and powers in writing.

republic
A government without a monarch; a government rooted in the consent of the governed, whose power is exercised by elected representatives responsible to the governed.

The Articles of Confederation

Barely a week after the Declaration of Independence was signed, the Second Continental Congress received a committee report entitled "Articles of Confederation and Perpetual Union." A **confederation** is a loose association of independent states that agree to cooperate on specified matters. In a confederation, the states retain their sovereignty, which means that each has supreme power within its borders. The central government is weak; it can only coordinate, not control, the actions of its sovereign states. Consequently, the individual states are strong.

The congress debated the **Articles of Confederation**, the compact among the thirteen original colonies that established the first government of the United States, for more than a year. The Articles were adopted by the Continental Congress on November 15, 1777, and finally took effect on March 1, 1781, following the required approval by all thirteen states. For more than three years, then, Americans had fought a revolution without an effective government. Raising money, troops, and supplies for the war had daunted and exhausted the leadership.

The Articles jealously guarded state sovereignty; their provisions clearly reflected the delegates' fears that a strong central government would resemble British rule. Article II, for example, stated, "Each state retains its sovereignty, freedom, and

confederation
A loose association of independent states that agree to cooperate on specified matters.

Articles of Confederation
The compact among the thirteen original states that established the first government of the United States.

independence, and every power, jurisdiction, and right, which is not by this Confederation expressly delegated to the United States, in Congress assembled."

Under the Articles, each state, regardless of its size, had one vote in the congress. Votes on financing the war and other important issues required the consent of at least nine of the thirteen states. The common danger, Britain, had forced the young republic to function under the Articles, but this first effort at government was inadequate to the task. The delegates had succeeded in crafting a national government that was largely powerless.

The Articles failed for at least four reasons. First, they did not give the national government the power to tax. As a result, the congress had to plead for money from the states to pay for the war and carry on the affairs of the new nation. A government that cannot reliably raise revenue cannot expect to govern effectively. Second, the Articles made no provision for an independent leadership position to direct the government (the president was merely the presiding officer of the congress). The omission was deliberate—the colonists feared the reestablishment of a monarchy—but it left the nation without a leader. Third, the Articles did not allow the national government to regulate interstate and foreign commerce. (When John Adams proposed that the confederation enter into a commercial treaty with Britain after the war, he was asked, "Would you like one treaty or thirteen, Mr. Adams?")[21]

Finally, the Articles could not be amended without the unanimous agreement of the congress and the assent of all the state legislatures; thus, each state had the power to veto any changes to the confederation.

The goal of the delegates who drew up the Articles of Confederation was to retain power in the states. This was consistent with republicanism, which viewed the remote power of a national government as a danger to liberty. In this sense alone, the Articles were a grand success. They completely hobbled the infant government.

Disorder Under the Confederation

Once the Revolution had ended and independence was a reality, it became clear that the national government had neither the economic nor the military power to function effectively. Freed from wartime austerity, Americans rushed to purchase goods from abroad. The national government's efforts to restrict foreign imports were blocked by exporting states, which feared retaliation from their foreign customers. Debt mounted and, for many, bankruptcy followed.

The problem was particularly severe in Massachusetts, where high interest rates and high state taxes were forcing farmers into bankruptcy. In 1786, Daniel Shays, a Revolutionary War veteran, marched on a western Massachusetts courthouse with fifteen hundred supporters armed with barrel staves and pitchforks: they were protesting against high taxes levied by the state to retire its wartime debt.[22] Later, they attacked an arsenal. Called Shays's Rebellion, the revolt against the established order continued into 1787. Massachusetts appealed to the confederation for help. Horrified by the threat of domestic upheaval, the congress approved a $530,000 requisition for the establishment of a national army. But the plan failed: every state except Virginia rejected the request for money. Finally, the governor of Massachusetts called out the militia and restored order.[23]

The rebellion demonstrated the impotence of the confederation and the urgent need to suppress insurrections and maintain domestic order. Proof to skeptics that Americans could not govern themselves, the rebellion alarmed all American leaders, with the exception of Jefferson. From Paris, where he was serving as American ambassador, he remarked, "A little rebellion now and then is a good thing; the tree of liberty must be refreshed from time to time with the blood of patriots and tyrants."[24]

From Confederation to Constitution

LO3 ★ Explain the major points of contention in the writing of the Constitution.

Order, the original purpose of government, was breaking down under the Articles of Confederation. The "league of friendship" envisioned in the Articles was not enough to hold the nation together in peacetime.

Some states had taken halting steps toward encouraging a change in the national government. In 1785, Massachusetts asked the congress to revise the Articles of Confederation, but the congress took no action. In 1786, Virginia invited the states to attend a convention at Annapolis, Maryland, to explore revisions aimed at improving commercial regulation. The meeting was both a failure and a success. Only five states sent delegates, but they seized the opportunity to call for another meeting—with a far broader mission—in Philadelphia the next year. That convention would be charged with devising "such further provisions as shall appear … necessary to render the constitution of the Federal Government adequate to the exigencies of the Union." The congress later agreed to the convention but limited its mission to "the sole and express purpose of revising the Articles of Confederation."[25]

Shays's Rebellion lent a sense of urgency to the task before the Philadelphia convention. The congress's inability to confront the rebellion was evidence that a stronger national government was necessary to preserve order and property—to protect the states from internal as well as external dangers. "While the Declaration was directed against an excess of authority," observed Supreme Court Justice Robert H. Jackson some one hundred fifty years later, "the Constitution [that followed the Articles of Confederation] was directed against anarchy."[26]

Twelve of the thirteen states named seventy-four delegates to convene in Philadelphia, the most important city in America, in May 1787. (Rhode Island, derisively renamed "Rogue Island" by a Boston newspaper, was the one exception. The state legislature sulkily rejected participating because it feared a strong national government.) Fifty-five delegates eventually showed up at the statehouse in Philadelphia, but no more than thirty were present at any one time during that sweltering spring and summer. The framers were not demigods, but many historians believe that such an assembly will not be seen again. Highly educated, they typically were fluent in Latin and Greek. Products of the Enlightenment, they relied on classical liberalism for the Constitution's philosophical underpinnings.

They were also veterans of the political intrigues of their states, and so were highly practical politicians who knew how to maneuver. In the words of a leading historian, "The framers built their Constitution with the bricks and mortar of political compromise."[27] Although well versed in ideas, they subscribed to the view expressed by one delegate that "experience must be our only guide, reason may mislead us."[28] Fearing for their fragile union, the delegates resolved to keep their proceedings secret. Theirs was a two-fold task: to build a stronger national government and to build a republican government, that is, one based on the consent of the people. Each task was daunting; both combined seemed irreconcilable.[29]

National Gallery of Art/Alamy

"Remember the Ladies"

Abigail Adams, the wife of Continental Congress delegate and future president John Adams, corresponded frequently with her powerful husband. In one such letter on the eve of independence she wrote, "I desire that you would Remember the Ladies, and be more generous and favorable to them. … If particular care and attention is not paid to the Ladies we are determined to foment a Rebellion, and will not hold ourselves bound by any Laws in which we have no Voice, or Representation."

The Constitutional Convention, at the time called the Federal Convention, officially opened on May 25. Within the first week, Edmund Randolph of Virginia had presented a long list of changes, suggested by fellow Virginian James Madison, that would replace the weak confederation of states with a powerful national government rather than revise it within its original framework. The delegates unanimously agreed to debate Randolph's proposal, called the **Virginia Plan**. Almost immediately, then, they rejected the idea of amending the Articles of Confederation, working instead to create an entirely new constitution.

The Virginia Plan

The Virginia Plan dominated the convention's deliberations for the rest of the summer, making several important proposals for a strong central government:

- That the powers of the government be divided among three separate branches: a **legislative branch**, for making laws; an **executive branch**, for enforcing laws; and a **judicial branch**, for interpreting laws.
- That the legislature consist of two houses. The first would be chosen by the people, the second by the members of the first house from among candidates nominated by the state legislatures.
- That each state's representation in the legislature be in proportion to the taxes it paid to the national government or in proportion to its free population.
- That an executive, consisting of an unspecified number of people, be selected by the legislature and serve for a single term.
- That the national judiciary include one or more supreme courts and other, lower courts, with judges appointed for life by the legislature.
- That the executive and a number of national judges serve as a council of revision, to approve or veto (disapprove) legislative acts. Their veto could be overridden by a vote of both houses of the legislature.
- That the scope of powers of all three branches be far greater than that assigned the national government by the Articles of Confederation and that the legislature be empowered to override state laws.

By proposing a powerful national legislature that could override state laws, the Virginia Plan clearly advocated a new form of government. It was to have a mixed structure, with more authority over the states and new authority over the people.

Madison was a monumental force in the ensuing debate on the proposals. He kept records of the proceedings that reveal his frequent and brilliant participation and give us insight into his thinking about freedom, order, and equality.

For example, his proposal that senators serve a nine-year term reveals his thinking about equality. Madison foresaw an increase "of those who will labor under all the hardships of life, and secretly sigh for a more equal distribution of its blessings. These may in time outnumber those who are placed above the feelings of indigence."[30] Power, then, could flow into the hands of the numerous poor. The stability of the senate, however, with its nine-year terms and election by the state legislatures, would provide a barrier against the "sighs of the poor" for more equality. Although most delegates shared Madison's apprehension about equality, the nine-year term was voted down.

The Constitution that emerged from the convention bore only a partial resemblance to the document Madison wanted to create. He endorsed seventy-one specific proposals, but he ended up on the losing side on forty of them.[31] And the parts of the Virginia Plan that were ultimately included in the Constitution were not adopted without challenge. Conflicts revolved primarily around the basis for representation in the legislature, the method of choosing legislators, and the structure of the executive branch.

Virginia Plan
A set of proposals for a new government, submitted to the Constitutional Convention of 1787; it included separation of the government into three branches, division of the legislature into two houses, and proportional representation in the legislature.

legislative branch
The lawmaking branch of government.

executive branch
The law-enforcing branch of government.

judicial branch
The law-interpreting branch of government.

The New Jersey Plan

When in 1787 it appeared that much of the Virginia Plan would be approved by the big states, the small states united in opposition. They feared that if each state's representation in the new legislature was based only on the size of its population, the states with large populations would be able to dominate the new government and the needs and wishes of the small states would be ignored. William Paterson of New Jersey introduced an alternative set of resolutions, written to preserve the spirit of the Articles of Confederation by amending rather than replacing them. The **New Jersey Plan** included the following proposals:

- That a single-chamber legislature have the power to raise revenue and regulate commerce.
- That the states have equal representation in the legislature and choose its members.
- That a multiperson executive be elected by the legislature, with powers similar to those proposed under the Virginia Plan but without the right to veto legislation.
- That a supreme tribunal be created, with a limited jurisdiction. (There was no provision for a system of national courts.)
- That the acts of the legislature be binding on the states—that is, that they be regarded as "the supreme law of the respective states," with the option of force to compel obedience.

After only three days of deliberation, the New Jersey Plan was defeated in the first major convention vote, 7–3. However, the small states had enough support to force a compromise on the issue of representation in the legislature. Table 3.1 compares the New Jersey Plan with the Virginia Plan.

New Jersey Plan
Submitted by the head of the New Jersey delegation to the Constitutional Convention, a set of nine resolutions that would have, in effect, preserved the Articles of Confederation by amending rather than replacing them.

The Great Compromise

The Virginia Plan provided for a two-chamber legislature, with representation in both chambers based on population. The idea of two chambers was never seriously challenged, but the idea of representation according to population stirred up heated and prolonged debate. The small states demanded equal representation for all states, but another vote rejected that concept for the House of Representatives. The debate continued. Finally, the Connecticut delegation moved that each state have an equal vote in the Senate. Still another poll showed that the delegations were equally divided on this proposal.

TABLE 3.1	Major Differences Between the Virginia Plan and the New Jersey Plan	
Characteristic	**Virginia Plan**	**New Jersey Plan**
Legislature	Two chambers	One chamber
Legislative power	Derived from the people	Derived from the states
Executive	Unspecified size	More than one person
Decision rule	Majority	Extraordinary majority
State laws	Legislature can override	National law is supreme
Executive removal	By Congress	By a majority of the states
Courts	National judiciary	No provision for national judiciary
Ratification	By the people	By the states

Great Compromise
Submitted by the Connecticut delegation to the Constitutional Convention, and thus also known as the Connecticut Compromise, a plan calling for a bicameral legislature in which the House of Representatives would be apportioned according to population and the states would be represented equally in the Senate.

A committee was created to resolve the deadlock. It consisted of one delegate from each state, chosen by secret ballot. After working straight through the Independence Day recess, the committee reported reaching the **Great Compromise** (sometimes called the Connecticut Compromise). Representation in the House of Representatives would be apportioned according to the population of each state. Initially, there would be fifty-six members. Revenue-raising acts would originate in the House. Most important, the states would be represented equally in the Senate, with two senators each. Senators would be selected by their state legislatures, not directly by the people. The deadlock broke when the Massachusetts delegation divided evenly, allowing the equal state vote to pass by the narrowest of margins, 5 states to 4.[32] The small states got their equal representation, the big states their proportional representation. The small states might dominate the Senate and the big states might control the House, but because all legislation had to be approved by both chambers, neither group would be able to dominate the other. To be perpetually assured of state equality, no amendment to the Constitution could violate the equal state representation principle.[33] If the meaning of democracy rests on the "one person, one vote" principle, then the state equality rule must be among the most undemocratic features of the U.S. Constitution.

Compromise on the Presidency

Conflict replaced compromise when the delegates turned to the executive branch. They did agree on a one-person executive, a president, but they disagreed on how the executive would be selected and what the term of office would be. The delegates distrusted the people's judgment; some feared that popular election of the president would arouse public passions. Consequently, the delegates rejected the idea. At the same time, representatives of the small states feared that election by the legislature would allow the big states to control the executive.

electoral college
A body of electors chosen by voters to cast ballots for president and vice president.

Once again, a committee composed of one member from each participating state was chosen to find a compromise. That committee fashioned the cumbersome presidential election system we still use today, the **electoral college**. (The Constitution does not use the expression *electoral college*.) Under this system, a group of electors would be chosen for the sole purpose of selecting the president and vice president. Each state legislature would choose a number of electors equal to the number of its representatives in Congress. Each elector would then vote for two people. The candidate with the most votes would become president, provided that the number of votes constituted a majority; the person with the next-greatest number of votes would become vice president. (The procedure was changed in 1804 by the Twelfth Amendment, which mandates separate votes for each office.) If no candidate won a majority, the House of Representatives would choose a president, with each state casting one vote.

The electoral college compromise eliminated the fear of a popular vote for president. At the same time, it satisfied the small states. If the electoral college failed to elect a president, which the delegates expected would happen, election by the House would give every state the same voice in the selection process. Finally, the delegates agreed that the president's term of office should be four years and that presidents should be eligible for reelection with no limit on the number of terms any individual president could serve. (The Twenty-Second Amendment, ratified in 1951, now limits the presidency to two terms.)

The delegates also realized that removing a president from office would be a serious political matter. For that reason, they involved both of the other two branches of government in the process. The House alone was empowered to charge a president with "Treason, Bribery, or other high Crimes and Misdemeanors" (Article II, Section 4), by a majority vote. The Senate was given the sole power to try the president on the House's charges. It could convict, and thus remove, a president only by a two-thirds vote (an **extraordinary majority**, a majority greater than the minimum of 50 percent plus one). And the chief justice of the Supreme Court was required to preside over the Senate trial. Only two presidents have been impeached by the House: Andrew Johnson and Bill Clinton; neither was convicted.

extraordinary majority
A majority greater than the minimum of 50 percent plus one.

The Final Product

LO4 ★ Explain the contribution of the Constitution to the American political tradition and the principles it establishes.

Once the delegates had resolved their major disagreements, they dispatched the remaining issues relatively quickly. A committee was then appointed to organize and write up the results of the proceedings. Twenty-three resolutions had been debated and approved by the convention; these were reorganized under seven articles in the draft constitution. The preamble, which was the last section to be drafted, begins with a phrase that would have been impossible to write when the convention opened. This single sentence contains four elements that form the foundation of the American political tradition:[34]

- *It creates a people:* "We the people of the United States" was a dramatic departure from a loose confederation of states.
- *It explains the reason for the Constitution:* "in order to form a more perfect Union" was an indirect way of saying that the first effort, the Articles of Confederation, had been inadequate.
- *It articulates goals:* "[to] establish Justice, insure domestic Tranquility, provide for the common defence, promote the general Welfare, and secure the Blessings of Liberty to ourselves and our Posterity"—in other words, the government exists to promote order and freedom.
- *It fashions a government:* "do ordain and establish this Constitution for the United States of America."

The Basic Principles

In creating the Constitution, the founders relied on four political principles— republicanism, federalism, separation of powers, and checks and balances—that together established a revolutionary new political order.

Republicanism is a form of government in which power resides in the people and is exercised by their elected representatives. The idea of republicanism may be traced to the Greek philosopher Aristotle (384–322 B.C.), who advocated a constitution that combined principles of both democratic and oligarchic government. The framers were determined to avoid aristocracy (rule by a hereditary class), monarchy (rule by one person), and direct democracy (rule by the people). A republic was both new and daring: no people had ever been governed by a republic on so vast a scale.

republicanism
A form of government in which power resides in the people and is exercised by their elected representatives.

federalism
The division of power between a central government and regional governments.

The framers themselves were far from sure that their government could be sustained. They had no model of republican government to follow; moreover, republican government was thought to be suitable only for small territories, where the interests of the public would be obvious and the government would be within the reach of every citizen. After the convention ended, Benjamin Franklin was asked what sort of government the new nation would have. "A republic," the old man replied, "if you can keep it."

Federalism is the division of power between a central government and regional governments. Citizens are thus subject to two different bodies of law. Federalism can be seen as standing between two competing government schemes. On the one side is unitary government, in which all power is vested in a central authority. On the other side stands confederation, a loose union of powerful states. In a confederation, the states surrender some power to a central government but retain the rest. The Articles of Confederation, as we have seen, divided power between loosely knit states and a weak central government. The Constitution also divides power between the states and a central government, but it confers substantial powers on a national government at the expense of the states.

According to the Constitution, the powers vested in the national and state governments are derived from the people, who remain the ultimate sovereigns. National and state governments can exercise their power over people and property within their spheres of authority. But at the same time, by participating in the electoral process or by amending their governing charters, the people can restrain both the national and the state governments if necessary to preserve liberty.

The Constitution lists the powers of the national government and the powers denied to the states. All other powers remain with the states. Generally, the states are required to give up only the powers necessary to create an effective national government; the national government is limited in turn to the powers specified in the Constitution. Despite the specific lists, the Constitution does not clearly describe the spheres of authority within which the powers can be exercised. As we will discuss in Chapter 4, limits on the exercise of power by the national government and the states have evolved as a result of political and military conflicts; moreover, the limits have proved changeable.

Separation of powers and checks and balances are two distinct principles, but both are necessary to ensure that one branch does not dominate the government. **Separation of powers** is the assignment of the lawmaking, law-enforcing, and law-interpreting functions of government to independent legislative, executive, and judicial branches, respectively. Separation of powers safeguards liberty by ensuring that all government power does not fall into the hands of a single person or group of people. However, the Constitution constrained majority rule by limiting the people's direct influence on the electoral process (see Figure 3.1). In theory, separation of powers means that one branch cannot exercise the powers of the other branches. In practice, however, the separation is far from complete. One scholar has suggested that what we have instead is "separate institutions sharing powers."[35]

Checks and balances is a means of giving each branch of government some scrutiny of and control over the other branches. The aim is to prevent the exclusive exercise of certain powers by any one of the three branches. For example, only Congress can enact laws. But the president (through the veto power) can cancel them, and the courts (by finding that a law violates the Constitution) can strike them down. The process goes on as Congress and the president sometimes begin the legislative process anew, attempting to reformulate laws to address the flaws identified by the Supreme Court in its decisions. In a "check on a check," Congress can override a president's

COMPARE WITH YOUR PEERS
MindTap® for American Government

Access The Constitution Forum: Polling Activity—Raising the Debt Ceiling.

separation of powers
The assignment of lawmaking, law-enforcing, and law-interpreting functions to separate branches of government.

checks and balances
A government structure that gives each branch some scrutiny of and control over the other branches.

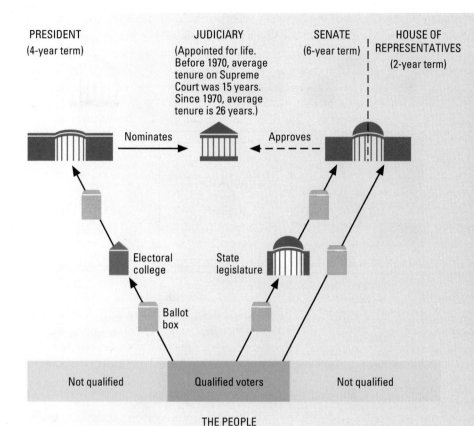

PRESIDENT
(4-year term)

JUDICIARY
(Appointed for life.
Before 1970, average
tenure on Supreme
Court was 15 years.
Since 1970, average
tenure is 26 years.)

SENATE
(6-year term)

HOUSE OF
REPRESENTATIVES
(2-year term)

Nominates →   ← Approves

Electoral
college

State
legislature

Ballot
box

Not qualified   Qualified voters   Not qualified

THE PEOPLE

**FIGURE 3.1 The Constitution
and the Electoral Process**

The framers were afraid of majority
rule, and that fear is reflected in the
electoral process for national office
described in the Constitution. The
people, speaking through the voters—
mostly white men who owned
property—participated directly only in
the choice of their representatives in
the House. The president and senators
were elected indirectly, through the
electoral college and state legislatures.
(Direct election of senators did not
become law until 1913, when the
Seventeenth Amendment was ratified.)
Judicial appointments are, and always
have been, far removed from
representative links to the people.
Judges are nominated by the president
and approved by the Senate.

Source: © Cengage Learning.

veto by an extraordinary (two-thirds) majority in each chamber. Congress is also
empowered to propose amendments to the Constitution, counteracting the courts'
power to invalidate. Figure 3.2 depicts the relationship between separation of powers
and checks and balances.

The Articles of the Constitution

In addition to the preamble, the Constitution contains seven articles. The first three
establish the separate branches of government and specify their internal operations
and powers. The remaining four define the relationships among the states, explain
the process of amendment, declare the supremacy of national law, and explain the
procedure for ratifying the Constitution.

Article I: The Legislative Article. In structuring their new government, the
framers began with the legislative branch because they considered lawmaking the
most important function of a republican government. Article I is the most detailed,
and therefore the longest, of the articles. It grants substantial but limited legislative
power to Congress (Article I begins: "All legislative Power herein granted. ..."). It
defines the bicameral (two-chamber) character of Congress and describes the internal
operating procedures of the House of Representatives and the Senate. Section 8 of
Article I articulates the principle of **enumerated powers**, which means that Congress
can exercise only the powers that the Constitution assigns to it. Eighteen powers are
enumerated; the first seventeen are specific powers. For example, the third clause of
Section 8 gives Congress the power to regulate interstate commerce. (One of the chief

**CONNECT
WITH YOUR CLASSMATES**
MindTap™ for American Government

Access The Constitution Forum:
Discussion—The Constitution
and Law Making.

enumerated powers
The powers explicitly granted
to Congress by the
Constitution.

FIGURE 3.2 **Separation of Powers and Checks and Balances**

Separation of powers is the assignment of lawmaking, law-enforcing, and law-interpreting functions to the legislative, executive, and judicial branches, respectively. The phenomenon is illustrated by the diagonal from upper left to lower right in the figure. Checks and balances give each branch some power over the other branches. For example, the executive branch possesses some legislative power, and the legislative branch possesses some executive power. These checks and balances are listed outside the diagonal.

Source: © Cengage Learning.

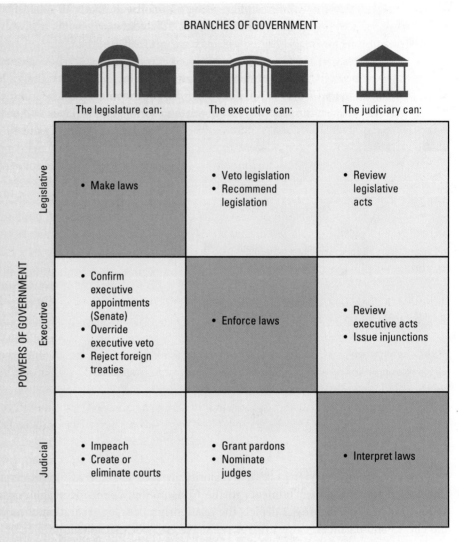

BRANCHES OF GOVERNMENT

POWERS OF GOVERNMENT

	The legislature can:	The executive can:	The judiciary can:
Legislative	• Make laws	• Veto legislation • Recommend legislation	• Review legislative acts
Executive	• Confirm executive appointments (Senate) • Override executive veto • Reject foreign treaties	• Enforce laws	• Review executive acts • Issue injunctions
Judicial	• Impeach • Create or eliminate courts	• Grant pardons • Nominate judges	• Interpret laws

shortcomings of the Articles of Confederation was the lack of a means to cope with trade wars between the states. The solution was to vest control of interstate commerce in the national government.)

The last clause in Section 8, known as the **necessary and proper clause** (or the elastic clause), gives Congress the means to execute the enumerated powers (see the Appendix). This clause is the basis of Congress's **implied powers**—those powers that Congress needs to execute its enumerated powers. For example, the power to levy and collect taxes (clause 1) and the power to coin money and regulate its value (clause 5), when joined with the necessary and proper clause (clause 18), imply that Congress has the power to charter a bank. Otherwise, the national government would have no means of managing the money it collects through its power to tax. Implied powers clearly expand the enumerated powers conferred on Congress by the Constitution.

Article II: The Executive Article. Article II grants executive power to a president. The article establishes the president's term of office, the procedure for electing the president by means of electors, the qualifications for becoming president, and the president's duties and powers. The last include acting as commander in chief of the

necessary and proper clause
The last clause in Section 8 of Article I of the Constitution, which gives Congress the means to execute its enumerated powers. This clause is the basis for Congress's implied powers. Also called the *elastic clause*.

implied powers
Those powers that Congress needs to execute its enumerated powers.

military; making treaties (which must be ratified by a two-thirds vote in the Senate); and appointing government officers, diplomats, and judges (again, with the advice and consent of the Senate).

The president also has legislative powers—part of the constitutional system of checks and balances. For example, the Constitution requires that the president periodically inform Congress of "the State of the Union" and of the policies and programs that the executive branch intends to advocate in the coming year. Today, this is done annually in the president's State of the Union address. Under special circumstances, the president can also convene or adjourn Congress.

The duty to "take Care that the Laws be faithfully executed" in Section 3 has provided presidents with a reservoir of power. President Richard Nixon tried to use this power when he refused to turn over the Watergate tapes despite a judicial subpoena in a criminal trial. He claimed broad executive privilege, an extension of the executive power implied in Article II. But the Supreme Court rejected his claim, arguing that it violated the separation of powers, because the decision to release or withhold information in a criminal trial is a judicial, not an executive, function.

Article III: The Judicial Article. The third article was left purposely vague. The Constitution established the Supreme Court as the highest court in the land. But beyond that, the framers were unable to agree on the need for a national judiciary or on its size, its composition, or the procedures it should follow. They left these issues to Congress, which resolved them by creating a system of federal (that is, national) courts, separate from the state courts.[36]

Unless they are impeached, federal judges serve for life. They are appointed to indefinite terms "during good Behaviour," and their salaries cannot be reduced while

How Many Pens Does It Take to Sign a Bill into Law?

Answer: It depends on the number of people a president wants to thank. The president gives his approval to legislation by signing it into law. Beginning in the 1960s, the bill-signing ceremony became an art form, garnering much press attention. The president would typically employ many pens in small strokes for his signature and then distribute the pens as souvenirs to the people instrumental in the bill's passage. Here President Barack Obama picks up the first pen (left), signs a portion of his signature (middle), then jokes about the multiple pens he will use to complete his signature on the American Recovery and Reinvestment Act, Tuesday, February 17, 2009, during a ceremony at the Denver Museum of Nature and Science (right). We wonder whether the pens were manufactured in the United States.

they hold office. These stipulations reinforce the separation of powers; they see to it that judges are independent of the other branches and that they do not have to fear retribution for their exercise of judicial power.

Congress exercises a potential check on the judicial branch through its power to create (and eliminate) lower federal courts. Congress can also restrict the power of the federal courts to decide cases. And, as we have noted, the president appoints, with the advice and consent of the Senate, the justices of the Supreme Court and the judges of the lower federal courts. Since the 1980s, especially, the judicial appointment process has become highly politicized, with both Democrats and Republicans accusing each other of obstructionism.

Article III does not explicitly give the courts the power of **judicial review**, that is, the authority to invalidate congressional or presidential actions because they violate the Constitution. That power has been inferred from the logic, structure, and theory of the Constitution and from important court rulings, some of which we discuss in subsequent chapters.

The Remaining Articles. The remaining four articles of the Constitution cover a lot of ground. Article IV requires that the judicial acts and criminal warrants of each state be honored in all other states, and it forbids discrimination against citizens of one state by another state. This provision promotes equality; it keeps the states from treating outsiders differently from their own citizens. For example, suppose Smith and Jones both reside in Illinois, and an Illinois court awards Smith a judgment of $100,000 against Jones. Jones moves to Alaska, hoping to avoid payment. Rather than force Smith to bring a new lawsuit against Jones in Alaska, the Alaska courts give full faith and credit to the Illinois judgment, enforcing it as their own. The origin of Article IV can be traced to the Articles of Confederation.

Article IV also allows the addition of new states and stipulates that the national government will protect the states against foreign invasion and domestic violence.

Article V specifies the methods for amending (changing) the Constitution and guarantees equal state representation in the Senate. We will have more to say about this amendment process shortly.

An important component of Article VI is the **supremacy clause**, which asserts that when the Constitution, national laws, and treaties conflict with state or local laws, the first three take precedence over the last two. The stipulation is vital to the operation of federalism (and it remains a source of contention within the EU). In keeping with the supremacy clause, Article VI requires that all national and state officials, elected or appointed, take an oath to support the Constitution. The article also mandates that religious affiliation or belief cannot be a prerequisite for holding government office.

Finally, Article VII describes the ratification process, stipulating that approval by conventions in nine states would be necessary for the Constitution to take effect.

The Framers' Motives

Some argue that the Constitution is essentially a conservative document written by wealthy men to advance their own interests. One distinguished historian who wrote in the early 1900s, Charles A. Beard, maintained that the delegates had much to gain from a strong national government.[37] Many held government securities dating from the Revolutionary War that had become practically worthless under the Articles of Confederation. A strong national government would protect their property and pay off the nation's debts.

judicial review
The power to declare congressional (and presidential) acts invalid because they violate the Constitution.

supremacy clause
The clause in Article VI of the Constitution that asserts that national laws take precedence over state and local laws when they conflict.

Beard's argument, that the Constitution was crafted to protect the economic interests of this small group of creditors, provoked a generation of historians to examine the existing financial records of the convention delegates. Their scholarship has largely discredited his once-popular view.[38] For example, it turns out that seven of the delegates who left the convention or refused to sign the Constitution held public securities worth more than twice the total of the holdings of the thirty-nine delegates who did sign. Moreover, the most influential delegates owned no securities. And only a few delegates appear to have directly benefited economically from the new government.[39] Still, there is little doubt about the general homogeneity of the delegates or about their concern for producing a stable economic order that would preserve and promote the interests of some more than others.

What did motivate the framers? Surely economic considerations were important, but they were not the major issues. The single most important factor leading to the Constitutional Convention was the inability of the national or state governments to maintain order under the loose structure of the Articles of Confederation. Certainly, order involved the protection of property, but the framers had a broader view of property than their portfolios of government securities. They wanted to protect their homes, their families, and their means of livelihood from impending anarchy.

Although they disagreed bitterly on the structure and mechanics of the national government, the framers agreed on the most vital issues. For example, three of the most crucial features of the Constitution—the power to tax, the necessary and proper clause, and the supremacy clause—were approved unanimously without debate; experience had taught the delegates that a strong national government was essential if the United States were to survive. The motivation to create order was so strong, in fact, that the framers were willing to draft clauses that protected the most undemocratic of all institutions: slavery.

The Slavery Issue

The institution of slavery was well ingrained in American life at the time of the Constitutional Convention, and slavery helped shape the Constitution, although it is mentioned nowhere by name in it. (According to the first national census in 1790, nearly 18 percent of the population—697,000 people—lived in slavery.) It is doubtful, in fact, that there would have been a Constitution if the delegates had had to resolve the slavery issue, for the southern states would have opposed a constitution that prohibited slavery. Opponents of slavery were in the minority, and they were willing to tolerate its continuation in the interest of forging a union, perhaps believing that the issue could be resolved another day.

The question of representation in the House of Representatives brought the slavery issue close to the surface of the debate at the Constitutional Convention, and it led to the Great Compromise. Representation in the House was to be based on population. But who counted in the population? States with large slave populations wanted all their inhabitants, slave and free, counted equally; states with few slaves wanted only the free population counted. The delegates agreed unanimously that in apportioning representation in the House and in assessing direct taxes, the population of each state was to be determined by adding "the whole Number of free Persons" and "three fifths of all other Persons" (Article I, Section 2). The phrase "all other Persons" is, of course, a substitute for "slaves."

The three-fifths formula had been used by the 1783 congress under the Articles of Confederation to allocate government costs among the states. The rule reflected the view that slaves were less efficient producers of wealth than free people, not that slaves were three-fifths human and two-fifths personal property.[40]

The three-fifths clause gave states with large slave populations (the South) greater representation in Congress than states with small slave populations (the North). If all slaves had been included in the count, the slave states would have had 50 percent of the seats in the House, an outcome that would have been unacceptable to the North. Had none of the slaves been counted, the slave states would have had 41 percent of House seats, which would have been unacceptable to the South. The three-fifths compromise left the South with 47 percent of the House seats, a sizable minority, but in all likelihood a losing one on slavery issues.[41] The overrepresentation resulting from the South's large slave populations translated into greater influence in selecting the president as well, because the electoral college was based on the size of the states' congressional delegations. The three-fifths clause also undertaxed states with large slave populations.

Another issue centered on the slave trade. Several southern delegates were uncompromising in their defense of the slave trade; other delegates favored prohibition. The delegates compromised, agreeing that the slave trade would not be ended before twenty years had elapsed (Article I, Section 9). Finally, the delegates agreed, without serious challenge, that fugitive slaves would be returned to their masters (Article IV, Section 2).

In addressing these points, the framers in essence condoned slavery. Tens of thousands of Africans were forcibly taken from their homes and sold into bondage. Many died on the journey to this distant land, and those who survived were brutalized and treated as less than human. Clearly, slavery existed in stark opposition to the idea that all men are created equal. Although many slaveholders, including Jefferson and Madison, agonized over it, few made serious efforts to free their own slaves. Most Americans seemed indifferent to slavery and felt no embarrassment at the apparent contradiction between the Declaration of Independence and slavery. Do the framers deserve contempt for their toleration and perpetuation of slavery? The most prominent founders—George Washington, John Adams, and Thomas Jefferson— expected slavery to wither away. A leading scholar of colonial history has offered a defense of their inaction: the framers were simply unable to transcend the limitations of the age in which they lived.[42]

Nonetheless, the eradication of slavery proceeded gradually in certain states. Opposition to slavery on moral or religious grounds was one reason. Economic forces, such as a shift in the North to agricultural production that was less labor intensive, were a contributing factor, too. By 1787, Connecticut, Massachusetts, Pennsylvania, Rhode Island, and Vermont had abolished slavery or provided for gradual emancipation. No southern states followed suit, although several enacted laws making it easier for masters to free their slaves. The slow but perceptible shift on the slavery issue in many states masked a volcanic force capable of destroying the Constitutional Convention and the Union.

Selling the Constitution

LO5 ★ Describe the actions taken to ensure the ratification of the Constitution.

Nearly four months after the Constitutional Convention opened, the delegates convened for the last time, on September 17, 1787, to sign the final version of their handiwork. Because several delegates were unwilling to sign the document, the last paragraph was craftily worded to give the impression of unanimity: "Done in

Convention by the Unanimous Consent of the States present." Before it could take effect, the Constitution had to be ratified by a minimum of nine state conventions. The support of key states was crucial. In Pennsylvania, however, the legislature was slow to convene a ratifying convention. Pro-Constitution forces became so frustrated at this dawdling that they broke into a local boardinghouse and hauled two errant legislators through the streets to the statehouse so the assembly could schedule the convention.

The proponents of the new charter, who wanted a strong national government, called themselves Federalists. The opponents of the Constitution were quickly dubbed Antifederalists. They claimed, however, to be the true federalists because they wanted to protect the states from the tyranny of a strong national government. Elbridge Gerry, a vocal Antifederalist, called his opponents "rats" (because they favored ratification) and maintained that he was an "antirat."[43] Such is the Alice-in-Wonderland character of political discourse. Whatever they were called, the viewpoints of these two groups formed the bases of the first American political parties, as well as several enduring debates that politicians have wrestled with as they have attempted to balance the tradeoffs between freedom, order, and equality.

The *Federalist* Papers

The press was the mass medium of the eighteenth century. Newspapers and commentaries became a battlefield of words, filled with extravagant praise or vituperative condemnation of the proposed constitution. Beginning in October 1787, an exceptional series of eighty-five New York newspaper articles defending the Constitution appeared under the title *The Federalist: A Commentary on the Constitution of the United States*. These partisan essays bore the pen name Publius (for a Roman consul and defender of the Republic, Publius Valerius, who was later known as Publicola); they were written primarily by James Madison and Alexander Hamilton, with some assistance from John Jay. Reprinted extensively during the ratification battle, the *Federalist* papers have far greater influence today when read as dispassionate analyses on the meaning of the Constitution and the political theory it embodies rather than as persuasive efforts to win ratification from New Yorkers.[44]

Not to be outdone, the Antifederalists offered their own intellectual basis for rejecting the Constitution. In several essays, the most influential published under the pseudonyms Brutus and Federal Farmer, the Antifederalists attacked the centralization of power in a strong national government, claiming it would obliterate the states, violate the social contract of the Declaration of Independence, and destroy liberty in the process. They defended the status quo, maintaining that the Articles of Confederation established true federal principles.[45]

Of all the *Federalist* papers, the most magnificent and most frequently cited is *Federalist* No. 10, written by James Madison. He argued that the proposed constitution was designed "to break and control the violence of faction." "By a faction," Madison wrote, "I understand a number of citizens, whether amounting to a majority or minority of the whole, who are united and actuated by some common impulse of passion, or of interest, adverse to the rights of other citizens, or to the permanent and aggregate interests of the community." No one has improved upon Madison's lucid and compelling argument, and it remains the touchstone on the problem of factions to this day.

What Madison called factions are today called interest groups or even political parties. According to Madison, "The most common and durable source of factions has been the various and unequal distribution of property." Madison was concerned not with reducing inequalities of wealth (which he took for granted) but with controlling the seemingly inevitable conflict that stems from them. The Constitution, he argued, was well constructed for this purpose.

Through the mechanism of representation, wrote Madison, the Constitution would prevent a "tyranny of the majority" (mob rule). The people would control the government not directly but indirectly through their elected representatives. And those representatives would have the intelligence and the understanding to serve the larger interests of the nation. Moreover, the federal system would require that majorities form first within each state and then organize for effective action at the national level. This and the vastness of the country would make it unlikely that a majority would form that would "invade the rights of other citizens."

The purpose of *Federalist* No. 10 was to demonstrate that the proposed government was not likely to be dominated by any faction. Contrary to conventional wisdom, Madison argued, the key to mending the evils of factions is to have a large republic—the larger, the better. The more diverse the society, the less likely it is that an unjust majority can form. Madison certainly had no intention of creating a majoritarian democracy; his view of popular government further was much more consistent with the model of pluralist democracy discussed in Chapter 2.

Madison pressed his argument from a different angle in *Federalist* No. 51. Asserting that "ambition must be made to counteract ambition," he argued that the separation of powers and checks and balances would control efforts at tyranny from any source. If power is distributed equally among the three branches, he argued, each branch will have the capacity to counteract the others. In Madison's words, "usurpations are guarded against by a division of the government into distinct and separate departments." Because legislative power tends to predominate in republican governments, legislative authority is divided between the Senate and the House of Representatives, which have different methods of election and terms of office. Additional protection arises from federalism, which divides power "between two distinct governments"—national and state—and subdivides "the portion allotted to each … among distinct and separate departments." Madison called this arrangement of power, divided as it was across and within levels of government, a "compound republic."

The Antifederalists wanted additional separation of powers and additional checks and balances, which they maintained would eliminate the threat of tyranny entirely. The Federalists believed that such protections would make decisive national action virtually impossible. But to ensure ratification, they agreed to a compromise.

A Concession: The Bill of Rights

Despite the eloquence of the *Federalist* papers, many prominent citizens, including Thomas Jefferson, were unhappy that the Constitution did not list basic civil liberties—the individual freedoms guaranteed to citizens. The omission of such a list—known as a bill of rights—was the chief obstacle to the adoption of the Constitution by the states. (Seven of the eleven state constitutions that were written in the first five years of independence included such a list.) The colonists had just rebelled against the British government to preserve their basic freedoms. Why did the proposed Constitution not spell out those freedoms?

The answer was rooted in logic, not politics. Because the national government was limited to those powers that were granted to it and because no power was granted to abridge the people's liberties, a list of guaranteed freedoms was not necessary. In *Federalist* No. 84, Hamilton went even further, arguing that the addition of a bill of rights would be dangerous. To deny the exercise of a nonexistent power might lead to the exercise of a power that is not specifically denied. For example, to declare that the national government shall make no law abridging free speech might suggest that the national government could prohibit activities in unspecified areas (such as divorce), which are the states' domain. Because it is not possible to list all prohibited powers, wrote Hamilton, any attempt to provide a partial list would make the unlisted areas vulnerable to government abuse.

But logic was no match for fear. Many states agreed to ratify the Constitution only after George Washington suggested adding a list of guarantees through the amendment process. Well in excess of one hundred amendments were proposed by the states. These were eventually narrowed to twelve, which were approved by Congress and sent to the states. Ten became part of the Constitution in 1791, after securing the approval of the required three-fourths of the states. Collectively, the ten amendments are known as the **Bill of Rights**. They restrain the national government from tampering with fundamental rights and civil liberties, and emphasize the limited character of the national government's power (see Table 3.2).

Bill of Rights
The first ten amendments to the Constitution. They prevent the national government from tampering with fundamental rights and civil liberties, and emphasize the limited character of national power.

TABLE 3.2   The Bill of Rights

The first ten amendments to the Constitution are known as the Bill of Rights. The following is a list of those amendments, grouped conceptually. For the actual order and wording of the Bill of Rights, see the Appendix.

Guarantees	Amendment
Guarantees for Participation in the Political Process	
No government abridgment of speech or press; no government abridgment of peaceable assembly; no government abridgment of petitioning government for redress.	1
Guarantees Respecting Personal Beliefs	
No government establishment of religion; no government prohibition of free religious exercise.	1
Guarantees of Personal Privacy	
Owner's consent necessary to quarter troops in private homes in peacetime; quartering during war must be lawful.	3
Government cannot engage in unreasonable searches and seizures; warrants to search and seize require probable cause.	4
No compulsion to testify against oneself in criminal cases.	5
Guarantees Against Government's Overreaching	
Serious crimes require a grand jury indictment; no repeated prosecution for the same offense; no loss of life, liberty, or property without due process; no taking of property for public use without just compensation.	5
Criminal defendants will have a speedy public trial by impartial local jury; defendants are informed of accusation; defendants may confront witnesses against them; defendants may use judicial process to obtain favorable witnesses; defendants may have legal assistance for their defense.	6
Civil lawsuits can be tried by juries if controversy exceeds $20; in jury trials, fact finding is a jury function.	7
No excessive bail; no excessive fines; no cruel and unusual punishment.	8
Other Guarantees	
The people have the right to bear arms.	2
No government trespass on unspecified fundamental rights.	9
The states or the people retain all powers not delegated to the national government or denied to the states.	10

Ratification

The Constitution officially took effect upon its ratification by the ninth state, New Hampshire, on June 21, 1788. However, the success of the new government was not ensured until July 1788, by which time the Constitution had been ratified by the key states of Virginia and New York after lengthy debate.

The reflection and deliberation that attended the creation and ratification of the Constitution signaled to the world that a new government could be launched peacefully. The French observer Alexis de Tocqueville (1805–1859) later wrote:

> That which is new in the history of societies is to see a great people, warned by its lawgivers that the wheels of government are stopping, turn its attention on itself without haste or fear, sound the depth of the ill, and then wait for two years to find the remedy at leisure, and then finally, when the remedy has been indicated, submit to it voluntarily without its costing humanity a single tear or drop of blood.[46]

Constitutional Change

LO6 ★ Explain the procedures required to amend the Constitution.

The founders realized that the Constitution would have to be changed from time to time. To this end, they specified a formal amendment process, and one that was used almost immediately to add the Bill of Rights. With the passage of time, the Constitution has also been altered through judicial interpretation and changes in political practice.

The Formal Amendment Process

The amendment process has two stages: proposal and ratification; both are necessary for an amendment to become part of the Constitution. The Constitution provides two alternatives for completing each stage (see Figure 3.3). Amendments can be proposed by a two-thirds vote in both the House of Representatives and the Senate or by a national convention, summoned by Congress at the request of two-thirds of the state legislatures. All constitutional amendments to date have been proposed by the first method; the second has never been used.

A proposed amendment can be ratified by a vote of the legislatures of three-fourths of the states or by a vote of constitutional conventions held in three-fourths of the states. Congress chooses the method of ratification. It has used the state convention method only once, for the Twenty-first Amendment, which repealed the Eighteenth Amendment (prohibition of intoxicating liquors). Congress may, in proposing an amendment, set a time limit for its ratification. Beginning with the Eighteenth Amendment, but skipping the Nineteenth, Congress has set seven years as the limit for ratification.

Note that the amendment process requires the exercise of extraordinary majorities (two-thirds and three-fourths). The framers purposely made it difficult to propose and ratify amendments (although nowhere near as difficult as under the Articles of Confederation). They wanted only the most significant issues to lead to constitutional change. Note, too, that the president plays no formal role in the process.

FIGURE 3.3 Amending the Constitution

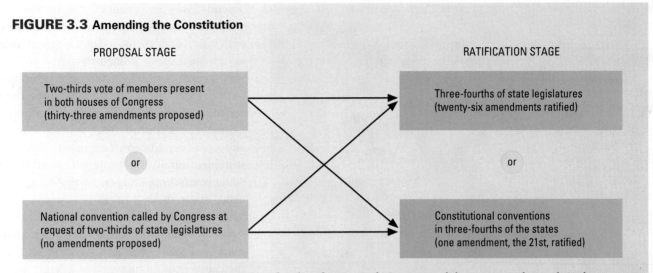

Amending the Constitution requires two stages: proposal and ratification. Both Congress and the states can play a role in the proposal stage, but ratification is a process that must be fought in the states themselves. Once a state has ratified an amendment, it cannot retract its action. However, a state may reject an amendment and then reconsider its decision.

Source: © Cengage Learning.

Presidential approval is not required to amend the Constitution, although the president's political influence affects the success or failure of any amendment effort.

Calling a national convention to propose an amendment has never been tried, and the method raises several thorny questions. For example, the Constitution does not specify the number of delegates who should attend, the method by which they should be chosen, or the rules for debating and voting on a proposed amendment. Confusion surrounding the convention process has precluded its use, leaving the amendment process in congressional hands.[47] The major issue is the limits, if any, on the business of the convention. Remember that the convention in Philadelphia in 1787, charged with revising the Articles of Confederation, drafted an entirely new charter. Would a national convention called to consider a particular amendment be within its bounds to rewrite the Constitution? No one really knows.

Most of the Constitution's twenty-seven amendments were adopted to reflect changes in political thinking. The first ten amendments (the Bill of Rights) were the price of ratification, but they have been fundamental to our system of government. The last seventeen amendments fall into three main categories: they make public policy, they correct deficiencies in the government's structure, or they promote equality. One attempt to make public policy through a constitutional amendment was disastrous. The Eighteenth Amendment (1919) prohibited the manufacture or sale of intoxicating beverages, extinguishing the fifth largest industry in the nation. This amendment and the Thirteenth, barring the ownership of slaves, were the only provisions to limit the activities of citizens.[48] Prohibition lasted fourteen years and was an utter failure. Gangsters began bootlegging liquor, people died from drinking homemade spirits, and millions regularly broke the law by drinking anyway. Congress had to propose another amendment in 1933 to repeal the Eighteenth. The states ratified this amendment, the Twenty-first, in less than ten months, less time than it took to ratify the Fourteenth Amendment, guaranteeing citizenship, due process, and equal protection of the laws.

Since 1787, about 10,000 constitutional amendments have been introduced; only a fraction has survived the proposal stage. Once Congress has approved an

AP Images

"We Want Beer": A Common Refrain

"We want beer" may be a popular refrain at tailgating parties and on certain college campuses today, but it was the basis of political protest in October 1932 when more than 20,000 protesters, many of them women, demanded repeal of the Eighteenth Amendment. The amendment, which was ratified in 1919, banned the manufacture, sale, and transportation of alcoholic beverages. The amendment was spurred by moral and social reform groups, such as the Women's Christian Temperance Union, founded by Evanston, Illinois, resident Frances Willard in 1874. The amendment proved to be an utter failure. People continued to drink, but their alcohol came from illegal sources.

amendment, its chances for ratification are high. The Twenty-seventh Amendment, which prevents members of Congress from voting themselves immediate pay increases, was ratified in 1992. It had been submitted to the states in 1789 without a time limit for ratification, but it languished in a political netherworld until 1982, when a University of Texas student, Gregory D. Watson, stumbled upon the proposed amendment while researching a paper. At that time, only eight states had ratified the amendment. Watson earned a C for the paper; his professor remained unconvinced that the amendment was still pending. [49] Watson took up the cause, prompting renewed interest in the amendment. In May 1992, ratification by the Michigan legislature provided the decisive vote, 203 years after congressional approval of the proposed amendment.[50] Only six amendments submitted to the states have failed to be ratified.

Interpretation by the Courts

In the famous case of *Marbury* v. *Madison* (1803), the Supreme Court declared that the courts have the power to nullify government acts that conflict with the Constitution. This is the power of judicial review. (We will elaborate on judicial review in Chapter 14.) The exercise of judicial review forces the courts to interpret the Constitution. In a way, this makes a lot of sense. The judiciary is the law-interpreting branch of the government; as the supreme law of the land, the Constitution is fair game for judicial interpretation. It is problematic, in theory at least, that the Constitution does not expressly authorize courts to exercise this power. Judicial review is the courts' main check on the other branches of government. But in interpreting the Constitution, the courts cannot help but give new meaning to its provisions. This is why judicial interpretation is a principal form of constitutional change.

What guidelines should judges use in interpreting the Constitution? For one thing, they must realize that the usage and meaning of many words have changed during the past two hundred years. Judges must be careful to think about what the words meant at the time the Constitution was written. Some insist that they must also consider the original intent of the framers—not an easy task. Of course, there are records of the Constitutional Convention and of the debates surrounding ratification. But there are also many questions about the completeness and accuracy of those records, even Madison's detailed notes. And at times, the framers were deliberately vague in writing the document. This may reflect lack of agreement on, or universal understanding of, certain provisions in the Constitution. Some scholars and judges maintain that the search for original meaning is hopeless and that contemporary notions of constitutional provisions must hold sway. Critics say that this approach comes perilously close to amending the Constitution as judges see fit, transforming law interpreters into lawmakers. Still other scholars and judges maintain that judges face the unavoidable challenge of balancing 200-year-old constitutional principles against the demands of modern society.[51] Whatever the approach, unelected judges with effective life tenure run the risk of usurping policies established by the people's representatives.

Political Practice

The Constitution is silent on many issues. It says nothing about political parties or the president's cabinet, for example, yet both have exercised considerable influence in American politics. Some constitutional provisions have fallen out of use. The electors in the electoral college, for example, were supposed to exercise their own judgment in voting for the president and vice president. Today, the electors function simply as a rubber stamp, validating the outcome of election contests in their states.

Meanwhile, political practice has altered the distribution of power without changes in the Constitution. The framers intended Congress to be the strongest branch of government. But the president has come to overshadow Congress. Presidents such as Abraham Lincoln and Franklin Roosevelt used their formal and informal powers imaginatively to respond to national crises. And their actions paved the way for future presidents, most recently George W. Bush, to enlarge further the powers of the office.

The framers could scarcely have imagined an urbanized nation of 317 million people stretching across a landmass some 3,000 miles wide, reaching halfway over the Pacific Ocean, and stretching past the Arctic Circle. Never in their wildest nightmares could they have foreseen the destructiveness of nuclear weaponry or envisioned its effect on the power to declare war. The Constitution empowers Congress to consider and debate this momentous step. But with nuclear annihilation perhaps only minutes away and terrorist threats a real if unpredictable prospect since September 11, 2001, the legislative power to declare war is likely to give way to the president's power to wage war as the nation's commander in chief. Strict adherence to the Constitution in such circumstances could destroy the nation's ability to protect itself.

 # An Evaluation of the Constitution

LO7 ★ Evaluate the extent to which the Constitution reflects and embodies the principles of majoritarian or pluralist democracy.

The U.S. Constitution is one of the world's most praised political documents. It is the oldest written national constitution and one of the most widely copied, sometimes word for word. It is also one of the shortest, consisting of about 4,300 words (not counting the amendments, which add 3,100 words). The brevity of the Constitution may be one of its greatest strengths. As we noted earlier, the framers simply laid out a structural framework for government; they did not describe relationships and powers in detail. For example, the Constitution gives Congress the power to regulate "Commerce … among the several States" but does not define interstate commerce.

Such general wording allows interpretation in keeping with contemporary political, social, and technological developments. Air travel, for instance, unknown in 1787, now falls easily within Congress's power to regulate interstate commerce.

The generality of the U.S. Constitution stands in stark contrast to the specificity of most state constitutions and the constitutions of many emerging democracies. The California constitution, for example, provides that "fruit and nut-bearing trees under the age of four years from the time of planting in orchard form and grapevines under the age of three years from the time of planting in vineyard form ... shall be exempt from taxation" (Article XIII, Section 12). Because they are so specific, most state constitutions are much longer than the U.S. Constitution. The longest by far is the Alabama constitution, which is more than 300,000 words. That's longer than *Moby-Dick* or the Bible.

For a long period, newly emerging nations viewed the U.S. Constitution and the ideals it embodied as a model worth emulating. But recent evidence reveals that the U.S. Constitution has become a dimming beacon for others to follow (see "Freedom, Order, Equality, and Different Strokes for Different Folks").

Freedom, Order, Equality, and Different Strokes for Different Folks

Back in 1987, on the occasion of the 200th birthday of the U.S. Constitution, *Time* magazine observed that "of the 170 countries that exist today, more than 160 have written charters modeled directly or indirectly on the U.S. version." But today, that same constitution has lost some of its mojo. A detailed empirical study of 729 constitutions adopted by 188 countries from 1946 to 2006 reveals a different picture. In the 1960s and 1970s, democratic constitutions became similar to the U.S. Constitution, but then reversed course in the 1980s and 1990s. And by the first few years of the twenty-first century, the departures became more pronounced such that for the most recent period for which there is evidence, "the constitutions of the world's democracies are, on average, less familiar to the U.S. Constitution now than they were at the end of World War II."

Reasons for this shift abound. The U.S. Constitution is concise and old; it also guarantees few rights; and, as some Supreme Court justices have advocated, the document should be interpreted according to its meaning when it was crafted in 1787. These possible explanations may suggest that the U.S. Constitution has little appeal to new nations. And the Constitution's declining influence may simply be an extension of a general decline in American power and prestige.

One of the study authors pithily summarized a central reason for the declining trend: "Nobody wants a copy of Windows 3.1." Supreme Court justice Ruth Bader Ginsburg echoed this sentiment in a 2012 interview on Egyptian television: "I would not look to the United States Constitution if I were drafting a constitution in the year 2012."

Of course, we should remember that constitutions offer only paper guarantees, so despite their high purpose and grand promises, what matters most is whether the guarantees they enshrined will be observed in practice.

The figure on the facing page details the most common provisions in the constitutions of 188 countries in 1946 and 2006. The provisions in the U.S. Constitution appear in **bold**.

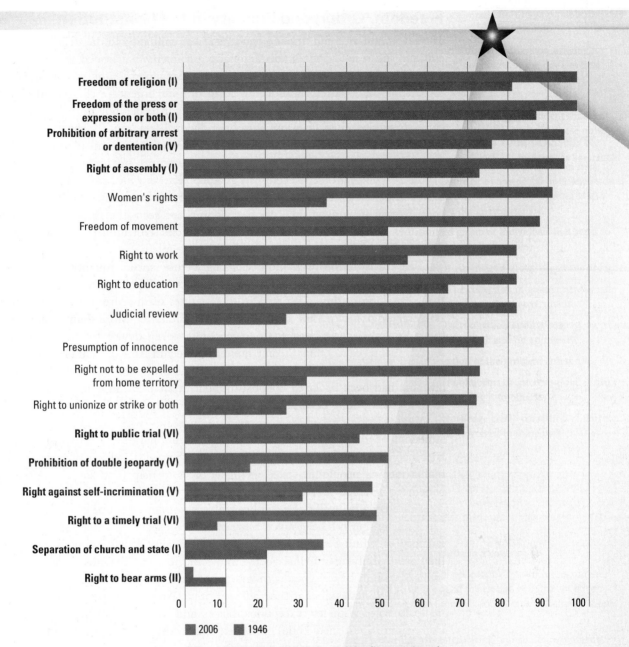

BOLD = explicit U.S. constitutional rights (by amendment).

Percentage of 188 constitutions containing selected provisions.

Sources: Adam Liptak, "Sidebar: 'We the People' Loses Appeal With People Around the World," *New York Times*, 7 February 2012, p. A1; David S. Law and Mila Versteeg, "The Declining Influence of the United States Constitution," *New York University Law Review*, Vol. 87, No. 3, pp. 762–858 (June 2012); John Greenwald, Alastair Matheson, and Bing W. Wong, "A Gift to All Nations," *Time*, 6 July 1987, Vol. 130, pp. 92–95.

Critical Thinking Which provisions of the U.S. Constitution have the most appeal in other countries? Which ones have the least appeal? What popular provisions lie outside the U.S. Constitution? Which provision has grown most in appeal in the period from 1946 to 2006? Only one provision has lost appeal. Which one? Speculate on the reasons for the growth and decline in these provisions.

Freedom, Order, and Equality in the Constitution

The revolutionaries' first try at government was embodied in the Articles of Confederation. The result was a weak national government that leaned too much toward freedom at the expense of order. Deciding that the confederation was beyond correcting, the revolutionaries chose a new form of government—a compound or *federal* government—that was strong enough to maintain order but not so strong that it could dominate the states or infringe on individual freedoms. In short, the Constitution provided a judicious balance between order and freedom. It paid virtually no attention to equality. (Recall that the equality premise in the Declaration of Independence was meant for the colonists as a people, not as individuals.)

Consider social equality. The Constitution never mentioned the word *slavery*, a controversial issue even then. In fact, as we have seen, the Constitution implicitly condones slavery in the wording of several articles. Not until the ratification of the Thirteenth Amendment in 1865 was slavery prohibited.

The Constitution was designed long before social equality was ever even thought of as an objective of government. In fact, in *Federalist* No. 10, Madison held that protection of the "diversities in the faculties of men from which the rights of property originate" is "the first object of government." More than a century later, the Constitution was changed to incorporate a key device for the promotion of social equality—a national income tax. The Sixteenth Amendment (1913) gave Congress the power to collect an income tax; it was proposed and ratified to replace a law that had been declared unconstitutional in an 1895 Supreme Court case. The income tax had long been seen as a means of putting into effect the concept of progressive taxation, in which the tax rate increases with income. The Sixteenth Amendment gave progressive taxation a constitutional basis.[52] Progressive taxation later helped promote social equality through the redistribution of income; that is, higher-income people are taxed at higher rates to help fund social programs that benefit low-income people.

Social equality itself has never been, and is not now, a prime constitutional value. The Constitution has been much more effective in securing order and freedom. Nor did the Constitution take a stand on political equality. It left voting qualifications to the states, specifying only that people who could vote for "the most numerous Branch of the State Legislature" could also vote for representatives to Congress (Article I, Section 2). Most states at that time allowed only taxpaying or property-owning white males to vote. With few exceptions, blacks and women were universally excluded from voting. These inequalities have been rectified by several amendments.

Political equality expanded after the Civil War. The Fourteenth Amendment (adopted in 1868) guaranteed all persons, including blacks, citizenship. The Fifteenth Amendment (ratified in 1870) declared that "race, color, or previous condition of servitude" could not be used to deny citizens the right to vote. This did not automatically give blacks the vote; some states used other mechanisms to limit black enfranchisement. The Nineteenth Amendment (adopted in 1920) opened the way for women to vote by declaring that sex could not be used to deny citizens the right to vote. The Twenty-fourth Amendment (adopted in 1964) prohibited the poll tax (a tax that people had to pay to vote and that tended to disenfranchise poor blacks) in presidential and congressional elections. The Twenty-sixth Amendment (adopted in 1971) declared that age could not be used to deny citizens eighteen years or older the right to vote. One other amendment expanded the Constitution's grant of political equality. The Twenty-third Amendment (adopted in 1961) allowed residents of Washington, D.C., who are not citizens of any state, to vote for president.

The Constitution and Models of Democracy

Think back to our discussion of the models of democracy in Chapter 2. Which model does the Constitution fit: pluralist or majoritarian? Actually, it is hard to imagine a government framework better suited to the pluralist model of democracy than the Constitution of the United States. It is also hard to imagine a document more at odds with the majoritarian model. Consider Madison's claim, in *Federalist* No. 10, that government inevitably involves conflicting factions. This concept coincides perfectly with pluralist theory (see Chapter 2). Then recall his description in *Federalist* No. 51 of the Constitution's ability to guard against concentration of power in the majority through separation of powers and checks and balances. This concept—avoiding a single center of government power that might fall under majority control—also fits perfectly with pluralist democracy.

The delegates to the Constitutional Convention intended to create a republic, a government based on majority consent; they did not intend to create a democracy, which rests on majority rule. They succeeded admirably in creating that republic. In doing so, they also produced a government that developed into a democracy—but a particular type of democracy. The framers neither wanted nor got a democracy that fit the majoritarian model. They may have wanted, and they certainly did create, a government that conforms to the pluralist model.

Master the Topic of The Constitution with MindTap™ for American Government

REVIEW MindTap™ **for American Government**
Access Key Term Flashcards for Chapter 3.

TEST YOURSELF MindTap™ **for American Government**
Take the Wrap It Up Quiz for Chapter 3.

STAY CURRENT MindTap™ **for American Government**
Access the KnowNow blog and customized RSS for updates on current events.

STAY FOCUSED MindTap™ **for American Government**
Complete the Focus Activities for The Constitution.

Summary

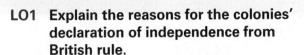

LO1 Explain the reasons for the colonies' declaration of independence from British rule.

- The Constitution was the end product of a revolutionary movement aimed at preserving existing liberties. The movement began with the Declaration of Independence, which proclaimed that everyone is entitled to certain rights and invoked the principle of equality of

peoples. The conflict was also a civil war that divided communities and families.

LO2 Identify the factors that led to the failure of the Confederation.

- After independence, a government was needed to replace the British monarchy. The Americans chose a republic and defined the structure of that republic in the Articles of Confederation. Although the

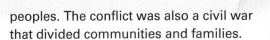

Articles guaranteed the states the independence they coveted, they were a failure: they left the central government too weak to deal with disorder and insurrection.

LO3 Explain the major points of contention in the writing of the Constitution.

- The Constitutional Convention was fraught with debate over the strength of government at the state versus the national level and the nature of the presidency. To resolve these conflicts, compromises were carefully crafted that all delegates could support, even if only reluctantly.

LO4 Explain the contribution of the Constitution to the American political tradition and the principles it establishes.

- The Constitution that finally emerged replaced a loose union of powerful states with a strong but still limited national government, incorporating four political principles: republicanism, federalism, separation of powers, and checks and balances. It also established a system of checks and balances, giving each branch some scrutiny of and control over the others.

LO5 Describe the actions taken to ensure the ratification of the Constitution.

- A major stumbling block to ratification of the Constitution proved to be its failure to list the individual liberties the Americans had fought to protect against the potential tyranny of a stronger central government. With the promise to add a bill of rights, the Constitution was ratified.

LO6 Explain the procedures required to amend the Constitution.

- The founders recognized that the Constitution would need to be amended to serve the changing needs of the citizenry. They therefore enumerated different formal methods for amending the document. In practice, the Constitution has also been modified through the courts and through changes in political practice.

LO7 Evaluate the extent to which the Constitution reflects and embodies the principles of majoritarian or pluralist democracy.

- The Constitution was designed to strike a balance between order and freedom. While the framers did not set out to create a democracy, they nevertheless produced a democratic form of government. The framers also wanted a balance between the powers of the national government and those of the states, the exact nature of which would be contested for many years to come.

Chapter Quiz

LO1 Explain the reasons for the colonies' declaration of independence from British rule.

1. Why did the colonies begin to protest against the British government, and what forms did this protest take?
2. What principles underpin the Declaration of Independence?

LO2 Identify the factors that led to the failure of the Confederation.

1. Why did the delegates to the Second Continental Congress seek to retain power in the states versus creating a strong central government?
2. Provide four reasons that help explain why the Articles of Confederation failed.

LO3 **Explain the major points of contention in the writing of the Constitution.**

1. What were the primary differences between the Virginia and New Jersey Plans?
2. What major compromises did the drafting of the Constitution entail?

LO4 **Explain the contribution of the Constitution to the American political tradition and the principles it establishes.**

1. Which powers are provided to Congress through the necessary and proper clause, and why are these important?
2. How did the Constitution originally address the institution of slavery?

LO5 **Describe the actions taken to ensure the ratification of the Constitution.**

1. Who were the Federalists and Antifederalists, and what were their main points of disagreement?
2. What is the Bill of Rights, and whose rights is it guaranteed to protect?

LO6 **Explain the procedures required to amend the Constitution.**

1. What are the two methods through which constitutional changes can be proposed, and what are the two methods for ratifying those changes?
2. What are the guidelines used by judges for interpreting the Constitution?

LO7 **Evaluate the extent to which the Constitution reflects and embodies the principles of majoritarian or pluralist democracy.**

1. What values does the Constitution secure? What values were not priorities at the time the Constitution was drafted?
2. Does the government created by the Constitution reflect the pluralist or majoritarian model of democracy?

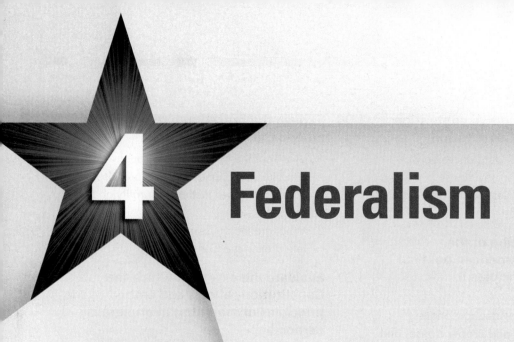

4 Federalism

Learning Outcomes

LO1 Compare and contrast the two theories of federalism used to describe the American system of government.

LO2 Identify and explain each of the four forces that stimulate changes in the relationship between the national and state governments.

LO3 Describe the role of ideology in shaping federalism.

LO4 Describe the influence of federalism on elections at the state and national levels.

LO5 Describe the role of local government in a federal system and illustrate how national, state, and local governments sometimes interact.

LO6 Analyze the role of federalism in American trade policy and in other nations around the world.

LO7 Discuss the changing relationship between federalism and pluralism.

 WATCH & LEARN MindTap™ for American Government

Watch a brief "What Do You Know?" video summarizing Federalism.

AP Images/Tom LoBianco

Since the early 2000s, public school students in the United States have taken more and more standardized tests in elementary and high school. Have you ever wondered who decides the topics that appear on these tests or how the questions are chosen? Who do you think should decide? Your teachers and members of your local school board? State legislators? Leaders in the national government?

Debates about academic expectations and student testing have intensified due to the development of the Common Core State Standards in reading and math. They emerged from efforts led by the National Governors' Association and the Council of Chief State School Officers, which represents state education agency leaders, along with support from the nonprofit organization Achieve, national foundations, and encouragement by the federal government. By 2014, forty-four states and the District of Columbia had adopted the standards and were busy crafting policies and other initiatives to help their school districts and schools implement them.

"I believe the Common Core State Standards may prove to be the single greatest thing to happen to public education in America since *Brown* v. *Board of Education*," said Arne Duncan, U.S. Secretary of Education, in a speech on June 2, 2013.[1] Yet less than one year

later, in March 2014, Indiana governor Mike Pence (pictured here with students) signed a new state law voiding the Common Core, which legislators in the Hoosier State previously had adopted in 2010. In explaining this reversal, Pence said in a press release, "I believe our students are best served when decisions about education are made at the state and local level. By signing this legislation, Indiana has taken an important step forward in developing academic standards that are written by Hoosiers, for Hoosiers, and are uncommonly high, and I commend members of the General Assembly for their support."[2]

The development of the Common Core and ongoing discussions about it reveal the disagreements that exist across the country about the proper role that national, state, and local officials should play in governing the nation's schools. Although the U.S. Constitution declares that the national government was created, among other things, to "promote the general Welfare," which arguably could include helping to educate the population, the nation's founding document never mentions education or schools. Yet schooling is a major topic, often spelled out in great detail, in the constitutions that govern each of the nation's fifty states. Strictly speaking, national officials did not participate in the writing of the Common Core standards, but the national government's financial and rhetorical support for them led some skeptics to wonder if Duncan and the federal education department nevertheless were too deeply involved and therefore had threatened state authority.

Debates about the Common Core reflect different views on the respective **sovereignty**, or the quality of being supreme in power or authority, of national and state governments. In this chapter, we examine American federalism in theory and in practice. Is the division of power between the nation and states a matter of constitutional principle or practical politics? How does the balance of power between the nation and states relate to the conflicts between freedom and order and between freedom and equality? How does federalism influence American relations with other countries and domestic politics in nations around the world? Does federalism reflect the pluralist or the majoritarian model of democracy?

sovereignty
The quality of being supreme in power or authority.

LISTEN & LEARN
MindTap™ for American Government

Access Read Speaker to listen to Chapter 4.

★ Theories and Metaphors

LO1 ★ Compare and contrast the two theories of federalism used to describe the American system of government.

The delegates who met in Philadelphia in 1787 were supposed to repair weaknesses in the Articles of Confederation. Instead, they tackled the problem of making one nation out of thirteen independent states by doing something much more radical: they wrote a new constitution and invented a new political form—federal government—that combined features of a confederacy with features of unitary government (see Chapter 3). Under the principle of **federalism**, two or more governments exercise power and authority over the same people and the same territory.

Still, this new national government did not intrude explicitly into the states' domain. The new constitution granted Congress express authority for only one service within the states, the creation of a postal system. Powers were meant to be exclusive or shared. For example, the governments of the United States and Pennsylvania share certain powers (the power to tax, for instance), but other powers belong exclusively to one or the other. As James Madison wrote in *Federalist* No. 10, "The federal Constitution forms a happy combination … [of] the great and aggregate interests being referred to the national, and the local and particular to state governments." So the power to coin money belongs to the national government, but the power to grant divorces remains a state prerogative. By contrast, authority over state militias may sometimes belong to the national government and sometimes to the states. The history of American federalism reveals that it has not always been easy to draw a line between what is "great and aggregate" and what is "local and particular."*

Nevertheless, federalism offered a solution to the problem of diversity in America. Citizens feared that without a federal system of government, majorities with different interests and values from different regions would rule them. Federalism also provided a new political model.

The history of American federalism is full of attempts to capture its true meaning in an adjective or a metaphor. By one reckoning, scholars have generated nearly five hundred ways to describe federalism.[3] Perhaps this is not surprising given one

federalism
The division of power between a central government and regional governments.

---

*The phrase Americans commonly use to refer to their central government—*federal government*—muddies the waters even more. Technically, we have a federal system of government, which encompasses both the national and state governments. To avoid confusion from here on, we use the term *national government* rather than *federal government* when we are talking about the central government.

scholar's view that the American federal system is "subject to constant reinterpretation. It is long on change and confusion and very low on fixed, generally accepted principles."[4] Still, before complicating the picture too much, it will be useful to focus on two common representations of the system: dual federalism and cooperative federalism.

Dual Federalism

The term **dual federalism** sums up a theory about the proper relationship between the national government and the states. The theory has four essential parts. First, the national government rules by enumerated powers only. Second, the national government has a limited set of constitutional purposes. Third, each government unit—nation and state—is sovereign within its sphere. And, fourth, the relationship between nation and states is best characterized by tension rather than cooperation.[5]

Dual federalism portrays the states as powerful components of the federal system—in some ways, the equals of the national government. Under dual federalism, the functions and responsibilities of the national and state governments are theoretically different and practically separate from each other. Of primary importance in dual federalism are **states' rights**, which reserve to the states or to the people all rights not specifically conferred on the national government by the Constitution. According to the theory of dual federalism, a rigid wall separates the nation and the states. After all, if the states created the nation, by implication they can set limits on the activities of the national government. Proponents of states' rights believe that the powers of the national government should be interpreted narrowly.

Debates about states' rights often emerge over differing interpretations of a given national government policy or proposed policy. Whether the Constitution has delegated to the national government the power to make such policy or whether it remains with the states or the people is often an open and difficult question to answer. States' rights supporters insist that the activities of Congress should be confined to the enumerated powers. They support their view by quoting the Tenth Amendment: "The powers not delegated to the United States by the Constitution, nor prohibited by it to the States, are reserved to the States respectively, or to the people." Conversely, those people favoring national action frequently point to the Constitution's elastic clause, which gives Congress the **implied powers** needed to execute its enumerated powers.

Regardless of whether one favors national action or states' rights, political scientists use a metaphor to describe the idea of dual federalism. They call it *layer-cake federalism* (see Figure 4.1), in which the powers and functions of the national and state governments are as separate as the layers of a cake. Each government is supreme in its own layer, its own sphere of action. The two layers are distinct, and the dimensions of each layer are fixed by the Constitution.

Cooperative Federalism

Cooperative federalism, a phrase coined in the 1930s, is a different theory of the relationship between the national and state governments. It acknowledges the increasing overlap between state and national functions and rejects the idea of separate spheres, or layers, for the states and the national government. Cooperative federalism has three elements. First, national and state agencies typically undertake government functions jointly rather than exclusively. Second, the nation and states routinely share power. And third, power is not concentrated at any government level or in any

dual federalism
A view holding that the Constitution is a compact among sovereign states, so that the powers of the national government and the states are clearly differentiated.

states' rights
The idea that all rights not specifically conferred on the national government by the U.S. Constitution are reserved to the states.

implied powers
Those powers that Congress needs to execute its enumerated powers.

cooperative federalism
A view holding that the Constitution is an agreement among people who are citizens of both state and nation, so there is much overlap between state powers and national powers.

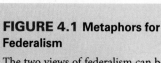

FIGURE 4.1 Metaphors for Federalism

The two views of federalism can be represented graphically.

Source: © Cengage Learning.

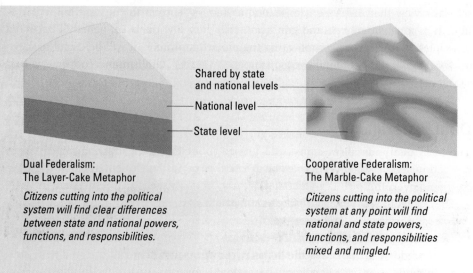

Shared by state and national levels
National level
State level

Dual Federalism:
The Layer-Cake Metaphor

Citizens cutting into the political system will find clear differences between state and national powers, functions, and responsibilities.

Cooperative Federalism:
The Marble-Cake Metaphor

Citizens cutting into the political system at any point will find national and state powers, functions, and responsibilities mixed and mingled.

agency; the fragmentation of responsibilities gives people and groups access to many venues of influence.

The bakery metaphor used to describe this type of federalism is a marble cake (see Figure 4.1).* The national and state governments do not act in separate spheres; they are intermingled in vertical and diagonal strands and swirls. In short, their functions are mixed in the American federal system. Critical to this theory is an expansive view of the Constitution's supremacy clause (Article VI), which specifically subordinates state law to national law and charges every government official with disregarding state laws that are inconsistent with the Constitution, national laws, or treaties.

Some scholars argue that the layer-cake metaphor has never accurately described the American political structure.[6] In practice, the national and state governments have many common objectives and have often cooperated to achieve them. In the nineteenth century, for example, cooperation, not separation, made it possible to develop transportation systems, such as canals, and to establish state land-grant colleges.

A critical difference between the theories of dual and cooperative federalism is the way they interpret two sections of the Constitution that define the relationship between the national and state governments. Article I, Section 8, lists the enumerated powers of Congress and then concludes with the **elastic clause**, which gives Congress the power to "make all Laws which shall be necessary and proper for carrying into Execution the foregoing Powers" (see Chapter 3). The Tenth Amendment reserves for the states or the people powers not assigned to the national government or denied to the states by the Constitution. Dual federalism postulates an inflexible elastic clause and a spacious Tenth Amendment. Cooperative federalism postulates a flexible elastic clause and confines the Tenth Amendment to a self-evident, obvious truth.

Although the Constitution establishes a kind of federalism, the actual and proper balance of power between the nation and states has always been more a matter of debate than of formal theory. Three broad principles help to underscore why. First, rather than operating in a mechanical fashion, American federalism is a flexible and dynamic system. The Constitution's inherent ambiguities about federalism, some of which we have already discussed, generate constraints but also opportunities for

elastic clause
The last clause in Article I, Section 8, of the Constitution, which gives Congress the means to execute its enumerated powers. This clause is the basis for Congress's implied powers. Also called the necessary and proper clause.

---

*A marble cake is a rough mixture of yellow and chocolate cake batter resembling marble stone. If you've never seen or eaten a slice of marble cake, imagine mixing a swirl of vanilla and chocolate soft-freeze ice cream.

politicians, citizens, and interest groups to advance their priorities. Second, because of this flexibility, both elected and appointed officials across levels of government often make policy decisions based on pragmatic considerations without regard to theories of what American federalism should look like. Third, there is a growing recognition among public officials and citizens that public problems (such as questions involving tradeoffs between freedom, order, and equality) cut across governmental boundaries. In sum, politics and policy goals rather than pure theoretical or ideological commitments about federalism tend to dominate decision making.

Federalism's Dynamics

LO2 ★ Identify and explain each of the four forces that stimulate changes in the relationship between the national and state governments.

In order to grasp how American federalism operates in practice, one must know more than simply the powers that the Constitution assigns the different levels of government. Real understanding stems from recognizing the forces that can prompt changes in relationships between the national government and the states. In this section, we focus on four specific forces: national crises and demands, judicial interpretations, the expansion of grants-in-aid, and the professionalization of state governments.

National Crises and Demands

The elastic clause of the Constitution gives Congress the power to make all laws that are "necessary and proper" to carry out its responsibilities. By using this power in combination with its enumerated powers, Congress has increased the scope of the national government tremendously during the previous two centuries. The greatest changes have come about in times of crisis and national emergencies, such as the Civil War; the world wars; the aftermath of September 11, 2001; and the economic recession that began in December 2007 and persisted into President Obama's first term. As an example, consider an even more dramatic economic crisis, the Great Depression of the 1930s.

The Great Depression placed dual federalism in repose. The problems of the Depression proved too extensive for either state governments or private businesses to handle, so the national government assumed much responsibility for providing relief and pursuing economic recovery. Under the New Deal, President Franklin D. Roosevelt's response to the Depression, Congress enacted various emergency programs designed to stimulate economic activity and help the unemployed. Many measures required national and state governments to cooperate. For example, the national government offered money to support state relief efforts; however, to receive these funds, states were usually required to provide administrative supervision or contribute some money of their own.[7]

Some call the New Deal era revolutionary. Clearly, the period was critical in reshaping federalism in the United States. The national and state governments had cooperated before, but the extent of their interactions during President Franklin Roosevelt's administration was unprecedented. In addition, the size of the national government and its budget increased tremendously. But perhaps the most significant change was in the way Americans thought about their problems and the role of the national government in solving them. Difficulties that people at one time would have considered personal or local were now viewed as national problems requiring national solutions. The general welfare, broadly defined, became a legitimate concern of the national government.

In other respects, however, the New Deal was not so revolutionary. For example, Congress did not claim any new powers to address the nation's economic problems. Rather, the national legislature simply used its constitutional powers to suit the circumstances. Arguably those actions were consistent with the overall purpose of the U.S. Constitution, which, as the preamble states, was designed in part to "insure domestic Tranquility … [and] promote the general Welfare."

More recently, concerns over terrorist attacks on U.S. soil have expanded national power. In the month after the events of September 11, 2001, Congress swiftly passed and the president signed into law the USA-PATRIOT Act. (USA-PATRIOT is an acronym for Uniting and Strengthening America by Providing Appropriate Tools Required to Intercept and Obstruct Terrorism.) Among other provisions, the law expanded significantly the surveillance and investigative powers of the Department of Justice. After some disagreement about its structure and organization, federal policymakers created the Department of Homeland Security in 2002, a new department that united over twenty previously separate federal agencies under a common administrative structure. In a move to further expand domestic surveillance activities, President George W. Bush gave approval to wiretaps without warrants of American citizens suspected of terrorist ties. In 2011, President Barack Obama signed a four-year extension of the act's key provisions.[8]

The role of the national government has also grown as it has responded to needs and demands that state and local governments were unwilling or unable to meet. To address the severe economic downturn saddling the nation, President Obama proposed and Congress quickly passed a $787 billion economic stimulus package in February 2009, known as the American Recovery and Reinvestment Act. No Republicans in the House of Representatives and only three Republicans in the Senate voted for the legislation, a clear signal of the charged partisan atmosphere in Washington. The stimulus package offered substantial direct aid to states, which were beleaguered by the recession, in the form of Medicaid payments, extended unemployment benefits, school and infrastructure spending, and other grants. Several Republican governors initially rejected the money, but their bluster receded as furious state legislators in both parties demanded the much needed funds. All governors eventually signed on.[9]

Judicial Interpretation

How federal courts have interpreted the Constitution and federal law is another factor that has influenced the relationship between the national government and the states. The U.S. Supreme Court, the umpire of the federal system, settles disagreements over the powers that national and state leaders claim by deciding whether the actions of either are unconstitutional (see Chapter 14). In the nineteenth and early twentieth centuries, the Supreme Court often decided in favor of the states. Then, for nearly sixty years, from 1937 to 1995, the Court almost always supported the national government in contests involving the balance of power between nation and states. After 1995, a conservative U.S. Supreme Court tended to favor states' rights, but not without some notable and important exceptions. Exploring the Court's federalism jurisprudence provides a useful window on changes to the system that have transpired since the nation's founding.

Ends and Means. Early in the nineteenth century, the nationalist interpretation of federalism prevailed over states' rights. In 1819, under Chief Justice John Marshall (1801–1835), the Supreme Court expanded the role of the national government in the landmark case of *McCulloch* v. *Maryland*. The Court was asked to decide whether Congress had the power to establish a national bank and, if so, whether states had the power to tax that bank. In a unanimous opinion that Marshall authored, the Court conceded that Congress had only the powers conferred on it by the Constitution, which nowhere mentioned banks. However, Article I granted Congress the authority to enact all laws "necessary and proper" to the execution of Congress's enumerated powers. Marshall adopted a broad interpretation of this elastic clause: "Let the end be legitimate, let it be within the scope of the constitution, and all means which are appropriate, which are plainly adapted to that end, which are not prohibited, but consist with the letter and spirit of the constitution, are constitutional."

The Court clearly agreed that Congress had the power to charter a bank. But did the states (in this case, Maryland) have the power to tax the bank? Arguing that "the power to tax involves the power to destroy," Marshall insisted that a state could not tax the national government because the bank represents the interests of the whole nation; a state may not tax those it does not represent. Therefore, a state tax that interferes with the power of Congress to make law is void.[10] Marshall was embracing cooperative federalism, which sees a direct relationship between the people and the national government, with no need for the states to act as intermediaries. The framers of the Constitution did not intend to create a meaningless document, he reasoned. Therefore, they must have meant to give the national government all the powers necessary to carry out its assigned functions, even if those powers are only implied.

Especially from the late 1930s to the mid-1990s, the Supreme Court's interpretation of the Constitution's **commerce clause** was a major factor that increased the national government's power. The third clause of Article I, Section 8, states that "Congress shall have Power … To regulate Commerce … among the several States." In early Court decisions, beginning with *Gibbons* v. *Ogden* in 1824, Chief Justice Marshall interpreted the word *commerce* broadly to include virtually every form of commercial activity. But later courts would take a narrower view of that power.

Roger B. Taney became chief justice in 1836, and during his tenure (1836–1864), the Court's federalism decisions began to favor the states. The Taney Court took a more restrictive view of commerce and imposed firm limits on the powers of the national government. As Taney saw it, the Constitution spoke "not only in the same words, but with the same meaning and intent with which it spoke when it came from the hands of its framers and was voted on and adopted by the people of the United States."[11] In the infamous *Dred Scott* decision (1857), for example, the Court decided that Congress had no power to prohibit slavery in the territories. The judicial winds shifted again during the Great Depression. After originally disagreeing with FDR's and the Congress's position that the economic crisis was a national problem that demanded national action, the Court, with no change in personnel, began to alter its course in 1937 and upheld several major New Deal measures. Perhaps the Court was responding to the 1936 election returns (Roosevelt won reelection in a landslide, and the Democrats commanded a substantial majority in Congress), which signified the voters' endorsement of the use of national policies to address national problems. Or perhaps the Court sought to defuse the president's threat to enlarge the Court with justices sympathetic to his views ("The switch in time that saved nine," rhymed one observer). In any event, the Court abandoned its effort to maintain a rigid boundary between national and state power.[12]

commerce clause
The third clause of Article I, Section 8, of the Constitution, which gives Congress the power to regulate commerce among the states.

The Umpire Adjusts the Strike Zone. In the 1990s, a series of important U.S. Supreme Court rulings involving the commerce clause suggested that the states' rights position was gaining ground once more. The Court's 5–4 ruling in *United States* v. *Lopez* (1995) held that Congress exceeded its authority under the commerce clause when it enacted a law in 1990 banning the possession of a gun in or near a school. A conservative majority, headed by Chief Justice William H. Rehnquist, who joined the Court as a Richard Nixon appointee and was promoted to chief by Ronald Reagan, concluded that having a gun in a school zone "has nothing to do with 'commerce' or any sort of economic enterprise, however broadly one might define those terms." Justices Sandra Day O'Connor, Antonin Scalia, Anthony Kennedy, and Clarence Thomas—all appointed by Republicans as well—joined in Rehnquist's opinion, putting the brakes on congressional power.[13]

Another piece of gun-control legislation, known as the Brady bill, produced similar eventual results. Congress enacted this law in 1993. It mandated the creation by November 1998 of a national system to check the background of prospective gun buyers to weed out, among others, convicted felons and those with mental illness. In the meantime, the law created a temporary system that called for local law enforcement officials to perform background checks and report their findings to gun dealers in their community. Several sheriffs challenged the law.

The Supreme Court agreed with the sheriffs, delivering a double-barreled blow to the local-enforcement provision. In *Printz* v. *United States* (1997), the Court concluded that Congress could not require local officials to implement a regulatory scheme imposed by the national government. In language that seemingly invoked dual federalism, Justice Antonin Scalia, writing for the five-member conservative majority, argued that locally enforced background checks violated the principle of dual sovereignty by allowing the national government "to impress into its service—and at no cost to itself—the police officers of the 50 States." In addition, he wrote, the scheme violated the principle of separation of powers by congressional transfer of the president's responsibility to faithfully execute national laws to local law enforcement officials.[14]

Federalism's Shifting Scales. In what appeared to signal the continuation of a pro–states' rights trajectory, in 2000 the justices struck down congressional legislation that had allowed federal court lawsuits for money damages for victims of crimes "motivated by gender." The Court held that the Violence Against Women Act violated both the commerce clause and Section 5 of the Fourteenth Amendment. Chief Justice Rehnquist, speaking for the five-person majority, declared that "the Constitution requires a distinction between what is truly national and what is truly local."[15]

But just as an umpire's strike zone can be ambiguous—is it knees to belt or knees to letters?—the Court during the last fifteen years has veered from its states' rights direction on federalism. Perhaps the best-known decision in this vein is *Bush* v. *Gore*, the controversial Supreme Court decision resolving the 2000 presidential election. That tight election did not result in an immediate winner because the race in Florida was too close to call. Florida courts, interpreting Florida election law, had ordered ballot recounts, but a divided Supreme Court ordered a halt to the process and gave George W. Bush the victory.

In two subsequent death penalty cases, the Court reflected the ambiguity and dynamic nature that frequently characterize the American federal system. In 2002, the Court concluded that states lacked the power to execute a defendant who was mentally disabled, reasoning that because many states had deemed such a practice inappropriate, "evolving standards of decency" in the nation suggested it was time to halt the practice.[16] In 2005, the Court again relied on evolving standards of decency to strike down a state death penalty for seventeen-year-olds.[17] In both cases, the

Court acted against the policy of individual states by asserting national power to declare that the death penalty in such circumstances amounted to cruel and unusual punishment and thus violated the Constitution.

Grants-in-Aid

Since the 1960s, the national government's use of financial incentives has rivaled its use of legislation and court decisions as a means of influencing its relationship with state governments. Simultaneously, state and local governments have increasingly looked to Washington for money. Leaders at these lower levels of government have attempted to push their own initiatives by getting leverage from new national interest in numerous policy areas. Thus, if governors can somehow convince national policy-makers to adopt laws that buttress state priorities, then these state officials can advance their own ideas even as Washington's power appears to grow. Through a sort of back-and-forth process of negotiation and debate, the dynamics of the American federal system are revealed yet again. The principal arena where many of these interactions occur is in debates over federal grants-in-aid.

A **grant-in-aid** is money paid by one level of government to another level of government, or sometimes to a nongovernmental organization, to be spent for a given purpose. Most grants-in-aid come with standards or requirements prescribed by Congress and accompanying regulations developed by federal agencies that administer the funds. Many grants-in-aid are awarded on a matching basis; that is, a recipient government must make some contribution of its own, which the national government then matches. For example, the nation's primary health-care law for low-income people, Medicaid, requires states to contribute a portion of the funds to help run the program. Grants-in-aid take two general forms: categorical grants and block grants.

Categorical grants target specific purposes, and restrictions on their use typically leave the recipient government relatively little formal discretion. Recipients today include state governments, local governments, and public and private nonprofit organizations. There are two kinds of categorical grants: formula grants and project grants. As their name implies, **formula grants** are distributed according to specific rules that define who is eligible for the grant and how much each eligible applicant will receive. The formulas may weigh factors such as state per capita income, number of school-age children, urban population, and number of families below the poverty line. Most grants, however, are **project grants**, although the total amount of money they provide often can be quite small. Project grants are awarded through a competitive application process and have focused on several policy areas including health (substance abuse and HIV-AIDS programs); natural resources and the environment (radon, asbestos, and toxic pollution); and education, training, and employment (for disabled, homeless, and elderly persons). Sometimes national policy combines formula and project grants into a single program. An example is the Community Development Block Grant, which uses formulas to allocate funds to states and then has states administer competitions to distribute funds to their localities.[18]

In contrast to categorical grants, Congress awards **block grants** for broad, general purposes. They allow recipient governments considerable freedom to decide how to spend the money. Whereas a categorical grant promotes a specific activity—say, developing an ethnic heritage studies curriculum in public schools—a block grant might be earmarked only for elementary, secondary, and vocational education more generally. The state or local government receiving the block grant then chooses the specific educational programs to fund with it. The recipient might use some money to support ethnic heritage studies and some to fund consumer education programs.

grant-in-aid
Money provided by one level of government to another level of government, or sometimes to a nongovernmental organization, to be spent for a given purpose.

categorical grants
Grants-in-aid targeted for a specific purpose by either formula or project.

formula grants
Categorical grants distributed according to a particular set of rules, called a formula, that specifies who is eligible for the grants and how much each eligible applicant will receive.

project grants
Categorical grants awarded on the basis of competitive applications submitted by prospective recipients to perform a specific task or function.

block grants
Grants-in-aid awarded for general purposes, allowing the recipient great discretion in spending the grant money.

Or the recipient might choose to put all the money into consumer education programs and spend nothing on ethnic heritage studies.

Grants-in-aid are a method of redistributing income. Money is collected by the national government from the taxpayers of all fifty states. The money is then funneled back to state and local governments. Many grants have worked to reduce gross inequalities among states and their residents. But the formulas used to redistribute income are not impartial; they are highly political, established through a process of congressional horse-trading.

Although grants-in-aid have been a policy tool of the national government since the early twentieth century, they grew at an astonishing pace in the 1960s, when grant spending doubled every five years. Into the 1970s and 1980s, Presidents Nixon and Reagan were strong advocates for redistributing money back to the states, and political support for such redistribution has remained strong. Controlling for inflation, in 1990 the national government returned $198 billion to the states. By 2010, the amount had increased to $527 billion.[19] The main trend, as illustrated in Figure 4.2, is an enormous growth in health-care spending, which now exceeds 50 percent of all national grant funds to the states.

Whatever its form or purpose, grant money comes with strings attached. Some strings are there to ensure that recipients spend the money as the law specifies; other regulations are designed to evaluate how well the grant is working. To these ends, the national government may stipulate that recipients follow certain procedures. The national government may also attach restrictions designed to achieve some broad national goal not always closely related to the specific purpose of the grant. Consider the issue of drunk driving, for example.

FIGURE 4.2 Trends in National Government Grants to States and Localities, Fiscal Year (FY) 1980 to 2013

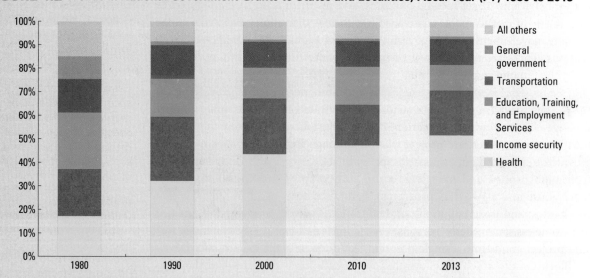

National government grants to states and localities vary substantially. In 1980, grants to support education, training, and employment services programs accounted for the biggest slice of the national government pie. In 1990, grants for health programs, reflecting the expanding costs of Medicaid, took the biggest slice, accounting for more than 30 percent of all national government grant funds to state and local governments. In 2000, health grants exceeded 43 percent of all such national government spending. By 2013, despite a downturn in the overall budget, health grants consumed more than 50 percent of national government grant funds to the states, yet another indicator of the health-care challenges confronting the nation.

Source: Historical Tables, *Budget of the United States Government*, FY2015, Table 12.3, http://www.gpo.gov/fdsys/pkg/BUDGET-2015-TAB/pdf/BUDGET-2015-TAB.pdf.

The use of highway construction funds has proved an effective means to induce states to accept national standards. Congress threatened to reduce millions of dollars in these funds if states did not agree to prohibit the purchase or consumption of alcoholic beverages by persons under the age of twenty-one. Some states objected, yet the Supreme Court upheld this condition in *South Dakota* v. *Dole* (1987), and by 1988 every state had approved legislation setting twenty-one as the minimum drinking age.

More recently, a new and potentially limiting principle to the exercise of national power arose in the legal challenges to the Affordable Care Act. A 2012 blockbuster showdown in the Supreme Court produced a slim 5–4 victory for the act's proponents on the basis of the national government's taxing power, upholding the "individual mandate." On the specific issue of grants to the states, however, by a 7–2 vote, the justices held that the national government could not threaten states with the complete loss of federal funding for Medicaid should states refuse to comply with the act's Medicaid expansion.[20] That expansion was a key part of the law, which its proponents assumed all states would accept.[21] As Figure 4.3 shows, however, as of early

FIGURE 4.3 **Status of State Acceptance of the Affordable Care Act's Medicaid Expansion, June 2014**

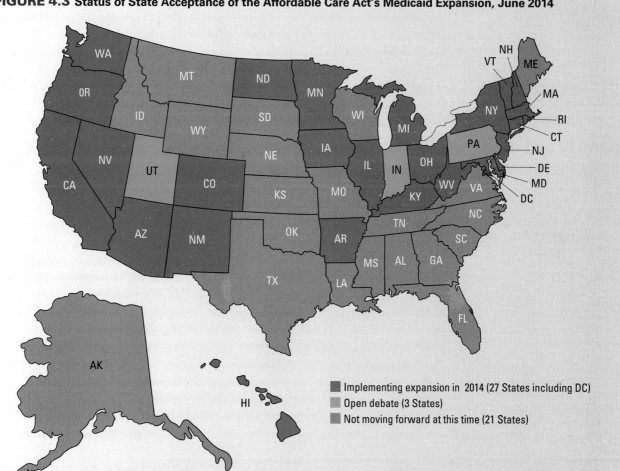

Medicaid is the nation's primary program to provide health care to people with low incomes. A provision in the Affordable Care Act expanded the program to better cover the uninsured. States were not required to accept the expansion, however, and, as the map shows, there remains much disagreement across the states about whether to do so.

Source: Kaiser Family Foundation, "Current Status of State Medicaid Expansion Decisions," http://kff.org/health-reform/slide/current-status-of-the-medicaid-expansion-decision/.

2014 not all states agreed, and the Supreme Court's decision allowed them to decline to participate without threatening the Medicaid dollars they previously had been receiving.

Professionalization of State Governments

A final important factor that has produced dynamic changes in the American federal system is that state governments have become more capable policy actors than they were in the past. While political scientists generally agree that the rise of competitive party politics in the South (see Chapter 8), the growth of money in elections (Chapter 9), and the expansion of the interest group system (Chapter 10) have all produced significant changes in American politics, nevertheless many scholars and students rarely consider the expanded capabilities of state governments in the same light. That oversight is important, especially given how far the states have come during the past four decades and how their progress has influenced the shape of American federalism.

It was not long ago that states were described as the weak links in the American policy system. Despite the crucial role that they played in the nation's founding and the legacy of dual federalism, observers both inside and outside the government were skeptical of their ability to contribute actively and effectively to national progress in the post–World War II era. In an oft-quoted book published in 1967, former North Carolina governor Terry Sanford leveled heavy criticisms at the states, calling them ineffective, indecisive, and inattentive organizations that, without reforms, would lose their relevance in an increasingly complicated nation and world.[22]

But since the 1960s especially, states have become more capable and forceful policy actors. These changes have created better policy outcomes that have benefited citizens across the United States while simultaneously contributing to dynamic changes in the American federal system. If the situation was so bleak less than five decades ago, what has happened since then? Several factors account for the change in perspective.[23]

First, the states have made many internal changes that have improved their capabilities. Governors, state legislators, and the agencies that support their work now employ more capably trained, experienced, and often specialized policy staff rather than part-time assistants with responsibilities across numerous policy areas. Second, legislatures now meet more days during the year, and elected officials in states receive higher salaries, a change that has helped attract more highly qualified people to run for state office. Third, the increasing ability of states to raise revenue, as a result of state tax and budgetary reforms that have transpired since the 1960s, has also given states greater leverage in designing and directing policy. This contrasts with previous generations, where local property taxes played a more significant role in relation to state budget and tax policy. And, fourth, the unelected officials who work in state departments and administer state programs in areas such as transportation, social services, and law enforcement have become better educated.

As evidence of the dynamic relationships between the national government and the states, changes in national policy have also helped the states develop. Many federal grants-in-aid include components designed explicitly to foster capacity-building measures in state governments. Because the national government recognizes—often for political or practical reasons—that several of its domestic initiatives depend on capable implementation from state actors, members of

Congress and presidents often design national laws with these capacity-building elements in mind.

Although state government capabilities have improved, states still face significant problems and challenges. In some ways, the states have been victims of their own success. Now that state capitals have become more viable venues where citizens and interest groups can agitate for their causes, the states have begun to face ever-increasing demands. Those requests can strain state administrators and legislative or gubernatorial staffs, who, while better educated and equipped than their predecessors, still struggle to set priorities and please their constituents.

Ideology, Policymaking, and American Federalism

LO3 ★ Describe the role of ideology in shaping federalism.

As the previous section illustrated, American federalism appears to be in constant motion. This is due in large part to what some political scientists call **policy entrepreneurs**: citizens, interest groups, and officials inside government who attempt to persuade others to accept a particular view of the proper balance of freedom, order, and equality. The American federal system provides myriad opportunities for interested parties to push their ideas.

policy entrepreneurs
Citizens, members of interest groups, or public officials who champion particular policy ideas.

In essence, the existence of national and state governments—specifically, their executive, legislative, and judicial branches and their bureaucratic agencies—offers these entrepreneurs venues where they can attempt to influence policy and politics. Sometimes when doors are closed in one place, opportunities may be available elsewhere, a process that researchers call "venue shopping."[24] The most creative of these entrepreneurs can work at multiple levels of government simultaneously, sometimes coordinating with one another to score political and policy victories.

In this section, we explore how views about American federalism can influence the nation's politics and policy. We also relate these issues to our ongoing discussion of political ideology, which we introduced in Chapter 1 (see Figure 1.2).

Ideology, Policymaking, and Federalism in Theory

To begin, recall the theories of dual and cooperative federalism mentioned earlier. Those models of the nation's federal system help capture some of what could be considered conventional wisdom about political ideology and federalism—in particular, the views of conservatives and liberals. In their efforts to limit the scope of the national government, conservatives are often associated with dual federalism. In contrast, it is often said that liberals, believing that one function of the national government is to bring about equality, are more likely to support the cooperative approach and more activism from Washington. Let's explore each of these general claims in a bit more detail.

People often describe conservatives as believing that different states have different problems and resources and that returning control to state governments would improve policymaking. States would be free to experiment with alternative ways to confront their problems. States would compete with one another. And people would be free to choose the state government they preferred by simply voting with their feet and moving. An additional claim frequently attributed to the conservative approach

Federalism in Global Politics

Working for the Public

The national government in the United States employs about 2 million people. But if we factor in individuals employed through grants and contracts that the national government supports, the number of national government employees balloons to around 15 million. When we factor in all public employees at the national, state, and local levels, we get a greater sense of the presence of government in our lives. Figure A compares the number of public sector workers at all levels controlling for population across several countries. In this comparison, public sector employment is approximately 71 workers for every 1,000 Americans. This is about average across all the countries compared. Public sector employment in the United States is roughly half of that in Norway and Sweden, much smaller countries with substantial public welfare programs. Public sector employment in the United States is greater than that in countries such as Germany and Japan.

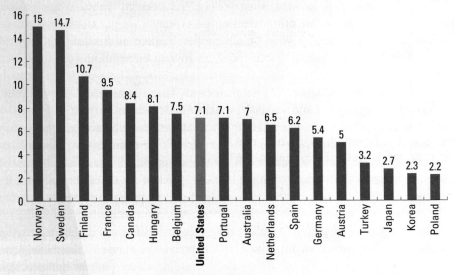

Figure A. Public Sector Employment as a Percentage of Total Population (2005)

The distribution of public sector employment between the national level on the one hand and the state and local levels on the other produces a different picture (see Figure B). By far, most public sector workers in the United States are

to federalism is that the national government is too remote, too tied to special interests, and not responsive to the public at large. The national government overregulates and tries to promote too much uniformity. States are closer to the people and better able to respond to specific local needs.

In contrast, others often argue that what conservatives hope for, liberals fear. Liberals remember, so the argument goes, that the states' rights model allowed extreme political and social inequalities and that it supported racism. Blacks and city dwellers were often left virtually unrepresented by white state legislators who disproportionately

found at the state and local levels. Higher state and local employment is also characteristic of other federal systems, such as those of Australia, Germany, and Canada. So if you ponder the question "Where is my government?" a postal worker would satisfy the national government part of the answer. Local government employees are far more numerous, working at the firehouse, the police station, or your local public school.

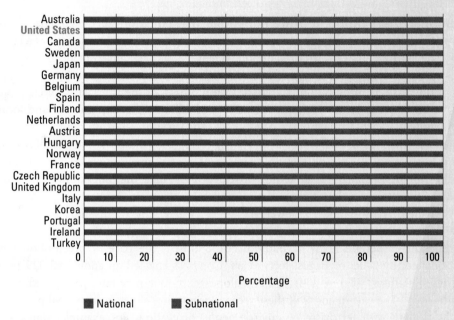

Figure B. Distribution of Employment Between the National and Subnational Levels of Government (2005)

Sources: Adam Sheingate, "Why Can't Americans See the State?" *The Forum* 7, no. 4 (2010): 1–14; Paul C. Light, "The New True Size of Government," *Organizational Performance Initiative: Research Brief, Number 2* (Robert F. Wagner Graduate School of Public Service, New York University, August 2006), p. 11.

Critical Thinking The size of the public sector and its distribution across national, state, and local governments vary considerably across countries. Why might some nations prefer to employ more people in the national government, while others prefer to have more employed by state and local governments?

served rural interests. The conclusion is that liberals believe the states remain unwilling or unable to protect civil rights or attend to their citizens' needs, whether those citizens are consumers seeking protection from business interests, defendants requiring guarantees of due process of law, or poor people seeking a minimum standard of living. The national government is uniquely positioned, many liberals contend, to help create important floors of support, be they in access to health care, housing, or other essential needs. That argument suggests a preference for an active national government and cooperative federalism.

Nutrition Facts

Serving Size ¾ cup (31g)
Servings Per Container about 11

Amount Per Serving	Cinnamon Toast Crunch	with ½ cup skim milk
Calories	130	170
Calories from Fat	30	30
	% Daily Value**	
Total Fat 3g*	**5%**	**5%**
Saturated Fat 0.5g	**2%**	**2%**
Trans Fat 0g		
Polyunsaturated Fat 0.5g		
Monounsaturated Fat 2g		
Cholesterol 0mg	**0%**	**1%**
Sodium 220mg	**9%**	**12%**
Potassium 45mg	**1%**	**7%**
Total Carbohydrate 25g	**8%**	**10%**
Dietary Fiber 1g	**4%**	**4%**
Sugars 10g		
Other Carbohydrate 14g		
Protein 1g		
Vitamin A	10%	15%
Vitamin C	10%	10%
Calcium	10%	25%
Iron	25%	25%
Vitamin D	10%	25%
Thiamin	25%	30%
Riboflavin	25%	35%
Niacin	25%	25%
Vitamin B6	25%	25%
Folic Acid	25%	25%
Vitamin B12	25%	35%
Phosphorus	4%	15%
Magnesium	2%	6%
Zinc	25%	30%
Copper	2%	2%

* Amount in cereal. A serving of cereal plus skim milk provides 3g total fat, less than 5mg cholesterol, 280mg sodium, 250mg potassium, 30g total carbohydrate (16g sugars) and 5g protein.

** Percent Daily Values are based on a 2,000 calorie diet. Your daily values may be higher or lower depending on your calorie needs:

		Calories	2,000	2,500
Total Fat	Less than		65g	80g
Sat Fat	Less than		20g	25g
Cholesterol	Less than		300mg	300mg
Sodium	Less than		2,400mg	2,400mg
Potassium			3,500mg	3,500mg
Total Carbohydrate			300g	375g
Dietary Fiber			25g	30g

Sarah-Maria Vischer/The Image Works

Label Me

Food labeling follows a single national standard today as a result of the Nutrition Labeling and Education Act of 1990. The act preempted states from imposing different labeling requirements.

Ideology, Policymaking, and Federalism in Practice

Despite refrains such as "liberals love the national government" and "conservatives favor states' rights," these simplifications are only sometimes correct and, in fact, are often misleading. Recall our admonition from Chapter 1 that to grasp the differences between conservatives and liberals, one needs to understand not only these general labels but also the purposes of government under discussion. One illustration emerges from debates over the federal preemption of state power.

National Intervention in State Functions. The power of Congress to enact laws by which the national government assumes complete or partial responsibility for a state government function is called **preemption**. When the national government shoulders a new government function, it restricts the discretionary power of the states.

Congressional prohibition of state or local taxation of the Internet is an example of complete preemption.[25] It represents a loss of billions of dollars to state and local governments. Partial preemption occurs with the enactment of minimum national standards that states must meet if they wish to regulate the field. The Do Not Call Implementation Act of 2003 is an example of partial preemption. States retained authority to regulate telemarketing provided they met the minimum standards spelled out by the act.[26]

Preemption is a modern power. Congress passed only twenty-nine preemptive acts before 1900. In the ensuing sixty years, Congress preempted the power of states to legislate in certain areas an additional 153 times. The pace of preemption has accelerated. By 2000, or in just forty years, Congress enacted an additional 329 preemption statutes.[27] From 2001 to 2005 alone, sixty-four new laws preempted state authority.[28] The vast majority of these recent preemption efforts were partial preemptions dealing with terrorism or environmental protection. For example, states are now forbidden to issue licenses to carriers of hazardous materials without a determination by the secretary of transportation that the person is not a security risk. This is a provision in the USA-PATRIOT Act.

Congressional preemption statutes infringe on state powers in two ways: through mandates and restraints. A **mandate** is a requirement that a state undertake an activity or provide a service, in keeping with minimum national standards. A mandate might require that states remove specified pollutants from public drinking water supplies, for example. In contrast, a **restraint** forbids state governments from exercising a certain power. A restraint might prohibit states from dumping sewage into the ocean.

The increased use of preemption has given birth to a new theory of federalism. The pressure to expand national power inherent in cooperative federalism has reduced the national government's reliance on fiscal tools such as grants-in-aid. Instead, the national government has come to rely on regulatory tools such as mandates and restraints to ensure the supremacy of federal policy. According to this view, cooperative federalism has morphed into **coercive federalism**.[29]

Constraining Unfunded Mandates. State and local government officials have long objected to the national government's practice of imposing requirements without providing the financial support needed to satisfy them. For example, the provisions in the Americans with Disabilities Act require nearly all American business owners to make their business premises available to disabled customers, without providing any funds for the cost of reconstruction or additional interior space. By 1992, more than 170 congressional acts had established partially or wholly unfunded mandates.[30]

One of the early results of the Republican-led 104th Congress (1995–1997) was the Unfunded Mandates Relief Act of 1995. The legislation requires the Congressional

Budget Office to prepare cost estimates of any newly proposed national legislation that would impose more than $50 million a year in costs on state and local governments or more than $100 million a year in costs on private business. It also requires a cost analysis of the impact of new agency regulations on governments and private businesses. (It is important to note that the Relief Act does not apply to legislation protecting constitutional rights and civil rights or to antidiscrimination laws.)

In practice, the law has been merely a speed bump rather than a blockade.[31] Its critics argue that large proportions of state budgets still must cover the costs of programs imposed by the national government. For example, the National Conference of State Legislatures estimated that Real ID, a federally mandated program that imposes security, authentication, and issuance standards for states to issue driver's licenses and identification cards, will cost $11 billion through 2012.[32] To pay for the program, states may be forced to raise fees or taxes on their constituents. Through coercive federalism, the national government now calls the tune for still more activities that were once the sole province of individual states. But coercion has limits, as the legislative debates and the Supreme Court's review of the Affordable Care Act both illustrate. While the Court limited the federal government's ability to force states to accept the Medicaid expansion, legislators crafting the law also allowed states to opt out of creating a health exchange where their residents could buy insurance by including language in the law stating that the national government would be responsible for establishing exchanges in states that chose not to establish them.

★ Federalism and Electoral Politics

LO4 ★ Describe the influence of federalism on elections at the state and national levels.

In addition to affecting the shape of American public policy, federalism plays a significant role in electoral politics. We have much more to say about elections in Chapter 9. For now, we focus on the ways that federalism is related to state and national election outcomes.

National Capital–State Capital Links

State capitals often serve as proving grounds for politicians who aspire to national office. After gaining experience in a state legislature or serving in a statewide elected position (governor or attorney general, for example), elected officials frequently draw on that experience in making a pitch for service in the U.S. House, the Senate, or even the White House. The role that state political experience can play in running for president seems to have become increasingly important in recent decades. Consider that since 1976, four of the previous six candidates to be elected to the highest office in the land had formerly served as governors: Jimmy Carter (Georgia), Ronald Reagan (California), Bill Clinton (Arkansas), and George W. Bush (Texas). George H. W. Bush and Barack Obama are the exceptions, although Obama had been a state legislator in Illinois. Today, several prominent members of Congress also have past experience in statewide offices. Examples as of 2014 are Senator Lamar Alexander (Rep.), former governor of Tennessee; Senator Mark Warner (Dem.) and Senator Tim Kaine (Dem.), both former governors of Virginia; and Senator Bill Nelson (Rep.) of Florida, who formerly was a state legislator as well as Florida's state treasurer, insurance commissioner, and fire marshall.

preemption
The power of Congress to enact laws by which the national government assumes total or partial responsibility for a state government function.

mandate
A requirement that a state undertake an activity or provide a service, in keeping with minimum national standards.

restraint
A requirement prohibiting a state or local government from exercising a certain power.

coercive federalism
A view holding that the national government may impose its policy preferences on the states through regulations in the form of mandates and restraints.

CONNECT WITH YOUR CLASSMATES
MindTap™ for American Government

Access the Federalism Forum: Discussion—Patient Protection and the Affordable Care Act.

Official White House Photo by Pete Souza

Born to Run?

In October 2012, President Obama (Dem.) and New Jersey Governor Chris Christie (Rep.) toured areas of the Garden State that had been devastated by Hurricane Sandy, here meeting with residents at the Brigantine Beach Community Center. Still, even during such a national emergency, discussions of electoral politics lingered. Some pundits and party insiders wondered if the governor's praise of Obama and federal help, on the eve of the 2012 elections, was perhaps too friendly and might undermine Christie's own future stature in the GOP should he choose to run for president in 2016.

One should not underestimate the value of previous political experience in attempting to mount a campaign for national office. In addition to learning the craft of being a politician, experience in state politics can be critically important for helping a candidate to develop a network of contacts, die-hard constituents, and potential fundraisers. Past governors also have the benefit of being plugged into organizations such as the National Governors' Association and the Republican and Democratic governors' groups, which can help to cultivate national name recognition, friendships, and a reputation in Washington. Finally, considering that presidential elections are really a series of fifty different state-level contests, given the structure of the electoral college, a candidate for the White House can benefit tremendously from a friendly governor who can mobilize his or her own political network on the candidate's behalf.

If state-level experience and friends can sometimes catapult an individual to national office, once secure in Congress or the White House, national-level politicians frequently return to the states to stump for local favorites. In 2013, for example, President Obama campaigned for his fellow Democrat, Terry McAuliffe, who was running for governor in Virginia, which holds state elections in odd-numbered years. Virginia has become an increasingly competitive state in national presidential politics and helped Obama secure the White House in 2008 and 2012.[33] With Obama's help, McAuliffe won that contest.

Congressional Redistricting

Perhaps even more important than activities on the campaign trail is the decennial process of congressional redistricting, which reveals crucial connections between federalism and the nation's electoral politics. Most generally, **redistricting** refers to the process of redrawing boundaries for electoral jurisdictions. Redistricting becomes an extremely high-stakes game in the two years after each decennial national census in the United States. During that window of time, the U.S. Census Bureau produces and releases updated population counts for the nation. Those numbers are used to determine the number of seats, apportioned based on population, that each state will have in the U.S. House.

While it is relatively straightforward to determine how many seats each state will have, drawing the new district lines is a hugely complicated and political process. Even in states that may not have lost or gained seats but have had population shifts—some areas grow at a rapid rate while others lose population, for example—the task of redistricting carries huge stakes because it happens once per decade and because state legislatures typically draw the lines that define the congressional districts in their states.

redistricting
The process of redrawing boundaries for electoral jurisdictions to reflect changes in population.

An important way that federalism has influenced redistricting is through a process called *preclearance*. Under Section 5 of the Voting Rights Act, several states have been required to submit their redistricting plans to the U.S. Department of Justice for approval. The process is quite complicated, but in essence it requires that states show how their proposed plans will not be "retrogressive in purpose or effect," meaning they will not dilute minority voting strength. Given the recent U.S. Supreme Court decision *Shelby County* v. *Holder* (2013), the future influence of Section 5 is uncertain. In a 5–4 decision, the Court left Section 5 untouched, but instead determined that the process used to decide whether preclearance was necessary, a process outlined in Section 4 of the act, was unconstitutional because, the majority reasoned, it relied on outdated information and methods. This decision means that if Section 5 is to empower the national government to subject states to preclearance, Congress will have to rewrite Section 4. Political observers see that outcome as doubtful, given the highly polarized climate in Congress and the extremely high stakes associated with redistricting.[34]

AP Images/Austin American Statesman, Larry Kolvoord

Drawing Lines in the Texas Sand

Texas state senators José Rodriguez, (Dem., left) and Steve Ogden (Rep., right) discuss proposed redistricting maps in the state legislature on June 6, 2011. As one of the largest states in the nation, Texas holds thirty-six seats in the U.S. House.

Federalism and the American Intergovernmental System

LO5 ★ Describe the role of local government in a federal system and illustrate how national, state, and local governments sometimes interact.

So far, this chapter has focused on the links between the national and state governments in the federal system, the two levels of government that the Constitution explicitly recognizes. As the United States has evolved since its founding, thousands of local governments have emerged as well. It is worth considering these local units because they help to illustrate the third main principle that we outlined near the beginning of this chapter: a growing recognition among public officials and citizens that public problems cut across governmental boundaries. The **intergovernmental system** is the term that researchers use to characterize the overall collection of national, state, and local governments in the United States. This is a much broader concept than the idea of federalism, which, strictly speaking and in the usage of the founders, refers only to the relationship between the national government and the states. As a practical matter, finding the right mix of national, state, and local involvement to address public problems is a perennial concern that challenges even the most pragmatic and experienced public officials.

intergovernmental system
The collection of governments made up of national, state, and local units of government.

Thousands of Governments

Based on data from 2012, the U.S. Census Bureau estimates that in addition to the one national government and fifty state governments, the United States is home to over 90,000 local governments of different sorts.[35] These governments are mainly the product of the previous century of American history, with nearly all coming into existence during the 1900s.

Americans are citizens of both a nation and a state, and they also come under the jurisdiction of various local government units. These units include **municipal governments**, the governments of cities and towns. Municipalities, in turn, are located in (or may contain or share boundaries with) counties, which are administered by **county governments**. (Sixteen states further subdivide counties into *townships* as units of government.) Most Americans also live in a **school district**, which is responsible for administering local elementary and secondary educational programs and in most states cut across county boundaries. People may also be served by one or more **special districts**, government units created to perform particular functions, typically when those functions, such as fire protection and water purification and distribution, spill across ordinary jurisdictional boundaries. Examples of special districts are the Port Authority of New York and New Jersey, the Chicago Sanitation District, and the Southeast Pennsylvania Transit Authority. Together, school districts and special districts add more than 50,000 units of government to the mix.

Local governments are created by state governments, either in their constitutions or through legislation. This means that their organization, powers, responsibilities, and effectiveness vary considerably from state to state. About forty states endow their cities with various forms of **home rule**—the right to enact and enforce legislation in certain administrative areas. Home rule gives cities a measure of self-government and freedom of action. In contrast, county governments, which are the main units of local government in rural areas, tend to have little or no legislative power. Instead, they ordinarily serve as administrative units, performing the specific duties assigned to them under state law, such as maintaining roads and administering health programs.

How can individuals be expected to make sense of this maze of governments? And do these governments really benefit ordinary citizens?

In theory at least, one advantage of localizing government is that it brings government closer to the people who can participate in the political process and have a direct influence on policy. Localized government conjures visions of informed citizens deciding their own political fate—the traditional New England town meeting, repeated across the nation. From this perspective, overlapping governments appear compatible with a majoritarian view of democracy.

The reality is somewhat different, however. Studies have shown that people are much less likely to vote in local elections than in national elections.[36] In fact, voter turnout in local contests tends to be quite low (although the influence of individual votes is thus much greater), in part because these races tend to have little publicity, and often, when the races are nonpartisan, candidates' names are not associated with party labels, which deprives voters of an easy cue in deciding for whom to vote. Furthermore, the fragmentation of powers, functions, and responsibilities among national, state, and local governments makes government as a whole seem complicated and frequently incomprehensible or inaccessible to ordinary people. In addition, most people have little time to devote to public affairs, which can be very time-consuming. These factors tend to discourage individual citizens from pursuing politics and augment the influence of organized groups, which have the resources—time, money, and know-how—

municipal governments
The government units that administer a city or town.

county governments
The government units that administer a county.

school districts
The government units that administer elementary and secondary schools and programs.

special districts
Government units created to perform particular functions, especially when those functions are best performed across jurisdictional boundaries.

home rule
The right to enact and enforce legislation locally.

to sway policymaking (see Chapter 10) or to rally their supporters to vote in local elections where very few other voters bother to turn out. Instead of bringing government closer to the people and reinforcing majoritarian democracy, the system's enormous complexity tends to encourage pluralism.

Still, the large number of governments makes it possible for government to respond to the diversity of conditions across the country. States and cities differ enormously in population, size, economic resources, climate, and other characteristics—the diverse elements that French political philosopher Montesquieu argued should be considered in formulating laws for a society. Smaller political units are better able to respond to particular local conditions and can generally do so more quickly than larger units. Nevertheless, smaller units may not be able to muster the economic resources to meet some challenges, as occurred in 2012 with Hurricane Sandy, which devastated the northeast. And in a growing number of policy areas, from education to environmental protection to welfare provision, citizens have come to see the advantages of coordinating efforts and sharing burdens across levels of government.

Kevin Moloney/The New York Times/Redux

Whose Rules?

Grand Staircase–Escalante National Monument in southern Utah was established by presidential decree in 1996. It sits on 1.7 million acres of austere and rugged land. The decree irked local residents, who had hoped for greater industrial development, which is now barred. They have fought back by claiming ownership of hundreds of miles of dirt roads, dry washes, and riverbeds in the monument. The conflicting signs illustrate the controversy. On the left, the local government, Kane County, approves use of all-terrain vehicles. On the right, the national government signals just the opposite.

Crosscutting Responsibilities

The national government continues to support other governments in the intergovernmental system. Yet spending pressures on state and local governments are enormous. The public demands better schools, harsher sentences for criminals (and more prisons to hold them), more and better day care for children, and nursing home assistance for the elderly. Bolstered by a strong national economy, many states cut income and business taxes in 2006. Other states provided local property tax relief. However, the deep and lengthy recession that began in 2008, and whose aftermath still persists, has added extra strains on state finances. During the deepest trough of the downturn, a majority of states reported their revenues had been hurt by the housing sector slump. Most, if not all, saw declines in their real estate transfer or recording taxes. Higher oil prices provided Alaska with a budget surplus, but that was the exception. With high unemployment, lower property values, fewer property sales, and general economic sluggishness, tax revenues failed to match state expenditures. And, unlike the national government's budget, state budgets must balance each year, which requires states either to cut services, raise taxes, or borrow money when shortfalls exist. Needless to say, these are not popular options. As another way to bolster their finances, some states have taken the dramatic move of leasing large public assets to private investors, who then can profit from them for the duration of the lease. Examples include the City of Chicago leasing its parking meters and the state of Indiana leasing the Indiana toll road.[37]

John Munson/Star Ledger/Corbis

Cooperating Cops

Police forces at the national, state, and local level have separate and overlapping spheres of responsibility. Here members of the New York Police Department and the Joint Terrorism Task Force of the Federal Bureau of Investigation raid a New Jersey apartment in 2010. The occupants were suspected to have had ties to terrorism suspect Mohamed Hamoud Alessa, who was arrested before getting on a plane at New York's JFK Airport. In 2011, Alessa and another suspect, Carlos Eduardo Almonte, pleaded guilty in federal court to conspiracy to murder individuals on behalf of a foreign terrorist group. In 2013, they were sentenced to twenty-two and twenty years in prison, respectively.

In addition to ongoing policy development and financing the activities of government, sometimes crises press different levels of government into duty together. A tragic turn of events in October 2002 provides a case in point. During that month, the Washington, D.C., metropolitan area found itself under siege from what appeared to be random, yet chillingly precise, attacks from a rifle-wielding sniper. Before the assailants were captured, ten people were killed and four others injured. Law enforcement agents also suggested that the Washington killings may have been related to similar murders in Alabama and Louisiana.

Officials at all levels of government in several states participated in what became a massive hunt for the killers. Although many citizens were pleased to see such a comprehensive effort to halt the shootings, inevitably turf battles emerged among the various jurisdictions involved, as officials in national, state, and local government jockeyed with one another, sometimes to push for their own theories of how the case was unfolding, and, inevitably given the bright spotlight on the whole affair, to score political points with their constituents and the public at large.[38]

Federalism and the International System

LO6 ★ Analyze the role of federalism in American trade policy and in other nations around the world.

In today's increasingly interconnected world, it is perhaps not surprising that federalism is more than simply a local curiosity for U.S. citizens. The dynamics of American federalism, in addition to helping shape the nation's politics, have begun to have more noticeable impacts in the international arena as well. And federalism as a system of government and governance is becoming increasingly important across the globe.

American Federalism and Trade Policy

American federalism can have important impacts on how the United States deals with other nations, even in areas that clearly seem to be the prerogative of the national government. Trade policy is one good example.

Article I, Section 8, of the U.S. Constitution declares that the legislative branch shall have the power "to regulate Commerce with foreign Nations," and Section 10 prohibits individual states from entering "into any Treaty, Alliance, or Confederation," or, without Congress's consent, from laying "any Imposts or Duties on Imports or Exports, except what may be absolutely necessary for executing its inspection Laws." These constitutional provisions provide the national government, but not the states, with significant justification and formal authority to develop foreign trade agreements and regulate imports and exports.

Despite what appears to be a clear constitutional mismatch between national and state officials on trade, state leaders do develop and advance their own trade agendas. In fact, trade policy has a noticeable intergovernmental component. In summarizing developments in state politics, two scholars have noted that states have become more aggressive in establishing their own outposts, so to speak, in other countries.[39] Today, all fifty states have international trade directors, and these officials coordinate several activities through an umbrella group called the State International Development Organizations (SIDO), an affiliate of the Council of State Governments. Additionally, approximately forty states maintain offices overseas to promote their interests in foreign nations.[40]

The involvement of state and local governments in trade-related matters has taken a new twist as concerns about international terrorism have increased. In part of the national response to the attacks on September 11, 2001, the next year Congress passed and President Bush signed the U.S. Maritime Transportation Security Act, which, among other things, charged the U.S. Coast Guard with shepherding a process to develop a national system designed to protect the nation's ports. Although every port has a Coast Guard officer assigned to be the captain of the port, the authority to make decisions about port operations can include independent port authorities, as well as state and local governments. Because no two ports are alike, with some receiving goods from distant markets, others hosting major cruise lines that serve tourists, and others serving as the termination points for oil and gas pipelines, the Coast Guard has had to accommodate a diverse set of state and local interests as it has tried to tighten port security.[41]

Federalism Across the Globe

Supreme Court Justice Anthony Kennedy once observed that "federalism was our Nation's own discovery. The Framers split the atom of sovereignty. It was the genius of their idea that our citizens would have two political capacities, one state and one federal, each protected from incursion by the other."[42] Federalism is not an obsolete nineteenth-century form of government inappropriate in the contemporary world. In fact, the concept of the *nation-state*, developed in the seventeenth century, may be heading for the dustbin. (A *nation-state* is a country with defined and recognized boundaries whose citizens have common characteristics, such as race, religion, customs, and language.)

Some scholars have noted that we may be moving from a world of sovereign nation-states to a world of diminished state sovereignty and increased interstate linkages of a constitutionally federal character. Among the nearly 200 politically sovereign states in the world today, 24 are federations that together embrace about 2.5 billion people, or 40 percent of the world population. Almost 500 constituent or federated states serve as the building blocks of these 24 federations.[43] New versions of the federal idea continue to arise. Countries like Iraq and Sudan are transitioning to federalism, and others such as Sri Lanka and South Sudan are considering adoption of a federal system.[44]

Iraq's experience after the 2003 invasion by U.S. and coalition forces has revealed the challenges inherent in designing a system of government based on federalism. In October 2005 the Iraqi people approved a new constitution that established a federal system with separate legislative, executive, and judicial functions. Former U.S. Ambassador to Croatia Peter Galbraith, a critic of the Bush administration's Iraq policy but a strong defender of the new constitution, has argued that "the constitution reflects the reality of the nation it is meant to serve." "There is," he says, "no meaningful Iraqi identity. In the north, you've got a pro-Western Kurdish population. In the south, you've got a Shiite majority that wants a 'pale version of an Iranian state.' And in the center you've got a Sunni population that is nervous about being trapped in a system in which it would be overrun."[45]

The challenge of democracy for Iraq is to find that delicate balance ensuring enough regional autonomy to satisfy ethnic or religious solidarity but not so much autonomy as to splinter the entire enterprise. American views of democracy may

Freedom, Order, or Equality

Freedom v. Order: Federalism and the Nation's Borders

Arizona governor Jan Brewer (Rep.) meets with President Obama (Dem.) at the White House on June 3, 2010, after Arizona's passage of SB 1070.

In an international system defined by the existence of nation-states, a major policy goal of every country is to maintain the integrity of its international borders. Unlike movement within the United States, where citizens are not required to prove their identities as they move between states, government officials will ask people to present their passports upon entering or leaving a country. These checks are designed to prevent people from moving across national borders who are unable to prove their identities, who are breaking the law in some way, such as bringing illegal goods or smuggling people into or out of a nation, or who may be wanted by law enforcement officials for crimes they have committed.

Debates over immigration policy and the movement of people across borders have prompted clashes between national and state officials. One way to understand these debates is to see them as a conflict between freedom versus order.

For years, Arizonans have borne the burden of illegal immigrants who have sought work and opportunity in the United States, burdens that intensified during the recession of 2007–2009.[1] In 2010, under Governor Jan Brewer, the state legislature adopted a law, SB 1070, taking immigration matters into its own hands. The law was both broad and strict; it went far beyond efforts in other states to address the problem of illegal immigration. More significantly, it went further than the U.S. government has chosen to go. In short, the governor, asserted that the state itself should have the freedom to act more aggressively to combat illegal immigration. This assertion of state power challenged the federal claim that it maintained sovereignty to police the nation's borders.

U.S. law requires foreigners who are not citizens living in the United States, called aliens, to register with the government and carry their registration papers.[2] SB 1070 took this requirement a step further by criminalizing the failure to carry the necessary papers. The new law obligated the police to determine a person's immigration status, when practicable during a "lawful stop, detention or arrest," if

complicate the situation. An Iraq that emulates America's free-style democracy may promote the seeds of its own destruction by giving every zealot a forum. But constraining Iraqi democracy by ruling some extreme viewpoints out of bounds may call into question one of the reasons America intervened in Iraq in the first place: to plant a viable democracy in the Middle East.

While less dramatic than the events in Iraq, the continent of Europe has experienced stresses of its own as its countries have attempted to live together as a more

there is reasonable suspicion that the person is an illegal alien. The law also cracked down on those who hire, transport, or shelter illegal aliens.[3]

The national government sued Arizona in federal court. The United States rested its case on federalism grounds: the Constitution and laws of the United States place the matter of immigration and maintaining orderly borders solely in the hands of the national government. The states remain duty-bound under the Constitution's supremacy clause (Article VI) to bow to national authority.

Just one day before the law was to go into effect, federal judge Susan Bolton blocked its main provisions, including the requirement that police check the immigration status of those arrested or stopped. Her reasoning adopted the position of the United States: principles of federalism give exclusive power over immigration matters to the national government, trumping state efforts at regulating or enforcing national immigration laws as in Arizona.[4] Arizona appealed, but Bolton's decision withstood the challenge.[5] Arizona then appealed to the Supreme Court of the United States, which accepted the case for review and heard arguments from the parties in April 2012. Less than three months later, the Court handed down its ruling.

In a 5–3 decision, the justices invalidated all but one of SB 1070's provisions because they interfered with the national government's role in setting immigration policy. But the Court upheld, at least for now, the part of the law that instructs law enforcement officials to check a person's immigration status if there is a reasonable suspicion that a person is in the country illegally. The justices left matters open for further review should actual practice under this "show-me-your-papers" provision raise new constitutional challenges.[6]

Critical Thinking How would you explain why the federal government appears to support dual federalism on the issue of immigration enforcement, but embraces cooperative federalism in other policy areas, such as provision of social services?

---

[1]Daniel B. Wood, "Opinion Polls Show Broad Support for Tough Arizona Immigration Law," *The Christian Science Monitor*, 30 April 2010, http://www.csmonitor/com/USA/Society/2010/0430/Opinionpolls-show-broad-support-for-tough-Arizona-immigration-law.Daniel B. Wood, "Opinion Polls Show Broad Support for Tough Arizona Immigration Law," *The Christian Science Monitor*, 30 April 2010, http://www.csmonitor/com/USA/Society/2010/0430/Opinionpolls-show-broad-support-for-tough-Arizona-immigration-law.
[2]8 U.S.C. § 1302 and § 1304(e).
[3]SB 1070, http://www.azleg.govlegtext/49leg/2r/bills/sb1070s.pdf.
[4]*United States* v. *Arizona*, 703 F.Supp.2d 980 (2010).
[5]*United States* v. *Arizona*, 641 F.3d 339 (2011).
[6]*Arizona* v. *United States*, 567 U.S. (2012).

unified whole. The bumpy road toward the creation of a European superstate—in either a loose confederation or a binding federation—demonstrates the potential and the limits of federalism to overcome long-held religious, ethnic, linguistic, and cultural divisions. The economic integration of such a superstate has created the Euro, an alternative to the globe's dominant currency, the U.S. dollar. And the creation of a single and expanding European market now serves as a magnet for buyers and sellers. The political unification of Europe seems to be more difficult to attain due to the resistance of some national populations and the lack of overall budgetary control, but European governments have not been dissuaded from their goal. They have found a new path—through the treaty—to circumvent the requirement of popular ratification and step closer to the goal of a unified Europe with its own unique federal structure.

Federalism and Pluralism

LO7 ★ Discuss the changing relationship between federalism and pluralism.

At the nation's founding, the federal system of government in the United States was designed to allay citizens' fears that they might be ruled by a majority in a distant region with whom they did not necessarily agree or share interests. By recognizing the legitimacy of the states as political divisions, the federal system also recognizes the importance of diversity. The existence and cultivation of diverse interests are the hallmarks of pluralism.

The two main competing theories of federalism that we have discussed both support pluralism, but in somewhat different ways. Dual federalism aims to maintain important powers in the states and to protect those powers from an aggressive or assertive national government. This theory recognizes the importance of state and national standards, but maintains that not all policy areas should be considered the same; some are more amenable to decision making and standards closer to home, while others are more appropriately national. Preserving this variety at the state level allows the people, if not a direct vote in policymaking, at least a choice of policies under which to live.

In contrast, cooperative federalism sees relations between levels of government in more fluid terms and is perfectly willing to override state standards for national ones depending on the issues at stake. Yet this view of federalism, while more amenable to national prerogatives, is highly responsive (at least in theory) to all manner of pressures from groups and policy entrepreneurs, including pressure at one level of government from those that might be unsuccessful at others. By blurring the lines of national and state responsibility, this type of federalism encourages petitioners to try their luck at whichever level of government offers them the best chance of success, or simultaneously to mount diverse sets of strategies across levels of government.

The national government has come to rely increasingly on its regulatory power to shape state policies. Through mandates and restraints, the national government has exercised a coercive form of federalism. This direction with policies flowing from Washington to the state and local levels signals a shift from a pluralist to a majoritarian model.

Master the Topic of Federalism with MindTap™ for American Government

 REVIEW MindTap™ for American Government
Access Key Term Flashcards for Chapter 4.

 STAY CURRENT MindTap™ for American Government
Access the KnowNow blog and customized RSS for updates on current events.

 TEST YOURSELF MindTap™ for American Government
Take the Wrap It Up Quiz for Federalism.

 STAY FOCUSED MindTap™ for American Government
Complete the Focus Activities for Federalism.

Summary

LO1 Compare and contrast the two theories of federalism used to describe the American system of government.

- The government framework outlined in the Constitution reflects the original thirteen states' fear of a powerful central government and frustrations that the Articles of Federation produced. The division of powers sketched in the Constitution turns over "great and aggregate" matters to the national government, leaving "local and particular" concerns to the states. The product—federalism—was a new form of government that acknowledged the diversity of interests and values in America.

- Although federalism comes in many varieties, two types stand out because they capture valuable differences between the original and modern visions. Dual, or layer-cake, federalism wants to retain a strong separation between state and national powers, which, in essence, provides the states with a protective buffer against national encroachments. Cooperative, or marble-cake, federalism sees national and state governments working together to solve national problems. In its own way, each view supports the pluralist model of democracy.

LO2 Identify and explain each of the four forces that stimulate changes in the relationship between the national and state governments.

- National crises and demands from citizens frustrated with the responsiveness of state governments, judicial interpretations of the proper balance between states and the national government, changes in the system of grants-in-aid, and the professionalism of state governments have all contributed to changes in American federalism.

LO3 Describe the role of ideology in shaping federalism.

- Although it is common to associate conservative views with dual federalism and liberal views with the cooperative model, the ambiguity with which federalism is treated in the Constitution makes it difficult to pin clear ideological labels on particular theories of federalism. In practice, the combination of ideology and the specific policy context—that is, how one prioritizes freedom, order, and equality—rather than ideology alone drives conceptions of the proper nation–state balance.

LO4 Describe the influence of federalism on elections at the state and national levels.

- Federalism plays a significant role in electoral politics, at both the state and national levels. Many national-level politicians have prior political experience in state government, and they often return to the states to stump for local favorites. Federalism also shapes the politics of drawing congressional boundaries. The interactions between Justice Department officials and the state legislators responsible for preclearance underscore the strong connections between federalism and the redistricting process, although that connection may be shifting due to a recent Supreme Court decision in 2013.

LO5 Describe the role of local government in a federal system and illustrate how national, state, and local governments sometimes interact.

- While in principle local governments bring politics closer to individuals, the reality is that most citizens are less engaged in local than in national politics. Organized groups, with the time and resources to understand the minutiae of government at each level, are the most successful at influencing local policy. Despite having specific jurisdictions, national, state, and local governments often must coordinate and work together in developing policies, financing government activities, and dealing with crises.

LO6 Analyze the role of federalism in American trade policy and in other nations around the world.

- The influence of American federalism extends outside the country's borders. In international trade policy, for example, states have many channels through which they can advance particular agendas, despite the more prominent general role that national government has in foreign policy. Further, in securing the transport of goods into and out of the nation, all members of the intergovernmental system participate. Looking across the globe, the United States is not the sole federal country in the world. Of the nearly 200 politically sovereign states in the world today, 24 are federations, which are made up of almost 500 constituent or federated states. As a framework for government, federalism is becoming increasingly important in the world.

LO7 Discuss the changing relationship between federalism and pluralism.

- Because federalism recognizes the importance of diversity and the existence of multiple sources of authority, this type of government most clearly reflects the pluralist model. Still, the national government's regulatory power casts a coercive shadow over all state governments. This model of coercive federalism reflects the continuing ebb and flow of power moving from states to nation.

Chapter Quiz

LO1 Compare and contrast the two theories of federalism used to describe the American system of government.

1. What is federalism, and what were the difficulties that it sought to overcome?
2. Define dual and cooperative federalism, and explain the metaphors used to describe them.

LO2 Identify and explain each of the four forces that stimulate changes in the relationship between the national and state governments.

1. Explain how the Supreme Court's interpretations of the commerce clause have influenced the national government's power.

2. How have national grants to the states and the states' own internal developments influenced changes in federalism?

LO3 Describe the role of ideology in shaping federalism.

1. Why can it be difficult to associate conservatives or liberals with particular types of federalism?
2. What are unfunded mandates, and why might conservatives or liberals sometimes favor them and sometimes oppose them?

LO4 Describe the influence of federalism on elections at the state and national levels.

1. What skills can a prior experience in state politics provide for aspiring national-level politicians?
2. What is redistricting, and in what ways can federalism influence the redistricting process?

LO5 Describe the role of local government in a federal system and illustrate how national, state, and local governments sometimes interact.

1. What are the advantages of localized government in theory, and how do these materialize in practice?
2. Why does crisis often lead to cooperation among the different levels of government?

LO6 Analyze the role of federalism in American trade policy and in other nations around the world.

1. Describe two mechanisms through which states can influence the movement of goods into and out of the United States.
2. What are some of the challenges to forming federal systems in countries or regions outside of the United States?

LO7 Discuss the changing relationship between federalism and pluralism.

1. How do dual and cooperative forms of federalism support pluralism?
2. In what way is American federalism shifting toward a majoritarian model?

5

Public Opinion and Political Socialization

Learning Outcomes

LO1 Distinguish the various roles played by public opinion in majoritarian and pluralist democracy.

LO2 Critique polling as a method for measuring public opinion and identify skewed, bimodal, and normal distributions of opinion.

LO3 Explain the influence of the agents of early socialization—family, school, community, and peers—on political learning.

LO4 Compare and contrast the effects of education, income, region, race, ethnicity, religion, and gender on public opinion.

LO5 Define the concept of ideology, describe the liberal–conservative continuum, and assess the influence of ideology on public opinion.

LO6 Assess the impact of knowledge, self-interest, and leadership on political opinions.

 WATCH & LEARN MindTap° for American Government

Watch a brief "What Do You Know?" video summarizing Public Opinion and Political Socialization.

AP Images/Stacy Bengs

At midnight on August 1, 2013, Margaret Miles and Cathy ten Broeke became the first gay couple to get married in Minneapolis. Their 5-year-old son got to stay up way past a kindergartener's bedtime to take part in the historic occasion. Nearly a year earlier, voters in Minnesota made history as well by being the first in the country to reject a proposed constitutional amendment to ban gay marriage. That same year, voters in three other states voted to legalize gay marriage. These election outcomes represented a dramatic reversal from just eight years earlier, when voters in fourteen states amended their constitutions to prohibit same-sex marriages.[1]

Perhaps no other issue in modern American politics has seen such swift changes in public sentiment as that of gay rights. For most of American history, all states had laws against sodomy, which made same-sex sexual relations a felony. As recently as 1995, Americans were evenly divided over whether such sexual relations between consenting adults should be legal. The Supreme Court invalidated anti-sodomy laws in 2003, and since then, the percentage of Americans saying that same-sex relations should be legal has risen to sixty-three. In 1996, when Gallup first started asking Americans if gay marriage should have the same legal status as traditional marriage, only 27 percent of Americans said yes. By 2014, 54 percent said yes, a 100 percent increase in just eighteen years. Change has occurred among people of all backgrounds; across age, gender, religion, partisan identification, and race, public opinion has become more supportive of gay rights.[2]

Among individuals who used to oppose gay marriage but now support it, the most common reason they give for changing their mind is having family, friends, or acquaintances who are gay. Thus, one reason why Americans have become more supportive of gay rights is that over time, more and more Americans have gay people in their lives. In 1993, only 22 percent of Americans said they had a close friend or family member who was gay. Today, 65 percent do.[3] Research confirms that having a close friend or family member who is gay is a strong predictor of support for marriage equality, on par with party, ideology, and religion.[4]

Despite this broad increase in support, gaps remain in how Americans of different backgrounds feel about gay rights. For instance, while 66 percent of people born after 1981 support gay marriage, only 35 percent of people born between 1928 and 1945 do. Likewise, a majority of whites are in favor, compared to 38 percent of blacks. Differences exist by party, ideology, gender, religion, and region as well.[5]

The case of public opinion on gay rights illustrates the complex interactions that routinely take place between the public and policy outcomes. Changes in public opinion appear to have preceded widespread policy change, just as the majoritarian model of democracy demands. In 2011, only six states allowed gay marriage. As of this writing, gay marriage is legal or soon to be legal in 26 states and the District of Columbia. Another 4 states were affected by a 2014 Supreme Court action that lets the decision of lower courts overturning their bans go into effect. That action means as many as 30 states could soon allow gay marriage. But noteworthy events, such as the first legalization of gay marriage in Massachusetts in 2003 and the Supreme Court's decision on anti-sodomy laws, occurred well before most Americans voiced support for such changes. Court challenges and organized interests spurred those events, which then provoked national debates about gay rights, just as the pluralist model of democracy would expect.

As both public opinion and policy move toward favoring marriage equality, attention is turning to other controversial topics, such as whether the federal government should prohibit employment discrimination against gays, how to ensure that the rights of transgendered people are protected, and whether individuals with religious objections to gay relationships can discriminate against gays and lesbians, such as when a Colorado baker refused to make a cake for a gay couple's wedding reception.[6] As new issues such as these arise, opinions fluctuate and familiar tensions between pluralism and majoritarianism, as well as among freedom, order, and equality, take shape.

LISTEN & LEARN

MindTap for American Government

Access Read Speaker to listen to Chapter 5.

public opinion
The collective attitudes of citizens concerning a given issue or question.

Public opinion is simply the collective attitude of the citizens on a given issue or question. The history of public thinking on gay rights reveals several characteristics of public opinion:

1. *The public's attitudes toward a given government policy can vary over time, often dramatically.* Opinions about gay rights have moved in the direction of favoring equality over order and have changed quickly in recent years.

2. *Public opinion places boundaries on allowable types of public policy.* In the early 2000s, voters themselves approved of bans on gay marriage in several states, often enshrining such bans in their state constitutions. As opinions have changed, so have state and national policies regarding marriage equality.

3. *If asked by pollsters, citizens are willing to register opinions on matters outside their experience.* Although only 9 percent of Americans have a close friend or family member who is transgender, 20 percent say that transgender people do not face much discrimination in the United States.[7]

4. *Governments tend to respond to public opinion.* As the public has grown more supportive of gay rights, other policies have changed in addition to gay marriage. The federal government eliminated its ban on having openly gay Americans serve in the military in 2011. That same year, the Obama administration said it would no longer defend the Defense of Marriage Act (DOMA), a law that prevented the federal government from recognizing same-sex marriages. In 2013, the Supreme Court struck down most of DOMA, paving the way for married same-sex couples to enjoy the same federal benefits as heterosexual couples, such as Social Security survivor's benefits and family medical leave.[8]

5. *The government sometimes does not do what the people want.* A solid majority of Americans, including 79 percent of Democrats and 61 percent of Republicans, favor legislation that would protect gays and lesbians from employment discrimination.[9] Nonetheless, the Employment Nondiscrimination Act (ENDA) has stalled in Congress for years.

The last two conclusions bear on our understanding of the majoritarian and pluralist models of democracy discussed in Chapter 2. Here, we probe more deeply into the nature, shape, depth, and formation of public opinion in a democratic government. What is the place of public opinion in a democracy? How do people acquire their opinions? What are the major lines of division in public opinion? How do individuals' ideology and knowledge affect their opinions?

Homosexuality in Global Politics

Around the world, gay rights have been advancing quickly. Fifteen countries allow same-sex marriage; most of them have only done so for a few years. In the United States, state-level policy on same-sex marriage has been changing rapidly as well. Attitudes about whether homosexuality should be accepted by society are changing, yet they vary widely from country to country. As the graph here illustrates, attitudes in the United States resemble attitudes of people in Latin America more than those of people in western Europe, Canada, and Australia. According to these data, people in western Europe are most accepting of homosexuality while people in Asia and Africa are least accepting.

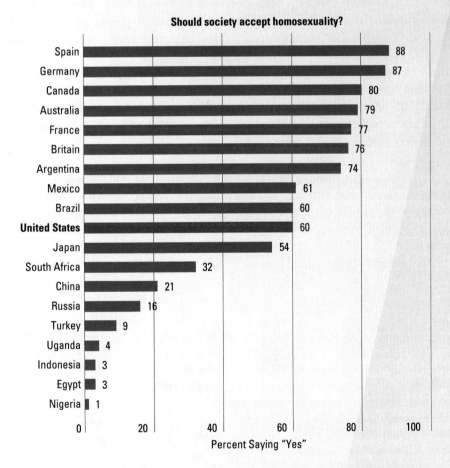

Should society accept homosexuality?

Country	Percent Saying "Yes"
Spain	88
Germany	87
Canada	80
Australia	79
France	77
Britain	76
Argentina	74
Mexico	61
Brazil	60
United States	60
Japan	54
South Africa	32
China	21
Russia	16
Turkey	9
Uganda	4
Indonesia	3
Egypt	3
Nigeria	1

Source: "The Global Divide on Homosexuality," Pew Research Global Attitudes Project, 2013.

Critical Thinking What American values underlie public opinion about homosexuality? Why might attitudes across the globe be changing on this issue?

Public Opinion and the Models of Democracy

LO1 ★ Distinguish the various roles played by public opinion in majoritarian and pluralist democracy.

COMPARE WITH YOUR PEERS

MindTap™ **for American Government**

Access the Public Opinion and Political Socialization Forum: Polling Activity— New York Times Instant Polls.

Opinion polling, which involves interviewing a sample of citizens to estimate public opinion as a whole, is such a common feature of contemporary life that we often forget it is a modern invention, dating only from the 1930s. In fact, survey methodology did not become a powerful research tool until the advent of computers in the 1950s. Before polling became a common part of the American scene, politicians, journalists, and everyone else could argue about what the people wanted, but no one really knew. Before the 1930s, observers of America had to guess at national opinion by analyzing newspaper stories, politicians' speeches, voting returns, and travelers' diaries. What if pollsters had been around when the colonists declared their independence from Britain in July 1776? We might have learned (as some historians estimate) that "40 percent of Americans supported the Revolution, 20 percent opposed it, and 40 percent tried to remain neutral."[10]

When no one really knows what the people want, how can the national government be responsive to public opinion? As we discussed in Chapter 3, the founders wanted to build public opinion into our government structure by allowing the direct election of representatives to the House and apportioning representation there according to population. The attitudes and actions of the House of Representatives, the framers thought, would reflect public opinion, especially on the crucial issues of taxes and government spending.

Bills passed by a majority of elected representatives do not necessarily reflect the opinion of a majority of citizens, a fact that would not have bothered the framers because they never intended to create a full democracy, a government completely responsive to majority opinion. Although they wanted to provide for some consideration of public opinion, they had little faith in the ability of the masses to make public policy.

The majoritarian and pluralist models of democracy differ greatly in their assumptions about the role of public opinion in democratic government. According to the classic majoritarian model, the government should do what a majority of the public wants. Americans tend to prefer this perspective—polls routinely show that most Americans think that representatives should follow the majority will of their constituency, even if the representative personally thinks that a different course of action is best.[11] In contrast, pluralists argue that the public as a whole seldom demonstrates clear, consistent opinions on the day-to-day issues of government. Pluralists recognize, however, that subgroups within the public do express opinions on specific matters—often and vigorously. The pluralist model requires that government institutions allow the free expression of opinions by these "minority publics." Democracy is at work when the opinions of many different publics clash openly and fairly over government policy.

Should policymakers follow the will of the majority? Or should they pay most attention to politically engaged groups who are deeply involved in certain issues? This debate has existed for some time, but modern polling has made the will of the majority easier to determine, which potentially increases the stakes of failing to enact its wishes. One expert said, "Surveys produce just what democracy is supposed to produce—equal representation of all citizens."[12] Indeed, research shows that public opinion in the polling era has had a strong influence on policy outcomes.[13] At the same time, because government policy sometimes runs against majority opinion, the majoritarian model is considered by some to be an inaccurate description of reality. For example, even though research shows public opinion influences policy outcomes, when opinions of the richest Americans differ from the opinions of everyone else, policy changes are more likely to reflect the views of the wealthy.[14]

The two models of democracy make different assumptions about public opinion. The majoritarian model assumes that a majority of the people holds clear, consistent opinions on government policy. The pluralist model assumes that the public is often uninformed and ambivalent about specific issues, and opinion polls frequently support that claim. For example, in January 2014, only 54 percent of Americans correctly knew that the Affordable Care Act prohibits companies from denying health insurance to people because of any illnesses they may have.[15] Possessing incorrect information can go on to shape attitudes about the policy itself, which, in turn, can influence the actions of legislators. Would it not be better, some argue, to pay more attention to the preferences of citizens and organizations that are most knowledgeable about, and most involved in, each policy domain?

With this overview of debates about the role of public opinion in the democratic process in place, we now move on to addressing questions about the foundations of public opinion. How do polls measure public opinion? What principles, if any, do people use to organize their beliefs and attitudes about politics? How do individuals form their political opinions? Under what conditions does the public meet the high standards set forth in the majoritarian model of democracy, and when does it fall short?

Joe Heller, www.hellertoon.com

Rocky Mountain High

Like gay rights, attitudes about marijuana have changed significantly in the past few decades. Pollsters have been asking Americans whether pot should be legal since the 1960s. Data collected in 2013 marked the first time that a majority (52 percent) responded that marijuana should be legal. And as with gay rights, Americans of all backgrounds have become more supportive over time. Gaps still remain, however, with men, young people, and Democrats more likely than women, older people, and Republicans to favor legalization.

Source: "Majority Now Supports Legalizing Marijuana," Pew Research Center for People and the Press, 4 April 2013.

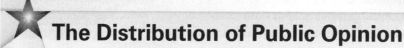

The Distribution of Public Opinion

LO2 ★ Critique polling as a method for measuring public opinion and identify skewed, bimodal, and normal distributions of opinion.

A government that tries to respond to public opinion soon learns that people seldom think alike. To understand and then act on the public's many attitudes and beliefs, government must pay attention to the way public opinion is distributed among the choices on a given issue. In particular, government must analyze the shape and the stability of that distribution. Understanding how polls work is the first step.

Measuring the Distribution of Public Opinion

How can a pollster tell what the nation thinks by talking to only a few hundred people? The answer lies in the statistical theory of sampling. Briefly, the theory holds that a sample of individuals selected by chance from any population is representative of that population. This means that the traits of the individuals in the sample—their attitudes, beliefs, and sociological characteristics—reflect the traits of the whole population. Sampling theory does not claim that a sample exactly matches the population, only that it reflects the population with some predictable degree of accuracy. Think of a blood test. If your doctor wants to measure your cholesterol level, she does not need to remove all of your blood. She fills one small tube, the contents of which offer a good reflection of the rest of the blood in your body. Sampling works similarly, in theory at least. In reality, ensuring that the test tube of the American public that is included in a survey represents the broader population can be very challenging.

Three important factors determine the accuracy of a sample. The first is how the sample is selected. For maximum accuracy, the individuals in the sample must be chosen randomly. Randomly does not mean "at whim," however; it means that every individual in the population has the same chance of being selected.

For a population as large and widespread as that of the United States, pollsters typically divide the country into geographical regions. Then they randomly choose areas and sample individuals who live within those areas. Today, most polls conducted by the mass media are done by telephone, with computers randomly dialing numbers within predetermined calling areas. Random dialing ensures that even people with unlisted numbers are called. Most media outlets ensure that they include cell phone numbers in their sampling, since a growing segment of the population (especially younger Americans) only has a cell phone.

A second factor that affects accuracy is the size of the sample. The larger the sample is, the more accurately it represents the population. For example, a sample of six hundred randomly selected individuals is accurate to within (plus or minus) five percentage points 95 percent of the time.

The third factor that affects the accuracy of sampling is the amount of variation in the population. If there were no variation, every sample would reflect the population's characteristics with perfect accuracy, such as if 100 percent of Americans approved of how the president was handling his job. The greater the variation is within the population, the greater is the chance that one random sample will be different from another, such as if 46 percent of Americans approved of the president. In that case, one poll might find 48 percent approved while another might find that only 45 percent approved.[16]

The Gallup Poll and most other national polls usually survey about fifteen hundred individuals and are accurate to within three percentage points 95 percent of the time (for example, "48 percent approval, plus or minus three percentage points"). As shown in Figure 5.1, the predictions of the Gallup Poll for nineteen presidential elections since 1936 have deviated from the voting results by less than 1.0 percentage point. Even this

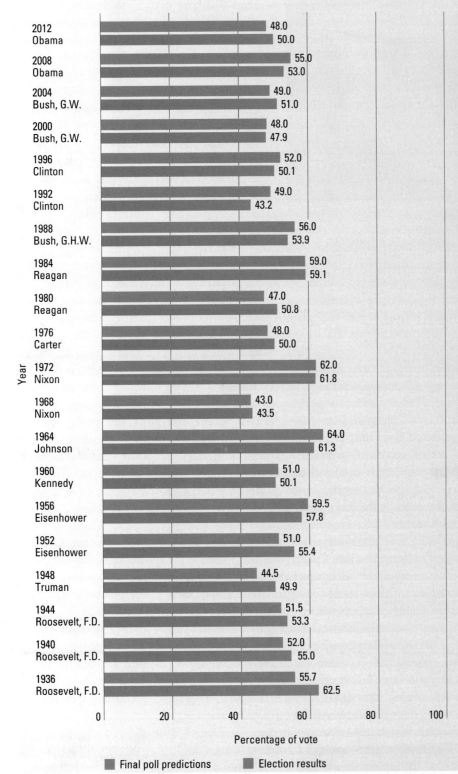

FIGURE 5.1 Gallup Poll Accuracy

One of the nation's oldest polls was started by George Gallup in the 1930s. The accuracy of the Gallup Poll in predicting presidential elections over time is charted here. Although not always on the mark, its predictions have been fairly close. Gallup's final prediction for the 2000 election declared the race "too close to call." Indeed, the race in the electoral college remained too close to call for weeks after the election. The poll was most notably wrong in 1948, when it predicted that Thomas Dewey, the Republican candidate, would defeat the Democratic incumbent, Harry Truman, underestimating Truman's vote by 5.4 percentage points. In 1992, the Gallup Poll was off by a larger margin, but this time it identified the winner: Bill Clinton. Just prior to the 2012 election, Gallup predicted that the popular vote would split 50 to 49 in favor of Mitt Romney. The vote did split 50 to 48, but in favor of Barack Obama. Still, Gallup was close.

Source: Gallup Editors, "Romney 49%, Obama 48% in Gallup's Final Election Survey," November 5, 2012. Copyright © 2012 Gallup, Inc. All rights reserved. Reproduced by permission.

Chart data (Final poll predictions / Election results):

Year	Final poll predictions	Election results
2012 Obama	48.0	50.0
2008 Obama	55.0	53.0
2004 Bush, G.W.	49.0	51.0
2000 Bush, G.W.	48.0	47.9
1996 Clinton	52.0	50.1
1992 Clinton	49.0	43.2
1988 Bush, G.H.W.	56.0	53.9
1984 Reagan	59.0	59.1
1980 Reagan	47.0	50.8
1976 Carter	48.0	50.0
1972 Nixon	62.0	61.8
1968 Nixon	43.0	43.5
1964 Johnson	64.0	61.3
1960 Kennedy	51.0	50.1
1956 Eisenhower	59.5	57.8
1952 Eisenhower	51.0	55.4
1948 Truman	44.5	49.9
1944 Roosevelt, F.D.	51.5	53.3
1940 Roosevelt, F.D.	52.0	55.0
1936 Roosevelt, F.D.	55.7	62.5

Year (vertical axis) — Percentage of vote (horizontal axis: 0, 20, 40, 60, 80, 100)

■ Final poll predictions   ■ Election results

Stop the Presses! Oops, Too Late...

As the 1948 election drew near, few people gave President Harry Truman a chance to defeat his Republican opponent, Thomas E. Dewey. Polling was still new, and almost all the early polls showed Dewey far ahead. Most organizations simply stopped polling weeks before the election. The *Chicago Daily Tribune* believed the polls and proclaimed Dewey's victory before the votes were counted. Here, the victorious Truman triumphantly displays the most embarrassing headline in American politics. Later, it was revealed that the few polls taken closer to election day showed Truman catching up to Dewey. Clearly, polls estimate the vote only at the time they are taken.

Bettmann/Corbis

small margin of error can mean an incorrect prediction in a close election. But for the purpose of estimating public opinion on political issues, a sampling error of three percentage points is acceptable.

Poll results can be wrong because of problems that have nothing to do with sampling. Survey questions are prone to random error because interviewers are likely to obtain superficial responses from busy respondents who say anything, quickly, to get rid of them. The way in which survey questions are worded can also change the results. For instance, referring to "Obamacare" as opposed to "the Affordable Care Act" decreases support for the health reform law.[17] But despite the potential for error, modern polling has told us a great deal about public opinion in America.

Shape of the Distribution

The results of public opinion polls are often displayed in graphs such as those in Figure 5.2. The height of the columns indicates the percentage of those polled who gave each response, identified along the baseline. The shape of the opinion distribution depicts the pattern of all the responses when counted and plotted. The figure depicts three patterns of distribution: skewed, bimodal, and normal.

Figure 5.2a plots the percentages of respondents surveyed in 2012 who favored or opposed imposing the death penalty for a person convicted of murder. The most frequent response ("favor") is called the *mode*. The mode produces a prominent "hump" in this distribution. The relatively few respondents who didn't know or were opposed to the death penalty lie to one side, in its "tail." Such an asymmetrical distribution is called a **skewed distribution**.

Figure 5.2b plots responses when participants were asked whether Obama's health-care reform law (see Chapter 18) will improve the quality of health-care services. These responses fall into a **bimodal distribution**: respondents generally chose two categories with equal frequency, dividing almost evenly over whether the law will make the quality of care better or worse; 17 percent remain in the middle.

Figure 5.2c shows how respondents to a national survey in 2012 were distributed along a liberal–conservative continuum. Its shape resembles what statisticians call a **normal distribution**—a symmetrical, bell-shaped spread around a single mode, or most frequent response. Here, the mode ("moderate") lies in the center. Fewer people tended to classify themselves in each category toward the liberal and conservative extremes, though conservatives did outnumber liberals in 2012.

When public opinion is normally distributed on an issue, the public tends to support a moderate government policy on that issue. It will also tolerate policies that fall slightly to the left or to the right as long as they do not stray too far from the

skewed distribution
An asymmetrical but generally bell-shaped distribution (of opinions); its mode, or most frequent response, lies off to one side.

bimodal distribution
A distribution (of opinions) that shows two responses being chosen about as frequently as each other.

normal distribution
A symmetrical bell-shaped distribution (of opinions) centered on a single mode, or most frequent response.

FIGURE 5.2 Three Distributions of Opinion

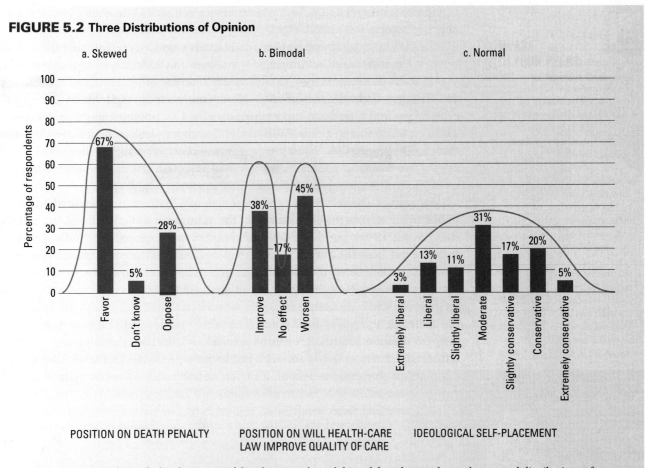

Here we superimpose three idealized patterns of distribution—skewed, bimodal, and normal—on three actual distributions of responses to survey questions. Although the actual responses do not match the ideal shapes exactly, the match is close enough that we can describe the distribution of (a) thoughts on the death penalty as skewed, (b) opinions on whether health-care reform will improve care as bimodal, and (c) ideological attitudes as approximately normal.

Source: 2012 American National Election Study, undertaken in collaboration by Stanford University and the University of Michigan, face-to-face sample.

moderate center. In contrast, when opinion is sharply divided in a bimodal distribution, as it is over Obama's health-care reform, there is great potential for political conflict. A skewed distribution, on the other hand, indicates that most respondents share the same opinion. If the public does not feel intensely about the issue, however, politicians can sometimes discount a skewed distribution of opinion. This is what has happened with the death penalty. Although most people favor capital punishment, it is not a burning issue for them. Thus, politicians can skirt the issue without serious consequences.

Stability of the Distribution

A **stable distribution** shows little change over time. Public opinion on important issues can change, but it is sometimes difficult to distinguish a true change in opinion from a difference in the way a question is worded. When different questions on the same issue produce similar distributions of opinion, the underlying attitudes are stable. When the same question (or virtually the same question) produces

stable distribution
A distribution (of opinions) that shows little change over time.

significantly different responses over time, an actual shift in public opinion probably has occurred.

People's ideological and partisan orientations tend to represent fairly stable distributions. Chapter 1 argued for using a two-dimensional ideological typology based on the trade-offs of freedom for equality and freedom for order. However, most opinion polls ask respondents to place themselves along only a single liberal–conservative dimension, which tends to force libertarians and communitarians into the middle category. Since surveying the American public about ideology began, the ideological distribution of the public has been skewed toward conservatism. When asked specifically about the role of government in particular policy areas, however, Americans often prefer the more liberal option to the conservative option.[18]

Sometimes changes occur within subgroups that are not reflected in overall public opinion. Americans aged 17–24, for example, were more liberal in the 1970s than in the 1980s, but they have since turned more liberal and today are much more liberal than the general public (see Figure 5.3). Moreover, public opinion in America is capable of massive change over time, even on issues that were once highly controversial, as in the case of gay rights discussed at the start of this chapter.

In trying to explain how political opinions are formed and how they change, political scientists cite the process of political socialization, the influence of cultural factors, and the interplay of ideology and knowledge. In the next several sections, we examine how these elements combine to create and influence public opinion.

FIGURE 5.3 Are Young People More Liberal Than Their Parents and Grandparents?

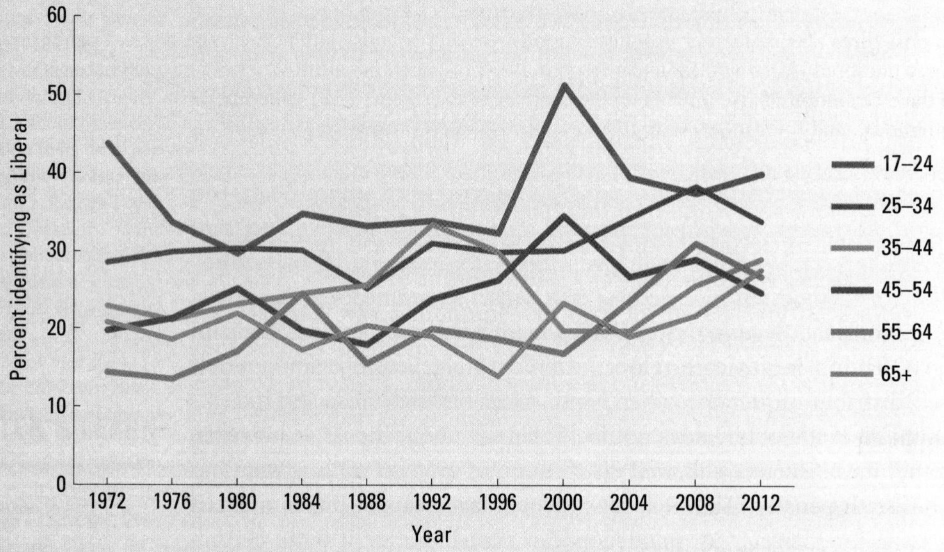

Are you more liberal than your parents and your grandparents? Many young people are. But when you become a parent and a grandparent yourself, chances are that you will become more conservative and your children and grandchildren will be more liberal than you. As this graph shows, Americans aged 17–24 are consistently more liberal than older Americans. The tendency to become more conservative as one ages is called a life cycle effect. As people become more entrenched in their communities and have more responsibilities, they tend to prefer the status quo and adopt a more conservative outlook. Generational effects are also evident here, with young people during the Reagan years showing less liberalism than young people during the presidencies of George W. Bush and Barack Obama.

Sources: American National Election Studies Cumulative Data File, 1972–2008; American National Election Studies 2012 Time Series Study.

Political Socialization

LO3 ★ Explain the influence of the agents of early socialization—family, school, community, and peers—on political learning.

Public opinion is grounded in political values. People acquire their values through **political socialization**, a complex process through which individuals become aware of politics, learn political facts, and form political values. Think for a moment about your political socialization. What is your earliest memory of a president? When did you first learn about political parties? If you identify with a party, how did you decide to do so? If you do not, why don't you? Who was the first liberal or conservative you ever met? Do you and your parents have a similar political outlook?

Obviously, the paths to political awareness, knowledge, and values vary among individuals, but most people are exposed to the same sources of influence, or agents of socialization, especially from childhood through young adulthood: family, school, community, peers, and the media.

> **political socialization**
> The complex process by which people acquire their political values.

The Agents of Early Socialization

Like psychologists, scholars of political socialization place great emphasis on early learning. Both groups point to two fundamental principles that characterize early learning:[19]

- *The primacy principle.* What is learned first is learned best.
- *The structuring principle.* What is learned first structures later learning.

The extent of the influence of any socializing agent depends on the extent of our exposure to it, our communication with it, and our receptivity to it. Because most people learn first from their family, the family tends to be an important agent of political socialization.

Family. In most cases, exposure, communication, and receptivity are highest in parent–child relationships. From their parents, children learn a wide range of values—social, moral, religious, economic, and political—that help shape their opinions. It is not surprising, then, that most people link their earliest memories of politics with their family. Moreover, when parents are interested in politics and maintain a favorable home environment for studying public affairs, they influence their children to become politically interested and informed.

One of the most politically important things that many children learn from their parents is party identification, a phenomenon known as the *transmission model* of partisanship. They learn party identification in much the same way as they do religion. Children (very young children, anyway) imitate their parents. When parents share the same religion, children are almost always raised in that faith. When parents are of different religions, their children are more likely to follow one or the other than to choose an entirely different religion. Similarly, parental influence on party identification is greater when both parents strongly identify with the same party.[20] Transmission doesn't just occur because parents and children live in the same environment and share the same race, class, and other social characteristics. Over and above these similarities, the way in which parents do or do not talk about politics in the home exerts a strong influence on how children acquire political views. Children whose partisanship is transmitted from their parents also exhibit higher levels of partisan stability throughout their lives compared to children whose views were not shaped by their parents.

School. Schools have also been shown to influence political learning. Here, however, we have to distinguish between elementary and secondary schools, on the one hand, and institutions of higher education, on the other. Elementary schools prepare children in a number of ways to accept the social order. They introduce authority figures outside the family: the teacher, principal, police officer. They also teach the nation's slogans and symbols: the Pledge of Allegiance, the national anthem, national heroes, and holidays. And they stress the norms of group behavior and democratic decision making: respecting the opinions of others, voting for class officers. In the process, they teach youngsters about the value of political equality. Children do not always understand the meaning of the patriotic rituals and behaviors they learn in elementary school. In fact, much of this early learning—in the United States and elsewhere—is more indoctrination than education. By the end of the eighth grade, however, children begin to distinguish between political leaders and government institutions. They become more aware of collective institutions, such as Congress and elections, than do younger children, who tend to focus on the president and other single figures of government authority. In sum, most children emerge from elementary school with a sense of national pride and an idealized notion of American government.

Although many secondary schools emphasize citizens' rights in addition to their responsibilities, high schools also attempt to build "good citizens." Field trips to the state legislature or the city council impress students with the majesty and power of government institutions. But secondary schools also offer more explicit political content in their curricula, including courses in recent U.S. history, civics, and American government. Teachers challenge students to think critically about American government and politics and focus on teaching civic responsibilities. The end product is a greater awareness of the political process and of the most prominent participants in that process. Students who have been taught skills such as letter writing and debating are more likely to participate in politics.[21]

Political learning at the college level can be much like that in high school, or it can be quite different. The degree of difference is greater if professors (or the texts they use) encourage their students to question authority. Questioning dominant political values does not necessarily mean rejecting them. For example, this text encourages you to recognize that freedom and equality, two values idealized in our culture, often conflict. It also invites you to think of democracy in terms of competing institutional models, one of which challenges the idealized notion of democracy. These alternative perspectives are meant to teach you about American political values, not to subvert those values. College courses that are intended to stimulate critical thinking have the potential to introduce students to political ideas that are radically different from those they bring to class. However, some specialists in socialization contend that taking particular courses in college has little effect on attitude change, which is more likely to come from sustained interactions with classmates who hold different views.[22]

Community and Peers. Your community and your peers are different but usually overlapping groups. Your community is the people of all ages with whom you come in contact because they live or work near you. Peers are your friends, classmates, and coworkers. Usually they are your age and live or work within your community.

The makeup of a community has a lot to do with how the political opinions of its members are formed. Homogeneous communities—those whose members are similar in ethnicity, race, religion, or occupation—can exert strong pressures on both children and adults to conform to the dominant attitude. For example, if all your neighbors praise the candidates of one party and criticize the candidates of the other, it is difficult to voice or even hold a dissenting opinion. Additionally, white Americans who live in diverse communities are more prone to hold less favorable attitudes about racial and ethnic minorities (and about policies related to race and ethnicity), unless the community diversity leads to the formation of genuine friendships across racial lines.[23]

For both children and adults, peer groups sometimes provide a defense against community pressures. Adolescent peer groups are particularly effective protection against parental pressures. In adolescence, children rely on their peers to defend their dress and their lifestyle, not their politics. At the college level, however, peer group influence on political attitudes often grows substantially, sometimes fed by new information that clashes with parental beliefs.

Continuing Socialization

Political socialization continues throughout life. As parental and school influences wane in adulthood, peer groups (neighbors, coworkers, club members) assume a greater importance in promoting political awareness and developing political opinions. For example, the extent to which politics is discussed in the workplace can shape public opinion. Research indicates that workplaces offer a valuable opportunity to interact with people who have differing political perspectives. Such encounters lead people to be more tolerant of different points of view. Alternatively, workplaces in which most people share the same partisan outlook can lead people to become more extreme in their political views.[24]

Because adults usually learn about political events from the mass media—newspapers, magazines, television, radio, and the Web—the media emerge as socialization agents. Older Americans are more likely to rely on newspaper and television news for political information, while younger Americans are more likely to turn to the Internet. The mass media are so important in the political socialization of both children and adults that we devote a whole chapter—Chapter 6—to a discussion of their role.

Regardless of how people learn about politics, they gain perspective on government as they grow older. They are likely to measure new candidates (and new ideas) against those they remember. Their values also change, increasingly reflecting their own self-interest. As voters age, for example, they begin to see more merit in government spending for Social Security than they did when they were younger. Generational differences in values and historical experience translate into different public policy preferences. Finally, political education comes simply through exposure and familiarity. One example is voting, which people do with increasing regularity as they grow older: it becomes a habit.

Social Groups and Political Values

LO4 ★ Compare and contrast the effects of education, income, region, race, ethnicity, religion, and gender on public opinion.

No two people are influenced by precisely the same socialization agents or in precisely the same way. Each individual experiences a unique process of political socialization and forms a unique set of political values. Still, people with similar backgrounds do share similar experiences, which means they tend to develop similar political opinions. In this section, we examine the ties between people's social background and their political values. In the process, we examine the ties between background and values by looking at responses to two questions posed by the 2012 American National Election Study (ANES).[25] Many questions in the survey tap the freedom-versus-order or freedom-versus-equality dimensions. The two we chose serve to illustrate the analysis of ideological types. These specific questions do not define or exhaust the typology; they merely illustrate it.

The first question dealt with abortion. The interviewer said, "There has been some discussion about abortion during recent years. Which opinion on this page best agrees with your view?":

1. "By law, abortion should never be permitted" [12 percent agreed].
2. "The law should permit abortion only in cases of rape, incest, or when the woman's life is in danger" [28 percent agreed].
3. "The law should permit abortion for reasons other than rape, incest, or danger to the woman's life, but only after the need for the abortion has been clearly established" [18 percent agreed].
4. "By law, a woman should be able to obtain an abortion as a matter of personal choice" [43 percent agreed].[26]

Those who chose the last category most clearly valued individual freedom over order imposed by government. Evidence shows that pro-choice respondents also tend to have concerns about broader issues of social order, such as the role of women and the legitimacy of alternative lifestyles.[27]

The second question posed by the 2012 ANES pertained to the role of government in guaranteeing employment:

> Some people feel the government in Washington should see to it that every person has a job and a good standard of living. Suppose that these people are at one end of the scale.... Others think the government should just let each person get ahead on his own. Suppose these people were at the other end.... Where would you put yourself on this scale, or haven't you thought much about this?

Excluding respondents who "hadn't thought much" about this question, 28 percent wanted the government to provide every person with a good standard of living, and 23 percent were undecided. That left 49 percent who wanted the government to let people "get ahead" on their own. These respondents valued freedom over government efforts to promote equality.

Together it seems that most people are inclined to value freedom over order or equality. About 61 percent felt that the government should permit abortions in many, if not all, instances while only 39 percent felt government should forbid or severely restrict abortions, and a near-majority thinks people should get ahead on their own efforts without much government aid. However, differences in attitudes emerged for both issues when the respondents were grouped by socioeconomic factors: education, income, region, race, religion, and sex. The differences are shown in Figure 5.4 as positive and negative deviations from the national average for each question. Bars that extend to the right identify groups that are more likely than most other Americans to sacrifice freedom for order (on the left-hand side of the figure) or equality (on the right-hand side). Next, we examine the opinion patterns more closely for each socioeconomic group.

FIGURE 5.4 How Groups Differ on Two Questions of Order and Equality

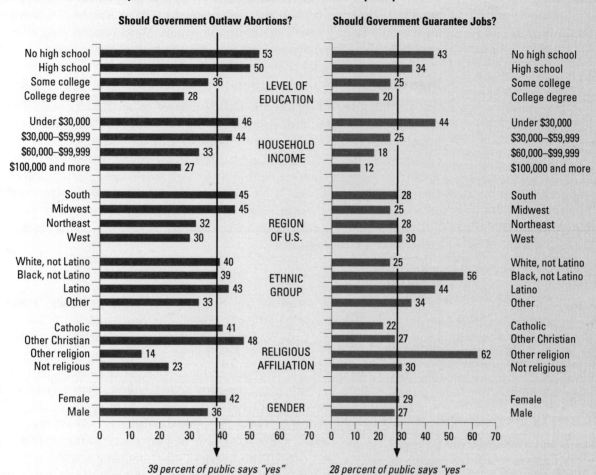

Two questions—one posing the dilemma of freedom versus order (regarding government limits on abortion) and the other the dilemma of freedom versus equality (regarding government guarantees of employment)—were asked of a national sample in 2012. Public opinion across the nation as a whole was divided on each question. These two graphs show how respondents in several social groups deviated from the national mean for each question.

Source: Data from the 2012 American National Election Study, undertaken in collaboration by Stanford University and the University of Michigan. Data are from face-to-face interviews and use weights provided by the ANES.

Education

Education increases people's awareness and understanding of political issues. Higher education also promotes tolerance of unpopular opinions and behavior and invites citizens to see issues in terms of civil rights and liberties.[28] This result is clearly shown in the left-hand column of Figure 5.4, which shows that people with less education are more likely to support outlawing abortions, while those with more education view abortion as a matter of a woman's choice.[29] When confronted with a choice between personal freedom and social order, college-educated individuals tend to choose freedom.

With regard to the role of government in reducing income inequality, the right-hand column in Figure 5.4 shows that people with less education favor government action to guarantee jobs and a good standard of living. Those with more education oppose government action, favoring freedom over equality. You might expect better educated people to be humanitarian and to support government programs to help the needy. However, because educated people tend to be wealthier, they would be taxed more heavily for such government programs. Moreover, they may believe that it is unrealistic to expect government to make such economic guarantees.

Income

In many countries, differences in social class, based on social background and occupation, divide people in their politics.[30] In the United States, the majority of citizens regard themselves as "middle class." Yet, as Figure 5.4 shows, wealth is linked to opinions favoring a limited government role in promoting both equality and order. Those with lower incomes are more likely to favor government guarantees of employment and living conditions. Those with incomes under $60,000 also favor outlawing abortions more than those earning over $60,000. For both issues, wealth and education tend to have a similar effect on opinion: the groups with more education and higher income favor freedom.

Region

Early in our country's history, regional differences were politically important—important enough to spark a civil war between the North and South. For nearly a hundred years after the Civil War, regional differences continued to affect American politics. The moneyed Northeast was thought to control the purse strings of capitalism. The Midwest was long regarded as the stronghold of isolationism in foreign affairs. The South was virtually a one-party region, almost completely Democratic. And the individualistic West pioneered its own mixture of progressive politics.

In the past, differences in wealth fed cultural differences between these regions. In recent decades, however, the movement of people and wealth away from the Northeast and Midwest to the Sunbelt states in the South and Southwest has equalized the per capita income of the various regions. One result of this equalization is that the formerly "solid South" is no longer solidly Democratic. In fact, the South has tended to vote for Republican presidential candidates since 1968, and the majority of southern congressmen are now Republicans. Political differences between the South and the rest of the country today are often rooted in attitudes about racial politics and social issues in addition to attitudes about the economy.[31]

Figure 5.4 shows public opinion on both an economic and a social issue in the four major regions of the United States. It shows that differences are more pronounced on the social issue: people in the South and Midwest were more likely to favor restricting abortion than people in the Northeast or the West, yet regional differences were minimal regarding government efforts to ensure a decent standard of living.

Ethnicity and Race

Over the course of American history, individuals of diverse ethnic and racial backgrounds have differed with respect to political values and opportunities. In the early twentieth century, the major ethnic minorities in America were composed of immigrants from Ireland, Italy, Germany, Poland, and other European countries who came to the United States in waves during the late 1800s and early 1900s. These immigrants entered a nation that had been founded by British settlers more than a hundred years earlier. They found themselves in a strange land, usually without money and unable to speak the language. Moreover, their religious backgrounds—mainly

Catholic and Jewish—differed from that of the predominantly Protestant earlier set-tlers. These urban ethnics and their descendants became part of the great coalition of Democratic voters that President Franklin Roosevelt forged in the 1930s. And for years after, the European ethnics supported liberal candidates and causes more strongly than the original Anglo-Saxon immigrants did.[32]

From the Civil War through the civil rights movement of the 1950s and 1960s, African Americans fought to secure basic political rights such as the right to vote. Ini-tially mobilized by the Republican Party—the party of Lincoln—following the Civil War, African Americans forged strong ties with the Democratic Party during the New Deal era. Today, African Americans are still more likely to support liberal candi-dates and identify with the Democratic Party. African Americans constitute 13 per-cent of the population, with sizable voting blocs in northern cities and in southern states like Mississippi, Georgia, and Louisiana. Over 93 percent of African Americans voted for Obama in 2008 and 2012.[33]

According to the U.S. Census Bureau, non-Hispanic whites comprised 63 percent of the population in 2012. The country is projected to become majority-minority by 2043.[34] Latinos, people of Latin American origin, now make up the largest minority group in the United States: 16.9 percent in 2012. They consist of both whites and nonwhites and are commonly but inaccurately regarded as a racial group. Latinos are projected to be 31 percent of the population in 2060.[35] At the national level, Latinos (consisting of groups as different as Cubans, Mexicans, Dominicans, and Puerto Ricans) have lagged behind African Americans in mobilizing and gaining political office. However, they constitute 46 percent of the population in New Mexico and 38 percent in California and Texas—where they have fared better in politics.[36] Like Afri-can Americans, Latinos tend to align with the Democratic Party. Over 70 percent of Latino voters voted for Obama in 2012.[37]

Both Asians and Native Americans account for another 6 percent of the popula-tion (5 percent Asian; 1 percent Native American). Like other minority groups, their political impact is greatest in cities or regions where they are concentrated and greater in number. For instance, Asian Americans constitute 39 percent of the population in Hawaii and 13 percent in California; Native Americans make up 12 percent of the population of California and 9 percent of Oklahoma.[38] The Asian population in the country overall is expected to increase to 8.2 percent by 2060 while the Native American population is expected to remain the same.[39] Studying the political attitudes of both of these groups is often difficult due to their small number, linguistic diversity, and geographic dispersion. Nonetheless, Asians, like other nonwhites, display a clear preference for Democrats over Republicans, with roughly 73 percent of Asian American voters voting for Obama in 2012.[40] Informa-tion on Native Americans' voting preferences is harder to come by, but estimates suggest that they too vote heavily Democratic.[41]

Members of minority groups often differ from whites in their attitudes on issues that pertain to equality.[42] The reasons are twofold.[43] First, racial minorities (excepting second-generation Asians) tend to have lower **socioeconomic status**, a measure of social condition that includes education, occupational status, and income. Second, minorities have been targets of prejudice and discrimination and have benefited from government actions in support of equality. The right-hand column in Figure 5.4 clearly shows the effects of race on the freedom–equality issue. All minority groups, particularly African Americans, are much more likely than whites to favor govern-ment action to improve economic opportunity. The abortion issue produces less dif-ference, although Latinos favor government restrictions on abortion more than other groups.[44]

socioeconomic status
Position in society, based on a combination of education, occupational status, and income.

**CONNECT
WITH YOUR CLASSMATES**
MindTap™ for American Government

Access the Public opinion and
Political Socialization Forum:
Discussion—How Religion
Shapes Public Opinion.

Religion

Religion is another factor that can have a significant impact on public opinion. Today, 48 percent of the population is Protestant or non-Catholic Christian, 22 percent is Catholic, and fewer than 2 percent is Jewish. Just under 20 percent of Americans today claim to be "unaffiliated" with respect to religion, a figure that has grown rapidly in the twenty-first century.[45] Less than 1 percent of the population was Muslim in 2010, a figure that is expected to rise to about 1.7 percent by 2030.[46] For many years, analysts found strong and consistent differences in the political opinions of Protestants, Catholics, and Jews.[47] Protestants were more conservative than Catholics, and Catholics tended to be more conservative than Jews. There have been few surveys of the Muslim population in the United States, though one recent study found that Muslim Americans are more likely to favor "big government" than the rest of the population, and largely consider themselves Democrats.[48]

Stephen Morton/Stringer/Getty Images

Word of God?

A person's religiosity may be as important as his or her denominational identification in predicting political opinions. One measure of people's religiosity in a Christian-Judaic society is their opinion about the Bible. When asked about the nature of the Bible in 2012, about 34 percent of respondents said it was the actual word of God and should be taken literally. About 46 percent regarded it as the word of God but believed it should not be taken literally, and 20 percent viewed it as written by men. Among those who believe that the Bible was written by men, 45 percent say that global warming is mainly a product of human activity; among those who believe the Bible is the word of God and should be taken literally, that figure drops to 20 percent. People who think the Bible was written by men were also fifty points more likely than people who say it should be taken literally to believe that abortion should be legal as a matter of personal choice.

Source: 2012 American National Election Study, undertaken in collaboration by Stanford University and the University of Michigan, face-to-face sample.

As Figure 5.4 indicates, such broad religious groupings affect attitudes about economic equality and social order. Protestants ("Other Christian") favor government action to limit abortion even more than Catholics. Non-Christians and people who are not religious overwhelmingly favor a woman's right to choose. Differences among religious subgroups have emerged across many contemporary social and political issues. Evangelical Protestants are more likely than members of other religious groups to oppose gay marriage and support the death penalty while favoring the right to life over abortion. Evangelicals and Jews are more likely to express support for Israel in Middle Eastern politics. Religious beliefs have been at the center of national and local debates over issues such as stem cell research, climate change, and the teaching of evolution or creationism as the appropriate explanation for the development of life on Earth.[49]

Gender

Men and women differ with respect to their political opinions on a broad array of social and political issues, though their views are similar on the two items depicted in Figure 5.4. Surveys show that women are consistently more supportive than men are of gay marriage, environmental policies, and government spending for social programs. They are consistently less supportive of the death penalty and of going to war.[50] Contemporary politics is marked by a "gender gap": women tend to identify with the Democratic Party more than men do (see Figure 8.5 on p. 225), and they are much more likely than men to vote for Democratic presidential candidates. In the 2012 general election, Barack Obama won the support of 55 percent of female voters but only 45 percent of male voters.[51]

From Values to Ideology

LO5 ★ Define the concept of ideology, describe the liberal–conservative continuum, and assess the influence of ideology on public opinion.

We have just seen that differences in groups' responses to two survey questions reflect those groups' value choices between freedom and order and between freedom and equality. But to what degree do people's opinions on specific issues reflect their explicit political ideology (the set of values and beliefs they hold about the purpose and scope of government)? Political scientists generally agree that ideology influences public opinion on specific issues; they have much less consensus on the extent to which people think explicitly in ideological terms. They also agree that the public's ideological thinking cannot be categorized adequately in conventional liberal–conservative terms.

The Degree of Ideological Thinking in Public Opinion

Although politicians and the media frequently use the terms *liberal* and *conservative*, many voters tend not to use ideological concepts when discussing politics. For years, surveys have shown that when voters are asked to explain the meaning of the terms "liberal" or "conservative," they often respond with dictionary definitions rather than explicitly political terms. They say that liberals are generous (a *liberal* portion) and conservatives are cautious (a *conservative* estimate). They also say that liberals tend to prefer spending money while conservatives prefer saving money. Very few mention "degree of government involvement" in describing liberals and conservatives.[52]

Ideological labels are technical terms used in analyzing politics, and most citizens don't play that sport. But if you want to play, you need suitable equipment. Scales and typologies, despite their faults, are essential for classification. No analysis, including the study of politics, can occur without classifying the objects being studied. The tendency to use ideological terms in discussing politics grows with increased education, which helps people understand political issues and relate them to one another.

People's personal political socialization experiences can also lead them to think ideologically. For example, children raised in strong union households may be taught to distrust private enterprise and value collective action through government.

True ideologues hold a consistent set of values and beliefs about the purpose and scope of government, and they tend to evaluate candidates in ideological terms. Some people respond to questions in ways that seem ideological but are not because they do not understand the underlying principles. For example, most respondents dutifully comply when asked to place themselves somewhere on a liberal–conservative continuum. The result, as shown earlier in Figure 5.2c, is an approximately normal distribution centering on "moderate," the modal category, which contains 31 percent of all respondents. But many people settle on moderate (a safe choice) when they do not clearly understand the alternatives. When allowed to say, "I haven't thought much about it," 22 percent of respondents in the survey acknowledged that they had not thought much about ideology and were excluded from the distribution.[53] The extent of ideological thinking in America, then, is even less than it might seem from responses to questions asking people to describe themselves as liberals or conservatives.[54] Nonetheless, the majority of Americans do identify themselves as either liberal or conservative.

The Quality of Ideological Thinking in Public Opinion

What people's ideological self-placement means in the twenty-first century is not clear. At one time, the liberal–conservative continuum represented a single dimension: attitudes toward the scope of government activity. Liberals were in favor of more government action to provide public goods, and conservatives were in favor of less. This simple distinction is not as useful today. Many people who call themselves liberal no longer favor government activism in general, and many self-styled conservatives no longer oppose it in principle. As a result, many people have difficulty deciding whether they are liberal or conservative, whereas others confidently choose identical points on the continuum for entirely different reasons. People describe themselves as liberal or conservative because of the symbolic value of the terms as much as for reasons of ideology.[55]

Studies of the public's ideological thinking find that two themes run through people's minds when they are asked to describe liberals and conservatives. One theme associates liberals with change and conservatives with tradition. It corresponds to the distinction between liberals and conservatives on the exercise of freedom and the maintenance of order, a distinction confirmed in research that finds that liberals tend to be more supportive of civil liberties and free speech than conservatives.[56]

The other theme has to do with equality. The conflict between freedom and equality was at the heart of President Roosevelt's New Deal economic policies in the 1930s, which included Social Security (see Chapter 18). The policies expanded the interventionist role of the national government to promote greater economic equality, and attitudes toward government intervention in the economy served to distinguish liberals from conservatives for decades afterward.[57] Attitudes toward government interventionism still underlie opinions about domestic *economic* policies. Liberals support intervention to promote economic equality; conservatives favor less government intervention and more individual freedom in economic activities. Conservatives, however, think differently about government action on *social* policies. (See "Freedom, Order, or Equality: Freedom v. Order: The Tea Party.")

Chapter 1 proposed an alternative system of ideological classification based on people's relative evaluations of freedom, order, and equality. It described liberals as people who believe that government should promote equality, even if some freedom is lost in the process, but who oppose surrendering freedom to government-imposed order. Conservatives do not necessarily oppose equality but put a higher value on freedom than on equality when the two conflict. Yet conservatives are not above restricting freedom when threatened with the loss of order. So both groups value freedom, but one is more willing to trade freedom for equality, and the other is more inclined to trade freedom for order. If you have trouble thinking about these trade-offs on a single dimension, you are in good company. The liberal–conservative continuum presented to survey respondents takes a two-dimensional concept and squeezes it into a one-dimensional format.[58]

Freedom, Order, or Equality

Freedom v. Order: The Tea Party

"I'll have tea with a generous helping of order." Tea party supporters tout their love of freedom and opposition to government interventions—especially concerning government spending. But tea party supporters favor limits to freedom on some key issues. The figure below compares the attitudes of tea party supporters, opponents, and those who neither support nor oppose the tea party on two questions in which freedom and order conflict: support for the death penalty and support for policies that require local police to determine the immigration status of people they think might be undocumented immigrants. It shows that when freedom and order conflict, tea party supporters are much more likely than other Americans to come down on the side of order.

This preference for order suggests that tea party support is motivated not just by government spending, but also by broad concerns about the social changes occurring in the United States, including ethnic and religious diversity, greater acceptance of gays and lesbians, and an expanded presence of women in leadership roles. Tea partiers, it has been argued, seek to preserve the place of whites, Christians, men, and heterosexuals at the top of the social hierarchy, and are willing to support government intervention in order to do so.

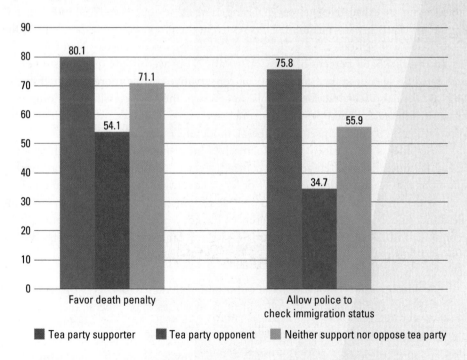

Sources: 2012 American National Election Study; Christopher Parker and Matt Barreto, *Change They Can't Believe In: The Tea Party and Reactionary Politics in America* (Princeton University Press, 2013).

Critical Thinking Which ideological tendency best characterizes tea party supporters: Liberal, Conservative, Libertarian, or Communitarian?

Ideological Types in the United States

Our ideological typology in Chapter 1 (see Figure 1.2, p. 23) classifies people as Liberals if they favor freedom over order and equality over freedom. (Here, capital letters signify our ideological classification; lowercase signifies ideological self-placement.) Conversely, Conservatives favor freedom over equality and order over freedom. Libertarians favor freedom over both equality and order—the opposite of Communitarians.[59] By cross tabulating people's answers to the two questions from the 2012 ANES about freedom versus order (abortion) and freedom versus equality (government job guarantees), we can classify respondents according to their ideological tendencies. As shown in Figure 5.5, a substantial portion of respondents falls within each of the quadrants.* This finding indicates that people do not make decisions about government activity according to a one-dimensional ideological continuum. If they did, responses to the two questions would correlate and cluster diagonally in the Liberal and Conservative boxes. In fact, the correlation is virtually zero (r = −.07). People's preferences for government action depend on what the action targets.

The Libertarian pattern occurred most frequently (26 percent), with the Liberals (20 percent) and Conservatives (19 percent) being represented about equally. Communitarians (10 percent) were least common (the totals do not sum up to 100 percent because some respondents picked the middle category on the question about guaranteeing jobs). The size of the groups, which was determined by the particular questions, is not as important as the fact that the population divided into four significant groups in answering the questions. Indeed, the results resemble earlier findings by other researchers who conducted more exhaustive analyses involving more survey questions.[60] Of more interest are the pie charts in each quadrant. They represent the proportion of respondents in the same survey who self-described as liberal, moderate, or conservative (see Figure 5.2c).

In Figure 5.5, 68 percent of our Conservatives (answering the questions on order and equality) also described *themselves* as conservatives, while more than half of our Liberals were also self-described liberals. In contrast, those we classified as Communitarian or Libertarian according to the order and equality questions showed less consistency in classifying themselves as liberal, moderate, or conservative.

Respondents who readily locate themselves on a single dimension running from liberal to conservative often go on to contradict their self-placement when answering questions that trade freedom for either order or equality. A two-dimensional typology such as that in Figure 5.5 allows us to analyze responses more meaningfully.[61] A single dimension does not fit their preferences for government action concerning both economic and social issues. One reason so many Americans classify themselves as conservative on a one-dimensional scale is that they have no option to classify themselves as libertarian.

The ideological typology reflects important differences between diverse social groups. Blacks and Hispanics are more likely than whites to be Liberal; men are more likely than women to be Libertarian; and people with higher degrees tend to be Libertarian while people with only a high school diploma are more likely to split between Liberal and Conservative. Regional differences are small among the types, with Libertarians being the most common type everywhere except the Midwest, where Conservatives were most common. Liberals were most prominent in the West. People who are not religious were most likely to be classified as Libertarian, and Protestants were

---

*Remember, however, that these categories—like the letter grades A, B, C, and D for courses—are rigid. The respondents' answers to both questions varied in intensity but were reduced to a simple yes or no to simplify this analysis. Many respondents would cluster toward the center of Figure 5.5 if their attitudes were represented more sensitively.

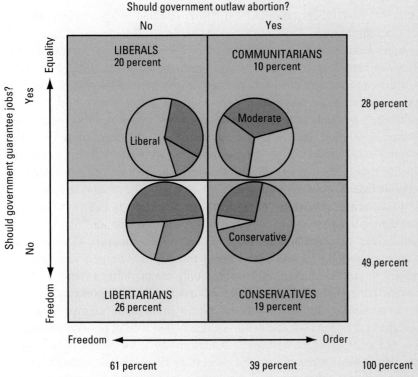

FIGURE 5.5 Respondents Classified by Ideological Tendencies

In the 2012 election survey, respondents were asked whether abortion should be outlawed by government or a matter of personal choice, and whether government should guarantee people a job and a good standard of living or people should get ahead on their own. (The questions are given verbatim on p. 130.) These two questions presented choices between freedom and order and between freedom and equality. People's responses to the two questions showed no correlation, demonstrating that these value choices cannot be explained by a one-dimensional liberal–conservative continuum. Instead, their responses can be analyzed more usefully according to four different ideological types. Note that totals do not sum to 100 percent because some people picked the middle category on the question about guaranteeing jobs. The pie charts in the center show the proportion of each group self-describing themselves as liberal, moderate, or conservative on the traditional one-dimensional scale.

Source: Data from the 2012 American National Election Study, undertaken in collaboration by Stanford University and the University of Michigan. Data are from face-to-face interviews and use weights provided by the ANES.

most likely to be Conservative. Finally, the poor were most likely to be classified as Liberal, while the affluent were solidly Libertarian.

This more refined analysis of political ideology explains why even Americans who pay close attention to politics might find it difficult to locate themselves on the liberal–conservative continuum: they are liberal on some issues and conservative on others. Forced to choose along just one dimension, they opt for the middle category, moderate. However, our analysis indicates that many people who classify themselves as liberal or conservative do fit these two categories in our typology. There is value, then, in the liberal–conservative distinction as long as we understand its limitations.

 Forming Political Opinions

LO6 ★ Assess the impact of knowledge, self-interest, and leadership on political opinions.

We have seen that people acquire their political values through socialization and that different social groups develop different sets of political values. We have also learned that some people, but only a minority, think about politics ideologically, holding a consistent set of political attitudes and beliefs. But how do those who are not ideologues—in other words, most citizens—form political opinions? Are most people well informed about politics? What can we say about the quality of public opinion in America?

Political Knowledge

In the United States today, education is compulsory (usually to age sixteen), and the literacy rate is relatively high. The country boasts an unparalleled network of colleges and universities. American citizens can obtain information from a variety of news sources. They can keep abreast of national and international affairs through live coverage of world events via satellite from virtually everywhere in the world. But how much do they know about politics?

In a comprehensive study of political knowledge two decades ago, two political scientists collected 3,700 individual survey items that measured some type of factual knowledge about public affairs.[62] They focused on over two thousand items that clearly dealt with political facts, such as knowledge of political institutions and processes, contemporary public figures, political groups, and policy issues. They found that "many of the basic institutions and procedures of government are known to half or more of the public, as are the relative positions of the parties on many major issues."[63]

Current surveys of political knowledge report mixed findings. Consider Pew Research Center's News IQ Survey, administered two or three times a year. In 2013, Pew researchers found that majorities answered only six of thirteen items correctly. Over 70 percent knew that the Federal Reserve is responsible for monetary policy as opposed to tax or trade policy, while only 49 percent could identify Egypt on a map. But is 49 percent high or low? All else being equal, a higher level of political knowledge is better, but if Pew researchers had asked Americans to locate Egypt on a map in 2010, before that country's revolution, the percentage of people answering correctly surely would have been much lower. Actual events, and media coverage of those events, can signal what is important to the public and lead to increased information levels.[64]

But perhaps simply calling and asking people if they can recall information like the name of the secretary of state is not the best way to measure political knowledge. Two researchers conducted an experiment where some people were given a full day to report back their answers to a political knowledge survey. People who were given more time to answer scored somewhat higher than people who had to answer on the spot. The study's authors concluded that in this day and age, people have a range of tools at their disposal, thanks to the Internet, where they can find out what they need to know when they need to know it. Today's wired and interconnected lifestyle means that the public is perhaps more competent regarding political affairs than traditional surveys indicate.[65]

As much as people know about some political facts, the public shows less knowledge on some matters that are critical to public policy. In 2011, for example, 58 percent of Americans thought that most immigrants in the United States are undocumented, when in reality, only about a third are. Most Americans also grossly overestimated the percentage of the population that is foreign-born: the average estimate was 39 percent while the true figure is closer to 13 percent.[66] Why are such misperceptions so widespread? Portrayals of Latinos in the media are one culprit. When asked in a 2012 study to recall the kind of roles they have seen Latinos play on television, the most common responses were "criminal," "gardener," and "maid," all of which are associated with an underground economy. That same study included an experiment that found that people who were exposed to negative media portrayals of Latinos were more likely than other people to agree that the term "illegal immigrant" applies well to Latinos.[67]

Although some studies have shown that the *collective* opinion of the public can be interpreted as stable and meaningful—because random ignorance balances off both sides of an issue[68]—the public is simply misinformed on some important issues. Moreover, individuals who strongly believe in certain causes may ignore information that questions their beliefs. Even worse, upon being told that their beliefs are incorrect, some people hold on to their incorrect beliefs even more, a phenomenon called the *backfire effect*. For instance, researchers found that ideological conservatives became more likely to think that Iraq had weapons of mass destruction (WMD) before the 2003 Iraq War *after* they were told that subsequent investigations concluded that Iraq did not have WMD.[69] In their minds, they argued against the evidence presented to them, which strengthened their incorrect beliefs.

The American public, it seems, is not as politically knowledgeable as a pure majoritarian model of democracy would demand. The public's store of information about the structure of American government and about current affairs is far from ideal, and people can be very resistant to new information that might challenge their existing beliefs. But when people are given more time to think about it, and when the news media indicates that new issues are important, levels of political information among the American public rise.

Costs, Benefits, and Cues

Perhaps people do not think in ideological terms or know a wide variety of political facts, but they can tell whether a policy is likely to directly help or hurt them. The **self-interest principle** states that people choose what benefits them personally.[70] Self-interest affects how people form opinions on policies with clear costs and benefits.[71] Tax payers tend to prefer low taxes to high taxes. Smokers tend to oppose bans on smoking in public places. Gun owners are less likely to support handgun control. People who are well-off financially tend to be less supportive of redistributive social welfare policies than people who are less well-off.

self-interest principle
The implication that people choose what benefits them personally.

In some cases, individuals are unable to determine personal costs or benefits. This tends to be true of foreign policy, which few people interpret in terms of personal benefits. Here, many people have no opinion, or their opinions are not firmly held and can change quite easily given almost any new information. Attitudes about foreign policy are also powerfully shaped by longstanding predispositions. For example, when it seemed as if the United States might intervene militarily in Syria's civil war in 2013, party and gender were strongly associated with people's preferences: Republicans and men were more likely than Democrats and women to support possible airstrikes.[72]

In other cases, opinions are driven more by what is considered to be in the nation's interest rather than what people think is in their own interest. Such **sociotropic responses** are particularly common with regard to how the economy affects attitudes during elections. Opinions about whether the nation is doing well or not are often more influential over candidate preferences than attitudes about one's own economic standing. It is believed, however, that sociotropic preferences form because people use their ideas about the national condition to help them figure out what to expect in their own lives.[73]

sociotropic responses
Opinions about how the country as a whole is doing affect political preferences more strongly than one's own personal circumstance.

Public opinion that is not based on a complicated ideology may also emerge from the skillful use of cues. Individuals may use heuristics—mental shortcuts that require hardly any information—to make fairly reliable political judgments.[74] For instance, citizens can use political party labels to compensate for low information about the policy positions of candidates. Voters may have well-developed expectations or stereotypes about political parties that structure the way they evaluate candidates and process new information.[75] They assume that Democrats and Republicans differ from each other in predictable ways. Stereotypes about other groups in society, such as women and minorities, can also influence people's political preferences.[76] Similarly, citizens take cues from trusted government officials and interest groups regarding the wisdom of bills pending in Congress or the ideology of Supreme Court nominees.

Political Leadership

Public opinion on specific issues is molded by political leaders, journalists, and policy experts. Politicians serve as cue givers to members of the public. Citizens with favorable views of a politician may be more likely to support his or her values and policy agenda; similarly, unfavorable views of a politician can dampen policy support. In an experiment conducted during the 2008 presidential campaign, 52 percent of Democrats supported a proposal to reform immigration when no party or candidate was mentioned in the policy description, but only 33 percent of Democrats supported it when it was described as being supported by John McCain, the Republican candidate. Similarly, 66 percent of Republicans opposed the proposal when no candidate was mentioned, and opposition jumped to 90 percent when the policy was attributed to Barack Obama.[77]

Politicians routinely make appeals to the public on the basis of shared political ideology and self-interest. They share information about social trends, policy options, and policy implementation. Competition and controversy among political elites provide the public with a great deal of information. But politicians are well aware that citizen understanding and support for an issue depend on its framing. In **issue framing**, politicians (and interest groups) define the way that issues are presented, selectively invoking values or recalling history in the presentation. For example, opinion leaders might frame a reduction in taxes as "returning money to the people" or, quite differently, as "reducing government services." Politicians and other leaders can frame issues to change or reinforce public opinion. Such framing is sometimes referred to as "spin," and "spin doctors" are those who stand ready to reinforce or elaborate on the spin inherent in the framing.[78]

The ability of political leaders to influence public opinion has been enhanced enormously by the growth of the broadcast media, especially television.[79] The majoritarian model of democracy assumes that government officials respond to public opinion, and evidence exists to confirm that such responsiveness does occur. But it is also true that political leaders will try to educate or sway the public and convince them to agree that particular courses of action are best.[80] Such attempts to guide public preferences raise important questions about how much potential there is for public opinion to be manipulated by political leaders through the mass media. We examine the relationships among the mass media, political leaders, and the public in the next chapter.

issue framing
The way that politicians or interest group leaders define an issue when presenting it to others.

Master the Topic of Public Opinion and Political Socialization with MindTap™ for American Government

 REVIEW MindTap™ for American Government
Access Key Term Flashcards for Chapter 5.

 TEST YOURSELF MindTap™ for American Government
Take the Wrap It Up Quiz for Chapter 5.

 STAY CURRENT MindTap™ for American Government
Access the KnowNow blog and customized RSS for updates on current events.

 STAY FOCUSED MindTap™ for American Government
Complete the Focus Activities for Public Opinion and Political Socialization.

Summary

LO1 Distinguish the various roles played by public opinion in majoritarian and pluralist democracy.

- Public opinion is more important to the majoritarian model of democracy than the pluralist model.

LO2 Critique polling as a method for measuring public opinion and identify skewed, bimodal, and normal distributions of opinion.

- At their best, public opinion polls represent the views of the American population as a whole, but there are many challenges to ensuring that polls are generalizable. The shape of the distribution of opinion (skewed, bimodal, or normal) indicates how sharply the public is divided. Bimodal distributions harbor the greatest potential for political conflict. The stability of a distribution over time indicates how settled people are in their opinions.

LO3 Explain the influence of the agents of early socialization—family, school, community, and peers—on political learning.

- People form their values through the process of political socialization. The most important socialization agents in childhood and young adulthood are family, school, community, and peers. Among adults, the workplace is a powerful socialization agent.

LO4 Compare and contrast the effects of education, income, region, race, ethnicity, religion, and gender on public opinion.

- Members of the same social group tend to experience similar socialization processes and thus to adopt similar values, which means people in different social groups tend to have different opinions.

LO5 Define the concept of ideology, describe the liberal–conservative continuum, and assess the influence of ideology on public opinion.

- Most people do not think about politics in ideological terms but readily classify themselves along a liberal–conservative continuum, with many choosing the middle category, moderate. Others choose the moderate category because they have liberal views on some issues and conservative views on others. Their political orientation is better captured by a two-dimensional framework that analyzes ideology according to the values of freedom, order, and equality, which classifies people as Liberals, Conservatives, Libertarians, and Communitarians.

LO6 Assess the impact of knowledge, self-interest, and leadership on political opinions.

- Surveys show that the public does moderately well on quizzes of political facts, but people sometimes misunderstand critical issues in public policy and can reject evidence that runs counter to their beliefs. Citizens use party labels and cues from elected officials to compensate for their lack of detailed political knowledge. Citizens also respond to the way in which issues are framed when forming their views. The way in which issues are presented to the public through the media can therefore be very important in shaping the relationship between public opinion and political action.

Chapter Quiz

LO1 **Distinguish the various roles played by public opinion in majoritarian and pluralist democracy.**

1. What does the majoritarian model assume about the nature of public opinion?
2. What does the pluralist model assume about public opinion?

LO2 **Critique polling as a method for measuring public opinion and identify skewed, bimodal, and normal distributions of opinion.**

1. Describe three factors that can affect the accuracy of a sample used in a public opinion poll.
2. Explain the differences among a skewed distribution of opinions, a bimodal distribution, and a normal distribution.

LO3 **Explain the influence of the agents of early socialization—family, school, community, and peers—on political learning.**

1. How do the primary principle and the structuring principle affect political learning?
2. What is the transmission model of partisan identification?

LO4 **Compare and contrast the effects of education, income, region, race, ethnicity, religion, and gender on public opinion.**

1. Which social grouping—education, income, region, race, ethnicity, religion, or gender—

appears to have the strongest effect on attitudes toward government's role in maintaining order, such as outlawing abortions?
2. Which social grouping appears to have the strongest effect on attitudes toward government's role in promoting equality, such as guaranteeing jobs?

LO5 **Define the concept of ideology, describe the liberal–conservative continuum, and assess the influence of ideology on public opinion.**

1. On which types of issues do liberals tend to support government interventionism? On which types of issues do they oppose it?
2. Why might Americans with a high degree of political engagement have trouble determining whether they are liberal or conservative?

LO6 **Assess the impact of knowledge, self-interest, and leadership on political opinions.**

1. What evidence shows that people know little about politics—or, conversely, that they know a lot about government and political affairs?
2. Using the concept of issue framing, pick a political issue and illustrate how Democratic and Republican candidates present it differently to voters.

6 The Media

Learning Outcomes

LO1 Trace the evolution of the mass media in the United States and evaluate the impact of new technologies on journalism.

LO2 Evaluate the effect of privately owned mass media on the quality of political communication in the United States.

LO3 Follow the evolution of government regulation of the media and identify the challenges that new media technologies present to existing regulations.

LO4 Analyze the role of the media in political socialization and the acquisition of political knowledge.

LO5 Assess the impact of the media on democratic values and politics in the United States.

 WATCH & LEARN MindTap™ for American Government
Watch a brief "What Do You Know?" video summarizing Media and Politics.

When Hurricane Sandy devastated the northeastern United States in 2012, people around the world learned about the extent of the damage by watching the news, reading newspapers, and going online. For those Americans trapped by floodwaters and left in the dark by power outages, traditional sources of news were of little use. Instead, mobile devices and social media allowed them to learn about developments in their area and even contribute to the news themselves. While some information posted was inaccurate, public officials and news outlets used Twitter to direct citizens to emergency shelters, respond to their distress calls, and inform them if their water was safe to drink.[1]

Twitter proved to be particularly helpful to residents of Newark, New Jersey, where then-Mayor (now U.S. Senator) Cory Booker personally responded to their tweets for help, including hand-delivering diapers to one family. When one resident complained that he was running out of Hot Pockets, Booker provided some much-needed comic relief, tweeting, "I believe in you. I know this is a problem you can handle," which prompted the parent company of Hot Pockets to donate hundreds of free microwavable sandwiches to the city.[2]

Hurricane Sandy wasn't Booker's first time using Twitter to communicate with Newark's citizens. In 2010, he used Twitter after a blizzard to find residents who needed help, personally showing up at some homes to shovel snow. In 2012, after rescuing a woman from a burning building, he tweeted about it on his way to the hospital for smoke inhalation. The story of Newark's superhero mayor and his savvy use of social media proved too good to pass up by traditional outlets; these incidents garnered substantial amounts of coverage in places like *Time*, *People*, *USA Today*, and network news.[3]

The use of social media during blizzards and hurricanes illustrates how news consumption is no longer a passive, one-way exercise. Journalists, government, and citizens now interact with each other routinely, with each actor producing and receiving information from the other. While most Americans still get most of their news from journalists at traditional outlets, we are in the midst of an era of great change in political communication. Politicians can bypass journalists altogether, going directly to YouTube or Facebook instead of issuing a press release or holding a news conference before a pack of reporters.

Journalists still play a critical role in the media landscape, and news transmitted by social media has its greatest impact when it is also covered by traditional news. But technological change has generated a range of important questions about the role of the media in American democracy, such as: What is to become of traditional journalism? Who is and is not a journalist? Throughout the twentieth century, a journalist was a trained professional who reported the news to the public after an editor determined that the story met standards of accuracy and objectivity. Today, that understanding of journalistic behavior is in the throes of change.

Some observers argue that the new media frontier is a threat to democracy. Traditional journalism conducts investigative reporting, follows up on stories once they are no longer on the front page, and sends journalists to report on foreign events and on state and city politics.[4] Journalistic norms of objectivity and accountability provide readers with accurate information that allows them to draw their own conclusions about current affairs. When citizens turn instead to opinion blogs and Twitter feeds, the market for traditional journalism is threatened, and the important services it contributes to the public good could disappear.

On the other side are people who find the new frontier in journalism exciting and democratizing. They argue that the amount of depth and context readers can find about any topic is a huge advance from the limited amount of information that was available when journalists were constrained by the length of a news show or printed article. As one writer put it, "Today's readers have access to far more high-quality coverage than they have time to read."[5] News sites that exist primarily on the Web, such as ProPublica, The Huffington Post, and Politico have won Pulitzer Prizes. Champions of new media also say that mobile technology and social networking allow information to reach ever broader audiences.[6]

People on both sides agree on three things. First, the changes—and challenges—facing traditional journalism are here to stay; we cannot put the Internet genie back in the bottle. Second, the media continue to play a critical role in the democratic process. Third, this critical role demands that we carefully and continually study the impact of the rapidly changing media environment.

In this chapter, we describe the origin, growth, and change of the media; assess their objectivity; and examine their influence on politics. How have the various media promoted or frustrated democratic ideals over time? How is technology challenging our conception of the role of the media in democratic politics? How do patterns of media ownership and regulation affect the tradeoffs among freedom, order, and equality? Who uses which media, and what do they learn? What new problems or possibilities flow from globalization of the news media?

★ The Development of the Mass Media in the United States

LO1 ★ Trace the evolution of the mass media in the United States and evaluate the impact of new technologies on journalism.

LISTEN & LEARN
MindTap for American Government

Access Read Speaker to listen to Chapter 6.

Communication is essential in a representative democracy. Elected officials need to inform the citizenry of their actions such that the people can effectively give their consent to be governed by the politicians of their choice. Likewise, citizens need to be able to communicate their wants and needs to elected officials such that those officials are able to provide adequate representation to their constituents.

Communication is simply the process of transmitting information from one individual or group to another. *Mass communication* is the process by which information

The News Fairy?

While the Internet may be gaining in popularity as a source of news, many Internet news sites rely on traditional media sources for their information. These sites, such as Google News, are known as news aggregators. If newspapers fail, news aggregators will too.

is transmitted to large, heterogeneous, widely dispersed audiences. The term **mass media** refers to the means for communicating to these audiences. Traditionally, the mass media has been divided into two types: print and broadcast. *Print media*, such as newspapers, communicate information through the publication of words and pictures on paper. *Broadcast media*, such as radio and television, communicate information electronically, through sounds and images. The Internet has made the distinction between print and broadcast media problematic, as newspapers and magazines now have an online presence that provides video clips to accompany news articles, and television and radio news programs have websites that provide text. Moreover, most of these sites provide opportunities for the public to comment and thus disseminate their own perspective. More so now than at any other time in history, the opportunities for genuine two-way flows of information between citizens and government are possible thanks to the interactivity of the Internet. It is now a central component of an ever evolving mass media, which is a collection of technologies with the dual capability of reflecting and shaping our political views.

The media are not the only connection between citizens and government. As we discussed in Chapter 5, various agents of socialization (especially schools) function as "linkage mechanisms" that promote such communication. In later chapters, we discuss other mechanisms for communication: voting, political parties, campaigning, and interest groups. The media, however, are the only linkage mechanisms that specialize in communication.

mass media
The means employed in mass communication; traditionally divided into print media and broadcast media.

Although this chapter concentrates on five prominent mass media—newspapers, magazines, radio, television, and the Internet—political content can also be transmitted through other mass media, such as music and movies. Popular musicians often express political ideas in their music. In 2011, for example, Lady Gaga released the single "Born This Way," and created the Born This Way Foundation as a vehicle for combating bullying, an effort that garnered her a meeting with top aides at the White House regarding anti-bullying initiatives.[7]

Motion pictures often convey intense political messages. Michael Moore's *Sicko*, a 2007 Oscar-nominated documentary, was a blistering attack on the health-care system in the United States. One poll found that nearly half of Americans had either seen or heard of the movie one month after its release, and of those, nearly half said that the film made them more likely to think that health-care reform was needed.[8]

Although the record and film industries sometimes convey political messages, they are primarily in the business of entertainment. Our focus here is on mass media in the news industry. Figure 6.1 plots the increase in the number of Americans with access to radios, televisions, and the Internet from 1920 to the present. The growth of the country, technological inventions, and shifting political attitudes about the scope of government, as well as trends in entertainment, have shaped the development of the news media in the United States.[9]

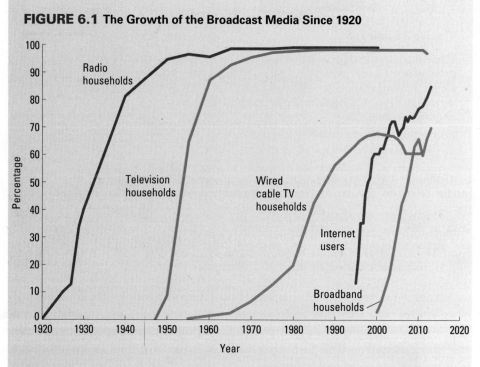

FIGURE 6.1 The Growth of the Broadcast Media Since 1920

The media environment in the United States has changed dramatically over time. This graph shows the percentage of all households or adults using a particular media technology: radio, television, cable TV, Internet, or broadband. In 1950, for instance, only 9 percent of all households had a television set. Within five years, almost two-thirds of all American households owned a television set. In 1995, only 14 percent of all adults reported using the Internet. Today around 85 percent of adults report using the Internet.

Sources: Early data on radio, television, and cable TV came from Northwestern University's Media Information Center. Additional data on radio households in the 1920s and 1930s are reported by Steve Craig, "How America Adopted Radio," *Journal of Broadcasting and Electronic Media* 48 (June 2004): 179–195. For recent data, Pew Internet & American Life Project (www.pewinternet.org), and Stanley and Niemi, *Vital Statistics on American Politics*, 2013–2014 (2013).

Newspapers

When the Revolutionary War broke out in 1775, thirty-seven newspapers (all weeklies) were publishing in the colonies.[10] They had small circulations, so they were not really mass media but group media read by elites. The first newspapers were mainly political organs, financed by parties and advocating party causes. Newspapers did not move toward independent ownership and large circulations until the 1830s, once publishers discovered they could raise revenue through advertising instead of relying on parties.

By 1880, 971 daily newspapers and 8,633 weekly newspapers and periodicals were published in the United States. Most larger cities had many newspapers: New York had twenty-nine; Philadelphia, twenty-four; and San Francisco, twenty-one. Competition for readers grew fierce among the big-city dailies. Toward the end of the nineteenth century, imaginative publishers courted readers by entertaining them with photographs, comic strips, sports sections, advice columns, and stories of sex and crime.

By the 1960s, under pressure from both radio and television, competition among big city dailies had nearly disappeared. New York had only three papers left by 1969, a pattern repeated in every large city in the country. By 2009, only twenty-six U.S. towns or cities had two or more competing dailies under separate ownership.[11] The net result is that newspaper circulation as a percentage of the U.S. population has dropped by 59 percent since 1947.[12] Some argue that the lack of competition mid-century is part of what allowed the journalistic norms of objectivity and accuracy to emerge; without having to pander to readers through sensationalism, reporters could focus on quality and depth.[13]

The daily paper with the largest circulation in 2012 (about 2.3 million copies) was the *Wall Street Journal*, followed by *USA Today* (1.7 million). *The New York Times*, which many journalists consider the best newspaper in the country, sold 1.6 million daily copies, placing it third in circulation (see Figure 6.2). In comparison, *People Magazine*, which carries stories about celebrities, had a circulation of about 3.5 million.[14] Neither the *Times* nor the *Wall Street Journal* carries comic strips, which no doubt limits their mass appeal. They also print more political news and analyses than most readers want.

While circulation of printed papers has declined, news readership is actually up, with many readers accessing newspapers online. In order to stay in business and avoid laying off journalists, more and more newspapers are requiring readers to pay for unlimited access to the news online. Many of these so-called paywalls have been successful, like that of the *Wall Street Journal* and the *New York Times*. Other news outlets, however, have found that when they institute a paywall, readers just go elsewhere. News organizations are continually struggling to find ways to earn both readers and revenue in the digital age.[15]

Magazines

Magazines differ from newspapers not only in the frequency of their publication but also in the nature of their coverage. News-oriented magazines cover the news in a more specialized manner than do daily newspapers and are often forums for opinions, not strictly news. The earliest public affairs magazines were founded in the mid-1800s, and two—*The Nation* and *Harper's*—are still publishing today. Such magazines were often politically influential, especially in framing arguments against slavery and later in publishing exposés of political corruption. Even magazines with limited readerships can wield political power. Magazines may influence **attentive policy elites**—group leaders who follow news in specific areas—and thus influence mass opinion indirectly through a **two-step flow of communication**.

attentive policy elites
Leaders who follow news in specific policy areas.

two-step flow of communication
The process in which a few policy elites gather information and then inform their more numerous followers, mobilizing them to apply pressure to government.

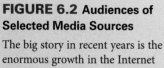

FIGURE 6.2 Audiences of Selected Media Sources

The big story in recent years is the enormous growth in the Internet news audience. The print version of the *New York Times*, for instance, has a circulation of 1.6 million people. Yet over 30 million people visit the paper's website for news every month. Some major news magazines (published weekly) have more readers than newspapers do, but newspapers are published daily and there are more of them.

Source: Pew Research Center's Project for Excellence in Journalism, "The State of the News Media, 2013," http://www.stateofthemedia.org/.

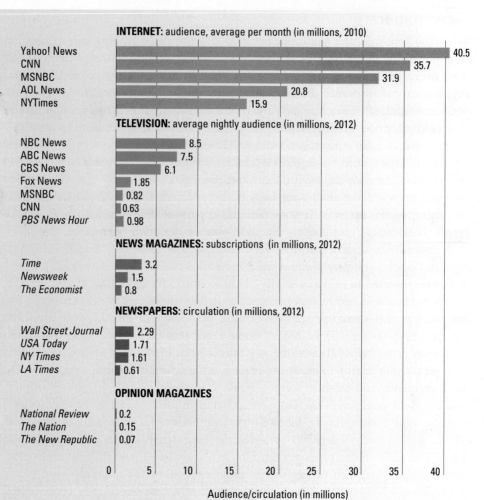

INTERNET: audience, average per month (in millions, 2010)

Yahoo! News	40.5
CNN	35.7
MSNBC	31.9
AOL News	20.8
NYTimes	15.9

TELEVISION: average nightly audience (in millions, 2012)

NBC News	8.5
ABC News	7.5
CBS News	6.1
Fox News	1.85
MSNBC	0.82
CNN	0.63
PBS News Hour	0.98

NEWS MAGAZINES: subscriptions (in millions, 2012)

Time	3.2
Newsweek	1.5
The Economist	0.8

NEWSPAPERS: circulation (in millions, 2012)

Wall Street Journal	2.29
USA Today	1.71
NY Times	1.61
LA Times	0.61

OPINION MAGAZINES

National Review	0.2
The Nation	0.15
The New Republic	0.07

Audience/circulation (in millions)

As scholars originally viewed the two-step flow, it conformed to the pluralist model of democracy. Once group leaders (for instance, union or industry leaders) became informed of political developments, they informed their more numerous followers, mobilizing them to apply pressure on government. Today, according to a revised interpretation of the two-step flow concept, policy elites are more likely to influence public opinion and other leaders by airing their views in the media. In this view, public deliberation on issues is mediated by these professional communicators who frame the issues in the media for popular consumption—that is, they define the way that issues will be viewed, heard, or read.[16]

Only one weekly news magazine—*Time* (founded in 1923)—enjoys big circulation numbers in the United States (3.2 million copies in 2012). Overall, news magazine circulation has declined in recent years much as newspaper circulation has. Once popular as a news weekly, *Newsweek* (founded in 1933) saw a 32 percent decline in circulation from 2009 to 2010. In 2012, *Newsweek* ceased its print publication and is now available only online. Despite these troubles, the magazine publishes in five languages and continues to operate domestic and international bureaus.

In contrast to these mainstream publications, there are also explicitly political magazines such as *The National Review* and *The Weekly Standard* that are aimed at the audience of policy elites more than the general public.

Radio

Regularly scheduled, continuous radio broadcasting began in 1920 on stations KDKA in Pittsburgh and WWJ in Detroit. Both stations claim to be the first commercial station, and both broadcast returns of the 1920 election of President Warren G. Harding. The first radio network, the National Broadcasting Company (NBC), was formed in 1926. Soon four networks were on the air, transforming radio into a national medium by linking thousands of local stations. Americans were quick to purchase and use this new technology (see Figure 6.1). Millions of Americans heard President Franklin D. Roosevelt deliver his first "fireside chat" in 1933.

Because the public could sense reporters' personalities over radio in a way they could not in print, broadcast journalists quickly became household names. Edward R. Murrow, one of the most famous radio news personalities, broadcast news of the merger of Germany and Austria by short-wave radio from Vienna in 1938 and during World War II gave stirring reports of German air raids on London.

Today there are nearly fifteen thousand licensed broadcast radio stations.[17] Despite the advent of iTunes, Internet radio, and podcasts, nine out of ten Americans listen to a traditional AM/FM radio every week.[18] Radio listeners often tune into stations that have news and talk radio formats, and the audience for talk radio continues to grow. The audience of talk radio is more Republican because the majority of talk radio hosts, like Rush Limbaugh, are conservative.[19] Talk radio shows have been criticized for polarizing politics by publicizing extreme views.[20]

Television

Experiments with television began in France in the early 1900s. By 1940, twenty-three television stations were operating in the United States. Two stations broadcast the returns of Roosevelt's 1940 reelection.[21] By 1950, ninety-eight stations covered the major population centers of the country, although only 9 percent of households had televisions (see Figure 6.1).

The first coast-to-coast broadcast came in 1951: President Harry Truman's address to delegates at the Japanese peace treaty conference in San Francisco. That same year, Democratic senator Estes Kefauver of Tennessee called for television coverage of his committee's investigation into organized crime. For weeks, people with televisions invited their neighbors to watch underworld crime figures answering questions before the camera. And Kefauver became one of the first politicians to benefit from television coverage. Previously unknown and representing a small state, he won many of the 1952 Democratic presidential primaries and became the Democrats' vice-presidential candidate in 1956.

Many early anchors of television network news programs came to the medium

MPI/Stringer/Archive Photos/Getty Images

Watching the President on Television

Television revolutionized presidential politics by allowing millions of voters to look closely at the candidates' faces and judge their personalities in the process. This close-up of John Kennedy during a debate with Richard Nixon in the 1960 campaign showed Kennedy to good advantage. In contrast, close-ups of Nixon made him look as though he needed a shave. Kennedy won one of the closest elections in history; his good looks on television may have made the difference.

already famous through their experience on radio. Now that the news audience could see the broadcasters as well as hear them, networks built their evening news around an "anchorman" chosen to inspire trust in viewers.

By 2012, the United States had more than thirteen hundred commercial and three hundred public television stations, and virtually every household (97 percent) had a television (and the vast majority had two or more sets).[22] Today, television claims the biggest news audience of all media outside the Internet. The three broadcast networks still have large audiences, but millions of viewers have drifted to more opinionated cable networks, especially MSNBC on the left and Fox News on the right. In fact, cable news is becoming a bit of a throwback; more and more it seems analogous to the early newspapers, which were blatantly political organizations. Research suggests that with viewers today having unprecedented choices, people who are more interested in politics increasingly desire partisan shows, while people who are less interested in politics simply avoid news programming altogether. Moreover, some research indicates that people who watch partisan news become more extreme in their political views. Still, some researchers have disputed citizens' "mass migration" from traditional media, concluding instead that these newer venues supplement rather than displace print and broadcast sources. Others also contend that viewers of partisan news are already quite partisan themselves, and that the shows they watch do not make them more extreme.[23]

The Internet

What we today call the Internet began in 1969 when, with support from the U.S. Defense Department's Advanced Research Projects Agency, computers at four universities were linked to form ARPANET, which connected thirty-seven universities by 1972. New communications standards developed in 1983 allowed these networks to be linked, creating the Internet. At first, the Internet was used mainly to transmit e-mail among researchers. In 1991, European physicists devised a standardized system for encoding and transmitting a wide range of materials, including graphics and photographs, over the Internet. The World Wide Web (WWW) was born, and both personal and mass communication would never be the same. Now anyone with Internet access can read text, view images, and download data from websites worldwide. In January 1993 there were only fifty websites in existence. Today there are over 860 million sites and over 2.75 billion Web users worldwide.[24]

The development of wireless technology and mobile devices such as smartphones and tablets has further extended the reach of electronic information. By 2013, 56 percent of American adults had smartphones (including a whopping 79 percent of people age 18 to 24). Thirty-five percent of American adults had tablet computers, up from just 9 percent in 2009. All news outlets with a presence on the Web are increasingly challenged to determine the best ways in which to make their information available on such devices.[25] (See "Mobile Media in Global Politics.")

It did not take long for the Internet to be incorporated into politics, and today virtually every government agency and political organization has its own website. Many private citizens also operate their own websites on politics and public affairs. An estimated 14 percent of Internet users have a so-called **blog** (for weblog); according to a survey of bloggers, about 35 percent of them discuss politics on their blogs.[26] A growing segment of the public also engages in news conversations through social media like Twitter and Facebook. These digital communications regularly influence news reporting and politics. As noted at the start of this chapter,

AP Images/Jason DeCrow

Laugh and Learn

Many people learn about politics by watching comedians like Jon Stewart, the host of *The Daily Show*. Almost 30 percent of adults surveyed said that they learned about the 2008 political campaign from comedy shows like *The Daily Show, The Colbert Report,* or *Saturday Night Live.* Studies show that watching *The Daily Show* can improve people's ability to learn real facts about politics and current affairs.

Source: Michael A. Xenos and Amy B. Becker, "Moments of Zen: Effects of *The Daily Show* on Information Seeking and Political Learning," *Political Communication* 26 (2009): 317–332.

blog
A form of newsletter, journal, or "log" of thoughts for public reading, usually devoted to social or political issues and often updated daily. The term derives from weblog.

Mobile Media in Global Politics

Ever since iPhones were introduced in 2007, worldwide adoption of smartphones has soared. Just since 2011, smartphone adoption in the United States rose from 35 percent to 56 percent. As the figure below shows, citizens in many countries far outpace the United States in terms of smartphone adoption, including United Arab Emirates (74 percent), Singapore (72 percent), and Sweden (63 percent). Other countries, such as India (13 percent) and Brazil (26 percent), still have fairly low rates of smartphone usage. The rapid adoption of this technology, along with the advent of social networking, has raised important questions about the nature and role of the news media in the political process.

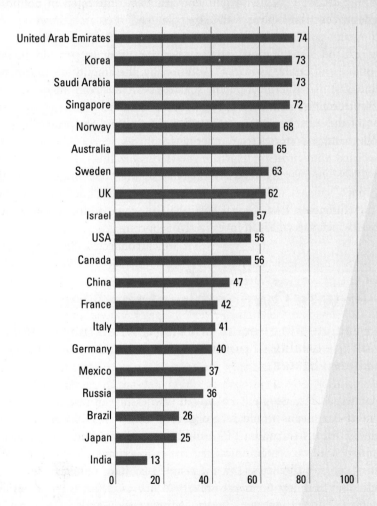

Source: Our Mobile Planet, Google.com.

Critical Thinking How might the content and quality of news accessed on a mobile device differ from that of news accessed in a newspaper or on television?

Newark Mayor Cory Booker's use of Twitter earned him national media attention, which helped propel him to the U.S. Senate. Another example is from July 2012, when a video was posted on YouTube about a film made by an Egyptian-American that mocked the Muslim prophet Muhammad. At the time, the video garnered little attention. But two months later, an Egyptian TV host began discussing the clip. Other news stations throughout the world began discussing the film as well, which led to anti-American protests across the globe.[27] As these examples illustrate, the influence of information conveyed through new media platforms on the course of politics is often largely indirect, influencing the types of stories that get picked up by the "mainstream media."

As we noted at the start of this chapter, some observers fear that the new media landscape will lead to a "wild west atmosphere" in which untrained private individuals can broadcast what they wish online to millions of readers without professional, organizational, or legal concerns about its source.[28] Research, however, shows the most prominent political bloggers are professional journalists from traditional news organizations and that the most popular news sites generally provide the same news in their offline and online formats.[29] Additionally, the amount of information available online is so vast that most people still rely on mainstream media institutions to help them determine which news is real and important.[30]

Some of the most common sources for news online are primarily aggregators, which collect and post stories from other news sources, such as Google News, or websites associated with print or television news organizations, such as the *New York Times* or CNN. Online-only news ventures that do their own original reporting command a much smaller audience, but their presence continues to grow. Such sites include the Huffington Post, Global Post (which focuses on international news), and ProPublica (which specializes in investigative reporting).[31]

Private Ownership of the Media

LO2 ★ Evaluate the effect of privately owned mass media on the quality of political communication in the United States.

In the United States, people take private ownership of the media for granted. Indeed, most Americans would regard government ownership of the media as an unacceptable threat to freedom that would interfere with the marketplace of ideas and result in one-way communication: from government to citizens. When the government controls the news flow, the people may have little chance to learn what the government is doing or to pressure it to behave differently. Certainly that is true in China. The Chinese government employs thousands of Internet police to prevent "subversive content" from being disseminated to its nearly 600 million Web users. If an Internet user in China searches for "democracy movements," she is met with a screen that reads, "Page cannot be displayed." Every year on June 4, the anniversary of a government crackdown on pro-democracy demonstrators in Tiananmen Square in 1989, activists try to outsmart the censors. They try, for instance, to come up with new ways to highlight the date, including 0.8*8 (which equals 6.4) and May 35 (four days after May 31), and replace censored images with absurd re-creations of the 1989 protests that have included inflatable ducks and Legos.[32]

In other Western democracies, the print media are privately owned, but the broadcast media often are not. In the United States, except for about three hundred public television stations (out of about seventeen hundred total) and one thousand public radio stations (out of over fifteen thousand), the broadcast media are privately owned.[33]

The Consequences of Private Ownership

Private ownership of the media gives the news industry in America more political freedom than any other in the world, but it also makes the media more dependent on advertising revenues to cover costs and make a profit. Because advertising rates are tied to audience size, news operations in America must appeal to the audiences they serve.

Much of the content of newspapers is advertising. After fashion reports, sports, comics, and so on, only a relatively small portion of any newspaper is devoted to news of any sort and only a fraction of that news—

Ducking the Censors

Pro-democracy activists in China are constantly challenged to find creative ways to evade government censors. This image of ducks in place of tanks in an iconic photo of a pro-democracy protestor was posted on China's version of Twitter in 2013. Soon enough, however, searches for "big yellow duck" were also censored.

excluding stories about fires, murder trials, and the like—can be considered political. In terms of volume, the entertainment content offered by the mass media in the United States can vastly overshadow the news content. In other words, the media function more to entertain than provide news. Entertainment increases the audience, which increases advertising revenues. The profit motive creates constant pressure to increase the ratio of entertainment to news or to make the news itself more entertaining.

You might think that a story's political significance, educational value, or social importance determines whether the media cover it. The truth is that most potential news stories are not judged by such grand criteria. The primary criterion of a story's **newsworthiness** is usually its audience appeal, which is judged according to its potential impact on readers or listeners, its degree of sensationalism (exemplified by violence, conflict, disaster, or scandal), its treatment of familiar people or life situations, its close-to-home character, and its timeliness.[34] As Figure 6.3 shows, the content of news coverage often consists of topics that have little to do with elections, foreign affairs, government, or the economy.

newsworthiness
The degree to which a news story is important enough to be covered in the mass media.

The importance of audience appeal has led the news industry to calculate its audience carefully. Additionally, the media try to increase ratings by tailoring the delivery or content of their news to the desires of their audience. Within the news industry, the process has been termed market-driven journalism—both reporting news and running commercials geared to a target audience.[35] For example, nearly 60 percent of network evening news viewers are over fifty years old, which is why these shows nearly always feature a health-related story and run one or more commercials related to prescription drugs.[36]

More citizens report watching local news than national news, and local news epitomizes market-driven journalism by matching audience demographics to advertising revenue while slighting news about government, policy, and public affairs.[37]

FIGURE 6.3 Getting the News: Consider the Source

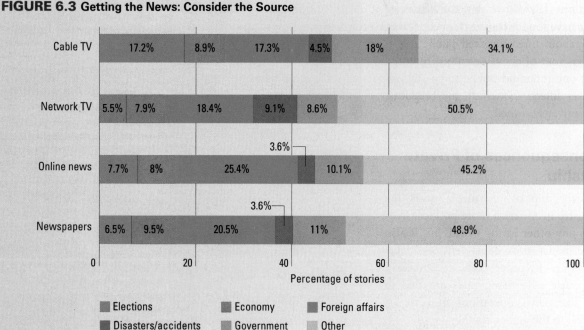

An analysis of over 50,000 news stories in 2011 (from the front pages of newspapers, major news programs, and Internet sites) shows that just a few categories dominated the news: elections, the economy, government, and foreign affairs. Cable TV was particularly devoted to election coverage, while online news sites and newspapers provided the most extensive coverage of foreign affairs. In all of these media, however, the category "other" predominates, reflecting the market-driven character of news media content.

Source: "A Year in the News Interactive, 2011," Pew Project for Excellence in Journalism, http://stateofthemeda.org/2012/year-in-the-news-3/.

Local television newscasts across the nation practice a "hook-and-hold" approach. They hook viewers at the start by airing alarming stories about crime, accidents, fires, and disasters. The middle of the broadcast has informative news about business, science, and politics that are not considered good viewing. To hold viewers to the end, stations tease them by promising soft topics on pop culture, human interest, or health. As a result, local news broadcasts across the country look much the same.[38]

At the national level, the nightly news broadcasts were once the crown jewels of independent broadcasting companies—ABC, CBS, and NBC—and valued for their public service. Now these broadcasts are cogs in huge corporate conglomerates. The Walt Disney Company, for example, owns ABC. NBC was owned by General Electric for years, but merged with the cable company Comcast in 2011, which has created a massive television conglomerate.[39] The merger highlights the fact that television nightly news is no longer a public service, but a profit center. Nonetheless, the financial reports from network news broadcasts are not good.

infotainment
A mix of information and diversion oriented to personalities or celebrities, not linked to the day's events, and usually unrelated to public affairs or policy; often called "soft news."

From 1980 to 2012, ABC, CBS, and NBC suffered severe losses in their primetime programming audience, dropping from about 42 million viewers per night to 15.1 million—despite an increase in population.[40] Increasingly, viewers turned to watching cable stations instead of network programs, or they turned away from news altogether. Audience declines brought declining profits and cutbacks in news budgets. As parent corporations demand that news programs "pay their way," networks succumb to **infotainment**—a mix of information and diversion oriented to personalities or celebrities, not linked to the day's events, and usually unrelated to public affairs or policy.[41] Over 12 million people tune in for morning shows such as NBC's *Today Show* that have long mixed news and celebrity interviews.

The Concentration of Private Ownership

Media owners can make more money by increasing their audience or by acquiring additional publications or stations. As illustrated by the NBC-Comcast merger discussed earlier, there has been a trend toward concentrated ownership of the media, increasing the risk that a few owners could control the news flow to promote their own interests—much as political parties influenced the content of the earliest American newspapers. In fact, the number of independent newspapers has declined as newspaper chains (owners of two or more newspapers in different cities) have acquired more newspapers. The Gannett chain, which owns *USA Today*, owns over eighty daily newspapers throughout the United States.[42] Research suggests that newspapers owned by publicly traded chains are more likely than other newspapers to resort to negative and positive spins on the news (as opposed to remaining neutral in tone) in order to attract more readers and thus, increase profits. While owners of privately held papers also care about profits, they seem more willing to promote journalistic integrity, even if it might hinder the bottom line.[43]

Some observers argue that since newspapers are under relentless financial stress, they should consider rejecting the for-profit model and instead operate as nonprofits. As nonprofits, newspapers would be financed through endowments, charitable donations, dues-paying members, and even the government, similar to how PBS and NPR operate on television and radio today. To date, a number of nonprofit news organizations have emerged; some focus on local issues, others on national issues, and others track policy-specific issues, such as health care. But no major newspaper has switched to the nonprofit model yet.[44]

At first glance, concentration of ownership does not seem to be a problem in the television industry. Although there are only three major networks, the networks usually do not own their affiliates. Most communities in the United States have a choice of multiple stations. As with newspapers, however, chains sometimes own television stations in different cities, and ownership sometimes extends across different media. Rupert Murdoch's News Corporation is one of the world's largest media companies. Even after creating a separate company for its newspapers in 2012, the company still owns the Fox network, twenty-seven local Fox stations, several film companies and cable channels, and more.[45]

Government Regulation of the Media

LO3 ★ Follow the evolution of government regulation of the media and identify the challenges that new media technologies present to existing regulations.

Although most of the mass media in the United States are privately owned, they do not operate free of government regulation. Broadcast media operate under more stringent regulations than print media, initially because of technical aspects of broadcasting. Lately, debates about government regulation of the Internet have become common. In general, government regulation of the mass media addresses three aspects of their operation: technical considerations, ownership, and content.

Technical and Ownership Regulations

In the early days of radio, stations that operated on similar frequencies in the same area often jammed each other's signals, and no one could broadcast clearly. At the broadcasters' insistence, Congress passed the Federal Radio Act (1927), which declared that the public owned the airwaves and private broadcasters could use them only by obtaining a license from the Federal Radio Commission. Thus, government regulation of broadcasting was not forced on the industry by socialist politicians; capitalist owners sought it to impose order on the use of the airwaves (thereby restricting others' freedom to enter broadcasting).

Seven years later, Congress passed the Federal Communications Act of 1934, a more sweeping law that created the **Federal Communications Commission (FCC)**, which has five members (no more than three from the same political party) nominated by the president for terms of five years. The commissioners can be removed from office only through impeachment and conviction. The FCC is thus an independent regulatory commission insulated from political control by either the president or Congress. (We discuss independent regulatory commissions in Chapter 13.) By law, its vague mandate is to "serve the public interest, convenience, and necessity." The FCC sets social, economic, and technical goals for the communications industry and deals with philosophical issues of regulation versus deregulation.[46] Today, the FCC's charge includes regulating interstate and international communications by radio, television, telephone, telegraph, cable, and satellite.

For six decades, the communications industry was regulated under the basic framework of the 1934 law that created the FCC. Pressured by businesses that wanted to exploit new electronic technologies, such as computers and satellite transmissions, Congress overhauled existing regulations in the Telecommunications Act of 1996.

The new law relaxed limitations on media ownership. For example, broadcasters were previously limited to owning only twelve television stations and forty radio stations. The 1996 law eliminated limits on the number of television stations one company may own, just as long as their coverage didn't extend beyond 35 percent of the market nationwide. As a result, CBS, Fox, and NBC doubled or tripled the number of stations that they owned.[47] The 1996 law also set no national limits for radio ownership and relaxed local limits. In its wake, Clear Channel Communications, Inc. which owned thirty-six stations, gobbled up over eleven hundred, including all six stations serving Minot, North Dakota.[48] In addition, the FCC allowed local and long-distance telephone companies to compete with one another and to sell television services.[49]

The FCC also regulates the Internet but has struggled to keep up with the changing role of the Internet in American life. Since Congress has not passed any laws that outline the role of the FCC with respect to the Internet, the FCC does not have jurisdiction to regulate content, although Internet service providers (ISPs) are subject to standing antimonopoly laws.[50] Nonetheless, the FCC has become involved in the regulation of emerging technologies, as issues of ownership, access, and cross-platform content have arisen. For instance, should regulations that apply to broadcast news also apply to the news program's website? What about when information from that website is transmitted through wireless communications to a mobile device instead of to a desktop computer via broadband? As one scholar put it, "The new communications technologies require a far more complete rethinking of the scope and purpose of federal regulation than has happened thus far."[51] In the absence of congressional action clarifying the role of the FCC with respect to the Internet, policies and rules will evolve and be challenged bit by bit (see "Freedom, Order, Equality, and … Net Neutrality").

Federal Communications Commission (FCC)
An independent federal agency that regulates interstate and international communication by radio, television, telephone, telegraph, cable, and satellite.

Freedom, Order, or Equality

Freedom, Order, Equality, and ... Net Neutrality

Should Comcast or Verizon be allowed to charge consumers who stream movies on Netflix more for their Internet service than consumers who just use e-mail and surf the Web? Should these Internet service providers (ISPs) be able to block consumers from even accessing sites like YouTube since streaming video eats up so much bandwidth and clogs Internet traffic? These questions are at the heart of current debates about *net neutrality*.

ISPs argue that as private companies, they should be free to set up their businesses as they see fit. They say they want to provide relief from Internet congestion and that establishing the equivalent of first-class mail delivery should be their prerogative. As the graph below indicates, Netflix and YouTube alone accounted for over 50 percent of Internet traffic during peak hours in 2013.

In 2014, a federal appeals court ruled that because the Federal Communications Commission (FCC) has classified broadband as *an information service*, ISPs cannot be prohibited from charging for more bandwidth or blocking access to otherwise legal sites.* Supporters of net neutrality say data-intensive information should not be available only to the affluent and that ISPs should not be allowed to determine which sites consumers can access.

When private companies operate within the basic infrastructure that is considered essential to modern democratic life, the government may restrict their freedom to operate as they wish, thus promoting equality of access and order to how the infrastructure is managed. Accordingly, Congress gave the FCC authority to regulate telecommunications. But should ISPs be regulated as one of these so-called *common carriers* that provide "basic telecommunications infrastructure"?**

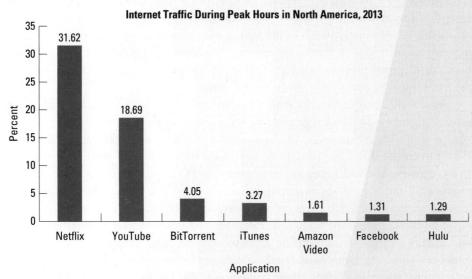

Internet Traffic During Peak Hours in North America, 2013

Source: Global Internet Phenomena Snapshot: 2H 2013; North America Fixed Access; https://www.sandvine.com/trends/global-internet-phenomena/.

---

*Edward Wyatt Lee, "Court Rejects Equal Access Rule for Internet Providers," *New York Times*, 14 January 2014.

**Timothy Lee, "Net Neutrality Is on Trial in Washington: Here's What You Need to Know," *Washington Post*, 10 September 2013.

The net neutrality debate involves clashes between the freedom of ISPs to develop their own business plans and their desire for order in the face of Internet congestion, and equality of access to information among the public. Now that the Internet is an essential medium for news transmission, it is arguably in the public interest to ensure that citizens can find information about politics in the most efficient and equitable way possible. Whether that requires more—or less—government regulation remains unsettled.

Critical Thinking Which types of companies, organizations, and groups do you think are most likely to be in favor of having the FCC promote net neutrality? Which ones are most likely to oppose it?

Regulation of Content

The First Amendment to the Constitution prohibits Congress from abridging the freedom of the press. Over time, the press has come to mean all media, and the courts have decided many cases that define how far freedom of the press extends under the law. Chapter 15 discusses the most important of these cases. Although the courts have had difficulty defining obscenity, they have not permitted obscene expression under freedom of the press. In 1996, however, a federal court overturned an attempt to limit transmission of "indecent" (not obscene) material on the Internet, calling the attempt "profoundly repugnant to First Amendment principles." [52]

Usually the courts strike down government attempts to restrain the press from disseminating the information, reports, or opinions it finds newsworthy. One notable exception concerns strategic information during wartime: the courts have supported censorship of information such as the sailing schedules of troop ships or the planned movements of troops in battle. Otherwise, they have recognized a strong constitutional case against press censorship. This stand has given the United States some of the freest, most vigorous news media in the world.

Because the broadcast media are licensed to use the public airwaves, they have been subject to some additional regulation of the content of their news coverage beyond what is applied to other media. The basis for the FCC's regulation of content lies in its charge to ensure that radio (and, later, television) stations would "serve the public interest, convenience, and necessity." For years, the FCC operated under three rules to promote the public interest concerning political matters. The *fairness doctrine* obligated broadcasters to provide fair coverage of all views on public issues. The *equal opportunities rule* (also known as the equal time rule) required any broadcast station that gave or sold time to a candidate for a public office to make an equal amount of time available under the same conditions to all other candidates for that office. The *reasonable access rule* required that stations make their facilities available for the expression of conflicting views on issues by all responsible elements in the community.

COMPARE WITH YOUR PEERS

MindTap™ for American Government

Access The Constitution Forum: Polling Activity—Fair and Balanced Media.

In 1987, the FCC repealed the *fairness doctrine*. Prior to its repeal, the news media tended to avoid controversial and partisan issues for fear of being in violation. Once broadcasters were no longer required to cover all views, they could express ideological viewpoints.[53] The National Association of Broadcasters says that the elimination of the fairness doctrine has played a large role in the proliferation of news and opinion alternatives now available to media consumers.[54] Indeed, some observers suggest that there might be too much diversity among news sources today and that the variation in content and quality is contributing to a population that is less informed and more polarized.[55]

Note that these content regulations were never imposed on the print media. And as noted earlier, the Internet has thus far been free from content regulations as well. In fact, one aspect of a free press is its ability to champion causes that it favors without having to argue the case for the other side. The broadcast media have traditionally been treated differently because they were licensed by the FCC to operate as semi-monopolies. With the rise of one-newspaper cities and towns, however, competition among television stations is greater than among newspapers in virtually every market area. Advocates of dropping all FCC content regulations argue that the broadcast media should be just as free as other media to decide which candidates they endorse and which issues they support.

Functions of the Mass Media for the Political System

LO4 ★ Analyze the role of the media in political socialization and the acquisition of political knowledge.

Most journalists consider "news" (at least hard news) to be an important event that happened within the past twenty-four hours. A presidential news conference or a suicide bombing qualifies as news. Who decides what is important? The media, of course. In this section, we discuss how the media cover political affairs, what they choose to report (what becomes "news"), who follows the news, and what they remember and learn from it. We are interested in four specific functions the mass media serve for the political system: *reporting* the news, *interpreting* the news, *setting the agenda* for government action, and *socializing* citizens about politics. Each one has important implications for the connections citizens forge with the political process.[56]

Reporting the News

All major news media seek to cover political events with firsthand reports from journalists on the scene. Because so many significant political events occur in the nation's capital, Washington has an immense press presence, with over 5,000 journalists in the congressional press corps alone.[57] Roughly fifty additional reporters are admitted to the White House press briefing room.[58] Since 1902, when President Theodore Roosevelt first provided space in the White House for reporters, the press has had special access to the president (though as Figure 6.4 shows, the number of presidential news conferences with reporters has declined in recent administrations). The media's relationship with the president is mediated primarily through the Office of the Press Secretary.

To meet daily deadlines, White House correspondents rely heavily on information they receive from the president's staff, each piece carefully crafted in an attempt to control the story. The most frequent form is the news release—a prepared text distributed to reporters in the hope that they will use it verbatim. A daily news briefing enables reporters to question the press secretary about news releases and allows television correspondents time to prepare their stories and film for the evening newscast. A news conference involves questioning high-level officials in the executive branch—including the president.[59] Occasionally, information is given "on background,"

FIGURE 6.4 More News = Less Talk?

As press conferences have become more formal and scripted, they have also become less frequent. When journalists and the president had more of a collegial relationship, press conferences were common. Except for Bill Clinton, modern presidents are clustered at the bottom of this graph, which shows the number of presidential press conferences in the first year in office since 1922.

Sources: "The Frequency of the Message Is Medium," *CQ Weekly Online* 27 (July 2009): 1755. Copyright © 2009 by CQ-ROLL CALL GROUP. Reproduced with permission of CQ-ROLL CALL GROUP via Copyright Clearance Center.

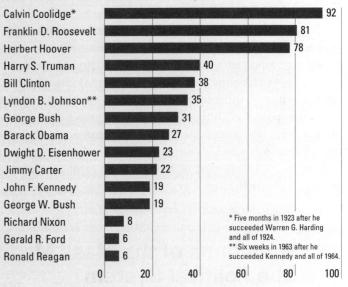

Presidential news conferences in the first year of office

Calvin Coolidge*	92
Franklin D. Roosevelt	81
Herbert Hoover	78
Harry S. Truman	40
Bill Clinton	38
Lyndon B. Johnson**	35
George Bush	31
Barack Obama	27
Dwight D. Eisenhower	23
Jimmy Carter	22
John F. Kennedy	19
George W. Bush	19
Richard Nixon	8
Gerald R. Ford	6
Ronald Reagan	6

* Five months in 1923 after he succeeded Warren G. Harding and all of 1924.
** Six weeks in 1963 after he succeeded Kennedy and all of 1964.

meaning the information can be quoted, but reporters cannot identify the source. A vague reference—"a senior official says"—is all right. Information disclosed "off the record" cannot even be printed. Journalists who violate these well-known rules risk losing their welcome.

Most news about Congress comes from press releases issued by its 535 members, from congressional reports, and, increasingly, from the members' own social networking accounts. Coverage of policy debates typically mirrors the intensity with which congressional actors seek to promote them.[60] A journalist can therefore report on Congress without inhabiting its press galleries. In an effort to save money in the face of tough times, many newspapers have cut the size of their Washington staff or eliminated it entirely.

Congress banned microphones and cameras from its chambers until 1979, when the House permitted live coverage. Televised broadcasts of the House were surprisingly successful, thanks to C-SPAN (the Cable-Satellite Public Affairs Network), which feeds to most cable systems across the country and has a cult-like following among hundreds of thousands of regular viewers.[61] To share in the exposure, the Senate began television coverage in 1986. Occasionally, an event captured on C-SPAN becomes a major news story. In 2009, for example, Representative Alan Grayson (D-Fla.) argued on the floor of the House that the Republican health-care plan had two options: stay healthy or die quickly. The C-SPAN coverage was picked up on YouTube, which then led to days of commentary by pundits. It also led to a fundraising boon: in the two weeks following the broadcast, Grayson's reelection campaign raised over $150,000 from one website alone.[62] But the national attention helped his opponent too, and Grayson lost his 2010 reelection bid (though he won again in 2012). This phenomenon of having a fiery quote picked up by the media, which then generates a spike in fundraising for the speaker (and often for his or her opponent as well), has been termed a "money blurt."[63]

In addition to these recognized sources of news, reporters occasionally benefit from leaks of information released by officials who are guaranteed anonymity. Officials may leak news to interfere with others' political plans or to float ideas ("trial balloons") past the public and other political leaders to gauge their reactions.

Interpreting and Presenting the News

Media executives, news editors, and prominent reporters function as **gatekeepers** in directing the news flow: they decide which events to report and how to handle the elements in those stories.[64] They not only select what topics go through the gate but also are expected to uphold standards of careful reporting and principled journalism. The rise of the Internet has made more information and points of view available to the public, but the Internet also can spread factual errors and rumors. The Internet has no gatekeepers, and thus no constraints on its content.[65] Most journalists think the Internet has made journalism better, mostly because it is a powerful research tool and its ability to deliver information quickly promotes competition.[66]

A parade of unconnected one-minute news stories, flashing across the television screen every night, would boggle the eyes and minds of viewers. To make televised news understandable and to hold viewers' attention, editors and producers concentrate on individuals because individuals have personalities (political institutions do not—except for the presidency). A study of network news coverage of the president, Congress, and the Supreme Court in 2008–2009 found that 66 percent of the stories were about the presidency, compared with 28 percent on Congress and just 6 percent on the Supreme Court.[67]

During elections, the focus on personalities encourages **horse race journalism,** in which media coverage becomes primarily a matter of which candidate is leading in the polls and who has raised the most money. Study after study of news coverage of presidential elections find that horse race coverage dominates and that horse race content increases as election day approaches. Journalists cover the horse race because it offers new material daily, whereas the candidates' programs remain the same.[68] Voters, however, say they want more attention on issues and less on the horse race. After the 2012 election, Americans rated the performance of the press lower than that of the candidates, parties, pollsters, and campaign consultants.[69]

Aside from the day-to-day flow of information from government institutions and the regularity (and frequency) of elections, journalists are drawn to **media events—** situations that are too "newsworthy" to pass up. The media have been described as having an "alarm mode," in which it seems like every news outlet is drawn to a story to the extent that virtually every other issue gets ignored, and a "patrol mode," in which journalists remain focused on the story even after the initial burst of attention has subsided. Once another alarm goes off, the patrol mode ends and attention shifts elsewhere.[70] In late 2013, the alarm sounded when the Obama administration's health-care website healthcare.gov opened for business but was riddled with glitches. For weeks, the media were in patrol mode, devoting sustained attention to the website debacle, seemingly at the expense of everything else. Television is particularly partial to events that have visual impact. Organized protests and fires, for example, "show well" on television, so television covers them. As Figure 6.3 shows, network news was much more likely to include stories of disasters and accidents in 2011 than other media.

Where the Public Gets Its News. Until the early 1960s, most people got more of their news from newspapers than from any other source. Television nudged out newspapers as the public's major source of news in the early 1960s and has since remained dominant. According to one recent report, 69 percent of Americans name television as their primary source for news. Twenty-eight percent cite newspapers as their primary news source, while 50 percent say they turn to the Internet most.

gatekeepers
Media executives, news editors, and prominent reporters who direct the flow of news.

horse race journalism
Election coverage by the mass media that focuses on which candidate is ahead rather than on national issues.

media event
A situation that is so "newsworthy" that the mass media are compelled to cover it. Candidates in elections often create such situations to garner media attention.

People in this survey were allowed to mention two sources, making it clear that the public consults multiple sources of news during the day—perhaps reading the paper at breakfast, checking the Internet at work, and ending the day watching television news. Additionally, over 30 percent of people under age forty report getting the news on social networks. Around 85 percent of Americans use the Internet, mostly people under age sixty-five and with at least a high school diploma. Whites and blacks are also more likely to be Internet users than Latinos.[71]

Media Influence on Knowledge and Opinions. If, as surveys indicate, most Americans read or hear the news each day, how much political information do they absorb? By all accounts, not much. A national survey in the fall of 2013 asked respondents thirteen questions about current events, including which states allow for gay marriage and the percentage of women serving in Congress. Only half of the respondents got more than half of the questions right.[72] Another recent poll asked Americans to name the heads of state for Cuba, Great Britain, Russia, Mexico, and Germany, as well as the U.S. secretary of state; only 2 percent of respondents could name all six leaders, and 18 percent of Americans could not name any.[73]

Numerous studies have found that those who rely on television for their news score lower on tests of knowledge about public affairs than those who rely on print media. Among media researchers, this finding has led to the **television hypothesis**—the belief that television is to blame for the low level of citizens' knowledge about public affairs.[74] This belief has a reasonable basis. We know that television tends to squeeze issues into short fragments, which makes it difficult to explain candidates' positions. Television also tends to cast abstract issues in personal terms to generate the visual content that the medium needs. Thus, viewers may become more adept at visually identifying the candidates and describing their personal habits than at outlining their positions on complex issues. Finally, because they are regulated by the FCC, television networks may be more concerned than newspapers about being fair and equal in covering the candidates. Research suggests, however, that newspapers differ from television less in content of coverage than in the amount; newspapers simply cover campaigns more extensively and intensively than television.[75] Whatever the explanation, the technological wonders of television may have contributed little to citizens' knowledge of public affairs. It may even discourage respect for different opinions since it tends to emphasize drama and conflict between political opponents.[76] It can also lead people to be less trusting of government.[77]

How the media cover the news can either exacerbate or diminish socioeconomic differences in levels of political knowledge. When the news is presented with lots of expert commentary—which tends to involve jargon and complex explanations—those who are more affluent and educated learn more from news coverage than those Americans who are less well off. But when the news is presented in a more contextual fashion—which tends to focus on the historical and factual background of an issue—socioeconomic differences in political knowledge diminish. Contextual information "gives meaning to what otherwise might seem like disconnected events and helps people understand why issues and problems deserve their attention."[78] In our age of the 24/7 news cycle, however, there is a tendency to provide contextual information when an event is new (in the so-called alarm mode) but to rely on expert commentary in subsequent coverage (the patrol mode). As a result, people who do not pay attention to an issue right from the start might lose a valuable chance to learn about it, since journalists quickly move on to covering experts' views on the latest developments.

television hypothesis
The belief that television is to blame for the low level of citizens' knowledge about public affairs.

News is also often communicated to the public via entertainment instead of journalism. So-called **soft news** refers to general entertainment programming that often includes discussions of political affairs. Programs such as *The Daily Show*, *The Tonight Show*, *The Today Show*, and *The View* all provide citizens with soft news. Research on the impact of soft news on the citizenry is mixed. Attention to soft news can improve people's levels of political knowledge and even help them identify which politicians best match their own political preferences. But it can also lead people to be more cynical about politicians and the political process.[79]

Americans overwhelmingly believe that the media exert a strong influence on their political institutions, and nearly nine out of ten Americans believe that the media strongly influence public opinion.[80] However, measuring the extent of media influence on public opinion is difficult. Because few of us learn about political events except through the media, it could be argued that the media create public opinion simply by reporting events. Consider the killing of Osama bin Laden and the subsequent seven-point rise in President Obama's approval rating.[81] Determining how much of that change was due to the actual event and how much was due to the way in which it was covered by the media is extremely difficult.

Setting the Political Agenda

Despite the media's potential for influencing public opinion, most scholars believe that the media's greatest influence on politics is in their power to set the **political agenda**—a list of issues that people identify as needing government attention. Those who set the political agenda define which issues government decision makers should discuss and debate. Like a tree that falls in the forest without anyone around to hear it, an issue that does not get on the political agenda will not get any political attention. Sometimes the media force the government to confront issues once buried in the scientific community, such as global warming. Other times the media move the government to deal with unpleasant social issues, such as wrongful execution of the death penalty. However, the media can also keep high on the agenda issues that perhaps should attract fewer public resources.[82]

Crime is a good example. Local television news covers crime twice as much as any other topic.[83] Given that fear of crime today is about the same as it was in the mid-1960s, are the media simply reflecting a constantly high crime rate?[84] Actually, crime rates dropped from the 1980s until very recently.[85] As one journalist said, "Crime coverage is not editorially driven; it's economically driven. It's the easiest, cheapest, laziest news to cover."[86] Moreover, crime provides good visuals. ("If it bleeds, it leads.") So despite the falling crime rate, the public encounters a continuing gusher of crime news and, as a result, a relatively high fear of crime.

The media's ability to influence public opinion by defining "the news" makes politicians eager to influence media coverage. Politicians attempt to affect not only public opinion but also the opinions of other political leaders. The president receives a daily digest of news and opinion from many sources, and top government leaders closely monitor the major national news sources.

The mass media have become a network for communicating among attentive elites, all trying to influence one another. If the White House is under pressure on some policy matter, for example, it might supply a high executive official to appear on one of the Sunday morning talk shows, such as *Face the Nation* (CBS). These programs draw less than half the audience of the network news shows, but engage the guest in lengthy discussions. The White House's goal is to influence the thinking of other insiders, who faithfully watch the program, as much as to influence the opinions of the relatively

soft news
General entertainment programming that often includes discussions of political affairs.

political agenda
A list of issues that need government attention.

**CONNECT
WITH YOUR CLASSMATES**
MindTap for American Government

Access the Media and Politics Forum: Discussion—Influence of the Media on Policy.

Obama Goes All In

With comprehensive immigration reform stalled in Washington, President Obama went public in January 2013 by giving a speech at a majority Hispanic high school in Las Vegas. Hispanics make up an increasing share of the electorate, so reaching out them on this issue is a strategy the administration has hoped would put pressure on Republicans to start making progress on immigration reform.

Jason Reed/Reuters

small number of ordinary citizens who watch as well.[87] Of course, other political leaders appear on these programs, and their criticism of the administration's policies emboldens others to be critical too.

Presidents use other indirect means to try to influence political elites. In the strategy known as going public, the president travels around the country speaking to Americans directly about his policy agenda (see Chapter 12 for more on going public). The goal is twofold: first, to generate media coverage of the speaking event; and, second, to motivate citizens to pressure their representatives to support the president's agenda. The strategy of going public has become more common over time. Barack Obama attempted this strategy in 2013, when he traveled to Colorado and Connecticut to give speeches about gun control. He blatantly acknowledged his strategy of appealing to Americans in states that were the sites of mass shootings in the hopes of advancing legislation in Congress, saying, "Congress is only going to act on [proposed reforms] if they hear from you—the American people."[88]

going public
A strategy whereby a president seeks to influence policy elites and media coverage by appealing directly to the American people.

Socializing the Citizenry

The mass media act as important agents of political socialization, in addition to those described in Chapter 5.[89] Young people who rarely follow the news by choice nevertheless acquire political values through the entertainment function of the media. From the 1930s to the early 1950s, children learned from dramas and comedies on the radio; now they learn from television and other electronic media. The average eight- to eighteen-year-old in America consumes over seven hours of media per day—and sees a lot of sex and hears countless swear words in prime time.[90] What children learned from radio was quite different from what they are learning now, however. In the golden days of radio, youngsters listening to the popular radio drama *The Shadow* heard repeatedly that "crime does not pay ... the *Shadow* knows!" In program after program—*Dragnet*, *Junior G-Men*, *Gangbusters*—the message never varied: criminals are bad; the police are good; criminals get caught and are severely punished for their crimes.

Television today does not portray the criminal justice system in the same way, even in police dramas. Consider programs such as *Blue Bloods*, *Justified*, and *Hawaii Five-O*, which are among the recent crop of shows that portray law enforcement officers and government agents as lawbreakers. Certainly, one cannot easily argue that years of television messages conveying distrust of law enforcement, disrespect for the criminal justice system, and violence help prepare law-abiding citizens.

Some scholars argue that the most important effect of the mass media, particularly television, is to reinforce the hegemony, or dominance, of the existing culture and order. According to this argument, social control functions not through institutions of force (police, military, and prisons) but through social institutions, such as the media, that cause people to accept "the way things are."[91] By displaying the lifestyles of the rich and famous, for example, the media induce the public to accept the unlimited accumulation of private wealth. Similarly, the media socialize citizens to value "the American way," to be patriotic, to back their country, "right or wrong."

So the media play contradictory roles in the process of political socialization. On the one hand, they promote popular support for government by joining in the celebration of national holidays, heroes' birthdays, political anniversaries, and civic accomplishments. On the other hand, the media erode public confidence by detailing politicians' extramarital affairs, airing investigative reports of possible malfeasance in office, and even showing television dramas about crooked cops.[92]

Evaluating the Media in Government

LO5 ★ Assess the impact of the media on democratic values and politics in the United States.

Are the media fair or biased in reporting the news? What contributions do the media make to democratic government? What effects do they have on the pursuit of freedom, order, and equality?

Is Reporting Biased?

News reports are presented as objective reality, yet critics of modern journalism contend that the news is filtered through the ideological biases of the media owners and editors (the gatekeepers) and the reporters themselves. Even citizens tend to be skeptical of the news and have become even more so over time (see Figure 6.5). Research suggests that as the parties have become more polarized (see Chapter 11) and as the presence of opinionated journalism has proliferated, political leaders increasingly go to ideologically friendly media outlets in order to criticize the rest of the media as an institution (former vice presidential candidate Sarah Palin took to calling the mainstream media the "lame stream" media). This elite criticism of the media in turn leads to greater skepticism of the press among the public. Their skepticism is consequential because people who distrust the media have been shown to be more resistant to learning new information about objective national events, such as changing economic conditions.[93]

The argument that news reports are politically biased has two sides. On the one hand, news reporters are often criticized for tilting their stories in a liberal direction, promoting social equality and undercutting social order.[94] On the other hand, wealthy and conservative media owners are suspected of preserving inequalities and reinforcing the existing order by serving a relentless round of entertainment that numbs the public's capacity for critical analysis.[95] Let's evaluate these arguments, looking first at reporters.

Although the picture is far from clear, available evidence seems to confirm the charge of liberal leanings among reporters in the major news media. In a 2007 survey of journalists, 32 percent of the national press considered themselves "liberal," compared with only 8 percent who said they were "conservative."[96] Content analysis of the tone of ABC, CBS, and NBC network coverage of presidential campaigns from 1988 to 2004 concluded that Democratic candidates received more "good press" than Republicans in every election but 1988, when the Republican candidate,

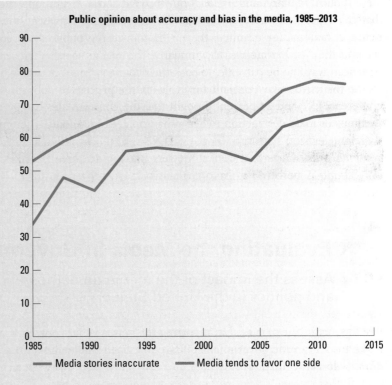

FIGURE 6.5 Rising Distrust in Accuracy and Objectivity of the Press

Over time, people have been asked whether news organizations generally get the facts straight or whether their stories and reports are often inaccurate. They have also been asked if they think that news organizations deal fairly with all sides or whether they tend to favor one side. The graph here shows that the public increasingly sees the news media as inaccurate and biased, especially in the past few years.

Sources: "Press Widely Criticized but Trusted More than Other Information Sources: Views of the News Media: 1985–2011," Report by Pew Research Center for People and the Press, September 22, 2011. Copyright © 2011 by Pew Research Center. Reproduced by permission. Source for 2013: Pew Research Center, p. 15, http://www.people-press.org/2013/08/08/amid-criticism-support-for-medias-watchdog-role-stands-out/.

George H. W. Bush, benefited from better press.[97] However, one news medium—talk radio—is dominated by conservative views. Rush Limbaugh alone broadcasts to more than 15 million listeners. Other prominent conservative radio hosts—such as Sean Hannity—reach millions more.[98] The top independent and liberal talk show hosts, in contrast, have audiences of fewer than 3 million listeners.

The counterargument is that working journalists in the national and local media often conflict with their own editors, who tend to be more conservative.[99] Editors, in their function as gatekeepers, tend to tone down reporters' liberal leanings by editing their stories or not placing them well in the medium. Newspaper publishers are also free to endorse candidates. In twelve of seventeen elections from 1948 to 2012, newspaper editorials favored the Republican candidate. In the 2012 election, 45 percent of newspapers endorsed Mitt Romney, 41 percent endorsed Barack Obama, and 14 percent did not issue an endorsement.[100]

In congressional elections, incumbents—as opposed to challengers—enjoy much more news coverage simply from holding office and issuing official statements. Non-campaign news coverage leads to greater incumbent name recognition at election time, particularly for members of Congress (see Chapter 11). This coverage effect is independent of any bias in reporting on campaigns. For more prominent offices such as the presidency, however, a different news dynamic may come into play. When a powerful incumbent runs for reelection, journalists may feel a special responsibility to counteract his or her advantage by putting the opposite partisan spin on the news.[101] An analysis of news stories appearing during the general election in 2012 found that when stories about the horse race were excluded, the tone of coverage about Barack Obama and Mitt Romney was similar: 32 percent of stories about both candidates were negative, while 15 percent of stories about Obama and 14 percent about Romney were positive.[102]

Of course, bias in reporting is not limited to election campaigns, and different media may reflect different understandings of political issues. An important series of surveys about perceptions of the Iraq war were taken over the summer of 2003, after Bush had announced the end of combat. Substantial portions of the public held erroneous understandings of the war. For example, 27 percent in the September survey thought that world opinion supported the U.S. war against Iraq (when world opinion opposed the war), 21 percent thought that Iraq had been directly involved in the 9/11 attack (which our government never claimed and President Bush denied at a news conference),[103] and 24 percent thought that the United States had already found Iraqi weapons of mass destruction (when it had not). Respondents who relied on the commercial television networks (Fox, CBS, ABC, CNN, or NBC) held the most misperceptions, with 45 percent of Fox viewers making all three mistakes compared with only about 15 percent for the other networks. Just 9 percent of those who relied on print media erred on all three facts. Broadcast media per se were not to blame, for a scant 4 percent of PBS viewers or listeners to National Public Radio were wrong on all items.[104] Newspapers can display biases too. One study found that newspapers devote more attention to high unemployment when the president's party differs from the papers' partisan endorsement history.[105]

The mere act of choosing to cover some stories while not covering others can also be seen as bias, and in that sense, some degree of bias is inevitable. Those with an optimistic perspective on today's fractured and voluminous media environment maintain that now more than ever, it is possible to find some type of coverage on nearly any topic from nearly any political viewpoint. Such availability puts more pressure on citizens to act as their own editors and learn how to judge whether the information they find is complete and backed up with sufficient evidence.[106] That, however, is a tall order.

Contributions to Democracy

As noted earlier, in a democracy, communication must move in two directions: from government to citizens and from citizens to government. In fact, political communication in the United States mostly goes from government to citizens by passing through the media. The point is important because news reporters tend to be highly critical of politicians; they consider it their job to search for inaccuracies in fact and weaknesses in argument—practicing **watchdog journalism**.[107] Some observers have characterized the news media and the government as adversaries—each mistrusting the other, locked in competition for popular favor while trying to get the record straight. Despite public concerns about the media (see Figure 6.5), recent polling finds that 68 percent of Americans say that the media perform the watchdog function well by preventing public officials from doing things that should not be done.[108]

The mass media transmit information in the opposite direction by reporting citizens' reactions to political events and government actions. The press has traditionally reflected public opinion (and often created it) in the process of defining the news and suggesting courses of government action. But the media's role in reflecting public opinion has become more refined in the information age. Since the 1820s, newspapers conducted straw polls of dubious quality that matched their own partisan inclinations.[109] After commercial polls (such as the Gallup Poll) were established in the 1930s, newspapers began to report more reliable readings of public opinion. By the 1960s, the media began to conduct their own surveys. *The New York Times*, for example, has conducted its own polls at a rate of roughly one poll per month since 2003.[110] Regularly reporting about public opinion is one of the most obvious ways in which the media can tell a story to their consumers—elites and ordinary Americans alike—about what the public believes at any point in time.

watchdog journalism
Journalism that scrutinizes public and business institutions and publicizes perceived misconduct.

Citizens and journalists both complain that heavy reliance on polls during election campaigns causes the media to emphasize the horse race and slights the discussion of issues. But the media also use their polling expertise for other purposes, such as gauging support for going to war and for balancing the budget. Their net effect has been to generate more accurate knowledge of public opinion and to report that knowledge to public officials as well as to the public. Decades of public opinion research confirm that public opinion often influences policy, a clear indication of government functioning according to the majoritarian model of democracy.[111]

Effects on Freedom, Order, and Equality

The media in the United States have played an important role in advancing equality. Throughout the civil rights movement of the 1950s and 1960s, the media gave national coverage to conflict in the South as black children tried to attend white schools or civil rights workers were beaten and even killed in the effort to register black voters. Partly because of this media coverage, civil rights moved up on the political agenda, and coalitions formed in Congress to pass new laws promoting racial equality.

In general, the mass media offer spokespersons for any disadvantaged group an opportunity to state their case before a national audience and to work for a place on the political agenda. In 2011, Pulitzer Prize–winning journalist Jose Antonio Vargas wrote a moving story for the *New York Times Magazine* in which he "came out" as an undocumented immigrant who had been brought to the United States by his mother when he was a child. He had previously worked for the *Washington Post* and many other news outlets, getting by for years with false documentation. Coming forward threatened his ability to continue working in the United States and raised the possibility of deportation, but it also put a dramatic national spotlight on debates about the DREAM Act, which would allow people who came to the country illegally as children to naturalize (see Chapter 18 for more on the DREAM Act).[112]

Although the media are willing to encourage government action to promote equality at the cost of some personal freedom, journalists resist government attempts to infringe on freedom of the press to promote order.[113] While the public tends to support a free press in theory, public support is not universal and wavers in practice. For example, when asked whether it is more important "that the government be able to censor news stories it feels threaten national security OR that the news media be able to report stories they feel are in the national interest," about one-third in a 2006 national survey favored government censorship.[114]

The media's ability to report whatever they wish and whenever they wish certainly erodes efforts to maintain order. For example, sensational media coverage of terrorist acts gives terrorists the publicity they seek, and portrayals of violence on television can encourage copycat crimes. In 2013, government officials criticized media reports about leaked information regarding surveillance programs run by the National Security Agency, charging that coverage of their complex monitoring programs would weaken public and international trust and threaten national security.[115] Freedom of the press is a noble value and one that has been important to democratic government. But we should not ignore the fact that democracies sometimes pay a price for pursuing it without qualification. At the same time, the disruption of order is not always a bad thing. As we saw in 2011 when revolutionary struggles to overthrow authoritarian regimes spread across the Middle East, new media technologies allow for information to be communicated freely in ways that can enable citizens to make their preferences known in dramatic fashion.

Master the Topic of Media and Politics with MindTap™ for American Government

 REVIEW MindTap™ **for American Government**
Access Key Term Flashcards for Chapter 6.

 TEST YOURSELF MindTap™ **for American Government**
Take the Wrap It Up Quiz for Chapter 6.

 STAY CURRENT MindTap™ **for American Government**
Access the KnowNow blog and customized RSS for updates on current events.

 STAY FOCUSED MindTap™ **for American Government**
Complete the Focus Activities for Media and Politics.

Summary

LO1 Trace the evolution of the mass media in the United States and evaluate the impact of new technologies on journalism.

- The mass media transmit information to large, heterogeneous, and widely dispersed audiences through print, broadcasts, and the Internet. The mass media have traditionally been divided into print and broadcast formats, but the rise of digital communications has created a more complicated landscape, rendering this traditional distinction problematic.

LO2 Evaluate the effect of privately owned mass media on the quality of political communication in the United States.

- The mass media in the United States are privately owned and in business to make money, which they do mainly by selling space or airtime to advertisers. The concern with profit leads both print and electronic media to determine which events are newsworthy on the basis of audience appeal.

LO3 Follow the evolution of government regulation of the media and identify the challenges that new media technologies present to existing regulations.

- The broadcast media operate under technical, ownership, and content regulations imposed by the government. The regulation of media content is minimal and has largely been confined to broadcast media. Comprehensive policy regarding regulation of Internet news has yet to be developed, resulting in clashes between the FCC, Congress, and media corporations.

LO4 Analyze the role of the media in political socialization and the acquisition of political knowledge.

- The main function of the mass media is entertainment, but the media also perform the political functions of reporting news, interpreting news, setting the political agenda, and socializing citizens about politics. Today, gatekeepers (publishers and editors) have less control over what counts as news. Americans get more news from television than from newspapers, and an increasing number of citizens turn to the Internet.

- Despite heavy exposure to news, the ability of most people to retain much political information is low. The media's most important effect on public opinion is in setting the country's political agenda. The media play more subtle, contradictory roles in political socialization, both promoting and undermining certain political and cultural values.

LO5   Assess the impact of the media on democratic values and politics in the United States.

- Reporters from the national media tend to be more liberal than the public while editors and publishers tend to be more conservative.

- From the standpoint of majoritarian democracy, one of the most important roles of the media is to facilitate communication from the people to the government through the reporting of public opinion polls. The media can promote equality, drawing national attention to disadvantaged groups that lack other political resources. They can also disrupt order, spreading information about events that challenge the status quo.

Chapter Quiz

LO1   Trace the evolution of the mass media in the United States and evaluate the impact of new technologies on journalism.

1. How has the development of the Internet challenged the traditional division between print and broadcast media?
2. Discuss ways in which the mainstream media still matters despite the rise of the Internet, blogs, and social networking as means of transmitting news.

LO2   Evaluate the effect of privately owned mass media on the quality of political communication in the United States.

1. How does the concept of newsworthiness affect the content of the news?
2. List concerns associated with the concentration of media ownership.

LO3   Follow the evolution of government regulation of the media and identify the challenges that new media technologies present to existing regulations.

1. Define the FCC and explain the role it plays in regulating the mass media.
2. What has been the effect of the elimination of the fairness doctrine?

LO4   Analyze the role of the media in political socialization and the acquisition of political knowledge.

1. Which media format is associated with higher levels of political knowledge?
2. What do most scholars believe is the media's greatest influence on politics?

LO5   Assess the impact of the media on democratic values and politics in the United States.

1. Identify the charges behind the claims that the media are liberal and/or that the media are conservative.
2. Discuss whether the media tend to advance order versus equality. What about order versus freedom?

7 Participation and Voting

Learning Outcomes

LO1 Define political participation and distinguish among types of participation.

LO2 Identify examples of unconventional participation in American history and evaluate their effectiveness.

LO3 Distinguish between supportive acts and influencing acts of political participation.

LO4 Trace the expansion of suffrage in the United States and assess the impact of expanded suffrage on voting turnout.

LO5 Identify the factors that affect political participation, especially voting.

LO6 Evaluate the relationship between the values of freedom, equality, and order and political participation in American democracy.

LO7 Identify the purposes elections serve and explain the relationship between elections and majoritarian and pluralist models of democracy.

 WATCH & LEARN MindTap· for American Government
Watch a brief "What Do You Know?" video
summarizing Voting.

The concept of participatory democracy (see page 32) urges that citizens decide important questions directly by voting, and many American states do decide such issues as gay marriage, abortion, gambling, and immigration by direct vote. In 2013, eleven northern counties in Colorado even voted (unsuccessfully) on seceding from the state. Could individual states vote freely to secede from the United States—as Scotland recently voted on leaving the United Kingdom?

In 1707, the kingdoms of Scotland and England were joined together as the United Kingdom of Great Britain and Northern Ireland. Over the last three centuries, many Scots chafed at London's parliamentary rule. In 1999, Scotland gained its own parliament and the right to legislate on domestic matters. Nevertheless, the Scottish National Party (SNP) in the 2011 parliamentary election pushed for a referendum on complete independence.

The SNP won and organized the referendum. Many prominent Scots backed the idea, including actor Sean Connery (famous as James Bond) who sported a "Scotland Forever" tattoo on his forearm. However, Scottish polls regularly showed roughly 45 percent opposed to independence, about one-third in favor, and the rest undecided.

Although strongly opposed to Scottish independence, the UK government, led by the Conservative Party, decided to allow the referendum. On September 18, 2014, the Scots voted and rejected independence by a vote of 55 to 45 percent.

Although the referendum provided a democratic answer to a long-standing issue, Britain risked its territorial integrity by allowing it. Perhaps the Conservative Party believed that the polls insured a satisfying result. Perhaps the government allowed the vote because its Conservative Prime Minister, David Cameron, proposed his own nationwide referendum for 2017 on Britain's membership in the European Union.

Holding a popular vote is a democratic method of settling a controversial issue, but it is also a risky one. What if President Lincoln had permitted the southern states to vote on secession before the Civil War? Could war between the non-slave United States of America and the slave-owning Confederate States of America have been avoided for long?

Although American states, Britain, and other countries have allowed citizens to decide important issues by direct vote, the U.S. Constitution does not provide for national referenda. Some regard this omission as a fault; others see it as a virtue. Nevertheless, American citizens participate in government in many other ways besides voting.

In this chapter, we consider various forms of popular participation in politics. We begin by distinguishing between conventional forms of political participation and unconventional forms that still comply with democratic government. Then we evaluate the nature and extent of both types of participation in American politics. Next, we study the expansion of voting rights and voting as the major mechanism for mass participation in politics. Finally, we examine the extent to which the various forms of political participation serve the values of freedom, equality, and order and the majoritarian and pluralist models of democracy.

 Democracy and Political Participation

LO1 ★ Define political participation and distinguish among types of participation.

Government ought to be run by the people. That is the democratic ideal in a nutshell. But how much and what kind of citizen participation are necessary for democratic government? Neither political theorists nor politicians, neither idealists nor realists, can agree on an answer. Champions of direct democracy believe that if citizens do not participate directly in government affairs, making government decisions themselves, they should give up all pretense of living in a democracy. More practical observers contend that people can govern indirectly, through their elected representatives. And they maintain that choosing leaders through elections—formal procedures for voting—is the only workable approach to democracy in a large, complex nation.

Elections are a necessary condition of democracy, but they do not guarantee democratic government. Before the collapse of communism, the former Soviet Union regularly held elections in which more than 90 percent of the electorate turned out to vote, but the Soviet Union did not function as a democracy because there was only one political party. Both the majoritarian and pluralist models of democracy rely on voting to varying degrees, but both models expect citizens to participate in politics in other ways. For example, they expect citizens to discuss politics, form interest groups, contact public officials, campaign for political parties, run for office, and even protest government decisions.

political participation
Actions of private citizens by which they seek to influence or support government and politics.

We define **political participation** as "those activities of citizens that attempt to influence the structure of government, the selection of government officials, or the policies of government."[1] This definition embraces both conventional and unconventional forms of political participation. In plain language, conventional behavior is behavior that is acceptable to the dominant culture in a given situation. Wearing a swimsuit at the beach in the United States is conventional; wearing one at a formal dance is not. Displaying campaign posters in front yards is conventional; spray-painting political slogans on buildings is not.

conventional participation
Relatively routine political behavior that uses institutional channels and is acceptable to the dominant culture.

Figuring out whether a particular political act is conventional or unconventional can be difficult. We find the following distinction useful:

- **Conventional participation** is a relatively routine behavior that uses the established institutions of representative government, especially campaigning for candidates and voting in elections.

unconventional participation
Relatively uncommon political behavior that challenges or defies established institutions and dominant norms.

- **Unconventional participation** is a relatively uncommon behavior that challenges or defies established institutions or the dominant culture (and thus is personally stressful to participants and their opponents).

Voting and writing letters to public officials illustrate conventional political participation; staging sit-down strikes in public buildings and chanting slogans outside officials' windows are examples of unconventional participation. Other democratic forms of participation, such as political demonstrations, can be conventional (carrying signs outside an abortion clinic) or unconventional (linking arms to prevent entrance). Various forms of unconventional participation are often used by powerless groups to gain political benefits while working within the system.[2]

Terrorism is an extreme and problematic case of unconventional political behavior. Indeed, the U.S. legal code defines **terrorism** as "premeditated, politically motivated violence perpetrated against noncombatant targets by sub-national groups or clandestine agents, usually intended to influence an audience."[3] Timothy McVeigh, a decorated veteran of the 1991 Gulf War, bombed the federal building in Oklahoma City in 1995, taking 168 lives. McVeigh said he bombed the building because the federal government had become a police state hostile to gun owners, religious sects, and patriotic militia groups.[4] In 2001, al Qaeda carried out the infamous 9/11 attack on New York and Washington, D.C., killing almost 3,000 Americans and foreign nationals. Political goals motivated both acts of terrorism. McVeigh acted because of domestic politics, al Qaeda because of international politics. Although terrorist acts are political acts by definition, they do not qualify as political participation because terrorists do not seek to influence government but to destroy it.

Methods of unconventional political behavior, in contrast, are used by disadvantaged groups that resort to them in lieu of more conventional forms of participation used by most citizens. These groups accept government while seeking to influence it. Let us look at both unconventional and conventional political participation in the United States.

terrorism
Premeditated, politically motivated violence perpetrated against noncombatant targets by subnational groups or clandestine agents.

★ Unconventional Participation

LO2 ★ Identify examples of unconventional participation in American history and evaluate their effectiveness.

On Sunday, March 7, 1965, a group of about six hundred people attempted to march fifty miles from Selma, Alabama, to the state capitol at Montgomery to show their support for voting rights for blacks. (At the time, Selma had fewer than five hundred registered black voters, out of fifteen thousand eligible.)[5] Alabama governor George Wallace declared the march illegal and sent state troopers to stop it. The two groups met at the Edmund Pettus Bridge over the Alabama River at the edge of Selma. The peaceful marchers were disrupted and beaten by state troopers and deputy sheriffs—some on horseback—using clubs, bullwhips, and tear gas. The day became known as Bloody Sunday.

The march from Selma was a form of unconventional political participation. Marching fifty miles in a political protest is certainly not common; moreover, the march challenged the existing institutions that prevented blacks from voting. But they had been prevented from participating conventionally—voting in elections—for many decades, and they chose this unconventional method to dramatize their cause.

The march ended in violence because Governor Wallace would not allow even this peaceful mode of unconventional expression. The brutal response to the marchers helped the rest of the nation understand the seriousness of the civil rights problem in the South. Unconventional participation is stressful and occasionally violent, but sometimes it is worth the risk. In 2010, thousands of blacks and whites solemnly but triumphantly reenacted the march on its forty-fifth anniversary.

March for Freedom, Forty-Five Years Later

On Sunday, March 7, 2010, thousands marched across the Edmund Pettus Bridge outside Selma, Alabama, to commemorate the "Bloody Sunday" forty-five years earlier when people were beaten during a voting rights protest.

Support for Unconventional Participation

Unconventional political participation has a long history in the United States.[6] The Boston Tea Party of 1773, in which American colonists dumped three cargoes of British tea into Boston Harbor, was only the first in a long line of violent protests against British rule that eventually led to revolution. Yet we know less about unconventional than conventional participation. The reasons are twofold. First, since it is easier to collect data on conventional practices, they are studied more frequently. Second, political scientists are simply biased toward institutionalized, or conventional, politics. In fact, some basic works on political participation explicitly exclude any behavior that is "outside the system."[7] One major study of unconventional political action asked people whether they had engaged in or approved of three types of political participation other than voting: signing petitions, joining boycotts, and attending demonstrations.[8] As shown in Figure 7.1, only signing petitions was clearly regarded as conventional, in the sense that the behavior was widely practiced.

The marchers in Selma, although peaceful, were demonstrating against the established order. If we measure conventional participation according to the proportion of

FIGURE 7.1 **What Americans Think Is Conventional Political Behavior**

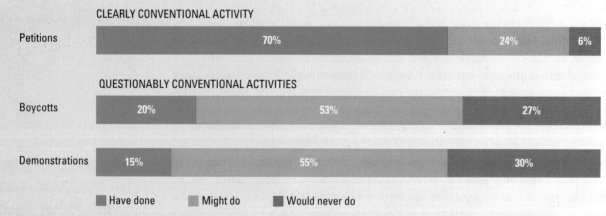

CLEARLY CONVENTIONAL ACTIVITY

| Petitions | 70% | 24% | 6% |

QUESTIONABLY CONVENTIONAL ACTIVITIES

| Boycotts | 20% | 53% | 27% |

| Demonstrations | 15% | 55% | 30% |

■ Have done ■ Might do ■ Would never do

A survey presented Americans with three forms of political participation outside the electoral process and asked whether they "have done," "might do," or "would never do" any of them. The respondents approved overwhelmingly of signing petitions, which was widely done and rarely ruled out. Even attending demonstrations (a right guaranteed in the Constitution) would "never" be done by 30 percent of the respondents. Boycotting products was less objectionable and more widely practiced. According to this test, attending demonstrations and boycotting products are only marginally conventional forms of political participation in the United States.

Source: 2005–2008 World Values Survey. The World Values Survey Association, based in Stockholm, conducts representative surveys in nations across the world. See http://www.worldvaluessurvey.org.

people who disapprove of the act, most demonstrations border on the unconventional, involving relatively few people. The same goes for boycotting products—for example, refusing to buy lettuce or grapes picked by nonunion farm workers. Demonstrations and boycotts are problem cases in deciding what is and is not conventional political participation.

The Effectiveness of Unconventional Participation

Vociferous antiabortion protests have discouraged many doctors from performing abortions, but they have not led to outlawing abortions. Does unconventional participation ever work (even when it provokes violence)? Yes. The unconventional activities of civil rights workers produced notable successes. Dr. Martin Luther King, Jr., led the 1955 Montgomery bus boycott (prompted by Rosa Parks's refusal to surrender her seat to a white man), which sparked the civil rights movement. He used **direct action** to challenge specific cases of discrimination, assembling crowds to confront businesses and local governments and demanding equal treatment in public accommodations and government. The civil rights movement organized more than 1,000 such newsworthy demonstrations nationwide—387 in 1965 alone.[9] And like the march in Selma, many of these protests provoked violent confrontations between whites and blacks.

Denied the usual opportunities for conventional political participation, minorities used unconventional politics to pressure Congress to pass a series of civil rights laws in 1957, 1960, 1964, and 1968—each one in some way extending national protection against discrimination by reason of race, color, religion, or national origin. (The 1964 act also prohibited discrimination in employment on the basis of sex.)

In addition, the Voting Rights Act of 1965 placed some state electoral procedures under federal supervision, protecting the registration of black voters and increasing their voting rate, especially in the South, where much of the violence occurred. Black protest activity—both violent and nonviolent—has also been credited with increased welfare support for blacks in the South. The civil rights movement showed that social change can occur even when it faces violent opposition at first. In 1970, fewer than fifteen hundred blacks served as elected officials in the United States. In 2006, the number was more than nine thousand, and over five thousand Hispanics held elected office.[10] In 2008, Barack Obama became the first African American to be elected president of the United States.

Although direct political action and the politics of confrontation can work, using them requires a special kind of commitment. Studies show that direct action appeals most to those who both distrust the political system and have a strong sense of political efficacy—the feeling that they can do something to affect political decisions. Whether this combination of attitudes produces behavior that challenges the system depends on the extent of organized group activity. The civil rights movement of the 1960s was backed by numerous organizations across the nation.

The decision to use unconventional behavior also depends on the extent to which individuals develop a group consciousness—identification with their group and awareness of its position in society, its objectives, and its intended course of action. These characteristics were present among blacks and young people in the mid-1960s and are strongly present today among blacks and, to a lesser degree, among Latinos. Indeed, some researchers contend that black consciousness has heightened both African Americans' distrust of the political system and their sense of individual efficacy, generating more political participation by poor blacks than by poor whites.

direct action
Unconventional participation that involves assembling crowds to confront businesses and local governments to demand a hearing.

Antiwar Protest, 2013

Fearful of being drawn into another conflict as in Iraq and Afghanistan, a majority of Americans opposed military intervention in Syria to topple the Asad regime.

Unconventional Participation Around the World

Although most Americans disapprove of using certain forms of participation to protest government policies, cross-national surveys show that U.S. citizens are about as likely to take direct action in politics as citizens of European democracies. A study comparing American respondents with those in eight other countries—Britain, Canada, France, Germany, Italy, Japan, Russia, and Sweden—found that Americans are just as likely as citizens of other countries to vote, sign a petition, be interested in politics, or boycott products—but they are less likely to join demonstrations.[11] So compared with citizens in other nations, Americans are not markedly apathetic.

Is something wrong with a political system if citizens resort to unconventional, and often disapproved-of, methods of political participation? To answer this question, we must first learn how much citizens use conventional methods of participation.

★ Conventional Participation

LO3 ★ Distinguish between supportive acts and influencing acts of political participation.

A practical test of the democratic nature of any government is whether citizens can affect its policies by acting through its institutions—meeting with public officials, supporting candidates, and voting in elections. If people must operate outside government institutions to influence policymaking, as civil rights workers had to do in the South, the system is not democratic. Citizens should not have to risk their life and property to participate in politics, and they should not have to take direct action to force the government to hear their views. The objective of democratic institutions is to make political participation conventional—to allow ordinary citizens to engage in relatively routine, nonthreatening behavior to get the government to heed their opinions, interests, and needs.

In a democracy, for a group to gather at a statehouse or city hall to dramatize its position on an issue—say, a tax increase—is not unusual. Such a demonstration is a form of conventional participation. The group is not powerless, and its members are not risking their personal safety by demonstrating. But violence can erupt between opposing groups demonstrating in a political setting, such as between pro-life and pro-choice groups. Circumstances, then, often determine whether organized protest is or is not conventional. In general, the less that the participants anticipate a threat, the more likely it is that the protest will be conventional.

Conventional political behaviors fall into two major categories: actions that show support for government policies and those that try to change or influence policies.

Supportive Behavior

Supportive behavior is action that expresses allegiance to country and government. Reciting the Pledge of Allegiance and flying the American flag on holidays show support for both the country and, by implication, its political system. Such ceremonial activities usually require little effort, knowledge, or personal courage; that is, they demand little initiative on the part of the citizen. The simple act of turning out to vote is in itself a show of support for the political system. Other supportive behaviors, such as serving as an election judge in a nonpartisan election or organizing a holiday parade, demand greater initiative.

At times, people's perception of patriotism moves them to cross the line between conventional and unconventional behavior. In their eagerness to support the American system, they break up a meeting or disrupt a rally of a group they believe is radical or somehow "un-American." Radical groups may threaten the political system with wrenching change, but superpatriots pose their own threat by denying to others the nonviolent means of dissent.

supportive behavior
Action that expresses allegiance to government and country.

Influencing Behavior

Citizens use **influencing behavior** to modify or even reverse government policy to serve political interests. Some forms of influencing behavior seek particular benefits from government; other forms have broad policy objectives.

influencing behavior
Behavior that seeks to modify or reverse government policy to serve political interests.

Particular Benefits. Some citizens try to influence government to obtain benefits for themselves, their immediate families, or close friends. For example, citizens might pressure their alderman to rebuild the curbs on their street or vote against an increase in school taxes, especially if they have no children. Serving one's self-interest through the voting process is certainly acceptable to democratic theory. Each individual has only one vote, and no single voter can wrest particular benefits from government through voting unless a majority of the voters agrees.

Political actions that require considerable knowledge and initiative are another story. Individuals or small groups who influence government officials to advance their self-interest—for instance, to obtain a lucrative government contract—may secretly benefit without others knowing. Those who quietly obtain particular benefits from government pose a serious challenge to a democracy. Pluralist theory holds that groups ought to be able to make government respond to their special problems and needs. In contrast, majoritarian theory holds that government should not do what a majority does not want it to do—if the majority knew what was happening. A majority of citizens might very well not want the government to do what any particular person or group seeks if it is costly to other citizens.

Citizens often ask for special services from local government. Such requests may range from contacting the city forestry department to remove a dead tree in front of a house to calling the county animal control center to deal with a vicious dog in the neighborhood. Studies of such "contacting behavior" find that it tends not to be empirically related to other forms of political activity. In other words, people who complain to city hall do not necessarily vote. Contacting behavior is related to socioeconomic status: people of higher socioeconomic status are more likely to contact public officials.

Americans demand much more of their local government than of the national government. Although many people value self-reliance and individualism in national politics, most people expect local government to solve a wide range of social problems. A study of residents of Kansas City, Missouri, found that more than 90 percent thought the city had a responsibility to provide services in thirteen areas, including maintaining parks, setting standards for new home construction, demolishing vacant and unsafe buildings, ensuring that property owners clean up trash and weeds, and providing bus service. The researcher noted that "it is difficult to imagine a set of federal government activities about which there would [be] more consensus."[12] Citizens can also mobilize against a project. Dubbed the "not in my back yard," or NIMBY, phenomenon, such a mobilization occurs when citizens pressure local officials to stop undesired projects from being located near their homes.

Finally, contributing money to a candidate's campaign is another form of influencing behavior. Here, too, the objective can be particular or broad benefits, although determining which is which can sometimes be difficult. Several points emerge from this review of "particularized" forms of political participation. First, approaching government to serve one's particular interests is consistent with democratic theory because it encourages participation from an active citizenry. Second, particularized contact may be a unique form of participation, not necessarily related to other forms of participation such as voting. Third, such participation tends to be used more by citizens who are advantaged in terms of knowledge and resources. Fourth, particularized participation may serve private interests to the detriment of the majority.

Broad Policy Objectives. We come now to what many scholars have in mind when they talk about political participation: activities that influence the selection of government personnel and policies. Here, too, we find behaviors that require little initiative (such as voting) and others that require high initiative (attending political meetings, persuading others how to vote).

Even voting intended to influence government policies is a low-initiative activity. Such "policy voting" differs from voting to show support or to gain special benefits in its broader influence on the community or society. Obviously, this distinction is not sharp: citizens vote for several reasons—a mix of allegiance, particularized benefits, and policy concerns. In addition to policy voting, many other low-initiative forms of conventional participation—wearing a candidate's T-shirt, visiting a candidate's website, posting a bumper sticker—are also connected with elections. In the next section, we focus on elections as a mechanism for participation. For now, we simply note that voting to influence policy is usually a low-initiative activity. As we discuss later, it actually requires more initiative to register to vote in the United States than to vote on election day. It is much easier to e-mail or text members of Congress than to vote.

Other types of participation designed to affect broad policies require high initiative. Running for office requires the most (see Chapter 9). Some high-initiative activities, such as attending party meetings and working on campaigns, are associated with the electoral process; others, such as attending legislative hearings and sending e-mails to Congress, are not. Although many nonelectoral activities involve making personal contact, their objective is often to obtain government benefits for some group of people—farmers, the unemployed, children, oil producers. In fact, studies of citizen contacts in the United States show that about two-thirds deal with broad social issues and only one-third are for private gain.[13] Few people realize that using the court system is a form of political participation, a way for citizens to press for their rights in a democratic society. Although most people use the courts to serve their particular interests, some also use them, as we discuss shortly, to meet broad objectives. Going to court demands high personal initiative.[14] It also requires knowledge of the law or the financial resources to afford a lawyer.

People use the courts for both personal benefit and broad policy objectives. A person or group can bring a **class action suit** on behalf of other people in similar circumstances. Lawyers for the National Association for the Advancement of Colored People pioneered this form of litigation in the famous school desegregation case *Brown* v. *Board of Education* (1954).[15] They succeeded in getting the Supreme Court to outlaw segregation in public schools, not just for Linda Brown, who brought the suit in Topeka, Kansas, but also for all others "similarly situated"—that is, for all other black students who wanted to attend desegregated schools. Participation through the courts is usually beyond the means of individual citizens, but it has proved effective for organized groups, especially those that have been unable to gain their objectives through Congress or the executive branch. Sometimes such court challenges help citizens without their knowing it. In 2009, Capital One (whose TV slogan is "What's in your wallet?") settled a class action suit over its credit cards, agreeing to drop contract language requiring customer disputes to be handled through binding arbitration instead of the legal system.[16]

Individual citizens can also try to influence policies at the national level by participating directly in the legislative process. One way is to attend congressional hearings, which are open to the public and are occasionally held outside Washington, D.C. Especially after World War II, the national government sought to increase citizen involvement in creating regulations and laws by making information on government activities available to interested parties. For example, government agencies were required to publish all proposed and approved regulations in the daily *Federal Register* and to make government documents available to citizens on request.

More recently, the Internet has allowed electronic access to information, allowing citizens to participate in government from their own homes. A comprehensive survey of national government websites reported 1,489 domains and 1,013 websites from 56 agencies.[17] Today, citizens can search the *Federal Register* online.[18] The government website USA.gov helps people find information online and offers video tutorials on standard topics. However, the private site GovTrack.us provides easier access to congressional voting records than the government site Thomas.gov. Private sites also monitor more contentious issues. The Center for Responsible Politics covers campaign finance, lobbyists' spending, and other forms of political influence.[19] The National Institute on Money in State Politics covers similar ground for the states.[20] OMB Watch focuses on government spending and the budget deficit, while the Institute for Truth in Accounting lobbies to reduce the national debt.[21]

class action suit
A legal action brought by a person or group on behalf of a number of people in similar circumstances.

Conventional Participation in America

You may know someone who has testified at a congressional or administrative hearing or closely monitors governmental actions on the Internet, but the odds are that you do not. Such participation is high-initiative behavior. Relatively few people—only those with high stakes in the outcome of a decision—are willing to participate in this way. How often do Americans contact government officials and engage in other forms of conventional political participation compared with citizens in other countries?

The most common form of political behavior in most industrial democracies is voting for candidates. The rate of voting is known as **voter turnout**, the percentage of eligible voters who actually vote in a given election. Voting eligibility is hard to determine across American states, and there are different ways to estimate voter turnout.[22] However measured, voting for candidates in the United States is less common than it is in other countries, as demonstrated in Figure 7.2. When voter turnout in the United

voter turnout
The percentage of eligible citizens who actually vote in a given election.

FIGURE 7.2 Voter Turnout in European and American Elections

Compared with turnout rates in fifteen established European nations, voter turnout for American presidential elections ranks below all but three countries, and turnout for American congressional elections ranks below all of them. The European data show the percentage of the voting-age population voting in the most recent parliamentary election prior to 2014. The American data show voters as percentages of the eligible voting-age population that voted in the 2012 presidential election and the 2010 congressional election. Turnout in U.S. elections tends to average about fifteen points higher in presidential years than in congressional years.

Sources: International IDEA, "Voter Turnout," http://elections.gmu.edu/index.html; and United States Elections Project, http://elections.gmu.edu/voter_turnout.htm.

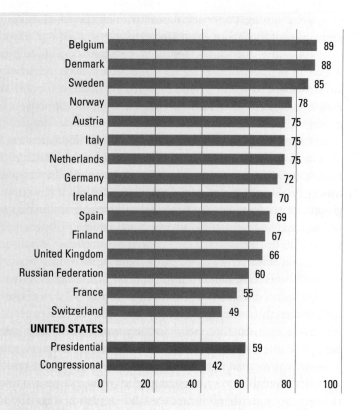

Country	Turnout
Belgium	89
Denmark	88
Sweden	85
Norway	78
Austria	75
Italy	75
Netherlands	75
Germany	72
Ireland	70
Spain	69
Finland	67
United Kingdom	66
Russian Federation	60
France	55
Switzerland	49
UNITED STATES	
Presidential	59
Congressional	42

States is compared with voting in fifteen other countries, the United States ranks at the bottom of the pack. This is a political paradox. On one hand, Americans are as likely as citizens in other democracies to engage in various forms of political participation. But when it comes to voting, the hand that casts the ballot, Americans rank dead last.

Other researchers noted this paradox and wrote, "If, for example, we concentrate our attention on national elections we will find that the United States is the least participatory of almost all other nations." But looking at the other indicators, they found that "political apathy, by a wide margin, is lowest in the United States. Interestingly, the high levels of overall involvement reflect a rather balanced contribution of both ... conventional and unconventional politics."[23] Clearly, low voter turnout in the United States constitutes a puzzle, to which we will return.

 Participating Through Voting

LO4 ★ Trace the expansion of suffrage in the United States and assess the impact of expanded suffrage on voting turnout.

The heart of democratic government lies in the electoral process. Whether a country holds elections—and if so, what kind—constitutes the critical difference between democratic and nondemocratic governments. Elections institutionalize mass participation in democratic government according to the three normative principles of procedural democracy discussed in Chapter 2: electoral rules specify *who* is allowed to vote, *how much* each person's vote counts, and *how many* votes are needed to win.

Again, elections are formal procedures for making group decisions. *Voting* is the act individuals engage in when they choose among alternatives in an election. **Suffrage** and **franchise** both mean the right to vote. By formalizing political participation through rules for suffrage and for counting ballots, electoral systems allow large numbers of people, who individually have little political power, to wield great power. Electoral systems decide collectively who governs and, in some instances, what government should do.

The simple act of holding elections is less important than the specific rules and circumstances that govern voting. According to democratic theory, everyone should be able to vote. In practice, however, no nation grants universal suffrage. All countries have age requirements for voting, and all disqualify some inhabitants on various grounds: lack of citizenship, criminal record, mental incompetence, and others. What is the record of enfranchisement in the United States?

suffrage
The right to vote. Also called the *franchise.*

franchise
The right to vote. Also called *suffrage.*

Expansion of Suffrage

The United States was the first country to provide for general elections of representatives through "mass" suffrage, but the franchise was far from universal. When the Constitution was framed, the idea of full adult suffrage was too radical to consider seriously. Instead, the framers left the issue of enfranchisement to the states, stipulating only that individuals who could vote for "the most numerous Branch of the State Legislature" could also vote for their representatives to the U.S. Congress (Article I, Section 2).

Initially, most states established taxpaying or property-holding requirements for voting. Virginia, for example, required ownership of twenty-five acres of settled land or five hundred acres of unsettled land. The original thirteen states began to lift such requirements after 1800. Expansion of the franchise accelerated after 1815, with the admission of new "western" states (Indiana, Illinois, Alabama), where land was more plentiful and widely owned. By the 1850s, the states had eliminated almost all taxpaying and property-holding requirements, thus allowing the working class—at least its white male members—to vote. Extending the vote to blacks and women took longer.

The Enfranchisement of Blacks. The Fifteenth Amendment, adopted shortly after the Civil War, prohibited the states from denying the right to vote "on account of race, color, or previous condition of servitude." However, the states of the old Confederacy worked around the amendment by reestablishing old voting requirements (poll taxes, literacy tests) that worked primarily against blacks. Some southern states also cut blacks out of politics through a cunning circumvention of the amendment. Because the amendment said nothing about voting rights in private organizations, these states denied blacks the right to vote in the "private" Democratic primary elections held to choose the party's candidates for the general election. Because the Democratic Party came to dominate politics in the South, the "white primary" effectively disenfranchised blacks, despite the Fifteenth Amendment. Finally, in many areas of the South, the threat of violence kept blacks from the polls.

The extension of full voting rights to blacks came in two phases, separated by twenty years. In 1944, the Court decided in *Smith* v. *Allwright* that laws preventing blacks from voting in primary elections were unconstitutional, holding that party primaries are part of the continuous process of electing public officials.[24] The Voting Rights Act of 1965, which followed Selma's Bloody Sunday by less than five months, suspended discriminatory voting tests. It also authorized federal registrars to register voters in seven southern states, where less than half of the voting-age population had registered to vote in the 1964 election. For good measure, the Supreme Court ruled in

FIGURE 7.3 Voter Registration in the South, 1960, 1980, 2000, and 2008

As a result of the Voting Rights Act of 1965 and other national actions, black voter registration in the eleven states of the old Confederacy nearly doubled between 1960 and 1980. By 2008, there was very little difference between the voting registration rates of white and black southern voters.

Sources: Data for 1960 and 1980 are from U.S. Bureau of the Census, *Statistical Abstract of the United States, 1982–1983* (Washington, D.C.: U.S. Government Printing Office, 1983), p. 488; data for 2000 and 2008 come from the U.S. Census Bureau, *Current Population Reports*, P20, Table 3.

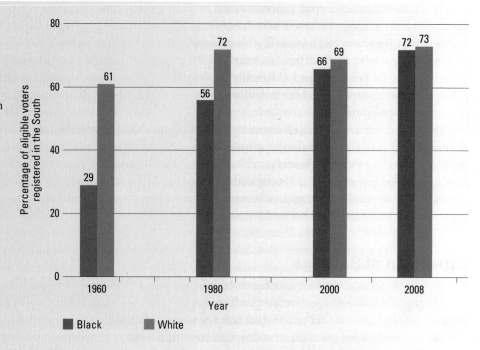

1966 in *Harper* v. *Virginia State Board of Elections* that state poll taxes are unconstitutional.[25] Although long in coming, these actions by the national government to enforce political equality in the states dramatically increased the registration of southern blacks (see Figure 7.3).

Acknowledging that the Voting Rights Act had dramatically changed voting patterns in the South, the Supreme Court voted 5–4 in 2013 to strike down a key part of the 1965 Voting Rights Act requiring nine southern states to get national approval to change their election laws. That decision permitted some states to enforce new voter identification laws, which Washington had previously blocked.

The Enfranchisement of Women. The enfranchisement of women in the United States is a less sordid story than enfranchisement of blacks but still nothing to be proud of. Women had to fight long and hard to win the right to vote. Until 1869, women could not vote anywhere in the world.[26] American women began to organize to obtain suffrage in the mid-1800s. Known then as *suffragettes,* the early feminists initially had a limited effect on politics.* Their first major victory did not come until 1869, when Wyoming, still a territory, granted women the right to vote. No state followed suit until 1893, when Colorado enfranchised women.

In the meantime, the suffragettes became more active. In 1884, they formed the Equal Rights Party and nominated Belva A. Lockwood, a lawyer (who could not herself vote), as the first woman candidate for president.[27] Between 1896 and 1918, twelve other states gave women the vote. Most of these states were in the West, where pioneer women often departed from traditional women's roles. Nationally, the women's suffrage movement intensified, often resorting to unconventional political behaviors (marches, demonstrations), which occasionally led to violent attacks from men and even other women. In 1919, Congress finally passed the Nineteenth Amendment, which prohibits states from denying the right to vote "on account of sex." The amendment was ratified

---

*The term *suffragist* applied to a person of either sex who advocated extending the vote to women, while *suffragette* was reserved for women who did so militantly.

The Fight for Women's Suffrage ... and Against It

Militant suffragettes demonstrated outside the White House prior to ratification of the Nineteenth Amendment to the Constitution, which gave women the right to vote. Congress passed the proposed amendment in 1919, and it was ratified by the required number of states in time for the 1920 presidential election. Suffragettes' demonstrations were occasionally disrupted by men—and other women—who opposed extending the right to vote to women.

in 1920, in time for the November election. A survey of Chicago voters in 1923 found that 75 percent of the men voted in the presidential election but only 46 percent of the women. Among women nonvoters, 11 percent cited "disbelief in woman's voting"; less than 2 percent cited "objection from husband."[28]

Evaluating the Expansion of Suffrage in America. The last major expansion of suffrage in the United States took place in 1971, when the Twenty-sixth Amendment lowered the voting age to eighteen. For most of its history, the United States has been far from the democratic ideal of universal suffrage. The United States initially restricted voting rights to white male taxpayers or property owners, and wealth requirements lasted until the 1850s. Through demonstrations and a constitutional amendment, women won the franchise only two decades before World War II. Through civil war, constitutional amendments, court actions, massive demonstrations, and congressional action, blacks finally achieved full voting rights only two decades after World War II. Our record has more than a few blemishes.

But compared with other countries, the United States looks pretty democratic.[29] Women did not gain the vote on equal terms with men until 1921 in Norway; 1922 in the Netherlands; 1944 in France; 1946 in Italy, Japan, and Venezuela; 1948 in Belgium; and 1971 in Switzerland. Women are still not universally enfranchised. Among the Arab monarchies, Kuwait granted full voting rights to women in 2005. In 2011, Saudi Arabia finally announced that women could vote in municipal elections—beginning in 2015. Of course, no one at all can vote in the United Arab Emirates. In South Africa, blacks, who outnumber whites by more than four to one, were not allowed to vote freely in elections until 1994. With regard to voting age, about 85 percent of the world's countries allow eighteen-year-olds to vote. About fifteen countries set the minimum age at twenty or twenty-one. Fewer than ten allow persons under age eighteen to vote—including Austria, which allows voting at sixteen.[30]

When judged against the rest of the world, the United States, which originated mass participation in government through elections, has as good a record of providing for political equality in voting rights as other democracies and a better record than many others.

Voting on Policies

Disenfranchised groups have struggled to gain voting rights because of the political power that comes with suffrage. Belief in the ability of ordinary citizens to make political decisions and to control government through the power of the ballot box was strongest in the United States during the Progressive era, which began around 1900 and lasted until about 1925. **Progressivism** was a philosophy of political reform that trusted the goodness and wisdom of individual citizens and distrusted "special interests" (railroads, corporations) and political institutions (traditional political parties, legislatures).

The leaders of the Progressive movement were prominent politicians (former president Theodore Roosevelt, Senator Robert La Follette of Wisconsin) and eminent scholars (historian Frederick Jackson Turner, philosopher John Dewey). Not content to vote for candidates chosen by party leaders, the Progressives championed the **direct primary**—a preliminary election, run by the state governments, in which the voters choose the party's candidates for the general election. Wanting a mechanism to remove elected candidates from office, the Progressives backed the **recall**, a special election initiated by a petition signed by a specified number of voters. Although about twenty states provide for recall elections, this device is rarely used. Only a few statewide elected officials have actually been unseated through recall. Indeed, only one state governor had ever been unseated until 2003, when California voters threw out Governor Gray Davis in a bizarre recall election that placed movie actor Arnold Schwarzenegger in the governor's mansion. In 2012, Wisconsin voters also sought to recall Republican governor Scott Walker but failed.

The Progressives also championed the power of the masses to propose and pass laws, approximating citizen participation in policymaking that is the hallmark of direct democracy.[31] They developed two voting mechanisms for policymaking that are still in use:

- A **referendum** is a direct vote by the people on either a proposed law or an amendment to a state constitution. The measures subject to popular vote are known as propositions. Twenty-four states permit popular referenda on laws, and all but Delaware require a referendum for a constitutional amendment. Most referenda are placed on the ballot by legislatures, not voters.
- The **initiative** is a procedure by which voters can propose a measure to be decided by the legislature or by the people in a referendum. The procedure involves gathering a specified number of signatures from registered voters (usually 5 to 10 percent of the total in the state) and then submitting the petition to a designated state agency. Twenty-four states provide for some form of voter initiative.

Figure 7.4 shows the West's affinity for these democratic mechanisms. In 2012, voters in thirty-eight states decided on 174 ballot propositions, most placed there by state legislatures, not citizen initiatives.[32] Voters approved most propositions, including ones in Colorado and Washington on legalizing possession and use of marijuana. In the off-year election of 2013, only six states voted on thirty-one propositions.[33] Most were approved, including one in Colorado that permitted taxing marijuana sales.

What conclusion can we draw about the Progressives' legacy of mechanisms for direct participation in government? One seasoned journalist paints an unimpressive picture. He notes that an expensive "industry" developed in the 1980s that makes money circulating petitions and then managing the large sums of money needed to run a campaign to approve (or defeat) a referendum. In 1998, opponents of a measure to allow casino gambling on Native American land in California spent $25.8 million. This huge sum, however, paled in comparison to the $66.2 million spent during the campaign by the tribes that supported the measure. The initiative passed.[34]

progressivism
A philosophy of political reform based on the goodness and wisdom of the individual citizen as opposed to special interests and political institutions.

direct primary
A preliminary election, run by the state government, in which the voters choose each party's candidates for the general election.

recall
The process for removing an elected official from office.

referendum
An election on a policy issue.

initiative
A procedure by which voters can propose an issue to be decided by the legislature or by the people in a referendum. It requires gathering a specified number of signatures and submitting a petition to a designated agency.

FIGURE 7.4 Westward Ho!

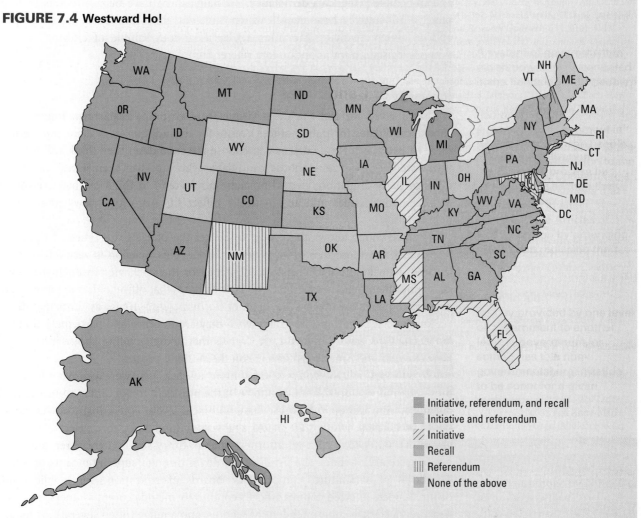

Initiative, referendum, and recall
Initiative and referendum
Initiative
Recall
Referendum
None of the above

This map shows quite clearly the western basis of the initiative, referendum, and recall mechanisms intended to place government power directly in the hands of the people. Advocates of "direct legislation" sought to bypass entrenched powers in state legislatures. Established groups and parties in the East dismissed them as radicals and cranks, but they gained the support of farmers and miners in the Midwest and West. The Progressive forces usually aligned with Democrats in western state legislatures to enact their proposals, often against Republican opposition.

Source: Initiative & Referendum Institute at http://iandrinstitute.org/statewide_i%26r.htm.

Clearly, citizens can exercise great power over government policy through the mechanisms of the initiative and the referendum. What is not clear is whether these forms of direct democracy improve on the policies made by elected representatives.[35] However, recent research has shown that—especially in midterm elections, which are characterized by low turnout—ballot measures tend to increase voting turnout, knowledge of issues, and campaign contributions to interest groups.[36] If the Internet had been around during their era, Progressives certainly would have endorsed it as a mechanism of direct democracy. At an elementary level, the Internet allows ordinary citizens who seek to initiate legislation to collect on petitions the thousands of signatures needed to place the proposal on the ballot. Pioneering websites, such as iSolon.org, aim at "exploring and advancing opportunities for democratic reform brought about by new information technologies," and the Brookings Institution proposes ways that social media can improve citizen engagement in political campaigns

and invigorate American democracy.[37] Finally, there have been attempts to implement "deliberative democracy," which involves thorough deliberation of policy
options (often involving the Internet) by a random sample of citizens who then
propose legislation for adoption in a referendum.[38]

Voting for Candidates

We have saved for last the most visible form of political participation: voting to
choose candidates for public office. Voting for candidates serves democratic government in two ways. First, citizens can choose the candidates they think will best serve
their interests. If citizens choose candidates who are "like themselves" in personal
traits or party affiliation, elected officials should tend to think as their constituents
do on political issues and automatically reflect the majority's views when making
public policy.

Second, voting allows the people to reelect the officials they guessed right about
and to kick out those they guessed wrong about. This function is very different from
the first. It makes public officials accountable for their behavior through the reward-
and-punishment mechanism of elections. It assumes that officeholders are motivated to
respond to public opinion by the threat of electoral defeat. It also assumes that the voters know what politicians are doing while they are in office and participate actively in
the electoral process. We look at the factors that underlie voting choice in Chapter 9.
Here, we examine Americans' reliance on the electoral process.

In national politics, voters seem content to elect just two executive officers—the
president and vice president—and to trust the president to appoint a cabinet to round
out his administration. But at the state and local levels, voters insist on selecting all
kinds of officials. Every state elects a governor (and forty-three elect a lieutenant
governor). Forty-four elect an attorney general; thirty-seven, a treasurer; and thirty-
five, a secretary of state. The list goes on, down through superintendents of schools,
secretaries of agriculture, comptrollers, boards of education, and public utilities
commissioners. Elected county officials commonly include commissioners, a sheriff, a
treasurer, a clerk, a superintendent of schools, and a judge (often several). At the local
level, voters elect all but about 600 of 15,300 school boards across the nation.[39]
Instead of trusting state and local chief executives to appoint lesser administrators (as
we do for more important offices at the national level), we expect voters to choose
intelligently among scores of candidates they meet for the first time on a complex
ballot in the polling booth.

Around the world, the number of countries holding regular, free, and fair elections has been rising (see "Electoral Democracy in Global Politics"). In the American
version of democracy, our laws recognize no limit to voters' ability to make informed
choices among candidates and thus to control government through voting. The reasoning seems to be that elections are good; therefore, more elections are better, and
the most elections are best. By this thinking, the United States clearly has the best
and most democratic government in the world because it is the undisputed champion
at holding elections. The author of a study that compared elections in the United
States with elections in twenty-six other democracies concluded:

> No country can approach the United States in the frequency and variety of
> elections, and thus in the amount of electoral participation to which its citi-
> zens have a right. No other country elects its lower house as often as every
> two years, or its president as frequently as every four years. No other country
> popularly elects its state governors and town mayors; no other has as wide a
> variety of nonrepresentative offices (judges, sheriffs, attorneys general, city

treasurers, and so on) subject to election.... The average American is entitled to do far more electing—probably by a factor of three or four—than the citizen of any other democracy.[40]

However, we learned from Figure 7.2, Voter Turnout in European and American Elections (p. 188), that the United States ranks at the bottom of fifteen European countries in voter turnout in national elections. How do we square low voter turnout with Americans' devotion to elections as an instrument of democratic government? To complicate matters further, how do we square low voter turnout with the fact that Americans seem to participate in politics in various other ways?

Electoral Democracy in Global Politics

Nations are "electoral democracies" if they have (1) a competitive, multiparty system; (2) universal adult suffrage; (3) regularly contested free elections; and (4) free election campaigns—according to Freedom House. The Washington-based organization has scored nations over the last four decades, during which the spread of electoral democracies can be analyzed in three stages: (1) the period from 1974 to 1989 depicts a "third wave" of democratization (the others were in 1828–1926 and 1943–1962) caused by social modernization and international influences, (2) the boom from 1989 to 1994 was sparked by the collapse of communism, and (3) a plateau was reached after 1995.

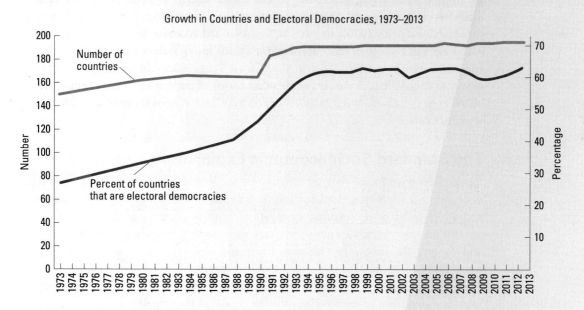

Growth in Countries and Electoral Democracies, 1973–2013

Sources: Larry Diamond, *The Spirit of Democracy* (New York: Times Books, 2008), p. 22 and Appendix, Table 2. Freedom House supplied data after 2007. See http://www.freedomhouse.org/sites/default/files/Electoral%20Democracy%20Numbers%2C%20FIW%201989-2014.pdf.

Critical Thinking The proportion of electoral democracies appears to have "maxed out" below two-thirds of the world's nations. Why?

Explaining Political Participation

LO5 ★ Identify the factors that affect political participation, especially voting.

As explained, political participation can be unconventional or conventional, can require little or much initiative, and can serve to support the government or influence its decisions. Researchers have found that people who take part in some form of political behavior often do not take part in others. For example, citizens who contact public officials to obtain special benefits may not vote regularly, participate in campaigns, or even contact officials about broader social issues. In fact, because particularized contacting serves individual rather than public interests, it is not even considered political behavior by some people.

This section examines some factors that affect the more obvious forms of political participation, with particular emphasis on voting. The first task is to determine how much patterns of participation vary within the United States over time.

Patterns of Participation over Time

Did Americans become more politically apathetic in the 2000s than they were in the 1960s? Generally not, as plots of several measures of participation from 1952 through 2012 show little variation over time in the percentage of citizens who were interested in election campaigns, talked to others about voting, worked for candidates, or attended party meetings. The only substantial dip in participation occurred in voter turnout during the 1970s and 1980s. Turnout did increase to 1960s levels in 2004 and 2008, but even then voter turnout was much lower than in most European countries. Not only is voter turnout in the United States relatively low, but also turnout over two decades has decreased while other forms of participation have remained stable or even increased. What is going on? Who votes? Who does not? Why? And does it really matter?

The Standard Socioeconomic Explanation

Researchers have found that socioeconomic status is a good indicator of most types of conventional political participation. People with more education, higher incomes, and white-collar or professional occupations tend to be more aware of the effect of politics on their lives, to know what can be done to influence government actions, and to have the necessary resources (time and money) to take action. So they are more likely to participate in politics than are people of lower socioeconomic status. This relationship between socioeconomic status and conventional political involvement is called the **standard socioeconomic model** of participation.[41]

standard socioeconomic model
A relationship between socioeconomic status and conventional political involvement: people with higher status and more education are more likely to participate than those with lower status.

Unconventional political behavior is related to socioeconomic status, and in much the same way. Those who protest against U.S. government policies tend to be better educated. Moreover, this relationship holds in other countries too. One scholar notes: "Protest in advanced industrial democracies is not simply an outlet for the alienated and deprived; just the opposite often occurs."[42] In one major way, however, those who engage in unconventional political behavior differ from those who participate more conventionally: protesters tend to be younger.

Obviously, socioeconomic status does not account for all the differences in the ways people choose to participate in politics, even for conventional participation.

Another important variable is age. Younger people are more likely to take part in demonstrations or boycotts and less likely to participate in conventional politics.[43] Younger people engage in more voluntary and charitable activities, but older Americans are more likely to vote, identify with the major political parties, and contact public officials.[44] Voting rates tend to increase as people grow older, until about age sixty-five, when physical infirmities begin to lower rates again.[45]

Two other variables—race and gender—have been related to participation in the past, but as times have changed, so have those relationships. Blacks, who had very low participation rates in the 1950s, now participate at rates comparable to whites when differences in socioeconomic status are taken into account.[46] Women also exhibited low participation rates in the past, but gender differences in political participation have virtually disappeared.[47] (The one exception is in attempting to persuade others how to vote, which women are less likely to do than men.)[48] Recent research on the social context of voting behavior has shown that married men and women are more likely to vote than those of either sex living without a spouse.[49]

Of all the social and economic variables, education is the strongest single factor in explaining most types of conventional political participation. A major study on civic participation details the impact of education:

> It affects the acquisition of skills; it channels opportunities for high levels of income and occupation; it places individuals in institutional settings where they can be recruited to political activity; and it fosters psychological and cognitive engagement with politics.[50]

Figure 7.5 shows the striking relationship between level of formal education and various types of conventional political behavior. The strong link between education and electoral participation raises questions about low voter turnout in the

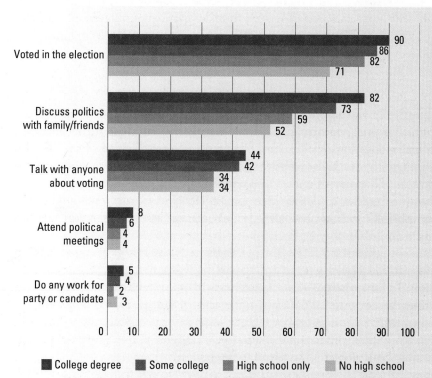

FIGURE 7.5 Effects of Education on Political Participation

Education has a powerful effect on political participation in the United States. These data from a 2012 sample show that level of education is directly related to five different forms of conventional political participation. (Respondents tend to overstate whether they voted.)

Source: This analysis was based on the 2012 American National Election Time Series Study (Ann Arbor, Mich., and Palo Alto, Calif.: University of Michigan and Stanford University).

United States, both over time and relative to other democracies. The fact is that the proportion of individuals with college degrees is greater in the United States than in other countries. Moreover, that proportion has been increasing steadily. Why, then, is voter turnout in elections so low? And why has it been dropping over time?

Low Voter Turnout in America

Economists wonder why people vote at all. In economic models of rational behavior, individuals avoid actions that have no payoff, and elections are rarely so close that an individual voter decides an outcome.[51] Unlike economists, political scientists wonder why citizens fail to vote. Voting is a low-initiative form of participation that can satisfy all three motives for political participation: showing allegiance to the nation, obtaining particularized benefits, and influencing broad policy. How then do we explain the decline in voter turnout in the United States?

The Decline in Voting over Time. The graph of voter turnout in Figure 7.6 shows that turnout in presidential elections was higher in the 1950s and 1960s than in the 1970s, 1980s, and 1990s, but it increased somewhat in 2004 and 2008.[52] The downward trend began with a sizable drop between the 1968 and 1972 elections. During this period (in 1971, actually) Congress proposed and the states ratified the

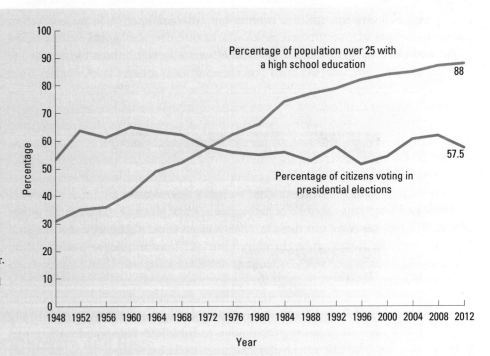

FIGURE 7.6 The Decline of Voter Turnout: An Unsolved Puzzle

Education strongly predicts the likelihood of voting in the United States. The percentage of adult citizens with a high school education or more has grown steadily since the end of World War II, but the overall rate of voter turnout trended downward from 1960 to 1996 and is still below the levels two decades after the war. Why turnout decreased as education increased is an unsolved puzzle in American voting behavior.

Sources: U.S. Census Bureau, Statistical Abstract 1962 and Statistical Abstract 2010, "Table A-1. Years of School Completed by People 25 Years and Over, by Age and Sex: Selected Years 1940 to 2008;" Kevin Liptak, "Report Shows Turnout Lower than 2008 and 2004," CNN Blog, November 8, 2012; and Harold W. Stanley and Richard G. Niemi, Vital Statistics on American Politics, 2009–2010 (Washington, D.C.: CQ Press, 2009), Table 1.1. The percentage voting in elections is based on the eligible voter population, not the voting-age population.

Twenty-sixth Amendment, which expanded the electorate by lowering the voting age from twenty-one to eighteen. Because people younger than twenty-one are much less likely to vote, their eligibility actually reduced the overall national turnout rate (the percentage of those eligible to vote who actually vote). Although young nonvoters inevitably vote more often as they grow up, observers estimate that the enfranchisement of eighteen-year-olds accounts for about one or two percentage points in the total decline in turnout since 1952. Nevertheless, that still leaves more than ten percentage points to be explained in the lower rates since 1972.[53]

Voter turnout has declined in most established democracies since the 1980s, but not as much as in the United States. Given that educational levels are increasing virtually everywhere, the puzzle is why turnout has decreased instead of increased. Many researchers have tried to solve this puzzle. Some attribute most of the decline to changes in voters' attitudes toward politics: beliefs that government is no longer responsive to citizens, that politicians are too packaged, that campaigns are too long.[54] Another is a change in attitude toward political parties, along with a decline in the extent to which citizens identify with a political party (a topic we discuss in Chapter 8).[55] According to these psychological explanations, voter turnout in the United States is not likely to increase until the government does something to restore people's faith in the effectiveness of voting—with or without political parties.

According to the age explanation, turnout in the United States is destined to remain a percentage point or two below its highs of the 1960s because of the lower voting rate of citizens younger than twenty-one. Turnout rates do increase as young people age, which suggests that voting is habit forming.[56] In 2004, almost 49 percent of those eighteen to twenty-nine years old turned out to vote.[57] In 2008, the Obama campaign made a special appeal to young voters, and youth voter turnout increased to 52 percent.[58] Young people actually voted about one point more in 2012 although the overall turnout declined.

U.S. Turnout versus Turnout in Other Countries. Scholars cite two factors to explain the low voter turnout in the United States compared with that in other countries. First are the differences in voting laws and administrative machinery. In a few countries, voting is compulsory, and obviously turnout is extremely high. But other methods can encourage voting: declaring election days to be public holidays or providing a two-day voting period. In 1845, Congress set election day for the first Tuesday after the first Monday in November, but a reform group—called "Why Tuesday?"— wants Congress to change election day to a weekend.[59]

Furthermore, nearly every other democratic country places the burden of registration on the government rather than on the individual voter. This is important. Voting in the United States is a two-stage process, and the first stage (going to the proper officials to register) has required more initiative than the second stage (going to the polling booth to cast a ballot). In most American states, the registration process has been separate from the voting process in terms of both time (usually voters had to register weeks in advance of an election) and geography (often voters had to register at the county courthouse, not their polling place). The nine states that do allow citizens to register and vote on the same day have consistently higher voter participation rates.[60] Turnout is higher in Oregon, where everyone votes by mail.[61] No state votes by Internet, yet. In 2009, the city of Honolulu claimed to hold the first all-digital election—voting online or by phone—but it involved only about 115,000 voters.[62]

**CONNECT
WITH YOUR CLASSMATES**
MindTap™ for American Government

Access the Voting Forum:
Discussion—Election Day.

**COMPARE
WITH YOUR PEERS**
MindTap™ for American Government

Access the Voting Forum:
Polling Activity—Voter Registration.

Regardless of voting ease, registration procedures for eligibility often are obscure, requiring potential voters to call around to find out what to do. People who move (and younger people move more frequently) have to reregister. In short, although voting requires little initiative, registration usually has required high initiative. If we compute voter turnout on the basis of those who are registered to vote, about 80 percent of Americans vote, a figure that moves the United States to the middle (but not the top) of all democratic nations.

Besides burdensome registration procedures, another factor usually cited to explain low turnout in American elections is the lack of political parties that mobilize the vote of particular social groups, especially lower-income and less educated people. American parties do make an effort to get out the vote, but neither party is as closely linked to specific groups as are parties in many other countries, where certain parties work hand in hand with specific ethnic, occupational, or religious groups. Research shows that strong party–group links can significantly increase turnout.[63] One important study claims that "changing mobilization patterns by parties, campaigns, and social movements accounts for at least half of the decline in electoral participation since the 1960s."[64]

Other research suggests that although well-funded, vigorous campaigns mobilize citizens to vote, the effect depends on the type of citizens, the nature of the election, and (yes) the weather.[65] Highly educated, low-income citizens are more likely to be stimulated to vote than are less educated, high-income citizens, but lower-class citizens can be more easily mobilized to vote in presidential elections than in non-presidential elections.[66] Some thought that the Internet would invite new classes of people to participate in politics, but well-educated and high income people are even more apt to participate online.[67] Citizens are more likely to turn out to vote when the elections are competitive or close.[68] One study observed that college students' decision to register and vote in their home state or in their college state depended in part on which had the more competitive races.[69]

To these explanations for low voter turnout in the United States—the traditional burden of registration and the lack of strong party–group links—we add another. Although the act of voting requires low initiative, the process of learning about the scores of candidates on the ballot in American elections requires a great deal of initiative. Some people undoubtedly fail to vote simply because they feel inadequate to the task of deciding among candidates for the many offices on the ballot in U.S. elections.

Teachers, newspaper columnists, and public affairs groups tend to worry a great deal about low voter turnout in the United States, suggesting that it signifies some sort of political sickness—or at least that it gives us a bad mark for democracy. Some others who study elections closely seem less concerned. One scholar argues:

> Turnout rates do not indicate the amount of electing—the frequency ... the range of offices and decisions, the "value" of the vote—to which a country's citizens are entitled.... Thus, although the turnout rate in the United States is below that of most other democracies, American citizens do not necessarily do less voting than other citizens; most probably, they do more.[70]

Despite such words of assurance, the nagging thought remains that turnout ought to be higher, so various organizations mount get-out-the-vote campaigns before elections. Civic leaders often back the campaigns because they value voting for its contribution to political order.

Participation and Freedom, Equality, and Order

LO6 ★ Evaluate the relationship between the values of freedom, equality, and order and political participation in American democracy.

As we have seen, Americans do participate in government in various ways and to a reasonable extent, compared with citizens of other countries. What is the relationship of political participation to the values of freedom, equality, and order?

Participation and Freedom

From the standpoint of normative theory, the relationship between participation and freedom is clear. Individuals should be free to participate in government and politics in the way they want and as much as they want. And they should be free not to participate as well. Ideally, all barriers to participation (such as restrictive voting registration and limitations on campaign expenditures) should be abolished, as should any schemes for compulsory voting. According to the normative perspective, we should not worry about low voter turnout because citizens should have the freedom not to vote as well as to vote.

In theory, freedom to participate also means that individuals should be able to use their wealth, connections, knowledge, organizational power (including sheer numbers in organized protests), or any other resource to influence government decisions, provided they do so legally. Of all these resources, the individual vote may be the weakest—and the least important—means of exerting political influence. Obviously, then, freedom as a value in political participation favors those with the resources to advance their own political self-interest.

Participation and Equality

The relationship between participation and equality is also clear. Each citizen's ability to influence government should be equal to that of every other citizen, so that differences in personal resources do not work against the poor or the otherwise disadvantaged.[71] Elections, then, serve the ideal of equality better than any other means of political participation. Formal rules for counting ballots—in particular, one person, one vote—cancel differences in resources among individuals.

At the same time, groups of people who have few resources individually can combine their votes to wield political power. Various European ethnic groups exercised this type of power in the late nineteenth and early twentieth centuries, when their votes won them entry to the sociopolitical system and allowed them to share in its benefits. More recently, blacks, Hispanics, homosexuals, and those with disabilities have used their voting power to gain political recognition. However, minorities often have had to use unconventional forms of participation to win the right to vote. As two major scholars of political participation put it, "Protest is the great equalizer, the political action that weights intensity as well as sheer numbers."[72]

Participation and Order

The relationship between participation and order is complicated. Some types of participation (pledging allegiance, voting) promote order and so are encouraged by those

Freedom, Order, or Equality?

Do citizens in a region have the right to secede from a nation? Most Americans support President Abraham Lincoln for fighting the Civil War "to save the Union."[73] By placing the nation's territorial integrity above southern citizens' desire to determine their future, Lincoln valued political order above freedom. Some fifty years later, Woodrow Wilson reversed presidential priorities. By proposing that the 1918 World War I peace treaty provide for self-determination of peoples, Wilson chose freedom over order. The treaty created new nations from subject peoples, and Wilson's principle of self-determination became incorporated into the United Nations Charter.

The freedom versus order conflict was revisited in March 2014, after a popular revolt in Ukraine ousted its corrupt and pro-Russian president. That infuriated Russian President Vladimir Putin and the Russian-speaking majority in Ukraine's Crimean peninsula, home of Russia's Black Sea fleet. Putin sent additional troops to Crimea, which hastily organized a referendum on joining Russia. Ethnic minorities boycotted the vote, but over 90 percent of those who voted chose to join Russia. President Barack Obama opposed the referendum, arguing for Ukrainian territorial integrity (consistent with President Lincoln). President Putin backed the vote, claiming self-determination (consistent with President Wilson).

In 2008, ironically, the American and Russian arguments had been reversed. The majority Albanian population in the Serbian province of Kosovo had revolted against Serbian rule. NATO bombed Serbian forces to stop killings of Albanians. With NATO peace-keeping forces on its ground, Kosovo's parliament voted for independence from Serbia. The United States and most European nations quickly

who value order; other types promote disorder and so are discouraged. Many citizens—men and women alike—even resisted giving women the right to vote for fear of upsetting the social order by altering the traditional roles of men and women.

Both conventional and unconventional participation can lead to the ouster of government officials, but the regime—the political system itself—is threatened more by unconventional participation. To maintain order, the government has a stake in converting unconventional participation to conventional participation whenever possible. We can easily imagine this tactic being used by authoritarian governments, but democratic governments also use it. According to documents obtained after September 11, 2001, the FBI not only increased surveillance of groups with suspected ties to foreign terrorists but also began monitoring other groups that protested public policies.[74]

Popular protests can spread beyond original targets. Think about student unrest on college campuses during the Vietnam War. In private and public colleges alike, thousands of students stopped traffic, occupied buildings, destroyed property, boycotted classes, disrupted lectures, staged guerrilla theater, and behaved in other unconventional ways to protest the war, racism, capitalism, the behavior of their college

recognized Kosovo as a new nation. Russia and most Slavic nations did not—and still do not. Today, the United States and the European Union do not recognize Crimea as part of Russia.

Uriel Sinai/The New York Times/Redux

Crimean citizen after voting on joining Russia.

Critical Thinking Two famous American presidents took opposing positions on citizens' rights to self-determination. Were both correct?

presidents, the president of the United States, the military establishment, and all other institutions. (We are not exaggerating here. Students did such things at our home universities after members of the National Guard shot and killed four students at a demonstration at Kent State University in Ohio on May 4, 1970.)

Confronted by civil strife and disorder in the nation's institutions of higher learning, Congress took action. On March 23, 1971, it enacted and sent to the states the proposed Twenty-sixth Amendment, lowering the voting age to eighteen. Three-quarters of the state legislatures had to ratify the amendment before it became part of the Constitution. Astonishingly, thirty-eight states (the required number) complied by July 1, establishing a new speed record for ratification and cutting the old record nearly in half.[75] (Ironically, voting rights were not high on the list of students' demands.)

Testimony by members of Congress before the Judiciary Committee stated that the eighteen-year-old vote would "harness the energy of young people and direct it into useful and constructive channels," to keep students from becoming "more militant" and engaging "in destructive activities of a dangerous nature."[76] As one observer argued, the right to vote was extended to eighteen-year-olds not because young people demanded it but because "public officials believed suffrage expansion to be a means of institutionalizing youths' participation in politics, which would, in turn, curb disorder."[77]

Participation and the Models of Democracy

LO7 ★ Identify the purposes elections serve and explain the relationship between elections and majoritarian and pluralist models of democracy.

Ostensibly, elections are institutional mechanisms that implement democracy by allowing citizens to choose among candidates or issues. But elections also serve several other important purposes:[78]

- Elections socialize political activity. They transform what might otherwise consist of sporadic, citizen-initiated acts into a routine public function. That is, the opportunity to vote for change encourages citizens to refrain from demonstrating in the streets. This helps preserve government stability by containing and channeling away potentially disruptive or dangerous forms of mass political activity.
- Elections institutionalize access to political power. They allow ordinary citizens to run for political office or to play an important role in selecting political leaders. Working to elect a candidate encourages the campaign worker to identify problems or propose solutions to the newly elected official.
- Elections bolster the state's power and authority. The opportunity to participate in elections helps convince citizens that the government is responsive to their needs and wants, which reinforces its legitimacy.

Participation and Majoritarianism

Although the majoritarian model assumes that government responsiveness to popular demands comes through mass participation in politics, majoritarianism views participation rather narrowly. It favors conventional, institutionalized behavior—primarily voting in elections. Because majoritarianism relies on counting votes to determine what the majority wants, its bias toward equality in political participation is strong. Clearly, a class bias in voting exists because of the strong influence of socioeconomic status on turnout. Simply put, better-educated, wealthier citizens are more likely to participate in elections, and get-out-the-vote campaigns cannot counter this distinct bias.[79] Because it favors collective decisions formalized through elections, majoritarianism has little place for motivated, resourceful individuals to exercise private influence over government actions.

Majoritarianism also limits individual freedom in another way: its focus on voting as the major means of mass participation narrows the scope of conventional political behavior by defining which political actions are "orderly" and acceptable. By favoring equality and order in political participation, majoritarianism goes hand in hand with the ideological orientation of communitarianism (see Chapter 1).

Participation and Pluralism

Resourceful citizens who want the government's help with problems find a haven in the pluralist model of democracy. A decentralized and organizationally complex form of government allows many points of access and accommodates various forms of conventional participation in addition to voting. For example, wealthy people and well-funded groups can afford to hire lobbyists to press their interests in Congress. In one view of pluralist democracy, citizens are free to ply and wheedle public officials to further their own selfish visions of the public good. From another viewpoint, pluralism offers citizens the opportunity to be treated as individuals when dealing with the government, to influence policymaking in special circumstances, and to fulfill (insofar as possible in representative government) their social potential through participation in community affairs.

Master the Topic of Voting with MindTap™ for American Government

REVIEW MindTap™ **for American Government**
Access Key Term Flashcards for Chapter 7.

TEST YOURSELF MindTap™ **for American Government**
Take the Wrap It Up Quiz for Chapter 7.

STAY CURRENT MindTap™ **for American Government**
Access the KnowNow blog and customized RSS for updates on current events.

STAY FOCUSED MindTap™ **for American Government**
Complete the Focus Activities for Voting.

Summary

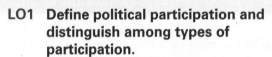

LO1 Define political participation and distinguish among types of participation.

- Most people participate in politics in conventional ways—voting and using established institutions of representative government. Some participate in unconventional ways that challenge established institutions.

LO2 Identify examples of unconventional participation in American history and evaluate their effectiveness.

- The Boston Tea Party of 1773 that protested British rule was an early instance of unconventional participation in America.

Citizens who marched for civil rights in the late 1950s and early 1960s succeeded in changing laws through unconventional political participation.

LO3 Distinguish between supportive acts and influencing acts of political participation.

- Citizens often unconsciously participate in politics, for example by reciting the Pledge of Allegiance and flying the flag on holidays, which constitute supportive behavior. More consciously, citizens engage in high-initiative influencing behavior when they seek to modify or reverse government policy.

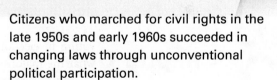

LO4 Trace the expansion of suffrage in the United States and assess the impact of expanded suffrage on voting turnout.

- Although the United States was the first country to hold elections with mass suffrage, only white male property holders could vote initially. Constitutional amendments after the Civil War gave blacks the right to vote, but they were systematically blocked from voting until the Voting Rights Act of 1965 and subsequent court decisions. Women did not get the right to vote nationwide until the Nineteenth Amendment passed in 1920. Progressive reforms—the initiative and referendum—facilitated voting on state policies, but citizens cannot vote on national policies in a referendum.

LO5 Identify the factors that affect political participation, especially voting.

- According to the standard socioeconomic model, increasing political participation is linked to increases in education, wealth, and occupational status. Voting turnout in the United States presents a puzzle, because voting turnout has remained flat or even declined while education has increased. Cited causes of low voting turnout are registration requirements, lack of strong parties to mobilize votes, and too frequent elections.

LO6 Evaluate the relationship between the values of freedom, equality, and order and political participation in American democracy.

- Freedom holds that people should be able to participate in politics as much (or as little) as they want and should be able to use all their resources in the process. Equality holds that each citizen's ability to influence government should be no greater than any other's, which is formally true in voting but not in influencing how others vote. Order is generally promoted by conventional participation but undercut by unconventional participation.

LO7 Identify the purposes elections serve and explain the relationship between elections and majoritarian and pluralist models of democracy.

- The majoritarian model assumes that government responds to popular demands expressed through conventional participation, primarily elections. The pluralist model encourages other forms of participation to influence government, including well-financed efforts to persuade both voters and officials.

Chapter Quiz

LO1 Define political participation and distinguish among types of participation.

1. What distinguishes conventional from unconventional political participation?
2. Is terrorism a form of political participation?

LO2 Identify examples of unconventional participation in American history and evaluate their effectiveness.

1. Does unconventional political participation produce results? Give an historical example both ways.

2. Are Americans more or less likely than Europeans to engage in unconventional participation?

LO3 Distinguish between supportive acts and influencing acts of political participation.

1. Cite an example of supportive political behavior and an example of influencing political behavior.
2. How can suing in court constitute a form of political behavior?

LO4 **Trace the expansion of suffrage in the United States and assess the impact of expanded suffrage on voting turnout.**

1. Compare the expansion of suffrage in the United States with that in most other democracies.
2. Compare voter turnout in the United States with turnout in other Western democracies.

LO5 **Identify the factors that affect political participation, especially voting.**

1. What is meant by the "standard socioeconomic model" for explaining political participation? Compared with the level of education in the United States, has voting turnout fulfilled the standard socioeconomic model?
2. Which requires more citizen initiative, to register to vote or to vote itself? Why, and why does it matter?

LO6 **Evaluate the relationship between the values of freedom, equality, and order and political participation in American democracy.**

1. Which value—freedom, equality, or order—is best served by voting as a form of participation and why?
2. How can political participation both serve and undermine order?

LO7 **Identify the purposes elections serve and explain the relationship between elections and majoritarian and pluralist models of democracy.**

1. What purposes are served by elections other than selecting candidates or deciding issues?
2. Which model of democracy—majoritarian or pluralist—is better served by elections and why?

8 ★ Political Parties

Learning Outcomes

LO1 Define political party and list the functions performed by parties in democratic government.

LO2 Outline the history of the U.S. political party system.

LO3 Explain why two parties dominate the history of American politics.

LO4 Compare and contrast the Democratic and Republican parties on the basis of ideology and organization.

LO5 Identify the principles of responsible party government and evaluate their role in majoritarian democracy.

 WATCH & LEARN MindTap° **for American Government**
Watch a brief "What Do You Know?" video summarizing Political Parties.

© Morphart Creations inc/Shutterstock.com

In the 1871 book, *Alice's Adventures in Wonderland*, Alice delighted readers by coping with all sorts of fantastic creatures. In the book's sequel, *Through the Looking Glass*, Alice encountered a curious pair of identical twins, Tweedledum and Tweedledee, who were "standing under a tree, each with an arm round the other's neck." She could tell them apart only "because one of them had 'DUM' embroidered on his collar, and the other 'DEE.'" Although Tweedledum and Tweedledee looked alike, they didn't seem to agree on much and loved to fight between themselves. However, they didn't fight very furiously, and not about anything consequential.

For decades during the nineteenth and twentieth centuries, observers of American politics characterized the Democratic and Republican parties as Tweedledum and Tweedledee. Composed mainly of well-to-do white men, the two parties looked much alike, disagreed over politics, and loved to contest elections. However, they seldom clashed over truly consequential issues. In fact, most politicians would have been as comfortable in office either as a "Dum" or as a "Dee." As late as 1996, Green Party presidential candidate Ralph Nader said that "deciding between President Bill Clinton and Republican Senator Bob Dole was like choosing between Tweedle-dum and Tweedle-dee."[1]

However true that characterization might have been during the nineteenth or twentieth century, it is not true in the first decades of the twenty-first century. The Democratic and Republican political parties today are *very* different in composition, and they clash furiously over consequential issues of government policy. Moreover, few Democratic politicians today would be comfortable as Republicans, and vice versa.

LISTEN & LEARN
MindTap™ **for American Government**

Access Read Speaker to listen to Chapter 8.

U.S. politics is characterized by a two-party system. The Democratic and Republican parties have dominated national and state politics for almost 150 years. Their domination is more complete than that of any pair of parties in any other democratic government. Although all democracies have some form of multiparty politics, very few have a stable two-party system. Even Britain, whose politics have been dominated for decades by the Labour and Conservative parties, has an important third party—the Liberal Democrats—who gained enough seats in parliament to join the Conservatives in a governing coalition. Most people take the U.S. two-party system for granted, not realizing that it is arguably the most distinctive feature of American politics.

Why do we have any political parties? What functions do they perform? How did we become a nation of Democrats and Republicans? Do these parties truly differ in their platforms and behavior? Are parties really necessary for democratic government, or do they just get in the way of citizens and their government? In this chapter, we answer these questions by examining political parties, perhaps the most misunderstood element of American politics.

 Political Parties and Their Functions

LO1 ★ Define political party and list the functions performed by parties in democratic government.

According to democratic theory, the primary means by which citizens control their government is voting in free elections. Most Americans agree that voting is important. Of those surveyed after the 2012 presidential campaign, 79 percent felt that elections make the government "pay attention to what the people think."[2] Americans are not nearly as supportive of the role played by our major political parties in elections, however. Asked in 2013 whether the "Republican and Democratic parties do an adequate job of representing the American people," only 24 percent thought they performed adequately.[3]

Nevertheless, Americans are quick to condemn as "undemocratic" countries that do not regularly hold elections contested by political parties. In truth, Americans have a love–hate relationship with political parties. They believe that parties are necessary for democratic government; at the same time, they think parties are somehow obstructionist and not to be trusted. This distrust is particularly strong among younger voters. To better appreciate the role of political parties in democratic government, we must understand exactly what parties are and what they do.

What Is a Political Party?

political party
An organization that sponsors candidates for political office under the organization's name.

nomination
Designation as an official candidate of a political party.

A **political party** is an organization that sponsors candidates for political office *under the organization's name.* The italicized part of this definition is important. True political parties select individuals to run for public office through a formal **nomination** process, which designates them as the parties' official candidates. This activity distinguishes the Democratic and Republican parties from interest groups, such as the AFL-CIO and the National Association of Manufacturers. Both of these interest groups support candidates, but they do not nominate them to run as their avowed representatives. If they did, they would be transformed into political parties. Because the so-called tea party does not nominate its own candidates, it is not a political party. True, five congressional candidates in 2010 managed to list themselves on the ballot under the tea party label, but none were endorsed by significant tea party groups and all lost. In short, the sponsoring of candidates, designated as representatives of the organization, is what defines an organization as a party.

Most democratic theorists agree that a modern nation-state cannot practice democracy without at least two political parties that regularly contest elections. In fact, the link between democracy and political parties is so firm that many people define democratic government in terms of competitive party politics.[4] A former president of the American Political Science Association held that even for a small nation, "democracy is impossible save in terms of parties."[5]

Party Functions

Parties contribute to democratic government through the functions they perform for the **political system**—the set of interrelated institutions that link people with government. Four of the most important party functions are nominating candidates for election to public office, structuring the voting choice in elections, proposing alternative government programs, and coordinating the actions of government officials.

Nominating Candidates. Question: Is *every* American citizen qualified to hold public office? A few scholars have thought they were and proposed that government positions be filled "randomly"—that is, through lotteries.[6] Most observers, however, hold that political leadership requires certain abilities (if not special knowledge or public experience) and that not just anyone should be entrusted to hold government office. The question then becomes, Who should be chosen among those who offer to lead? Without political parties, voters would confront a bewildering array of self-nominated candidates, each seeking votes on the basis of personal friendships, celebrity status, or name recognition. Parties can provide a form of quality control for their nominees through the process of peer review. Party insiders, the nominees' peers, usually know the strengths and faults of potential candidates much better than average voters do and thus can judge their suitability for representing the party. Founders of the Internet site, americanselect.org, thought that average voters would do better.

In nominating candidates, parties often do more than pass judgment on potential office seekers; sometimes they recruit talented individuals to become candidates. In this way, parties help not only to ensure a minimum level of quality among candidates who run for office but also to raise the quality of those candidates.

Structuring the Voting Choice. Political parties help democratic government by structuring the voting choice—reducing the number of candidates on the ballot to those who have a realistic chance of winning. Established parties—those with experience in contesting elections—acquire a following of loyal voters who guarantee the party's candidates a predictable base of votes. The ability of established parties to mobilize their supporters discourages nonparty candidates from running for office and new parties from forming. Consequently, the realistic choice is between candidates offered by the major parties, reducing the amount of new information that voters need to choose their leaders. Of course, parties seek to structure the voting choice in a way that helps their candidates win.

Contrast the voting decision in our stable competitive two-party system (and the outcome) with Russian voters' choices in their December 2011 parliamentary election to the State Duma, the lower house of the Russian Federation. The Russian ballot listed seven parties. Three parties failed to receive at least 7 percent of the

political system
A set of interrelated institutions that link people with government.

parliamentary vote and thus won no seats. The four that did had been seated in the previous parliament. United Russia, Prime Minister Vladimir Putin's party, lost seventy-seven seats but still emerged as the majority party. Election observers (and many Russian citizens) viewed the elections as fraudulent. Even in honest elections, however, the presence of multiple parties tends to split opposition to a dominant regime and prevent alternation in power. Two-party systems tend to promote citizens' ability to replace government leaders.

Proposing Alternative Government Programs. Parties help voters choose among candidates by proposing alternative programs of government action—the general policies their candidates will pursue if they gain office. In a stable party system, even if voters know nothing about the qualities of the parties' candidates, they can vote rationally for the candidates of the party that has policies they favor. The specific policies advocated vary from candidate to candidate and from election to election. However, the types of policies advocated by candidates of one party tend to differ from those proposed by candidates of other parties. Although there are exceptions, candidates of the same party tend to favor policies that fit their party's underlying political philosophy, or ideology. Parties in multiparty systems tend to propose more varied and specific programs than parties offer in two-party systems.

In many countries, parties' names, such as Conservative and Socialist, reflect their political stance. The Democrats and Republicans have ideologically neutral names, but many minor parties in the United States have used their names to advertise their policies—for example, the Libertarian Party, the Socialist Party, and the Green Party.[7] The neutrality of the two major parties' names suggests that their policies are similar. This is not true. As we shall see, they regularly adopt very different policies in their platforms.

Coordinating the Actions of Government Officials. Finally, party organizations help coordinate the actions of public officials. A government based on the separation of powers, such as that of the United States, divides responsibilities for making public policy. The president and the leaders of the House and Senate are not required to cooperate with one another. Political party organizations are the major means for bridging the separate powers to produce coordinated policies that can govern the country effectively. Parties do this in two ways. First, candidates' and officeholders' political fortunes are linked to their party organization, which can bestow and withhold favors. Second, and perhaps more important in the United States, members of the same party in the presidency, the House, and the Senate tend to share political principles and thus often voluntarily cooperate in making policy.

Depending on how members view their party, parties differ in how they perform these functions. Two main views prevail. The eighteenth-century thinker Edmund Burke defined a party as "a body of men united for promoting by their joint endeavours the national interest upon some particular principle in which they are all agreed."[8] To Burke, people unite in a party in order to enact agreed policies. In contrast, the mid-twentieth-century economist Anthony Downs defined a party as "a team of men seeking to control the governing apparatus by gaining office in a duly constituted election."[9] To Downs, people unite in a party to get elected. In recent years Republicans have tended to act like Burkeans. For example, they nominated candidates who catered to their conservative base but who often lost in general elections. Democrats have more consistently acted like Downsians, backing policies more popular with ideologically moderate voters. This may explain why Republican presidential candidates won fewer votes than Democrats in five of the last six elections.

So why do we have parties? One expert notes that successful politicians in the United States need electoral and governing majorities and that "no collection of ambitious politicians has long been able to think of a way to achieve their goals in this democracy save in terms of political parties."[10]

★ A History of U.S. Party Politics

LO2 ★ Outline the history of the U.S. political party system.

The two major U.S. parties are among the oldest in the world. In fact, the Democratic Party, founded in 1828 but with roots reaching back to the late 1700s, has a strong claim to being the oldest party in existence. Its closest rival is the British Conservative Party, formed in 1832, two decades before the Republican Party was organized in 1854. Several generations of citizens have supported the Democratic and Republican parties, and they are part of American history. They have become institutionalized in our political process.

The Preparty Period

Today we think of party activities as normal, even essential, to American politics. It was not always so. The Constitution makes no mention of political parties, and none existed when the Constitution was written in 1787. It was common then to refer to groups pursuing some common political interest as factions. Although *factions* were seen as inevitable in politics, they were also considered dangerous.[11] One argument for adopting the Constitution—proposed in *Federalist* No. 10 (see Chapter 3)—was that its federal system would prevent factional influences from controlling the government.

Factions existed even under British rule. In colonial assemblies, supporters of the governor (and thus of the Crown) were known as *Tories* or *Loyalists*, and their opponents were called *Whigs* or *Patriots*. After independence, the arguments over whether to adopt the Constitution produced a different alignment of factions. Those who backed the Constitution were loosely known as *Federalists*, their opponents as *Antifederalists*. At this stage, the groups could not be called parties because they did not sponsor candidates for election.

Elections then were vastly different from elections today. The Constitution provided for the president and vice president to be chosen by an **electoral college**—a body of electors who met in the capitals of their respective states to cast their ballots. Initially, in most states, the legislatures, not the voters, chose the electors (one for each senator and representative in Congress). Presidential elections in the early years of the nation, then, actually were decided by a handful of political leaders. (See Chapter 9 for a discussion of the electoral college in modern presidential politics.) Often they met in small, secret groups, called **caucuses**, to propose candidates for public office. Typically, they were composed of like-minded members of state legislatures and Congress. This was the setting for George Washington's election as the first president in 1789.

We can classify Washington as a Federalist because he supported the Constitution, but he was not a factional leader and actually opposed factional politics. His immense prestige, coupled with his political neutrality, left Washington unopposed for the office of president, and he was elected unanimously by the electoral college. During Washington's administration, however, the political cleavage sharpened between those who favored a stronger national government and those who wanted a less powerful,

electoral college
A body of electors chosen by voters to cast ballots for president and vice president.

caucus
A closed meeting of the members of a political party to decide questions of policy and the selection of candidates for office.

more decentralized national government. The first group, led by Alexander Hamilton, proclaimed themselves *Federalists*. The second group, led by Thomas Jefferson, called themselves *Republicans*. (Although they used the same name, they were not the Republicans we know today.) The Jeffersonians chose the name *Republicans* to distinguish themselves from the "aristocratic" tendencies of Hamilton's Federalists. The Federalists countered by calling the Republicans the *Democratic Republicans*, attempting to link Jefferson's party to the disorder (and beheadings) in the French Revolution, led by "radical democrats."

The First Party System: Federalists and Democratic Republicans

Washington was reelected president unanimously in 1792, but his vice president, John Adams, was opposed by a candidate backed by the Democratic Republicans. This brief skirmish foreshadowed the nation's first party struggle over the presidency. Disheartened by the political split in his administration, Washington spoke out against "the baneful effects" of parties in his farewell address in 1796. Nonetheless, parties already existed in the political system, as Figure 8.1 shows. In the election of 1796, the Federalists supported Vice President John Adams to succeed Washington as president. The Democratic Republicans backed Thomas Jefferson for president but could not agree on a vice-presidential candidate. In the electoral college, Adams won seventy-one votes to Jefferson's sixty-eight, and both ran ahead of other candidates. At that time, the Constitution provided that the presidency would go to the candidate who won the most votes in the electoral college, with the vice presidency going to the runner-up (like a school election). So Adams, a Federalist, had to accept Jefferson, a Democratic Republican, as his vice president. Obviously, the Constitution did not anticipate a presidential contest between candidates from opposing political parties.

The party function of nominating candidates emerged more clearly in the election of 1800. Both parties caucused in Congress to nominate candidates for president and vice president. The result was the first true party contest for the presidency. The Federalists nominated John Adams and Charles Pinckney; the Democratic Republicans nominated Thomas Jefferson and Aaron Burr. Although the Democratic Republican candidates (Jefferson and Burr) won the electoral vote, the new party organization worked too well. According to the Constitution, each elector had to vote by ballot for two persons. *All* Democratic Republican electors unanimously cast both votes for Jefferson and for Burr. The presidency was to go to the candidate with the most votes, but due to party discipline the top two candidates were tied! Although Jefferson was the party's presidential candidate and Burr its vice-presidential candidate, the Constitution empowered the House of Representatives to choose either one of them as president. After seven days and thirty-six ballots, the House decided in favor of Jefferson.

The Twelfth Amendment, ratified in 1804, prevented a repeat of the troublesome election outcomes of 1796 and 1800. It required the electoral college to vote separately for president and vice president, implicitly recognizing that parties would nominate different candidates for the two offices.

The election of 1800 marked the beginning of the end for the Federalists, who lost the next four elections. By 1820, the Federalists were no more. The Democratic Republican candidate, James Monroe, was reelected in the first presidential contest without party competition since Washington's time. (Monroe received all but one electoral vote, reportedly cast against him so that Washington would remain the only president ever elected unanimously.) Ironically, the lack of partisan competition under Monroe, in what was dubbed the "Era of Good Feelings," also fatally weakened

FIGURE 8.1 The Two-Party System in American History

1789	*Washington unanimously elected president*				
1792	*Washington unanimously reelected*				**PREPARTY PERIOD**
1796	Federalist *Adams*	Democratic Republican			
1800	—	*Jefferson*			
1804	—	*Jefferson*			**FIRST PARTY SYSTEM**
1808	—	*Madison*			
1812	—	*Madison*			
1816	—	*Monroe*			
1820		*Monroe*			**"ERA OF GOOD FEELINGS"**
1824		*J. Q. Adams*			
1828		Democratic *Jackson*		National Republican	
1832		*Jackson*		Whig	
1836		*Van Buren*		—	
1840	**SECOND PARTY SYSTEM**	—		*Harrison*	
1844		*Polk*			
1848		—		*Taylor*	
1852		*Pierce*		—	
1856		*Buchanan*		Republican	
1860	Constitutional Union Southern Democrat	—		*Lincoln*	
1864		—		*Lincoln*	
1868		—		*Grant*	
1872		—		*Grant*	
1876	**THIRD PARTY SYSTEM**	—		*Hayes*	
1880		—		*Garfield*	
1884		*Cleveland*			
1888	**Rough Balance**	—		*Harrison*	
1892		*Cleveland*		—	
1896		—	Populist	*McKinley*	
1900		—		*McKinley*	
1904		—		*Roosevelt, T.*	
1908		—		*Taft*	
1912	**Republican Dominance**	*Wilson*	Progressive	—	
1916		*Wilson*			
1920		—		*Harding*	
1924		—	Progressive	*Coolidge*	
1928		—		*Hoover*	
1932		*Roosevelt, F. D.*		—	
1936		*Roosevelt, F. D.*		—	
1940		*Roosevelt, F. D.*		—	
1944		*Roosevelt, F. D.*		—	
1948	**Democratic Dominance**	*Truman*	States' Rights	—	
1952		—		*Eisenhower*	
1956		—		*Eisenhower*	
1960		*Kennedy*		—	
1964		*Johnson*		—	
1968		—	American Independent	*Nixon*	
1972		—		*Nixon*	
1976		*Carter*		—	
1980		—	Independent	*Reagan*	
1984		—		*Reagan*	
1988	**Rough Balance**	—		*Bush, G. H. W.*	
1992		*Clinton*	Independent	—	
1996		*Clinton*	Reform	—	
2000		—	Green	*Bush, G. W.*	
2004		—		*Bush, G. W.*	
2008		*Obama*		—	
2012		*Obama*		—	

Over time, the American party system has undergone a series of wrenching transformations. Since 1856, the Democrats and the Republicans have alternated irregularly in power, each party enjoying a long period of dominance.

Source: © Cengage Learning.

his party, the Democratic Republicans. Lacking competition, the Democratic Republicans neglected their function of nominating candidates. In the 1824 election, the party caucus's nominee was challenged by three other Democratic Republicans, including John Quincy Adams and Andrew Jackson, who together won 70 percent of the popular and electoral vote.

Although Jackson won more of the popular vote and electoral vote than Adams, he did not win the necessary majority in the electoral college. The House of Representatives again had to decide the winner. It chose the second-place John Quincy Adams (from the established state of Massachusetts) over the voters' choice, Jackson (from the frontier state of Tennessee). The factionalism among the leaders of the Democratic Republican Party became so intense that the party split in two.

The Second Party System: Democrats and Whigs

The Jacksonian faction of the Democratic Republican Party represented the common people in the expanding South and West, and its members took pride in calling themselves simply Democrats. Jackson ran again for the presidency as a Democrat in 1828, a milestone that marked the beginning of today's Democratic Party. That election was also the first mass election in U.S. history. In earlier elections, few people were entitled to vote. States began to drop restrictive requirements for voting after 1800, and voting rights for white males expanded even faster after 1815 (see Chapter 7). With the expansion of suffrage, more states began to allow voters, rather than state legislatures, to choose the presidential electors. Although voters had directly chosen many presidential electors in 1824, the total votes cast in that election numbered fewer than 370,000. By 1828, relaxed requirements for voting (and the use of popular elections to select presidential electors in more states) had increased the vote by more than 300 percent, to more than 1.1 million.

As the electorate expanded, the parties changed. No longer could a party rely on a few political leaders in the state legislatures to control votes in the electoral college. Parties now needed to campaign for votes cast by hundreds of thousands of citizens. Recognizing this new dimension of the nation's politics, the parties responded with a new method for nominating presidential candidates. Instead of selecting candidates in a closed caucus of party representatives in Congress, the parties devised the **national convention**. At these gatherings, delegates from state parties across the nation would choose candidates for president and vice president and adopt a statement of policies called a **party platform**. The Anti-Masonic Party, which was the first "third" party in American history to challenge the two major parties for the presidency, called the first national convention in 1831. The Democrats adopted the convention idea in 1832 to nominate Jackson for a second term, as did their new opponents that year, the National Republicans.

The label *National Republicans* applied to John Quincy Adams's faction of the former Democratic Republican Party. However, the National Republicans did not become today's Republican Party. Adams's followers called themselves National Republicans to signify their old Federalist preference for a strong national government, but the symbolism did not appeal to the voters, and the National Republicans lost to Jackson in 1832.

Elected to another term, Jackson began to assert the power of the nation over the states (acting more like a National Republican than a Democrat). His policies drew new opponents, who started calling him "King Andrew." A coalition made up of former National Republicans, Anti-Masons, and Jackson haters formed the Whig Party in 1834. The name referred to the English Whigs, who opposed the powers of the British

national convention
A gathering of delegates of a single political party from across the country to choose candidates for president and vice president and to adopt a party platform.

party platform
The statement of policies of a national political party.

throne; the implication was that Jackson was governing like a king. For the next thirty years, Democrats and Whigs alternated in the presidency. However, the issues of slavery and sectionalism eventually destroyed the Whigs from within. Although the party had won the White House in 1848 and had taken 44 percent of the vote in 1852, the Whigs were unable to field a presidential candidate in the 1856 election.

The Current Party System: Democrats and Republicans

In the early 1850s, antislavery forces (including some Whigs and antislavery Democrats) began to organize. At meetings in Jackson, Michigan, and Ripon, Wisconsin, they recommended the formation of a new party, the Republican Party, to oppose the extension of slavery into the Kansas and Nebraska territories. This party, founded in 1854, continues as today's Republican Party.

The Republican Party entered its first presidential election in 1856. It took 33 percent of the vote, and its candidate, John Frémont, carried eleven states—all in the North. Then, in 1860, the Republicans nominated Abraham Lincoln. The Democrats were deeply divided over the slavery issue and split into two parties. The Northern Democrats nominated Stephen Douglas. The Southern Democrats ran John Breckinridge. A fourth party, the Constitutional Union Party, nominated John Bell. Breckinridge won every southern state. Lincoln took 40 percent of the popular vote and carried every northern state.

The election of 1860 is considered the first of four critical elections under the current party system.[12] A **critical election** is marked by a sharp change in the existing patterns of party loyalty among groups of voters. Moreover, this change in voting patterns, which is called an **electoral realignment,** does not end with the election but persists through several subsequent elections.[13] The election of 1860 divided the country politically between the northern states, whose voters mainly voted Republican, and the southern states, which were overwhelmingly Democratic. The victory of the North over the South in the Civil War cemented Democratic loyalties in the South.

For forty years, from 1880 to 1920, no Republican presidential candidate won even one of the eleven states of the former Confederacy. The South's solid Democratic record earned it the nickname the "Solid South." (Today's students may be puzzled, for the South has been "solid" for Republicans throughout their lifetimes.[14] That was not true prior to 1950, and the change is addressed below.) The Republicans did not puncture the Solid South until 1920, when Warren G. Harding carried Tennessee. The Republicans won five southern states in 1928, when the Democrats ran the first Catholic candidate, Al Smith. Republican presidential candidates won no more southern states until 1952, when Dwight Eisenhower broke the pattern of Democratic dominance in the South—ninety years after that pattern had been set by the Civil War.

Eras of Party Dominance Since the Civil War

The critical election of 1860 established the Democratic and Republican parties as the dominant parties in our two-party system. In a **two-party system,** most voters are so loyal to one or the other of the major parties that independent candidates or candidates from a third party (which means any minor party) have little chance of winning office. Third-party candidates tend to be more successful at the local or state level. Since the current two-party system was established, relatively few minor-party candidates have won election to the U.S. House, even fewer have won election to the Senate, and none has won the presidency.

critical election
An election that produces a sharp change in the existing pattern of party loyalties among groups of voters.

electoral realignment
The change in voting patterns that occurs after a critical election.

two-party system
A political system in which two major political parties compete for control of the government. Candidates from a third party have little chance of winning office.

The voters in a given state, county, or community are not always equally divided in their loyalties between the Republicans and the Democrats. In some areas, voters typically favor the Republicans, whereas voters in other areas prefer the Democrats. When one party in a two-party system regularly enjoys support from most voters in an area, it is called the *majority party* in that area; the other is called the *minority party*. Since the inception of the current two-party system, four periods (1860–1894, 1896–1930, 1932–1964, and 1968 to the present) have characterized the balance between the two major parties at the national level.

A Rough Balance: 1860–1894. From 1860 through 1894, the Grand Old Party (or GOP, as the Republican Party is sometimes called) won eight of ten presidential elections, which would seem to qualify it as the majority party. However, some of its success in presidential elections came from its practice of running Civil War heroes and from the North's domination of southern politics. Seats in the House of Representatives are a better guide to the breadth of national support. An analysis shows that the Republicans and Democrats won an equal number of congressional elections, each controlling the chamber for nine sessions between 1860 and 1894.

A Republican Majority: 1896–1930. A second critical election, in 1896, transformed the Republican Party into a true majority party. Grover Cleveland, a Democrat, occupied the White House, and the country was in a severe depression. The Republicans nominated William McKinley, governor of Ohio and a conservative, who stood for a high tariff against foreign goods and sound money tied to the value of gold. Rather than tour the country seeking votes, McKinley ran a sedentary campaign from his Ohio home.

The Democrats, already in trouble because of the depression, nominated the fiery William Jennings Bryan. In stark contrast to McKinley, Bryan advocated the free and unlimited coinage of silver, which would mean cheap money and easy payment of debts through inflation. Bryan was also the nominee of the young Populist Party, an agrarian protest party that had proposed the free-silver platform Bryan adopted. Conservatives, especially businesspeople, were aghast at the Democrats' radical turn, and voters in the heavily populated Northeast and Midwest surged toward the Republican Party, many of them permanently. McKinley carried every northern state east of the Mississippi. The Republicans also won the House, and they retained their control of it in the next six elections.

The election of 1896 helped solidify a Republican majority in industrial America and forged a link between the Republican Party and business. In the subsequent electoral realignment, the Republicans emerged as a true majority party. The GOP dominated national politics—controlling the

Library of Congress Prints and Photographs Division Washington, D.C

William Jennings Bryan: When Candidates Were Orators

Today, televised images of a candidate waving his hands and shouting to an audience would look silly. But candidates once had to resort to such tactics to be effective with large crowds. One of the most commanding orators around the turn of the twentieth century was William Jennings Bryan (1860–1925), whose stirring speeches extolling the virtues of the free coinage of silver were music to the ears of thousands of westerners and southern farmers.

presidency, the Senate, and the House—almost continuously from 1896 until the Wall Street crash of 1929, which burst big business's bubble and launched the Great Depression.*

A Democratic Majority: 1932–1964.

The Republicans' majority status ended in the critical election of 1932 between incumbent president Herbert Hoover and the Democratic challenger, Franklin Delano Roosevelt. Roosevelt promised new solutions to unemployment and the economic crisis of the Great Depression. His campaign appealed to labor, middle-class liberals, and new European ethnic voters. Along with Democratic voters in the Solid South, urban workers in the North, Catholics, Jews, and white ethnic minorities formed "the Roosevelt coalition." The relatively few blacks who voted at that time tended to remain loyal to the Republicans—"the party of Lincoln."

Roosevelt was swept into office in a landslide, carrying huge Democratic majorities with him into the House and Senate to enact his liberal activist programs. The electoral realignment reflected by the election of 1932 made the Democrats the majority party. Not only was Roosevelt reelected in 1936, 1940, and 1944, but also Democrats held control of both houses of Congress in most sessions from 1933 through 1964. The only exceptions were Republican control of the House and Senate in 1947 and 1948 (under President Truman) and in 1953 and 1954 (under President Eisenhower). The Democrats also won the presidency in seven of nine elections. Moreover, national surveys from 1952 through 1964 show that Americans of voting age consistently and decidedly favored the Democratic Party.

A Rough Balance: 1968 to the Present.

Scholars agree that an electoral realignment occurred after 1964, and some attribute the realignment to the turbulent election of 1968, sometimes called the fourth critical election.[15] The Republican Richard Nixon won in a very close race by winning five of the eleven southern states in the old Confederacy, while Democrat Hubert Humphrey won only one. The other five states were won by George Wallace, the candidate of the American Independent Party, made up primarily of southerners who defected from the Democratic Party. Wallace won no states outside the South.

Since 1968, Republican candidates for president have run very well in southern states and tended to win election—Nixon (twice), Reagan (twice), G. H. W. Bush, and G. W. Bush (twice). The record of party control of Congress has been more mixed since 1968. Democrats have controlled the House for most of the sessions, while the parties have split control of the Senate almost evenly. Therefore, the period since 1968 rates as a "rough balance" between the parties, much like the period from 1860 to 1894. Today, both parties nationally are fairly close in electoral strength. However, the North–South coalition of Democratic voters forged by Roosevelt in the 1930s has completely crumbled. Two southern scholars wrote:

> It is easy to forget just how thoroughly the Democratic party once dominated southern congressional elections. In 1950 there were no Republican senators from the South and only 2 Republican representatives out of 105 in the southern House delegation.... A half-century later Republicans constituted *majorities* of the South's congressional delegations—13 of 22 southern senators and 71 of 125 representatives.[16]

---

*The only break in the GOP domination was in 1912, when Teddy Roosevelt's Progressive Conservative Party split from the Republicans, allowing Democrat Woodrow Wilson to win the presidency and giving the Democrats control of Congress, and again in 1916 when Wilson was reelected.

electoral dealignment
A lessening of the importance of party loyalties in voting decisions.

Although party loyalty within regions has shifted inexorably, the Democratic coalition of urban workers and ethnic minorities still seems intact, if weakened. Indeed, rural voters have become decidedly more Republican.[17] Some scholars say that in the 1970s and 1980s, we were in a period of **electoral dealignment**, in which party loyalties became less important to voters as they cast their ballots. Others counter that partisanship increased in the 1990s in a gradual process of realignment not marked by a single critical election.[18] We examine the influence of party loyalty on voting in the next chapter, after we look at the operation of our two-party system.

The American Two-Party System

LO3 ★ Explain why two parties dominate the history of American politics.

Our review of party history in the United States has focused on the two dominant parties. But we should not ignore the special contributions of certain minor parties, among them the Anti-Masonic Party, the Populists, and the Progressives of 1912. In this section, we study the fortunes of minor, or third, parties in American politics. We also look at why we have only two major parties, explain how federalism helps the parties survive, and describe voters' loyalty to the two major parties today.

Minor Parties in America

Minor parties have always figured in party politics in America. Most minor parties in our political history have been one of four types:[19]

- *Bolter parties* are formed by factions that have split off from one of the major parties. Seven times in the thirty-eight presidential elections from the Civil War to 2012, disgruntled leaders have "bolted the ticket" and challenged their former parties by forming new parties.* Bolter parties have occasionally won significant proportions of the vote. However, with the exception of Teddy Roosevelt's Progressive Party in 1912 and the possible exception of George Wallace's American Independent Party in 1968, bolter parties have not affected the outcome of presidential elections.

- *Farmer-labor parties* represented farmers and urban workers who believed that they, the working class, were not getting their share of society's wealth. The People's Party, founded in 1892 and nicknamed the "Populist Party," was a prime example of a farmer-labor party. The Populists won 8.5 percent of the vote in 1892 and also became the first third party since 1860 to win any electoral votes. Flushed by success, it endorsed William Jennings Bryan, the Democratic candidate, in 1896. When he lost, the party quickly faded. Farm and labor groups revived many Populist ideas in the Progressive Party in 1924, which nominated Robert La Follette for the presidency. Although the party won 16.6 percent of the popular vote, it carried only La Follette's home state of Wisconsin and died in 1925. In 1944, however, the

---

*The seven candidates who bolted from their former parties and ran for president on a third-party ticket were Theodore Roosevelt (1912), Robert La Follette (1924), Henry A. Wallace (1948), Strom Thurmond (1948), George Wallace (1968), John Anderson (1980), and Pat Buchanan (2000). Thurmond and both Wallaces had been Democrats; the others had originally been elected to office as Republicans. Note that Harry Truman won reelection in 1948 despite facing opposition from former Democrats running as candidates of other parties.

Minnesota Farmer-Labor Party merged with the Democrats to form the Democratic Farmer-Labor (DFL) Party. The DFL is Minnesota's Democratic Party today.

- *Parties of ideological protest* go further than farmer-labor parties in criticizing the established system. These parties reject prevailing doctrines and propose radically different principles, often favoring more government activism. The Socialist Party has been the most successful party of ideological protest. Even at its high point in 1912, however, it garnered only 6 percent of the vote, and Socialist candidates for president have never won a single state. Nevertheless, the Socialist Party persists, fielding a presidential ticket again in 2012. In recent years, protest parties have tended to come from the right, arguing against government action in society. Such is the program of the Libertarian Party, which stresses freedom over order and equality (see page 20). In contrast, the Green Party protests from the left, favoring government action to preserve the environment. Together, the Libertarian and Green parties polled just over 1 percent of the total vote for their presidential candidates in 2012. Although both parties together ran nearly two hundred congressional candidates, they won relatively few votes (see Figure 8.2) and no seats.

- *Single-issue parties* are formed to promote one principle, not a general philosophy of government. The Anti-Masonic parties of the 1820s and 1830s, for example, opposed Masonic lodges and other secret societies. The Free Soil Party of the 1840s and 1850s worked to abolish slavery. The Prohibition Party, the most durable example of a single-issue party, was founded to oppose the consumption of alcoholic beverages, but recently its platform has taken conservative positions: favoring right-to-life, limiting immigration, and urging withdrawal from the World Bank. Prohibition candidates consistently won from 1 to 2 percent of the vote in nine presidential elections between 1884 and 1916, and the party has run candidates in every presidential election since, usually winning only a trickle of votes.

America has a long history of third parties that operate on the periphery of our two-party system. Minor parties form primarily to express some voters' discontent with choices offered by the major parties and to work for their own objectives within the electoral system.[20]

How have minor parties fared historically? As vote getters, they have not performed well. However, bolter parties have twice won more than 10 percent of the vote. (Although Ross Perot won 19 percent of the vote in 1992, he ran as an independent. When he created the Reform Party and ran as its candidate in 1996, he won only 8 percent.)[21] More significantly, the Republican Party originated in 1854 as a

The Libertarian Party, http://www.lp.org

A Third-Party Theme

The Libertarian Party values freedom above both order and equality. Founded in 1971, the party has run presidential candidates in every election since 1972. It was most successful in 1980, when Libertarian Ed Clark won about 920,000 votes, which was 1.06 percent of all votes cast. In 2012, Libertarian Gary Johnson won more votes (about 1,155,000), but they were only 0.97 percent of the total. Ron Paul, its 1988 presidential candidate, was elected to Congress in 1996 as a Republican. His son, Rand Paul, was elected to the Senate also as a Republican. None of the hundreds of Libertarian candidates in recent congressional elections was elected. Nevertheless, the Libertarian Party's website justifiably describes itself as "America's third largest and fastest growing political party." That says something about the state of third parties in the United States.

FIGURE 8.2 Party Candidates for the U.S. House in the 2014 Election

In 2014, as in other recent elections, the Democratic and Republican parties each ran candidates for the House of Representatives in about 90 percent of the 435 congressional districts. Of minor parties, only the Libertarian Party, the best-organized minor party in the nation, ran candidates in more than one hundred districts. In most of those districts, however, the Libertarian candidates usually got about 3 percent of the vote when they ran. All other minor parties ran fewer candidates than the Libertarians.

Sources: Candidate data come from *Ballot Access News*, 30 (October 1, 2014), p. 4; estimated percentage of votes cast come from Pew Research Center, at http://www.pewresearch.org/facttank/2014/11/05/as-gop-celebrates-win-no-sign-of-narrowing-gender-age-gaps/.

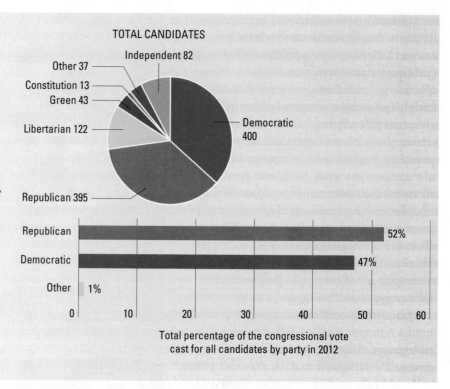

TOTAL CANDIDATES

Independent 82
Other 37
Constitution 13
Green 43
Libertarian 122
Democratic 400
Republican 395

Republican   52%
Democratic   47%
Other   1%

0   10   20   30   40   50   60

Total percentage of the congressional vote cast for all candidates by party in 2012

single-issue third party opposed to slavery in the nation's new territories. In its first election, in 1856, the party came in second, displacing the Whigs. (Undoubtedly, the Republican exception to the rule has inspired the formation of other hopeful third parties.) Although surveys repeatedly show over half the public saying they want a third major party, voters tend not to support them at the polls.[22]

As policy advocates, minor parties have a slightly better record. At times, they have had a real effect on the policies adopted by the major parties. Women's suffrage, the graduated income tax, and the direct election of senators all originated with third parties. Of course, third parties may fail to win more votes simply because their policies lack popular support. The Democrats learned this lesson in 1896, when they adopted the Populists' free-silver plank in their own platform. Both their candidate and their platform went down to defeat, hobbling the Democratic Party for decades. Beginning around the 1930s, third-party voting began to decline. Research attributes the decline to the Democratic Party's leftward shift to encompass issues raised by minor parties.[23]

Most important, minor parties function as safety valves. They allow those who are unhappy with the status quo to express their discontent within the system, to contribute to the political dialogue. Surely this was the function of Ralph Nader as the Green Party candidate in 2000, when it won 2.7 percent of the vote. (By drawing votes from Democrat Al Gore in key states, Nader also denied Gore a victory over George Bush in the closest popular vote in history.) If minor parties and independent candidates are indicators of discontent, what should we make of the numerous minor parties, detailed in Figure 8.3, which took part in the 2012 election? Not much. The number of third parties that contest elections is less important than the total number of votes they receive. Despite the presence of numerous minor parties in every presidential election, the two major parties usually collect more than 95 percent of the vote, as they did in 2012 despite challenges from candidates of other parties. In the 2010 congressional elections, the tea party movement blew off steam within the Republican Party by backing more conservative candidates. In that sense, it acted like a minor party, as a safety valve.

FIGURE 8.3 Candidates and Parties in the 2012 Presidential Election

CANDIDATE AND PARTY*	TOTAL POPULAR VOTE	PERCENTAGE OF POPULAR VOTE
Barack Obama (Democratic)	65,915,796	0.51
Mitt Romney (Republican)	60,933,500	0.47
Gary Johnson (Libertarian)	1,275,971	0.0099
Jill Stein (Green)	469,628	0.0036
Virgil Goode (Constitution)	122,388	0.00
Roseann Barr (Peace and Freedom)	67,326	0.00
Rocky Anderson (Justice)	43,018	0.00
Tom Hoefling (America's)	40,628	0.00
Randall Terry (Independent)	13,105	0.00
Richard Duncan (Independent)	12,557	0.00
Peta Lindsay (Socialism and Liberation)	7,791	0.00
Chuck Baldwin (Kansas Reform)	5,017	0.00
Will Christensen (Oregon constitution)	4,453	0.00
Stewart Alexander (Socialist)	4,405	0.00
James Harris (Socialist workers)	4,117	0.00
Thomas Stevens (Objectivist)	4,091	0.00
Jim Carlson (Grassroots)	3,149	0.00
Merlin Miller (American third position)	2,875	0.00
Samm Tittle (We the people)	2,701	0.00
Jill Reed (Twelve positions)	2,572	0.00
Gloria La Riva (Socialism and liberation)	1,608	0.00
Jerry Litzel (Independent)	1,279	0.00
Jerry White (Socialist equality)	1,094	0.00
Dean Morstad (Constitutional government)	1,027	0.00
Barbara Washer (Mississippi reform)	1,016	0.00
Jeff Boss (NSA Did 911)	1,007	0.00
Andre Barnett (Reform)	956	0.00
Jack Fellure (Prohibition)	518	0.00
Total	129,085,403	

*Party designations varied in some states.

In addition to the candidates of the two major parties, twenty-six other candidates ran in various states under banners of more than a dozen parties. All of them together, however, captured less than 2 percent of the total vote.

Source: Federal Election Commission at http://www.fec.gov/pubrec/fe2012/2012pres.pdf.

Why a Two-Party System?

The history of party politics in the United States is essentially the story of two parties that have alternating control of the government. With relatively few exceptions, Americans conduct elections at all levels within the two-party system. Nevertheless, surveys show that about half of the population today think that the United States needs a third party. Why does the United States have only two major parties? Other democratic countries usually have multiparty systems, but they typically involve more than three parties. In truth, a political system with three relatively equal parties has never existed over a length of time in any country, for it is inherently unstable.[24]

The two most convincing explanations for the two-party system in the United States lie (1) in its electoral system and (2) in our historical pattern of political socialization. Consider first the electoral system, which sets the "rules of the game" under which the parties play. Think of a U.S. election as a prizefight between two boxers. If a third boxer enters the ring, two gang up on one. In the typical U.S. election, two or more candidates contest each office, and the winner is the single candidate who collects the most votes, whether those votes constitute a majority or not. That rule tends to put only two candidates in the ring in the first place, resulting in the inherent instability of three-party systems. The two principles of *single winners* chosen by a *simple plurality* of votes produce an electoral system known as **majority representation** (despite its reliance on pluralities rather than majorities). Think about how American states choose representatives to Congress. A state entitled to ten representatives is divided into ten congressional districts, and each district elects one representative. Almost always, the ten representatives are Democrats and Republicans. Majority representation of voters through single-member districts is also a feature of most state legislatures.

Alternatively, a legislature might be chosen through a system of **proportional representation**, which awards legislative seats to each party in proportion to the total number of votes it wins in an election. Under this system, the state might hold a single statewide election for all ten seats, with multiple parties presenting their rank ordered lists of ten candidates. Voters could vote for the party list they preferred, and the party's candidates would be elected from the top of each list, according to the proportion of votes won by the party. Thus, if a party got 30 percent of the vote in this example, its first three candidates would be elected.[25]

Although this form of election may seem strange, more democratic countries use it than use our system of majority representation. Proportional representation tends to produce (or perpetuate) several parties because each can win enough seats nationwide to wield some influence in the legislature. In contrast, our system of elections forces interest groups of all sorts to work within the two major parties, for only one candidate in each race stands a chance of being elected under plurality voting. Therefore, the system tends to produce only two parties. Moreover, the two major parties benefit from state laws that automatically list candidates on the ballot if their party won a sizable percentage of the vote in the previous election. These laws discourage minor parties, which usually have to collect thousands of signatures to get on a state ballot.[26]

The rules of our electoral system may explain why only two parties tend to form in specific election districts, but why do the same two parties (Democratic and Republican) operate within every state? The contest for the presidency is the key to this question. A candidate can win a presidential election only by amassing a majority of electoral votes from across the entire nation. Presidential candidates try to win votes under the same party label in each state in order to pool their electoral votes in the electoral college. The presidency is a big enough political prize to induce parties to harbor uncomfortable coalitions of voters (southern white Protestants allied with northern Jews and blacks in the Democratic Party, for example) just to win the electoral vote and the presidential election.

The American electoral system may force U.S. politics into a two-party mold, but why must the same two parties reappear from election to election? In fact, they do not. The earliest two-party system pitted the Federalists against the Democratic Republicans. A later two-party system involved the Democrats and the Whigs. More than 135 years ago, the Republicans replaced the Whigs in what is our two-party system today. But with modern issues so different from the issues then, why do the Democrats and Republicans persist? This is where the second explanation, political socialization, comes into play. The two parties persist simply because they have persisted. After more than one hundred years of political socialization, the two parties today have such a head start in structuring the vote that they discourage challenges from new parties. Third parties

majority representation
The system by which one office, contested by two or more candidates, is won by the single candidate who collects the most votes.

proportional representation
The system by which legislative seats are awarded to a party in proportion to the vote that party wins in an election.

still try to crack the two-party system from time to time, but most have had little success. In truth, the two parties in power also write laws that make it hard for minor parties to get on the ballot, such as requiring petitions with thousands of signatures.[27]

The Federal Basis of the Party System

Focusing on contests for the presidency is a convenient and informative way to study the history of American parties, but it also oversimplifies party politics to the point of distortion. By concentrating only on presidential elections, we tend to ignore electoral patterns in the states, where elections often buck national trends. Even during its darkest defeats for the presidency, a party can still claim many victories for state offices. Victories outside the arena of presidential politics give each party a base of support that keeps its machinery oiled and ready for the next contest.[28]

Party Identification in America

The concept of **party identification** is one of the most important in political science. It signifies a voter's sense of psychological attachment to a party (which is not the same thing as voting for the party in any given election). Scholars measure party identification simply by asking, "Do you usually think of yourself as a Republican, a Democrat, an independent, or what?"[29] Voting is a behavior; identification is a state of mind. For example, millions of southerners voted for Eisenhower for president in 1952 and 1956 but continued to consider themselves Democrats. Again in the 1980s, millions of voters temporarily became "Reagan Democrats." Across the nation, more people identify with one of the two major parties than reject a party attachment. The proportions of self-identified Republicans, Democrats, and independents (no party attachment) in the electorate since 1952 are shown in Figure 8.4. Three significant points stand out:

party identification
A voter's sense of psychological attachment to a party.

- The proportion of Republicans and Democrats combined has exceeded that of independents in every year.
- The proportion of Democrats has consistently exceeded that of Republicans but has shrunk over time.
- The proportion of independents has nearly doubled over the period.

Although party identification predisposes citizens to vote for their favorite party, other factors may convince them to choose the opposition candidate. If they vote against their party often enough, they may rethink their party identification and eventually switch. Apparently, this rethinking has gone on in the minds of many southern Democrats over time. In 1952, about 70 percent of white southerners thought of themselves as Democrats, and fewer than 20 percent thought of themselves as Republicans. In 2012, white southerners were only 24 percent Democratic, whereas 35 percent were Republican and 41 percent were independent.[30] Much of the nationwide growth in the proportion of Republicans and independents (and the parallel drop in the number of Democrats) stems from changes in party preferences among white southerners and from migration of northerners, which translated into substantial gains in the proportion of Republicans.

Who are the self-identified Democrats and Republicans in the electorate? Figure 8.5 shows party identification by various social groups in 2012. The effects of socioeconomic factors are clear. People who have lower incomes and less education are more likely to think of themselves as Democrats rather than as Republicans. However, citizens with advanced degrees (such as college faculty) are more Democratic. The cultural factors of religion and ethnicity produce even sharper differences between the

FIGURE 8.4 Distribution of Party Identification, 1952–2012

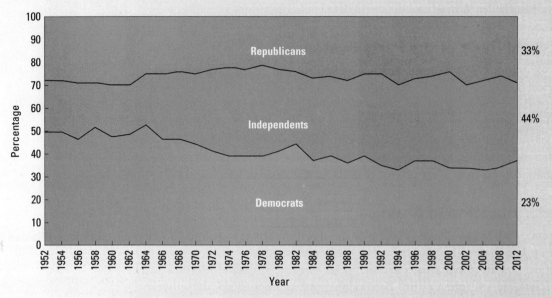

In every presidential election since 1952, voters across the nation have been asked, "Generally speaking, do you usually think of yourself as a Republican, a Democrat, an independent, or what?" Most voters think of themselves as either Republicans or Democrats, but the proportion of those who think of themselves as independents has increased over time. The size of the Democratic Party's majority has also shrunk. Nevertheless, most Americans today still identify with one of the two major parties, and Democrats still outnumber Republicans.

Sources: Data for 1952 to 2008 come from the American National Election Studies Guide to Public Opinion and Electoral Behavior, http://www.electionstudies. org/nesguide/nesguide.htm. The 2012 figure is from the 2012 ANES Time Series tabulated at the Survey Documentation and Analysis website, http://sda.berkeley.edu/archive.htm. The few respondents (typically under 5 percent) who gave other answers were excluded from the graph.

parties. Those who are unaffiliated with a religious group are strongly Democratic compared with those affiliated with religious groups but are mainly independent. Non-Hispanic whites are markedly more Republican than those in other ethnic groups. Finally, American politics has a gender gap: more women tend to be Democrats than men, and (although not shown here) this gap seems to widen with women's greater education.[31] The youngest citizens are more apt to be Democrats than Republicans, but most are independents. People tend to acquire party identification as they age.

The influence of region on party identification has changed over time, and strong regional differences no longer exist. Because of the high proportion of blacks in the South, it is still predominantly Democratic (in party identity, but not in voting because of lower turnout among low-income blacks). Despite the erosion of Democratic strength in the South, we still see elements of Roosevelt's old Democratic coalition of different socioeconomic groups. Perhaps the major change in that coalition has been the replacement of white European ethnic groups by blacks, attracted by the Democrats' backing of civil rights legislation in the 1960s leading to the critical election of 1968.

Nonwhites in general have become more Democratic than Republican today, as the ethnic composition of the United States is inexorably becoming less white. Estimated at 65 percent in 2010, the non-Latino white population is projected to be only 58 percent in 2030. The Latino and nonwhite share of the population, estimated at 36 percent in 2010, is projected to be 44 percent by 2030.[32] Given that blacks, Asians, and Latinos are strongly Democratic, the Republican Party faces problems in the partisan implications of demographic change.

FIGURE 8.5 Party Identification by Social Groups

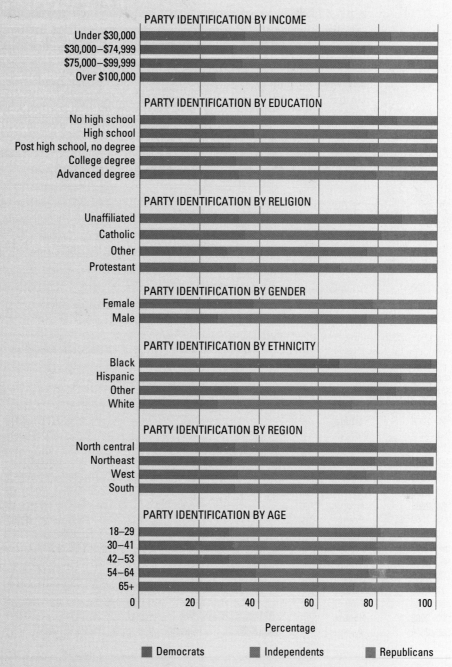

Respondents to a 2012 survey were grouped by seven socioeconomic criteria—income, education, religion, gender, ethnicity, region, and age—and analyzed according to their self-descriptions as Democrats, independents, or Republicans. As income increases, people are more likely to vote Republican. The same is true for education, except for those with advanced degrees. Protestants are far more likely to be Republican than those without religious affiliation, while women, Hispanics, and all nonwhite groups are more likely to be Democrats. Party identification varies relatively little by region. The main effect of age was to reduce the proportion of independents as respondents grew older. Younger citizens who tend to think of themselves as independents are likely to develop an identification with one party or the other as they mature.

Source: Data come from the January 11–16, 2012 survey by the Pew Research Center for the People & the Press, kindly supplied by Senior Researcher, Dr. Leah Melani Christian. Rounding errors were adjusted to total to 100 percent for each group.

Studies show that about half of all Americans adopt their parents' party. But it often takes time for party identification to develop. The youngest group of voters is most likely to be independent, but people in their thirties and forties, who were socialized during the Reagan and first Bush presidencies, are more Republican. The oldest group not only is strongly Democratic but also shows the greatest partisan commitment (fewest independents), reflecting the fact that citizens become more interested in politics as they mature.[33] While partisanship has been declining in the United States, that is true elsewhere too.

Political Partying in Global Politics

As shown earlier in Figure 8.4, the proportion of Americans who identify with the Republican or Democratic parties has declined over time, while the proportion of independents has increased. This chart shows a similar decline in formal party members for most European countries where citizens formally belong to political parties. Among nineteen European countries that provide available data over time, only Greece and Spain show an increase in party members as a percentage of the electorate. (Similar data exist for party identification in European countries.) Citizens everywhere seem less likely to party.

Gain (green) or loss (red) in party members as a percent of the electorate over years shown

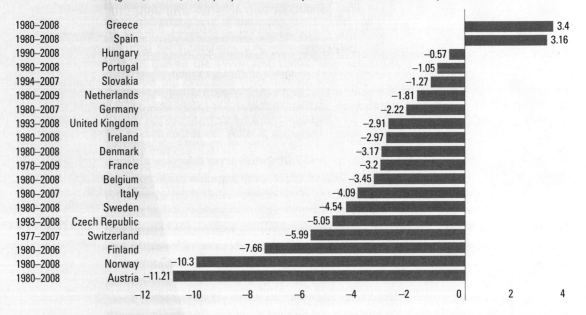

Years	Country	Value
1980–2008	Greece	3.4
1980–2008	Spain	3.16
1990–2008	Hungary	−0.57
1980–2008	Portugal	−1.05
1994–2007	Slovakia	−1.27
1980–2009	Netherlands	−1.81
1980–2007	Germany	−2.22
1993–2008	United Kingdom	−2.91
1980–2008	Ireland	−2.97
1980–2008	Denmark	−3.17
1978–2009	France	−3.2
1980–2008	Belgium	−3.45
1980–2007	Italy	−4.09
1980–2008	Sweden	−4.54
1993–2008	Czech Republic	−5.05
1977–2007	Switzerland	−5.99
1980–2006	Finland	−7.66
1980–2008	Norway	−10.3
1980–2008	Austria	−11.21

Sources: Ingrid van Biezen, Peter Mair, and Thomas Poguntke, "Going, Going, … Gone? The Decline of Party Membership in Contemporary Europe," *European Journal of Political Research*, 51 (January 2012): 24–56. © 2011 Ingrid van Biezen, Peter Mair, and Thomas Poguntke, *European Journal of Political Research*. © 2011 European Consortium for Political Research. Reproduced by permission.

Critical Thinking Does the decline in party membership suggest an increase or a decrease in political participation? Is that good or bad for democratic government?

Americans tend to find their political niche and stay there.[34] The enduring party loyalty of American voters tends to structure the vote even before an election is held, and even before the candidates are chosen. In Chapter 9, we will examine the extent to which party identification determines voting choice. But first we will explore whether the Democratic and Republican parties have any significant differences between them.

Party Ideology and Organization

LO4 ★ Compare and contrast the Democratic and Republican parties on the basis of ideology and organization.

George Wallace, a disgruntled Democrat who ran for president in 1968 on the American Independent Party ticket, complained that "there isn't a dime's worth of difference" between the Democrats and Republicans (like Tweedledum and Tweedledee described at the start of this chapter). Decades earlier, humorist Will Rogers said, "I am not a member of any organized political party—I am a Democrat." Wallace's comment was made in disgust, Rogers's in jest. Wallace was wrong; Rogers was close to being right. Here we will dispel the myth that the parties do not differ significantly on issues and explain how they are organized to coordinate the activities of party candidates and officials in government.

Differences in Party Ideology

George Wallace notwithstanding, there is more than a dime's worth of difference between the two parties. In fact, the difference amounts to many billions of dollars— the cost of the different government programs each party supports. Democrats are more disposed to government spending to advance social welfare (and hence to promote equality) than are Republicans. And social welfare programs cost money, a lot of money. Republicans decry massive social spending, but they are not averse to spending billions of dollars for the projects they consider important, among them national defense. Ronald Reagan portrayed the Democrats as big spenders, but his administration spent more than $1 trillion for defense. His Strategic Defense Initiative (the missile defense program labeled "Star Wars") cost billions before it was curtailed under the Democrats.[35] Although President George W. Bush introduced a massive tax cut, he also revived spending on missile defense, backed a $400 billion increase in Medicare, and proposed building a space platform on the moon for travel to Mars. One result was a huge increase in the budget deficit and a rare *Wall Street Journal* editorial against the 2003 GOP "spending spree."[36] Reflecting the influence of the tea party, however, the Republican Party in 2012 fervently opposed government spending, whereas Democrats still supported spending for social programs and to stimulate the economy.

Involved and Uninvolved Voters. As discussed in Chapter 5, relatively few ordinary voters think about politics in ideological terms. Party activists often do, however. Figure 8.6 compares all voters with party identifiers classified by their political involvement. "Involved" identifiers said that they cared "a lot" about the 2012 presidential candidates; the "uninvolved" cared less. The middle of the graph shows 42 percent of all voters describing themselves as conservative versus 31 percent liberal. Uninvolved Democrats and Republicans differ somewhat more, with uninvolved Republicans being far more conservative. The ideological gap, however, becomes a

FIGURE 8.6 Ideologies of Involved and Uninvolved Party Voters in 2012

The Democratic and Republican parties differ substantially in their ideological centers of gravity, especially when party identifiers are classified according to their political involvement. Involved Democrats and Republicans were those who cared "a lot" about the 2012 presidential candidates. Uninvolved Democrats and Republicans cared less. Virtually none of the involved Republican identifiers described themselves as liberal, while almost all said they were conservative. Nearly half of involved Democrats described themselves as liberal.

Source: January 12, 2012 Pew Survey.

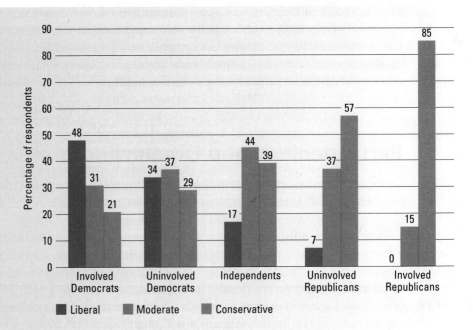

yawning chasm between involved Democrats, 48 percent of whom were liberal, versus involved Republicans, 85 percent being conservative.

Platforms: Freedom, Order, and Equality. Surveys of voters' ideological orientation may merely reflect differences in their personal self-image rather than actual differences in party ideology. For another test of party philosophy, we can look to the platforms adopted at party conventions. Although many people feel that party platforms don't matter very much, several scholars have demonstrated, using different approaches, that winning parties tend to carry out much of their platforms when in office.[37] One study matched the parties' platform statements from 1948 to 1985 against subsequent allocations of program funds in the federal budget. Spending priorities turned out to be quite closely linked to the platform emphases of the party that won control of Congress, especially if the party also controlled the presidency.[38]

Party platforms also matter a great deal to the parties' convention delegates—and to the interest groups that support the parties.[39] The wording of a platform plank often means the difference between victory and defeat for factions within a party. Delegates fight not only over ideas but also over words.

The platforms adopted at both parties' conventions in 2012 were similar in length (about 26,000 words for the Democrats and 31,000 for the Republicans) but strikingly different in content. The Republicans mentioned "free" or "freedom" more than three times as often (73 to 19), while the Democrats referred to "equal" or "equality" or "inequality" more than four times as much (23 to 4). Republicans talked more about order than Democrats, mentioning "crime" or "criminals" more often (33 to 26) and swamping the Democrats with talk about "marriage" (21 to 4) and "abortion" (20 to 4). Republicans also drummed on "spending" almost five times as frequently (29 to 6), while Democrats talked more about "discrimination" (18 to 9 mentions).

Different but Similar. The Democrats and the Republicans have very different ideological orientations. Yet many observers claim that the parties are really quite similar in ideology compared to the different parties of other countries. Although

Freedom, Order, or Equality?

Freedom v. Order v. Equality in Party Platforms

As discussed in the text, the 2012 platforms of the Republican and Democratic parties made strikingly different references to freedom, order, and equality. Republicans were almost four times as likely to mention "free" or "freedom" and five times as likely to invoke images of order by mentioning "marriage" or "abortion." Democrats, however, were almost six times as likely to use "equal" or "equality."

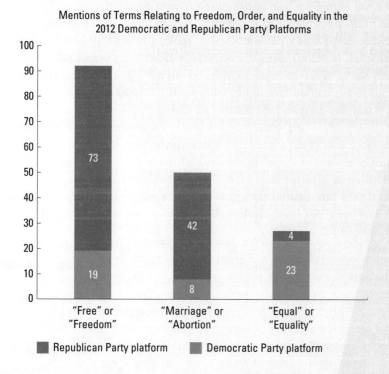

Mentions of Terms Relating to Freedom, Order, and Equality in the 2012 Democratic and Republican Party Platforms

■ Republican Party platform   ■ Democratic Party platform

Source: Personal research using 2012 party platforms at http://www.janda.org/politxts/PartyPlatforms/listing.html.

Critical Thinking Do the two parties' usage of these terms in their platforms match or contradict the ideological images that they project?

both Republicans and Democrats favor a market economy over a planned economy more than parties elsewhere, Republicans do so more strongly than Democrats. A major cross-national study of party positions in Western countries since 1945 concludes that the United States experiences "a form of party competition that is as ideologically (or non-ideologically) driven as the other countries we have studied."[40]

National Party Organization

Most casual observers would agree with Will Rogers's description of the Democrats as an unorganized political party. It used to apply to the Republicans too, but this has changed since the 1970s, at least at the national level. Bear in mind the distinction between levels of party structure. American parties parallel our federal system: they have separate national and state organizations (and functionally separate local organizations, in many cases).

At the national level, each major party has four main organizational components:

- *National convention.* Every four years, each party assembles thousands of delegates from the states and U.S. territories (such as Puerto Rico and Guam) in a national convention for the purpose of nominating a candidate for president. This presidential nominating convention is also the supreme governing body of the party. It determines party policy through the platform, formulates rules to govern party operations, and designates a national committee, which is empowered to govern the party until the next convention.

national committee
A committee of a political party composed of party chairpersons and party officials from every state.

- *National committee.* The **national committee**, which governs each party between conventions, is composed of party officials representing the states and territories, including the chairpersons of their party organizations. The Republican National Committee (RNC) has about 150 members, consisting of the national committeeman, national committeewoman, and a chairperson from each state and from the District of Columbia, Guam, Puerto Rico, and the Virgin Islands. The Democratic National Committee (DNC) has approximately 450 elected and appointed members, including, in addition to the national committee members and party chairs, members representing auxiliary organizations. The chairperson of each national committee is usually chosen by the party's presidential nominee and then duly elected by the committee. If the nominee loses the election, the national committee usually replaces the nominee's chairperson.

party conferences
A meeting to select party leaders and decide committee assignments, held at the beginning of a session of Congress by Republicans or Democrats in each chamber.

- *Congressional party conferences.* At the beginning of each session of Congress, the Republicans and Democrats in each chamber hold separate **party conferences** (the House Democrats call theirs a caucus) to select their party leaders and decide committee assignments. The party conferences deal only with congressional matters and have no structural relationship to each other and none with their national committees.

congressional campaign committee
An organization maintained by a political party to raise funds to support its own candidates in congressional elections.

- *Congressional campaign committees.* Democrats and Republicans in the House and Senate also maintain separate **congressional campaign committees,** each of which raises its own funds to support its candidates in congressional elections. The separation of these organizations from the national committee tells us that the national party structure is loose; the national committee seldom gets involved with the election of any individual member of Congress. Moreover, even the congressional campaign organizations merely supplement the funds that senators and representatives raise on their own to win reelection.

It is tempting to think of the national party chairperson as sitting at the top of a hierarchical party organization that not only controls its members in Congress but also issues orders to the state committees and on down to the local level. Few ideas could be more wrong.[41] In fact, the RNC and DNC do not even really direct or control the crucial presidential campaigns. Prospective nominees hire their own campaign staffs during the party primaries to win delegates who will support them for nomination at the party conventions. Successful nominees then keep their winning staffs to contest the general election. The main role of a national committee is to support its candidate's personal campaign staff in the effort to win.

In this light, the national committees appear to be relatively useless organizations—as reflected in the 1964 book about them, *Politics Without Power.*[42] For many years, their role was essentially limited to planning for the next party convention. The committee would select the site, invite the state parties to attend, plan the program, and so on. Beginning in the 1970s, however, the roles of the DNC and RNC began to expand—but in different ways.

The Democratic story was dramatic. During the Vietnam War in 1968, an unpopular President Lyndon Johnson was challenged for renomination by prominent Democrats, including Senators Robert F. Kennedy and Eugene McCarthy. On March 31, after primary elections had begun, Johnson chose not to run for reelection. His vice president, Hubert Humphrey, then announced his candidacy. A month later, Senator Kennedy was assassinated. Although Humphrey did not enter a single primary, he won the nomination over McCarthy at a riotous convention angry at the war and the role of party bosses in picking Humphrey. In an attempt to open the party to broader participation, a party commission formulated new guidelines for selecting delegates to the next convention in 1972. These guidelines promised party members a "full, meaningful and timely opportunity" to participate in the process. To comply with the new guidelines, many states used more open procedures, electing convention delegates in party primaries.

While the Democrats were busy in the 1970s with *procedural* reforms, the Republicans were making *organizational* reforms.[43] The RNC did little to open up its delegate selection process; Republicans were not inclined to impose quotas on state parties through their national committee. Instead, the RNC strengthened its fundraising, research, and service roles. Republicans acquired their own building and their own computer system, and in 1976 they hired the first full-time chairperson in the history of either national party. (Until then, the chairperson had worked part-time.) The new RNC chairman, William Brock, expanded the party's staff, launched new publications, held seminars, conducted election analyses, and advised candidates for state and legislative offices—things that national party committees in other countries had been doing for years. By the 2000 election, campaign finance analysts noted, American parties had become "an important source of funding in the race for the White House."[44]

The vast difference between the Democratic and Republican approaches to reforming the national committees shows in the funds raised by the DNC and RNC during election campaigns. Even though Republicans traditionally raised more campaign money than Democrats, they no longer relied on a relatively few wealthy contributors. As a matter of fact, the Republicans received more of their funds in small contributions (less than $100), mainly through direct-mail solicitation, than the Democrats. Until the 2008 election, the RNC raised far more money than the DNC, from many more citizens, as part of its long-term commitment to improving its organizational services. Beginning in 2002, however, significant changes occurred in how political parties could collect money to finance their activities. These campaign finance reforms are discussed in Chapter 9.

According to a major study of presidential party building, all Republican presidents, from Eisenhower through G. W. Bush, supported their national committee's organization efforts in order to build a Republican majority in the electorate. In contrast, Democratic presidents from Kennedy through Clinton "were not out to build a new majority but to make use of the one they had."[45] They tended to exploit, not build, the party organization. Obama fell back into the traditional pattern during his first term. By using his party to generate publicity for his administration's policy agenda while neglecting its organizational capacities at the state and local levels, Obama's behavior tended to parallel that of his Democratic predecessors.

State and Local Party Organizations

At one time, both major parties were firmly anchored by powerful state and local party organizations. Big-city party organizations, such as the Democrats' Tammany Hall in New York City and the Cook County Central Committee in Chicago, were called *party machines*.

party machine
A centralized party organization that dominates local politics by controlling elections.

A **party machine** was a centralized organization that dominated local politics by controlling elections—sometimes by illegal means, often by providing jobs and social services to urban workers in return for their votes. The patronage and social service functions of party machines were undercut when the government expanded unemployment compensation, aid to families with dependent children, and other social services. As a result, most local party organizations lost their ability to deliver votes and thus to determine the outcome of elections. However, machines remained strong in certain areas. In Nassau County, New York, for example, suburban Republicans showed that they could run a machine as well as urban Democrats.[46]

The individual state and local organizations of both parties vary widely in strength, but recent research has found that "neither the Republican nor Democratic party has a distinct advantage with regard to direct campaign activities."[47] Whereas once both the RNC and the DNC were dependent for their funding on "quotas" paid by state parties, now the funds flow the other way. In addition to money, state parties also received candidate training, poll data and research, and campaigning instruction.[48] The national committees have also taken a more active role in congressional campaigns.[49] In the 2009–2010 congressional election cycle, the national party campaign committees transferred over $50 million to state and local parties.[50]

Decentralized but Growing Stronger

COMPARE WITH YOUR PEERS
MindTap® for American Government

Access the Political Parties Forum: Discussion—Hurricane Sandy and Politics.

Although the national committees have gained strength over the past three decades, American political parties are still among the most decentralized parties in the world.[51] Not even the president can count on loyalty from the legislative members of his party. Consider the 2009 congressional vote on reforming health care, President Obama's most important policy initiative. Although the Democrats held 258 seats in the House, the bill passed only 220–215, as 39 Democrats (15 percent) voted against it. Although all Democrats voted for the bill to reach the 60 votes needed for passage in the Senate (all 39 Republicans opposed it), some Democratic senators demanded and got changes before backing the president's plan.

In 2013, the Republican Speaker of the House of Representatives, John Boehner, also had trouble commanding loyalty from his majority in the chamber. According to a moderate Republican congressman, about two dozen hardcore conservatives among the House Republicans constrained Boehner "on what he can deliver."[52] The 234 House Republicans were reportedly divided among different party factions: only about 44 members regularly supported the GOP leadership, but others—including more than 60 aligned with the tea party movement—held to their own demands.[53] Speaker Boehner lashed out at these hardline groups, saying, "They're pushing our members into places where they don't want to be."[54]

Decentralization of power has always been the most distinguishing characteristic of American political parties. Moreover, the rise in the proportion of citizens who style themselves as independents suggests that our already weak parties are in further decline.[55] But there is evidence that our political parties *as organizations* are enjoying a period of resurgence. Indeed, both national parties have "globalized" their organizations, maintaining branches in over a dozen nations.[56] Both parties' national committees have never been better funded or more active in grassroots campaign activities.[57]

And more votes in Congress are being decided along party lines. (See Chapter 11 for a discussion of the rise of party voting in Congress since the 1970s.) In fact, a specialist in congressional politics has concluded, "When compared to its predecessors of the past half-century, the current majority party leadership is more involved and more decisive in organizing the party and the chamber, setting the policy agenda, shaping legislation, and determining legislative outcomes."[58] However, the American parties have traditionally been so weak that these positive trends have not altered their basic character.[59] American political parties are still so organizationally diffuse and decentralized that they raise questions about how well they link voters to the government.

The Model of Responsible Party Government

LO5 ★ Identify the principles of responsible party government and evaluate their role in majoritarian democracy.

According to the majoritarian model of democracy, parties are essential to making the government responsive to public opinion. In fact, the ideal role of parties in majoritarian democracy has been formalized in the four principles of **responsible party government**:[60]

1. Parties should present clear and coherent programs to voters.
2. Voters should choose candidates on the basis of party programs.
3. The winning party should carry out its program once in office.
4. Voters should hold the governing party responsible at the next election for executing its program.

How well do these principles describe American politics? You've learned that the Democratic and Republican platforms are different and that they are much more ideologically consistent than many people believe. So the first principle is being met fairly well.[61] To a lesser extent, so is the third principle: once parties gain power, they usually try to do what they said they would do. As Obama's attempt to reform health care showed, however, not every party member will necessarily support the party's position. Moreover, the Republicans, who won control of the House of Representatives in the 2010 congressional election, failed to carry out their pledge to repeal Obama's health-care legislation, blocked by a Democratic Senate.

One can ask whether the model of responsible party government is suited to the American political system. Because governmental power is divided among the House, Senate, and president, a party must control all three components to carry out its program. In national surveys, people only favor one-party control of the presidency and Congress if their party is in control. Otherwise, a majority favors divided government or thinks it makes no difference.[62]

From the standpoint of democratic theory and responsible parties, the real question involves principles 2 and 4: Do voters really pay attention to party platforms and policies when they cast their ballots?[63] And if so, do voters hold the governing party responsible at the next election for delivering, or failing to deliver, on its pledges? To answer these questions, we must consider in greater detail the parties' role in nominating candidates and structuring the voters' choices in elections. At the conclusion of Chapter 9, we will return to evaluating the role of political parties in democratic government.

responsible party government
A set of principles formalizing the ideal role of parties in a majoritarian democracy.

CONNECT WITH YOUR CLASSMATES
MindTap⁻ **for American Government**

Access the Political Parties Forum: Discussion—Working Together After Elections.

Master the Topic of Political Parties with MindTap™ for American Government

REVIEW MindTap® for American Government
Access Key Term Flashcards for Chapter 8.

TEST YOURSELF MindTap® for American Government
Take the Wrap It Up Quiz for Chapter 8.

STAY CURRENT MindTap® for American Government
Access the KnowNow blog and customized RSS for updates on current events.

STAY FOCUSED MindTap® for American Government
Complete the Focus Activities for Political Parties.

Summary

LO1 Define political party and list the functions performed by parties in democratic government.

- Political parties perform four important functions: nominating candidates, structuring the voting choice, proposing alternative government programs, and coordinating the activities of government officials. Political parties have been performing these four functions longer in the United States than in any other country.

LO2 Outline the history of the U.S. political party system.

- The Democratic Party, founded in 1828, is the world's oldest political party. The Republican Party emerged as a major party after the 1856 election. Our two-party system has been marked by four critical elections: The election of 1860 established the Republicans as the major party in the North and the Democrats as the dominant party in the South. The election of 1896 strengthened the link between the Republican Party and business interests in the Northeast and Midwest, making it the majority party nationally for more than three decades. The election of 1932 during the Great Depression transformed the Democrats into the majority party for more than three decades. The election of 1968 ended the Democrats' domination of national politics, as Republican presidential candidates ran well in the South.

LO3 Explain why two parties dominate the history of American politics.

- Minor parties have contributed ideas to the Democratic and Republican platforms but have not enjoyed much electoral success in America. Our two-party system is perpetuated by two principles of our electoral system: single-member districts and plurality rule. The political socialization process causes most Americans to identify with either the Democratic or the Republican Party. Over the last sixty years, voters have been leaving the Democratic Party and becoming independents. Still, Democrats nationally outnumber Republicans, and together they outnumber independents.

LO4 Compare and contrast the Democratic and Republican parties on the basis of ideology and organization.

- Democratic identifiers and activists are more likely to describe themselves as liberal; Republican identifiers and activists tend to be conservative. Democratic Party platforms stress equality over freedom; Republican platforms stress freedom but also emphasize the importance of restoring social order. Organizationally, the Republicans have recently become the stronger party at both the national and state levels, and both parties are showing signs of resurgence. Nevertheless, both parties are still very decentralized compared with parties in other countries.

LO5 Identify the principles of responsible party government and evaluate their role in majoritarian democracy.

- According to the four principles of responsible party government, parties should present clear programs to voters and voters should choose candidates on the basis of party programs. The winning party should carry out its program, and voters should hold the party responsible for doing so. However, citizens tend not to pay much attention to platforms when voting.

Chapter Quiz

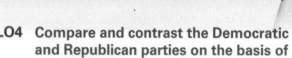

LO1 Define political party and list the functions performed by parties in democratic government.

1. How does a political party differ from an interest group?
2. What are the major functions of political parties?

LO2 Outline the history of the U.S. political party system.

1. How did the Twelfth Amendment to the Constitution affect how parties nominated presidential candidates?
2. How did the second party system differ from the first?

LO3 Explain why two parties dominate the history of American politics.

1. How does an electoral system based on majority representation favor two parties compared with one based on proportional representation?
2. What does "party identification" mean, how is it measured, and how stable has it been in America since the 1950s?

LO4 Compare and contrast the Democratic and Republican parties on the basis of ideology and organization.

1. How do the Democratic and Republican parties' platforms differ in invoking the concepts of freedom, order, and equality?
2. To what extent do the national committees of the Democratic and Republican parties control their parties' presidential campaigns?

LO5 Identify the principles of responsible party government and evaluate their role in majoritarian democracy.

1. Describe the ideal role of parties in majoritarian democracy and assess how American politics fits this ideal.
2. Is there any evidence that the two major American political parties fulfill the first principle of responsible party government?

9 Nominations, Elections, and Campaigns

Learning Outcomes

LO1 Describe how election campaigns have changed over time.

LO2 Explain the procedures followed in the nomination of both congressional and presidential candidates.

LO3 Describe the function of the electoral college and formulate arguments for and against the electoral vote system.

LO4 Analyze the American election campaign process in terms of political context, financial resources, and strategies and tactics for reaching the voters.

LO5 Assess the effects of party identification, political issues, and candidate attributes on voter choice.

LO6 Explain the significance of candidate-centered as opposed to party-centered election campaigns for both majoritarian and pluralist democracy.

 WATCH & LEARN MindTap for American Government

Watch a brief "What Do You Know?" video summarizing Elections and Campaigning for Office.

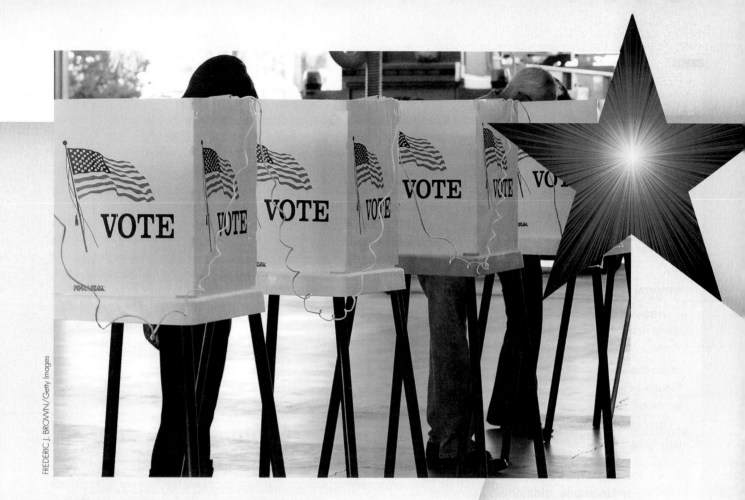

FREDERIC J. BROWN/Getty Images

The United States schedules its general elections according to planetary movement. In early November, after the Earth has traveled four times around the sun, we hold a presidential election. The timing is predictable but has little to do with politics.[1] Predictability does carry some advantages for political stability, but it also has some negative consequences. A major negative is the multiyear length of our presidential election campaigns. For example, presidential hopefuls in both parties began planning for the 2016 election right after the 2012 election—four years in advance. If elections were not held strictly according to the calendar, how else could a nation plan for them?

More countries across the world (and far more western European countries) hold general elections according to the needs of politics—according to voters' attitudes toward the government. In the typical European model, countries hold general elections to parliament following which the winning parties form governments. Although some countries limit the duration that governments can hold office, elections seldom occur on a predictable schedule. They are typically held either after governments lose their parliamentary support or when prime ministers judge it advantageous to hold elections to maintain, or perhaps increase, their parliamentary majorities.

So if you think that American presidential election campaigns last too long, blame the Constitution for fixing them according to the calendar every four years. Presidential hopefuls merely respond to the calendar as do Olympic hopefuls. Athletes know that the Olympic games are held every four years, so they begin training for them years ahead. Because politicians know that presidential elections will be held every four years, they too begin preparing for them four years early.

You may also think that general elections themselves are held too frequently and that voters have to make too many voting decisions. In truth, American voters do carry a heavier burden than most other voters. Whereas the American electorate votes every two years, electorates elsewhere vote less frequently. For example, the United States held eight general elections every two years from 2000 to 2014. During the same period, Britain and France held only three, Germany and Italy four, and Canada five.

Moreover, in the United States, an election is "general" in the sense that it includes various levels of government. Every two years, American voters are asked to choose among scores of candidates running for many different public offices at the local, state, and national levels. In most other countries, an election is "general" only in the sense that all parliamentary seats

237

are up for election. Individual voters only need to choose among slates of candidates offered by competing parties or among a limited number of candidates seeking seats in the voters' districts. The voters' burden is less both in how frequently they are required to go to the polls and also in terms of the complexity of choices they are asked to make.

In this chapter, we probe more deeply into elections in the United States. We study how candidates are nominated in and the factors that are important in causing voters to favor one nominee over another. We consider the role of election campaigns and how they have changed over time. We also address these important questions: How well do election campaigns inform voters? How important is money in conducting a winning campaign? What are the roles of party identification, issues, and candidate attributes in influencing voters' choices and thus election outcomes? How do campaigns, elections, and parties fit into the majoritarian and pluralist models of democracy?

LISTEN & LEARN
MindTap® for American Government

Access Read Speaker to listen to Chapter 9.

The Evolution of Campaigning

LO1 ★ Describe how election campaigns have changed over time.

Voting in free elections to choose leaders is the main way that citizens control government. As discussed in Chapter 8, political parties help structure the voting choice by reducing the number of candidates on the ballot to those who have a realistic chance of winning or who offer distinctive policies. An **election campaign** is an organized effort to persuade voters to choose one candidate over others competing for the same office. An effective campaign requires sufficient resources to acquire and analyze information about voters' interests, develop a strategy and matching tactics for appealing to these interests, deliver the candidate's message to the voters, and get them to cast their ballots.

election campaign
An organized effort to persuade voters to choose one candidate over others competing for the same office.

In the past, political parties conducted all phases of the election campaign. As recently as the 1950s, state and local party organizations "felt the pulse" of their rank-and-file members to learn what was important to the voters. They chose the candidates and then lined up leading officials to support them and to ensure big crowds at campaign rallies. They also prepared buttons, banners, and newspaper advertisements that touted their candidates, proudly named under the prominent label of the party. Finally, candidates relied heavily on the local precinct and county party organizations to contact voters before elections, to mention their names, to extol their virtues, and—most importantly—to make sure their supporters voted, and voted correctly.

Today, candidates seldom rely much on political parties to conduct their campaigns. How do candidates learn about voters' interests now? By contracting for public opinion polls, not by asking the party. How do candidates plan their campaign strategy and tactics? By hiring political consultants to devise clever sound bites (brief, catchy phrases) that will capture voters' attention on television, not by consulting party headquarters. How do candidates deliver their messages to voters? By conducting media campaigns, not by counting on party regulars to canvass the neighborhoods. Beginning with the 2004 election, presidential and congressional candidates have also relied heavily on the Internet to raise campaign funds and mobilize supporters.

Increasingly, election campaigns have evolved from being party centered to being candidate centered.[2] This is not to say that political parties no longer have a role to play in campaigns, for they do. As noted in Chapter 8, the Democratic National Committee now exercises more control over the delegate selection process than it did before 1972. Since 1976, the Republicans have greatly expanded their national organization and fundraising capacity. But whereas the parties virtually ran election campaigns prior to the 1960s, now they exist mainly to support candidate-centered campaigns by providing services or funds to their candidates. National party organizations also lost influence in conducting campaigns after a 2010 Supreme Court decision (discussed below) that allowed other political organizations to fund candidates. Nevertheless, we will see that the party label is usually a candidate's prime attribute at election time.

Perhaps the most important change in American elections is that candidates don't campaign just to get elected anymore. Due to the Progressive movement in the 1920s that championed use of the direct primary to select party candidates (see page 192), candidates must campaign for *nomination* as well. As we said in Chapter 8, nominating candidates to run for office under the party label is one of the main functions of political parties. Party organizations once controlled that function. Even Abraham Lincoln served only one term in the House of Representatives before the party transferred the nomination for his House seat to someone else.[3] For most important offices today, however, candidates are no longer nominated by the party organization but *within* the party. Except when recruiting prominent individuals to challenge entrenched incumbents, party leaders seldom choose candidates; they merely organize and supervise the election process by which party voters choose the candidates. Because almost all aspiring candidates must first win a primary election to gain their party's nomination, those who would campaign for election must first campaign for nomination.

Nominations

LO2 ★ Explain the procedures followed in the nomination of both congressional and presidential candidates.

The distinguishing feature of the nomination process in American party politics is that it usually involves an election by party voters. National party leaders do not choose their party's nominee for president or even its candidates for House and Senate seats. Virtually no other political parties in the world nominate candidates to the national legislature through party elections.[4] In more than half the world's parties, local party leaders choose legislative candidates, and their national party organization must usually approve these choices.

Democrats and Republicans nominate their candidates for national and state offices in varying ways across the country, because each state is entitled to make its own laws governing the nomination process. (This is significant in itself, for political parties in most other countries are largely free of laws stating how they must select their candidates.)[5] We can classify nomination practices by the types of party elections held and the level of office sought.

Nomination for Congress and State Offices

In the United States, almost all aspiring candidates for major offices are nominated through a **primary election**, a preliminary election conducted within the party to

primary election
A preliminary election conducted within a political party to select candidates who will run for public office in a subsequent election.

select its candidates. Some forty states use primary elections alone to nominate candidates for all state and national offices, and primaries figure in the nomination processes of all the other states. The rules governing primary elections vary greatly by state, and they can change between elections. Hence, it is difficult to summarize the types of primaries and their incidence. Every state uses primary elections to nominate candidates for statewide office, but a few also use party conventions to place names on the primary ballots and some allow minor parties to nominate candidates in conventions.[6] The nomination process, then, is highly decentralized, resting on the decisions of thousands, perhaps millions, of the party rank and file who participate in primary elections.

In both parties, only about half of the regular party voters (about one-quarter of the voting-age population) bother to vote in a given primary, although the proportion varies greatly by state and contest. Early research on primary elections concluded that Republicans who voted in their primaries were more conservative than those who did not, whereas Democratic primary voters were more liberal than other Democrats. Some research disputed this finding, but recent studies suggest that primary voters are unrepresentative of the ideological orientation of other party voters.[7]

Some studies support another interpretation: although party activists who turn out for primaries and caucuses are not representative of the average party member, they subordinate their own views to select candidates "who will fare well in the general election."[8] Within the Republican Party in the 2010 election, however, the tea party movement worked to nominate strongly conservative House and Senate candidates over more moderate and arguably more electable candidates. Tea party choices fared better in House elections than in Senate elections, which some notable tea party candidates lost. Noting that losing candidates tended to be chosen in conventions dominated by tea party activists, establishment GOP leaders sought to end that route to nomination in 2014. One Republican leader in Virginia said, "If the goal is actually to win elections, holding more primaries would be a good start."[9] Perhaps the most significant fact about primary elections in American politics today is the decline in competition for party nominations. One major study found that only "about 25 percent of statewide candidates face serious primary competition."[10]

There are four major types of primary elections, and variants of each type have been used frequently across all states to nominate candidates for state and congressional offices. At one end of the spectrum are **closed primaries**, in which voters must register their party affiliation to vote on that party's potential nominees. At the other end are **open primaries**, in which any voter, regardless of party registration or affiliation, can choose either party's ballot. In between are **modified closed primaries**, in which individual state parties decide whether to allow those not registered with either party to vote with their party registrants, and **modified open primaries**, in which all those not already registered with a party can choose any party ballot and vote with party registrants.

For decades, Louisiana—historically a Democratic state—has used a "blanket primary," which listed all candidates (usually Democrats) on a single ballot. The top two vote-getters ran again in a general election; if one got over 50 percent, that candidate won automatically. Recently voters in two-party states Washington (2004) and California (2010) approved a variant of the blanket primary, called the "top-two." It is open to all candidates, with the top two vote-getters standing for the general election. Brief experience with this "top-two" primary system shows that winning candidates virtually always come from the two major parties.[11] Limited research on its use to date in California shows that the new system has not delivered on its

closed primaries
Primary elections in which voters must declare their party affiliation before they are given the primary ballot containing that party's potential nominees.

open primaries
Primary elections in which voters need not declare their party affiliation and can choose one party's primary ballot to take into the voting booth.

modified closed primaries
Primary elections that allow individual state parties to decide whether they permit independents to vote in their primaries and, if so, for which offices.

modified open primaries
Primary elections that entitle independent voters to vote in a party's primary.

backers' claims. Turnout in top-two primary elections in 2012 was less than usual, not more, and candidates were not measurably less polarized, perhaps even more polarized.[12] Indeed, researchers have found limited effects of the types of primaries generally on candidates' ideologies—at least at the state level.[13]

Most scholars believe that the type of primary held in a state affects the strength of its party organizations. Open primaries weaken parties more than closed primaries, for they allow voters to float between parties rather than require them to work within one. But the differences among types of primaries are much less important than the fact that our parties have primaries at all—that parties choose candidates through elections. This practice originated in the United States and largely remains peculiar to us. Placing the nomination of party candidates in the hands of voters rather than party leaders is a key factor in the decentralization of power in American parties, which contributes more to pluralist than to majoritarian democracy.

Nomination for President

The decentralized nature of American parties is readily apparent in how presidential hopefuls must campaign for their party's nomination for president. Each party formally chooses its presidential and vice-presidential candidates at a national convention held every four years in the summer prior to the November election. Until the 1960s, party delegates chose their party's nominee right at the convention, sometimes after repeated balloting over several candidates who divided the vote and kept anyone from getting the majority needed to win the nomination. In 1920, for example, the Republican National Convention deadlocked over two leading candidates after nine ballots. Party leaders then met in a "smoke-filled room" and compromised on Warren G. Harding, who won on the tenth ballot. Harding was not among the leading candidates and had won only a single primary (in his native Ohio). The last time that either party needed more than one ballot to nominate its presidential candidate was in 1952, when the Democrats took three ballots to nominate Adlai E. Stevenson. The Republicans that year nominated Dwight Eisenhower on only one ballot, but he won in a genuine contest with Senator Robert Taft. So Eisenhower also won his nomination on the convention floor.

Although 1952 was the last year a nominating majority was engineered by delegates inside the hall, delegates at the Democratic convention in 1960 and the Republican convention in 1964 also resolved uncertain outcomes. So did the 1968 Democratic convention, which critics charged was rigged. After President Lyndon Johnson unexpectedly announced on March 31, 1968, that he would not seek reelection, Democratic Party leaders at the summer's Chicago convention anointed his Vice President Hubert Humphrey as the party's nominee—although Humphrey had not run in a single primary. (See page 219.) The ensuing riots at the convention and in the streets led to fundamental reforms in the delegate selection process in both parties beginning with the 1972 presidential election.

Prior to 1972, major party organizations dominated the presidential nominating process; there were few primaries, short campaigns, limited media coverage, and open conventions—during which the assembled delegates actually chose the nominee. The reverse has been true in every convention since. Both parties' nominating conventions now simply ratify the results of a complex process for selecting the convention delegates. Most minor parties still choose their presidential candidates in national conventions. In 2012, a nonpartisan organization, Americans Elect, experimented with nominating presidential candidates online but failed because not enough voters participated.

presidential primary
A special primary election used to select delegates to attend the party's national convention, which in turn nominates the presidential candidate.

caucus/convention
A method used to select delegates to attend a party's national convention. Generally, a local meeting selects delegates for a county-level meeting, which in turn selects delegates for a higher-level meeting; the process culminates in a state convention that actually selects the national convention delegates.

front-loading
States' practice of moving delegate selection primaries and caucuses earlier in the calendar year to gain media and candidate attention.

Selecting Convention Delegates. No national legislation specifies how the state parties must select delegates to their national conventions. Instead, state legislatures have enacted a bewildering variety of procedures, which often differ for Democrats and Republicans in the same state. The most important distinction in delegate selection is between the presidential primary and the local caucus. In 2012, both major parties in more than thirty states used primaries to select delegates to their presidential nominating conventions, and both parties in fewer than twenty states selected delegates through a combination of local caucuses and state conventions.[14]

A **presidential primary** is a special primary held to select delegates to attend a party's national nominating convention. Party supporters typically vote for the candidate they favor as their party's nominee for president, and candidates win delegates according to various formulas. Democratic presidential primaries are *proportional*, meaning that candidates win delegates in rough proportion to the votes they win. Specifically, candidates who win at least 15 percent of the vote divide the state's delegates in proportion to the percentage of their primary votes. Prior to 2012, most Republican primaries followed the *winner-take-all* principle, which gives all the state's delegates to the candidate who wins a plurality of its vote. For 2012, however, some states adopted proportional rules for Republican primaries. Analyses expected that the rule changes would prolong the race for the party's nomination, because the leading candidate could not gobble up a majority of the delegates from states that held early primaries. In fact, the last two challengers to Mitt Romney, the eventual Republican presidential nominee, did not withdraw until May.

The **caucus/convention** method of delegate selection has several stages. It begins with local meetings, or caucuses, of party supporters to choose delegates to attend a larger subsequent meeting, usually at the county level. Most delegates selected in the local caucuses openly back one of the presidential candidates. The county meetings select delegates to a higher level. The process culminates in a state convention, which selects the delegates to the national convention.

Primary elections were first used to select delegates to nominating conventions in 1912. Heralded as a party "reform," primaries spread like wildfire.[15] By 1916, a majority of delegates to both conventions were chosen through party elections, but presidential primaries soon dropped in popularity. From 1924 through 1960, rarely were more than 40 percent of the delegates to the national conventions chosen through primaries. Protests at the 1968 Democratic National Convention (see Chapter 8) sparked rule changes in the national party that required more "open" procedures for selecting delegates. Voting in primaries seemed the most open procedure. By 1972, this method of selection accounted for about 60 percent of the delegates at both party conventions. Now the parties in almost forty states rely on presidential primaries of some form, which generate about 80 percent of the delegates.

Because most delegates selected in primaries are publicly committed to specific candidates, one usually can tell before a party's summer nominating convention who is going to be its nominee. Starting in 1972, we began learning the nominee's identity earlier and earlier, thanks to **front-loading** of delegate selection. This term describes the tendency during the past two decades for states to move their primaries earlier in the calendar year to gain attention from the media and the candidates. Some states moved their primaries back for the 2012 primary season. Whereas half the Republican delegates had been chosen by February 5 in 2008, half were not selected until April 24 in 2012.

Campaigning for the Nomination. The process of nominating party candidates for president is a complex, drawn-out affair that has no parallel in any other nation. Would-be presidents announce their candidacy and begin campaigning many months before the first convention delegates are selected. Soon after one election ends, prospective candidates quietly begin lining up political and financial support for their likely race nearly four years later. This early, silent campaign has been dubbed the *invisible primary*. (See Figure 9.1 for dates when presidential hopefuls announced their candidacies—and their withdrawals.)

By historical accident, two small states, Iowa and New Hampshire, became the testing ground of candidates' popularity with party voters. Accordingly, each basks in the media spotlight once every four years. The legislatures of both states are committed to leading the delegate selection process in their own way—Iowa using party caucuses and New Hampshire a direct primary—ensuring their states' share of national publicity and their bids for political history. The Iowa caucuses and the New Hampshire primary have served different functions in the presidential nominating process. The contest in Iowa, attended by party activists, has traditionally tended to winnow out candidates,

FIGURE 9.1 From Many to Two: Presidential Hopefuls Starting and Dropping Out

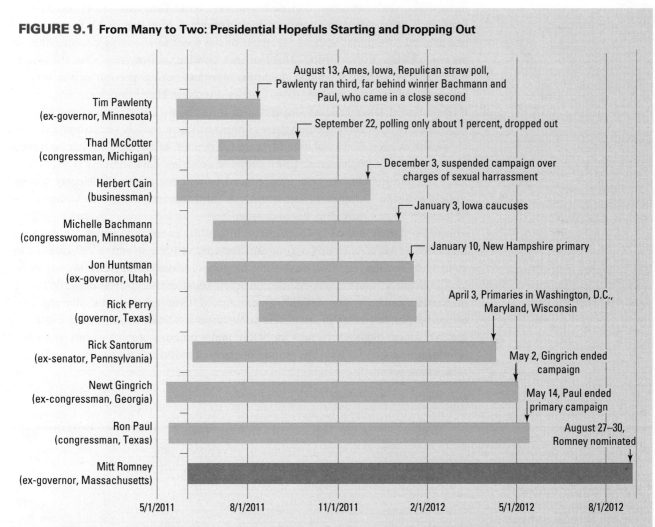

Over three hundred candidates filed with the Federal Election Commission (FEC) to run for president in 2012. The graph lists the ten Republicans who filed with the FEC as presidential candidates and who received significant early attention. As usual, some candidates withdrew before the delegate selection process began and others dropped out afterward for lack of support. By late January, only four hopefuls were competing in the numerous televised debates.

Source: © Cengage Learning.

narrowing the field. The New Hampshire primary, typically held a week later, tests the Iowa front-runners' appeal to ordinary party voters, which foreshadows their likely strength in the general election. Because voting takes little effort by itself, more citizens are likely to vote in primaries than to attend caucuses, which can last for hours. In 2012, about 6.5 percent of the voting-age population participated in both parties' Iowa caucuses, whereas about 31 percent voted in both New Hampshire primaries.[16] These turnout rates were about half of those in 2008, when both parties had hot contests for the presidential nomination. In 2012, only the Republican Party featured caucus and primary contests.

From 1920 to 1972, New Hampshire's primary election led the nation in selecting delegates to the parties' summer conventions. But in 1972 Iowa chose its convention delegates in caucuses held even earlier. Since then, Iowa and New Hampshire agreed to be first in their methods of delegate selection.[17] As usual, the two states in 2012 fulfilled their role in winnowing down the field of presidential hopefuls.

Seven notables stood for the Iowa Republican caucuses on January 3, 2012. In alphabetical order, they were Michele Bachmann, Newt Gingrich, Jon Huntsman, Ron Paul, Rick Perry, Mitt Romney, and Rick Santorum. (See Figure 9.1 for candidates' background.) Romney (with 24.5 percent of the vote) was initially declared the winner, only to lose to Santorum (24.5 percent) by a handful of votes after the recount. Bachmann (who had depended on Iowa) won less than 5 percent of the vote and dropped out the next day. A week later in the New Hampshire primary, Romney won decisively, taking almost 40 percent of the vote, with Paul second at 23 percent. Huntsman (who had counted on New Hampshire) won only 17 percent and dropped out two days later. Perry (who had less than 1 percent of the vote in New Hampshire after getting only 10 percent in Iowa) dropped out a few days later.

Thus, the Republican field was reduced to four for the third delegate selection contest in South Carolina on January 31. A third winner emerged as Gingrich took 40 percent of the vote, but his star faded ten days later when Romney decisively defeated Gingrich in the Florida primary. In ensuing contests, Romney and Santorum alternated as winners, setting up a protracted contest for convention delegates chosen in forty primaries over 168 days—the longest presidential primary season in history.[18] When Santorum dropped out on April 10, after the Maryland and Wisconsin primaries, Romney's nomination was guaranteed; Gingrich and Paul lingered a little before bowing to Romney's inevitable convention nomination. Requiring prospective presidential candidates to campaign before many millions of party voters in scores of primaries and hundreds of thousands of party activists in caucus states has several consequences:

- *When no incumbent in the White House is seeking reelection, the presidential nominating process becomes contested in both parties.* This is what occurred in 2008, when twelve Republicans and ten Democrats met the Federal Election Commission (FEC) requirements for electronic filing of their presidential campaigns. In the complex mix of caucus and primary methods that states use to select convention delegates, timing and luck can affect who wins, and even an outside chance of success ordinarily attracts a half-dozen or so plausible contestants in either party lacking an incumbent president. Expect about a dozen hopefuls in each party seeking nomination for the 2016 presidential election.

- *An incumbent president usually encounters little or no opposition for renomination within the party.* Thus, Obama was routinely renominated in 2012, but challenges can occur. In 1992, President George Herbert Walker Bush faced fierce opposition for the Republican nomination from Pat Buchanan. In 1968,

President Lyndon Johnson faced such hostility within the Democratic Party that he declined to seek renomination.

- *Many hopefuls seek the presidential nomination of the opposition party.* In 2012, twelve notable Republicans filed with the FEC as presidential candidates along with hundreds (yes) of others not so notable.
- *The Iowa caucuses and New Hampshire primaries do matter.* Since the first Iowa caucus in 1972, eleven candidates in each party have won presidential nominations. All of the eleven Republican nominees were first in either Iowa or New Hampshire, as were nine of the Democrats.
- *Candidates eventually favored by most party identifiers usually win their party's nomination.*[19] There have been only two exceptions to this rule since 1936, when poll data first became available: Adlai E. Stevenson in 1952 and George McGovern in 1972.[20] Both were Democrats; both lost impressively in the general election.
- *Candidates who win the nomination do so largely on their own and owe little or nothing to the national party organization, which usually does not promote a candidate.* In fact, Jimmy Carter won the nomination in 1976 against a field of nationally prominent Democrats, although he was a party outsider with few strong connections to the national party leadership. Barack Obama won in 2008 against Hillary Clinton, who had strong ties to Democratic Party leaders.

CONNECT WITH YOUR CLASSMATES MindTap™ for American Government

Access the Elections Forum: Discussion—Bringing the Party Together After Primaries.

Elections

LO3 ★ Describe the function of the electoral college and formulate arguments for and against the electoral vote system.

By national law, all seats in the House of Representatives and one-third of the seats in the Senate are filled in a **general election** held in early November in even-numbered years. Every state takes advantage of the national election to fill some of the nearly 500,000 state and local offices across the country, which makes the election even more "general." When the president is chosen every fourth year, the election is identified as a presidential election. The intervening elections are known as *congressional, midterm,* or *off-year elections.*

general election
A national election held by law in November of every even-numbered year.

Presidential Elections and the Electoral College

In contrast to almost all other offices in the United States, the presidency does not go automatically to the candidate who wins the most votes. In fact, George W. Bush won the presidency in 2000 despite receiving fewer popular votes than Al Gore. Instead, a two-stage procedure specified in the Constitution decides elections for the president; it requires selection of the president by a group (college) of electors representing the states. Technically, we elect a president not in a national election but in a *federal* election.

The Electoral College: Structure. Surprising as it might seem, the term *electoral college* is not mentioned in the Constitution and is not readily found in books on American politics prior to World War II. One major dictionary defines a college as "a body of persons having a common purpose or shared duties."[21] The electors who choose the president of the United States became known as the electoral college largely during the twentieth century. Eventually, this term became incorporated into statutes relating to presidential elections, so it has assumed a legal basis.[22]

According to the Constitution (Article II, Section 1) each of the fifty states is entitled to one elector for each of its senators (100 total) and one for each of its representatives (435 votes total), totaling 535 electoral votes. In addition, the Twenty-third Amendment to the Constitution awarded three electoral votes (the minimum for any state) to the District of Columbia, although it elects no voting members of Congress. The total number of electoral votes therefore is 538. The Constitution specifies that a candidate needs a majority of electoral votes, or 270 today, to win the presidency. If no candidate receives a majority, the election is thrown into the House of Representatives. The House votes by state, with each state casting one vote. The candidates in the House election are the top three finishers in the general election. A presidential election has gone to the House only twice in American history, in 1800 and 1824, before a stable two-party system had developed.

Electoral votes are apportioned among the states according to their representation in Congress, which depends largely on their population. Because of population changes recorded by the 2010 census, the distribution of electoral votes among the states changed between the 2008 and 2012 presidential elections. Figure 9.2 shows the distribution of electoral votes for the 2012 election, indicating which states have lost and gained electoral votes. The clear pattern is the systemic loss of people and electoral votes in the north-central and eastern states and the gain in the western and southern states.

The Electoral College: Politics. In 1789, the first set of presidential electors was chosen under the new Constitution. Only three states chose their electors by direct popular vote, while state legislatures selected electors in the others. Selection by state legislature remained the norm until 1792. Afterward, direct election by popular vote became more common, and by 1824 voters chose electors in eighteen of twenty-four states. Since 1860, all states have selected their electors through popular vote once they entered the Union.[23] In the disputed 2000 presidential election, the Republican Florida state legislature threatened to resolve the dispute in favor of Bush by selecting its electors itself. There was precedent to do so, but it was a pre–Civil War precedent.

Of course, the situation in Florida was itself unprecedented due to the extremely close election in 2000. Voters nationwide favored the Democratic candidate, Al Gore, by a plurality of approximately 500,000 votes out of 105 million cast. But the presidential election is a *federal* election. A candidate is not chosen president by national popular vote but by a majority of the states' electoral votes. In every state but Maine and Nebraska, the candidate who wins a plurality of its popular vote—whether by 20 votes or 20,000 votes—wins all of the state's electoral votes. Gore and his Republican opponent, George W. Bush, ran close races in many states across the nation. Not counting Florida, Gore had won 267 electoral votes, just three short of the 270 he needed to claim the presidency.

But in Florida, which had twenty-five electoral votes in 2000, the initial vote count showed an extremely close race, with Bush ahead by the slimmest of margins. If Bush outpolled Gore by just a single vote, Bush could add its 25 electoral votes to the 246 he won in the other states, for a total of 271. That was just one more than the number needed to win the presidency. Gore trailed Bush by only about 2,000 votes, close enough to ask for a recount. But the recount proved difficult due to different

FIGURE 9.2 Population Shifts and Political Gains and Losses Since 1960

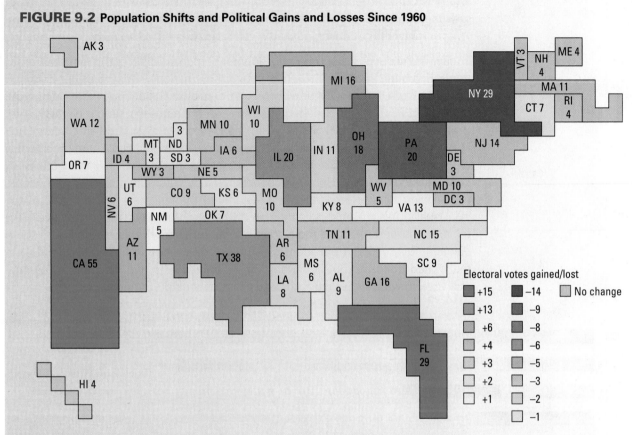

If the states were sized according to their electoral votes for the 2012 presidential election, the nation might resemble this map, on which states are drawn according to their population, based on the 2010 census. Each state has as many electoral votes as its combined representation in the Senate (always two) and the House (which depends on population). Although New Jersey is much smaller in area than Montana, New Jersey has far more people and is thus bigger in terms of "electoral geography." The coloring on this map shows the states that have gained electoral votes since 1960 (in shades of green) and those that have lost electoral votes (in shades of purple). States that have not had the number of their electoral votes changed since 1960 are blue. This map clearly reflects the drain of population (and seats in Congress) from the north-central and eastern states to the western and southern states. California, with two senators and fifty-three representatives in the 2012 election, will have fifty-five electoral votes for presidential elections until 2024, when reapportionment follows the 2020 census.

ballots and different methods for counting them. After more than a month of ballot counting, recounting, more recounting, lawsuits, court decisions—and the Republican legislature's threat to select the electors on its own to ensure Bush's victory—Bush was certified as the winner of Florida's 25 *electoral* votes by a mere 537 *popular* votes. So ended one of the most protracted, complicated, and intense presidential elections in American history.[24]

The Electoral College: Abolish It? As shown in "Presidential Elections in Global Politics," more presidential elections are being held by more nations across the world, but very few elect presidents using an electoral college. Between 1789 and 2000, about seven hundred proposals to change the electoral college scheme were introduced in Congress.[25] Historically, polls have shown public opinion opposed to the electoral college.[26] Following the 2000 election, letters flooded into newspapers, urging anew that the system be changed.[27]

**COMPARE
WITH YOUR PEERS**
 for American Government

Access the Elections Forum:
Polling Activity—Presidential
Election Process.

Presidential Elections in Global Politics

Today, many nations elect their presidents, and do so differently from how presidents had been chosen. This chart shows how nations chose presidents in 405 elections from 1946 to 2010. Only eleven presidential elections were held in the postwar 1940s and most presidents then were elected by simple plurality vote. Argentina and the United States were the only countries to use an electoral college. As more countries became democratic over the decades, more presidential elections occurred—135 in the 2000s. In that recent decade, only thirty-one elections decided the presidency by a simple plurality vote. In eighty-seven elections, the winning candidate had to win a majority of the vote cast, not a simple plurality. Usually, this meant holding a second ballot some days later. In twelve elections, a qualified majority (more than a simple majority) was needed. The three elections that chose a president by an electoral college in the 2000s were all in the United States (2000, 2004, and 2008). Ireland held two elections by alternative vote, in which voters ranked candidates by their preferences.

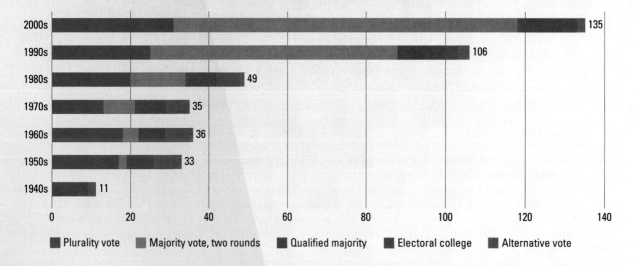

Source: Nils-Christian Bormann and Matt Golder, "Democratic Electoral Systems Around the World, 1946–2011," *Electoral Studies*, 32 (2013): 360–369.

Critical Thinking According to the Constitution, candidates must win a majority of the electoral votes (270 out of 538) to claim the presidency. Suppose only a plurality of the vote was needed to become president. How might this simple change affect American politics? Would it advantage or disadvantage minor parties? Would the change be desirable or undesirable?

To evaluate the criticisms, one must first distinguish between the electoral "college" and the "system" of electoral votes. Strictly speaking, the electoral college is merely the set of individuals empowered to cast a state's electoral votes. In a presidential election, voters don't actually vote for a candidate; they vote for a slate of little-known electors (their names are often not on the ballot) pledged to one of the candidates. Most critics hold that the founding fathers argued for a body of electors because they did not trust people to vote directly for candidates. But one scholar contends that the device of independent electors was adopted by the Constitutional Convention as a compromise between those who favored having legislatures cast the states' electoral votes for president and those who favored direct popular election.[28] The electoral college allowed states to choose, and—as described in Chapter 8—all states gravitated to direct election of electors by 1860. Occasionally (but rarely), electors break their pledges when they assemble to cast their written ballots at their state capitol in December (electors who do so are called "faithless electors"). Indeed, this happened in 2004, when one of the ten Minnesota electors voted not for Democrat John Kerry, who won the state, but for his running mate, John Edwards. Electors vote by secret ballot, so no one knew which one voted for Edwards instead of Kerry.[29] Such aberrations make for historical footnotes but do not affect outcomes. Today, voters have good reason to oppose a body of electors to translate their decision, and few observers defend the electoral college itself.

The more troubling criticism centers on the electoral vote *system*, which makes for a federal rather than a national election. Many reformers favor a majoritarian method for choosing the president—by nationwide direct popular vote. They argue that it is simply wrong to have a system that allows a candidate who wins the most popular votes nationally to lose the election. Until 2000, that situation had not occurred since 1888, when Grover Cleveland won the popular vote but lost the presidency to Benjamin Harrison in the electoral college. During all intervening elections, the candidate winning a plurality of the popular vote also won a majority of the electoral vote. In fact, the electoral vote generally operated to magnify the margin of victory, as Figure 9.3 shows. Some scholars argued that this magnifying effect increased the legitimacy of presidents-elect who failed to win a majority of the popular vote, which happened in the elections of Kennedy, Nixon (first time), Clinton (both times), and certainly George W. Bush (first time).

The 2000 election proved that defenders of the electoral vote system can no longer claim that a federal election based on electoral votes yields the same outcome as a national election based on the popular vote. However, three lines of argument support selecting a president by electoral votes rather than by popular vote. First, if one supports a federal form of government as embodied within the Constitution, then one may defend the electoral vote system because it gives small states more weight in the vote: they have two senators, the same as large states. Second, if one favors presidential candidates campaigning on foot and in rural areas (needed to win most states) rather than campaigning via television to the one hundred most populous market areas to win the popular vote, then one might favor the electoral vote system.[30] Third, if you do not want to risk a *nationwide* recount in a close election (multiplying by fifty the counting problems in Florida in 2000), then you might want to keep the current system. So switching to selecting the president by popular vote has serious implications, which explains why Congress has not moved quickly to amend the Constitution.

Congressional Elections

In a presidential election, the candidates for the presidency are listed at the top of the ballot, followed by the candidates for other national offices and those for state and local offices. A voter is said to vote a **straight ticket** when she or he chooses the same party's candidates for all the offices. A voter who chooses candidates from different parties is said to vote a **split ticket**. About half of all voters say they split their tickets,

straight ticket
Voting for a single party's candidates for all the offices.

split ticket
Voting for candidates from different parties for different offices.

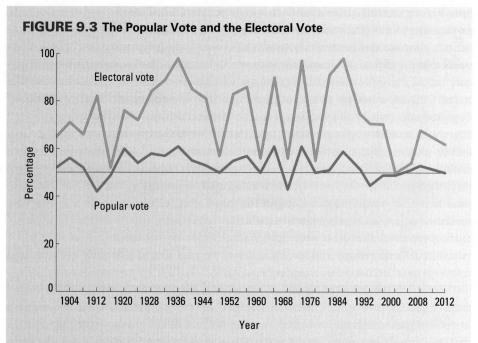

FIGURE 9.3 The Popular Vote and the Electoral Vote

Strictly speaking, a presidential election is a federal election, not a national election. A candidate must win a majority (270) of the nation's total electoral vote (538). A candidate can win a plurality of the popular vote and still not win the presidency. Until 2000, the last time a candidate won most of the popular votes but did not win the presidency was in 1888. In every election between these two, the candidate who won a plurality of the popular vote won an even larger proportion of the electoral vote. So the electoral vote system magnified the winner's victory and thus increased the legitimacy of the president-elect. As we learned from the 2000 election, that result is not guaranteed.

Source: Harold W. Stanley and Richard G. Niemi, *Vital Statistics on American Politics, 2011–2012* (Washington, D.C.: CQ Press, 2014).

and the proportion of voters who chose a presidential candidate from one party and a congressional candidate from the other has varied between 15 and 30 percent since 1952.[31] In the 1970s and 1980s, the common pattern was to elect a Republican as president while electing mostly Democrats to Congress. This produced a divided government, with the executive and legislative branches controlled by different parties (see Chapter 12). In the mid-1990s, the electorate flipped the pattern, electing a Democratic president but a Republican Congress.

Until the 1994 election, Democrats had maintained a lock on congressional elections for decades, winning a majority of House seats since 1954 and controlling the Senate for all but six years during that period. Republicans regularly complained that inequitable districts drawn by Democrat-dominated state legislatures had denied them their fair share of seats. For example, the Republicans won 46 percent of the congressional vote in 1992 but gained only 40 percent of the seats. Despite the Republicans' complaint, election specialists note that sizable discrepancies between votes won and seats won are the inevitable consequence of **first-past-the-post elections**—a British term for elections conducted in single-member districts that award victory to the candidate with the most votes. In all such elections worldwide, the party that wins the most votes tends to win more seats than projected by its percentage of the vote.* In 2012,

first-past-the-post elections
A British term for elections conducted in single-member districts that award victory to the candidate with the most votes.

---

*If you have trouble understanding this phenomenon, think of a basketball team that scores, on average, 51 percent of the total points in all the games it plays. That team usually wins more than just 51 percent of the games because it tends to win the close games.

therefore, the Republicans benefited from the electoral mathematics. They won just 48 percent of the congressional vote to the Democrats' 46 percent, but Republicans won 54 percent of the seats. These recent election results reveal no evidence of Democratic malapportionment of congressional districts. Both parties have enjoyed, and suffered, the mathematics of first-past-the-post elections.

Heading into the 2014 congressional elections, Republicans anticipated keeping control of the House of Representatives and winning control of the Senate by campaigning against Democratic President Obama as a failed leader. The Republican strategy worked, as exit polls showed 55 percent of the voters disapproving Obama's performance. Republicans increased their majority in the House and won a small majority in the Senate for the first time since 2008. Beginning with the 2015 Congress, Republicans controlled both houses of Congress. As Obama served out his term, the nation faced two years of divided government.

Campaigns

LO4 ★ Analyze the American election campaign process in terms of political context, financial resources, and strategies and tactics for reaching the voters.

Election campaigns can be analyzed according to their political context, the financial resources available for conducting the campaign, and the strategies and tactics that underlie the dissemination of information about the candidate.

The Political Context

The two most important structural factors that face each candidate planning a campaign are the office the candidate is seeking and whether he or she is the incumbent (the current officeholder running for reelection) or the challenger (who seeks to replace the incumbent). Incumbents usually enjoy great advantages over challengers, especially in elections to Congress. Most congressional elections today are not very competitive. Of 2,175 congressional elections in the 2000s, only 41 (1.9 percent) were decided by 2 percentage points or fewer.[32] As explained in Chapter 11, incumbents in the House of Representatives are almost impossible to defeat, historically winning more than 95 percent of the time.[33] Incumbent senators are somewhat more vulnerable. An incumbent president is also difficult to defeat—but not impossible. Democrat Jimmy Carter was defeated for reelection in 1980, as was Republican George H. W. Bush in 1992. Of course, a nonincumbent will always triumph in an **open election**, one lacking an incumbent because of a resignation, death, or constitutional requirement.

Every candidate for Congress must also examine the characteristics of the state or district, including its physical size and the sociological makeup of its electorate. In general, the bigger and more populous the district or state and the more diverse the electorate, the more complicated and costly is the campaign. Obviously, running for president means conducting a huge, complicated, and expensive campaign. After losing the 2008 Republican presidential nomination to John McCain and after McCain lost the general election to Obama, Romney used funds remaining in his 2008 campaign chest to plan a billion-dollar campaign in 2012.[34] By 2010, Romney had a network of state organizations to supply funds for his presidential run.[35]

Despite talk about the decreased influence of party affiliation on voting behavior, the party preference of the electorate is an important factor in the context of a

open election
An election that lacks an incumbent.

Access the Campaigning for Office Forum: Discussion—Electing Incumbents.

campaign. It is easier for a candidate to get elected when her or his party matches the electorate's preference, in part because raising the money needed to conduct a winning campaign is easier. Challengers for congressional seats, for example, get far less money from organized groups than do incumbents and must rely more on their personal funds and raising money from individual donors. So where candidates represent the minority party, they have to overcome not only a voting bias but also a funding bias. Finally, significant political issues—such as economic recession, personal scandals, and war—not only affect a campaign but also can dominate it and even negate such positive factors as incumbency and the advantages of a strong economy. In 2012, Republicans attacked Obama for presiding over a weak economy and for passing the health-care legislation they derided as "Obamacare." Republicans revived these issues in campaigning for the 2014 congressional elections.

Financing

Regarding election campaigns, former House Speaker Thomas ("Tip") O'Neill said, "There are four parts to any campaign. The candidate, the issues of the candidate, the campaign organization, and the money to run the campaign with. Without money you can forget the other three."[36] Money pays for office space, staff salaries, cell phones, computers, travel expenses, campaign literature, and, of course, advertising in the mass media. A successful campaign requires a good campaign organization and a good candidate, but enough money will buy the best campaign managers, equipment, transportation, research, and consultants—making the quality of the organization largely a function of money. That may be true, but money alone does not ensure a successful campaign. Initially in the campaign season, President Obama raised more campaign funds than all the candidates seeking the Republican nomination, but by the summer months, Mitt Romney's fundraising had caught up with and exceeded Obama's. From all sources, Romney's campaign spent $1.2 billion versus Obama's $1.1 billion over the entire 2012 presidential election campaign.[37]

No one can run a successful presidential campaign without raising a great deal of money. Regulations of campaign financing for state elections vary according to the state. Campaign financing for federal elections is regulated by national legislation.

Regulating Campaign Financing. Early campaign financing laws had various flaws, and none provided for adequate enforcement. In 1971, during a period of party reform, Congress passed the Federal Election Campaign Act (FECA), which limited media spending and imposed stringent new rules for full reporting of campaign contributions and expenditures. The need for strict legislation soon became clear. In 1968, before FECA was enacted, House and Senate candidates reported spending $8.5 million on their campaigns. In 1972, with FECA in force, the same number of candidates admitted spending $88.9 million—ten times as much.[38]

Financial misdeeds during Nixon's 1972 reelection campaign forced major amendments to the original FECA in 1974. The new legislation created the **Federal Election Commission (FEC)**, an independent agency of six members appointed by the president with approval of the Senate. No more than three members may come from the same party, and their six-year appointments are staggered over time so that no one president appoints the entire commission. The FEC is charged with enforcing limits on financial contributions to national campaigns, requiring full disclosure of campaign spending, and administering the public financing of presidential campaigns, which began with the 1976 election.

Federal Election Commission (FEC)
A bipartisan federal agency of six members that oversees the financing of national election campaigns.

The law also condoned the creation of **political action committees (PACs)** by corporations, labor unions, or "nonconnected" groups that could, under limits, collect money and contribute it to campaigns for federal office—that is, Congress and the presidency. (The role of PACs in congressional elections is discussed at length in Chapter 10.)

Some people opposed any limits on campaign contributions, viewing money as "free speech" and challenging the 1974 limits under the First Amendment. Although the Supreme Court upheld limits on contributions in 1976, it struck down limits on *spending* by individuals or organizations made independently on behalf of a national candidate—holding that such spending constituted free speech, protected under the First Amendment. It also limited the FEC to regulate only advertisements advocating a candidate's election or defeat with such words as "vote for" or "vote against."[39] The 1974 FECA (with minor amendments) governed national elections for almost three decades.

As campaign spending increased, some members of Congress spoke piously about strengthening campaign finance laws but feared altering the process that elected them. In 2002 a bill introduced by Republican senator John McCain (Arizona) and Democratic senator Russell Feingold (Wisconsin) finally passed as the Bipartisan Campaign Reform Act (BCRA; pronounced "bikra"). BCRA was fiercely challenged from several sources, including Republican conservatives who attacked McCain for limiting contributions and weakening the party. Nevertheless, the law was upheld by the Supreme Court in 2003 and took effect for the 2004 election.

In general, BCRA raised the old limits on individual spending and indexed them for inflation in future years. Here are the major BCRA limitations for 2013–2014 contributions by individuals, adjusted for inflation:

- $2,600 to a specific candidate in a separate election during a two-year cycle (primaries, general, and runoff elections count as separate elections);
- $10,000 per year to each state party or political committee;
- $32,400 per year to any national party committee;
- $5,000 per year to any PAC.

Note that the 2002 law did not raise the $5,000 contribution limit for PACs, which many thought already had too much influence in elections, and did not index PAC contributions for inflation. That law also limited the total amount that donors could contribute in one election cycle, which in 2013–2014 was $48,000 to all candidates and $74,600 to all parties and political committees—capped at $123,200 for both.

BCRA also banned large so-called soft-money contributions to national political parties. Ostensibly given for capital improvements and operating expenses, these funds were often channeled to state parties for electoral campaigns. It also banned organizations from running issue ads that named candidates in the weeks before an election. However, BCRA allowed issue-advocacy groups, called **527 committees** (after Section 527 of the Internal Revenue Code, which makes them tax-exempt organizations), to spend unlimited amounts for media advertising, as long as they did not expressly advocate a candidate's election or defeat. Spending by 527 committees increased from $151 million in 2002 to $489 million in 2008.[40]

Within a decade after the 2002 McCain–Feingold BCRA campaign funding limitations went into effect, a more conservative Supreme Court gutted almost all limitations. In 2007, it struck down BCRA's ban of issue ads run before elections, which opened the door to massive independent campaign spending by nonparty groups. Many no longer organized as 527 committees, which were required to report their

political action committee (PAC)
An organization that collects campaign contributions from group members and donates them to candidates for political office.

527 committees
Committees named after Section 527 of the Internal Revenue Code; they enjoy tax-exempt status in election campaigns if they are unaffiliated with political parties and take positions on issues, not specific candidates.

501(c)4 social welfare organizations
Groups named after Section 501 of the Internal Revenue Code that operate for promotion of social welfare; they are exempt from reporting donors if they spend most of their funds on issues, not candidates.

donors to the FEC, but as **501(c)4 social welfare organizations**, exploiting a legal loophole excusing them from disclosing donors.[41]

In January 2010 a bitterly divided Supreme Court departed from its precedents and ruled against BCRA's ban on spending by corporations in candidate elections.[42] Conservatives viewed its decision in *Citizens United* v. *Federal Election Commission* as defending freedom of speech,[43] while liberals saw it as opening the door to the corrupting influence of corporate money.[44] Beginning with the 2010 election, corporations, unions, and trade associations were free to run ads directly advocating a candidate's election for the first time since 1907, when Congress first banned using general corporate funds in federal election campaigns.[45] In the 2010 elections, for example, the Service Employees International Union spent over $15 million and the National Rifle Association spent over $7 million.

In March 2010, an Appeals court applied the *Citizens United* ruling in *SpeechNow.org* v. *FEC*, a decision that expanded the influence of private money in elections. It legalized a new category of funding organizations: "independent expenditures only political committees" or "Super PACs." If political committees make only independent expenditures and do not give money to candidates, they can accept funds in unlimited amounts to spend independently on election campaigns.[46] Unlike the $5,000 limit on contributions to PACs, there is no limit on contributions to Super PACs. While Super PACs must periodically disclose donations from individuals and for-profit groups, they need not disclose donations from nonprofit groups.[47]

By early 2012, Super PACs aligned with each of the Republican presidential candidates had spent more than $40 million. "Restore Our Future," the main Super PAC supporting Romney, raised $20 million and outspent the Romney campaign itself 2 to 1.[48] Ostensibly, Super PAC expenditures were supposed to have "no connection" with the official campaigns of candidates they were backing—despite the fact that Super PACs were often run by candidates' former campaign officials and political cronies. For example, the director of the Romney-oriented "Restore Our Future" Super PAC was Carl Forti, who ran Romney's 2008 presidential campaign. To parody what the law allowed, Stephen Colbert of Comedy Central's cable show, *The Colbert Report*, legally named Jon Stewart, his business partner at Comedy Central's *The Daily Show*, to run Colbert's own Super PAC, "Americans for a Better Tomorrow, Tomorrow."[49]

Super PACs quickly raised unprecedented amounts of money. By February, FEC filings identified fourteen individuals or corporations who had each given at least $1 million to "Restore Our Future," which backed Romney, while a Nevada casino owner and his wife gave $10 million to "Winning Our Future," which supported Gingrich.[50] "American Crossroads," a Super PAC dedicated to the defeat of Obama, got $12 million from billionaire Harold C. Simmons. Realizing that Republican Super PACs would raise huge sums, President Obama reversed his opposition to Super PACs in February and endorsed "Priorities USA Action," founded by two former White House aides. Comedian Bill Maher quickly gave it $1 million. And the number of Super PACs exploded as the campaign proceeded. By July 12, 2012, 548 Super PACs had registered with the Federal Election Commission.[51] According to the Center for Responsive Politics, all types of nonparty groups (Super PACs, 527 committees, 501(c)4 organizations, etc.) spent over $1.2 billion—66 percent by conservative groups and 31percent by liberal groups—during the 2011–2012 election cycle.[52]

AP Images/Comedy Central, Kristopher Long

A Laughing Matter: Money in Politics

In the summer of 2011, Stephen Colbert, host of Comedy Central's *The Colbert Report*, created a Super PAC, "Americans for a Better Tomorrow, Tomorrow." When Colbert decided to run in the South Carolina primary to be president of South Carolina, his Super PAC spending would not be "independent" of his candidacy. So on January 12, 2012, he surrendered its control to his business partner, Jon Stewart, host of Comedy Central's *The Daily Show*. On January 30, after the primary, Colbert wrestled control back. View the videos for those dates at www.colbertnation.com— especially that for January 12, which laughingly explains the letter of the law.

Then in the 2014 case, *McCutcheon et al.* v. *FEC*, the Court struck down *all* limits on contributions to candidates, parties, and political committees—eliminating the 2002 BCRA cap of $123,200 for the 2013–2014 campaign. Although the Court kept the limits on contributions to individual candidates, it freed rich individuals to give to the maximum for as many candidates, parties, and political groups as they wished to support. Technically, there still were limits to campaign contributions, but they had little effect on wealthy donors.

COMPARE WITH YOUR PEERS
MindTap‑ for American Government

Access the Campaigning for Office Forum: Polling Activity— Super PACs and Elections.

Public Financing of Presidential Campaigns. The 1974 FECA provided for public funding of campaigns for presidential elections but not congressional elections. During the primary season, a presidential candidate could qualify for public funds by raising at least $5,000 in each of twenty states from private donations of no more than $250 each. The FEC matched these donations up to one-half of a preset spending limit—indexed for inflation—for each qualifying candidate. Candidates who raised up to $22.8 million in private funds would have that amount matched by up to $22.8 million in public funds, subject to the limitation that they could not spend more than the combined amount of $45.6 million in their primary campaigns.

From 1976 through 1992, all major candidates seeking their party's presidential nomination accepted public matching funds for their primary election campaigns and thus adhered to the spending limits. But candidates found that they could raise more money privately to spend in their primary campaigns. Wealthy publisher Steve Forbes declined public funds in 1996 and again in 2000, when George W. Bush also raised his own primary funds. In 2004, Bush and Democratic hopefuls Howard Dean and John Kerry all declined public money for their primary campaigns. In 2008, only six of the nineteen candidates who participated in both parties' primary debates relied on public funds.[53] By August 2012, only Libertarian presidential candidate Gary Johnson, Green Party candidate Jill Stein, and Buddy Roemer—who sought the nomination of the online organization, Americans Elect—had applied for and qualified for public matching funds.[54]

The public funding program for presidential elections in November operated somewhat differently. First, the campaign spending limit was double that for primary elections. Second, candidates who accepted public funds had no need to raise matching funds privately. They were simply reimbursed by the government up to the spending limit (indexed to inflation), which was $91.2 million in 2012. Candidates who accepted public funds could spend no more than that.

From 1976 to 2004, every major party nominee for president had accepted public funds (and spending limits) for the general election. In 2008, Republican candidate John McCain agreed to accept public funds, thus limiting his campaign spending to $84.1 million for the general election. Compare that with the $220 million McCain raised just to win the nomination. Democratic candidate Obama refused public funds for both and raised $750 million to McCain's total of $304 million.[55] In 2012, neither party's candidate accepted public funds.

Private Financing of Congressional Campaigns. One might think that a party's presidential campaign would be closely coordinated with its congressional campaigns. However, campaign funds go to the presidential candidate, not to the party, and the national committee does not run the presidential campaign. Presidential candidates may join congressional candidates in public appearances for mutual benefit, but presidential campaigns are usually isolated—financially and otherwise—from congressional campaigns.

Candidates for national office raised and spent more than $7 billion during the primary and general election campaigns in the 2011–2012 election cycle. Obama and

McCain together raised over $1.3 billion—not counting money raised by Super PACs—while 1,500 candidates in primary and general election campaigns for the U.S. Congress raised $1.8 billion more.[56] Most congressional candidates were competing for the 435 seats in the House; only 34 Senate seats were up for election. Nevertheless, individual Senate candidates raised relatively more money because they had to compete in larger districts (states) rather than individual House districts, which average about 675,000 people.

Future Trends in Campaign Finance. Public funding of presidential campaigns was intended to equalize candidate spending as well as to limit it. After successfully equalizing and limiting spending for decades, public funding faces its abandonment and demise. Today, prominent presidential candidates find that they can raise far more money for their campaigns than provided by public funding. Two major fundraising methods have made a huge difference. The first is the rise of contribution bundlers who collect legal campaign donations from individuals ($2,500 for the primary and $2,500 for the general elections in 2012) and then deliver the bundled donations to the candidate. Just as the 2010 *Citizens United* decision gave rise to Super PACs, it also gave rise to "super bundlers." Now fundraising professionals could collect from individual citizens $5,000 contributions to candidates, $5,000 contributions to PACs, and *unlimited* amounts for Super PACs simultaneously. For the first time, they could also collect *unlimited* contributions to PACs from corporations, which previously could not contribute to campaigns.[57] The second method of fundraising is through the Internet, and it is even more lucrative. Among all Republican presidential hopefuls in February 2012, only Mitt Romney had raised more money ($56 million) than Ron Paul ($26 million).[58] However, most of Romney's contributions ranged between $1,000 and $2,500. Most of Paul's contributions were under $200 and collected over the Internet.[59]

Although BCRA did ban national party committees from raising huge sums of soft money, it did not reduce the amount of money raised (and spent) for presidential campaigns. At least raising money on the Internet has a grassroots basis, in contrast to using money bundlers. But trying to prevent people from spending money to influence elections and politics is like trying to stop water flooding into a basement. Like water, money seeps around barriers. If people could no longer give massively to political parties, they gave to independent groups that campaigned for candidates separate from the parties. Due to the Supreme Court's 5–4 decision in *Citizens United*, citizens—especially wealthy ones—can contribute as much as they want to Super PACs to influence elections. (See "Freedom, Order, or Equality? Freedom v. Equality in Campaign Finance.") The money genie has escaped from the public funding bottle, and future candidates for president are unlikely to accept the public funding limits imposed by the 1974 Federal Election Campaign Act.

Strategies and Tactics

In a military campaign, *strategy* is the overall scheme for winning the war, whereas *tactics* involve the conduct of localized hostilities. In an election campaign, strategy is the broad approach used to persuade citizens to vote for the candidate, and tactics determine the content of the messages and the way they are delivered. Three basic strategies, which campaigns may blend in different mixes, are as follows:

- A *party-centered strategy*, which relies heavily on voters' partisan identification as well as on the party's organization to provide the resources necessary to wage the campaign;

Freedom, Order, or Equality?

Freedom v. Equality in Campaign Finance

"Freedom of speech" is guaranteed in the Constitution. Because the Supreme Court regards spending money on political campaigns as a form of speech, it closely scrutinizes limits on campaign spending. The 2002 Bipartisan Campaign Reform Act restricted spending on campaigns. In a series of cases from 2007 to 2014, the Court struck down BCRA's limits. In 2007, the Court ended BCRA's ban on issue ads before elections, allowing outside groups to spend freely on campaigns. The Court's 2010 decision allowed unlimited contributions to Super PACs, and in 2014 it lifted all limits on total donations to candidates, parties, and political committees. Accordingly, wealthy people manage to contribute as much money as they wish to influence elections. This graph identifies the eight persons (or families) who donated over $5 million to Super PACs, political parties, and other political groups during the 2011–2012 election cycle. The $198 million they contributed accounted for almost 25 percent of the $828 million raised by all Super PACs in 2011–2012. Of course, each member of these families can cast only one vote, the same as any other citizen.

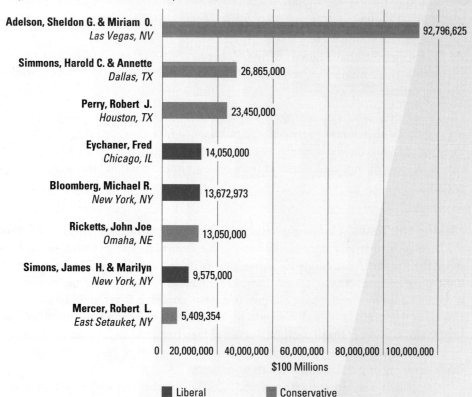

Source: Center for Responsive Politics, http://www.opensecrets.org/outsidespending/donor_stats.php?cycle=2012&type=I.

Critical Thinking The First Amendment of the Constitution states, "Congress shall make no laws ... abridging the freedom of speech." Is spending money on election campaigns a form of speech?

- An *issue-oriented strategy*, which seeks support from groups that feel strongly about various policies;
- A *candidate-oriented strategy*, which depends on the candidate's perceived personal qualities, such as experience, leadership ability, integrity, independence, and trustworthiness.

The campaign strategy must be tailored to the political context of the election. Clearly, a party-centered strategy is inappropriate in a primary because all contenders have the same party affiliation. Research suggests that a party-centered strategy is best suited to voters with little political knowledge.[60] How do candidates learn what the electorate knows and thinks about politics, and how can they use this information? Candidates today usually turn to pollsters and political consultants, of whom there are hundreds. Well-funded candidates can purchase a "polling package" that includes:

- A benchmark poll, which provides "campaign information about the voting preferences and issue concerns of various groups in the electorate and a detailed reading of the image voters have of the candidates in the race";
- Focus groups, consisting of ten to twenty people "chosen to represent particular target groups (e.g., Latinos)[61] the campaign wants to reinforce or persuade ... led in their discussion by persons trained in small-group dynamics," giving texture and depth to poll results;
- A trend poll "to determine the success of the campaigns in altering candidate images and voting preferences";
- Tracking polls that begin in early October, "conducting short nightly interviews with a small number of respondents, keyed to the variables that have assumed importance."[62]

Professional campaign managers can use information from such sources to settle on a strategy that mixes party affiliation, issues, and images in its messages.[63] In major campaigns, the mass media disseminate these messages to voters through news coverage, advertising, and Internet services—around which a new industry has grown.

Making the News. Campaigns value news coverage by the media for two reasons: the coverage is free, and it seems objective to the audience. If news stories do nothing more than report the candidate's name, that is important, for name recognition by itself often wins elections. To get favorable coverage, campaign managers cater to reporters' deadlines and needs. Getting free news coverage is yet another advantage that incumbents enjoy over challengers, for incumbents can command attention simply by announcing political decisions—even if they had little to do with them. Members of Congress are so good at this, says one observer, that House members have made news organizations their "unwitting adjuncts."[64]

Campaigns vary in the effectiveness with which they transmit their messages through the news media. Effective tactics recognize the limitations of both the audience and the media. The typical voter is not deeply interested in politics and has trouble keeping track of multiple themes supported with details. By the same token, television is not willing to air lengthy statements from candidates. As a result, news coverage is often condensed to sound bites only a few seconds long. The media often use the metaphor of a horse race in covering politics in the United States. In 2008, more than half the national news stories on television, in print, and online dealt with the horse race.[65] Ironically, evidence suggests that the national media focus more on campaign tactics and positioning than the state or local media do.[66] One longtime student of the media contends that reporters both enliven and simplify campaigns by describing them in terms of four basic scenarios: *bandwagons, losing ground, the front-runner*, and *the likely loser*.[67] Once the opinion polls show weakness or strength in a candidate, reporters dust off the appropriate story line.

The more time the press spends on the horse race, the less attention it gives to campaign issues. In fact, recent studies have found that in some campaigns, voters get more information from television ads than they do from television news.[68] Ads are more likely to be effective in low-visibility campaigns below the presidential level because the voters know less about the candidates at the outset and there is little "free" news coverage of the campaigns.[69]

Advertising the Candidate. In all elections, the first objective of paid advertising is name recognition. The next is to promote candidates by extolling their virtues. Finally, campaign advertising can have a negative objective: to attack one's opponent or play on emotions.[70] But name recognition is usually the most important. Studies show that many voters cannot recall the names of their U.S. senators or representatives, but they can recognize their names on a list—as on a ballot. Researchers attribute the high reelection rate for members of Congress mainly to high name recognition (see Chapter 11). Name recognition is the key objective during the primary season even in presidential campaigns, but other objectives become salient in advertising for the general election.

At one time, candidates for national office relied heavily on newspaper advertising; today, they overwhelmingly use the electronic media—primarily television. Political ads convey more substantive information than many people believe, but the amount varies by campaign. In his comprehensive study of campaign advertising in the last seven presidential elections, Darrell West found that political ads tended to mention candidates' policy preferences more in 1984, 1988, 1992, and 2000 and candidates' personal qualities more in 1996, 2004, and 2008.[71] In 1996, Bill Clinton drew fire for lack of "honesty and integrity"; in 2004, John Kerry was attacked for "flip-flopping" on issues and for false "heroism" in Vietnam; and in 2008 Obama was criticized for inexperience and in 2012 for "gutting welfare reform." In turn, Romney was attacked as "catering to the rich at the expense of the middle class."[72]

Other scholars have cautioned that the policy positions put forward in campaign ads may be misleading, if not downright deceptive.[73] West found that the 2012 presidential campaign showed "the highest level of campaign negativity in the post–World War II era. Not only were most of the advertisements negative in tone, many of them were highly misleading or characterized by false appeals."[74] Not all negatively toned ads qualify as *attack ads*, which advocate nothing positive. In 2012, television attack ads predominated in states prior to Republican caucuses or primary elections. Most were run by Super PACs, which spent 72 percent of their money on negative ads, compared with 27 percent spent by candidates' own campaigns.[75]

The term *contrast ads* describes those that both criticize an opponent and advocate policies of the sponsoring candidate.[76] A review of recent studies found that, ironically, both attack and contrast ads "actually carry more policy information than pure advocacy ads."[77] Regardless of whether people learn from political ads, scholars found, advertising does "a great deal to persuade potential voters" who viewed ads compared with those not seeing the ads.[78]

The media often inflate the effect of prominent ads by reporting them as news, which means that citizens are about as likely to see controversial ads during the news as in the ads' paid time slots. Although negative ads do convey information, some studies suggest that negative ads produce low voter turnout.[79] However, recent research shows that the existing level of political mistrust is more important than the negativity of the ads.[80] Moreover, negative ads seem to work differently for challengers (who show a tendency to benefit from them) than for incumbents (who tend to do better with more positive campaigns).[81] If these findings seem confusing, that's essentially the state of research on negative ads.[82] Researchers reviewing studies say that the connection between reality and perceptions is complex. Campaigns seen as negative by scholars are not necessarily viewed that way by voters.[83]

Using the Internet. The Internet debuted in presidential campaigns in 1992, when Democratic candidate Jerry Brown, former (and current) governor of California, sent e-mail messages to supporters.[84] Two decades later in 2012, campaigns used the Internet to "microtarget" voters, sending specific messages to computer screens of selected viewers.[85] As in online marketing, visits to campaign websites generate information for providers who slip digital markers or "cookies" into the users' computers. That information is matched with other user information (e.g., make of car) stored in a huge database. Campaign consultants then match those data with voting records, turnout, and party registration (but not voting choice, which is protected). Then they can frame ads targeted at visitors to conservative (or liberal) websites who shop for Lexus (or Ford) cars, who are registered Republicans (or Democrats), and who are frequent voters. Consultants can produce targeted Internet ads cheaply, transmit them with little expense, and—very importantly—send them quickly in reaction to breaking news.

Candidates like the Internet because it is fast, easy to use, and cheap—saving mailing costs and phone calls. Nevertheless, relatively few people get campaign news via the Internet. A national survey in January 2012 asked respondents whether they "learned something" about the presidential campaign or candidates from various news sources. Most people named some form of television (cable news, 36 percent; local TV news, 32 percent; network news, 26 percent), and only 25 percent named the Internet.[86] Although the survey was early in the primary season, 72 percent of respondents reported hearing or seeing campaign commercials, whereas only 16 percent received e-mails, 15 percent visited a candidate's website, and only 6 percent followed the candidate on Twitter or Facebook. Political "insiders," however, burn up the airwaves tweeting about their campaign prowess.

Despite the increased reliance on the Internet by candidates for campaigning and fundraising, only about 10 percent of the ad budgets in 2012 was devoted to digital commercials.[87] Because Internet users seek out what they want to view, the best way to reach average voters is still through local broadcast television.

Explaining Voting Choice

LO5 ★ Assess the effects of party identification, political issues, and candidate attributes on voter choice.

Why do people choose one candidate over another? That is not easy to determine, but there are ways to approach the question. Individual voting choices can be analyzed as products of both long-term and short-term forces. Long-term forces operate throughout a series of elections, predisposing voters to choose certain types of candidates. Short-term forces are associated with particular elections; they arise from a combination of the candidates and issues of the time. Party identification is by far the most important long-term force affecting U.S. elections. The most important short-term forces are candidates' attributes and their policy positions.

Party Identification

Ever since the presidential election of 1952, when the University of Michigan's National Election Studies began, we have known that more than half the electorate decides how to vote before the party conventions end in the summer.[88] And voters who make an early voting decision generally vote according to their party identification. Despite frequent comments in the media about the decline of partisanship in voting behavior, party identification again had a substantial effect on the presidential vote in 2012, as Figure 9.4 shows. Each party's candidates, Barack Obama and Mitt Romney, won around 90 percent of self-described partisans of their party, with independents splitting their votes slightly in favor of Romney.

This is a common pattern in presidential elections. The winner holds nearly all the voters who identify with his party. The loser holds most of his fellow Democrats or Republicans, but some percentage defects to the winner, a consequence of short-term forces—the candidates' attributes and the issues—surrounding the election. The winner usually gets most of the independents, who split disproportionately for him, also because of short-term forces. In 2012, the electorate favored the Democratic candidate. But as shown in Figure 8.4 on page 224, Democrats have consistently outnumbered Republicans over the past fifty years. Why, then, have Republican candidates won more presidential elections since 1952 than Democrats? For one thing, Democrats do not turn out to vote as consistently as Republicans do. For another, Democrats tend to defect more readily from their party. Defections are sparked by the candidates' attributes and the issues, which have usually favored Republican presidential candidates since 1952.

Prior to the 2012 election, polls showed strong relationships between ethnicity and party identification. By a margin of about ten percentage points, non-Hispanic whites described themselves more as Republicans than Democrats. In contrast, blacks were more likely to identify as Democrats by about eight points. Hispanics were Democratic more than three to one, but Hispanics were less likely than whites or blacks to be registered and to vote.

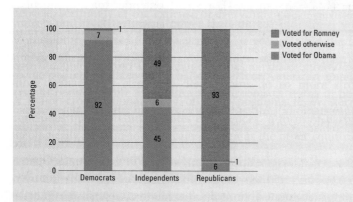

FIGURE 9.4 Effect of Party Identification on the Vote, 2012

The 2012 election showed that party identification still plays a key role in voting behavior. The chart shows the results of exit polls of thousands of voters as they left hundreds of polling places across the nation on election day. Voters were asked what party they identified with and how they voted for president. Those who identified with one of the two parties voted strongly for their party's candidate.

Source: Data from *Wall Street Journal*, online report, November 7, 2012, "Exit Polls: Casting Ballots in 2012."

Hope Renewed

President Barack Obama and Vice President Joe Biden were re-elected to another term in 2012, despite the nation's high unemployment rate and its huge national debt.

SHAWN THEW/EPA/Landov

Hope Denied

Republican presidential candidate, Mitt Romney, and his running mate, Representative Paul Ryan, won only 47 percent of the popular vote to 51 percent for Obama and Biden. According to exit polls, Romney and Ryan took almost 60 percent of the vote from whites, but the Democrats won over 70 percent from blacks, Hispanics, and Asians and 60 percent of voters from 18 to 29 years of age.

Jamie Sabau/Getty Images News/Getty Images

Issues and Policies

Candidates exploit issues that they think are important to voters. Challengers usually campaign by pointing out problems—unemployment, inflation, war, civil disorders, corruption—and promising to solve them. Incumbents compile a record in office (for better or worse) and thus try to campaign on their accomplishments. In 2012, the overriding campaign issue was the economy. With about 20 million Americans unemployed, the unemployment rate stuck at about eight percentage points, and the government facing a trillion-dollar budget deficit and more than $10 trillion in national debt, Republican challenger Romney faulted President Obama for his handling of the economy. President Obama could justifiably claim that economic conditions were better than when he took office, but Romney contended that he could do better because of his business background.

Candidates' Attributes

Candidates' attributes are especially important to voters who lack good information about a candidate's past performance and policy stands—which means most of us. Without such information, voters search for clues about the candidates to try to predict their behavior in office. Some fall back on their personal beliefs about religion, gender, and race in making political judgments. Such stereotypic thinking accounts for the patterns of opposition and support met by, among others, a Catholic candidate for president (John Kennedy), a woman candidate for vice president (Geraldine Ferraro in 1984), a black contender for a presidential nomination (Jesse Jackson in 1984 and 1988), the first Jewish vice-presidential candidate of a major party (Joe Lieberman in 2000), the first African American presidential candidate (Barack Obama in 2008), and the first Mormon candidate (Mitt Romney in 2012).

National surveys taken a week before the 2012 election showed that voters had more favorable opinions of President Barack Obama than his Republican opponent, Mitt Romney. However, only about half the electorate approved of the job that Obama was doing as president.

Evaluating the Voting Choice

Choosing among candidates according to their personal attributes might be an understandable approach, but it is not rational voting, according to democratic theory. According to that theory, citizens should vote according to the candidates' past performance and proposed policies. Voters who choose between candidates on the basis of their policies are voting on the issues, a behavior that fits the idealized conception of democratic theory. However, issues, candidates' attributes, and party identification all figure in the voting decision, and scholars have incorporated these factors in statistical models to explain voting.

Unfortunately for democratic theory, many studies of presidential elections show that issues are less important to voters than either party identification or the candidates' attributes. One exception occurred in 1972, when voters perceived George McGovern as too liberal for their tastes and issue voting exceeded party identification.[89] Later research found an increase in policy-based voting.[90] Although party voting has declined somewhat since the 1950s, the relationship between voters' positions on the issues and their party identification is clearer and more consistent today. For example, Democratic Party identifiers are now more likely than Republican identifiers to describe themselves as liberal, and they are more likely than Republican identifiers to favor government spending for Social Security and health care. The more closely party identification is aligned with ideological orientation, the more sense it makes to vote by party. Over the last four decades, as shown in Figure 9.5, the alignment of party and ideology has increased in congressional voting such that the fit is almost perfect. Virtually all Democrats in the House of Representatives have more liberal voting records than virtually all Republicans, who have more conservative records.

Campaign Effects

If party identification is the most important factor in the voting decision and is also resistant to short-term changes, there are definite limits to the capacity of a campaign

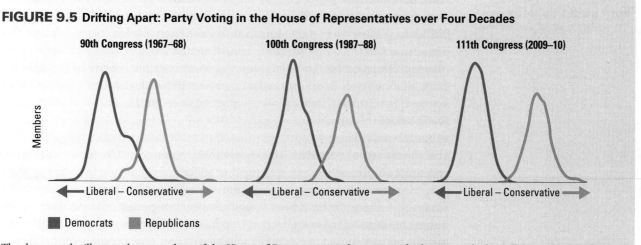

FIGURE 9.5 Drifting Apart: Party Voting in the House of Representatives over Four Decades

The three graphs illustrate how members of the House of Representatives have grown further apart ideologically over the past four decades. The base line estimates the representatives' liberal—conservative ideology as computed from hundreds of roll call votes in each congress. In the mid-1960s, some Republicans had more liberal voting records than Democrats, and some Democrats voted more as conservatives—a few being very conservative. By the late 1980s, the overlap had shrunk considerably. By 2009–2010, almost all Democrats were liberals and all Republicans were conservative.

Source: The graphs were kindly provided by Royce Carroll, Rice University. For the methodology, see http://voteview.com/dwnomin.htm. Reproduced by permission.

to influence the outcome of elections.[91] In a close election, however, changing just a few votes means the difference between victory and defeat, so a campaign can be decisive even if its effects cannot be disentangled.

The Television Campaign. Because of the propensity of television news shows to offer only sound bites, candidates cannot rely on television news to get their message out. In 2008, remarks from the two major presidential candidates on network news programs averaged only 8.9 seconds, about a second less than in the 1988 election, when sound bite timing began.[92] In truth, the networks devoted about as much airtime to the presidential campaign as in the past, but they did not give the candidates themselves much time to speak. In the average presidential campaign story, reporters spoke about 74 percent of the time compared with the candidates' 11 percent. No wonder that presidential candidates volunteer to appear on entertainment television shows: they get the chance to talk to the public![93]

Although candidates seek free coverage on news and entertainment programs, they fight their election campaigns principally through television advertisements. Both parties understand that a presidential election is not truly a national election to be fought across the nation but a *federal* election whose outcome would be decided in certain "battleground" or "swing" states.[94] The Obama and Romney television campaigns differed on approach, spending, and effectiveness. Obama used professional ad buyers, while Romney relied on one person who placed commercials on a targeted week-to-week basis, which proved to be more costly, and in some states even reached fewer viewers.[95]

Entering the 2012 election, Obama's strategists knew that even if he won all of the same states as in 2008, he would lose six electoral votes because of reapportionment. But he would still have more than the 270 votes needed for reelection. Obama could count on 246 electoral votes from the twenty states that voted Democratic in 2004 and 2008, but Republicans could count on only 180 votes from twenty-two states that favored them both years. A total of 112 electoral votes rested with nine states that voted for Bush in 2004 but for Obama in 2008. Given that many white working-class voters had soured on Obama, Republicans hoped to pick up many of the nine: Colorado, Florida, Indiana, Iowa, Ohio, Nevada, New Mexico, North Carolina, and Virginia. Both campaigns focused on those states. On election night, Obama's campaign proved to be more successful, winning seven of the nine states, losing to Romney only in Indiana and narrowly in North Carolina. Obama outpolled Romney only 51 to 47 percent in the popular vote but his 332 electoral votes were 62 percent of the total of 538.

The Presidential Debates. In 1960, John F. Kennedy and Richard Nixon held the first televised presidential debate, but debates between the two Democratic and Republican presidential nominees were not used again until 1976. Since then, candidate debates in some form have been a regular feature of presidential elections, although sitting presidents have been reluctant to debate except on their own terms. Both campaign staffs agreed to three presidential debates and one vice-presidential debate in October. Surveyed after the first debate (watched by almost 70 million people), viewers overwhelmingly thought a confident, articulate Romney outperformed a distracted Obama. Afterwards, Romney began to erode Obama's lead in the polls. The vice-presidential debate between Paul Ryan and an animated Joe Biden perked up Democratic enthusiasm somewhat. Although Obama marginally outperformed Romney in most polls after the last two debates, Romney clearly benefited from them, virtually erasing Obama's lead heading into the November election.

Campaigns, Elections, and Parties

LO6 ★ Explain the significance of candidate-centered as opposed to party-centered election campaigns for both majoritarian and pluralist democracy.

Election campaigns today tend to be highly personalized, candidate centered, and conducted outside the control of party organizations. The increased use of electronic media, especially television, has encouraged candidates to personalize their campaign messages; at the same time, the decline of party identification has decreased the power of party-related appeals. Although the party affiliations of the candidates and the party identifications of the voters jointly explain a good deal of electoral behavior, party organizations are not central to elections in America, and this situation has implications for democratic government.

Parties and the Majoritarian Model

According to the majoritarian model of democracy, parties link people with their government by making government responsive to public opinion. Chapter 8 outlined the model of responsible party government in a majoritarian democracy. This model holds that parties should present clear and coherent programs to voters, that voters should choose candidates according to the party programs, that the winning party should carry out its programs once in office, and that voters should hold the governing party responsible at the next election for executing its program. As noted in Chapter 8, the Republican and Democratic parties do follow the model because they formulate different platforms and tend to pursue their announced policies when in office. The weak links in this model of responsible party government are those that connect candidates to voters through campaigns and elections.

You have not read much in this book about the role of the party platform in nominating candidates, conducting campaigns, or explaining voters' choices. In nominating presidential candidates, basic party principles (as captured in the party platform) do interact with the presidential primary process, and the candidate who wins enough convention delegates through the primaries will surely be comfortable with any platform that her or his delegates adopt. But House and Senate nominations are rarely fought over the party platform. And thoughts about party platforms usually are virtually absent from campaigning and from voters' minds when they cast their ballots. Although voters care little about party platforms, platforms reflect party ideology, and Democrats and Republicans in Congress today are divided sharply over ideology. As shown in Figure 9.5, there was almost no overlap between House Democrats and Republicans concerning ideology in their voting records in 2009–2010. The pattern was similar among senators, but not as sharply defined. Members of Congress may be behaving "responsibly" when voting cohesively according to their ideology, but they are probably not responding to the majority of the voters, who are ideologically more moderate.

Parties and the Pluralist Model

The way parties in the United States operate is more in keeping with the pluralist model of democracy than the majoritarian model. Our parties are not the basic mechanism through which citizens control their government; instead, they function more as two giant interest groups. The parties' interests lie in electing and reelecting their candidates and in enjoying the benefits of public office. In past elections, the parties cared little about the positions or ideologies favored by their candidates for Congress or state offices. Within today's Republican Party, tea party groups work actively to nominate candidates that are suitably conservative. Perhaps to a lesser extent, liberal groups like MoveOn.org push to nominate and elect suitably progressive candidates.

Some scholars believe that stronger parties would strengthen democratic government, even if they could not meet all the requirements of the responsible party model.[96] Our parties already perform valuable functions in structuring the vote along partisan lines and in proposing alternative government policies, but stronger parties might also be able to play a more important role in coordinating government policies after elections. Fulfilling that role, however, presumes that the same party controls the House, the Senate, and the presidency. Under the common situation of divided government—when different parties control different branches—strong parties may simply block coordinated policies. At present, the decentralized nature of the nominating process and campaigning for office offer many opportunities for organized groups outside the parties to identify and back candidates who favor their interests. Although this is in keeping with pluralist theory, it is certain to frustrate majority interests on occasion.

Master the Topics of Elections and Campaigning for Office with MindTap™ for American Government

 REVIEW MindTap™ for American Government
Access Key Term Flashcards for Chapter 9.

 TEST YOURSELF MindTap™ for American Government
Take the Wrap It Up Quiz for Chapter 9.

 STAY CURRENT MindTap™ for American Government
Access the KnowNow blog and customized RSS for updates on current events.

 STAY FOCUSED MindTap™ for American Government
Complete the Focus Activities for Elections and Campaigning for Office.

Summary

LO1 Describe how election campaigns have changed over time.

- Campaigning has evolved from a party-centered to a candidate-centered process.

LO2 Explain the procedures followed in the nomination of both congressional and presidential candidates.

- Using primary elections to nominate candidates tends to decentralize power in American political parties. The successful

candidate for public office must campaign first to win the party nomination, then to win the general election. Democratic and Republican nominations for president are not decided at the parties' national conventions but determined in advance through the complex process of selecting delegates pledged to particular candidates. Party nominees can legitimately say that they won through their own efforts and owe little to the party organization.

However, candidates cannot win the nomination unless they have broad support within the party.

LO3 Describe the function of the electoral college and formulate arguments for and against the electoral vote system.

- The need to win a majority of votes in the electoral college structures presidential elections. Only twice in more than 100 years has a candidate won a majority of the popular vote and lost in the electoral college; the last time was in 2000. In fact, the electoral college usually magnifies the victory margin of the winning candidate. Since World War II, one party has often won the presidency, while the other party controlled one or more chambers of Congress. Such divided government has interfered with party control of government.

LO4 Analyze the American election campaign process in terms of political context, financial resources, and strategies and tactics for reaching the voters.

- Money is essential in running a modern campaign for major office. Serious attempts to control campaign finance began in 1974 with passage of the Federal Election Campaign Act, which established the Federal Election Commission (FEC). The law restricted campaign contributions by corporations and labor unions and set limits on contributions by individuals. Court decisions in 2010 allowed unlimited contributions by corporations, labor unions, and individuals to influence elections as long as the expenditures were "uncoordinated" with candidates or parties. These decisions gave rise to Super PACs that raised and spent millions of dollars in the 2012 general election. Public funding for presidential elections began with the 1976 election, but by 1996 some candidates learned that they could raise more money privately than

provided through public funds. In 2012, no major candidate seeking the presidency sought public funding. The government does not provide funding for congressional campaigns, so candidates must raise contributions from individuals or PACs.

LO5 Assess the effects of party identification, political issues, and candidate attributes on voter choice.

- Voting choice can be analyzed in terms of party identification, candidates' attributes, and policy positions. Party identification is the most important long-term factor in shaping the voting decision, but few candidates rely on it in their campaigns— relying instead on personalized campaigns that stress their attributes and policies. Short-term factors stemming from a combination of the candidates and issues in the election can solidify support from one candidate's partisans nationally, encourage defections from the other's partisans, and capture a majority of the independents. Overall, presidential campaigns are not national but federal elections, and the winning candidate assembles an electoral vote majority by winning traditionally loyal states plus enough swing states.

LO6 Explain the significance of candidate-centered as opposed to party-centered election campaigns for both majoritarian and pluralist democracy.

- The way that nominations, campaigns, and elections are conducted in America is out of keeping with the ideals of responsible party government that fit the majoritarian model of democracy. In particular, campaigns and elections do not function to link parties strongly to voters, as the model posits. American parties are better suited to the pluralist model of democracy, which sees them as major interest groups competing with lesser groups to further their own interests.

Chapter Quiz

LO1 **Describe how election campaigns have changed over time.**

1. Candidates once relied on their parties to run election campaigns; on whom do they rely today?
2. What main role do political parties perform in an election campaign?

LO2 **Explain the procedures followed in the nomination of both congressional and presidential candidates.**

1. What is the difference between an "open" and "closed" party primary? Which weakens political parties?
2. Describe the different methods used to select delegates to a party's national nominating convention.

LO3 **Describe the function of the electoral college and formulate arguments for and against the electoral vote system.**

1. What is the difference between the electoral college and the electoral vote system?
2. Explain why a presidential election is a federal election, not a national election.

LO4 **Analyze the American election campaign process in terms of political context, financial resources, and strategies and tactics for reaching the voters.**

1. By what reasoning has the Supreme Court struck down attempts to regulate campaign finance?

2. Explain how the Court's 2010 decision in the *Citizens United* case has led to increased spending in federal election campaigns.

LO5 **Assess the effects of party identification, political issues, and candidate attributes on voter choice.**

1. Historically, which has the greater effect on voting for president, party identification or the candidates' issue positions?
2. What are "battleground states" in presidential elections, and why are they important?

LO6 **Explain the significance of candidate-centered as opposed to party-centered election campaigns for both majoritarian and pluralist democracy.**

1. How well do political parties fulfill the expectations of the responsible model of party government set forth at the end of the preceding chapter on political parties?
2. Do American political parties operate more in keeping with the majoritarian or pluralist models of democracy?

10 Interest Groups

Learning Outcomes

LO1 Identify the different roles that interest groups play in our political system.

LO2 Analyze the role played by entrepreneurs in interest group formation.

LO3 Identify the various resources available to interest groups and evaluate their role in interest group performance.

LO4 Compare and contrast different types of lobbying.

LO5 Evaluate whether the interest group system biases the public policymaking process.

 WATCH & LEARN MindTap™ for American Government
Watch a brief "What Do You Know?" video summarizing Interest Groups.

AP Images/Jason Getz

Too often the nation is shocked by the act of a demented gunman walking into a building and massacring a number of people who just happen to be in the wrong place at the wrong time. This happened in Aurora, Colorado, where a gunman walked into a midnight screening of a Batman movie and used multiple guns to kill twelve people and injure another seventy. At Virginia Tech University, a gunman walked into one of the school's dorms and shot two students to death; he then proceeded to an academic building where he opened fire in a classroom. Thirty-two were left dead.

Horrific as these events were, the Newtown shootings seemed to reach a new level of depravity. In this small Connecticut town, twenty-year-old Adam Lanza went to the Sandy Hook Elementary School and murdered twenty first-graders and six school staff. He then killed himself. Americans struggled with the horrific image of Lanza opening fire with a semiautomatic rifle in a roomful of six-year-olds.

The national revulsion led, as these tragedies typically do, to calls for tighter restrictions on the purchase of guns. The Second Amendment to the Constitution says the "right of the people to keep and bear Arms shall not be infringed." Yet, even this broad liberty is subject to some regulation, and purchasers of weapons at a gun store must go through a back-ground check to see if they've committed a serious crime or run up against a few other restrictions. In the wake of Newtown, proposed legislation in Congress, backed by President Obama, would have put an end to an inconsistency in current law whereby people purchasing firearms at gun shows and on the Internet are not subject to a background check.

The public is strongly in favor of tightening restrictions so that mentally ill or convicted criminals are prohibited from purchasing guns. In one poll, 92 percent said they favored universal background checks (see Figure 10.1). Other measures to try to regulate guns have lower levels of support. Still, if we had a system of government based on majority public opinon, the Newtown bill would likely have passed overwhelmingly. And yet it failed in the Senate and no other new legislation emerged.

The reason why public opinion did not carry the day is because many gun owners believe the regulation of gun ownership is a step toward a confiscation of guns by a too strong national government. Such views are embodied by the National Rifle Association (NRA), the nation's preeminent gun rights lobby, which fought vigorously against the Newtown legislation. The organization is wealthy, supported financially by the gun industry, and has a huge membership of

FIGURE 10.1 Strong Views on Background Checks

In the wake of the Newtown massacre, support rose for legislation mandating background checks for gun shows and Internet purchases. Public support for other gun control measures is much more mixed. People who oppose gun control efforts tend to be more intense about their views than those who support gun control.

Source: "Gun Policy: Universal Background Checks and Armed Guards, January 11–15, 2012," CBS News/*New York Times* Poll, http://www.scribd.com/doc/120711121/CBS-News-New-York-Times-Poll.

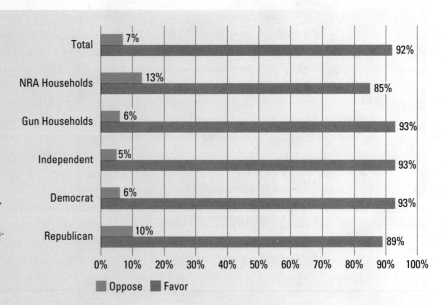

	Oppose	Favor
Total	7%	92%
NRA Households	13%	85%
Gun Households	6%	93%
Independent	5%	93%
Democrat	6%	93%
Republican	10%	89%

5 million. More than anything else, what's critical is that its membership is impassioned and is willing to vote against any legislator, no matter the party, if he or she votes in favor of a gun control bill. In responding to the call for universal registration, the leader of the NRA, Wayne LaPierre, said "The only thing that stops a bad guy with a gun is a good guy with a gun."

Thus, in the end, what mattered most was not overall public opinion but the intensity of opinion by the two opposing sides. Those who favor gun control tend not to feel as strongly as those who oppose it. For opponents of gun control, it is a matter of freedom—the freedom to own and carry a gun in line with what they believe is an ironclad Constitutional guarantee.[1]

LISTEN & LEARN

MindTap™ **for American Government**

Access Read Speaker to listen to Chapter 10.

In this chapter, we look at the central dynamic of pluralist democracy: the interaction of interest groups and government. In analyzing the process by which interest groups and lobbyists come to speak on behalf of different groups, we focus on several questions. How do interest groups form? Whom do they represent? What tactics do they use to convince policymakers that their views are best for the nation? Is the interest group system biased in favor of certain types of people? If so, what are the consequences?

Interest Groups and the American Political Tradition

LO1 ★ Identify the different roles that interest groups play in our political system.

interest group
An organized group of individuals that seeks to influence public policy. Also called a *lobby*.

An **interest group** is an organized body of individuals who share some political goals and try to influence public policy decisions. Among the most prominent interest groups in the United States are the AFL-CIO (representing labor union members), the American Farm Bureau Federation (representing farmers), the Business Round-table (representing big business), and Common Cause (representing citizens concerned with reforming government). Interest groups are also called **lobbies**, and their representatives are referred to as **lobbyists**.

Interest Groups: Good or Evil?

A recurring debate in American politics concerns the role of interest groups in a democratic society. Are interest groups a threat to the well-being of the political system, or do they contribute to its proper functioning? A favorable early evaluation of interest groups can be found in the writings of Alexis de Tocqueville, a French visitor to the United States in the early nineteenth century. During his travels, Tocqueville marveled at the array of organizations he found, and he later wrote that "Americans of all ages, all conditions, and all dispositions, constantly form associations."[2] Tocqueville was suggesting that the ease with which we form organizations reflects a strong democratic culture.

Yet other early observers were concerned about the consequences of interest group politics. Writing in the *Federalist* papers, James Madison warned of the dangers of "factions," the major divisions in American society. In *Federalist* No. 10, written in 1787, Madison said it was inevitable that substantial differences would develop between factions. It was only natural for farmers to oppose merchants, tenants to oppose landlords, and so on. Madison further reasoned that each faction would do what it could to prevail over other factions, that each basic interest in society would try to persuade the government to adopt policies that favored it at the expense of others. He noted that the fundamental causes of faction were "sown in the nature of man."[3]

But Madison argued against trying to suppress factions. He concluded that factions can be eliminated only by removing our freedoms because "Liberty is to faction what air is to fire."[4] Instead, Madison suggested that relief from the self-interested advocacy of factions should come only through controlling the effects of that advocacy. The relief would be provided by a democratic republic in which government would mediate among opposing factions. The size and diversity of the nation as well as the structure of government would ensure that even a majority faction could never come to suppress the rights of others.[5]

How we judge interest groups—as "good" or "evil"—may depend on how strongly we are committed to freedom or equality (see Chapter 1). People dislike interest groups in general because they do not offer equal representation to all; some sectors of society are better represented than others. In a poll, four out of five respondents indicated that they believe it is common for lobbyists to bribe members of Congress.[6] Recent filings with Congress listed $3.3 billion in annual spending on lobbying, and as Figure 10.2 shows, individual lobbies spend vast sums as they try to influence legislation.[7] Interest groups have recently enjoyed unparalleled growth; many new groups have formed, and old ones have expanded. Apparently we distrust interest groups as a whole, but we like those that represent our views. Stated more bluntly, we hate lobbies—except those that speak on our behalf.

The Roles of Interest Groups

The "evil" side of interest group politics is all too apparent. Each group pushes its own selfish interests, which, despite the group's claims to the contrary, are not always in the best interest of other Americans. The "good" side of interest group advocacy may not be so clear. How do the actions of interest groups benefit our political system?[8]

lobby
See *interest group*.

lobbyist
A representative of an interest group.

COMPARE WITH YOUR PEERS
MindTap for American Government

Access the Interest Groups Forum: Polling Activity—Regulating Interest Groups.

FIGURE 10.2 Investing in Public Policy

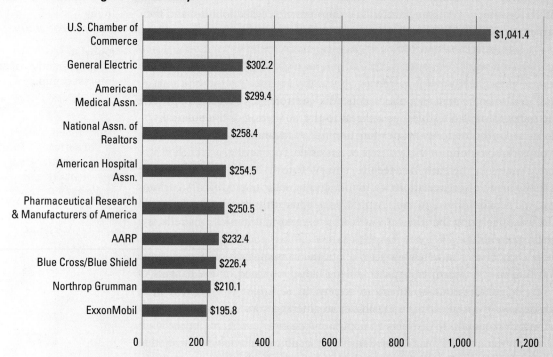

Lobbying expenditures (in millions of dollars) 1998–2013

This list of the top ten spenders on lobbying for the period between 1998 and 2013 demonstrates the vast sum of money spent to influence public policy. The top spenders are, not surprisingly, predominantly business-related interest groups as a change in public policy can result in a business making or losing hundreds of millions of dollars. The Chamber of Commerce's figure reflects a huge effort to defeat the Affordable Care Act.

Source: Center for Responsive Politics, "Top Spenders," http://www.opensecrets.org/lobby/top.php?showYear=a &indexType=s.

Representation. Interest groups represent people before their government. Just as a member of Congress represents a particular constituency, so does a lobbyist. A lobbyist for the National Association of Broadcasters, for example, speaks for the interests of radio and television broadcasters when Congress or a government agency is considering a relevant policy decision.

Whatever the political interest—the cement industry, Social Security, endangered species—it helps to have an active lobby operating in Washington. Members of Congress represent a multitude of interests, some of them conflicting, from their own districts and states. Government administrators, too, are pulled in different directions and have their own policy preferences. Interest groups articulate their members' concerns, presenting them directly and forcefully in the political process.

Participation. Interest groups are vehicles for political participation. They provide a means by which like-minded citizens can pool their resources and channel their energies into collective political action. People band together because they know it is much easier to get government to listen to a group than to an individual. One farmer fighting against a new pesticide proposal in Congress probably will not get very far, but thousands of farmers united in an organization stand a much better chance of getting policymakers to consider their needs. Interest groups not only facilitate participation; they stimulate it as well. By asking people to write to their member of

CONNECT WITH YOUR CLASSMATES
MindTap™ **for American Government**

Access the Interest Groups Forum: Discussion—Participation in Interest Groups.

Congress or take other action, lobbies get people more involved in the political process than they otherwise would be.

Education. As part of their efforts to lobby government and increase their membership, interest groups help educate their members, the public at large, and government officials. To gain the attention of the policymakers they are trying to educate, interest groups need to provide them with information that is not easily obtained from other sources. Lobbyists are apparently quite good at this: 65 percent of congressional staffers told university researchers that meetings with lobbyists representing corporations were helpful.[9]

Agenda Building. In a related role, interest groups bring new issues into the political limelight through a process called **agenda building**. American society has many problem areas, but public officials are not addressing all of them. Through their advocacy, interest groups make the government aware of problems and then try to see to it that something is done to solve them.[10] Labor unions, for example, have historically played a critical role in gaining attention for problems that were being systematically ignored. As Figure 10.3 shows, however, union membership has declined significantly over the years. As private sector employment in unionized industries has fallen, union membership among municipal government employees has become the largest sector of unionized workers.[11]

agenda building
The process by which new issues are brought into the political limelight.

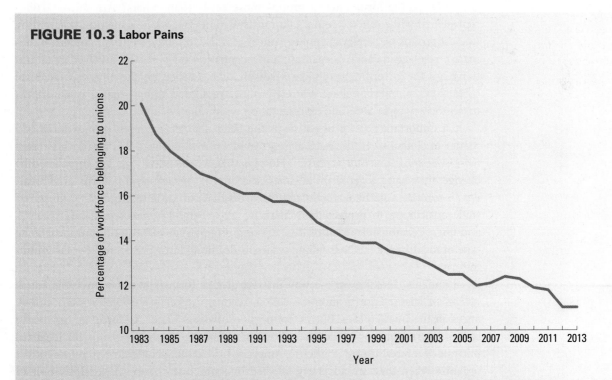

FIGURE 10.3 Labor Pains

Over the years, many manufacturing jobs in the United States have migrated overseas to developing countries where workers earn lower wages. That may be good for consumers (cheaper wages mean lower-cost products), but it has been bad for labor unions because workers in heavy industry have traditionally been the most likely to be unionized. Service sector workers like restaurant employees have been much harder for unions to organize.

Source: Bureau of Labor Statistics.

program monitoring
Keeping track of government programs; usually done by interest groups.

Program Monitoring. Finally, interest groups engage in **program monitoring**. Lobbies follow government programs that are important to their constituents, keeping abreast of developments in Washington and the communities where the policies are implemented. When a program is not operating as it should, concerned interest groups push administrators to change it in ways that promote the groups' goals. They also draw attention to proposals that are circulating before governmental bureaucracies. When Trout Unlimited, a lobby representing sport fishermen, learned that a gold mine was proposed near Bristol Bay in Alaska, it immediately went to the Environmental Protection Agency to stop the mining before it began so as to protect a salmon fishery there.[12]

Interest groups do, then, play some positive roles in their pursuit of self-interest. But we should not assume that the positive side of interest groups neatly balances the negative. Questions remain about the overall influence of interest groups on public policymaking. Most important, are the effects of interest group advocacy being controlled, as Madison believed they should be?

How Interest Groups Form

LO2 ★ Analyze the role played by entrepreneurs in interest group formation.

Do some people form interest groups more easily than others? Are some factions represented while others are not? Pluralists assume that when a political issue arises, interest groups with relevant policy concerns begin to lobby. Policy conflicts are ultimately resolved through bargaining and negotiation between the involved organizations and the government. Unlike Madison, who dwelled on the potential for harm by factions, pluralists believe interest groups are a good thing—that they contribute to democracy by broadening representation within the system.

An important part of pluralism is the belief that new interest groups form as a matter of course when the need arises. David Truman outlines this idea in his classic work *The Governmental Process.*[13] He says that when individuals are threatened by change, they band together in an interest group. For example, if government threatens to regulate a particular industry, the firms that compose that industry will start a trade association to protect their financial well-being. Truman sees a direct cause-and-effect relationship in all of this: existing groups stand in equilibrium until some type of disturbance (such as falling wages or declining farm prices) forces new groups to form.

Truman's thinking on the way interest groups form is like the "invisible hand" notion of laissez-faire economics: self-correcting market forces will remedy imbalances in the marketplace. But in politics, no invisible hand, no force, automatically causes interest groups to develop. Truman's disturbance theory paints an idealized portrait of interest group politics in America. In real life, people do not automatically organize when they are adversely affected by some disturbance. A good example of "nonorganization" can be found in Herbert Gans's book *The Urban Villagers.*[14] Gans, a sociologist, moved into the West End, a low-income neighborhood in Boston, during the late 1950s. The neighborhood had been targeted for urban redevelopment; the city was planning to replace old buildings with modern ones. This meant that the people living there—primarily poor Italian Americans who very much liked their neighborhood—would have to move.

Being evicted is a highly traumatic experience, so the situation in the West End certainly qualified as a bona fide disturbance according to Truman's scheme of interest group formation. Yet the people of the West End barely put up a fight to save their neighborhood. Residents remained largely unorganized; soon they were moved, and the buildings in the neighborhood were demolished.

Disturbance theory clearly fails to explain what happened (or didn't happen) in Boston's West End. An adverse condition or change does not automatically mean that an interest group will form. What, then, is the missing ingredient? Political scientist Robert Salisbury says that the quality of interest group leadership may be the crucial factor.[15]

Interest Group Entrepreneurs

Salisbury likens the role of an interest group leader to that of an entrepreneur in the business world. An entrepreneur is someone who starts new enterprises, usually at considerable personal financial risk. Salisbury says that an **interest group entrepreneur**, or organizer, succeeds or fails for many of the same reasons a business entrepreneur succeeds or fails. The interest group entrepreneur must have something attractive to "market" in order to convince people to join.[16] Potential members must be persuaded that the benefits of joining outweigh the costs. Someone starting a new union, for example, must convince workers that the union can win them wages high enough to more than offset membership dues. The organizer of an ideological group must convince potential members that the group can effectively lobby the government to achieve their particular goals.

interest group entrepreneur
An interest group organizer or leader.

The development of the United Farm Workers union shows the importance of leadership in the formation of an interest group. The union is made up of men and women who pick crops in California and other parts of the country. These pickers—predominantly poor, uneducated Mexican Americans—perform backbreaking work in the hot growing season.

Their chronically low wages and deplorable living conditions made the farm workers prime candidates for organization into a labor union. And throughout the twentieth century, various unions tried to organize them. Yet for many reasons, including distrust of union organizers, intimidation by employers, and lack of money to pay union dues, all failed. Then, in 1962, the late Cesar Chavez, a poor Mexican American, began to crisscross the Central Valley of California, talking to workers and planting the idea of a union. Chavez had been a farm worker himself (he first worked as a picker at the age of ten), and he was well aware of the difficulties that lay ahead for his newly organized union.

After a strike against grape growers failed in 1965, Chavez changed his tactic of trying to build a stronger union merely by recruiting a larger membership. Copying the civil rights movement, Chavez and his followers marched 250 miles to the state capitol in Sacramento to demand help from the governor. The march and other nonviolent tactics began to draw sympathy from people who had no direct involvement in farming. Seeing the movement as a way to help poor members of the church, Catholic clergy were a major source of support. This support gave the charismatic Chavez greater credibility, and his followers cast him in the role of spiritual as well as political leader.[17]

Chavez subsequently called for a boycott, and a small but significant number of Americans stopped buying grapes. The growers, who had bitterly fought the union, were finally hurt economically. Under this and other economic pressures, they eventually agreed to recognize and bargain with the United Farm Workers. The union then helped its members with the wage and benefit agreements it was able to negotiate.

Who Is Being Organized?

Cesar Chavez is a good example of the importance of leadership in the formation of a new interest group. Despite many years of adverse conditions, efforts to organize farm workers had failed. The dynamic leadership of Cesar Chavez is what seems to have made the difference.

But another important element is at work in the formation of interest groups. The residents of Boston's West End and the farm workers in California were poor, uneducated or undereducated, and politically inexperienced—factors that made it extremely difficult to organize them into interest groups. If they had been well-to-do, educated, and politically experienced, they probably would have banded together immediately. People who have money, are educated, and know how the system operates are more confident that their actions can make a difference.[18] Together, these attributes give people more incentive to devote their time and ample resources to organizing and supporting interest groups.

Every existing interest group has its own history, but the three variables just discussed can help explain why groups may or may not become fully organized. First, an adverse change or disturbance can contribute to people's awareness that they need political representation. However, this alone does not ensure that an organization will form, and organizations have formed in the absence of a disturbance. Second, the quality of leadership is critical in the organization of interest groups. Some interest group entrepreneurs are more skilled than others at convincing people to join their organizations. Third, the higher the socioeconomic level of potential members is, the more likely they are to know the value of interest groups and to participate in politics by joining them.

Finally, not all interest groups have real memberships. In this sense "group" is a misnomer; some lobbying organizations are institutions that lack members but are affected by public policy and establish lobbying offices or hire lobbyists to represent them before government. Universities and hospitals, for example, don't have members but are well represented before government. Texas A&M University spent $900,000 on lobbying expenses during 2013; the University of California spent $638,000. For-profit colleges such as the Corinthian Colleges, Apollo Education Group, and DeVry, Inc., also spent heavily. In the case of these for-profit enterprises, their lobbyists are trying to fend off adverse government regulations while protecting the financial interests of shareholders.[19]

Because wealthy and better-educated Americans are more likely to form and join lobbies, they seem to have an important advantage in the political process. Nevertheless, as the United Farm Workers' case shows, poor and uneducated people are also capable of forming interest groups. The question that remains, then, is not *whether* various opposing interests are represented but *how well* they are represented. In terms of Madison's premise in *Federalist* No. 10, are the effects of faction—in this case, the advantages of the wealthy and well educated—being controlled? Before we can answer this question about how interest groups affect the level of political equality in our society, we need to turn our attention to the resources available to interest groups.

 ## Interest Group Resources

LO3 ★ Identify the various resources available to interest groups and evaluate their role in interest group performance.

The strengths, capabilities, and influence of an interest group depend in large part on its resources. A group's most significant resources are its members, lobbyists, and money, including funds that can be contributed to political candidates. The sheer quantity of a group's resources is important, and so is the wisdom with which its resources are used.

Members

One of the most valuable resources an interest group can have is a large, politically active membership. If a lobbyist is trying to convince a legislator to support a particular bill, having a large group of members who live in the legislator's home district or state is tremendously helpful. A legislator who has not already taken a firm position on a bill might be swayed by the knowledge that voters back home are kept informed by interest groups of his or her votes on key issues. The American Association of Retired Persons (AARP) has a membership of 40 million, making it a feared interest group in Washington.

Members give an organization not only the political muscle to influence policy but also financial resources. The more money an organization can collect through dues and contributions, the more people it can hire to lobby government officials and monitor the policymaking process. Greater resources also allow an organization to communicate with its members more and to inform them better. And funding helps a group maintain its membership and attract new members.

Attracting New Members. All membership groups are constantly looking for new adherents to expand their resources and clout. Groups that rely on ideological appeals have a special problem because the competition in most policy areas is intense. People concerned about the environment, for example, can join a seemingly infinite number of local, state, and national groups. The National Wildlife Federation, Environmental Defense, the Natural Resources Defense Council, Friends of the Earth, the National Audubon Society, the Wilderness Society, and the Sierra Club are just some of the national organizations that lobby on environmental issues. Groups try to distinguish themselves from competitors by concentrating on a few key issues and developing a reputation as the most involved and knowledgeable about them. The Sierra Club, one of the oldest and largest environmental groups, has long had a focus on protecting national parks. Some smaller organizations, such as Defenders of Wildlife and the Rainforest Action Network, have found a sufficient number of members to support their advocacy. Organizations in a crowded policy area must differentiate themselves from the competition and then aggressively market what they have to offer to potential contributors.

The Internet has become an increasingly important means of soliciting new members.[20] Compared to direct mail—an interest group sending a letter and supporting material via old fashioned "snail mail"—e-mail is much cheaper. E-mail directed to prospects may entice them to go to the organization's website to learn more and, possibly, make a contribution. Ideological citizen groups depend heavily on Internet traffic to gain new supporters.

Interest groups also use social-networking sites like Facebook for fundraising. There's no shortage of "Friends of [fill in the blank]"—postings that ask visitors to that page to make a generous contribution. These are typically ideological groups, and many try to tap the idealism of the generally youthful clientele of networking sites. The effectiveness of using social-networking sites to build interest group membership is not yet clear.

The Free-Rider Problem. Interest groups' use of aggressive marketing suggests that getting people who sympathize with a group's goals to join and support it with their contributions is difficult. Economists call this difficulty the **free-rider problem**, but we

free-rider problem
The situation in which people benefit from the activities of an organization (such as an interest group) but do not contribute to those activities.

Karen Bleier/AFP/Getty Images/Newscom

An Aggressive Chamber

Most business groups and professional associations try to maintain positive relations with both political parties. The national Chamber of Commerce, however, has been a relentless critic of the Obama administration and helped lead the charge against the Affordable Care Act (see Figure 10.2).

might call it, more colloquially, the "Let-George-do-it problem."[21] Funding for public television stations illustrates the dilemma. Almost all agree that public television, which survives in large part through viewers' contributions, is of great value. But only a fraction of those who watch public television contribute on a regular basis. Why? Because people can watch the programs whether they contribute or not. The free rider has the same access to public television as the contributor.

The same problem crops up for interest groups. When a lobbying group wins benefits, those benefits are not restricted to the members of the organization. For instance, if the U.S. Chamber of Commerce convinces Congress to enact a policy benefiting business, all businesses will benefit, not just those that actually pay the membership dues of the lobbying group. Thus, some executives may feel that their corporation doesn't need to spend the money to join the U.S. Chamber of Commerce, even though they might benefit from the group's efforts; they prefer instead to let others shoulder the financial burden.

The free-rider problem increases the difficulty of attracting paying members, but it certainly does not make the task impossible.[22] Many people realize that if everyone decides to let someone else do it, the job simply will not get done.[23] Millions of Americans contribute to interest groups because they are concerned about an issue or feel a responsibility to help organizations that work on their behalf. Also, many organizations offer membership benefits that have nothing to do with politics or lobbying. Business **trade associations**, for example, are a source of information about industry trends and effective management practices; they organize conventions at which members can learn, socialize, and occasionally find new customers or suppliers. An individual firm in the electronics industry may not care that much about the lobbying done by the American Chemistry Council, but it may have a vital interest in the information about marketing and manufacturing that the organization provides. Successful interest groups are adept at supplying the right mix of benefits to their target constituency.

trade association
An organization that represents firms within a particular industry.

Lobbyists

Some of the money that interest groups raise is used to pay lobbyists who represent the organizations before the government. Lobbyists make sure that people in government know what their members want and that their organizations know what the government is doing. For example, when an administrative agency issues new regulations, lobbyists are right there to interpret the content and implications of the regulations for rank-and-file members. As one lobbyist put it, "a large portion of what we do is educate our clients."[24]

Lobbyists can be full-time employees of their organization or employees of public relations or law firms who are hired on retainer. As noted earlier, when hiring a lobbyist, an interest group looks for someone who knows her or his way around Washington. Lobbyists are valued for their experience and their knowledge of how government operates. Karen Ignagni, the chief lobbyist for America's Health Insurance Plans, an industry trade group, was at the center of the negotiations over the Obama administration's health reform proposal. Ignagni's experience, vast knowledge of health care, and skills as a bargainer made her a formidable presence as Congress struggled to formulate a bill that could pass. The stakes for the insurance companies were enormous as industry executives worried that a government-run insurance plan could cost them customers. Ignagni's stature is such that she is paid $1.6 million annually.[25]

So lucrative is lobbying that many representatives and senators go through the "revolving door" and take such jobs when they leave Congress.[26] After one recent session, seventy-seven former members of Congress who were defeated for re-election or left voluntarily were subsequently tracked as to their new occupation. Of the seventy-seven, thirty-two (42 percent) had taken jobs with a firm that lobbies.[27] One of those was Christopher Dodd, a former Democratic senator from Connecticut. Dodd was hired by the Motion Picture Association of America, which represents six major Hollywood studios. His major task was to lead the fight against "digital theft" and improve access to China. His thirty-six-year career in Congress gave him innumerable contacts around Washington; he's someone who gets his phone calls returned.[28]

Many lobbyists have a law degree and find their legal backgrounds useful in bargaining and negotiating over laws and regulations. Because of their location, many Washington law firms are drawn into lobbying. Expanding interest group advocacy has created a boon for Washington law firms. At Patton Boggs, a top Washington firm, partners earn around $750,000 a year.[29] Corporations without their own Washington office rely heavily on law firms to lobby for them before the national government.

The stereotype of lobbyists portrays them as people of dubious ethics because they trade on their connections and may hand out campaign donations to candidates for office as well as raise money for legislators. Lobbying is a much maligned profession, but the lobbyist's primary job is not to trade on favors or campaign contributions. It is rather to pass information on to both their employers and to policymakers. Lobbyists provide government officials and their staffs with a constant flow of data that support their organizations' policy goals. Lobbyist Elizabeth Moeller said of her job, "Finally, my nerdiness can pay off."[30] And those in government find it valuable to compare the information they receive from lobbyists against their own understanding of an issue. As one congressional committee staffer noted, lobbyists "can explain the impact of our ideas on the real world."[31]

Lobbyists also try to build a compelling case for their goals, showing that the "facts" dictate that a particular change be made or avoided. What lobbyists are really trying to do, of course, is to convince policymakers that their data deserve more attention and are more accurate than those presented by opposing lobbyists.

Political Action Committees

One of the organizational resources that can make a lobbyist's job easier is a **political action committee (PAC)**. PACs pool campaign contributions from group members and donate the money to candidates for political office. As noted in Chapter 9, under federal law, a PAC can give as much as $5,000 to a candidate for Congress for each separate election. There were over 7,000 PACs of all types active during the 2011–2012 campaign cycle. For the 2012 election, PACs gave $420 million to candidates for the House and Senate.[32]

political action committee (PAC)
An organization that pools campaign contributions from group members and donates those funds to candidates for political office.

Brussels Sprouts in Global Politics

The European Union (EU) is now the world's largest economy. The twenty-eight countries that make up the EU are tied together both politically and economically. Most essentially, trade barriers between these countries have been largely eliminated. For example, Italy cannot place a tariff (essentially a tax) on imports of olive oil from Greece even though it might like to do so as a means of protecting its own producers. This elimination of trade barriers has created a dynamic, integrated marketplace for European commerce.

Beyond its borders, the EU is the largest trading partner for the United States. U.S. companies must abide by EU product standards and trade rules if they are to do business in these twenty-eight countries. Moreover, the increasing globalization of the world's economies leads many American companies to focus heavily on international trade. As such, they need representation before EU policymaking bodies as the laws and regulations formulated there affect their businesses. American law and lobbying firms have seen this business opportunity and many branch offices have sprouted up in Brussels, Belgium, in recent years (see the map on the following page.). Brussels is home to the European Commission, the regulatory and administrative arm of the EU, and it also serves as one of the two homes of the European Parliament.

Covington & Burling, one of the best known lobbying-focused law firms in Washington, has a significant presence in Brussels. Among its clients are the oil giant Chevron, Microsoft, and the Pharmaceutical Research and Manufacturers of America. Much of what American lobbying firms do in Brussels is to work to harmonize regulations affecting the same industry on both continents. The EU has increasingly moved toward tighter regulations in the areas of consumer and environmental protection. An American chemical manufacturer, for example, might find that the tolerance level for a particular ingredient in a pesticide is lower in the EU than in the United States. This difference could necessitate two separate manufacturing processes.

The Brussels lobbying offices follow a strategy commonly found in the United States: hire former high-ranking government employees and let them use their connections to get their foot in the door of government offices. Covington & Burling employs Jean De Ruyt, a Belgian who previously worked in an important position at the EU.

A PAC can be the campaign-wing affiliate of an existing interest group or a wholly independent or nonconnected group. Super PACs tend to be strictly campaign instruments and are discussed in Chapter 9. The majority of PACs are small and donate only modest amounts, but the largest fifty PACs contributing to congressional campaigns gave a minimum of at least $2 million in aggregate donations.[33] Many PACs are large enough to gain recognition for the issues they care about. Among the largest for the 2012 congressional elections were the Letter Carriers Political Action Fund ($5.8 million in contributions), the National Association of Realtors ($4.7 million), and the National Beer Wholesalers Association ($4.0 million).[34] Super PAC spending was vast, but reporting requirements are not the same as for conventional PACs and cannot easily be disaggregated on the congressional level.[35] Lobbyists believe that campaign contributions help significantly

Just how many lobbyists are working in Brussels is not clear as there is no rule requiring lobbyists or their firms to identify themselves in the Transparency Registry, a voluntary directory of those working to influence EU policymakers. One estimate is that there are 40,000 lobbyists either working in Brussels or sometimes coming there for advocacy purposes. Brussels is starting to look a lot like Washington, where lobbyists like to position their offices near where policymakers are located.

Not surprisingly, lobbyists like to position their offices close to where policymakers are located. The size of the blue dots reflects the density of lobbying firms, American and otherwise, at particular addresses in Brussels. The largest clusters are adjacent to EU buildings.

Sources: Eric Lipton and Danny Hakim, "Lobbying Bonanza as Firms Try to Influence European Union," *New York Times*, 19 October 2013; David Vogel, *The Politics of Precaution* (Princeton, N.J.: Princeton University Press, 2012); and Justin Greenwood and Joanna Dreger, "The Transparency Register: A European Vanguard of Strong Lobbying Regulation?" *Interest Groups & Advocacy* 2 (2013): 139–162.

Critical Thinking In what ways is lobbying at the EU similar to lobbying in Washington? Why is the EU so important to American firms and industries?

when they are trying to gain an audience with a member of Congress. Members of Congress and their staffers generally are eager to meet with representatives of their constituencies, but their time is limited. However, a member of Congress or staffer would find it difficult to turn down a lobbyist's request for a meeting if the PAC of the lobbyist's organization had made a significant campaign contribution in the previous election. Lobbyists also regard contributions as a form of insurance in case of issues that might arise unexpectedly. As one scholar put it, the donations are given to protect "against unforeseen future dangers as the policymaking process develops."[36]

Typically, PACs, like most other interest groups, are highly pragmatic and adaptable organizations; pushing a particular political philosophy takes second place to achieving immediate policy goals.[37] Although many corporate executives strongly believe in a free-market economy, for example, their company PACs tend to hold congressional candidates to a much more practical standard and will donate to legislators of various ideological and partisan stripes. The goal of bipartisan contributions is to enhance access, no matter who is in power. Labor unions are an exception to this, donating almost exclusively to Democrats. Nonconnected PACs are highly ideological and tend to give to either conservatives or liberals.

Critics charge that PAC contributions influence public policy, yet political scientists have not been able to document any consistent link between campaign donations and the way members of Congress vote on the floor of the House and Senate.[38] The problem is this: Do PAC contributions influence votes in Congress, or are they just rewards for legislators who would vote for the group's interests anyway because of their long-standing ideology? How do we determine the answer to this question? Simply looking for the influence of PACs in the voting patterns of members of Congress may be shortsighted; influence can also be felt before bills get to the floor of the full House or Senate for a vote. Some sophisticated research shows that PAC donations do seem to influence what goes on in congressional committees.[39] Despite the advantages that organizations with ample resources have through PACs, there are those who defend the current system, emphasizing that interest groups and their members should have the freedom to participate in the political system through campaign donations.

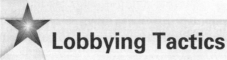

★ Lobbying Tactics

LO4 ★ Compare and contrast different types of lobbying.

When an interest group decides to try to influence the government on an issue, its staff and officers must develop a strategy, which may include several tactics aimed at various officials or offices. Some tactics are utilized far more frequently than others, but all together, the tactics should use the group's resources as effectively as possible.

We turn here to the different types of lobbying tactics. Keep in mind that lobbying extends beyond the legislative branch. Groups can seek help from the courts and administrative agencies as well as from Congress. Moreover, interest groups may have to shift their focus from one branch of government to another. After a bill becomes a law, for example, a group that lobbied for the legislation will probably try to influence the administrative agency responsible for implementing the new law. Some policy decisions are left unresolved by legislation and are settled through regulations. Interest groups try to influence policy through court suits as well, though litigation can be expensive, and opportunities to go to court may be narrowly structured. Lobbying Congress and agencies is more common.

Direct Lobbying

direct lobbying
Attempts to influence a policymaker through personal contact with that individual.

Direct lobbying relies on personal contact with policymakers. This interaction occurs when a lobbyist meets with a member of Congress, an agency official, or a staff member. In their meetings, lobbyists usually convey their arguments by providing data about a specific issue. If a lobbyist from a chamber of commerce, for example, meets with a member of Congress about a bill the chamber backs, the lobbyist does not say (or even suggest), "Vote for this bill, or our people in the district will vote against you in the next election." Instead, the lobbyist might say, "If this bill is passed, we're going to see hundreds of new jobs created back home." The representative has no trouble at all figuring out that a vote for the bill can help in the next election.

Personal lobbying is a day-in, day-out process. It is not enough simply to meet with policymakers just before a vote or a regulatory decision. Lobbyists must maintain contact with congressional and agency staffers, constantly providing them with pertinent data. In their meetings with policymakers and through other tactics, lobbyists are trying to frame the issue at hand in terms most beneficial to their point of view. Is a gun-control bill before Congress a policy that would make our streets and schools safer from deranged, violent individuals who should not have access to guns—or is it a bill aimed at depriving law-abiding citizens of their constitutional right to bear arms? Research has shown that once an issue emerges, it is very difficult for lobbyists to reframe it—that is, to influence journalists and policymakers alike to view the issue in a new light.[40] Mindful of how the image of their industry could change in the wake of the Newtown massa-

Christian Science Monitor/Getty Images

A Meeting with the Senator

In this day and age, lobbyists don't actually lobby in a *lobby*. Here Senator Kelly Ayotte (R.-New Hampshire) meets with some lobbyists in the Senate Reception Room in the Capitol.

cre, the makers of video games initiated a strong lobbying campaign in Washington. The video game manufacturers were concerned that real-world violence might be linked in people's minds to the violence in the most popular games. Among those that lobbyists from the industry trade association met with was Vice President Joseph Biden.[41]

Testifying at committee hearings is a tactic that allows the interest group to put its views on record and make them widely known. Although testifying is one of the most visible parts of lobbying, it is generally considered window dressing as it does little by itself to persuade members of Congress. Another direct but somewhat different approach is legal advocacy. Using this tactic, a group tries to achieve its policy goals through litigation. Claiming some violation of law, a group will file a lawsuit and ask that a judge make a ruling that will benefit the organization.

Grassroots Lobbying

Grassroots lobbying involves an interest group's rank-and-file members and may include people outside the organization who sympathize with its goals. Grassroots tactics, such as letter-writing campaigns and protests, are often used in conjunction with direct lobbying by Washington representatives. Letters, e-mails, faxes, and telephone calls from a group's members to their representatives in Congress or to agency administrators add to a lobbyist's credibility in talks with these officials. Policymakers are more concerned about what a lobbyist says when they know that constituents are really watching their decisions.

Group members—especially influential members (such as corporation presidents or local civic leaders)—occasionally go to Washington to lobby. More ordinary citizens can have an impact too. Research shows that grassroots activity by women's groups is related to passage of legislation aimed at gender equality.[42]

grassroots lobbying
Lobbying activities performed by rank-and-file interest group members and other supporters.

Jahi Chikwendiu/The Washington Post via Getty Images

New Starring Role for Clooney: Getting Arrested

Groups protesting the Sudanese government's blockade of humanitarian aid to those starving in the country were after media coverage when they asked a number of celebrities to participate in civil disobedience outside Sudan's embassy in Washington. Popular film actor George Clooney had traveled to Sudan and witnessed the crisis there firsthand. He made a short speech to the assembled crowd and was arrested shortly thereafter. He did not serve any significant time in jail, but his participation led to a great deal of press coverage on the Sudanese crisis.

John Moore/Getty Images

Angry and Organized

Over the past few years, conservatives have become increasingly concerned about undocumented immigrants. Many conservative citizen groups have been highly vocal in trying to attract attention to the problem, such as these demonstrators in Denver. This group went out onto the streets on April 15, the day taxes are due, to add emphasis to their argument that illegal immigration has economic consequences.

The most common grassroots tactic is letter writing. "Write your member of Congress" is not just a slogan for a civics test. Legislators are highly sensitive to the content of their mail. Interest groups often launch letter-writing campaigns through their regular publications or special alerts. They may even provide sample letters and the names and addresses of specific policymakers. The Internet facilitates mobilization as an interest group office can communicate instantaneously with its members and followers and at virtually no cost through e-mail.

If people in government seem unresponsive to conventional lobbying tactics, a group might resort to some form of political protest. A protest or demonstration, such as picketing or marching, is designed to attract media attention to an issue. Protesters hope that television and newspaper coverage will help change public opinion and make policymakers more receptive to their group's demands. When Republicans in the Ohio State Legislature brought up a bill in 2011 restricting the collective bargaining rights of municipal unions there, it was greeted with widespread demonstrations by union members and sympathizers. The legislation was still passed, but angry union members succeeded in getting an initiative put on a statewide ballot and the law was overturned by the voters.

The main drawback to protesting is that policymaking is a long-term, incremental process, and a demonstration is short-lived. It is difficult to sustain anger and activism among group supporters—to keep large numbers of people involved in protest after protest.[43] A notable exception was the civil rights demonstrations of the 1960s, which were sustained over a long period. National attention focused not only on the widespread demonstrations but also on the sometimes violent confrontations between protesters and white law enforcement officers. For example, the use of police dogs and high-power fire hoses against blacks marching in Alabama in the early 1960s angered millions of Americans who saw footage of the confrontations on television. By stirring public opinion, the protests hastened the passage of the Civil Rights Act of 1964 and the Voting Rights Act of 1965.

Freedom, Order, or Equality

Freedom v. Equality: We Are the 99%!

"We are the 99%" is the slogan of the Occupy Wall Street movement. Perhaps it's more accurate to say that it *was* the slogan for the Occupy movement as it has largely disappeared.

Occupy Wall Street began in the fall of 2011 when young, liberal activists pitched tents and occupied Zuccotti Park in the area of Manhattan where Wall Street is located. It was an imaginative protest as an encampment is an unusual political tactic, and it drew national attention. The protesters chose the Wall Street location because they wanted to demonstrate their anger and disgust at the growing inequality between the very rich (the 1 percent) and the rest of the country (the 99 percent). Given the growing income inequality in the United States, the issue resonated with many Americans who, while not ready to pitch a tent themselves, were sympathetic to the protesters.

The attention paid to the Wall Street protesters stimulated Occupy efforts across the country. Encampments sprung up in Boston, Los Angeles, Philadelphia, Oakland, and many other American cities. The movement spread internationally, too, with cities such as Berlin and London gaining encampments.

Like a shooting star, however, Occupy quickly faded from sight. It never transformed itself into a set of interest groups with a firm organizational structure and a clear lobbying strategy. First and foremost, it failed because it was hyper-democratic. The ethos of Occupy was that all were equal and that the collective members of the tent camp should make decisions instead of a single leader or a leadership council. The locus of each camp's internal government were general assemblies. The various Occupys seemed structurally incapable of generating any advocacy campaigns beyond an occasional march or street protest.

Because each Occupy was organized horizontally rather than hierarchically, there was no one person or persons who spoke for the group of protesters in any one city. Consequently, journalists were reduced to asking random activists at the sites what they wanted from government. What they heard was a wide variety of complaints about government. Some wanted the Federal Reserve Board abolished, while others said fracking for oil was the problem. To the degree there was any unifying theme, it was resentment of the nation's banking system. There was never a common reform offered to rein in the financial sector; rather, what was communicated was resentment toward the freedom of the marketplace to generate high levels of inequality of wealth. In short, Occupy adherents seemed to feel that freedom had so overpowered equality as a societal goal that the American way of life is threatened. Not surprisingly, many regarded Occupy's criticism as hopelessly naïve and were quick to point out how the freedom of our market-based economy has produced a high standard of living in the United States.

What Occupy needed was a political entrepreneur to harness all the energy and passion of a great many Americans who feel disillusioned and disaffected. Meanwhile tent camps became increasingly untenable as winter approached. Before winter hit, however, the police, hesitant to take on the protesters at first out of fear of inciting a confrontation, eventually forced many of the camps to fold

up. Since no Occupy organizational structure had been formed outside of the camps, there was nothing to replace this vibrant but fragile movement. Indeed, as one scholar put it, Occupy turned out to be "more moment than movement."

Yet, in its own way, Occupy helped to catalyze debate over income inequality. Since the time of the tents, there has been increasing discussion of the disparities between the 1 percent and the 99 percent. Occupy is only one reason for this, but it's clear that Occupy did leave behind a legacy if not a lobbying presence.

Sources: Todd Gitlin, *Occupy Nation* (New York: It Books, 2012); Mattathias Schwartz, "Pre-Occupied: The Origins and Future of Occupy Wall Street," *New Yorker*, 28 November 2011; and Craig Calhoun, "Occupy Wall Street in Perspective," *British Journal of Sociology* 64 (2013).

Critical Thinking Was the encampment strategy effective for the Occupy Wall Street movement? Looking back, how might the Occupy movement have increased its chances of sustaining itself over a longer period of time?

Information Campaigns

As the strategy of the civil rights movement shows, interest groups generally feel that public backing adds strength to their lobbying efforts. And because all interest groups believe they are absolutely right in their policy orientation, they think that they will get that backing if they can only make the public aware of their position and the evidence supporting it. To this end, interest groups launch **information campaigns**, which are organized efforts to gain public backing by bringing their views to the public's attention. The underlying assumption is that public ignorance and apathy are as much a problem as the views of competing interest groups. Various means are used to combat apathy. Some are directed at the larger public; others are directed at smaller audiences with long-standing interest in an issue.

Public relations is one information campaign tactic. A public relations campaign might involve sending speakers to meetings in various parts of the country, producing pamphlets and handouts, taking out newspaper and magazine advertising, or establishing websites. When cell phone service provider AT&T took steps to take over T-Mobile, another provider, it found that the Department of Justice was resistant on antitrust grounds. If the AT&T and T-Mobile merger went through, 75 percent of the cell phone market would be controlled by just two companies, Verizon and the newly expanded AT&T. AT&T launched a public relations campaign with ads in the *Washington Post* and other Washington-based political publications. Despite spending $40 million in advertising related to the merger, it failed to change the government's mind and abandoned its effort to absorb T-Mobile.[44]

Sponsoring research is another way interest groups press their cases. When a group believes that evidence has not been fully developed in a certain area, it may commission research on the subject. In the controversy over illegal immigration, studies have proliferated as interest groups push their position forward. Lobbies on opposing sides of the issue have publicized research on matters such as the impact of illegal immigration on the overall economy, whether immigrants drive down wages, and whether undocumented aliens take jobs away from citizens who would otherwise fill them.

information campaign
An organized effort to gain public backing by bringing a group's views to public attention.

Information campaigns may affect public opinion, which, presumably, will influence policymakers. However, research has shown that the public's priorities are not systematically reflected in the lobbying priorities of interest groups. Figure 10.4 shows the responses of citizens when the Gallup Poll asked them what they thought was the most important problem facing the United States. Those responses show little relationship to the issues that lobbyists were working on at the same time.

Coalition Building

A final aspect of lobbying strategy is **coalition building**, in which several organizations band together for the purpose of lobbying. Such joint efforts conserve or make more effective use of the resources of groups with similar views. Most coalitions are informal arrangements that exist only for the purpose of lobbying on a single issue. Coalitions most often form among groups that work in the same policy area and have

coalition building
The banding together of several interest groups for the purpose of lobbying.

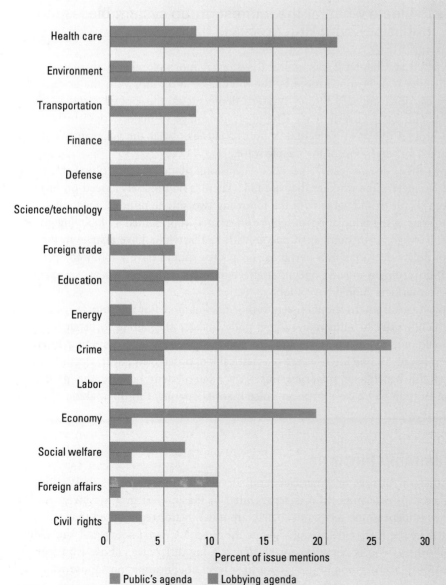

FIGURE 10.4 The Lobbying Agenda versus the Public's Agenda

The figures for the lobbying agenda come from research by the authors listed at the end of this note. They interviewed a random sample of lobbyists and asked them what issue they were working at that time. Corresponding data for the public for the same year come from the Gallup Poll. Its question was "What is the most important problem facing the country today?"

Source: Adapted from David C. Kimball, Frank R. Baumgartner, Jeffrey M. Berry, Marie Hojnacki, and Beth L. Leech, "Who Cares About the Lobbying Agenda?" paper presented at the annual meeting of the American Political Science Association, Seattle, WA, September 2011. Copyright © 2012 by Palgrave Macmillan. Reproduced by permission.

similar constituencies, such as environmental groups or feminist groups. When an issue arises that several such groups agree on, they are likely to develop a coalition.

Yet coalitions often extend beyond organizations with similar constituencies and similar outlooks. Environmental groups and business groups are often thought of as dire enemies. But some businesses support the same goals as environmental lobbies because it is in their self-interest.[45] For example, companies in the business of cleaning up toxic waste sites have worked with environmental groups to strengthen the Superfund program, the government's primary weapon for dealing with dangerous waste dumps. Lobbyists see an advantage in having a diverse coalition. In the words of one lobbyist, "You can't do anything in this town without a coalition. I mean the first question [from policymakers] is, 'Who supports this?'"[46]

 ## Is the System Biased?

LO5 ★ Evaluate whether the interest group system biases the public policymaking process.

As we noted in Chapter 2, our political system is more pluralist than majoritarian. Policymaking is determined more by the interaction of groups with the government than by elections. Indeed, among Western democracies, the United States is one of the most pluralistic governments. The great advantage of majoritarianism is that it is built around the most elemental notion of fairness: what the government does is determined by what most of the people want.

How, then, do we justify the policy decisions made under a pluralist system? How do we determine whether they are fair? There is no precisely agreed-on formula, but most people would agree with the following two simple notions. First, all significant interests in the population should be adequately represented by lobbying groups. That is, if a significant number of people with similar views have a stake in the outcome of policy decisions in a particular area, they should have a lobby to speak for them. If government makes policy that affects farmers who grow wheat, for example, then wheat farmers should have a lobby.

Second, government should listen to the views of all major interests as it develops policy. Lobbies are of little value unless policymakers are willing to listen to them. We should not require policymakers to balance perfectly all competing interests, however, because some interests are diametrically opposed. Moreover, elections inject some of the benefits of majoritarianism into our system because the party that wins an election will have a stronger voice than its opponent in the making of public policy.

Membership Patterns

Public opinion surveys of Americans and surveys of interest groups in Washington can be used to determine who is represented in the interest group system. A clear pattern is evident: some sectors of society are much better represented than others.[47] As noted in the earlier discussions about the Boston West Enders and the United Farm Workers, who is being organized makes a big difference. Those who work in business or in a profession, those with a high level of education, and those with high incomes are the most likely to belong to interest groups. Even middle-income people are much more likely to join interest groups than are those who are poor.

Douglas Graham/Roll Call/Getty Images

AP Images/Charles Rex Arbogast

Experience Counts

Lobbyists are valued for the connections and having worked for the President of the United State can lead to a lucrative career in lobbying. Jim Messina, former Deputy Chief of Staff, left the White House to start his own lobbying firm, the Messina Group. Stephanie Cutter, Deputy Campaign Manager for Obama in 2012, also started her own lobbying shop, Precision Strategies.

One survey of interest groups is revealing, finding that "the 10 percent of adults who work in an executive, managerial, or administrative capacity are represented by 82 percent" of the organizations that in one way or another engage in advocacy on economic issues. In contrast, "organizations of or for the economically needy are a rarity." Thus, in terms of membership in interest groups, there is a profound bias in favor of those who are well-off financially.[48]

Citizen Groups

Because the bias in interest group membership is unmistakable, should we conclude that the interest group system is biased overall? Before reaching that determination, we should examine another set of data. The actual population of interest groups in Washington surely reflects a class bias in interest group membership, but that bias may be modified in an important way. Some interest groups derive support from sources other than their membership. Thus, although they have no welfare recipients as members, the Center for Budget and Policy Priorities and the Children's Defense Fund have been effective long-term advocates working on behalf of the poor. Poverty groups gain their financial support from philanthropic foundations, government grants, corporations, and wealthy individuals.[49] Given the large numbers of Americans who benefit from welfare and social service programs, poor people's lobbies are not numerous enough. Nevertheless, the poor are represented by these and other organizations (such as labor unions and health lobbies) that regard the poor as part of the constituency they must protect. In short, although the poor are seriously underrepresented in our system, the situation is not as bad as interest group membership patterns suggest.

Another part of the problem of membership bias has to do with free riders. The interests that are most affected by free riders are broad societal problems, such as the environment and consumer protection, in which literally everyone can be considered as having a stake in the outcome. We are all consumers, and we all care about the environment. But the greater the number of potential members of a group, the more likely it is that individuals will decide to be free riders because they believe that plenty of others can offer financial support to the organization.

Environmental and consumer interests were long underrepresented in the Washington interest group community. In the 1960s, however, a strong citizen group

citizen group
Lobbying organization built around policy concerns unrelated to members' vocational interests.

movement emerged. **Citizen groups** are lobbying organizations built around policy concerns unrelated to members' vocational interests. People who join Environmental Defense do so because they care about the environment, not because it lobbies on issues related to their profession. If that group fights for stricter pollution control requirements, it doesn't further the financial interests of its members. The benefits to members are largely ideological and aesthetic. In contrast, a corporation fighting the same stringent standards is trying to protect its economic interests. A law that requires a corporation to install expensive antipollution devices can reduce stockholders' dividends, depress salaries, and postpone expansion. Although both the environmental group and the corporation have valid reasons for their stands, their motives are different. Despite the free-rider problem and corporate opposition, citizen groups have had an impressive impact on public policy, with environmental and consumer groups achieving many changes they've lobbied for.[50]

Business Mobilization

Business has always been well represented in Washington. When Congress considers a bill or an agency is formulating a regulation, the stakes for individual corporations and industries can be enormous. Samsung, the South Korean electronics giant, spent $800,000 in lobbying in one recent year. This sounds like a huge sum—and it is—but in light of the firm's annual revenues of $179 billion, this $800,000 is but a tiny drop in its bucket.[51] In the last analysis lobbying by business is "an investment strategy."[52]

The health-care industry illustrates the level of involvement by business in Washington lobbying. Government regulation is a hugely important factor in determining health-care profits. Through reimbursement formulas for Medicare, Medicaid, and other health-care programs funded by Washington, the national government limits what providers can charge. The new Obama health-care reform mandates additional areas of government regulation. As this regulatory activity has grown, more and more health-care trade associations (like the American Hospital Association) and professional associations (like the American Nurses Association) have come to view Washington lobbying as increasingly significant to the well-being of their members. The number of such lobbies has skyrocketed, and health-care lobbyists cluster around Washington like locusts. Today there are 3,000 registered lobbyists in Washington working for health-care entities.[53] Aggregate spending by health-care lobbies in 2013 was $480 million. Hundreds of millions more were contributed to candidates for Congress by health-care concerns.[54]

The advantages of business are enormous. As Figure 10.5 illustrates, there are more business lobbies (corporations and trade associations) than any other type. Professional associations—the American Dental Association, for example—tend to represent business interests as well. Beyond the numbers of groups are the superior resources of business, including lobbyists, researchers, campaign contributions, and well-connected chief executive officers. Business lobbyists, for example, are much more likely to participate in lobbying administrative agencies on proposed regulations.[55] Whereas citizen groups can try to mobilize their individual members, trade associations can mobilize the corporations that are members of the organization.

Yet the resource advantages of business make it easy to overlook the obstacles that business faces in the political arena. To begin with, business is often divided, with one industry facing another. Cable companies and phone companies have frequently tangled over who will have access to what markets. And even if an industry is unified, it may face strong opposition from labor or citizen groups—sectors that have substantial resources too, even if they don't match up to those of businesses. If

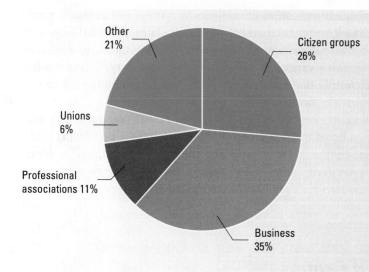

Other
21%

Citizen groups
26%

Unions
6%

Professional
associations 11%

Business
35%

FIGURE 10.5 Interest Group Participants

One large-scale study of lobbying in Washington documented the pattern of participation by interest groups on close to a hundred issues before the federal government. Business-related groups (corporations and trade associations) made up the largest segment of all lobbies, and citizen groups constituted roughly a quarter of all organizations.

Source: Frank R. Baumgartner, Jeffrey M. Berry, Marie Hojnacki, David C. Kimball, and Beth L. Leech, *Lobbying and Policy Change* (Chicago: University of Chicago Press, 2009), p. 9. Copyright © 2009 University of Chicago Press. Reproduced by permission.

both sides have sufficient resources to put up a battle, simply having more money or lobbyists than the other side is unlikely to determine the outcome.[56]

Even though business does not always get its way, or is divided among itself, the affluent and business interests are in the best position to influence policymakers. The aggregate advantages of representation and resources are substantial and give this sector a powerful say in policymaking.[57]

Reform

If the interest group system is biased, should the advantages of some groups some-how be eliminated or reduced? This is hard to do. In an economic system marked by great differences in income, great differences in the degree to which people are organized are inevitable. Moreover, as James Madison foresaw, limiting interest group activity is difficult without limiting fundamental freedoms. The First Amendment guarantees Americans the right to petition their government, and lobbying, at its most basic level, is a form of organized petitioning.

Still, some sectors of the interest group community may enjoy advantages that are unacceptable. If it is felt that the advantages of some groups are so great that they affect the equality of people's opportunity to be heard in the political system, then restrictions on interest group behavior can be justified on the grounds that the disadvantaged must be protected. Pluralist democracy is justified on exactly these grounds: all constituencies must have the opportunity to organize, and competition between groups as they press their case before policymakers must be fair.

Some critics charge that a system of campaign finance that relies so heavily on PACs undermines our democratic system. They claim that access to policymakers is purchased through the wealth of some constituencies. PAC donations come disproportionately from business and professional interests. It is not merely a matter of wealthy interest groups showering incumbents with donations; members of Congress aggressively solicit donations from PACs. Although observers disagree on whether PAC money actually influences policy outcomes, agreement is widespread that PAC donations give donors better access to members of Congress.

As noted in Chapter 9, in 2010 the Supreme Court ruled in the *Citizens United* case that government may not restrict corporations and unions from spending money in candidate elections.[58] The *Citizens United* ruling has facilitated the formation of so-called Super PACs without the contribution limits of normal PACs. Huge contributions to these organizations were used on behalf of candidates in the 2012 election. Sheldon Adelson and his wife alone contributed more than $90 million to a number of Super PACs. Adelson owns casinos, a heavily regulated industry.[59] Concern has emerged that the large contributions to the Super PACs by corporations and unions will add to the advantages they already have in the political process.

Although some minor reforms have been passed in recent years, the laws surrounding lobbying have altered interest group politics very little. Upon taking office in 2009, President Obama promised to "change the culture of Washington" in terms of the cozy relationship between lobbyists and policymakers. His words were surely sincere, but six years later the culture remained unchanged.

Master the Topics of Interest Groups
MindTap™ for American Government

REVIEW MindTap™ **for American Government**
Access Key Term Flashcards for Chapter 10.

TEST YOURSELF MindTap™ **for American Government**
Take the Wrap It Up Quiz for Chapter 10.

STAY CURRENT MindTap™ **for American Government**
Access the KnowNow blog and customized RSS for updates on current events.

STAY FOCUSED MindTap™ **for American Government**
Complete the Focus Activities for Interest Groups.

Summary

LO1 Identify the different roles that interest groups play in our political system.

- Interest groups play many important roles in our political process: representation, participation, education, agenda building, and program monitoring. They are a means by which citizens can participate in politics, and they communicate their members' views to those in government. Interest groups make positive contributions, yet the interest group system remains unbalanced, with some segments of society (particularly business, the wealthy, and the educated) considerably better organized than others. Suppressing interest groups, though, runs against our First Amendment freedoms.

LO2 Analyze the role played by entrepreneurs in interest group formation.

- Interest groups are organizations, and they do not form just because a constituency has a need. An organizer or political "entrepreneur" must convince potential members to join. Not all constituencies are created equal in terms of a propensity to join an interest group. Those high in social class are much more likely to join; those in a lower social class are much more challenging to organize.

LO3 Identify the various resources available to interest groups and evaluate their role in interest group performance.

- The strength and influence of an interest group depends heavily on the group's resources, which include its membership, lobbyists, and political action committees (PACs). Interest group efforts to attract members are made more difficult because of the free-rider problem. Among the most important resources for interest groups are their lobbyists, who have the responsibility for communicating what the organization wants policymakers to know. PACs can facilitate access to policymakers.

LO4 Compare and contrast different types of lobbying.

- Direct lobbying relies on personal contact with policymakers in the legislative and administrative branches. It also includes filing court suits in the legal system. Grassroots lobbying can involve both

rank-and-file members communicating with policymakers through letter-writing campaigns and political protests. Common tactics of information campaigns are public relations efforts and sponsoring research.

LO5 Evaluate whether the interest group system biases the public policymaking process.

- Strong growth in the citizen group sector has brought more effective representation on behalf of environmental and consumer interests. Business mobilization has enhanced the advantages already possessed by business in the political system. Little meaningful reform has been enacted to try to change the status quo of interest group politics.

Chapter Quiz

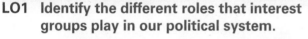

LO1 Identify the different roles that interest groups play in our political system.

1. On balance, are interest groups beneficial to the political system or are they harmful?
2. What roles do interest groups play in American politics?

LO2 Analyze the role played by entrepreneurs in interest group formation.

1. What is an interest group "entrepreneur"?
2. What factors influence the success of an effort to organize a new interest group?

LO3 Identify the various resources available to interest groups and evaluate their role in interest group performance.

1. What is the "free-rider problem"?
2. In our governmental system, what role do lobbyists play?

LO4 Compare and contrast different types of lobbying.

1. How does direct lobbying differ from grassroots lobbying?
2. How do information campaigns work?

LO5 Evaluate whether the interest group system biases the public policymaking process.

1. What advantages does business possess in the lobbying world, and are citizen groups effective counterweights to business groups?
2. Overall, is the interest group system a biased one?

11 Congress

Learning Outcomes

LO1 Explain the structure and powers of Congress as envisioned by the framers and enumerated in the Constitution.

LO2 Analyze the factors that affect the way voters elect members of Congress.

LO3 Describe the ways in which issues get on the congressional agenda.

LO4 Differentiate among the types of congressional committees and evaluate the role of the committee system in the legislative process.

LO5 Identify the leadership structure of the legislative branch and assess the rules and norms that influence congressional operations.

LO6 Appraise the components of the legislative environment that affect decision making in Congress.

LO7 Consider whether members of Congress should vote according to the majority views of their constituents.

LO8 Assess the elements that characterize Congress as a pluralist or majoritarian system.

 WATCH & LEARN MindTap™ **for American Government**
Watch a brief "What Do You Know?" video summarizing Congress.

After the 2012 elections, Republicans retained control of the House of Representatives while Democrats held on to the Senate. With different political parties leading different chambers of Congress, it can be difficult for opposing sides to come together to pass legislation. But the 113th Congress took the challenge of compromise to new heights, earning the dubious distinction of being the "least productive Congress ever."[1] In its first year, the 113th Congress enacted only fifty-eight laws, less than the previous post-WWII low of eighty-eight, set back in 1995. From the 1940s to the 1990s, the average amount of legislation enacted in the first year of a new Congress was closer to 200, but this number has been falling.

The inability of the opposing parties in Congress to agree on how to address issues of the day came to a head in October 2013, when they could not agree on how to extend the nation's spending plan, and the government shut down for sixteen days. The major sticking point was President Obama's health-care law (see Chapter 18). The Republican-led House would not authorize congressional spending unless funding for the law was delayed. The Democrat-led Senate rebuffed attempts to deny the funds. Eventually, enough Republicans agreed to reopen the government,

and government spending was restored. During the shutdown, nonessential public employees could not go to work, student loan processing stopped, food safety inspections halted, passport and visa applications were not reviewed, national parks and museums closed, and more. To the dismay of many, the panda cam at the National Zoo went dark. More importantly, cancer patients in experimental drug trials run by the government had to delay treatment. The list of people and places affected during the shutdown was long.

In a majoritarian government, the policies supported by the majority are expected to become a reality. But when one party controls the House and another the Senate, it can be hard to determine what the majority view even is. Even when one party has the luxury of controlling both chambers, Congress is still slow to act; the majority encounters many obstacles in its way. First, Congress is embedded in a system of separation of powers, which means that even with enough votes to move legislation through both chambers, the president still has to agree before a bill becomes law.

Second, representatives have to answer to their own constituents as well as to their party leadership. Several Republican members of Congress were elected by campaigning against government spending, which created pressure to be responsive to the segment of the electorate that sent them to Washington. While acknowledging the national unpopularity of the shutdown, some lawmakers claimed that their constituents wanted them to resist compromise. As Todd Rokita (R-Ind.) said, "As far as I'm concerned, we're doing exactly what our constituents asked us to do ... take a stand against Obamacare and against big government."[2]

In addition to these enduring obstacles to lawmaking, other factors have made passing legislation even harder in recent years. First, each political party has become more ideologically cohesive over the past sixty years.[3] Before, some Republican lawmakers were liberal and some Democrats were conservative. Today, however, there is little ideological overlap between the parties, which means there is less room for finding common ground across party lines. Second, belonging to the same party does not guarantee agreement on key issues of the day or even on the notion of compromise itself, a fact that has made it difficult for Republicans to agree on legislative strategy in recent years. Their activist base, particularly supporters aligned with the tea party, has threatened (often successfully) to oust incumbents and replace them with more conservative candidates. One prominent example is when House majority leader Eric Cantor (R-Va.) lost his primary in June 2014 to a tea party-backed challenger, who claimed that Cantor was not conservative enough for the district. This internal division has resulted in newer Republican representatives who are even further away from the ideological center.[4] Finally, from the 1930s to the 1990s, the House and Senate were controlled by Democrats, with only a few exceptions. The party's dominance encouraged Republicans to accept compromise if they wanted any of their preferences enacted into law. But since 1994, the majority changed hands three times in the House and four times in the Senate. These days, it seems that the majority hangs in the balance with each election, which reduces incentives to compromise for fear of giving the other side a legislative victory on which to campaign.[5]

So while a party would prefer to be the majority in Congress rather than the minority, being the majority party rarely means that the party has smooth sailing in enacting its agenda. And if the majority party fails, the minority party has a compelling theme for the next election.

LISTEN & LEARN
MindTap™ **for American Government**

Access Read Speaker to listen to Chapter 11.

In this chapter, we'll examine majoritarian politics through the prism of the two congressional parties. We'll look at how the forces of pluralism work against majoritarian policymaking. We'll turn our attention to the procedures and norms that have traditionally facilitated bargaining and compromise in Congress, which are key to understanding how the House and Senate operate. We'll discuss Congress's relations with the executive branch, and we'll analyze how the legislative process affects public policy. We begin by asking how the framers envisioned Congress.

The Origin and Powers of Congress

LO1 ★ Explain the structure and powers of Congress as envisioned by the framers and enumerated in the Constitution.

The framers of the Constitution wanted to keep power from being concentrated in the hands of a few, but they were also concerned with creating a Union strong enough to overcome the weaknesses of the government that had operated under the

Articles of Confederation. They argued passionately about the structure of the new government. In the end, they produced a legislative body that was as much of an experiment as the new nation's democracy.

The Great Compromise

The U.S. Congress has two chambers: the House of Representatives and the Senate. A bill cannot become law unless it is passed in identical form by both chambers. Recall from Chapter 3 that during the drafting of the Constitution, small states wanted all the states to have equal representation, and more populous states wanted representation based on population. The Great Compromise broke the deadlock: small states would receive equal representation in the Senate, but the number of each state's representatives in the House would be based on population and the House would have the sole right to originate revenue-related legislation.

Each state has two senators, who serve six-year terms of office. Terms are staggered so that one-third of the Senate is elected every two years. When it was ratified, the Constitution directed that senators be chosen by the state legislatures. However, the Seventeenth Amendment, adopted in 1913, provided for the direct election of senators by popular vote. From the beginning, the people have directly elected members of the House of Representatives. They serve two-year terms, and all House seats are up for election at the same time.

There are 435 members of the House of Representatives. Because each state's representation in the House is in proportion to its population, the Constitution provides for a national census every ten years; population shifts are handled by the **reapportionment** (redistribution) of seats among the states after each census is taken. Since recent population growth has been centered in the Sunbelt, Texas and Florida have gained seats, while the Northeast and Midwest states like New York and Illinois have lost them. Each representative is elected from a particular congressional district within his or her state, and each district elects only one representative. The districts within a state must be roughly equal in population.

reapportionment
Redistribution of representatives among the states, based on population change. The House is reapportioned after each census.

Duties of the House and Senate

Although the Great Compromise provided for considerably different schemes of representation for the House and Senate, the Constitution gives them similar legislative tasks. They share many powers, among them the powers to declare war, raise an army and navy, borrow and coin money, regulate interstate commerce, create federal courts, establish rules for the naturalization of immigrants, and "make all Laws which shall be necessary and proper for carrying into Execution the foregoing Powers."

Yet the constitutional duties of the two chambers are different in some ways. As noted in Chapter 3, the House alone has the right to originate revenue bills. In practice, this power is of limited consequence because both the House and Senate must approve all bills. The House of Representatives has the power of **impeachment**: the power formally to charge the president, vice president, and other "civil officers" of the national government with serious crimes. The Senate is empowered to act as a court to try impeachments, with the chief justice of the Supreme Court presiding. A two-thirds majority vote of the senators present is necessary for conviction. Prior to President Clinton's impeachment in 1998, only one sitting president, Andrew Johnson, had been impeached, and in 1868 the Senate came within a single vote of finding him guilty. Clinton was accused of both perjury and obstruction of justice concerning his relationship with a White House intern, but was acquitted by the

impeachment
The formal charging of a government official with "treason, bribery, or other high crimes and misdemeanors."

Senate. The House Judiciary Committee voted to recommend impeachment of President Richard Nixon because of his involvement in the cover-up of a scandal known as Watergate, but before the full House could vote, Nixon resigned from office.

The Constitution gives the Senate the power to approve major presidential appointments (such as to federal judgeships, ambassadorships, and cabinet posts) and treaties with foreign nations. The president is empowered to make treaties but must submit them to the Senate for approval by a two-thirds majority. Because of this requirement, a president must at times try to convince a doubting Senate of the worth of a particular treaty. Shortly after World War I, President Woodrow Wilson submitted to the Senate the Treaty of Versailles, which contained the charter for the proposed League of Nations. Wilson had attempted to convince the Senate that the treaty deserved its support; when the Senate refused to approve the treaty, Wilson suffered a severe setback as he had made the treaty his highest priority.

Despite the long list of congressional powers in the Constitution, the question of which powers are appropriate for Congress has generated substantial controversy. For example, although the Constitution gives Congress the sole power to declare war, presidents have initiated military action on their own. And at times, the courts have found that congressional actions have usurped the rights of the states.

COMPARE WITH YOUR PEERS

MindTap™ **for American Government**

Access The Congress Forum: Polling Activity—The Power to Declare War.

Electing Congress

LO2 ★ Analyze the factors that affect the way voters elect members of Congress.

If Americans are not happy with the job Congress is doing, they can use their votes to say so. With congressional elections every two years, voters have frequent opportunities to express themselves.

The Incumbency Effect

incumbent
A current officeholder.

Congressional elections offer voters a chance to show their approval of Congress's performance by reelecting **incumbents** or to demonstrate their disapproval by "throwing the rascals out."[6] The voters do more reelecting than rascal throwing. The reelection rate is astonishingly high: in the majority of elections since 1950, more than 90 percent of all House incumbents have held on to their seats (see Figure 11.1). In the 2012 congressional elections, only eight Democrats and sixteen Republicans were voted out of office, giving each chamber a reelection rate above 95 percent. Most House elections aren't even close; in most recent elections, over 70 percent of House incumbents have won reelection by margins of greater than 60 percent of the vote.[7] Senate elections are more competitive, but incumbents still have a high reelection rate.

These findings may seem surprising, since the public does not hold Congress as a whole in especially high esteem. In the past few years, Americans have been particularly critical of Congress (see Figure 11.2). One reason Americans hold Congress in disdain is that they regard it as overly influenced by interest groups. A struggling economy and persistent partisan disagreements within Congress have also reduced people's confidence in the institution.[8]

Redistricting. One explanation for the incumbency effect centers on redistricting— the way states redraw House districts after a census-based reapportionment.[9] It is

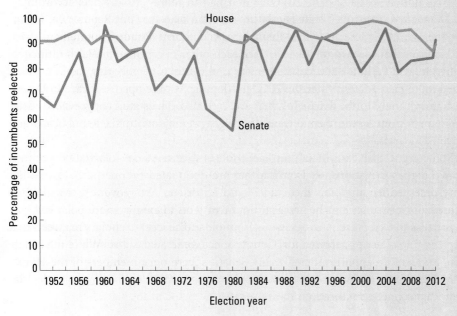

FIGURE 11.1 Incumbents: Life Is Good

Despite the public's dissatisfaction with Congress in general, incumbent representatives win reelection at an exceptional rate. Incumbent senators aren't quite as successful but still do well. Voters seem to believe that their own representatives and senators don't share the same foibles that they attribute to other members of Congress.

Sources: Various sources for 1950–2006. For 2008 and 2010, Harold W. Stanley and Richard G. Niemi (eds.), *Vital Statistics on American Politics*, 2011–2012 (Washington, D.C.: CQ Press, 2011), pp. 43–44.

entirely possible for the states to draw the new districts to benefit the incumbents of one or both parties. Altering district lines for partisan advantage is commonly called **gerrymandering**.

Gerrymandering has been practiced since at least the early 1800s.[10] With new computer software, gerrymandering is reaching new heights of precision. Precinct voting data can easily be used to manipulate boundary lines and produce districts that enhance or damage a candidate's or party's chances.[11] After the 2010 census, for

gerrymandering
Redrawing a congressional district to intentionally benefit one political party.

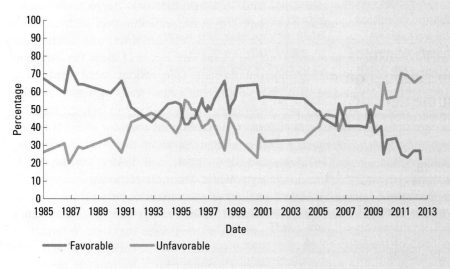

Favorable   Unfavorable

FIGURE 11.2 We Love Our Incumbents, but Congress Itself Stinks

Despite the reelection rate of incumbents reflected in Figure 11.1, public approval of Congress is far less positive. Favorability ratings have never been particularly high, but opinion has turned decidedly negative in recent years. Citizens don't believe that the House and Senate are facing up to the nation's problems.

Source: Figure 3-7, Rating of Congress, 1985–2013. In H. W. Stanley and R. G. Niemi (eds.), *Vital Statistics on American Politics* 2013–2014 (Washington, D.C.: CQ Press). Retrieved from http://library.cqpress.com/vsap/vsap11_fig3-7.

example, Illinois lost a seat in Congress and had to redraw its districts accordingly. The Democratic-controlled state legislature passed a plan that put Republican incumbent Joe Walsh's home in fellow Republican incumbent Randy Hultgren's district, which meant that the two men had to face each other in a primary. Walsh ultimately decided to avoid a bitter and costly primary and run in a neighboring district, which leaned more Democratic. After the 2012 election, he lost the open seat race to Democrat Tammy Duckworth, while Hultgren was reelected. The state's congressional delegation went from eleven Republicans and eight Democrats to six Republicans and twelve Democrats.[12]

Some argue that gerrymandering contributes to increasing polarization between the two parties in the House. Districts that are dominated by one party or another have some tendency to be more ideologically driven. Moreover, representatives elected from new districts after reapportionment tend to exhibit more polarized voting patterns than representatives elected from older districts.[13] Scholars maintain that the polarizing effect of gerrymandering has affected the Senate too. While the Senate doesn't undergo reapportionment, many Senators were once members of the House. Their experiences in that polarized body, it is argued, continue to affect their legislative behavior once they move on to the Senate.[14]

Name Recognition. Holding office brings with it some important advantages. First, incumbents develop significant name recognition among voters simply by being members of Congress. Representatives have press secretaries who help with name recognition through their efforts to get publicity for the activities and speeches of their bosses. Another resource available to members of Congress is the *franking privilege*—the right to send mail at taxpayer expense. Mailings work to make constituents aware of their legislators' names, activities, and accomplishments. In 2012, members of Congress sent out $24.8 million worth of mail, which often consists of "glossy productions filled with flattering photos and lists of the latest roads and bridges the lawmaker has brought home to the district."[15]

Under current franking regulations, information about the representative's personal life and political campaign cannot be included in official mailings and websites, and mailings can only target constituents who live in the representatives' districts. Both chambers have established rules limiting the type of information that members can send out through their official social networking accounts, but actual franking regulations do not cover social media.[16] In fact, the franking manual posted on the website of the House of Representatives as of this writing was published in 1998, well before the advent of new media. Yet these platforms enable representatives to communicate with people well beyond their own geographic constituency and have been used to send information about sporting events, their health, and even their shopping trips.[17] By 2012, 90 percent of members of Congress had Facebook accounts and 83 percent had Twitter accounts.[18]

 **ChuckGrassley** ✔
@ChuckGrassley   👤▾ 🐦 Follow

Fred and I hit a deer on hiway 136 south of Dyersville. After I pulled fender rubbing on tire we continued to farm. Assume deer dead

 Reply   Retweet   Favorite

Twitter

Assume Deer Dead

Today, members of Congress go well beyond the use of franking to keep their constituents informed about their activities. Some even tweet about their personal misadventures, such as when Senator Chuck Grassley (R-Ia.) informed followers about an unfortunate encounter with a deer. Social media allow members of Congress to connect with people all over the world, not just their constituents. Such technological developments challenge traditional limitations placed on the use of taxpayer funds for congressional outreach.

Technology has changed the way constituents communicate with representatives as well. In 1997, constituents sent 30.5 million pieces of communication to their representatives; by 2007, they sent 491.6 million. This communication revolution is due to the rise of electronic media and further helps to promote the name recognition that incumbents enjoy.[19]

Casework. Much of the work performed by the large staffs of members of Congress is **casework**—services for constituents, such as tracking down a Social Security check or directing the owner of a small business to the appropriate federal agency. Many congressional staffers are employed primarily as caseworkers. Thus, the very structure of congressional offices is built around helping constituents. One caseworker on a staff may be a specialist on immigration, another on veterans' benefits, another on Social Security, and so on. Legislators devote much of their office budget to casework because they assume that when they provide assistance to a constituent, that constituent will be grateful. Not only will that person probably vote for the legislator in the next election, but he or she is also sure to tell family members and friends how helpful the representative or senator was. "Casework is all profit," says one congressional scholar.[20]

casework
Solving problems for constituents, especially problems involving government agencies.

Campaign Financing. Anyone who wants to challenge an incumbent needs solid financial backing. Challengers must spend large sums of money to run a strong campaign with an emphasis on advertising—an expensive but effective way to bring their name and record to the voters' attention. But here too the incumbent has the advantage. Challengers have difficulty raising funds because they have to overcome contributors' doubts about whether they can win. In the 2012 elections, incumbents raised 53 percent of all money contributed to campaigns for election to the House and the Senate. Only 22 percent went to challengers (those running for open seats received the rest).[21]

Political action committees (PACs) show a strong preference for incumbents (see Chapter 10). They tend not to want to risk offending an incumbent by giving money to a long-shot challenger. The attitude of the American Medical Association's PAC is fairly typical. "We have a friendly incumbent policy," says its director. "We always stick with the incumbent if we agree with both candidates."[22]

Successful Challengers. Clearly, the deck is stacked against challengers. Yet some challengers do beat incumbents. How? The opposing party and unsympathetic PACs may target incumbents who seem vulnerable because of age, lack of seniority, a scandal, or unfavorable redistricting. Some incumbents appear vulnerable because they were elected by a narrow margin, or the ideological and partisan composition of their district does not favor their holding the seat. Vulnerable incumbents also bring out higher-quality challengers—individuals who have held elective office previously and are capable of raising adequate funds. Experienced challengers are more likely to defeat incumbents than are amateurs with little background in politics.[23] Senate challengers have a higher success rate than House challengers because they are generally higher-quality candidates. Often they are governors or members of the House who enjoy high name recognition and can attract significant campaign funds because they are regarded as credible candidates.

2014 Election. In all but two midterm elections in the post-WWII era, the president's party lost seats in the House of Representatives. The 2014 midterms continued this pattern. With some races too close to call as of this writing, Republicans gained 14 seats in the House, leaving them with the majority. The big story of the election involved the Senate, where Republicans gained control. It was the fifth time since 1980 that the Senate majority changed hands. As of this writing, Republicans gained 7 seats, giving them 52 seats overall. Despite Republican gains, incumbents of both parties enjoyed success. Only 13 Democrats and 2 Republicans were voted out of office. The reelection rate was over 95 percent for the House and over 87 percent for the Senate. Although there will be many new faces in Congress and both chambers will be controlled by Republicans, compromise could remain elusive: Democrats in the Senate have the filibuster, and the Democratic president has the veto.

Whom Do We Elect?

The people we elect to Congress are not a cross-section of American society. Although over half of the American labor force works in blue-collar jobs, someone currently employed as a blue-collar worker rarely wins a congressional nomination. Most members of Congress are upper-class professionals—lawyers and businesspeople—and, at last count, 50 percent are millionaires.[24]

Women and minorities have long been underrepresented in elective office, although both groups have increased their representation in Congress over time. Twenty women served in the Senate in the 2013–2014 session, a record number that made it necessary to expand the women's restroom![25] This is a historic high, but nowhere near the proportion of women to men in the population at large. One reason that the number of women in Congress lags behind their proportion in the population is that as women develop professionally, they are not recruited or encouraged to run in the same way that men are.[26] (See "Women in Legislatures in Global Politics" for a comparison of the representation of women in national legislatures.) In recent years, Congress has become more diverse in other ways as well, including religion and sexual orientation. The 113th Congress included six members who were Muslim, Hindu, or Buddhist, as well as seven who were gay or lesbian, leading the *Washington Post* to declare it "the most diverse in history."[27]

Other members of Congress don't necessarily ignore the concerns of women and minorities.[28] Yet many women and minorities believe that only members of their own group—people who have experienced what they have experienced—can truly represent their interests. This is a belief in **descriptive representation**—the view that a legislature

CONNECT WITH YOUR CLASSMATES
MindTap™ for American Government

Access The Congress Forum: Discussion—Representation in Congress.

descriptive representation
A belief that constituents are most effectively represented by legislators who are similar to them in such key demographic characteristics as race, ethnicity, religion, or gender.

The Millionaires' Club

In 2013, Representative Darrell Issa (R-Calif.) was the richest lawmaker in Congress, with an estimated net worth of $464 million. While 50 percent of lawmakers are millionaires, only about 4.5 percent of Americans can say the same.

Source: "Personal Finances," opensecrets.org/pfds/, 7 January 2014.

Alex Wong/Getty Images News/Getty Images

Women in Legislatures in Global Politics

Compared with other countries, the United States has substantially fewer women serving in the legislature. This figure includes fifteen European countries as well as fifteen countries from the Americas (North America, Central America, and South America) as of November 2013. Ranked by the percentage of women in the lower house of the national legislature, the European countries include, on average, a significantly higher percentage of women than the legislatures of countries in the Western Hemisphere. The United States ranks near the bottom, with women making up only 17.9 percent of the representatives in the House.

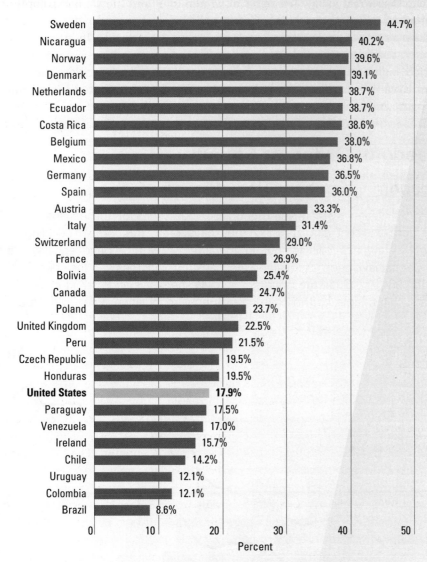

Source: Inter-Parliamentary Union, http://www.ipu.org/wmn-e/classif.htm.

Critical Thinking How might the laws passed in countries with more female legislators differ from laws passed in countries with fewer female legislators? How might the percentage of women in office affect how women (and men) feel about government?

racial gerrymandering
The drawing of a legislative district to maximize the chance that a minority candidate will win election.

should resemble the demographic characteristics of the population it represents.[29] The power of descriptive representation was on display in 2013. With seven women serving on the Senate Armed Services Committee, the issue of how the military handles sexual assault cases received significant legislative and media attention. A major defense bill that became law that year included strict new provisions, and female senators continue to press for additional reforms.[30]

It is difficult to promote the descriptive representation of women since women do not live in geographically concentrated areas. But since many racial minorities do live in concentrated areas, the use of **racial gerrymandering** has helped bring about a more racially diverse legislature (see "Freedom, Order, or Equality: Freedom v. Equality: Redistricting"). In 1993, however, the Supreme Court ruled that racial gerrymandering could violate the rights of whites. In *Shaw* v. *Reno*, the majority ruled in a split decision that a North Carolina district that meandered 160 miles from Durham to Charlotte was an example of "political apartheid." In effect, the Court ruled that racial gerrymandering segregated blacks from whites instead of creating districts built around contiguous communities.[31] In a later decision, the Supreme Court ruled that the "intensive and pervasive use of race" to protect incumbents and

Freedom, Order, or Equality

Freedom v. Equality: Redistricting

Every ten years, state governments use the results of the census to redraw their congressional district lines. They have great freedom in deciding where district boundaries will lie, but in the interest of promoting equality, certain regulations have been imposed on the states by Congress and the courts.

In 1964, the Supreme Court ruled in *Wesberry* v. *Sanders* that all House districts within a state had to have roughly equal population. Prior to this decision,

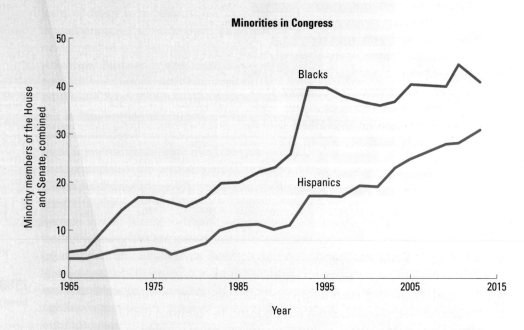

Source: H. W. Stanley and R. G. Niemi (eds.), *Vital Statistics on American Politics* 2013–2014 (Washington, D.C.: CQ Press), Table 5.2.

promote political gerrymandering violated the Fourteenth Amendment and Voting Rights Act of 1965.[32] In 2001, just before the redistricting from the 2000 census was to begin in the individual states, the Court modified its earlier decisions by declaring that race was not an illegitimate consideration in drawing congressional boundaries as long as it was not the "dominant and controlling" factor.[33]

Racial gerrymandering has been less effective for Hispanics. Hispanic representation is only about half that of blacks, even though there are slightly more Hispanics in the United States than blacks. One reason for this inequity is that Hispanics tend not to live in such geographically concentrated areas as do blacks. Another reason is that an estimated 23.2 percent of adult Hispanics living in the United States are ineligible to vote because they are not American citizens.[34]

Although this movement over time to draw districts that work to elect minorities has clearly increased the number of black and Hispanic legislators, almost all of whom are Democrats, it has also helped the Republican Party. As more Democratic voting minorities have been packed into some districts, their numbers have diminished in others, leaving the remaining districts not merely "whiter" but also more Republican than they would have otherwise been.[35]

states often drew districts that had over two and three times the number of people than other districts, which the Courts ruled to be a violation of the principle of "one person, one vote."

During the 1980s, both Congress and the Supreme Court affected the freedom of states to draw district lines as they wish by promoting descriptive representation for blacks and Hispanics. When Congress amended the Voting Rights Act in 1982, it encouraged states to draw districts that concentrated minorities together so that black and Hispanic candidates would have a better chance of being elected to office. The Supreme Court decision in *Thornburg* v. *Gingles* in 1986 also pushed states to concentrate minorities in House districts. After the 1990 census was the first time states redrew House boundaries with the intent of creating districts with majority-minority populations. This effort led to a roughly 50 percent increase in the number of black candidates elected to the House. In 2013, there were 114 majority-minority districts in the country (26 percent of all districts), sixty-nine of them with minority representatives.

Debates about the extent to which racial considerations are necessary when drawing district lines or whether they constitute an undue restriction on both state sovereignty and on the voting rights of white voters continue to emerge with every round of redistricting.

Source: H. W. Stanley and R. G. Niemi (eds.), *Vital Statistics on American Politics* 2013–2014 (Washington, D.C.: CQ Press, 2013).

Critical Thinking Are there ways to promote racial equality and diversity in Congress that do not conflict with state freedoms in determining how congressional district lines are drawn? What advantages or disadvantages might there be in eliminating state districts altogether and having each voter vote for all of the state's representatives?

How Issues Get on the Congressional Agenda

LO3 ★ Describe the ways in which issues get on the congressional agenda.

The formal legislative process begins when a member of Congress introduces a *bill*, a proposal for a new law. In the House, members drop bills in the "hopper," a mahogany box near the rostrum where the Speaker presides. Senators give their bills to a Senate clerk or introduce them from the floor. But before a bill can be introduced to solve a problem, someone must perceive that a problem exists or that an issue needs to be resolved. In other words, the problem somehow must find its way onto the congressional agenda.

Many issues Congress works on seem to have been around forever. Foreign aid, the national debt, and Social Security have come up in just about every recent session of Congress. Other issues emerge more suddenly, especially those that are the product of technological change.[36] The issue of "cybersecurity" is one example. Not long ago, the term did not even exist. But today, the possibility that a cyberattack could disrupt the nation's economy and security is very real. In 2013, the House passed the Cybersecurity Enhancement Act, which included provisions aimed at easing communication between the government and technology companies and funding cybersecurity research. However, the bill did not come to a vote in the Senate, and President Obama threatened a veto, citing insufficient civil liberties protections for the personal information of American citizens. Determining how to balance freedom and order in an age of cyber warfare has only been on the agenda for a short time, but is likely to stay on the agenda for some time.[37]

New issues reach the congressional agenda in many ways. Sometimes a highly visible event focuses national attention on a problem. When a gunman killed twenty-six children and staffers at Sandy Hook Elementary School in Newtown, Connecticut, in 2012, Congress quickly took up the issue of gun control. Within months, nine gun provisions were voted on in the Senate, though partisan divisions prevented them from becoming law.[38] Presidential support can also move an issue onto the agenda quickly. The media attention paid to the president gives him enormous opportunity to draw the nation's attention to problems he believes need some form of government action.

Within Congress, party leaders and committee chairs have the opportunity to move issues onto the agenda, but they rarely act capriciously. They often bide their time, waiting for other members of Congress to learn about an issue as they attempt to gauge the level of support for some kind of action. At times, the efforts of an interest group spark awareness of an issue and support for action.

The Lawmaking Process and the Importance of Committees

LO4 ★ Differentiate among the types of congressional committees and evaluate the role of the committee system in the legislative process.

The process of writing bills and getting them enacted is relatively simple in the sense that it follows a series of specific steps. What complicates the process is the many ways legislation can be treated at each step. Here, we examine the straightforward process by which laws are made. In the next few sections, we discuss some of the complexities of that process.

After a bill is introduced in either house, it is assigned to the committee with jurisdiction over that policy area (see Figure 11.3). A banking bill, for example, would

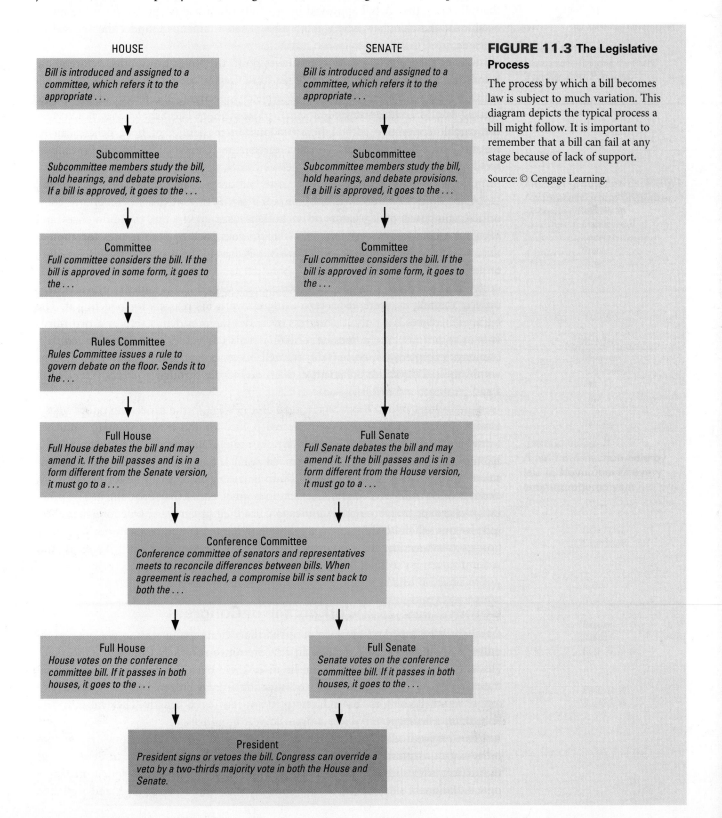

FIGURE 11.3 The Legislative Process

The process by which a bill becomes law is subject to much variation. This diagram depicts the typical process a bill might follow. It is important to remember that a bill can fail at any stage because of lack of support.

Source: © Cengage Learning.

be assigned to the Financial Services Committee in the House or to the Banking, Housing, and Urban Affairs Committee in the Senate. When a committee considers a piece of legislation assigned to it, the bill is usually referred to a subcommittee. The subcommittee may hold hearings, and legislative staffers may do research on the bill. The original bill usually is modified or revised; if passed in some form, it is sent to the full committee. A bill approved by the full committee is sent to the entire membership of the chamber, where it may be debated, amended, and either passed or defeated.

Bills coming out of House committees go to the Rules Committee before going before the full House membership. The Rules Committee attaches a rule to the bill that governs the coming floor debate, typically specifying the length of the debate and types of amendments House members can offer. The Senate does not have a comparable committee, although restrictions on the length of floor debate can be reached through unanimous consent agreements (see the "Rules of Procedure" section later in this chapter).

Even if both houses of Congress pass a bill on the same subject, the Senate and House versions are often different from each other. In that case, a conference committee, composed of legislators from both houses, works out the differences and develops a compromise version. This version goes back to both houses for another floor vote. If both chambers approve the bill, it goes to the president for his signature or veto.

When the president signs a bill, it becomes law. If the president **vetoes** (disapproves) the bill, he sends it back to Congress with his reasons for rejecting it. The bill then becomes law only if Congress overrides the president's veto by a two-thirds vote in each house. If the president neither signs nor vetoes the bill within ten days (Sundays excepted) of receiving it, the bill becomes law. But if Congress adjourns within the ten days, the president can let the bill die through a *pocket veto*, by not signing it.

The content of a bill can be changed at any stage of the process in either house. Lawmaking in Congress has many access points for those who want to influence legislation. This openness tends to fit within the pluralist model of democracy. As a bill moves through Congress, it is amended again and again, in a search for a consensus that will get it enacted and signed into law. The process can be tortuously slow, and it is often fruitless. Derailing legislation is much easier than enacting it. The process gives groups frequent opportunities to voice their preferences. One foreign ambassador stationed in Washington aptly described the twists and turns of our legislative process this way: "In the Congress of the U.S., it's never over until it's over. And when it's over, it's still not over."[39]

veto
The president's disapproval of a bill that has been passed by both houses of Congress. Congress can override a veto with a two-thirds vote in each house.

Committees: The Workhorses of Congress

President Woodrow Wilson once observed that "Congress in session is Congress on public exhibition, whilst Congress in its committee-rooms is Congress at work."[40] His words are as true today as when he wrote them over 100 years ago. A speech on the Senate floor, for example, may convince the average citizen, but it is less likely to influence other senators. Indeed, few of them may even hear it. The real nuts and bolts of lawmaking go on in the congressional committees.

The House and Senate are divided into committees for the same reason that other large organizations are broken into departments or divisions: to develop and use expertise in specific areas. At Apple, for example, different groups of people design iPhones and iPads, write software, assemble hardware, and sell the company's products. Each task requires an expertise that may have little to do with the others. Likewise, in Congress, decisions on weapons systems require a special knowledge that is of little relevance to decisions on reimbursement formulas for health insurance. It makes sense for some members of Congress to spend more time examining defense issues, becoming increasingly expert on the topic, while others concentrate on health matters. Eventually, all members of Congress vote on each bill that emerges from committees. Those who are not on a particular committee depend on committee members to examine the issues thoroughly, make compromises as necessary, and bring forward a sound piece of legislation that has a good chance of being passed.

Standing Committees. There are several different kinds of congressional committees, but the **standing committee** is predominant. Standing committees are permanent committees that specialize in a particular area—for example, the House Judiciary Committee or the Senate Foreign Relations Committee. Most of the day-to-day work of drafting legislation takes place in the sixteen standing Senate committees and twenty-one standing House committees. Typically, sixteen to twenty senators serve on each standing Senate committee, and around forty members serve on each standing committee in the House. The proportions of Democrats and Republicans on a standing committee are controlled by the majority party in each house. The majority gives the minority a percentage of seats that, in theory, approximates the minority party's percentage in the entire chamber. However, the majority party usually gives itself enough of a cushion to ensure that it can control each committee.

Standing committees are often broken down further into subcommittees. For instance, the Senate Foreign Relations Committee has seven subcommittees, covering different regions of the world and issues such as human rights. Subcommittees exist for the same reason parent committees exist: members acquire expertise by continually working within the policy area. Typically, members of the subcommittee are the dominant force in shaping the content of a bill.

Other Committees. Members of Congress can also serve on joint, select, and conference committees. A **joint committee** is composed of members of both chambers. Like standing committees, the four joint committees are concerned with particular policy areas. The Joint Economic Committee, for instance, analyzes the country's economic policies. Joint committees are much weaker than standing committees because they typically cannot report bills to the House or Senate. Their role is that of fact finding and publicizing problems and issues that fall within their jurisdiction.

A **select committee** is a temporary committee created for a specific purpose. Congress establishes select committees to deal with special circumstances or with issues that either overlap or fall outside the areas of expertise of standing committees. In 2011, the Joint Select Committee on Deficit Reduction was created and charged with issuing recommendations by November of that year for reducing the deficit. It was dubbed a "supercommittee" by the media because it included members from both the House and Senate (three members from each party in each chamber).

A **conference committee** is also a temporary committee, created to work out differences between the House and Senate versions of a specific piece of legislation. Its members are appointed from the standing committees or subcommittees from each house that originally crafted and reported the legislation.

standing committee
A permanent congressional committee that specializes in a particular policy area.

joint committee
A committee made up of members of both the House and the Senate.

select committee
A temporary congressional committee created for a specific purpose and disbanded after that purpose is fulfilled.

conference committee
A temporary committee created to work out differences between the House and Senate versions of a specific piece of legislation.

Conference committees are not always used, however, to reconcile differing bills. Often, informal negotiations between committee leaders in the House and Senate resolve differences. The increasing partisan conflict between Democrats and Republicans often results in a compromise bill devised solely by the majority party (when a single party controls both chambers).

Congressional Expertise and Seniority

Once appointed to a committee, a representative or senator has great incentive to remain there and gain expertise because influence increases with expertise. Influence also grows in a more formal way, with **seniority**, or years of consecutive service, on a committee. In their quest for expertise and seniority, members tend to stay on the same committees. Within each committee, the senior member of the majority party usually becomes the committee chair. Other senior members of the majority party become subcommittee chairs, whereas their counterparts from the minority party gain influence as ranking minority members.

The way in which committees and subcommittees are led and organized within Congress is significant because much public policy decision making takes place there. The first step in drafting legislation is to collect information on the issue. Committee staffers research the problem, and committees hold hearings to take testimony from witnesses who have some special knowledge of the subject.

At times, committee hearings are more theatrical than informational, designed to draw public attention to them and to offer the majority party a chance to express its views. In 2011, Peter King, the Republican chair of the House Homeland Security Committee who once claimed that there are "too many mosques in the country" and that most are run by extremists, convened highly publicized hearings purportedly aimed at discovering whether American Muslims were becoming increasingly radicalized.[41] Democrats denounced the hearings as inflammatory and as harmful to U.S. relations with the Muslim world. One observer of the contentious hearings wrote, "Mostly, it was the committee itself that appeared to be on trial."[42]

The meetings at which subcommittees and committees actually debate and amend legislation are called *markup sessions*. In some committees, the chair, the ranking minority member, and others work hard, in formal committee sessions and in informal negotiations, to find a middle ground on issues that divide committee members in order to reach consensus. In other committees, members exhibit strong ideological and partisan sentiments. However, committee and subcommittee leaders prefer to find ways to overcome ideological and partisan divisions so that they can build compromise solutions that will appeal to the broader membership of their house. The skill of

seniority
Years of consecutive service on a particular congressional committee.

Game On
Famous people often testify before congressional committees in the hopes that their star power will influence legislation. Weeks after winning the national NBA championship in 2013, basketball star Ray Allen of the Miami Heat testified before a Senate committee to argue in favor of preserving a funding program for research into type 1 diabetes, a disease that affects his son, Walker.

committee leaders in assembling coalitions that produce legislation that can pass on the floor of their house is critically important. When committees are mired in disagreement, they lose power.

Oversight: Following Through on Legislation

There is general agreement in Washington that knowledge is power. For Congress to retain influence over the programs it creates, it must be aware of how the agencies responsible for them are administering them. To that end, committees engage in **oversight**, reviewing agencies' operations to determine whether they are carrying out policies as Congress intended.

As the executive branch has grown and policies and programs have become increasingly complex, oversight has become more difficult. On a typical weekday, agencies issue more than a hundred pages of new regulations. Even with the division of labor in the committee system, determining how good a job an agency is doing in implementing a program is no easy task.

Congress performs its oversight function in several different ways. The most visible is the hearing. Hearings may be part of a routine review or can occur when a problem with a program or with an agency's administrative practices emerges. For example, when the new health-care website, healthcare.gov, was unveiled in 2013, it became clear that it was riddled with problems and people were unable to use it to sign up for health insurance. Committees in both chambers launched investigations, calling government officials and website contractors to testify in order to uncover what went wrong.

Another way Congress keeps track of what departments and agencies are doing is by requesting reports on specific agency practices. When majority control in Congress switches from one party to another, committees become more aggressive in investigating ethical lapses and policy problems of the opposing party. After becoming the majority in the House in 2011, for example, Republicans held hearings on a range of issues, including Obama's energy policies and the role of the United States during March 2011 airstrikes against Libya by the NATO alliance.

Oversight is often stereotyped as a process in which angry legislators bring some administrators before television cameras at a hearing and proceed to dress them down for some scandal or mistake. Some of this does go on, but the pluralist side of Congress ensures that at least some members of a committee are advocates of the programs they oversee because those programs serve their constituents back home. Members of the House and Senate Agriculture Committees, for example, both Democrats and Republicans, want farm programs to succeed. Thus, most oversight is aimed at trying to find ways to improve programs and is not directed at efforts to discredit them. In short, Congress engages in oversight because it is an extension of their efforts to control public policy.

oversight
The process of reviewing the operations of an agency to determine whether it is carrying out policies as Congress intended.

Majoritarian and Pluralist Views of Committees

Government by committee vests significant power in the committees and subcommittees of Congress—and especially their leaders. This is particularly true in the House, which has more decentralized patterns of influence than the Senate and is more restrictive about letting members amend legislation on the floor. Committee members can bury a bill by not reporting it to the full House or Senate. Many of them also make up the conference committees charged with developing compromise versions of bills.

In some ways, the committee system enhances the force of pluralism in American politics. Representatives and senators are elected by the voters in their particular districts and states, and they tend to seek membership on the committees that make the decisions most important to their constituents. Members from farm areas, for example, want membership on the House and Senate Agriculture Committees, while urban liberals like committees that handle social programs. As a result, committee members tend to represent constituencies with a strong interest in the committee's policy area and are predisposed to write legislation favorable to those constituencies.

Committees have a majoritarian aspect as well, as most committees reflect the general ideological profiles of the two parties' congressional contingents.[43] For example, Republicans on individual House committees tend to vote like all other Republicans in the House. Moreover, even if a committee's views are not in line with those of the full membership, it is constrained in the legislation it writes because bills cannot become law unless they are passed by the parent chamber and the other house. Consequently, in formulating legislation, committees anticipate what other representatives and senators will accept. The parties within each chamber also have means of rewarding members who are loyal to party priorities. Party committees and the party leadership within each chamber make committee assignments and respond to requests for transfers from less prestigious to more prestigious committees. Those who vote in line with the party get better assignments.[44]

Leaders and Followers in Congress

LO5 ★ Identify the leadership structure of the legislative branch and assess the rules and norms that influence congressional operations.

Above the committee chairs is another layer of authority in Congress. The party leaders in each house work to maximize the influence of their own party while keeping their chamber functioning smoothly and efficiently. The operation of the two houses is also influenced by the rules and norms that each chamber has developed over the years.

The Leadership Task

Republicans and Democrats elect party leaders in both chambers who are charged with overseeing institutional procedures, managing legislation, fundraising, and communicating with the press. In the House, the majority party's leader is the **Speaker of the House**. The Speaker is a constitutional officer, but the Constitution does not list the Speaker's duties.[45] The majority party in the House also has a majority leader, who helps the Speaker guide the party's policy program through the legislative process, and a majority whip, who keeps track of the vote count and rallies support for legislation on the floor. The minority party is led by a minority leader who is assisted by the minority whip.

The Constitution makes the vice president of the United States the president of the Senate. But in practice the vice president rarely visits the Senate, unless there is a possibility of a tie vote, in which case he can break the tie. The *president pro tempore* (president "for the time"), elected by the majority party, is supposed to chair the Senate in the vice president's absence, but by custom this constitutional position is

Speaker of the House
The presiding officer of the House of Representatives.

entirely honorary. The title is typically assigned to the most senior member of the majority party.

The real power in the Senate resides in the **majority leader**. As in the House, the top position in the opposing party is that of minority leader. Technically, the majority leader does not preside over Senate sessions (members rotate in the president pro tempore's chair), but he or she does schedule legislation, in consultation with the minority leader. More broadly, party leaders play a critical role in getting bills through Congress. The most significant function that leaders play is steering the bargaining and negotiating over the content of legislation. When an issue divides their party, their house, the two houses, or their house and the White House, the leaders try to work out a compromise.

Much of what leaders do each day is meet with other members of their chamber to try to strike deals that will yield a majority on the floor. It is often a matter of finding out whether one faction is willing to give up a policy preference in exchange for another concession. Beyond trying to engineer trade-offs that will win votes, the party leaders must persuade others (often powerful committee chairs) that theirs is the best deal possible. Former Speaker Dennis Hastert used to say, "They call me the Speaker, but … they really ought to call me the Listener."[46]

It is often difficult for party leaders to control rank-and-file members because they have independent electoral bases in their districts and states and receive most of their campaign funds from nonparty sources. Yet party leaders can be aggressive about enforcing party discipline, either by threatening to withdraw support for policy issues near and dear to the defectors or by rewarding those members who toe the

majority leader
The head of the majority party in the Senate; the second-highest ranking member of the majority party in the House.

George Tames/The New York Times/Redux

The Johnson Treatment

When he was Senate majority leader in the 1950s, Lyndon Johnson was well known for his style of interaction with other members. In this unusual set of photographs, we see him applying the "Johnson treatment" to Senator Theodore Francis Green (D-R.I.). Washington journalists Rowland Evans and Robert Novak offered the following description of the treatment: "Its tone could be supplication, accusation, cajolery, exuberance, scorn, tears, complaint, the hint of threat. It was all of these together. It ran the gamut of human emotions. Its velocity was breathtaking and it was all in one direction. Interjections from the target were rare. Johnson anticipated them before they could be spoken. He moved in close, his face a scant millimeter from his target, his eyes widening and narrowing, his eyebrows rising and falling. From his pockets poured clippings, memos, statistics. Mimicry, humor, and the genius of analogy made The Treatment an almost hypnotic experience and rendered the target stunned and helpless."

Source: Quote from Rowland Evans and Robert Novak, *Lyndon B. Johnson: The Exercise of Power* (New York: New American Library, 1966), p. 104.

party line. When House Republicans had a chance to meet with Obama in the White House in June 2011, the leadership selected freshman Reid Ribble as one of a handful of members who would be able to question the president directly. Ribble was chosen, in part, because "he had never crossed the G.O.P. leadership on anything important."[47] Republican members who had dissented in the past, it was decided, were free to figure out on their own how to have face time with the president.

Rules of Procedure

The operations of Congress are structured by both formal rules and informal norms of behavior. Rules in each chamber are mostly matters of parliamentary procedure. For example, they govern the scheduling of legislation, outlining when and how certain types of legislation can be brought to the floor. Rules also govern the introduction of floor amendments. In the House, amendments must be directly relevant to the bill at hand; in the Senate, except in certain, specified instances, amendments that are not relevant can be proposed.

As noted earlier, an important difference between the two chambers is the House's use of its Rules Committee to govern floor debate. Lacking a similar committee to act as a "traffic cop" for legislation, the Senate relies on unanimous consent agreements to set the starting time and length of debate. If one senator objects, a bill is stalled. Senators do not routinely object to unanimous consent agreements, however, because they will need them when bills of their own await scheduling.

If a senator wants to stop a bill badly enough, she or he may start a **filibuster** and try to talk the bill to death. By historical tradition, the Senate gives its members the right of unlimited debate. During a 1947 debate, Idaho Democrat Glen Taylor "spoke for 8½ hours on fishing, baptism, Wall Street, and his children." The record for holding the floor belongs to South Carolina Republican Strom Thurmond for a twenty-four-hour, eighteen-minute marathon in 1957.[48] In the House, no member is allowed to speak for more than an hour without unanimous consent.

After a 1917 filibuster by a small group of senators killed President Wilson's bill to arm merchant ships—a bill favored by a majority of senators—the Senate adopted **cloture**, a means of limiting debate. It takes the votes of sixty senators to invoke cloture. To signal one's intent to filibuster, a senator issues a **hold**, which is a letter requesting that a bill be held from floor debate. In response to a hold, the majority party can take the legislation off the table, try to compromise with the obstructionist lawmaker, or hold a cloture vote.

In today's Congress, the mere threat of a filibuster is common, which means that a bill often needs the support of sixty senators instead of a simple majority in order to pass. It has been argued that filibuster threats have become more common because "the workload of the Senate has increased to the point that wasting time is more costly than accepting the outcome of a cloture vote."[49] In other words, senators are just too busy to wait around while filibustering senators take to the floor. So senators have become more willing to threaten obstruction, knowing that the result will most likely be a cloture vote. Given today's high level of partisan polarization (see Figure 11.4), cloture votes often result in victory for the obstructionist. This "60-vote Senate" is often criticized for its ability to thwart the principle of majority rule and to make the legislative process even slower than was originally intended.[50]

In 2013, Senate Democrats became so frustrated with minority filibusters that they enacted a rare change to Senate rules, eliminating the use of filibusters for the confirmation of presidential nominees for the federal courts and executive positions

filibuster
A delaying tactic, used in the Senate, that involves speechmaking to prevent action on a piece of legislation.

cloture
The mechanism by which a filibuster is cut off in the Senate.

hold
A letter requesting that a bill be held from floor debate.

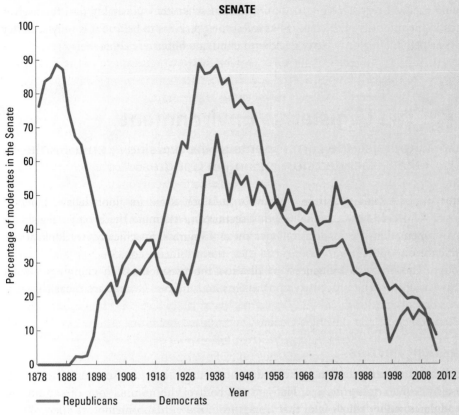

SENATE

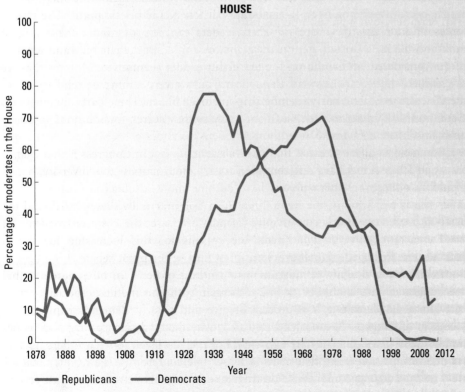

HOUSE

FIGURE 11.4 Disappearing Moderates

For much of the twentieth century, Congress relied on bipartisanship—the two parties working together—in policymaking. This often meant that the moderates of both parties were central to the development of legislation as they coalesced around the most workable compromise. More recently, behavior has turned more partisan. Increasingly, members of each party vote with each other and against the position of the other party, and each party is mainly comprised of politicians of the same ideological orientation. These graphs show the percentage of representatives and senators who can be considered moderate based on their voting records. Today, moderates have all but disappeared.

Source: http://voteview.com/political_polarization.asp.

(except in the case of nominees for the Supreme Court). Republicans argued that Democrats will regret having made this change when they inevitably find themselves back in the minority. The change has led some observers to believe it is only a matter of time before a majority party decides to eliminate filibusters altogether.

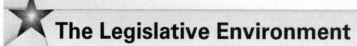

★ The Legislative Environment

LO6 ★ Appraise the components of the legislative environment that affect decision making in Congress.

After legislation emerges from committee, it is scheduled for floor debate. How do legislators decide how to vote? In this section, we examine the broader legislative environment that affects decision making in Congress. Specifically, we look at the influence on legislators of political parties, the president, constituents, and interest groups. The first two influences, parties and the president, push Congress toward majoritarianism. The other two, constituents and interest groups, are pluralist influences on policymaking.

Political Parties

The national political parties might appear to have limited resources at their disposal to influence lawmakers. They do not control the nominations of candidates. Candidates receive the bulk of their funds from individual contributors and political action committees, not from the national parties. Nevertheless, parties are strong forces in the legislative process.[51] Party leaders can help or hinder the efforts of rank-and-file legislators to get on the right committees, get their bills and amendments considered, and climb on the leadership ladder themselves. Moreover, as we saw earlier, the Democrats and Republicans on a given committee tend to reflect the views of the entire party membership in the chamber. Thus, party members on a committee often act as agents of their party as they search for solutions to policy problems.

The most significant reason that parties are important in Congress is that Democrats and Republicans have different ideologies.[52] Both parties have diversity, but as Figure 11.4 illustrates, both parties have become more ideologically cohesive over time. The liberal wing of the Republican Party has practically disappeared, and the party is unified around a conservative agenda. Likewise, the conservative wing of the Democratic Party has declined. The reasons for this increasing ideological homogeneity within the parties are a matter of intense academic debate.[53]

Traditionally, one of the most important norms of behavior in Congress is that individual members should be willing to bargain with one another, especially across party lines. Policymaking is a process of give and take; it demands compromise. Members of Congress are not expected to violate their conscience on policy issues simply to strike a deal. They are expected, however, to listen to what others have to say and to make every effort to reach a reasonable compromise. Few policy matters are so clear-cut that compromise destroys one's position. Yet over the past several years, as the parties have become more polarized, compromises between them have become ever more difficult to achieve. The inability to compromise threatens majoritarianism, especially in the Senate, as minority factions can produce stalemate after stalemate.

The President

Unlike members of Congress, the president is elected by voters across the entire nation. It can thus be argued that the president has a better claim to representing the nation than does any single member of Congress or even Congress as a whole. As such, presidents try to capitalize on their popular election and usually act as though they are speaking for the majority.

During the twentieth century, the public's expectations of what the president can accomplish in office grew enormously. We now expect the president to be our chief legislator: to introduce legislation on major issues and use his influence to push bills through Congress. This is much different from our early history, when presidents felt constrained by the constitutional doctrine of separation of powers and had to have members of Congress work confidentially for them during legislative sessions.[54]

Today, the White House is openly involved not only in the writing of bills but also in their development as they wind their way through the legislative process. If the White House does not like a bill, it tries to work out a compromise with legislators to have it amended. To monitor Congress and lobby for the administration's policies, many legislative liaison personnel work for the executive branch. On issues of the greatest importance, the president himself may meet with legislators directly. During the government shutdown in 2013 described at the start of this chapter, President Obama met personally with Republicans in both the House and the Senate and tried to negotiate a deal that would reopen the government.[55]

Although members of Congress grant presidents a leadership role in proposing legislation, they jealously guard the power of Congress to debate, shape, and pass or defeat any legislation the president proposes. Congress often clashes sharply with the president.

Constituents

Constituents are the people who live and vote in a legislator's district or state. Their opinions are a crucial part of the legislative decision-making process. As much as members of Congress want to please their party's leadership or the president by going along with their preferences, they have to think about what the voters back home want. If they displease enough people by the way they vote, they might lose their seat in the next election.

Constituents' influence contributes to pluralism because the diversity of America is mirrored by the geographical basis of representation in Congress. A representative from Los Angeles needs to be sensitive to issues of particular concern to constituents whose backgrounds are Korean, Vietnamese, Indian, Hispanic, African American, or Jewish. A representative from Montana will have few such constituents but must pay particular attention to issues involving minerals and mining. Such constituencies push and pull Congress in many different directions.

At all stages of the legislative process, the interests of the voters are on the minds of members of Congress. As they decide what to spend time on and how to vote, they weigh how different courses of action will affect their constituents' views of them, and the degree to which they feel they should follow constituency preferences.[56]

constituents
People who live and vote in a government official's district or state.

Interest Groups

As we pointed out in Chapter 10, interest groups are one way constituents influence Congress. Because they represent a vast array of vocational, regional, and ideological groupings within our population, interest groups exemplify pluralist politics. Interest groups press members of Congress to take a particular course of action, believing sincerely that what they prefer is also best for the country. Legislators are attentive to interest groups not because of an abstract commitment to pluralist politics but because these organizations represent citizens, some of whom live back home in their district or state.

Lobbies are an indispensable source of information for members of Congress. They are also important contributors to and fundraisers for campaigns. Periodic scandals raise concern, however, about potential conflicts of interest and whether legislators do special favors for lobbyists in exchange for campaign contributions or even for personal gain.[57] More common are the entirely legal campaign contributions that individual lobbyists and PACs make to legislators (see Chapter 10). Interest groups don't believe that contributions will necessarily get them what they want, but they certainly expect that significant donations will give them greater access to legislators. And access is the first step toward influencing the process.

With all these strong forces constraining legislators, it's easy to believe that they function solely in response to these external pressures. Legislators, however, bring their own views and life experiences to Congress. The issues they choose to work on and the way they vote reflect these personal values too.[58] But to the degree that the four external sources of influence on Congress—parties, the president, constituents, and interest groups—do influence legislators, they push them in both majoritarian and pluralist directions.

The Dilemma of Representation

LO7 ★ Consider whether members of Congress should vote according to the majority views of their constituents.

When candidates for Congress campaign, they routinely promise to work hard for their district's or state's interests. When they get to Washington, though, they all face a troubling dilemma: what their constituents want may not be what the people across the nation want.

Presidents and Shopping Bags

In doing the research for his book *Home Style*, political scientist Richard Fenno accompanied several representatives as they worked and interacted with constituents in their home district. On one of Fenno's trips, one representative said, "I spent fifteen minutes on the telephone with the president this afternoon. He had a plaintive tone in his voice and he pleaded with me." His side of the issue had prevailed over the president's, and he was elated by the victory. When Fenno and the representative got into their awaiting car, the representative saw the back seat piled high with campaign paraphernalia: shopping bags printed with his name and picture. "Back to this again," he sighed.[59]

Every member of Congress lives in two worlds: the world of presidents and the world of constituents. A typical week in the life of a representative means working in Washington, then boarding a plane and flying back to the home district. There, the representative spends time meeting with individual constituents and talking to civic groups, church gatherings, business associations, labor unions, and others. A 2013 study found that 78 percent of representatives surveyed said they spent at least forty weekends per year in their districts.[60]

Members of Congress are often criticized for being out of touch with the people they are supposed to represent. This charge does not seem justified. Legislators work extraordinarily hard at keeping in touch with voters and finding out what is on their constituents' minds. The problem is how to act on that knowledge.

Trustees or Delegates?

Are members of Congress bound to vote the way their constituents want them to vote, even if it means voting against their conscience? Some say no. They argue that legislators must be free to vote in line with what they think is best. This view has long been associated with the eighteenth-century English political philosopher Edmund Burke (1729–1797). Burke, who served in Parliament, told his constituents in Bristol that "you choose a member, indeed; but when

Brandon Thibodeaux/The New York Times/Redux

Have You Seen This Man?

Traditionally, members of Congress would travel to their home districts during recesses and talk with constituents. Yet as Congress has become more polarized, these meetings have gotten increasingly contentious, so much so that fewer and fewer representatives have been having them. In 2013, constituents of Rep. Pete Sessions (R-Tex.) held a meeting without him and brought a poster of a milk carton indicating that he was missing.

you have chosen him, he is not a member of Bristol, but he is a member of *Parliament*."[61] Burke reasoned that representatives are sent by their constituents to vote as they think best. As **trustees**, representatives are obligated to consider the views of their constituents, but they are not obligated to vote according to those views if they think they are misguided.

Others hold that legislators should represent the majority view of their constituents—that they are **delegates** with instructions from the people at home on how to vote on critical issues. Delegates, unlike trustees, must be prepared to vote against their own preferences. During the fight over President Obama's healthcare reform, Representative Joseph Cao knew he would be in a bind. As a Republican representing a heavily Democratic and black district in Louisiana in which 25 percent of people lacked health insurance, he was torn between his party on the one hand and the desires of his constituents on the other. He ultimately voted for the first reform bill (the only Republican to do so) but against the final version. In the 2010 election, he was one of only two sitting Republicans to be defeated.[62]

Given the conflicts between the trustee and delegate models of representation, it is not surprising that Congress is not clearly a body of either delegates or trustees. Research has shown, however, that members of Congress are more likely to take the delegate role on issues that are of great concern to their constituents.[63] But much of the time, what constituents really want is not clear. Many issues are not highly visible back home. Some issues may cut across the constituency, affecting constituents in different ways. Or constituents may only partially understand them. For such issues, no delegate position is obvious.

trustee
A representative who is obligated to consider the views of constituents but is not obligated to vote according to those views if he or she believes they are misguided.

delegate
A legislator whose primary responsibility is to represent the majority view of his or her constituents, regardless of his or her own view.

Pluralism, Majoritarianism, and Democracy

LO8 ★ Assess the elements that characterize Congress as a pluralist or majoritarian system.

The dilemma that individual members of Congress face in adopting the role of either delegate or trustee has broad implications for the way our country is governed. When legislators act as delegates, congressional policymaking is more pluralistic, and policies reflect the bargaining that goes on among lawmakers who speak for different constituencies. When legislators act as trustees and vote their consciences, policymaking becomes less tied to the narrower interests of districts and states. But even here there is no guarantee that congressional decision making reflects majority interests. True majoritarian legislatures require a paramount role for political parties.

We end this chapter with a short discussion of pluralism versus majoritarianism in Congress. But first, to establish a frame of reference, we look at a more majoritarian type of legislature: the parliament.

Parliamentary Government

parliamentary system
A system of government in which the chief executive is the leader whose party holds the most seats in the legislature after an election or whose party forms a major part of the ruling coalition.

In our system of government, the executive and legislative functions are divided between a president and a Congress, each elected separately. Most other democracies—such as Britain—have parliamentary governments. In a **parliamentary system**, the chief executive is the legislative leader whose party holds the most seats in the legislature after an election or whose party forms a major part of the ruling coalition. For instance, in Great Britain, voters do not cast a ballot for prime minister. They vote only for their member of Parliament and thus influence the choice of prime minister only indirectly, by voting for the party they favor in the local district election. Parties are unified, and in Parliament, legislators vote for their party's position, giving voters a strong and direct means of influencing public policy. Where there is a multiple party system (as opposed to just two parties), a governing coalition must sometimes be formed from an alliance of multiple parties.

In a parliamentary system, power is concentrated in the legislature because the leader of the majority party is also the head of the government. Moreover, parliamentary legislatures are usually composed of only one house or have a second chamber that is much weaker than the other. Parliamentary governments usually do not have a court that can invalidate acts of the parliament. Under such a system, the government is in the hands of the party that controls the parliament. With no separation of government powers, checks on government action are few. These governments fit the majoritarian model of democracy to a much greater extent than a separation-of-powers system.

Pluralism versus Majoritarianism in Congress

The U.S. Congress is often criticized for being too pluralist and not majoritarian enough. The federal budget deficit provides a case in point. Americans are often deeply concerned about the big deficits that plague our national budgets. Both Democrats and Republicans in Congress repeatedly call for reductions in those deficits. But when spending bills come before Congress, legislators' concern turns to what the bills would do for their district or state.

Until 2011, appropriations bills often included **earmarks**, pork barrel projects that benefited specific districts or states that were added to spending bills without debate. In 2011, both parties banned earmarks. Lawmakers, however, still try to get funding for bridges, beach replenishment, and other local projects, but now they have to do more to convince other members of Congress that the projects have merit. Doing so often entails making the case that the projects in question serve the national interest, typically through the job creation or economic development that such projects allegedly produce.

Some members of Congress have been calling for the return of earmarks, claiming that they allow for the exchange of political favors, which enables legislation to move forward. The "least productive Congress ever," they argue, could use a little grease in the wheels to get things done. As Representative Tom Cole (R-Okla.) put it, the ban on earmarks removes "all incentive for people to vote on things that are tough."[64] Additionally, members of Con-

Everything Is Better with Bacon

Distributional policies allocate resources to a specific constituency. Previously, Congress often allocated resources through earmarks. Now that the parties have banned earmarks, representatives have to be more creative in finding ways to divert federal dollars to projects in their districts. Their addiction to local spending projects stems, in part, from contradictory messages from voters, who dislike "wasteful" projects but expect their representative to "bring home the bacon."

gress want to secure projects and programs that will benefit their constituents and help them at election time. To win approval of such projects, members must be willing to vote for other legislators' projects in turn. Such a system promotes pluralism. Survey data suggest that voters like earmarks too, at least in principle if not in name. A 2010 survey asked Americans if certain candidate qualities would make them more or less likely to vote for a particular congressional candidate. Among the eight qualities in the survey, the only one that a majority of Americans said would make them more likely to vote for someone was "has a record of bringing government projects and money to your district." So despite Americans' dislike of so-called wasteful government spending, they still place great pressure on their own representatives to direct federal spending back home.[65]

Proponents of pluralism also argue that the makeup of Congress generally reflects that of the nation—that different members of Congress represent farm areas, low income inner cities, industrial areas, and so on. They point out that America itself is pluralistic, with a rich diversity of economic, social, religious, and racial groups, and even if one's own representatives and senators don't represent one's particular viewpoint, it's likely that someone in Congress does.

Whatever the shortcomings of pluralism, institutional reform aimed at reducing legislators' concern for individual districts and states is difficult. Members of Congress resist any structural changes that might weaken their ability to gain reelection. Nevertheless, the growing partisanship in Congress represents a trend toward greater majoritarianism. As both parties have become more ideologically homogeneous, there is greater unity around policies. To the degree that voters correctly recognize the differences between the parties and are willing to cast their ballots on

earmarks
Federal funds appropriated by Congress for use on local projects.

that basis, increasing majoritarianism will constrain pluralism in Congress. Ironically, once in office legislators weaken the incentive for constituents to vote based on ideology. The congressional system is structured to facilitate casework and to fund pork barrel spending. Both of these characteristics of the modern Congress work to enhance each legislator's reputation in his or her district or state. In short, the modern Congress is characterized by strong elements of both majoritarianism and pluralism.

Master the Topic of The Congress with MindTap™ for American Government

 REVIEW MindTap™ for American Government
Access Key Term Flashcards for Chapter 11.

 TEST YOURSELF MindTap™ for American Government
Take the Wrap It Up Quiz for Chapter 11.

 STAY CURRENT MindTap™ for American Government
Access the KnowNow blog and customized RSS for updates on current events.

 STAY FOCUSED MindTap™ for American Government
Complete the Focus Activities for The Congress.

Summary

LO1 Explain the structure and powers of Congress as envisioned by the framers and enumerated in the Constitution.

- In designing the legislative branch, the framers wanted a strong union but also wanted to prevent the concentration of power. The Senate consists of two senators from each state elected for six-year terms. The House has 435 members, with each state's representation in proportion to its population. Shared powers include the power to declare war, raise an army and navy, borrow and coin money, regulate interstate commerce, create federal courts, establish rules for the naturalization of immigrants, and make laws. Specific to the Senate are the powers to confirm presidential appointments, ratify treaties, and try cases of impeachment. The House

has the power to initiate revenue bills and to impeach.

LO2 Analyze the factors that affect the way voters elect members of Congress.

- Many factors create an electoral advantage for incumbents, including name recognition, casework, campaign fundraising, and weak challengers. The American population is less wealthy and less diverse than members of Congress, though Congress has become more diverse over time.

LO3 Describe the ways in which issues get on the congressional agenda.

- The congressional agenda includes both recurrent issues, such as the national debt and foreign aid, and new issues that may emerge as a result of some highly visible event.

LO4 Differentiate among the types of congressional committees and evaluate the role of the committee system in the legislative process.

- The process by which a bill becomes a law follows a series of specific steps, but the different ways legislation can be treated at each step complicates the process. There are four types of congressional committees: standing, joint, select, and conference; standing committees, which specialize in a particular area of legislation, are predominant. The committee system fosters expertise; representatives and senators who know the most about particular issues have the most influence over them.

LO5 Identify the leadership structure of the legislative branch and assess the rules and norms that influence congressional operations.

- Party leaders in the House and Senate are charged with overseeing institutional procedures, managing legislation, fundraising, and communicating with the press. The majority party leader in the House is the Speaker, who shapes the House agenda and leadership. The vice president of the United States is president of the Senate, but the Senate majority leader exercises the real power in the Senate. Formal rules of procedure structure operations in Congress, while informal norms guide members' behavior.

LO6 Appraise the components of the legislative environment that affect decision making in Congress.

- Political parties, the president, constituents, and interest groups all influence how members of Congress decide issues. Political parties and the president push Congress toward majoritarianism; interest groups exercise a pluralist influence on policymaking; constituents can push representatives in both directions.

LO7 Consider whether members of Congress should vote according to the majority views of their constituents.

- Bargaining and compromise play important roles in Congress. Some find this disquieting. They want less deal making and more adherence to principle. This thinking is in line with the desire for a more majoritarian democracy. Others defend the current system, arguing that the United States is a large, complex nation, and the policies that govern it should be developed through bargaining among various interests.

LO8 Assess the elements that characterize Congress as a pluralist or majoritarian system.

- There is no clear-cut answer to whether a majoritarian or a pluralist legislative system provides better representation for voters. Our system is a mix of pluralism and majoritarianism. It serves minority interests that might otherwise be neglected or even harmed by an unthinking or uncaring majority. At the same time, members of Congress work to represent the broader interests of the American people.

Chapter Quiz

LO1 Explain the structure and powers of Congress as envisioned by the framers and enumerated in the Constitution.

1. How is the number of congressional representatives elected from each state determined?
2. Name the powers that are unique to the House of Representatives and those that are unique to the Senate.

LO2 Analyze the factors that affect the way voters elect members of Congress.

1. What factors contribute to the high reelection rates of congressional incumbents?
2. What does the term descriptive representation mean?

LO3 Describe the ways in which issues get on the congressional agenda.

1. What might bring an issue to the forefront of the congressional agenda?

LO4 Differentiate among the types of congressional committees and evaluate the role of the committee system in the legislative process.

1. Outline the typical process by which a bill becomes a law.
2. Define standing, joint, and select committees and explain the primary role of each one.

LO5 Identify the leadership structure of the legislative branch and assess the rules and norms that influence congressional operations.

1. Who serves as Speaker of the House, and what roles does the Speaker serve?
2. What are the most significant functions performed by the House and Senate leaders?

LO6 Appraise the components of the legislative environment that affect decision making in Congress.

1. How do political parties and the president push Congress toward majoritarian democracy?
2. How do constituents and interest groups exercise a pluralist influence on policymaking?

LO7 Consider whether members of Congress should vote according to the majority views of their constituents.

1. How do members of Congress who see themselves as trustees view their roles?
2. How do members of Congress who see themselves as delegates view their responsibility to their constituents?

LO8 Assess the elements that characterize Congress as a pluralist or majoritarian system.

1. Why is a parliamentary system more majoritarian than a separation-of-power system?
2. What accounts for the growing majoritarianism in Congress?

12 The Presidency

Learning Outcomes

LO1 Assess whether the constitutional powers of the president form a strong basis for the modern presidency.

LO2 Illustrate how claims of inherent powers augment the formal powers of the presidency.

LO3 Assess the role played by the various executive branch institutions as resources for an effective president.

LO4 Defend the argument that "Presidential power is the power to persuade."

LO5 Compare and contrast the different roles that the president plays as national leader.

LO6 Analyze the role of the president within the context of the changing nature of global politics.

 WATCH & LEARN MindTap® for American Government

Watch a brief "What Do You Know?" video summarizing The Presidency.

A Majeed/AFP/Getty Images

When Barack Obama replaced George W. Bush as president, he inherited the "war on terror." Those whose hatred toward the United States leads them to violence intended to kill and maim Americans do not dress in military uniforms, march in battalions with rifles pointed skyward, or fight in tanks or planes. In small groups, blending in with the population in native garb, they typically set off hidden bombs or ambush targets with small arms.

The fight against al Qaeda, the terrorist organization responsible for the attacks on the United States on September 11, 2001, and similar groups, is based on counterinsurgency strategies. Small American units, utilizing intelligence pointing to the location of terrorists, attempt to kill them before they can initiate any further actions. At the core of current U.S. counterinsurgency warfare are drones, pilotless planes with technologically sophisticated electronic equipment, that hover above targets and fire missiles when a controller in the United States is satisfied that a target is fixed in the computerized bombsights aboard the plane. Such was the case in January 2013 when a drone began tracking a double cab pickup truck in rural Pakistan. Two missiles launched from the drone struck the truck and all six aboard were blown apart.

One of those killed was Mullah Nazir, a local warlord known to be part of a terrorist network.[1]

The decision to kill Nazir and those around him was ultimately made by President Obama. Intelligence experts make recommendations, but Obama has insisted that he approve such kills. Aides say Obama makes sure he is in the administrative loop on these decisions not because he questions his military leaders' judgment but because he feels that as president he should take moral responsibility for these actions of war.[2] Under Obama's watch, drones have been used in Afghanistan, Yemen, and Somalia, in addition to Pakistan.

Obama's personal involvement may be noble, but there are troubling questions about the morality of drone strikes. Intelligence can pinpoint the whereabouts of particular terrorists who are under surveillance but can't identify all who may be in physical proximity to the targeted individual. In many instances, innocent bystanders have been killed by missiles from a drone. This includes children, wives, and, generally, people who have the misfortune of being in the wrong place at the wrong time.[3]

Congress plays little role in overseeing drone strikes, and Obama is very much both judge and jury. From his point of view, the killing of innocent bystanders is abhorrent; but so are the actions taken by terrorists who plant car bombs and ignite a suicide vest in a crowded marketplace. The president surely rationalizes the use of drones as a matter of killing them before they kill us.

Obama has been criticized from within this country and from abroad and has said he is curtailing the use of drones.[4] Yet since there are no government data issued on drone usage, it is unclear just what has changed. Drones are still used. The president of the United States still sits at his desk and makes judgments as to whose history of terrorism or credible threats of terrorism merit a bomb being dropped upon them.

LISTEN & LEARN
MindTap for American Government

Access Read Speaker to listen to Chapter 12.

All presidents face a daunting set of challenges. They are expected to offer solutions to national problems, whether waging a war or reviving a failing economy. As the nation's major foreign diplomat and commander in chief of the armed forces, they are held responsible for the security and status of America in the world. Our presidents are the focal point for the nation's hopes and disappointments.

This chapter analyzes presidential leadership, looking at how presidents try to muster majoritarian support for their domestic goals and how they must function today as global leaders. What are the powers of the presidency? How is the president's advisory system organized? What are the ingredients of strong presidential leadership: character, public relations, or a friendly Congress? Finally, what are the particular issues and problems that presidents face in foreign affairs?

The Constitutional Basis of Presidential Power

LO1 ★ Assess whether the constitutional powers of the president form a strong basis for the modern presidency.

When the presidency was created, the colonies had just fought a war of independence; their reaction to British domination had focused on the autocratic rule of King George III. Thus, the delegates to the Constitutional Convention were extremely wary of unchecked power and were determined not to create an all-powerful, dictatorial presidency.

The delegates' fear of a powerful presidency was counterbalanced by their desire for strong leadership. The Articles of Confederation, which did not provide for a single head of state, had failed to bind the states together into a unified nation (see Chapter 3). In addition, the governors of the individual states had generally proved to be inadequate leaders because they had few formal powers. The new nation was conspicuously weak; its Congress had no power to compel the states to obey its legislation. The delegates knew they had to create some type of effective executive office. Their task was to provide for national leadership without allowing opportunity for tyranny.

Initial Conceptions of the Presidency

Debates about the nature of the office began. Should there be one president or a presidential council or committee? Should the president be chosen by Congress and remain largely subservient to that body? The delegates gave initial approval to a plan that called for a single executive, chosen by Congress for a seven-year term and ineligible for reelection.[5] But some delegates continued to argue for a strong president who would be elected independently of the legislative branch.

The final structure of the presidency reflected the checks-and-balances philosophy that had shaped the entire Constitution. In the minds of the delegates, they had imposed important limits on the presidency through the powers specifically delegated to Congress and the courts. Those counterbalancing powers would act as checks, or controls, on presidents who might try to expand the office beyond its proper bounds.

The Powers of the President

The requirements for the presidency are set forth in Article II of the Constitution: the president must be a U.S.-born citizen, at least thirty-five years old, who has lived in the United States for a minimum of fourteen years. Article II also sets forth the responsibilities of presidents. In view of the importance of the office, the constitutional description of the president's duties is surprisingly brief and vague. This vagueness has led to repeated conflict about the limits of presidential power.

The delegates undoubtedly had many reasons for the lack of precision in Article II. One likely explanation was the difficulty of providing and at the same time limiting presidential power. Furthermore, the framers of the Constitution had no model—no existing presidency—on which to base their description of the office. And, ironically, their description of the presidency might have been more precise if they had had less confidence in George Washington, the obvious choice for the first president. According to one account of the Constitutional Convention, "when Dr. Franklin predicted on June 4 that 'the first man put at the helm will be a good one,' every delegate knew perfectly well who that first good man would be."[6] The delegates had great trust in Washington; they did not fear that he would try to misuse the office.

The major duties and powers that the delegates listed for Washington and his successors can be summarized as follows:

- *Serve as administrative head of the nation.* The Constitution gives little guidance on the president's administrative duties. It states merely that "the executive Power shall be vested in a President of the United States of America" and that "he shall take Care that the Laws be faithfully executed." These imprecise directives have been interpreted to mean that the president is to supervise and offer leadership to various departments, agencies, and programs created by Congress. In practice, a chief executive spends much more time making policy decisions for his cabinet departments and agencies than enforcing existing policies.
- *Act as commander in chief of the military.* In essence, the Constitution names the president as the highest-ranking officer in the armed forces. But it gives Congress the power to declare war. The framers no doubt intended Congress to control the president's military power; nevertheless, presidents have initiated military action without the approval of Congress.
- *Veto legislation.* The president can **veto** (disapprove) any bill or resolution enacted by Congress, with the exception of joint resolutions that propose constitutional amendments. Congress can override a presidential veto with a two-thirds vote in each house.
- *Appoint various officials.* The president has the authority to appoint federal court judges, ambassadors, cabinet members, other key policymakers, and many lesser officials. Many appointments are subject to Senate confirmation.
- *Make treaties.* With the "Advice and Consent" of at least two-thirds of those senators voting at the time, the president can make treaties with foreign powers. The president is also to "receive Ambassadors," a phrase that presidents have interpreted to mean the right to recognize other nations formally.

veto
The president's formal disapproval of a bill that has been passed by both houses of Congress. Congress can override a veto with a two-thirds vote in each house.

The Expansion of Presidential Power

LO2 ★ Illustrate how claims of inherent powers augment the formal powers of the presidency.

The framers' limited conception of the president's role has given way to a considerably more powerful interpretation. In this section, we discuss how presidential power has expanded as presidents have exercised their explicit constitutional responsibilities and boldly interpreted the ambiguities of the Constitution. First, we look at the ways in which formal powers, such as veto power, have been increasingly used over time. Second, we turn to claims that presidents make about "inherent" powers implicit in the Constitution. Finally, we discuss congressional grants of power to the executive branch.

Formal Powers

The Constitution clearly involves the president in the policymaking process through his veto power, his ability to report to Congress on the state of the Union, and his role as commander in chief. Over time, presidents have become more aggressive in their use of these formal powers. Vetoes, for instance, have become much more frequent, particularly when presidents face a Congress dominated by the opposing political party. The first sixteen presidents, from Washington to Lincoln, issued a total of 59 vetoes. Dwight Eisenhower issued 181 vetoes over the course of his two terms; Ronald Reagan vetoed legislation 78 times. Through 2013 Barack Obama vetoed only two bills sent to him by Congress. Not counting President James Garfield, who served less than a year, this was the least amount since Abraham Lincoln.[7] The ability to veto legislation gives the president power even when he doesn't issue many vetoes. Veto threats shape legislation because members of Congress anticipate vetoes and modify legislation to avoid them. If a president does veto a bill and there is not enough support to override the president's veto, Congress may be forced to rewrite the bill, making concessions to the president's point of view.

Modern presidents have also taken a much more active role in setting the nation's policy agenda, and it is now expected that they will enter office with clear policy goals and work with their party in Congress to pass legislation. Most controversial has been the president's use of his power as commander in chief. Several modern presidents have used their power as commander in chief to enter into foreign conflicts without appealing to Congress for a formal declaration of war. The entire Vietnam War was fought without a congressional declaration of war. Complicating this issue is the nature of modern warfare. When the United States began fighting guerilla forces in Afghanistan, there was no Taliban nation to declare war against.

The Inherent Powers

Several presidents have expanded the power of the office by taking actions that exceeded commonly held notions of the president's proper authority. These men justified what they had done by saying that their actions fell within the **inherent powers** of the presidency. From this broad perspective, presidential power derives not only from those duties clearly outlined in Article II but also from inferences that may be drawn from the entire Constitution.

COMPARE WITH YOUR PEERS

MindTap for American Government

Access The Presidency Forum: Polling Activity—Presidential Veto Power.

inherent powers
Authority claimed by the president that is not clearly specified in the Constitution. Typically, these powers are inferred from the Constitution.

When a president claims a power that has not been considered part of the chief executive's authority, he forces Congress and the courts either to acquiesce to his claim or to restrict it. For instance, President Bush unilaterally established military commissions to try alleged enemy combatants captured in Afghanistan and Iraq and held at the U.S. naval base at Guantánamo Bay, Cuba. In 2006, the U.S. Supreme Court ruled that the military commissions were illegal, and the Bush administration was forced to go to Congress for the authorization to establish new commissions with new trial procedures.[8]

When presidents succeed in claiming a new power, they leave to their successors the legacy of a permanent expansion of presidential authority. During the Civil War, for example, Abraham Lincoln instituted a blockade of southern ports, thereby committing acts of war against the Confederacy without the approval of Congress. Lincoln said the urgent nature of the South's challenge to the Union forced him to act without waiting for congressional approval. His rationale was simple: "Was it possible to lose the nation and yet preserve the Constitution?"[9] In other words, Lincoln circumvented the Constitution to save the nation. Subsequently, Congress and the Supreme Court approved Lincoln's actions. That approval gave added legitimacy to the theory of inherent powers, a theory that over time has transformed the presidency.

Today, presidents routinely issue **executive orders**, presidential directives that carry the force of law.[10] The Constitution does not explicitly grant the president the power to issue an executive order. Sometimes presidents use them to see that the laws are "faithfully executed." This was the case when President Dwight Eisenhower ordered the Arkansas National Guard into service in Little Rock, Arkansas, to enforce court orders to desegregate the schools. But many times presidents issue executive orders by arguing that they may take actions in the best interest of the nation so long as the law does not directly prohibit these actions. Executive orders are issued for a wide variety of purposes, from administrative reorganization to civil rights. For instance, Harry Truman issued an executive order to end racial segregation in the armed services.

executive orders
Presidential directives that create or modify laws and public policies, without the direct approval of Congress.

The boundaries of the president's inherent powers have been sharply debated since the September 11, 2001, attacks upon the United States.[11] In response to an ongoing threat of terrorism, President Bush secretly authorized the National Security Agency (NSA) to wiretap telephone calls, without a warrant, between people within the United States and people overseas with suspected links to terrorism. When NSA contractor Edward Snowden stole documents from the security agency and then leaked some of them to the press in 2013, it was President Obama who came under criticism for secret surveillance. As we explain more fully in Chapter 15, the NSA runs a "metadata" program that gathers the records of phone calls made by ordinary Americans. The NSA says it is looking for suspicious patterns and not listening in on our individual calls. The president defended the program as one means of trying to stop terrorists before they harm us and acknowledged that the NSA program may need to be circumscribed.[12]

Congressional Delegation of Power

Presidential power grows when presidents successfully challenge Congress, but in many instances, Congress willingly delegates power to the executive branch. As the American public pressures the national government to solve various problems, Congress, through a process called **delegation of powers**, gives the executive branch more responsibility to administer programs that address those problems. One example of delegation of congressional power occurred in the 1930s, during the Great

delegation of powers
The process by which Congress gives the executive branch the additional authority needed to address new problems.

Depression, when Congress gave Franklin Roosevelt's administration wide latitude to do what it thought was necessary to solve the nation's economic ills.

When Congress concludes that the government needs flexibility in its approach to a problem, the president is often given great freedom in how or when to implement policies. Richard Nixon was given discretionary authority to impose a freeze on wages and prices in an effort to combat escalating inflation. If Congress had been forced to debate the timing of the freeze, merchants and manufacturers would surely have raised their prices in anticipation of the event. Instead, Nixon was able to act suddenly, imposing the freeze without warning. (We discuss congressional delegation of authority to the executive branch in more detail in Chapter 13.)

At other times, however, Congress believes that too much power has accumulated in the executive branch, and it enacts legislation to reassert congressional authority. During the 1970s, many representatives and senators agreed that presidents were exercising power that rightfully belonged to the legislative branch, and therefore Congress's role in the American political system was declining. The most notable reaction was the enactment of the War Powers Resolution (1973), which was directed at ending the president's ability to pursue armed conflict without explicit congressional approval. (We discuss the War Powers Resolution later in this chapter.)

The Executive Branch Establishment

LO3 ★ Assess the role played by the various executive branch institutions as resources for an effective president.

Although we elect a single individual as president, it would be a mistake to ignore the extensive staff and resources of the entire executive branch of government. The president has a White House staff that helps him formulate policy. The vice president is another resource; his duties within the administration vary according to his relationship with the president. The president's cabinet secretaries—the heads of the major departments of the national government—play a number of roles, including the critical function of administering the programs that fall within their jurisdictions. Effective presidents think strategically about how best to use the resources available to them. Each must find ways to organize structures and processes that best suit his management style.

The Executive Office of the President

The president depends heavily on key aides. They advise him on crucial political choices, devise the general strategies the administration will follow in pursuing congressional and public support, and control access to the president to ensure that he has enough time for his most important tasks. Consequently, he needs to trust and respect these top staffers; many in a president's inner circle of assistants are longtime associates. The president's personal staff constitutes the White House Office.

Presidents typically have a chief of staff, who may be a first among equals or, in some administrations, the unquestioned leader of the staff. President Obama's first chief of staff, Rahm Emanuel (now the mayor of Chicago), earned a reputation for in-your-face aggressiveness. He pushed and prodded and was relentless in trying to gain cooperation from members of Congress and other executive branch officials. His profane manner led one of his two brothers to give him a sign for his

White House desk that says, "Undersecretary for Go ___ Yourself."[13] Ultimately, Emanuel was effective, though, because Obama gave him broad authority to act on his behalf. Hamilton Jordan, President Carter's chief of staff, was at the other end of the spectrum: Carter did not give him the authority to administer the White House with a strong hand and, not surprisingly, Jordan was not terribly effective.

Presidents also have a national security adviser to provide daily briefings on foreign and military affairs and longer-range analyses of issues confronting the administration. Similarly, the president has the Council of Economic Advisers and the National Economic Council to report on the state of the economy and advise the president on the best way to promote economic growth. Senior domestic policy advisers help determine the administration's basic approach to areas such as health, education, and social services.

Below these top aides are the large staffs that serve them and the president. These staffs are organized around certain specialties. Some staff members work on political

Pete Souza/Reuters/White House/Landov

Captured!

After American special operations forces helicoptered into Pakistan to pursue September 11 mastermind Osama bin Laden, the Navy Seals wore helmet-mounted cameras as they assaulted bin Laden's compound. This allowed President Obama, the tension evident in his face, to watch the operation in real time on a monitor in the Situation Room at the White House.

matters, such as communicating with interest groups, maintaining relations with ethnic and religious minorities, and managing party affairs. One staff deals exclusively with the media (sixty-nine people in the Obama White House).[14] Another group, the legislative liaison staff, lobbies Congress for the administration. The large Office of Management and Budget (OMB) analyzes budget requests, is involved in the policymaking process, and examines agency management practices. This extended White House executive establishment, including the White House Office, is known as the **Executive Office of the President**. The Executive Office employs around 2,000 individuals and has an annual budget of $500 million.[15]

No one agrees about a "right way" for a president to organize his White House staff, but scholars have identified three major advisory styles.[16] Franklin Roosevelt exemplified the first system: a competitive management style. He organized his staff so that his advisers had overlapping authority and differing points of view. Roosevelt used this system to ensure that he would get the best possible information, hear all sides of an argument, and still be the final decision maker in any dispute. Dwight Eisenhower, a former general, best exemplifies a hierarchical staff model. His staff was arranged with clear lines of authority and a hierarchical structure that mirrored a military command. This places fewer demands on presidential time and energy, since the president does not participate in the details of policy discussion. Bill Clinton had more of a collegial staffing arrangement, a loose staff structure that gave many top staffers direct access to him. Clinton himself was immersed in the details of the policymaking process and brainstormed with his advisers. He was much less likely to delegate authority to others.

No matter the president, White House staffs are always full of smart and highly aggressive individuals who inevitably begin to squabble over authority. In the first years of the Obama presidency, top female staffers became increasingly angry over a sense that they

Executive Office of the President
The president's executive aides and their staffs; the extended White House executive establishment.

were being marginalized by more influential staffers, notably Emanuel and Lawrence Summers, Obama's leading economic adviser. Their dissatisfaction was eventually communicated to the president and Obama responded by holding a dinner for the top women in the White House. When they sat down at the table, Obama said, "I really want you guys to talk to me about this openly."[17] How much this meeting improved the situation is unclear.

Above all, a president must ensure that staff members feel comfortable telling him things he may not want to hear. Telling the president of the United States he is misguided on something is not an easy thing to do. Journalists writing about George W. Bush's White House have painted him as temperamental and sometimes hostile toward aides who brought him bad news.[18] George Stephanopoulos, a close aide to President Clinton, acknowledged frankly in his memoirs that he was too eager to ingratiate himself with Clinton because he saw himself in a competitive position with other staff aides. In retrospect, he realizes that he should have confronted Clinton early in the 1992 campaign about his infidelity. But, says Stephanopoulos, "I needed Clinton to see me as his defender, not his interrogator, which made me, of course, his enabler."[19]

The Vice President

The most important duty of the vice president is to take over the presidency in the event of presidential death, disability, impeachment, or resignation. Traditionally, vice presidents were not used in any important advisory capacity. Before passage of the Twenty-fifth Amendment to the Constitution in 1965, vice presidents who became president due to the death of their predecessor did not even select a new vice president.

Vice presidents have traditionally carried out political chores—campaigning, fundraising, and "stroking" the party faithful. This is often the case because vice-presidential candidates are chosen for reasons that have more to do with the political campaign than with governing the nation. Presidential candidates often choose vice-presidential candidates who appeal to a different geographic region or party coalition. Sometimes they even join forces with a rival from their political primary campaign. New Englander John Kennedy chose Texan Lyndon Johnson. Conservative Ronald Reagan selected George H. W. Bush, his more moderate rival in the Republican primaries. President Carter broke the usual pattern of relegating the vice president to political chores, relying heavily on his VP, Walter Mondale. Carter was wise enough to recognize that Mondale's experience in the Senate could be of great value to him, especially because Carter had never held national office. Al Gore played a significant role in the Clinton administration and was one of the president's most influential advisers. George W. Bush's vice president, Dick Cheney, was even more influential than his predecessors. Cheney was a powerful presence in the

RJ Sangosti/The Denver Post/Getty Image

Next in Line

Vice President Joe Biden is next in line to the presidency should something happen to President Barack Obama. Biden was a Senator from Delaware for 36 years before he ran with Obama in 2008. In the Senate he served on the Foreign Relations and Judiciary committees and wrote legislation such as the 1994 Violence Against Women Act. He twice pursued the Democratic nomination for President but was unsuccessful.

development of Bush's foreign policy agenda, championing the war in Iraq. Vice President Joe Biden has been a loyal and dogged defender of the Obama presidency. Most notable about the vice president's term in office, perhaps, is that Biden pushed the president by publicly embracing marriage equality. Although Obama had been growing increasingly uncomfortable with his stated opposition to gay marriage, the vice president's reversal of his own position on the issue made it difficult for Obama as he didn't want to say his own vice president was wrong. Obama soon came out in favor of marriage equality.[20]

The Cabinet

The president's **cabinet** is composed of the heads of the departments of the executive branch and a small number of other key officials, such as the head of the OMB and the ambassador to the United Nations. The cabinet has expanded greatly since George Washington formed his first cabinet, which contained an attorney general and the secretaries of state, treasury, and war. Clearly, the growth of the cabinet to fifteen departments reflects an increase in government responsibility and intervention in areas such as energy, housing, and, most recently, homeland security.

In theory, the members of the cabinet constitute an advisory body that meets with the president to debate major policy decisions. In practice, however, cabinet meetings have been described as "vapid non-events in which there has been a deliberate nonexchange of information as part of a process of mutual nonconsultation."[21] Why is this so? First, the cabinet has become rather large. Counting department heads, other officials of cabinet rank, and presidential aides, it is a body of at least twenty people—a size that many presidents find unwieldy for the give-and-take of political decision making. Second, most cabinet members have limited areas of expertise and cannot contribute much to deliberations in policy areas they know little about. The secretary of defense, for example, would probably be a poor choice to help decide important issues of agricultural policy. Third, the president often chooses cabinet members because of their reputations or to give his cabinet some racial, ethnic, geographic, gender, or religious balance, not because they are personally close to the president or easy for him to work with.

Finally, modern presidents do not rely on the cabinet to make policy because they have such large White House staffs, which offer most of the advisory support they need. And in contrast to cabinet secretaries, who may be pulled in different directions by the wishes of the president and those of their clientele groups, staffers in the White House Office are likely to see themselves as being responsible to the president alone. More broadly, presidents use their personal staff and the large Executive Office of the President to centralize control over the entire executive branch.[22] The vast size of the executive branch and the number and complexity of decisions that must be made each day pose a challenge for the White House. Each president must be careful to appoint people to top administration positions who are not merely competent but also passionate about the president's goals and skillful enough to lead others in the executive branch to fight for the president's program instead of their own agendas.

cabinet
A group of presidential advisers; the heads of the executive departments and other key officials.

Presidential Leadership

LO4 ★ Defend the argument that "Presidential power is the power to persuade."

A president's influence comes not only from his assigned responsibilities but also from his political skills and from how effectively he uses the resources of his office.

His leadership is a function of his own character and skill, as well as the political environment in which he finds himself. Does he work with a congressional majority that favors his policy agenda? Are his goals in line with public opinion? Does he have the interpersonal skills and strength of character to be an effective leader?

Table 12.1 provides two rankings of U.S. presidents. One is based on a Gallup Poll of ordinary Americans; the other is based on a C-SPAN survey of fifty-eight prominent historians and professional observers of the presidency. In this section, we look at the factors that affect presidential performance—both those that reside in the person of the individual president and those that are features of the political context that he inherits. Why do some presidents rank higher than others?

Presidential Character

How does the public assess which presidential candidate has the best judgment and whether a candidate's character is suitable to the office? Americans must make a broad evaluation of the candidates' personalities and leadership styles. Although it's difficult to judge, character matters. One of Lyndon Johnson's biographers argues that Johnson had trouble extricating the United States from Vietnam because of

TABLE 12.1 Presidential Greatness

This table provides two "top twelve" lists of American presidents. The first ranking comes from a Gallup Poll that asked ordinary Americans to name whom they regard as the greatest U.S. president. The second ranking comes from a survey of historians and observers of the presidency, who rated presidents according to their abilities, such as public persuasion, crisis leadership, economic management, moral authority, and relations with Congress. Although the rank order is different, nine presidents appear on both lists. Ordinary Americans are more likely to name recent presidents—Carter, Clinton, and George W. Bush—with whom they have had direct experience.

Gallup Poll Ratings		Historians' Ratings	
Rank	**President**	**Rank**	**President**
1	Abraham Lincoln	1	Abraham Lincoln
2	Ronald Reagan	2	Franklin Roosevelt
3	John F. Kennedy	3	George Washington
4	Bill Clinton	4	Theodore Roosevelt
5	Franklin Roosevelt	5	Harry Truman
6	George Washington	6	Woodrow Wilson
7	Harry Truman	7	Thomas Jefferson
8	George W. Bush	8	John F. Kennedy
9	Theodore Roosevelt	9	Dwight Eisenhower
10	Dwight Eisenhower	10	Lyndon Johnson
11	Thomas Jefferson	11	Ronald Reagan
12	Jimmy Carter	12	James K. Polk

Sources: Gallup Poll results are reported by Lydia Saad, "Lincoln Resumes Position as Americans' Top-Rated President," 19 February 2007, http://www.gallup.com. Copyright © 2010 Gallup, Inc. All rights reserved. The content is used with permission; however, Gallup retains all rights of republication. The historians' ranking is reported by the C-SPAN survey of Presidential Leadership 2000, www.americanpresidents.org/survey/historians/overall.asp. Copyright © 2000 C-SPAN.

insecurities about his masculinity. Johnson wanted to make sure he "was not forced to see himself as a coward, running away from Vietnam."[23] It's hard to know for sure whether this psychological interpretation is valid. Clearer, surely, is the tie between President Nixon's character and Watergate. Nixon had such an exaggerated fear of what his "enemies" might try to do to him that he created a climate in the White House that nurtured the Watergate break-in and subsequent cover-up.

Presidential character was at the forefront of national politics when it was revealed that President Clinton engaged in a sexual relationship with Monica Lewinsky, a White House intern half his age. Many argued that presidential authority is irreparably damaged when the president is perceived as personally untrustworthy or immoral. Yet despite the disgust and anger that Clinton's actions provoked, most Americans remained unconvinced that his behavior constituted an impeachable offense. The buoyant economy and the public's general satisfaction with Clinton's leadership strongly influenced the country's views on the matter. A majority of the House of Representatives voted to impeach him on the grounds of perjury and obstructing justice, but the Senate did not have the two-thirds majority necessary to convict Clinton, so he remained in office.

AP Images/Jorge Saenz

The Odd Couple

Former presidents Bill Clinton and George W. Bush don't see eye-to-eye on much, but they put differences aside when President Obama asked them to go to Haiti after the devastating earthquake in January 2010. Officially they were there to assess the damage to the country, but a more urgent purpose for the two presidents' visit was to encourage private donations to help Haiti rebuild.

Scholars have identified personality traits such as strong self-esteem and emotional intelligence that are best suited to leadership positions like the American presidency.[24] In the media age, it often proves difficult to evaluate a candidate's personality when everyone tries to present himself or herself in a positive light. Even so, voters repeatedly claim that they care about traits such as leadership, integrity, and competence when casting their ballots.[25]

The President's Power to Persuade

In addition to desirable character traits, individual presidents must have the interpersonal and practical political skills to get things done. A classic analysis of the use of presidential resources is offered by Richard Neustadt in his book *Presidential Power*. Neustadt develops a model of how presidents gain, lose, or maintain their influence. His initial premise is simple enough: "Presidential power is the power to persuade."[26] Presidents, for all their resources—a skilled staff, extensive media coverage of presidential actions, the great respect the country holds for the office—must depend on others' cooperation to get things done. Harry Truman echoed Neustadt's premise when he said, "I sit here all day trying to persuade people to do the things they ought to have sense enough to do without my persuading them. ... That's all the powers of the President amount to."[27]

Ability in bargaining, dealing with adversaries, and choosing priorities, according to Neustadt, separates above-average presidents from mediocre ones. A president must make wise choices about which policies to push and which to put aside until he can find more support. President Nixon described such decisions as a lot like poker. "I knew when to get out of a pot," said Nixon. "I didn't stick around when I didn't have the cards."[28] The president must decide when to accept compromise and when to stand on principle. He must know when to go public and when to work behind the scenes.

A president's political skills can be important in affecting outcomes in Congress. The president must choose his battles carefully and then try to use the force of his personality and the prestige of his office to forge an agreement among differing factions. When President Lyndon Johnson needed House Appropriations chair George Mahon (D-Tex.) to support him on an issue, he called Mahon on the phone and emphasized the value of Mahon's having a good long-term relationship with him. Speaking slowly to let every point sink in, Johnson told Mahon, "I know one thing … I know I'm right on this. … I know I mean more to you, … and Lubbock [Texas], … and your district, … and your State,—and your grandchildren, than Charlie Halleck [the Republican House leader] does."[29]

At the same time, there are real limits to the ability of a president to use his personal resources to persuade recalcitrant legislators, especially those of the opposition party. The opposition party may actually want to do what it can to make the president look bad, rather than helping him accomplish his legislative goals. For presidents, the more important skill may not be bargaining with legislators but forming and timing his legislative agenda.

The President and the Public

A familiar aspect of the modern presidency is the effort presidents devote to mobilizing public support for their programs. A president uses televised addresses (and the media coverage surrounding them), remarks to reporters, and public appearances to speak directly to the American people and convince them of the wisdom of his policies. Scholars have coined the phrase "going public" to describe situations where the president "forces compliance from fellow Washingtonians by going over their heads to appeal to their constituents."[30] Rather than bargain exclusively with a small number of party and committee leaders in Congress, the president rallies broad coalitions of support as though undertaking a political campaign.

Since public opinion is a resource for modern presidents, they pay close attention to their standing in the polls. Presidents closely monitor their approval ratings or "popularity," which is a report card on how well they are performing their duties. Presidential popularity is typically at its highest during a president's first year in office. This "honeymoon period" affords the president a particularly good opportunity to use public support to get some of his programs through Congress. Over time, economic conditions exert an enormous impact on a president's approval rating (see Figure 12.1).[31]

Scholarly research demonstrates that energetic and well-planned efforts by presidents to influence public opinion are likely to have little effect. As political scientist George Edwards concludes, "Presidents cannot reshape the contours of the political landscape to pave the way for change."[32] Perhaps the most difficult obstacle presidents face is a lack of serious attention by the public. The vast majority of Americans have limited interest in policymaking and a presidential speech may fall on deaf ears. Even a televised address to the nation carried by major networks may be ignored.

FIGURE 12.1 It All Goes Back to the Economy

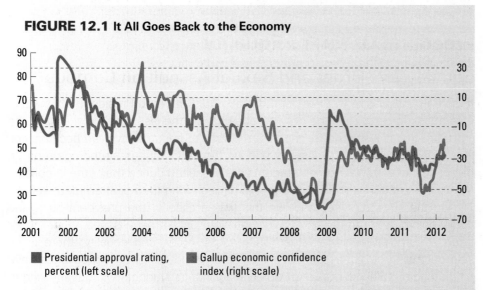

The economy is always critical to each president's standing with the American public. As shown here for the Bush and Obama years, each president's approval rating closely tracks a composite index of economic conditions as measured by the Gallup Poll. There are fluctuations reflecting events other than economic conditions, of course, but over time, there is a strong correlation between popularity and economic performance.

Source: Lydia Saad, "Obama's Job Approval Tied to Economic Confidence in 2012," *Gallup Poll*, 19 March 2012. http://www.gallup.com. Copyright © 2012 Gallup, Inc. All rights reserved. The content is used with permission; however, Gallup retains all rights of republication.

As former White House aide David Gergen put it, presidential speeches and statements "wash over the public. They are dull, gray prose, eminently forgettable."[33]

President Obama's endeavor to convince the American public to back his program for health-care reform is a case in point. Throughout the spring, summer, and fall of 2009, Obama worked continually to rally public opinion to his side. Through speeches, forums, press interviews, and other efforts, he labored to make Americans understand the benefits of the program. He failed to move opinion, and his own popularity declined during this time.[34] Unemployment and the continuing recession were the primary causes of his sagging popularity, but unfavorable attitudes toward the health-care proposal may have contributed to his problems as well.[35] Like presidents before him, Obama found that the so-called bully pulpit for rallying Americans isn't so bully after all.[36] (See "Freedom, Order, or Equality: Equality *and* Order and Sexual Assault on Campus.")

The president's power to persuade seems more potent within his own party.[37] Obama was effective at prodding his Democrats in Congress to support his proposal, which eventually passed. Legislators' own chances of reelection can be influenced by a president's public standing in his own party. Still, presidents are right to be wary of backing legislation that the voters back home don't like. Presidential persuasion may make the difference when a vote looms in Congress.

Presidents' obsessive concern with public opinion can be defended as a means of furthering majoritarian democracy: the president tries to gauge what the people want so that he can offer policies that reflect popular preferences. As discussed in Chapter 2, responsiveness to the public's views is a bedrock principle of democracy, and presidents should respond to public opinion as well as try to lead it. Some believe that presidents are too concerned about their popularity and are unwilling to champion unpopular causes or take principled stands that may affect their poll ratings. Yet research shows

Freedom, Order, or Equality

Equality *and* Order and Sexual Assault on Campus

It isn't a typical issue for presidents to take up. But when President Obama created a task force to examine how colleges handle the issue of sexual assault, he indicated that it was time for the White House to become involved because colleges weren't making this issue a priority. Sexual assault is all too common on campuses: one in five women students are assaulted during their time in college. Seven percent of male students admit to having committed or attempted rape.

On the surface, it seemed like this was a case of the president using the "bully pulpit" to try to galvanize public opinion. Unlike many issues, where there is a tradeoff between the values of freedom, order, and equality, there is no side defending sexual assault. Nor are there advocates of letting colleges have the autonomy to handle cases of violence against its students without any kind of government oversight. Sexual assault is one of those issues on which everyone is aligned in terms of core values yet generating change is still challenging. And changing the behavior of college students is no easy task.

Rather than trying to mobilize public opinion, Obama used the authority of the federal government to push colleges to do more to create a climate where students understand what constitutes assault and what constitutes consent. Students also need to know that they will be dealt with harshly should they be found guilty of assault. A critical problem is that women often feel that the authorities at their college are not interested in punishing male assailants. Often, women fail to report assaults because they fear the trauma of being questioned skeptically. Although victims can always choose to go to the police instead, many opt for college investigations as they are unsure of what evidence may be necessary to implicate an assailant, may not want to face the possibility of a public trial, or may have more trust in their college than a city's or town's police department.

The Obama plan focuses on enforcing civil rights law. Sexual violence and sexual harassment are forms of discrimination and, according to the Department of Education, Obama's initiative "was the first time any administration has called out sexual violence as a civil rights issue." The White House strategy puts pressure on colleges to improve the methods by which complaints are handled. It asks colleges to systematically test students' attitudes and awareness of sexual assault; to promote intervention by bystanders to stop misconduct in its tracks; and to better train the college personnel who interact with victims, ensuring that students are treated in a respectful, sensitive, and confidential manner.

that presidents don't always follow public opinion and, instead, push many proposals and policies that reflect their own priorities rather than the public's.[38] Commenting on the presidential polls that first became widely used during his term, Harry Truman said, "I wonder how far Moses would have gone if he'd taken a poll in Egypt?"[39]

The Political Context

One thing we learn from the health-care case is that the strategy of leading by courting public opinion has considerable risks. Since it is not easy to move public opinion, presidents who plan to use it as leverage in dealing with Congress are left highly vulnerable

Mark Wilson/Getty Images News/Getty Images

The federal government has powerful tools that can be used to punish schools that don't adopt adequate procedures. For example, it can deny federal funds to schools not in compliance with provisions of the law. Thus, it seems likely that schools will respond to the White House effort, especially those that have already been criticized by the Department of Education. Whether the actual incidence of sexual violence on campus will decrease remains to be seen. Nevertheless, the Obama administration felt moved to act out of a concern for both order and equality.

Sources: *Not Alone: The First Report of the White House Task Force to Protect Students from Sexual Assault* (Washington, D.C.: The White House, 2014); Jackie Calmes, "Obama Seeks to Raise Awareness of Rape on Campus," *New York Times*, 22 January 2014; Nick Anderson and Katie Zezima, "White House Issues Report on Steps to Prevent Sexual Assaults on College Campuses," *Washington Post*, 29 April 2014; Nick Anderson, "Sexual Violence Probes at Colleges Arise from Obama Push on Civil Rights Issues," *Washington Post*, 3 May 2014; and Kristin Lombardi, *A Lack of Consequences for Sexual Assault* (Washington, D.C.: Center for Public Integrity, 2010).

Critical Thinking Is sexual assault the type of issue on which a president is likely to have an impact?

if public support for their position does not materialize. Some presidents have the benefit of working on legislation while their own political party has a majority in both chambers of Congress. Others are fortunate to serve when the economy is good. Still others have large election victories that facilitate greater policy achievements.

Partisans in Congress. Generally, presidents have their greatest success in Congress during the period immediately following their inauguration, which is also the peak of their popularity. One of the best predictors of presidential success in

Congress is the number of fellow partisans in Congress, particularly whether the president's party has a majority in each chamber. Presidential success in Congress is measured by how often the president wins his way on congressional roll call votes on which he takes a clear position. George W. Bush's success rate hovered around 75 percent during his first six years in office with a Republican Congress. After the Democrats won control of Congress in 2006, his success rate fell to 38 percent.[40] With large majorities in both the House and the Senate during his first two years in office, Barack Obama did very well with Congress and got major pieces of legislation such as the economic stimulus package and the health-care plan enacted. After Republicans captured control of the House of Representatives in the 2010 election, his success in Congress declined precipitously.

The American political system poses a challenge for presidents and their policy agendas because the president is elected independently of Congress. Often this leads to **divided government**, with one party controlling the White House and the other party controlling at least one house of Congress. This may seem politically schizophrenic, with the electorate saying one thing by electing a president from one party and another by its vote for legislators of the other party. This does not appear to bother the American people, however, as divided government is fairly common.

Scholars are divided about the impact of divided government. Increasingly, though, partisanship is seen as contributing to **gridlock**, a situation in which government is incapable of acting on important policy issues.[41] As noted in Chapter 11, in recent years, there has been a pattern of increasingly partisan voting in Congress: Republicans voting in a relatively unified pattern while Democrats also vote in an increasingly unified manner.[42] Adding to the poisonous atmosphere that creates disincentives for members of Congress to work across the aisle and for opposition members to work with the White House is the constant vitriol on cable political networks, on talk radio, and in the blogosphere.[43] When President Obama invited Republican Speaker of the House John Boehner and Republican Senate leader Mitch McConnell to the White House for a social evening to watch a screening of the movie, *Lincoln*, they turned him down. Observers believe they didn't want the criticism that would come from their partisan base.[44] Nevertheless, political scientists do not regard this as a permanent state of affairs and hold out hope for at least a modest increase in bipartisan policymaking.[45]

Elections. In his farewell address to the nation, Jimmy Carter lashed out at the interest groups that had plagued his presidency. Interest groups, he said, "distort our purposes because the national interest is not always the sum of all our single or special interests." Carter noted the president's singular responsibility: "The president is the only elected official charged with representing all the people."[46] Like all other presidents, Carter quickly recognized the dilemma of majoritarianism versus pluralism after he took office. The president must try to please countless separate constituencies while trying to do what is best for the whole country.

It is easy to stand on the sidelines and say that presidents should always try to follow a majoritarian path, pursuing policies that reflect the preferences of most citizens. However, simply by running for office, candidates align themselves with particular segments of the population. As a result of their electoral strategy, their identification with activists in their party, and their own political views, candidates come into office with an interest in pleasing some constituencies more than others.

As the election campaign proceeds, each candidate tries to win votes from different groups of voters through his stand on various issues. Because issue stances can cut both ways—attracting some voters but driving others away—candidates may try to finesse an issue by being deliberately vague. Candidates sometimes hope that

---

divided government
The situation in which one party controls the White House and the other controls at least one house of Congress.

gridlock
A situation in which government is incapable of acting on important issues.

voters will put their own interpretations on ambiguous stances. If the tactic works, the candidate will attract some voters without offending others.

But candidates cannot be deliberately vague about all issues. A candidate who is noncommittal on too many issues appears wishy-washy. And future presidents do not build their political careers without working strongly for and becoming associated with important issues and constituencies. Moreover, after the election is over, the winning candidate wants to claim that he has been given an electoral mandate, or endorsement, by the voters to carry out the policy platform on which he campaigned. Newly chosen presidents make a majoritarian interpretation of the electoral process, claiming that their electoral victory is an expression of the direct will of the people. For such a claim to be credible, the candidate must have emphasized some specific issues during the campaign and offered some distinctive solutions. Reelection to a second term might seem to be a powerful endorsement or continuing mandate; typically, however, popularity drops lower than in the first term (see Figure 12.2). Even so, political scientists have found that the underlying fundamentals are more important than specific campaign promises or campaign tactics.[47] These "fundamentals" are the state of the economy, the popularity of the sitting president, whether the country is at war (and how popular that war is), and the degree to which the public just feels like it's "time for a change."[48]

Political Party Systems. An individual president's election is just one in a series of contests between the major political parties in the United States. As noted in Chapter 8, American political history is marked by eras in which one of the major political parties tends to dominate national-level politics, consistently capturing the presidency and majorities in the Senate and House of Representatives. Scholars of the American presidency have noted that presidential leadership is shaped by the president's relationship to the dominant political party and its policy agenda.

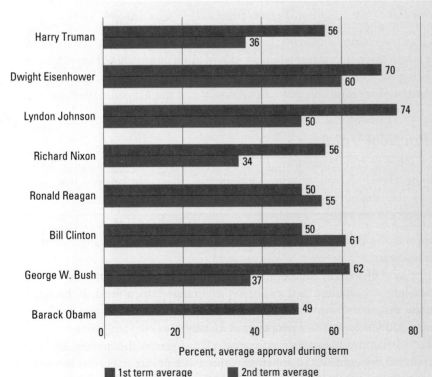

FIGURE 12.2 Second Term Fatigue

For those presidents who are elected to a second term, popularity tends to slide after their reelection. These figures are the average approval ratings in the Gallup Poll for each four-year term. Five of seven postwar presidents saw their popularity lower in the second term. Presidents Reagan and Clinton bucked this trend. Barack Obama's second term has not yet run its full course but at this writing his average approval rating is lower than his first term.

Source: Andrew Duga, "U.S. Presidents Typically Less Popular in Second Term," *Gallup Poll*, 11 January 2013, www.Gallup.com.

Presidential leadership is determined in part by whether the president is a member of the dominant political party and whether the public policies and political philosophy associated with his party have widespread support. A president will have a greater opportunity to change public policy when he is in the majority and the opposing political party is perceived to be unable to solve major national problems. Presidents who are affiliated with the dominant political party have larger majorities in Congress and more public support for their party's policy agenda.

Presidents who come to power right after critical elections have the most favorable environment for exerting strong presidential leadership. Franklin Roosevelt, for instance, came to office when the Republican Party was unable to offer solutions to the economic crisis of the Great Depression. He enjoyed a landslide victory and large Democratic majorities in Congress, and he proposed fundamental changes in government and public policy. The weakest presidents are those, like Herbert Hoover, who are constrained by their affiliation with a political party that is perceived to stand for worn-out ideas. Democratic presidents like Truman and Johnson, who followed FDR, were also well positioned to achieve policy success and further their party program since they were affiliated with the dominant New Deal coalition. Republicans Eisenhower and Nixon faced different leadership challenges: they needed to cultivate the support of voters and legislators in both parties in order to achieve a successful legislative program.

The President as National Leader

LO5 ★ Compare and contrast the different roles that the president plays as national leader.

With an election behind him and the resources of his office at hand, a president is ready to lead the nation. Although not every president's leadership is acclaimed, each president enters office with a general vision of how government should approach policy issues. During his term, a president spends much of his time trying to get Congress to enact legislation that reflects his general philosophy and specific policy preferences.

From Political Values …

Presidents differ greatly in their views of the role of government. Lyndon Johnson had a strong liberal ideology concerning domestic affairs. He believed that government has a responsibility to help disadvantaged Americans. Johnson described his vision of justice in his inaugural address:

> Justice was the promise that all who made the journey would share in the fruits of the land.
>
> In a land of wealth, families must not live in hopeless poverty. In a land rich in harvest, children just must not go hungry. In a land of healing miracles, neighbors must not suffer and die untended. In a great land of learning and scholars, young people must be taught to read and write.
>
> For [the] more than thirty years that I have served this nation, I have believed that this injustice to our people, this waste of our resources, was our real enemy. For thirty years or more, with the resources I have had, I have vigilantly fought against it.[49]

Johnson used *justice and injustice* as code for *equality and inequality*. He used those words six times in his speech; he used *freedom* only twice. Johnson used his popularity, his skills, and the resources of his office to press for a "just" America—a "Great Society."

To achieve his Great Society, Johnson sent Congress an unprecedented package of liberal legislation. He launched projects such as the Job Corps (which created centers and camps offering vocational training and work experience to youths aged sixteen to twenty-one), Medicare (which provided medical care for the elderly), and the National Teacher Corps (which paid teachers to work in impoverished neighborhoods). Supported by huge Democratic majorities in Congress during 1965 and 1966, he had tremendous success getting his proposals through. Liberalism was in full swing.

In 1985, exactly twenty years after Johnson's inaugural speech, Ronald Reagan took his oath of office for the second time. Addressing the nation, Reagan reasserted his conservative philosophy. He emphasized freedom, using the term fourteen times, and failed to mention justice or equality once. In the following excerpt, we have italicized the term freedom for easy reference:

Different Visions

Lyndon Johnson and Ronald Reagan had strikingly different visions of American democracy and what their goals should be as president. Johnson was committed to equality for all, and major civil rights laws are among the most important legacies of his administration. He is pictured here signing the 1964 Civil Rights Act. Reagan was devoted to reducing the size of government so as to enhance freedom. He worked hard to reduce both taxes and spending.

> By 1980, we knew it was time to renew our faith, to strive with all our strength toward the ultimate in individual *freedom* consistent with an orderly society. ... We will not rest until every American enjoys the fullness of *freedom*, dignity, and opportunity as our birthright. ... Americans ... turned the tide of history away from totalitarian darkness and into the warm sunlight of human *freedom*. ...
>
> Let history say of us, these were golden years—when the American Revolution was reborn, when *freedom* gained new life, when America reached for her best. ... *Freedom* and incentives unleash the drive and entrepreneurial genius that are at the core of human progress. ... From new *freedom* will spring new opportunities for growth. ... Yet history has shown that peace does not come, nor will our *freedom* be preserved by goodwill alone. There are those in the world who scorn our vision of human dignity and *freedom*. ... Human *freedom* is on the march, and nowhere more so than in our own hemisphere. *Freedom* is one of the deepest and noblest aspirations of the human spirit. ... America must remain *freedom*'s staunchest friend, for *freedom* is our best ally. ... Every victory for human *freedom* will be a victory for world peace. ... One people under God, dedicated to the dream of *freedom* that He has placed in the human heart.[50]

Reagan turned Johnson's philosophy on its head, declaring that "government is not the solution to our problem. Government is the problem." During his presidency,

Reagan worked to undo many welfare and social service programs and cut funding for programs such as the Job Corps and food stamps. By the end of his term, there had been a fundamental shift in federal spending, with sharp increases in defense spending and "decreases in federal social programs [which] served to defend Democratic interests and constituencies."[51]

... to Policy Agenda

The roots of particular policy proposals, then, can be traced to the more general political ideology of the president. Presidential candidates outline that philosophy of government during their campaign for the White House as they attempt to mobilize voters and interest groups. After the election, presidents and their staffs continue to identify and track support among different kinds of voters as they decide how to translate their general philosophy into concrete legislative proposals.

When the hot rhetoric of the presidential campaign meets the cold reality of what is possible in Washington, the newly elected president must make some hard choices about what to push for during the coming term. There is some urgency early in an administration as the public mood of the nation can turn sharply against the president's ideological orientation (see Figure 12.3). These choices are reflected in the bills the president submits to Congress, as well as in the degree to which he works for their passage. The president's bills, introduced by his allies in the House and Senate, always receive a good deal of initial attention.

The president's role in legislative leadership is largely a twentieth-century phenomenon. A critical change came with Franklin Roosevelt. With the nation in the midst of the Great Depression, Roosevelt began his first term in 1933 with an ambitious array of legislative proposals. During the first one hundred days Congress was in session, it enacted fifteen significant laws, including the Agricultural Adjustment Act, the act creating the Civilian Conservation Corps, and the National Industrial

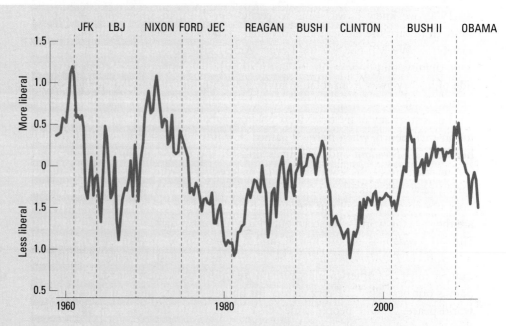

FIGURE 12.3
Ideological Swings

The ideological mood of the nation is measured through a battery of survey questions tapping respondents' attitudes toward government spending and related issues. In this chart, the higher the trend line, the more liberal the public mood is at the time. Note that the ideological swing does not always match the political orientation of the president. For example, the public became less liberal after electing liberal Bill Clinton.

Source: John Sides and Lynn Vavreck, *The Gamble* (Princeton, N.J.: Princeton University Press, 2013), p. 229.

Recovery Act. Never before had a president demanded—and received—so much from Congress. Roosevelt's legacy was that the president would henceforth provide aggressive leadership of Congress through his own legislative program.

Chief Lobbyist

When Franklin D. Roosevelt and Harry Truman first became heavily involved in preparing legislative packages, political scientists typically described the process as one in which "the president proposes and Congress disposes." In other words, once the president sends his legislation to Capitol Hill, Congress decides what to do with it. When the opposition party controls at least one house of Congress, the president can propose all the legislation he wants, but the process has to be collaborative if Congress is to pass some semblance of what was initially proposed.

Over time presidents have become increasingly active in all stages of the legislative process, not just in proposing bills. Most critically, the president is expected to do all that he can to push legislation through. The president's efforts to influence Congress are reinforced by the work of his legislative liaison staff. All departments and major agencies have legislative specialists as well. These department and agency people work with the White House liaison staff to coordinate the administration's lobbying on major issues.

The **legislative liaison staff** is the communications link between the White House and Congress. As a bill slowly makes its way through Congress, liaison staffers advise the president or a cabinet secretary on the problems that emerge. They specify what parts of a bill are in trouble and may have to be modified or dropped. They tell their boss what amendments are likely to be offered, which members of Congress need to be lobbied, and what the bill's chances for passage are with or without certain provisions. Decisions on how the administration will respond to such developments must then be reached. For example, when the Reagan White House realized that it was still a few votes short of victory on a budget bill in the House, it reversed its opposition to a sugar price support bill. This attracted the votes of representatives from Louisiana and Florida, two sugar-growing states, for the budget bill. The White House would not call what happened a deal, but it noted that "adjustments and considerations" had been made.[52] Still, not all demands from legislators can be met.

A certain amount of the president's job consists of stereotypical arm twisting—pushing reluctant legislators to vote a certain way. The president also talks to legislators to seek their advice and takes soundings from committee chairs on what proposals can get through and what must be modified or abandoned. During Obama's first four months in office, four hundred representatives and senators were brought to the White House to speak to the president or attend meetings or other events.[53] Yet most day-in, day-out interactions between the White House and Congress tend to be more mundane, with the liaison staff trying to build support by working cooperatively with legislators.

The White House also works directly with interest groups in its efforts to build support for legislation. Presidential aides hope key lobbyists will activate the most effective lobbyists of all: the voters back home. Interest groups can quickly reach the constituents who are most concerned about a bill, using their communications network to mobilize members to write, call, or e-mail their members of Congress. There are so many interest groups in our pluralist political system that they could easily overload the White House with their demands. Consequently, except for those groups most important to the president, lobbies tend to be granted access only when the White House needs them to activate public opinion. During the titanic struggle over

legislative liaison staff
Those people who act as the communications link between the White House and Congress, advising the president or cabinet secretaries on the status of pending legislation.

health-care legislation, the Obama White House knew it needed a great deal of interest group support. It cut a number of deals with the insurance and pharmaceutical industries to make the president's proposal more palatable to them.

Agreement with Congress cannot always be reached, and sometimes Congress may pass a bill the president opposes. In such a case, the president may veto the bill and send it back to Congress; as noted earlier, Congress can override a veto with a two-thirds majority of those voting in each house. Presidents use their veto power sparingly, but having it in their arsenal increases their bargaining leverage with members of Congress.

Party Leader

Part of the president's job is to lead his party.[54] This is very much an informal duty, with no prescribed tasks. In this respect, American presidents are considerably different from European prime ministers, who are the formal leaders of their party in the national legislature, as well as the head of their government. In the American system, a president and members of his party in Congress can clearly take very different positions on the issues before them.

As Congress has turned more partisan, presidents have focused more on leadership of their own party rather than trying to bridge differences between the two parties.[55] With less of a moderate middle to work with in Congress, a president needs to work hard to unify his party around his priorities. Increasingly, the public regards presidents as partisan leaders rather than unifying national leaders. Polls show that Americans have evaluated recent presidents, notably Ronald Reagan, Bill Clinton, George W. Bush, and Barack Obama, through a largely partisan prism. Republican identifiers love Republican presidents and despise Democratic ones. Likewise, Democratic identifiers like presidents of their own party and are contemptuous of Republican ones (see Figure 12.4).

FIGURE 12.4 The Partisan Structure of Public Opinion

How we evaluate a president's performance is strongly shaped by our own partisan predisposition. As illustrated here with Barack Obama, a president's approval scores in surveys of the public are highly correlated with partisan affiliation. Obama's approval among Democrats has remained strong throughout his term, but he has weak approval among Republicans. During George W. Bush's term, the pattern was reversed: Democrats were highly critical, while Republicans were more supportive.

Source: Gary C. Jacobson, "How the Economy and Partisanship Shaped the 2012 Presidential and Congressional Elections," *Political Science Quarterly* 128 (Spring 2013): 6.

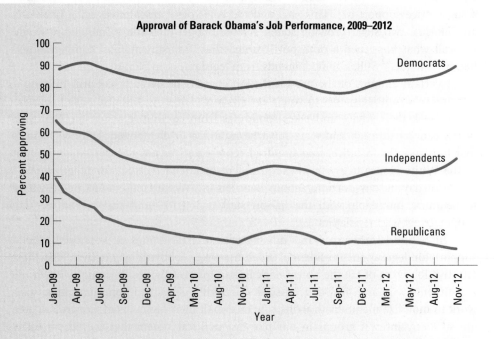

The president himself has become the "fundraiser in chief" for his party. Since presidents have a vital interest in more members of their party being elected to the House and Senate, they have a strong incentive to spend time raising money for congressional candidates. All incumbent presidents travel frequently to fundraising dinners in different states, where they are the main attraction. Donors pay substantial sums—$1,000 a ticket is common—to go to such a dinner. In addition to helping elect more members of his party, a not-so-small by-product for the president is the gratitude of legislators. It's a lot harder to say no to a president's request for help on a bill when he spoke at your fundraiser during the last election.

The President as World Leader

LO6 ★ Analyze the role of the president within the context of the changing nature of global politics.

The president's leadership responsibilities extend beyond Congress and the nation to the international arena. Each administration tries to further what it sees as the country's best interests in its relations with allies, adversaries, and the developing countries of the world. In this role, the president must be ready to act as diplomat and crisis manager.

Foreign Relations

From the end of World War II until the late 1980s, presidents were preoccupied with containing communist expansion around the globe. Truman and Korea, Kennedy and Cuba, Johnson and Nixon and Vietnam, and Reagan and Nicaragua are just some examples of presidents and the communist crosses they had to bear. Presidents not only used overt and covert military means to fight communism but also tried to reduce tensions through negotiations. President Nixon made particularly important strides in this regard, completing an important arms control agreement with the Soviet Union and beginning negotiations with China, with which the United States had had no formal diplomatic relations.

With the collapse of communism in the Soviet Union and Eastern Europe, American presidents entered a new era in international relations, but they are still concerned with three fundamental objectives. First is national security, the direct protection of the United States and its citizens from external threats. National security has been highlighted since the September 11 terrorist attacks. After U.S. intelligence sources pinpointed the hiding place of Osama bin Laden in Pakistan, a special forces operation was carried out during which Navy Seals stormed his compound and shot him to death. President Obama received an immediate boost in the public's estimation of him by appearing to be effective in keeping Americans safe.[56]

Committing military force to pursue American foreign policy objectives is a highly risky endeavor. President Obama was put in a difficult position when a democracy movement erupted in Egypt, challenging the rule of Hosni Mubarak. Mubarak was a dictator but a staunch American ally in a volatile region. Obama chose to distance the United States from Mubarak, assuming (correctly, as it turned out) that a revolution would succeed and Mubarak would fall.

Second is fostering a peaceful international environment. Presidents work with international organizations like the United Nations and the North Atlantic Treaty Organization (NATO) to seek an end to regional conflicts throughout the world.

In some cases, like the ongoing dispute between Palestinians and Israelis, the United States has played a central role in mediating conflict and facilitating bargaining between opposing sides. In other cases, presidents send the U.S. military to participate in multinational peace-keeping forces to ensure stability, enforce negotiated peace plans, and monitor democratic elections. The United States may impose trade sanctions to discourage human rights violations.

A third objective is the protection of U.S. economic interests. The new presidential job description places much more emphasis on managing economic relations with the rest of the world. Trade relations are an especially difficult problem because

German Leadership in Global Politics

The serious economic downturn that began in the United States in September of 2008 has had an even greater impact on Europe. The financial devastation persists there even as the United States continues to gradually improve. Italy and Spain went into catastrophic decline and remain depressed. The economies of France and England have sputtered, and they are struggling to stay out of another recession. Though a relatively small economy, Greece went bankrupt, and its inability to pay its bills threatened the viability of the euro, the currency used in much of Europe.

Through these travails, the German economy has remained strong and the country has played a crucial role in holding the European Union (EU) together as political strains caused by individual countries' debt grew. But it is more than Germany's well-functioning economy that facilitates the country's leadership of Europe. In addition, Angela Merkel, the head of its government, has been a steadfast leader who is widely respected both in and outside of Europe.

Merkel grew up in what used to be communist East Germany. She earned a doctorate in physical chemistry but left science for politics when the communist government collapsed there in 1989 and West Germany and East Germany became one country. She became an activist in the Christian Democratic Party (CDU), the leading conservative party in Germany, and was elected to the Bundestag, the German legislature, in 1990. Merkel worked her way up the party hierarchy and was elected chancellor in 2005. (Germany has a parliamentary form of government, so she won the position when her party and a coalition partner gained a majority of seats in the Bundestag.) Merkel was the first woman to win election as the chancellor of Germany.

Merkel won reelection in 2009 and then won a convincing third term in 2013. Merkel's appeal does not come from charisma; rather, she comes across as steady and calm. She is perceived as forceful but at the same time is seen as one whose leadership is dependent on her ability to persuade rather than aggressively push those countries, parties, and interest groups that do not initially line up behind her. She demonstrated enormous skill in keeping Greece's bankruptcy from derailing the EU. Greece needed loans to keep its government going, but German voters were staunchly opposed to any of their tax dollars going to a European Union fund to bail out a country characterized by considerable corruption and a failure to collect much of the tax money owed by its citizens. Germany's largest newspaper ran a front page headline that read "Greeks Want Our Money." Merkel firmly voiced the rank-and-file German's opposition to a bailout while quietly helping to forge a compromise that eventually worked to stabilize Greece.

presidents must balance the conflicting interests of foreign countries (many of them allies), the interests of particular American industries, the overall needs of the American economy, and the demands of the legislative branch.

Constitutional Ambiguities

At the outset of this chapter, we enumerated the constitutional powers of the presidency. We noted that the president is the commander in chief of the military and that he can make treaties with other nations. Yet the Constitution also confers powers on

© 360b/Shutterstock.com

Serious challenges confront Merkel as she charts Germany's future course. Although its economy is stronger than the rest of the EU, growth is still restrained by the poor performance of other European countries, which cannot afford to purchase as many German goods as they could during good times. Germany's population is also poised to actually decline in number unless there is significant immigration into the country. Yet immigration is controversial in Germany, especially relating to Turks who have emigrated there. Nevertheless, there seems to be faith in Germany that Merkel will lead them through these perilous times.

Sources: "Viewpoints: Angela Merkel's Record," *BBC News*, 22 September 2013, http://www.bbc.com/news/world-europe-24157440; Kate Connolly and Philip Oltermann, "German Election: Angela Merkel Secures Historic Third Win," *The Guardian*, 22 September 2013, http://www.theguardian.com/world/2013/sep/22/angela-merkel-wins-third-term-germany; and "Coalition Deal: Merkel Reaches Agreement on Next Government," *Spiegel Online*, 27 November 2013, http://www.spiegel.de/international/germany/merkel-reaches-agreement-to-form-new-german-government-a-935934.html.

Critical Thinking How might you compare the leadership styles of Barack Obama and Angela Merkel? In what ways might executive leadership in Germany differ from that in the United States?

the legislative branch that give it considerable authority over the military and the nation's conduct of foreign policy.

Without mentioning the term *foreign policy*, the Constitution establishes that Congress is empowered to:

- legislate.
- declare war.
- raise revenue and dispense funds.
- support, maintain, govern, and regulate the army and navy.
- call out the state militias to repel invasions.
- regulate commerce with foreign nations.
- define and punish piracy and offenses against the law of nations.

In addition the Senate alone is give the power to:

- give advice and consent to treaties made by the president.
- give advice and consent to the appointment of ambassadors and various other public officials involved in foreign policy.

These are considerable powers and they engender a great deal of ambiguity. Although the president is commander in chief, Congress has the power to declare war. But if the nation is attacked, does the president need to wait on Congress? Congress has actually made a formal declaration of war just five times.[57] Yet the United States has been involved in military conflicts far more times than that. The Constitution leaves much unsaid, and the overlap in powers between the two branches is intentional as we know that the framers' underlying theory of government was that there should be checks and balances.

Over time many of the questions of which branch holds what kinds of power in foreign and military affairs have been resolved; others, like the war power, remain controversial. Still, even though both branches have established significant authority in foreign policy, the president has parlayed constitutional provisions plus laws passed by Congress, Supreme Court decisions, and precedents created by bold action, to become the leading actor in this broad realm of government.

Congress has relied on its own powers to influence foreign policy. Using its legislative authority, Congress can involve the nation in programs of international scope or limit the actions of the executive branch. Probably most important, Congress has used the power of the purse (appropriations) to provide funds for the activities it supports—and to prohibit or restrict funds for those it opposes. In the end, sometimes Congress and the president are collaborators in foreign policy; other times they are antagonists.

The War Powers Resolution. As commander in chief of the armed forces, several presidents have committed American troops in emergency situations, thus involving the United States in undeclared wars. America's undeclared wars, police actions, and similar interventions have outnumbered its formal, congressionally declared wars by about forty to one. Since the last declared war ended in 1945, over 100,000 American members of the military have died in locations ranging from Korea and Vietnam to Grenada, Somalia, Iraq, and Afghanistan.

Reacting to controversy over the undeclared war in Vietnam, Congress passed the War Powers Resolution in 1973 over President Richard Nixon's veto. Nixon believed that the new law infringed upon the authority of the president. Congress, however, came to realize that it had abandoned its constitutional duty to decide whether the country goes to war. The large number of casualties in Vietnam, and the divisiveness that ensued in the country as our commitment there grew, made Congress appear to have shirked responsibility.

The **War Powers Resolution** requires that the president "consult" with Congress in "every possible instance" before involving U.S. troops in hostilities and notify Congress within forty-eight hours of committing troops to a foreign intervention. If troops are deployed, they may not stay for more than sixty days without congressional approval (although the president may take up to thirty days more to remove them "safely"). Some critics of the legislation claimed that it did not restrict presidential power as much as extend a free hand to wage war for up to sixty days. The War Powers Resolution has not constrained presidents as they've learned to adapt to its requirements. However, it has forced Congress to go on record in support of various military interventions.

After September 11, 2001, President George W. Bush had to work within the War Powers Resolution to build his "global coalition against terrorism." Congress promptly authorized the president to "use all necessary and appropriate force against those nations, organizations or persons he determines planned, authorized, committed or aided the terrorist attacks … or harbored such organizations or persons."[58] Bush relied on this joint resolution to attack al Qaeda in Afghanistan and to defeat the Taliban regime there in late 2001, prior to the Taliban's resurgence in 2006.

A year later, Congress was not as quick to support the president's use of military force against Saddam Hussein in Iraq. Although a war resolution passed with strong support in both chambers, it was opposed by more than half the Democrats in the House and nearly half in the Senate.

The Senate's Treaty Power. The Senate alone provides "advice and consent" on **treaties**—agreements between two or more countries. It gives much more consent than rejection. Over the course of the nation's history, the Senate has approved over 1,500 treaties while rejecting just 21.[59] Some of the defeats have been historically significant, however, establishing the Senate as a force in foreign policy. At the end of World War I, Democratic President Woodrow Wilson proposed and championed a plan for an international organization—the League of Nations—in the hopes of eliminating future wars. To enter the League, however, Wilson's treaty had to be approved by two-thirds of the Senate. Wilson, an idealistic, international liberal, was opposed by a group of mostly Republican, internationally conservative senators. After eight months of debate, the Senate rejected his treaty, and the United States never joined the League of Nations. Some attribute the weakness of the League of Nations, which failed to prevent a second world war, to the absence of the United States.

In the early days of World War II, President Franklin D. Roosevelt and British prime minister Winston Churchill revived Wilson's idea for collective security and proposed a new international organization—the United Nations—after the war. By the time the UN treaty went to the Senate in the summer of 1945, Roosevelt had died. It fell to President Harry Truman, also a Democrat and mindful of Wilson's failure with the League of Nations, to win acceptance of the UN treaty by a Republican-controlled Senate.

A two-thirds agreement in the Senate is a challenge, ever more so in the highly partisan atmosphere today. Presidents often find it more expedient to reach agreement with another country through an **executive agreement**, a pact between heads of countries concerning their joint activities. The Supreme Court has ruled that executive agreements are within the inherent powers of the president and have the legal status of treaties.[60] Executive agreements must conform to the Constitution, existing treaties, and the laws of Congress.[61] Unlike treaties, they do not require Senate

War Powers Resolution
An act of Congress that forces that body to decide whether a commitment of troops into a war zone is permissible.

treaty
A legal agreement between two or more countries.

executive agreement
A pact between the heads of two countries.

approval. Until 1972 the texts of these agreements did not even have to be reported to Congress. Legislation passed that year required the president to send copies to the House and Senate Foreign Relations committees. This requirement has not seriously affected the use of executive agreements, which has escalated dramatically, outnumbering treaties by about ten to one since the 1930s.[62]

Most executive agreements deal with minor bureaucratic business that would not interest a busy Senate. On occasion, presidents have resorted to executive agreements on important issues that were unlikely to win Senate consent. In 1992, President George H. W. Bush negotiated the North American Free Trade Agreement (NAFTA) with Canada and Mexico that facilitated free trade among the three countries by reducing national tariffs on imported goods. This plan, which reflected a free-market international libertarian ideology, was widely favored by economists but bitterly opposed by trade protectionists and international conservatives.

As presidents have expanded their role in the foreign policy drama, the Senate has sought to enlarge its part, interpreting quite broadly its power to "advise and consent" on presidential appointments to offices involved in foreign affairs. Senators have used confirmation hearings to prod the administration toward particular policy stands.

Making Foreign Policy: Organization and Cast

Although American foreign policy originates within the executive branch, the organizational structure for policymaking is created and funded by Congress and is subject to congressional oversight. There are a number of large and critically important departments, agencies, and bureaus that formulate and implement foreign and defense policy.

The State Department. During its very first session in 1789, Congress created the Department of Foreign Affairs as the government's first executive department. It became the State Department, and since its establishment, it has assisted the president in formulating American foreign policy, executing policy decisions, and monitoring foreign governments throughout the world. The department's head, the secretary of state, is the highest-ranking official in the cabinet. Hillary Clinton, wife of former President Bill Clinton, was President Obama's secretary of state during his first term. Her stature in that position helped to vault her into a leading position for the Democratic Party's nomination for president in 2016.

Like other executive departments, the State Department is staffed by both political appointees and permanent employees selected under the civil service merit system. Political appointees include deputy secretaries and undersecretaries of state and some—but not all—ambassadors. Permanent employees include approximately four thousand foreign service officers, at home and abroad, who staff and service U.S. embassies and consulates throughout the world. They have primary responsibility for representing the United States to the rest of the world and caring for American citizens and interests abroad.

The State Department also lacks a strong domestic constituency to exert pressure in support of its policies. The Department of Agriculture, by contrast, can mobilize farmers to support its activities, and the Department of Defense can count on help from defense industries and veterans' groups. In a pluralist democracy, the lack of a natural constituency is a serious drawback for an agency or department. Exacerbating this problem is the changing character of global political issues.

The Defense Department. The U.S. system of government is characterized by civilian control of the military. Its head, the secretary of defense, is a cabinet member with authority over the entire military establishment. The role of the defense secretary depends in part on the individual's vision of the job and willingness to use the tools available. Strong secretaries, such as Robert McNamara (under Kennedy and Johnson), wield significant power. President George W. Bush chose Donald Rumsfeld, who had previously served as secretary of defense under President Ford but who clashed with secretary of state Colin Powell over planning and handling the Iraq war.

Below the defense secretary are the civilian secretaries of the army, navy, and air force; below them are the military commanders of the individual branches of the armed forces, who make up the Joint Chiefs of Staff. The Joint Chiefs meet to coordinate military policy among the different branches; they also serve as the primary military advisers to the president, the secretary of defense, and the National Security Council, helping to shape policy positions on matters such as alliances, plans for nuclear and conventional war, and arms control and disarmament.

The National Security Council. The National Security Council (NSC) is made up of a group of advisers who help the president mold a coherent approach to foreign policy by integrating and coordinating details of domestic, foreign, and military affairs that relate to national security. The statutory members of the NSC are the president, the vice president, and the secretaries of state and defense. Each president designates other members of the NSC as he sees fit. NSC discussions can cover a wide range of issues, such as the formulation of U.S. policy in the Middle East. In theory, at least, NSC discussions offer the president an opportunity to solicit advice and allow key participants in the foreign policymaking process to keep abreast of the policies and capabilities of other departments. In practice, the role played by the NSC has varied considerably under different presidents. Truman and Kennedy seldom met with it; Eisenhower and Nixon brought it into much greater prominence.

The Intelligence Community. Conducting an effective foreign policy requires accurate information—termed "intelligence"—in international affairs.[63] Raw data on foreign countries, observations of politics abroad, and inside information are merged into finished intelligence for policymakers through activities spread across seventeen agencies in the executive branch known informally as the intelligence community.[64] The best known of these agencies is the Central Intelligence Agency (CIA). Before World War II, the United States had no permanent agency specifically charged with gathering intelligence about the actions and intentions of foreign powers. After the war, when America began to play a much greater international role and feared the spread of communism, Congress created the CIA to collect information and to draw on intelligence activities in other departments and agencies.

Most material obtained by the CIA comes from readily available sources: statistical abstracts, books, and newspapers. The agency's Intelligence Directorate is responsible for these overt (open) activities in collecting and processing information. The CIA's charter also empowers it "to perform such other functions and duties related to intelligence affecting the national security as the National Security Council shall direct." This vague clause has been used to justify the agency's covert (secret) activities undertaken in foreign countries by its Operations Directorate. These activities have included espionage, coups, assassination plots, wiretaps, interception of mail, and infiltration of protest groups.

Covert operations raise both moral and legal questions for a democracy. Allen Dulles, President Eisenhower's CIA director, once called these operations "an essential part of the free world's struggle against communism." Are they equally important in a post–Cold War world? Can they be reconciled with the principle of checks and balances in American government? When government engages in clandestine actions, are the people able to hold their government accountable for its actions? After the attack on the United States by al Qaeda terrorists in 2001, most Americans came to believe that the United States needed to be aggressive in seeking out terrorists before they strike.

After the September 11 attacks, there was widespread recognition that our intelligence gathering operations had failed. Although various intelligence agencies had information about al Qaeda, it was never pieced together into an understanding of what was planned. In response, Congress passed the Intelligence Reform and Terrorism Prevention Act of 2004. It amended the 1947 National Security Act, partially restructured the intelligence community, and created an Office of Director of National Intelligence to coordinate all intelligence activities. Since so much of what these agencies do is secret, it's difficult to evaluate whether this administrative reform has actually improved the coordination and performance of the intelligence community.

One part of the intelligence community that has generated a great deal of criticism for its spying activities is the National Security Agency (NSA). Using satellites, supercomputers, and other high-tech equipment, it conducts surveillance around the world. It was created to spy on foreign governments but as noted earlier in this chapter, controversy erupted when it was revealed that the NSA was spying on Americans by gathering phone records.

Ralph Crane/Time Life Pictures/Getty Images

Crisis in Camelot

In October 1962, people gathered in the electronics section of a store to watch President Kennedy address the nation on the Cuban missile crisis. When the United States learned that the Soviet Union was placing missile bases in Cuba, Kennedy demanded that the Soviets remove their missiles, and he ordered a naval blockade. After seven days, Soviet leader Nikita Khrushchev complied with Kennedy's demands, and direct conflict between the two major superpowers was avoided. Cuba's leader at that time, Fidel Castro, had seized power in 1959 and aligned himself with the Soviet Union during the Cold War.

Crisis Management

Periodically the president faces a grave situation in which conflict is imminent or a small conflict threatens to explode into a larger war. Because handling such episodes is a critical part of the presidency, citizens may vote for candidates who project careful judgment. One reason for Barry Goldwater's crushing defeat in the 1964 election was his warlike image and rhetoric, which scared many Americans. Fearing that Goldwater would be too quick to resort to nuclear weapons, they voted for Lyndon Johnson instead.

A president must be able to exercise good judgment and remain cool in crisis situations. Henry Kissinger, secretary of state during the Nixon years, notes, "Historians rarely do justice to the psychological stress on a policymaker."[65] John Kennedy's behavior during the Cuban missile crisis of 1962 has become a model of effective crisis management. When the United States learned that the Soviet Union had placed missiles containing nuclear warheads in Cuba, Kennedy saw those missiles as an unacceptable threat to U.S. security. He asked a group of senior aides, including top people from the

Pentagon, to advise him on feasible military and diplomatic responses. Kennedy considered an invasion of Cuba and air strikes against the missiles but eventually chose a less dangerous response: a naval blockade. He also privately signaled to Soviet leader Nikita Khrushchev that if the Soviet Union withdrew its missiles from Cuba, the United States would remove American missiles from Turkey.[66] Although the Soviet Union complied, the world held its breath for a short time over the very real possibility of a nuclear war.

What guidelines determine what a president should do in times of crisis? Drawing on a range of advisers and opinions is one. Not acting in unnecessary haste is another. A third is having a well-designed, formal review process with thorough analysis and open debate. A fourth guideline is rigorously examining the reasoning underlying all options to ensure that their assumptions are valid. When President Kennedy backed a CIA plan for a rebel invasion of Cuba by expatriates hostile to Fidel Castro, he did not know that its chances for success were based on unfounded assumptions of immediate uprisings by the Cuban population. Had Kennedy been more aggressive in questioning intelligence officials, he might have chosen to stop the operation. The invasion by a hapless and poorly equipped rebel group went ahead, only to be crushed immediately by the Cuban army. This resulted in an enormous embarrassment for the United States and a stain on Kennedy's reputation.

Master the Topic of The Presidency with 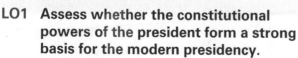 for American Government

REVIEW MindTap™ for American Government
Access Key Term Flashcards for Chapter 12.

STAY CURRENT MindTap™ for American Government
Access the KnowNow blog and customized RSS for updates on current events.

TEST YOURSELF MindTap™ for American Government
Take the Wrap It Up Quiz for Chapter 12.

STAY FOCUSED MindTap™ for American Government
Complete the Focus Activities for The Presidency.

Summary

LO1 **Assess whether the constitutional powers of the president form a strong basis for the modern presidency.**

- Presidential leadership is shaped by the president's ability to bargain, persuade, and make wise choices. Over time, presidential power has grown as presidents have interpreted their constitutional authority more broadly. At the same time, there are substantial constraints on presidents, notably Congress, which may have very different goals. The formal powers of the presidency are set forth in Article II of the Constitution.

LO2   Illustrate how claims of inherent powers augment the formal powers of the presidency.

- Informal powers, those not explicitly stated in the Constitution, complement a president's formal powers. A significant source of the growth in presidential power derives from Congress's delegation of authority to the executive branch.

LO3   Assess the role played by the various executive branch institutions as resources for an effective president.

- The president is surrounded by a staff of advisors who provide support and analysis of pending decisions and of broader strategic direction. The primary components of the presidential advisory system are the president's personal staff, the Executive Office of the President, the vice president, and the cabinet.

LO4   Defend the argument that "Presidential power is the power to persuade."

- A part of a president's power is his power to persuade. A president's relationship with the public is highly influenced by Americans' evaluation of his performance in office. A president's ability to get things done is largely contingent on political factors, particularly the relative division of the two parties in Congress.

LO5   Compare and contrast the different roles that the president plays as national leader.

- Leadership is structured by vision, and vision reflects a president's ideological orientation. Over time, presidents have come to play a critical role in preparing a package of proposals (an agenda) for introduction in Congress. They then lobby for those proposals. Presidents are also leaders of their party, offering direction in terms of policy as well as engaging in more mundane activities, such as raising campaign money for congressional allies.

LO6   Analyze the role of the president within the context of the changing nature of global politics.

- Presidents not only lead the United States but also are important leaders of formal and informal alliances among democracies. The president sits atop a vast set of bureaucracies that aid him in making foreign and defense policy decisions.

Chapter Quiz

LO1   Assess whether the constitutional powers of the president form a strong basis for the modern presidency.

1. What is the underlying philosophy that guided the framers in determining the power of the presidency and, indeed, in structuring the entire Constitution?
2. What are the major formal powers of the presidency as listed in Article II of the Constitution?

LO2   Illustrate how claims of inherent powers augment the formal powers of the presidency.

1. Why have the powers of the presidency grown over time?

2. What are the differences between formal powers and inherent powers?

LO3   Assess the role played by the various executive branch institutions as resources for an effective president.

1. What constitutes the Executive Office of the President?
2. Why does the cabinet not play a major role as a *body* of advisors?

LO4   Defend the argument that "Presidential power is the power to persuade."

1. How might presidential character affect presidential performance?
2. What are the contextual factors that can influence the course of a presidency?

LO5 Compare and contrast the different roles that the president plays as national leader.

1. What fundamental political values distinguish the differences between conservative Republican presidents and liberal Democratic ones?

2. How does a president work to influence Congress?

LO6 Analyze the role of the president within the context of the changing nature of global politics.

1. What are the president's primary responsibilities in terms of leadership in foreign affairs?

2. What guidelines should a president follow in making decisions during crises or urgent situations?

13 The Bureaucracy

Learning Outcomes

LO1 Define the concept of bureaucracy, explain the role of organizations in the administration of the nation's laws, examine the reasons for the growth of the bureaucratic state, and assess arguments for and against its continued expansion.

LO2 Describe the organization of the executive branch, the role of the civil service, and the bureaucracy's responsiveness to presidential control.

LO3 Describe the roles of administrative discretion and rule-making authority in the execution of administrative policymaking.

LO4 Analyze how incrementalism and bureaucratic culture affect policymaking.

LO5 Identify obstacles to effective policy implementation.

LO6 Compare the strengths and weaknesses of reform efforts aimed at increasing the effectiveness of the bureaucracy's performance.

 WATCH & LEARN MindTap° for American Government

Watch a brief "What Do You Know?" video summarizing The Bureaucracy.

Carol Kohen/Cultura RM/Alamy; David R. Frazier Photolibrary, Inc./Alamy; AP Images/M. Spencer Green

The Obama administration's most impressive achievement has been passage of the far-reaching Affordable Care Act. Its most conspicuous failure has been the initial implementation of the Affordable Care Act.

The Affordable Care Act, also known as Obamacare or the ACA, was unusually ambitious, creating a method of bringing health insurance to all Americans who lack coverage (47 million were uninsured in 2012).[1] The ACA is nothing short of a revolution in health-care coverage. And yet, despite its importance to the administration, its full activation roughly two and one-half years after its enactment was, in the words of the normally staid New York Times, "a disaster."[2]

The "disaster" was the website (Healthcare.gov) where individuals lacking insurance select a policy. The site was designed as an exchange where customers shop among competing plans. Once registered on the website, the user can compare plans and also find out if the government will provide them with a subsidy to help pay for the insurance.

When the federal website opened on October 1, 2013, it just flat out failed. Relatively few of the millions who went to Healthcare.gov were able to register as customers. Unable to register, individuals weren't able to access the insurance exchange to evaluate plans

available to residents of their state. The website meltdown was an enormous embarrassment for the administration. Yet, despite the complexity and scale of the ACA, the computer problems were not inevitable. President Obama said plainly, "We created [a] problem we didn't need to create."[3]

What went wrong? A review of what happened reveals numerous problems, but they all relate in one way or another to *organizational* failures. Different parts of the government worked poorly with other parts of the government. The overall effort was ineffectively coordinated and various pieces of software initially failed to work with other segments of Healthcare.gov software. A key problem was that a "systems integrator" was not put in place during the creation of the site and many bugs in the software were not recognized until Healthcare.gov went live.

There was plenty of blame to go around, starting with the president, who was slow to react to the website's failure. Secretary of Health and Human Services (HHS) Kathleen Sebelius, who has since left the administration, had the most direct supervisory responsibility and it's clear that she underestimated the complexity of the task and misunderstood the manner in which the work should have been organized. Some of the outside contractors who wrote computer code performed badly.

Changes were made. Jeffrey Zients, a highly skilled administrator, was brought in to manage repairs. A software company was hired to coordinate the debugging of the website. Within a couple of months, the site was functioning well, and by the time the enrollment period for 2014 ended, more than 8 million Americans had signed up for coverage, matching the initial estimate prior to the ACA's launch. But it's not "all's well that ends well." The problems with the website eroded confidence in the government and in a program designed to provide health insurance to all Americans.

LISTEN & LEARN

MindTap™ **for American Government**

Access Read Speaker to listen to Chapter 13.

In this chapter, we examine how bureaucracies like HHS operate and address many of the central dilemmas of American political life. Bureaucracies represent what Americans dislike about government, yet our interest groups lobby them to provide us with more of the services we desire. We say we want smaller, less intrusive government, but different constituencies value different agencies of government and fight fiercely to protect those bureaucracies' budgets. This enduring conflict once again represents the majoritarian and pluralist dimensions of American politics.

 Organization Matters

LO1 ★ Define the concept of bureaucracy, explain the role of organizations in the administration of the nation's laws, examine the reasons for the growth of the bureaucratic state, and assess arguments for and against its continued expansion.

bureaucracy
A large, complex organization in which employees have specific job responsibilities and work within a hierarchy of authority.

A nation's laws and policies are administered, or put into effect, by various departments, agencies, bureaus, offices, and other government units, which together are known as its *bureaucracy*. **Bureaucracy** actually means any large, complex organization in which employees have specific job responsibilities and work within a hierarchy of authority. The employees of these government units, who are quite knowledgeable within their narrow areas, have become known somewhat derisively as **bureaucrats**.

bureaucrats
Employees of a bureaucracy, usually meaning a government bureaucracy.

We study bureaucracies because they play a central role in the governments of modern societies. In fact, organizations are a crucial part of any society, no matter how elementary it is. Even a preindustrial tribe is an organization. It has a clearly defined leader (a chief), senior policymakers (elders), a fixed division of labor (some hunt, some cook, some make tools), an organizational culture (religious practices, initiation rituals), and rules of governance (what kind of property belongs to families and what belongs to the tribe). How that tribe is organized is not merely a quaint aspect of its evolution; it is critical to the survival of its members in a hostile environment.

The organization of modern government bureaucracies also reflects their need to survive. The environment in which modern bureaucracies operate, filled with conflicting political demands and the ever-present threat of budget cuts, is no less hostile than that of preindustrial tribes. The way a given government bureaucracy is organized also reflects the particular needs of its clients. The bottom line, however, is that the manner in which any bureaucracy is organized affects how well it can accomplish its tasks.

Different approaches to fighting German submarines in World War II vividly demonstrate the importance of organization. At the beginning of the war, German submarines, or U-boats, were sinking American merchant ships off the East Coast of

America at a devastating rate. One U-boat commander wrote that his task was so easy that "all we had to do was press the button." In contrast, the British had a great deal of success in defending their ships in the North Atlantic from U-boats.

The British navy used a highly centralized structure to quickly pool all incoming information on U-boat locations and just as quickly pass on what it had learned to commanders of antisubmarine ships and planes and to convoys. In contrast, the U.S. Navy's operations structure was decentralized, leaving top-line managers to decide for themselves how to allocate their resources. No one unit was coordinating anti-submarine warfare. When the U.S. Navy finally adopted a system similar to the British navy's, its success against the U-boats improved dramatically. In the eighteen months before it changed its system, the U.S. Navy sank just thirty-six U-boats. In the first six months with its centralized structure, seventy-five U-boats were destroyed.[4]

Clearly organization matters. The ways in which bureaucracies are structured to perform their work directly affect their ability to accomplish their tasks. Unfortunately, "if organization matters, it is also the case that there is no one best way of organizing."[5] Highly centralized organization, like the British navy's approach to combating U-boats, may not always be the best approach to solving a bureaucracy's performance problems. In some instances, it's surely better to give local managers the flexibility to tailor their own solutions to the unique problems they face in their community or state. The study of bureaucracy, then, centers on finding solutions to the many different kinds of problems that large government organizations face.

The Development of the Bureaucratic State

A common complaint voiced by Americans is that the national bureaucracy is too big and tries to accomplish too much. To the average citizen, the national government may seem like an octopus—its long arms reach just about everywhere. Ironically, compared to other Western democracies, the size of the U.S. government is proportionally smaller (see "The Size of Government in Global Politics").

American government seems to have grown unchecked since the start of the twentieth century. As one observer noted wryly, "The assistant administrator for water and hazardous materials of the Environmental Protection Agency [presides] over a staff larger than Washington's entire first administration."[6] Yet even during George Washington's time, bureaucracies were necessary. No one argued then about the need for a postal service to deliver mail or a treasury department to maintain a system of currency.

However, government at all levels (national, state, and local) has grown enormously over time, for several major reasons. A principal cause of government expansion is the increasing complexity of society. George Washington did not have an assistant administrator for water and hazardous materials because he had no need for one. The National Aeronautics and Space Administration (NASA) was not necessary until rockets were invented.

Another reason government has grown is that the public's attitude toward business has changed. Throughout most of the nineteenth century, there was little or no government regulation of business. Business was generally autonomous, and any government intervention in the economy that might limit that autonomy was considered inappropriate. This attitude began to change toward the end of the nineteenth century as more Americans became aware that the end product of a laissez-faire approach was not always highly competitive markets that benefited consumers. Instead, businesses sometimes formed oligopolies, such as the infamous "sugar trust," a small group of companies that controlled virtually the entire sugar market.

The Size of Government in Global Politics

Compared with other Western democracies, the U.S. government turns out to be relatively small. Measuring the size of government is difficult, but one way is to calculate government expenditures as a proportion of all economic activity. By this standard, the size of the U.S. government is relatively small. Virtually all other advanced industrialized democracies have larger government sectors. Typically these countries pay for all of their citizens' health care through government insurance, and this is a significant difference with the United States. Taxes are often higher, too, to reflect the cost of more robust government services.

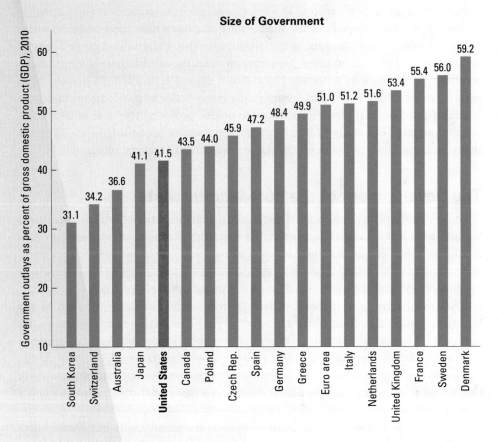

Size of Government

Government outlays as percent of gross domestic product (GDP), 2010

South Korea	31.1
Switzerland	34.2
Australia	36.6
Japan	41.1
United States	41.5
Canada	43.5
Poland	44.0
Czech Rep.	45.9
Spain	47.2
Germany	48.4
Greece	49.9
Euro area	51.0
Italy	51.2
Netherlands	51.6
United Kingdom	53.4
France	55.4
Sweden	56.0
Denmark	59.2

Source: Workforall.net.

Critical Thinking What are the underlying reasons why budgets in democracies differ so greatly?

Gradually government intervention came to be accepted as necessary to protect the integrity of markets. And if government was to police unfair business practices effectively, it needed administrative agencies. During the twentieth century, new bureaucracies were organized to regulate specific industries. Among them are the Securities and Exchange Commission (SEC), which oversees securities trading, and the Food and

Drug Administration (FDA), which tries to protect consumers from unsafe food, drugs, and cosmetics. Through bureaucracies such as these, government has become a referee in the marketplace, developing standards of fair trade, setting rates, and licensing individual businesses for operation. As new problem areas have emerged, government has added new agencies, further expanding the scope of its activities.

General attitudes about government's responsibilities in the area of social welfare have changed too. An enduring part of American culture is the belief in self-reliance. People are expected to overcome adversity on their own, to succeed on the basis of their own skills and efforts. Yet certain segments of our population are believed to deserve government support, because we either particularly value their contribution to society or have come to believe that they cannot realistically be expected to overcome adversity on their own.

This belief goes as far back as the nineteenth century. The government provided pensions to Civil War veterans because they were judged to deserve financial support. Later, programs to help mothers and children were developed. Further steps toward income security came in the wake of the Great Depression, when the Social Security Act became law, creating a fund that workers pay into and then collect income from during old age. In the 1960s, the government created Head Start, Medicare, and Medicaid, programs designed to help minorities, the elderly, and the poor. As the government made these new commitments, it also made new bureaucracies and expanded existing ones.

Can We Reduce the Size of Government?

For many Americans, government is unpopular: they have little confidence in its capabilities and feel that it wastes money and is out of touch with the people. They want a smaller government that costs less and performs better.

Most of the national government is composed of large bureaucracies, so if government is to become smaller, bureaucracies will have to be eliminated or reduced in size. Everyone wants to believe that we can shrink government by eliminating unnecessary bureaucrats. Although efficiencies can be found, serious budget cuts also require serious reductions in programs. Not surprisingly, presidents and members of Congress face opposition when they try to cut specific programs. The national government often engages in a bit of a shell game, modestly reducing the number of bureaucrats (which is popular) without reducing government programs (which is politically risky). (See Figure 13.1.) The government often turns over the former bureaucrats' jobs to nonprofit or private contractors who do the same job but are not technically government employees.

Beneath the common rhetoric that government needs to be smaller and more efficient, serious efforts to shrink the bureaucracy have varied considerably. Ideological differences between the two parties and the gyrating size of the national budget deficit have shaped the debate. Democrats and liberals generally prefer a more expansive government, one committed to providing social services to those citizens who need them. Republicans and conservatives generally prefer smaller government, one requiring more self-reliance on the part of citizens. Liberals also favor a more active government in regulating the economy, while conservatives want government to play less of a role in supervising the economy. At the beginning of his presidency, Barack Obama and the Democratic Congress expanded government across a number of fronts. Most notably, bureaucracies were created to administer new programs for health care and for oversight of the financial services industry. The sagging economy and gains by the Republicans in the 2010 elections led to greater concern about

FIGURE 13.1 The Bureaucracy No One Likes

No one likes to pay taxes, but tax collection is an essential function of government. The Internal Revenue Service (IRS) has the task of not only collecting taxes but also making sure that individuals and businesses pay what they actually owe. Not surprisingly, it's not a terribly popular agency as there's no pro-tax collection lobby or constituency to promote it. Consequently, it's vulnerable to budget cutting and as this chart shows, the number of employees has been forced down by smaller budgets even though the IRS's functions have not been reduced. As a consequence, fewer audits of taxpayers are being conducted, and this may diminish the disincentive to cheat on one's taxes: there is less chance of being caught.

Sources: Michael Kranish, "IRS: America's Feared and Failing Agency," *Boston Globe*, 17 February 2014; Stephen Ohlemacher, "Chances of Getting Audited by IRS Lowest in Years," *Associated Press*, 14 April 2014, http://bigstory.ap.org/article/chances-getting-audited-irs-lowest-years-0.

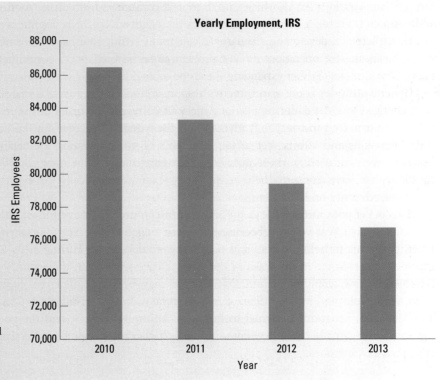

the national debt, and legislation was passed to reduce government spending by $1.2 trillion over the next ten years.[7]

The tendency for big government to endure over the longer term reflects the tension between majoritarianism and pluralism. Even when the public as a whole wants a smaller national government, that sentiment can be undermined by the strong desire of different segments of society for government to continue performing some valuable function for them. Lobbies that represent these segments work strenuously to convince Congress and the administration that certain agencies' funding is vital and that any cuts ought to come out of other agencies' budgets.

Bureaus and Bureaucrats

LO2 ★ Describe the organization of the executive branch, the role of the civil service, and the bureaucracy's responsiveness to presidential control.

We often think of the bureaucracy as a monolith. In reality, the bureaucracy in Washington is a disjointed collection of departments, agencies, bureaus, offices, and commissions—each a bureaucracy in its own right.

The Organization of Government

By examining the basic types of government organizations, we can better understand how the executive branch operates. In our discussion, we pay particular attention to the relative degree of independence of these organizations and to their relationship with the White House.

Departments. The biggest units of the executive branch are **departments**, covering broad areas of government responsibility. As noted in Chapter 12, the secretaries (heads) of the departments, along with a few other key officials, form the president's cabinet. The current cabinet departments are State, Treasury, Defense, Interior, Agriculture, Justice, Commerce, Labor, Health and Human Services, Housing and Urban Development, Transportation, Energy, Education, Veterans Affairs, and Homeland Security (see Figure 13.2). Each of these massive organizations is broken down into subsidiary agencies, bureaus, offices, and services.

Independent Agencies. Within the executive branch are many **independent agencies** that are not part of any cabinet department. They stand alone and are controlled to varying degrees by the president. Some, among them the Central Intelligence Agency (CIA), are directly under the president's control. Others, such as the Federal Communications Commission, are structured as **regulatory commissions**. Each commission is run by a small number of commissioners (usually an odd

departments
The biggest units of the executive branch, covering a broad area of government responsibility. The heads of the departments, or secretaries, form the president's cabinet.

independent agencies
Executive agencies that are not part of a cabinet department.

regulatory commissions
Agencies of the executive branch of government that control or direct some aspect of the economy.

FIGURE 13.2 Bureaucrats at Work

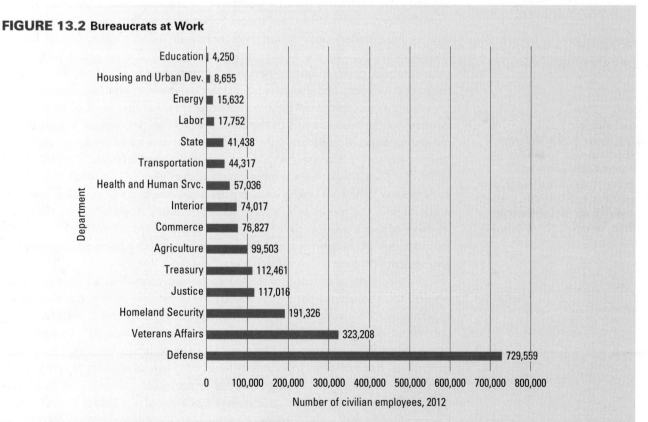

The size of the cabinet departments varies dramatically. That more than 1 million civilians are employed in the departments of Defense, Homeland Security, and Veterans Affairs is a reflection of the centrality of national security and war in recent American history. At the opposite end of the spectrum is the tiny Department of Education, with fewer than five thousand employees, despite the common rhetoric about the need to improve education.

Source: Office of Personnel Management, Data, Analysis & Documentation, Federal Employment Reports, Employment and Trends—September 2012, Table 2—Comparison of Total Civilian Employment of the Federal Government by Branch, Agency, and Area Aa of June 2012 and September 2012, http://www.opm.gov/policy-data-oversight/data-analysis-documentation/federal-employment-reports/employment-trends-data/2012/september/table-2/.

number, to prevent tie votes) appointed to fixed terms by the president. Some commissions were formed to guard against unfair business practices. Others were formed to protect the public from unsafe products. Although presidents don't have direct control over these regulatory commissions, they can strongly influence their direction through their appointments of new commissioners.

Government Corporations. Finally, Congress has also created a small number of **government corporations**. These executive branch agencies perform services that theoretically could be provided by the private sector, but Congress has decided that the public is better served when these organizations have some link with the government. For example, the national government maintains the postal service as a government corporation because it feels that Americans need low-cost, door-to-door service for all kinds of mail, not just for profitable routes or special services. In some instances, the private sector does not have enough financial incentive to provide an essential service. This is the case with the financially troubled Amtrak passenger train line.

The Civil Service

The national bureaucracy is staffed by roughly 2.8 million civilian employees, who account for 2 percent of the U.S. workforce.[8] Americans have a tendency to stereotype all government workers as faceless paper pushers, but the public sector workforce is quite diverse. Government workers include forest rangers, Federal Bureau of Investigation (FBI) agents, typists, foreign service officers, computer programmers, policy analysts, public relations specialists, security guards, librarians, administrators, engineers, plumbers, and people from literally hundreds of other occupations.

An important feature of the national bureaucracy is that most of its workers are hired under the requirements of the **civil service**. The civil service was created after the assassination of President James Garfield, who was killed by an unbalanced and dejected job seeker. Congress responded by passing the Pendleton Act (1883), which established the Civil Service Commission (now the Office of Personnel Management). The objective of the act was to reduce patronage—the practice of filling government positions with the president's political allies or cronies. The civil service fills jobs on the basis of merit and sees to it that workers are not fired for political reasons. Over the years, job qualifications and selection procedures have been developed for most government positions.

The tidal wave of criticism of the federal bureaucracy—that it's unresponsive, too big, and too inefficient—has raised concerns that the government has become a less appealing place to work. As one study concluded, "The federal bureaucracy became the symbol of big government's problems—rarely of its success."[9] In recent years, surveys have shown that morale on the part of bureaucrats working for the federal government has declined. Only roughly four in ten federal workers believe that doing their jobs well will result in being rewarded or promoted.[10] (See Figure 13.3.) Part of the problem with morale is that Congress has enacted significant budget cuts that have resulted in staff reductions; at the same time there have been no corresponding cuts in the work that must be handled by bureaucracies. Fortunately, there's been no evidence of a decline in the quality of work done by federal bureaucrats.

Presidential Control over the Bureaucracy

Civil service and other reforms have effectively insulated the vast majority of government workers from party politics.[11] An incoming president can appoint only

government corporations
Government agencies that perform services that might be provided by the private sector but that either involve insufficient financial incentive or are better provided when they are somehow linked with government.

civil service
The system by which most appointments to the federal bureaucracy are made, to ensure that government jobs are filled on the basis of merit and that employees are not fired for political reasons.

FIGURE 13.3 A Discouraged Workforce

Percentage of the federal workforce who believe that they will be rewarded or promoted for doing their jobs well.

Morale among federal government employees has been falling. Indeed, the most recent survey shows the lowest level of job satisfaction since the surveys began in 2003. Budget cuts have led to a shrinking workforce which, in turn, means more work per remaining employee (or work that doesn't get done). Salaries have also lagged.

Source: *Satisfaction with Performance-Based Rewards and Advancement*, Partnership for Public Service, June 2013, http://bestplacestowork.org/BPTW/index.php.

about three thousand people to jobs in his administration, less than 1 percent of all executive branch employees. These presidential appointees fill the top policy-making positions in government, and about a thousand of the president's appointees require Senate confirmation.[12] Each new president, then, establishes an extensive personnel review process to find appointees who are both politically compatible and qualified in their field. Although the president selects some people from his campaign staff, most political appointees have not been campaign workers. Instead, cabinet secretaries, assistant secretaries, agency heads, and the like tend to be drawn directly from business, universities, nonprofits, and government itself.

Presidents find that the bureaucracy is not always as responsive as they might like, for several reasons. Principally, pluralism can pull agencies in a direction other than that favored by the president. The Department of Transportation may want to move toward more support for mass transit, but politically it cannot afford to ignore the preferences of highway builders. An agency administrator must often try to broker a compromise between conflicting groups rather than pursue a position that holds fast and true to the president's ideology. Bureaucracies must also follow—at least in general terms—the laws governing the programs they are entrusted with, even if the president doesn't agree with some of those statutes. In this regard, bureaucracies are full of experienced careerists who are effective at running their programs. It is difficult for political appointees to ignore the careerists' preferences because of their long experience in the agency.[13]

Even with the constraints imposed by interest group preferences and by what the statutes require, presidents still have considerable influence over agency policymaking. They appoint administrators sympathetic to their policy goals who work to adapt the president's philosophy to both pending issues and new initiatives. Presidential aides review agency policymaking to ensure that it is in line with their preferences, often setting up a process requiring agencies to submit draft regulations to a White House office like the Office of Management and Budget.

Congress always has the prerogative to override regulations that it doesn't like or that it feels distort its intent. When a president faces a Congress controlled by the opposition party, this constraint is more significant. When the president's party also controls both houses, it is much easier for him to implement regulations that are in line with his preferences. Whatever party controls Congress, the White House and agency administrators have an incentive to consult with committee chairs to minimize conflict and gain a sense of what might provoke a hostile response on the part of a committee overseeing a particular agency. A committee can punish an agency by cutting its budget, altering a key program, or (for Senate committees) holding up confirmation of a nominee to a top agency post.

Administrative Policymaking: The Formal Processes

LO3 ★ Describe the roles of administrative discretion and rule-making authority in the execution of administrative policymaking.

Many Americans wonder why agencies sometimes actually make policy rather than merely carry it out. Administrative agencies are, in fact, authoritative policymaking bodies, and their decisions on substantive issues are legally binding on the citizens of this country.

Administrative Discretion

What are executive agencies set up to do? To begin with, cabinet departments, independent agencies, and government corporations are creatures of Congress. Congress creates a new department or agency by enacting a law that describes the organization's mandate, or mission. As part of that mandate, Congress grants the agency the authority to make certain policy decisions. Congress recognized long ago that it has neither the time nor the technical expertise to make all policy decisions. Thus, agencies are seen as a better means of managing uncertainty.[14] Ideally, Congress sets general guidelines for policy and expects agencies to act within those guidelines.[15] The latitude that Congress gives agencies to make policy in the spirit of their legislative mandate is called **administrative discretion**.

administrative discretion
The latitude that Congress gives agencies to make policy in the spirit of their legislative mandate.

Critics of the bureaucracy frequently complain that agencies are granted too much discretion because Congress commonly gives vague directives in its initial enabling legislation. Congress charges agencies with protecting "the public interest" but leaves them to determine on their own what policies best serve the public.

The breadth of agency discretion is illustrated by the FDA. Its mandate is, essentially, to protect Americans from unsafe products and unsavory business practices. This gives it enormous powers.[16] In 2013, for example, it proposed rules largely banning trans fats from foods. Trans fats are used in many popular prepared foods such as microwave popcorn, cake frosting, and frozen pizzas. They are popular with manufacturers of these kinds of foods because they are relatively inexpensive and work well in the production process. Medical research has shown, however, that trans fats are linked to heart disease.[17] Nevertheless, removing them from the marketplace is a burden to manufacturers and will cost them money to find acceptable replacements.

Congress grants the broadest discretion to those agencies that are involved in domestic and global security. Both the FBI and the CIA have enjoyed a great deal of freedom from formal and informal congressional constraints because of the legitimate need for secrecy in their operations. In the post-9/11 era, additional discretion has accrued to security-related agencies.[18]

Rule Making

Agencies exercise their policymaking discretion through formal administrative procedures, usually rule making. **Rule making** is the administrative process that results in the issuance of regulations. **Regulations** are rules that guide the operation of government programs. When an agency issues regulations, it is using the discretionary authority granted to it by Congress to implement a program or policy enacted into law. Rule making itself follows procedural guidelines requiring that proposed regulations first be published so that interested parties—typically interest groups—have a chance to comment on them, making any recommendations they see as appropriate.

Because they are authorized by congressional statutes, regulations have the effect of law. When Congress created the Department of Transportation in 1966, it was given authority to write regulations relevant to the safety, accessibility, and efficiency of various transportation industries. Controversy has swirled for years around a practice of airlines to keep passengers on board an aircraft that has pulled away from the gate but cannot take off (usually due to inclement weather). Horror stories abound. In August 2009, an ExpressJet flight with forty-seven passengers on board stayed overnight on the tarmac at the airport in Rochester, New York. It doesn't take long before a plane runs out of food and water and bathrooms become fouled.

Rolf Adlercreutz/Alamy

Tarmac Hell

Flying these days has its share of challenges, but government regulation has resulted in some modest improvements. The airlines' practice of keeping passengers on their plane on the tarmac while waiting for bad weather to clear is now subject to restrictions. If an airline keeps a plane on the tarmac for more than three hours, it is subject to a heavy fine.

Whenever Congress threatened to enact a "passenger bill of rights" to forbid such unconscionable tarmac delays, the airlines promised to improve their service. At the end of 2009, however, the Department of Transportation announced a new set of rules, limiting tarmac waits to no more than three hours. If that much time elapses, the plane must return to the gate and give passengers the option of deplaning. Airlines claimed there would be unintended consequences and even longer delays as ground crews removed luggage and searched for bags belonging to passengers who deplaned.[19] The new rule, however, has worked well, and according to one report, "controllable tarmac delays [have] all but vanished."[20]

The regulatory process is controversial because regulations often require individuals and corporations to act against their own self-interest. The airline regulations are a classic case of freedom versus order. The airline companies believed they needed the greater freedom to conduct business in a way that they found most efficient. Consumer groups preferred that the government put more of a premium on maintaining order (preserving the health and well-being of passengers). Administrative rule making gives agencies flexibility as they try to find a balance between conflicting pressures.

rule making
The administrative process that results in the issuance of regulations by government agencies.

regulations
Administrative rules that guide the operation of a government program.

COMPARE WITH YOUR PEERS
MindTap™ for American Government

Access The Bureaucracy Forum: Polling Activity—Bureaucracy and Regulation.

Administrative Policymaking: Informal Politics

LO4 ★ Analyze how incrementalism and bureaucratic culture affect policymaking.

When an agency is considering a new regulation and all the evidence and arguments have been presented, how does an administrator reach a decision? Because policy decisions typically address complex problems that lack a single satisfactory solution, these decisions rarely exhibit mathematical precision and efficiency.

The Science of Muddling Through

In his classic analysis of policymaking, "The Science of Muddling Through," Charles Lindblom compared the way policy might be made in the ideal world with the way it is formulated in the real world.[21] The ideal, rational decision-making process, according to Lindblom, begins with an administrator's tackling a problem by ranking values and objectives. After clarifying the objectives, the administrator thoroughly considers all possible solutions to the problem. He or she comprehensively analyzes alternative solutions, taking all relevant factors into account. Finally, the administrator chooses the alternative that appears to be the most effective means of achieving the desired goal and solving the problem.

Lindblom claims that this "rational-comprehensive" model is unrealistic. Policymakers have great difficulty defining precise values and goals. Administrators at the U.S. Department of Energy, for example, want to be sure that supplies of home heating oil are sufficient each winter. At the same time, they want to reduce dependence on foreign oil. Obviously, the two goals are not fully compatible. How should these administrators decide which goal is more important? And how should they relate them to the other goals of the nation's energy policy?

Real-world decision making parts company with the ideal in another way: the policy selected cannot always be the most effective means to the desired end. Even if a tax at the gas pump is the most effective way to reduce gasoline consumption during a shortage, motorists' anger would make this theoretically "right" decision politically difficult. So the "best" policy is often the one on which most people can agree. However, political compromise may mean that the government is able to solve only part of a problem.

Finally, critics of the rational-comprehensive model point out that policymaking can never be based on truly comprehensive analyses. A secretary of energy cannot possibly find the time to read a comprehensive study of all alternative energy sources and relevant policy considerations for the future. A truly thorough investigation of the subject would produce thousands of pages of text. Instead, administrators usually rely on short staff memos that outline a limited range of feasible solutions to immediate problems. Time is of the essence, and problems are often too pressing to wait for a complete study. According to Lindblom, policymaking tends to be characterized by **incrementalism**, with policies and programs changing bit by bit, step by step. Decision makers are constrained by competing policy objectives, opposing political forces, incomplete information, and the pressures of time. They choose from a limited number of feasible options that are almost always modifications of existing policies rather than wholesale departures from them.

Because policymaking proceeds by means of small modifications of existing policies, it is easy to assume that incrementalism describes a process that is intrinsically conservative, sticking close to the status quo.[22] Yet even if policymaking moves in small steps, those steps may all be in the same direction. Over time, a series of incremental changes can significantly alter a program. Moreover, although Lindblom offered a more realistic portrayal of the policymaking process, incrementalism is not ubiquitous. There are a minority of cases where decisions are made that move a policy in a significantly new direction. The Obama administration's intervention to resuscitate a collapsing banking industry could not accurately be labeled an incremental change, even though in the past the government has on occasion intervened to shore up an industry in trouble. The staggering sums the government loaned to failed or fragile financial institutions and the level of control the government exerted were without real precedent. It's certainly true that virtually all policy changes have antecedents in current policy, but some changes are considerable in scope.[23]

incrementalism
Policymaking characterized by a series of decisions, each typically instituting modest change.

The Culture of Bureaucracy

How an agency makes decisions and performs its tasks is greatly affected by the people who work there: the bureaucrats. Americans often find their interactions with bureaucrats frustrating because bureaucrats are inflexible (they go by the book) or lack the authority to get things done. Top administrators too can become frustrated with the bureaucrats who work for them.

Why do people act bureaucratically? Individuals who work for large organizations cannot help but be affected by the culture of bureaucracy.[24] Part of that culture is the development of **norms**, an organization's informal, unwritten rules that guide individual behavior. For example, the Individuals with Disabilities Act (IDEA) requires that every child with qualifying disabilities receive an Individualized Education Plan that provides for the necessary, appropriate services. However, school administrators implementing this law frequently offer families fewer services than the law arguably calls for. The reason is not that school administrators don't want to do the maximum for disabled children but that they don't have enough money to provide all services to all qualifying students in their school or district. Norms develop about how to allocate scarce resources even though the law assumes adequate services will be offered.[25]

Bureaucracies are often influenced in their selection of policy options by the prevailing customs, attitudes, and expectations of the people working within them. Departments and agencies commonly develop a sense of mission, where a particular objective or a means for achieving it is emphasized. The Army Corps of Engineers, for example, is dominated by engineers who define the agency's objective as protecting citizens from floods by building dams. There could be other objectives, and there are certainly other methods of achieving this one, but the engineers promote the solutions that fit their conception of what the agency should be doing.

When Leon Panetta became head of the CIA in 2009, he faced an especially delicate and difficult task in trying to change behavior in a bureaucracy with a powerful sense of mission.[26] During the war on terror under the Bush administration, many suspected terrorists who were captured were taken to secret prisons and subjected to waterboarding and other forms of torture. Some of these people were truly evil, while others were not terrorists but victims of mistaken identity. For Panetta, the challenge was more than developing new legal standards to replace the ones that permitted torture. Rather, he had to change the mindset of the agency.[27]

Sometimes we get frustrated with government bureaucrats because we believe that the norms of their agencies have made them timid and too ready to fall back on written rules. We may see formal rules as too cumbersome and requiring too much delay before action can be taken.[28] Bureaucracies can be slow and require a great deal of paperwork before action can be taken but, at the same time, written rules are in place to prevent bureaucrats from acting arbitrarily, impulsively, or without doing the review of evidence necessary to make the most intelligent decision.

norms
An organization's informal, unwritten rules that guide individual behavior.

★ Problems in Implementing Policy

LO5 ★ Identify obstacles to effective policy implementation.

The development of policy in Washington is the end of one phase of the policy-making cycle and the beginning of another. After policies have been developed, they

implementation
The process of putting specific policies into operation.

must be implemented. **Implementation** is the process of putting specific policies into operation. Ultimately, bureaucrats must convert policies on paper into policies in action. It is important to study implementation because policies do not always do what they were designed to do.

Implementation may be difficult because the policy to be carried out is not clearly stated. Policy directives to bureaucrats sometimes lack clarity and leave them with too much discretion. Implementation can also be problematic because it often involves many different agencies and different layers of government. Take, for example, the case of reducing air pollution in Los Angeles, a city that was afflicted with horrible smog. In 1977 Congress amended the Clean Air Act, which among other things shifted a great deal of responsibility to state, regional, and local institutions. The Environmental Protection Agency (EPA) still retained much authority and continued to issue regulations specifying standards. To implement these regulations in the Los Angeles region, the state of California created the South Coast Air Quality Management District. However, considerable jurisdiction over many sources of pollution lay with another body, the California Air Resources Board. Implementation also involved many city governments in the Los Angeles basin along with a number of transportation agencies.

Despite these challenges of divided responsibilities, considerable progress was made in reducing pollution and smog. But the national government then changed regulatory philosophies, and in 1993 the EPA issued a new set of instructions. The new approach was to move away from "command and control" regulations (basically orders to be carried out) to market incentives. Both businesses and consumers were to be offered incentives to move toward less polluting technologies. Progress in reducing pollution was made through this approach as well. Los Angeles is now at the beginning of a third approach, one aimed at "sustainability." This approach aims at achieving an equilibrium in which pollution is offset by gains that improve the environment. In one analyst's words, this "would be a fundamental transformation in what Los Angelenos value in their personal and professional lives."[29] The implementation challenges are no less daunting.

Effective implementation takes time as processes must be established and continually improved so all stakeholders can negotiate and communicate effectively. There's a great deal of trial and error as bureaucrats learn what works and what doesn't, and what's efficient and what is too costly or too slow.

Clearly the sheer complexity of public policy problems makes implementation a challenge. The more organizations and levels of government involved, the more difficult it is to coordinate implementation. Moreover, many policies are implemented at the last stage not by government bureaucracies but by nonprofit or for-profit organizations hired

Steve Starr/Corbis News/CORBIS

L.A. Story

No U.S. city is more identified with air pollution than Los Angeles (pictured here in 1993). Over the years, different levels of government have cooperated in developing various approaches to improving the quality of air in the L.A. area. Implementation of these policies has been complex, but while there's still pollution in Los Angeles, there is progress and the air is cleaner than it was when this picture was taken.

under a contract to deliver a specific service.[30] As will be discussed in the next section, "outsourcing" of government programs is very common. Government agencies devise, fund, and oversee programs but hire some other entity to run them. That adds another layer of participants and more opportunities for miscommunication, poor performance, and coordination problems.

Beyond complexity is the challenge of government capacity.[31] Sometimes government simply doesn't have the resources to address the problem at hand. It's easy for a president to declare a war on drugs, but it would take far more resources than government realistically has at its disposal to seriously erode illegal drug use. With the best of intentions, government may take on tasks not well suited to bureaucracies. For example, to fight poverty and to create more stable home environments for young children, the federal government funds the Family Expectations program. It's designed for young couples (married or not) with children with the intent of increasing the chances of them staying together. The program runs thirteen weeks and participants are ostensibly taught how to be better partners and better parents. However, the program has been a failure. Compared to a control group of couples receiving no intervention, the participants in Family Expectations have actually shown less likelihood of staying together.[32]

Unfortunately, obstacles to effective implementation can create the impression that nothing the government does succeeds, but programs can and do work. Problems in implementation demonstrate why patience and continual analysis are necessary ingredients of successful policymaking.

© iStockphoto.com/SandraKim

Government Fails to Deliver

The federal government's Family Expectations program was designed to help young couples manage the stress of parenthood. Despite the best of intentions, the program failed to help couples stay together. Apparently nurturing and maintaining relationships is beyond what the government is capable of doing.

Reforming the Bureaucracy: More Control or Less?

LO6 ★ Compare the strengths and weaknesses of reform efforts aimed at increasing the effectiveness of the bureaucracy's performance.

As we saw at the beginning of this chapter, organization matters. How bureaucracies are designed directly affects how effective they are in accomplishing their tasks. People in government constantly tinker with the structure of bureaucracies, trying to find ways to improve their performance. Administrative reforms have taken many different approaches as criticism of government has mounted.

In recent years, three basic approaches to reforming the bureaucracy have attracted the most attention. First, advocates of *deregulation* envision eliminating layers of bureaucracy and reducing the rules that govern business markets with the market forces of supply and demand. Let consumer preferences dictate what products and services are offered. A second approach is directed at waste and inefficiency in

**CONNECT
WITH YOUR CLASSMATES**
MindTap™ for American Government

Access The Bureaucracy Forum: Discussion—Bureaucracy at Work.

government and promotes *competition* so that government services are offered by the lowest bidder from the public or private sector. Instead of a bureaucracy having a monopoly over a particular task, create incentives for that bureaucracy to continually find ways of doing the job more cheaply, thus saving the taxpayers money. Third, a range of reforms focuses on measuring agency performance. Instituting clear *performance standards* and holding bureaucrats accountable for meeting those standards should improve the quality and efficiency of government services.

Deregulation

regulation
Government intervention in the workings of a business market to promote some socially desired goal.

deregulation
A bureaucratic reform by which the government reduces its role as a regulator of business.

Many people believe that government is too involved in **regulation**, intervening in the natural working of business markets to promote some social goal. For example, government might regulate a market to ensure that products pose no danger to consumers. Through **deregulation**, the government reduces its role and lets the natural market forces of supply and demand take over. Conservatives have championed deregulation because they see freedom in the marketplace as the best route to an efficient and growing economy. Indeed, nothing is more central to capitalist philosophy than the belief that the free market will efficiently promote the balance of supply and demand. Considerable deregulation took place in the 1970s and 1980s, notably in the airline, trucking, financial services, and telecommunications industries.

In telecommunications, for example, consumers used to have no role in choosing a telephone vendor—one could call on the Bell system or not call at all. After an out-of-court settlement broke up the Bell system in 1982, AT&T was awarded the right to sell the long-distance services that had previously been provided by that system, but it now had to face competition from newly emergent long-distance carriers. Deregulation for local phone service followed some years later, and consumers have benefited from the vigorous competition for their business in both realms. Few sectors of the economy have shown as much innovation and appeal as today's smartphones like iPhones and Droids, which are essentially small computers that can be put in a pocket, backpack, or purse.

Deciding on an appropriate level of deregulation is especially difficult for health and safety issues. Companies within a particular industry may legitimately claim that health and safety regulations are burdensome, making it difficult for them to earn sufficient profits or compete effectively with foreign manufacturers. But the FDA's drug licensing procedures illustrate the potential danger of deregulating such policy areas. The thorough and lengthy process that the FDA uses to evaluate drugs has as its ultimate validation the thalidomide case. The William S. Merrell Company purchased the license to market this sedative, already available in Europe, and filed an application with the FDA in 1960. The company then began

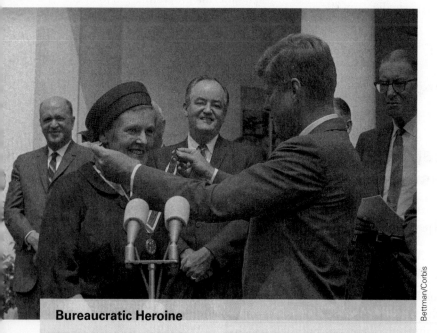

Bettman/Corbis

Bureaucratic Heroine

The government recognized Dr. Frances Kelsey's courageous work to keep thalidomide off the American market with the President's Award for Distinguished Federal Civilian Service. The medal is being affixed here by President John F. Kennedy in 1962. In 2010, the Food and Drug Administration awarded its first annual Frances Kelsey Award to honor a staff member of the agency. Its first recipient: ninety-eight-year-old Dr. Frances Kelsey.

a protracted fight with an FDA bureaucrat, Dr. Frances Kelsey, who was assigned to evaluate the thalidomide application. She demanded that the company abide by all FDA drug testing requirements, despite the fact that the drug was already in use in other countries. She and her superiors resisted pressure from the company to bend the rules a little and expedite approval. Before Merrell had conducted all the FDA tests, news came pouring in from Europe that some women who had taken thalidomide during pregnancy were giving birth to babies without arms, legs, or ears. Strict adherence to government regulations protected Americans from the same tragic consequences.

Some agencies have tried to move beyond rules that simply increase or decrease the amount of government control to regulatory processes that offer firms flexibility in meeting standards while at the same time protecting health and safety concerns. For example, the EPA has instituted flexible caps on air pollution at some manufacturing plants. Instead of having to request permits on new equipment and processes, plants are given an overall pollution cap and can decide on their own how to meet that limit.[33]

Efforts aimed at making organizations, typically corporations, more transparent and accountable in their actions are also gaining favor as another regulatory approach. For example, food manufacturers are now required to disclose information in packaging labels as to the quantity of fats and various other ingredients in the product. At the same time, the internal deliberations of bureaucracies formulating regulatory or deregulatory initiatives are often shrouded in mystery.[34]

Who controls the government makes a huge difference in the level and type of regulation. When a Democrat controls the White House, there is sure to be a more forceful stance toward regulation as presidential appointees in the agencies reflect the incumbent's philosophy.[35] More broadly, there was a surge in regulations after Obama took over (see Figure 13.4). There may have been many factors that contributed to this trend, but as one analysis put it, "the new aggressiveness reflects the new cops on the beat."[36] In contrast, Republican presidents are prone

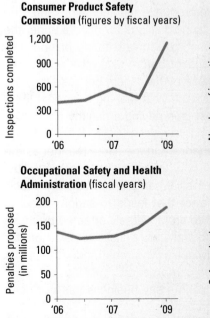

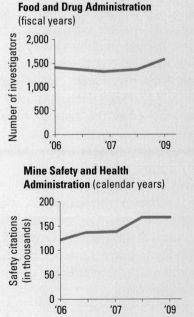

FIGURE 13.4 It Makes a Difference

Control over the White House makes an enormous difference in the way regulatory agencies perform their duties. With Democrat Barack Obama in the White House, agencies followed his lead and moved aggressively on health and safety issues. Under President George W. Bush, agencies relied more on the free market to solve policy problems.

Source: Eric Lipton, "With Obama Regulations Are Back in Fashion," *New York Times*, 23 May 2010.

to place more emphasis on freedom, and agencies under their control will regulate less.

Even though deregulation is seen as a means of promoting innovation and efficient economic markets, the government continues to expand its regulatory reach. One reason is that new problems are always emerging. For example, Google is developing a car that drives itself. If and when it's brought to market, it seems inconceivable that the government would not develop regulations intended to make sure that the complex technology underlying such cars is safe.[37] Another reason why agencies continue to extend their regulatory reach is that American businesses operate in an increasingly globalized marketplace. U.S. companies wanting to sell their products in Europe must comply with European Union (EU) regulatory standards; consequently U.S. agencies sometimes believe it's best to harmonize regulations with

Freedom, Order, or Equality

Freedom, Order, and Tanning

A tanned body has long been seen as a sign of health and beauty. If it's not summer or you don't have time to sun yourself at the beach or in the backyard, a convenient option is a tanning salon. Lying under the ultraviolet lamps can turn white skin to brown.

Unfortunately, tanning lamps turn white skin to brown by essentially damaging the skin. (The same is true of tanning from the sun.) The damage is more than skin deep. Among those who use tanning beds or booths, there is a considerably heightened chance of developing melanoma (skin cancer). And skin cancer can metastasize and ultimately turn fatal.

Tanning is especially popular among young, white, non-Hispanic women. Thirty percent of young white high school-age women report going to a tanning parlor at least once a year. Seventeen percent go frequently. Some become addicted.

Due to the dangers of tanning, many states regulate tanning salons in some form or another. California, for example, bans tanning salons for minors under the age of eighteen. Thirty-three states have chosen to regulate these businesses, often by requiring minors to obtain parental consent before using the services of a tanning studio. State governments focus on use by teenagers because they are less likely to understand the health risks associated with tanning and most likely to feel physically invincible. The state's interest is in having a healthy population and not one in which there are unnecessary cancers.

The federal government does not regulate tanning in the same manner as the states do, but under the Affordable Care Act, it now taxes use of tanning studios. Customers have a 10 percent tax added to their bill when they utilize such a facility. This tax is justified as a deterrent to behavior that leads to serious medical problems. All of us who pay for health insurance are adversely affected by those who must be treated for skin cancer. Or more bluntly, we all have to pay more for our health insurance to cover the costs of individuals who must undergo serious and costly treatments for melanoma and related complications.

Despite this new tax, owners of tanning parlors say business has not been affected. The popularity of tanning has not been dimmed.

those of the EU.[38] The federal government also acts at times to set a national standard when different states have set different standards in a policy area where Washington has heretofore abstained from regulating. There are still many areas, however, where the states regulate but Washington doesn't (see "Freedom, Order, or Equality: Freedom, Order, and Tanning").

A strong case can be made for deregulated business markets, in which free and unfettered competition benefits consumers and promotes productivity. The strength of capitalist economies comes from the ability of individuals and firms to compete freely in the marketplace, and the regulatory state places restrictions on this freedom. But without regulation, nothing ensures that marketplace participants will act responsibly. Achieving the right balance between protecting citizens, maintaining orderly markets, and promoting free markets is elusive.

© iStockphoto.com/Vigold

Sources: "Indoor Tanning Restrictions for Minors," National Conference of State Legislatures, March, 2014, http://www.ncsl.org/research/health/indoor-tanning-restrictions.aspx; Karen Kaplan, "Young White Women Still Embrace Indoor Tanning Despite Cancer Risks," *Los Angeles Times*, 19 August 2013, http://articles.latimes.com/2013/aug/19/science/la-sci-sn-indoor-tanning-cancer-white-women-20130819; and Erin Kim, "Obamacare's 'Tanning Tax' Is Here to Stay," CNNMoney, 28 June 2012, http://money.cnn.com/2012/06/28/pf/taxes/tanning-tax/.

Critical Thinking What is the justification for government regulating this business sector through both taxation and restrictions on consumers?

Competition and Outsourcing

Conservative critics of government have long complained that bureaucracies should act more like businesses, meaning they should try to emulate private sector practices that promote efficiency and innovation. Many recent reformers advocate something more drastic: unless bureaucracies can demonstrate that they are as efficient as the private sector, turn those agencies' functions over to the private sector. Underlying this idea is the belief that competition will make government more dynamic and more responsive to changing environments and will weaken the ability of labor unions to raise wages beyond those of nonunion employees.

One widespread adaptation of competitive bidding to administer government programs has come in the area of social services. Over time government welfare programs have increasingly emphasized social services—giving people training and non-cash support—rather than income maintenance (cash support). Social services are labor intensive, and state and local governments have found it efficient to outsource programs to nongovernmental organizations, principally nonprofit organizations like community health centers and day-care centers for elderly persons. For-profit companies compete for the grants and contracts that the government awards through competitive grants or bidding. For example, the for-profit company Maximus is contracted by a number of state agencies responsible for child support to locate noncustodial parents to establish paternity or enforce payments to a custodial parent.[39]

This movement toward **competition and outsourcing** continues to grow. More and more government jobs are open to bidding from nongovernment competitors, and sometimes a government bureau or office competes for the jobs and programs that they used to "own." As the number of federal government employees has declined while the population of Americans increases, some wonder if our country is building a "hollow state." By this, critics mean a government that is distinct from the programs it funds, disengaged from interaction with the people it serves.

competition and outsourcing
Procedures that allow private contractors to bid for jobs previously held exclusively by government employees.

Performance Standards

Another approach to improving the bureaucracy's performance is to focus on performance: To what degree does any individual agency accomplish the objectives that have been set for it? In this view, each agency is held accountable for reaching quantifiable goals each year or budget cycle. Under such a system, congressional and White House overseers examine each agency to see if it meets its objectives, and they reward or punish agencies accordingly. As one scholar noted, this is a philosophy of "making the managers manage."[40]

A major initiative to hold agencies accountable for their performance is the **Government Performance and Results Act**. Passed by Congress, it requires each agency to identify specific goals, adopt a performance plan, and develop quantitative indicators of agency progress in meeting its goals. The law requires that agencies publish reports with performance data on each measure established. This is no small challenge.[41] A case in point is the Healthy Start program funded by the Health Resources and Services Administration (HRSA) and intended to improve infant mortality rates and infant health generally. Among the specific goals are increasing the number of mothers receiving prenatal care during the first trimester and reducing the number of low-weight births. These are measurable, and the hospitals and health centers receiving federal funding for Healthy Start must report the appropriate data to HRSA. More complicated is the degree to which this program makes a difference since infant health can be influenced by many factors.[42]

Government Performance and Results Act
A law requiring each government agency to implement quantifiable standards to measure its performance in meeting stated program goals.

Another problem is that since agencies set their own goals and know they'll be judged on meeting them, they may select indicators where they know they'll do best.[43] Or if standards that have been set prove to be too difficult to achieve, standards may be lowered, sometimes under the guise of "reform," to make them work better. The Department of Education's No Child Left Behind program was envisioned as a means for forcing underperforming schools to raise their students up to the reading and math standards prescribed for each grade level. Although the law is that of the national government, states were allowed to implement the program in their own way. Over time, many states reduced their standards because their schools could not improve enough to meet the model guidelines of a national test of students. In short, performance-based management runs the risk of perverting an agency's incentives toward what it can achieve rather than what would be most valuable to achieve.

Despite the relative appeal of these different approaches to improving the bureaucracy, each has serious shortcomings. There is no magic bullet. The commitment of the government to solve a problem is far more important than management techniques. Still, to return to a theme that we began with, organization does matter. Trying to find ways of improving the bureaucracy is important because bureaucracies affect people's lives, and enhancing their performance, even at the margins, has real consequences.

Master the Topic of The Bureaucracy with MindTap™ for American Government

REVIEW MindTap™ **for American Government**
Access Key Term Flashcards for Chapter 13.

TEST YOURSELF MindTap™ **for American Government**
Take the Wrap It Up Quiz for Chapter 13.

STAY CURRENT MindTap™ **for American Government**
Access the KnowNow blog and customized RSS for updates on current events.

STAY FOCUSED MindTap™ **for American Government**
Complete the Focus Activities for The Bureaucracy.

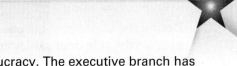

Summary

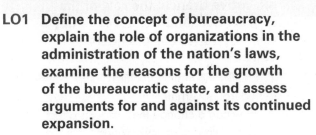

LO1 **Define the concept of bureaucracy, explain the role of organizations in the administration of the nation's laws, examine the reasons for the growth of the bureaucratic state, and assess arguments for and against its continued expansion.**

- As the scope of government activity has grown during the twentieth and early twenty-first centuries, so too has the bureaucracy. The executive branch has evolved into a complex set of departments and independent agencies. The way in which the various bureaucracies are organized matters a great deal because their structure affects their ability to carry out their tasks. Shrinking the government, though popular in the abstract, is difficult to enact because individual programs are popular with individual constituencies.

LO2   Describe the organization of the executive branch, the role of the civil service, and the bureaucracy's responsiveness to presidential control.

- The executive branch is organized around cabinet departments, independent agencies, and a small number of government corporations. Almost all civilian employees of the federal government are protected by civil service employment requirements. Presidents have some control over the bureaucracy, but such authority is constrained by a number of factors.

LO3   Describe the roles of administrative discretion and rule-making authority in the execution of administrative policymaking.

- Administrative discretion is delegated to agencies by the Congress because Congress recognizes that it does not have the staff, time, and expertise to make all the decisions necessary in each policy area. The formulation of regulations follows a formal, legal process termed rule making. Regulations set forth policy and are not mere details of administrative processes.

LO4   Analyze how incrementalism and bureaucratic culture affect policymaking.

- A rational-comprehensive model of administrative policymaking is unrealistic.

Instead, agencies make policy through incremental steps. The behavior of bureaucrats is shaped by bureaucratic culture—the norms and informal practices that characterize the internal workings of the organization.

LO5   Identify obstacles to effective policy implementation.

- Implementation is the process by which policies formulated by bureaucracies are put into practice. Lack of clarity in policy directives, involvement of many agencies at different levels of government, time constraints, and the sheer complexity of public policy problems are some of the challenges to effective implementation.

LO6   Compare the strengths and weaknesses of reform efforts aimed at increasing the effectiveness of the bureaucracy's performance.

- Deregulation is a reduction in the level of supervision of a business market or other activity by a government bureaucracy. Recent efforts by government to improve the performance of bureaucracies include competition and outsourcing and setting performance standards.

Chapter Quiz

LO1   Define the concept of bureaucracy, explain the role of organizations in the administration of the nation's laws, examine the reasons for the growth of the bureaucratic state, and assess arguments for and against its continued expansion.

1. Why has the bureaucracy grown over the years?
2. What are the obstacles to reducing the size of government?

LO2   Describe the organization of the executive branch, the role of the civil service, and the bureaucracy's responsiveness to presidential control.

1. Identify the major structural components of the federal government.
2. How can a change in presidents affect administrative policymaking?

LO3 **Describe the roles of administrative discretion and rule-making authority in the execution of administrative policymaking.**

1. Why does Congress give agencies significant discretion?
2. What is rule making?

LO4 **Analyze how incrementalism and bureaucratic culture affect policymaking.**

1. What is incrementalism?
2. Compare and contrast formal and informal influences on policymaking.

LO5 **Identify obstacles to effective policy implementation.**

1. What is involved in the implementation of policies?

2. What are some of the challenges in implementing policy directives formulated by Washington agencies?

LO6 **Compare the strengths and weaknesses of reform efforts aimed at increasing the effectiveness of the bureaucracy's performance.**

1. What are the potential benefits as well as the negative consequences of deregulation?
2. Why might performance standards be ineffective?

14 The Courts

Learning Outcomes

LO1 Define judicial review, explain the circumstances under which it was established, and assess the significance of the authority it gave the courts.

LO2 Outline the organization of the U.S. court system and identify the principal functions of courts at each tier of the system.

LO3 Describe the process by which cases are both accepted for review and decided by the U.S. Supreme Court and analyze the role played by judicial restraint and judicial activism in judicial decisions.

LO4 Explain how judges at different levels of the federal court system are nominated and confirmed to the federal bench.

LO5 Examine the impact, influence, and acceptance of decisions on issues of national importance by an institution unaccountable to the electorate.

LO6 Evaluate the decision-making authority of the federal judiciary within the context of both majoritarian and pluralist democracy.

 WATCH & LEARN MindTap™ **for American Government**
Watch a brief "What Do You Know?" video summarizing The Judiciary.

© Gary Blakeley/Shutterstock.com

When U.S. Supreme Court Chief Justice Fred M. Vinson died unexpectedly on September 8, 1953, his colleague Associate Justice Felix Frankfurter commented, "This is the first solid piece of evidence I've ever had that there really is a God."[1] Frankfurter—a lifelong agnostic—despised Vinson as a leader and disliked him as a person. Vinson's sudden death would bring a new colleague— and perhaps new hope—to the school desegregation cases known collectively as *Brown* v. *Board of Education*. The issue of segregated schools had arrived in the Supreme Court in late 1951. Although the Court had originally scheduled oral argument for October 1952, the justices elected a postponement until December and merged several similar cases. When a law clerk expressed puzzlement at the delay, Frankfurter explained that the Court was holding the cases for the outcome of the national election in 1952. "I thought the Court was supposed to decide without regard to elections," declared the clerk. "When you have a major social political issue of this magnitude," replied Frankfurter, "we do not think this is the time to decide it."[2]

The justices were at loggerheads following the December argument, with Vinson unwilling to inval-

idate racial segregation in public education. Because the justices were not ready to reach a decision, they scheduled the cases for reargument the following year. The justices asked the attorneys to address the history of the Fourteenth Amendment and the potential remedies if the Court ruled against segregation.

Frankfurter's caustic remark about Vinson's death reflected the critical role Vinson's replacement would play when the Court again tackled the desegregation issue. In his first appointment to the nation's highest court, President Dwight D. Eisenhower chose California's Republican governor, Earl Warren, as chief justice. The president would later regret his choice.

When the Court heard the reargument of *Brown* v. *Board of Education* in late 1953, the new chief justice led his colleagues from division to unanimity on the issue of public school segregation. Unlike his predecessor, Warren began the secret conference to decide the segregation issue with a strong statement: that segregation was contrary to the Thirteenth, Fourteenth, and Fifteenth Amendments to the Constitution. "Personally," remarked the new chief justice, "I can't see how today we can justify segregation based solely on race."[3] Moreover, if the Court were to uphold segregation, he argued, it could do so only on the theory that blacks were inherently inferior to whites. As the discussion proceeded, Warren's opponents were cast in the awkward position of appearing to support racism.

Five justices were clearly on Warren's side, making six votes; two were prepared to join the majority if Warren's reasoning satisfied them. With only one clear holdout, Warren set about the task of responding to his colleagues' concerns. In the months that followed, he met with them individually in their chambers, reviewing the decision and the justification that would accompany it. Finally, in April 1954, Warren approached Justice Stanley Reed, whose vote would make the opinion unanimous. "Stan," said the chief justice, "you're all by yourself in this now. You've got to decide whether it's really the best thing for the country." Ultimately, Reed joined the others. On May 17, 1954, the Supreme Court unanimously ruled against racial segregation in public schools, signaling the end of legally created or government-enforced segregation of the races in the United States.[4]

LISTEN & LEARN
MindTap™ for American Government

Access Read Speaker to listen to Chapter 14.

Judges confront conflicting values in the cases before them, and in crafting their decisions, they—especially Supreme Court justices—make policy. Their decisions become the precedents other judges use to rule in similar cases. One judge in one court makes public policy to the extent that she or he influences other decisions in other courts.

The power of the courts to shape public policy creates a difficult problem for democratic theory. According to that theory, the power to make law resides only in the people or the people's elected representatives. When judges undo the work of elected majorities (which was surely the case with government-sponsored racial segregation), they risk depriving the people of the right to make the laws or to govern themselves.

Court rulings—especially Supreme Court rulings—extend far beyond any particular case. Judges are students of the law, but they remain human beings. They have their own opinions about the values of freedom, order, and equality. And although all judges are constrained by statutes and precedents from imposing their personal will on others through their decisions, some judges are more prone than others to interpreting the law in the light of their own beliefs.

America's courts are deeply involved in the life of the country and its people. Some courts, such as the Supreme Court, make fundamental policy decisions vital to the preservation of freedom, order, and equality. Through checks and balances, the elected branches link the courts to democracy, and the courts link the elected branches to the Constitution. But does this system work? Can the courts exercise political power within the pluralist model? Or are judges simply sovereigns in black robes, making decisions independent of popular control? In this chapter, we examine these questions by exploring the role of the courts in American political life.

National Judicial Supremacy

LO1 ★ Define judicial review, explain the circumstances under which it was established, and assess the significance of the authority it gave the courts.

Section 1 of Article III of the Constitution creates "one supreme Court." The founders were divided on the need for other national courts, so they deferred to Congress the decision to create a national court system. Those who opposed the creation of national courts believed that such a system would usurp the authority of state courts.[5] Congress considered the issue in its first session and, in the Judiciary Act of 1789, gave life to a system of federal (that is, national) courts that would coexist with the courts in each state but be independent of them. Federal judges would also be independent of popular influences because the Constitution provided for their lifetime appointment.

In the early years of the Republic, the federal judiciary was not a particularly powerful branch of government. It was especially difficult to recruit and keep Supreme Court justices. They spent much of their time as individual traveling judges ("riding circuit"); disease and poor transportation were everyday hazards. The justices met as the Supreme Court only for a few weeks in February and August.[6] John Jay, the first chief justice, refused to resume his duties in 1801 because he concluded that the Court could not muster the "energy, weight, and dignity" to contribute to national affairs.[7] Several distinguished statesmen refused appointments to the Court, and

Lollapalooza of a Line

With no video allowed in the courtroom, the hottest ticket in Washington, D.C., for 2012 was a seat in the Supreme Court to hear arguments examining the constitutionality of the Obama administration's signature legislative achievement, the Affordable Care Act. The Court, under Chief Justice John G. Roberts, Jr., seemed to be embracing political conflict when it agreed to decide the constitutionality of Obamacare before the 2012 presidential election.

several others, including Oliver Ellsworth, the third chief justice, resigned. But a period of profound change began in 1801 when President John Adams appointed his secretary of state, John Marshall, to the position of chief justice.

Judicial Review of the Other Branches

Shortly after Marshall's appointment, the Supreme Court confronted a question of fundamental importance to the future of the new republic: If a law enacted by Congress conflicts with the U.S. Constitution, which should prevail? The question arose in the case of *Marbury* v. *Madison* (1803), which involved a controversial series of last-minute political appointments.[8]

The case began in 1801 when the Adams administration designated an obscure Federalist, William Marbury, as a justice of the peace in the District of Columbia. Marbury and several others were appointed to government posts created by the Federalist-controlled Congress in the last days of John Adams's presidency, but the appointments were never completed. The newly arrived Jefferson administration had little interest in delivering the required documents; qualified Jeffersonians would welcome the jobs.

To secure their jobs, Marbury and the other disgruntled appointees invoked an act of Congress to obtain the necessary papers. The act authorized the Supreme Court to issue orders against government officials. Marbury and the others sought such an order in the Supreme Court against the new secretary of state, James Madison, who held the crucial documents. Chief Justice Marshall observed that Marbury was clearly entitled to his job. However, Marshall faced a dilemma: On the one hand, if the Court

The Supreme Court of the United States

Chief Justice John Marshall

John Marshall (1755–1835) clearly ranks as the Babe Ruth of the Supreme Court. Both Marshall and the Bambino transformed their respective games and became symbols of their institutions. Scholars now recognize both men as originators—Marshall of judicial review and Ruth of the modern age of baseball. (FIAT JUSTITIA is Latin for "Let justice be done.")

judicial review
The power to declare congressional (and presidential) acts invalid because they violate the Constitution.

agreed with Marbury, Jefferson would likely not comply, thus making the Court look powerless. On the other hand, if the Court agreed with Madison, the Court would appear impotent for failing to side with Marbury who rightfully deserved his appointment. Cleverly, the chief justice found a way out of his dilemma.

Marshall observed that the act of Congress that Marbury invoked to sue in the Supreme Court posed a conflict with Article III of the U.S. Constitution, which did not authorize such suits. In February 1803, the Court delivered its opinion.*

Must the Court follow the law or the Constitution? (The Constitution remains silent on this question.) The High Court held, in Marshall's forceful argument, that the Constitution was "the fundamental and paramount law of the nation" and that "an act of the legislature, repugnant to the constitution, is void." In other words, when an act of the legislature conflicts with the Constitution—the nation's highest law—that act is invalid.

Marshall's argument vested in the judiciary the power to weigh the validity of congressional acts:

> It is emphatically the province and duty of the judicial department to say what the law is. Those who apply the rule to particular cases, must of necessity expound and interpret that rule.... So if a law be in opposition to the constitution; if both the law and the constitution apply to a particular case, so that the court must either decide that case conformably to the law, disregarding the constitution; or conformably to the constitution, disregarding the law; the court must determine which of these conflicting rules governs the case. This is of the very essence of judicial duty.[9]

By invalidating the law that gave Marbury access to the Court for his rightful claim, John Marshall secured the Court's power to strike down acts of Congress and at the same time avoided a confrontation with the Jefferson administration that would leave it ineffectual. Marbury never got his job, but the decision in *Marbury* v. *Madison* firmly established the Supreme Court's power of **judicial review**—the power to declare congressional acts invalid if they violate the Constitution.** Subsequent cases extended the power to cover presidential acts as well.[10]

Marshall expanded the potential power of the Supreme Court to equal or exceed the power of the other branches of government. Should a congressional act (or, by implication, a presidential act) conflict with the Constitution, the Supreme Court claimed the power to declare the act void. The judiciary would be a check on the legislative and executive branches, consistent with the principle of checks and balances embedded in the Constitution. Although Congress and the president may sometimes wrestle with the constitutionality of their actions, judicial review gave the Supreme Court the final word on the meaning of the Constitution. The exercise of judicial review—an appointed branch's checking of an elected branch in the name of the Constitution—appears to run counter to democratic theory. But in more than two hundred years of practice, the Supreme Court has invalidated nearly 180 provisions

---

*Courts publish their opinions in volumes called reporters. Today, the *United States Reports* is the official reporter for the U.S. Supreme Court. For example, the Court's opinion in the case of *Brown* v. *Board of Education* is cited as 347 U.S. 483 (1954). This means that the opinion in *Brown* begins on page 483 of Volume 347 in *United States Reports*. The citation includes the year of the decision, in this case, 1954. Before 1875, the official reports of the Supreme Court were published under the names of private compilers. For example, the case of *Marbury* v. *Madison* is cited as 1 Cranch 137 (1803). This means that the case is found in Volume 1, compiled by reporter William Cranch, starting on page 137, and that it was decided in 1803.

**The Supreme Court had earlier upheld an act of Congress in *Hylton* v. *United States* (3 Dallas 171 [1796]). *Marbury* v. *Madison* was the first exercise of the power of a court to invalidate an act of Congress.

of national law. Only a small number have had great significance for the political system.[11] The Constitution provides mechanisms to override judicial review (constitutional amendments) and to control excesses of the justices (impeachment), but these steps are more theoretical than practical. In addition, the Court can respond to the continuing struggle among competing interests (a struggle that is consistent with the pluralist model) by reversing itself. It has done so only about 240 times in its entire history.[12]

Although the Constitution did not spell out judicial review of Congress and the president, it did provide such power over state and local government. When such laws conflict with the Constitution or national laws or treaties, the federal courts can invalidate them. That's because the Supremacy Clause obligates state judges to follow the Constitution, national laws, and treaties when state law conflicts with them. Moreover, the Supreme Court ruled that it had final authority to review state court decisions calling for the interpretation of national law.[13] In time, the Supreme Court would use its judicial review power in nearly twelve hundred instances to invalidate state and local laws, on issues as diverse as abortion, the death penalty, the rights of the accused, and reapportionment.[14]

The Exercise of Judicial Review

These early cases, coupled with other historic decisions, established the components of judicial review:

- The power of the courts to declare national, state, and local laws invalid if they violate the Constitution
- The supremacy of national laws or treaties when they conflict with state and local laws
- The role of the Supreme Court as the final authority on the meaning of the Constitution

This political might—the power to undo decisions of the elected branches of the national and state governments—lay in the hands of appointed judges, that is, people who were not accountable to the electorate. Did judicial review square with democratic government?

Alexander Hamilton had foreseen and tackled the problem in *Federalist* No. 78. Writing during the ratification debates surrounding the adoption of the Constitution (see Chapter 3), Hamilton maintained that despite the power of judicial review, the judiciary would be the weakest of the three branches of government because it lacked the strength of the sword or the purse. The judiciary, wrote Hamilton, had "neither FORCE nor WILL, but merely judgment."

Although Hamilton was defending legislative supremacy, he argued that judicial review was an essential barrier to legislative oppression.[15] He recognized that the power to declare government acts void implied the superiority of the courts over the other branches. But this power, he contended, simply reflects the will of the people, declared in the Constitution, as opposed to the will of the legislature, expressed in its statutes. Judicial independence, guaranteed by lifetime tenure and protected salaries, frees judges from executive and legislative control, minimizing the risk of deviation from the law established in the Constitution. If judges make a mistake, the people or their elected representatives have the means to correct the error, through constitutional amendments and impeachment.

Their lifetime tenure does free judges from the direct influence of the president and Congress. And although mechanisms to check judicial power are in place, these mechanisms require extraordinary majorities and remain rarely used. When they exercise the power of judicial review, then, judges can and occasionally do operate counter to majoritarian rule by invalidating the actions of the people's elected representatives.

The Organization of Courts

LO2 ★ Outline the organization of the U.S. court system and identify the principal functions of courts at each tier of the system.

The American court system is complex, partly as a result of our federal system of government. Each state runs its own court system, and no two states' courts are identical. In addition, we have a system of courts for the national government. The national, or federal, courts coexist with the state courts. All court systems have pyramid-like structures with a layer of trial courts at the bottom, frequently a layer of intermediate appeals courts in the middle, and a single high appeals court at the very top. Individuals and entities fall under the jurisdiction of both court systems. They can sue or be sued in either system, depending mostly on what their case is about. Litigants file nearly all cases (95 percent) in state courts. State trial courts receive on average one civil, domestic relations, criminal, juvenile, or traffic case for every three citizens. The volume of state court cases has remained steady at about 106 million, according to the most recent data, dwarfing federal court cases, which amount to about 432,000 a year. Viewed another way, for every case in federal court, state courts handle about 250 cases.[16]

Some Court Fundamentals

Courts are full of mystery to citizens uninitiated in their activities. Lawyers, judges, and seasoned observers understand the language, procedures, and norms associated with legal institutions. Let's start with some fundamentals.

Criminal and Civil Cases. A crime is a violation of a law that forbids or commands an activity. Legislatures create, amend, and repeal criminal laws. Penal codes record these laws and the punishments for violating them. All state penal codes criminalize murder, rape, and arson. A few states decriminalize some activities— marijuana use, for example—that other state still consider criminal. Because crime is a violation of public order, the government prosecutes **criminal cases**. Maintaining public order through the criminal law is largely a state and local function. Criminal cases brought by the national government represent only a small fraction of all criminal cases prosecuted in the United States. In theory, the national penal code is limited by the principle of federalism. The code aims at activities that fall under the delegated and implied powers of the national government, enabling the government, for example, to criminalize tax evasion or the use of computers and laser printers to counterfeit money, bank checks, or even college transcripts.

Fighting crime is popular, and politicians sometimes outbid one another in their efforts to get tough on criminals. National crime-fighting measures have begun to usurp areas long viewed to be under state authority. Since 1975, Congress has added hundreds of new federal criminal provisions covering a wide range of activities once

criminal cases
Court cases involving a crime, or violation of public order.

thought to be within the states' domain, including carjacking, willful failure to pay child support, and crossing state lines to engage in gang-related street crime.[17]

Courts decide both criminal and civil cases. **Civil cases** stem from disputed claims to something of value. Disputes arise from accidents, contractual obligations, and divorce, for example. Often the parties disagree over tangible issues (possession of property, custody of children), but civil cases can involve more abstract issues too (the right to equal accommodations, compensation for pain and suffering). The government can be a party to civil disputes, called on to defend its actions or to allege wrongdoing.

civil cases
Court cases that involve a private dispute arising from such matters as accidents, contractual obligations, and divorce.

Procedures and Policymaking. Most civil and criminal cases never go to trial. In the overwhelming majority of criminal cases, the defendant's lawyer and the prosecutor **plea bargain**, negotiating the severity and number of charges to be brought against the defendant. In a civil case, one side may only be using the threat of a lawsuit to exact a concession from the other. Often the parties settle (or resolve the dispute between themselves) because of the uncertainties in litigation. Though rare, settlement can occur even at the level of the Supreme Court. And sometimes the initiating parties (the plaintiffs in civil cases) may simply abandon their efforts, leaving disputes unresolved.

plea bargain
A defendant's admission of guilt in exchange for a less severe punishment.

When cases are neither settled nor abandoned, they end with an *adjudication*, a court judgment resolving the parties' claims and enforced by the government. When trial judges adjudicate cases, they may offer written reasons to support their decisions. When the issues or circumstances of cases are novel, judges may publish *opinions*, explanations justifying their rulings.

Judges make policy in two different ways. The first is through their rulings on matters that no existing legislation addresses. Such rulings set precedents that judges rely on in future, similar cases. We call this body of rules the **common, or judge-made, law**. The roots of the common law lie in the English legal system. Common-law domains include property and torts (injuries or wrongs to the person or property of another). The second area of judicial lawmaking involves the application of statutes enacted by legislatures. The judicial interpretation of legislative acts is called *statutory construction*. The proper application of a statute is not always clear from its wording. To determine how a statute should be applied, judges look for the legislature's intent, reading reports of committee hearings and debates. If these sources do not clarify the statute's meaning, the court does so. With or without legislation to guide them, judges look to the relevant opinions of higher courts for authority to decide the issues before them.

common, or judge-made, law
Legal precedents derived from previous judicial decisions.

Like the state courts, the federal courts are organized in three tiers, as a pyramid. At the bottom of the pyramid are the **U.S. district courts**, where litigation begins. In the middle are the **U.S. courts of appeals**. At the top is the Supreme Court of the United States. To *appeal* means to take a case to a higher court. The courts of appeals and the Supreme Court are appellate courts; with few exceptions, they review only cases that have already been decided in lower courts. Most federal courts hear and decide a wide array of civil and criminal cases.

U.S. district courts
Courts within the lowest tier of the three-tiered federal court system; courts where litigation begins.

U.S. courts of appeals
Courts within the second tier of the three-tiered federal court system, to which decisions of the district courts and federal agencies may be appealed for review.

The U.S. District Courts

There are ninety-four federal district courts in the United States. Each state has at least one district court, and no district straddles more than one state.[18] In 2013, there were 678 full-time federal district judgeships, and they received over 376,000 new criminal and civil cases.[19]

The district courts are the entry point for the federal court system. When trials occur in the federal system, they take place in the federal district courts. Here is where witnesses testify, lawyers conduct cross-examinations, and judges and juries decide the fate of litigants. More than one judge may sit in each district court, but each case is tried by a single judge, sitting alone. U.S. magistrate judges assist district judges, but they lack independent judicial authority. Magistrate judges have the power to hear and decide minor offenses and conduct preliminary stages of more serious cases. District court judges appoint magistrate judges for eight-year (full-time) or four-year (part-time) terms. As of 2013, there were 531 full-time and 43 part-time and other magistrate judge positions.[20]

Sources of Litigation. Today the authority of U.S. district courts extends to the following:

- Federal criminal cases, as defined by national law (for example, robbery of a nationally insured bank or interstate transportation of stolen securities)
- Civil cases, brought by individuals, groups, or the government, alleging violation of national law (for example, failure of a municipality to implement pollution-control regulations required by a national agency)
- Civil cases brought against the national government (for example, a vehicle manufacturer sues the motor pool of a government agency for its failure to take delivery of a fleet of new cars)
- Civil cases between citizens of different states when the amount in controversy exceeds $75,000 (for example, when a citizen of New York sues a citizen of Alabama in a U.S. district court in Alabama for damages stemming from an auto accident that occurred in Alabama)

The U.S. Courts of Appeals

All cases resolved in a U.S. district court and all decisions of federal administrative agencies can be appealed to one of the twelve regional U.S. courts of appeals. These courts, with 179 full-time judgeships, received 56,000 new cases in 2013.[21] Each appeals court hears cases from a geographical area known as a *circuit*. The U.S. Court of Appeals for the Seventh Circuit, for example, is located in Chicago; it hears appeals from the U.S. district courts in Illinois, Wisconsin, and Indiana. The United States is divided into twelve circuits.*

Appellate Court Proceedings. Appellate court proceedings are public, but they usually lack courtroom drama. There are no jurors, witnesses, or cross-examinations; these are features only of the trial courts. Appeals are based strictly on the rulings made and procedures followed in the trial courts. Suppose, for example, that in the course of a criminal trial, a U.S. district judge allows the introduction of evidence that convicts a defendant but was obtained under questionable circumstances. The defendant can appeal on the grounds that the evidence was obtained in the absence of a valid search warrant and so was inadmissible. The issue on appeal is the admissibility of the evidence, not the defendant's guilt or innocence. If the appellate court agrees with the trial judge's decision to admit the evidence, the conviction stands. If the appellate court disagrees with the trial judge and rules that the evidence is inadmissible, the defendant must be retried without the incriminating evidence or be released.

---

*The thirteenth court, the U.S. Court of Appeals for the Federal Circuit, is not a regional court. It specializes in appeals involving patents, contract claims against the national government, and federal employment cases.

The courts of appeals are regional courts. They usually convene in panels of three judges to render judgments. The judges receive written arguments known as *briefs* (which are also sometimes submitted in trial courts). Often the judges hold oral hearings to question the lawyers to probe their arguments.

Precedents and Making Decisions. Following review of the briefs and, in many appeals, oral arguments, the three-judge panel meets to reach a judgment. One judge attempts to summarize the panel's views, although each judge remains free to disagree with the judgment or the reasons for it. When an appellate opinion is published, its influence can reach well beyond the immediate case. For example, a lawsuit turning on the meaning of the Constitution produces a ruling, which then serves as a **precedent** for subsequent cases; that is, the decision becomes a basis for deciding similar cases in the future in the same way. Thus, judges make public policy to the extent that they influence decisions in other courts. Although district judges sometimes publish their opinions, it is the exception rather than the rule. At the appellate level, however, precedent requires that opinions be written.

Making decisions according to precedent is central to the operation of our legal system, providing continuity and predictability. The bias in favor of existing decisions is captured by the Latin expression *stare decisis*, which means "let the decision stand." But the use of precedent and the principle of **stare decisis** do not make lower-court judges cogs in a judicial machine. "If precedent clearly governed," remarked one federal judge, "a case would never get as far as the Court of Appeals: the parties would settle."[22]

Judges on the courts of appeals direct their energies to correcting errors in district court proceedings and interpreting the law (in the course of writing opinions). When judges interpret the law, they often modify existing laws. In effect, they are making policy. Judges are politicians in the sense that they exercise political power, but the black robes that distinguish judges from other politicians signal constraints on their exercise of power.

precedent
A judicial ruling that serves as the basis for the ruling in a subsequent case.

stare decisis
Literally, "let the decision stand"; decision making according to precedent.

★ The Supreme Court

LO3 ★ Describe the process by which cases are both accepted for review and decided by the U.S. Supreme Court and analyze the role played by judicial restraint and judicial activism in judicial decisions.

Above the west portico of the Supreme Court building are inscribed the words EQUAL JUSTICE UNDER LAW. At the opposite end of the building, above the east portico, are the words JUSTICE THE GUARDIAN OF LIBERTY. The mottos reflect the Court's difficult task: achieving a just balance among the values of freedom, order, and equality. Consider how these values came into conflict in two controversial issues the Court has faced.

Flag burning as a form of political protest pits the value of order, or the government's interest in maintaining a peaceful society, against the value of freedom, including the individual's right to vigorous and unbounded political expression. In two flag-burning cases, the Supreme Court affirmed constitutional protection for unbridled political expression, including the emotionally charged act of desecrating a national symbol.[23] Because under a pluralist system no decision is ever truly final, the flag-burning decisions hardly quelled the demand for laws to punish flag desecration.

In 2006, Congress inched ever so close to a constitutional amendment banning flag desecration. The proposal passed by more than a two-thirds vote in the House but failed by a single vote in the Senate.

School desegregation pits the value of equality against the value of freedom. In *Brown v. Board of Education* (1954), the Supreme Court carried the banner of racial equality by striking down state-mandated segregation in public schools. The decision helped launch a revolution in race relations in the United States. The justices recognized the disorder their decision would create in a society accustomed to racial bias, but in this case, equality clearly outweighed freedom. Twenty-four years later, the Court was still embroiled in controversy over equality when it ruled that race could be a factor in university admissions (to diversify the student body).[24] Having secured equality for blacks, the Court in 2003 faced the charge by white students who sought admission to the University of Michigan that it was denying whites the freedom to compete for admission. A slim Court majority concluded that the equal protection clause of the Fourteenth Amendment did not prohibit the narrowly tailored use of race as a factor in law school admissions but rejected the automatic use of racial categories to award fixed points toward undergraduate admissions.[25] Michigan voters responded by adopting a state constitutional amendment in 2006 banning the use of race or sex considerations in public education. Affirmative action advocates sued the state, arguing that the state amendment violated the Equal Protection Clause of the U.S. Constitution. In 2014, the Roberts Court upheld the amendment by a vote of 6 to 2, declaring that courts possess no authority to set aside state laws that commit such policy determinations to the voters.[26] (See Chapter 16.)

The Supreme Court makes national policy. Because its decisions have far-reaching effects on all of us, it is vital that we understand how it reaches those decisions. With this understanding, we can better evaluate how the Court fits within our model of democracy.

original jurisdiction
The authority of a court to hear a case before any other court does.

The Supreme Court of the United States

The Supreme Court, 2014 Term: The Lineup

The justices of the Supreme Court of the United States. Seated are (left to right) Clarence Thomas, Antonin Scalia, Chief Justice John G. Roberts, Jr., Anthony Kennedy, and Ruth Bader Ginsburg. Standing are Sonia Sotomayor, Stephen J. Breyer, Samuel A. Alito, and Elena Kagan.

Access to the Court

All litigants must follow rules of access to bring a case to the Supreme Court. To succeed, lawyers must be sensitive to the justices' policy and ideological preferences. The notion that anyone can take a case all the way to the Supreme Court is true only in theory, not fact.

The Supreme Court's cases come from two sources. A few arrive under the Court's **original jurisdiction**, conferred by Article III, Section 2, of the Constitution, which gives the Court the power to hear and decide "all Cases affecting Ambassadors, other public Ministers and Consuls, and those in which a State shall be Party." Cases falling under the Court's original jurisdiction are tried and decided in the Court itself; the cases begin and end there. For example, the Court is the first and only forum in which legal disputes between states are resolved. It hears few original jurisdiction cases today, however, usually referring them to a special master, often a retired judge, who reviews the parties' contentions and recommends a resolution that the justices are free to accept or reject.

Most cases enter the Supreme Court from the U.S. courts of appeals or the state courts of last resort. This is the Court's **appellate jurisdiction**. These cases have been tried, decided, and reexamined as far as the law permits in other federal or state courts. The Court exercises judicial power under its appellate jurisdiction only because Congress gives it the authority to do so. Congress may change (and, perhaps, eliminate) the Court's appellate jurisdiction. This is a powerful but rarely used weapon in the congressional arsenal of checks and balances.

Litigants in state cases who invoke the Court's appellate jurisdiction must satisfy two conditions. First, the case must have reached the end of the line in the state court system. Litigants cannot jump at will from a state to a federal court. Second, the case must raise a **federal question**, that is, an issue covered by the Constitution, federal laws, or national treaties. But even cases that meet both of these conditions do not guarantee review by the Court.

Since 1925, the Court has exercised substantial (today, nearly complete) control over its **docket**, or agenda (see Figure 14.1). The Court selects a handful of cases (about eighty) for full consideration from the nine thousand requests filed each year. These requests take the form of petitions for certiorari, in which a litigant seeking review asks the Court "to become informed" of the lower-court proceeding. For the vast majority of cases, the Court denies the petition for certiorari, leaving the decision of the lower court undisturbed. No explanations accompany these denials, so they have little or no value as Court rulings.

appellate jurisdiction
The authority of a court to hear cases that have been tried, decided, or reexamined in other courts.

federal question
An issue covered by the U.S. Constitution, national laws, or U.S. treaties.

docket
A court's agenda.

FIGURE 14.1 Access to and Decision Making in the U.S. Supreme Court

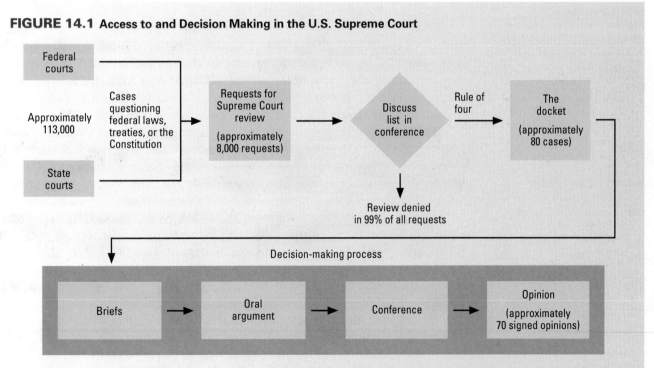

State and national appeals courts churn out thousands of decisions each year. Only a fraction ends up on the Supreme Court's docket. This chart sketches the several stages leading to a decision from the High Court.

Source: John G. Roberts, Jr., "The 2013 Year-End Report on the Federal Judiciary," http://www.supremecourt.gov/publicinfo/year-end/2013yearendreport.pdf.

With advance preparation by their law clerks, who screen petitions and prepare summaries, all nine justices make these judgments at secret weekly conferences.[27] During the conferences, justices vote on previously argued cases and consider which new cases to add to the docket. The chief justice circulates a "discuss list" of worthy petitions. Cases on the list are then subject to **the rule of four**, a practice by custom that permits four of the nine justices to grant review of a case. Though it takes only four votes to place a case on the docket, it may ultimately take an enormous leap to garner a fifth, and deciding, vote on the merits of the appeal. This is especially true if the Court is sharply split ideologically. Thus, a minority of justices in favor of an appeal may oppose review if they are not confident the outcome will be to their satisfaction.[28]

It is important to note that business cases represent a substantial portion of the Court's docket, though they receive far less attention than cases addressing social issues such as same-sex marriage, affirmative action, and school prayer. Business disputes are less emotional and the issues more technical. But business cases involve billions of dollars, have enormous consequences for the economy, and affect people's lives more often than the social issues that tend to dominate public debate and discussion.[29]

The Solicitor General

Why does the Court decide to hear certain cases but not others? The best evidence scholars have adduced suggests that agenda setting depends on the individual justices, who vary in their decision-making criteria, and on the issues raised by the cases. Occasionally justices weigh the ultimate outcome of a case when granting or denying review. At other times, they grant or deny review based on disagreement among the lower courts or because delay in resolving the issues would impose alarming economic or social costs.[30] The solicitor general plays a vital role in the Court's agenda setting.

The **solicitor general** represents the national government before the Supreme Court, serving as the hinge between an administration's legal approach and its policy objectives. Appointed by the president, the solicitor general is the third-ranking official in the U.S. Department of Justice (after the attorney general and the deputy attorney general). Today, the solicitor general is Donald B. Verrilli, Jr., who succeeded Elena Kagan, the first woman to hold the office. President Obama tapped Kagan to replace Supreme Court Justice John Paul Stevens, who retired in June 2010.

The solicitor general's duties include determining whether the government should appeal lower-court decisions; reviewing and modifying, when necessary, the briefs filed in government appeals; and deciding whether the government should file an **amicus curiae brief*** in any appellate court.[31] The objective is to create a cohesive program for the executive branch in the federal courts.

Solicitors general play two different, and occasionally conflicting, roles. First, they are advocates for the president's policy preferences; second, as officers of the Court, they traditionally defend the institutional interests of the national government.

Solicitors general usually act with considerable restraint in recommending to the Court that a case be granted or denied review. By recommending only cases of general importance, they increase their credibility and their influence.

By carefully selecting the cases it presses, the solicitor general's office usually maintains a very impressive record of wins in the Supreme Court. Solicitors general are a "formidable force" in the process of setting the Supreme Court's agenda.[32] Their influence in bringing cases to the Court and arguing them there has earned them the informal title of "the tenth justice."

---

the rule of four
An unwritten rule that requires at least four justices to agree that a case warrants consideration before it is reviewed by the U.S. Supreme Court.

solicitor general
The third highest official of the U.S. Department of Justice, and the one who represents the national government before the Supreme Court.

amicus curiae brief
A brief filed (with the permission of the court) by an individual or group that is not a party to a legal action but has an interest in it.

---

*Amicus curiae is Latin for "friend of the court." Amicus briefs can be filed with the consent of all the parties or with the permission of the court. They allow groups and individuals who are not parties to the litigation but have an interest in it to influence the court's thinking and, perhaps, its decision.

Decision Making

Once the Court grants review, attorneys submit written arguments (briefs). The justices follow an unwritten rule to avoid discussing cases with one another before oral argument. Should the rule be violated, the justices will inform their colleagues in an effort to avoid "little cliques or cabals or little groups that lobby each other before [argument]."[33] Oral argument, typically limited to thirty minutes for each side, is the first time the justices know what their colleagues might be thinking. From October through April, the justices spend two to three hours a day, five or six days a month, hearing arguments. Experience seems to help. Like the solicitor general, seasoned advocates enjoy a greater success rate, regardless of the party they represent.[34] The justices like crisp, concise, conversational presentations; they disapprove of attorneys who read from a prepared text. Some justices are aggressive, relentless questioners who frequently interrupt the lawyers; others are more subdued. In a 1993 free speech case, an attorney who offered an impassioned plea on the facts of the case was soon "awash in a sea of judicial impatience that at times seemed to border on anger.... 'We didn't take this case to determine who said what in the cafeteria,'" snapped one justice.[35]

The Court now releases oral argument transcripts on its website on the day of argument, and it releases recordings at the end of the week. In 2012, the Court scheduled a whopping 6.5 hours of argument in three cases challenging the constitutionality of the Affordable Care Act (also known as Obamacare) and took the extra step of sharing the audio with the public on each day rather than waiting until the end of the week. But the Court continues to ban tweets and blog posts from the courtroom itself, where computers, mobile phones, and tablets remain off-limits.

Court protocol prohibits the justices from addressing one another directly during oral arguments, but they often debate obliquely through the questions they pose to the attorneys. The justices reach no collective decision at the time of oral arguments. They reach a tentative decision only after they have met in conference.

Our knowledge of the dynamics of decision making on the Supreme Court is all secondhand. Only the justices attend the Court's weekly conferences. By tradition, the justices first shake hands prior to conference and to going on the bench, a gesture of harmony. The handshaking was introduced by Melville Fuller when he was chief justice from 1888 to 1910.[36] The chief justice then begins the presentation of each case with a discussion of it and his vote, which is followed by a discussion and vote from each of the other justices, in order of their seniority on the Court. Justice Antonin Scalia, who joined the Court in 1986, remarked that "not much conferencing goes on." By *conferencing*, Scalia meant efforts to persuade others to change their views by debating points of disagreement. "To call our discussion of a case a conference," he said, "is really something of a misnomer. It's much more a statement of the views of each of the nine Justices, after which the totals are added and the case is assigned" for an opinion.[37]

Judicial Restraint and Judicial Activism

How do the justices decide to vote on a case? According to some scholars, legal doctrines and previous decisions explain their votes. This explanation, which is consistent with the majoritarian model, anchors the justices closely to the law and minimizes the contribution of their personal values. This view is embodied in the concept of **judicial restraint**, which maintains that the people's elected representatives, not judges, should make the laws. Judges are said to exercise judicial restraint when they defer to decisions of other governmental actors. Other scholars contend that the value preferences and resulting ideologies of the justices provide a more powerful interpretation of their voting.[38] This view is embodied in the concept of **judicial activism**,

judicial restraint
A judicial philosophy by which judges tend to defer to decisions of the elected branches of government.

judicial activism
A judicial philosophy by which judges tend not to defer to decisions of the elected branches of government, resulting in the invalidation or emasculation of those decisions.

which maintains that judges should not give deference to the elected branches but should use their judicial power to promote the judges' preferred social and political goals. The concept of judicial activism and its cognate, judicial restraint, has many strands, and scholars sometimes disagree on its many meanings.[39] But at its core, all would agree that judges are activists when their decisions run counter to the will of the other branches of government, in effect substituting their own judgment for the judgment of the people's representatives. By interjecting personal values into court decisions, activist judging is more consistent with the pluralist model.

The terms *judicial restraint* and *judicial activism* describe different relative degrees of judicial assertiveness. Judges acting according to an extreme model of

Freedom, Order, and Equality: Judicial Activism or Judicial Restraint?

Conservatives like to link judicial activism to liberalism. But that bond is hardly fixed; conservative judges can be activists too. One well-known example tends to upend that association. In *Bush* v. *Gore*, the Supreme Court resolved the contentious 2000 presidential election, which was essentially tied, handing victory to the Republicans. This suggested to many critics that conservative jurists can also be judicial activists, promoting their preferred political goals. Had a majority deferred to the Florida courts on the issue of a recount, the decision would have been hailed as an example of judicial restraint. But overturning the Florida courts and delivering a victory for the Republicans labeled the majority in *Bush* v. *Gore* as conservative judicial activists.

In an effort at greater precision, scholars have used the overturning of legislation as a yardstick for judicial activism; the results are somewhat surprising. Looking solely at the direction of the invalidations in Figure 14.A, the Warren Court is most active and the Roberts Court the most restrained. However, a more refined examination of the evidence looks at individual justice votes in Figure 14.B. The evidence below makes the case. Conservative laws tend to be invalidated by liberal justices, and liberal laws tend to be invalidated by conservative justices. Today, the conservative bent of the Roberts Court makes it a friendly forum to

FIGURE 14.A

		Overturning Laws	Percent of invalidations that went in a liberal direction
		Percent of cases that invalidated federal, state, or local laws	
Earl Warren	1953–69	7.1	91
Warren E. Burger	1969–86	8.9	88
William H. Rehnquist	1986–2005	6.4	71
John G. Roberts, Jr.	2005–13	3.8	59

Source: Figure A, Adam Liptak, "How Activist Is the Supreme Court?" *New York Times*, 13 October 2013, p. SR4.

judicial restraint would never question the validity of duly enacted laws but would defer to the superiority of other government institutions in construing the laws. Judges acting according to an extreme model of judicial activism would be an intrusive and ever-present force that would dominate other government institutions. Actual judicial behavior lies somewhere between these two extremes.

How activist is the Supreme Court today? The Court led by Chief Justice John G. Roberts, Jr., has struck down parts of a federal law regulating campaign spending, and parts of the Voting Rights Act and the Defense of Marriage Act. But a look at the overall record across many Courts produces a more nuanced view (see "Freedom, Order, and Equality: Judicial Activism or Judicial Restraint?").

challenge liberal laws. So expect more cases to give today's conservatives a chance to "swing for the fences."

FIGURE 14.B

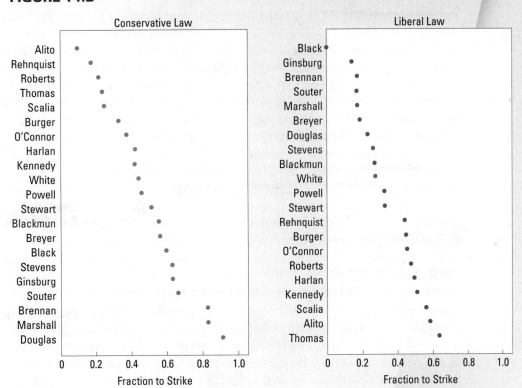

Source: Figure B, Lee Epstein and Andrew D. Martin, "Is the Roberts Court Especially Activist?" *Emory Law Journal* 61 (2012): 742.

Critical Thinking Conservative justices tend to vote against liberal policies and liberals tend to vote against conservative policies. But justices are supposed to be above politics. Offer an argument that justifies this apparent contradiction. (*Hint:* What practices come into play when nominating and confirming candidates for the High Court?)

judgment
The judicial decision in a court case.

argument
The heart of a judicial opinion; its logical content separated from facts, rhetoric, and procedure.

concurrence
The agreement of a judge with the Supreme Court's majority decision, for a reason other than the majority reason.

dissent
The disagreement of a judge with a majority decision.

Judgment and Argument. The voting outcome is the **judgment**, the decision on who wins and who loses. The justices often disagree not only on the winner and loser, but also on the reasons for their judgment. This should not be surprising, given nine independent minds and issues that can be approached in several ways. Voting in the conference does not end the justices' work or resolve their disagreements. Votes remain tentative until the Court issues an opinion announcing its judgment.

After voting, the justices in the majority must draft an opinion setting out the reasons for their decision. The **argument** is the kernel of the opinion—its logical content, as distinct from supporting facts, rhetoric, and procedures. If all justices agree with the judgment and the reasons supporting it, the opinion is unanimous. Agreement with a judgment for different reasons from those set forth in the majority opinion is called a **concurrence**. Or a justice can **dissent** if she or he disagrees with a judgment. Both concurring and dissenting opinions may be drafted, in addition to the majority opinion.

The Opinion. After the conference, the chief justice or most senior justice in the majority (in terms of years of service on the Court) decides which justice will write the majority opinion. He or she may consider several factors in assigning the crucial opinion-writing task, including the prospective author's workload, expertise, public opinion, and (above all) ability to hold the majority together. (Remember that the votes are only tentative at this point.) On the one hand, if the drafting justice holds an extreme view on the issues in a case and is not able to incorporate the views of more moderate colleagues, those justices may withdraw their votes. On the other hand, assigning a more moderate justice to draft an opinion could weaken the argument on which the opinion rests. Opinion-writing assignments can also be punitive. Justice Harry Blackmun once commented, "If one's in the doghouse with the Chief [former Chief Justice Warren Burger], he gets the crud."[40]

Opinion writing is the justices' most critical function. It is not surprising, then, that they spend much of their time drafting opinions. The justices usually call on their law clerks—top graduates of the nation's elite law schools—to help them prepare opinions and carry out other tasks. The commitment can be daunting. All of the justices now rely on their clerks to shoulder substantial responsibilities, including the initial drafts of opinions.[41]

The writing justice distributes a draft opinion to all the justices, who then read it and circulate their criticisms and suggestions. An opinion may have to be rewritten several times to accommodate colleagues who remain unpersuaded by the draft. Justice Felix Frankfurter was a perfectionist; some of his opinions went through thirty or more drafts. Justices can change their votes, and perhaps alter the judgment, until the decision is officially announced. Often, the most controversial cases pile up as coalitions on the Court vie for support or sharpen their criticisms. When the Court announces a decision, the justices who wrote the opinion read or summarize their views in the courtroom.

Justices in the majority frequently try to muffle or stifle dissent to encourage institutional cohesion. Since the mid-1940s, however, unity has been more difficult to obtain.[42] Gaining agreement from the justices today is akin to negotiating with nine separate law firms. It may be more surprising that the justices ever agree. In 2006, for example, the Court spoke without dissent in more than half of its cases. The conservative shift occasioned by the appointments of Roberts and Alito has infused cohesion among dissenters, who have tended to join a single opinion. And the Court's genteel etiquette appears strained as once collegial justices voice their views publicly and forcefully from the bench.[43]

The justices remain aware of the slender foundation of their authority, which rests largely on public respect. That respect is tested whenever the Court ventures into controversial areas. Banking, slavery, and Reconstruction policies embroiled the Court in the nineteenth century. Freedom of speech and religion, racial equality, the right to privacy, the 2000 election, and the extent of presidential power have led the Court into controversy in the past sixty years.

The Chief Justice

The chief justice is only one of nine justices, but he has several important functions based on his authority. Apart from his role in forming the docket and directing the Court's conferences, the chief justice can also be a social leader, generating solidarity within the group. Sometimes a chief justice can embody intellectual leadership. Finally, the chief justice can provide policy leadership, directing the Court toward a general policy position. Perhaps only John Marshall could lay claim to possessing social, intellectual, and policy leadership. Warren E. Burger, who resigned as chief justice in 1986, was reputed to be a lackluster leader in all three areas.[44] When presiding at the conference, the chief justice can control the discussion of issues, although independent-minded justices are not likely to acquiesce to his views. Moreover, justices today rarely engage in a debate of the issues in the conference. Rather, they communicate by memoranda, not e-mail; they use their law clerks as ambassadors between justices' chambers and, in effect, "run the Court without talking to one another."[45]

Judicial Recruitment

LO4 ★ Explain how judges at different levels of the federal court system are nominated and confirmed to the federal bench.

Neither the Constitution nor national law imposes formal requirements for appointment to the federal courts. Once appointed, district and appeals judges must reside in the district or circuit to which they are appointed. The president appoints judges to the federal courts, and all nominees must be confirmed by majority vote in the Senate. Congress sets, but cannot lower, a judge's compensation. In 2014, salaries were as listed below.

Chief justice of the Supreme Court	$255,500
Associate Supreme Court justices	244,400
Courts of appeals judges	211,200
District judges	199,100
Magistrate judges	183,172

Source: © Cengage Learning.

By comparison, in 2013, the average salary of a state supreme court judge was about $158,000. The average for a state trial judge was about $142,000.[46] Although annual compensation for equity partners in major law firms exceeds $1 million, employment prospects for new lawyers have tanked since the recession that began in 2008 with median starting salaries for lawyers in private practice dropping by

35 percent compared to 2009.[47] Still, Supreme Court law clerks entering private practice will earn more than the justices who hired them. This prompted Supreme Court Justice Antonin Scalia to urge bright students to choose other professions, such as engineering and teaching. "Society cannot afford to have such a huge proportion of its best minds going into the law," said Scalia.[48]

In more than half the states, the governor appoints the state judges, often in consultation with judicial nominating commissions. In many of these states, voters decide whether the judges should be retained in office. Other states select their judges by partisan, nonpartisan, or (rarely) legislative election.[49] In some states, nominees must be confirmed by the state legislature. Contested elections for judgeships are on the rise, and at the extreme, such contests may call a judge's impartiality into question. In 2009, the U.S. Supreme Court ruled that the newly elected chief justice of the West Virginia Supreme Court, Brent Benjamin, had to disqualify himself from deliberations in a case involving a coal company chief executive who had spent $3 million to elect Benjamin.[50] Most other countries appoint their judges, making the United States an outlier nation (see "Judicial Selection in Global Politics").

The Appointment of Federal Judges

One of the great prizes of any presidency is the ability to appoint federal judges. These are lifetime appointments, enabling presidents to extend their legacies well beyond their terms of office. As of July 2014, President Obama has appointed a total of 273 federal judges; 29 nominations await Senate action and 61 vacancies have yet to be filled. An additional 22 announced vacancies will occur before the end of Obama's presidency.*[51]

Judicial vacancies occur when sitting judges resign, retire, or die. Vacancies also arise when Congress creates new judgeships to handle increasing caseloads. In both cases, the president nominates a candidate, who must be confirmed by the Senate. Under President Obama, the Office of White House Counsel is deeply involved in this screening process. The president also had the help of the Justice Department, primarily through its Office of Legal Policy, which screens candidates before the formal nomination, subjecting serious contenders to FBI investigation. The White House and the Justice Department formed a Judicial Selection Committee as part of this vetting process. The White House and the Senate vie for control in the approval of district and appeals court judges.

The "Advice and Consent" of the Senate. For district and appeals court vacancies, the nomination "must be acceptable to the home state senator from the president's party"[52] (or to the state's House delegation from the president's party if no senator is from the president's party). The Judicial Selection Committee consults extensively with home state senators from which the appointment will be made.[53] Senators' influence is greater for appointments to district court than for appointments to the court of appeals.

This practice, called **senatorial courtesy**, forces presidents to share the nomination power with members of the Senate. The Senate will not confirm a nominee who is opposed by the senior senator from the nominee's state if that senator is a member of the president's party. The Senate does not actually reject the candidate. Instead, the senator whose state is the source of the nomination fails to return a **blue slip** to

senatorial courtesy
A norm under which a nomination must be acceptable to the home state senator from the president's party.

blue slip
The failure of a senator to return a blue slip signals the end of the road for a judicial nomination.

---

*As of 2014, fifteen federal judges have been impeached. Of these, eight were convicted in the Senate and removed from office. The most recent to be forced to leave office was Judge G. Thomas Porteous, Jr., who was impeached by the House and convicted by the Senate in 2010.

Judicial Selection in Global Politics

The United States is an outlier nation, at least when it comes to the way we select judges. In at least half of the U.S. states, judges run for election. In fact, nearly 90 percent of all state judges face the voters. This practice is in stark contrast to the rest of the world, where governments appoint their judges, either by the executive branch (with or without recommendations from a judicial selection commission), by the judicial selection commission itself, or by the legislative branch. In a few countries, the civil service offers a professional career path leading to a judgeship. In these countries, the route to a judgeship rests on examinations and school programs. In only two nations—Switzerland and Japan—judicial elections hold sway, but only in a very limited way: (1) Some smaller Swiss cantons (subnational units) elect judges, and (2) appointed justices of the Japanese Supreme Court may face retention elections, though scholars regard the practice as a mere formality. Hans A. Linde, a retired justice of the Oregon Supreme Court, captured the essence of the American exception when he observed: "To the rest of the world, American adherence to judicial elections is as incomprehensible as our rejection of the metric system."

The table here shows the judicial selection process used in countries around the world. Some countries use more than one method; the table lists the primary one.

Executive Appointment Without Commission	Executive Appointment with Commission	Appointment by Commission	Legislative Appointment	Career Judiciary
Afghanistan	Albania	Algeria	China	Czech Republic
Argentina	Canada	Andorra	Cuba	France
Australia	Dominican Republic	Angola	Laos	Germany
Bangladesh	England	Bulgaria	Macedonia	Italy
Belarus	Greece	Croatia	Montenegro	Japan
Belgium	Namibia	Cyprus	Poland	
Cambodia	Russia	Israel	Portugal	
Chad	Scotland	Lebanon	Spain	
Egypt	South Africa	Mexico	Turkey	
New Zealand	Ukraine	Rwanda		
Uzbekistan	Zimbabwe	Yemen		

Source: Based on Adam Liptak, "American Exception: Rendering Justice, with One Eye on Re-election," *New York Times*, 25 May 2008, http://www.nytimes.com/2008/05/25/us/25exception.html?pagewanted=1&_r=1.

Critical Thinking What changes, if any, would you implement to the way in which the United States appoints federal judges? Be sure to justify any change as an improvement over the status quo or explain why the status quo is better than the alternatives.

the Senate Judiciary Committee. In this case, the chairman of the committee, which reviews all judicial nominees, will not schedule a confirmation hearing, effectively killing the nomination.

Although the Justice Department is still sensitive to senatorial prerogatives, senators can no longer submit a single name to fill a vacancy. The department searches for acceptable candidates and polls the appropriate senator for her or his reaction to them. President George H. W. Bush asked Republican senators to seek more qualified female and minority candidates. Bush made progress in developing a more diverse bench, and President Clinton accelerated the change.[54] President George W. Bush improved the Republican track record in appointing women and minorities but still lagged behind Clinton. President Obama now ranks at the top in appointing more women during his tenure compared to his predecessors.[55]

The Senate Judiciary Committee conducts a hearing for judicial nominees. The committee chair exercises a measure of control in the appointment process that goes beyond senatorial courtesy. If a nominee is objectionable to the chair, he or she can delay a hearing or hold up other appointments until the president and the Justice Department find an alternative. Such behavior does not win a politician much influence in the long run, however. So committee chairs of the president's party are usually loath to place obstacles in a president's path, especially when they may want presidential support for their own policies and constituencies.

Beginning with the Carter administration, judicial appointments below the Supreme Court have proved a new battleground, with a growing proportion of nominees not confirmed and increasing delays in the process. These appointments were once viewed as presidential and party patronage, but that old-fashioned view has given way to a focus on the president's policy agenda through judicial appointments. This perspective has enlarged the ground on which senators have opposed judicial nominees to include matters of judicial policy (for example, abortion) and theory (for example, delving into a nominee's approach when interpreting the meaning of a statute). Beginning in 2003, Democratic senators used the filibuster to prevent confirmation votes for judicial candidates they deemed "outside the mainstream." This behavior provoked ire from the majority Republicans, who threatened to end the filibuster practice entirely. The parties reached an uneasy compromise in 2005 to invoke a judicial filibuster only for "extraordinary circumstances," but that compromise seems to have dissolved in 2011 when the Republicans began employing the judicial filibuster to scuttle Obama nominees.[56] But the turnabout-is-fair-play game ran out of steam in late 2013 when Senate Democrats changed the rules to require a simple majority (rather than 60 votes) to end debate for all but Supreme Court nominations. Now for the first time in several years, judges appointed by Democrats outnumber judges appointed by Republicans.[57]

The American Bar Association. The American Bar Association (ABA), the biggest organization of lawyers in the United States, has been involved in screening candidates for the federal bench since 1946.[58] Its role is defined by custom, not law. At the president's behest, the ABA's Standing Committee on the Federal Judiciary routinely rates prospective appointees using a three-value scale: "well qualified," "qualified," and "not qualified." The association no longer has advance notice of possible nominees. The George W. Bush administration considered the ABA too liberal, posing an unnecessary impediment to the confirmation of conservative judges.[59] Nonetheless, the association continued to evaluate the professional qualifications of nominees after they were nominated. President Obama restored the ABA's prenomination review in 2009.[60]

Recent Presidents and the Federal Judiciary

Since the presidency of Jimmy Carter, chief executives have tended—more or less—to make appointments to the federal courts that are more diverse in racial, ethnic, and gender terms than in previous administrations. President Bill Clinton took the lead on diversity. For the first time in history, more than half of the president's judicial appointments were women or minorities. Clinton's chief judge selector, Assistant Attorney General Eleanor Acheson, followed through on Clinton's campaign pledge to make his appointees "look like America." That approach has continued with President Obama's picks (see Figure 14.2).

The racial and ethnic composition of the parties themselves helps explain much of the variation between the appointments of presidents of different parties. It seems clear that political ideology, not demographics, lies at the heart of judicial appointments. Presidents are likely to appoint judges who share similar values.[61]

Appointment to the Supreme Court

The announcement of a vacancy on the High Court usually causes quite a stir. Campaigns for Supreme Court seats are commonplace, although the public rarely

FIGURE 14.2 The Changing Makeup of the Federal Courts

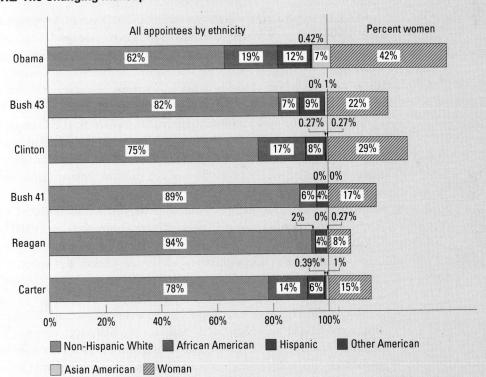

*Note: Frank Howell Seay did not discover his Native American heritage until after judicial appointment.

President Obama has appointed more than 250 federal judges. Their racial, ethnic, and gender makeup stands in contrast to previous presidents with more Hispanics, African American, Asian, and women judges than any of his predecessors. Obama's picks come closer to the ethnic and gender composition of the population.

Source: Brookings, http://www.brookings.edu/~/media/research/files/papers/2009/8/federal%20judiciary%20wheeler/08_federal_judiciary_wheeler.pdf; Source for Obama stats: http://www.whitehouse.gov/share/judicial-nominations.

sees them. Hopefuls contact friends in the administration and urge influential associates to do the same on their behalf. Some candidates never give up hope. Judge John J. Parker, whose nomination to the Court was defeated in 1930, tried in vain to rekindle interest in his appointment until he was well past the age—usually the early sixties—that appointments are made.[62]

The president is not shackled by senatorial courtesy when it comes to nominating a Supreme Court justice. However, appointments to the Court attract more intense public scrutiny than do lower-level appointments, effectively narrowing the president's options and focusing attention on the Senate's advice and consent.

Of the 155 men and 5 women nominated to the Court, 11 names have been withdrawn, and 25 have failed to receive Senate confirmation. (Seven confirmed justices declined to serve.)[63] Only six such fumbles have occurred since 1900. The last one was George W. Bush's nomination of Harriet Miers in 2005 to fill the vacancy created by the retirement of Sandra Day O'Connor. Miers, who was White House counsel, withdrew her candidacy after coming under withering criticism, largely from conservatives, for her lack of clarity on issues likely to come before the Court.

The most important factor in the rejection of a nominee is partisan politics. At least sixteen candidates lost their bids for appointment because the presidents who nominated them were considered likely to become lame ducks: the opposing party in control of the Senate anticipated victory for its candidate in an upcoming presidential race and sought to deny the incumbent president an important political appointment.[64]

Eighteen of the twenty-five successful Supreme Court nominees since 1950 have had prior judicial experience in federal or state courts. This tendency toward "promotion" from within the judiciary may be based on the idea that a judge's previous opinions are good predictors of his or her future opinions on the High Court. After all, a president is handing out a powerful lifetime appointment, so it makes sense to want an individual who is sympathetic to his views. Judges holding lifetime appointments are likely to state their views frankly in their opinions. In contrast, the policy preferences of High Court candidates who have been in legal practice or in political office can only be guessed at, based on the conjecture of professional associates or on speeches they have given to local Rotary Clubs, on the floor of a legislature, and elsewhere.

After a vacancy drought of more than eleven years, President George W. Bush put his stamp on the Supreme Court with two appointments in 2005. He nominated federal judge John G. Roberts, Jr., in July 2005 to replace Associate Justice Sandra Day O'Connor (after the withdrawal of Harriet Miers). But with the death of Chief Justice William H. Rehnquist in September, Bush withdrew Roberts's nomination as associate justice and resubmitted him for the position of chief justice. Roberts was confirmed 78–22. Democrats were evenly split: 22 for and 22 against. Bush then nominated federal judge Samuel A. Alito for the seat vacated by O'Connor. His confirmation hearing was far more contentious, with the Democrats aiming to paint him as "outside the mainstream." The effort failed, as did a last-minute call to filibuster the nomination. Alito was confirmed by the Senate by a narrow margin, 58–42 (nearly all Democrats were opposed), and he took his seat as the 110th justice in January 2006.

The results of the Roberts and Alito appointments were soon apparent. In the 2006 Term (October 2006 to June 2007), the first full term with Roberts and Alito on the bench, the Court moved in a decidedly conservative direction. One-third of all the cases were decided by 5–4 votes, almost triple the proportion of close votes from the previous term. In each case, Justice Anthony Kennedy cast the deciding vote.

CONNECT WITH YOUR CLASSMATES
MindTap® for American Government

Access The Judiciary Forum: Discussion—Supreme Court Confirmation Process.

He joined the majority in all twenty-four 5–4 decisions, siding more often with his conservative colleagues. Subsequently, Kennedy has left his mark by authoring the majority opinion or providing the deciding vote across a range of hot-button issues: declaring the death penalty unconstitutional for the rape of a child, ensuring Guantánamo detainees a constitutional right to challenge their detention in federal courts, supporting a constitutional right for individuals to own a gun for personal use, and removing restrictions on corporate spending in election campaigns.

The hearts of many a lawyer and loyal Democrat fluttered when Justice David H. Souter announced his decision to retire from the Supreme Court effective June 29, 2009. This gave President Obama the opportunity to appoint a second woman to the Supreme Court, federal judge Sonia Sotomayor of New York. Sotomayor, the first Latina to be nominated to the Court, possessed a sterling résumé with a compelling personal story. Raised by her widowed mother in a Bronx housing project, Sotomayor went on to earn top honors at Princeton and distinction at Yale Law School. She spent years as a federal prosecutor and in private legal practice before she was appointed by Republican president George H. W. Bush to the federal district court in 1992. President Bill Clinton appointed her to the federal appellate court in 1998.

Republicans on the Senate Judiciary Committee tried to derail Sotomayor's nomination, pouring over everything she had written or said. Some senators focused on a comment she made in 2001, that a wise Latina woman "would more often than not reach a better conclusion than a white male who hasn't lived that life."[65] In opposing Sotomayor, some Republicans risked the ire of Hispanic voters, whose role in American politics is destined to grow. By 2050, the percentage of Hispanics in the population is expected to increase from 15 to 30 percent.

Sotomayor deflected the attacks and stuck to her well-rehearsed script, declaring that her core guiding principle was "fidelity to the law." That bromide kept her opponents at bay. In the end, she was confirmed by a vote of 68 to 31, largely along party lines. Given her record as a moderate, Sotomayor's appointment will not be a game changer since she replaced a moderate justice.

President Obama filled a second seat when moderate justice John Paul Stevens announced in April 2010 that he would retire at the end of the current term in June 2010. President Obama nominated Elena Kagan, his solicitor general, to fill the spot. In a departure from recent practice, Obama did not find his choice in the minor leagues of the federal judiciary. Rather, Kagan made her mark as a law professor and law school administrator (and a coveted clerkship with Supreme Court Justice Thurgood Marshall). In a 1995 book review, Kagan wrote that confirmation hearings were "a vapid and hollow charade."[66] But when it was her turn to be interrogated by the Senate Judiciary Committee, she chose the well-worn path of avoiding

Paul J. Richards/AFP/Getty Images

Welcome to the Club!

Chief Justice John G. Roberts, Jr. (right), congratulated Elena Kagan (left), after administering the judicial oath to Kagan on August 7, 2010, making her the 112th justice of the U.S. Supreme Court. (Jeffrey Minear, counselor to the chief justice, held the Bible.) In prepared remarks afterward, Kagan pledged to support judicial restraint and a "modest" role for the Court.

answers to serious questions. Her bromide: the Court's role "must … be a modest one—properly deferential to the decisions of the American people and their elected representatives."[67] The Senate confirmed Kagan by a vote of 63 to 37. On August 7, 2010, she became the 112th justice—and the fourth woman—to serve on the Court.

The Consequences of Judicial Decisions

LO5 ★ Examine the impact, influence, and acceptance of decisions on issues of national importance by an institution unaccountable to the electorate.

Judicial rulings represent the tip of the iceberg in terms of all the legal conflicts and disputes that arise in this country. Most cases never surface in court. The overwhelming majority of lawsuits end without a court judgment. Many civil cases are settled, or the parties give up, or the courts dismiss the suits because they are beyond the legitimate bounds of judicial resolution. Most criminal cases end in a plea bargain, with the defendant admitting his or her guilt in exchange for a less severe punishment. Only about 10 percent of criminal cases in the federal district courts are tried; an equally small percentage of civil cases are adjudicated.

Furthermore, the fact that a judge sentences a criminal defendant to ten years in prison or a court holds a company liable for billions in damages does not guarantee that the defendant will lose his or her freedom or the company will give up any assets. In the case of the criminal defendant, the road of seeking an appeal following trial and conviction is well traveled and, if nothing else, serves to delay the day when he or she must go to prison. In civil cases as well, an appeal may be filed to delay the day of reckoning.

Supreme Court Rulings: Implementation and Impact

When the Supreme Court makes a decision, it relies on others to implement it—to translate policy into action. How a judgment is implemented depends in good measure on how it was crafted. Remember that the justices, in preparing their opinions, must work to hold their majorities together, to gain greater, if not unanimous, support for their arguments. This forces them to compromise in their opinions, to moderate their arguments, which introduces ambiguity into many of the policies they articulate. Ambiguous opinions affect the implementation of policy. For example, when the Supreme Court issued its unanimous order in 1955 to desegregate public school facilities "with all deliberate speed,"[68] judges who opposed the Court's policy dragged their feet in implementing it. In the early 1960s, the Supreme Court prohibited prayers and Bible reading in public schools. Yet state court judges and attorneys general reinterpreted the High Court's decision to mean that only compulsory prayer or Bible reading was unconstitutional and that state-sponsored voluntary prayer or Bible reading was acceptable.[69]

Because the Supreme Court confronts issues freighted with deeply felt social values or fundamental political beliefs, its decisions have influence beyond the immediate parties in a dispute. The Court's decision in *Roe* v. *Wade*, legalizing abortion, generated heated public reaction. The justices were barraged with thousands of angry letters. Groups opposing abortion vowed to overturn the decision; groups favoring the freedom to obtain an abortion moved to protect the right they had won. Within eight months of the decision, more than two dozen constitutional amendments had been introduced in Congress, although none managed to carry the extraordinary majority required for passage. Still, the antiabortion faction achieved a modest victory with the passage of a provision forbidding the use of national government funds for abortions except when the woman's life is in jeopardy. (Since 1993, the exception has also included victims of rape or incest.)

Abortion opponents have also directed their efforts at state legislatures, hoping to load abortion laws with enough conditions to discourage women from terminating their pregnancies. For example, one state required that women receive detailed information about abortions, then wait at least twenty-four hours before consenting to the procedure. The information listed every imaginable danger associated with abortion and included a declaration that fathers are liable to support their children financially. A legal challenge to these new restrictions reached the Supreme Court, and in 1989, it abandoned its strong defense of abortion rights.[70] The Court continued to support a woman's right to abortion, but in yet other legal challenges, it recognized the government's power to further limit the exercise of that right.[71] In 2000, in a 5–4 vote, it struck down a state law banning late-term abortions. But in 2007, the Roberts Court reversed course and in a 5–4 vote upheld a nearly identical federal late-term abortion ban.[72]

Public Opinion and the Supreme Court

Democratic theorists have a difficult time reconciling a commitment to representative democracy with a judiciary that is not accountable to the electorate yet has the power to undo legislative and executive acts. The difficulty may simply be a problem for theorists, however. The policies coming from the Supreme Court, although lagging years behind public opinion, rarely seem out of line with the public's ideological choices.[73] Surveys in several controversial areas reveal that an ideologically balanced Court seldom departs from majority sentiment or trends.[74] "What history shows," wrote Professor Barry Friedman in the most recent and thorough study in this area, "is assuredly not that Supreme Court decisions always are in line with popular opinion, but rather that they come into line with one another over time."[75] That alignment has yet to materialize nearly five decades later on the issue of school prayer, since the Court struck down the recitation of a nondenominational public school prayer in 1961.[76] A majority of Americans then and now do not agree with the Court's position. And so long as much of the public continues to want prayer in schools, the controversy will continue.

New research has shed valuable light on public knowledge and understanding of the judiciary. It turns out that Americans know more about the Supreme Court than pundits had previously acknowledged. As citizens gain knowledge about the judiciary, they are at the same time confronted with important symbols of judicial power such as the wearing of judicial robes, the use of a privileged form of address (e.g., "Your Honor"), and the requirement to rise when judges enter a court room. These symbols tend to emphasize a special role for the courts. "To know more about courts may not be to love them," wrote James L. Gibson and Gregory A. Caldeira, "but to know them is to learn and think that they are different from other political institutions (and often therefore more worthy of trust, respect, and legitimacy)."[77]

Americans today remain divided on the Supreme Court's approval with results now hovering at the low end since polling on this issue began in 2000. In 2009, the Gallup Poll showed that nearly six out of ten Americans were much more likely to approve than disapprove of the job the Supreme Court is doing.[78] Oddly, Court

Justices at Bat

At his confirmation hearings in 2005 to become the seventeenth chief justice of the United States, John G. Roberts, Jr., declared, "[I]t's my job to call balls and strikes and not to pitch or bat." But bat he did, moving the Court in a more conservative direction in 2010 and in 2014 by voting in landmark 5–4 decisions to strike down campaign finance regulation in place for more than forty years and tying money to free speech.

approval surged for Democrats and declined for Republicans even as the Court continued its conservative direction. By 2014, the Court's public approval rating hovered at 47 percent. Approval among Democrats and Independents fell to 44 percent, while approval among Republicans increased dramatically from 30 percent to 51 percent.[79]

The judicial process is imperfect, so it is not surprising that the Court will continue to step into minefields of public criticism. In 2005 the Court ruled that the Constitution did not forbid a city from taking private property for private development.[80] The outrage across the ideological spectrum was enormous and immediate. State legislatures and courts acted swiftly to give greater protection to private property. This was strong evidence that the Court's measured opinion was out of step with conventional wisdom. And while the Court sidestepped a direct challenge to California's Proposition 8 (defining marriage in the state constitution in strictly monogamous, heterosexual terms), the outcome in the lower courts made gay marriage a fact in California. At the national level in 2013, the Court struck down a portion of the Defense of Marriage Act, a federal law that sought to avoid legal recognition of gay marriage.

★ The Courts and Models of Democracy

LO6 ★ Evaluate the decision-making authority of the federal judiciary within the context of both majoritarian and pluralist democracy.

How far should judges stray from existing statutes and precedents? Supporters of the majoritarian model would argue that the courts should adhere to the letter of the law, that judges must refrain from injecting their own values into their decisions. If the law places too much (or not enough) emphasis on equality or order, the elected legislature, not the courts, can change the law. In contrast, those who support the pluralist model maintain that the courts are a policymaking branch of government. It is thus legitimate for the individual values and interests of judges to mirror group interests and preferences and for judges to attempt consciously to advance group interests as they see fit. However, judges at all levels find it difficult to determine when, where, and how to proceed.

The argument that our judicial system fits the pluralist model gains support from a legal procedure called the **class action**. A class action is a device for assembling the

class action
A procedure by which similarly situated litigants may be heard in a single lawsuit.

claims or defenses of similarly situated individuals so that they can be heard in a single lawsuit. A class action makes it possible for people with small individual claims and limited financial resources to aggregate their claims and resources and thus make a lawsuit viable. The class action also permits the case to be tried by representative parties, with the judgment binding on all. Decisions in class action suits can have broader impact than decisions in other types of cases. Since the 1940s, class action suits have been the vehicles through which groups have asserted claims involving civil rights, legislative apportionment, and environmental problems. For example, schoolchildren have sued (through their parents) under the banner of class action to rectify claimed racial discrimination on the part of school authorities, as in *Brown* v. *Board of Education.*

Abetting the class action is the resurgence of state supreme courts' fashioning policies consistent with group preferences. Informed Americans often look to the U.S. Supreme Court for protection of their rights and liberties. In many circumstances, that expectation is correct. But state courts may serve as the staging areas for legal campaigns to change the law in the nation's highest court. They also exercise substantial influence over the policies that affect citizens daily, including the rights and liberties enshrined in state constitutions, statutes, and common law.[81]

Furthermore, state judges need not look to the U.S. Supreme Court for guidance on the meaning of certain state rights and liberties. If a state court chooses to rely solely on national law in deciding a case, that case is reviewable by the U.S. Supreme Court. But a state court can avoid review by the U.S. Supreme Court by basing its decision solely on state law or by plainly stating that its decision rests on both state and federal law. If the U.S. Supreme Court is likely to render a restrictive view of a constitutional right and the judges of a state court are inclined toward a more expansive view, the state judges can use the state ground to avoid Supreme Court review. In a period when the nation's highest court is moving in a decidedly conservative direction, some state courts have become safe havens for liberal values. And individuals and groups know where to moor their policies.

The New Jersey Supreme Court has been more aggressive than most other state supreme courts in following its own liberal constitutional path. It has gone further than the U.S. Supreme Court in promoting equality at the expense of freedom by prohibiting discrimination against women by private employers and by striking down the state's public school financing system, which had perpetuated vast disparities in public education within the state. The court has also preferred freedom over order in protecting the right to terminate life-support systems and in protecting free speech against infringement.[82] The New Jersey judges have charted their own path, despite the similarity in language between sections of the New Jersey Constitution and the U.S. Constitution. And the New Jersey judges have parted company with their national cousins even when the constitutional provisions at issue were identical.[83]

For example, the U.S. Supreme Court has ruled that warrantless searches of curbside garbage are constitutionally permissible. Both the New Jersey Constitution and the U.S. Constitution bar unreasonable searches and seizures. Yet in a decision expanding constitutional protections, the New Jersey court ruled that police officers need a search warrant before they can rummage through a person's trash. The court claimed that the New Jersey Constitution offers a greater degree of privacy than the U.S. Constitution. Because the decision rested on an interpretation of the state constitution, the existence of a similar right in the national charter had no bearing. The New Jersey court cannot act in a more restrictive manner than the U.S. Supreme Court allows, but it can be—and is—less restrictive.[84] State supreme courts can turn to their own state constitutions to "raise the ceiling of liberty above the floor created by the federal Bill of Rights."[85]

When judges reach decisions, they pay attention to the views of other courts—and not just those above them in the judicial hierarchy. State and federal court opinions are the legal storehouse from which judges regularly draw their ideas. Often the issues that affect individual lives—property, family, contracts—are grist for state courts, not federal courts. For example, when a state court faces a novel issue in a contract dispute, it will look at how other state courts have dealt with the problem. (Contract disputes are not a staple of the federal courts.) And if courts in several states have addressed an issue and the direction of the opinion is largely one-sided, the weight and authority of those opinions may move the court in that direction.[86] Courts that confront new issues with cogency and clarity are likely to become leaders of legal innovation.

State courts continue to serve as arenas for political conflict, with litigants, individually or in groups, vying for their preferred policies. The multiplicity of the nation's court system, with overlapping state and national responsibilities, provides alternative points of access for individuals and groups to present and argue their claims. This description of the courts fits the pluralist model of government.

Master the Topic of The Judiciary with MindTap™ for American Government

 REVIEW MindTap™ for American Government
Access Key Term Flashcards for Chapter 14.

 TEST YOURSELF MindTap™ for American Government
Take the Wrap It Up Quiz for Chapter 14.

 STAY CURRENT MindTap™ for American Government
Access the KnowNow blog and customized RSS for updates on current events.

 STAY FOCUSED MindTap™ for American Government
Complete the Focus Activities for The Judiciary.

Summary

LO1 Define judicial review, explain the circumstances under which it was established, and assess the significance of the authority it gave the courts.

• Section 1 of Article III of the Constitution creates "one supreme Court," although in its early years the federal judiciary was not a particularly powerful branch of government. With the establishment of judicial review, the Supreme Court's power came to equal or potentially exceed the other branches. The principle of checks and balances can restrain judicial power through several means, such as constitutional amendments and impeachment. But restrictions on that power have been infrequent, leaving the federal courts to exercise considerable influence through judicial review and statutory construction.

LO2 Outline the organization of the U.S. court system and identify the principal functions of courts at each tier of the system.

• The federal court system has three tiers. At the bottom are the district courts, where litigation begins and most disputes end. In the middle are the courts of appeals. At the top is the Supreme Court. The ability of judges to make policy increases as they move up the pyramid from trial courts to appellate courts to the Supreme Court. The American legal system functions with a bias that favors existing decisions. This notion of stare decisis ("let the decision stand") provides continuity and predictability to the legal process.

LO3 Describe the process by which cases are both accepted for review and decided by the U.S. Supreme Court and analyze the role played by judicial restraint and judicial activism in judicial decisions.

- The Supreme Court harmonizes conflicting interpretations of national law and articulates constitutional rights. The Supreme Court is free to draft its agenda through the discretionary control of its docket. It is helped at this crucial stage by the solicitor general, who represents the executive branch of government before the Court. The solicitor general's influence with the justices affects their choice of cases to review. Given their capacity to accept, consider, and render opinions on issues of national import, the justices on the Supreme Court exercise real political power.

LO4 Explain how judges at different levels of the federal court system are nominated and confirmed to the federal bench.

- Political allegiance and complementary values are necessary conditions for appointment by the president to the coveted position of judge. The president and senators from the same party share appointment power in the case of federal district and appellate judges. The president has more leeway in nominating Supreme Court justices, although all nominees must be confirmed by the Senate. Recent presidents have made efforts to make the federal courts more diverse in racial, ethnic, and gender terms. When it comes

to Supreme Court appointments, however, partisan politics is the most important factor affecting which nominees are confirmed.

LO5 Examine the impact, influence, and acceptance of decisions on issues of national importance by an institution unaccountable to the electorate.

- Courts inevitably fashion policy, for each of the states and for the nation. Because the Supreme Court deals with issues that often reflect deeply felt values or political beliefs, the impact of its decisions often extends well beyond the parties in dispute. The crafting of a majority decision often means that justices must moderate their arguments and compromise in their opinions, which can reduce their overall impact on policy implementation. The relationship between the Supreme Court and public opinion is rarely highly contentious. In fact, the Court's decisions tend to come in line with the views of the general public over time.

LO6 Evaluate the decision-making authority of the federal judiciary within the context of both majoritarian and pluralist democracy.

- The courts provide multiple points of access for individuals to pursue their preferences. Furthermore, class action enables people with small individual claims and limited financial resources to pursue their goals in court, reinforcing the pluralist model. As the U.S. Supreme Court marches in a more conservative direction, some state supreme courts have become safe havens for more liberal policies on civil rights and civil liberties and for legal innovation generally. The state court systems have overlapping state and national responsibilities, offering groups and individuals additional access points to present and argue their claims.

Chapter Quiz

LO1 **Define judicial review, explain the circumstances under which it was established, and assess the significance of the authority it gave the courts.**

1. Why was the decision in *Marbury* v. *Madison* so important for the Supreme Court?
2. What are the components of judicial review?

LO2 **Outline the organization of the U.S. court system and identify the principal functions of courts at each tier of the system.**

1. List the different areas over which the U.S. district courts have authority.
2. What is precedent, and how is it used in the court system?

LO3 **Describe the process by which cases are both accepted for review and decided by the U.S. Supreme Court and analyze the role played by judicial restraint and judicial activism in judicial decisions.**

1. What are the two ways that cases arrive at the Supreme Court?
2. Distinguish between judicial restraint and judicial activism as approaches to decision making.

LO4 **Explain how judges at different levels of the federal court system are nominated and confirmed to the federal bench.**

1. How does the practice of senatorial courtesy affect the judicial appointment process?
2. Using the confirmation of a recent Supreme Court justice, explain why the appointment process to the Supreme Court can be politically contentious.

LO5 **Examine the impact, influence, and acceptance of decisions on issues of national importance by an institution unaccountable to the electorate.**

1. What factors affect the impact that Supreme Court decisions can have on policy?
2. Why are many Supreme Court decisions considered ambiguous in nature?

LO6 **Evaluate the decision-making authority of the federal judiciary within the context of both majoritarian and pluralist democracy.**

1. How does a class action make a lawsuit viable?
2. In what way can state courts diverge from the U.S. Supreme Court on specific decisions?

15 Order and Civil Liberties

Learning Outcomes

LO1 Explain the role of the Bill of Rights in protecting civil liberties and civil rights.

LO2 Identify the mechanisms that guarantee freedom of religion.

LO3 Identify the free-expression clauses and describe the scope of their protection.

LO4 Discuss the controversy over the Second Amendment and explain how Supreme Court rulings have addressed that debate.

LO5 Explain the process by which the Supreme Court extended the protections of the Bill of Rights to the local and state levels of government.

LO6 Explain how the Supreme Court interpreted the Ninth Amendment to broaden the individual's constitutional protection of personal privacy beyond the language in the Bill of Rights, a right not enumerated in the Constitution.

 WATCH & LEARN MindTap for American Government

Watch a brief "What Do You Know?" video summarizing Civil Liberties.

AP Images/File/Patrick Semansky

How many friends have you texted or e-mailed today? Did your messages include any deep personal secrets or your own views on controversial issues in your school, town, or the nation? Or consider this: Have you ever attended a party where your friends have snapped embarrassing photos of themselves—or perhaps you!—and texted them to others or tweeted them to their social networks? How would you feel if you discovered that your cell phone company or Internet provider were making it possible for government officials to monitor and capture those electronic exchanges, and even store them in federal databases?

Every day, billions of cell phone calls, text messages, pictures, and videos stream across the nation's and the world's communications systems. Flowing within this veritable ocean of information are undercurrents of activity that government officials believe they can use to help track down and apprehend some of the U.S.'s most committed enemies. Just as citizens have embraced the medium of electronic communications for connecting to friends and family, government officials in the National Security Agency (NSA), for example, also have recognized the "big data" potential that such exchanges offer.

Therein lies one of the contemporary challenges of democracy: How to ensure that citizens' liberties to develop and privately share ideas remain protected while simultaneously preserving the government's ability to maintain order by apprehending those who would do great harm.

Following the September 11 attacks, that balance tipped toward maintaining order. But in recent years, citizens and some elected officials, assisted by high-profile leakers of national secrets, have generated much pushback against government monitoring of individual communications. Major revelations have emerged since Edward Snowden, a former NSA contractor, obtained what some estimates suggest was more than 1.7 million classified items, including records of NSA efforts to monitor personal communications of Americans and world leaders.[1] Snowden shared these data with the media, and reporters have used them to describe the NSA's surveillance activities.

Some members of both major political parties have defended the NSA's work, in particular its "metadata" program, stating that it provides background information needed to "connect the dots" to identify potential threats.[2] Defenders of privacy who believe that people expressing their views should reasonably expect to be free from government monitoring have objected, calling these efforts a threat to the Constitution. They question the ultimate value of the NSA's information gathering, which the *Washington Post* has reported amounts to the retrieval of 1.7 billion e-mails, phone calls, and other communications each day.[3]

In the American political system, courts often resolve such controversies. How well do the courts respond to clashes that pit freedom against order or freedom against equality? Is freedom, order, or equality ever unconditional? In this chapter, we explore some value conflicts that the judiciary has resolved. You will be able to judge from the decisions in these cases whether the American government has met the challenge of democracy by finding the appropriate balance between freedom and order and between freedom and equality.

LISTEN & LEARN
MindTap for American Government

Access Read Speaker to listen to Chapter 15.

The value conflicts described in this chapter revolve around claims or entitlements that rest on law. Although we concentrate on conflicts over constitutional issues, the Constitution is not the only source of people's rights. Governments at all levels create rights through laws written by legislatures and regulations issued by bureaucracies.

We begin this chapter with the Bill of Rights and the freedoms it protects. Then we take a closer look at the role of the First Amendment in the original conflict between freedom and order. Next, we turn to the Fourteenth Amendment and the limits it places on the states. We then examine the Ninth Amendment and its relationship to issues of personal autonomy. In Chapter 16, we will look at the Fourteenth Amendment's promise of equal protection, which sets the stage for the modern dilemma of government: the struggle between freedom and equality.

The Bill of Rights

LO1 ★ Explain the role of the Bill of Rights in protecting civil liberties and civil rights.

You may remember from Chapter 3 that, at first, the framers of the Constitution did not include a list of individual liberties—a bill of rights—in the national charter. They believed that a bill of rights was not necessary because the Constitution spelled out the extent of the national government's power. But during the ratification debates, it became clear that the omission of a bill of rights was the most important obstacle to the adoption of the Constitution by the states. Eventually, the First Congress approved twelve amendments and sent them to the states for ratification. In 1791, the states ratified ten of the twelve amendments, and the nation had a bill of rights.

The Bill of Rights imposed limits on the national government but not on the state governments.* During the next seventy-seven years, litigants pressed the Supreme Court to extend the amendments' restraints to the states, but the Court refused until well after the adoption of the Fourteenth Amendment in 1868. Before then, protection from repressive state government had to come from state bills of rights.

The U.S. Constitution guarantees Americans numerous liberties and rights. In this chapter we explore a number of them. We will define and distinguish civil

---

*Congress considered more than one hundred amendments in its first session. One that was not approved would have limited power of the states to infringe on the rights of conscience, speech, press, and jury trial in criminal cases. James Madison thought this amendment was the "most valuable" of the list, but it failed to muster a two-thirds vote in the Senate.

Library of Congress

Russell Curtis/Science Source

To Pledge or Not to Pledge, That Is the Question

Every day, students across the United States stand, place their right hands over their hearts, and recite the Pledge of Allegiance while facing the American flag. The pledge exercise began in 1892, when Francis Bellamy proposed the right-hand-extended gesture to accompany the Pledge of Allegiance, which he authored. President Franklin D. Roosevelt instituted the hand-over-heart gesture in 1943 to avoid confusion with the Roman salute (right hand extended) used by the Italian fascists and quickly copied by the German Nazis. The picture on the left shows March 1943 grade school students saluting the flag. The picture on the right shows contemporary grade school students saluting the flag.

Some students hold religious beliefs that conflict with saluting the flag or reciting the pledge. In its 1943 ruling in *West Virginia Board of Education* v. *Barnette*, the U.S. Supreme Court upheld the right of students with religious objections to refuse to recite the pledge or salute the flag. From time to time, that ruling has been ignored or forgotten in some communities.

liberties and civil rights. (On some occasions, we use the terms interchangeably.) **Civil liberties**, sometimes referred to as "negative rights," are freedoms that are guaranteed to the individual. The guarantees take the form of restraints on government. For example, the First Amendment declares that "Congress shall make no law … abridging the freedom of speech." Civil liberties declare what the government cannot do.

In contrast, civil rights, sometimes called "positive rights," declare what the government must do or provide. **Civil rights** are powers and privileges that are guaranteed to the individual and protected against arbitrary removal at the hands of the government or other individuals. The right to vote and the right to a jury trial in criminal cases are civil rights embedded in the Constitution. Today, civil rights also embrace laws that further certain values. The Civil Rights Act of 1964, for example, furthered the value of equality by establishing the right to nondiscrimination in public accommodations and the right to equal employment opportunity. (See Table 15.1 for examples of positive and negative rights in U.S. and U.N. contexts.) Civil liberties are the subject of this chapter; we discuss equality-focused civil rights and their ramifications in Chapter 16.

The Bill of Rights lists both civil liberties and civil rights. When we refer to the rights and liberties of the Constitution, we mean the protections that are enshrined in the Bill of Rights and the first section of the Fourteenth Amendment.[4] The list includes freedom of religion, freedom of speech and of the press, the rights to assemble peaceably and to petition the government, the right to bear arms, the rights of the criminally accused, the requirement of due process, and the equal protection of the laws.

Although the idea of a written enumeration of rights seems entirely natural to Americans today, not all nations, including other advanced democratic societies, maintain a bill of rights. Unlike the United States, for example, Britain has no single document or law known as "the constitution." Instead, it has an "unwritten constitution"— a combination of important documents and laws passed by Parliament (the British

civil liberties
Freedoms guaranteed to individuals taking the form of restraint on government.

civil rights
Powers or privileges guaranteed to individuals and protected from arbitrary removal at the hands of government or individuals.

CONNECT WITH YOUR CLASSMATES
MindTap· for American Government

Access the Civil Liberties Forum: Discussion—Eighth Amendment Rights.

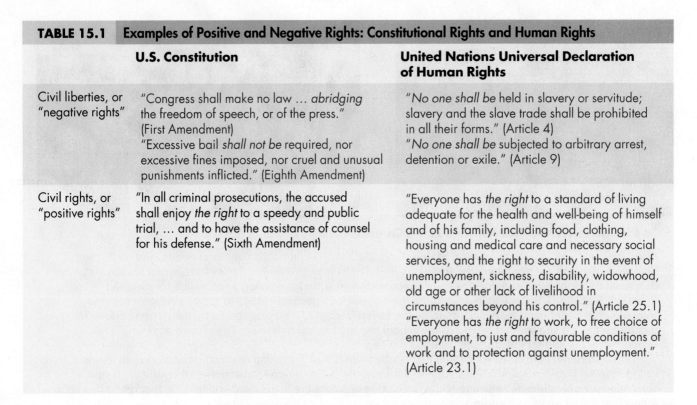

TABLE 15.1	Examples of Positive and Negative Rights: Constitutional Rights and Human Rights	
	U.S. Constitution	**United Nations Universal Declaration of Human Rights**
Civil liberties, or "negative rights"	"Congress shall make no law … *abridging* the freedom of speech, or of the press." (First Amendment) "Excessive bail *shall not be* required, nor excessive fines imposed, nor cruel and unusual punishments inflicted." (Eighth Amendment)	"*No one shall be* held in slavery or servitude; slavery and the slave trade shall be prohibited in all their forms." (Article 4) "*No one shall be* subjected to arbitrary arrest, detention or exile." (Article 9)
Civil rights, or "positive rights"	"In all criminal prosecutions, the accused shall enjoy *the right* to a speedy and public trial, … and to have the assistance of counsel for his defense." (Sixth Amendment)	"Everyone has *the right* to a standard of living adequate for the health and well-being of himself and of his family, including food, clothing, housing and medical care and necessary social services, and the right to security in the event of unemployment, sickness, disability, widowhood, old age or other lack of livelihood in circumstances beyond his control." (Article 25.1) "Everyone has *the right* to work, to free choice of employment, to just and favourable conditions of work and to protection against unemployment." (Article 23.1)

legislature), court decisions, customs, and conventions. Britain's "constitution" has no existence apart from ordinary law. A 2008 report by a joint committee of Parliament endorsed the idea of a consensus-based U.K. Bill of Rights and Freedoms emphasizing civil liberties rather than civil rights. In 2011, the U.K. Bill of Rights Commission opened up the debate to the public, launching a consultation with citizens on whether the country should have a bill of rights. The Commission published its final report in 2012, unable to agree on a path forward and leaving the question open for future debate.[5]

Some additional distinctions will prove useful in this and subsequent chapters. Persons possess *rights*, and governments possess *powers*. If governments may lawfully regulate a person's behavior (for example, requiring that you possess a valid license to drive a car), then that behavior is a privilege. Thus, you do not have a right to drive, but merely a *privilege* subject to reasonable restrictions by government. Although some rights may be spelled out in absolute language, generally no right is absolute. However, government limitations on rights are exceptional: they require a higher burden of proof and must be minimal in scope.[6]

 # Freedom of Religion

LO2 ★ Identify the mechanisms that guarantee freedom of religion.

Congress shall make no law respecting an establishment of religion, or prohibiting the free exercise thereof.

Religious freedom was important to the colonies and later to the states. That importance is reflected in its position among the ratified amendments that we know as the Bill of Rights: first, in the very first amendment. The First Amendment guarantees freedom of religion in two clauses: the **establishment clause**, which prohibits laws sponsoring or supporting religion, and the **free-exercise clause**, which prevents the government from interfering with religious practice. Together, they ensure that the government can neither promote nor inhibit religious beliefs or practices.

At the time of the Constitutional Convention, many Americans, especially in New England, maintained that government could and should foster religion, specifically Protestantism. However, many more Americans agreed that this was an issue for state governments, that the national government had no authority to meddle in religious affairs. The religion clauses were drafted in this spirit.[7]

The Supreme Court has refused to interpret the religion clauses definitively. The result is an amalgam of rulings, which collectively maintain that freedom to believe is unlimited, but freedom to practice a belief can be limited. Religion cannot benefit directly from government actions (for example, government cannot make contributions to churches or synagogues), but it can benefit indirectly from those actions (for example, government can supply books on secular subjects for use in all schools—public, private, and parochial).

Religion plays an important role in the lives of many Americans. Compared to people in Western Europe, for example, the vast majority of Americans say that religion is important in their lives, and high percentages also attest that belief in God is essential for being a moral person.[8] (See Figure 15.1.) Majoritarians might argue, then, that government should support religion. They would agree that the establishment clause bars government support of a single faith, but they might maintain that government should support all faiths. Such support would be consistent with what the majority wants and true to the language of the Constitution, they would say. In its decisions, the Supreme Court has rejected this interpretation of the establishment clause, leaving itself open to charges of undermining democracy. Those charges may be true with regard to majoritarian democracy, but the Court can justify its protection in terms of the basic values of democratic government.

establishment clause
The first clause in the First Amendment, which forbids government establishment of religion.

free-exercise clause
The second clause in the First Amendment, which prevents the government from interfering with the exercise of religion.

FIGURE 15.1 Percent of Respondents in the U.S. and Western Europe Saying Religion Is "Very Important," 2002–2011

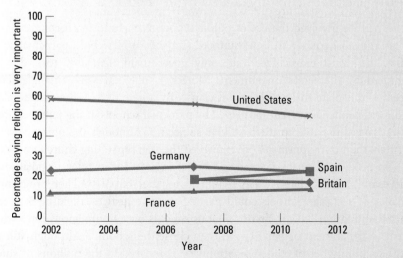

Source: Pew Research Center Global Attitudes Project, "The American Western-European Values Gap," 29 February 2012, http://www.pewglobal.org/2011/11/17/the-american-western-european-values-gap/.

The Establishment Clause

The provision that "Congress shall make no law respecting an establishment of religion" bars government sponsorship or support of religious activity. The Supreme Court has consistently held that the establishment clause requires government to maintain a position of neutrality toward religions and to maintain that position in cases that involve choices between religion and nonreligion. However, the Court has never interpreted the clause as barring all assistance that incidentally aids religious institutions, rendering the resulting legal landscape incoherent.[9]

Government Support of Religion. In 1879, the Supreme Court contended, quoting Thomas Jefferson, that the establishment clause erected "a wall of separation between church and State."[10] That wall was breached somewhat in 1947, when the justices upheld a local government program that provided free transportation to parochial school students.[11] The breach seemed to widen in 1968, when the Court held constitutional a government program in which parochial school students borrowed state-purchased textbooks.[12] The objective of the program, reasoned the majority, was to further educational opportunity. The students, not the schools, borrowed the books, and the parents, not the church, realized the benefits.

But in 1971, in **Lemon v. Kurtzman,*** the Court struck down a state program that would have helped pay the salaries of teachers hired by parochial schools to give instruction in secular subjects.[13] The justices proposed a three-pronged test for determining the constitutionality of government programs and laws under the establishment clause:

- They must have a secular purpose (such as lending books to parochial school students).
- Their primary effect must not be to advance or inhibit religion.
- They must not entangle the government excessively with religion.

The program in *Lemon* did not satisfy the last prong. The government would have had to monitor the program constantly, thus ensuring an excessive entanglement with religion. The *Lemon* test, as it became known, governed the Supreme Court's interpretation of such cases for twenty-five years. Then in 1997, the Court dramatically loosened its application of the test in a case reminiscent of the one that gave rise to it. The future of the test now seems uncertain.

The case involved the use of public school teachers to teach congressionally mandated remedial courses to disadvantaged students in New York parochial schools. This time, the Court emphasized that only government *neutrality* toward religion was required by the First Amendment. Moreover, only *excessive* entanglements will be deemed to violate the establishment clause. By a vote of 5–4, the Court held that religion was neither hindered nor helped by parochial schools' using public school teachers at taxpayers' expense to teach secular subjects.[14] Although the opinion was narrowly written, the Court appears to have lowered the wall separating church and state.

In 2002, the Court provided additional support for its tolerant position regarding the establishment clause when it upheld a state school-voucher program in which secular or sectarian schools could participate. The justices, dividing 5–4, maintained that the program did not favor religious schools over nonreligious ones when the aid went to the student or parent who then chose the school.[15] Although still reaching a very small number of students nationwide compared to the millions of students who attend public schools, similar programs have expanded across the country since the

---

*Key cases are highlighted in bold, and a list of key cases appears at the end of the chapter.

Court's ruling. During the 2013–2014 school year, for example, school vouchers served more than 115,000 students across eleven states and the District of Columbia.[16]

Consider another thorny issue. Does the display of religious artifacts on public property violate the establishment clause? In *Lynch* v. *Donnelly* (1984), the Court said no, by a vote of 5–4.[17] At issue was a publicly funded nativity scene on public property, surrounded by commercial symbols of the Christmas season such as Santa and his sleigh. Although he conceded that a crèche has religious significance, Chief Justice Warren E. Burger, writing for the majority, maintained that the display had a legitimate secular purpose: the celebration of a national holiday. Second, the display did not have the primary effect of benefiting religion; the religious benefits were "indirect, remote and incidental." And third, the display led to no excessive entanglement of religion and government. The justices hinted at a relaxation of their interpretation of the establishment clause by asserting an "unwillingness to be confined to any single test or criterion in this sensitive area." The upshot of *Lynch* was an acknowledgment of the religious heritage of the majority of Americans, although the Christmas holiday is a vivid reminder to religious minorities and the nonreligious of their separateness from the dominant Christian culture.

The *Lynch* decision led to a proliferation of closely decided and confusing cases testing the limits of government-sponsored religious displays. A pair of cases in 2005 involved a forty-year-old monument displaying the Ten Commandments on the Texas state capitol and a display of the Ten Commandments in two Kentucky county courthouses. In separate 5–4 rulings, the justices declined to apply the *Lemon* test but upheld the Texas display because of the monument's "secular purpose";[18] and, on the same day, the Court applied the *Lemon* test to strike down the Kentucky courthouse displays because they were not integrated into a secular presentation and so had a primarily religious purpose.[19]

The Court continued to struggle with the limits of government entanglement with religious symbols. In 2010, a badly splintered 5–4 ruling in *Salazar* v. *Buono* generated six separate opinions holding that a five-by-eight-foot cross—originally made of wood but more recently made of four-inch metal pipe—erected by the Veterans of Foreign Wars on federal land to honor World War I veterans did not violate the establishment clause.[20] The federal government faced a dilemma: leaving the cross in place would violate the establishment clause, but removing the cross would show "disrespect for those the cross was seen as honoring," wrote Justice Anthony M. Kennedy for the majority. The solution at issue in the case was a land swap in which the government traded the public land for private property, enabling the cross to remain. But the land trade could be viewed as promoting religion, argued Justice John Paul Stevens in dissent. Such cases are sure to continue as the Court's majority coalition moves in a more conservative direction.

Prayer in School and Other Settings. The Supreme Court has consistently equated prayer in public schools with government support of religion. In 1962, it struck down the daily reading of this twenty-two-word nondenominational prayer in New York's public schools: "Almighty God, we acknowledge our dependence upon Thee, and we beg Thy blessings upon us, our parents, our teachers and our country." Justice Hugo L. Black, writing for a 6–1 majority, held that official state approval of prayer was an unconstitutional attempt on the part of the state to establish a religion. This decision, in **Engel v. Vitale**, drew a storm of protest that has yet to subside.[21]

The following year, the Court struck down a state law calling for daily Bible reading and recitation of the Lord's Prayer in Pennsylvania's public schools.[22] The school district defended the reading and recitation on the grounds that they taught literature, perpetuated traditional institutions, and inculcated moral virtues. But the Court held that the state's involvement violated the government's constitutionally imposed neutrality in matters of religion.

Gretchen Ertl/The New York Times/Redux

A Standout in Her Class

Jessica Ahlquist took a brave stand in her Cranston, Rhode Island, high school by objecting to the display of a Christian prayer in the school auditorium. She was ostracized by her classmates and community, but with the help of the American Civil Liberties Union, she prevailed in federal court. When asked by a reporter if she empathized with those who wanted to retain the prayer banner, she replied: "It's almost like making a child get a shot even though they don't want to. It's for their own good. I feel like they might see it as a very negative thing right now, but I'm defending their Constitution, too."

In 1992, the Court struck down the offering of nonsectarian prayers at official public school graduations. In a 5–4 decision, the Court held that government involvement creates "a state-sponsored and state-directed religious exercise in a public school."[23] The justices said that the establishment clause means that government may not conduct a religious exercise in the context of a school event.

Yet the issue of school prayer remains. In 2008, the Indian River school district in Sussex County, Delaware, agreed to revise its policies that had tolerated Christian prayer at school functions in clear violation of prior Supreme Court rulings. The settlement, which arose from a lawsuit by two Jewish families, created enormous ill will. One family was forced to move after facing threats and harassment when Christian community members viewed the lawsuit as an effort to limit their free exercise of religion.[24] Soon thereafter, tensions arose over a similar challenge at Cranston High School West in Rhode Island. For forty-nine years, an eight-by-four-foot banner hung in the school auditorium bore the Christian prayer beseeching, "Our Heavenly Father, grant us each day the desire to do our best, to grow mentally and morally as well as physically, to be kind and helpful." The prayer continued for a few more lines before concluding with "Amen." Sixteen-year-old junior Jessica Ahlquist, an avowed atheist, objected to the prayer and, with the assistance of the American Civil Liberties Union, sought the banner's removal. The town was divided over the matter, and Jessica was ostracized for her advocacy. Yet in January 2012, federal judge Roger R. Lagueux ruled that the prayer violated the principle of government neutrality in religion and ordered the permanent removal of the banner.[25]

Religious training during public school is out-of-bounds, but religious training after school now passes constitutional muster. In 2001, the Supreme Court ruled that public schools must open their doors to after-school religious activities on the same basis as other after-school programs such as the debate club. To do otherwise would constitute viewpoint discrimination in violation of the free speech clause of the First Amendment.

Public schools are not the only government institutions where controversies over prayer have reached the nation's highest court. In 2014, the Supreme Court examined a different version of public prayer in *Town of Greece* v. *Galloway*. In 1999, the Town Board of Greece, New York, began a tradition of having a local religious leader open its meeting with a prayer. All such prayers from 1999–2007 were offered by individuals expressing a Christian faith, sometimes explicitly in the context of their remarks, in contrast to using more religiously inclusive language. Susan Galloway, a town resident, sued arguing that the practice violated the establishment clause. In a 5–4 decision, the Court rejected Galloway's claim and pointed to the tradition of legislatures across the country beginning their sessions with a prayer, which the majority did not find to be coercive. The dissenters argued that the town's practices marginalized followers of faiths other than Christianity, and in doing so violated the establishment clause by expressing a preference for one particular religion.[26]

The establishment clause creates a problem for government. Support for all religions at the expense of nonreligion seems to pose the least risk to social order. Tolerance of the dominant religion at the expense of other religions risks minority discontent, but support for no religion (neutrality between religion and nonreligion) risks majority discontent.

The Free-Exercise Clause

The free-exercise clause of the First Amendment states that "Congress shall make no law … prohibiting the free exercise [of religion]." The Supreme Court has struggled to avoid absolute interpretations of this restriction and thus avoid its complement, the establishment clause. An example: suppose Congress grants exemptions from military service to individuals who have religious scruples against war. These exemptions could be construed as a violation of the establishment clause because they favor some religious groups over others. But if Congress forced conscientious objectors to fight—to violate their religious beliefs—the government would run afoul

Praying Before Legislating

Reverend Kevin Kisler from the Covenant Orthodox Presbyterian Church helps to start the Greece Town Board meeting with a prayer. Although some people believe that divine intervention could help to improve the legislative process, others have argued that beginning such meetings with a moment of prayer violates the establishment clause of the First Amendment. The U.S. Supreme Court disagreed with those critics and narrowly upheld the practice in a 5–4 decision in 2014.

of the free-exercise clause. In fact, Congress has granted military draftees such exemptions. But the Supreme Court has avoided a conflict between the establishment and free-exercise clauses by equating religious objection to war with any deeply held humanistic opposition to it. This solution leaves unanswered a central question: Does the free-exercise clause require government to grant exemptions from legal duties that conflict with religious obligations, or does it guarantee only that the law will be applicable to religious believers without discrimination or preference?[27]

In the free-exercise cases, the justices have distinguished religious beliefs from actions based on those beliefs. Beliefs are inviolate, beyond the reach of government control. But the First Amendment does not protect antisocial actions. Consider conflicting values about working on the Sabbath.

The modern era of free-exercise thinking began with **Sherbert v. Verner** (1963). Adeil Sherbert, a Seventh-Day Adventist, lost her mill job because she refused to work on Saturday, her Sabbath. She filed for unemployment compensation and was referred to another job, which she declined because it also required Saturday work. Because she declined the job, the state disqualified her from receiving unemployment benefits. In a 7–2 decision, the Supreme Court ruled that the disqualification imposed an impermissible burden on Sherbert's free exercise of religion. The First Amendment, declared the majority, protects observance as well as belief. A neutral law that burdens the free exercise of religion is subject to **strict scrutiny**. This means that the law may be upheld only if the government can demonstrate that (1) the law is justified by a "compelling governmental interest," (2) the law is narrowly tailored to achieve a legitimate goal, and

strict scrutiny
A standard used by the Supreme Court in deciding whether a law or policy is to be adjudged constitutional. To pass strict scrutiny, the law or policy must be justified by a "compelling governmental interest," must be narrowly tailored, and must be the least restrictive means for achieving that interest.

(3) the law in question is the least restrictive means for achieving that interest.[28] Scholars had long maintained that strict scrutiny was "strict in theory but fatal in fact." A recent empirical study debunked this claim, finding that in all strict scrutiny cases from 1990 to 2003, the federal courts upheld nearly one-third of the challenged laws.[29] The strict scrutiny standard sets a high bar but not an insurmountable one.

The *Sherbert* decision prompted religious groups and individual believers to challenge laws that conflict with their faith. We have seen how conflicts arise from the imposition of penalties for refusing to engage in religiously prohibited conduct. But conflicts may also arise from laws that impose penalties for engaging in religiously motivated conduct.[30] For example, neutral criminal laws apply to individuals who use illegal drugs as part of a religious ceremony; and, government may withhold unemployment benefits from workers who have been dismissed from their jobs because they used illegal drugs in a religious ceremony.[31]

Courts continue to face the challenge of line-drawing between religious belief and religious conduct as they determine the limits of the free-exercise clause. In fact, this tension was the source of a recent court challenge to the Affordable Care Act, also known as "Obamacare." In oral argument in November 2013, the Supreme Court heard *Sebelius* v. *Hobby Lobby Stores*. In that case, the Green family, owners of Hobby Lobby, an arts and crafts chain with 500 locations and 13,000 employees, argued that the Affordable Care Act's requirement that employer-based health insurance plans provide coverage for contraceptives violated the free-exercise clause of the First Amendment and the Religious Freedom Restoration Act of 1993 (RFRA). The Greens contended they have organized their business around their Christian faith and they argued that requiring them to support insurance coverage for contraception would violate their constitutional rights, implying that corporations, in addition to individuals, can claim rights under the free-exercise clause. A divided Supreme Court held 5–4 in favor of Hobby Lobby. Justice Alito's majority opinion agreed that the RFRA did apply to corporations, and further that the religious exemptions that the Department of Health and Human Services has issued to religious nonprofit institutions in implementing the law also should apply to private for-profit organizations like Hobby Lobby. Writing for the dissenters, Justice Ginsburg argued that the majority's opinion conflicted with prior Supreme Court reasoning, and that its RFRA interpretation was incorrect because for-profit corporations, by definition, are not considered religious organizations under the law.[32]

Freedom of Expression

LO3 ★ Identify the free-expression clauses and describe the scope of their protection.

> Congress shall make no law … abridging the freedom of speech, or of the press; or the right of the people peaceably to assemble, and to petition the Government for a redress of grievances.

James Madison introduced the original versions of the speech clause and the press clause of the First Amendment in the House of Representatives in June 1789. One early proposal provided that "the people shall not be deprived of their right to speak, to write, or to publish their sentiments, and the freedom of the press, as one of the great bulwarks of liberty, shall be inviolable." That version was rewritten several times, then merged with the religion and peaceable assembly clauses to yield the First Amendment.

The spare language of the First Amendment seems perfectly clear: "Congress shall make no law … abridging the freedom of speech, or of the press." Yet a majority of the Supreme Court has never agreed that this "most majestic guarantee" is absolutely inviolable.[33] Historians have long debated the framers' intentions regarding these **free-expression clauses**, the press and speech clauses of the First Amendment. The dominant view is that the clauses confer a right to unrestricted discussion of public affairs.[34] Other scholars, examining much the same evidence, conclude that few, if any, of the framers clearly understood the clause; moreover, they insist that the First Amendment does not rule out prosecution for seditious statements (statements inciting insurrection).[35]

free-expression clauses
The press and speech clauses of the First Amendment.

The license to speak freely does not move multitudes of Americans to speak out on controversial issues. Americans have woven subtle restrictions into the fabric of our society: the risk of criticism or ostracism by family, peers, or employers tends to reduce the number of people who test the limits of free speech to individuals ready to bear the burdens. As Mark Twain once remarked, "It is by the goodness of God that in our country we have three unspeakably precious things: freedom of speech, freedom of conscience, and the prudence never to practice either of them."[36]

Today, the clauses are deemed to bar most forms of **prior restraint**—censorship before publication as well as after-the-fact prosecution for political and other discourse. The Supreme Court has evolved two approaches to the resolution of claims based on the free-expression clauses. First, government can regulate or punish the advocacy of ideas, but only if it can prove an intent to promote lawless action and demonstrate that a high probability exists that such action will occur.[37] Second, government may impose reasonable restrictions on the means for communicating ideas, restrictions that can incidentally discourage free expression. Hence, people have the right to protest but not if their physical presence would block the entrance to an occupied public building. Governments around the world have different views on what constitutes speech that is a threat to public safety, including views that would be offensive in democratic societies, as our discussion of China and the Internet in this chapter illustrates (see "Order and Civil Liberties in Global Politics: Internet Censorship in China").

prior restraint
Censorship before publication.

Suppose, for example, that a political party advocates nonpayment of personal income taxes. Government cannot regulate or punish that party for advocating tax nonpayment because the standards of proof—that the act be directed at inciting or producing imminent lawless action and that the act be likely to produce such action—do not apply. But government can impose restrictions on the way the party's candidates communicate what they are advocating. Government can bar them from blaring messages from loudspeakers in residential neighborhoods at 3:00 A.M.

Freedom of Speech

The starting point for any modern analysis of free speech is the **clear and present danger test**, formulated by Justice Oliver Wendell Holmes in the Supreme Court's unanimous decision in *Schenck v. United States* (1919). Charles T. Schenck and his fellow defendants were convicted under a federal criminal statute for attempting to disrupt World War I military recruitment by distributing leaflets claiming that conscription was unconstitutional. The government believed this behavior threatened the public order. At the core of the Court's opinion, Holmes wrote, was the view that

clear and present danger test
A means by which the Supreme Court has distinguished between speech as the advocacy of ideas, which is protected by the First Amendment, and speech as incitement, which is not protected.

> the character of every act depends upon the circumstances in which it is done. … The most stringent protection of free speech would not protect a man in falsely shouting fire in a theatre, and causing a panic. … The question

Order and Civil Liberties in Global Politics: Internet Censorship in China

Autocratic leaders around the world have gambled that their hold on power relies upon their ability to maintain order at all costs, which includes curtailing individual freedoms that citizens in democratic nations often take for granted. Global developments in communication have made it more difficult for these regimes to keep their grip, as their opponents have found increasing outlets for promoting their ideas.

The development of the Internet and social networking sites have been a boon for democratic movements across the globe. Members of the Green Movement in Iran, for example, used social media and other sites to transmit images of government violence following the disputed 2009 election in which Iranian President Mahmoud Ahmadinejad was declared the victor. As one author noted, "The Green movement remains the first major world event broadcast worldwide almost entirely via social media."* Similarly, uprisings during the Arab Spring of 2011 prompted an explosion of social media activity. Researchers at the University of Washington found, for example, when Hosni Mubarak resigned as president of Egypt, the number of tweets coming from that nation rose dramatically from 2,300 per day to 230,000 per day.**

Autocratic regimes are aware of how the freedom to communicate online can threaten their survival. In attempting to insulate themselves from criticism, some of these governments have made aggressive efforts to silence such exchanges of information by blocking Internet traffic or pushing back with their own aggressive media campaigns to brand their critics as traitors and threats to national order.

Recent research by political scientists has revealed how China has used more subtle techniques to control the flow of online information that the nation's

---

*Jared Keller, "Evaluating Iran's Twitter Revolution," *The Atlantic*, 18 June 2010.

**Catherine O'Donnell, "New Study Quantifies Use of Social Media in Arab Spring," University of Washington News Release, 12 September 2011, http://www.washington.edu/news/2011/09/12/new-study-quantifies-use-of-social-media-in-arab-spring/.

---

in every case is whether the words used are used in such circumstances and are of such a nature as to create *a clear and present danger* that they will bring about the substantive evils that Congress has a right to prevent. It is a question of proximity and degree. When a nation is at war many things that might be said in time of peace are such a hindrance to its effort that their utterance will not be endured so long as men fight, and that no court could regard them as protected by any constitutional right [emphasis added].[38]

Because the actions of the defendants in *Schenck* were deemed to create a clear and present danger to the United States at that time, the Supreme Court upheld the defendants' convictions. The clear and present danger test helps distinguish between the advocacy of ideas, a protected right, and incitement, which is not protected. However, Holmes later frequently disagreed with a majority of his colleagues in applying the test. In an oft-quoted dissent in *Abrams* v. *United States* (1919), Holmes revealed

leaders believe poses potential threats to the communist regime's security.[†] The authors call China's efforts possibly "the most extensive effort to selectively censor human expression ever implemented." To study China's online censorship, the researchers developed an ingenious data collection procedure that allowed them to pull from the Internet millions of posts to Chinese social media sites before the government's censors could erase them. That allowed the researchers to compare the presence of information before and after the censors had an opportunity to pull down posts that they disliked.

The study's main findings showed that the government's censors do allow some free expression of opposing views, but simultaneously they act quickly to take down other views that they perceive to be a threat to order. How does the government decide which criticisms should be allowed to stay and which are too threatening? The researchers showed that the regime is most wary of communications that are critical of the government *and* have the potential to spark broader collective action against it. Posts to social media sites that critique the government, sometimes with much vitriol, but do not appear to have the potential to spur wider action were ignored by censors.

As the study's authors note in their conclusion, the government's effort to quash mobilizing speech while allowing individual critics to voice their opinions means that "the Chinese people are individually free but collectively in chains." In other words, while Chinese leaders may identify the presence of online government criticism as evidence that their efforts pose no threat to free expression, the research findings reveal a careful and subtle form of repression that is crafted to maintain order and ensure the survival of the nation's one-party state.

> **Critical Thinking** How might critics of the Chinese government use the research findings described above to adjust their strategies and tactics as they attempt to use electronic media to mobilize others?

[†]Gary King, Jennifer Pan, and Margaret E. Roberts, "How Censorship in China Allows Government Criticism but Silences Collective Expression," *American Political Science Review* 107 (May 2013): 326–343.

his deeply rooted resistance to the suppression of ideas. The majority had upheld Jacob Abrams's criminal conviction for distributing leaflets that denounced the war and U.S. opposition to the Russian Revolution. Holmes wrote:

> When men have realized that time has upset many fighting faiths, they may come to believe … that the ultimate good desired is better reached by free trade in ideas—that the best test of truth is the power of the thought to get itself accepted in the competition of the market, and that truth is the only ground upon which their wishes safely can be carried out. That at any rate is the theory of our Constitution.[39]

In 1925, the Court issued a landmark free-expression decision in *Gitlow* v. *New York*.[40] Benjamin Gitlow was arrested for distributing copies of a "left-wing manifesto" that called for the establishment of socialism through strikes and working-class uprisings of any form. Gitlow was convicted under a state criminal anarchy law; Schenck and Abrams had been convicted under a federal law. For the first time, the Court assumed that the First Amendment speech and press provisions applied to the states through the due process clause of the Fourteenth Amendment. Still, a majority of the justices affirmed Gitlow's conviction. Justices Holmes and Louis D. Brandeis argued in dissent that Gitlow's ideas did not pose a clear and present danger. "Eloquence may set fire to reason," conceded the dissenters. "But whatever may be thought of the redundant discourse before us, it had no chance of starting a present conflagration."

The protection of advocacy faced yet another challenge in 1948, when eleven members of the Communist Party were charged with violating the Smith Act, a federal law making the advocacy of force or violence against the United States a criminal offense. The leaders were convicted, although the government introduced no evidence that they had actually urged people to commit specific violent acts. The Supreme Court mustered a majority for its decision to uphold the convictions under the act, but it could not get a majority to agree on the reasons in support of that decision. The biggest bloc, of four justices, announced the plurality opinion in 1951, arguing that the government's interest was substantial enough to warrant criminal penalties.[41] The justices interpreted the threat to the government to be the gravity of the advocated action, "discounted by its improbability." In other words, a single soapbox orator advocating revolution stands little chance of success. But a well-organized, highly disciplined political movement advocating revolution in the tinderbox of unstable political conditions stands a greater chance of success. In broadening the "clear and present danger" test to the "grave and probable danger" test, the Court held that the government was justified in acting preventively rather than waiting until revolution was about to occur.

By 1969, the pendulum had swung back in the other direction: the justices began to put more emphasis on freedom. That year, in ***Brandenburg v. Ohio***, a unanimous decision widened the freedom of speech to new boundaries.[42] Clarence Brandenburg, the leader of the Ohio Ku Klux Klan, had been convicted under a state law for advocating racial strife at a Klan rally. His comments, which had been filmed by a television crew, included threats against government officials.

The Court reversed Brandenburg's conviction because the government had failed to prove that the danger was real. The Court went even further and declared that threatening speech is protected by the First Amendment unless the government can prove that such advocacy is "directed to inciting or producing imminent lawless action and is likely to incite or produce such action." The ruling offered wider latitude for the expression of political ideas than ever before in the nation's history.

The United States stands alone when it comes to protection for hateful speech. Several democratic nations—including Canada, England, France, Germany, the Netherlands, South Africa, Australia, and India—have laws or have signed international conventions banning such speech. Nazi swastikas and flags are forbidden for sale in Israel and France but not in the United States. Anyone who denies the Holocaust in Canada, Germany, and France is subject to criminal prosecution but not in the United States. Some scholars have begun to urge a relaxation of our stringent speech protections because we now live "in an age when words have inspired acts of mass murder and terrorism."[43]

Symbolic Expression. Symbolic expression, or nonverbal communication, generally receives less protection than pure speech. But the courts have upheld certain types of symbolic expression. ***Tinker v. Des Moines Independent County School District*** (1969) involved three public school students who wore black armbands to school to protest the Vietnam War. Principals in their school district had prohibited the wearing of armbands on the grounds that such conduct would provoke a disturbance; the district suspended the students. The Supreme Court overturned the suspensions. Justice Abe Fortas declared for the majority that the principals had failed to show that the forbidden conduct would substantially interfere with appropriate school discipline:

> Undifferentiated fear or apprehension of disturbance is not enough to overcome the right to freedom of expression. Any departure from absolute regimentation may cause trouble. Any variation from the majority's opinion may inspire fear. Any word spoken, in class, in the lunchroom, or on the campus, that deviates from the views of another person may start an argument or cause a disturbance. But our Constitution says we must take this risk.[44]

Symbolic expression continues to be an important issue that courts have considered, and their judgments about it now must tackle free speech in new arenas. Consider, for example, the now common act of "liking" a person or organization on Facebook. Is clicking a Facebook site's thumbs-up icon protected symbolic speech under the First Amendment? This question arose when Daniel Ray Carter, Jr., an employee in the local sheriff's office in Hampton, Virginia, liked the page of a candidate who in 2011 was running for sheriff against his current boss. Carter claimed that upon learning of his support for the challenger, incumbent Hampton sheriff B. J. Roberts became "incensed" and approximately one month after Roberts won the election, Carter was fired.[45] He claimed that Roberts's actions violated his First Amendment rights. In a much-watched lower-court decision, the U.S. Court of Appeals for the 4th Circuit agreed. In its decision, issued in 2013, the three-judge panel wrote that liking a Facebook page "is the Internet equivalent of displaying a political sign in one's front yard, which the Supreme Court has held is substantive speech."

Order versus Free Speech: Fighting Words and Threatening Expression.
Fighting words are a notable exception to the protection of free speech. In *Chaplinsky* v. *New Hampshire* (1942), Walter Chaplinsky, a Jehovah's Witness, convicted under a state statute for calling a city marshal a "God-damned racketeer" and "a damned fascist" in a public place, appealed to the Supreme Court.[46] The Supreme Court upheld Chaplinsky's conviction on the theory that **fighting words**—words that "inflict injury or tend to incite an immediate breach of the peace"—do not convey ideas and thus are not subject to First Amendment protection.

The Court sharply narrowed the definition of fighting words just seven years later. Arthur Terminiello, a suspended Catholic priest from Alabama and a vicious anti-Semite, addressed the Christian Veterans of America, a right-wing extremist group, in a Chicago hall. Terminiello called the jeering crowd of fifteen hundred angry protesters outside the hall "slimy scum" and ranted on about the "communistic, Zionistic" Jews of America, evoking cries of "kill the Jews" and "dirty kikes" from his listeners. The crowd outside the hall heaved bottles, bricks, and rocks, while the police attempted to protect Terminiello and his listeners inside. Finally, the police arrested Terminiello for disturbing the peace.

Terminiello's speech was far more incendiary than Walter Chaplinsky's. Yet the Supreme Court struck down Terminiello's conviction on the ground that provocative speech, even speech that stirs people to anger, is protected by the First Amendment. "Freedom of speech," wrote Justice William O. Douglas in the majority opinion, "though not absolute ... is nevertheless protected against censorship or punishment, unless shown likely to produce a clear ... and present danger of a serious substantive evil that rises far above public inconvenience, annoyance, or unrest."

fighting words
Speech that is not protected by the First Amendment because it inflicts injury or tends to incite an immediate disturbance of the peace.

This broad view of protection brought a stiff rebuke in Justice Robert Jackson's dissenting opinion:

> The choice is not between order and liberty. It is between liberty with order and anarchy without either. There is danger that, if the court does not temper its doctrinaire logic with a little practical wisdom, it will convert the constitutional Bill of Rights into a suicide pact.[47]

The times seem to have caught up with the idealism that Jackson criticized in his colleagues. In ***Cohen* v. *California*** (1971), a nineteen-year-old department store worker expressed his opposition to the Vietnam War by wearing a jacket in the hallway of a Los Angeles County courthouse emblazoned with the words "FUCK THE DRAFT. STOP THE WAR." The young man, Paul Cohen, was charged in 1968 under a California statute that prohibits "maliciously and willfully disturb[ing] the peace and quiet of any neighborhood or person [by] offensive conduct." He was found guilty and sentenced to thirty days in jail. On appeal, the U.S. Supreme Court reversed Cohen's conviction.

The Court reasoned that the expletive he used, while provocative, was not directed at anyone in particular; besides, the state presented no evidence that the words on Cohen's jacket would provoke people in "substantial numbers" to take some kind of physical action. In recognizing that "one man's vulgarity is another's lyric," the Supreme Court protected two elements of speech: the emotive (the expression of emotion) and the cognitive (the expression of ideas).[48]

Order versus Free Speech: When Words Hurt. The First Amendment protects a person's ability to address matters of public importance even if the speech is hurtful. But speech of a purely private matter receives less protection. What happens when the speech in question contains a mix of public and private matters?

For more than twenty years, members of the Westboro Baptist Church have picketed funerals to communicate their belief that God punishes the United States and its military for tolerating homosexuality. Displaying signs that read, "Thank God for dead soldiers" and "Fag troops," the church pastor and a handful of members picketed the funeral of Marine Lance Corporal Matthew Snyder. Matthew's father was deeply offended by the picketing and sued the pastor and the church for the intentional infliction of emotional distress. He won a judgment of $5 million, which a federal appeals court reversed. Snyder appealed to the U.S. Supreme Court.

In ***Snyder* v. *Phelps*** (2011), the Supreme Court affirmed the appeals court ruling supporting the free-expression rights of the church and its pastor on the grounds that the messages displayed concerned a matter of public importance and were delivered from public property. Writing for the eight-member majority, Chief Justice John G. Roberts, Jr., concluded that the signs unequivocally addressed public concerns and the picketers congregated on public land. Moreover, the ideas expressed, though hateful, could not be censored on the grounds that they were offensive.

Equality and Free Speech. Recall from Chapter 9 that in 2010, the Supreme Court held in ***Citizens United* v. *Federal Election Commission*** that corporations and labor unions may spend freely but transparently to advocate the election or defeat of political candidates. The Court further expanded the ability of citizens to make financial contributions to candidates in its 2013 ruling in *McCutcheon* v. *Federal Election Commission*.[49] In a 5–4 decision, the justices found unconstitutional FEC rules limiting the total amount of money over the two-year federal election cycle that individuals could contribute to federal candidates. While limits on specific contributions to candidates could remain, the aggregate limits on contributions that had been in place—$48,600 to all federal candidates and $74,600 to party committees—violated the First Amendment. Illustrating the Court's sharp and lingering disagreement over the issue of campaign finance, dating back to the 2010 *Citizens United* decision, Justice Stephen Breyer issued a rare dissent from the bench, arguing that "If the court in *Citizens United* opened a door, today's decision may well open a floodgate," which Breyer suggested would increase the influence of money in elections.[50]

We can make sense of the *Citizens United* and *McCutcheon* cases and the vast array of free speech cases through the prism of freedom and equality. On the one hand, freedom of speech promotes the interest of political equality by assuring that speech rights apply to everyone (anarchists, flag burners, communists, and others with marginal or unorthodox views). On the other hand, freedom of speech serves the interest of political liberty by removing government restrictions on political speech, including limits on corporate or union speech. In the *Citizens United* and *McCutcheon* decisions, political liberty trumped political equality, allowing the wealthy few to have the loudest voice among the many.[51]

Freedom of the Press

The First Amendment guarantees that government "shall make no law ... abridging the freedom ... of the press." Although the free press guarantee was originally adopted as a restriction on the national government, since 1931 the Supreme Court has held that it applies to state and local governments as well.

The ability to collect and report information without government interference was (and still is) thought to be essential to a free society. The print media continue to use and defend the freedom conferred on them by the framers. However, the electronic media have had to accept some government regulation stemming from the scarcity of broadcast frequencies (see Chapter 6).

Defamation of Character. Libel is the written defamation of character.* A person who believes his or her name and character have been harmed by false statements in a publication can institute a lawsuit against the publication and seek monetary compensation for the damage. Such a lawsuit can impose limits on freedom of expression; at the same time, false statements impinge on the rights of individuals. In a landmark decision in **New York Times v. Sullivan** (1964), the Supreme Court declared that freedom of the press takes precedence—at least when the defamed individual is a public official.[52] The Court unanimously agreed that the First Amendment protects the publication of all statements—even false ones—about the conduct of public officials, except statements made with actual malice (with knowledge that they are false or in reckless disregard for their truth or falsity).

Three years later, the Court extended this protection to apply to suits brought by any public figure, whether a government official or not. **Public figures** are people who assume roles of prominence in society or thrust themselves to the forefront of public controversies, including officials, actors, writers, and television personalities. These people must show actual malice on the part of the publication that printed false statements about them. Because the burden of proof is so great, few plaintiffs prevail. And freedom of the press is the beneficiary.

public figures
People who assume roles of prominence in society or thrust themselves to the forefront of public controversy.

Prior Restraint and the Press. As discussed above, in the United States, freedom of the press has primarily meant protection from prior restraint, or censorship. The Supreme Court's first encounter with a law imposing prior restraint on a

---

*Slander is the oral defamation of character. The durability of the written word usually means that libel is a more serious accusation than slander.

Evelyn Hockstein/For The Washington Post/Getty Images for Ellsberg.
Mark Wilson/Getty Images News/Getty Images for Manning

Following in His Footsteps

Daniel Ellsberg (left), who leaked the Pentagon Papers to the *New York Times*, has called Bradley Manning (right, today known as Chelsea Manning) a hero for disclosing classified government documents to the media that described U.S. efforts in Iraq and Afghanistan. Despite protests from others, including Ellsberg, who here is being arrested at a demonstration supporting Manning's actions, Manning was convicted in July 2013 for violating the Espionage Act and sentenced to thirty-five years of confinement.

newspaper was in *Near* v. *Minnesota* (1931).[53] In Minneapolis, Jay Near published a scandal sheet in which he attacked local officials, charging that they were in league with gangsters.[54] Minnesota officials obtained an injunction to prevent Near from publishing his newspaper, under a state law that allowed such action against periodicals deemed "malicious, scandalous, and defamatory."

The Supreme Court struck down the law, declaring that prior restraint places an unacceptable burden on a free press. Chief Justice Charles Evans Hughes forcefully articulated the need for a vigilant, unrestrained press: "The fact that the liberty of the press may be abused by miscreant purveyors of scandal does not make any the less necessary the immunity of the press from previous restraint in dealing with official misconduct." Although the Court acknowledged that prior restraint may be permissible in exceptional circumstances, it did not specify those circumstances, nor has it yet done so.

Consider another case, which occurred during wartime, when the tension between government-imposed order and individual freedom is often at a peak. In 1971, Daniel Ellsberg, a special assistant in the Pentagon's Office of International Security Affairs, delivered portions of a classified U.S. Department of Defense study to the *New York Times* and the *Washington Post*. By making the documents public, he hoped to discredit the Vietnam War and thereby end it. The U.S. Department of Justice sought to restrain the *Times* and the *Post* from publishing the documents, which became known as the Pentagon Papers, contending that their publication would prolong the war and embarrass the government. The case was quickly brought before the Supreme Court, which delayed its summer adjournment to hear oral arguments.

Three days later, in a 6–3 decision in **New York Times v. United States** (1971), the Court concluded that the government had not met the heavy burden of proving that immediate, inevitable, and irreparable harm would follow publication of the documents.[55] The majority expressed its view in a brief, unsigned opinion; individual and collective concurring and dissenting views added nine additional opinions to the decision. Two justices maintained that the First Amendment offers absolute protection against government censorship, no matter what the situation. But the other justices left the door ajar for the imposition of prior restraint in the most extreme and compelling of circumstances. The result was hardly a ringing endorsement of freedom of the press or a full affirmation of the public's right to all the information that is vital to the debate of public issues.

Freedom of Expression versus Maintaining Order. The courts have consistently held that freedom of the press does not override the requirements of law enforcement. A grand jury called on a Louisville, Kentucky, reporter who had researched and written an article about drug-related activities to identify people he had seen in possession of marijuana or in the act of processing it. The reporter refused to testify, maintaining that freedom of the press shielded him from this inquiry. In a closely divided decision, the Supreme Court in 1972 rejected this position.[56] The Court declared that no exception, even a limited one, is permissible to the rule that all citizens have a duty to give their government whatever testimony they are capable of giving.

Consider a very different setting in the 1988 case of a St. Louis high school principal who deleted articles on divorce and teenage pregnancy from the school's newspaper on the grounds that the articles invaded the privacy of students and families who were the focus of the stories. Three student editors filed suit in federal court, claiming that the principal had violated their First Amendment rights. They argued that the principal's censorship interfered with the newspaper's function as a public forum, a role protected by the First Amendment. The principal maintained that the newspaper was just an extension of classroom instruction and thus was not protected by the First Amendment.

AP Images/Evan Vucci

Hey Dudes, Let's Protest

Students rally on the steps of the U.S. Supreme Court to demonstrate their support for Joseph Frederick, who was suspended from high school when he held up a banner declaring "Bong Hits 4 Jesus" at a school outing in Juneau, Alaska. Frederick lost. Party on.

In a 5–3 decision, the Supreme Court upheld the principal's actions in sweeping terms. Educators may limit speech within the confines of the school curriculum, including speech that might seem to bear the approval of the school, provided their actions serve any "valid educational purpose." Student expression beyond school property took a hit in 2007 when an increasingly conservative Supreme Court upheld the suspension of a high school student in Juneau, Alaska, who had displayed a banner ("Bong Hits 4 Jesus") at an outside school event. School officials may prohibit speech, wrote Chief Justice John G. Roberts, Jr., if it could be interpreted as promoting illegal drug use.[57]

The Rights to Assemble Peaceably and to Petition the Government

The final clause of the First Amendment states that "Congress shall make no law … abridging … the right of the people peaceably to assemble, and to petition the Government for a redress of grievances." The roots of the right of petition can be traced to the Magna Carta, the charter of English political and civil liberties granted by King John at Runnymede in 1215. The right of peaceable assembly arose much later. The framers meant that the people have the right to assemble peaceably *in order to* petition the government. Today, however, the right to assemble peaceably is equated with the right to free speech and a free press, independent of whether the government is petitioned. Precedent has merged these rights and made them indivisible.[58] Government cannot prohibit peaceful political meetings and cannot brand as criminals those who organize, lead, and attend such meetings.[59]

The clash of interests in cases involving these rights illustrates the continuing nature of the effort to define and apply fundamental principles. The need for order and stability has tempered the concept of freedom. And when freedom and order conflict, the justices of the Supreme Court, who are responsible only to their consciences, strike the balance. Such clashes are certain to occur again and again. Freedom and order conflict when public libraries become targets of community censors, when religious devotion interferes with military service, and when individuals and groups express views or hold beliefs at odds with majority sentiment.

The constitutional right to free association frequently becomes threatened during times of crisis. For example, the national government decided, after the September 11 terrorist attacks, to forgo some liberties in order to secure greater order, through bipartisan passage of the USA-PATRIOT Act. This landmark law greatly expanded the ability of law enforcement and intelligence agencies to tap phones, monitor Internet traffic, and conduct other forms of surveillance in pursuit of terrorists. In 2006, Congress extended, with a few minor changes, sixteen expiring provisions of the act.

Shortly after the bill became law, then–Attorney General John Ashcroft declared, "Let the terrorists among us be warned: If you overstay your visa—even by one day— we will arrest you. If you violate a local law, you will be put in jail and kept in custody as long as possible. We will use every available statute. We will seek every prosecutorial advantage. We will use all our weapons within the law and under the Constitution to protect life and enhance security for America."[60] In this shift toward order, civil libertarians worry. "These new and unchecked powers could be used against American citizens who are not under criminal investigation," said Gregory T. Nojeim, associate director of the American Civil Liberties Union's Washington office.[61]

Such worries have manifested themselves in recent court cases that are testing the government's ability to infringe upon individual rights. One collection of cases involves challenges from members of the Muslim community in the northeast who claim that their businesses and mosques were the subject of unconstitutional police surveillance that violated their right to peaceably assemble. In New York City, for example, shortly after the September 11 attacks, the New York Police Department (NYPD) established a surveillance unit that gathered extensive data on the region's Muslim community. The plaintiffs have called these actions unconstitutional spying, whereas the government has defended the practice. In 2014, the NYPD eliminated that special unit, yet cases are still pending in court regarding its actions.[62]

 The Right to Bear Arms

LO4 ★ Discuss the controversy over the Second Amendment and explain how Supreme Court rulings have addressed that debate.

The Second Amendment declares:

> A well-regulated militia, being necessary to the security of a free State, the right of the people to keep and bear arms, shall not be infringed.

This amendment has created a hornet's nest of problems for gun-control advocates and their opponents. Gun-control advocates assert that the amendment protects the right of the states to maintain *collective* militias. Gun-use advocates assert that the amendment protects the right of *individuals* to own and use guns. There are good arguments on both sides.

Federal firearms regulations did not come into being until Prohibition, so the Supreme Court had little to say on the matter before then. In 1939, however, a unanimous Court upheld a 1934 federal law requiring the taxation and registration of machine guns and sawed-off shotguns. The Court held that the Second Amendment protects a citizen's right to own ordinary militia weapons; sawed-off shotguns did not qualify for protection.[63]

In 2008, the Court squarely considered whether the Second Amendment protects an individual's right to gun ownership or is simply a right tied to service in a militia. **District of Columbia v. Heller** was a challenge to the strictest gun-control statute in the country. It barred private possession of handguns and required the disassembly or use of trigger locks on rifles and shotguns. In a landmark decision, the Court ruled 5–4 that there is a personal constitutional right to keep a loaded handgun at home for self-defense. Justice Antonin Scalia, writing for the conservative majority, acknowledged the problem of handgun violence. "But the enshrinement of constitutional rights," declared Scalia, "necessarily takes certain policy choices off the table. … It is not the role of this court to pronounce the Second Amendment extinct."[64]

The ruling overturned the ban, but it left a host of issues unanswered. Here are three:

1. The Court expressly left open whether the individual right to keep and bear arms in the Second Amendment should be brought into or incorporated into the Fourteenth Amendment to apply against the states. (The District of Columbia is a creation of the federal government; it is not a state.)

2. The justices suggested that personal handgun possession did not extend to unusual weapons like submachine guns or assault rifles, but that issue was not squarely before them.

3. The opinion did not set out the standard that would be used to evaluate future challenges to gun regulations that stop short of prohibition.

The Court addressed only the first of these issues in **McDonald v. Chicago** (2010), leaving the matter of gun regulation for another day.[65] In five separate opinions covering more than 200 pages, the justices held, 5–4, that an individual's right to bear arms is fundamental and cannot be prohibited by state or local government. The majority could not agree on the exact Fourteenth Amendment clause that enabled this application. Four justices—Chief Justice John G. Roberts, Jr., and Associate Justices Antonin Scalia, Anthony M. Kennedy, and Samuel A. Alito, Jr.—argued that the due process clause served this function. Justice Clarence Thomas maintained that the quiescent privileges and immunities clause should carry the freight.

AP Images/Rich Pedroncelli

Rallying for a Right

Second Amendment activists gathered around the country on April 19, 2010, also known as Patriots Day, to demonstrate the right to bear arms. The date commemorates the battles of Lexington and Concord during the Revolutionary War. One protester wore his holstered unloaded pistol while attending such a rally in Sacramento, California. He and others objected to a proposed state law that would ban gun owners from openly carrying unloaded guns in public. In June 2010, the U.S. Supreme Court held that state and local governments may not forbid individual gun ownership. The Court has yet to decide how far government may go in regulating it.

Since 2010, the Court has declined to hear other cases that could have further clarified the constitutional protections that the Second Amendment provides. In 2014, for example, the justices refused to hear challenges to lower court rulings that let stand restrictions on ownership of certain kinds of guns for people under age twenty-one. One such lower court ruling had affirmed a Texas law that prohibited most eighteen- to twenty-year-olds (excluding those in the military) from obtaining a permit to carry a handgun. The other involved a federal law that prevented licensed dealers of firearms from selling handguns to people under age twenty-one. Gun rights advocates had urged the Court to hear these cases, but the justices denied their pleas, leaving these restrictions in place.[66]

Applying the Bill of Rights to the States

LO5 ★ Explain the process by which the Supreme Court extended the protections of the Bill of Rights to the local and state levels of government.

The major purpose of the Constitution was to structure the division of power between the national government and the state governments. Even before it was amended, the Constitution set some limits on both the nation and the states with regard to citizens' rights. It barred both governments from passing **bills of attainder**, laws that make an individual guilty of a crime without a trial. It also prohibited them from enacting **ex post facto laws**, which declare an action a crime after it has been performed. And it barred both nation and states from impairing the **obligation of contracts**, the obligation of the parties in a contract to carry out its terms.

Although initially the Bill of Rights seemed to apply only to the national government, various litigants pressed the claim that its guarantees also applied to the states. In response to one such claim, Chief Justice John Marshall affirmed what seemed plain from the Constitution's language and "the history of the day" (the events surrounding the Constitutional Convention): the provisions of the Bill of Rights served only to limit national authority. "Had the framers of these amendments intended them to be limitations on the powers of the state governments," wrote Marshall in 1833, "they would have ... expressed that intention."[67]

Change came with the Fourteenth Amendment, which was adopted in 1868. The due process clause of that amendment is the linchpin that holds the states to the provisions of the Bill of Rights.

The Fourteenth Amendment: Due Process of Law

> Section 1.... No State shall make or enforce any law which shall abridge the privileges or immunities of citizens of the United States; nor shall any State deprive any person of life, liberty, or property, without due process of law.

Most freedoms protected in the Bill of Rights today function as limitations on the states. And many of the standards that limit the national government serve equally to limit state governments. The changes have been achieved through the Supreme Court's interpretation of the due process clause of the Fourteenth Amendment: "nor shall any State deprive any person of life, liberty, or property, without due process of law." The clause has two central meanings. First, it requires the government to adhere to appropriate procedures. For example, in a criminal trial, the government must establish the

bill of attainder
A law that pronounces an individual guilty of a crime without a trial.

ex post facto law
A law that declares an action to be criminal after it has been performed.

obligation of contracts
The obligation of the parties to a contract to carry out its terms.

defendant's guilt beyond a reasonable doubt. Second, it forbids unreasonable government action. For example, at the turn of the twentieth century, the Supreme Court struck down a state law that forbade bakers from working more than sixty hours a week. The justices found the law unreasonable under the due process clause.[68]

The Supreme Court has used the first meaning of the due process clause as a sponge, absorbing or incorporating the procedural specifics of the Bill of Rights and spreading or applying them to the states. The history of due process cases reveals that unlikely litigants often champion constitutional guarantees and that freedom is not always the victor.

The Fundamental Freedoms

In 1897, the Supreme Court declared that the states are subject to the Fifth Amendment's prohibition against taking private property without providing just compensation.[69] The Court reached that decision by absorbing the prohibition into the due process clause of the Fourteenth Amendment, which explicitly applies to the states. Thus, one Bill of Rights protection—but only that one—applied to both the states and the national government, as illustrated in Figure 15.2. In 1925, the Court assumed that the due process clause protected the First Amendment speech and press liberties from impairment by the states.[70]

The inclusion of other Bill of Rights guarantees within the due process clause faced a critical test in **Palko v. Connecticut** (1937).[71] Frank Palko had been charged with homicide in the first degree. He was convicted of second-degree murder, however, and sentenced to life imprisonment. The state of Connecticut appealed and won a new trial; this time, Palko was found guilty of first-degree murder and sentenced to death. Palko appealed the second conviction on the grounds that it violated the

FIGURE 15.2 The Selective Incorporation of the Bill of Rights

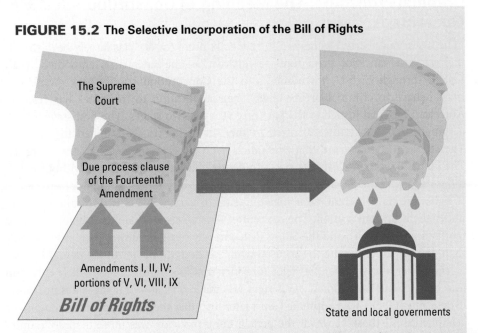

The Supreme Court has used the due process clause of the Fourteenth Amendment as a sponge, absorbing most of the provisions in the Bill of Rights and applying them to state and local governments. All provisions in the Bill of Rights apply to the national government.

© Cengage Learning.

protection against double jeopardy guaranteed to him by the Fifth Amendment. This protection applied to the states, he contended, because of the Fourteenth Amendment's due process clause.

The Supreme Court upheld Palko's second conviction. In his opinion for the majority, Justice Benjamin N. Cardozo formulated principles that were to guide the Court's actions for the next three decades. He reasoned that some Bill of Rights guarantees, such as freedom of thought and speech, are fundamental and that these fundamental rights are absorbed by the Fourteenth Amendment's due process clause and are therefore applicable to the states. These rights are essential, argued Cardozo, because "neither liberty nor justice would exist if they were sacrificed." Trial by jury and other rights, although valuable and important, are not essential to liberty and justice and therefore are not absorbed by the due process clause. "Few would be so narrow or provincial," Cardozo claimed, "as to maintain that a fair and enlightened system of justice would be impossible" without these other rights. In other words, only certain provisions of the Bill of Rights—the "fundamental" provisions—were absorbed selectively into the due process clause and made applicable to the states. Because protection against double jeopardy was not one of them, Palko died in Connecticut's electric chair in 1938.

The next thirty years saw slow but perceptible change in the standard for determining whether a Bill of Rights guarantee was fundamental. The reference point changed from the idealized "fair and enlightened system of justice" in *Palko* to the more realistic "American scheme of justice" thirty years later.[72] Case after case tested various guarantees that the Court found to be fundamental. By 1969, when *Palko* was finally overturned, the Court had found most of the Bill of Rights applicable to the states. (Recall that the Court made the Second Amendment's "right to keep and bear arms" fully applicable to the states in 2010.)

Criminal Procedure: The Meaning of Constitutional Guarantees

"The history of liberty," remarked Justice Felix Frankfurter, "has largely been the history of observance of procedural safeguards."[73] The safeguards embodied in the Fourth through Eighth Amendments to the Constitution specify how government must behave in criminal proceedings. Their application to the states has reshaped American criminal justice in the past fifty years in two stages. The first stage was the judgment that a guarantee asserted in the Bill of Rights also applied to the states. The second stage required that the judiciary give specific meaning to the guarantee. The courts could not allow the states to define guarantees themselves without risking different definitions from state to state—and thus differences among citizens' rights. If rights are fundamental, their meaning cannot vary. But life is not quite so simple under the U.S. Constitution. The concept of federalism is sewn into the constitutional fabric (see Chapter 4), and the Supreme Court has recognized that there may be more than one way to prosecute the accused while heeding his or her fundamental rights.

Consider, for example, the right to a jury trial in criminal cases, which is guaranteed by the Sixth Amendment. This right was made obligatory for the states in *Duncan* v. *Louisiana* (1968). The Supreme Court later held that the right applied to all nonpetty criminal cases—those in which the penalty for conviction was more than six months' imprisonment.[74] But the Court did not require that state juries have twelve members, the number required for federal criminal proceedings. The Court permits jury size to vary from state to state, although it has set the minimum number at six. Furthermore, it has not imposed on the states the federal requirement of a unanimous jury verdict. As a result, even today, many states do not require unanimous verdicts for criminal convictions. Some observers question whether criminal defendants in these states enjoy the same rights as defendants in unanimous-verdict states.

In contrast, the Court left no room for variation in its definition of the fundamental right to an attorney, also guaranteed by the Sixth Amendment. Clarence Earl Gideon was a penniless vagrant accused of breaking into and robbing a pool hall. Because Gideon could not afford a lawyer, he asked the state to provide him with legal counsel for his trial. The state refused and subsequently convicted Gideon and sentenced him to five years in the Florida State Penitentiary. From his cell, Gideon appealed to the U.S. Supreme Court, claiming that his conviction should be struck down because the state had denied him his Sixth Amendment right to counsel.[75]

In its landmark decision in **Gideon v. Wainwright** (1963), the Court set aside Gideon's conviction and extended to defendants in state courts the Sixth Amendment right to counsel.[76] The state retried Gideon, who this time had the assistance of a lawyer, and the court found him not guilty.

In subsequent rulings that stretched over more than a decade, the Court specified at which points in the course of criminal proceedings a defendant is entitled to a lawyer (from arrest to trial, appeal, and beyond). These pronouncements are binding on all states. In state as well as federal proceedings, the government must furnish legal assistance to those who do not have the means to hire their own attorney.

During this period, the Court also came to grips with another procedural issue: informing suspects of their constitutional rights. Without this knowledge, procedural safeguards are meaningless. Ernesto Miranda was arrested in Arizona in connection with the kidnapping and rape of an eighteen-year-old woman. After the police questioned him for two hours and the woman identified him, Miranda confessed to the crime. An Arizona court convicted him based on that confession—although he was never told that he had the right to counsel and the right not to incriminate himself. Miranda appealed his conviction, which was overturned by the Supreme Court in 1966.[77]

The Court based its decision in **Miranda v. Arizona** on the Fifth Amendment privilege against self-incrimination. According to the Court, the police had forced Miranda to confess during in-custody questioning, not with physical force but with the coercion inherent in custodial interrogation without counsel. The Court said that warnings are necessary to dispel that coercion. The Court does not require warnings if a person is only held in custody without being questioned or is only questioned without being arrested. But in *Miranda*, the Court found the combination of custody and interrogation sufficiently intimidating to require warnings before questioning. These statements are known today as the **Miranda warnings**:

- You have the right to remain silent.
- Anything you say can be used against you in court.
- You have the right to talk to a lawyer of your own choice before questioning.
- If you cannot afford to hire a lawyer, a lawyer will be provided without charge.

In each area of criminal procedure, the justices have had to grapple with two steps in the application of constitutional guarantees to criminal defendants: the extension of a right to the states and the definition of that right. In *Duncan*, the issue was the right to jury trial, and the Court allowed variation in all states. In *Gideon*, the Court applied the right to counsel uniformly in all states. Finally, in *Miranda*, the Court declared that all governments—national, state, and local—have a duty to inform suspects of the full measure of their constitutional rights. In one of its most important cases in 2000, the Court reaffirmed this protection in a 7–2 decision, holding that *Miranda* had "announced a constitutional rule" that Congress could not undermine through legislation.[78]

Miranda warnings
Statements concerning rights that police are required to make to a person before he or she is subjected to in-custody questioning.

Freedom, Order, or Equality

Freedom v. Order: Marijuana Legalization and Enforcement of the Controlled Substances Act

The Controlled Substances Act (CSA) is one of the nation's primary drug enforcement laws. It contains many provisions that either regulate or ban the production, importation, possession, and use of different substances. Specifically, the law contains five "schedules," which define different classes of substances. Schedule I substances, the law notes, are potentially the most threatening because they are likely to be abused, or have no widely accepted medical or other use that is safe. Examples include drugs such as LSD and heroin. Schedule I also includes marijuana.

One of the main motivations behind the CSA is a belief that drug use and abuse undermine society. People who become addicted to drugs frequently are unable to succeed in school, hold a job, and be productive. In worst-case scenarios, drug use can cause easily preventable deaths, stoke violence, and provide funds to criminal organizations that traffic in illegal substances.

Although such concerns strike many people as warranted for certain drugs, opinions are changing about marijuana and its classification as a Schedule I substance. As the accompanying graphic shows, since the late 1990s public support for legalizing marijuana has increased. The year 2013 was the first in which the Gallup organization has found majorities of Americans favoring legalization. The use of marijuana for medical purposes also has become more popular, and citizen referendums in Colorado and Washington have legalized its recreational use. Thus, there exists new momentum for advocates who believe marijuana should no longer be classified as an illegal drug, giving it a status comparable to alcohol.

These emerging practices and the evolution of the public's views about marijuana have created challenges for officials in the U.S. Department of Justice (DOJ) and the department's U.S. attorneys stationed across the country who enforce the CSA. The demands of the law combined with these dynamic forces in society have produced a tension between the government's interest in maintaining order and the freedom of citizens to take into their bodies substances of their own choosing. The CSA remains the law of the land, yet more and more citizens have been using marijuana for medical purposes and for recreational ones in Colorado and Washington. How has the DOJ responded? Very carefully.

In August 2013, Deputy Attorney General James Cole distributed a memo to U.S. attorneys across the country attempting to clarify the government's position.* Cole affirmed that "marijuana is a dangerous drug and that the illegal distribution

---

*U.S. Department of Justice, Memo, Guidance Regarding Marijuana Enforcement, 29 August 2013, http://www.justice.gov/iso/opa/resources/3052013829132756857467.pdf.

The problems in balancing freedom and order can be formidable. A primary function of government is to maintain order. What happens when the government infringes on individuals' freedom for the sake of order? Consider the guarantee in the Fourth Amendment: "The right of the people to be secure in their persons, houses, papers, and effects, against unreasonable searches and seizures, shall not be violated." The Court made this right applicable to the states in *Wolf* v. *Colorado* (1949).[79]

and sale of marijuana is a serious crime" before explaining that the department "is committed to enforcement of the CSA consistent with those determinations." He then noted that, historically, the federal government has collaborated with state government partners in narcotics enforcement, and that recent efforts in some states to legalize marijuana use have influenced that relationship. As a result, Cole advised the U.S. attorneys to monitor closely new state plans to regulate the use of marijuana. As long as those states "have also implemented strong and effective regulatory and enforcement systems," Cole believed they would be "less likely to threaten the federal [enforcement] priorities," which include curtailing marijuana's use as a revenue source for criminals, gangs, and cartels.

In short, Cole's memo reveals the complicated challenge of democracy that government attorneys must manage as they attempt to balance the need to maintain order, via enforcement of the CSA, while simultaneously recognizing the desire that some citizens have for the freedom to use marijuana in ways that they believe poses no threat to others.

Americans' View on Legalizing Marijuana
Do you think the use of marijuna should be made legal, or not?

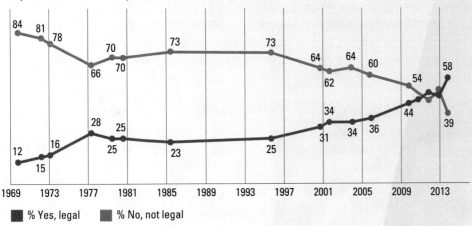

■ % Yes, legal   ■ % No, not legal

Source: Art Swift, "For First Time, Americans Favor Legalizing Marijuana," GALLUP Politics, October, 22, 2013, http://www.gallup.com/poll/165539/first-time-americans-favor-legalizing-marijuana.aspx.

Critical Thinking Suppose that the federal government were deciding between these two strategies for removing marijuana from Schedule I of the CSA: Remove it for all states or only remove it for states that prove they can regulate marijuana effectively. What would be some persuasive arguments for and against each strategy?

Following the reasoning in *Palko*, the Court found that the core of the amendment—security against arbitrary police intrusion—is a fundamental right and that citizens must be protected from illegal searches by state and local governments. But how? The federal courts had long followed the **exclusionary rule**, which holds that evidence obtained from an illegal search and seizure cannot be used in a trial. If that evidence is critical to the prosecution, the case dissolves. But the Court refused to apply the

exclusionary rule
The judicial rule that states that evidence obtained in an illegal search and seizure cannot be used in trial.

exclusionary rule to the state courts. Instead, it allowed the states to decide on their own how to handle the fruits of an illegal search. The decision in *Wolf* stated that obtaining evidence by illegal means violated the Constitution and that states could fashion their own rules of evidence to give effect to this constitutional decree. The states were not bound by the exclusionary rule.

The justices considered the exclusionary rule again twelve years later, in *Mapp* v. *Ohio*.[80] An Ohio court had found Dolree Mapp guilty of possessing obscene materials after an admittedly illegal search of her home for a fugitive. The Ohio Supreme Court affirmed her conviction, and she appealed to the U.S. Supreme Court. Mapp's attorneys argued for a reversal based primarily on freedom of expression, contending that the First Amendment protected the confiscated materials. However, the Court elected to use the decision in *Mapp* to give meaning to the constitutional guarantee against unreasonable search and seizure. In a 6–3 decision, the justices declared that "all evidence obtained by searches and seizures in violation of the Constitution is, by [the Fourth Amendment], inadmissible in a state court." Ohio had convicted Mapp illegally; the evidence should have been excluded.

The decision was historic. It placed the exclusionary rule under the umbrella of the Fourth Amendment and required all levels of government to operate according to the provisions of that amendment. Failure to do so could result in the dismissal of criminal charges against guilty defendants.

Mapp launched a divided Supreme Court on a troubled course of determining how and when to apply the exclusionary rule. For example, the Court has continued to struggle with police use of sophisticated electronic eavesdropping devices and searches of movable vehicles. In each case, the justices have confronted a rule that appears to handicap the police and to offer freedom to people whose guilt has been established by the illegal evidence. In the Court's most recent pronouncements, order has triumphed over freedom.

The struggle over the exclusionary rule took a new turn in 1984, when the Court reviewed *United States* v. *Leon*.[81] In this case, the police obtained a search warrant from a judge on the basis of a tip from an informant of unproven reliability. The judge issued a warrant without firmly establishing probable cause to believe the tip. The police, relying on the warrant, found large quantities of illegal drugs. The Court, by a vote of 6–3, established the **good faith exception** to the exclusionary rule. The justices held that the state could introduce at trial evidence seized on the basis of a mistakenly issued search warrant. The exclusionary rule, argued the majority, is not a right but a remedy against illegal police conduct. The rule is costly to society. It excludes pertinent valid evidence, allowing guilty people to go unpunished and generating disrespect for the law. These costs are justifiable only if the exclusionary rule deters police misconduct. Such a deterrent

good faith exception
An exception to the Supreme Court exclusionary rule, holding that evidence seized on the basis of a mistakenly issued search warrant can be introduced at trial if the mistake was made in good faith, that is, if all the parties involved had reason at the time to believe that the warrant was proper.

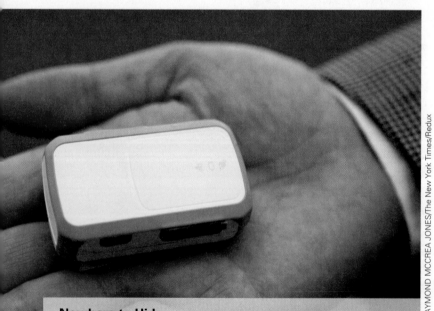

RAYMOND MCCREA JONES/The New York Times/Redux

Nowhere to Hide

Police in the District of Columbia placed a GPS tracking device like the one pictured here on Antoine Jones's Jeep without a court warrant. Jones was convicted of drug trafficking based in part on the evidence culled from monitoring the car's movements for twenty-eight days. On appeal, Jones argued that the use of the GPS device to track his movement amounted to a warrantless search in violation of the Fourth Amendment. In 2012, the Supreme Court agreed with Jones.

effect was not a factor in *Leon*: the police acted in good faith. Hence, the Court decided, there is a need for an exception to the rule.

The Court recognized another exception in 2006. When police search a home with a warrant, they have been required to "knock and announce" before entering. But the Supreme Court held that when the police admittedly fail to "knock and announce," the evidence obtained from such a search may still be admitted into evidence, thus creating a new exception to the exclusionary rule. The case was a close one: decided 5–4 with Justice Scalia writing the majority opinion and implying that the exclusionary rule should not be applied in other illegal search circumstances.[82] As a more conservative coalition has taken shape, the exclusionary rule has come under close scrutiny as the preference for order outweighs the value of freedom. In yet another exception, the Supreme Court held in 2009 that evidence obtained through police negligence would not bar the introduction of that evidence at trial.[83]

The electronic age has forced the Supreme Court to wrestle with other types of evidence and searches, as well. Consider the data stored on your cell phone. During or after an arrest, should police officers be able to search through photos, text messages, and other items stored in a phone's memory, much like they would search a suspect's jacket pockets, tote bag, or car? In 2014 a unanimous Supreme Court said no, unless the law enforcement officials first obtained a warrant to search the phone. Digital data are different than physical personal items, the justices argued, and so merit additional constitutional protections.[84]

The Ninth Amendment and Personal Autonomy

LO6 ★ Explain how the Supreme Court interpreted the Ninth Amendment to broaden the individual's constitutional protection of personal privacy beyond the language in the Bill of Rights, a right not enumerated in the Constitution.

> The enumeration in the Constitution, of certain rights, shall not be construed to deny or disparage others retained by the people.

The working and history of the Ninth Amendment remain an enigma; the evidence supports two different views: the amendment may protect rights that are not enumerated, or it may simply protect state governments against the assumption of power by the national government.[85] The meaning of the amendment was not an issue until 1965, when the Supreme Court used it to protect privacy, a right that is not enumerated in the Constitution.

Controversy: From Privacy to Abortion

In *Griswold v. Connecticut* (1965), the Court struck down, by a vote of 7–2, a seldom-enforced Connecticut statute that made the use of birth control devices a crime.[86] Justice Douglas, writing for the majority, asserted that the "specific guarantees in the Bill of Rights have penumbras [partially illuminated regions surrounding fully lit areas]" that give "life and substance" to broad, unspecified protections in the Bill of Rights. Several specific guarantees in the First, Third, Fourth, and Fifth Amendments create a zone of privacy, Douglas argued, and this zone is protected by

COMPARE WITH YOUR PEERS

MindTap° for American Government

Access the Civil Liberties Forum: Polling Activity—Privacy Rights.

the Ninth Amendment and is applicable to the states by the due process clause of the Fourteenth Amendment.

Three justices gave further emphasis to the relevance of the Ninth Amendment, which, they contended, protects fundamental rights derived from those specifically enumerated in the first eight amendments. This view contrasted sharply with the position expressed by the two dissenters, Justices Hugo Black and Potter Stewart. In the absence of some specific prohibition, they argued, the Bill of Rights and the Fourteenth Amendment do not allow judicial annulment of state legislative policies, even if those policies are abhorrent to a judge or justice.

Griswold established the principle that the Bill of Rights as a whole creates a right to make certain intimate, personal choices, including the right of married people to engage in sexual intercourse for reproduction or pleasure. This zone of personal autonomy, protected by the Constitution, was the basis of a 1973 case that sought to invalidate state antiabortion laws. But rights are not absolute, and in weighing the interests of the individual against the interests of the government, the Supreme Court found itself caught up in a flood of controversy that has yet to subside.

In **Roe v. Wade** (1973), the Court, in a 7–2 decision, declared unconstitutional a Texas law making it a crime to obtain an abortion except for the purpose of saving the woman's life.[87] Justice Harry A. Blackmun, who wrote the majority opinion, could not point to a specific constitutional guarantee to justify the Court's ruling. Instead, he based the decision on the right to privacy protected by the due process clause of the Fourteenth Amendment. In effect, state abortion laws were unreasonable and hence unconstitutional. The Court declared that in the first three months of pregnancy, the abortion decision must be left to the woman and her physician. In the interest of protecting the woman's health, states may restrict but not prohibit abortions in the second three months of pregnancy. Finally, in the last three months of pregnancy, states may regulate or even prohibit abortions to protect the life of the fetus, except when medical judgment determines that an abortion is necessary to save the woman's life. In all, the Court's ruling affected the laws of forty-six states.

The dissenters—Justices Byron R. White and William H. Rehnquist—were quick to assert what critics have frequently repeated since the decision: the Court's judgment was directed by its own dislikes, not by any constitutional compass. In the absence of guiding principles, they asserted, the majority justices simply substituted their views for the views of the state legislatures whose abortion regulations they invalidated.[88] In a 1993 television interview, Blackmun insisted that "*Roe* versus *Wade* was decided … on constitutional grounds."[89] It was as if Blackmun were trying, by sheer force of will, to turn back twenty years' worth of stinging objections to the opinion he had crafted.

A perceptible shift away from abortion rights materialized in *Webster* v. *Reproductive Health Services* (1989) after the composition of the Court had shifted in a more conservative direction with new appointments from President Ronald Reagan. The case was a blockbuster, attracting voluminous media coverage. In *Webster*, the Supreme Court upheld the constitutionality of a Missouri law that denied the use of public employees or publicly funded facilities in the performance of an abortion unless the woman's life was in danger.[90] Furthermore, the law required doctors to perform tests to determine whether fetuses twenty weeks and older could survive outside the womb. This was the first time that the Court upheld significant government restrictions on abortion.

The justices issued five opinions, but no single opinion captured a majority. Four justices (Blackmun, William J. Brennan, Jr., Thurgood Marshall, and John Paul Stevens) voted to strike down the Missouri law and hold fast to *Roe*. Four justices

(Kennedy, Rehnquist, Scalia, and White) wanted to overturn *Roe* and return to the states the power to regulate abortion. The remaining justice, Sandra Day O'Connor, avoided both camps. Her position was that state abortion restrictions are permissible provided they are not "unduly burdensome." She voted with the conservative plurality to uphold the restrictive Missouri statute on the grounds that it did not place an undue burden on women's rights. But she declined to reconsider (and overturn) *Roe*.

The Court has since moved cautiously down the road toward greater government control of abortion. In 1990, the justices split on two state parental notification laws. The Court struck down a state requirement that compelled unwed minors to notify both parents before having an abortion. In another case, however, the Court upheld a state requirement that a physician notify one parent of a pregnant minor of her intent to have an abortion. In both cases, the justices voiced widely divergent opinions, revealing a continuing division over abortion.[91]

With a clear conservative majority, the Court seemed poised to reverse *Roe* in 1992. But a new coalition—forged by Reagan appointees O'Connor and Kennedy, and George H. W. Bush appointee David H. Souter—reaffirmed *Roe* yet tolerated additional restrictions on abortions. In *Planned Parenthood* v. *Casey*, a bitterly divided bench opted for the O'Connor "undue burden" test. Eight years later, in 2000, O'Connor sided with a coalition of liberal and moderate justices in a 5–4 decision striking down a Nebraska law that had banned so-called partial-birth abortion, illustrating the Court's continuing and deep division on the abortion issue.[92]

Let's view the abortion controversy through our lens of value conflicts. Presidents try to appoint justices whose values coincide with their own. Justices appointed by conservative presidents Reagan and George H. W. Bush weakened abortion as a constitutional right, putting more weight on order. President Clinton's appointees (Ruth Bader Ginsburg and Stephen G. Breyer) fulfilled his liberal campaign promise to protect women's access to abortion from further assault, putting more weight on freedom. President George W. Bush's conservative appointees—John G. Roberts, Jr., and Samuel A. Alito, Jr.—have tipped the balance toward order. In 2007, the Court by a 5–4 vote upheld a federal law banning partial-birth abortion.[93] The law was nearly identical to the one struck down by the Court years before. Today, order trumps freedom. An ideological shift in the White House may be insufficient to produce a different result unless conservative justices leave the Court. And none have expressed the intention to do so.

Many groups defending or opposing abortion also have turned to state legislatures to advance their priorities. This approach has forced candidates for state office to debate the abortion issue and then translate electoral outcomes into legislation that restricts or protects abortion. In some states, for example, legislators have attempted to define in law that life begins at conception, making the fetus "a person" with constitutional and other legal protections. If the abortion issue is deeply felt by Americans, pluralist theory would predict that the strongest voices for or against abortion rights will mobilize the greatest support in the political arena.

Privacy, Personal Autonomy, and Sexual Orientation

The right-to-privacy cases may have opened a Pandora's box of divisive social issues. Does the right to privacy embrace private homosexual acts between consenting adults? Consider the case of Michael Hardwick, who was arrested in 1982 in his Atlanta bedroom while having sex with another man. In a standard approach to prosecuting homosexuals, Georgia charged him under a state criminal statute with the crime of sodomy, which means oral or anal intercourse. The police said that they had gone to his home to arrest him for failing to pay a fine for drinking in public. Although the prosecutor dropped the charges, Hardwick sued to challenge the law's constitutionality. He won in the lower courts, but the state pursued the case.

The conflict between freedom and order lies at the core of the case. "Our legal history and our social traditions have condemned this conduct uniformly for hundreds and hundreds of years," argued Georgia's attorney. Constitutional law, he continued, "must not become an instrument for a change in the social order." Hardwick's attorney, a noted constitutional scholar, said that government must have a more important reason than "majority morality to justify regulation of sexual intimacies in the privacy of the home." He maintained that the case involved two precious freedoms: the right to engage in private sexual relations and the right to be free from government intrusion in one's home.[94]

In a bitterly divided ruling in 1986, the Court held in *Bowers* v. *Hardwick* that the Constitution does not protect homosexual relations between consenting adults, even in the privacy of their own homes.[95] The logic of the findings in the privacy cases involving contraception and abortion would seem to have compelled a finding of a right to personal autonomy—a right to make personal choices unconstrained by government—in this case as well. But the 5–4 majority maintained that only heterosexual choices—whether and whom to marry, whether to conceive a child, whether to have an abortion—fall within the zone of privacy established by the Court in its earlier rulings. "The Judiciary necessarily takes to itself further authority to govern the country without express constitutional authority" when it expands the list of fundamental rights not rooted in the language or design of the Constitution, wrote Justice White, the author of the majority opinion.

The arguments on both sides of the privacy issue are compelling. This makes the choice between freedom and order excruciating for ordinary citizens and Supreme Court justices alike. At the conference to decide the merits of the *Bowers* case, Justice Lewis Powell cast his vote to extend privacy rights to homosexual conduct. Later, he switched sides and joined with his conservative colleagues, fashioning a new winning coalition. Four years after the *Bowers* decision, Powell revealed another change of mind: "I probably made a mistake," he declared, speaking of his decision to vote with the conservative majority.[96]

Justice White's majority opinion was reconsidered in 2003 when the Court heard a "carefully choreographed" challenge to a Texas law that criminalized homosexual but not heterosexual sodomy.[97] This time, in **Lawrence and Garner v. Texas**, a new coalition of six justices viewed the issue in a different light. May a majority use the power of government to enforce its views on the whole society through the criminal law? Speaking through Justice Kennedy, the Court observed "an emerging awareness that liberty gives substantial protection to adult persons in deciding how to conduct their private lives in matters pertaining to sex." Since the Texas law furthered no legitimate state interest but intruded into the intimate personal choices of individuals, the law was void. Kennedy along with four other justices then took the unusual step of reaching back in time to declare that the *Bowers* decision was wrong and should be overruled.[98]

Justice Antonin Scalia, joined by Chief Justice Rehnquist and Justice Clarence Thomas, issued a stinging dissent. Scalia charged the majority with "signing on to the homosexual agenda" aimed at eliminating the moral opprobrium traditionally attached to homosexual conduct. The consequence is that the Court would be departing from its role of ensuring that the democratic rules of engagement are observed. The challenge of democracy calls for the democratic process to sort out value conflicts whenever possible. And, according to Scalia, the majority has moved from its traditional responsibility of umpiring the system to favoring one side over another in the struggle between freedom and order.[99]

For groups dissatisfied with rulings from the nation's courts, the pluralist model provides one avenue for redress. State courts and state legislatures have demonstrated their receptivity to positions that are probably untenable in the federal courts. Pluralist mechanisms such as the initiative and the referendum offer countermeasures to judicial intervention. However, state-by-state decisions offer little comfort to Americans who believe the U.S. Constitution protects them in their most intimate decisions and actions, regardless of where they reside.

Master the Topic of Civil Liberties with MindTap™ for American Government

REVIEW MindTap™ **for American Government**
Access Key Term Flashcards for Chapter 15.

TEST YOURSELF MindTap™ **for American Government**
Take the Wrap It Up Quiz for Chapter 15.

STAY CURRENT MindTap™ **for American Government**
Access the KnowNow blog and customized RSS for updates on current events.

STAY FOCUSED MindTap™ **for American Government**
Complete the Focus Activities for Civil Liberties.

Summary

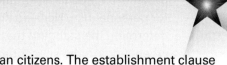

LO1 Explain the role of the Bill of Rights in protecting civil liberties and civil rights.

- When they established the new government of the United States, the states and the people compelled the framers, through the Bill of Rights, to protect their freedoms. The ten original amendments to the Constitution include both civil liberties and civil rights. In interpreting these ten amendments, the courts, especially the Supreme Court, have taken on the task of balancing freedom and order.

LO2 Identify the mechanisms that guarantee freedom of religion.

- The First Amendment protects several freedoms. The first of these, the freedom of religion, has long been important to

American citizens. The establishment clause demands government neutrality toward religions and between the religious and the nonreligious. This clause, instituted to protect all religious beliefs, has nonetheless sparked some controversy in its application. According to judicial interpretations of the free-exercise clause, religious beliefs are inviolable, but the Constitution does *not* protect antisocial actions in the name of religion. Extreme interpretations of the religion clauses could bring the clauses into conflict with each other.

LO3 Identify the free-expression clauses and describe the scope of their protection.

- Freedom of expression encompasses many freedoms, including freedom of speech, freedom of the press, and the right to assemble peaceably and to petition the government. Freedom of speech and freedom of the press have never been held to be absolute, but the courts have ruled that the Bill of Rights gives the people far greater protection than other freedoms. Press freedom has enjoyed broad constitutional protection because a free society depends on the ability to collect and report information without government interference. The rights to assemble peaceably and to petition the government stem from the guarantees of freedom of speech and of the press. Each freedom is equally fundamental, but the right to exercise them is not absolute.

LO4 Discuss the controversy over the Second Amendment and explain how Supreme Court rulings have addressed that debate.

- The nature and scope of the Second Amendment have long been a source of contention for gun-control advocates and their opponents. After nearly seventy years of silence, in 2008 the Supreme Court declared that the right to bear arms protects an individual's right to own a gun for personal use. New legal challenges will determine the standard that should apply when judging the appropriateness of gun regulations. For now, however, government may not prohibit individual gun ownership.

LO5 Explain the process by which the Supreme Court extended the protections of the Bill of Rights to the local and state levels of government.

- The adoption of the Fourteenth Amendment in 1868 extended the guarantees of the Bill of Rights to the states. The due process clause of the amendment became the vehicle for applying specific provisions of the Bill of Rights to the states. The Supreme Court has tolerated some variation from state to state in the meaning of certain constitutional rights. It has also imposed a duty on governments to inform citizens of their rights so that they are equipped to exercise them.

LO6 Explain how the Supreme Court interpreted the Ninth Amendment to broaden the individual's constitutional protection of personal privacy beyond the language in the Bill of Rights, a right not enumerated in the Constitution.

- As it has fashioned new fundamental rights from the Constitution, the Supreme Court has become embroiled in controversy. The right to privacy served as the basis for the right of women to terminate a pregnancy, which in turn suggested a right to personal autonomy. The abortion controversy is still raging, and the justices, relying in part on the abortion cases, have extended protections against state criminal prosecution of private consensual sexual behavior for homosexuals.
- By offering constitutional protection to certain public policies, some people worry that the courts may be threatening the democratic process that gives the people a voice in government through their elected representatives. Should elected representatives fail to heed the public, voters may act on their own as in states that have mechanisms such as the referendum or initiative.

Chapter Quiz

LO1 Explain the role of the Bill of Rights in protecting civil liberties and civil rights.

1. Why are civil liberties called "negative rights" and civil rights called "positive rights"?
2. Identify the liberties and rights that are enshrined in the Bill of Rights.

LO2 Identify the mechanisms that guarantee freedom of religion.

1. Which clause in the First Amendment formalizes the separation of church and state?
2. What aspect of religion does the First Amendment not protect?

LO3 Identify the free-expression clauses and describe the scope of their protection.

1. Define the clear and present danger test and explain how it is used in adjudicating cases of freedom of speech.
2. Explain what the right to peaceably assemble entails.

LO4 Discuss the controversy over the Second Amendment and explain how Supreme Court rulings have addressed that debate.

1. What distinguishes the interpretation of the Second Amendment by gun-control advocates from that of their opponents?

2. Does the Second Amendment pertain only to the national government, or to local and state governments as well?

LO5 Explain the process by which the Supreme Court extended the protections of the Bill of Rights to the local and state levels of government.

1. What is the due process clause, and how does it hold the states to the provisions of the Bill of Rights?
2. What are the *Miranda* warnings, and to which amendment are they related?

LO6 Explain how the Supreme Court interpreted the Ninth Amendment to broaden the individual's constitutional protection of personal privacy beyond the language in the Bill of Rights, a right not enumerated in the Constitution.

1. Which principle did the decision in *Griswold* v. *Connecticut* establish regarding the Bill of Rights as a whole?
2. In *Roe* v. *Wade*, what was the opinion of the majority of the justices? What was the argument of the dissenters?

KEY CASES

Lemon v. *Kurtzman* (religious establishment test, 1971)

Engel v. *Vitale* (public school prayer ban, 1962)

Sherbert v. *Verner* (religious free exercise, 1963)

Schenck v. *United States* (free speech, clear and present danger test, 1919)

Brandenburg v. *Ohio* (free speech, 1969)

Tinker v. *Des Moines Independent County School District* (symbolic speech, 1969)

Cohen v. *California* (free expression, 1971)

Snyder v. *Phelps* (public/private speech; emotional harm, 2011)

Citizens United v. *Federal Election Commission* (unlimited political campaign spending, 2010)

New York Times v. *Sullivan* (free press, 1964)

New York Times v. *United States* (prior restraint, 1971)

District of Columbia v. *Heller* (2008) and *McDonald* v. *Chicago* (right to bear arms, 2010)

Palko v. *Connecticut* (Applying the Bill of Rights to the States, 1937)

Gideon v. *Wainwright* (assistance of counsel, 1963)

Miranda v. *Arizona* (self-incrimination, 1966)

Griswold v. *Connecticut* (privacy, 1965)

Roe v. *Wade* (abortion, 1973)

Lawrence and Garner v. *Texas* (gay rights, 2003)

16 Equality and Civil Rights

Learning Outcomes

LO1 Explain why some discrimination may be benign while other forms of discrimination may be harmful.

LO2 Trace the Supreme Court rulings and state legislative efforts that prevented African Americans from achieving "equal protection of the laws."

LO3 Identify the Supreme Court decisions that dismantled school segregation and explain the significance of each.

LO4 Describe the circumstances under which the 1964 Civil Rights Act was passed and its evolving interpretation in subsequent Supreme Court decisions.

LO5 Evaluate the effect of the civil rights movement on other minority groups' struggles for equality.

LO6 Trace the evolution of women's legal rights beginning with laws based on protectionism and concluding with Supreme Court rulings prohibiting gender-based discrimination.

LO7 Compare and contrast the consequences that follow from policies aimed at equal opportunities versus those aimed at equal outcomes.

 WATCH & LEARN MindTap for American Government
Watch a brief "What Do You Know?" video summarizing Civil Rights.

AP Images/Danny Moloshok

Abigail Fisher was a senior at Stephen F. Austin High School in Sugar Land, Texas, when she applied for admission in 2008 to the University of Texas–Austin, the flagship of the state's university system. All Texas students who graduate in the top 10 percent of their classes must be admitted to the state university. Students falling short of this threshold may be admitted nonetheless according to a formula that takes into account the race of each applicant among several factors. The university denied Fisher admission. Fisher, who is white, contended that the government may not consider race in making such decisions. The university used race to hold her back, she argued, denying Fisher her freedom.

Fisher brought a lawsuit in federal court against the university, arguing that the inclusion of race in university admissions violates the equal protection clause of the Fourteenth Amendment to the U.S. Constitution. Fisher lost the first two rounds as federal courts applied the prevailing rules based on previous Supreme Court cases. These decisions fall under the umbrella of **affirmative action**, a wide range of programs, from special recruitment efforts to numerical quotas, aimed at expanding opportunities for minority groups and women. Universities justify the use of

racial preferences in admissions to assure a critical mass of diverse students. By pursuing diversity, public universities may do what the Constitution forbids: sort people on the basis of race.[1]

In a 7–1 decision in 2013, the Supreme Court decided Fisher v. University of Texas but only to the limited extent that the university had failed to meet the Court's "strict scrutiny" standard when reviewing its affirmative action policy. This is the most stringent standard to judge government action. It means that a government policy will be overruled unless the policy meets three requirements: (1) the policy in question furthers a compelling governmental interest; (2) the policy in question is narrowly tailored to achieve that interest; and (3) the policy in question is the least restrictive means to achieve that interest.

So far, Fisher has won a pyrrhic victory to end the race-preference policies at the university. In returning the case to the appeals court, the university had to demonstrate "that no workable race-neutral alternatives would produce the educational benefits of diversity."[2]

In effect, the Supreme Court tightened the reins on racial diversity policies. While the Court gave deference to the university's judgment that the *end* of

affirmative action
Any of a wide range of programs, from special recruitment efforts to numerical quotas, aimed at expanding opportunities for women and minority groups.

achieving a racially diverse student body is a compelling government interest, the justices would give no deference in assessing whether the *means* chosen by the university were narrowly tailored to achieve that end.

The appeals court reviewed Fisher's case in light of this sharpened policy. In a 2–1 decision, the court ruled in 2014 that the university's affirmative action policy met the narrow tailoring standard. Fisher said she would continue to press her case again in the highest court of the land.[3]

In yet a further tightening of the reins, the Court in 2014 upheld a Michigan constitutional amendment approved by 58 percent of voters that banned discrimination based on race, color, sex, or religion in admission to colleges, jobs, and other publicly funded institutions. In its 6–2 decision—Schuette v. BAMN—the Court declared that courts possess no authority to set aside state laws that commit such policy determinations to the voters.[4]

Why do affirmative action policies cast as efforts to achieve racial diversity generate opposition? Why do racial and other forms of unlawful discrimination persist in the United States despite laudable efforts to end them? The answer may appear deceptively simple. Laws and policies that promote equality inevitably come into conflict with demands for freedom. The conflict between freedom and equality intensifies when we recognize that Americans advocate competing conceptions of equality (see "Freedom, Order, and Two Conceptions of Equality").

In this chapter, we consider the different ideals of equality and the quest to realize them through government action. We begin with the struggle for racial equality, which continues to cast a long shadow in government policies. This struggle has served as a model for the diverse groups that chose to follow in the same path.

LISTEN & LEARN
MindTap® for American Government

Access Read Speaker to listen to Chapter 16.

Freedom, Order, and Two Conceptions of Equality

The Constitution commands that government shall not deny to any person "the equal protection of the laws." Two different concepts of equality thread through our laws today: formal equality and dynamic equality. *Formal equality* requires that government treat similarly situated individuals alike. For example, black and white applicants to state universities would be treated the same when it comes to admissions; gay couples would be treated like straight couples when it comes to marriage. *Dynamic equality* acknowledges the fact of real disparities between groups and bends to the weight of history. For example, in light of brutal state-sanctioned racial segregation policies that hobbled blacks for more than a century, we should make special allowances for blacks seeking university admissions to achieve the historic goal of equality. Viewed through the lens of ideology, conservatives seek formal equality in university admissions and dynamic equality on gay marriage. Liberals want the opposite: dynamic equality in university admissions and formal equality on gay marriage.[a]

Support for dynamic equality varies, revealing further tension. Most Americans support **equality of opportunity**, the idea that people should have an equal chance to develop their talents and that effort and ability should be rewarded equitably. This form of equality offers all individuals the same chance to get ahead; it glorifies personal achievement and free competition and allows everyone to play on a level field where the same rules apply to all. Special recruitment

equality of opportunity
The idea that each person is guaranteed the same chance to succeed in life.

efforts aimed at identifying qualified minority or female job applicants, for example, ensure that everyone has the same chance starting out. Low-bid contracting illustrates equality of opportunity because every bidder has the same chance to compete for work.

Americans remain less committed to **equality of outcome**, which means greater uniformity in social, economic, and political power among different social groups. For example, schools and businesses aim at equality of outcome when they allocate admissions or jobs on the basis of race, gender, or disability, which are unrelated to ability. (Some observers refer to these allocations as *quotas*; others call them *goals*. The difference is subtle. A quota *requires* that a specified proportional share of some benefit go to a favored group. A goal aims for proportional allocation of benefits, without requiring it.) The government seeks equality of outcome when it adjusts the rules to handicap some bidders or applicants and favor others. The vast majority of Americans, however, consistently favor low-bid contracting and merit-based admissions and employment over preferential treatment.[b] Recent survey results signal that Americans remain firmly against the preferential treatment of minorities,[c] even as they tend to be supportive of certain affirmative action policies.[d]

Some people believe that equality of outcome can occur in today's society only if we restrict the free competition that is the basis of equality of opportunity. In 1978, Supreme Court Justice Harry Blackmun articulated this controversial position on a divided bench: "In order to get beyond racism, we must first take account of race. There is no other way. And in order to treat some persons equally, we must treat them differently."[e] In 2007, Chief Justice John G. Roberts, Jr., cast the issue in reverse on a divided bench: "The way to stop discrimination on the basis of race is to stop discriminating on the basis of race."[f] In 2014, Justice Sonia Sotomayor, dissenting from the Court's decision to uphold a Michigan constitutional amendment banning racial preferences, riffed: "The way to stop discrimination on the basis of race is to speak openly and candidly on the subject of race, and to apply the Constitution with eyes open to the unfortunate effects of centuries of racial discrimination."[g]

equality of outcome
The concept that society must ensure that people are equal, and governments must design policies to redistribute wealth and status so that economic and social equality is actually achieved.

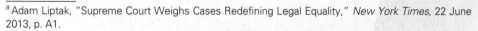

[a] Adam Liptak, "Supreme Court Weighs Cases Redefining Legal Equality," *New York Times*, 22 June 2013, p. A1.

[b] Jack Citrin, "Affirmative Action in the People's Court," *Public Interest* 122 (1996): 40–41; Sam Howe Verhovek, "In Poll, Americans Reject Means but Not Ends of Racial Diversity," *New York Times*, 14 December 1997, sec. 1, p. 1; and "Aid to Blacks and Minorities, 1970–2008," in *National Election Studies Guide to Public Opinion and Electoral Behavior*, http://www.electionstudies.org/nesguide/toptable/tab4b_4.htm.

[c] Jeffrey M. Jones, "In U.S., Most Reject Considering Race in College Admissions," 24 July 2013, http://www.gallup.com/poll/163655/reject-considering-race-college-admissions.aspx.

[d] Michael I. Norton and Samuel R. Sommers, "Whites See Racism as a Zero-Sum Game That They Are Now Losing," *Perspectives on Psychological Science* 6 (May 2011): 215–218, http://ase.tufts.edu/psychology/sommerslab/documents/raceinternortonsommers2011.pdf. See Pew Research Center, "Public Backs Affirmative Action, But Not Minority Preferences," http://www.pewresearch.org/2009/06/02/public-backs-affirmative-action-but-not-minority-preferences/.

[e] *Regents of the University of California* v. *Bakke*, 438 U.S. 265,407 (1978).

[f] *Parents Involved in Community Schools* v. *Seattle School District No. 1*, 551 U.S. 701 (2007).

[g] *Schuette* v. *BAMN*, 572 US. ___, 46 (2014).

The Supreme Court has yet to harmonize its controversial equality decisions under a single concept, and perhaps it is better off divided. By giving something to conservatives (reining in dynamic equality in matters of race) and something to liberals (applying formal equality to the law of marriage), the Court has temporized the two camps, avoiding all-out conflict.

Critical Thinking Explain whether a single definition of equality fits the pluralist or majoritarian model of democracy.

COMPARE WITH YOUR PEERS

MindTap for American Government

Access the Civil Rights Forum: polling Activity—Civil Rights Protection.

The Struggle for Racial Equality

LO1 ★ Explain why some discrimination may be benign while other forms of discrimination may be harmful.

The history of civil rights in the United States is primarily the story of a search for social and economic equality. This search has persisted for more than a century and is ongoing. It began with the battle for civil rights for black citizens, whose prior subjugation as slaves had roused the passions of the nation and brought about its bloodiest conflict, the Civil War. The struggle of blacks has been a beacon lighting the way for Native Americans, immigrant groups of which Latinos represent the largest component, women, people with disabilities, and homosexuals. Each of these groups has confronted **invidious discrimination**. Discrimination is simply the act of making or recognizing distinctions. When making distinctions among people, discrimination may be benign (that is, harmless) or invidious (harmful). For example, forbidding people from driving without a license is benign discrimination because proof that a person knows how to drive is a rational way to minimize accidents. Banning African American adults from driving would be invidious because its only possible justification would be unfairness or animus toward African American adults. Sometimes this harm has been subtle, and sometimes it has been overt. Sometimes it has even come from other minorities. Each group has achieved a measure of success in its struggle by pressing its interests on government, even challenging it. These challenges and the government's responses to them have helped shape our democracy.

Remember that **civil rights** are powers or privileges guaranteed to the individual and protected from arbitrary removal at the hands of the government or other individuals. Sometimes people refer to civil rights as "positive rights" (see Table 15.1, "Examples of Positive and Negative Rights: Constitutional Rights and Human Rights," on page 424). In this chapter, we concentrate on the rights guaranteed by the constitutional amendments adopted after the Civil War and by laws passed to enforce those guarantees. Prominent among them is the right to equal protection of the laws. This right remained a promise rather than a reality well into the twentieth century.

invidious discrimination
Discrimination against persons or groups that works to their harm and is based on animosity.

civil rights
Powers or privileges guaranteed to individuals and protected from arbitrary removal at the hands of government or individuals.

The Civil War Amendments

LO2 ★ Trace the Supreme Court rulings and state legislative efforts that prevented African Americans from achieving "equal protection of the laws."

The Civil War amendments were adopted to provide freedom and equality to black Americans. The Thirteenth Amendment, ratified in 1865, provided that

> neither slavery nor involuntary servitude … shall exist within the United States, or any place subject to their jurisdiction.

The Fourteenth Amendment was adopted three years later. It provides first that freed slaves are citizens:

> All persons born or naturalized in the United States, and subject to the jurisdiction thereof, are citizens of the United States and of the State wherein they reside.

As we saw in Chapter 15, it also prohibits the states from abridging the "privileges or immunities of citizens of the United States" or depriving "any person of life, liberty, or property, without due process of law." The amendment then goes on to guarantee equality under the law, declaring that no state shall

> deny to any person within its jurisdiction the equal protection of the laws.

The Fifteenth Amendment, adopted in 1870, added a measure of political equality:

> The right of citizens of the United States to vote shall not be denied or abridged by the United States or by any State on account of race, color, or previous condition of servitude.

American blacks were thus free and politically equal—at least according to the Constitution. But for many years, the courts sometimes thwarted the efforts of the other branches to protect their constitutional rights.

Congress and the Supreme Court: Lawmaking versus Law Interpreting

In the years after the Civil War, Congress went to work to protect the rights of black citizens. In 1866, lawmakers passed a civil rights act that gave the national government some authority over the treatment of blacks by state courts. This legislation was a response to the **black codes**, laws enacted by the former slave states to restrict the freedom of blacks. For example, vagrancy and apprenticeship laws forced blacks to work and denied them a free choice of employers. One section of the 1866 act that still applies today grants all citizens the right to make and enforce contracts; the right to sue others in court (and the corresponding ability to be sued); the duty and ability to give evidence in court; and the right to inherit, purchase, lease, sell, hold, or convey property. Later, in the Civil Rights Act of 1875, Congress attempted to guarantee blacks equal access to public accommodations (parks, theaters, and the like).

Although Congress enacted laws to protect the civil rights of black citizens, the Supreme Court weakened some of those rights. In 1873, the Court ruled that the Civil War amendments had not changed the relationship between the state and national governments.[5] State citizenship and national citizenship remained separate and distinct. According to the Court, the Fourteenth Amendment did not obligate the states to honor the rights guaranteed by U.S. citizenship.

black codes
Legislation enacted by former slave states to restrict the freedom of blacks.

In subsequent years, the Court's decisions narrowed some constitutional protections for blacks. In 1876, the justices limited congressional attempts to protect the rights of blacks.[6] A group of Louisiana whites had used violence and fraud to prevent blacks from exercising their basic constitutional rights, including the right to assemble peaceably. The justices held that the rights allegedly infringed on were not nationally protected rights and that therefore Congress was powerless to punish those who violated them. On the very same day, the Court ruled that the Fifteenth Amendment did not guarantee all citizens the right to vote; it simply listed grounds that could not be used to deny that right.[7] And in 1883, the Court struck down the public accommodations section of the Civil Rights Act of 1875.[8] The justices declared that the national government could prohibit only *government* action that discriminated against blacks; private acts of discrimination or acts of omission by a state were beyond the reach of the national government. For example, a person who refused to serve blacks in a private club was outside the control of the national government because the discrimination was a private—not a governmental—act. The Court refused to see racial discrimination as an act that the national government could prohibit. In many cases, the justices tolerated racial discrimination. In the process, they abetted **racism**, the belief that there are inherent differences among the races that determine people's achievement and that one's own race is superior to and thus has a right to dominate others.

The Court's decisions gave the states ample room to maneuver around civil rights laws. In the matter of voting rights, for example, states that wanted to bar black men from the polls simply used nonracial means to do so. One popular tool was the **poll tax**, first imposed by Georgia in 1877. This was a tax of $1 or $2 on every citizen who wanted to vote. The tax was not a burden for most whites. But many blacks were tenant farmers, deeply in debt to white merchants and landowners; they had no extra money for voting. Other bars to black suffrage included literacy tests, minimum education requirements, and a grandfather clause that restricted suffrage to men who could establish that their grandfathers were eligible to vote before 1867 (three years before the Fifteenth Amendment declared that race could not be used to deny individuals the right to vote).[9] White southerners also used intimidation and violence to keep blacks from the polls.

racism

A belief that human races have distinct characteristics such that one's own race is superior to, and has a right to rule, others.

poll tax

A tax of $1 or $2 on every citizen who wished to vote, first instituted in Georgia in 1877. Although it was no burden on most white citizens, it effectively disenfranchised blacks.

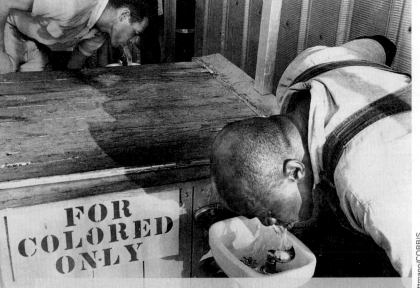

Bettmann/CORBIS

The Roots of Racial Segregation

From well before the Civil War, **racial segregation** had been a way of life in the South: blacks lived and worked separately from whites. After the war, southern states began to enact *Jim Crow* laws to reinforce segregation. (Jim Crow was a derogatory term for a black person.) Once the Supreme Court took the teeth out of the Civil Rights Act of 1875, such laws proliferated. They required blacks to live in separate (generally inferior) areas and restricted them to separate sections of hospitals; separate cemeteries; separate drinking and toilet facilities; separate schools; and separate sections of trains, jails, and parks.

Separate and Unequal

The Supreme Court gave constitutional protection to racial separation on the theory that states could provide "separate but equal" facilities for blacks. The facilities here appear equal, but the harm inherent in racial separation lies beneath the surface. Separating people by race is inherently unequal, declared the Supreme Court, in its landmark 1954 ruling, *Brown* v. *Board of Education*.

In 1892, Homer Adolph Plessy, who was seven-eighths Caucasian, took a seat in a "whites-only" car of a Louisiana train. He refused to move to the car reserved for blacks and was arrested. Plessy argued that Louisiana's law mandating racial segregation on its trains was an unconstitutional infringement on both the privileges and immunities guaranteed by the Fourteenth Amendment and its equal protection clause. The Supreme Court disagreed. The majority in **Plessy v. Ferguson*** (1896) upheld state-imposed racial segregation.[10] They based their decision on what came to be known as the **separate-but-equal doctrine**, which held that separate facilities for blacks and whites satisfied the Fourteenth Amendment as long as they were equal. (The Court majority used the phrase "equal but separate" to describe the requirement. Justice John Marshall Harlan's dissenting opinion cast the phrase as "separate but equal," the way we have come to refer to the doctrine.)

Three years later, the Supreme Court extended the separate-but-equal doctrine to the schools.[11] The justices ignored the fact that black educational facilities (and most other "colored-only" facilities) were far from equal to those reserved for whites.

By the end of the nineteenth century, legal racial segregation was firmly entrenched in the American South. Although constitutional amendments and national laws to protect equality under the law were in place, the Supreme Court's interpretation of those amendments and laws rendered them ineffective. Several decades would pass before any change was discernible.

separate-but-equal doctrine
The concept that providing separate but equivalent facilities for blacks and whites satisfies the equal protection clause of the Fourteenth Amendment.

 # The Dismantling of School Segregation

LO3 ★ Identify the Supreme Court decisions that dismantled school segregation and explain the significance of each.

Denied the right to vote and to be represented in the government, blacks sought access to power through other parts of the political system. The National Association for the Advancement of Colored People (NAACP), founded in 1909 by W. E. B. Du Bois and others, both black and white, with the goal of ending racial discrimination and segregation, took the lead in the campaign for black civil rights. The plan was to launch a two-pronged legal and lobbying attack on the separate-but-equal doctrine: first by pressing for fully equal facilities for blacks, then by proving the unconstitutionality of segregation. The process would be a slow one, but the strategies involved did not require a large organization or heavy financial backing; at the time, the NAACP had neither.**

Pressure for Equality ...

By the 1920s, the separate-but-equal doctrine was so deeply ingrained in American law that no Supreme Court justice would dissent from its continued application to racial segregation. But a few Court decisions offered hope that change would come. In 1935, Lloyd Gaines graduated from Lincoln University, a black college in Missouri, and applied to the state law school. The law school rejected him because he was black. Missouri refused to admit blacks to its all-white law school; instead, the state's policy was to pay the costs of blacks admitted to out-of-state law schools. With the support of the NAACP, Gaines appealed to the courts for admission to the University of Missouri Law School. In 1938, the

---

*Key cases are highlighted in bold, and a list of key cases appears at the end of the chapter.

**In 1939, the NAACP established an offshoot, the NAACP Legal Defense and Education Fund, to work on legal challenges while the parent organization concentrated on lobbying.

U.S. Supreme Court ruled that he must be admitted.[12] Under the *Plessy* ruling, Missouri could not shift to other states its responsibility to provide an equal education for blacks.

Later cases helped reinforce the requirement that segregated facilities must be equal in all major respects. One was brought by Heman Sweatt, again with the help of the NAACP. The all-white University of Texas Law School had denied Sweatt entrance because of his race. A federal court ordered the state to provide a black law school for him; the state responded by renting a few rooms in an office building and hiring two black lawyers as teachers. Sweatt refused to attend the school and took his case to the Supreme Court.[13]

The Court ruled on *Sweatt* v. *Painter* in 1950. The justices unanimously found that the facilities were inadequate: the separate "law school" provided for Sweatt did not approach the quality of the white state law school. The University of Texas had to give Sweatt full student status. But the Court avoided reexamining the separate-but-equal doctrine.

… and Pressure for Desegregation

These decisions suggested to the NAACP that the time was right for an attack on segregation itself. In addition, public attitudes toward race relations were slowly changing from the predominant racism of the nineteenth and early twentieth centuries toward greater tolerance. Black groups had fought with honor—albeit in segregated military units—in World War II. Blacks and whites were working together in unions and in service and religious organizations. Social change and court decisions suggested that government-imposed segregation was vulnerable.

President Harry S. Truman risked his political future with his strong support of blacks' civil rights. In 1947, he established the President's Committee on Civil Rights. The committee's report, issued later that year, became the agenda for the civil rights movement during the next two decades. It called for national laws prohibiting racially motivated poll taxes, segregation, and brutality against minorities and for guarantees of voting rights and equal employment opportunity. In 1948, Truman ordered the **desegregation** (the dismantling of authorized racial segregation) of the armed forces.

desegregation
The ending of authorized segregation, or separation by race.

In 1947, the U.S. Department of Justice had begun to submit briefs to the courts in support of civil rights. The department's most important intervention probably came in *Brown* v. *Board of Education*.[14] This case was the culmination of twenty years of planning and litigation on the part of the NAACP to invalidate racial segregation in public schools.

Linda Brown was a black child whose father had tried to enroll her in a white public school in Topeka, Kansas. The white school was close to Linda's home; the walk to the black school meant that she had to cross a dangerous set of railroad tracks. Brown's request was refused because of Linda's race. A federal district court found that the black public school was equal in quality to the white school in all relevant respects; therefore, according to the *Plessy* doctrine, Linda was required to go to the black public school. Brown appealed the decision.

Brown* v. *Board of Education reached the Supreme Court in late 1951. The justices delayed argument on the sensitive case until after the 1952 national election. *Brown* was merged with four similar cases into a class action, a device for combining the claims or defenses of similar individuals so that they can be tried in a single lawsuit (see Chapter 14). The class action was supported by the NAACP and coordinated by Thurgood Marshall, who would later become the first black justice to sit on the Supreme Court. The five cases squarely challenged the separate-but-equal doctrine. By all tangible measures (standards for teacher licensing, teacher–pupil ratios, library facilities), the two school systems in each case—one white, the other black—were equal. The issue was legal separation of the races.

On May 17, 1954, Chief Justice Earl Warren, who had only recently joined the Court, delivered a single opinion covering four of the cases. Warren spoke for a unanimous Court when he declared that "in the field of public education the doctrine of 'separate but equal' has no place. Separate educational facilities are inherently unequal,"[15] depriving the plaintiffs of the equal protection of the laws. Segregated facilities generate in black children "a feeling of inferiority ... that may affect their hearts and minds in a way unlikely ever to be undone."[16] In short, the nation's highest court found that state-imposed public school segregation violated the equal protection clause of the Fourteenth Amendment.

A companion case to *Brown* challenged the segregation of public schools in Washington, D.C.[17] Segregation there was imposed by Congress. The equal protection clause protected citizens only against state violations; no equal protection clause restrained the national government because the District of Columbia is not a state. It was unthinkable for the Constitution to impose a lesser duty on the national government than on the states. In this case, the Court unanimously decided that the racial segregation requirement was an arbitrary deprivation of liberty without due process of law, a violation of the Fifth Amendment. In short, the concept of liberty encompassed the idea of equality. The Court deferred implementation of the school desegregation decisions until 1955. Then, in **Brown v. Board of Education II**, it ruled that school systems must desegregate "with all deliberate speed" and assigned the task of supervising desegregation to the lower federal courts.[18]

Some states quietly complied with the *Brown* decree. Others did little to desegregate their schools. And many communities in the South defied the Court, sometimes violently. Some white business and professional people formed "white citizens' councils." The councils put economic pressure on blacks who asserted their rights by foreclosing on their mortgages and denying them credit at local stores. Georgia and North Carolina resisted desegregation by paying tuition for white students attending private schools. Virginia and other states ordered that desegregated schools be closed. This resistance, along with the Supreme Court's "all deliberate speed" order, placed a heavy burden on federal judges to dismantle what was the fundamental social order in many communities.[19] Gradual desegregation under *Brown* was in some cases no desegregation at all. In 1969, a unanimous Supreme Court ordered that the operation of segregated school systems stop "at once."[20]

Two years later, the Court approved several remedies to achieve integration, including

ullstein bild/The Image Works

Anger Erupts in Little Rock

In 1957, the Little Rock, Arkansas, school board attempted to implement court-ordered desegregation: nine black teenagers were to be admitted to Little Rock Central High School. Governor Orval Faubus ordered the National Guard to bar their attendance. A mob blocked a subsequent attempt by the students. Finally, President Dwight D. Eisenhower ordered federal troops to escort the students to the high school. Among them was fifteen-year-old Elizabeth Eckford (right). Hazel Bryan Massery (left) angrily taunted her from the crowd. This image seared the nation's conscience. The violence and hostility led the school board to seek a postponement of the desegregation plan. The Supreme Court, meeting in special session, affirmed the decision in *Brown* v. *Board of Education* and ordered the plan to proceed. Not to be outdone, Governor Faubus closed all public schools in 1958. They reopened the following year. Fifty years later, a federal judge declared Little Rock's schools desegregated.

de jure segregation
Government-imposed segregation.

de facto segregation
Segregation that is not the result of government influence.

busing, racial quotas, and the pairing or grouping of noncontiguous school zones. In *Swann* v. *Charlotte-Mecklenburg County Schools*, the Supreme Court affirmed the right of lower courts to order the busing of children to ensure school desegregation.[21] But these remedies applied only to **de jure segregation**, government-imposed segregation (for example, government assignment of whites to one school and blacks to another within the same community). Court-imposed remedies did not apply to **de facto segregation**, which is not the result of government action (for example, racial segregation resulting from residential patterns).

The busing of schoolchildren came under heavy attack in both the North and the South. Desegregation advocates saw busing as a potential remedy in many northern cities, where schools had become segregated as white families left the cities for the suburbs. This "white flight" had left inner-city schools predominantly black and suburban schools almost all white. Public opinion strongly opposed the busing approach, and Congress sought to impose limits on busing as a remedy to segregation. In 1974, a closely divided Court ruled that lower courts could not order busing across school district boundaries unless each district had practiced racial discrimination or school district lines had been deliberately drawn to achieve racial segregation.[22] This ruling meant an end to large-scale school desegregation in metropolitan areas.

The Civil Rights Movement

LO4 ★ Describe the circumstances under which the 1964 Civil Rights Act was passed and its evolving interpretation in subsequent Supreme Court decisions.

Although the NAACP concentrated on school desegregation, it also made headway in other areas. The Supreme Court responded to NAACP efforts in the late 1940s by outlawing whites-only primary elections in the South, declaring them to be in violation of the Fifteenth Amendment. The Court also declared segregation on interstate bus routes to be unconstitutional and desegregated restaurants and hotels in the District of Columbia. Despite these and other decisions that chipped away at existing barriers to equality, states still were denying black citizens political power, and segregation remained a fact of daily life. Moreover, power in Congress resided with southern Democrats who resisted efforts to pass civil rights legislation.[23]

Dwight D. Eisenhower, who became president in 1953, was not as concerned about civil rights as his predecessor had been. He chose to stand above the battle between the Supreme Court and those who resisted the Court's decisions. He even refused to reveal whether he agreed with the Court's decision in *Brown* v. *Board of Education*. "It makes no difference," Eisenhower declared, because "the Constitution is as the Supreme Court interprets it."[24] Eisenhower did enforce school desegregation when the safety of schoolchildren was involved, but he appeared unwilling to do much more to advance racial equality. That goal seemed to require the political mobilization of the people—black and white—in what is now known as the **civil rights movement**.

civil rights movement
The mass mobilization during the 1960s that sought to gain equality of rights and opportunities for blacks in the South and to a lesser extent in the North, mainly through nonviolent, unconventional means of participation.

Black churches served as the crucible of the movement. More than places of worship, they served hundreds of other functions. In black communities, the church was "a bulletin board to a people who owned no organs of communication, a credit union to those without banks, and even a kind of people's court."[25] Some of its preachers were motivated by fortune, others by saintliness. One would prove to be a modern day Moses.

Civil Disobedience

Rosa Parks, a black woman living in Montgomery, Alabama, sounded the first call to action. That city's Jim Crow ordinances were tougher than those in other southern cities, where blacks were required to sit in the back of the bus while whites sat in the front, both races converging as the bus filled with passengers. In Montgomery, bus drivers had the power to define and redefine the floating line separating blacks and whites: drivers could order blacks to vacate an entire row to make room for one white or order blacks to stand even when some seats were vacant. Blacks could not walk through the white section to their seats in the back; they had to leave the bus after paying their fare and reenter through the rear.[26] In December 1955, Parks boarded a city bus on her way home from work and took an available seat in the front of the bus; she refused to give up her seat when the driver asked her to do so. She was arrested and fined $10 for violating the city ordinance.

Montgomery's black community responded to Parks's arrest with a boycott of the city's bus system. A **boycott** is a refusal to do business with a company or individual as an expression of disapproval or a means of coercion. Blacks walked or carpooled or stayed at home rather than ride the city's buses. As the bus company moved close to bankruptcy and downtown merchants suffered from the loss of black business, city officials began to harass blacks, hoping to frighten them into ending the boycott. But Montgomery's black citizens now had a leader, a charismatic twenty-six-year-old Baptist minister named Martin Luther King, Jr. King urged the people to hold out, and they did. A year after the boycott began, a federal court ruled that segregated transportation systems violated the equal protection clause of the Constitution. The boycott had proved to be an effective weapon.

In 1957, King helped organize the Southern Christian Leadership Conference to coordinate civil rights activities. He was totally committed to nonviolent action to bring racial issues into the light. To that end, he advocated **civil disobedience**, the willful but nonviolent breach of unjust laws.

One nonviolent tactic was the sit-in. On February 1, 1960, four black freshmen from North Carolina Agricultural and Technical College in Greensboro sat down at a whites-only lunch counter. They were refused service by the black waitress, who said, "Fellows like you make our race look bad." The young men stayed all day and promised to return the next morning to continue what they called a "sit-down protest." Other students soon joined in, rotating shifts so that no one missed classes. Within two days, eighty-five students had flocked to the lunch counter. Although abused verbally and physically, the students would not move. Finally, they were arrested. Soon people held similar sit-in demonstrations throughout the South and then in the North.[27] The Supreme Court upheld the actions of the demonstrators, although the unanimity that had characterized its earlier decisions was gone. (In this decision, three justices argued that even bigots had the right to call on the government to protect their property interests.)[28]

The Civil Rights Act of 1964

In 1961, a new administration, headed by President John F. Kennedy, came to power. At first Kennedy did not seem to be committed to civil rights. But his stance changed as the movement gained momentum and as more and more whites became aware of the abuse being heaped on sit-in demonstrators, freedom riders (who protested unlawful segregation on interstate bus routes), and those who were trying to help blacks register to vote in southern states. Volunteers were being jailed, beaten, and even killed for advocating activities among blacks that whites took for granted.

boycott
A refusal to do business with a firm, individual, or nation as an expression of disapproval or as a means of coercion.

civil disobedience
The willful but nonviolent breach of laws that are regarded as unjust.

LBJ Library/Photo by Yoichi R. Okamoto

When Leaders Confer

Martin Luther King, Jr., was a Baptist minister who believed in the principles of nonviolent protest practiced by India's Mohandas (Mahatma) Gandhi. This photograph captures King at a meeting with President Lyndon Johnson and other civil rights leaders in the White House cabinet room on March 18, 1966. King later joked that he was instructed to reach the White House south gate by "irregular routes," chuckling that he "had to sneak in the back door." King, who won the Nobel Peace Prize in 1964, was assassinated in 1968 in Memphis, Tennessee.

In late 1962, President Kennedy ordered federal troops to ensure the safety of James Meredith, the first black to attend the University of Mississippi. In early 1963, Kennedy enforced the desegregation of the University of Alabama. In April 1963, television viewers were shocked to see civil rights marchers in Birmingham, Alabama, attacked with dogs, fire hoses, and cattle prods. (The idea of the Birmingham march was to provoke confrontations with white officials in an effort to compel the national government to intervene on behalf of blacks.) Finally, in June 1963, Kennedy asked Congress for legislation that would outlaw segregation in public accommodations.

Two months later, Martin Luther King, Jr., joined in a march on Washington, D.C. The organizers called the protest "A March for Jobs and Freedom," signaling the economic goals of black America. More than 250,000 people, black and white, gathered peaceably at the Lincoln Memorial to hear King speak. "I have a dream," the great preacher extemporized, "that my little children will one day live in a nation where they will not be judged by the color of their skin but by the content of their character."[29]

Congress had not yet enacted Kennedy's public accommodations bill when he was assassinated on November 22, 1963. His successor, Lyndon B. Johnson, considered civil rights his top legislative priority. Johnson's long congressional experience and exceptional leadership ability as Senate majority leader were put to good use in overcoming the considerable opposition to the legislation. Within months, Congress enacted the Civil Rights Act of 1964, which included a vital provision barring segregation in most public accommodations. This congressional action was in part a reaction to Kennedy's death. But it was also almost certainly a response to the brutal treatment of blacks throughout the South. Viewed from afar, it is probably fair to say that King's efforts were necessary but not sufficient to ensure passage of the law. But Johnson's legislative mastery made all the difference between success and failure.[30]

Congress had enacted civil rights laws in 1957 and 1960, but they dealt primarily with voting rights. The 1964 act was the most comprehensive legislative attempt ever to erase racial discrimination in the United States. Among its many provisions, the act

- Entitled all persons to "the full and equal enjoyment" of goods, services, and privileges in places of public accommodation, without discrimination on the grounds of race, color, religion, or national origin (the inclusion of "national origin" or place of birth would set in motion plans for immigration reform the following year)
- Established the right to equality in employment opportunities
- Strengthened voting rights legislation
- Created the Equal Employment Opportunity Commission (EEOC) and charged it with hearing and investigating complaints of job discrimination*
- Provided that funds could be withheld from federally assisted programs administered in a discriminatory manner

The last of these provisions had a powerful effect on school desegregation when Congress enacted the Elementary and Secondary Education Act in 1965. That act provided billions of federal dollars for the nation's schools; the threat of losing that money spurred local school boards to formulate and implement new plans for

---

*Since 1972, the EEOC has had the power to institute legal proceedings on behalf of employees who allege that they have been victims of illegal discrimination.

desegregation. The 1964 act faced an immediate constitutional challenge. Its opponents argued that the Constitution does not forbid acts of private discrimination—the position the Supreme Court itself had taken in the late nineteenth century. But this time, a unanimous Court upheld the law, declaring that acts of discrimination impose substantial burdens on interstate commerce and thus are subject to congressional control.[31]

In a companion case, Ollie McClung, the owner of a small restaurant, had refused to serve blacks. McClung maintained that he had the freedom to serve whomever he wanted in his own restaurant. The justices, however, upheld the government's prohibition of McClung's racial discrimination on the grounds that a substantial portion of the food served in his restaurant had moved in interstate commerce.[32] Thus, the Supreme Court vindicated the Civil Rights Act of 1964 by reason of the congressional power to regulate interstate commerce rather than on the basis of the Fourteenth Amendment. Since 1937, the Court had approved ever-widening authority to regulate state and local activities under the commerce clause. It was the most powerful basis for the exercise of congressional power in the Constitution. In 2012, the Court's conservative majority signaled a limit to this power, declaring that Congress may not regulate commercial "inactivity" to support the insurance mandate of the Obama administration's health-care law. But a coalition of four liberal justices plus Chief Justice John G. Roberts, Jr., upheld the law's constitutionality on Congress's power to tax and spend for the general welfare.[33]

President Johnson's goal was a "great society." Soon a constitutional amendment and a series of civil rights laws were in place to help him meet his goal:

- The Twenty-fourth Amendment, ratified in 1964, banned poll taxes in primary and general elections for national office.
- The Economic Opportunity Act of 1964 provided education and training to combat poverty.
- The Voting Rights Act of 1965 empowered the attorney general to send voter registration supervisors to areas in which fewer than half the eligible minority voters had been registered. This act has been credited with doubling black voter registration in the South in only five years.[34]
- The Fair Housing Act of 1968 banned discrimination in the rental and sale of most housing.

The Continuing Struggle over Civil Rights

In the decades that followed, it became clear that civil rights laws on the books do not ensure civil rights in action. In 1984, for example, the Supreme Court was called on to interpret a law forbidding sex discrimination in schools and colleges that receive financial assistance from the national government: Must the entire institution comply with the regulations, or only those portions of it that receive assistance?

In *Grove City College* v. *Bell*, the Court ruled that government educational grants to students implicate the institution as a recipient of government funds; therefore, it must comply with government nondiscrimination provisions. However, only the specific department or program receiving the funds (in Grove City's case, the financial aid program), not the whole institution, was barred from discriminating.[35] Athletic departments rarely receive such government funds, so colleges had no obligation to provide equal opportunity for women in their sports programs.

The *Grove City* decision had widespread effects because three other important civil rights laws were worded similarly. The implication was that any law barring discrimination on the basis of race, sex, age, or disability would be applicable only to

CONNECT WITH YOUR CLASSMATES
MindTap for American Government

Access the Civil Rights Forum: Discussion—Minority Rights Protection.

programs receiving federal funds, not to the entire institution. So a university laboratory that received federal research grants could not discriminate, but other departments that did not receive federal money could. The effect of *Grove City* was to frustrate enforcement of civil rights laws. In keeping with pluralist theory, civil rights and women's groups shifted their efforts to the legislative branch.

Congress reacted immediately, exercising its lawmaking power to check the law-interpreting power of the judiciary. Congress can revise national laws to counter judicial decisions; in this political chess game, the Court's move is hardly the last one. Legislators protested that the Court had misinterpreted the intent of the antidiscrimination laws, and they forged a bipartisan effort to make that intent crystal clear: if any part of an institution gets federal money, no part of it can discriminate. Their work led to the Civil Rights Restoration Act, which became law in 1988 despite a presidential veto by Ronald Reagan.

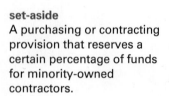

set-aside
A purchasing or contracting provision that reserves a certain percentage of funds for minority-owned contractors.

Although Congress tried to restore and expand civil rights enforcement, the Supreme Court weakened it again. The Court restricted minority contractor **set-asides** of state public works funds, an arrangement it had approved in 1980. (A set-aside is a purchasing or contracting provision that reserves a certain percentage of funds for minority-owned contractors.) The five-person majority held that past societal discrimination alone cannot serve as the basis for rigid quotas.[36]

Buttressed by Republican appointees, the Supreme Court continued to narrow the scope of national civil rights protections in a string of decisions that suggested the ascendancy of a new conservative majority more concerned with freedom than equality.[37] To counter the Court's changing interpretations of civil rights laws, liberals turned to Congress to restore and enlarge earlier Court decisions by writing them into law. The result was a comprehensive new civil rights bill. The Civil Rights Act of 1991 reversed or altered twelve Court decisions that had narrowed civil rights protections. The new law clarified and expanded earlier legislation and increased the costs to employers for intentional, illegal discrimination. Continued resentment generated by equal outcomes policies would move the battle back to the courts, however.

Civil Rights for Other Minorities

LO5 ★ Evaluate the effect of the civil rights movement on other minority groups' struggles for equality.

The civil rights movement has had an enormous effect on all minorities. Here we examine the civil rights struggles of four groups: Native Americans, immigrant groups (the largest of which are Latinos), people with disabilities, and homosexuals.

Native Americans

During the eighteenth and nineteenth centuries, the U.S. government took Indian lands, isolated Native Americans on reservations, and denied them political and social rights. The government's dealings with the Indians were often marked by violence and broken promises. The agencies responsible for administering Indian reservations kept Native Americans poor and dependent on the national government.

The national government switched policies at the beginning of the twentieth century, promoting assimilation instead of separation. The government banned the use of native languages and religious rituals; it sent Indian children to boarding schools and gave them non-Indian names. In 1924, Indians received U.S. citizenship. Until that time, they had been considered members of tribal nations whose relations with the U.S. government were determined by treaties. The Native American population suffered badly during the Great Depression, primarily because the poorest Americans were affected most severely but also because of the inept administration of Indian reservations. (Today, Native Americans make up less than 1 percent of the population.)

Anger bred of poverty, unemployment, and frustration with an uncaring government exploded in militant action in late 1969, when several American Indians seized Alcatraz Island, an abandoned island in San Francisco Bay. The group cited an 1868 Sioux treaty that entitled them to unused federal lands; they remained on the island for a year and a half. In 1973, armed members of the American Indian Movement seized eleven hostages at Wounded Knee, South Dakota, the site of an 1890 massacre of two hundred Sioux (Lakota) by U.S. cavalry troops. They remained there, occasionally exchanging gunfire with federal marshals, for seventy-one days, until the government agreed to examine the treaty rights of the Oglala Sioux.[38]

In 1946, Congress enacted legislation establishing an Indian claims commission to compensate Native Americans for land that had been taken from them. In the 1970s, the Native American Rights Fund and other groups used that legislation to win important victories in the courts. The tribes won the return of lands in the Midwest and in the states of Oklahoma, New Mexico, and Washington. In 1980, the Supreme Court ordered the national government to pay the Sioux $117 million plus interest for the Black Hills of South Dakota, which had been stolen from them a century before. The special status accorded Indian tribes in the Constitution has proved attractive to a new group of Indian leaders. Some of the 565 recognized tribes have successfully instituted casino gambling on their reservations, even in the face of state opposition to their plans. The tribes pay no taxes on their profits, which has helped them make gambling a powerful engine of economic growth for themselves and has given a once impoverished people undreamed-of riches and responsibilities. Congress has allowed these developments, provided that the tribes spend their profits on Indian assistance programs.

It is important to remember that throughout American history, Native Americans have been coerced physically and pressured economically to assimilate into the mainstream of white society. The destiny of Native Americans as viable groups with separate identities depends in no small measure on curbing their dependence on the national government.[39] The wealth created by casino gambling and other ventures funded with gambling profits may prove to be Native Americans' most effective weapon for regaining their heritage. (See Figure 16.1.)

Immigrant Groups

The Statue of Liberty stands at the entrance to New York harbor, a gift from the people of France to commemorate the centennial of the United States. It is an icon of the United States in the world, capturing the belief that this country is a beacon of liberty for countless immigrants far and wide. We are a nation of immigrants. But the truth is more complex. Until 1965, the laws that governed immigration were rooted in invidious discrimination. Liberty's beacon drew millions of undocumented immigrants. Efforts to stem this tide brought unanticipated consequences, but further reform has failed to stop the flow of undocumented immigrants to these shores.

For most of the first half of the twentieth century, immigration rules established a strict quota system that gave a clear advantage to Northern and Western Europeans and guaranteed that few Southern or Eastern Europeans, Asians, Africans, and Jews would enter the country by legal means. This was akin to the same unjustified

FIGURE 16.1 Wampum Winners: Native American and Commercial Gambling Revenue, 1990–2012

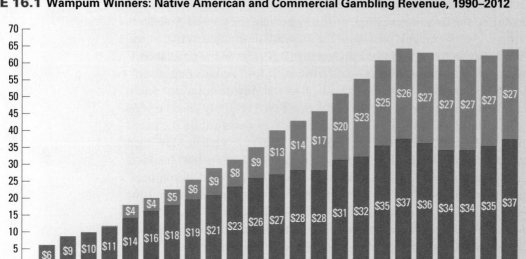

Most people imagine Las Vegas as the hub of American gambling, but it accounts for a mere 10 percent of all gambling revenue. In 2012, Native American gaming accounted for more than 37 percent of all such revenue. Revenue at Native American casinos grew from less than $1 billion in 1993 to $27 billion in 2012. Once-poor Native American tribes have now found a path to economic success.

Source: BofA Merrill Lynch Gloabl Research, NIGC, State gaming control boards.
Note: Native American gaming revenues not available for periods prior to 1993.

discrimination that had subjugated blacks since the end of the Civil War. In the same spirit that championed civil rights for African Americans, a once-reluctant Congress changed the rules to end discrimination on the basis of national origin. In 1965, President Lyndon Johnson signed a new immigration bill into law at the Statue of Liberty. Henceforth, the invidious quota system was gone; everyone was supposed to have an equal chance of immigrating to the United States. Upon signing the bill, Johnson remarked that there was nothing revolutionary about the law. "It will not reshape the structure of our daily lives or add importantly to either our wealth or our power." Within a few years, Johnson's prediction proved fundamentally wrong.

One purpose of the new law was to reunite families. It gave preference to relatives of immigrants already here, but since the vast majority of these legal immigrants came from Northern or Western Europe, the expectation was that reuniting families would continue the earlier preferences. Another provision gave preference in much smaller numbers to immigrants with much needed skills, such as doctors and engineers. It never occurred to the law's designers that African doctors, Indian engineers, Philippine nurses, or Chinese software programmers would be able to immigrate. Word trickled out to those newly eligible to come. Once here, these immigrants petitioned for their relatives to come. And those family members petitioned for yet others. As a result of this "chain migration," entire extended families established themselves in the United States, yet the law did nothing to staunch the flow of undocumented immigrants.

The demand for cheap labor in agriculture and manufacturing proved an enticing lure to many of the poor with access to America's southern border. The personal risk in crossing the border illegally was often outweighed by the possible gain in employment and a new, though illegal, start. There was no risk of imprisonment, merely a return to south of the border and perhaps another attempt to cross into a "promised land." During the post-1965 period, millions of men and women chose personal risk for the possibility of a better future.

In 1986, Congress sought to fix a system that by all accounts was broken. It sought to place the burden of enforcement on employers by imposing fines for hiring undocumented workers and then by offering amnesty to resident undocumented immigrants who were in the United States for at least five years. But lax government enforcement and ease in obtaining falsified worker documents such as a "green card" doomed the enforcement strategy. Undocumented immigrants continued to enter the United States, the majority from Mexico (see Figure 16.2).

By 2006, politicians were ready for another round of reform, motivated by over 11 million undocumented immigrants in the United States (triple the number since the previous reform effort twenty years earlier); state and local governments in border states that were hit hard for the cost of public services (for example, health and education) for undocumented immigrants; and the threat to national security in a post-9/11 world posed by porous, unguarded borders. While the public is opposed to undocumented immigrants obtaining driver's licenses or health care, it is important to note that in 2005, undocumented immigrants paid an estimated $7 billion in Social Security taxes with little or nothing in return from the government.

Frustration brought about by hard economic times tends to make undocumented immigrants easy targets. This is especially the case in Arizona, which experiences the

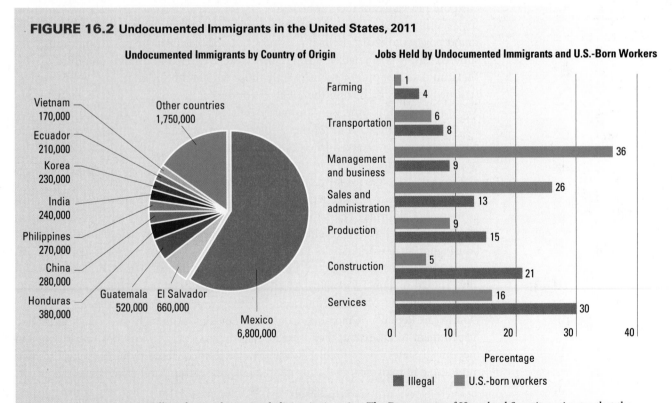

FIGURE 16.2 Undocumented Immigrants in the United States, 2011

Undocumented Immigrants by Country of Origin

- Vietnam 170,000
- Ecuador 210,000
- Korea 230,000
- India 240,000
- Philippines 270,000
- China 280,000
- Honduras 380,000
- Guatemala 520,000
- El Salvador 660,000
- Other countries 1,750,000
- Mexico 6,800,000

Jobs Held by Undocumented Immigrants and U.S.-Born Workers

	Illegal	U.S.-born workers
Farming	1	4
Transportation	6	8
Management and business	36	9
Sales and administration	26	13
Production	9	15
Construction	5	21
Services	16	30

Percentage

■ Illegal   ■ U.S.-born workers

In 2011, there were 40.4 million foreign-born people living in America. The Department of Homeland Security estimates that the undocumented immigrant population living in the United States increased to 11.1 million in January 2011 from 8.4 million in January 2000. Between 2000 and 2011, the undocumented population grew by 36 percent.

Sources: Michael Hoefer, Nancy Rytina, and Bryan C. Baker, "Estimates of the Unauthorized Immigrant Population Residing in the United States: January 2011," Office of Immigration Statistics of the DHS, March 2012, http://www.dhs.gov/xlibrary/assets/statistics/publications/ois_ill_pe_2011.pdf; and "A Nation of Immigrants" (Washington, D.C.: Pew Hispanic Center), http://pewhispanic.org/files/reports/2013/01/29/a-nation-of-immigrants/.

greatest number of illegal border crossings from Mexico and has a large Hispanic population. With a surge in violence resulting from drug smuggling and human trafficking at its border, the Arizona legislature—backed by strong public opinion—adopted the strictest state immigration law in the nation in 2010. Among its many provisions, the law made it a crime for an alien to be in Arizona without carrying legal documents and obligates the police to determine a person's immigration status if there is a reasonable suspicion that the person is an illegal alien. It also stepped up state and local law enforcement of federal immigration laws and cracked down on those sheltering, hiring, and transporting illegal aliens. In June 2012, the Supreme Court struck down three of the law's draconian provisions on federalism grounds—the Constitution vests exclusive power over naturalization and citizenship in the national government—but the Court upheld the part of the law that instructs law enforcement officials to check a person's immigration status when there is reasonable suspicion of the person's illegal status.[40]

Many Latinos have a rich and deep-rooted heritage in America, but until the 1920s, that heritage was largely confined to the southwestern states, particularly California. Then unprecedented numbers of Mexican immigrants came to the United States in search of employment and a better life. Businesspeople who saw in them a source of cheap labor welcomed them. Many Mexicans became farm workers; others settled mainly in crowded, low-rent, inner-city districts in the Southwest, forming their own barrios, or neighborhoods, within the cities, where they maintained the customs and values of their homeland.

Like blacks who had migrated to northern cities, most new Latino immigrants found poverty and discrimination. And like poor blacks and Native Americans, they suffered disproportionately during the Great Depression. About one-third of the Mexican American population (mainly those who had been migratory farm workers) returned to Mexico during the 1930s. World War II gave rise to another influx of Mexicans, who this time were primarily courted to work farms in California. But by the late 1950s, most farm workers—blacks, whites, and Hispanics—were living in poverty. Latinos who lived in cities fared little better. Yet millions of Mexicans continued to cross the border into the United States, both legally and illegally. The effect was to depress wages for farm labor in California and the Southwest.

In 1965, Cesar Chavez led a strike of the United Farm Workers union against growers in California. The strike lasted several years and eventually, in combination with a national boycott, resulted in somewhat better pay, working conditions, and housing for farm workers.

In the 1970s and 1980s, the Latino population continued to grow, and to grow rapidly. The 20 million Latinos living in the United States in the 1970s were still mainly Puerto Rican and Mexican American, but they were joined by immigrants from the Dominican Republic, Colombia, Cuba, and Ecuador. Although civil rights legislation helped them to an extent, they were among the poorest and least educated groups in the United States. Their problems were similar to those faced by other nonwhites, but most also had to overcome the further difficulty of learning and using a new language.

One effect of the language barrier is that voter registration and voter turnout among Hispanics are lower than among other groups. Today, there are thirty-three Hispanic majority congressional districts, ensuring a measure of representation. These majority minority districts remain under scrutiny as a result of Supreme Court decisions prohibiting race-based districting. Also, voter turnout depends on effective political advertising, and Hispanics have not been targeted as often as other groups with political messages in Spanish. Despite these stumbling blocks, Hispanics have started to exercise a measure of political power.

Hispanics occupy positions of power in national and local arenas. Hispanics or Latinos constitute about 16 percent of the population and 7 percent of Congress. The 113th Congress (2013–2014) convened with a diverse group of thirty-seven members of Hispanic descent: thirty-three in the House and four in the Senate. The National Hispanic Caucus of State Legislators, which has over 350 members, is an informal bipartisan group dedicated to voicing and advancing issues affecting Hispanic Americans at the state level. The appointment of Sonia Sotomayor to the U.S. Supreme Court in 2009, and the growing number of Hispanics appointed to the lower federal courts, signaled yet another milestone in the quest for equality for America's largest minority group. The Census Bureau estimates that by 2050, one-third of all residents will be Hispanic. With such growth will come greater political power.[41]

Americans with Disabilities

Minority status is not confined to racial and ethnic groups. After more than two decades of struggle, 43 million Americans with disabilities gained recognition in 1990 as a protected minority with the enactment of the Americans with Disabilities Act (ADA). The law extends the protections embodied in the Civil Rights Act of 1964 to people with physical or mental disabilities, including people with AIDS, alcoholism, and drug addiction. It guarantees them access to employment, transportation, public accommodations, and communication services.

The roots of the disabled rights movement stem from the period after World War II. Thousands of disabled veterans returned to a country and a society that were insensitive to their needs. Institutionalization seemed the best way to care for people with disabilities, but this approach came under increasing fire as people with disabilities and their families sought care at home.

Advocates for persons with disabilities found a ready model in the existing civil rights laws. Opponents argued that the changes mandated by the 1990 law (such as access for those confined to wheelchairs) could cost billions of dollars, but supporters replied that the costs would be offset by an equal or greater reduction in federal aid to people with disabilities, who would rather be working.

The law's enactment set off an avalanche of job discrimination complaints filed with the national government's discrimination watchdog agency, the EEOC. From 1997 to 2013, the EEOC had received about 19,000 ADA-related complaints annually. Curiously, most complaints came from already employed people, both previously and recently disabled. They charged that their employers failed to provide reasonable accommodations as required by the law. The disabilities cited most frequently were back problems, mental illness, heart trouble, neurological disorders, and substance abuse.[42]

A deceptively simple question lies at the heart of many ADA suits: What is the meaning of *disability*? According to the EEOC, a disability is "a physical or mental impairment that substantially limits one or more major life activities." This deliberately vague language has thrust the courts into the role of providing needed specificity, a path that politicians have feared to tread.[43]

Congress moved a step closer in 2008, passing a revision to the ADA. The legislation increased protections for people with disabilities by making it easier for workers to prove discrimination. The ADA Amendments Act of 2008 gives protection to people with epilepsy, diabetes, cancer, cerebral palsy, multiple sclerosis, and other ailments. Federal court decisions had denied protection under the ADA because the disabling conditions were controlled by medication or were in remission.

A change in the nation's laws, no matter how welcome, does not ensure a change in people's attitudes. Laws that end racial discrimination do not extinguish racism, and laws that ban biased treatment of people with disabilities cannot mandate their acceptance. But civil rights advocates predict that bias against people with disabilities, like similar biases against other minorities, will wither as they become full participants in society.

Gay Americans

June 27, 1969, marked the beginning of an often overlooked movement for civil rights in the United States. On that Friday evening, plainclothes officers of the New York City police force raided a gay bar in Greenwich Village known as the Stonewall Inn. The police justified the raid because of their suspicions that Stonewall had been operating without a proper liquor license. In response, hundreds of citizens took to the streets in protest. Violent clashes and a backlash against the police involving hundreds of people ensued for several nights, during which cries of "Gay power!" and "We want freedom!" could be heard. The event became known as the Stonewall Riots and served as the touchstone for the gay liberation movement in the United States.[44]

Stonewall led to the creation of several political interest groups that have fought for the civil liberties and civil rights of members of the gay and lesbian communities. One in particular, the National Gay and Lesbian Task Force, successfully lobbied the U.S. Civil Service Commission in 1973 to allow gay people to serve in public employment. With over a million members, the Human Rights Campaign, founded in 1980, is the largest civil rights organization seeking equality for lesbian, gay, bisexual, and transgender (LGBT) Americans. One of its current priorities is to seek passage of an employment nondiscrimination act to prevent U.S. citizens from being fired from their jobs for being gay.

Although once viewed as being on the fringe of American society, the gay community today maintains a visible presence in national politics. Seven openly gay members serve in the U.S. House of Representatives (113th Congress): Mike Michaud (D-Maine), Jared Polis (D-Col.), David Cicilline (D-R.I.), Sean Patrick Maloney (D-N.Y.), Mark Takano (D-Calif.), Mark Pokan (D-Wisc.), and Kyrsten Sinema (D-Ariz.). One openly gay member—Tammy Baldwin (D-Wisc.)—serves in the Senate.

Gays and lesbians have made significant progress since the early 1970s, but they still have a long way to go to enjoy the complete menu of civil rights now written into laws that protect other minority groups. Progress includes an end to the "don't ask, don't tell" policy enabling gays and lesbians to serve openly in the U.S. military.[45] And on May 9, 2012, Obama became the first sitting president to state that he supported same-sex marriage. While his was an explicitly personal endorsement of same-sex unions and therefore would have little immediate policy impact, the announcement was nonetheless hailed as "historic."[46]

In 2008, the California Supreme Court ruled 4–3 that same-sex couples have a state constitutional right to marry. State law and a statewide initiative approved in 2000 defined marriage as a union between a man and a woman. The ruling was celebrated in San Francisco's large gay community and denounced by religious and conservative groups throughout the state who supported a ballot initiative that would amend the state constitution to ban same-sex marriages and overturn the decision. Proposition 8 passed in 2008, overturning the ruling by defining marriage in the state constitution as a union between one man and one woman.

While conceding that Californians could define their own rules, attorney Theodore Olson argued that those rules could not take away a fundamental right. The case boiled down to marriage equality. Is marriage a fundamental constitutional right? If so, then everyone is entitled to exercise that right unless the government has compelling reasons to curtail it.[47] Many states do not adhere to Olson's logic. Thirty-one state constitutions ban legal recognition of same-sex unions; federal courts have declared eight such bans contrary to the equal protection clause of the Fourteenth Amendment. A showdown in the U.S. Supreme Court seems inevitable as states seek to protect their values enshrined in state constitutions against the demands for equality advanced by same-sex couples with increasing approval from a wider public. (See Figure 16.3.)

A federal appeals court overturned the California initiative in 2012 on the grounds that it violated the U.S. Constitution's equal protection clause. On further review, a sharply divided Supreme Court kicked the case out on technical grounds, which resulted in the legalization of gay marriage in California.[48]

Marriage equality under federal law took a major step forward in 2013 when the Supreme Court struck down part of the federal Defense of Marriage Act (DOMA) in the case of *United States v. Windsor*.[49] The provision of the act, passed in 1993, denied federal benefits to same-sex couples. For example, same-sex married couples were subject to higher estate taxes compared to other married couples. Federal laws contained hundreds of provisions—some minor, others not-that treated same—sex married couples differently. Justice Anthony Kennedy, writing for the

Justin Sullivan/Getty Images

Court Confronts California Clash

Same-sex marriage continues to provoke controversy. Here supporters of California's Proposition 8, which banned same-sex marriage in the state constitution, express their opposition to homosexuality at the federal courthouse in San Francisco where a federal appeals court heard arguments in late 2010 challenging the proposition's constitutionality. In February 2012, the court decided 2 to 1 that the provision violated the equal protection clause of the U.S. Constitution. It remains the law in California, but legal challenges continue for similar provisions in other states.

FIGURE 16.3 Marriage Equality and the Public

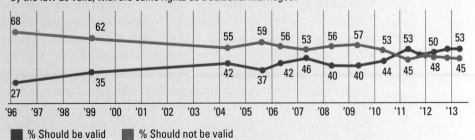

Do you think marriages between same-sex couples should or should not be recognized by the law as valid, with the same rights as traditional marriages?

| | '96 | '97 | '98 | '99 | '00 | '01 | '02 | '03 | '04 | '05 | '06 | '07 | '08 | '09 | '10 | '11 | '12 | '13 |

■ % Should be valid   ■ % Should not be valid

Note: Trend shown for polls in which same-sex marriage question followed question on gay/lesbian rights and relations
1996–2005 wording: "Do you think marriages between homosexuals ..."

Courts rarely manage to get out of step with public opinion. Sometimes, courts forge ahead in leading social change; oftentimes they lag behind. Given the surprisingly swift pace of social change on the matter of marriage equality, the courts appear closer to the prevailing sentiment as judged by the changing public attitude toward same-sex marriage.

Source: Jeffrey M. Jones, "Same-Sex Marriage Support Solidifies Above 50% in U.S.," 13 May 2013, http://www.gallup.com/poll/162398/sex-marriage-support-solidifies-above.aspx.

On my honor, I will do my best....

The Boy Scouts of America lifted its ban on gay scouts in 2014, but the organization continues to ban gays from serving as adult leaders. Jennifer Tyrrell (L) was removed from her position as den leader in 2012 for being gay. In this May 23, 2013 photo, Tyrrell hugs Pascal Tessier following passage of the policy at the Boy Scouts' National Annual Meeting in Grapevine, Texas. The Scouts, a private organization, can set its own membership standards, according to the Supreme Court's decision in Boy Scouts of America v. Dale (2000).

STRINGER/Reuters/Corbis

majority of five justices, held the DOMA provision unconstitutional under the Fifth Amendment's "due process" clause.

By 2014, a tide of lawsuits in the federal courts had swept away bans on same-sex marriage in a majority of the states. A last-ditch effort by the losing states to force Supreme Court review failed when the justices decided not to intervene. "Sometimes they [the justices] act by inaction," observed attorney Theodore Olson, encouraging further lawsuits in the remaining states that continue to ban such unions.[50]

A 2000 Supreme Court decision, **Boy Scouts of America v. Dale**, illustrates both the continuing legal struggles of gays and lesbians for civil rights and the modern conflict between freedom and equality. James Dale began his involvement in scouting in 1978 and ten years later achieved the esteemed rank of Eagle Scout. In 1989, he applied to and was accepted for the position of assistant scoutmaster of Troop 73 in New Jersey. Shortly after, in 1990, the Boy Scouts revoked Dale's membership in the organization when it learned that he had become a campus activist with the Rutgers University Lesbian/Gay Alliance. The Boy Scouts argued that because homosexual conduct was inconsistent with its mission, the organization enjoyed the right to revoke his membership. Dale argued that the Scouts' actions violated a New Jersey law that prohibited discrimination on the basis of sexual orientation in places of public accommodation. The U.S. Supreme Court resolved this conflict in a narrow 5–4 decision and sided with the Scouts. The majority opinion, authored by Chief Justice William H. Rehnquist, maintained that New Jersey's public accommodations law violated the Boy Scouts' freedom of association, outweighing Dale's claim for equal treatment. The dissenters, led by Justice John Paul Stevens, maintained that equal treatment outweighed free association. They reasoned that allowing Dale to serve as an assistant scoutmaster did not impose serious burdens on the Scouts or force the organization "to communicate any message that it does not wish to endorse."[51]

Gender and Equal Rights: The Women's Movement

LO6 ★ Trace the evolution of women's legal rights beginning with laws based on protectionism and concluding with Supreme Court rulings prohibiting gender-based discrimination.

Together with unconventional political activities such as protests and sit-ins, conventional political tools such as the ballot box and the lawsuit have brought minorities in

America a measure of equality. The Supreme Court, once responsible for perpetuating inequality for blacks, has expanded the array of legal tools available to all minorities to help them achieve social equality. Women, too, have benefited from this change.

Protectionism

Until the early 1970s, laws that affected the civil rights of women were based on traditional views of the relationship between men and women. At the heart of these laws was **protectionism**—the notion that women must be sheltered from life's harsh realities. Thomas Jefferson, author of the Declaration of Independence, believed that "were our state a pure democracy there would still be excluded from our deliberations women, who, to prevent deprivation of morals and ambiguity of issues, should not mix promiscuously in gatherings of men."[52] And "protected" they were, through laws that discriminated against them in employment and other areas. With few exceptions, women were also "protected" from voting until early in the twentieth century.

> **protectionism**
> The notion that women must be protected from life's cruelties; until the 1970s, the basis for laws affecting women's civil rights.

The demand for women's rights arose from the abolition movement and later was based primarily on the Fourteenth Amendment's prohibition of laws that "abridge the privileges or immunities of citizens of the United States." However, the courts consistently rebuffed challenges to protectionist state laws. In 1873, the Supreme Court upheld an Illinois statute that prohibited women from practicing law. The justices maintained that the Fourteenth Amendment had no bearing on a state's authority to regulate admission of members to the bar.[53]

Protectionism reached a peak in 1908, when the Court upheld an Oregon law limiting the number of hours women could work.[54] The decision was rife with assumptions about the nature and role of women, and it gave wide latitude to laws that "protected" the "weaker sex." It also led to protectionist legislation that barred women from working more than forty-eight hours a week and from working at jobs that required them to lift more than thirty-five pounds. (The average work week for men was sixty hours or longer.) In effect, women were locked out of jobs that called for substantial overtime (and overtime pay) and were shunted to jobs that men believed suited their abilities.

Protectionism can take many forms. Some employers hesitate to place women at risk in the workplace. Some have excluded women of child-bearing age from jobs that involve exposure to toxic substances that could harm a developing fetus. Usually such jobs offer more pay to compensate for their higher risk. Although they too face reproductive risks from toxic substances, men have experienced no such exclusions.

In 1991, the Supreme Court struck down a company's fetal protection policy in strong terms. The Court relied on amendments to the 1964 Civil Rights Act providing for only a very few narrow exceptions to the principle that unless some workers differ from others in their ability to work, they must be treated the same as other employees. "In other words," declared the majority, "women as capable of doing their jobs as their male counterparts may not be forced to choose between having a child and having a job."[55]

Political Equality for Women

With a few exceptions, women were not allowed to vote in this country until 1920. In 1869, Francis and Virginia Minor sued a St. Louis, Missouri, registrar for not allowing Virginia Minor to vote. In 1875, the Supreme Court held that the Fourteenth Amendment's privileges and immunities clause did not confer the right to vote on all citizens or require that the states allow women to vote.[56]

The decision clearly slowed the movement toward women's suffrage, but it did not stop it. In 1878, Susan B. Anthony, a women's rights activist, convinced a U.S. senator from California to introduce a constitutional amendment requiring that "the right of citizens of the United States to vote shall not be denied or abridged by the United States or by any State on account of sex." The amendment was introduced and voted down several times over the next twenty years. Meanwhile, as noted in Chapter 7, a number of states, primarily in the Midwest and West, did grant limited suffrage to women.

The movement for women's suffrage became a political battle to amend the Constitution. In 1917, police arrested 218 women from twenty-six states when they picketed the White House, demanding the right to vote. Nearly one hundred went to jail, some for days and others for months. The movement culminated in the adoption in 1920 of the **Nineteenth Amendment**, which gave women the right to vote. Its wording was that first suggested by Anthony.

The right of women to vote does not ensure that women representatives will be elected to public office. Meanwhile, the Supreme Court continued to act as the benevolent protector of women. Women entered the workforce in significant numbers during World War I and did so again during World War II, but they received lower wages than the men they replaced. Again, the justification was the "proper" role of women as mothers and homemakers. Because society expected men to be the principal providers, it followed that women's earnings were less important to the family's support. This thinking perpetuated inequalities in the workplace. Economic equality was closely tied to social attitudes. Because society expected women to stay at home, the assumption was that they needed less education than men did. Therefore, they tended to qualify only for low-paying, low-skilled jobs with little chance for advancement.

Nineteenth Amendment
The amendment to the Constitution, adopted in 1920, that ensures women of the right to vote.

Prohibiting Sex-Based Discrimination

The movement to provide equal rights to women advanced a step with the passage of the Equal Pay Act of 1963, which required equal pay for men and women doing similar work. However, state protectionist laws still had the effect of restricting women to jobs that men usually did not want. Where employment was stratified by sex, equal pay was an empty promise. To remove the restrictions of protectionism, women needed equal opportunity for employment. They got it in the Civil Rights Act of 1964 and later legislation.

The objective of the Civil Rights Act of 1964 was to eliminate racial discrimination in America. The original wording of Title VII of the act prohibited employment discrimination based on race, color, religion, and national origin—but not gender. In an effort to scuttle the provision during House debate, Democrat Howard W. Smith of Virginia proposed an amendment barring job discrimination based on sex. Smith's intention was to make the law unacceptable; his effort to ridicule the law brought gales of laughter to the debate. But Democrat Martha W. Griffiths of Michigan used Smith's strategy against him. With her support, Smith's amendment carried, as did the act.[57] Congress extended the jurisdiction of the EEOC to cover cases of invidious sex discrimination, or **sexism**.

Subsequent women's rights legislation was motivated by the pressure for civil rights, as well as by a resurgence of the women's movement, which had subsided in 1920 after the adoption of the Nineteenth Amendment. One particularly important law was Title IX of the Education Amendments of 1972, which prohibited sex discrimination in federally aided education programs. Another boost to women came from the Revenue Act of 1972, which provided tax credits for child-care expenses. In effect, the act subsidized parents with young children so that women could enter or

sexism
Invidious sex discrimination.

remain in the workforce. However, the high-water mark in the effort to secure women's rights was the equal rights amendment, as we shall explain shortly.

In 2007, a conservative Supreme Court tightened the rules over pay discrimination lawsuits under Title VII.[58] The case involved a woman who did not learn of the pay disparity with sixteen men in her office until years later because salary information is secret. But the law required her to file a complaint within 180 days of pay setting. The 5–4 decision prompted a bitter oral dissent by Justice Ruth Bader Ginsburg.

True to the pluralist character of American democracy, the Obama administration and a Democratic Congress reversed the 2007 decision by passing the Lilly Ledbetter Fair Pay Act. The act allows the filing of complaints beyond the 180-day period.[59] Pay equity for women still remains a hope, not a reality.

Stereotypes Under Scrutiny

After nearly a century of protectionism, the Supreme Court began to take a closer look at gender-based distinctions. In 1971, it struck down a state law that gave men preference over women in administering the estate of a person who died without naming an administrator.[60] The state maintained that the law reduced court workloads and avoided family battles; however, the Court dismissed those objections because they were not important enough to justify making gender-based distinctions between individuals. Two years later, the justices declared that paternalism operated to "put women not on a pedestal, but in a cage."[61] They then proceeded to strike down several laws that either prevented or discouraged departures from traditional sex roles. In 1976, the Court finally developed a workable standard for reviewing such laws: gender-based distinctions are justifiable only if they serve some important government purpose.[62]

The objective of the standard is to dismantle laws based on sexual stereotypes while fashioning public policies that acknowledge relevant differences between men and women. Perhaps the most controversial issue is the idea of comparable worth, which requires employers to pay comparable wages for different jobs, filled predominantly by one sex or the other, that are of about the same worth to the employer. Absent new legislation, the courts remain reluctant and ineffective vehicles for ending wage discrimination.[63] The courts have not been reluctant to extend to women the constitutional guarantees won by blacks. In 1994, the Supreme Court extended the Constitution's equal protection guarantee by forbidding the exclusion of potential jurors on the basis of their sex. In a 6–3 decision, the justices held that it is unconstitutional to use gender, and likewise race, as a criterion for determining juror competence and impartiality. "Discrimination in jury selection," wrote Justice Harry A. Blackmun for the majority, "whether based on race or on gender, causes harm to the litigants, the community, and the individual jurors who are wrongfully excluded from participation in the judicial process."[64] The 1994 decision completed a constitutional revolution in jury selection that began in 1986 with a bar against juror exclusions based on race.

In 1996, the Court spoke with uncommon clarity when it declared that the men-only admissions policy of the Virginia Military Institute (VMI), a state-supported military college, violated the equal protection clause of the Fourteenth Amendment. Virginia defended the school's policy on the grounds that it was preserving diversity among America's educational institutions.

In an effort to meet women's demands to enter VMI—and stave off continued legal challenges—Virginia established a separate-but-equal institution, the Virginia Women's Institute for Leadership (VWIL). The program was housed at Mary

Baldwin College, a private liberal arts college for women, and students enrolled in VWIL received the same financial support as students at VMI.

The presence of women at VMI would require substantial changes in the physical environment and the traditional close scrutiny of the students. Moreover, the presence of women would alter the manner in which cadets interact socially. Was the uniqueness of VMI worth preserving at the expense of women who could otherwise meet the academic, physical, and psychological stress imposed by the VMI approach?

In a 7–1 decision, the High Court voted no. Writing for a six-member majority in **United States v. Virginia**, Justice Ruth Bader Ginsburg applied a demanding test she labeled "skeptical scrutiny" to official acts that deny individuals rights or responsibilities based on their sex. "Parties who seek to defend gender-based government action," she wrote, "must demonstrate an 'exceedingly persuasive justification' for that action." Ginsburg declared that "women seeking and fit for a VMI-quality education cannot be offered anything less, under the State's obligation to afford them genuinely equal protection." Ginsburg went on to note that the VWIL program offered no cure for the "opportunities and advantages withheld from women who want a VMI education and can make the grade."[65] The upshot is that distinctions based on sex are almost as suspect as distinctions based on race. Three months after the Court's decision, VMI's board of directors finally voted 9–8 to admit women. This ended VMI's distinction as the last government-supported single-sex school. However, school officials made few allowances for women. Buzz haircuts and fitness requirements remained the standard for all students. "It would be demeaning to women to cut them slack," declared VMI's superintendent.[66]

The Equal Rights Amendment

Policies protecting women, based largely on gender stereotypes, have been woven into the legal fabric of American life. This protectionism has limited the freedom of women to compete with men socially and economically on an equal footing. However, the Supreme Court has been hesitant to extend the principles of the Fourteenth Amendment beyond issues of race. When judicial interpretation of the Constitution imposes a limit, then only a constitutional amendment can overcome it.

The National Women's Party, one of the few women's groups that did not disband after the Nineteenth Amendment was enacted, introduced the proposed **equal rights amendment (ERA)** in 1923. The ERA declared that "equality of rights under the law shall not be denied or abridged by the United States or any State on account of sex." It remained bottled up in committee in every Congress until 1970, when Representative Martha Griffiths filed a discharge petition to bring it to the House floor for a vote. The House passed the ERA, but the Senate scuttled it by attaching a section calling for prayer in the public schools.

A national coalition of women's rights advocates generated enough support to get the ERA through Congress in 1972. Its proponents then had seven years to get the amendment ratified by thirty-eight state legislatures, as required by the Constitution. By 1977, they were three states short of that goal, and three states had rescinded their earlier ratification. Then, in an unprecedented action, Congress extended the ratification deadline. It didn't help. The ERA died in 1982, still three states short of adoption.

Why did the ERA fail? There are several explanations. Its proponents mounted a national campaign to generate approval, while its opponents organized state-based anti-ERA campaigns. ERA proponents hurt their cause by exaggerating the

equal rights amendment (ERA) A failed constitutional amendment introduced by the National Women's Party in 1923, declaring that "equality of rights under the law shall not be denied or abridged by the United States or any State on account of sex."

amendment's effects; such claims only gave ammunition to the amendment's opponents. For example, the puffed-up claim that the amendment would make wife and husband equally responsible for their family's financial support caused alarm among the undecided. As the opposition grew stronger, especially from women who wanted to maintain their traditional role, state legislators began to realize that supporting the amendment involved risk. Given the exaggerations and counter-exaggerations, lawmakers ducked. Because it takes an extraordinary majority to amend the Constitution, it takes only a committed minority to thwart the majority's will.

Despite its failure, the movement to ratify the ERA produced real benefits. It raised the consciousness of women about their social position, spurred the formation of the National Organization for Women (NOW) and other large organizations, contributed to women's participation in politics, and generated important legislation affecting women.[67]

The failure to ratify the ERA stands in stark contrast to the quick enactment of many laws that now protect women's rights. Such legislation had little audible opposition. If years of racial discrimination called for government redress, then so did years of gender-based discrimination. Furthermore, laws protecting women's rights required only the amending of civil rights bills or the enactment of similar bills.

Some scholars argue that for practical purposes, the Supreme Court has implemented the equivalent of the ERA through its decisions. It has struck down distinctions based on sex and held that stereotyped generalizations about sexual differences must fall.[68] In recent rulings, the Court has held that states may require employers to guarantee job reinstatement to women who take maternity leave, that sexual harassment in the workplace is illegal, and that the existence of a hostile work environment may be demonstrated by a reasonable perception of abuse rather than by proven psychological injury.[69]

But the Supreme Court can reverse its decisions, and legislators can repeal statutes. Without an equal rights amendment, argue some feminists, the Constitution will continue to bear the sexist imprint of a document written by men for men. Until the ERA becomes part of the Constitution, said the late feminist Betty Friedan, "We are at the mercy of a Supreme Court that will interpret equality as it sees fit."[70]

 # Affirmative Action: Equal Opportunity or Equal Outcome?

LO7 ★ Compare and contrast the consequences that follow from policies aimed at equal opportunities versus those aimed at equal outcomes.

In his vision of a Great Society, President Johnson linked economic rights with civil rights and equality of outcome with equality of opportunity. "Equal opportunity is essential, but not enough," he declared. "We seek not just legal equity but human ability, not just equality as a right and a theory but equality as a fact and equality as a result."[71] This commitment led to affirmative action programs to expand opportunities for women, minorities, and people with disabilities.

Affirmative action is a commitment by a business, employer, school, or other public or private institution to expand opportunities for women, blacks, Hispanic Americans, and members of other minority groups. Affirmative action aims to overcome the effects of present and past discrimination. It embraces a range of public and private programs, policies, and procedures, including special recruitment, preferential treatment, and quotas in job training and professional education, employment, and the awarding of government contracts. The point of these programs is to move beyond equality of opportunity to equality of outcome.

Establishing numerical goals (such as designating a specific number of places in a law school for minority candidates or specifying that 10 percent of the work on a government contract must be subcontracted to minority-owned companies) is the most aggressive form of affirmative action, and it generates more debate and opposition than any other aspect of the civil rights movement. Advocates claim that such goal setting for college admissions, training programs, employment, and contracts will move minorities, women, and people with disabilities out of their second-class status. President Johnson explained why aggressive affirmative action was necessary:

> You do not take a person who for years has been hobbled by chains, liberate him, bring him up to the starting line of a race, and then say, "You are free to compete with all the others," and still justly believe that you have been completely fair. Thus, it is not enough just to open the gates of opportunity; all our citizens must have the ability to walk through those gates.[72]

Arguments for affirmative action programs (from increased recruitment efforts to quotas) tend to use the following reasoning: certain groups have historically suffered invidious discrimination, denying them educational and economic opportunities. To eliminate the lasting effects of such discrimination, the public and private sectors must take steps to provide access to good education and jobs. If the majority once discriminated to hold groups back, discriminating to benefit those groups is fair. Therefore, quotas are a legitimate means to provide a place on the ladder to success.[73]

Affirmative action opponents maintain that quotas for designated groups necessarily create invidious discrimination (in the form of reverse discrimination) against individuals who are themselves blameless. Moreover, they say, quotas lead to the admission, hiring, or promotion of the less qualified at the expense of the well qualified. In the name of equality, such policies thwart individuals' freedom to succeed.

Government-mandated preferential policies probably began in 1965 with the creation of the Office of Federal Contract Compliance. Its purpose was to ensure that all private enterprises doing business with the federal government complied with nondiscrimination guidelines. Because so many companies do business with the federal government, a large portion of the American economy became subject to these guidelines. In 1968, the guidelines required "goals and timetables for the prompt achievement of full and equal employment opportunity." By 1971, they called for employers to eliminate "underutilization" of minorities and women, which meant that employers had to hire minorities and women in proportion to the government's assessment of their availability.[74]

Preferential policies are seldom explicitly legislated. More often, such policies are the result of administrative regulations, judicial rulings, and initiatives in the private sector to provide a remedial response to specific discrimination or to satisfy new legal standards for proving nondiscrimination. Quotas or goals enable administrators to assess changes in hiring, promotion, and admissions policies. Racial quotas are an economic fact of life today. Employers engage in race-conscious preferential treatment to avoid litigation. Cast in value terms, equality trumps freedom.

Preferential Policies in Global Politics

Americans are not alone in their disagreements over preferential policies. Controversies, even bloodshed, have arisen where the government treats certain groups of citizens preferentially. One study found several common patterns among countries that had enacted preferential policies. Although begun as temporary measures, preferential policies tend to persist and even to expand to include more groups. The policies usually seek to improve the situation of disadvantaged groups as a whole, but they often benefit the better-off members of such groups more so than the worse-off members. Finally, preferential policies tend to increase antagonisms among different groups within a country.

Of course, there are variations across countries in terms of who benefits from such policies, what types of benefits are bestowed, and even the names of the policies. In India, such policies carry the label "positive discrimination." But that isn't the only way India differs from the United States when it comes to preferential policies.

Although India is the world's largest democracy, its society is rigidly stratified into groups called castes. The government forbids caste-based discrimination, but members of the lower castes (the lowest being the Dalits, or "untouchables") were historically restricted to the least prestigious and lowest-paying jobs. To improve their status, India has set aside government jobs for the lower castes, which make up half of India's population of 1 billion. India now reserves 27 percent of government jobs for the lower castes and an additional 23 percent for untouchables and remote tribe members. Gender equality has also improved since a 1993 constitutional amendment that set aside one-third of all seats in local government councils for women. By 2004, 900,000 women had been elected to public office, and 80,000 of them now lead local governing bodies. Positive discrimination in India has intensified tensions between the lower and upper castes. In 1990, soon after the new quotas were established, scores of young upper-caste men and women set themselves ablaze in protest. And when Indian courts issued a temporary injunction against the positive discrimination policies, lower-caste terrorists bombed a train and killed dozens of people. Adding further strain, a 2010 proposal to create a one-third set-aside for women in the parliament and state legislatures met stiff resistance from the political parties representing the lower castes. The Dalits viewed the proposal as a threat to their monopoly quota. Lower-caste women opposed the idea while feminists from higher-caste parties supported it. The issue in India is not the use of quotas but which group should benefit from quotas. No longer considered temporary, quotas there have become a fact of life. And while race-based affirmative action in the United States remains under threat, positive discrimination in India has become a vast system of political patronage providing rewards to the powerful rather than uplifting those in need.

All governments broker conflict to varying degrees. Under a majoritarian model, group demands could lead quickly to conflict and instability because majority rule leaves little room for compromise. A pluralist model allows different groups to get a piece of the pie. By parceling out benefits, pluralism mitigates disorder in the short term. But in the long term, repeated demands for increased

benefits can spark instability. A vigorous pluralist system should provide acceptable mechanisms (legislative, executive, bureaucratic, judicial) to vent such frustrations and yield new allocations of benefits.

Sources: Trudy Rubin, "Will Democracy Survive in India?" *Record* (Bergen County, N.J.), 19 January 1998, p. A12; Alex Spillius, "India's Old Warriors to Launch Rights Fight," *Daily Telegraph*, 20 October 1997, p. 12; Robin Wright, "World's Leaders: Men, 187, Women, 4," *Los Angeles Times*, 30 September 1997, p. A1; "Indian Eunuchs Demand Government Job Quotas," *Agence France Presse*, 22 October 1997; Juergen Hein and M. V. Balaji, "India's First Census of New Millennium Begins on February 9," *Deutsche Presse-Agentur*, 7 February 2001; Gillian Bowditch, "You Can Have Meritocracy or Equality, but Not Both," *Sunday Times*, Features Section: Scotland News, 19 January 2003, p. 21; Press Trust of India, "About a Million Women Elected to Local Bodies in India," 10 February 2004; Somini Sengupta, "Quotas to Aid India's Poor vs. Push for Meritocracy," *New York Times*, 23 May 2006, p. A3; "Caste in Doubt," *The Economist*, 12 June 2010, p. 46; and Gardiner Harris, "With Affirmative Action, India's Rich Gain School Slots Meant for Poor," *New York Times*, 8 October 2012, p. A4.

Critical Thinking Preferential policies have at times threatened to disrupt order in rigidly stratified societies. What are some of the risks associated with affirmative action? How do different institutional models address these risks? Which do you think matters more for bolstering group participation and opportunity: institutional or social change?

Reverse Discrimination

The Supreme Court confronted an affirmative action quota program for the first time in *Regents of the University of California* v. *Bakke*.[75] Allan Bakke, a thirty-five-year-old white man, had twice applied for admission to the University of California Medical School at Davis and was rejected both times. As part of the university's affirmative action program, the school had reserved sixteen places in each entering class of one hundred for qualified minority applicants in an effort to redress long-standing and unfair exclusion of minorities from the medical profession. Bakke's academic qualifications exceeded those of all the minority students admitted in the two years his applications were rejected. Bakke contended, first in the California courts and then in the Supreme Court, that he was excluded from admission solely on the basis of his race. He argued that the equal protection clause of the Fourteenth Amendment and the Civil Rights Act of 1964 prohibited this reverse discrimination.

The Court's decision in *Bakke* contained six opinions and spanned 154 pages, but no opinion commanded a majority. Despite the confusing multiple opinions, the Court struck down the school's rigid use of race, thus admitting Bakke, and it approved of affirmative action programs in education that use race as a plus factor (one of many such factors) but not as the sole factor. Thus, the Court managed to minimize white opposition to the goal of equality (by finding for Bakke) while extending gains for racial minorities through affirmative action.

True to the pluralist model, groups opposed to affirmative action continued their opposition in federal courts and state legislatures. They met with some success. The Supreme Court struck down government-mandated set-aside programs in the U.S. Department of Transportation.[76] Lower federal courts took this as a signal that other forms of affirmative action were ripe for reversal.

By 2003—twenty-five years after *Bakke*—the Supreme Court reexamined affirmative action in two cases, both challenging aspects of the University of Michigan's racial preferences policies. In *Gratz* v. *Bollinger*, the Court considered the university's undergraduate admissions policy, which conferred 20 points automatically to members of favored groups (100 points guaranteed admission). In a 6–3 opinion, Chief Justice William H. Rehnquist argued that such a policy violated the equal protection clause because it lacked the narrow tailoring required for permissible racial preferences and it failed to provide for individualized consideration of each candidate.[77] In the second case, *Grutter* v. *Bollinger*, the Court considered the University of Michigan's law school admissions policy, which gave preference to minority applicants with lower GPAs and standardized test scores over white applicants. This time, the Court, in a 5–4 decision authored by Justice Sandra Day O'Connor, held that the equal protection clause did not bar the school's narrowly tailored use of racial preferences to further a compelling interest that flowed from a racially diverse student body.[78] Since each applicant is judged individually on his or her merits, race remains only one among many factors that enter into the admissions decision.

The issue of race-based classifications in education arose again in 2007 when parents challenged voluntary school integration plans based on race in *Parents Involved in Community Schools* v. *Seattle School District No. 1*.[79] Chief Justice John G. Roberts, Jr., writing for the 5–4 majority on a bitterly divided bench, invalidated the plans, declaring that the programs were "directed only to racial balance, pure and simple," which the equal protection clause of the Fourteenth Amendment forbids. "The way to stop discrimination on the basis of race is to stop discriminating on the basis of race," he said.

Justice Anthony Kennedy, who cast the fifth and deciding vote, wrote separately to say that achieving racial diversity and avoiding racial isolation were "compelling interests" that schools could constitutionally pursue as long as they "narrowly tailored" their programs to avoid racial labeling and sorting of individual children.

Justice Stephen G. Breyer, writing for the minority and speaking from the bench, used pointed language, declaring, "This is a decision that the Court and the nation will come to regret." A sign of growing frustration among the justices is the increased frequency with which they have read their dissents aloud, a tactic used to express great distress with the majority opinion.

Recall Abigail Fisher's claim of reverse discrimination that began this chapter. While her case still remains pending, the Supreme Court has tightened the reins on public university racial diversity policies. The Court has also allowed states to amend their own constitutions limiting racial preference policies. Moving in small but deliberate steps, the Court is charting a course away from dynamic equality in matters of race and toward a policy of formal equality without completely rejecting government affirmative action policies.

The Politics of Affirmative Action

A comprehensive review of nationwide surveys conducted over the past twenty-five years reveals an unsurprising truth: that blacks favor affirmative action programs and whites do not. The gulf between the races was wider in the 1970s than it is today, but the moderation results from shifts among blacks, not whites. Perhaps the most important finding is that "whites' views have remained essentially unchanged over twenty-five years."[80]

How do we account for the persistence of equal outcomes policies? A majority of Americans have consistently rejected explicit race or gender preferences for the awarding of contracts, employment decisions, and college admissions, regardless of the groups such preferences benefit. Nevertheless, preference policies have survived and thrived under both Democrats and Republicans because they are attractive. They encourage unprotected groups to strive for inclusion. The list of protected groups includes African

KRISTOPHER SKINNER/Polaris/Newscom

The Price of Equality?

College Republicans at the University of California, Berkeley drive home the pernicious effect of equal outcomes policies by holding a bake sale with items priced according to race, ethnicity, or gender. Most of us would expect one price for everyone but in the view of some people, correcting for various forms of invidious discrimination poses unequal results, as in the bake sale example.

Americans, Hispanic Americans, Native Americans, Asian Pacific Americans, and subcontinent Asian Americans.[81] Politicians have a powerful motive—votes—to expand the number of protected groups and the benefits such policies provide. What was once the noble goal of righting the wrong of slavery runs the risk of transforming African Americans into just another interest group.

Recall that affirmative action programs began as temporary measures, ensuring a jump-start for minorities shackled by decades or centuries of invidious discrimination. For example, fifty years ago, minority racial identity was a fatal flaw on a medical or law school application. Today it is viewed as an advantage, encouraging applicants to think in minority-group terms. Thinking in group terms and conferring benefits on such grounds generates hostility from members of the majority, who see the deck stacked against them for no other reason than their race. It is not surprising that affirmative action has become controversial, since many Americans view it as a violation of their individual freedom.

Recall Lyndon Johnson's justification for equal outcomes policies. Though free to compete, a person once hobbled by chains cannot run a fair race. Americans are willing to do more than remove the chains. They will support special training and financial assistance for those who were previously shackled. The hope is that such efforts will enable once-shackled runners to catch up with those who have forged ahead. But Americans stop short at endorsing equal outcomes policies because they predetermine the results of the race.[82]

The conflict between freedom and equality will continue as other individuals and groups continue to press their demands through litigation and legislation. The choice will depend on whether and to what extent Americans still harbor deep-seated racial prejudice.

Master the Topic of Civil Rights with MindTap™ for American Government

REVIEW MindTap™ for American Government
Access Key Term Flashcards for Chapter 16.

TEST YOURSELF MindTap™ for American Government
Take the Wrap It Up Quiz for Chapter 16.

STAY CURRENT MindTap™ for American Government
Access the KnowNow blog and customized RSS for updates on current events.

STAY FOCUSED MindTap™ for American Government
Complete the Focus Activities for Civil Rights.

Summary

LO1 Explain why some discrimination may be benign while other forms of discrimination may be harmful.

- Discrimination simply means making distinctions; by itself discrimination is neither good nor evil. Some forms of discrimination are benign; we want government to engage in such discrimination. Some forms of government discrimination are invidious and violate our understanding of equality.

LO2 Trace the Supreme Court rulings and state legislative efforts that prevented African Americans from achieving "equal protection of the laws."

- Congress enacted the Civil War amendments—the Thirteenth, Fourteenth, and Fifteenth amendments—to provide full civil rights to black Americans. In the late nineteenth century, however, the Supreme Court interpreted the amendments very narrowly, declaring that they did not restrain individuals from denying civil rights to blacks and did not apply to the states. The Court's rulings in effect made racial segregation a fact of daily life for black Americans and enabled states in the American South to deny the vote to most blacks and to institutionalize racism. By the end of the nineteenth century, legal racial segregation was firmly entrenched in the American South.

LO3 Identify the Supreme Court decisions that dismantled school segregation and explain the significance of each.

- Through a series of court cases spanning two decades, the Court slowly dismantled segregation in the schools, thanks in large part to the efforts of the NAACP, which undertook a two-prong approach to dismantling the separate-but-equal doctrine. The battle for desegregation culminated in the *Brown* cases in 1954 and 1955, in which a now-supportive Supreme Court declared segregated schools to be inherently unequal and therefore unconstitutional. While the initial order to undertake desegregation with "all deliberate speed" was ambiguous enough to avoid desegregation in practice altogether, by 1969 the Supreme Court ordered that segregated school systems be dismantled "at once." The Court also upheld the use of busing in those school districts that had deliberately drawn boundaries to maintain racial segregation in schools.

LO4 Describe the circumstances under which the 1964 Civil Rights Act was passed and its evolving interpretation in subsequent Supreme Court decisions.

- Gains in other spheres of civil rights came more slowly. The motivating force was the civil rights movement, led by Martin Luther King, Jr., until his assassination in 1968. King's efforts, along with those of many others, helped to bring about the Civil Rights Act, which was passed in 1964 and upheld in the courts by reason of the congressional power to regulate interstate commerce. Other court decisions had the effect of frustrating the enforcement of civil rights. In order to counteract these decisions, Congress took the lead by instituting laws that expanded and clarified the scope of civil rights law.

LO5 Evaluate the effect of the civil rights movement on other minority groups' struggles for equality.

- Civil rights activism and the civil rights movement worked to the benefit of all minority groups—in fact, they benefited all Americans. Native Americans obtained some redress for past injustices, winning, for example, the return of lands in various states throughout the country. Immigrant groups press government for a stake in the American experience as they work to gain a better life in jobs that few citizens will do. Hispanics have come to recognize the importance of group action to achieve economic and political equality. By the mid-twenty-first century, they will be one-third of the population and possess greater political power. With enactment of the Americans with Disabilities Act (ADA) in 1990, disabled Americans won civil rights protections enjoyed by African Americans and others. Civil rights legislation removed the protectionism that was, in effect, legalized discrimination against women in education and employment. LGBT Americans aim to follow the same path, but their quest for equality remains unfinished.

LO6 Trace the evolution of women's legal rights beginning with laws based on protectionism and concluding with Supreme Court rulings prohibiting gender-based discrimination.

- Despite legislative advances in the area of women's rights, including the passing of the Nineteenth Amendment, the states did not ratify the equal rights amendment.

Legislation and judicial rulings implemented much of the amendment's provisions in practice. The Supreme Court now judges sex-based discrimination with "skeptical scrutiny," making distinctions based on sex almost as suspect as distinctions based on race.

LO7 Compare and contrast the consequences that follow from policies aimed at equal opportunities versus those aimed at equal outcomes.

- When programs make race the determining factor in awarding contracts, offering employment, or granting admission to educational institutions, the courts will be increasingly skeptical of their validity. However, the politics of affirmative action suggest that such programs are likely to remain persistent features on our political landscape. We can guarantee equal outcomes only if we restrict the free competition that is an integral part of equal opportunity. Many Americans object to policies that restrict individual freedom, such as quotas and set-asides that arbitrarily change the outcome of the race. The challenge of pluralist democracy is to balance the need for freedom with demands for equality.

Chapter Quiz

LO1 Explain why some discrimination may be benign while other forms of discrimination may be harmful.

1. Differentiate between equality of opportunity and equality of outcomes.
2. What is invidious discrimination? Provide examples of groups that have confronted this.

LO2 Trace the Supreme Court rulings and state legislative efforts that prevented African Americans from achieving "equal protection of the laws."

1. What was the purpose of the black codes?

2. Define the separate-but-equal doctrine and explain how it satisfied the Fourteenth Amendment while upholding racial segregation.

LO3 Identify the Supreme Court decisions that dismantled school segregation and explain the significance of each.

1. Why was the *Brown* v. *Board of Education* ruling so important for the fight against racial segregation?
2. What is the difference between de jure segregation and de facto segregation?

LO4 **Describe the circumstances under which the 1964 Civil Rights Act was passed and its evolving interpretation in subsequent Supreme Court decisions.**

1. Define civil disobedience and give two examples of it.
2. Identify the major provisions of the Civil Rights Act of 1964.

LO5 **Evaluate the effect of the civil rights movement on other minority groups' struggles for equality.**

1. Why was assimilation an ineffective tool for successfully integrating Native Americans with the rest of American society?
2. Who was Cesar Chavez, and what did he do to improve the living conditions of immigrant farm workers?

LO6 **Trace the evolution of women's legal rights beginning with laws based on protectionism and concluding with Supreme Court rulings prohibiting gender-based discrimination.**

1. How did protectionism promote the discrimination of women?
2. Define the concept of skeptical scrutiny.

LO7 **Compare and contrast the consequences that follow from policies aimed at equal opportunities versus those aimed at equal outcomes.**

1. Why are explicit quota policies generally unpopular with the public?
2. What might explain the persistence of affirmative action policies despite their unpopularity with the majority?

KEY CASES

Plessy v. *Ferguson* (racial segregation constitutional, 1896)

Brown v. *Board of Education* (racial segregation unconstitutional, 1954)

Brown v. *Board of Education II* (racial desegregation implementation, 1955)

United States v. *Windsor* (marriage equality under federal law, 2013)

Boy Scouts of America v. *Dale* (association rights, Boy Scouts versus gays, 2000)

United States v. *Virginia* (gender equality, 1996)

Regents of the University of California v. *Bakke* (affirmative action, 1978)

Gratz v. *Bollinger* (affirmative action in college admissions, 2003)

Grutter v. *Bollinger* (affirmative action in law school admissions, 2003)

Parents Involved in Community Schools v. *Seattle School District No. 1* (public school racial diversity, 2007)

17 Economic Policy

Learning Outcomes

LO1 Compare and contrast three theories of market economics: laissez-faire, Keynesian, and supply-side.

LO2 Describe the process by which the national budget is prepared and passed into law and the reforms undertaken by Congress to balance the budget.

LO3 Identify the objectives of tax policies and explain why tax reform is difficult.

LO4 Identify the major areas of government outlays and explain the role of incremental budgeting and uncontrollable spending on the growth of government spending.

LO5 Identify the origins of the income tax, trace the influence of government spending and taxing policies on inequality, and examine these policies from the majoritarian and pluralist perspectives.

 WATCH & LEARN MindTap® for American Government

Watch a brief "What Do You Know?" video summarizing Economic Policy.

"Blessed are the young, for they shall inherit the national debt," said former President Herbert Hoover to the Nebraska Republican Conference in January 1936.[1] Hoover had the misfortune of being president in 1929 when the stock market collapsed, and he lost the 1932 election to Franklin Delano Roosevelt. Hoover was addressing Republicans during the Great Depression in 1936. In that year, the gross debt for the national government (sometimes called the national debt, sometimes the federal debt) was estimated at $39.79 billion.[2] Despite the Great Depression and the increased national debt, President Roosevelt was overwhelmingly reelected.

More than seventy-five years later, the 1936 national debt of $39.7 billion seems paltry compared with our 2013 debt of $16,719 billion! (The National Debt Clock photo was taken earlier in 2013, when the debt was lower.) But that scary number does not take into account seventy-five years of population increase, economic growth, and inflation. A better way to compare levels of national debt over time is to express debt levels as percentages of gross domestic product (GDP—the total value of all goods and services produced in a given year). In 1936, our GDP was $84.9 billion.[3] As a percentage of GDP, the national debt then was only 39.8 percent. In 2013, our national debt was 72.1 percent of GDP.[4] Historically, our national debt as a percent of GDP had been even higher, rising over 100 from 1945 to 1947 and not dropping below 90 percent until 1950. So our nation can tolerate heavy debt without suffering a Great Depression. Like President Roosevelt, President Obama was reelected despite the nation's debt. Nevertheless, like heavy drinking and smoking, carrying a huge debt is not healthy.

How much of this debt do you owe? Let's do the math using round numbers. Dividing the 2013 national debt of $16,719 billion by the U.S. population of 318 million is about $53,000 per person. That is indeed bad news, but the good news is that not all the debt needs to be paid off. Nations—like families who borrow to buy homes and cars—are almost never debt-free. Since 1936, the national debt has averaged over 57 percent of the GDP, and it has never dropped below 30 percent. Regarding the national debt as a manageable problem leads one away from wailing in despair about the debt's magnitude to considering ways to pay it down.

As with household debt, our national debt should be reduced to avoid large annual interest payments, which limit spending for national needs. At present, the U.S. debt payments are relatively low due to historically low interest rates. However, interest rates will rise, and—as President Hoover implied—old people will die before the debt is paid down, leaving the task to the young. Young people may understand better how much money they will have tomorrow if they know more today about the economics of government. How does the national debt relate to the current budget deficit? How did the deficit grow so large and prove so difficult to control against the spending appetites of Congress? More concretely, how is the national budget formulated? How much control of the domestic economy can government really exercise through the judicious use of economic theory? How much is the economy influenced by events that lie outside governmental control? What effects do government taxing and spending policies have on the economy and on economic equality? We address these questions in this chapter. As we shall see, no one person or organization controls the American economy; multiple actors have a voice in economic conditions. And not all of these actors are public—or American.

LISTEN & LEARN
MindTap™ for American Government

Access Read Speaker to listen to Chapter 17.

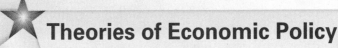

★ Theories of Economic Policy

LO1 ★ Compare and contrast three theories of market economics: laissez-faire, Keynesian, and supply-side.

Government efforts to control the economy rely on theories about how the economy responds to government taxing and spending policies and its control of the money supply. How policymakers tax and spend, and loosen and tighten interest rates, depends on their beliefs about how the economy functions and the proper role of government in the economy. The American economy is so complex that no one knows exactly how it works. Policymakers rely on economic theories to explain its functioning, and there are nearly as many theories as there are economists. Unfortunately, different theories (and economists) often predict different outcomes, sometimes due to different assumptions. Then too, abstract theories can clash with the real world. Still, despite disagreement among economists, knowledge of basic economics is necessary to understand how government approaches public policy.[5]

We are concerned here with economic policy in a market economy—one in which the prices of goods and services are determined through the interaction of sellers and buyers (that is, through supply and demand). This kind of economy is typical of the consumer-dominated societies of Western Europe and the United States. A nonmarket economy relies on government planners to determine both the prices of goods and the amounts that are produced. The old Soviet economy was a perfect example; the government owned and operated the major means of production.

Market economies are loosely called capitalist economies: they allow private individuals to own property; sell goods for profit in free, or open, markets; and accumulate wealth, called *capital*. Market economies often exhibit a mix of government and private ownership. For example, Britain has had more government-owned enterprises (railroads, broadcasting, and housing) than has the United States. China today contends that it has a *socialist market economy*, which depends on the private sector for economic growth but also directs and supports state-owned enterprises. Competing economic theories differ largely on how free they say the markets should be—in other words, on government's role in directing the economy (see "The National Debt in Global Politics").

The National Debt in Global Politics

Globalization produces economic interdependence among nations. Over the past five decades, Americans have been buying more goods and services from other countries than we are selling to them. Foreigners have been using their profits to buy U.S. government securities, thus acquiring increasing shares of the "public" debt portion, which totaled almost $12 trillion in 2013. (That number excludes almost $5 billion in intragovernmental debts. See page 502.) In effect, foreigners have been lending us money to buy their goods and services.

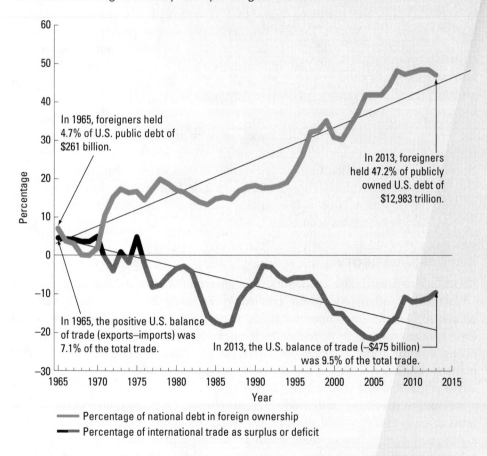

In 1965, foreigners held 4.7% of U.S. public debt of $261 billion.

In 2013, foreigners held 47.2% of publicly owned U.S. debt of $12,983 trillion.

In 1965, the positive U.S. balance of trade (exports–imports) was 7.1% of the total trade.

In 2013, the U.S. balance of trade (−$475 billion) was 9.5% of the total trade.

— Percentage of national debt in foreign ownership
— Percentage of international trade as surplus or deficit

Sources: Office of Management and Budget, "Table 4.7: Foreign Holdings of Federal Debt," in Analytical Perspectives: Budget of the U.S. Government, Fiscal Year 2015 (Washington, D.C.: U.S. Government Printing Office, 2014); and U.S. Census Bureau, Foreign Trade Division, "U.S. Trade in Goods and Services, Balance of Payments (BOP) Basis," http://www.census.gov/foreign-trade/statistics/historical/gands.txt.

Critical Thinking What consequences for American public policy might result from this disparity between the large amount of U.S. debt owned by foreigners and our negative trade balance with foreign countries?

Laissez-Faire Economics

The French term *laissez faire*, introduced in Chapter 1 and discussed again in Chapter 13, describes the absence of government control. The economic doctrine of laissez faire likens the operation of a free market to the process of natural selection. Economic competition weeds out the weak and preserves the strong. In the process, the economy prospers, and everyone eventually benefits.

Advocates of laissez-faire economics are fond of quoting Adam Smith's *The Wealth of Nations*. In his 1776 treatise, Smith argued that each individual, pursuing his own selfish interests in a competitive market, was "led by an invisible hand to promote an end which was no part of his intention." Smith's "invisible hand" has been used for two centuries to justify the belief that the narrow pursuit of profits serves the broad interests of society.[6] Strict advocates of laissez faire maintain that government interference with business tampers with the laws of nature, obstructing the workings of the free market. Mainstream economists today favor market principles but do recognize that "governments can sometimes improve market outcomes."[7] Within the last century, a companion principle, the **efficient market hypothesis**, has held that financial markets are informationally efficient—they quickly absorb all relevant information about securities into their prices. It implies that securities are priced and traded at their fair value, meaning that investors cannot "beat the market." If the market is rational, attempts to regulate it become irrational.[8]

Today, laissez-faire thought is associated with the "Austrian school" of economics. A leading theorist of the Austrian school, Friedrich Hayek, won the 1974 Nobel Prize for economics. In *Road to Serfdom*, Hayek warned that tyranny inevitably results from government control of economic decision making. In contemporary politics, Hayek is often cited by libertarians in defense of free-market capitalism and in opposition to Keynesian economics.

Keynesian Theory

According to laissez-faire economics, our government should have done nothing when markets across the world crashed in February 2008 and threatened our economy. Laissez-faire economics holds that government should do little about **economic depression** (a period of high unemployment and business failures); or raging **inflation** (price increases that decrease the value of currency); or—for that matter—**stagflation** (the joint occurrence of slow growth, unemployment, and inflation of the 1970s).

Since the beginning of the Industrial Revolution, capitalist economies have suffered through many cyclical fluctuations. Since 1857, the United States has experienced more than thirty of these **business cycles**: expansions and contractions of business activity, the first stage accompanied by inflation and the second stage by unemployment.[9] No widely accepted theory explained these cycles until the Great Depression of the 1930s.

That was when John Maynard Keynes, a British economist, theorized that business cycles stem from imbalances between aggregate demand and productive capacity. **Aggregate demand** is the total income that consumers, business, and government wish to spend on goods and services. **Productive capacity** is the total value of goods and services that can be produced when the economy is working at full capacity. The value of the goods and services actually produced is called the **gross domestic product (GDP)**. When demand exceeds productive capacity, people are

efficient market hypothesis
Financial markets are informationally efficient—they quickly absorb all relevant information about securities into their prices.

economic depression
A period of high unemployment and business failures; a severe, long-lasting downturn in a business cycle.

inflation
An economic condition characterized by price increases linked to a decrease in the value of the currency.

stagflation
The joint occurrence of slow growth, unemployment, and inflation.

business cycles
Expansions and contractions of business activity, the first accompanied by inflation and the second by unemployment.

aggregate demand
The total income that consumers, businesses, and government wish to spend for goods and services.

productive capacity
The total value of goods and services that can be produced when the economy works at full capacity.

gross domestic product (GDP)
The total value of the goods and services produced by a country during a year.

willing to pay more for available goods, which leads to price inflation. When productive capacity exceeds demand, producers cut back on their output of goods, which leads to unemployment. When many people are unemployed for an extended period, the economy is in a depression. Keynes theorized that government could stabilize the economy (and smooth out or eliminate business cycles) by controlling the level of aggregate demand.

Keynesian theory holds that aggregate demand can be adjusted through a combination of fiscal and monetary policies. **Fiscal policies**, which are enacted by the president and Congress, involve changes in government spending and taxing. When demand is too low, according to Keynes, government should either spend more itself, hiring people and thus giving them money, or cut taxes, giving people more of their own money to spend. When demand is too great, the government should either spend less or raise taxes, giving people less money to spend. **Monetary policies**, which are largely determined by the Federal Reserve Board, involve changes in the money supply and operate less directly on the economy. Increasing the amount of money in circulation increases aggregate demand and thus increases price inflation. Decreasing the money supply decreases aggregate demand and inflationary pressures.

Despite some problems with the assumptions of Keynesian theory, capitalist countries have widely adopted it in some form.[10] At one time or another, virtually all have used the Keynesian technique of **deficit financing**—spending in excess of tax revenues—to combat an economic slump. Because a slump lowers profits and wages, it reduces tax revenues—thus generating a budget deficit all by itself. Prior to Keynes, economists prescribed raising taxes and cutting spending to bring the budget back into balance. That only reduced aggregate demand and worsened the recession. The objective of deficit financing is to increase demand for goods and services, either directly by increasing government purchases or indirectly by cutting taxes to generate more after-tax income to spend. Most deficits are financed with funds borrowed through the issuing of government bonds, notes, or other securities. The theory holds that deficits can be paid off with budget surpluses after the economy recovers.

Because Keynesian theory requires government to play an active role in controlling the economy, it runs counter to laissez-faire economics. Before Keynes, no administration in Washington would shoulder responsibility for maintaining a healthy economy. In 1946, the year Keynes died, Congress passed an employment act establishing "the continuing responsibility of the national government to … promote maximum employment, production and purchasing power." The Employment Act of 1946, which reflected Keynesian theory, had a tremendous effect on government economic policy. Many people believe it was the primary source of "big government" in America. Even Richard Nixon, a conservative president, admitted in 1971 that "we are all Keynesians now," by accepting government responsibility for the economy. But not all conservatives buy into that philosophy. In a 2008 editorial, "We're All Keynesians Now," the *Wall Street Journal* deplored Bush's $168 billion fiscal stimulus package of tax rebates to forestall a recession as taking money from one pocket (those with high income) and handing it to another (those with low to moderate income).[11]

For economically oriented and ideologically committed partisans, the 2012 presidential contest turned into a slugfest between Keynes's supporters and those who followed Friedrich Hayek. Obama heralded the bailout of the auto industry (à la Keynes), whereas Mitt Romney wrote a 2008 op-ed piece, "Let Detroit Go Bankrupt"

Keynesian theory
An economic theory stating that the government can stabilize the economy—that is, can smooth business cycles—by controlling the level of aggregate demand, and that the level of aggregate demand can be controlled by means of fiscal and monetary policies.

fiscal policies
Economic policies that involve government spending and taxing.

monetary policies
Economic policies that involve control of, and changes in, the supply of money.

deficit financing
The Keynesian technique of spending beyond government income to combat an economic slump. Its purpose is to inject extra money into the economy to stimulate aggregate demand.

CONNECT WITH YOUR CLASSMATES
MindTap‾ for American Government

Access the Economic Policy Forum: Discussion—Government Intervention in the Economy.

Courtesy Emergent Order

Dueling Economists on YouTube

This image from a YouTube video portrays British economist John Maynard Keynes (left) and Austrian economist Friedrich Hayek (right). Keynes taught at Cambridge University but had enormous influence on American economics and government. Keynes's *The General Theory of Employment* (1936) advocated deficit spending during economic downturns to maintain employment. Keynesian theory fell out of favor in the 1980s, but Presidents Bush and Obama both embraced it to deal with the 2008 economic collapse. Hayek taught at the University of Chicago and elsewhere in the United States. His *The Road to Serfdom* (1944) argued that government intervention led to socialism and tyranny. Hayek's advocacy of free-market capitalism enjoyed popularity among Republicans in 2012 who objected to the government bailout of the auto industry. The ten-minute YouTube video, "Keynes vs. Hayek: Round Two," reflects their clashing views from a libertarian perspective. Ironically, Keynes and Hayek were colleagues at Cambridge briefly during World War II and respected each other's work.

Source: See Nicholas Wapshott, *Keynes Hayek: The Clash That Defined Modern Economics* (New York: W. W. Norton, 2011).

(à la Hayek). An observer outlined the issue: "A trillion-dollar Keynesian stimulus was quickly followed by a Hayekian wave of buyers' remorse that deemed that the swift reduction of the national debt was more important than giving jobs to the unemployed."[12] In November 2011, the Asia Society held a Keynes-Hayek debate on Park Avenue in New York between two teams of economists. The audience divided slightly in favor of Keynes afterward.[13] The hot topic, Keynes versus Hayek, generated YouTube videos, and new books appeared extolling both Keynes and Hayek.[14]

Monetary Policy

Although most economists accept Keynesian theory in its broad outlines, they depreciate its political utility. Some especially question the value of fiscal policies in controlling inflation and unemployment. They argue that government spending programs take too long to enact in Congress and to implement through the bureaucracy. As a result, jobs are created not when they are needed but years later, when the crisis may have passed and government spending needs to be reduced.

Also, government spending is easier to start than to stop because the groups that benefit from spending programs tend to defend them even when they are no longer needed. A similar criticism applies to tax policies. Politically, it is much easier to cut taxes than to raise them. In other words, Keynesian theory requires that governments be able to begin and end spending quickly and to cut and raise taxes quickly. But in the real world, these fiscal tools are easier to use in one direction than the other.

Recognizing these limitations of fiscal policies, **monetarists** argue that government can control the economy's performance simply by controlling the nation's money supply.[15] Staunch monetarists, like Nobel Laureate Milton Friedman, favor a long-range policy of small but steady growth in the amount of money in circulation rather than frequent manipulation of monetary policies.

Monetary policies in the United States are under the control of the **Federal Reserve System**, which acts as the country's central bank. Established in 1913, the Fed by law has three major goals: controlling inflation, maintaining maximum employment, and insuring moderate interest rates.[16] The Fed is not a single bank but a system of banks. At the top of the system is the board of governors, seven members appointed by the president for staggered terms of fourteen years. The president designates one member of the board to be its chairperson, who serves a four-year term

monetarists
Those who argue that government can effectively control the performance of an economy mainly by controlling the supply of money.

Federal Reserve System
The system of banks that acts as the central bank of the United States and controls major monetary policies.

that extends beyond the president's term of office. This complex arrangement was intended to make the board independent of the president and even of Congress. An independent board, the reasoning went, would be able to make financial decisions for the nation without regard to their political implications.[17] Following the Fed's bold actions taken to combat the financial crisis in 2008, however, members of Congress proposed auditing Fed decisions for the first time. By the summer of 2010, when President Obama signed a financial reform bill, the Fed was granted even greater powers to regulate large complex financial firms.[18]

The Fed controls the money supply, which affects inflation, in three ways. Most important, the Fed can sell and buy government securities (such as U.S. Treasury bills) on the open market. When the Fed sells securities, it takes money out of circulation, thereby making money scarce and raising the interest rate. When the Fed buys securities, the process works in reverse, lowering interest rates. The Fed also sets a target for the *federal funds rate*, which banks charge one another for overnight loans and which is usually cited when newspapers write, "The Fed has decided to lower [or raise] interest rates." Less frequently (for technical reasons), the Fed may change its *discount rate*, the interest rate that member banks have to pay to borrow money from a Federal Reserve bank. Finally, the Fed can change its *reserve requirement*, which is the amount of cash that member banks must keep on deposit in their regional Federal Reserve bank. An increase in the reserve requirement reduces the amount of money banks have available to lend.

Basic economic theory holds that interest rates should be raised to discourage borrowing and spending when the economy is growing too quickly (this combats inflation) and lowered when the economy is sluggish (thus increasing the money flow to encourage spending and economic growth). Historically, the Fed has adjusted interest rates to combat inflation rather than to stimulate economic growth, which would maximize employment. (A former Fed chairman once said its task was "to remove the punch bowl when the party gets going.")[19] That is, the Fed would dampen economic growth before it leads to serious inflation.

Accordingly, some charge that the Fed acts to further interests of the wealthy (who fear rampant inflation) more than interests of the poor (who fear widespread unemployment). Why so? Although all classes of citizens complain about increasing costs of living, inflation usually harms upper classes (creditors) more than lower classes (debtors). To illustrate, suppose someone borrows $20,000, to be repaid after ten years, during which the inflation rate was 10 percent. When the loan is due, the $20,000 borrowed is "worth" only $18,000. Debtors find the cheaper money easier to raise, and creditors are paid less than the original value of their loan. Hence, wealthy people fear severe inflation, which can erode the value of their saved wealth. As one Federal Reserve bank bluntly stated, "Debtors gain when inflation is unexpectedly high, and creditors gain when it is unexpectedly low."[20]

Formally, the president is responsible for the state of the economy, and voters hold him accountable. As the economy deteriorated in 2008, more people blamed President Bush for its poor performance than blamed Congress, multinational corporations, or financial institutions.[21] However, the president neither determines interest rates (the Fed does) nor controls spending (Congress does). In this respect, all presidents since 1913 have had to work with a Fed made independent of both the president and Congress, and all have had to deal with the fact that Congress ultimately controls spending. These restrictions on presidential authority are consistent with the pluralist model of democracy, but a president held responsible for the economy may not appreciate that theoretical argument.

Although the Fed's economic policies are not perfectly insulated from political concerns, they are sufficiently independent that the president is not able to control monetary policy without the Fed's cooperation. This means that the president cannot be held completely responsible for the state of the economy. Nevertheless, the public blames presidents for poor economic conditions and votes against them in elections. Naturally, a strong economy favors the incumbent party. When people are optimistic about the economic future and feel that they are doing well, they typically see no reason to change the party controlling the White House. But when conditions are bad or worsening, voters often decide to seek a change.

The Fed's activities are essential parts of the government's overall economic policy, but they lie outside the direct control of the president—and directly in the hands of the chair of the Federal Reserve Board. This makes the Fed chair a critical player in economic affairs and can create problems in coordinating economic policy. For example, the president might want the Fed to lower interest rates to stimulate the economy, but the Fed might resist for fear of inflation. Such policy clashes can pit the chair of the Federal Reserve Board directly against the president. So presidents typically court the Fed chair, even one who served a president of the other party.

Appointed Fed chair in 2006 by President Bush, Ben Bernanke replaced Alan Greenspan, who held the post for almost twenty years and was praised for overseeing an economy with low inflation, low unemployment, and strong growth. Greenspan, who believed that markets knew best and should be left unregulated (in keeping with the "efficient market hypothesis"), was later blamed for the financial crisis of 2008. Called before a House committee in October, Greenspan admitted that his "whole intellectual edifice collapsed in the summer," when banks held nearly worthless securities that had tumbled from dizzyingly high values.[22] Criticized for his complacency prior to the crisis, Bernanke acted boldly during it to rescue the economy, stretching the Fed's authority by arranging bank purchases, emergency loan programs, and the lowest interest rates in American history. In 2014, Janet Yellen replaced Bernanke, becoming the first woman to serve as Fed chair.

Historical evidence suggests that government can indeed slow down and smooth out the booms and busts of business cycles through active use of monetary and fiscal policies. From 1855 through World War II—prior to the active employment of Keynesian theory—the nation suffered through economic recessions 42 percent of the time, with each recession averaging twenty-one months. Since then and through June 2007, the nation was in a recession only 16 percent of the time, and the average duration lasted only ten months.[23] The recession that began in December 2007 lasted for 18 months, officially ending in June 2009. However, unemployment remained over 8 percent during most of the year prior to the 2012 presidential

The Federal Reserve

In 2014, the Senate confirmed President Obama's appointment of Janet Yellen as the first woman to chair the Federal Reserve System, succeeding Ben Bernanke. Dr. Yellen, a distinguished professor of economics at the University of California, Berkeley, had been vice-chair at the Fed for four years.

election. Under its new chair Janet Yellen, the Fed in 2014 seemed more concerned about persistent unemployment, which fell to just under 6 percent in October, than about inflation, which was only about 1 percent.

Supply-Side Economics

When Reagan came to office in 1981, he embraced a school of thought called **supply-side economics** to deal with the stagflation (both unemployment and inflation) that the nation was experiencing. Keynesian theory argues that inflation results when consumers, businesses, and governments have more money to spend than there are goods and services to buy. The standard Keynesian solution is to reduce demand (for example, by increasing taxes). Supply-siders argue that inflation can be lowered more effectively by increasing the supply of goods (that is, they stress the supply side of the economic equation). Specifically, they favor tax cuts to stimulate investment (which leads to the production of more goods) and less government regulation of business (again, to increase productivity—which they hold will yield more, not less, government revenue). Supply-siders also argue that the rich should receive larger tax cuts than the poor because the rich have more money to invest. The benefits of increased investment will then "trickle down" to working people in the form of additional jobs and income.

In a sense, supply-side economics resembles laissez-faire economics because it prefers fewer government programs and regulations and less taxation. Supply-siders believe that government interferes too much with the efforts of individuals to work, save, and invest. Inspired by supply-side theory, Reagan proposed (and got) massive tax cuts in the Economic Recovery Tax Act of 1981. The act reduced individual tax rates by 23 percent over a three-year period and cut the marginal tax rate for the highest income group from 70 to 50 percent. Reagan also launched a program to deregulate business. According to supply-side theory, these actions would generate extra government revenue, making spending cuts unnecessary to balance the budget. Nevertheless, Reagan also cut funding for some domestic programs, including Aid to Families with Dependent Children. Contrary to supply-side theory, he also proposed hefty increases in military spending. This blend of tax cuts, deregulation, cuts in spending for social programs, and increases in spending for defense became known, somewhat disparagingly, as *Reaganomics*.

How well did Reaganomics work? Inflation, which ran over 13 percent in 1981, was lowered to about 3 percent by 1983, but that was due mostly to Federal Reserve chair Paul Volcker raising interest rates to 20 percent. Although Reaganomics worked largely as expected in the area of industry deregulation, unemployment increased to 9.6 percent in 1983, and it failed massively to reduce the budget deficit. Contrary to supply-side theory, the 1981 tax cut was accompanied by a massive drop in tax revenues. Shortly after taking office, Reagan promised that his economic policies would balance the annual budget by 1984. In fact, lower tax revenues and higher defense spending produced the largest budget deficits to that time, as shown in Figure 17.1. Budget deficits continued until 1998, when a booming U.S. economy—plus increased tax rates—generated the first budget surplus since 1969. Economist Gregory Mankiw, advisor to President Bush, said that history failed to confirm the main conjecture of supply-side economics: that lower tax revenues would raise tax revenues: "When Reagan cut taxes after he was elected, the result was less tax revenue, not more."[24] Nevertheless, the supply-side idea that cutting taxes raises more revenue is still popular.[25]

supply-side economics
Economic policies aimed at increasing the supply of goods (as opposed to decreasing demand); consists mainly of tax cuts for possible investors and less regulation of business.

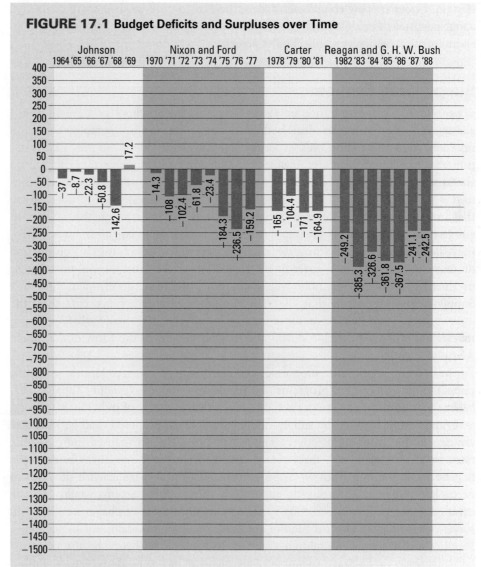

FIGURE 17.1 Budget Deficits and Surpluses over Time

This chart shows the actual deficits and surpluses in constant 2009 dollars incurred under administrations from Johnson to Obama. The deficits were enormous under Reagan, George H. W. Bush, and even during Clinton's early years. Budget deficits were eventually eliminated under Clinton and replaced by surpluses. Larger deficits appeared again under George W. Bush and Barack Obama.

Source: Executive Office of the President, *Budget of the United States Government, Fiscal Year 2015: Historical Tables* (Washington, D.C.: U.S. Government Printing Office, 2014), Table l.3.

Public Policy and the Budget

LO2 ★ Describe the process by which the national budget is prepared and passed into law and the reforms undertaken by Congress to balance the budget.

To most people, the national budget is B-O-R-I-N-G. To national politicians, it is an exciting script for high drama. The numbers, categories, and percentages that numb

FIGURE 17.1 (Continued)

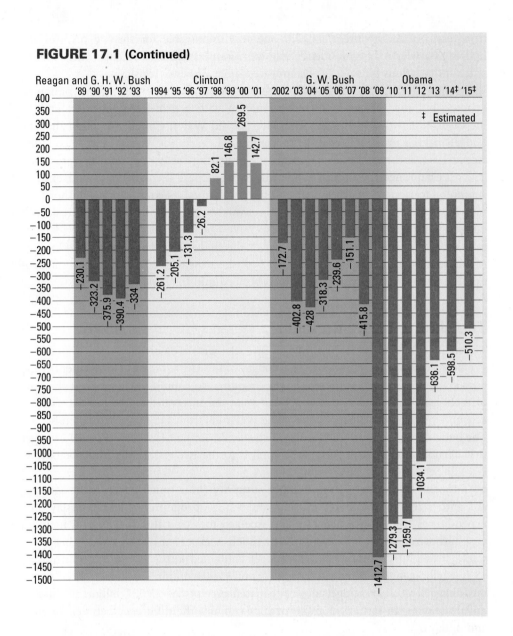

normal minds cause politicians' nostrils to flare and their hearts to pound. The budget is a battlefield on which politicians wage war over the programs they support.

Control of the budget is important to members of Congress because they are politicians, and politicians want to wield power, not watch someone else wield it. Also, the Constitution established Congress, not the president, as the "first branch" of government and the people's representatives. Unfortunately for Congress, the president has emerged as the leader in shaping the budget. Although Congress often disagrees with presidential spending priorities, it has been unable to mount a serious challenge to presidential authority by presenting a coherent alternative budget.

Today, the president prepares the budget, and Congress approves it. This was not always the case. Before 1921, Congress prepared the budget under its constitutional authority to raise taxes and appropriate funds. The budget was formed piecemeal by enacting a series of laws that originated in the many committees involved in the highly decentralized process of raising revenue, authorizing expenditures, and appropriating funds. Executive agencies even submitted their budgetary requests directly to

Congress, not to the president. No one was responsible for the big picture—the budget as a whole. The president's role was essentially limited to approving revenue and appropriations bills, just as he approved other pieces of legislation.

Congressional budgeting (such as it was) worked well enough for a nation of farmers, but not for an industrialized nation with a growing population and an increasingly active government. Soon after World War I, Congress realized that the budget-making process needed to be centralized. With the Budget and Accounting Act of 1921, it thrust the responsibility for preparing the budget onto the president. The act established the Bureau of the Budget to prepare the president's budget to be submitted to Congress each January. Congress retained its constitutional authority to raise and spend funds, but now Congress would begin its work with the president's budget as its starting point. And all executive agencies' budget requests had to be funneled for review through the Bureau of the Budget (which became the Office of Management and Budget in 1970); those consistent with the president's overall economic and legislative program were incorporated into the president's budget.

The Nature of the Budget

The national budget is complex. But its basic elements are not beyond understanding. We begin with some definitions. The Budget of the United States Government is the annual financial plan that the president is required to submit to Congress at the start of each year. It applies to the *next* **fiscal year**, the interval the government uses for accounting purposes. Currently, the fiscal year runs from October 1 to September 30. The budget is named for the year in which it *ends*, so the fiscal year (FY) 2015 budget that Obama submitted in early 2014 applied to the twelve months from October 1, 2014, to September 30, 2015.

Broadly, the budget defines **budget authority** (how much government agencies are authorized to spend on current and future programs); **budget outlays**, or expenditures (how much agencies are expected to spend this year, which includes past authorizations); and **receipts** (how much is expected in taxes and other revenues). President Obama's FY 2015 budget contained *authority* for expenditures of $3,969 billion, but it provided for *outlays* of $3,901 billion (including some previous obligations). His budget also anticipated receipts of $3,337 billion in current dollars, leaving an estimated *deficit* of $564 billion—the difference between receipts and outlays.

When the U.S. government runs a deficit, it borrows funds on a massive scale to finance its operation that fiscal year, thus limiting the supply of loanable funds for business investment. However, economists seemed more concerned about the accumulated government debt, not the annual deficit. A deficit in the annual budget is different from the **national debt**, which represents the sum of all unpaid government deficits. On April 3, 2014, the total national debt was $17.5 trillion.[26] Various "national debt clocks" calculate real-time estimates of the total national debt.[27] However, about $4.9 billion of the total debt then was "intragovernmental"—money that one part of the government owes to another part. Concerning the $16.6 trillion of "public" debt—money owed to lenders outside the government—almost 50 percent was held by institutions or individuals in other countries (see page 493). If foreign lenders were to stop financing America's governmental annual deficit and national debt, the economy could suffer a serious blow. During the 2008–2012 recession in Europe and the associated economic crises in Greece, Italy, Portugal, and Spain, foreign lenders fled to the safety of U.S. Treasury notes, buying them even at very low interest rates.[28]

fiscal year
The twelve-month period from October 1 to September 30 used by the government for accounting purposes. A fiscal year budget is named for the year in which it ends.

budget authority
The amounts that government agencies are authorized to spend for current and future programs.

budget outlays
The amounts that government agencies are expected to spend in the fiscal year.

receipts
For a government, the amount expected or obtained in taxes and other revenues.

national debt
The accumulated sum of past government borrowing owed to lenders outside the government.

Preparing the President's Budget

The budget that the president submits to Congress each winter is the end product of a process that begins the previous spring under the supervision of the **Office of Management and Budget (OMB)**. The OMB is located within the Executive Office of the President and is headed by a director appointed by the president, with the approval of the Senate. The OMB, with a staff of more than five hundred, is the most powerful domestic agency in the bureaucracy, and its director, who attends meetings of the president's cabinet, is one of the most powerful figures in government. The federal budget, with appendixes, is now available electronically on the OMB website.[29] Thousands of pages long, the budget contains more than numbers. It also explains individual spending programs in terms of national needs and agency objectives, and it analyzes proposed taxes and other receipts. Each year, reporters, lobbyists, and political analysts anxiously await publication of the president's budget, eager to learn his plans for government spending in the coming year.

The OMB initiates the budget process each spring by meeting with the president to discuss the economic situation and his budgetary priorities. It then sends broad budgeting guidelines to every government agency and requests their initial projection of how much money they will need for the next fiscal year. The OMB assembles this information and makes recommendations to the president, who then develops more precise guidelines describing how much each is likely to get. By summer, the agencies are asked to prepare budgets based on the new guidelines. By fall, they submit their formal budgets to the OMB, where budget analysts scrutinize agency requests, considering both their costs and their consistency with the president's legislative program. A lot of politicking goes on at this stage, as agency heads try to circumvent the OMB by pleading for their pet projects with presidential advisers and perhaps even the president himself.

Political negotiations over the budget may extend into the early winter—and often until it goes to the printer. The voluminous document looks very much like a finished product, but the figures it contains are not final. In giving the president the responsibility for preparing the budget in 1921, Congress simply provided itself with a starting point for its own work. And even with this head start, Congress has a hard time disciplining itself to produce a coherent, balanced budget.

Passing the Congressional Budget

The president's budget must be approved by Congress. Its process for doing so is a creaky conglomeration of traditional procedures overlaid with structural reforms. The cumbersome process has had difficulty producing a budget according to Congress's own timetable. Traditionally, the tasks of budget making were divided among a number of committees, a process that has been retained. Three types of committees are involved in budgeting:

- **Tax committees** are responsible for raising the revenues to run the government. The Ways and Means Committee in the House and the Finance Committee in the Senate consider all proposals for taxes, tariffs, and other receipts contained in the president's budget.
- **Authorization committees** (such as the House Armed Services Committee and the Senate Banking, Housing, and Urban Affairs Committee) have jurisdiction over particular legislative subjects. The House has about twenty committees that can authorize spending and the Senate about fifteen. Each pores over the portions of the budget that pertain to its area of responsibility. However, in recent years, power has shifted from the authorization committees to the appropriations committees.

Office of Management and Budget (OMB)
The budgeting arm of the Executive Office; prepares the president's budget.

tax committees
The two committees of Congress responsible for raising the revenue with which to run the government.

authorization committees
Committees of Congress that can authorize spending in their particular areas of responsibility.

appropriations committees
Committees of Congress that decide which of the programs passed by the authorization committees will actually be funded.

• **Appropriations committees** decide which of the programs approved by the authorization committees will actually be funded (that is, given money to spend). For example, the House Armed Services Committee might propose building a new line of tanks for the army, and it might succeed in getting this proposal enacted into law. But the tanks will never be built unless the appropriations committees appropriate funds for that purpose. Twelve distinct appropriations bills are supposed to be enacted each year to fund the nation's spending. Congress had trouble passing those too, and passed none of them before the end of the year in 2013.[30]

Two serious problems are inherent in a budgeting process that involves three distinct kinds of congressional committees. First, the two-step spending process (first authorization, then appropriation) is complex; it offers wonderful opportunities for interest groups to get into the budgeting act in the spirit of pluralist democracy. Second, because one group of legislators in each house plans for revenues and many other groups plan for spending, no one is responsible for the budget as a whole.

budget committees
One committee in each house of Congress that supervises a comprehensive budget review process.

Congressional Budget Office (CBO)
The budgeting arm of Congress, which prepares alternative budgets to those prepared by the president's OMB.

mandatory spending
In the Budget Enforcement Act of 1990, expenditures required by previous commitments.

discretionary spending
In the Budget Enforcement Act of 1990, authorized expenditures from annual appropriations.

entitlements
Benefits to which every eligible person has a legal right and that the government cannot deny.

In the 1970s, Congress created **budget committees** in each chamber to supervise a comprehensive budget review process. They were directed to pass annual budget resolutions setting spending targets and to work out differences in conferences. They were aided by a new **Congressional Budget Office (CBO)**, with a staff of more than two hundred, to supply budgetary expertise equal to the president's OMB. From 1976 to 2010, Congress usually passed the required budget resolutions but failed to pass *any* since.[31]

In 1990, Congress defined two types of spending: **mandatory spending** and **discretionary spending**. Spending is mandatory for programs that have become **entitlements** (such as Social Security and veterans' pensions), which provide benefits to individuals legally entitled to them and cannot be reduced without changing the law. Discretionary spending, including annual military expenditures, was subject to limits, or caps.

In 1997, President Clinton and Congress accomplished what most observers thought was beyond political possibility. They not only produced a balanced budget ahead of schedule but actually produced a budget surplus—the first surplus since 1969. In the early 2000s, President Bush and Republicans in Congress advocated using the budget surplus for large across-the-board tax cuts to return money to taxpayers.[32] Although the caps on discretionary spending helped balance the budget entering 2000, many members of Congress in both parties resented the caps' restrictions on their freedom to make fiscal decisions. Accordingly, Congress allowed the caps on discretionary spending to expire at the end of 2002.[33] Since 2002, the government has run budget deficits, not surpluses.

Repeated failures to eliminate annual budget deficits renewed calls for a constitutional amendment requiring Congress to balance the budget—as required by most state constitutions. Congressional proposals for a balanced budget amendment (BBA) were first introduced in 1936 and often since.[34] Republicans in Congress tend to favor a BBA as a means to limit spending, while Democrats oppose it for reasons similar to those given by most economists: a serious BBA would prevent the government from running a deficit to simulate the economy. Some conservatives feared that a BBA would increase the courts' role in deciding government spending cases certain to arise under it.[35] Others noted that Congress could pass balanced budgets if it wished without a constitutional requirement, which would only encourage Congress to work around the law to increase deficits. In 1985, a desperate Congress set annually decreasing deficit targets that would trigger automatic spending cuts if not met. Each year thereafter, Congress simply raised the targets to meet them. The law was an utter failure, and the deficit targets were eliminated in 1990.

Congress's failure to limit the national debt is similar and instructive. Prior to World War II, Congress limited indebtedness to $45 billion, only 10 percent above the existing debt of $40.4 billion.[36] Every time the debt neared its legal limit—over 100 times since 1940—Congress repeatedly raised the ceiling.[37] Under pressure from the tea party movement in 2011, congressional Republicans opposed raising the debt ceiling again, but financial groups within the Republican Party argued that failing to pay our debts would cause financial chaos.[38] Congress complied once more. Given that the debt ceiling causes so much partisan rancor and that only one other modern democracy (Denmark) legislates a similar debt ceiling, one wonders why it exists at all.[39]

Tax Policies

LO3 ★ Identify the objectives of tax policies and explain why tax reform is difficult.

So far, we have been concerned mainly with the spending side of the budget, for which appropriations must be enacted each year. The revenue side of the budget is governed by overall tax policy, which is designed to provide a continuous flow of income without annual legislation. A major text on government finance says that tax policy is sometimes changed to accomplish one or more of several objectives:

- To adjust overall revenue to meet budget outlays
- To make the tax burden more equitable for taxpayers
- To help control the economy by raising taxes (thus decreasing aggregate demand) or by lowering taxes (thus increasing demand)[40]

If those were the only objectives, the tax code might be simple, but tax policy also reflects two conflicting philosophies for distributing the costs of government: whether citizens should be taxed according to their ability to pay or for benefits they receive. Tax policy is further complicated because it is also used to advance social goals (such as home ownership through the deduction for mortgage interest) or to favor certain industries. To accommodate such deductions and incentives, the tax code (which is available over the Internet) runs over seven thousand pages.[41] Over 90 percent of the government revenue in FY 2015 was expected from three major sources: individual income taxes (46 percent), social insurance taxes (32 percent), and corporate income taxes (14 percent).[42] Because the income tax accounts for most government revenue, discussion of tax policy usually focuses on that source.

Reform

Tax reform proposals are usually so heavily influenced by interest groups looking for special benefits that they end up working against their original purpose.[43] Without question, the tax code is complex. Before 1987, people paid different tax rates depending on where they fit in fourteen income brackets. President Reagan backed a sweeping reform that reduced the number of brackets to two and the rate for the top bracket from 70 to 28 percent. By eliminating many tax brackets, the new tax policy approached the idea of a flat tax—one that requires everyone to pay at the same rate.

A flat tax has the appeal of simplicity, but it violates the principle of **progressive taxation**, under which the rich pay proportionately higher taxes than the poor. The ability to pay has long been a standard of fair taxation, and surveys show that citizens favor this idea in the abstract.[44] In practice, however, they have different opinions, as we will see.

progressive taxation
A system of taxation whereby the rich pay proportionately higher taxes than the poor; used by governments to redistribute wealth and thus promote equality.

Mike Simons/Stringer/Getty Images

We Gave at the Bureaucracy

One of many clerks working at the Cincinnati Internal Revenue Service Center in Covington, Kentucky, one of the ten centers operated by the Internal Revenue Service to process tax forms and taxpayer requests. Each processes millions of forms each year.

Nevertheless, most democratic governments rely on progressive taxation to redistribute wealth and thus promote economic equality. Although wealthy people finance redistributive programs, they also benefit if redistribution alleviates extreme inequalities and prevents poor people from revolting.

In general, the greater the number of tax brackets, the more progressive a tax can be, for higher brackets can be taxed at higher rates. To deal with a budget deficit in 1990, President George H. W. Bush violated his campaign pledge of "no new taxes" by creating a third tax rate, 31 percent, for those with the highest incomes. In 1993, Clinton created a fourth level, 39.6 percent, moving toward a more progressive tax structure, although still less progressive than before 1987. Both presidents acted to increase revenue to reduce a soaring deficit.

Campaigning for president, George W. Bush promised to cut taxes. Soon after his election, he got Congress to pass a complex $1.35 trillion tax cut, with a top personal tax rate of 35 percent. Intended to stimulate the economy, the tax cut also reduced the revenue needed to match government spending.[45] Budget deficits quickly returned under Bush, owing to reduced revenue, a downturn in the stock market, and unanticipated expenses for homeland defense and military action following the September 11 attacks on America. The deficit zoomed to over a trillion dollars (10 percent of GDP) in Bush's last budget (see Figure 17.1), which reflected costs of his $168 billion stimulus package and his $700 billion Troubled Assets Relief Program (TARP). The deficit grew further with Obama's $787 billion stimulus package in 2009 but began to decrease in 2010. Obama campaigned to restore the 39.6 percent tax bracket for those with the highest incomes and succeeded in 2013.

Comparing Tax Burdens

No one likes to pay taxes, so politicians find it popular to criticize the agency that collects taxes: the Internal Revenue Service. The income tax itself—and taxes in general—are also popular targets for U.S. politicians who campaign on getting government off the backs of the people. Is the tax burden on U.S. citizens truly too heavy? Compared with what? One way to compare tax burdens is to examine taxes over time in the same country; another is to compare taxes in different countries at the same time. By comparing taxes over time in the United States, we find that the income tax burden on U.S. citizens has actually decreased since the 1950s. The federal income tax rate for a family of four with the median household income was 20 percent in 1955 and 15 percent in 2013.[46] Another way to compare tax burdens is to examine tax rates in different countries. By nearly two to one, more respondents in a post-2000 national survey thought that Americans pay a higher percentage of their income in taxes than citizens in Western Europe.[47] They were flat wrong. Despite

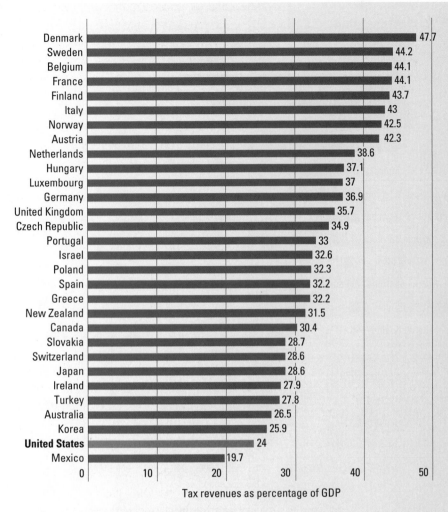

FIGURE 17.2 Tax Burdens in Thirty Countries

This graph compares tax burdens in 2011 in thirty countries as a percentage of gross domestic product (GDP), which is the market value of goods produced inside the country by workers, businesses, and government. The percentages encompass national, state, and local taxes and Social Security contributions. By this measure, the U.S. government extracts less in taxes from its citizens than do the governments of all Western democratic nations. At the top of the list stand Denmark and Sweden, well known for providing heavily for social welfare. Despite its low ranking in tax burden, the United States also supports the world's largest military force, to which it allocates about 4 percent of its GDP, or about 18 percent of its total expenditures.

Source: OECD, *Revenue Statistics 2013*, OECD Publishing, doi: 10.1787/rev_stats-2013-en-fr. Copyright © 2013 by Organization for Economic Development and Cooperation (OECD). Reproduced by permission.

Americans' complaints about high taxes, the U.S. tax burden is not large compared with that of other democratic nations. As shown in Figure 17.2, Americans' taxes are quite low in general compared with those in twenty-nine other democratic nations. Primarily because they provide their citizens with more generous social benefits (such as health care and unemployment compensation), almost every democratic nation taxes more heavily than the United States does.[48]

Spending Policies

LO4 ★ Identify the major areas of government outlays and explain the role of incremental budgeting and uncontrollable spending on the growth of government spending.

The FY 2015 budget projects spending over $3,901,000,000,000—that's almost $4 trillion (or $4,000 billion, if you prefer). Where does all that money go? Figure 17.3 breaks down the $3.9 trillion in proposed outlays in President Obama's FY 2015 budget by eighteen major governmental functions. The largest amount (22 percent of the total budget) was targeted for Social Security. From World War II to FY 1993, national

FIGURE 17.3 Federal Spending in FY 2015, by Function

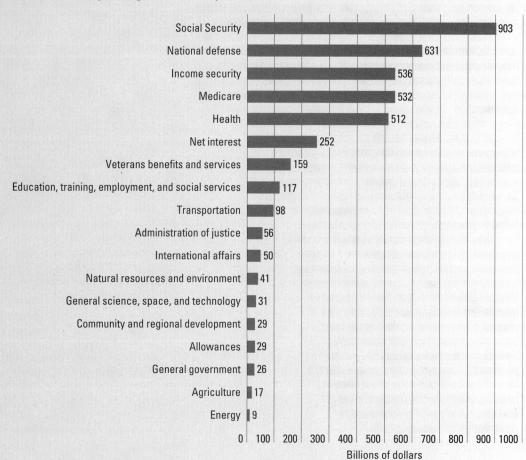

Federal budget authorities and outlays are organized into about twenty categories, some of which are mainly for bookkeeping purposes. This graph shows estimated outlays for each of eighteen substantive functions in President Obama's FY 2015 budget. The final budget differed somewhat from this distribution because Congress amended some of the president's spending proposals. The graph makes clear the huge differences among spending categories. Social Security alone accounts for 22 percent of the budget. Military spending costs 16 percent. Income security—housing, nutrition, and energy assistance to low-income persons—takes another 13 percent. Health costs (including Medicare) account for 26 percent more, and net interest consumes about 6 percent. This leaves only 16 percent for transportation, agriculture, justice, science, and energy—matters often regarded as important centers of government activity.

Source: Executive Office of the President, *Budget of the United States Government, Fiscal Year 2015: Historical Tables* (Washington, D.C.: U.S. Government Printing Office, 2014), Table 3.1.

defense (military spending) accounted for most spending under these categories, but it fell to second place after the collapse of communism and stayed there until FY 2015. Income security (mainly for housing assistance) and Medicare, the third and fourth largest categories, together account for almost 27 percent of all budgetary outlays. At 13 percent, the fifth category, health, includes research organizations such as the National Institutes of Health. Health and Medicare together account for about one-quarter of the budget, which underscores the importance of controlling the costs of health care. The sixth largest category is interest on the accumulated national debt, which alone consumes over 6 percent of all national government spending. Some people think that money spent on "foreign aid" is a huge drain on our treasury. However, the $50 billion outlay for international affairs constitutes under 1.5 percent of the total—and one-quarter of that is for the State Department and our embassies abroad.

Consider the relative shares of expenditures over time in broad categories, as in Figure 17.4. The effect of World War II is clear: spending for national defense rose sharply after 1940, peaked at about 90 percent of the budget in 1945, and fell to about 30 percent in peacetime. The percentage for defense rose again in the early 1950s, reflecting rearmament during the Cold War with the Soviet Union. Thereafter, defense's share of the budget decreased steadily (except for the bump during the Vietnam War in the late 1960s). This trend was reversed by the Carter administration in the 1970s and then shot upward during the Reagan presidency. Defense spending decreased under George H. W. Bush and continued to decline under Clinton. Following the September 11 attacks, President George W. Bush increased military spending 22 percent. Throughout his administration, military spending increased by 30 percent.[49] The Iraq war eventually cost over $800 billion and the war in Afghanistan over $700 billion.[50]

Government payments to individuals (e.g., Social Security checks) consistently consumed less of the budget than national defense until 1971. Since then, payments to individuals have accounted for the largest portion of the national budget, and they have been increasing. Net interest payments also increased substantially during the years of budget deficits. Pressure from payments for national defense, individuals, and interest on the national debt has squeezed all other government outlays.

There are two major explanations for the general trend of increasing government spending. One is bureaucratic, the other political.

FIGURE 17.4 National Government Outlays over Time

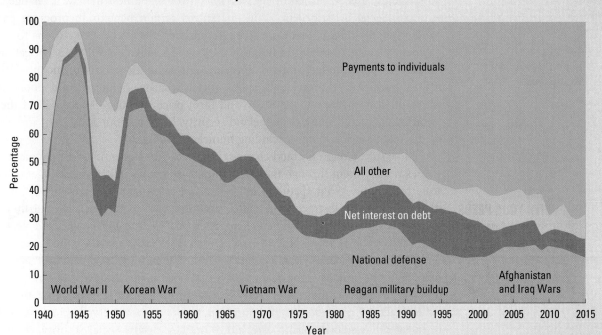

This chart plots the percentage of the annual budget devoted to four major expense categories over time. It shows that significant changes have occurred in national spending since 1940. During World War II, defense spending consumed more than 80 percent of the national budget. Defense again accounted for most national expenditures during the Cold War of the 1950s. Following the collapse of communism in the 1990s, the military's share of the budget declined but rose again with the war in Iraq. The major story, however, has been the growth in payments to individuals—for example, in the form of Social Security benefits, Medicare, health care, and various programs that provide a social safety net—including unemployment compensation.

Source: Executive Office of the President, *Budget of the United States Government, Fiscal Year 2015: Historical Tables* (Washington, D.C.: U.S. Government Printing Office, 2014), Table 6.1.

Incremental Budgeting ...

incremental budgeting
A method of budget making that involves adding new funds (an increment) onto the amount previously budgeted (in last year's budget).

The bureaucratic explanation for spending increases involves **incremental budgeting**: bureaucrats, in compiling their funding requests for the following year, traditionally ask for the amount they got in the current year plus some incremental increase to fund new projects. Because Congress has already approved the agency's budget for the current year, it pays little attention to the agency's current size (the largest part of its budget) and focuses instead on the extra money (the increment) requested for the next year. As a result, few agencies are ever cut back, and spending continually goes up.

Incremental budgeting generates bureaucratic momentum that continually raises spending. Once an agency is created, it attracts a clientele that defends its existence and supports its requests for extra funds year after year. Because budgeting is a two-step process, agencies that get cut back in the authorizing committees sometimes manage (assisted by their interest group clientele) to get funds restored in the appropriations committees—and if not in the House, then perhaps in the Senate. Often appropriations committees approve spending for a specific purpose, known as an **earmark**. The practice of earmarking funds for "congressional pork" has greatly increased since the early 1990s. Stung by criticism of the practice, Congress declared a moratorium on earmarks after the 2010 election, but some members are now repackaging them as "special funds" for which only their districts qualify.[51]

earmark
Federal funds appropriated by Congress for use on local projects.

... and Uncontrollable Spending

discretionary outlays
Payments made by legislators' choice and based on annual appropriations.

mandatory outlays
Payments that government must make by law.

Earmarks are examples of **discretionary outlays** that Congress can choose to make. Most spending is enshrined in law and uncontrollable unless the law is changed. For example, Social Security legislation guarantees certain benefits to program participants when they retire. Medicare and veterans' benefits also entitle citizens to certain payments. These represent **mandatory outlays**. In Obama's FY 2015 budget, about 65 percent of all budget outlays were uncontrollable or relatively uncontrollable—mainly payments to individuals under Social Security, Medicare, and public assistance; interest on the national debt; and farm price supports. About half of the rest went for national defense or homeland security, leaving about 15 percent for domestic discretionary spending—excluding homeland security.[52]

To be sure, Congress could change the laws to abolish entitlement payments, and it does modify them through the budgeting process. But politics argues against large-scale reductions. What spending cuts would be acceptable to or even popular with the public? In the abstract, voters favor cutting government spending, but they tend to favor maintaining government programs that help needy people and deal with important national problems. Substantial majorities favor spending the same or even more on Social Security, Medicare, education, job training, programs for poor children, and the military. In fact, when a national poll asked whether respondents thought federal spending should be "increased, decreased, or kept about the same" for eighteen different purposes—education, public schools, veterans' benefits, college financial aid, Medicare, health care, aid to the U.S. needy, Social Security, combating crime, infrastructure, environmental protection, scientific research, energy, agriculture, terrorism, military defense, unemployment aid, and aid to the world's needy—respondents favored increasing or keeping about the same level of spending for *every* purpose except military defense, unemployment aid, and aid to the world's needy.[53]

In truth, a perplexed Congress, trying to reduce the budget deficit, faces a public that favors funding most programs at even higher levels than those favored by most lawmakers.[54] Moreover, spending for the most expensive of these programs—Social Security and Medicare—is uncontrollable. Americans have grown accustomed to certain government benefits, but they do not like the idea of raising taxes to pay for them.

COMPARE WITH YOUR PEERS
MindTap™ for American Government

Access the Economic Policy Forum: Polling Activity—Reforming Social Security.

Taxing, Spending, and Economic Equality

LO5 ★ Identify the origins of the income tax, trace the influence of government spending and taxing policies on inequality, and examine these policies from the majoritarian and pluralist perspectives.

As we noted in Chapter 1, the most controversial purpose of government is to promote equality, especially economic equality. Promoting economic equality through government action comes about only at the expense of economic freedom. Wealthy people lose freedom to keep their money when government redistributes wealth from the rich to the poor through a progressive income tax. The goal is not to achieve equality of outcome but to reduce existing levels of inequality.

The national government introduced an income tax in 1862 to help finance the Civil War. That tax was repealed in 1871, and the country relied on revenue from tariffs on imported goods to finance the national government. The tariffs acted as a national sales tax imposed on all citizens, and many manufacturers—themselves taxed at the same rate as a laborer—grew rich from undercutting foreign competition.[55] Followers of a new political movement, the Populists (see Chapter 8), decried the inequities of wealth and called for a more equitable form of taxation, an income tax. An income tax law passed in 1894 was declared unconstitutional by the Supreme Court the next year. The Democratic Party and the Populists accused the Court of defending wealth against equal taxation and called for amending the Constitution to permit an income tax in their 1896 platforms. A bill to do so was introduced in 1909 and ratified in 1913 as the Sixteenth Amendment.

The Sixteenth Amendment gave government the power to levy a tax on individual incomes, and it has done so every year since 1914. From 1964 to 1981, people who reported taxable incomes of $100,000 or more were taxed at least 70 percent on all income above that figure or margin. Individuals with lower incomes paid taxes at progressively lower marginal rates. (Figure 17.5 shows how the top marginal rate has fluctuated over the years.) Let us look at the overall effect of government spending and tax policies on economic equality in America.

Government Effects on Economic Equality

We begin by asking whether government spending policies have any measurable effect on income inequality. Economists call a government payment to individuals through Social Security, unemployment insurance, food stamps, and other programs, such as agricultural subsidies, a **transfer payment**. Transfer payments need not always go to the poor. In fact, one problem with the farm program is that the wealthiest farmers have often received the largest subsidies. Nevertheless, most researchers have determined that transfer payments have had a definite effect on reducing income inequality.

According to the principle of progressive taxation, tax rates are supposed to take more revenue from the rich than from the poor. Although the effective rates have varied during the recent past, the wealthy were always taxed at higher rates than the poor, in line with the principle of progressive taxation. Some oppose progressive taxation as a tool for redistributing income rooted in an "obsession" with inequality.[56] They can point out that the richest 1 percent of taxpayers paid 35 percent of all federal individual income taxes in 2011.[57] Perhaps they paid so much because they made

transfer payment
A payment by government to an individual, mainly through Social Security or unemployment insurance.

FIGURE 17.5 The Ups and Downs of Top National Tax Rates

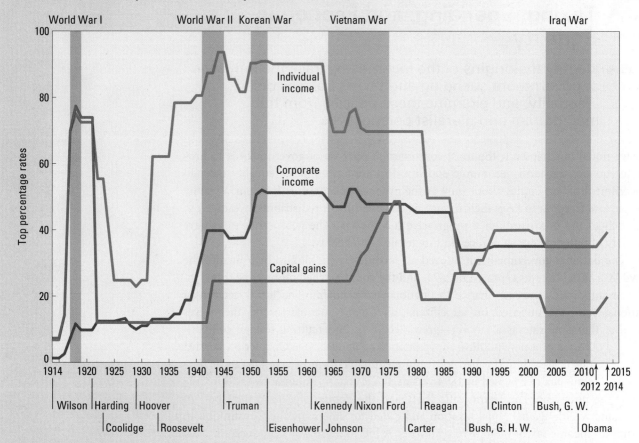

In 1913, the Sixteenth Amendment empowered the national government to collect taxes on income. Since then, the government has levied taxes on individual and corporate income and on capital gains realized by individuals and corporations from the sale of assets, such as stocks or real estate. Incomes above certain levels are taxed at higher rates than incomes below those levels. This chart, which lists only the maximum tax rates, shows that these top tax rates have fluctuated wildly over time, from less than 10 percent to more than 90 percent. (They tend to be highest during periods of war.) During the Reagan administration, the maximum individual income tax rate fell to the lowest level since the Coolidge and Hoover administrations in the late 1920s and 1930s. The top rate increased slightly for 1991, to 31 percent, during George H. W. Bush's administration and jumped to 39.6 percent for 1994 under Clinton. The top rate was reduced in stages to 35 percent by Bush's tax plans in 2001 and 2003, which expired at the end of 2012. Congress and Obama agreed to restore the rate of 39.6 percent in 2013 for individuals making over $400,000.

Sources: *Wall Street Journal*, 18 August 1986, p. 10. Copyright 1986 by Dow Jones & Company, Inc. Reproduced with permission of Dow Jones & Company, Inc., in the format textbook via Copyright Clearance Center. Additional data from the Tax Policy Center, which reports tax brackets for individual years at http://www.taxpolicycenter.org.

so much. If the richest 1 percent of all taxpayers took in 19 percent of all income in the nation (which they did), some think that they should pay twice that percentage in taxes (which they almost did).[58]

However, the national income tax is only part of the story. In some cases, poorer citizens pay a larger share of their income in taxes than wealthier citizens. "Stop Coddling the Super-Rich," wrote Warren Buffett. The third richest man in the world reported that he paid only 17.4 percent of his income in income taxes for 2010, while the average tax burden for the other twenty people in his office was 36 percent.[59] How can people in the lowest income group pay a higher percentage of their income in taxes than do those in the very highest group? In part, Buffett wrote, he made most of his money through capital gains on stocks, which were taxed at only 15 percent.

The full answer has to do with the combination of national, state, and local tax policies. Only the national income tax is progressive, with rates rising as income rises. The national payroll tax, which funds Social Security and Medicare, has two components—12.4 points go to Social Security and 2.9 to Medicare—for a total tax of 15.3 percent. The tax is regressive: its effective rate decreases as income increases beyond a certain point. Because employers typically pay half, the effective rate for taxpayers is usually 7.65 percent. However, the larger Social Security component is levied on only a set portion of a person's income (the first $113,100 in 2013), and there is no Social Security tax at all on wages over that amount. So the effective rate of the Social Security tax is higher for lower-income groups than for the very top group. In fact, 98 percent of employees in the lowest 20 percent paid more payroll tax than income tax, compared with only 16 percent of employees in the upper 20 percent.[60]

Most state and local sales taxes are equally regressive. Poor and rich usually pay the same flat rate on their purchases. But the poor spend almost everything they earn on purchases, which are taxed, whereas the rich are able to save. A study showed that the effective sales tax rate for the lowest income group was thus about 7 percent, whereas that for the top 1 percent was only 1 percent.[61]

In general, the nation's tax policies at all levels have historically favored not only those with higher incomes, but also the wealthy—those who draw income from capital (wealth) rather than labor—for example:

- There is no national tax at all on investments in certain securities, including municipal bonds (issued by local governments for construction projects).
- The tax on earned income (salaries and wages) is withheld from paychecks by employers under national law; the tax on unearned income (interest and dividends) is not.
- The tax on income from the sale of real estate or stocks (called capital gains) has typically been lower than the highest tax on income from salaries. (Income from selling property or from receiving stock dividends is taxed at 20 percent, while income from salaries for highly paid employees is taxed at almost twice that rate.)

Effects of Taxing and Spending Policies over Time

In 1967, at the beginning of President Johnson's Great Society programs, the poorest fifth of American families received 4 percent of the nation's income after taxes, whereas the richest fifth received 43.6 percent. Forty years later, after many billions of dollars had been spent on social programs, the income gap between the rich and poor had actually grown, as illustrated in "Freedom, Order, or Equality: Freedom v. Income Inequality." This is true despite the fact that many households in the lowest category had about one-third more wage-earners, mainly women, decades later.

In a capitalist system, some degree of inequality is inevitable. Is there some mechanism that limits how much economic equality can be achieved and prevents government policies from further equalizing income, no matter what is tried? To find out, we can look to other democracies to see how much equality they have been able to sustain. An international organization of developed nations analyzed data for twenty-two member countries in 2008. It found that the ratio of the income for the richest 10 percent of the population to the poorest 10 percent was lowest overall in the Nordic and many continental European countries.[62] The ratio rose to 10 to 1 in Italy, Japan, Korea, and Britain—and was around 14 to 1 in the United States, Israel, and Turkey. Only Mexico and Chile were more unequal than that. Other studies also show that our society has more economic inequality than other advanced nations. The question is, why?

Freedom, Order, or Equality

Freedom v. Income Inequality

In 2012, the 20 percent of U.S. families with the highest incomes received over 50 percent of all income, and their share has increased since 1967. This distribution of income is one of the most unequal among Western nations. At the bottom end of the scale, the poorest 20 percent of families received less than 4 percent of total family income, and their share has decreased over time.

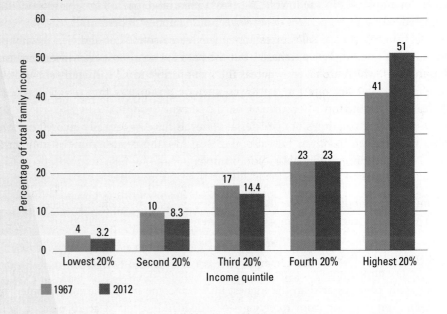

Source: U.S. Census Bureau, "Income, Poverty, and Health Insurance Coverage in the United States: 2012," Current Population Reports (Washington, D.C.: U.S. Government Printing Office, September 2013), Table A-3.

Critical Thinking Despite nearly fifty years of progressive taxation, high-income people took home a greater share of total income in 2012 than in 1967. What would explain that?

Democracy and Equality

Although the United States is a democracy that prizes political equality for its citizens, its record in promoting economic equality is not as good. In fact, its distribution of wealth—which includes not only income but also ownership of savings, housing, automobiles, stocks, and so on—is strikingly unequal. The wealthiest 1 percent of American families control almost 35 percent of the nation's household wealth (property, stock holdings, bank accounts).[63] Moreover, the distribution of wealth among ethnic groups is alarming. The typical white family has an annual income over 1.5 times that of both blacks and Hispanics.[64] If democracy means government "by the people," why aren't the people sharing more equally in the nation's wealth? If one of the supposed purposes of government is to promote equality, why are government policies not working that way?

One scholar theorizes that interest group activity in a pluralist democracy distorts government's efforts to promote equality. His analysis of pluralism sees "corporations and organized groups with an upper-income slant as exerting political power over and above the formal one-man-one-vote standard of democracy."[65] As argued in Chapter 10, the pluralist model of democracy rewards groups that are well organized and well funded.

What would happen if national tax policy were determined according to principles of majoritarian rather than pluralist democracy? Perhaps not much, if public opinion is any guide. In a string of Gallup polls from 1985 to 2013, clear majorities consistently said that the distribution of wealth is not fair and favor some redistribution—but the public is roughly evenly split on heavy taxes on the rich.[66] The people of the United States are not eager to redistribute wealth by increasing the only major progressive tax, the income tax. When polls asked over the years about replacing the progressive income tax with a flat tax or a national sales tax, most showed that a plurality of respondents preferred a flat tax, and almost as many favored a sales tax as the current income tax.[67] But a sales tax is a flat tax, paid by rich and poor at the same rate, and it would have a regressive effect on income distribution, promoting inequality. In one poll, the public also preferred a weekly $10 million national lottery to an increase in the income tax.[68] Because the poor are willing to chance more of their income on winning a fortune through lotteries than are rich people, lotteries (run by about forty states) also contribute to wealth inequality.[69]

Majoritarians might argue that most Americans fail to understand the inequities of the national tax system, which hides regressiveness in sales taxes and Social Security taxes. According to a national survey, Americans in the highest income categories (earning over $150,000 a year) understand the tax system much better than those at the lower income levels.[70] In Alabama, for example, income above $4,600 for a family of four went untaxed—meaning that most poor and all rich paid the same income tax, and the state relied mainly on sales and property taxes. In 2003, the conservative Republican governor of Alabama proposed a more progressive system of higher tax rates, mainly on the wealthy, only to have voters reject his reforms 2 to 1.[71] A black preacher and advocate of tax reform said that his parishioners like the (regressive) sales tax because they pay it in small increments.[72]

So majoritarians cannot argue that the public demands "fairer" tax rates that take from richer citizens to help poorer ones. If the public did, the lowest income families might receive a greater share of the national income than they do. Instead, economic policy is determined mainly through a complex process of pluralist politics that returns nearly half the national income to only 20 percent of the nation's families.

Master the Topic of Economic Policy with MindTap™ for American Government

 REVIEW MindTap™ for American Government
Access Key Term Flashcards for Chapter 17.

 TEST YOURSELF MindTap™ for American Government
Take the Wrap It Up Quiz for Chapter 17.

 STAY CURRENT MindTap™ for American Government
Access the KnowNow blog and customized RSS for updates on current events.

 STAY FOCUSED MindTap™ for American Government
Complete the Focus Activities for Economic Policy.

Summary

LO1 Compare and contrast three theories of market economics: laissez-faire, Keynesian, and supply-side.

- Laissez-faire economics holds that government should keep its hands off the economy. Keynesian theory holds that government should take an active role in dealing with inflation and unemployment, using fiscal and monetary policies to produce desired levels of aggregate demand. Supply-side economists, popular during the Reagan administration, focus on controlling the supply of goods and services rather than the demand for them.

- Economic growth in the United States during the mid- to late-1990s seemed to support the omniscience of free markets over government regulation. The financial crisis of 2008 and the accompanying recession led to a return to Keynesian principles. The continuing process of globalization has eroded government's ability to manage its own economy completely.

LO2 Describe the process by which the national budget is prepared and passed into law and the reforms undertaken by Congress to balance the budget.

- Congress alone prepared the budget until 1921, when it thrust the responsibility onto the president. In the 1970s, Congress sought to regain control of the process, creating a Congressional Budget Office and new House and Senate budget committees. Congress produced huge budget deficits in the 1980s fueled by tax cuts, increased military spending, and increased payments to individuals under entitlement programs, such as Social Security and Medicare. In 1985, Congress passed a law to reduce annual deficits in stages, through automatic across-the-board cuts if necessary, but Congress

simply increased the allowable deficits. In 1939, Congress set a ceiling for the national debt, but it always voted (over 100 times since) to increase the ceiling to accommodate the debt. Both examples of Congress's failure to control its own spending habits suggest that it would also circumvent any balanced budget amendment to the Constitution.

LO3 Identify the objectives of tax policies and explain why tax reform is difficult.

- Tax policies have several objectives: to adjust revenue to meet budget outlays; to make the tax burden more equitable for taxpayers; and to help control the economy by raising taxes. Tax reform is difficult because tax policies reflect two conflicting philosophies for distributing the costs of government: whether citizens should be taxed according to their ability to pay or for the benefits they receive.

- Despite public complaints about high taxes, current U.S. tax rates are lower than those in most other major countries and lower than they have been since the Great Depression of the 1930s. But even with the heavily progressive tax rates of the past, the national tax system has done little to redistribute income. Government transfer payments to individuals have helped reduce some income inequalities, but the distribution of income is less equal in the United States than in most major Western nations.

LO4 Identify the major areas of government outlays and explain the role of incremental budgeting and uncontrollable spending on the growth of government spending.

- Six categories consume about 85 percent of the FY 2015 budget: Social Security payments (the largest portion at 22 percent); national defense (18 percent);

income security and Medicare (almost 29 percent); health, which includes research organizations such as the National Institutes of Health, (10 percent); and interest on the national debt (6 percent). The remaining 15 percent is distributed among veteran's affairs, education, transportation, administration of justice, international affairs, natural resources, community development, science and technology, general government, agriculture, and energy.

LO5 **Identify the origins of the income tax, trace the influence of government spending and taxing policies on inequality, and examine these policies from the majoritarian and pluralist perspectives.**

- Pluralist democracy as practiced in the United States has allowed well-organized, well-financed interest groups to manipulate taxing and spending policies to their benefit. Taxing and spending policies in the United States are tipped in the direction of freedom rather than equality.

Chapter Quiz

LO1 **Compare and contrast three theories of market economics: laissez-faire, Keynesian, and supply-side.**

1. How does the "efficient market hypothesis" relate to laissez-faire economics?
2. How does the concept of "aggregate demand" relate to Keynesian economics?

LO2 **Describe the process by which the national budget is prepared and passed into law and the reforms undertaken by Congress to balance the budget.**

1. What is the difference between a budget authorization and an appropriation?
2. Distinguish between mandatory and discretionary spending.

LO3 **Identify the objectives of tax policies and explain why tax reform is difficult.**

1. What is the difference between a flat tax and a progressive tax? Which do you think is fairer?
2. Compared with other countries, how heavy is the tax burden in the United States?

LO4 **Identify the major areas of government outlays and explain the role of incremental budgeting and uncontrollable spending on the growth of government spending.**

1. Of the twenty or so categories of government functions, which consumes the most federal spending?
2. What percentage of the federal budget is consumed by foreign aid?

LO5 **Identify the origins of the income tax, trace the influence of government spending and taxing policies on inequality, and examine these policies from the majoritarian and pluralist perspectives.**

1. How much effect has national tax policy had on the distribution of family income over time?
2. What might happen if national tax policy were determined according to principles of majoritarian democracy and not pluralist democracy?

Policymaking and Domestic Policy

Learning Outcomes

LO1 Categorize different types of public policies and outline the process by which policies are formulated and implemented.

LO2 Trace the evolution of social welfare programs as a central element of public policy in the United States.

LO3 Describe the origins and evolution of Social Security as well as the funding and benefit issues facing the program.

LO4 Explain how poverty is defined and trace the evolution of public assistance programs designed to address it.

LO5 Differentiate among Medicare, Medicaid, and the Affordable Care Act of 2010 and explain how each program addresses the issues of health-care delivery.

LO6 Describe the role of the federal government in shaping education policy at the state and local government levels.

LO7 Assess alternative policies for addressing illegal immigration into the United States.

LO8 Explain how the issue of fairness shapes perspectives on government benefits.

 WATCH & LEARN MindTap for American Government
Watch a brief "What Do You Know?" video summarizing Domestic Policy.

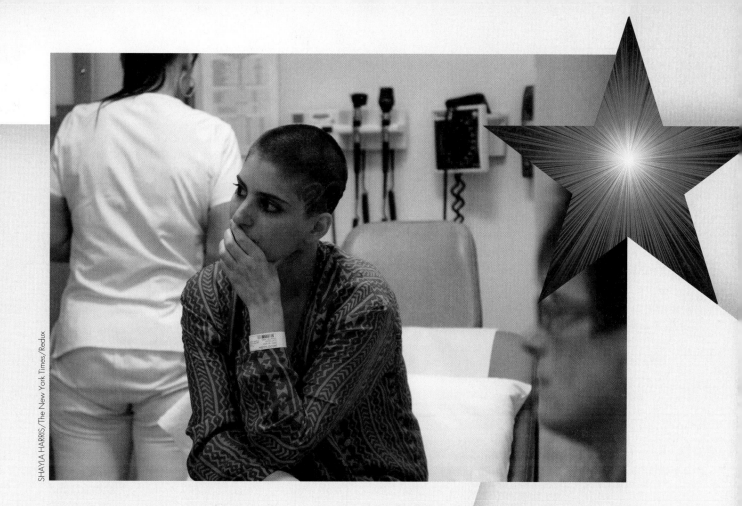

SHAYLA HARRIS/The New York Times/Redux

How can you pay your bills if you are too sick to work or if you need to spend your time taking care of a sick family member? This question is one faced by many Americans every year, especially those whose lives are affected by cancer. Approximately 41 percent of Americans will be diagnosed with some form of cancer in their lifetimes.[1] Drug treatment alone can cost in excess of $100,000 per year per patient. The total annual cost of treating cancer in the United States exceeds $124 billion.[2] Even people who have health insurance can end up paying significant amounts of money. One woman, Suleika Jaoaud, was twenty-two years old when she was diagnosed with a form of leukemia. Even with comprehensive insurance coverage provided by her father's plan, her family has incurred tens of thousands of dollars in expenses. During her first year of treatment, her insurance company paid over $1 million for her care. She and her mother were unable to work; Suleika because she was so ill and her mother because of the time needed to manage Suleika's care (including all of the paperwork).[3] The loss of income plus the added expenses that they and so many other families face only add to the hardship of cancer. One recent study found that cancer patients are over twice as likely as people without cancer to file for bankruptcy.[4]

The Affordable Care Act (ACA), passed in 2010 and implemented gradually, was designed to help people like Suleika. She has a serious and expensive health condition, and before the law was passed, insurance companies were able to deny her coverage on that basis alone. As of 2014, coverage cannot be denied due to illness. One recent study concluded that up to 50 percent of nonelderly Americans, including 24 percent of people under age eighteen and 35 percent of people aged eighteen to thirty-four, have at least one preexisting condition that previously would have been grounds for being denied coverage.[5] In order to offset the costs of having so many more people with expensive illnesses now getting insurance, the ACA requires all Americans to have health insurance. People under age twenty-six, like Suleika was at the time of her diagnosis, can remain on their parents' health plan, thanks to another provision of the law. About 3 million young people have taken advantage of this provision since it went into effect in 2010.[6]

Despite these apparent successes, debate about the ACA remains fierce. First is the philosophical debate about whether government even has the authority to require people to get insurance. Then come more technical debates about the effect of the law on government spending and individual tax burdens, the impact of the law on state-level finances and agencies, the quality (or lack thereof) of the law's implementation, and more. While it is tempting to conclude that a policy that allows people with serious conditions to get the treatment they need and avoid bankruptcy is one that should remain in effect, the policy realm of health care is complicated. The challenge of devising, implementing, and assessing a policy that protects the citizenry's standard of living while also satisfying other basic principles, such as federalism, the economic freedom of private employers and insurance providers, and the individual freedom of people to shun insurance coverage if they want to, is ongoing.

In modern democracies, many people feel that the government should provide basic social services so that no one's quality of life falls below a certain level. The notion that only the wealthy or the healthy have access to both routine and life-saving medical care is at odds with modern understandings of the role of government. Crafting public policies that promote the view that governments have such responsibilities without infringing on personal or economic freedoms is a task that policymakers continually face. If and when a policy is enacted, tracking its progress and determining whether it is achieving its goals without also incurring undesirable, unintended consequences is the next hurdle. Then, deciding what, if any, changes should be made to the policy starts the cycle again.

Previous chapters focused on individual institutions of government. Here we look at government more broadly and ask how policymaking takes place across institutions. We first identify different types of public policies and analyze stages in the policymaking process. We describe policymaking as an ongoing process, often without a clear start or finish. Policies are continually evaluated, altered, and reevaluated. Then we look at specific domestic policies, that is, government plans of action targeting concerns internal to the United States. These are among the most enduring and costly programs that the government has launched on behalf of its citizens. Four questions guide our inquiry: What are the broad contours of the policymaking process? What are the origins and politics of specific domestic policies? What are the effects of these policies once they are implemented? Are disagreements about policy really disagreements about values?

LISTEN & LEARN
MindTap° **for American Government**

Access Read Speaker to listen to Chapter 18.

public policy
A general plan of action adopted by the government to solve a social problem, counter a threat, or pursue an objective.

 Government Purposes and Public Policies

LO1 ★ Categorize different types of public policies and outline the process by which policies are formulated and implemented.

In Chapter 1, we noted that most citizens accept limitations on their personal freedom in return for various benefits of government. We defined the major purposes of government as maintaining order, providing public benefits, and promoting equality. Different governments place different values on each broad purpose, and those differences are reflected in their public policies. A **public policy** is a general plan of action adopted by a government to solve a social problem, counter a threat, or pursue an objective.

At times, governments choose not to adopt a new policy to deal with a troublesome situation; instead, they muddle through, hoping the problem will diminish in importance. This too is a policy decision because it chooses to maintain the status quo. Whatever their form and effectiveness, all policies are the means by which government pursues certain goals in specific situations. People disagree about public policies because they disagree about one or more of the following elements: the goals government should have, the means it should use to meet them, and how the situation at hand should be perceived.

The Policymaking Process

When people disagree on goals, that disagreement is often rooted in a difference in values. As emphasized throughout this book, such value conflict often involves pitting freedom against order or freedom against equality. Disputes involving values are hard to bridge since they reflect a basic worldview and go to the core of one's sense of right and wrong.

The problem of illegal drugs illustrates how different core values lead us to prefer different policies. Everyone agrees that government should address problems created by drugs. Yet views of what should be done differ sharply. Recall from Chapter 1 that libertarians prioritize individual freedom and want to limit government as much as possible. Many libertarians argue that drugs should be decriminalized; if people want to take drugs, they should be free to do so. If drug use were legal, crimes associated with the drug trade would evaporate. Conservatives emphasize order. In their minds, a safe and civilized society does not allow people to debase themselves through drug abuse, and the government should punish those who violate the law. Liberals promote treatment as a policy option. They regard addiction as a medical problem and believe that government should offer services that help addicts. Government should help people in need, they argue, and many drug offenders cannot pay for treatment because their drug habit has left them impoverished.

Types of Policies

Although values underlie choices, analysis of public policy does not usually focus explicitly on core beliefs. Political scientists often categorize policies by their objectives. One common purpose is to allocate resources so that some segment of society or region of the country can receive a service or benefit. We call these **distributive policies**. Pork barrel government projects discussed in Chapter 11 are distributive policies. One example of the distribution of resources toward a local project involves the roughly $50,000 that the National Endowment for the Arts gave to the Western Folklife Center for its annual Cowboy Poetry Festival in Elko, Nevada, in 2014. Some argue that the government should not distribute funds for such local projects. Others, such as Senate Majority Leader Harry Reid (D-Nev.), say that the funding preserves and celebrates the culture of the American West while also enhancing the region's economy, since the yearly festival generates millions in economic activity.[7]

distributive policies
Government policies designed to confer a benefit on a particular institution or group.

With distributional policies, all of us, by paying our taxes, support those who receive the benefit, presumably because that benefit works toward the common good, such as stronger security, modernized infrastructure, a cleaner environment, or a richer national culture. In contrast, **redistributional policies** are explicitly designed to take resources from one sector of society and transfer them to another, reflecting the core value of equality.

redistributional policies
Policies that take government resources, such as tax funds, from one sector of society and transfer them to another.

State-level tax policies offer prime examples of differing ways to think about redistribution. The recession of 2007–2009 led nearly all states to grapple with budget shortfalls and growing numbers of people in hardship. States looked to their tax codes in order to find ways to shore up revenue. Some states, like Connecticut, increased taxes on the wealthiest residents and cut taxes for low-income workers as a way to raise revenue and redistribute income. This approach views taxation as a shared sacrifice that helps people out of poverty (freeing them from government safety net programs) and spurs further economic activity. Other states, like Michigan, reduced tax credits for low-income workers in order to keep more funds for government programs and to finance tax cuts for businesses and corporations. This approach, which minimizes redistribution, views taxes on the wealthy and the business sector as a barrier to economic development. Taking this approach to its extreme, governors in Oklahoma and Kansas have both promoted eliminating their state income tax altogether (an option long practiced in a handful of other states). This plan would essentially require the rich and poor alike to pay the same dollar amount (but vastly different income *percentages*) in taxes through the sales tax.[8] (For public opinion on federal taxes, see Figure 18.1.)

Another policy approach is **regulation**. In Chapter 13, we noted that regulations are rules that guide the operation of government programs. When regulations apply to businesses, they are an attempt to structure the market in a particular way. Government becomes a referee, establishing rules that set boundaries on how businesses can operate. Prior to the twentieth century, the food industry was unregulated. Since then, both the Food and Drug Administration (FDA) and the U.S. Department of Agriculture have been created to regulate the production and marketing of food. In 2011, the government added to existing regulations by enacting the FDA Food Safety Modernization Act, which was motivated by several high-profile food recalls involving products such as spinach, eggs, and peanut butter. An investigation that followed a *Salmonella*

regulation
Government intervention in the workings of a business market to promote some socially desired goal.

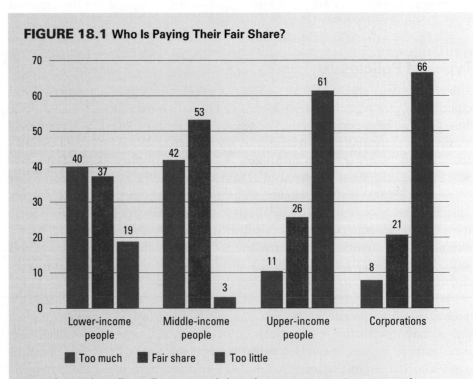

FIGURE 18.1 Who Is Paying Their Fair Share?

■ Too much   ■ Fair share   ■ Too little

According to the Gallup Poll, Americans believe that upper-income Americans and corporations pay too little in the way of taxes. Battles over federal income taxes confront nearly every president and every Congress.

Source: Gallup Poll, 4–14 April 2013.

outbreak tied to eggs revealed that the contaminated eggs had been exposed to rodents, flies, maggots, manure, and chicken innards. One provision of the new law empowers the FDA to issue its own recalls instead of relying on voluntary recalls from food producers. It also provides greater inspection authority to the FDA, in the hope of preventing unsafe foods from reaching consumers in the first place.[9]

Americans disagree over the extent to which markets should operate freely. Some believe government should be only minimally involved. Others believe markets need close supervision because competitive pressures lead businesses to cut corners on the safety of their products or the integrity of their conduct. On the one hand, the decisions on how to regulate or whether to reduce regulation (to *deregulate*) may involve technical questions and are best left to experts who work for the relevant bureaucratic agencies. What, for example, is a safe level of "rodent filth" to allow in curry powder?[10] On the other hand, regulation and deregulation are subject to the same pulls and pushes of the political process as distributional and redistributional policies. In the case of food safety, the new regulations were supported by major food producers including General Mills and Kraft Foods, while they were opposed by associations representing smaller farms, who feared that the new law would create an insurmountable degree of new regulations and paperwork for them.[11]

This framework of distributional, redistributional, and regulatory policies is rather general, and there are surely policy approaches that don't fit neatly into these categories.[12] Nevertheless, it is a useful prism to examine policymaking. Understanding the broad purposes of public policy allows a better evaluation of the tools necessary to attain these objectives.

Public Policy Tools

There are different ways of achieving public policy objectives. One policy tool is *incentives*. A fundamental element of human behavior is that we can be induced to do certain things if rewards become substantial enough. We should all give to charity simply because it is a generous act. But to promote more giving, the government provides tax deductions for people who donate to nonprofit charities. A taxpayer who makes a $1,000 donation to the Red Cross can subtract that amount from her taxable income when determining how much she owes in taxes. Although giving to charity is a good thing, there's no free lunch. Incentives like these constitute a *tax expenditure*. Since government loses revenue on the charity deduction, it must make up revenue elsewhere. This tax expenditure is quite substantial: over 80 percent of Americans donate to charity each year, totaling over $300 billion annually.[13]

The flip side of incentives are *disincentives*—policies that discourage particular behavior. A tax on pollution, for example, is a disincentive for a factory to continue using high-polluting manufacturing processes. Likewise, taxes on cigarettes are meant to discourage smoking.

Much of what policymakers want to accomplish cannot be done through incentives or disincentives. Rather than coaxing or discouraging behavior, it must take responsibility itself to establish a program. Government's largest expenditures—for health care, education, social services, and defense—come from government's direct payments to its employees or to vendors who implement programs.

Finally, a common policy tool is to set rules. Much of what government does in the form of regulation involves setting rules regarding what businesses or individuals can do in the marketplace, as in the case of food safety discussed earlier. The federal government constantly issues new or revised rules on a variety of policy questions. As of this writing, the FDA is considering whether to regulate electronic cigarettes as a tobacco product. The cigarettes contain nicotine and other chemicals, but are tobacco-free. Currently, businesses can decide for themselves whether e-cigarettes fall under their tobacco-free policies.[14]

A Policymaking Model

Clearly, different approaches to solving policy problems affect the policymaking process, but common patterns exist. We can separate the policymaking process into four stages: agenda setting, policy formulation, implementation, and policy evaluation. Figure 18.2 shows the four stages in sequence. Note, however, that the process does not end with policy evaluation. Policymaking is a circular process; the end of one phase is the beginning of another.

Agenda Setting. When we think of the political agenda, we usually think of the broad set of policy areas that are central to American life. This broad agenda changes over time as conditions change, though Americans routinely place the economy and education among the nation's top priorities.

Political scientists not only study what's on the agenda at any one time but also **agenda setting**, the part of the process in which problems are defined as political issues. Many problems confront Americans in their daily lives, but government is not actively working to solve them all. Consider Social Security. Today the old-age insurance program seems a hardy perennial of American politics, but it was not created until the New Deal. The problem of poverty among the elderly did not suddenly arise during the 1930s—there had always been poor people of all ages—but that is when inadequate income for the elderly was defined as a political problem. When the government begins to consider acting on an issue it previously ignored, we say that the issue has become part of the political agenda.

Why does a social problem become redefined as a political problem? There is no single reason; many factors stimulate new thinking about a problem. Sometimes highly visible events or developments push issues onto the agenda. Examples are great calamities (such as an oil spill, showing a need for safer offshore drilling rigs), the creation of new technology (such as the invention of mobile location technology, requiring privacy regulations), or irrational human behavior (such as airline hijackings, pointing to the need for greater airport security).[15] Whether a certain problem moves onto the agenda is also affected by who controls the government and by broad ideological shifts. Presidential and congressional candidates run for office promising to put neglected issues on the

agenda setting
The stage of the policymaking process during which problems get defined as political issues.

FIGURE 18.2 The Policymaking Process

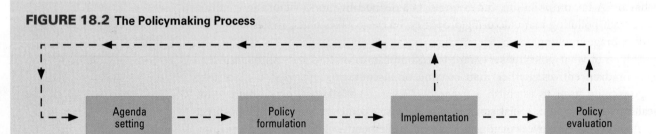

This model, one of many possible ways to depict the policymaking process, shows four stages. Feedback on program operations and performance from the last two stages stimulates new cycles of the process.

Source: © Cengage Learning.

agenda. The political parties also take up new issues to promote their candidates and respond to public opinion.

Part of the politics of agenda building is not just which new issues emerge and which issues decline in visibility, but the way the substantive problem at the heart of an issue is conceived. **Issue definition** is the way we think about a problem. Our conception of an issue is influenced by our own values and the way we see the political world. Interest groups and political parties try to persuade Americans to define issues in ways that are sympathetic to their cause. Ideological conservatives, for example, frame policy problems in terms of market approaches. If we accept that a market approach is better, then we'll shy away from government regulation.[16]

Citizens' views are also colored by what they regard as a government responsibility. Consider autism. If we define autism as a *disease*, then we might see a limited role for government—primarily as a funder of scientific research. But if we define autism as a *disability*, our issue definition will be broader. In the United States, persons with disabilities are guaranteed certain protections, and government has the responsibility to fight relevant forms of discrimination.[17] Many political battles are thus battles to define what the issue at hand is even about.

Droning On

The development of new technology often puts issues on the agenda. The Federal Aviation Administration is developing policy regulations for the domestic use of unmanned drones, a topic of new importance thanks to technological developments. The potential benefits of using drones in commercial sectors such as agriculture and package delivery need to be balanced against potential risks to safety and privacy.

Amazon/UPI/Newscom

issue definition
Our conception of the problem at hand.

The most likely form of change in issue definition occurs when an additional *frame* emerges, which happens when a new perspective comes to the fore. For example, for many years the dominant issue frames concerning the death penalty involved punishment and morality. Some argued that the death penalty is a just punishment for a heinous crime. Those on the other side argued that the death penalty was immoral—that the state didn't have the right to take a life. In the late 1990s, stories emerged in the press about people who were wrongly convicted and sentenced to death. DNA testing became an increasing source of exculpatory evidence. This so-called innocence frame became part of the debate over the death penalty, and public support for the death penalty began to drop.[18]

Since the emergence of a new frame can alter policymaking, interest groups make concerted efforts to reshape policy debate when the dominant frames work to their disadvantage. However, it is difficult for interest groups to reshape a debate.[19] Most change in issue framing is evolutionary and reflects both changes in the world and long-term interest group advocacy.

Policy Formulation. **Policy formulation** is the stage of the process in which formal policy proposals are developed and officials decide whether to adopt them. The most obvious kind of policy formulation is the proposal of a measure by the president or the development of legislation by Congress. Administrative agencies also formulate policy, through the regulatory process. Courts formulate policy too, when their decisions establish new interpretations of the law.

policy formulation
The stage of the policymaking process during which formal proposals are developed and adopted.

Although policy formulation is depicted in Figure 18.2 as a single stage, it actually takes place over several stages and across different levels of government. In 2013, Congress passed legislation requiring stricter oversight of compounding pharmacies (pharmacies that mix their own drugs) after a fatal outbreak of meningitis was linked to unsanitary compounding practices. Bureaucratic agencies then had to develop specific policies for implementing the law. If and when those policies are contested, courts will be called in to settle disputes.[20] Once the policy is in place for some time, it will be periodically evaluated and policymakers will consider further reforms.

As noted in Chapter 13, policy formulation is often *incremental*. As policies are debated, the starting point is the existing policy in that area, and if new policy is adopted, it is usually a modification of what was in place previously. One long-standing policy in the midst of incremental formulation involves fuel efficiency for cars and light trucks, known as Corporate Average Fuel Economy Standards (CAFE Standards). Such standards were first adopted by Congress in 1975, when the average gas mileage for a carmaker's fleet (passenger cars only) could not exceed 18 miles per gallon (mpg). These limits were designed to reduce energy consumption and carbon emissions. By 1990, that average had increased to 27.5 mpg. In 2012, the Environmental Protection Agency changed the standards again. By 2025, the average for a fleet's passenger cars will not be able to exceed 54.5 mpg. This dramatic increase in fuel standards represents a large change from previous limits, but it also represents a continuation and evolution of existing practices.[21]

Keep in mind that policy formulation is only the development of proposals designed to solve a problem. Some issues reach the agenda and stimulate new proposals but then fail to win enactment because political opposition mobilizes.

implementation
The process of putting specific policies into operation.

Implementation. Policies are not self-executing; **implementation** is the process by which they are carried out. When policies are enacted and when agencies issue regulations, government bodies must put those policies into effect. This process often involves multiple levels of government as well as actors in the private sector. After a major oil spill from the Deepwater Horizon rig in the Gulf of Mexico in 2010, government actors implemented the Oil Pollution Act of 1990, which requires "responsible parties" to establish a way to compensate victims who have suffered personally or professionally as a result of an oil spill. The BP oil company that operated the rig was thus responsible, but the government decided to take the lead in ensuring that the needs of victims were addressed. BP was ordered to establish a $20 billion fund, which was administered by a government-appointed "compensation czar." By December 2013, the government-run fund had paid out over $11 billion to individuals and businesses. In further response to the spill, the government is implementing provisions of the Clean Water Act, which involves charging BP for policy violations, such as negligence.[22]

Although it may sound technical, implementation is actually a very political process, involving a great deal of bargaining and negotiation among different groups of people in and out of government. The challenge of implementing complex policies in a federal system, with multiple layers of government, that is also a pluralistic system, with competing interests, seems daunting. Yet there are incentives for cooperation, not the least of which is to avoid blame if a policy fails. (We discuss coordination in more detail in the next section.)

policy evaluation
Analysis of a public policy so as to determine how well it is working.

Policy Evaluation. How does the government know whether a policy is working? In some cases, success or failure may be obvious, but at other times, experts in a specific field must tell government officials how well a policy is working. **Policy evaluation** is the analysis of the results of public policy. Although there is no one method of evaluating policy, evaluation draws heavily on research, including cost-effectiveness analysis and measurement of program outcomes. Such studies influence decisions on whether to continue, expand, alter, reduce, or eliminate programs.

Evaluation is part of the policymaking process because it helps identify problems that arise from current policy. In other words, evaluations provide **feedback** to policymakers on program performance. The dotted line in Figure 18.2 represents a feedback loop. Problems that emerge during implementation also provide feedback to policymakers. Feedback can be positive or negative.[23] Evaluation of how the U.S. State Department handled requests from Syrian refugees for asylum displays the feedback process. Decades ago, Congress passed legislation defining refugees and has since set broad guidelines for admittance, which are then implemented by executive agencies. In early 2014, the Senate held hearings to determine why only thirty-one Syrian refugees were admitted to the United States in 2013 when over 135,000 applied for asylum. During the hearings, Senators asked State Department officials about options for greater leniency within existing regulations and debated whether policy reform was needed in order to address the humanitarian crisis created by the Syrian civil war.[24]

Feedback reflects the dynamic nature of policymaking. By drawing attention to emerging problems, policy evaluation influences the political agenda. The end of the process—evaluating whether the policy is being implemented as it was envisioned—is the beginning of a new cycle of public policymaking.

Fragmentation, Coordination, and Issue Networks

The policymaking process encompasses many stages and includes different participants at each stage. Here we examine some forces that pull the government in different directions and make problem solving less coherent than it might otherwise be. We also look at some structural elements of American government that work to coordinate competing approaches to the same problems.

A single policy problem may be attacked in different ways by government for many reasons. At the heart of this **fragmentation** of policymaking is the fundamental nature of government in America. The separation of powers divides authority among the branches of the national government, and federalism divides authority among the national, state, and local levels of government. These multiple centers of power are a primary component of pluralist democracy. Different groups try to influence different parts of the government; no one entity completely controls policymaking.

Differing policies among the states and between the states and the federal government cause confusion because of the fragmented approach of the different levels of government. Frustrated because the federal government had taken no action regarding the poisoning of children who unknowingly drink out of containers of antifreeze, California and Oregon passed laws requiring manufacturers to add a bitter-tasting ingredient to the mix. But this legislation meant that different states required different things from manufacturers.[25]

Coordination of different elements of government is not impossible. Fragmentation often creates a productive pressure to rethink jurisdictions and to create incentives for coordination. In our federal system, for instance, states possess some degree of autonomy. American federalism is often lauded because the states can be "fifty laboratories" for developing policy alternatives. Yet this can be frustrating to the federal government because states may develop policies at odds with federal approaches.

feedback
Information received by policymakers about the effectiveness of public policy.

fragmentation
In policymaking, the phenomenon of attacking a single problem in different and sometimes competing ways.

Currently, states vary widely in their policies regarding the use of mobile devices while driving. Such distracted driving led to over 3,300 deaths and over 420,000 injuries in the United States in 2012. In response to this problem, some states have banned all handheld phone use by all drivers, some ban handheld phone use only for young drivers, most ban texting while driving, and some have practically no restrictions at all. To encourage coordination, the Distracted Driving Prevention Act has been introduced in Congress. It would encourage states to adopt laws that ban the use of handheld mobile devices while driving except in emergencies and navigation. States that fail to enact such laws would lose a portion of their federal transportation funds.[26]

The policy fragmentation created by federalism may be solved when an industry asks the national government to develop a single regulatory policy. In the antifreeze case discussed earlier, the state actions convinced the industry trade group that represents antifreeze manufacturers that it should drop its opposition to federal safety regulations.[27] Although an industry may prefer no regulation at all, it generally prefers one instead of fifty.

Another counterweight to fragmentation is the working relationships that develop among the many participants in the pluralist system. Suppose that Congress is considering amendments to the Clean Air Act. Because Congress does not function in a vacuum, other parts of government affected by the legislation participate in the process too. The Environmental Protection Agency (EPA) has an interest in the outcome because it will have to administer the law. The White House is concerned about legislation that affects such vital sectors of the economy as the steel and coal industries. Thus, officials from the EPA and the White House work with members of Congress and the appropriate committee staffs to try to ensure that their interests are protected. At the same time, lobbyists representing corporations, trade associations, and environmental groups try to influence Congress, agency officials, and White House aides. Experts from think tanks and universities might be asked to testify at hearings or to serve in an informal advisory capacity.

The various individuals and organizations that work in a policy area form a loosely knit community known as an **issue network**, where participants share expertise in a policy domain and interact frequently.[28] Such networks include members of Congress, committee staffers, agency officials, lawyers, lobbyists, consultants, scholars, and public relations specialists. Overall, a network can be quite large. One study identified over twelve hundred interest groups that had some contact with government officials in relation to health care over a five-year period.[29]

The common denominator in a network is not the same political outlook but policy expertise. Consider Medicare. The program is crucial to the health of the elderly, and with millions of baby boomers beginning to retire, it needs to be structured carefully to make sure there will be enough money available to care for them all. But to enter the political debate on Medicare requires specialized knowledge. For instance, what is the difference between "global capitation" and "fee for service"? "Advance directives" and "withholds for never events" may be grating jargon to the uninitiated, but they are meaningful terms to those in this network. In short, members of an issue network speak the same language. They understand the substance of policy, the way Washington works, and one another's viewpoints.

In a number of ways, issue networks promote pluralist democracy. They are open systems, populated by a wide range of interest groups. Decision making is not centralized in the hands of a few key players; policies are formulated in a participatory fashion. But there is still no guarantee that all relevant interests are represented, and

COMPARE WITH YOUR PEERS

MindTap for American Government

Access the Domestic Policy Forum: Polling Activity—The Clean Air Act.

issue network
A shared-knowledge group consisting of representatives of various interests involved in some particular aspect of public policy.

those with greater financial resources have an advantage. Nevertheless, issue networks provide access to government for a diverse set of competing interests and thus further the pluralist ideal.

Issue networks are an obstacle to achieving the majoritarian vision of how government should operate. The technical complexity of contemporary issues makes it difficult for the public at large to influence policy outcomes. The more complex an issue, the more elected officials must depend on the technocratic elite that comprise issue networks for policy guidance. Yet majoritarianism still influences policymaking. The broad contours of public opinion can be a dominant force on highly visible issues.[30] Elections, too, send messages to policymakers about the most widely discussed campaign issues. What issue networks have done, however, is facilitate pluralist politics in policy areas in which majoritarian influences are weak.

With this overview of the policymaking process in place, we now turn our attention to some of the largest, most expensive, and politically challenging domestic policy programs in the United States. We discuss how these programs became part of the political agenda and how they have been formulated, implemented, evaluated, and altered over time. We also illustrate how different perspectives on these programs highlight different values placed on freedom, order, and equality.

CONNECT WITH YOUR CLASSMATES
MindTap⁃ **for American Government**

Access the Domestic Policy Forum: Discussion—The Public's Impact on Policy Making.

The Development of the American Welfare State

LO2 ★ Trace the evolution of social welfare programs as a central element of public policy in the United States.

The most controversial purpose of government is to promote social and economic equality. To do so may conflict with the freedom of some citizens because it requires government action to redistribute income from rich to poor. This choice between freedom and equality constitutes the modern dilemma of government; it has been at the center of many conflicts in U.S. public policy since World War II. On one hand, most Americans believe that government should help the needy.[31] On the other hand, they do not want to sacrifice their own standard of living in order to do so.

At one time, governments confined their activities to the minimal protection of people and property—to ensuring security and order. Now, almost every modern nation is a **welfare state** serving as the provider and protector of individual well-being through economic and social programs. **Social welfare programs** are government programs designed to provide the minimum living conditions necessary for all citizens. Income for the elderly, health care, public assistance, and education are among the concerns addressed by government social welfare programs.

Social welfare policy is based on the premise that society has an obligation to meet the basic needs of its members. The term *welfare state* describes this protective role of government. To understand American social welfare policies, one must first understand the significance of a major event in U.S. history—the Great Depression—and the two presidential plans that extended the scope of government, the New Deal and the Great Society. Initiatives from these programs dominated national policy and established the idea that it is the role of the federal government to help meet the basic needs of its citizens until changes in the 1980s and 1990s produced retrenchment of the American welfare state.

welfare state
A nation in which the government assumes responsibility for the welfare of its citizens by providing a wide array of public services and redistributing income to reduce social inequality.

social welfare programs
Government programs that provide the minimum living standards necessary for all citizens.

The Great Depression and the New Deal

Great Depression
The longest and deepest setback the American economy has ever experienced. It began with the stock market crash on October 24, 1929, and did not end until the start of World War II.

Throughout its history, the U.S. economy has experienced alternating good and bad times, generally referred to as business cycles (see Chapter 17). The **Great Depression** was the longest and deepest setback that the American economy ever experienced. It began with the stock market crash on October 24, 1929, and did not end until the start of World War II. By 1933, one out of every four U.S. workers was unemployed, and millions more were underemployed. To put that in perspective, the annual U.S. unemployment rate since the end of World War II has never topped 10 percent.[32] The effect of the Great Depression on attitudes about the role of government and on the actual operation of governmental institutions is arguably without peer.

In the 1930s, the forces that stemmed earlier business declines were no longer operating. There were no more frontiers, no growth in export markets, no new technologies to boost employment. Unchecked, unemployment spread, and the crisis fueled itself. Workers who lost their income could not buy the food, goods, and services that kept the economy going. Private industry and commercial farmers produced more than they could sell profitably. Closed factories, surplus crops, and idle workers were the consequences. From 1929 to 1932, more than 44 percent of the nation's banks failed when unpaid loans exceeded the value of bank assets. Farm prices fell by more than half in the same period. Upon accepting the presidential nomination at the 1932 Democratic National Convention, Franklin Delano Roosevelt, then governor of New York, said: "I pledge you, I pledge myself to a new deal for the American people." Roosevelt did not specify the contents of his **New Deal**, but the term was applied to measures Roosevelt's administration undertook to stem the Depression. The most significant New Deal policy created the Social Security program, which is explained in detail later in this chapter. Overall, New Deal policies initiated a long-range trend toward government expansion.

New Deal
The measures advocated by the Franklin D. Roosevelt administration to alleviate the Depression.

The Great Society

After winning the 1964 presidential election in a landslide, Lyndon Baines Johnson (who became president in 1963 after President Kennedy was assassinated) entered

A Human Tragedy

The Great Depression idled millions of able-bodied Americans. By 1933, when President Herbert Hoover left office, about one-fourth of the labor force was out of work. Private charities were swamped with the burden of feeding the destitute. The hopeless men pictured on the left await a handout from a wealthy San Francisco matron known as the "White Angel," who provided resources for a bread line. Over eighty years later, roughly 15 percent of American families suffer from food insecurity and struggle to find enough to eat, as seen on the right.

Source: "Face the Facts USA," George Washington University, 30 October 2013.

1965 committed to pushing an aggressive and activist domestic agenda designed to foster equality. In his 1965 State of the Union address, President Johnson offered his own version of the New Deal: the **Great Society**, an array of programs designed to redress political, social, and economic inequality. In contrast to the New Deal, which was largely aimed at short-term relief, most of Johnson's programs targeted chronic ills requiring a long-term commitment by the government.

Central to the Great Society was the **War on Poverty**. The major weapon in this war was the Economic Opportunity Act (1964), which encouraged local programs to educate and train people for employment. Among them were college work-study programs, summer employment for high school and college students, loans to small businesses, a domestic version of the Peace Corps (called VISTA, for Volunteers in Service to America), educational enrichment and nutrition for preschoolers through Head Start, and legal services for the poor. The War on Poverty also saw the passage of the Food Stamp Act, which was a precursor to today's nationwide nutritional assistance program. The year 2014 marked the fiftieth anniversary of the War on Poverty. Some critics say that since the official poverty rate is at roughly the same level as when the War on Poverty began, the policies have not been successful and poverty won. Others contend that without our current antipoverty programs, the poverty rate would be considerably higher.[33]

Retrenchment and Reform

In the years following the Great Society era, critics seized on perceived shortcomings of the growing American welfare state. Perhaps these counterarguments were the predictable result of the high standards that President Johnson and his team had set, such as a promise to eliminate poverty in a decade. The fact that poverty persisted and had become more concentrated in areas that the Great Society had targeted (inner cities and rural areas) suggested to some observers that the effort was a failure.

Those arguments took hold in the late 1970s and helped Ronald Reagan capture the White House in 1980. Reagan's victory and reelection in 1984 forced a reexamination of social welfare policy. Reagan argued that to the extent that government should guarantee the well-being of less fortunate citizens, state and local governments could do so more efficiently than the national government. Congress, controlled by Democrats, blocked some of Reagan's proposed cutbacks, and many Great Society programs remained in force, although with less funding. The growth of social welfare that began with the New Deal ended with the Reagan administration. Then President Bill Clinton, a Democrat, entered office in 1993 hoping to reform social safety net programs while simultaneously protecting their basic elements. Charting that middle course became essential after 1994 when Republicans took control of Congress. By the end of Clinton's two terms, important reforms emerged in public assistance, which we describe later in this chapter. More recently, President Obama enacted the biggest welfare state reform since the New Deal, with the passage of the Affordable Care Act in 2010, also described later.

Social Security

LO3 ★ Describe the origins and evolution of Social Security as well as the funding and benefit issues facing the program.

Insurance protects against loss. Since the late nineteenth century, there has been a growing tendency for governments to offer **social insurance**, which is government-backed

Great Society
President Lyndon Johnson's broad array of programs designed to redress political, social, and economic inequality.

War on Poverty
A part of President Lyndon Johnson's Great Society program, intended to eradicate poverty within ten years.

social insurance
A government-backed guarantee against loss by individuals without regard to need.

protection against loss by individuals, regardless of need. Common forms of social insurance offer health protection and guard against losses from worker sickness, injury and disability, old age, and unemployment. The first social insurance in the United States was workers' compensation. Beginning early in the twentieth century, this insurance compensated workers who lost income because they were injured in the workplace.

Social insurance benefits are distributed to recipients without regard to their economic status. Old-age benefits, for example, are paid to workers—rich or poor—provided that they have enough covered work experience and have reached the required age. Thus, social insurance programs are examples of **entitlements**—benefits to which every eligible person has a legal right and that the government cannot deny. The largest entitlement program is **Social Security**.

Social Security is social insurance that provides economic assistance to people faced with unemployment, disability, or old age. In most social insurance programs, employees and employers contribute to a fund from which employees later receive payments. Contributions to two programs for social insurance in the United States are taken from workers' wages: Social Security and Medicare. The Social Security tax supports disability, survivors' benefits, and retirement benefits. Since 1990, this tax has been assessed at a rate of 6.2 percent, but was temporarily reduced to 4.2 percent during the recession of 2007–2009. In 2014, the tax was only assessed on the first $117,000 earned. The Medicare tax finances much (but not all) of the Medicare program and has been assessed at 1.45 percent of all wages since 1986.[34]

Origins of Social Security

The idea of Social Security came late to the United States. Most European nations adopted old-age insurance after World War I; many provided income support for the disabled and income protection for families after the death of the principal wage earner. In the United States, however, the needs of the elderly and the unemployed were left largely to private organizations and individuals. Although twenty-eight states had old-age assistance programs by 1934, neither private charities nor state governments could cope with the prolonged unemployment and distress of the Great Depression. It became clear that a national policy was necessary to deal with a national crisis.

In 1935, President Roosevelt signed the **Social Security Act**, which remains the cornerstone of the modern American welfare state. The act developed three approaches to the problem of dependence. The first provided social insurance in the form of old-age and surviving-spouse benefits and cooperative state–national unemployment assistance. To ensure that the elderly did not retire into poverty, it created a program to provide income to retired workers. An unemployment insurance program was also created to provide payments for a limited time to workers who were laid off or dismissed for reasons beyond their control.

The second approach provided aid to the destitute in the form of grants-in-aid to the states. It was the first national commitment to provide financial assistance to the needy aged, needy families with dependent children, the blind, and (since the 1950s) the permanently and totally disabled. The third approach provided health and welfare services through federal aid to the states. Included were health and family services for disabled children and orphans and vocational rehabilitation for the disabled.

How Social Security Works

Although the Social Security Act encompasses many components, when most people think of "Social Security," they have the retirement security element of the law in mind. Revenues for retirement security go into their own *trust fund* (each program contained

entitlements
Benefits to which every eligible person has a legal right and that the government cannot deny.

Social Security
Social insurance that provides economic assistance to persons faced with unemployment, disability, or old age. It is financed by taxes on employers and employees.

Social Security Act
The law that provided for Social Security and is the basis of modern American social welfare.

in the Social Security Act has a separate fund). The fund is administered by the Social Security Administration, an independent government agency. Trust fund revenue can be spent only for the old-age benefits program. Benefits, in the form of monthly payments, begin when an employee reaches retirement age, which is sixty-seven for people born in 1960 or later. People can retire as early as age sixty-two with reduced benefits.

Social Security taxes collected today pay the benefits of today's retirees with any surpluses held over to help finance the retirement of future generations. Thus, Social Security (and social insurance in general) is not a form of savings (your contributions are not set aside for your retirement); it is a pay-as-you-go tax system. Today's workers support today's program beneficiaries. Universal participation is thus essential. Government—the only institution with the authority to coerce—requires all employees and their employers to contribute, thereby imposing restrictions on freedom.

When the Social Security program began, it had many contributors and few beneficiaries. The program could therefore provide relatively large benefits with low taxes. In 1955, Social Security taxes of nearly 9 workers supported each beneficiary. Over time, this ratio has decreased, dropping to 2.8 workers for every beneficiary in 2013 (see Figure 18.3).[35] The solvency of the Social Security program will soon be tested. Based on projections from recent analyses, the program's assets will be exhausted by 2033.[36]

People who currently pay into the system receive retirement benefits financed by future participants. If the birthrate remains steady or grows, future wage earners can support today's contributors when they retire. And if the economy expands, there will be more jobs, more income, and a growing wage base to tax for benefits to retirees. But when the birthrate falls or mortality declines or the economy falters, then contributions decline and the financial status of the program suffers. With life expectancy in the United States roughly five years longer than it was when Social Security was created, some argue that it is time to increase the retirement age since retirees today benefit from the program for a longer period of time than was originally envisioned. If the retirement age had been indexed to life expectancy in 1935, the retirement age today would be around seventy-two.[37]

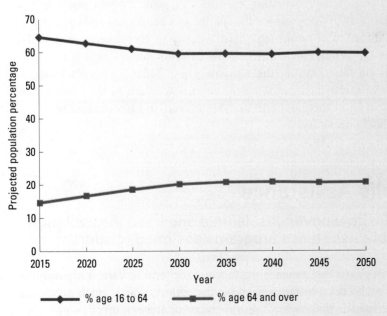

FIGURE 18.3 More Seniors, Fewer Workers

Between now and 2035, the percentage of the population aged sixteen to sixty-four is expected to decrease by 5.1 points while the percentage over sixty-five is expected to grow by 6.1 points. With a smaller percentage contributing to Social Security and a greater percentage receiving benefits, the financing of the program will be challenged. Debate over changes to the program boils down to two questions that politicians politely decline to answer: How soon will the national government change the current system, and how much will the government change it?

Source: Bureau of Census. "Resident Population Projections by Sex and Age: 2015 to 2050 [Quinquennially, as of July 1]," *ProQuest Statistical Abstract of the U.S. 2014 Online Edition*, ed. ProQuest, 2014.

Added to the demographic challenges facing Social Security is the fact that the rising cost of living means that payments to retirees need to increase as well in order for the program to achieve its aim of helping seniors avoid poverty. In 1972, Congress adopted automatic adjustments in benefits and in the dollar amount of contributors' wages subject to tax. The cost of living adjustment (COLA) is now based on changes in the Consumer Price Index. During the recession of 2007–2009, the Consumer Price Index did not rise, which resulted in no COLA in 2010 or 2011, marking the first time that benefits did not rise since adjustments were made automatic. In 2014, the COLA was 1.5 percent.[38]

Social Security Reform

Given the fund projections and demographic trends discussed earlier, concern over the future survival of Social Security runs high. For example, in 2011, 77 percent of Americans aged thirty to forty-four said that they were not confident that Social Security would have the money available to pay for their benefits when they retire.[39]

Repeated attempts to reform Social Security have failed to be enacted due to the tough choices involved. President George W. Bush advocated allowing individual workers to invest their own payroll taxes in the stock market in hopes of earning a higher rate of return than currently paid to the Social Security Trust Funds. However, people who wanted to stay in the current Social Security system could choose to do so.[40] But he was unable to generate enough support for the reform, since many Americans and lawmakers alike feared that privatizing the program would expose the elderly to too much risk of lost savings should the stock market decline. Bush left office with the Social Security program unchanged.

When Barack Obama took office in 2009, addressing the economic recession became his first priority; reforming Social Security was on the back burner. In fact, one of his key tools for combating the recession was to temporarily *reduce* Social Security payroll taxes.[41] In his 2014 budget plan, Obama proposed basing COLAs on *chained CPI* instead of on the traditional CPI. Chained CPI is an alternative measure of inflation, based on the assumption that as the price of goods rises, people look to save money by buying cheaper alternatives. Traditional CPI, on the other hand, does not factor in changes in people's buying habits. The Obama administration and Republicans in Congress support using chained CPI, which would result in lower COLAs, but Democrats in Congress see the change as a benefit cut and oppose it.[42]

Despite the difficulty of reforming Social Security in recent years, it is unlikely that Congress or the White House will ever let its fund run dry, which means that the issues of raising taxes, raising the retirement age, reducing benefit levels, and devising alternative means of controlling the fund will return to the agenda. Given the unpopularity of all of these options, decision makers will be reluctant to act until it becomes absolutely necessary.

 Public Assistance

LO4 ★ Explain how poverty is defined and trace the evolution of public assistance programs designed to address it.

public assistance
Government aid to individuals who can demonstrate a need for that aid.

Most people mean **public assistance** when they use the term *welfare*; it is government aid to individuals who demonstrate a need for that aid. Although much public assistance is directed toward those who lack the ability or the resources to provide for themselves or their families, the poor are not the only recipients of welfare.

Corporations, farmers, and college students are among the many recipients of government aid in the form of tax breaks, subsidized loans, and other benefits.

Public assistance programs instituted under the Social Security Act, apart from the retirement security components of the law, are known as *categorical assistance programs*. They include (1) old-age assistance for the needy elderly not covered by old-age pension benefits, (2) aid to the needy blind, (3) aid to needy families with dependent children, and (4) aid to the disabled. Adopted initially as stop-gap measures during the Great Depression, these programs have become entitlements. They are administered by the states, but most funding comes from the national government's general tax revenues. Because states also contribute to funding of their public assistance programs, the benefits and some standards that define eligibility can vary widely from state to state.

Poverty in the United States

Until 1996, the government imposed national standards on state welfare programs. It distributed funds to each state based on the proportion of its population living in poverty. That proportion is determined by a federally defined **poverty level**, or poverty threshold, which is the minimum cash income that will provide for a family's basic needs. The poverty level varies by family size and was originally calculated as three times the cost of a minimally nutritious diet for a given number of people over a given time period. The threshold was computed this way because research suggested that poor families of three or more persons spent approximately one-third of their income on food.[43] Today, the threshold is adjusted using the Consumer Price Index. The poverty threshold is what the Census Bureau uses to determine the number of people who live below the poverty line. In 2012, the poverty threshold for a family of four was a cash income below $23,492.[44] The Department of Health and Human Services uses a slightly different measure, called the poverty guideline, to determine the income level at which families qualify for government assistance.

poverty level
The minimum cash income that will provide for a family's basic needs; calculated using the Consumer Price Index.

The poverty level is only a rough measure for distinguishing the poor from the nonpoor. For instance, the poverty level has been fairly constant since the early 1970s, even though other indicators of well-being, like the infant mortality rate and the percentage of adults with a high school diploma, show dramatic improvement in that same time period.[45]

The poverty rate in the United States declined after the mid-1960s, rose slightly in the 1980s, then declined again. In 2012, the U.S. Census Bureau estimated that 46.5 million people, or roughly 15 percent of the population, were living in poverty.[46] That's up from 12.5 percent in 2007 before the recent recession began. Poverty was once a condition of old age, but Social Security changed that. Today, poverty is still related to age, but in the opposite direction: it is largely a predicament of the young. In 2012, 21.8 percent of persons under eighteen years old were in poverty, compared with about 9.1 percent of people over sixty-five.[47]

Over time, the proportion of income spent on food has declined as the costs of housing, child care, health care, and other expenses have increased. Policymakers have therefore considered different approaches to determine how much a family of four needs to live in the United States, but they have been reluctant to abandon a measure that has been in use since the 1960s. In 2009, officials from several agencies developed a supplemental poverty measure (SPM) that incorporates both cost of living changes across a wider range of goods and benefits from antipoverty programs. According to the SPM, the poverty rate in 2012 was closer to 16 percent, one point higher than the rate determined by the traditional measure.[48] We attach importance to the poverty-level figure, despite its inaccuracies, because it helps us assess how the American promise of equality stands up against the performance of our public policies.

Another trend in the United States, which we describe in Figure 18.4, is the concentration of poverty in households headed by single women. One in every two poor Americans resides in a family in which a woman is the head of the household. Researchers have labeled this trend toward greater poverty among women the **feminization of poverty**.

feminization of poverty
The term applied to the fact that a large percentage of all poor Americans are women or the dependents of women.

Welfare Reform

Critics of social welfare spending have long argued that antipoverty policies make poverty more attractive by removing incentives to work. During Reagan's campaign for the presidency, he blamed such policies for creating Cadillac-driving "welfare queens."[49] In 1996, the Republican-led Congress sought a fundamental revision of the welfare system and enlisted President Clinton in their cause. When Clinton signed the Personal Responsibility and Opportunity to Work Act into law that year, he abolished the sixty-one-year-old Aid to Families with Dependent Children (AFDC) program, which was created during the New Deal to provide cash assistance to poor families, and replaced it with the **Temporary Assistance for Needy Families (TANF)** program.

Temporary Assistance for Needy Families (TANF)
A 1996 national act that abolished the longtime welfare policy, Aid for Families with Dependent Children (AFDC). TANF gives the states much more control over welfare policy.

Critics of AFDC complained that government aid discouraged individuals from seeking work. The program was also unpopular. In 1994, 59 percent of Americans thought that "welfare recipients were taking advantage of the system."[50] Although originally established with widowed mothers in mind, AFDC grew rapidly beginning in the 1960s as divorce and single motherhood increased (see Figure 18.5). By the

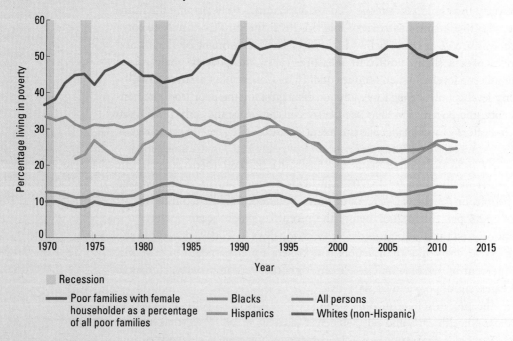

FIGURE 18.4 The Feminization of Poverty

Legend: Recession ▪; Poor families with female householder as a percentage of all poor families; Blacks; Hispanics; All persons; Whites (non-Hispanic)

The twentieth century brought extraordinary changes for women. Women won the right to vote and own property, and they gained some legal and social equality (see Chapter 16). But increases in rates of divorce and adolescent pregnancy have cast more women into the head-of-household role, a condition that tends to push women and children into poverty. In the absence of a national child-care policy, single women with young children face limited employment opportunities and lower wages in comparison to other workers. These factors have contributed to the feminization of poverty—the fact that a growing percentage of all poor Americans are women or the dependents of women.

Sources: Barbara Ehrenreich and Frances Fox Piven, "The Feminization of Poverty," *Dissent* (Spring 1984): 162–170; Harrell R. Rodgers, Jr., *Poor Women, Poor Families: The Economic Plight of America's Female-Headed Households*, 2nd ed. (Armonk, N.Y.: M. E. Sharpe, 1990); and U.S. Census Bureau, *Income, Poverty, and Health Insurance Coverage in the United States: 2012* (published 2013), Table 3 People in Poverty by Selected Characteristics: 2011 and 2012, http://www.census.gov/prod/2013pubs/p60-245.pdf.

time AFDC was abolished, 4 million adults and almost 9 million children were on welfare, and 24 million Americans were receiving food stamps. The end of AFDC significantly changed the lives of more than one-fifth of American families.

Under TANF, which devolves power to the states, adult recipients of welfare payments have to become employed within two years. The law places the burden of job training and creation on the states. Families can receive no more than a total of five years of benefits in a lifetime, and states can set a lower limit.[51]

How has welfare reform affected the states? In terms of funding, federal support for the law has been implemented through block grants, or a lump-sum, to the states totaling $16.5 billion per year. That money helps finance fifty different welfare systems. As in any other complicated piece of legislation, the process of writing regulations and offering guidance to help states implement the law has been an ongoing process. Overall, though, state leaders generally were pleased with the increased flexibility that TANF provided when compared to policy on the books prior to 1996. In 2011, nearly 29 percent of TANF funds went to direct cash assistance to poor families, 16.6 percent paid for child care, 9.4 percent covered employment programs, and 38 percent covered other services and programs aimed at helping low-income families.[52]

What about welfare recipients themselves? How have they fared under the law? As Figure 18.5 illustrates, the number of families on welfare has declined and remained relatively low when compared to the pre-TANF period. Large numbers of former welfare recipients were able to find steady work. One of the biggest fears of TANF's critics, that employers would find former welfare recipients undesirable employees and that there would be few jobs available in major urban areas, did not materialize.[53] As a result, Americans' opposition to welfare spending has declined in recent years, and their attitudes about welfare recipients have improved.[54]

Other trends are less promising. Despite former welfare recipients' increased levels of employment, most have not been able to find jobs that pay good wages and offer valuable benefits, such as health care. Thus, many former TANF recipients still live below or close to the poverty level. Moreover, studies have found that these jobs often require workers to have long commutes, which creates added stress as parents need to secure child care during their long workday.[55] Other challenges became acute

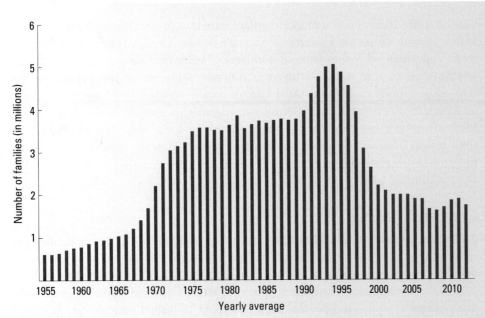

FIGURE 18.5 Families on Welfare, 1955–2012

Beginning in the 1950s, the number of families on welfare skyrocketed as divorce and single motherhood increased. The welfare rolls stabilized during the late 1970s but rose again in the early 1990s. The sharp decline at the end of the 1990s was a product of welfare reform and the demand for workers fueled by a strong domestic economy. Rolls increased somewhat during the 2007 recession.

Source: Department of Health and Human Services, Administration for Children and Families, "TANF Data and Reports," http://www.acf.hhs.gov/programs/ofa/programs/tanf/data-reports.

Supplemental Nutrition Assistance Program (SNAP) A federal program administered by the states that provides assistance for purchasing food to eligible beneficiaries.

during the recession that started in 2007. Many Americans hit hard by the recession were not helped by TANF. The problem is that the block grant funding is set to a fixed amount and does not change in response to increased need. Moreover, that fixed amount has not changed since TANF was first created. As a result, TANF cases did not increase much during the recession despite widespread job loss and hardship. As a point of comparison, the food stamp program known as **Supplemental Nutrition Assistance Program (SNAP)**, which gets increased funding when the need arises, saw a 45 percent increase in its participation rate from 2007 to 2009, whereas TANF participation only rose by 13 percent. With the dollar amount given to states unchanged and with needs rising, many states actually cut TANF benefits during the recession.[56]

TANF was due to be reauthorized in 2010. During the reauthorization process, Congress debates whether to make changes to both the funding levels and the rules that affect how and under what conditions the funds may be spent. TANF has not yet been formally reauthorized; instead Congress has been passing temporary measures to continue funding the program. When Congress finally turns its attention to TANF, the policy evaluation (recall Figure 18.2) will likely center on how the program fared during the recent recession. Although welfare reform was initially hailed as a success, the experiences of the past few years have led many people to conclude otherwise.

SNAP, like TANF, is run through a partnership between the federal government and the states, though the states do not have as much freedom in its administration as they do with TANF. In 2013, the program provided food aid to 47 million Americans, 72 percent of them in families with children. That year, the average benefit was $133 per month (or $4.45 per day; $1.48 per meal). In early 2014, President Obama signed into law a farm bill that included cutting $8.6 billion from the $82.5 billion program.[57]

★ Health Care

LO5 ★ Differentiate among Medicare, Medicaid, and the Affordable Care Act of 2010 and explain how each program addresses health-care delivery.

One important function of a modern welfare state is to protect the health of its population. How to do that is a source of constant debate. The United States is the only major industrialized nation without a universal health-care system. Rather, a patchwork system of care designed to cover different segments of the population has evolved over time. In addition to private insurance, which many Americans receive as a benefit of employment, government programs to provide health care include Medicare, primarily for the elderly; Medicaid, for the qualifying poor; and the Children's Health Insurance Program (CHIP), for children in needy families. This section discusses Medicare, Medicaid, and the Affordable Care Act (ACA) enacted by the Obama administration in 2010.

Cost and Access

To better understand the American system of health care and possibilities for reforms, it is important to consider two issues that animate the nation's health-care debate: access to care and cost. First, many Americans have no health insurance. In 2012, around 48 million Americans, roughly 15.4 percent, had no health insurance. The number of uninsured people varies according to factors such as age, race, and income. People aged nineteen to thirty-four are less likely to have insurance, as are

FIGURE 18.6 Poverty in the States

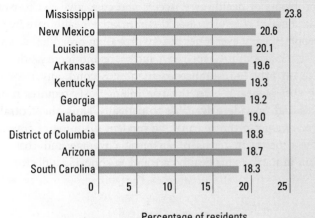

Percentage of residents
below poverty line

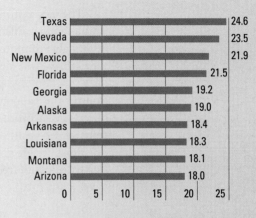

Percentage of residents
without health insurance

In 2012, 15 percent of all Americans lived below the poverty line; 15.4 percent had no health insurance. These national figures mask important differences across states. In New Hampshire, for example, only around 10 percent of the population lives in poverty; in Mississippi, nearly 24 percent of residents live in poverty. In Massachusetts and Vermont, fewer than 7 percent of state residents are without health insurance, yet a quarter of Texans don't have health insurance. Variations are due to state laws, social problems, immigration, and local job opportunities. In this figure, we list the top ten states according to the percentage of state residents who live below the poverty line and who are without health insurance (as of 2012).

Sources: U.S. Census Bureau, "Small Area Income and Poverty Estimates," 2012, http://www.census.gov/did/www/saipe/data/highlights/2012.html; and U.S. Census Bureau, "Health Insurance," http://www.census.gov/hhes/www/cpstables/032013/health/toc.htm.

African Americans, Hispanics, immigrants, and families with an income under $50,000. Figure 18.6 lists the states with the highest percentages of uninsured residents. About two-thirds of Americans with health insurance are insured through their employer or have some type of private plan. The practice of employers offering health insurance to their employees became widespread during World War II as employers searched for ways to attract workers in the face of wage controls. The remainder of insured Americans receives coverage through the government, with programs such as Medicaid, Medicare, and the military.[58]

Access to health care depends on more than having insurance. Many Americans with insurance are underinsured, with plans that do not adequately meet their true health-care needs. And even with adequate health insurance, many Americans lack easy access to doctors or hospitals. The supply of physicians in the United States simply does not meet the demand. Increasing the number of insured Americans might only make the problem worse. One study projects that with greater use of medical services, the United States will need 130,600 additional physicians by 2025.[59]

The second major issue confronting the nation's health-care system is cost. The health-care sector is a significant portion of the U.S. economy. In 2012, public and private spending on health care reached an all-time high of $2.8 trillion, which was 17.2 percent of gross domestic product (GDP).[60] Given the aging of the American population, coverage expansions due to the Affordable Care Act (described below), and the development of newer medical technologies, those numbers are projected to increase. By 2022, health care is expected to account for 19.9 percent of GDP.[61] Among advanced industrial nations, the United States spends the largest proportion of its economy on health care. In 2013, it spent more than nations with comprehensive systems of coverage, including Switzerland (11 percent of GDP), Germany (11.3 percent), and Canada (11.2 percent) (see "Health Spending in Global Politics").[62]

The two central problems of health care, access and cost, give rise to two goals and a familiar dilemma. First, any reform should democratize health care by making it available to more people, ideally everyone. But by providing broad access to medical care, we will increase the amount we spend on such care and increase the amount of regulations we place on private insurance companies. Second, any reform must control the ballooning cost of health care. But controlling costs requires restricting the range of procedures and providers available to patients. Thus, the central problems of the health-care issue go to the heart of the modern dilemma of government: we must weigh greater equality in terms of universal coverage and cost controls against a loss of freedom in markets for health care and in choosing a doctor.

Health Spending in Global Politics

Compared to other nations, the United States spends a great deal of money on health care. In 2013, the United States spent more than 17 percent of its gross domestic product on health care. What does spending on health care achieve? Looking just at longevity, life expectancy in developed nations reveals little variation. Babies born in the United States in 2013 can expect to live on average to almost seventy-nine. In contrast, babies born in Switzerland can expect to live past eighty-two, as can those born in Italy and Spain. Despite the fact that Americans outspend other nations on health care, the payoff in life expectancy has not been realized.

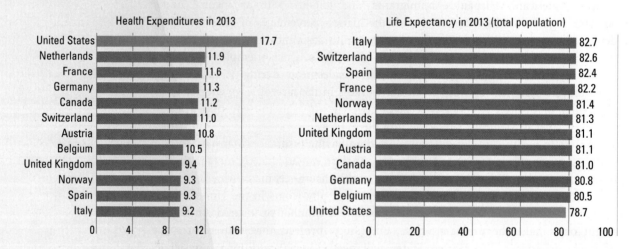

Health Expenditures in 2013

United States	17.7
Netherlands	11.9
France	11.6
Germany	11.3
Canada	11.2
Switzerland	11.0
Austria	10.8
Belgium	10.5
United Kingdom	9.4
Norway	9.3
Spain	9.3
Italy	9.2

Life Expectancy in 2013 (total population)

Italy	82.7
Switzerland	82.6
Spain	82.4
France	82.2
Norway	81.4
Netherlands	81.3
United Kingdom	81.1
Austria	81.1
Canada	81.0
Germany	80.8
Belgium	80.5
United States	78.7

Source: OECD Health Statistics 2013 - Frequently Requested Data, http://www.oecd.org/els/health-systems/oecdhealthdata2013-frequentlyrequesteddata.htm.

Critical Thinking What other factors besides spending might affect a society's life expectancy? Why might the United States rank highest on spending but comparatively low on life expectancy?

Over the past few decades, the health insurance industry has undergone tremendous change, and it continues to do so as these trade-offs become more acute. Most Americans used to carry what was called catastrophic care insurance, which provided hospital coverage for serious illnesses only. As the cost of medical care ballooned, health-care providers realized that preventing illness through regular physical examinations was cheaper than curing illnesses after onset. Thus, health insurance providers began to offer extended coverage of routine, preventive care in return for limiting an individual's freedom to choose when and what type of medical specialist to see. Health insurance providers also became increasingly concerned with the amount of risk they were taking on by providing insurance; they became more interested in covering healthy people who were likely to consume fewer services and less interested in covering people with existing—and expensive—medical conditions.

Medicare

In 1962, the Senate considered extending Social Security benefits to provide hospitalization and medical care for the elderly. Opponents were concerned that costs would soar without limit. Others echoed the fears of the American Medical Association (AMA), which saw any form of government-provided medical care as a step toward government control of medicine. Such opponents won the battle that day. Three years later, however, on the heels of Lyndon Johnson's victory in the 1964 election, the Social Security Act was amended to provide **Medicare**, a health insurance program for all people aged sixty-five and older.[63]

As early as 1945, public opinion supported some form of national health insurance, and President Harry Truman proposed such a program during his administration. However, that idea became entangled in Cold War politics—the growing crusade against communism in America.[64] The AMA, representing the nation's physicians, mounted and financed a campaign to link national health insurance (so-called socialized medicine) with socialism; the campaign was so successful that the prospect of a national health-care policy vanished.

Both proponents and opponents of national health insurance tried to link their positions to deeply rooted American values: advocates emphasized equality and fairness; opponents stressed freedom. In the absence of a clear mandate on the kind of insurance (publicly funded or private) the public wanted, the AMA was able to exert its political influence to prevent any national insurance at all.[65] After the 1960 election, however, the terms of the debate changed. It no longer focused on the clash between freedom and equality. Democrats cast the issue of health insurance in terms of providing assistance to the aged, a reframing that brought it back to the national agenda.[66]

On July 30, 1965, with Harry Truman at his side, President Johnson signed a bill that provided a number of health benefits to the elderly and the poor. One major provision created a compulsory hospitalization insurance plan for the elderly (known today as Part A of Medicare). In addition, the bill created voluntary government-subsidized insurance to cover physicians' fees (known today as Part B of Medicare). In 2011, almost 49 million people were enrolled in the program, which costs roughly $550 billion.[67]

Medicare is compulsory insurance that covers certain hospital services for people aged sixty-five and older. Workers pay a tax, and for certain parts of the program other than Part A, retirees pay premiums deducted from their Social Security payments. Payments for services are made by the government directly to participating hospitals and other qualifying facilities. Citizens with Medicare coverage may also possess private insurance for additional services that the program may not cover or may cover in less generous ways.

Medicare
A health insurance program serving primarily persons sixty-five and older.

The program still contains its original components, Parts A and B, but over the years, Medicare has expanded to cover more services. Today, Part A pays for care in facilities, such as inpatient hospital visits, care in skilled nursing facilities, and hospice. Part B pays for doctors' services and outpatient care. Services under Part A come at no cost to beneficiaries, but Part B services require participants to pay a monthly premium (just over $100 in 2014); the government pays the remaining cost of Part B.

In addition to the original Parts A and B, the program also offers supplemental plans, known as Medigap plans, that are run by private insurance companies and that seniors pay for through a premium, which varies by type of plan.

An important change in Medicare occurred in 2003 with the passage of the Medicare Prescription Drug, Improvement, and Modernization Act. Rather than a single program with simple rules, the drug plan (known as Part D) encouraged private insurers to offer competing plans. In some locations, seniors may have the option of thirty or more plans from which to choose, each with different costs, deductibles, participating pharmacies, and formularies (covered medications). Like other aspects of Medicare, the costs of the program continue to increase at rates in excess of the cost of living. In 2011, 12 percent of government spending on Medicare was devoted to the prescription plan (see later section on health-care reform for new provisions related to Medicare).[68]

Medicaid

Medicaid
A need-based comprehensive medical and hospitalization program.

Another important part of the nation's health-care patchwork is **Medicaid**, the main program to provide health care to low-income Americans. Like Medicare, it was the product of the Great Society, and was passed as another amendment to the Social Security Act. In 1965, the program was relatively small and enrolled 4 million people at an annual cost of $0.4 billion. It has since become a massive program, enrolling more than 60 million people.[69] The 2010 Affordable Care Act created additional expansions of the program, which went into effect in 2014.

The program's scope is vast. It insures one in three of the nation's children and millions of low-income adults and people with disabilities. It also pays for 40 percent of all childbirths.[70] Although Medicaid is designed primarily to cover citizens with low incomes, the pool of eligible people varies significantly across the country. That is because, unlike Medicare, which is solely a federal program, Medicaid is jointly run and financed by the federal government and the states. Federal law defines a certain minimum level of benefits that states must offer through Medicaid, but states vary in the criteria they use to define eligibility and in the types of services the program covers. Because Medicaid expenditures are typically one of the top expenses in state budgets (along with education), benefits are frequently cut when states experience difficult budgetary situations, as occurred during the recession of 2007–2009. Such cuts come despite the fact that more and more people rely on Medicaid during economic downturns.

Medicaid participants fall into four main groups: children under age twenty-one, adults (mainly pregnant women, parents, and other caregivers of children), those who are disabled, and those aged sixty-five and over (senior citizens can qualify for Medicare *and* Medicaid if their incomes fall below a certain level). Although their numbers are relatively small compared to other participants in the program, the disabled and elderly account for over half of Medicaid expenditures; the cost of the program is driven by the high cost of medical care for these two groups rather than other factors.[71]

The ACA expanded the pool of eligible beneficiaries in 2014 to include any adult earning up to 138 percent of the federal poverty level ($26,951 for a family of three in 2013). Originally, the health-care law required states to expand eligibility in this manner. Failure to do so would have resulted in the loss of all federal help paying for Medicaid. But the Supreme Court ruled in 2012 that such expansion can only be voluntary; the federal government cannot require it by threatening to remove such a significant portion of states' health-care funding. The threat, it was ruled, was too coercive. Under the ACA, the federal government will cover the cost of Medicaid expansion for the first three years. In subsequent years, the federal government will pay 90 percent of the bill. As of this writing, twenty-six states have opted to expand Medicaid eligibility. Of the remaining twenty-four states, twenty-one have refused expansion while three are undecided.[72] Even with the refusal of so many states, the expansion is certain to add to the size, scope, and cost of the program.

Health-Care Reform: The Affordable Care Act

In 2010, President Obama signed sweeping health-care reform legislation into law. The law is called the Patient Protection and Affordable Care Act, but has become known as the ACA and as "Obamacare." It has been described as the most wide-ranging policy change in a generation, comparable to the creation of Social Security. Its aim is to provide insurance to as many Americans as possible. To get the law passed, Obama had to scale back some initial ideas (such as offering a health insurance plan administered by the federal government), create new taxes, and ensure that federal funds would not be used to cover the costs of abortions. The legislative battle pitted arguments about equality of access to care against arguments about freedom from government intervention. The arguments about equality won the day, but battles about the scope of this legislation endure.

There are several notable aspects of the law, some of which were mentioned at the start of this chapter. People aged nineteen to twenty-five immediately became eligible to stay on their parents' insurance plans. By 2014, insurance providers could no longer deny people coverage because of preexisting conditions. To make it possible for insurers to pay for the needs of high-cost treatments, what is perhaps the most controversial aspect of the reform was added, namely that all individuals are required to have health insurance by 2014 or pay a fine (some are exempt from this so-called *individual mandate*, including Native Americans and people with religious objections). There are opportunities for people to get government subsidies to help them obtain coverage, and as noted earlier, the bill expands eligibility for Medicaid. It is estimated that by 2022, 93.1 percent of Americans will have health insurance.[73]

Individuals aren't the only ones subject to mandates under the ACA; employers are as well. By 2015, all employers with 100 or more employees must offer health insurance or pay a fine (employers with fifty to ninety-nine employees have until 2016). Tax credits are available to some small businesses that offer health plans to their workers. Finally, states were encouraged to set up insurance marketplaces, called *exchanges*, by 2014 where people and small businesses can shop for competitively priced health plans.[74] Residents lacking health insurance in the twenty-seven states that did not set up exchanges need to use a federally run marketplace if they do not already have health insurance through their employer. Twenty-one states have neither established exchanges nor opted to expand Medicaid. They are largely in the South and the Great Plains, and have Republican leadership at the state level.

Expanding Medicaid and providing subsidies for insurance coverage will cost the government hundreds of billions of dollars over the next several years, but the law also includes provisions that will help pay for it. In fact, the Congressional Budget Office has estimated that the bill will reduce deficits in the long run. The ACA places new taxes on high-cost health plans, places new Medicare taxes on wealthy

Americans, creates a new tax on indoor tanning, charges fees to employers and private health insurance companies, and reforms some aspects of Medicare spending (including the creation of an advisory board that can alter how Medicare is administered and the introduction of a program in which doctors are paid for the quality of treatment instead of the quantity). The state insurance exchanges are also expected to lower health-care costs; because private insurers will have new competition, insurance premiums are expected to decrease.[75]

That the ACA is not expected to add to the deficit has not silenced critics. For people wary of "big government," any program that results in more bureaucracy, more regulation, and more taxes is problematic. Additionally, many patients and hospitals harbor fears about how reforms to Medicare will play out despite assurances that benefits will not be affected. Others charge that even with government subsidies, many families will not be able to pay the insurance premiums that the law requires of them. The botched rollout of the federal marketplace (see Chapter 13) generated criticism that the federal government is simply not equipped to manage such a massive program successfully. Still others have raised concerns about whether the privacy of their medical and financial records will be protected sufficiently. Finally, other opponents simply charge that it is unconstitutional for the government to require that all individuals purchase health insurance, though the Supreme Court ruled otherwise (see "Freedom, Order, or Equality: Freedom v. Equality: Health Insurance"). Whether the alleged benefits or drawbacks of the ACA will come to pass still remains to be seen. With the rollout of the ACA in 2014, health-care policy in the United States is in a period of great transformation. Evaluation of the ACA's implementation will be

Freedom, Order, or Equality

Freedom v. Equality: Health Insurance

John Darkow/Cagle Cartoons

ongoing, and debates about the law will feature prominently in Washington and across the country for decades to come.

Elementary and Secondary Education

LO6 ★ Describe the role of the federal government in shaping education policy at the state and local government levels.

Although it is no less important, education is unlike the other public policies discussed in this chapter given that responsibility for schooling resides primarily in state and local governments in the United States. Since Horace Mann introduced mandatory public schooling in Massachusetts in the mid-nineteenth century, public schools have been an important part of local government. The federal government covers only around 10 percent of the nation's K–12 education bill.[76]

Concerns Motivating Change

Two main factors, related to freedom, order, and equality, have prompted greater federal involvement in the nation's elementary and secondary schools during the last half century.

Did your mother make you eat broccoli? A Supreme Court justice thinks that the government might. The Affordable Care Act made it illegal for private health insurance companies to deny people health care on the basis of preexisting medical conditions. The law also included a requirement that virtually everyone purchase health insurance by 2014, a provision known as the individual mandate. Several states filed lawsuits in federal court to contest the law. Some courts upheld the individual mandate and others rejected it. In June 2012, the Supreme Court ruled (5–4) that Congress has the authority to levy taxes. The fine for not buying insurance amounts to a tax; therefore, the mandate is constitutional. Despite this ruling, the provision remains controversial and unpopular: 68 percent of Americans surveyed in 2013 viewed the mandate unfavorably.* In his dissent, Justice Antonin Scalia argued that requiring individuals to purchase insurance means the government essentially has unlimited power and could require citizens to engage in all manner of commercial activity. Could it, he wondered, require Americans to buy broccoli? As his question illustrates, the case of the ACA and the individual mandate creates a dramatic clash between individual freedom and equal access to health care.

Critical Thinking Should the government be able to require that people buy health insurance? What constitutional arguments could be made for or against such a requirement?

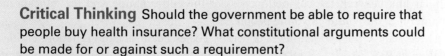

*Associated Press/Gfk Knowledge Networks Poll, Oct, 2013. Retrieved Jan-31-2014 from the iPOLL Databank, The Roper Center for Public Opinion Research, University of Connecticut. http://www.ropercenter.uconn.edu.ezproxy.library.tufts.edu/data_access/ipoll/ipoll.html.

Elementary and Secondary Education Act of 1965 (ESEA) The federal government's primary law to assist the nation's elementary and secondary schools. It emerged as part of President Lyndon Johnson's Great Society program.

Equity. The overriding and persistent concern has been educational equity. An important part of Lyndon Johnson's Great Society was the American belief that social and economic equality could be attained through equality of educational opportunity. The justices of the Supreme Court argued as much in their landmark decision in *Brown* v. *Board of Education* (1954). Legislatively, the **Elementary and Secondary Education Act of 1965 (ESEA)**, yet another product of the Great Society, was the first major federal effort to address educational equity in a systematic way. The law, which has been reauthorized periodically, provided direct national government aid to local schools in order to improve the educational opportunities of the economically disadvantaged.

The original law focused on economic disadvantage; later iterations recognized other groups, such as students for whom English is a second language and Native American students. A separate but related law, the Individuals with Disabilities Education Act (IDEA), is designed to improve educational opportunities for students of all ages (elementary school through college and graduate school) with physical or other disabilities.

Despite the federal policy, improvements in educational, and thus social and economic, equality have been elusive. Differences in student achievement between advantaged and disadvantaged groups have declined since the 1960s. However, gaps remain in test scores and in overall graduation rates.[77] These gaps are important because they tend to correlate with future educational and economic opportunities.[78]

National Security and Prosperity. Concern over educational achievement is not limited to issues of social equality at home. In an increasingly competitive global economy, countries are competing to offer—and attract—highly educated and skilled workers. Thus, a desire to keep the United States competitive with other nations, both economically and militarily, is one reason why education is considered a key public policy area.

The connection between national security and education is not new. It dates back at least to the 1950s when the Eisenhower administration promoted the National Defense Education Act of 1958 (NDEA). The law is considered to be a response to the Soviet Union's launch of a satellite known as *Sputnik*, the first such craft to orbit the earth. This Soviet success, which many interpreted to mean that the United States was losing the "brain race" against its rival, set off calls for improving the nation's stock of scientists and engineers, as well as its cadre of foreign language speakers, to counter the communist threat. Funding from the NDEA supported efforts in all of these areas at the elementary, secondary, and postsecondary levels.

A desire to improve American economic competitiveness has been the most recent force prompting greater efforts to improve the nation's education system. These concerns date back to the 1970s, when state governors realized the link between their own states' economic fortunes and the quality of their schools. These state-level concerns foreshadowed subsequent debates at the national level that forged a similar link between the competitiveness of the entire nation and the educational preparation of the country's young people.

These state- and national-level concerns coalesced in a famous report entitled *A Nation at Risk*, which was released in 1983 by the National Commission on Excellence in Education. The report charged that the nation's schools were inadequate and were getting worse. Its findings, along with improved data comparing American students with their international counterparts, through projects such as the Trends in International Mathematics and Science Study (TIMSS), created momentum for public officials to improve schools.

Values and Reform

At the center of debates over education is the dilemma of freedom versus equality. The American belief in equality is weighted toward equality of opportunity, and equality of opportunity depends on equal access to a good education. At the same time, Americans vehemently support their freedom to choose where to live, what kind of school they want their children to attend, and what their children will be taught while they are there.

As the national and international challenges we face grow in technological and scientific sophistication, the dilemmas of education reform will become more pressing. The questions of who will pay for reform, who will benefit, and how best to improve student learning came to a head in a major reauthorization of the ESEA, known as the **No Child Left Behind Act of 2001 (NCLB)**.

No Child Left Behind Act of 2001 (NCLB)
A reauthorization of the Elementary and Secondary Education Act during the George W. Bush presidency.

The No Child Left Behind Act of 2001. In 2000, Republican candidate George W. Bush made education one of the most important issues in his campaign for the White House, and with much fanfare, he signed the measure into law in January 2002.[79]

Although the law was technically a reauthorization of the ESEA, it also instituted far-reaching changes in education policy. Most significant among them was the law's requirement that states demonstrate that all of their students are performing at proficient levels in reading and math by 2014, leaving states free to determine their own standards of proficiency and means of assessment. Along the way, the law required schools to show that they were making "Adequate Yearly Progress" among all student groups, be they economically disadvantaged, weak in English language skills, or disabled.

NCLB was initially praised for highlighting educational inequality and asserting that all students deserve qualified teachers. But its implementation was controversial.[80] Critics charged that the emphasis on testing led teachers to "teach to the test" and ignore subjects that were not tested, like music and social studies. Others charged that the federal government did not spend enough money to help schools live up to the standards that it set. When the NCLB law came up for reauthorization in 2007, the Bush administration wanted to expand the law to include more testing and merit pay for teachers. Democrats in Congress opposed the new changes, however, and members of the House Education and Labor Committee could not agree on a compromise bill. NCLB was not reauthorized.

Common Core. In the meantime, the Obama administration granted waivers to forty states in order to free them from the proficiency guidelines of NCLB. In return, those states agreed to adopt a common set of academic standards and develop new systems for evaluating teacher effectiveness (a clear use of incentives as an important public policy tool).[81] During the Obama administration, forty-five states developed and adopted a set of *Common Core Standards*, which lays out a set of skills in math and English language arts that students are encouraged to master in each grade. The goals of the Common Core were to raise standards as well as promote consistency across states. From the start, the Common Core had critics. Some said the core still placed too much weight on testing; others said the federal government would be too involved in dictating state standards; others charged that the standards were developed without enough input from educators or the public. Some states have since relabeled their initiatives in order to distance themselves from the program. Examples include Iowa's "Iowa Core," and Florida's "Next Generation Sunshine State Standards."[82] Whether such changes are just cosmetic remains to be seen, as the new standards have only been newly implemented.

As states moved forward implementing the Common Core, Congress was still working on reauthorizing the ESEA. As of this writing, the House and Senate are working on competing bills. The chance of compromise appears slim, however, due to the widely different roles for the federal government that each chamber envisions, with House Republicans advancing a diminished role for the government, and with Senate Democrats preferring federal efforts to encourage coordination across states.

Perhaps nowhere are the challenges of fragmentation and coordination on display more than with education policy. The 2001 NCLB Act and subsequent debates illustrate the difficulties of coordinating efforts across the states, devising national objectives that still allow for local flexibility, and evaluating which aspects of a policy work and which ones need reform.

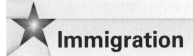 Immigration

LO7 ★ Assess alternative policies for addressing illegal immigration into the United States.

Along with health care and education, immigration is also central to the domestic policy agenda. Immigrants today make up around 13 percent of the population. It is estimated that about 11.1 million immigrants are here illegally, down from about 12 million in 2007.[83] Americans are divided over whether overall levels of immigration to the United States should be decreased or kept the same, but most agree that addressing the situation of illegal immigration in the United States is important.

Undocumented immigrants are among the poorest and most vulnerable individuals. Whereas roughly 15 percent of all Americans are without health insurance, 43.4 percent of foreign-born noncitizens lack health insurance, and 24.5 percent live below the poverty line. The rates for those noncitizens in the country illegally are even higher.[84] Should they have access to the benefits of the social welfare state such as health care and education? Should they be eligible to earn citizenship?

The United States didn't regulate immigration until the end of the nineteenth century, and it wasn't until 1924 that the concept of an "illegal immigrant" took hold. It was then that Congress enacted the Johnson-Reed Act, which set strict quotas on the number of immigrants permitted to enter the country and the nations from which they could come. Due to racist concerns about the dilution of American culture, the act favored immigration from western Europe and severely limited immigration from southern and eastern Europe and from Asia. These restrictions were significantly loosened by the Johnson administration in 1965, which is when the rate of legal and illegal immigration began to surge.

Foreigners who wish to work in the United States for an extended period of time need to apply for a permanent resident card, or "green card." Individuals with a green card are known as "legal permanent residents," and they may eventually apply to become U.S. citizens. In 2012, the United States granted permanent admission to 1 million noncitizens.[85] Priority is given to reuniting families, admitting workers in occupations with strong demand for labor, providing a refuge for people who face persecution in their home countries, and providing admission to people from a diverse set of countries.[86] Prior to the 1996 welfare reforms (discussed earlier in this chapter), legal immigrants were eligible for most public benefits on the same terms as citizens. The 1996 reforms, however, prohibited legal immigrants from participating in safety net programs such as SNAP, Medicaid, and TANF until they have been in the country for five years. States are free to enroll legal immigrants sooner, provided that state funds—and not federal funds—are used to supply the benefit.[87]

But it is undocumented immigrants who get the most attention in policy debates. If caught, they may be offered the chance to leave the country voluntarily, or they may be fined, imprisoned, deported, and prohibited from returning to the United States. In 2012, about 419,000 undocumented immigrants were deported, and around 230,000 left voluntarily.[88] Most undocumented immigrants in the United States come from Mexico and other Latin American countries. They tend to be geographically concentrated in western states and large urban areas, where they provide cheap labor in agriculture and manufacturing industries.

Undocumented immigrants have always been ineligible for the safety net programs discussed in this chapter (their American-born children are eligible), but they enroll in public schools and get treated in hospital emergency rooms, both of which come at a cost to American taxpayers. Most policy debates about illegal immigration focus on how best to increase border security with Mexico, how to get employers to stop hiring undocumented workers, and whether undocumented immigrants currently in the United States should be allowed to become legal residents and/or citizens. Since 2005, Congress and the Bush and Obama administrations have sought legislation that would allow undocumented immigrants in the United States to earn citizenship if they paid fines, passed English and civics exams, and remained employed, but every effort has stalled. Conservative groups charge that such legislation would give "amnesty" to people who had broken the law. Pro-immigrant groups have been concerned with proposals that would create a temporary worker program that allows people to work in the United States for a period of time and then forces them to return to their home country before reapplying for a temporary permit. Unions fear that legal temporary workers would drive down wages and take jobs away from American workers.

As of this writing, the Senate has passed a reform bill with bipartisan support. It would create a lengthy path to citizenship for undocumented immigrants living in the United States, increase the number of temporary visas available for highly skilled and agricultural guest workers, devote more resources to border security, and require employers to use E-Verify (a program that allows employers to check the immigration status of potential employees). The House of Representatives has yet to act.[89] Despite the lack of progress, majorities of the American public consistently support the major elements of the Senate bill, including the path to citizenship for undocumented immigrants.[90]

Another proposal that Americans generally support but that has stalled in Congress is the Development, Relief, and Education for Alien Minors (DREAM) Act. If passed, the act would allow undocumented immigrants

Marjorie Kamys Cotera/Bob Daemmrich Photography/Alamy

An Uncertain Path Ahead

Since the mid-1990s, anywhere from 500,000 to 1 million people become naturalized citizens each year. Today, there are over 18 million naturalized citizens in the United States. If comprehensive immigration reform becomes a reality, nearly 12 million undocumented immigrants could join their ranks. Their path, however, would take a minimum of thirteen years, according to some proposals.

Source: Emma Britz and Jeanne Batalova, "Frequently Requested Statistics on Immigrants and Immigration in the United States," Migration Information Source, January 2013.

who had been brought to the United States as children to become eligible for legalized status. With Congress unable to agree on the DREAM Act, President Obama issued an executive action in 2012, called Deferred Action for Childhood Arrivals (DACA), that directed federal immigration authorities to cease pursuing deportations for most undocumented immigrants who were brought to the United States as children. DACA also allows those immigrants to apply for a two-year work authorization. One year later, over 588,000 people applied for the change in status. Over 96 percent of the applications were approved.[91]

The Constitution grants Congress the authority to "establish a uniform rule of naturalization," which has been interpreted to grant jurisdiction of immigration policy solely to the federal government. Yet in the absence of federal action to address the pressing social needs that illegal immigration produces in social services, states have increasingly enacted their own policies on the issue (see Figure 18.7). Employers in several states must check workers' residency status with E-Verify and could be fined if they knowingly hire undocumented immigrants. Some states, such as California, have enacted immigrant-friendly legislation that allows undocumented immigrants to pay in-state tuition at public universities and get driver's licenses. Others, such as Arizona and Alabama, have enacted policies aimed at creating a climate that drives immigrants away. The Arizona law, for example, directs local law enforcement officials to check the immigration status of people they stop or arrest. In addition to raising fears that the law will promote racial profiling, some believe that only the federal government has the authority to engage in this type of immigration enforcement. In 2012, the Supreme Court ruled that states can direct law enforcement authorities to ask people to demonstrate whether they are in the country legally.[92]

FIGURE 18.7 Absent Federal Action, States Take on Immigration Reform

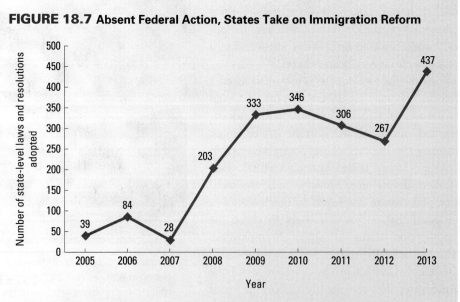

With immigration reform stalled at the federal level, state legislative activity to address issues that arise from immigration has increased dramatically. Some laws are considered immigration-friendly while others are considered hostile. Whether the states even have the jurisdiction to enact these policies is a matter of continuing debate.

Source: National Conference of State Legislatures, "State Laws Related to Immigration and Immigrants," http://www.ncsl.org/research/immigration/state-laws-related-to-immigration-and-immigrants.aspx.

Benefits and Fairness

LO8 ★ Explain how the issue of fairness shapes perspectives on government benefits.

As the policies examined here demonstrate, the national government provides many Americans and noncitizen residents with benefits. Some benefits are conditional. **Means-tested benefits** impose an income test to qualify. For example, Medicaid benefits are available to households with an income that falls below a designated threshold. **Non-means-tested benefits** impose no such income test; benefits such as Medicare and Social Security are available to all.

Some Americans question the fairness of non-means-tested benefits. Benefits are subsidies, and some people need them more than others do. If resources available for such benefits are limited, imposing means tests on more benefits has real allure. For example, historically, all elderly people received the same basic Medicare benefits, regardless of income, and all wage earners paid the same percentage in Medicare taxes. Fairness advocates maintain that the affluent should shoulder a higher share of Medicare costs, shifting more benefits to the low-income elderly. The ACA addresses some of this concern by increasing Medicare taxes for the wealthy. If the idea of shifting benefits gains support in the future, reform debates will focus on the income level below which a program will apply. Thus, the question of fairness is one more problem for policymakers to consider as they try to reform the nation's welfare state programs.

There are many other domestic policy areas that consume significant government resources and that merit attention when analyzing the complex processes by which policies are formulated, implemented, and evaluated. These policy areas include energy policy, the environment, science and technology, transportation, and food policy, just to name a few. As with the policies covered in this chapter, debates in these other areas often come down to differing perspectives on freedom and equality, involve coordination problems across levels of government, and are influenced by complex issue networks that are at the heart of the nation's pluralist system.

means-tested benefits
Conditional benefits provided by government to individuals whose income falls below a designated threshold.

non-means-tested benefits
Benefits provided by government to all citizens, regardless of income; Medicare and Social Security are examples.

Master the Topic of Domestic Policy with MindTap™ for American Government

 REVIEW MindTap™ for American Government
Access Key Term Flashcards for Chapter 18.

 TEST YOURSELF MindTap™ for American Government
Take the Wrap It Up Quiz for Chapter 18.

 STAY CURRENT MindTap™ for American Government
Access the KnowNow blog and customized RSS for updates on current events.

 STAY FOCUSED MindTap™ for American Government
Complete the Focus Activities for Domestic Policy.

Summary

LO1 Categorize different types of public policies and outline the process by which policies are formulated and implemented.

- Underlying policy choices are basic values—the core beliefs about how government should work. The basic objectives of government policy tend to be distributional, redistributional, and regulatory.

- The policymaking process consists of four broad stages: agenda setting, formulation, implementation, and evaluation. All three branches of the national government formulate policy, along with policy experts, interest groups, and trade organizations, who together form issue networks. Formulation often involves one of the following tools to achieve objectives: incentives and disincentives, direct provision of services, or rule setting. Implementation and evaluation influence agenda building because program shortcomings become evident during these stages. Thus, the process is circular, with the end often marking the beginning of a new round of policymaking. Policymaking stages are often marked by fragmentation and by efforts intended to achieve coordination.

LO2 Trace the evolution of social welfare programs as a central element of public policy in the United States.

- Many domestic policies that provide benefits to individuals and promote economic equality were instituted during the Great Depression and were expanded during President Johnson's Great Society agenda.

LO3 Describe the origins and evolution of Social Security as well as the funding and benefit issues facing the program.

- Today, the government plays an active role in providing benefits to the poor, the elderly, and the disabled, which reflects the social welfare function of the modern state.

LO4 Explain how poverty is defined and trace the evolution of public assistance programs designed to address it.

- Programs to aid the elderly and the poor have been transformed into entitlements, or rights that accrue to eligible persons. These programs have reduced poverty among some groups, especially the elderly. However, poverty retains a grip on certain segments of the population.

- Temporary Assistance for Needy Families (TANF) was a major overhaul of welfare policy. While initially considered a success for reducing the number of people on welfare and granting more flexibility to the states, recent national economic difficulties have led many to conclude that TANF is inadequate at combating poverty.

LO5 Differentiate among Medicare, Medicaid, and the Affordable Care Act of 2010 and explain how each program addresses health-care delivery.

- Recent health-care reform is a reflection of the modern dilemma of democracy: universal coverage and cost controls versus a loss of freedom in health-care choices.

LO6 Describe the role of the federal government in shaping education policy at the state and local government levels.

- Education is considered a critical public policy area among Americans, though it remains largely a state and local endeavor. The federal government's education policy centers on providing equal access to a good education for all Americans, often relying on incentives to help achieve these aims.

LO7 Assess alternative policies for addressing illegal immigration into the United States.

- While the federal government has long been interested in controlling the number of immigrants who are legal permanent residents, the problem of illegal immigration has only garnered national attention in the past few decades. In the absence of federal legislation addressing illegal immigration, many states have enacted their own policies.

LO8 Explain how the issue of fairness shapes perspectives on government benefits.

- Some government subsidy programs provide means-tested benefits, for

which eligibility hinges on income. Non-means-tested benefits are available to all, regardless of income. As the demand for such benefits exceeds available resources, their fairness becomes questioned. Departing from non-means-tested benefits in the name of fairness may very well be the next challenge of democracy.

Chapter Quiz

LO1 Categorize different types of public policies and outline the process by which policies are formulated and implemented.

1. Identify and explain at least two public policy tools used to achieve objectives.
2. What are the four main stages of the policymaking process?
3. What are issue networks? Do they reflect the pluralist or majoritarian model of democracy?

LO2 Trace the evolution of social welfare programs as a central element of public policy in the United States.

1. What are social welfare programs?
2. Summarize the emergence and goals of the New Deal.

LO3 Describe the origins and evolution of Social Security as well as the funding and benefit issues facing the program.

1. Why is the success of the Social Security program dependent on such factors as birth rate and life expectancy?
2. Discuss alternative proposed reforms to Social Security recently debated by policymakers.

LO4 Explain how poverty is defined and trace the evolution of public assistance programs designed to address it.

1. What is the current poverty rate, and what is the current poverty threshold?
2. What does TANF stand for, and how did this program change welfare policy?

LO5 Differentiate among Medicare, Medicaid, and the Affordable Care Act of 2010 and explain how each program addresses health-care delivery.

1. Define Medicare.
2. Explain how federalism shapes the administration and financing of Medicaid.
3. Identify at least three key features of the Affordable Care Act of 2010.

LO6 Describe the role of the federal government in shaping education policy at the state and local government levels.

1. Discuss how the dilemma of freedom versus equality shapes debates about education policy.
2. What was the main feature of the No Child Left Behind Act of 2001, and why has it been controversial?

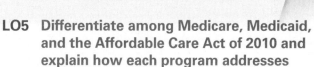

LO7 Assess alternative policies for addressing illegal immigration into the United States.

List central features of current policy debates for addressing illegal immigration that have been proposed by the federal government and/or by individual states.

LO8 Explain how the issue of fairness shapes perspectives on government benefits.

Contrast means-tested and non-means-tested benefits.

Appendix

The Declaration of Independence

In Congress, July 4, 1776

The unanimous Declaration of the thirteen United States of America

When in the course of human events, it becomes necessary for one people to dissolve the political bands which have connected them with another, and to assume, among the powers of the earth the separate and equal station to which the Laws of Nature and of Nature's God entitle them, a decent respect to the opinions of mankind requires that they should declare the causes which impel them to the separation.

We hold these truths to be self-evident, that all men are created equal, that they are endowed by their Creator with certain unalienable rights, that among these are life, liberty, and the pursuit of happiness. That to secure these rights, governments are instituted among men, deriving their just powers from the consent of the governed. That whenever any form of government becomes destructive of these ends, it is the right of the people to alter or to abolish it, and to institute new government, laying its foundation on such principles, and organizing its power in such form, as to them shall seem most likely to effect their safety and happiness. Prudence, indeed, will dictate that governments long established should not be changed for light and transient causes; and accordingly all experience hath shown, that mankind are more disposed to suffer, while evils are sufferable, than to right themselves by abolishing the forms to which they are accustomed. But when a long train of abuses and usurpations, pursuing invariably the same object evinces a design to reduce them under absolute despotism, it is their right, it is their duty, to throw off such government, and to provide new guards for their future security. Such has been the patient sufferance of these Colonies; and such is now the necessity which constrains them to alter their former systems of government. The history of the present King of Great Britain is a history of repeated injuries and usurpations, all having in direct object the establishment of an absolute tyranny over these States. To prove this, let facts be submitted to a candid world.

He has refused his assent to laws, the most wholesome and necessary for the public good.

He has forbidden his governors to pass laws of immediate and pressing importance, unless suspended in their operation till his assent should be obtained; and, when so suspended, he has utterly neglected to attend to them.

He has refused to pass other laws for the accommodation of large districts of people, unless those people would relinquish the right of representation in the legislature, a right inestimable to them, and formidable to tyrants only.

He has called together legislative bodies at places unusual, uncomfortable, and distant from the depository of their public records, for the sole purpose of fatiguing them into compliance with his measures.

He has dissolved representative houses repeatedly, for opposing, with manly firmness, his invasions on the rights of the people.

He has refused for a long time, after such dissolutions, to cause others to be elected; whereby the legislative powers, incapable of annihilation, have returned to the people at large for their exercise; the State remaining, in the meantime exposed to all the dangers of invasions from without and convulsions within.

He has endeavored to prevent the population of these States; for that purpose obstructing the laws for naturalization of foreigners; refusing to pass others to encourage their migration hither, and raising the conditions of new appropriations of lands.

He has obstructed the administration of justice, by refusing his assent to laws for establishing judiciary powers.

He has made judges dependent on his will alone, for the tenure of their offices, and the amount and payment of their salaries.

He has erected a multitude of new offices, and sent hither swarms of officers to harass our people, and eat out their substance.

He has kept among us, in times of peace, standing armies, without the consent of our legislatures.

He has affected to render the military independent of and superior to the civil power.

He has combined with others to subject us to a jurisdiction foreign to our constitution, and unacknowledged by our laws; giving his assent to their acts of pretended legislation: For quartering large bodies of armed troops among us; For protecting them, by a mock trial, from punishment for any murders which they should commit on the inhabitants of these states; For cutting off our trade with all parts of the world; For imposing taxes on us without our consent; For depriving us, in many cases, of the benefits of trial by jury; For transporting us beyond seas, to be tried for pretended offenses; For abolishing the free system of English laws in a neighboring province, establishing therein an arbitrary government, and enlarging its boundaries, so as to render it at once an example and fit instrument for introducing the same absolute rule into these Colonies; For taking away our Charters, abolishing our most valuable laws, and altering fundamentally the forms of our governments; For suspending our own Legislatures, and declaring themselves invested with power to legislate for us in all cases whatsoever.

He has abdicated government here, by declaring us out of his protection and waging war against us.

He has plundered our seas, ravaged our coasts, burned our towns, and destroyed the lives of our people.

He is at this time transporting large armies of foreign mercenaries to complete the works of death, desolation, and tyranny, already begun with circumstances of cruelty and perfidy scarcely paralleled in the most barbarous ages, and totally unworthy the head of a civilized nation.

He has constrained our fellow-citizens taken captive on the high seas to bear arms against their country, to become the executioners of their friends and brethren, or to fall themselves by their hands.

He has excited domestic insurrection among us, and has endeavored to bring on the inhabitants of our frontiers the merciless Indian savages, whose known rule of warfare is an undistinguished destruction of all ages, sexes, and conditions.

In every stage of these oppressions we have petitioned for redress in the most humble terms: our repeated petitions have been answered only by repeated injury. A prince whose character is thus marked by every act which may define a tyrant, is unfit to be the ruler of a free people.

Nor have we been wanting in our attentions to our British brethren. We have warned them, from time to time, of attempts by their Legislature to extend an unwarrantable jurisdiction over us. We have reminded them of the circumstances of our emigration and settlement here. We have appealed to their native justice and magnanimity, and we have conjured them by the ties of our common kindred to disavow these usurpations, which would inevitably interrupt our connections and correspondence. They too have been deaf to the voice of justice and of consanguinity. We must, therefore, acquiesce in the necessity, which denounces our separation, and hold them, as we hold the rest of mankind, enemies in war, in peace friends.

We, therefore, the Representatives of the United States of America, in General Congress assembled, appealing to the Supreme Judge of the world for the rectitude of our intentions, do, in the name, and by the authority of the good people of these Colonies, solemnly publish and declare, That these United Colonies are, and of right ought to be, FREE AND INDEPENDENT STATES; that they are absolved from all allegiance to the British Crown, and that all political connection between them and the State of Great Britain is, and ought to be, totally dissolved; and that, as Free and Independent States they have full power to levy war, conclude peace, contract alliances, establish commerce, and do all other acts and things which independent States may of right do. And for the support of this declaration, with a firm reliance on the protection of Divine Providence, we mutually pledge to each other our lives, our fortunes and our sacred honor.

JOHN HANCOCK
and fifty-five others

The Constitution of the United States of America*

[Preamble: outlines goals and effect]

We the people of the United States, in order to form a more perfect Union, establish Justice, insure domestic Tranquility, provide for the common defence, promote the general Welfare, and secure the Blessings of Liberty to ourselves and our Posterity, do ordain and establish this Constitution for the United States of America.

Article I

[The legislative branch]

[Powers vested]

Section 1 All legislative Powers herein granted shall be vested in a Congress of the United States, which shall consist of a Senate and a House of Representatives.

[House of Representatives: selection, term, qualifications, apportionment of seats, census requirement, exclusive power to impeach]

Section 2 The House of Representatives shall be composed of Members chosen every second Year by the people of the several States, and the Electors in each State shall have the Qualifications requisite for Electors of the most numerous Branch of the State Legislature.

No person shall be a Representative who shall not have attained to the Age of twenty five Years, and been seven Years a Citizen of the United States, and who shall not, when elected, be an Inhabitant of that State in which he shall be chosen.

---

*Passages no longer in effect are printed in italic type.

Representatives and direct Taxes shall be apportioned among the several States which may be included within this Union, according to their respective numbers, which shall be determined by adding to the whole Number of free Persons, including those bound to Service for a Term of Years and excluding Indians not taxed, three-fifths of all other Persons. The actual Enumeration shall be made within three Years after the first Meeting of the Congress of the United States, and within every subsequent Term of ten Years, in such Manner as they shall by Law direct. The number of Representatives shall not exceed one for every thirty Thousand, but each State shall have at Least one Representative; *and until such enumeration shall be made, the State of New Hampshire shall be entitled to choose three, Massachusetts eight, Rhode Island and Providence Plantations one, Connecticut five, New York six, New Jersey four, Pennsylvania eight, Delaware one, Maryland six, Virginia ten, North Carolina five, South Carolina five, and Georgia three.*

When vacancies happen in the Representation from any State, the Executive Authority thereof shall issue Writs of Election to fill such Vacancies.

The House of Representatives shall chuse their Speaker and other Officers; and shall have the sole Power of Impeachment.

[Senate: selection, term, qualifications, exclusive power to try impeachments]

Section 3 The Senate of the United States shall be composed of two Senators from each State, *chosen by the Legislature thereof,* for six years; and each Senator shall have one Vote.

Immediately after they shall be assembled in Consequence of the first Election, they shall be divided as equally as may be into three Classes. The Seats of the Senators of the first Class shall be vacated at the Expiration of the second Year, of the second Class at the expiration of the fourth Year, and of the third Class at the expiration of the sixth Year, so that one-third may be chosen every second Year; and if Vacancies happen by Resignation or otherwise, during the Recess of the Legislature of any State, the Executive thereof may make temporary Appointments until the next meeting of the legislature, which shall then fill such Vacancies.

No person shall be a Senator who shall not have attained to the Age of thirty Years, and been nine Years a Citizen of the United States, and who shall not, when elected, be an Inhabitant of that State for which he shall be chosen.

The Vice-President of the United States shall be President of the Senate, but shall have no Vote, unless they be equally divided.

The Senate shall choose their other officers, and also a President pro tempore, in the absence of the Vice-President, or when he shall exercise the Office of President of the United States.

The Senate shall have the sole Power to try all impeachments. When sitting for that purpose, they shall be on Oath or Affirmation. When the President of the United States is tried, the Chief Justice shall preside: and no Person shall be convicted without the Concurrence of two-thirds of the members Present.

Judgment in Cases of Impeachment shall not extend further than to removal from the Office, and disqualification to hold and enjoy any Office of honor, Trust or Profit under the United States: but the Party convicted shall nevertheless be liable and subject to Indictment, Trial, Judgment and Punishment, according to Law.

[Elections]

Section 4 The Times, Places and Manner of holding Elections for Senators and Representatives shall be prescribed in each State by the Legislature thereof; but the Congress may at any time by Law make or alter such regulations, except as to the Places of chusing Senators.

The Congress shall assemble at least once in every Year, and such meeting *shall be on the first Monday in December, unless they shall by Law appoint a different Day.*

[Powers and duties of the two chambers: rules of procedure, power over members]
Section 5 Each House shall be the Judge of the Elections, Returns and Qualifications of its own Members, and a Majority of each shall constitute a Quorum to do Business; but a smaller Number may adjourn from day to day, and may be authorized to compel the Attendance of absent Members, in such Manner, and under such Penalties as each House may provide.

Each House may determine the Rules of its proceedings, punish its Members for disorderly behaviour, and with the Concurrence of two thirds, expel a Member.

Each House shall keep a Journal of its Proceedings, and from time to time publish the same, excepting such Parts as may in their Judgment require Secrecy; and the Yeas and Nays of the Members of either House on any question shall, at the Desire of one fifth of those Present, be entered on the Journal.

Neither House, during the Session of Congress, shall, without the Consent of the other, adjourn for more than three days, nor to any other Place than that in which the two Houses shall be sitting.

[Compensation, privilege from arrest, privilege of speech, disabilities of members]
Section 6 The Senators and Representatives shall receive a Compensation for their services, to be ascertained by Law, and paid out of the Treasury of the United States. They shall in all Cases, except Treason, Felony and Breach of the Peace, be privileged from Arrest during their Attendance at the Session of their respective Houses, and in going to and returning from the same; and for any Speech or Debate in either House, they shall not be questioned in any other Place.

No Senator or Representative shall, during the Time for which he was elected, be appointed to any civil Office under the Authority of the United States, which shall have been created, or the Emoluments whereof shall have been increased, during such time; and no Person holding any Office under the United States, shall be a Member of either House during his Continuance in Office.

[Legislative process: revenue bills, approval or veto power of president]
Section 7 All bills for raising Revenue shall originate in the House of Representatives; but the Senate may propose or concur with Amendments as on other Bills.

Every Bill which shall have passed the House of Representatives and the Senate, shall, before it become a Law, be presented to the President of the United States; if he approve he shall sign it, but if not he shall return it with Objections to that House in which it originated, who shall enter the Objections at large on their journal, and proceed to reconsider it. If after such Reconsideration two thirds of that House shall agree to pass the Bill, it shall be sent, together with the Objections, to the other House, by which it shall likewise be reconsidered, and, if approved by two thirds of that house, it shall become a Law. But in all such Cases the Votes of both houses shall be determined by yeas and Nays, and the Names of the Persons voting for and against the Bill shall be entered on the journal of each House respectively. If any Bill shall not be returned by the President within ten Days (Sundays excepted) after it shall have been presented to him, the Same shall be a Law, in like Manner as if he had signed it, unless the Congress by their Adjournment prevent its Return, in which Case it shall not be a Law.

Every Order, Resolution, or Vote to which the Concurrence of the Senate and House of Representatives may be necessary (except on a question of Adjournment) shall be presented to the President of the United States; and before the Same shall take Effect, shall be approved by him, or being disapproved by him, shall be repassed by two thirds of the Senate and House of Representatives, according to the Rules and Limitations prescribed in the Case of a Bill.

[Powers of Congress enumerated]

Section 8 The Congress shall have Power

To lay and collect Taxes, Duties, Imposts, and Excises, to pay the Debts and provide for the common Defence and general Welfare of the United States; but all Duties, Imposts and Excises shall be uniform throughout the United States;

To borrow Money on the credit of the United States;

To regulate Commerce with foreign Nations, and among the several States, and with the Indian tribes;

To establish an uniform Rule of Naturalization, and uniform Laws on the subject of Bankruptcies throughout the United States;

To coin Money, regulate the Value thereof, and of foreign Coin, and fix the Standard of Weights and Measures;

To provide for the Punishment of counterfeiting the Securities and current Coin of the United States;

To establish Post Offices and post Roads;

To promote the Progress of Science and useful Arts by securing for limited Times to Authors and Inventors the exclusive Right to their respective Writings and Discoveries;

To constitute Tribunals inferior to the supreme Court;

To define and punish Piracies and Felonies committed on the high Seas, and offenses against the Law of Nations;

To declare War, grant Letters of Marque and Reprisal, and make Rules concerning Captures on Land and Water;

To raise and support Armies, but no Appropriation of Money to that Use shall be for a longer Term than two Years;

To provide and maintain a Navy;

To make rules for the Government and Regulation of the land and naval Forces;

To provide for calling forth the Militia to execute the Laws of the Union, suppress Insurrections, and repel Invasions;

To provide for organizing, arming, and disciplining the Militia, and for governing such Part of them as may be employed in the Service of the United States, reserving to the States respectively the Appointment of the Officers, and the Authority of training the Militia according to the discipline prescribed by Congress;

To exercise exclusive Legislation in all Cases whatsoever, over such District (not exceeding ten Miles square) as may, by cession of particular States, and the Acceptance of Congress, become the Seat of Government of the United States, and to exercise like Authority over all places purchased by the Consent of the Legislature of the State in which the Same shall be, for Erection of Forts, Magazines, Arsenals, dock-Yards, and other needful Buildings;—And

[Elastic clause]

To make all Laws which shall be necessary and proper for carrying into Execution the foregoing Powers, and all other powers vested by this Constitution in the Government of the United States, or in any Department or Officer thereof.

[Powers denied Congress]

Section 9 *The Migration or Importation of such persons as any of the States now existing shall think proper to admit, shall not be prohibited by the Congress prior to the Year 1808; but a Tax or duty may be imposed on such Importation, not exceeding $10 for each Person.*

The Privilege of the Writ of Habeas Corpus shall not be suspended, unless when in Cases of Rebellion or Invasion the public Safety may require it.

No Bill of Attainder or ex post facto Law shall be passed.

No Capitation, or other direct, Tax shall be laid, unless in Proportion to the Census or Enumeration herein before directed to be taken.

No Tax or Duty shall be laid on Articles exported from any State.

No Preference shall be given by any Regulation of Commerce or Revenue to the Ports of one State over those of another; nor shall Vessels bound to, or from, one State, be obliged to enter, clear, or pay Duties in another.

No Money shall be drawn from the Treasury, but in Consequence of Appropriations made by Law; and a regular Statement and Account of the receipts and Expenditures of all public Money shall be published from time to time.

No Title of Nobility shall be granted by the United States: And no Person holding any Office or Profit or trust under them, shall, without the Consent of the Congress, accept of any present, Emolument, Office, or Title, of any kind whatever, from any King, Prince, or foreign State.

[Powers denied the states]

Section 10 No State shall enter into any Treaty, Alliance, or Confederation; grant Letters of Marque and Reprisal; coin Money; emit Bills of Credit; make any Thing but gold and silver Coin a Tender in Payment of Debts; pass any Bill of Attainder, ex post facto law, or Law impairing the obligation of Contracts, or grant any Title of Nobility.

No State shall, without the Consent of Congress, lay any Imposts or Duties on Imports or Exports, except what may be absolutely necessary for executing its inspection Laws: and the net Produce of all duties and imposts, laid by any State on Imports or Exports, shall be for the Use of the Treasury of the United States; and all such Laws shall be subject to the Revision and Controul of the Congress.

No State shall, without the consent of Congress, lay any Duty of Tonnage, keep Troops or Ships of War in time of Peace, enter into any Agreement or Compact with another State, or with a foreign Power, or engage in War, unless actually invaded, or in such imminent Danger as will not admit of delay.

Article II

[The executive branch]

[The president: power vested, term, electoral college, qualifications, presidential succession, compensation, oath of office]

Section 1 The executive Power shall be vested in a President of the United States of America. He shall hold his Office during the Term of four Years, and, together with the Vice President, chosen for the same Term, be elected as follows:

Each State shall appoint, in such Manner as the Legislature thereof may direct, a Number of Electors, equal to the whole Number of Senators and Representatives to which the State may be entitled in the Congress; but no Senator or Representative, or Person holding an Office of Trust or Profit under the United States, shall be appointed an Elector.

The Electors shall meet in their respective States, and vote by Ballot for two Persons, of whom one at least shall not be an inhabitant of the same State with themselves. And they shall make a List of all the Persons voted for, and of the Number of Votes for each: which List they shall sign and certify, and transmit sealed to the Seat of Government of the United States, directed to the President of the Senate. The President of the Senate shall, in the presence of the Senate and House of Representatives, open all the Certificates, and the Votes shall then be counted. The Person having the greatest Number of Votes shall be the President, if such Number be a Majority of the whole number of Electors appointed; and if there be more than one who have such Majority, and have an equal Number of Votes, then the House of Representatives shall immediately chuse by Ballot one of them for President; and if no Person have a Majority, then from the five highest on the List said House shall in like Manner chuse the President. But in chusing the President the Votes shall be taken by States, the Representation from each State having one Vote; a quorum for this purpose shall consist of a Member or Members from two thirds of the States, and a Majority of all the States shall be necessary to a Choice. In every Case, after the Choice of the President, the person having the greatest Number of Votes of the Electors shall be the Vice President. But if there should remain two or more who have equal Votes, the Senate shall chuse from them by Ballot the Vice President.

The Congress may determine the Time of chusing the Electors and the Day on which they shall give their Votes; which Day shall be the same throughout the United States.

No person except a natural born Citizen, or a Citizen of the United States at the time of the Adoption of this Constitution, shall be eligible to the Office of President; neither shall any Person be eligible to that Office who shall not have attained to the age of thirty-five Years, and been fourteen Years a Resident within the United States.

In cases of the Removal of the President from Office or of his Death, Resignation, or Inability to discharge the Powers and Duties of the said Office, the same shall devolve on the Vice President, and the Congress may by law provide for the case of Removal, Death, Resignation, or inability, both of the President and Vice President, declaring what Officer shall then act as President, and such Officer shall act accordingly, until the Disability be removed, or a President shall be elected.

The President shall, at stated Times, receive for his Services, a Compensation, which shall neither be increased nor diminished during the Period for which he shall have been elected, and he shall not receive within that Period any other emolument from the United States, or any of them.

Before he enter on the Execution of his Office, he shall take the following Oath or Affirmation:—"I do solemnly swear (or affirm) that I will faithfully execute the Office of the President of the United States, and will to the best of my Ability preserve, protect and defend the Constitution of the United States."

[Powers and duties: as commander in chief, over advisers, to pardon, to make treaties and appoint officers]

Section 2 The President shall be Commander in Chief of the Army and Navy of the United States, and of the Militia of the several States, when called into the actual service of the United States; he may require the Opinion, in writing, of the principal Officer in each of the executive Departments, upon any Subject relating to the Duties of their respective Offices, and he shall have Power to grant Reprieves and Pardons for Offences against the United States, except in Cases of Impeachment.

He shall have Power, by and with the Advice and Consent of the Senate, to make Treaties, provided two-thirds of the Senators present concur; and he shall nominate, and by and with the Advice and Consent of the Senate, shall appoint Ambassadors, other public Ministers and Consuls, Judges of the supreme Court, and all other Officers of the United States, whose Appointments are not herein otherwise provided for, and which shall be established by Law: but Congress may by Law vest the Appointment of such inferior Officers, as they think proper, in the President alone, in the courts of Law, or in the Heads of Departments.

The President shall have Power to fill up all Vacancies that may happen during the Recess of the Senate, by granting Commissions which shall expire at the end of their next Session.

[Legislative, diplomatic, and law-enforcement duties]

Section 3 He shall from time to time give to the Congress Information of the State of the Union, and recommend to their Consideration such Measures as he shall judge necessary and expedient; he may, on extraordinary Occasions, convene both Houses, or either of them, and in Case of Disagreement between them, with Respect to the Time of Adjournment, he may adjourn them to such Time as he shall think proper; he shall receive Ambassadors and other public Ministers; he shall take Care that the Laws be faithfully executed, and shall Commission all the Officers of the United States.

[Impeachment]

Section 4 The President, Vice President and all civil Officers of the United States shall be removed from Office on Impeachment for, and on Conviction of, Treason, Bribery, or other high Crimes and Misdemeanors.

Article III

[The judicial branch]

[Power vested; Supreme Court; lower courts; judges]

Section 1 The judicial Power of the United States shall be vested in one supreme Court, and in such inferior Courts as the Congress may from time to time ordain and establish. The Judges, both of the supreme and inferior Courts, shall hold their Offices during good Behaviour, and shall, at stated Times, receive for their Services a Compensation which shall not be diminished during their Continuance in Office.

[Jurisdiction; trial by jury]

Section 2 The judicial Power shall extend to all Cases, in Law and Equity, arising under this Constitution, the Laws of the United States, and Treaties made, or which shall be made, under their Authority;—to all Cases affecting Ambassadors, other public Ministers and Consuls;—to all Cases of admiralty and maritime Jurisdiction;—to Controversies to which the United States shall be a Party;—to controversies between two or more States;—*between a State and Citizens of another State;*—between Citizens of different States—between Citizens of the same State claiming Lands under grants of different States, and between a State, or the Citizens thereof, and foreign States, Citizens or Subjects.

In all cases affecting Ambassadors, other public Ministers and Consuls, and those in which a State shall be Party, the supreme Court shall have original Jurisdiction. In all the other Cases before mentioned, the supreme Court shall have appellate Jurisdiction, both as to Law and Fact, with such Exceptions, and under such Regulations, as the Congress shall make.

The Trial of all Crimes, except in cases of Impeachment, shall be by Jury; and such Trial shall be held in the State where said Crimes shall have been committed; but when not committed within any State, the Trial shall be at such Place or Places as the Congress may by Law have directed.

[Treason: definition, punishment]

Section 3 Treason against the United States shall consist only in levying War against them, or in adhering to their Enemies, giving them Aid and Comfort. No

Person shall be convicted of Treason unless on the Testimony of two Witnesses to the same overt Act, or on confession in open Court.

The Congress shall have power to declare the Punishment of Treason, but no Attainder of Treason shall work Corruption of Blood, or Forfeiture except during the Life of the Person attainted.

Article IV

[States' relations]

[Full faith and credit]

Section 1 Full Faith and Credit shall be given in each State to the public Acts, Records, and judicial Proceedings of every other State. And the Congress may by general laws prescribe the Manner in which such Acts, Records, and Proceedings shall be proved, and the Effect thereof.

[Interstate comity, rendition]

Section 2 The Citizens of each State shall be entitled to all Privileges and Immunities of Citizens in the several States.

A Person charged in any State with Treason, Felony, or other Crime, who shall flee from Justice, and be found in another State, shall on Demand of the executive Authority of the State from which he fled, be delivered up, to be removed to the State having Jurisdiction of the Crime.

No person held to Service or Labor in one State, under the Laws thereof, escaping into another, shall, in consequence of any Law or Regulation therein, be discharged from such Service or Labor, but shall be delivered up on Claim of the Party to whom such Service or Labor may be due.

[New states]

Section 3 New States may be admitted by the Congress into this Union; but no new State shall be formed or erected within the Jurisdiction of any other State; nor any State be formed by the Junction of two or more States, or parts of States, without the Consent of the Legislatures of the States concerned as well as of the Congress.

The Congress shall have Power to dispose of and make all needful Rules and Regulations respecting the Territory or other Property belonging to the United States; and nothing in this Constitution shall be so construed as to Prejudice any Claims of the United States, or of any particular State.

[Obligations of the United States to the states]

Section 4 The United States shall guarantee to every State in this Union a Republican Form of Government, and shall protect each of them against Invasion; and on Application of the Legislature, or of the Executive (when the Legislature cannot be convened), against domestic Violence.

Article V

[Mode of amendment]

The Congress, whenever two-thirds of both Houses shall deem it necessary, shall propose Amendments to this Constitution, or, on the Application of the Legislatures of two-thirds of the several States, shall call a Convention for proposing Amendments, which, in either Case, shall be valid to all Intents and Purposes, as part of this Constitution, when ratified by the legislatures of three-fourths of the several States, or by Conventions in three-fourths thereof, as the one or the other

Mode of Ratification may be proposed by the Congress; Provided *that no Amendment which may be made prior to the Year One thousand eight hundred and eight shall in any Manner affect the first and fourth clauses in the Ninth Section of the first Article;* and that no State, without its Consent, shall be deprived of its equal suffrage in the Senate.

Article VI

[Prior debts, supremacy of Constitution, oaths of office]

All Debts contracted and Engagements entered into, before the Adoption of this Constitution, shall be as valid against the United States under this Constitution, as under the Confederation.

This Constitution, and the Laws of the United States which shall be made in Pursuance thereof; and all Treaties made, or which shall be made, under the Authority of the United States, shall be the supreme Law of the Land; and the judges in every State shall be bound thereby, anything in the Constitution or Laws of any State to the Contrary notwithstanding.

The Senators and Representatives before mentioned, and the Members of the several State Legislatures, and all executive and judicial Officers, both of the United States and of the several States, shall be bound by Oath or Affirmation to support this Constitution; but no religious test shall ever be required as a Qualification to any Office or public Trust under the United States.

Article VII

[Ratification]

The ratification of the Conventions of nine States shall be sufficient for the Establishment of this Constitution between the States so ratifying the Same.

Done in Convention by the Unanimous Consent of the States present, the seventeenth day of September in the Year of our Lord one thousand seven hundred and eighty-seven and of the Independence of the United States of America the twelfth. In WITNESS whereof We have hereunto subscribed our Names.

GEORGE WASHINGTON
and thirty-seven others

Amendments to the Constitution
[The first ten amendments—the Bill of Rights—were adopted in 1791.]

Amendment I

[Freedom of religion, speech, press, assembly]

Congress shall make no law respecting an establishment of religion, or prohibiting the free exercise thereof; or abridging the freedom of speech, or of the press; or the right of the people peaceably to assemble, and to petition the Government for a redress of grievances.

Amendment II

[Right to bear arms]

A well-regulated militia being necessary to the security of a free State, the right of the people to keep and bear arms shall not be infringed.

Amendment III

[Quartering of soldiers]

No Soldier shall, in time of peace, be quartered in any house without the consent of the Owner, nor in time of war, but in a manner to be prescribed by law.

Amendment IV

[Searches and seizures]

The right of the people to be secure in their persons, houses, papers, and effects, against unreasonable searches and seizures, shall not be violated, and no Warrants shall issue but upon probable cause, supported by Oath or Affirmation, and particularly describing the place to be searched, and the persons or things to be seized.

Amendment V

[Rights of persons: grand juries, double jeopardy, self-incrimination, due process, eminent domain]

No person shall be held to answer for a capital, or otherwise infamous crime, unless on a presentment or indictment of a Grand Jury, except in cases arising in the land or naval forces, or in the Militia, when in actual service in time of War or public danger; nor shall any person be subject for the same offense to be twice put in jeopardy of life or limb; nor shall be compelled in any criminal case to be a witness against himself, nor be deprived of life, liberty, or property, without due process of law; nor shall private property be taken for public use without just compensation.

Amendment VI

[Rights of accused in criminal prosecutions]

In all criminal prosecutions, the accused shall enjoy the right to a speedy and public trial, by an impartial jury of the State and district wherein the crime shall have been committed, which district shall have been previously ascertained by law, and to be informed of the nature and cause of the accusation; to be confronted with the witnesses against him; to have compulsory process for obtaining Witnesses in his favor, and to have the assistance of counsel for his defence.

Amendment VII

[Civil trials]

In Suits at common law, where the value in controversy shall exceed twenty dollars, the right of trial by jury shall be preserved, and no fact tried by a jury shall be otherwise reexamined in any Court of the United States, than according to the rules of the common law.

Amendment VIII

[Punishment for crime]

Excessive bail shall not be required, nor excessive fines imposed, nor cruel and unusual punishments inflicted.

Amendment IX

[Rights retained by the people]

The enumeration in the Constitution, of certain rights, shall not be construed to deny or disparage others retained by the people.

Amendment X

[Rights reserved to the states]

The powers not delegated to the United States by the Constitution, nor prohibited by it to the States, are reserved to the States respectively, or to the people.

Amendment XI

[Suits against the states; adopted 1798]

The Judicial power of the United States shall not be construed to extend to any suit in law or equity, commenced or prosecuted against one of the United States by Citizens of another state, or by Citizens or Subjects of any Foreign State.

Amendment XII

[Election of the president; adopted 1804]

The electors shall meet in their respective States, and vote by ballot for President and Vice-President, one of whom, at least, shall not be an inhabitant of the same state with themselves; they shall name in their ballots the person voted for as President, and in distinct ballots the person voted for as Vice-President, and they shall make distinct lists of all persons voted for as President, and of all persons voted for as Vice-President, and of the number of votes for each, which lists they shall sign and certify, and transmit sealed to the seat of government of the United States, directed to the President of the Senate;—the President of the Senate shall, in the presence of the Senate and House of Representatives, open all the certificates and the votes shall then be counted;—the person having the greatest number of votes for President shall be the President, if such number be a majority of the whole number of electors appointed; and if no person have such majority, then from the persons having the highest numbers not exceeding three on the list of those voted for as President, the House of Representatives shall choose immediately, by ballot, the President. But in choosing the President, the votes shall be taken by States, the representation from each State having one vote; a quorum for this purpose shall consist of a member or members from two-thirds of the States, and a majority of all the States shall be necessary to a choice. And if the House of Representatives shall not choose a President whenever the right of choice shall devolve upon them, before *the fourth day of March* next following, then the Vice-President shall act as President, as in the case of the death or other constitutional disability of the President.—The person having the greatest number of votes as Vice-President shall be the Vice-President, if such number be a majority of the whole number of electors appointed; and if no person have a majority, then from the two highest numbers on the list the Senate shall choose the Vice-President; a quorum for the purpose shall consist of two-thirds of the whole number of Senators, and a majority of the whole number shall be necessary to a choice. But no person constitutionally ineligible to the Office of President shall be eligible to that of Vice-President of the United States.

Amendment XIII

[Abolition of slavery; adopted 1865]

Section 1 Neither slavery nor involuntary servitude, except as a punishment for crime whereof the party shall have been duly convicted, shall exist within the United States, or any place subject to their jurisdiction.

Section 2 Congress shall have power to enforce this article by appropriate legislation.

Amendment XIV

[Adopted 1868]

[Citizenship rights; privileges and immunities; due process; equal protection]

Section 1 All persons born or naturalized in the United States, and subject to the jurisdiction thereof, are citizens of the United States and of the State wherein they reside. No State shall make or enforce any law which shall abridge the privileges or immunities of citizens of the United States; nor shall any State deprive any person of life, liberty, or property, without due process of law; nor deny to any person within its jurisdiction the equal protection of the laws.

[Apportionment of representation]

Section 2 Representatives shall be apportioned among the several States according to their respective numbers, counting the whole number of persons in each State, excluding Indians not taxed. But when the right to vote at any election for the choice of Electors for President and Vice-President of the United States, Representatives in Congress, the Executive and Judicial officers of a State, or the members of the Legislature thereof, is denied to any of the male inhabitants of such State, being twenty-one years of age and citizens of the United States, or in any way abridged, except for participation in rebellion, or other crime, the basis of representation therein shall be reduced in the proportion which the number of such male citizens shall bear to the whole number of male citizens twenty-one years of age in such State.

[Disqualification of Confederate officials]

Section 3 No person shall be a Senator or Representative in Congress, or Elector of President and Vice-President, or hold any Office, civil or military, under the United States, or under any State, who, having previously taken an oath, as a member of Congress, or as an officer of the United States, or as a member of any State legislature, or as an executive or judicial officer of any State, to support the Constitution of the United States, shall have engaged in insurrection or rebellion against the same, or given aid or comfort to the enemies thereof. Congress may, by a vote of two-thirds of each house, remove such disability.

[Public debts]

Section 4 The validity of the public debt of the United States, authorized by law, including debts incurred for payment of pensions and bounties for services in suppressing insurrection or rebellion, shall not be questioned. But neither the United States nor any State shall assume or pay any debt or obligation incurred in aid of insurrection or rebellion against the United States, or any claim for the loss of emancipation of any slave; but all such debts, obligations, and claims shall be held illegal and void.

[Enforcement]

Section 5 The Congress shall have power to enforce, by appropriate legislation, the provisions of this article.

Amendment XV

[Extension of right to vote; adopted 1870]

Section 1 The right of citizens of the United States to vote shall not be denied or abridged by the United States or by any State on account of race, color, or previous condition of servitude.

Section 2 The Congress shall have power to enforce this article by appropriate legislation.

Amendment XVI

[Income tax; adopted 1913]

The Congress shall have power to lay and collect taxes on incomes, from whatever source derived, without apportionment among the several States, and without regard to any census or enumeration.

Amendment XVII

[Popular election of senators; adopted 1913]

Section 1 The Senate of the United States shall be composed of two Senators from each State, elected by the people thereof, for six years; and each Senator shall have one vote. The electors in each State shall have the Qualifications requisite for electors of the most numerous branch of the State legislatures.

Section 2 When vacancies happen in the representation of any State in the Senate, the executive authority of such State shall issue writs of election to fill such vacancies: Provided, that the Legislature of any State may empower the executive thereof to make temporary appointments until the people fill the vacancies by election as the Legislature may direct.

Section 3 This amendment shall not be so construed as to affect the election or term of any Senator chosen before it becomes valid as part of the Constitution.

Amendment XVIII

[Prohibition of intoxicating liquors; adopted 1919, repealed 1933]

Section 1 After one year from the ratification of this article the manufacture, sale or transportation of intoxicating liquors within, the importation thereof into, or the exportation thereof from the United States and all territory subject to the jurisdiction thereof, for beverage purposes, is hereby prohibited.

Section 2 The Congress and the several States shall have concurrent power to enforce this article by appropriate legislation.

Section 3 This article shall be inoperative unless it shall have been ratified as an amendment to the Constitution by the legislatures of the several States, as provided by the Constitution, within seven years from the date of the submission thereof to the States by the Congress.

Amendment XIX

[Right of women to vote; adopted 1920]

Section 1 The right of citizens of the United States to vote shall not be denied or abridged by the United States or by any State on account of sex.

Section 2 The Congress shall have power to enforce this article by appropriate legislation.

Amendment XX

[Commencement of terms of office; adopted 1933]

Section 1 The terms of the President and Vice-President shall end at noon on the 20th day of January, and the terms of Senators and Representatives at noon on the

3d day of January, of the years in which such terms would have ended if this article had not been ratified; and the terms of their successors shall then begin.

Section 2 The Congress shall assemble at least once in every year, and such meetings shall begin at noon on the 3d day of January, unless they shall by law appoint a different day.

[Extension of presidential succession]

Section 3 If, at the time fixed for the beginning of the term of the President, the President-elect shall have died, the Vice-President-elect shall become President. If a President shall not have been chosen before the time fixed for the beginning of his term, or if the President-elect shall have failed to qualify, then the Vice-President-elect shall act as President until a President shall have qualified; and the Congress may by law provide for the case wherein neither a President-elect nor a Vice-President-elect shall have qualified, declaring who shall then act as President, or the manner in which one who is to act shall be selected, and such persons shall act accordingly until a President or Vice-President shall have qualified.

Section 4 The Congress may by law provide for the case of the death of any of the persons from whom the House of Representatives may choose a President whenever the right of choice shall have devolved upon them, and for the case of the death of any of the persons from whom the Senate may choose a Vice-President whenever the right of choice shall have devolved upon them.

Section 5 Sections 1 and 2 shall take effect on the 15th day of October following the ratification of this article.

Section 6 This article shall be inoperative unless it shall have been ratified as an amendment to the Constitution by the Legislatures of three-fourths of the several States within seven years from the date of its submission.

Amendment XXI

[Repeal of Eighteenth Amendment; adopted 1933]

Section 1 The eighteenth article of amendment to the Constitution of the United States is hereby repealed.

Section 2 The transportation or importation into any State, Territory, or Possession of the United States for delivery or use therein of intoxicating liquors, in violation of the laws thereof, is hereby prohibited.

Section 3 This article shall be inoperative unless it shall have been ratified as an amendment to the Constitution by conventions in the several States, as provided in the Constitution, within seven years from the date of submission thereof to the States by the Congress.

Amendment XXII

[Limit on presidential tenure; adopted 1951]

Section 1 No person shall be elected to the Office of President more than twice, and no person who has held the Office of President, or acted as President, for more than two years of a term to which some other person was elected President shall be elected to the Office of President more than once. But this article shall not apply to any person holding the Office of President when this article was proposed by the Congress, and shall not prevent any person who may be holding the Office of

President, or acting as President, during the term within which this article becomes operative from holding the Office of President or acting as President during the remainder of such term.

Section 2 This article shall be inoperative unless it shall have been ratified as an amendment to the Constitution by the legislatures of three-fourths of the several States within seven years from the date of its submission to the States by the Congress.

Amendment XXIII

[Presidential electors for the District of Columbia; adopted 1961]

Section 1 The District constituting the seat of Government of the United States shall appoint in such manner as the Congress may direct: A number of electors of President and Vice President equal to the whole number of Senators and Representatives in Congress to which the District would be entitled if it were a State, but in no event more than the least populous State; they shall be in addition to those appointed by the States, but they shall be considered for the purposes of the election of President and Vice President, to be electors appointed by a State; and they shall meet in the District and perform such duties as provided by the twelfth article of amendment.

Section 2 The Congress shall have the power to enforce this article by appropriate legislation.

Amendment XXIV

[Poll tax outlawed in national elections; adopted 1964]

Section 1 The right of citizens of the United States to vote in any primary or other election for President or Vice President, for electors for President or Vice President, or for Senator or Representative in Congress, shall not be denied or abridged by the United States or any State by reason of failure to pay any poll tax or other tax.

Section 2 The Congress shall have the power to enforce this article by appropriate legislation.

Amendment XXV

[Presidential succession; adopted 1967]

Section 1 In case of the removal of the President from Office or of his death or resignation, the Vice President shall become President.

[Vice-presidential vacancy]

Section 2 Whenever there is a vacancy in the Office of the Vice President, the President shall nominate a Vice President who shall take Office upon confirmation by a majority vote of both Houses of Congress.

Section 3 Whenever the President transmits to the President pro tempore of the Senate and the Speaker of the House of Representatives his written declaration that he is unable to discharge the powers and duties of his Office, and until he transmits to them a written declaration to the contrary, such powers and duties shall be discharged by the Vice President as Acting President.

[Presidential disability]

Section 4 Whenever the Vice President and a majority of either the principal officers of the executive departments or of such other body as Congress may by law provide, transmit to the President pro tempore of the Senate and the Speaker of the House of Representatives their written declaration that the President is unable to discharge the powers and duties of his Office, the Vice President shall immediately assume the powers and duties of the Office as Acting President.

Thereafter, when the President transmits to the President pro tempore of the Senate and the Speaker of the House of Representatives his written declaration that no inability exists, he shall resume the powers and duties of his Office unless the Vice President and a majority of either the principal officers of the executive department(s) or of such other body as Congress may by law provide, transmit within four days to the President pro tempore of the Senate and the Speaker of the House of Representatives their written declaration that the President is unable to discharge the powers and duties of his Office. Thereupon Congress shall decide the issue, assembling within forty-eight hours for that purpose if not in session. If the Congress, within twenty-one days after receipt of the latter written declaration, or, if Congress is not in session, within twenty-one days after Congress is required to assemble, determines by two-thirds vote of both Houses that the President is unable to discharge the powers and duties of his Office, the Vice President shall continue to discharge the same as Acting President; otherwise, the President shall resume the powers and duties of his Office.

Amendment XXVI

[Right of eighteen-year-olds to vote; adopted 1971]

Section 1 The right of citizens of the United States, who are eighteen years of age or older, to vote shall not be denied or abridged by the United States or by any State on account of age.

Section 2 The Congress shall have power to enforce this article by appropriate legislation.

Amendment XXVII

[Congressional pay raises; adopted 1992]

No law, varying the compensation for the services of the Senators and Representatives shall take effect, until an election of Representatives shall have intervened.

Glossary

A

administrative discretion The latitude that Congress gives agencies to make policy in the spirit of their legislative mandate.

affirmative action Any of a wide range of programs, from special recruitment efforts to numerical quotas, aimed at expanding opportunities for women and minority groups.

agenda building The process by which new issues are brought into the political limelight.

agenda setting The stage of the policymaking process during which problems get defined as political issues.

aggregate demand The total income that consumers, businesses, and government wish to spend for goods and services.

amicus curiae brief A brief filed (with the permission of the court) by an individual or group that is not a party to a legal action but has an interest in it.

anarchism A political philosophy that opposes government in any form.

appellate jurisdiction The authority of a court to hear cases that have been tried, decided, or reexamined in other courts.

appropriations committees Committees of Congress that decide which of the programs passed by the authorization committees will actually be funded.

argument The heart of a judicial opinion; its logical content separated from facts, rhetoric, and procedure.

Articles of Confederation The compact among the thirteen original states that established the first government of the United States.

attentive policy elites Leaders who follow news in specific policy areas.

authorization committees Committees of Congress that can authorize spending in their particular areas of responsibility.

autocracy A system of government in which the power to govern is concentrated in the hands of one individual.

B

Bill of Rights The first ten amendments to the Constitution. They prevent the national government from tampering with fundamental rights and civil liberties, and emphasize the limited character of national power.

bill of attainder A law that pronounces an individual guilty of a crime without a trial.

bimodal distribution A distribution (of opinions) that shows two responses being chosen about as frequently as each other.

black codes Legislation enacted by former slave states to restrict the freedom of blacks.

block grants Grants-in-aid awarded for general purposes, allowing the recipient great discretion in spending the grant money.

blog A form of newsletter, journal, or "log" of thoughts for public reading, usually devoted to social or political issues and often updated daily. The term derives from weblog.

blue slip The failure of a senator to return a blue slip signals the end of the road for a judicial nomination.

boycott A refusal to do business with a firm, individual, or nation as an expression of disapproval or as a means of coercion.

budget authority The amounts that government agencies are authorized to spend for current and future programs.

budget committees One committee in each house of Congress that supervises a comprehensive budget review process.

budget outlays The amounts that government agencies are expected to spend in the fiscal year.

bureaucracy A large, complex organization in which employees have specific job responsibilities and work within a hierarchy of authority.

bureaucrats Employees of a bureaucracy, usually meaning a government bureaucracy.

business cycles Expansions and contractions of business activity, the first accompanied by inflation and the second by unemployment.

C

cabinet A group of presidential advisers; the heads of the executive departments and other key officials.

capitalism The system of government that favors free enterprise (privately owned businesses operating without government regulation).

casework Solving problems for constituents, especially problems involving government agencies.

categorical grants Grants-in-aid targeted for a specific purpose by either formula or project.

caucus A closed meeting of the members of a political party to decide questions of policy and the selection of candidates for office.

caucus/convention A method used to select delegates to attend a party's national convention. Generally, a local meeting selects delegates for a county-level meeting, which in turn selects delegates for a higher-level meeting; the process culminates in a state convention that actually selects the national convention delegates.

checks and balances A government structure that gives each branch some scrutiny of and control over the other branches.

citizen group Lobbying organization built around policy concerns unrelated to members' vocational interests.

civil cases Court cases that involve a private dispute arising from such matters as accidents, contractual obligations, and divorce.

civil disobedience The willful but nonviolent breach of laws that are regarded as unjust.

civil liberties Freedoms guaranteed to individuals taking the form of restraint on government.

civil rights Powers or privileges guaranteed to individuals and protected from arbitrary removal at the hands of government or individuals.

civil rights movement The mass mobilization during the 1960s that sought to gain equality of rights and opportunities for blacks in the South and to a lesser extent in the North, mainly through nonviolent, unconventional means of participation.

civil service The system by which most appointments to the federal bureaucracy are made, to ensure that government jobs are filled on the basis of merit and that employees are not fired for political reasons.

class action A procedure by which similarly situated litigants may be heard in a single lawsuit.

clear and present danger test A means by which the Supreme Court has distinguished between speech as the advocacy of ideas, which is protected by the First Amendment, and speech as incitement, which is not protected.

closed primaries Primary elections in which voters must declare their party affiliation before they are given the primary ballot containing that party's potential nominees.

cloture The mechanism by which a filibuster is cut off in the Senate.

coalition building The banding together of several interest groups for the purpose of lobbying.

coercive federalism A view holding that the national government may impose its policy preferences on the states through regulations in the form of mandates and restraints.

commerce clause The third clause of Article I, Section 8, of the Constitution, which gives Congress the power to regulate commerce among the states.

common, or judge-made, law Legal precedents derived from previous judicial decisions.

communism A political system in which, in theory, ownership of all land and productive facilities is in the hands of the people, and all goods are equally shared. The production and distribution of goods are controlled by an authoritarian government.

communitarians Those who are willing to use government to promote both order and equality.

competition and outsourcing Procedures that allow private contractors to bid for jobs previously held exclusively by government employees.

concurrence The agreement of a judge with the Supreme Court's majority decision, for a reason other than the majority reason.

confederation A loose association of independent states that agree to cooperate on specified matters.

conference committee A temporary committee created to work out differences between the House and Senate versions of a specific piece of legislation.

Congressional Budget Office (CBO) The budgeting arm of Congress, which prepares alternative budgets to those prepared by the president's OMB.

congressional campaign committee An organization maintained by a political party to raise funds to support its own candidates in congressional elections.

conservatives Those who are willing to use government to promote order but not equality.

constituents People who live and vote in a government official's district or state.

conventional participation Relatively routine political behavior that uses institutional channels and is acceptable to the dominant culture.

cooperative federalism A view holding that the Constitution is an agreement among people who are citizens of both state and nation, so there is much overlap between state powers and national powers.

county governments The government units that administer a county.

criminal cases Court cases involving a crime, or violation of public order.

critical election An election that produces a sharp change in the existing pattern of party loyalties among groups of voters.

D

de facto segregation Segregation that is not the result of government influence.

de jure segregation Government-imposed segregation.

Declaration of Independence Drafted by Thomas Jefferson, the document that proclaimed the right of the colonies to separate from Great Britain.

deficit financing The Keynesian technique of spending beyond government income to combat an economic slump. Its purpose is to inject extra money into the economy to stimulate aggregate demand.

delegate A legislator whose primary responsibility is to represent the majority view of his or her constituents, regardless of his or her own view.

delegation of powers The process by which Congress gives the executive branch the additional authority needed to address new problems.

democracy A system of government in which, in theory, the people rule, either directly or indirectly.

democratic socialism A socialist form of government that guarantees civil liberties such as freedom of speech and religion. Citizens determine the extent of government activity through free elections and competitive political parties.

democratization A process of transition as a country attempts to move from an authoritarian form of government to a democratic one.

departments The biggest units of the executive branch, covering a broad area of government responsibility. The heads of the departments, or secretaries, form the president's cabinet.

deregulation A bureaucratic reform by which the government reduces its role as a regulator of business.

descriptive representation A belief that constituents are most effectively represented by legislators who are similar to them in such key demographic characteristics as race, ethnicity, religion, or gender.

desegregation The ending of authorized segregation, or separation by race.

direct action Unconventional participation that involves assembling crowds to confront businesses and local governments to demand a hearing.

direct lobbying Attempts to influence a legislator's vote through personal contact with the policymaker.

direct primary A preliminary election, run by the state government, in which the voters choose each party's candidates for the general election.

discretionary outlays Payments made by legislators' choice and based on annual appropriations.

discretionary spending In the Budget Enforcement Act of 1990, authorized expenditures from annual appropriations.

dissent The disagreement of a judge with a majority decision.

distributive policies Government policies designed to confer a benefit on a particular institution or group.

divided government The situation in which one party controls the White House and the other controls at least one house of Congress.

docket A court's agenda.

dual federalism A view holding that the Constitution is a compact among sovereign states, so that the powers of the national government and the states are clearly differentiated.

E

earmark Federal funds appropriated by Congress for use on local projects.

economic depression A period of high unemployment and business failures; a severe, long-lasting downturn in a business cycle.

efficient market hypothesis Financial markets are informationally efficient—they quickly absorb all relevant information about securities into their prices.

e-government Online communication channels that enable citizens to easily obtain information from government and facilitate the expression of opinions to government officials.

elastic clause The last clause in Article I, Section 8, of the Constitution, which gives Congress the means to execute its enumerated powers. This clause is the basis for Congress's implied powers. Also called the *necessary and proper clause*.

election campaign An organized effort to persuade voters to choose one candidate over others competing for the same office.

electoral college A body of electors chosen by voters to cast ballots for president and vice president.

electoral dealignment A lessening of the importance of party loyalties in voting decisions.

electoral realignment The change in voting patterns that occurs after a critical election.

Elementary and Secondary Education Act of 1965 (ESEA) The federal government's primary law to assist the nation's elementary and secondary schools. It emerged as part of President Lyndon Johnson's Great Society program.

elite theory The view that a small group of people actually makes most of the important government decisions.

entitlements Benefits to which every eligible person has a legal right and that the government cannot deny.

enumerated powers The powers explicitly granted to Congress by the Constitution.

equal rights amendment (ERA) A failed constitutional amendment introduced by the National Women's Party in 1923, declaring that "equality of rights under the law shall not be denied or abridged by the United States or any State on account of sex."

equality of opportunity The idea that each person is guaranteed the same chance to succeed in life.

equality of outcome The concept that society must ensure that people are equal, and governments must design policies to redistribute wealth and status so that economic and social equality is actually achieved.

establishment clause The first clause in the First Amendment, which forbids government establishment of religion.

ex post facto law A law that declares an action to be criminal after it has been performed.

exclusionary rule The judicial rule that states that evidence obtained in an illegal search and seizure cannot be used in trial.

executive agreement A pact between the heads of two countries.

executive branch The law-enforcing branch of government.

Executive Office of the President The president's executive aides and their staffs; the extended White House executive establishment.

executive orders Presidential directives that create or modify laws and public policies, without the direct approval of Congress.

extraordinary majority A majority greater than the minimum of 50 percent plus one.

F

Federal Communications Commission (FCC) An independent federal agency that regulates interstate and international communication by radio, television, telephone, telegraph, cable, and satellite.

Federal Election Commission (FEC) A bipartisan federal agency of six members that oversees the financing of national election campaigns.

federal question An issue covered by the U.S. Constitution, national laws, or U.S. treaties.

Federal Reserve System The system of banks that acts as the central bank of the United States and controls major monetary policies.

federalism The division of power between a central government and regional governments.

feedback Information received by policymakers about the effectiveness of public policy.

feminization of poverty The term applied to the fact that a large percentage of all poor Americans are women or the dependents of women.

fighting words Speech that is not protected by the First Amendment because it inflicts injury or tends to incite an immediate disturbance of the peace.

filibuster A delaying tactic, used in the Senate, that involves speechmaking to prevent action on a piece of legislation.

first-past-the-post elections A British term for elections conducted in single-member districts that award victory to the candidate with the most votes.

fiscal policies Economic policies that involve government spending and taxing.

fiscal year The twelve-month period from October 1 to September 30 used by the government for accounting purposes. A fiscal year budget is named for the year in which it ends.

501(c)4 social welfare organizations Groups named after Section 501 of the Internal Revenue Code that operate for promotion of social welfare; they are exempt from reporting donors if they spend most of their funds on issues, not candidates.

527 committees Committees named after Section 527 of the Internal Revenue Code; they enjoy tax-exempt status in election campaigns if they are unaffiliated with political parties and take positions on issues, not specific candidates.

formula grants Categorical grants distributed according to a particular set of rules, called a *formula*, that specifies who is eligible for the grants and how much each eligible applicant will receive.

fragmentation In policymaking, the phenomenon of attacking a single problem in different and sometimes competing ways.

franchise The right to vote. Also called *suffrage*.

freedom from Immunity, as in *freedom from want*.

freedom of An absence of constraints on behavior, as in *freedom of speech* or *freedom of religion*.

free-exercise clause The second clause in the First Amendment, which prevents the government from interfering with the exercise of religion.

free-expression clauses The press and speech clauses of the First Amendment.

free-rider problem The situation in which people benefit from the activities of an organization (such as an interest group) but do not contribute to those activities.

front-loading States' practice of moving delegate selection primaries and caucuses earlier in the calendar year to gain media and candidate attention.

G

gatekeepers Media executives, news editors, and prominent reporters who direct the flow of news.

general election A national election held by law in November of every even-numbered year.

gerrymandering Redrawing a congressional district to intentionally benefit one political party.

globalization The increasing interdependence of citizens and nations across the world.

going public A strategy whereby a president seeks to influence policy elites and media coverage by appealing directly to the American people.

good faith exception An exception to the Supreme Court exclusionary rule, holding that evidence seized on the basis of a mistakenly issued search warrant can be introduced at trial if the mistake was made in good faith, that is, if all the parties involved had reason at the time to believe that the warrant was proper.

government The legitimate use of force to control human behavior; also, the organization or agency authorized to exercise that force.

government corporations Government agencies that perform services that might be provided by the private sector but that either involve insufficient financial incentive or are better provided when they are somehow linked with government.

Government Performance and Results Act A law requiring each government agency to implement quantifiable standards to measure its performance in meeting stated program goals.

grant-in-aid Money provided by one level of government to another level of government, or sometimes to a non-governmental organization, to be spent for a given purpose.

grassroots lobbying Lobbying activities performed by rank-and-file interest group members and other supporters.

Great Compromise Submitted by the Connecticut delegation to the Constitutional Convention, and thus also known as the Connecticut Compromise, a plan calling for a bicameral legislature in which the House of Representatives would be apportioned according to population and the states would be represented equally in the Senate.

Great Depression The longest and deepest setback the American economy has ever experienced. It began with the stock market crash on October 24, 1929, and did not end until the start of World War II.

Great Society President Lyndon Johnson's broad array of programs designed to redress political, social, and economic inequality.

gridlock A situation in which government is incapable of acting on important issues.

gross domestic product (GDP) The total value of the goods and services produced by a country during a year.

H

hold A letter requesting that a bill be held from floor debate.

home rule The right to enact and enforce legislation locally.

horse race journalism Election coverage by the mass media that focuses on which candidate is ahead rather than on national issues.

I

impeachment The formal charging of a government official with "treason, bribery, or other high crimes and misdemeanors."

implementation The process of putting specific policies into operation.

implied powers Those powers that Congress needs to execute its enumerated powers.

incremental budgeting A method of budget making that involves adding new funds (an increment) onto the amount previously budgeted (in last year's budget).

incrementalism Policymaking characterized by a series of decisions, each instituting modest change.

incumbent A current officeholder.

independent agencies Executive agencies that are not part of a cabinet department.

inflation An economic condition characterized by price increases linked to a decrease in the value of the currency.

influencing behavior Behavior that seeks to modify or reverse government policy to serve political interests.

information campaign An organized effort to gain public backing by bringing a group's views to public attention.

infotainment A mix of information and diversion oriented to personalities or celebrities, not linked to the day's events, and usually unrelated to public affairs or policy; often called "soft news."

inherent powers Authority claimed by the president that is not clearly specified in the Constitution. Typically, these powers are inferred from the Constitution.

initiative A procedure by which voters can propose an issue to be decided by the legislature or by the people in a referendum. It requires gathering a specified number of signatures and submitting a petition to a designated agency.

interest group An organized group of individuals that seeks to influence public policy; also called a *lobby*.

interest group entrepreneur An interest group organizer or leader.

intergovernmental system The collection of governments made up of national, state, and local units of government.

invidious discrimination Discrimination against persons or groups that works to their harm and is based on animosity.

issue definition Our conception of the problem at hand.

issue framing The way that politicians or interest group leaders define an issue when presenting it to others.

issue network A shared-knowledge group consisting of representatives of various interests involved in some particular aspect of public policy.

J

joint committee A committee made up of members of both the House and the Senate.

judgment The judicial decision in a court case.

judicial activism A judicial philosophy by which judges tend not to defer to decisions of the elected branches of government, resulting in the invalidation or emasculation of those decisions.

judicial branch The law-interpreting branch of government.

judicial restraint A judicial philosophy by which judges tend to defer to decisions of the elected branches of government.

judicial review The power to declare congressional (and presidential) acts invalid because they violate the Constitution.

K

Keynesian theory An economic theory stating that the government can stabilize the economy—that is, can smooth business cycles—by controlling the level of aggregate demand, and that the level of aggregate demand can be controlled by means of fiscal and monetary policies.

L

laissez faire An economic doctrine that opposes any form of government intervention in business.

legislative branch The lawmaking branch of government.

legislative liaison staff Those people who act as the communications link between the White House and Congress, advising the president or cabinet secretaries on the status of pending legislation.

liberalism The belief that states should leave individuals free to follow their individual pursuits.

liberals Those who are willing to use government to promote equality but not order.

libertarianism A political ideology that is opposed to all government action except as necessary to protect life and property.

libertarians Those who are opposed to using government to promote either order or equality.

lobby See *interest group.*

lobbyist A representative of an interest group.

M

majoritarian model of democracy The classical theory of democracy in which government by the people is interpreted as government by the majority of the people.

majority leader The head of the majority party in the Senate; the second-highest ranking member of the majority party in the House.

majority representation The system by which one office, contested by two or more candidates, is won by the single candidate who collects the most votes.

majority rule The principle—basic to procedural democratic theory—that the decision of a group must reflect the preference of more than half of those participating; a simple majority.

mandate A requirement that a state undertake an activity or provide a service, in keeping with minimum national standards.

mandatory outlays Payments that government must make by law.

mandatory spending In the Budget Enforcement Act of 1990, expenditures required by previous commitments.

mass media The means employed in mass communication; traditionally divided into print media and broadcast media.

means-tested benefits Conditional benefits provided by government to individuals whose income falls below a designated threshold.

media event A situation that is so "newsworthy" that the mass media are compelled to cover it. Candidates in elections often create such situations to garner media attention.

Medicaid A need-based comprehensive medical and hospitalization program.

Medicare A health insurance program serving primarily persons sixty-five and older.

minority rights The benefits of government that cannot be denied to any citizen by majority decisions.

Miranda warnings Statements concerning rights that police are required to make to a person before he or she is subjected to in-custody questioning.

modified closed primaries Primary elections that allow individual state parties to decide whether they permit independents to vote in their primaries and, if so, for which offices.

modified open primaries Primary elections that entitle independent voters to vote in a party's primary.

monetarists Those who argue that government can effectively control the performance of an economy mainly by controlling the supply of money.

monetary policies Economic policies that involve control of, and changes in, the supply of money.

municipal governments The government units that administer a city or town.

N

national committee A committee of a political party composed of party chairpersons and party officials from every state.

national convention A gathering of delegates of a single political party from across the country to choose candidates for president and vice president and to adopt a party platform.

national debt The accumulated sum of past government borrowing owed to lenders outside the government.

national sovereignty A political entity's externally recognized right to exercise final authority over its affairs.

necessary and proper clause The last clause in Section 8 of Article I of the Constitution, which gives Congress the means to execute its enumerated powers. This clause is the basis for Congress's implied powers. Also called the *elastic clause.*

New Deal The measures advocated by the Franklin D. Roosevelt administration to alleviate the Depression.

New Jersey Plan Submitted by the head of the New Jersey delegation to the Constitutional Convention, a set of nine resolutions that would have, in effect, preserved the Articles of Confederation by amending rather than replacing them.

newsworthiness The degree to which a news story is important enough to be covered in the mass media.

Nineteenth Amendment The amendment to the Constitution, adopted in 1920, that ensures women of the right to vote.

No Child Left Behind Act of 2001 (NCLB) A reauthorization of the Elementary and Secondary Education Act during the George W. Bush presidency.

nomination Designation as an official candidate of a political party.

non-means-tested benefits Benefits provided by government to all citizens, regardless of income; Medicare and Social Security are examples.

normal distribution A symmetrical bell-shaped distribution (of opinions) centered on a single mode, or most frequent response.

norms An organization's informal, unwritten rules that guide individual behavior.

O

obligation of contracts The obligation of the parties to a contract to carry out its terms.

Office of Management and Budget (OMB) The budgeting arm of the Executive Office; prepares the president's budget.

oligarchy A system of government in which power is concentrated in the hands of a few people.

open election An election that lacks an incumbent.

open primaries Primary elections in which voters need not declare their party affiliation and can choose one party's primary ballot to take into the voting booth.

order Established ways of social behavior. Maintaining order is the oldest purpose of government.

original jurisdiction The authority of a court to hear a case before any other court does.

oversight The process of reviewing the operations of an agency to determine whether it is carrying out policies as Congress intended.

P

parliamentary system A system of government in which the chief executive is the leader whose party holds the most seats in the legislature after an election or whose party forms a major part of the ruling coalition.

participatory democracy A system of government where rank-and-file citizens rule themselves rather than electing representatives to govern on their behalf.

party conferences A meeting to select party leaders and decide committee assignments, held at the beginning of a session of Congress by Republicans or Democrats in each chamber.

party identification A voter's sense of psychological attachment to a party.

party machine A centralized party organization that dominates local politics by controlling elections.

party platform The statement of policies of a national political party.

plea bargain A defendant's admission of guilt in exchange for a less severe punishment.

pluralist model of democracy An interpretation of democracy in which government by the people is taken to mean government by people operating through competing interest groups.

police power The authority of a government to maintain order and safeguard citizens' health, morals, safety, and welfare.

policy entrepreneurs Citizens, members of interest groups, or public officials who champion particular policy ideas.

policy evaluation Analysis of a public policy so as to determine how well it is working.

policy formulation The stage of the policymaking process during which formal proposals are developed and adopted.

political action committee (PAC) An organization that collects campaign contributions from group members and donates them to candidates for political office.

political agenda A list of issues that need government attention.

political equality Equality in political decision making: one vote per person, with all votes counted equally.

political ideology A consistent set of values and beliefs about the proper purpose and scope of government.

political participation Actions of private citizens by which they seek to influence or support government and politics.

political party An organization that sponsors candidates for political office under the organization's name.

political socialization The complex process by which people acquire their political values.

political system A set of interrelated institutions that links people with government.

poll tax A tax of $1 or $2 on every citizen who wished to vote, first instituted in Georgia in 1877. Although it was no burden on most white citizens, it effectively disenfranchised blacks.

poverty level The minimum cash income that will provide for a family's basic needs; calculated using the Consumer Price Index.

precedent A judicial ruling that serves as the basis for the ruling in a subsequent case.

preemption The power of Congress to enact laws by which the national government assumes total or partial responsibility for a state government function.

presidential primary A special primary election used to select delegates to attend the party's national convention, which in turn nominates the presidential candidate.

primary election A preliminary election conducted within a political party to select candidates who will run for public office in a subsequent election.

prior restraint Censorship before publication.

procedural democratic theory A view of democracy as being embodied in a decision-making process that involves universal participation, political equality, majority rule, and responsiveness.

productive capacity The total value of goods and services that can be produced when the economy works at full capacity.

program monitoring Keeping track of government programs; usually done by interest groups.

progressive taxation A system of taxation whereby the rich pay proportionately higher taxes than the poor; used by governments to redistribute wealth and thus promote equality.

progressivism A philosophy of political reform based on the goodness and wisdom of the individual citizen as opposed to special interests and political institutions.

project grants Categorical grants awarded on the basis of competitive applications submitted by prospective recipients to perform a specific task or function.

proportional representation The system by which legislative seats are awarded to a party in proportion to the vote that party wins in an election.

protectionism The notion that women must be protected from life's cruelties; until the 1970s, the basis for laws affecting women's civil rights.

public assistance Government aid to individuals who can demonstrate a need for that aid.

public figures People who assume roles of prominence in society or thrust themselves to the forefront of public controversy.

public goods Benefits and services, such as parks and sanitation, that benefit all citizens but are not likely to be produced voluntarily by individuals.

public opinion The collective attitudes of citizens concerning a given issue or question.

public policy A general plan of action adopted by the government to solve a social problem, counter a threat, or pursue an objective.

R

racial gerrymandering The drawing of a legislative district to maximize the chance that a minority candidate will win election.

racial segregation Separation from society because of race.

racism A belief that human races have distinct characteristics such that one's own race is superior to, and has a right to rule, others.

reapportionment Redistribution of representatives among the states, based on population change. The House is reapportioned after each census.

recall The process for removing an elected official from office. Eighteen states allow recall.

receipts For a government, the amount expected or obtained in taxes and other revenues.

redistributional policies Policies that take government resources, such as tax funds, from one sector of society and transfer them to another.

redistricting The process of redrawing political boundaries to reflect changes in population.

referendum An election on a policy issue.

regulation Government intervention in the workings of a business market to promote some socially desired goal.

regulations Administrative rules that guide the operation of a government program.

regulatory commissions Agencies of the executive branch of government that control or direct some aspect of the economy.

representative democracy A system of government where citizens elect public officials to govern on their behalf.

republic A government without a monarch; a government rooted in the consent of the governed, whose power is exercised by elected representatives responsible to the governed.

republicanism A form of government in which power resides in the people and is exercised by their elected representatives.

responsible party government A set of principles formalizing the ideal role of parties in a majoritarian democracy.

responsiveness A decision-making principle, necessitated by representative government, that implies that elected representatives should do what the majority of people wants.

restraint A requirement prohibiting a state or local government from exercising a certain power.

rights The benefits of government to which every citizen is entitled.

rule making The administrative process that results in the issuance of regulations by government agencies.

rule of four An unwritten rule that requires at least four justices to agree that a case warrants consideration before it is reviewed by the U.S. Supreme Court.

S

school districts The government units that administer elementary and secondary schools and programs.

select committee A temporary congressional committee created for a specific purpose and disbanded after that purpose is fulfilled.

self-interest principle The implication that people choose what benefits them personally.

senatorial courtesy A norm under which a nomination must be acceptable to the home state senator from the president's party.

seniority Years of consecutive service on a particular congressional committee.

separate-but-equal doctrine The concept that providing separate but equivalent facilities for blacks and whites satisfies the equal protection clause of the Fourteenth Amendment.

separation of powers The assignment of lawmaking, law-enforcing, and law-interpreting functions to separate branches of government.

set-aside A purchasing or contracting provision that reserves a certain percentage of funds for minority-owned contractors.

sexism Invidious sex discrimination.

skewed distribution An asymmetrical but generally bell-shaped distribution (of opinions); its mode, or most frequent response, lies off to one side.

social contract theory The belief that the people agree to set up rulers for certain purposes and thus have the right to resist or remove rulers who act against those purposes.

social equality Equality in wealth, education, and status.

social insurance A government-backed guarantee against loss by individuals without regard to need.

Social Security Social insurance that provides economic assistance to persons faced with unemployment, disability, or old age. It is financed by taxes on employers and employees.

Social Security Act The law that provided for Social Security and is the basis of modern American social welfare.

social welfare programs Government programs that provide the minimum living standards necessary for all citizens.

socialism A form of rule in which the central government plays a strong role in regulating existing private industry and directing the economy, although it does allow some private ownership of productive capacity.

socioeconomic status Position in society, based on a combination of education, occupational status, and income.

sociotropic responses Opinions that indicate attitudes about how the country as a whole is doing affect political preferences more strongly than one's own personal circumstance.

soft news General entertainment programming that often includes discussions of political affairs.

solicitor general The third highest official of the U.S. Department of Justice, and the one who represents the national government before the Supreme Court.

sovereignty The quality of being supreme in power or authority.

Speaker of the House The presiding officer of the House of Representatives.

special districts Government units created to perform particular functions, especially when those functions are best performed across jurisdictional boundaries.

split ticket Voting for candidates from different parties for different offices.

stable distribution A distribution (of opinions) that shows little change over time.

stagflation The joint occurrence of slow growth, unemployment, and inflation.

standard socioeconomic model A relationship between socioeconomic status and conventional political involvement: people with higher status and more education are more likely to participate than those with lower status.

standing committee A permanent congressional committee that specializes in a particular policy area.

stare decisis Literally, "let the decision stand"; decision making according to precedent.

states' rights The idea that all rights not specifically conferred on the national government by the U.S. Constitution are reserved to the states.

straight ticket Voting for a single party's candidates for all the offices.

strict scrutiny A standard used by the Supreme Court in deciding whether a law or policy is to be adjudged constitutional. To pass strict scrutiny, the law or policy must be justified by a "compelling governmental interest," must be narrowly tailored, and must be the least restrictive means for achieving that interest.

substantive democratic theory The view that democracy is embodied in the substance of government policies rather than in the policymaking procedure.

suffrage The right to vote. Also called the *franchise.*

Supplemental Nutrition Assistance Program (SNAP) A federal program administered by the states that provides assistance for purchasing food to eligible beneficiaries.

supply-side economics Economic policies aimed at increasing the supply of goods (as opposed to decreasing demand); consists mainly of tax cuts for possible investors and less regulation of business.

supportive behavior Action that expresses allegiance to government and country.

supremacy clause The clause in Article VI of the Constitution that asserts that national laws take precedence over state and local laws when they conflict.

T

tax committees The two committees of Congress responsible for raising the revenue with which to run the government.

television hypothesis The belief that television is to blame for the low level of citizens' knowledge about public affairs.

Temporary Assistance for Needy Families (TANF) A 1996 national act that abolished the longtime welfare policy, Aid for Families with Dependent Children (AFDC). TANF gives the states much more control over welfare policy.

terrorism Premeditated, politically motivated violence perpetrated against noncombatant targets by subnational groups or clandestine agents.

totalitarianism A political philosophy that advocates unlimited power for the government to enable it to control all sectors of society.

trade association An organization that represents firms within a particular industry.

transfer payment A payment by government to an individual, mainly through Social Security or unemployment insurance.

treaty A legal agreement between two or more countries.

trustee A representative who is obligated to consider the views of constituents but is not obligated to vote according to those views if he or she believes they are misguided.

two-party system A political system in which two major political parties compete for control of the government. Candidates from a third party have little chance of winning office.

two-step flow of communication The process in which a few policy elites gather information and then inform their more numerous followers, mobilizing them to apply pressure to government.

U

unconventional participation Relatively uncommon political behavior that challenges or defies established institutions and dominant norms.

universal participation The concept that everyone in a democracy should participate in governmental decision making.

U.S. courts of appeals Courts within the second tier of the three-tiered federal court system, to which decisions of the district courts and federal agencies may be appealed for review.

U.S. district courts Courts within the lowest tier of the three-tiered federal court system; courts where litigation begins.

V

veto The president's disapproval of a bill that has been passed by both houses of Congress. Congress can override a veto with a two-thirds vote in each house.

Virginia Plan A set of proposals for a new government, submitted to the Constitutional Convention of 1787; it included separation of the government into three branches, division of the legislature into two houses, and proportional representation in the legislature.

voter turnout The percentage of eligible citizens who actually vote in a given election.

W

War on Poverty A part of President Lyndon Johnson's Great Society program, intended to eradicate poverty within ten years.

War Powers Resolution An act of Congress that forces that body to decide whether a commitment of troops into a war zone is permissible.

watchdog journalism Journalism that scrutinizes public and business institutions and publicizes perceived misconduct.

welfare state A nation in which the government assumes responsibility for the welfare of its citizens by providing a wide array of public services and redistributing income to reduce social inequality.

Notes

Chapter 1

1. U.S Census Bureau, http://www.census.gov/hhes/www/poverty/data/threshld/thresh64.
2. U.S. Census Bureau, http://www.census.gov/hhes/povmeas/publications/measureofpoverty.pdf.
3. Austin Nichols, "Poverty in the United States," *Urban Institute*, 12 September 2012, http://www.urban.org/UploadedPDF/412653-Poverty-in-the-United-States.pdf.
4. U.S. Census Bureau, http://www.census.gov/hhes/www/income/data/historical/inequality/index.html, Table F-2.
5. Historical data from the U.S. Census on median income is conveniently tabulated at http://www.davemanuel.com/median-household-income.php.
6. 2012 American National Election Time Series Study, undertaken in collaboration by Stanford University and the University of Michigan.
7. There are more elaborate definitions. A recent book defines globalization as "the intensification of cross-national interactions that promote the establishment of trans-national structures and the global integration of cultural, economic, environmental, political, technological and social processes on global, supranational, national, regional and local levels," in Axel Dreher, Noel Gaston, and Pim Martens, *Measuring Globalisation: Gauging Its Consequences* (New York: Springer, 2008), p. 15.
8. Mark Andreas Kayser, "How Domestic Is Domestic Politics? Globalization and Elections," *Annual Review of Political Science* 10 (2007): 341–362.
9. Thomas Biersteker and Cynthia Weber (eds.), *State Sovereignty as Social Construct* (Cambridge: Cambridge University Press, 1996), p. 12. For distinctions among four different types of sovereignty, see Stephen D. Krasner, "Abiding Sovereignty," *International Political Science Review* 22 (July 2001): 229–251.
10. Jess Bravin, "U.S. to Pull Out of World Court on War Crimes," *Wall Street Journal*, 6 May 2002, p. A4.
11. Tom Hundley, "Europe Seeks to Convert U.S. on Death Penalty," Chicago Tribune, 26 June 2000, p. 1; and Salim Muwakkil, "The Capital of Capital Punishment," *Chicago Tribune*, 12 July 1999, p. 18.
12. *Liberalism* constitutes a nebulous doctrine for theorists. Louis Hartz, in his classic *The Liberal Tradition in America* (New York: Harcourt, Brace & World, 1955), says it is an "even vaguer term" than feudalism (pp. 3–4). David G. Smith calls it "too ecumenical and too pluralistic to be called, properly, an ideology" in *The International Encyclopedia of the Social Sciences* (New York: Macmillan and Free Press, 1968), 9:276. More recently, Robert Eccleshall admitted that "in everyday usage," liberalism "often stands for little more than a collection of values and principles which no decent person would reject" but then proceeds to find substance in an "incoherent doctrine." In Political *Ideologies: An Introduction*, 3rd ed. (London: Routledge, 2003), p. 18.
13. Karl Marx and Friedrich Engels, *Critique of the Gotha Programme* (New York: International Publishers, 1938), p. 10. Originally written in 1875 and published in 1891.
14. CNN, "Same Sex Marriage in the United States," http://www.cnn.com/interactive/us/map-same-sex-marriage/index.html.
15. One scholar holds that *freedom* came from northern European languages, and liberty from Latin, and the words originally had opposite meanings. Liberty meant separation and freedom meant connection.

See David Hackett Fischer, *Liberty and Freedom: A Visual History of America's Founding Ideas* (New York: Oxford University Press, 2005), pp. 1–15.
16. For a philosophical analysis, see Robert E. Goodin and Frank Jackson, "Freedom from Fear," *Philosophy and Public Affairs* 35 (2007): 249–265.
17. See the argument in Amy Gutman, *Liberal Equality* (Cambridge: Cambridge University Press, 1980), pp. 9–10.
18. See John H. Schaar, "Equality of Opportunity and Beyond," in *Equality, NOMOS IX*, ed. J. Roland Pennock and John W. Chapman (New York: Atherton Press, 1967), pp. 228–249.
19. Lyndon Johnson, "To Fulfill These Rights," commencement address at Howard University, 4 June 1965, http://www.hpol.org/record.asp?id=54.
20. Jean Jacques Rousseau, *The Social Contract and Discourses*, trans. G. D. H. Cole (New York: Dutton, 1950), p. 5.
21. Andrew Dugan, "More Say Crime Is Serious Problem in U.S. than Locally," Gallup Poll Report, 1 November 2013.
22. Tamara Audi and Gary Fields, "L.A. Is Latest City to See Crime Drop," *Wall Street Journal*, 7 January 2010, p. A8.
23. Milton Friedman, *Capitalism and Freedom* (Chicago: University of Chicago Press, 1962).
24. Joseph Khan, "Anarchism, the Creed That Won't Stay Dead," *New York Times*, 5 August 2000, p. A15.
25. For a similar approach, see Scott Keeter and Gregory A. Smith, "In Search of Ideologues in America," Pew Research Center for the People & the Press, 11 April 2006, http://pewresearch.org/pubs/17/in-search-of-ideologues-in-america.
26. The communitarian category was labeled "populist" in the first four editions of this book. We have relabeled it for two reasons. First, we believe that *communitarian* is more descriptive of the category. Second, we recognize that the term populist has been used increasingly to refer to the political styles of presidential hopefuls as diverse as Pat Buchanan (2000), Ralph Nader (2000, 2004, 2008), and Herman Cain (2012). In this sense, a populist appeals to mass resentment against those in power. Given the debate over what populist really means, we decided to use communitarian, a less familiar term with fewer connotations. See Michael Kazin, *The Populist Persuasion: An American History* (New York: Basic Books, 1995).
27. Keeter and Smith call this grouping "Populist."
28. The communitarian movement was founded by a group of ethicists and social scientists who met in Washington, D.C., in 1990 at the invitation of sociologist Amitai Etzioni and political theorist William Galston to discuss what they viewed as the declining state of morality and values in the United States. Etzioni became the leading spokesperson for the movement. See his *Rights and the Common Good: The Communitarian Perspective* (New York: St. Martin's Press, 1995), pp. iii–iv. The communitarian political movement should be distinguished from communitarian thought in political philosophy, which is associated with theorists such as Alasdair MacIntyre, Michael Sandel, and Charles Taylor, who wrote in the late 1970s and early 1980s. In essence, communitarian theorists criticized liberalism, which stressed freedom and individualism, as excessively individualistic. Their fundamental critique was that liberalism slights the values of community life. See Allen E. Buchanan, "Assessing the

Communitarian Critique of Liberalism," *Ethics* 99 (July 1989): 852–882; and Patrick Neal and David Paris, "Liberalism and the Communitarian Critique: A Guide for the Perplexed," *Canadian Journal of Political Science* 23 (September 1990): 419–439. Communitarian philosophers attacked liberalism over the inviolability of civil liberties. In our framework, such issues involve the trade-off between freedom and order. Communitarian and liberal theorists differ less concerning the trade-off between freedom and equality. See William R. Lund, "Communitarian Politics and the Problem of Equality," *Political Research Quarterly* 46 (September 1993): 577–600. But see also Susan Hekman, "The Embodiment of the Subject: Feminism and the Communitarian Critique of Liberalism," *Journal of Politics* 54 (November 1992): 1098–1119.

29. Etzioni, *Rights and the Common Good*, p. iv; and Etzioni, "Communitarian Solutions/What Communitarians Think," *Journal of State Government* 65 (January–March 1992): 9–11. For a critical review of the communitarian program, see Jeremiah Creedon, "Communitarian Manifesto," *Utne Reader* (July–August 1992): 38–40.

30. Etzioni, "Communitarian Solutions/What Communitarians Think,". 10; and Dana Milbank, "Catch-Word for Bush Ideology; 'Communitarianism' Finds Favor," *Washington Post*, 1 February 2001, p. A1. See also Lester Thurow, "Communitarian vs. Individualistic Capitalism," in Etzioni, *Rights and the Common Good*, pp. 277–282. Note, however, that government's role in dealing with issues of social and economic inequality is far less developed in communitarian writings than is its role in dealing with issues of order. In the same volume, an article by David Osborne, "Beyond Left and Right: A New Political Paradigm" (pp. 283–290), downplays the role of government in guaranteeing entitlements.

31. Researchers who have studied populations in Western and Eastern Europe find that the model fits citizens in Western Europe better than those in Eastern Europe. See Hulda Thorisdottir, John T. Jost, Ido Liviatan, and Patrick E. Shrout, "Psychological Needs and Values Underlying Left-Right Political Orientation: Cross-National Evidence from Eastern and Western Europe," *Public Opinion Quarterly* 71 (Summer 2007): 175–203.

Chapter 2

1. Julia Preston, "Young Immigrants Turn Focus to President," *New York Times*, 24 February 2014.

2. "U.S. Deported Around 369,000 in 2013," *New America Media*, 9 January 2014, http://newamericamedia.org/2014/01/us-deported-around-369000-immigrants-in-2013.php.

3. "Immigration," CNN/ORC Poll, January 31–February 2, 2014, from *PollingReport.com*, http://pollingreport.com/immigration.htm.

4. This estimate is based on ongoing research on comparative political parties by Kenneth Janda.

5. Richard F. Fenno, Jr., *The President's Cabinet* (New York: Vintage, 1959), p. 29.

6. Carole Pateman, "Participatory Democracy Revisited," *Perspectives on Politics* 10 (March 2012): 7–19.

7. Robert A. Dahl, *Democracy and Its Critics* (New Haven, Conn.: Yale University Press, 1989), pp. 13–23.

8. http://www.portlandoregon.gov/oni/.

9. Shaun Bowler, Todd Donovan, and Jeffrey A. Karp, "Enraged or Engaged? Preferences for Direct Citizen Participation in Affluent Democracies," *Political Research Quarterly* 60 (September 2007): 351–361.

10. Jeffrey M. Berry, Kent E. Portney, and Ken Thomson, *The Rebirth of Urban Democracy* (Washington, D.C.: Brookings Institution, 1993), p. 77.

11. Steven Goldsmith, "An Old-Fashioned Mayor on the Forefront of Innovation," *Governing*, 6 September 2012, http://www.governing.com/blogs/bfc/col-boston-mayor-tom-menino-office-new-urban-mechanics.html; and Edward L. Glaeser, "New Urban Mechanics, Keep Tinkering," *Boston Globe*, 9 January 2014.

12. Donald F. Norris and Christopher G. Reddick, "Local E-Government in the United States: Transformation or Incremental Change?" *Public Administration Review* 73 (2012): 165–175.

13. Christopher Wlezien and Stuart N. Soroka, "Inequality in Policy Responsiveness?" in *Who Gets Represented?* eds. Peter K. Ennis and Christopher Wlezien (New York: Russell Sage Foundation, 2011), pp. 285–310.

14. Dietrich Rueschemeyer, "Addressing Inequality," *Journal of Democracy* 15 (October 2004): 76–90.

15. Russell J. Dalton, Doh C. Shin, and Willy Jou, "Popular Conceptions of the Meaning of Democracy" (Irvine: Center for the Study of Democracy, University of California, Irvine, 18 May 2007), http://escholarship.org/uc/item/2j74b860.

16. "Initiative, Referendum, and Recall," National Conference of State Legislatures, http://www.ncsl.org/research/elections-and-campaigns/initiative-referendum-and-recall-overview.aspx.

17. Sabrina Tavernise and Steven Greenhouse, "Ohio Vote on Labor Is Parsed for Omens," *New York Times*, 9 November 2011.

18. Melissa Eddy and Stephen Castle, "Swiss Immigration Vote Raises Alarm Across Europe," *New York Times*, 10 February 2014; and Alexandre Afonso, "Why the Swiss Voted to Cap Immigration," *Washington Post*, 10 February 2014, http://www.washingtonpost.com/blogs/monkey-cage/wp/2014/02/10/why-the-swiss-voted-to-cap-immigration.

19. Gallup Poll, "More Americans Plugged Into Political News," 28 September 2009, http://www.gallup.com/poll/123203/Americans-Plugged-Into-Political-News.aspx.

20. Robert A. Dahl, *Pluralist Democracy in the United States* (Chicago: Rand McNally, 1967), p. 24.

21. Kay Lehman Schlozman, Sidney Verba, and Henry E. Brady, *The Unheavenly Chorus: Unequal Political Voice and the Broken Promise of American Democracy* (Princeton, N.J.: Princeton University Press, 2012).

22. The classic statement on elite theory is C. Wright Mills, *The Power Elite* (New York: Oxford University Press, 1956).

23. Jeffrey A. Winters and Benjamin I. Page, "Oligarchy in the United States?" *Perspectives on Politics* 7 (December 2009): 731–751.

24. Benjamin I. Page, Larry M. Bartels, and Jason Seawright, "Democracy and the Policy Preferences of Wealthy Americans," *Perspectives on Politics* 11 (March 2013): 51–73.

25. Martin Gilens, *Affluence and Influence* (Princeton, N.J.: Princeton University Press, 2012).

26. Powerful arguments on the subtlety of elite domination can be found in Peter Bachrach and Morton S. Baratz, "Two Faces of Power," *American Political Science Review* 56 (December 1962): 947–952; and John Gaventa, *Power and Powerlessness* (Urbana: University of Illinois Press, 1980).

27. Nicholas Confessore, "Financier Plans Big Ad Campaign on Climate Change," *New York Times*, 18 February 2014, http://www.nytimes.com/2014/02/18/us/politics/financier-plans-big-ad-campaign-on-environment.html?hpw&rref=politics.

28. Frank R. Baumgartner, Jeffrey M. Berry, Marie Hojnacki, David C. Kimball, and Beth L. Leech, *Lobbying and Policy Change* (Chicago: University of Chicago Press, 2009).

29. See Larry M. Bartels, *Unequal Democracy* (Princeton, N.J.: Princeton University Press, 2009).

30. Michael Coppedge, John Gerring, et al., "Conceptualizing and Measuring Democracy: A New Approach," *Perspectives on Politics* 9 (June 2011): 247–267.

31. See, for example, David Beetham, Edzia Carvalho, Todd Landman, and Stuart Weir (eds.), *Assessing the Quality of Democracy: A Practical Guide* (Stockholm: International Institute for Democracy and Electoral Assistance, 2008), http://www.idea.int/publications/aqd/index.cfm.

32. *Freedom in the World 2014* (Washington, D.C.: Freedom House, 2014), p. 1, http://www.freedomhouse.org/report/freedom-world-2014/release-booklet.

33. Michael Albertus and Victor Menaldo, "Coercive Capacity and the Prospects for Democratization," *Comparative Politics* 44 (January 2012): 151–169.

34. The classic treatment of the conflict between freedom and order in democratizing countries is Samuel P. Huntington, *Political Order in Changing Societies* (New Haven, Conn.: Yale University Press, 1968).

35. See Henry Teune, "The Consequences of Globalization on Local Democracy: An Assessment" (paper presented at the International Political Science Association, Durban, South Africa, July 2003); *Human Development Report 2002: Deepening Democracy in a Fragmented World* (New York: United Nations, 2002), pp. 51–61; Yi Feng, *Democracy, Governance, and Economic Performance: Theory and Evidence* (Cambridge, Mass.: MIT Press, 2003), pp. 296–299; and Adam Przeworski and Fernando Limongi, "Modernization: Theories and Facts," *World Politics* 49 (January 1997): 155–183.

36. David Chandler, "Democracy Unbound? Non-Linear Politics and the Politicization of Everyday Life," *European Journal of Social Theory* 17 (February 2014): 42–59.

37. Ellen Barry and Betwa Sharma, "After Fleeing Violence, Many Indian Muslims Refuse to Return Home," *New York Times*, 3 January 2014, http://www.nytimes.com/2014/01/04/world/asia/uttar-pradesh-religious-violence.html.

38. Gilens, *Affluence and Influence*; and Schlozman, Verba, and Brady, *The Unheavenly Chorus*.

39. See Nolan McCarty, Keith T. Poole, and Howard Rosenthal, *Polarized America* (Cambridge, Mass.: MIT Press, 2006); and Steven S. Smith, *Party Influence in Congress* (New York: Cambridge University Press, 2007).

40. Joseph Bafumi and Michael C. Herron, "Leapfrog Representation and Extremism: A Study of American Voters and Their Members of Congress," *American Political Science Review* 104 (August 2010): 519–542; and Theda Skocpol and Vanessa Williamson, *The Tea Party and the Remaking of Republican Conservatism* (New York: Oxford University Press, 2012).

41. Jeffrey M. Berry and Sarah Sobieraj, *The Outrage Industry: Political Opinion Media and the New Incivility* (New York: Oxford University Press, 2014).

Chapter 3

1. Introductory speech by President V. Giscard d'Estaing to the Convention on the Future of Europe, 28 February 2002, http://gandalf.aksis.uib.no/brit/EXPORT-EU-Constitution/Export-Document-CONV/CONV-004-02-03-05-EN/ANNEX4ChairmanoftheEuropeanConvention,Mr.html.

2. Günter Burghardt, "The Development of the European Constitution from the U.S. Point of View," in Esther Brimmer (ed.), *The European Union Constitutional Treaty: A Guide for Americans* (Washington, D.C.: Center for Transatlantic Relations, Johns Hopkins University, 2004).

3. Patricia Kowsmann, "New Hurdle for Resolving Euro Crisis: Constitutions," *Wall Street Journal*, 36 September 2013.

4. Stephen Castle, "Europeans Planning for Less Unanimity," *New York Times*, 3 January 2012, p. A4.

5. Samuel Eliot Morison, *Oxford History of the American People* (New York: Oxford University Press, 1965), p. 172.

6. Richard Walsh, *Charleston's Sons of Liberty: A Study of the Artisans, 1763–1789* (Columbia: University of South Carolina Press, 1959).

7. Mary Beth Norton, *Liberty's Daughters* (Boston: Little, Brown, 1980), pp. 155–157.

8. Joseph J. Ellis, *Revolutionary Summer: The Birth of American Independence* (New York: Knopf, 2013). pp. 20–22.

9. Morison, *Oxford History*, p. 204.

10. Ellis, *Revolutionary Summer*, p. 35.

11. David McCullough, *John Adams* (New York: Simon & Schuster, 2001).

12. John Plamentz, *Man and Society*, rev. ed., ed. M. E. Plamentz and Robert Wokler, vol. 1, *From the Middle Ages to Locke* (New York: Logan, 1992), pp. 216–218.

13. Pauline Maier, *American Scripture: Making the Declaration of Independence* (New York: Knopf, 1997), pp. 133–134.

14. Jack N. Rakove (ed.), *The Annotated U.S. Constitution and Declaration of Independence* (Boston: Belknap Press of Harvard University Press, 2009), p. 23.

15. Joseph Ellis, *American Sphinx: The Character of Thomas Jefferson* (New York: Vintage Books, 1998), p. 59.

16. Maya Jasanoff, *Liberty's Exiles* (New York: Knopf, 2011), p. 9.

17. Charles H. Metzger, *Catholics and the American Revolution: A Study in Religious Climate* (Chicago: Loyola University Press, 1962).

18. Extrapolated from U.S. Department of Defense, *Selected Manpower Statistics, FY 1982* (Washington, D.C.: U.S. Government Printing Office, 1983), Table 2-30, p. 130; and U.S. Bureau of the Census, 1985 *Statistical Abstract of the United States* (Washington, D.C.: U.S. Government Printing Office, 1985), Tables 1 and 2, p. 6.

19. Jasanoff, *Liberty's Exiles*, pp. 10–12.

20. McCullough, *John Adams*, pp. 165–385.

21. Joseph T. Keenan, *The Constitution of the United States* (Homewood, Ill.: Dow-Jones-Irwin, 1975).

22. Rakove, *Annotated U.S. Constitution*, p. 30.

23. David P. Szatmary, *Shays' Rebellion: The Making of an Agrarian Insurrection* (Amherst: University of Massachusetts Press, 1980), pp. 82–102.

24. As cited in Morison, *Oxford History*, p. 304.

25. "The Call for the Federal Constitutional Convention, Feb. 21, 1787," in *The Federalist*, ed. Edward M. Earle (New York: Modern Library, 1937), p. 577.

26. Robert H. Jackson, *The Struggle for Judicial Supremacy* (New York: Knopf, 1941), p. 8.

27. David Brian Robertson, *The Original Compromise: What the Constitution's Framers Were Really Thinking* (New York: Oxford University Press, 2013), p.4.

28. John Dickinson of Delaware, as quoted in Morison, *Oxford History*, p. 270.

29. Robertson, *ibid.*

30. Catherine Drinker Bowen, *Miracle at Philadelphia* (Boston: Little, Brown, 1966), p. 122.

31. Forrest McDonald, *Novus Ordo Seclorum: The Intellectual Origins of the Constitution* (Lawrence: University Press of Kansas, 1985), pp. 205–209.

32. It may be overstating the case to refer to this small shift as "a compromise," as there was hardly consensus or general agreement, but that is how historians have characterized it.

33. U.S. Constitution, Article V.

34. Donald S. Lutz, "The Preamble to the Constitution of the United States," *This Constitution* 1 (September 1983): 23–30.

35. Charles O. Jones, "The Separated Presidency—Making It Work in Contemporary Politics," in *The New American Political System*, 2nd ed., ed. Anthony King (Washington, D.C.: American Enterprise Institute, 1990).

36. Gordon S. Wood, *Empire of Liberty* (New York: Oxford, 2009), Chapter 11.

37. Charles A. Beard, *An Economic Interpretation of the Constitution of the United States* (New York: Macmillan, 1913).

38. Leonard W. Levy, *Constitutional Opinions* (New York: Oxford University Press, 1986), p. 101.

39. Robert E. Brown, *Charles Beard and the Constitution* (Princeton, N.J.: Princeton University Press, 1956); Levy, *Constitutional Opinions*, pp. 103–104; Forrest McDonald, *We the People: Economic Origins of the Constitution* (Chicago: University of Chicago Press, 1958).

40. Compare Eugene D. Genovese, *The Political Economy of Slavery: Studies in the Economics and Society of the Slave South* (Middletown, Conn.: Wesleyan University Press, 1989), and Robert William Fogel, *Without Contract or Consent: The Rise and Fall of American Slavery* (New York: Norton, 1989).

41. Robert A. Goldwin, letter to the editor, *Wall Street Journal*, 30 August 1993, p. A11.

42. Bernard Bailyn, *Faces of Revolution: Personalities and Themes in the Struggle for American Independence* (New York: Knopf, 1990), pp. 221–222.

43. Walter Berns, *The First Amendment and the Future of Democracy* (New York: Basic Books, 1976), p. 2.

44. Pauline Maier, *Ratification: The People Debate the Constitution, 1787–1788* (New York: Simon & Schuster, 2010).

45. Herbert J. Storing, ed., *The Complete Anti-Federalist*, 7 vols. (Chicago: University of Chicago Press, 1981).

46. Alexis de Tocqueville, *Democracy in America*, ed. J. P. Mayer and Max Lerner (1835–1839, reprint, New York: Harper & Row, 1966), p. 102.

47. Russell L. Caplan, *Constitutional Brinkmanship: Amending the Constitution by National Convention* (New York: Oxford University Press, 1988), p. 162.

48. Daniel Okrent, *Last Call: The Rise and Fall of Prohibition* (New York: Scribners, 2010), p. 3.

49. Seth Lipsky, *The Citizen's Constitution: An Annotated Guide* (New York: Basic Books, 2009), p. 286.

50. Richard L. Berke, "1789 Amendment Is Ratified but Now the Debate Begins," *New York Times*, 8 May 1992, p. A1.

51. The interpretation debate is fully explored in John H. Garvey and T. Alexander Aleinikoff, *Modern Constitutional Theory: A Reader*, 5th ed. (Minneapolis, Minn.: West Publishing Co., 2004). A classic statement on judicial decision making, composed before he became a member of the U.S. Supreme Court in 1932, is Benjamin N. Cardozo's *The Nature of the Judicial Process* (New Haven, Conn.: Yale University Press, 1921).

52. Jerold L. Waltman, *Political Origins of the U.S. Income Tax* (Jackson: University Press of Mississippi, 1985), p. 10.

Chapter 4

1. "Duncan Pushes Back on Attacks on Common Core Standards," U.S. Department of Education Press Release, 25 June 2013, http://www.ed.gov/news/speeches/duncan-pushes-back-attacks-common-core-standards.

2. "Governor Pence Signs Bill Taking Indiana Out of Common Core," Governor Events Calendar for IN.GOV, 24 March 2014, http://www.in.gov/activecalendar/EventList.aspx?view=EventDetails&eventidn=164408&information_id=197968&type=&syndicate=syndicate.

3. William H. Stewart, *Concepts of Federalism* (Lanham, Md.: University Press of America, 1984).

4. Martha Derthick, *Keeping the Compound Republic: Essays on American Federalism* (Washington, D.C.: Brookings Institution Press, 2001), p. 153.

5. Edward Corwin, "The Passing of Dual Federalism," *University of Virginia Law Review* 36 (1950): 1–24.

6. See Daniel J. Elazar, *The American Partnership* (Chicago: University of Chicago Press, 1962); Morton Grodzins, *The American System* (Chicago: Rand McNally, 1966).

7. James T. Patterson, *The New Deal and the States: Federalism in Transition* (Princeton, N.J.: Princeton University Press, 1969).

8. Lisa Mascaro, "Patriot Act Provisions Extended Just in Time," *Los Angeles Times*, 27 May 2011, http://articles.latimes.com/2011/may/27/nation/la-na-patriot-act-20110527.

9. John Dinan and Shama Gamkhar, "The State of American Federalism 2008–2009: The Presidential Election, the Economic Downturn, and the Consequences for Federalism," *Publius: The Journal of Federalism* 39, no. 3 (2009): 369–407.

10. *McCulloch* v. *Maryland*, 4 Wheat. 316 (1819).

11. *Dred Scott* v. *Sandford*, 19 How. 393, 426 (1857).

12. Jeff Shesol, *Supreme Power: Franklin Roosevelt vs. the Supreme Court* (New York: W.W. Norton, 2010).

13. *United States* v. *Lopez*, 514 U.S. 549 (1995).

14. *Printz* v. *United States*, 521 U.S. 898 (1997).

15. *United States* v. *Morrison*, 120 S. Ct. 1740 (2000).

16. *Atkins* v. *Virginia*, 536 U.S. 304 (2002).

17. *Roper* v. *Simmons*, 343 U.S. 551 (2005).

18. Brian K. Collins and Brian J. Gerber, "Redistributive Policy and Devolution: Is State Administration a Road Block (Grant) to Equitable Access to Federal Funds?" *Journal of Public Administration Research and Theory* 16 (2006): 613–632.

19. Historical Tables, *Budget of the United States Government, FY2012* (Washington, D.C.: U.S. Government Printing Office, 2012), Table 12.1.

20. *National Federation of Independent Business* v. *Sebelius*, 567 U.S. (2012).

21. The Kaiser Family Foundation, "The Role of Medicaid in State Economies and the ACA," *Issue Brief*, November 2013, http://kaiserfamilyfoundation.files.wordpress.com/2013/11/8522-the-role-of-medicaid-in-state-economies-looking-forward-to-the-aca.pdf.

22. Terry Sanford, *Storm over the States* (New York: McGraw-Hill, 1967).

23. David M. Hedge, *Governance and the Changing American States* (Boulder, Colo.: Westview Press, 1998).

24. Frank R. Baumgartner and Bryan D. Jones, *Agendas and Instability in American Politics* (Chicago: University of Chicago Press, 1993).

25. Internet Tax Freedom Act Amendment Act of 2007.

26. Joseph Zimmerman, "Congressional Preemption during the George W. Bush Administration," *Publius* 37 (2007): 432–452

27. Ibid., p. 436.

28. Ibid., p. 432.

29. John Kincaid, "American Federalism: The Third Century," *Annals of the American Academy of Political and Social Science* 509 (1990): 139–152.

30. "Unfunded Federal Mandates," *Congressional Digest* (March 1995): 68.

31. Paul Posner, "The Politics of Coercive Federalism," *Publius: The Journal of Federalism* 37 (2007): 390–412.

32. National Conference of State Legislatures, "State Legislatures Face Unsettled Conditions in 2008," *NCSL News*, 14 December 2007, http://www.ncsl.org/default.aspx?tabid1/416893.

33. Associated Press, "Obama Campaigning for Terry McAuliffe in Virginia," *The Huffington Post*, 3 November 2013, http://www.huffingtonpost.com/2013/11/03/obama-terry-mcauliffe_n_4208306.html.

34. *Shelby County* v. *Holder*, 570 U.S. (2013).

35. U.S. Census Bureau, 2012 *Census of Governments*, https://www.census.gov/govs/cog/.

36. Nancy Burns, *The Formation of American Local Governments: Private Values in Public Institutions* (New York: Oxford University Press, 1994), pp. 11–13; Garrick L. Percival, Mary Currin-Percival, Shaun Bowler, and Henk van der Kolk, "Taxing, Spending, and Voting: Voter Turnout Rates in Statewide Elections in Comparative Perspective," *State and Local Government Review* 39, no. 3 (2007): 131–143.

37. John B. Gilmour, "The Indiana Toll Road Lease as an Intergenerational Cash Transfer," *Public Administration Review* 72, no. 6 (2012): 856–864.

38. CNN, "Sniper Attacks: A Trail of Terror," 2002, http://web.archive.org/web/20031208191803/www.cnn.com/SPECIALS/2002/sniper/.

39. Cynthia J. Bowling and Deil S. Wright, "Public Administration in the Fifty States: A Half-Century Administrative Revolution," *State and Local Government Review* 30, no. 1 (1998) pp. 52–64.

40. For more information from the Council of State Governments, see http://www.csg.org/pubs/capitolideas/july_august_2011/ForeignTrade.aspx.

41. John D. Donahue and Mark H. Moore (eds.), *Ports in a Storm: Public Management in a Turbulent World* (Washington, DC: Brookings, 2012).

42. *U.S. Term Limits* v. *Thornton*, 514 U.S. 779 (1995).

43. Ann L. Griffiths and Karl Nerenberg (eds.), *Handbook of Federal Countries* (Montreal and Kingston, Canada: McGill-Queens University Press, 2005).

44. Information available at the *Forum of Federations*, http://www.forumfed.org/en/federalism/by_country/index.php.

45. David Brooks, "Divided They Stand," *New York Times*, 25 August 2005.

Chapter 5

1. "Same Sex Marriage, State by State," Pew Research Religion and Public Life Project, 6 January 2014, http://features.pewforum.org/same-sex-marriage-state-by-state/; and "Midnight Same-Sex Marriage Ceremonies at Mpls City Hall," Minnesota Public Radio, 1 August 2013, http://minnesota.publicradio.org/display/web/2013/08/01/news/same-sex-marriage-minneapolis-photos.

2. Margaret Canaday, "We Colonials: Sodomy Laws in America," *The Nation*, 22 September 2008; Lydia Saad, "U.S. Acceptance of Gay/Lesbian Relations Is the New Normal," Gallup.com, 14 May 2012; Lydia Saad, "In U.S., 52% Back Law to Legalize Gay Marriage in 50 States," Gallup.com, 29 July 2013; and "Changing Attitudes on *Gay* Marriage," Pew Research Religion and Public Life Project, June 2013, http://features.pewforum.org/same-sex-marriage-attitudes/index.php.

3. Robert Jones, Daniel Cox, and Juhem Navarro-Rivera, "A Shifting Landscape: A Decade of Change in American Attitudes about Same-sex Marriage and LGBT Issues," Public Religion Research Institute, 26 February 2014, http://publicreligion.org/research/2014/02/2014-lgbt-survey/.

4. Amy Becker, "Determinants of Public Support for Same-Sex Marriage: Generational Cohorts, Social Contact, and Shifting Attitudes," *International Journal of Public Opinion Research* 24, no. 4 (2012): 524–533.

5. "Gay Marriage: Key Data Points from Pew Research," Pew Research Center, 11 June 2013.

6. Ashby Jones, "Judge Rules Colorado Bakery Discriminated Against Gay Couple," *Wall Street Journal*, 6 December 2013.

7. Jones, Cox, and Navarro-Rivera, "A Shifting Landscape."

8. "The Supreme Court Ruling on the Defense of Marriage Act: What It Means," Lambda Legal, http://www.lambdalegal.org/publications/after-doma-summary.

9. Jones, Cox, and Navarro-Rivera, "A Shifting Landscape."

10. E. Wayne Carp, "If Pollsters Had Been Around during the American Revolution" (letter to the editor), *New York Times*, 17 July 1993, p. 10.

11. See, for example, "Tea Party Image Turns More Negative," Pew Research Center for People and the Press, 16 October, 2013.

12. Sidney Verba, "The Citizen as Respondent: Sample Surveys and American Democracy," *American Political Science Review* 90 (March 1996): 3. For a historical discussion of the search for the "average" citizen, see Sarah E. Igo, *The Averaged American: Surveys, Citizens, and the Making of a Mass Public* (Cambridge, Mass.: Harvard University Press, 2007).

13. Robert Shapiro, "Public Opinion and American Democracy," *Public Opinion Quarterly* 75, no. 5 (2011): 982–1017.

14. Martin Gilens, *Affluence and Influence: Economic Inequality and Political Power in America* (Princeton, NJ: Princeton University Press, 2012).

15. "Kaiser Health Tracking Poll: January 2014," Kaiser Family Foundation, 30 January 2014, http://kff.org/health-reform/poll-finding/kaiser-health-tracking-poll-january-2014/.

16. For a detailed discussion of the challenges of achieving a representative random sample, see D. Sunshine Hillygus, "The Practice of Survey Research: Changes and Challenges," in *New Directions in Public Opinion* ed. Adam J. Berinsky (New York: Routledge, 2012), pp. 32–51.

17. Peter Grier, "'Obamacare' vs. 'Affordable Care Act': Does the Name Matter?" *Christian Science Monitor*, 29 November 2013.

18. See, for example, Christopher Ellis and James Stimson, *Ideology in America* (New York: Cambridge University Press, 2012).

19. Steven A. Peterson, *Political Behavior: Patterns in Everyday Life* (Newbury Park, Calif.: Sage, 1990), pp. 28–29. See also David O. Sears and Christia Brown, "Childhood and Adult Political Development," in *Oxford Handbook of Political Psychology*, 2nd ed., ed. David O. Sears, Leonie Huddy, and Jack Levy (New York: Oxford University Press, 2013).

20. Stephen E. Frantzich, *Political Parties in the Technological Age* (New York: Longman, 1989); and M. K. Jennings, L. Stoker, & J. Bowers, J., "Politics across Generations: Family Transmission Reexamined," *Journal of Politics* 71 (2009): 782–799.

21. Cliff Zukin et al., *A New Engagement: Political Participation, Civic Life, and the Changing American Citizen* (New York: Oxford University Press, 2006), pp. 142–144.

22. Janie S. Steckenrider and Neal E. Cutler, "Aging and Adult Political Socialization: The Importance of Roles and Transitions," in *Political Learning in Adulthood: A Sourcebook of Theory and Research*, ed. Roberta S. Sigel (Chicago: University of Chicago Press, 1989), pp. 56–88.

23. See, for example, Christopher Ellison, Heeju Shin, and David Leal, "The Contact Hypothesis and Attitudes Toward Latinos in the United States," *Social Science Quarterly* 92, no. 4 (2011): 938–958.

24. Diana Mutz and Jeffery Mondak. "The Workplace as a Context for Cross-Cutting Political Discourse." *Journal of Politics* 68, no. 1 (2006): 140–155; and David Jones, "The Polarizing Effect of a Partisan Workplace," *PS: Political Science & Politics* 46, no. 1 (2013): 67–73.

25. The American National Election Studies are jointly done by Stanford University and the University of Michigan, with funding by the National Science Foundation. Data reported here are from the ANES face-to-face interviews only. Responses are weighted using weights provided by the ANES. The 1 percent of respondents who did not answer this question was removed from subsequent discussions of this question.

26. Other scholars have analyzed opinion on abortion using six questions from the General Social Survey. See R. Michael Alvarez and John Brehm, "American Ambivalence toward Abortion Policy," *American Journal of Political Science* 39 (1995): 1055–1082; and Elizabeth Adell Cook, Ted G. Jelen, and Clyde Wilcox, *Between Two Absolutes: Public Opinion and the Politics of Abortion* (Boulder, Colo.: Westview Press, 1992). Percentages reported here do not sum to 100 due to rounding.

27. Although some people view the politics of abortion as "single-issue" politics, the issue has broader political significance. In their book on the subject, Cook, Jelen, and Wilcox say, "Although embryonic life is one important value in the abortion debate, it is not the only value at stake." They contend that the politics is tied to alternative sexual relationships and traditional roles of women in the home, which are "social order" issues. *See Between Two Absolutes*, pp. 8–9.

28. Russell J. Dalton, *The Good Citizen* (Washington, D.C.: Congressional Quarterly Press, 2008), Chap. 5.

29. Ibid., p. 50.

30. See the exchange between Ronald Inglehart and Scott C. Flanagan, "Value Change in Industrial Societies," *American Political Science Review* 81 (December 1987): 1289–1319.

31. For analysis of regional trends over time, see Larry Bartels, "What's the Matter with *What's the Matter with Kansas*," *Quarterly Journal of Political Science* 1 (2006): 201–226.

32. Nathan Glazer, "The Structure of Ethnicity," *Public Opinion* 7 (October–November 1984): 4.

33. According to CNN Exit Polls, available at http://www.cnn.com/election/2012/results/race/president.

34. "U.S. Census Bureau Projections Show a Slower-Growing, Older, More Diverse Nation Half a Century from Now," 12 December 2012, http://www.census.gov/newsroom/releases/archives/population/cb12-243.html.

35. Ibid. Note that the terms "Latino" and "Hispanic" are used interchangeably.

36. Anna Brown and Mark Hugo Lopez, "Mapping the Latino Population, by State, County, and City," Pew Hispanic Center, 29 August 2013.

37. CNN Exit Polls.

38. "The Asian Population: 2010," and "The American Indian and Alaska Native Population: 2010," U.S. Census Bureau.

39. "U.S. Census Bureau Projections Show a Slower-Growing, Older, More Diverse Nation Half a Century From Now."

40. CNN Exit Polls.

41. See, for example, "Obama Draws Nearly 90% of Native Vote," 31 October 2008, https://nativevotewa.wordpress.com/2008/10/31/obama-draws-nearly-90-of-native-vote/.

42. Michael Dawson, Black Visions: *The Roots of Contemporary African American Political Ideologies* (Chicago: University of Chicago Press, 2001); John Garcia, *Latino Politics in America* (Lanham, Md.: Rowman & Littlefield, 2003); Thomas Kim, *The Racial Logic of Politics: Asian Americans and Party Competition* (Philadelphia: Temple University Press, 2007); Pei-te Lien, M. Margaret Conway, and Janelle Wong, *The Politics of Asian Americans* (New York: Routledge, 2004); and Katherine Tate, *Black Faces in the Mirror: African Americans and Their Representatives in the U.S. Congress* (Princeton, N.J.: Princeton University Press, 2003).

43. Glazer, "Structure of Ethnicity," p. 5; and Dennis Chong and Dukhong Kim, "The Experiences and Effects of Economic Status among Racial and Ethnic Minorities," *American Political Science Review* 100 (August 2006): 335–351.

44. For a thorough analysis of political views broken down by race and ethnicity, see Gary Segura and Shaun Bowler, *The Future is Ours: Minority Politics, Political Behavior, and the Multiracial Era of American Politics* (Washington, D.C. Congressional Quarterly Press, 2012).

45. "Nones on the Rise," Pew Research Religion and Public Life Project, 9 October 2012.

46. "The Future of the Global Muslim Population," Pew Research Religion and Public Life Project, January 2011.

47. See David C. Leege and Lyman A. Kellstedt (eds.), *Rediscovering the Religious Factor in American Politics* (Armonk, N.Y.: M. E. Sharpe, 1993); and "Many Americans Uneasy with Mix of Religion and Politics," Pew Forum on Religion and Public Life, 24 August 2006, http://pewforum.org/docs/DocID=153.

48. "A Portrait of Muslim Americans," Pew Research Center for People and the Press, 30 August 2011, http://www.people-press.org/2011/08/30/a-portrait-of-muslim-americans/.

49. For more on religion and public opinion, see The Public Religion Research Institute, http://publicreligion.org/.

50. See, for example, "The Gender Gap: Three Decades Old, as Wide as Ever," Pew Research Center for People and the Press, 29 March 2012.

51. CNN Exit Polls.

52. Angus Campbell, Philip E. Converse, Warren E. Miller, and Donald E. Stokes, *The American Voter* (New York: Wiley, 1960); Michael Lewis-Beck, et al., *The American Voter Revisited* (Ann Arbor: University of Michigan Press, 2008); Marjorie Connelly, "A 'Conservative' Is (Fill in the Blank)," *New York Times*, 3 November 1996, sec. 4, p. 5; and Robert Erikson and Kent Tedin, *American Public Opinion*, 8th ed. (Boston: Pearson Longman, 2011).

53. American National Election Study, 2012.

54. However, citizens can have ideologically consistent attitudes toward candidates and perceptions about domestic issues without thinking about politics in explicitly liberal and conservative terms. See William Jacoby, "The Structure of Ideological Thinking in the American Electorate," *American Journal of Political Science* 39:2 (1995): 314–335.

55. Ellis and Stimson, *Ideology in America*.

56. James L. Gibson, "Measuring Political Tolerance and General Support for Pro-Civil Liberties Policies: Notes and Cautions," *Public Opinion Quarterly* 77(S1) (2013): 45–68.

57. Herbert Asher, *Presidential Elections and American Politics*, 5th ed. (Upper Saddle River, N.J.: International Thomson Publishing Group, 1997).

58. Milton Rokeach also proposed a two-dimensional model of political ideology grounded in the terminal values of freedom and equality. See *The Nature of Human Values* (New York: Free Press, 1973), especially Chap. 6. Rokeach found that positive and negative references to the two values permeate the writings of socialists, communists, fascists, and conservatives and clearly differentiate the four bodies of writing from one another (pp. 173–174). However, Rokeach built his two dimensional model around only the values of freedom and equality; he did not deal with the question of freedom versus order.

59. In our framework, opposition to abortion is classified as a communitarian position. However, the communitarian movement led by Amitai Etzioni adopted no position on abortion (personal communication from Vanessa Hoffman by e-mail, in reply to a query of 5 February 1996).

60. William S. Maddox and Stuart A. Lilie, *Beyond Liberal and Conservative: Reassessing the Political Spectrum* (Washington, D.C.: Cato Institute, 1984), p. 68. From 1993 to 1996, the Gallup Organization, in conjunction with CNN and *USA Today*, asked national samples two questions: (1) whether individuals or government should solve our country's problems and (2) whether the government should promote traditional values. Gallup constructed a similar ideological typology from responses to these questions and found a similar distribution of the population into four groups. See Gallup's "Final Top Line" for 12–15 January 1996, pp. 30–31. For another typology that goes beyond liberal and conservative, see "Beyond Red vs. Blue: The Political Typology," Pew Research Center for People and the Press, 4 May 2011.

61. The same conclusion was reached in a major study of British voting behavior. See Hilde T. Himmelweit et al., *How Voters Decide* (New York: Academic Press, 1981), pp. 138–141. See also Aaron Wildavsky, "Choosing Preferences by Constructing Institutions: A Cultural Theory of Preference Formation," *American Political Science Review* 81 (March 1987): 13; and Stanley Feldman and Christopher Johnston, "Understanding Political Ideology" (paper presented at the annual meeting of the American Political Science Association, Toronto, Canada, 2009).

62. Michael X. Delli Carpini and Scott Keeter, *What Americans Know about Politics and Why It Matters* (New Haven, Conn.: Yale University Press, 1996).

63. Ibid., p. 269. For more on this topic, see Scott L. Althaus, *Collective Preferences in Democratic Politics: Opinion Surveys and the Will of the People* (New York: Cambridge University Press, 2003).

64. "What the Public Knows—In Words, Pictures, Maps and Graphs," Pew Research Center for People and the Press, 5 September 2013.

65. Markus Prior and Arthur Lupia, "Money, Time, and Political Knowledge: Distinguishing Quick Recall and Political Learning Skills," *American Journal of Political Science* 52, no. 1 (2008): 169–183.

66. Eben Harrell, "How We See Immigration—and Why We're Wrong," *Time*, 3 February 2011, http://content.time.com/time/world/article/0,8599,2045932,00.html#ixzz1DedBU3i5/.

67. "The Impact of Media Stereotypes on Opinions and Attitudes Towards Latinos," National Hispanic Media Coalition and Latino Decisions, September 2012, http://www.latinodecisions.com/blog/2012/09/18/how-media-stereotypes-about-latinos-fuel-negative-attitudes-towards-latinos/; and Mark Koba, "$2 Trillion Underground Economy May Be Recovery's Savior," CNBC.com, 24 April 2013.

68. Benjamin I. Page and Robert Y. Shapiro, *The Rational Public* (Chicago: University of Chicago Press, 1992).

69. Brendan Nyhan and Jason Reifler, "When Corrections Fail: The Persistence of Political Misperceptions," *Political Behavior* 32, no. 2 (2010): 303–330. Also see Brendan Nyhan, Jason Reifler, and Peter A. Ubel, "The Hazards of Correcting Myths about Health Care Reform," *Medical Care* 51, no. 2 (2013): 127–132; and Brenan Nyhan, Jason Reifler, Sean Richey, and Gary Freed, "Effective Messages in Vaccine Promotion: A Randomized Trial," *Pediatrics*, forthcoming.

70. Self-interest is often posed as the major alternative to choice based on general orientations such as political ideology and moral values. A significant literature exists on the limitations of self-interest in explaining political life. See Jane J. Mansbridge (ed.), *Beyond Self-Interest* (Chicago: University of Chicago Press, 1990).

71. Richard D. Dixon et al., "Self-Interest and Public Opinion toward Smoking Policies," *Public Opinion Quarterly* 55 (1991): 241–254; David O. Sears and Jack Citrin, *Tax Revolt: Something for Nothing in California* (Cambridge, Mass.: Harvard University Press, 1985); and Robin Wolpert and James Gimpel, "Self-Interest, Symbiotic Politics, and Public Attitudes toward Gun Control," *Political Behavior* 20 (1998): 241–262.

72. "Public Opinion Runs Against Syrian Airstrikes," Pew Research Center for People and the Press, 3 September 2013.

73. For two classic investigations of self-interest and sociotropic responses, see Donald R. Kinder and D. Roderick Kiewiet, "Sociotropic Politics: The American Case," *British Journal of Political Science* 11, no. 2 (1981): 129–161; David O. Sears, et al. "Self-interest vs. Symbolic Politics in Policy Attitudes and Presidential Voting," *American Political Science Review* 74, no. 3 (1980): 670–684.

74. Henry Brady and Paul Sniderman, "Attitude Attribution: A Group Basis for Political Reasoning," *American Political Science Review* 79 (1985): 1061–1078; Samuel Popkin, *The Reasoning Voter*, 2nd ed. (Chicago: University of Chicago Press, 1994); and P. Sniderman, R. Brody, and P. Tetlock, *Reasoning and Choice* (Cambridge: Cambridge University Press, 1991). Psychologists have tended to emphasize the distorting effects of heuristics. See D. Kahneman, P. Slovic, and A. Tversky (eds.), *Judgment under Uncertainty: Heuristics and Biases* (Cambridge: Cambridge University Press, 1982); and R. Nisbett and L. Ross, *Human Inference: Strategies and Shortcomings of Social Judgment* (Englewood Cliffs, N.J.: Prentice-Hall, 1980).

75. Wendy M. Rahn, "The Role of Partisan Stereotypes in Information Processing about Political Candidates," *American Journal of Political Science* (1993): 472–496.

76. See, for example, LaFleur Stephens and Andrea Benjamin, "I Get So Emotional: Race, Gender, and Candidate Evaluations," paper presented at the Annual Meeting of the American Political Science Association, Chicago, Ill. 2013.

77. Stephen P. Nicholson, "Polarizing Cues," *American Journal of Political Science* 56, no. 1 (2012): 52–66.

78. On framing, see Dennis Chong and James N. Druckman, "Framing Public Opinion in Competitive Democracies," *American Political Science Review* 101 (November 2007): 637–655; James N. Druckman, "Political Preference Formation: Competition, Deliberation, and the (Ir)relevance of Framing Effects," *American Political Science Review* 98 (November 2004): 671–686; and Michael W. Wagner, "The Utility of Staying on Message: Competing Partisan Frames and Public Awareness of Elite Differences on Political Issues," *The Forum* 5, no. 3 (2007), http://www.be-press.com/forum/vol15/iss3/art8.

79. Benjamin I. Page, Robert Y. Shapiro, and Glenn R. Dempsey, "What Moves Public Opinion?" *American Political Science Review* 81 (March 1987): 23–43.

80. Lawrence R. Jacobs and Robert Y. Shapiro, *Politicians Don't Pander* (Chicago: University of Chicago Press, 2000).

Chapter 6

1. Timothy Clary, "Social Media a News Source and Tool During Superstorm Sandy," cbsnews.com, 30 October 2012.

2. Rachel Tepper, "Cory Booker, Newark Mayor, Gets Hundreds of Free Hot Pockets for the City," *Huffington Post*, 8 November 2012.

3. Anjali Mullany, "Sore-backed Newark Mayor Cory Booker Uses Twitter to Rescue Citizens, Dig Out Cars, Deliver Diapers," *New York Daily News*, 28 December 2010; and Nick Carbone, "Cory Booker Reminds Us All He's Still a Superhero," Time.com, 13 April 2012.

4. Alex S. Jones, *Losing the News*, http://losingthenews.com/.

5. Matthew Yglesias, "American Journalism Has Never Been Healthier Than It Is Today," Slate.com, 19 March 2013.

6. Richard Davis, *Typing Politics: The Role of Blogs in American Politics* (New York: Oxford University Press, 2009); Tom Price, "Future of Journalism," *CQ Researcher* 19, No. 12 (27 March 2009): 273–295; and Pew Project for Excellence in Journalism, http://www.stateofthe media.org/2009/narrative_online_audience.php?media=58:cat=2.

7. Gil Kaufman, "Lady Gaga Visits with White House to Discuss Bullying," 7 December 2011, http://www.mtv.com.

8. "Michael Moore's *Sicko*: Broad Reach and Impact Even without the Popcorn?" Press release from Kaiser Family Foundation, 27 August 2007, http://www.kff.org/kaiserpolls/pomr082707nr.cfm.

9. See Markus Prior, *Post-Broadcast Democracy: How Media Choice Increases Inequality in Political Involvement and Polarizes Elections* (New York, NY: Cambridge University Press, 2007); and Bill Kovach and Tom Rosenstiel, *Blur: How to Know What's True in the Age of Information Overload* (New York: Bloomsbury, 2010).

10. S. N. D. North, *The Newspaper and Periodical Press* (Washington, D.C.: U.S. Government Printing Office, 1884), p. 27. This source provides much of the information reported here about newspapers and magazines before 1880. Also see Jonathan Ladd, *Why Americans Hate the Media and How It Matters* (Princeton, N.J.: Princeton University Press, 2011).

11. Editor & Publisher, *International Year Book, 2009* (New York: Editor & Publisher, 2009), p. xi.

12. Harold W. Stanley and Richard G. Niemi (eds.), *Vital Statistics on American Politics, 2011–2012* (Washington, D.C.: CQ Press, 2012), p. 160. For a brief history of the newspaper business, see Paul E. Steiger, "Read All about It: How Newspapers Got into Such a Fix and Where They Go from Here," *Wall Street Journal*, 29–30 December 2007, p. 1.

13. See Ladd, *Why Americans Hate the Media and How It Matters*, pp. 48–52.

14. "The Top 25 Consumer Magazines for June 2013," Alliance for Audited Media, http://www.auditedmedia.com/.

15. "Yet Another Newspaper Paywall Goes Bust," www.techdirt.com, 14 August 2013.

16. On framing in the media, see Stephen D. Reese, Oscar H. Gandy, Jr., and August E. Grant (eds.), *Framing Public Life: Perspectives on Media and Our Understanding of the Social World* (Mahwah, N.J.: Erlbaum, 2001). More generally on how leaders mediate public deliberation on issues, see Doris A. Graber, *Media Power in Politics*, 7th ed. (Washington, D.C.: CQ Press, 2005).

17. Federal Communications Commission, http://hraunfoss.fcc.gov/edocs_public/attachmatch/DOC-315231A1.pdf.

18. See radio statistics at *The State of the News Media 2013*, http://www.stateofthenewsmedia.org.

19. Ibid.; and Jeffrey M. Berry and Sarah Sobieraj, *The Outrage Industry: Political Opinion Media and the New Incivility* (Oxford University Press, 2014).

20. Berry and Sobieraj, *The Outrage Industry*; David Barker and Kathleen Knight, "Political Talk Radio and Public Opinion," *Public Opinion Quarterly* 64 (Summer 2000): 149–170; and David C. Barker, *Rushed to Judgment: Talk Radio, Persuasion, and American Political Behavior* (New York: Columbia University Press, 2003).

21. Dana R. Ulloth, Peter L. Klinge, and Sandra Eells, *Mass Media: Past, Present, Future* (St. Paul, Minn.: West, 1983), p. 278.

22. "TV Basics," Television Bureau of Advertising, http://www.tvb.org/media/file/TV_Basics.pdf; and "Frequently Asked Questions," Corporation for Public Broadcasting, http://www.cpb.org/aboutpb/faq/stations.html.

23. Douglas Ahers, "News Consumption and the New Electronic Media," *Harvard International Journal of Press/Politics* 11 (Winter 2006): 29–52; Bill Carter, "CNN Last in TV News on Cable," *New York Times*, 27 October 2009, http://www.nytimes.com/2009/10/27/business/media/27rating.html?emc=etal; Prior, *Post-Broadcast Democracy*; Matthew Levendusky, *How Partisan Media Polarize America* (Chicago: University of Chicago Press, 2013); and Kevin Arcenaux and Martin Johnson, *Changing Minds or Changing Channels? Partisan News in an Age of Choice* (Chicago: University of Chicago Press, 2013).

24. "January 2014 Web Server Survey," Netcraft.com; International Telecommunication Union, http://www.itu.int/en/ITU-D/Statistics/Pages/stat/default.aspx.

25. All data reported here come from the Pew Internet and American Life Project, http://www.pewinternet.org.

26. Richard Davis, *Typing Politics* (New York: Oxford University Press, 2009); Technorati State of the Blogosphere 2008, http://technorati.com/blogging/feature/state-of-the-blogosphere-2008; and "What Internet Users Do Online," Pew Internet & American Life Project, Trend Data, http://www.pewinternet.org/Static-Pages/Trend-Data-%28Adults%29.aspx.

27. Rick Gladstone, "Anti-American Protests Flare Beyond the Mideast," *New York Times*, 14 September 2012.

28. Katharine Q. Seelye, "Take That, Mr. Newsman!" *New York Times*, 1 January 2006, p. C1; and David Coursey, "You Be the Judge: Are Bloggers Journalists?" forbes.com, 2 January 2012.

29. Matthew Hindman, *The Myth of Digital Democracy* (Princeton, N.J.: Princeton University Press, 2009); and Diana Mutz and Lori Young, "Communication and Public Opinion," *Public Opinion Quarterly* 75 (December 2011): 1018–1044.

30. Henry Farrell, "Why Glenn Greenwald's New Media Venture Is a Big Deal," *Washington Post*, 17 October 2013.

31. Note that in 2010, Yahoo! News began offering some original news reporting in addition to its usual aggregation.

32. Jennifer Lai, "'Big Yellow Duck,' 'May 35th,' and Other Words You Can't Use On China's Twitter Today," Slate.com, 4 June 2013.

33. "Frequently Asked Questions," Corporation for Public Broadcasting, http://www.cpb.org/aboutpb/faq/stations.html; Total number of stations found at, Federal Communications Commission, http://transition.fcc.gov/Daily_Releases/Daily_Business/2014/db0108/DOC-325039A1.pdf.

34. Doris A. Graber, *Mass Media and American Politics*, 8th ed. (Washington, D.C.: CQ Press, 2010), pp. 84–87. See also W. Lance Bennett, *News: The Politics of Illusion*, 3rd ed. (White Plains, N.Y.: Longman, 1996), Chap. 2.

35. John H. McManus, *Market-Driven Journalism: Let the Citizen Beware?* (Thousand Oaks, Calif.: Sage, 1994), p. 85.

36. "In Changing News Landscape, Even Television is Vulnerable," Report by Pew Research Center for People and the Press, 27 September 2012.

37. "The Changing TV News Landscape," *The State of the News Media 2013*, stateofthemedia.org.

38. David D. Kurplus, "Bucking a Trend in Local Television News," Journalism 4 (2003): 77–94.

39. Bill Carter and Brian Stelter, "In NBC Universal Bid, Comcast Seeks an Empire," *New York Times*, 1 October 2009, http://www.nytimes.com/2009/10/02/business/media/02nbc.html.

40. "Network: By the Numbers," *State of the News Media 2013*.

41. Thomas E. Patterson, *Doing Well and Doing Good: How Soft News and Critical Journalism Are Shrinking the News Audience and Weakening Democracy—and What News Outlets Can Do about It* (Cambridge, Mass.: Harvard University, Joan Shorenstein Center for Press, Politics, and Public Policy, 2000), pp. 2–5.

42. "Our Company," www.gannett.com.

43. Johanna Dunaway, "Media Ownership and Story Tone in Campaign News," *American Politics Research* 41, No. 1 (2013): 24–53.

44. Price, "Future of Journalism;' and' Amy Mitchell, et al., "Nonprofit Journalism: A Growing but Fragile Part of the U.S. News System," Pew Research Journalism Project, www.journalism.org, 10 June 2013.

45. "Who Owns What," *Columbia Journalism Review*, http://www.cjr.org/resources/index.php.

46. Graber, *Mass Media and American Politics*, pp. 41–43.

47. Matthew Rose and Joe Flint, "Behind Media-Ownership Fight, an Old Power Struggle Is Raging," *Wall Street Journal*, 15 October 2003, p. 1. In 2003 the Federal Communications Commission (FCC) voted to increase the percentage share of the market to 45 percent. In 2007, the FCC ruled that no company can control more than 30 percent of the cable television market and relaxed newspaper-broadcast cross-ownership rules in the nation's twenty largest media markets. See Stephen Labaton, "F.C.C. Reshapes Rules Limiting Media Industry," *New York Times*, 19 December 2007, p. A1.

48. Jennifer Lee, "On Minot, N.D., Radio, a Single Corporate Voice," *New York Times*, 31 March 2003, p. C7.

49. For a clear summary of very complex developments, see Robert B. Horowitz, "Communications Regulations in Protecting the Public Interest," in *The Institutions of American Democracy: The Press*, ed. Geneva Overholser and Kathleen Hall Jamieson (New York: Oxford University Press, 2005), pp. 284–302.

50. Graber, *Mass Media and American Politics*, p. 42.

51. Graber, *Mass Media and American Politics*, p. 342.

52. Jared Sandberg, "Federal Judges Block Censorship on the Internet," *Wall Street Journal*, 13 June 1996, p. B1.

53. Robert Entman, *Democracy without Citizens: Media and the Decay of American Politics* (New York: Oxford University Press, 1989), pp. 103–108; and John Leland, "Why the Right Rules the Radio Waves," *New York Times*, 8 December 2003, sec. 4, p. 7.

54. Wes Allison, "Are Democrats Really Trying to Hush Rush?" *St. Petersburg Times*, 20 February 2009, p. 1A.

55. See Prior, *Post-Broadcast Democracy*; and Jason Gainous and Kevin Wagner, *Rebooting American Politics: The Internet Revolution* (Lanham, Md.: Rowman and Littlefield, 2011). For a discussion of the prevalence and possible consequence of incivility among fragmented media sources, see Berry and Sobieraj, *The Outrage Industry*.

56. For an alternative view of the functions of the media, see Graber, *Mass Media and American Politics*, pp. 5–11.

57. Harold W. Stanley and Richard G. Niemi (eds.), *Vital Statistics on American Politics, 2011–2012* (Washington, D.C.: CQ Press, 2012), p. 161.

58. For a view from the point of view of a reporter who covered Washington for over sixty years, see Helen Thomas, *Watch-dogs of Democracy? The Waning Washington Press Corps and How It Has Failed the Public* (New York: Scribner, 2006).

59. For a discussion of the Bush years, see Scott McClellan, *What Happened: Inside the Bush White House and Washington's Culture of Deception* (New York: Public Affairs Books, 2008). For a discussion of Obama, see Adriel Bettelheim, "Meeting the Press Less Than Half Way," *CO Weekly Online*, 20 July 2009, pp. 1700–1701, http://library.cqpress.com/cqweekly/weeklyreport1 11-000003170492.

60. Patrick Sellers, *Cycles of Spin: Strategic Communication in the U.S. Congress* (New York: Cambridge University Press: 2010), p. 198.

61. Warren Weaver, "C-SPAN on the Hill: 10 Years of Gavel to Gavel," *New York Times*, 28 March 1989, p. 10; and Francis X. Clines, "C-SPAN Inventor Offers More Politics Up Close," *New York Times*, 31 March 1996, p. 11.

62. ActBlue, "Alan Grayson," http://www.actblue.com/entity/ fundraisers/18665.

63. Dan Eggen and T.W. Farnam, "Michelle Bachmann, Others, Raise Millions for Political Campaigns with 'Money Blurts'," *Washington Post*, 19 June 2011.

64. Jon Garfunkel, "The New Gatekeepers Part 1: Changing the Guard," Civilities: Media Structures Research, 4 April 2005, http://civilities.net/TheNewGatekeepers-Changing.

65. Gainous and Wagner, *Rebooting American Politics*.

66. "Press Going Too Easy on Bush," *The State of the News Media 2007*, http://www.stateofthemedia.org.

67. Graber, *Mass Media and American Politics*, p. 259. For weekly content analysis of news topics, see the Project for Excellence in Journalism's "News Coverage Index," http://www.journalism.org.

68. Stephen J. Farnsworth and S. Robert Lichter, "The Nightly News Nightmare Revisited: Network Television's Coverage of the 2004 Presidential Election,"(paper presented at the annual meeting of the Washington, D.C. American Political Science Association, 2005; "Contest Lacks Content," *Media Tenor* 1 (2005): 12–15; Cristina Alsina, Philip John Davies, and Bruce Gronbeck, "Preference Poll Stories in the Last 2 Weeks of Campaign 2000," *American Behavioral Scientist* 44, No. 12 (2001): 2288–2305; C. Anthony Broh, "Horse Race Journalism: Reporting the Polls in the 1976 Presidential Election," *Public Opinion Quarterly* 44 (1980): 514–529; and David Paletz, Jonathan Short, Helen Baker, Barbara Cookman Campbell, Richard Cooper, and Rochelle Oeslander, "Polls in the Media: Content, Credibility, and Consequences," *Public Opinion Quarterly* 44 (1980): 495–513.

69. "Low Marks for the 2012 Election," Pew Research Center for People and the Press, 15 November 2012.

70. Amber Boydstun, *Making the News: Politics, the Media, and Agenda Setting* (Chicago: University of Chicago Press, 2013).

71. "Amid Criticism, Support for Media's Watchdog Role Stands Out," Pew Research Center for People and the Press, 8 August 2013; *State of the Media 2013*; and "Demographics of Internet Users," Pew Internet and American Life Project, April 2013 survey, http://www.pewinternet.org.

72. "What the Public Knows—In Words, Pictures, Maps, and Graphs," Pew Research Center for People and the Press, 5 September 2013.

73. Jeffrey Jones, "Gallup Quizzes Americans on Knowledge of World Leaders," 20 February 2006, Gallup News Service, http://www.gallup.com.

74. W. Russell Neuman, Marion R. Just, and Ann N. Crigler, *Common Knowledge: News and the Construction of Political Meaning* (Chicago: University of Chicago Press, 1992), p. 10. See also Debra Gersh Hernandez, "Profile of the News Consumer," *Editor & Publisher*, 18 January 1997, pp. 6, 7. For a more optimistic assessment of television's instructional value, see Doris A. Graber, *Processing Politics: Learning from Television in the Internet Age* (Chicago: University of Chicago Press, 2001), esp. pp. 120–128. Another negative note is sounded by Alan B. Krueger, "Economic Scene," *New York Times*, 1 April 2004, p. C2.

75. James N. Druckman, "Media Matter: How Newspapers and Television News Cover Campaigns and Influence Voters," *Political Communication* 22 (October–December 2005): 463–481. For a complementary study finding that television news has little effect on campaign learning, see Stephen C. Craig, James G. Kane, and Jason Gainous, "Issue-Related Learning in a Gubernatorial Campaign: A Case Study," *Political Communication* 22 (October–December 2005): 483–503.

76. Diana Mutz, "Effects of 'In-Your-Face' Television Discourse on Perceptions of a Legitimate Opposition," *American Political Science Review* 101 (November 2007): 621–635.

77. James Avery, "Videomalaise or Virtuous Circle? The Influence of the News Media on Political Trust," *International Journal of Press/Politics* 14, No. 4 (2009): 410–433.

78. Jennifer Jerit, "Understanding the Knowledge Gap: The Role of Experts and Journalists," *The Journal of Politics* 71, No. 2 (2009): 444.

79. Jody Baumgartner and Jonathan Morris, "The Daily Show Effect: Candidate Evaluations, Efficacy, and American Youth," *American Politics Research* 34 (2006): 341–367; Michael Parkin, "Taking Late Night Comedy Seriously," *Political Research Quarterly* 63 (2010): 3–15; Xiaoxia Cao, "Hearing It from Jon Stewart," *International Journal of Public Opinion Research* 22 (2010): 26–46; Matthew A. Baum, "Sex, Lies, and War: How Soft News Brings Foreign Policy to the Inattentive Public," *American Political Science Review* 96 (2002): 91–110; and Matthew A. Baum and Angela S. Jamison, "The Oprah Effect: How Soft News Helps Inattentive Citizens Vote Consistently," *Journal of Politics* 68 (2006): 946–959.

80. Mutz and Young, "Communication and Public Opinion."

81. Lydia Saad, "Obama's Approval Bump Hasn't Transferred to 2012 Prospects," http://www.gallup.com, 11 May 2011, accessed on 6 January 2012.

82. Maxwell McCombs, "The Agenda-Setting Function of the Press," in Overholser and Jamieson, *Institutions of American Democracy*, pp. 156–168.

83. Danilo Yanich, "Kids, Crime, and Local TV News," report of the Local TV News Media Project, January (Newark: University of Delaware, 2005). See also Jeremy H. Lipschultz and Michael L. Hilt, *Crime and Local Television News: Dramatic, Breaking, and Live from the Scene* (Mahwah, N.J.: Erlbaum, 2002).

84. See data on fear of crime at the General Social Survey, http://www3.norc.org/GSS+Website/.

85. Leger, Donna, "Violent Crime Rises for Second Consecutive Year," *USA Today*, 24 October 2013.

86. Lawrie Mifflin, "Crime Falls, but Not on TV," *New York Times*, 6 July 1997, sec. 4, p. 4.

87. John Tierney, "Talk Shows Prove Key to White House," *New York Times*, 21 October 2002, p. A13.

88. Samuel Kernell, *Going Public: New Strategies of Presidential Leadership*, 4th ed. (Washington D.C.: CQ Press, 2006); and Anne-Marie Adams, "President Obama Visits Hartford—Urges Audience to Let Congress Hear Strong Voice on Gun Control," *The Hartford Guardian*, 9 April 2013.

89. Doris Graber reviews some studies of socially undesirable effects on children and adults in *Processing Politics*, pp. 91–95, and in *Mass Media and American Politics*.

90. Moreover, much of what children see is advertisements. See "Study: Almost 20% of Kid TV Is Ad-Related," *Chicago Tribune*, 22 April 1991, p. 11. See also Stephen Seplow and Jonathan Storm, "Reviews Mixed on Television's Effect on Children," *St. Paul Pioneer Press*, 28 December 1997, p. 9A; Nell Minow, "Standards for TV Language Rapidly Going Down the Tube," *Chicago Tribune*, 7 October 2003, sec. 5, p. 2; and "Generation M2," Report by the Kaiser Family Foundation, January 2010, http://www.kff.org/entmedia/upload/8010.pdf.

91. Douglas Kellner, *Television and the Crisis of Democracy* (Boulder, Colo.: Westview Press, 1990), p. 17.

92. James Fallows, *Breaking the News: How the Media Undermine American Democracy* (New York: Pantheon Books, 1996). Also see Paul Gronke and Timothy Cook, "Disdaining the Media," *Political Communication* 24 (July 2007): 259–281.

93. Ladd, *Why Americans Hate the Media and How It Matters*.

94. See Bernard Goldberg, *Bias: A CBS Insider Exposes How the Media Distort the News* (Washington, D.C.: Regnery Publishing, 2002); and Ann Coulter, *Slander: Liberal Lies about the American Right* (New York: Crown, 2002).

95. See Eric Alterman, *What Liberal Media? The Truth about Bias and the News* (New York: Basic Books, 2003); and Al Franken, *Lies and the Liars Who Tell Them … a Fair and Balanced Look at the Right* (New York: Penguin, 2003).

96. Pew Research Center of the People and the Press, "Financial Woes Now Overshadow All Other Concerns for Journalists," 17 March 2008, http://people-press.org/reports/pdf/403.pdf.

97. Farnsworth and Lichter, "The Nightly News Nightmare Revisited," p. 31.

98. Berry and Sobieraj, *The Outrage Industry*; and "Audio: By the Numbers," *The State of the News Media 2013*, http://stateofthemedia.org.

99. *The People, the Press, and Their Leaders* (Washington, D.C.: Times-Mirror Center for the People and the Press, 1995). See also Pew Research Center, "Self Censorship: How Often and Why," a survey of nearly three hundred journalists and news executives in February–March 2000, released 30 April 2000.

100. Harold W. Stanley and Richard G. Niemi, *Vital Statistics on American Politics, 2013–2014* (Washington, D.C.: CQ Press, 2013).

101. Maura Clancey and Michael J. Robinson, "General Election Coverage: Part I," *Public Opinion* 7 (December–January 1985): 54. Also see Pew Research Center, "Striking the Balance, Audience Interests, Business Pressures and Journalists' Values," 30 March 1999, http://people-press.org/reports/display.php3?ReportK>=67.

102. "Winning the Media Campaign 2012", Pew Research Center Project for Excellence in Journalism, 2 November 2012.

103. Bob Kemper, "Bush: No Iraqi Link to Sept. 11," *Chicago Tribune*, 18 September 2003, pp. 1–6.

104. Steven Kull and others, "Misperceptions, the Media, and the Iraq War," Program on International Policy Attitudes (PIPA), 2 October 2003, http://www.pipa.org.

105. Valentino Larcinese, Ricardo Puglisi, and James Snyder, Jr, "Partisan Bias in Economic News: Evidence on the Agenda-Setting Behavior of U.S. Newspapers," *Journal of Public Economics* 95 (2011): 1178–1189.

106. See Bill Kovach and Tom Rosentstiel, *Blur: How to Know What's True in the Age of Information Overload*.

107. W. Lance Bennett and William Serrin, "The Watchdog Role," in Overholser and Jamieson, *Institutions of American Democracy*, pp. 169–188.

108. "Amid Criticism, Support for Media's Watchdog Role Stands Out," Pew Research Center for People and the Press, 8 August 2013.

109. For a historical account of efforts to determine voters' preferences before modern polling, see Tom W. Smith, "The First Straw? A Study of the Origin of Election Polls," *Public Opinion Polling* 54 (Spring 1990): 21–36. See also Susan Herbst, *Numbered Voices: How Opinion Polling Has Shaped American Politics* (Chicago: University of Chicago Press, 1993), Chap. 4.

110. See New York Times Polls at http://topics.nytimes.com/top/reference/timestopics/subjects/n/newyorktimes-poll-watch/index.html.

111. Robert Shapiro, "Public Opinion and American Democracy," *Public Opinion Quarterly* 75 (2011): 982–1017. But for a critique of the class bias inherent in government responsiveness to polls, see Martin Gilens, *Affluence and Influence: Economic Inequality and Political Power in America* (Princeton, NJ: Princeton University Press, 2012).

112. Jose Antonio Vargas, "My Life as an Undocumented Immigrant," *New York Times Magazine*, 22 June 2011.

113. William Schneider and I. A. Lewis, "Views on the News," *Public Opinion* 8 (August–September 1985): 6–11, 58–59. For similar findings from a 1994 study, see Times-Mirror Center for the People and the Press, "Mixed Message about Press Freedom on Both Sides of the Atlantic," press release, 16 March 1994, p. 65. See also Thomas E. Patterson, "News Decisions: Journalists as Partisan Actors" (paper presented at the annual meeting of the American Political Science Association, 1996), p. 21.

114. Pew Research Center for the People and the Press, News Interest Final Topline, 1–5 February 2006, http://peoplepress.org/reports/display.php3?ReportID=270.

115. Barton Gellman, Aaron Blake, and Greg Miller, "Edward Snowden Comes Forward as Source of NSA Leaks," *Washington Post*, 9 June 2013.

Chapter 7

1. M. Margaret Conway, *Political Participation in the United States*, 3rd ed. (Washington, D.C.: CQ Press, 2000), p. 3.

2. Michael Lapsky, "Protest as a Political Resource," *American Political Science Review* 62 (December 1968): 1145.

3. U.S. Department of State, "Patterns of Global Terrorism 2001" (Washington, D.C.: U.S. Department of State, May 2002), p. 17. The definition is contained in Title 22 of the U.S. Code, Section 2656f(d). On the problem of defining terrorism, see Walter Laquer, *No End to War: Terrorism in the 21st Century* (New York: Continuum International, 2003), esp. the appendix.

4. Lou Nichel and Dan Herbeck, *American Terrorist: Timothy McVeigh and the Oklahoma City Bombing* (New York: HarperCollins, 2001), pp. 350–354.

5. William E. Schmidt, "Selma Marchers Mark 1965 Clash," *New York Times*, 4 March 1985.

6. Frances Fox Piven, *Challenging Authority: How Ordinary People Change America* (Lanham, Md.: Rowman & Littlefield, 2006).

7. See Sidney Verba and Norman H. Nie, *Participation in America: Political Democracy and Social Equality* (New York: Harper & Row, 1972), p. 3.

8. 2005-2008 World Values Survey. The World Values Survey Association, based in Stockholm, conducts representative surveys in nations across the world. See http://www.worldvaluessurvey.org.

9. Jonathan D. Casper, *Politics of Civil Liberties* (New York: Harper & Row, 1972), p. 90.

10. U.S. Census Bureau, 2010 *Statistical Abstract*, http://www.census.gov/compendia/statab/cats/elections/elected_public_official scharacteristics.html.

11. International Social Survey Programme, 2004 Citizenship Survey.

12. Elaine B. Sharp, "Citizen Demand Making in the Urban Context," *American Journal of Political Science* 28 (November 1984): 654–670, esp. pp. 654, 665.

13. Verba and Nie, *Participation in America*, p. 67; and Sharp, "Citizen Demand Making," p. 660.

14. See Joel B. Grossman et al., "Dimensions of Institutional Participation: Who Uses the Courts and How?" *Journal of Politics* 44 (February 1982): 86–114; and Frances Kahn Zemans, "Legal Mobilization: The Neglected Role of the Law in the Political System," *American Political Science Review* 77 (September 1983): 690–703.

15. *Brown* v. *Board of Education*, 347 U.S. 483 (1954).

16. "Capital One Settles Litigation over Card Disputes," http://www.dailyherald.com/story/?id=345003.

17. .gov Reform Task Force, "State of the Federal Web Report," 16 December 2011, http://www.usa.gov/webreform/state-of-the-web.pdf.

18. The *Federal Register* is available via the Federal Digital System, http://www.gpo.gov/fdsys/.

19. http://www.opensecrets.org.

20. http://www.followthemoney.org.

21. http://www.ombwatch.org and http://truthinaccounting.org.

22. See Michael P. MacDonald and Samuel L. Popkin, "The Myth of the Vanishing Voter," *American Political Science Review* 95 (December 2001): 963–974. Traditionally, turnout had been computed by dividing the number of voters by the voting-age population (VAP), which included noncitizens and ineligible felons. Recent research excludes these groups, computing the *eligible* voting-age population, or VEP. Using VEP in estimating voter turnout has revised the U.S. turnout rates upward by three to five points in elections since 1980. See http://elections.gmu.edu for the comparison. For a study of felon disenfranchisement, see Jeff Manza and Christopher Uggen, *Locked Out: Felon Disenfranchisement and American Democracy* (New York: Oxford University Press, 2006).

23. Max Kaase and Alan Marsh, "Political Action: A Theoretical Perspective," in *Political Action: Mass Participation in Five Western Democracies*, ed. Samuel H. Barnes and Max Kaase (Beverly Hills, Calif.: Sage, 1979), p. 168.

24. *Smith* v. *Allwright*, 321 U.S. 649 (1944).

25. *Harper* v. *Virginia State Board of Elections*, 383 U.S. 663 (1966).

26. Everett Carll Ladd, *The American Polity* (New York: Norton, 1985), p. 392.

27. Gorton Carruth et al. (eds.), *The Encyclopedia of American Facts and Dates* (New York: Crowell, 1979), p. 330. For an eye-opening account of women's contributions to politics before gaining the vote, see Robert J. Dinkin, *Before Equal Suffrage: Women in Partisan Politics from Colonial Times to 1920* (Westport, Conn.: Greenwood Press, 1995).

28. Jodie T. Allen, "Reluctant Suffragettes: When Women Questioned Their Right to Vote," Pew Research Center, 18 March 2009, http://pewresearch.org/pubs/1156/women-reluctant-voters-after-suffrage-19th-amendment.

29. Ivor Crewe, "Electoral Participation," in *Democracy at the Polls: A Comparative Study of Competitive National Elections*, ed. David Butler, Howard R. Penniman, and Austin Ranney (Washington, D.C.: American Enterprise Institute, 1981), pp. 219–223.

30. International IDEA, "Frequently Asked Questions," http://www.idea.int/vt/faq.cfm#9.%20Which%20is%20the%20minimum%20voting%20age?

31. For an early history, see Thomas Goebel, *A Government by the People: Direct Democracy in America, 1890–1940* (Chapel Hill: University of North Carolina Press, 2007).

32. Initiative and Referendum Institute, "Ballotwatch," November 2012, http://www.iandrinstitute.org/BW%202012-3%20Election%20results%20v1.pdf.

33. Initiative and Referendum Institute, "Ballotwatch," December 2013, http://www.iandrinstitute.org/BW%202013-1%20Election%20results.pdf.

34. David S. Broder, *Democracy Derailed: Initiative Campaigns and the Power of Money* (New York: Harcourt, 2000); and David S. Broder, "A Snake in the Grass Roots," *Washington Post*, 26 March 2000, pp. B1, B2.

35. One could also select special bodies of citizens to decide policies. One scholar proposes creating large "citizens assemblies" consisting of randomly selected citizens statistically representative of the population to decide very critical issues. See James H. Snider, "Using Citizens Assemblies to Reform the Process of Democratic Reform," Joan Shorenstein Center on the Press, Politics and Public Policy, Spring 2008.

36. Caroline J. Tolbert, Ramona S. McNeal, and Daniel A. Smith, "Enhancing Civic Engagement: The Effect of Direct Democracy on Political Participation and Knowledge," *State Politics and Policy Quarterly* 3 (Spring 2003): 23–41. For a more critical look at initiatives as undermining representative government, see Bruce E. Cain and Kenneth P. Miller, "The Populist Legacy: Initiatives and the Undermining of Representative Government," in *Dangerous Democracy? The Battle over Ballot Initiatives in America*, ed. Larry J. Sabato, Howard R. Ernst, and Bruce A. Larson (Lanham, Md.: Rowman & Littlefield, 2001), pp. 33–62. For the role of interest groups in ballot issue campaigns, see Robert M. Alexander, *Rolling the Dice with State Initiatives* (Westport, Conn.: Praeger, 2002).

37. See http://www.isolon.org/ and http://www.brookings.edu/opinions/2011/0628_social_media_west.aspx.

38. Mark E. Warren and Hilary Pearse (eds.), *Designing Deliberative Democracy: The British Columbia Citizens' Assembly* (New York: Cambridge University Press, 2008).

39. Data on the elected state officials come from *The Book of the States 2013* (Lexington, Ky.: Council of State Governments, 2013). Estimates of the number of elected school board members come from *Chicago Tribune*, 10 March 1985.

40. Crewe, "Electoral Participation," p. 232. A rich literature has grown to explain turnout across nations. See Pippa Norris, *Democratic Phoenix: Reinventing Political Activism* (Cambridge: Cambridge University Press, 2002), Chap. 3; and Mark N. Franklin, "The Dynamics of Electoral Participation," in *Comparing Democracies 2: New Challenges in the Study of Elections and Voting*, ed. Lawrence LeDuc, Richard G. Niemi, and Pippa Norris (London: Sage, 2002), pp. 148–168.

41. Verba and Nie, *Participation in America*, p. 13.

42. Russell J. Dalton, *Citizen Policies*, 3rd ed. (New York: Seven Bridges, 2002), pp. 67–68. For the argument that greater economic inequality leads to greater political inequality, see Frederick Solt, "Economic Inequality and Democratic Political Engagement," *American Journal of Political Science* 52 (January 2008): 48–60.

43. Russell J. Dalton, The *Good Citizen: How a Younger Generation Is Reshaping American Politics* (Washington, D.C.: Congressional Quarterly Press, 2008).

44. Cliff Zukin et al., *A New Engagement?* (New York: Oxford University Press, 2006), pp. 188–191.

45. For a concise summary of the effect of age on voting turnout, see William H. Flanigan and Nancy H. Zingale, *Political Behavior of the American Electorate*, 11th ed. (Washington, D.C.: CQ Press, 2005).

46. Ibid., pp. 46–47.

47. M. Margaret Conway, Gertrude A. Steuernagel, and David W. Ahern, *Women and Political Participation: Cultural Change in the Political Arena* (Washington, D.C.: CQ Press, 1997), pp. 79–80.

48. Ronald B. Rapoport, "The Sex Gap in Political Persuading: Where the 'Structuring Principle' Works," *American Journal of Political Science* 25 (February 1981): 32–48. Perhaps surprisingly, research fails to show any relationship between a wife's role in her marriage and her political activity. See Nancy Burns, Kay Lehman Schlozman, and Sidney Verba, "The Public Consequences of Private Inequality: Family Life and Citizen Participation," *American Political Science Review* 91 (June 1997): 373–389.

49. Bruce C. Straits, "The Social Context of Voter Turnout," *Public Opinion Quarterly* 54 (Spring 1990): 64–73.

50. Sidney Verba, Kay Lehman Scholzman, and Henry E. Brady, *Voice and Equality: Civic Voluntarism in American Politics* (Cambridge, Mass.: Harvard University Press, 1995), p. 433.

51. Stephen J. Dubner and Steven D. Levitt, "Why Vote?" *New York Times Magazine*, 6 November 2005, pp. 30–31. The classic formulation of the rational choice theory of turnout is Anthony Downs, *An Economic Theory of Democracy* (New York: Harper and Row, 1957). For an empirical test of economic models, see David Levine and Thomas Palfry, "The Paradox of Voter Participation? A Laboratory Study," *American Political Science Review* 101 (February 2007): 143–158.

52. Associated Press, "Voter Turnout Tops Since 1968," *St. Paul Pioneer Press*, 14 December 2008, p. A4

53. Stephen D. Shaffer, "A Multivariate Explanation of Decreasing Turnout in Presidential Elections, 1960–1976," *American Journal of Political Science* 25 (February 1981): 68–95; and Paul R. Abramson and John H. Aldrich, "The Decline of Electoral Participation in America," *American Political Science Review* 76 (September 1981): 603–620. However, one scholar argues that this research suffers because it looks only at voters and nonvoters in a single election. When the focus shifts to people who vote sometimes but not at other times, the models do not fit so well. See M. Margaret Conway and John E. Hughes, "Political Mobilization and Patterns of Voter Turnout" (paper presented at the annual meeting of the American Political Science Association, Washington, D.C., September 1993).

54. See Jack Doppelt and Ellen Shearer, *America's No-Shows: Non-voters* (Washington, D.C.: Medill School of Journalism, 2001); Thomas E. Patterson, The Vanishing Voter (New York: Vintage Books, 2003); and Deborah J. Brooks and John Geer, "Beyond Negativity: The Effects of Incivility on the Electorate," *American Journal of Political Science* 51 (January 2007): 1–16.

55. Some scholars argue that Americans generally have become disengaged from social organizations (not just political parties), becoming more likely to act "alone" than to participate in group activities. See Robert D. Putnam, *Bowling Alone: The Collapse and Revival of American Community* (New York: Simon & Schuster, 2000).

56. See Eric Pultzer, "Becoming a Habitual Voter: Inertia, Resources, and Growth in Young Adulthood," *American Political Science Review* (March 2002): 41–56; Alan S. Gerber, Donald P. Green, and Ron

Shachar, "Voting May Be Habit-Forming: Evidence from a Randomized Field Experiment," *American Journal of Political Science* (July 2003): 540–550; and David Dreyer Lassen, "The Effect of Information on Voter Turnout: Evidence from a Natural Experiment," *American Journal of Political Science* 49 (January 2005): 103–111. For the argument that turnout may be genetic, see Charles Q. Choi, "The Genetics of Politics," *Scientific American*, November 2007.

57. Center for Information and Research on Civil Learning and Engagement (CIRCLE) at the University of Maryland School of Public Policy, "The 2004 Youth Vote," http://www.civicyouth.org.

58. For the latest analysis of voting trends in the United States, see the research done by Michael McDonald, http://elections.gmu.edu/voter_turnout.htm.

59. Visit the Why Tuesday? website at http://www.whytuesday.org.

60. "High Turnout with Iowa's Election Day Registration Law," http://www.866ourvote.org/newsroom/news?id=0191.

61. Ruth Goldway, "The Election Is in the Mail," *New York Times*, 6 December 2006; and Randal C. Archibold, "Mail-in Voters Become the Latest Prize," *New York Times*, 14 January 2008.

62. "Hawaii's Internet Vote Is 1st in Nation," *St. Paul Pioneer Press*, 24 May 2009, p. 5A

63. Recent research finds that "party contact is clearly a statistically and substantively important factor in predicting and explaining political behavior." See Peter W. Wielhouwer and Brad Lockerbie, "Party Contacting and Political Participation, 1952–1990" (paper presented at the annual meeting of the American Political Science Association, Chicago, 1992), p. 14 Of course, parties strategically target the groups that they want to see vote in elections. See Peter W. Wielhouwer, "Strategic Canvassing by Political Parties, 1952–1990," *American Review of Politics* 16 (Fall 1995): 213–238.

64. Steven J. Rosenstone and John Mark Hansen, *Mobilization, Participation, and Democracy in America* (New York: Macmillan, 1993), p. 213.

65. For the differences between national and local elections, see J. Eric Oliver and Shang E. Ha, "Vote Choice in Suburban Elections," *American Political Science Review* 101 (August 2007): 393–408; and Brad T. Gomez, Thomas G. Hansford, and George A. Krause, "The Republicans Should Pray for Rain: Weather, Turnout, and Voting in U.S. Presidential Elections," *Journal of Politics* 69 (August 2007): 649–663.

66. See Robert A. Jackson, "Voter Mobilization in the 1986 Midterm Election," *Journal of Politics* 55 (November 1993): 1081–1099; Kim Quaile Hill and Jan E. Leighley, "Political Parties and Class Mobilization in Contemporary United States Elections," *American Journal of Political Science* 40 (August 1996): 787–804; and Janine Parry et al., "Mobilizing the Seldom Voter: Campaign Contact and Effects in High Profile Elections," *Political Behavior* 30 (March 2008): 97–113.

67. Aaron Smith, "Civic Engagement Online: Politics as Usual," Pew Internet & American Life Project, 1 September 2009, http://pewresearch.org/pubs/1328/online-political-civic-engagement-activity.

68. Nonprofit Voter Engagement Network, "America Goes to the Polls: A Report on Voter Turnout in the 2006 Election," http://www.nonprofitvote.org.

69. Richard Niemi and Michael Hanmer, "Voter Registration and Turnout among College Students" (paper presented at the annual meeting of the American Political Science Association, 2006). Students at Northwestern University in 2008 were more likely to register and vote absentee if they came from a "swing" state. See Kim Castle, Janice Levy, and Michael Peshkin, "Local and Absentee Voter Registration Drives on a College Campus," CIRCLE Working Paper 66, October 2009.

70. Crewe, "Electoral Participation," p. 262.

71. For research showing that economic inequality depresses political engagement of the citizenry, see Frederick Solt, "Economic Inequality and Democratic Political Engagement," *American Journal of Political Science* 52 (2008): 48–60.

72. Barnes and Kaase, *Political Action*, p. 532.

73. Eric Lichtblau, "F.B.I. Watched Activist Groups, New Files Show," *New York Times*, 20 December 2005, p. 1

74. 1971 *Congressional Quarterly Almanac* (Washington, D.C.: CQ Press, 1972), p. 475.

75. Benjamin Ginsberg, *The Consequences of Consent: Elections, Citizen Control, and Popular Acquiescence* (Reading, Mass.: Addison-Wesley, 1982), p. 13.

76. Ibid., pp. 13–14.

77. Ibid., pp. 6–7.

78. Some people have argued that the decline in voter turnout during the 1980s served to increase the class bias in the electorate because people of lower socioeconomic status stayed home. But later research has concluded that "class bias has not increased since 1964." Jan E. Leighley and Jonathan Nagler, "Socioeconomic Class Bias in Turnout, 1964–1988: The Voters Remain the Same," *American Political Science Review* 86 (September 1992): 734 Nevertheless, Rosenstone and Hansen, in *Mobilization, Participation, and Democracy in America*, say, "The economic inequalities in political participation that prevail in the United States today are as large as the racial disparities in political participation that prevailed in the 1950s. America's leaders today face few incentives to attend to the needs of the disadvantaged" (p. 248).

79. "My paramount object in this struggle *is* to save the Union, and is *not* either to save or to destroy slavery." From Abraham Lincoln's August 22, 1862, letter to Horace Greeley, at http://www.abrahamlincolnonline.org/lincoln/speeches/greeley.htm.

Chapter 8

1. Comment by Judy Woodruff on the PBS *News Hour*, 12 October 2011, http://www.pbs.org/newshour/rundown/this-weeks-republican-presidential-candidate/.

2. The American National Election 2012 Time Series Study, http://www.electionstudies.org.

3. Gallup Poll 3–6, October 2013. N=1,028 adults nationwide.

4. See, for example, Peter Mair, "Comparing Party Systems," in *Comparing Democracies 2: New Challenges in the Study of Elections and Voting*, ed. Lawrence LeDuc, Richard G. Niemi, and Pippa Norris (London: Sage, 2002), pp. 88–107.

5. E. E. Schattschneider, *Party Government* (New York: Holt, 1942).

6. See Lyn Carson and Brian Martin, *Random Selection in Politics* (Westport, Conn.: Praeger, 1999). They say: "The assumption behind random selection in politics is that just about anyone who wishes to be involved in decision making is capable of making a useful contribution, and that the fairest way to ensure that everyone has such an opportunity is to give them an equal chance to be involved" (p.4).

7. See James M. Snyder, Jr., and Michael M. Ting, "An Informational Rationale for Political Parties," *American Journal of Political Science* 46 (January 2002): 90–110. They formalize the argument that political parties acquire "brand names" that help voters make sense of politics.

8. Edmund Burke, *Thoughts on the Cause of the Present Discontents* (1770).

9. Anthony Downs, *An Economic Theory of Democracy* (New York: HarperCollins, 1957), p. 25.

10. John H. Aldrich, *Why Parties? The Origin and Transformation of Political Parties in America* (Chicago: University of Chicago Press, 1995), p. 296.

11. See John Kenneth White and Daniel M. Shea (eds.), *New Party Politics: From Jefferson and Hamilton to the Information Age* (Boston: Bedford/St. Martin's, 2000), for essays on the place of political parties in American history.

12. See Jerome M. Clubb, William H. Flanigan, and Nancy H. Zingale, *Partisan Realignment: Voters, Parties, and Government in American History* (Beverly Hills, Calif.:: Sage, 1980), p. 163. Once central to the analysis of American politics, the concept of critical elections has been discounted by some scholars in recent years. See Larry M. Bartels,

"Electoral Continuity and Change," *Electoral Studies* 17 (September 1998): 301–326; and David R. Mayhew, *Electoral Realignments: A Critique of an American Genre* (New Haven, Conn.: Yale University Press, 2002). However, the concept has been defended by other scholars. See Peter F. Nardulli, "The Concept of a Critical Realignment, Electoral Behavior, and Political Change," *American Political Science Review* 89 (March 1995): 10–22; and Norman Schofield, Gary Miller, and Andrew Martin, "Critical Elections and Political Realignments in the USA: 1860–2000," *Political Studies* 51 (2003): 217–240.

13. See Gerald M. Pomper, "Classification of Presidential Elections," *Journal of Politics* 29 (August 1967): 535–566. See also Walter Dean Burnham, *Critical Elections and the Mainsprings of American Politics* (New York: Norton, 1970). Decades later, an update of Gerald Pomper's analysis of presidential elections through 1996 determined that 1960, 1964, and 1968 all had realigning characteristics. See Jonathan Knuckley, "Classification of Presidential Elections: An Update," *Polity* 31 (Summer 1999): 639–653.

14. See Ronald Brownstein, "For GOP, a Southern Exposure," *National Journal Online*, http://www.nationaljournal.com/njonline/no_20090523_3656.php?.

15. In "Realignment in Presidential Politics: South and North?" (paper presented at the Citadel Symposium on Southern Politics, 4–5 March 2004), William Crotty argues that a political realignment definitely occurred in the South around 1968 that affected presidential politics and national voting behavior.

16. Earl Black and Merle Black, *The Rise of Southern Republicans* (Cambridge, Mass.: Harvard University Press, 2002), pp. 2–3.

17. Seth C. McKeen, "Rural Voters and the Polarization of American Presidential Elections," *PS: Political Science and Politics* 41 (January 2008): 101–108.

18. Jeffrey M. Stonecash, *Political Parties Matter: Realignment and the Return of Partisan Voting* (Boulder, Colo.: Lynne Rienner, 2006), pp. 129–130.

19. The discussion that follows draws heavily on Austin Ranney and Willmoore Kendall, *Democracy and the American Party System* (New York: Harcourt, Brace, 1956), Chapter 18, Chapter 19. For later analyses of multiparty politics in America, see Steven J. Rosenstone, Roy L. Behr, and Edward H. Lazarus, *Third Parties in America: Citizen Response to Major Party Failure*, 2nd ed. (Princeton, N.J.: Princeton University Press, 1996); and John F. Bibby and L. Sandy Maisel, *Two Parties—or More?* (Boulder, Colo.: Westview Press, 1998).

20. J. David Gillespie, *Politics at the Periphery: Third Parties in a Two-Party America* (Columbia: University of South Carolina Press, 1993). Surveys of public attitudes toward minor parties are reported in Christian Coller, "Trends: Third Parties and the Two-Party System," *Public Opinion Quarterly* 60 (Fall 1996): 431–449. For a spirited defense of having a strong third party in American politics, see Theodore J. Lowi, "Toward a More Responsible Three-Party System: Deregulating American Democracy," in *The State of the Parties*, 4th ed., ed. John C. Green and Rick Farmer (Lanham, Md.: Rowman & Littlefield, 2003), pp. 354–377. For an analysis of third-party presidential campaigns in 2008, see Brian J. Brox, "Running Nowhere: Third Party Presidential Campaigns in 2008" (paper presented at the annual meeting of the Midwest Political Science Association, Chicago, 3–6 April 2008).

21. Ronald B. Rapoport and Walter J. Stone, *Three's a Crowd: The Dynamics of Third Parties, Ross Perot, and Republican Resurgence* (Ann Arbor: University of Michigan Press, 2005).

22. In a June 18–29, 2008, Pew Research Center Poll, 56 percent of the respondents agreed that "we should have a third major political party in this country in addition to the Democrats and Republicans." See also Shigeo Hirano and James M. Snyder, Jr., "The Decline of Third-Party Voting in the United States," *The Journal of Politics* 69 (February 2007): 1–16.

23. Shigeo Hirano and James M. Snyder, Jr., "The Decline of Third-Party Voting in the United States," *Journal of Politics* 69 (February 2007): 1–6. See also Rapoport and Stone, *Three's a Crowd*.

24. In his study of party systems, Jean Blondel noticed that most three-party systems had two major parties and a much smaller third party, which he called two-and-a-half-party systems. (Britain, for example, has two major parties—Labour and Conservative—and a smaller Social Democratic Party. Germany has followed a similar pattern.) Blondel said, "While it would seem theoretically possible for three-party systems to exist in which all three significant parties were of about equal size, there are in fact no three-party systems of this kind among Western democracies." He concluded that "genuine three-party systems do not normally occur because they are essentially transitional, thus unstable, forms of party systems." See his "Types of Party System," in *The West European Party System*, ed. Peter Mair (New York: Oxford University Press, 1990), p. 305.

25. See Douglas J. Amy, *Real Choices, New Voices: The Case for Proportional Representation in the United States*, 2nd ed. (New York: Columbia University Press, 2002).

26. The most complete report of these legal barriers is contained in monthly issues of *Ballot Access News*, http://www.ballot-access.org. State laws and court decisions may systematically support the major parties, but the U.S. Supreme Court seems to hold a more neutral position toward major and minor parties. See Lee Epstein and Charles D. Hadley, "On the Treatment of Political Parties in the U.S. Supreme Court, 1900–1986," *Journal of Politics* 52 (May 1990): 413–432; and E. Joshua Rosenkranz, *Voter Choice 96: A 50-State Report Card on the Presidential Elections* (New York: New York University School of Law, Brennan Center for Justice, 1996), p. 24.

27. Samuel Issacharoff, Pamela S. Karlan, and Richard H. Pildes, *The Law of Democracy*, rev. 2nd ed. (New York: Foundation Press, 2002), pp. 417–436.

28. See James Gimpel, *National Elections and the Autonomy of American State Party Systems* (Pittsburgh, Pa.: University of Pittsburgh Press, 1996).

29. Measuring the concept of party identification has had its problems. For insights into the issues, see R. Michael Alvarez, "The Puzzle of Party Identification," *American Politics Quarterly* 18 (October 1990): 476–491; and Donald Philip Green and Bradley Palmquist, "Of Artifacts and Partisan Instability," *American Journal of Political Science* 34 (August 1990): 872–902

30. This breakdown used data from the 2012 Pew Research Center survey.

31. Susan Page, "Highly Educated Couples Often Split on Candidates," *USA Today*, 18 December 2002, pp.1–2.

32. U.S. Census, "Table 1a, Projected Population of the United States, by Race and Hispanic Origin: 2000 to 2050," http://www.census.gov/population/www/projections/usinterimproj.

33. The relationship between age and party identification is quite complicated, but research finds that it becomes more stable as people age. See Elias Dinas and Mark Franklin, "The Development of Partisanship during the Life-Course" (paper presented at the Midwest Political Science Association 67th Annual National Conference, Palmer House Hilton, Chicago, 2 April 2009), http://www.allacademic.com/meta/p363000_index.html.

34. Two scholars on voting behavior describe partisanship as "the feeling of sympathy for and loyalty to a political party that an individual acquires—sometimes during childhood—and holds through life, often with increasing intensity." See William H. Flanigan and Nancy H. Zingale, *Political Behavior of the American Electorate*, 10th ed. (Washington, D.C.: CQ Press, 2002), p. 60.

35. Bill Keller, "As Arms Buildup Eases, U.S. Tries to Take Stock," *New York Times*, 14 May 1985; and Ed Gillespie and Bob Schellhas, *Contract with America* (New York: Times Books, 1994), p. 107.

36. "The GOP's Spending Spree," *Wall Street Journal*, 25 November 2003, p. A18.

37. See, for example, Gerald M. Pomper, *Elections in America* (New York: Dodd, Mead, 1968); Benjamin Ginsberg, "Election and Public Policy," *American Political Science Review* 70 (March 1976): 41–50; and Jeff Fishel, *Presidents and Promises* (Washington, D.C.: CQ Press, 1985).

38. Ian Budge and Richard I. Hofferbert, "Mandates and Policy Outputs: U.S. Party Platforms and Federal Expenditures," *American Political Science Review* 84 (March 1990): 111–131.

39. See Terri Susan Fine, "Economic Interests and the Framing of the 1988 and 1992 Democratic and Republican Party Platforms," *American Review of Politics* 16 (Spring 1995): 79–93.

40. Ian Budge et al., *Mapping Policy Preferences: Estimates for Parties, Electors, and Governments 1945–1998* (Oxford: Oxford University Press, 2001), p. 49.

41. See Ralph M. Goldman, *The National Party Chairmen and Committees: Factionalism at the Top* (Armonk, N.Y.: M. E. Sharpe, 1990). The subtitle is revealing.

42. Cornelius P. Cotter and Bernard C. Hennessy, *Politics without Power: The National Party Committees* (New York: Atherton Press, 1964).

43. Phillip A. Klinkner, "Party Culture and Party Behavior," in *The State of the Parties*, 3rd ed., ed. Daniel M. Shea and John C. Green (Lanham, Md.: Rowman & Littlefield, 1999), pp. 275–287; and Phillip A. Klinkner, *The Losing Parties: Out-Party National Committees, 1956–1993* (New Haven, Conn.: Yale University Press, 1994).

44. "Take the Lead: Political Parties and the Financing of the 2000 Presidential Election," in *The State of the Parties*, 4th ed., ed. John C. Green and Rick Farmer (Lanham, Md.: Rowman & Littlefield, 2003), p. 97; and Klinkner, *The Losing Parties*.

45. Daniel J. Galvin, *Presidential Party Building: Dwight D. Eisenhower to George W. Bush* (Princeton, N.J.: Princeton University Press, 2010), pp. ix–x.

46. Dan Barry, "Republicans on Long Island Master Science of Politics," *New York Times*, 8 March 1996, p. A1S. Recent research suggests that when both major parties have strong organizations at the county level, the public has more favorable attitudes toward the parties. See John J. Coleman, "Party Organization Strength and Public Support for Parties," *American Journal of Political Science* 40 (August 1996): 805–824.

47. John Frendreis et al., "Local Political Parties and Legislative Races in 1992," in Shea and Green, *The State of the Parties*, p. 139.

48. Raymond J. La Raja, "State Parties and Soft Money: How Much Party Building?" in Green and Farmer, *The State of the Parties*, p. 146.

49. Robert Biersack, "Hard Facts and Soft Money: State Party Finance in the 1992 Federal Elections," in Shea and Green, *The State of the Parties*, p. 114.

50. Federal Election Commission, *National Party Transfers to State/Local Party Committees, January 1, 2009–December 31, 2010*, http://www.fec.gov/press/bkgnd/cf_summary_info/2010prt_fullsum/10_ptytransfersye2010.pdf.

51. See the evidence presented in Robert Harmel and Kenneth Janda, *Parties and Their Environments* (New York: Longman, 1982), Chapter 5; and the more recent assessment in Nicol C. Rae, "Be Careful What You Wish For: The Rise of Responsible Parties in American National Politics," *Annual Review of Political Science* 10 (2007): 169–191.

52. Jonathan Weisman and Ashley Parker, "A Committed Group of Conservatives Outflanks the House Leadership," *New York Times*, 2 October 2013, p. A14.

53. "The Factions in the House of Representatives," *New York Times*, 20 October 2013, p. 20.

54. Andrew Taylor, "Fed-up Boehner Lashes Out at Right Wing," *Minneapolis StarTribune*, 13 December 2013, p. A3.

55. Martin P. Wattenberg, *The Decline of American Political Parties, 1952–1994* (Cambridge, Mass.: Harvard University Press, 1996).

56. Taylor Dark III, "The Rise of a Global Party? American Party Organizations Abroad," *Party Politics* 9 (March 2003): 241–255.

57. In 1996, the Democratic National Committee mounted an unprecedented drive to organize up to sixty thousand precinct captains in twenty states, while the new Republican candidate for U.S. senator from Illinois, Al Salvi, fired his own campaign manager and replaced him with someone from the National Republican Senatorial Campaign Committee. See Sue Ellen Christian, "Democrats Will Focus on Precincts," *Chicago Tribune*, 29 June 1996; and Michael Dizon, "Salvi Fires Top Senate Race Aides," *Chicago Tribune*, 24 May 1996, sec. 2, p. 3.

58. Barbara Sinclair, "The Congressional Party: Evolving Organizational, Agenda-Setting, and Policy Roles," in *The Parties Respond: Changes in American Parties and Campaigns*, 3rd ed., ed. L. Sandy Maisel (Boulder, Colo.: Westview Press, 1998), p. 227.

59. David M. Farrell, "Political Parties in a Changing Campaign Environment," in *Handbook of Party Politics*, ed. Richard S. Katz and William Crotty (London: Sage, 2006), p. 124.

60. The model is articulated most clearly in a report by the American Political Science Association, "Toward a More Responsible Two-Party System," *American Political Science Review* 44 (September 1950): Part II. See also Gerald M. Pomper, "Toward a More Responsible Party System? What, Again?" *Journal of Politics* 33 (November 1971): 916–940. See also the seven essays in the symposium "Divided Government and the Politics of Constitutional Reform," *PS: Political Science and Politics* 24 (December 1991): 634–657.

61. Within the American states, parties also differ on policies, but to varying degrees. See John H. Aldrich and James S. Coleman Battista, "Conditional Party Government in the States," *American Journal of Political Science* 46 (January 2002): 164–172.

62. Jeffrey M. Jones, "Americans Lack Consensus on Desirability of Divided Gov't," *Gallup Poll Report*, 10 June 2010.

63. Recent research finds that voters do differentiate between policies backed by the president and by congressional candidates. See David R. Jones and Monika L. McDermott, "The Responsible Party Government Model in House and Senate Elections," *American Journal of Political Science* 48 (January 2004): 1–12.

Chapter 9

1. For a philosophical discussion of "temporal properties" of American elections, see Dennis F. Thompson, "Election Time: Normative Implications of the Electoral Process in the United States," *American Political Science Review* 98 (February 2004): 51–64.

2. David Menefree-Libey, *The Triumph of Campaign-Centered Politics* (New York: Chatham House, 2000).

3. Stephen E. Frantzich, *Political Parties in the Technological Age* (New York: Longman, 1989), p. 105.

4. Reuven Y. Hazan and Gideon Rahat, *Democracy Within Parties: Candidate Selection Methods and Their Political Consequences* (Oxford: Oxford University Press, 2010). See also Krister Lundell, "Determinants of Candidate Selection: The Degree of Centralization in Comparative Perspective," *Party Politics* 10 (January 2004): 25–47.

5. Kenneth Janda, "Adopting Party Law," in *Political Parties and Democracy in Theoretical and Practical Perspectives* (Washington, D.C.: National Democratic Institute for International Affairs, 2005). This is a series of research papers.

6. *The Book of the States, 2013* (Lexington, Ky.: Council of State Governments, 2013), Table 6.3.

7. Karen M. Kaufmann, James G. Gimpel, and Adam H. Hoffman, "A Promise Fulfilled? Open Primaries and Representation," *Journal of Politics* 65 (May 2003): 457–476.

8. James A. McCann, "Presidential Nomination Activists and Political Representation: A View from the Active Minority Studies," in *Pursuit of the White House: How We Choose Our Presidential Nominees*, ed. William G. Mayer (Chatham, N.J.: Chatham House, 1996), p. 99.

9. Jeremy W. Peters and Jonathan Martin, "G.O.P. Weighs Limiting Clout of Right Wing," *New York Times* 7 November 2013, p. 1 and A18.

10. James M. Snyder, Jr., et al., "The Decline of Competition in U.S. Primary Elections, 1908-2004" (unpublished paper, MIT, Cambridge, Mass., June 2005), p. 22.

11. "Ninth Circuit Upholds Washington Top-Two System," *Ballot Access News* 27 (1 February 2012): 1–2; and "California Primary," *Ballot Access News* 28 (1 July 2012): 4.

12. Richard Winger, "California Experience with Top-Two During 2013," *Ballot Access News* (1 January 2014): 3; Richard Winger, "Five New Papers Issued on Relationships between Primary Systems and Polarization," *Ballot Access News* (1 September 2013): 1–3.

13. E. McGhee, S. Masket, B. Shor, S. Rogers, and N. McCarty, "A Primary Cause of Partisanship? Nomination Systems and Legislator Ideology," *American Journal of Political Science* (2013) doi:10.1111/ajps.12070.

14. See "The Green Papers" http://www.thegreenpapers.com for information on state methods of delegate selection in 2012.

15. Alan Ware, *The American Direct Primary: Party Institutionalization and Transformation in the North* (Cambridge: Cambridge University Press, 2002). Ware argues that the primary system resulted less from the reform movement than the unwieldy nature of the caucus/convention system for nominating candidates.

16. These figures, calculated for voting-eligible population (VEP), come from elections. http://elections.gmu.edu/voter_turnout.htm. VEP is lower than voting-age population (VAP) because VEP excludes those ineligible to vote, usually noncitizens and felons.

17. Richard L. Berke, "Two States Retain Roles in Shaping Presidential Race," *New York Times*, 29 November 1999, p. 1; and Leslie Wayne, "Iowa Turns Its Presidential Caucuses into a Cash Cow, and Milks Furiously," *New York Times*, 5 January 2000, p. A16. See also Adam Nagourney, "Iowa Worries about Losing Its Franchise," *New York Times*, 18 January 2004, sec. 4, p. 3.

18. "Presidential Primary Season Is Longer Than Ever," *Ballot Access News* 27 (November 2011): 6.

19. One scholar holds that early popularity is more important for Republican presidential hopefuls. See D. Jason Berggren, "Two Parties, Two Types of Nominees, Two Paths to Winning a Presidential Nomination, 1972–2004," *Presidential Studies Quarterly* 37 (June 2007): 203–227.

20. See James R. Beniger, "Winning the Presidential Nomination: National Polls and State Primary Elections, 1936–1972," *Public Opinion Quarterly* 40 (Spring 1976): 22–38.

21. *The American Heritage Dictionary of the English Language*, 4th ed. (Boston: Houghton Mifflin, 2000), p. 362. Indeed, the entry on "Electoral College" in the 1989 Oxford English Dictionary does not note any usage in American politics up to 1875, when it cites a reference in connection with the Germanic Diet.

22. References to the electoral college in the U.S. Code can be found through the Legal Information Institute website, http://www4.law.cornell.edu/uscode/3/ch1.html.

23. Michael Nelson, *Congressional Quarterly's Guide to the Presidency* (Washington, D.C.: CQ Press, 1989), pp. 155–156. Colorado selected its presidential electors through the state legislature in 1876, but that was the year it entered the Union.

24. Who would have become president if the 538 electoral votes had been divided equally, at 269 each? According to the Constitution, the House of Representatives would have chosen the president, for no candidate had a majority. One way to avoid tied outcomes in the future is to create an odd number of electoral votes. To do this, one scholar proposes making the District of Columbia a state. That would give Washington three electoral votes—the same number as it has now without congressional representation. The Senate would increase to 102 members, while the House would remain fixed at 435. (Presumably, Washington's seat would come from one of the other states after decennial reapportionment.) This clever solution would produce an electoral college of 537, an odd number that could not produce a tie between two candidates. See David A. Crockett, "Dodging the

25. Bullet: Election Mechanics and the Problem of the Twenty-third Amendment," *PS: Political Science and Politics* 36 (July 2003): 423–426.

25. Shlomo Slonim, "The Electoral College at Philadelphia: The Evolution of an Ad Hoc Congress for the Selection of a President," *Journal of American History* 73 (June 1986): 35. For a recent critique and proposal for reform, see David W. Abbott and James P. Levine, *Wrong Winner: The Coming Debacle in the Electoral College* (New York: Praeger, 1991). For a reasoned defense, see Walter Berns (ed.), *After the People Vote: A Guide to the Electoral College* (Washington, D.C.: American Enterprise Institute, 1992). For a detailed analysis of a congressional failure to enact proportional distribution of state electoral votes, see Gary Bugh, "Normal Politics and the Failure of the Most Intense Effort to Amend the Presidential Election System" (paper presented at the annual meeting of the Northeastern Political Science Association, Boston, 2006).

26. Lydia Saad, "Americans Would Swap Electoral College for Popular Vote," *Gallup Poll Report*, 24 October 2011.

27. For the most recent review, see Gary Bugh (ed.), *Electoral College Reform: Challenges and Possibilities* (Burlington, Vt.: Ashgate, 2010).

28. Walter Berns (ed.), *After the People Vote*, pp. 45–48. The framers had great difficulty deciding how to allow both the people and the states to participate in selecting the president. This matter was debated on twenty-one different days before they compromised on the electoral college, which, Slonim says, "in the eyes of its admirers…represented a brilliant scheme for successfully blending national and federal elements in the selection of the nation's chief executive" ("The Electoral College at Philadelphia," p. 58).

29. Observers suspect that the vote for Edwards instead of Kerry was cast by error. See http://news.minnesota.publicradio.org/features/2004/12/13_ap_electors.

30. See Alexis Simendinger, James A. Barnes, and Carl M. Cannon, "Pondering a Popular Vote," *National Journal*, 18 November 2000, pp. 3650–3656

31. Harold W. Stanley and Richard G. Niemi, *Vital Statistics on American Politics, 2011–2012* (Washington, D.C.: CQ Press, 2011), Table 3.10.

32. Nate Silver and Andrew Gelman, "No Country for Close Calls," *New York Times*, 19 April 2009, p. WK11.

33. See Edward I. Sidlow, *Challenging the Incumbent: An Underdog's Undertaking* (Washington, D.C.: CQ Press, 2004), for the engaging account of the unsuccessful 2000 campaign by a young political scientist, Lance Pressl, against the most senior Republican in the House, Phil Crane, in Illinois' Sixth District. Sidlow's book invites readers to ponder what the high reelection rate of incumbents means for American politics.

34. Frank Phillips, "Romney Paves Way for Possible '12 Run," Boston Globe (8 December 2008), http://www.boston.com/news/nation/articles/2008/12/08/romney_paves_way_for_possible_12_run/.

35. Michal Luo, "Romney, Weighing Run, Leans on State PACs," *New York Times*, 21 November 2010, p. 17.

36. Quoted in E. J. Dionne, Jr., "On the Trail of Corporation Donations," *New York Times*, 6 October 1980.

37. Center for Responsive Politics, http://www.opensecrets.org/pres12/#out.

38. Federal Election Commission, *The First Ten Years: 1975–1985* (Washington, D.C.: Federal Election Commission, 14 April 1985), p. 1.

39. Michael J. Malbin, "Assessing the Bipartisan Campaign Reform Act," in *The Election After Reform: Money, Politics and the Bipartisan Campaign Reform Act*, ed. Michael J. Malbin (Lanham, Md.: Rowman & Littlefield, 2006).

40. "527 Advocacy Spending," Opensecrets.org, http://www.opensecrets.org/527s/index.php.

41. Brody Mullins, "Stealthy Groups Shake Up Races," *Wall Street Journal*, 4 February 2008, p. A12.

42. Adam Liptak, "Justices, 5-4, Reject Corporate Campaign Spending Limit," *New York Times*, 22 January 2010, pp. A1, A16.

43. Editorial, "A Free Speech Landmark," *Wall Street Journal*, 22 January 2010, p. A18.

44. Editorial, "The Court's Blow to Democracy," *New York Times*, 22 January 2010, p. A20.

45. "Changing the Rules," *Wall Street Journal*, 22 January 2010, p. A6.

46. *SpeechNow.org* v. *FEC*, 599 F.3d 686 (D.C. Circuit, 26 March 2010). See also http://www.fec.gov/press/press2011/FEC_Joint_Statement-Nov3.pdf.

47. "With New Political Committees, Possible Channels for Unlimited, Anonymous Donations," *New York Times*, 16 October 2011, p. 24.

48. Tom Hamburger and Melanie Mason, "PACs Upend, Outspend Pack," *Chicago Tribune*, 1 January 2012, p. 23.

49. See the Federal Election Commission Advisory Opinion of June 30, 2011, http://www.fec.gov/press/press2011/20110630openmeeting.shtml.

50. Nicholas Confessore, Michael Luo, and Mike McIntire, "In G.O.P. Race, a New Breed of Superdonor," *New York Times*, 22 February 2012, pp. A1, A14.

51. See the FEC's listing of Independent Expenditure-Only groups, http://www.fec.gov/press/press2011/ieoc_alpha.shtml.

52. "2012 Outside Spending, by Groups," http://www.opensecrets.org/outsidespending/summ.php?cycle=2012&disp=O&type=A&chrt=V.

53. James A. Barnes, "Matching Funds, R.I.P.," *National Journal*, 26 April 2008, p. 75.

54. "Federal Election Commission Certifies Federal Matching Funds for Jill Stein for President," *Federal Election Committee News Release*, 28 August 2012.

55. Federal Election Commission, "2008 Presidential Campaign Financial Activity Summarized," News Release, 8 June 2009.

56. Federal Election Commission, "FEC Summarizes Campaign Activity for the 2011–2012 Election Cycle," News Release, 19 April 2013.

57. Dan Eggen, "The 2012 Election Brings a New Kind of Fundraiser: The Super Bundler," *Washington Post*, 16 August 2011.

58. "2012 Presidential Candidate Fundraising Summary," Center for Responsive Politics, OpenSecrets.org, http://www.opensecrets.org/pres12/index.php?ql3.

59. "PostPolitics: Campaign 2012, Campaign Finance Explorer," *Washington Post*, http://www.washingtonpost.com/wp-srv/special/politics/campaign-finance/.

60. According to Brian F. Schaffner and Matthew J. Streb, less educated respondents are less likely to express a vote preference when party labels are not available. See "The Partisan Heuristic in Low-Information Elections," *Public Opinion Quarterly* 66 (Winter 2002): 559–581.

61. See Matt A. Barreto et al., "Bulls Eye or Ricochet? Ethnically Targeted Campaign Ads in the 2008 Election" (paper presented at the Chicago Area Behavioral Workshop, Evanston, Ill., 8 May 2009); and Michael G. Hagenand and Robin Kolodny, "Microtargeting Campaign Advertising on Cable Television" (paper presented at the annual meeting of the Midwest Political Science Association, Chicago, 3–6 April 2008).

62. See Eric W. Rademacher and Alfred J. Tuchfarber, "Preelection Polling and Political Campaigns," in Bruce I. Newman, *Handbook of Political Marketing* (Thousand Oaks, CA: Sage Publications. 1999), pp. 197–221.

63. Bruce I. Newman, "A Predictive Model of Voter Behavior," in Newman, *Handbook of Political Marketing*, pp. 259–282.

64. Timothy E. Cook, *Making Laws and Making News: Media Strategies in the U.S. House of Representatives* (Washington, D.C.: Brookings Institution, 1989).

65. Stephen J. Farnsworth and S. Robert Lichter, *The Nightly News Nightmare: Media Coverage of U.S. Presidential Elections, 1988–2008* (Lanham, Md.: Rowman & Littlefield, 2010), p. 52.

66. Julianne F. Flowers, Audrey A. Haynes, and Michael H. Crispin, "The Media, the Campaign, and the Message," *American Journal of Political Science* 47 (April 2003): 259–273.

67. Ann N. Crigler, Marion R. Just, and Timothy E. Cook, "Local News, Network News and the 1992 Presidential Campaign" (paper presented at the annual meeting of the American Political Science Association, Washington, D.C., September 1993), p. 9.

68. Stephen Ansolabehere and Shanto Iyengar, *Going Negative: How Political Advertisements Shrink and Polarize the Electorate* (New York: Free Press, 1995), p. 145.

69. Darrell M. West, *Air Wars: Television Advertising in Election Campaigns, 1952–2004*, 4th ed. (Washington, D.C.: CQ Press, 2010), p. 23.

70. Ted Brader, "Striking a Responsive Chord: How Political Ads Motivate and Persuade Voters by Appealing to Emotions," *American Journal of Political Science* 49 (April 2005): 388–405.

71. Darrell M. West, *Air Wars: Television Advertising in Election Campaigns, 1952–2009*, 5th ed. (Washington, D.C.: CQ Press, 2010), pp. 51–52.

72. Darrell M. West, *Air Wars: Television Advertising in Election Campaigns, 1952–2012*, 6th ed. (Washington, D.C.: CQ Press, 2014), p. 70.

73. This theme runs throughout Kathleen Hall Jamieson's *Dirty Politics: Deception, Distraction, and Democracy* (New York: Oxford University Press, 1992). See also John Boiney, "You Can Fool All of the People … Evidence on the Capacity of Political Advertising to Mislead" (paper presented at the annual meeting of the American Political Science Association, Washington, D.C., September 1993).

74. West, *Air Wars*, 6th ed., p. 70.

75. T. W. Farnam, "Study: Negative Campaign Ads Much More Frequent, Vicious Than in Primaries Past," *Washington Post*, 20 February 2012, http://www.washingtonpost.com/politics/study-negativecampaign-ads-much-more-frequent-vicious-than-in-primaries-past/2012/02/14/gIQAR7ifPR_story.html.

76. Kathleen Hall Jamieson, Paul Waldman, and Susan Sheer, "Eliminate the Negative? Categories of Analysis for Political Advertisements," in *Crowded Airwaves: Campaign Advertising in Elections*, ed. James A. Thurber, Candice J. Nelson, and David A. Dulio (Washington, D.C.: Brookings Institution Press, 2000), p. 49.

77. David A. Dulio, Candice J. Nelson, and James A. Thurber, "Summary and Conclusions," in Thurber, Nelson, and Dulio, *Crowded Airwaves*, p. 172. Laboratory research found that even "uncivil" exchanges between candidates can be handled by the public. See Deborah Jordan Brooks and John G. Geer, "Beyond Negativity: The Effects of Incivility on the Electorate," *American Journal of Political Science* 51 (January 2007): 1–16.

78. Gregory A. Huber and Kevin Arceneaux, "Identifying the Persuasive Effects of Presidential Advertising," *American Journal of Political Science* 51 (2007): 957–977.

79. Ansolabehere and Iyengar, *Going Negative*, p. 112.

80. West, however, takes issue with the Ansolabehere and Iyengar analysis in *Going Negative*, saying that turnout is more dependent on mistrust than on negativity of ads. See West, *Air Wars*, 5th ed., pp. 71–72.

81. Richard R. Lau and Gerald M. Pomper, "Effectiveness of Negative Campaigning in U.S. Senate Elections," *American Journal of Political Science* 46 (January 2002): 47–66.

82. Richard R. Lau, Lee Sigelman, and Ivy Brown Rovner, "The Effects of Negative Political Campaigns: A Meta-Analytic Reassessment," *Journal of Politics* 69 (November 2007): 1176–1209.

83. Lee Sigelman and Mark Kugler, "Why Is Research on the Effects of Negative Campaigning So Inconclusive? Understanding Citizens' Perceptions of Negativity," *Journal of Politics* 65 (February 2003): 142–160; and Richard R. Lau, Lee Sigelman, and Ivy Brown Rovner, "The Effects of Negative Political Campaigns: A Meta-Analytic Reassessment," *The Journal of Politics* 69 (November 2007): 1176–1209.

84. The information on early campaign websites comes from Jill Zuckerman, "Candidates Spin Web of Support on Cybertrail," *Chicago Tribune*, 3 December 2003, p. 13.

85. Tanzina Vega, "Online Data Helping Campaigns Customize Ads," *New York Times*, 21 February 2012, pp. 1–13.

86. "Cable Leads the Pack as Campaign News Source," Pew Research Center for the People and the Press, 7 February 2012, http://www.people-press.org/files/legacy-pdf/2012%20Communicating% 20 Release.pdf.

87. West, *Air Wars*, 6th ed., p. 29.

88. See the website for the American National Election Studies, http://www.electionstudies.org.

89. Michael M. Gant and Norman R. Luttbeg, *American Electoral Behavior* (Itasca, Ill.: Peacock, 1991), pp. 63–64.

90. Martin Gilens, Jynn Vavreck, and Martin Cohen, "The Mass Media and the Public's Assessments of Presidential Candidates, 1952–2000," Journal of Politics 69 (November 2007): 1160–1175.

91. For a thorough review of studies on campaign effects, see Rian J. Brox and Daron R. Shaw, "Political Parties, American Campaigns, and Effects on Outcomes," in Katz and Crotty, *Handbook of Party Politics*, pp. 146–150.

92. Farnsworth and Lichter, *The Nightly News Nightmare*, p. 64.

93. Matthew A. Baum, "Talking the Vote: Why Presidential Candidates Hit the Talk Show Circuit," *American Journal of Political Science* 49 (April 2005): 213–234.

94. Electorates tend to be more engaged by campaigning in "battleground" states. See James G. Gimpel et al., "Battleground States versus Blackout States: The Behavioral Implications of Modern Presidential Campaigns," *Journal of Politics* 69 (August 2007): 786–797.

95. West, *Air Wars*, 6th ed., p. 31.

96. But for a contrary view, see Nicol C. Rae, "Be Careful What You Wish For: The Rise of Responsible Parties in American National Politics," *Annual Review of Political Science* 10 (2007): 169–191.

Chapter 10

1. Robert Draper, "Inside the Power of the N.R.A.," *New York Times Magazine*, 12 December 2013; Chris Cillizza, "A Story of the NRA's Influence—in 2 Charts," *Washington Post*, 19 December 2012; "National Rifle (Selling) Association," *New York Times*, 20 December 2012; "11 Days to Inaug; NRA Membership Surges …" *Politico Playbook*, 10 January 2013; "9 in 10 Back Universal Gun Background Checks," CBS News, 17 January 2013, http://www.cbsnews.com/news/9-in-10-back-universal-gun-background-checks/.

2. Alexis de Tocqueville, *Democracy in America, 1835–1839*, ed. Richard D. Heffner (New York: Mentor Books, 1956), p. 198.

3. *The Federalist Papers* (New York: Mentor Books, 1961), p. 79.

4. Ibid., p. 78.

5. See Robert A. Dahl, *A Preface to Democratic Theory* (Chicago: University of Chicago Press, 1956), pp. 4–33.

6. Pew Research Center for the People and the Press, 1–5 February 2006, http://www.pollingreport.com/politics.htm.

7. "Lobbying Database," Center for Responsive Politics, http://www.opensecrets.org/lobby/.

8. This discussion follows from Jeffrey M. Berry and Clyde Wilcox, *The Interest Group Society*, 5th ed. (New York: Longman, 2009), pp. 7–8.

9. Megan Wilson, "Poll: Congressional Staffers Find Lobbyist Chats Helpful," *The Hill*, 10 June 2013, http://thehill.com/business-a-lobbying/304519-poll-congressional-staffers-find-lobbyist-chats-helpful.

10. See Frank R. Baumgartner, "Interest Groups and Agendas," in *The Oxford Handbook of American Political Parties and Interest Groups*, ed. L. Sandy Maisel and Jeffrey M. Berry (Oxford, UK: Oxford University Press, 2010), pp. 519–533.

11. Terry Moe, *Special Interest* (Washington, D.C.: Brookings Institution Press, 2011); and "Union Members—2012," Bureau of Labor Statistics, 23 January 2013, http://www.bls.gov/news.release/union2.nr0.htm.

12. Juliet Eilperin and Tom Hamburger, "For Obama's Ex-Aides, It's Time to Cash in on Experience," *Washington Post*, 30 May 2013, http://www.washingtonpost.com/politics/for-obamas-ex-aides-its-time-to-cash-in-on-experience/2013/05/30/a649ccde-c867-11e2-9245-773c0123c027_story.html.

13. David B. Truman, *The Governmental Process* (New York: Knopf, 1951).

14. Herbert Gans, *The Urban Villagers* (New York: Free Press, 1962).

15. Robert H. Salisbury, "An Exchange Theory of Interest Groups," *Midwest Journal of Political Science* 13 (February 1969): 1–32.

16. See Mancur Olson, Jr., *The Logic of Collective Action* (New York: Schocken, 1968).

17. Marshall Ganz, *Why David Sometimes Wins* (New York: Oxford University Press, 2009).

18. Kay Lehman Schlozman, Sidney Verba, and Henry E. Brady, *The Unheavenly Chorus: Unequal Political Voice and the Broken Promise of American Democracy* (Princeton, N.J.: Princeton University Press, 2012).

19. "Education: Lobbying, 2013," Center for Responsive Politics, http://www.opensecrets.org/industries/lobbying.php?cycle=2014&ind=W04.

20. See David Karpf, *The MoveOn Effect* (New York: Oxford University Press, 2012).

21. See Olson, *The Logic of Collective Action*.

22. Gunnar Trumbull, *Strength in Numbers* (Cambridge, Mass.: Harvard University Press, 2012).

23. On the underlying motivation to contribute, see Hahrie Hahn, *Moved to Action* (Stanford, Calif.: Stanford University Press, 2009).

24. Beth L. Leech, *Lobbyists at Work* (New York: Apress, 2013), p. 19.

25. "Health Lobbyist Has Great Sway," Associated Press, 24 May 2009.

26. Timothy M. LaPira and Herschel F. Thomas, "Revolving Door Lobbying and Interest Representation," *Interest Groups & Advocacy* (forthcoming); and Eilperin and Hamburger, "For Obama's Ex-Aides."

27. Eric Lipton, "Ex Lawmaker Still Working for Old Allies," *New York Times*, 6 August 2011; and Eric Lipton and Ben Protess, "Law Doesn't End Revolving Door on Capitol Hill," *New York Times*, 1 February 2014, http://dealbook.nytimes.com/2014/02/01/law-doesnt-end-revolving-door-on-capitol-hill/?_php=true&_type=blogs&_r=0.

28. Ethan Smith and Brody Mullins, "Studios Tap Dodd to Lead Lobbying," *Wall Street Journal*, 2 March 2011; and "Official: Chris Dodd to Lead MPAA," *The Hollywood Reporter*, 1 March 2011, http://www.hollywoodreporter.com/news/official-chris-dodd-lead-mpaa-162817.

29. Elizabeth Olson, "After a Merger Falls Through, Patton Boggs Keeps Looking," *New York Times*, 10 January 2014.

30. Suzy Khimm, "Transformers," *New Republic*, 24 December 2008, p. 13.

31. Robert G. Kaiser, *Act of Congress* (New York: Knopf, 2013), p. 152.

32. "FEC Summarizes Campaign Activity of the 2011–2012 Election Cycle," Federal Election Commission, April 19, 2013, http://www.fec.gov/press/press2013/20130419_2012-24m-Summary.shtml.

33. "Top 50 PACs by Contributions to Candidates and Other Committees," 2011–2012 Election Data Summaries, Table 4c, Federal Election Commission, http://www.fec.gov/press/summaries/2012/ElectionCycle/24m_PAC.shtml.

34. Ibid.

35. "Super PACs," 2012 Election Cycle, Center for Responsive Politics, http://www.opensecrets.org/pacs/superpacs.php?cycle=2012.

36. Rogan Kersh, "To Donate or Not to Donate?" (paper delivered at the annual meeting of the American Political Science Association, Philadelphia, August 2003), p. 2.

37. Michael M. Franz, *Choices and Changes* (Philadelphia: Temple University Press, 2008).

38. One study concludes, "Scholars have struggled to document the impact of campaign contributions, but with inconsistent results." Frank R. Baumgartner, Jeffrey M. Berry, Marie Hojnacki, David C. Kimball, and Beth L. Leech, *Lobbying and Policy Change* (Chicago: University of Chicago Press, 2009), p. 193.

39. Marie Hojnacki and David Kimball, "PAC Contributions and Lobbying Access in Congressional Committees," *Political Research*

Quarterly 54 (March 2001): 161–180; John R. Wright, "Contributions, Lobbying, and Committee Voting in the U.S. House of Representatives," *American Political Science Review* 84 (June 1990): 417–438; and Richard L. Hall and Frank W. Wayman, "Buying Time: Money Interests and the Mobilization of Bias in Congressional Committees," *American Political Science Review* 84 (September 1990): 797–820.

40. Baumgartner et al., *Lobbying and Policy Change*, pp. 166–189.

41. Eric Lichtblau, "Makers of Violent Video Games Marshal Support to Fend Off Regulation," *New York Times*, 12 January 2013.

42. S. Laurel Weldon, *When Protest Makes Policy* (Ann Arbor: University of Michigan Press, 2011), pp. 57–81.

43. For a more optimistic assessment of protest politics, see Andrew S. McFarland, *Boycotts and Dixie Chicks* (Boulder, Colo.: Paradigm, 2011).

44. Jim Puzzanghera, "AT&T Finds Big-Money Lobbying, Ad Efforts Don't Always Pay Off," *Los Angeles Times*, 21 December 2011, http:// articles.latimes.com/2011/dec/21/business/la-fi-att-regulators-20111221; and Shira Ovide, "AT&T Sets Ad Blitz in Capital," *Wall Street Journal*, 20 September 2011.

45. On competition and cooperation among Washington lobbies, see Thomas T. Holyoke, *Competitive Interests* (Washington, D.C.: Georgetown University Press, 2011).

46. Dara Z. Strolovitch, *Affirmative Advocacy* (Chicago: University of Chicago Press, 2007), p. 181.

47. See Schlozman, Verba, and Brady, *The Unheavenly Chorus*; and Matt Grossman, *The Not-So-Special Interests* (Stanford, Calif.: Stanford University Press, 2012).

48. Kay Lehman Schlozman, Traci Burch, and Samuel Lampert, "Still an Upper-Class Accent?" (paper presented at the annual meeting of the American Political Science Association, September 2004), pp. 16, 25.

49. Such nonprofits have obstacles created by their status as tax-deductible public charities. See Jeffrey M. Berry with David F. Arons, *A Voice for Nonprofits* (Washington, D.C.: Brookings Institution, 2003).

50. See Jeffrey M. Berry and Kent E. Portney, "Sustainability and Interest Group Participation in City Politics," *Sustainability* 5 (2013): 2077–2097; and Trumbull, *Strength in Numbers*.

51. Michelle Quinn, "Samsung's Lobbying Grows with its Market Share," *Politico*, 28 January, 2013, http://www.politico.com/story/2013/01/samsungs-lobbying-grows-with-its-market-share-86784.html; and "Fortune Global 500," http://money.cnn.com/magazines/fortune/global500/2013/full_list/?iid=G500_sp_full.

52. Thomas B. Edsall, "Kill Bill," http://opinionator.blogs.nytimes.com/2013/05/22/kill-bill/.

53. "Health Care Lobbyists Rise to Power," CBS News, 20 October 2009, http://www.cbsnews.com/news/health-care-lobbyists-rise-to-power/.

54. Center for Responsive Politics, http://www.opensecrets.org/lobby/top.php?indexType=c&showYear=2013; and http://www.opensecrets.org/lobby/lm_health.php.

55. Jason Webb Yackee and Susan Webb Yackee, "A Bias towards Business? Assessing Interest Group Influence on the U.S. Bureaucracy," *Journal of Politics* 68 (February 2006): 128–139.

56. Baumgartner et al., *Lobbying and Policy Change*, pp. 190–214. On the power of the status quo, see Amy McKay, "Negative Lobbying and Policy Outcomes," *American Politics Research* 40 (January 2012): 116–146.

57. Martin Gilens, *Affluence and Influence* (Princeton, N.J.: Princeton University Press, 2012).

58. *Citizens United* v. *Federal Election Commission*, 558 U.S. (2010).

59. Theodore Meyer, "How Much Did Sheldon Adelson Really Spend on Campaign 2012?" *ProPublica*, 21 (December 2012), http://www.propublica.org/article/how-much-did-sheldon-adelson-really-spend-on-campaign-2012.

Chapter 11

1. David Welna, "Congress is on Pace to Be Least Productive Ever," NPR, 24 December 2013, http://www.npr.org/2013/12/24/256696665/congress-is-on-pace-to-be-the-least-productive-ever; Matt Viser, "This Congress Going Down as Least Productive," *Boston Globe*, 4 December 2013, http://www.bostonglobe.com/news/politics/2013/12/04/congress-course-make-history-least-productive/kGAVEBskUeqCB0htOUG9GI/story.html.

2. Michael Young, "Indiana Congressman Rokita Says Voters Want Government Shutdown," *The Purdue Review*, http://www.purduereview.com/politics/indiana-congressman-rokita-says-voters-want-government-shutdown/.

3. See "The Political Polarization of the Congressional Parties," at http://voteview.com/political_polarization.asp.

4. Meredith Shiner, "Boehner: Speaker of the Unruly," *CQ Weekly*, 10 September 2012, pp. 1830–1834).

5. Frances Lee, "Making Laws and Making Points: Senate Governance in an Era of Uncertain Majorities," *The Forum* 9 No. 4, DOI: 10.2202/1540-8884.1488.

6. Monika McDermott and David Jones, "Do Public Evaluations of Congress Matter? Retrospective Voting in Congressional Elections," *American Politics Research* 31, No. 2 (2003): 155–177.

7. Harold W. Stanley and Richard G. Niemi (eds.), *Vital Statistics on American Politics, 2011–2012* (Washington, D.C.: CQ Press, 2011), pp. 46–47.

8. For more on public opinion about Congress, see John Hibbing and Elizabeth Theiss-Morse, *Congress as Public Enemy: Public Attitudes toward American Political Institutions* (Cambridge: Cambridge University Press, 1995); John Hibbing and Elizabeth Theiss-Morse, *Stealth Democracy: Americans' Beliefs about How Government Should Work* (Cambridge: Cambridge University Press, 2002); and David Jones and Monika McDermott, *Americans, Congress, and Democratic Responsiveness* (Ann Arbor: University of Michigan Press, 2010).

9. Alan Abramowitz, Brad Alexander, and Matthew Gunning, "Incumbency, Redistricting, and the Decline of Competition in U.S. House Elections," *Journal of Politics* 68 (February 2006): 75–88.

10. Gary W. Cox and Jonathan N. Katz, *Elbridge Gerry's Salamander* (Cambridge: Cambridge University Press, 2002).

11. Micah Altman, Karin MacDonald, and Michael McDonald, "Pushbutton Gerrymanders? How Computing Has Changed Redistricting," in *Party Lines*, ed. Thomas E. Mann and Bruce E. Cain (Washington, D.C.: Brookings Institution, 2005), pp. 51–66; and Mark Monmonier, *Bushmanders and Bullwinkles* (Chicago: University of Chicago Press, 2001).

12. Steven Yaccino, "Illinois Redistricting Forces Republican Face-Off," *New York Times*, 21 September 2011, http://thecaucus.blogs.nytimes.com/2011/09/21/illinois-redistricting-forces-republican-face-off/.

13. Thomas E. Mann, "Polarizing the House of Representatives: How Much Does Gerrymandering Matter?" in *Red and Blue Nation*, ed. Pietro S. Nivola and David W. Brady (Washington, D.C.: Brookings Institution and Hoover Institution, 2006), pp. 263–283; and Sean Theriault, *Party Polarization in Congress* (New York: Cambridge University Press, 2011). For a contrasting view, see Nolan McCarty, Keith Poole, and Howard Rosenthal, "Does Gerrymandering Cause Polarization?" *American Journal of Political Science* 53, No. 3 (2009): 666–680.

14. Sean Theriault and David Rhode, "The Gingrich Senators and Party Polarization in the U.S. Senate," *Journal of Politics* 73, No. 4 (2011): 1011–1024. Note that this article claims that it is Senate *Republicans* who had served in the House who have been the main polarizing agent in the Senate.

15. Dennis Conrad, "House Spends Big on Home Mailings," *Boston Globe*, 28 December 2007, p. A2; and Matthew Eric Glassman, "Congressional Franking Privilege: Background and Recent Legislation," *CRS Report for Congress*, 10 April 2013.

16. Sherri Greenberg, "Congress and Social Media," Lyndon B. Johnson School of Public Affairs, University of Texas at Austin. 2012, http://www.utexas.edu/lbj/cpg/docs/research_congress_social_media.pdf.

17. Jordan Fabian, "Critics Say Franking Rules Should Change to Suit the Age of Twitter," *The Hill*, 14 October 2009, http://thehill.com/homenews/senate/62969-critics-say-franking-rules-should-change-fortwitter; Alex Katz, "Not Much Tweeting from Mass. Delegation," *The Boston Globe*, 4 November 2011, http://bostonglobe.com/news/nation/2011/11/03/not-much-tweeting-from-mass-delegation/bR5jndH4Y2eoIBWNnNoc4H/story.html; and Jennifer Moire, "Survey: U.S. Congressmen Really Like Facebook," http://www.allfacebook. com/facebook-like-congress-us-2011-07. Also see http://tweetcongress.org/, which tracks tweets sent by members of Congress.

18. Matthew Eric Glassman, Jacob Straus, and Colleen Shogan. "Social Networking and Constituent Communications: Members' Use of Twitter and Facebook During a Two-Month Period in the 112th Congress," *CRS Report for Congress*, 22 March 2013, Social-Media-Use-by-Congress-CRS-March-2013.pdf.

19. Collen J. Shogan, "Blackberries, Tweets, and YouTube: Technology and the Future of Communicating with Congress," *PS: Political Science and Politics* 43, No. 2 (April 2010): 231–233.

20. Morris P. Fiorina, as cited in Roger H. Davidson and Walter J. Oleszek, *Congress and Its Members*, 11th ed. (Washington, D.C.: CQ Press, 2008), p. 144.

21. Center for Responsive Politics, "Incumbent Advantage: 2012 Election Cycle," http:// http://www.opensecrets.org/bigpicture/incumbs.php.

22. Larry Sabato, *PAC Power* (New York: Norton, 1984), p. 72.

23. Gary Jacobson, *The Politics of Congressional Elections*, 8th ed. (Pearson, 2013).

24. Katie Long, "Most Members of Congress are Millionaires," slate.com, 9 January 2014.

25. Emily Heil, "Senate Women's Restroom Expanding to Accommodate Historic Numbers," *Washington Post*, 12 June 2013.

26. Jennifer L. Lawless and Richard L. Fox, *It Still Takes a Candidate*, rev. ed. (New York: Cambridge University Press, 2010).

27. Jeremy Peters, "Openly Gay, and Openly Welcomed in Congress," *New York Times*, 25 January 2013; Jennifer Manning, "Membership of the 113th Congress: A Profile," *CRS Report for Congress*, 6 December 2013; and Rosalind Helderman, "The 113th Congress Is the Most Diverse in History," *Washington Post*, 3 January 2013.

28. See Beth Reingold, *Representing Women* (Chapel Hill, N.C.: University of North Carolina Press, 2000); and Michele L. Swers, *The Difference Women Make* (Chicago: University of Chicago Press, 2002).

29. Hanna Fenichel Ptikin, *The Concept of Representation* (Berkeley: University of California Press, 1967), pp. 60–91; and Jane Mansbridge, "Should Blacks Represent Blacks and Women Represent Women? A Contingent 'Yes,'" *Journal of Politics* 61 (1999): 628–657.

30. Philip Rucker, "Obama Signs Defense Law, Calls It a 'Welcome Step' toward Closing Guantanamo Bay Prison," *Washington Post*, 26 December 2013.

31. *Shaw* v. *Reno*, 509 U.S. 630 (1993).

32. *Bush* v. *Vera*, 116 S. Ct. 1941 (1996).

33. *Easley* v.*Cromartie*, 532 U.S. 234 (2001).

34. Ana Gonzalez-Barrera and Jeffery Passel, "An Awakened Giant: The Hispanic Electorate Is Likely to Double by 2013," *Pew Hispanic Center Report*, 14 November 2012.

35. See David Lublin, *The Paradox of Representation* (Princeton, N.J.: Princeton University Press, 1997). See, *contra*, Kenneth W. Shotts, "Does Racial Redistricting Cause Conservative Policy Outcomes?" *Journal of Politics* 65 (2003): 216–226.

36. See Frank R. Baumgartner et al., *Advocacy and Policy Change* (Chicago: University of Chicago Press, 2009).

37. Peter Kasperowicz, "House to Take Up Cybersecurity Bills Next Week," *The Hill*, 12 April 2013;"Rep. Lapinksi's Cybersecurity Enhancement Act Passes House," http://www.lipinski.house.gov/press-releases/rep-lipinskis-cybersecurity-enhancement-act-passes-house1/, 17 April 2013.

38. Staff, CQ Roll Call, "Senate Rejects Most Gun Bill Amendments," *CQ Weekly*, 22 April 2013.

39. David Shribman, "Canada's Top Envoy to Washington Cuts Unusually Wide Swath," *Wall Street Journal*, 29 July 1985, p. 1.

40. Woodrow Wilson, *Congressional Government* (Boston: Houghton Mifflin, 1885), p. 79.

41. David Fahrenthold and Michelle Boorstein, "Rep. Peter King's Muslim Hearings: A Key Moment in an Angry Conversation," *Washington Post*, 9 March 2011, http://www.washingtonpost.com/wp-dyn/content/article/2011/03/09/AR2011030902061.html?sid=ST2011031002070.

42. Alessandra Stanely, "Terror Hearing Puts Lawmakers in Harsh Light," *New York Times*, 10 March, 2011, http://www.nytimes.com/2011/03/11/arts/television/at-muslim-hearing-finger-pointing-andtears.html?_r=1&ref=politics.

43. See Steven S. Smith, *Party Influence in Congress* (New York: Cambridge University Press, 2007).

44. Gary W. Cox and Mathew D. McCubbins, *Legislative Leviathan* (Berkeley: University of California Press, 1993); and Keith Krehbiel, *Information and Legislative Organization* (Ann Arbor: University of Michigan Press, 1992).

45. Matthew N. Green, *The Speaker of the House* (New Haven, Conn.: Yale University Press, 2010).

46. Jonathan Franzen, "The Listener," *New Yorker*, 6 October 2003, p. 85.

47. Robert Draper, "How Kevin McCarthy Wrangles the Tea Party in Washington," *New York Times*, 17 July 2011.

48. Charles O. Jones, *The United States Congress* (Homewood, Ill.: Dorsey Press, 1982), p. 322.

49. Gregory Kroger, *Filibustering: A Political History of Obstruction in the House and Senate* (Chicago: Chicago University Press, 2010), p. 133.

50. Norman Ornstein, "Our Broken Senate," *The American*, May/April 2008, http://www.american.com/archive/2008/march-april-magazine-contents/our-broken-senate; and Barbara Sinclair, "The 60 Vote Senate," in *U.S. Senate Exceptionalism*, ed. Bruce Oppenheimer (Columbus: Ohio State University Press, 2002), pp. 241–261.

51. Gary W. Cox and Mathew D. McCubbins, *Setting the Agenda: Responsible Party Government in the U.S. House of Representatives* (New York: Cambridge University Press, 2005); and Smith, *Party Influence in Congress*.

52. These ideologies affect policy outcomes as well as the structure of the institution itself. See Nelson Polsby, *How Congress Evolves: Social Bases of Institutional Change* (New York: Oxford University Press, 2004).

53. See, for example, Sean Theriault, *Party Polarization in Congress* (New York: Cambridge University Press, 2008); Sean Theriault, *The Gingrich Senators* (New York: Oxford University Press, 2013); Thomas Mann and Norman Ornstein, *It's Even Worse than It Looks* (New York: Basic Books, 2013); Frances Lee, *Beyond Ideology: Politics, Principles, and Partisanship in the U.S. Senate* (Chicago: University of Chicago Press, 2009); and Hans Noel, *Political Ideologies and Political Parties in America* (New York: Cambridge University Press, 2014).

54. James Sterling Young, *The Washington Community* (New York: Harcourt, Brace, 1964).

55. Tom Cohen and Greg Botelho, "Obama, Boehner Agree All Sides Should Keep Talking," *CNN*, 12 October 2013, http://www.cnn.com/2013/10/11/politics/shutdown-showdown/.

56. Joshua D. Clinton, "Representation in Congress: Constituents and Roll Calls in the 106th House," *Journal of Politics* 68 (May 2006): 397–409.

57. See John Cochran, "The Influence Implosion," *CQ Weekly*, 16 January 2006, p. 174; and Susan Ferrechio, "2005 Legislative Summary: House Ethics Investigations," *CQ Weekly*, 2 January 2006, p. 31.

58. Barry C. Burden, *The Personal Roots of Representation* (Princeton, N.J.: Princeton University Press, 2007).

59. Richard F. Fenno, Jr., *Home Style* (Boston: Little, Brown, 1978), p. xii.

60. "Life in Congress: The Member Perspective," Congressional Management Foundation Report, 11 March 2013, http://www.congressfoundation.org/projects/life-in-congress/the-member-perspective.

61. Louis I. Bredvold and Ralph G. Ross (eds.), *The Philosophy of Edmund Burke* (Ann Arbor: University of Michigan Press, 1960), p. 148.

62. "In Congress, Voting Your Own Way and Paying for It," *National Public Radio*, 18 July 2011, http://www.npr.org/2011/07/18/138473342/in-congress-voting-your-own-way-and-paying-for-it.

63. Warren E. Miller and Donald E. Stokes, "Constituency Influence in Congress," *American Political Science Review* 57 (March 1963): 45–57.

64. Erin Kelly, "Some Want Earmarks Back to Help Congress Pass Bills," *USA Today*, 29 October 2013.

65. "Possible Negatives for Candidates: Vote for Bank Bailout, Palin Support," Pew Center for People and the Press, 6 October 2010, http://www.people-press.org/2010/10/06/possible-negatives-forcandidates-vote-for-bank-bailout-palin-support/.

Chapter 12

1. David Wood, "Drone War Expansion Sparks Questions about Effectiveness, Oversight in Obama's Second Term," *Huffington Post*, 16 January 2013, http://www.huffingtonpost.com/2013/01/16/drone-war-obama_n_2454901.html.

2. Jo Becker and Scott Shane, "Secret 'Kill List' Proves a Test of Obama's Principles and Will," *New York Times*, 29 May 2012, http://www.nytimes.com/2012/05/29/world/obamas-leadership-in-war-on-al-qaeda.html?pagewanted=all.

3. *Between a Drone and Al-Qaeda: The Civilian Costs of US Targeted Killings in Yemen* (Washington, D.C.: Human Rights Watch, 2013).

4. Peter Baker, "Pivoting from a War Footing, Obama Acts to Curtail Drones," *New York Times*, 23 May 2013, http://www.nytimes.com/2013/05/24/us/politics/pivoting-from-a-war-footing-obama-acts-to-curtail-drones.html.

5. Clinton Rossiter, *1787: The Grand Convention* (New York: Mentor, 1968), p. 148.

6. Ibid., pp. 190–191.

7. United States Senate, "Summary of Bills Vetoed, 1789-Present," http://www.senate.gov/reference/Legislation/Vetoes/vetoCounts.htm.

8. *Hamdan* v. *Rumsfeld*, 548 U.S. 557 (2006).

9. Wilfred E. Binkley, *President and Congress*, 3rd ed. (New York: Vintage, 1962), p. 155.

10. William G. Howell, *Power without Persuasion: The Politics of Direct Presidential Action* (Princeton, N.J.: Princeton University Press, 2003); Kenneth R. Mayer, *With the Stroke of a Pen: Executive Orders and Presidential Power* (Princeton, N.J.: Princeton University Press, 2001); and Adam Warber, *Executive Orders and the Modern Presidency* (Boulder, Colo.: Lynne Rienner, 2005).

11. See Jack Goldsmith, *Power and Constraint* (New York: Norton, 2012).

12. Charlie Savage, "Obama to Call for End to N.S.A.'s Bulk Data Collection," *New York Times*, 24 March 2014, http://www.nytimes.com/2014/03/25/us/obama-to-seek-nsa-curb-on-call-data.html; and Ryan Lizza, "State of Deception," *New Yorker*, 16 December 2013.

13. Noam Scheiber, "The Chief," *New Republic*, 25 March 2010, pp. 17–21; and Ryan Lizza, "The Gatekeeper," *New Yorker*, 2 March 2009, pp. 24–29.

14. George G. Edwards III, *Overreach* (Princeton, N.J.: Princeton University Press, 2012), p. 36.

15. *The 2012 Statistical Abstract*, Table 499, "Federal Civilian Employment by Branch and Agency: 1990–2010," http://www.census.gov/compendia/statab/2012/tables/12s0499.pdf; and Table 472, "Federal Budget Outlays by Agency: 1990–2011," http://www.census.gov/compendia/statab/2012/tables/12s0472.pdf.

16. Richard Tanner Johnson, *Managing the White House* (New York: Harper & Row, 1974); and John P. Burke, *The Institutional Presidency* (Baltimore: Johns Hopkins University Press, 1992).

17. Ron Suskind, *Confidence Men* (New York: Harper, 2011), p. 351.

18. Dan Froomkin, "Now They Tell Us," *Washington Post*, 12 September 2005, http://busharchive.froomkin.com/BL2005091200806_pf.html.

19. George Stephanopoulos, *All Too Human* (Boston: Back Bay Books, 1999), p. 61.

20. Jo Becker, "Mr. President, How Can We Help You Evolve More Quickly," *New York Times Magazine*, 16 April 2014.

21. Edward Weisband and Thomas M. Franck, *Resignation in Protest* (New York: Penguin, 1975), p. 139, quoted in Thomas E. Cronin, *The State of the Presidency*, 2nd ed. (Boston: Little, Brown, 1980), p. 253.

22. In his memoir, *Duty* (New York: Knopf, 2014), Obama's secretary of defense Robert Gates details his fights with the White House staff and demonstrates how his relationship with the President was affected by Obama's advisory structure.

23. Doris Kearns, *Lyndon Johnson and the American Dream* (New York: Signet, 1977), p. 363.

24. James David Barber, *Presidential Character*, 4th ed. (Englewood Cliffs, N.J.: Prentice Hall, 1992); Fred I. Greenstein, *The Presidential Difference: Leadership Style from FDR to Clinton* (Princeton, N.J.: Princeton University Press, 2000); and David G. Winter, "Things I've Learned about Personality from Studying Political Leadership at a Distance," *Journal of Personality* 73 (2005): 557–584.

25. Donald Kinder, "Presidential Character Revisited," in *Political Cognition*, ed. Richard Lau and David O. Sears (Hillsdale, N.J.: Erlbaum, 1986), pp. 233–255; W. E. Miller and J. M. Shanks, *The New American Voter* (Cambridge, Mass.: Harvard University Press, 1996); and Frank Newport and Joseph Carroll, "Analysis: Impact of Personal Characteristics on Candidate Support," *Gallup News Service*, 13 March 2007, http://www.gallup.com.

26. Richard E. Neustadt, *Presidential Power* (New York: Wiley, 1980), p. 10.

27. Ibid., p. 9.

28. Chad Roedemeier, "Nixon Kept Softer Self Off Limits, Tape Shows," *Boston Globe*, 8 July 2000, p. A4.

29. Terry Sullivan, "I'll Walk Your District Barefoot" (paper presented at the MIT Conference on the Presidency, Cambridge, Mass., 29 January 2000), p. 6. See also Robert A. Caro, *The Passage of Power* (New York: Knopf, 2012), pp. 484–502 and pp. 552–557.

30. Samuel Kernell, *Going Public: New Strategies of Presidential Leadership*, 4th ed. (Washington, D.C.: CQ Press, 2007).

31. On Americans' tendency to be disappointed in their presidents, see Richard Waterman, Carol L. Silva, and Hank Jenkins-Smith, *The Presidential Expectations Gap* (Ann Arbor: University of Michigan Press, 2014).

32. George C. Edwards III, *The Strategic President* (Princeton, N.J.: Princeton University Press, 2009), p. 188.

33. David Gergen, *Eyewitness to Power* (New York: Simon & Schuster, 2000), as quoted in Edwards. *Overreach*, p. 49.

34. Jeffrey M. Jones, "Obama Job Approval at 51% After Healthcare Vote," Gallup Poll, 25 March 2010, http://www.gallup.com/poll/126989/Obama-Job-Approval-51-After-Healthcare-Vote.aspx.

35. Gary C. Jacobson, "The Republican Resurgence in Congress," *Political Science Quarterly* 126 (Spring 2011): 27–52.

36. The term comes from Theodore Roosevelt's break with the past to campaign for his policies as president. Up until that time presidents tended to refrain from public outreach. Doris Kearns Goodwin, *The Bully Pulpit* (New York: Simon & Schuster, 2013).

37. Francis Lee, *Beyond Ideology* (Chicago: University of Chicago Press, 2009).

38. B. Dan Wood, *The Myth of Presidential Representation* (New York: Cambridge University Press, 2009); and Lawrence C. Jacobs and Robert Y. Shapiro, *Politicians Don't Pander* (Chicago: University of Chicago Press, 2000).

39. David McCullough, *Truman* (New York: Simon & Schuster, 1992), p. 914.

40. Clea Benson, "Presidential Support: The Power of No," *Congressional Quarterly Weekly Report*, 14 January 2008, p. 137.

41. Sarah Binder, "Congress in the Rearview Mirror," *Washington Post*, 31 December 2013, http://www.washingtonpost.com/blogs/monkey-cage/wp/2013/12/31/congress-in-the-rearview-mirror/.

42. Sean M. Theriault, *Party Polarization in Congress* (New York: Cambridge University Press, 2008); and Nolan McCarty, Keith T. Poole, and Howard Rosenthal, *Polarized America* (Cambridge, Mass.: MIT Press, 2008).

43. Jeffrey M. Berry and Sarah Sobieraj, *The Outrage Industry: Political Opinion Media and the New Incivility* (New York: Oxford University Press, 2014).

44. David Remnick, "Going the Distance," *New Yorker*, 27 January 2014, p. 51.

45. Jane Mansbridge and Cathie Jo Martin, eds., *Negotiating Agreement in Politics* (Washington: D.C: American Political Science Association, 2013), https://www.apsanet.org/negotiatingagreement/.

46. "Prepared Text of Carter's Farewell Address," *New York Times*, 15 January 1981, p. B10.

47. John Sides and Lynn Vavreck, *The Gamble* (Princeton, N.J.: Princeton University Press, 2013).

48. On the "time-for-a-change" variable, see Alan I. Abramowitz, "Forecasting the 2008 Election with the Time-for-Change Model," *PS: Political Science and Politics* 41 (October 2008): 691–695.

49. *Public Papers of the President*, Lyndon B. Johnson, 1965, vol. 1 (Washington, D.C.: U.S. Government Printing Office, 1966), p. 72.

50. "Transcript of Second Inaugural Address by Reagan," *New York Times*, 22 January 1985, p. 72. For a historical study of how presidents use the symbol of freedom, see Kevin Coe, "The Language of Freedom in the American Presidency, 1933–2006," *Presidential Studies Quarterly* 37 (September 2007): 375–398.

51. Kevin Phillips, *The Politics of Rich and Poor* (New York: Random House, 1990), p. 88.

52. Seth King, "Reagan, in Bid for Budget Votes, Reported to Yield on Sugar Prices," *New York Times*, 27 June 1981, p. A1.

53. Matt Bai, "Taking the Hill," *New York Times Magazine*, 7 June 2009, p. 35.

54. Sidney M. Milkis, Jesse H. Rhodes, and Emily J. Charnock, "What Happened to Post-Partisanship? Barack Obama and the New American Party System," *Perspectives on Politics* 10 (March 2012): 57–76.

55. Richard M. Skinner, "George W. Bush and the Partisan Presidency," *Political Science Quarterly* 123 (Winter 2008–2009): 605–622; and Milkis et al., "What Happened to Post-Partisanship?"

56. Lydia Saad, "Majority in U.S. Say Bin Laden's Death Makes America Safer," *Gallup Poll*, 4 May 2011, http://www.gallup.com/poll/147413/Majority-Say-Bin-Laden-Death-Makes-America-Safer.aspx.

57. John Yoo, who worked in the Office of Legal Counsel for President George W. Bush, distinguishes between the power to "declare" war, given to Congress, and the power to "make" war, which inheres in the president, in *Crisis and Command: The History of Executive Power from George Washington to George W. Bush* (New York: Kaplan Publishing, 2009).

58. Miles A. Pomper, "In for the Long Haul," *CO Weekly Report*, 15 September 2001, p. 2118.

59. "The Senate's Role in Treaties," United States Senate, http://www.senate.gov/artandhistory/history/common/briefing/Treaties.htm.

60. *United States v. Curtiss-Wright Export Corporation*, 299 U.S. 304 (1936); *United States v. Belmont*, 301 U.S. 324 (1937); and Jack C. Plano and Roy Olton, *The International Relations Dictionary* (New York: Holt, Rinehart and Winston, 1969), p. 149.

61. Plano and Olton, *The International Relations Dictionary*, p. 149.

62. Lyn Ragsdale, *Vital Statistics on the Presidency* (Washington, D.C.: CQ Press, 1998), pp. 317–319. After 1984, government reports eliminated the clear distinction between treaties and executive agreements, making it difficult to determine the ratio. Indeed, other nations have criticized the reluctance of the United States to sign binding treaties. See Barbara Crossette, "Washington Is Criticized for Growing Reluctance to Sign Treaties," *New York Times*, 4 April 2002, p. A5.

63. Paul R. Pillar, *Intelligence and U.S. Foreign Policy* (New York: Columbia University Press, 2011).

64. Office of the Direcctor of National Intelligence, http://www.dni.gov/index.php.

65. Robert Jervis, "Why Intelligence and Policymakers Clash," *Political Science Quarterly* 125 (Summer 2010): 125.

66. Ernest R. May and Philip D. Zelikow (eds.), *The Kennedy Tapes: Inside the White House during the Cuban Missile Crisis* (Cambridge, Mass.: Harvard University Press, 1997), pp. 498–499, 498–501, 512–513, 663–666.

Chapter 13

1. "Key Facts about the Uninsured Population," Henry J. Kaiser Family Foundation, 26 September 2013, http://kff.org/uninsured/fact-sheet/key-facts-about-the-uninsured-population/.

2. Sheryl Gay Stolberg and Michael D. Shear, "Inside the Race to Rescue a Health Care Site, and Obama," *New York Times*, 30 November 2013, http://www.nytimes.com/2013/12/01/us/politics/inside-the-race-to-rescue-a-health-site-and-obama.html?_r=0.

3. Stolberg and Shear, "Inside the Race."

4. Malcolm Gladwell, "The Talent Myth," *New Yorker*, 22 July 2002, p. 32.

5. James Q. Wilson, *Bureaucracy* (New York: Basic Books, 1989), p. 25.

6. Bruce D. Porter, "Parkinson's Law Revisited: War and the Growth of American Government," *Public Interest* 60 (Summer 1980): 50.

7. Binyamin Applebaum and Annie Lowrey, "For Deficit Panel, Failure Cuts Two Ways," *New York Times*, 21 November 2011, http:// www.nytimes.com/2011/11/22/us/politics/behind-deficit-panelsfailure-a-surprise.html.

8. United States Census Bureau, *2012 Statistical Abstract*, "Federal Civilian Employment and Annual Payroll" (Table 496).

9. Joel D. Aberbach and Bert A. Rockman, *In the Web of Politics* (Washington, D.C.: Brookings Institution, 2000), p. 162.

10. *Satisfaction with Performance-Based Rewards and Advancement*, Partnership for Public Service, June, 2013, http://bestplacestowork.org/BPTW/index.php.

11. On the challenges of trying to loosen the strictures and protections of civil service, see Norma Riccucci and Frank J. Thompson, "The New Public Management, Homeland Security, and the Politics of Civil Service Reform," *Public Administration Review* 68 (September–October 2008): 877–890.

12. *A Survivor's Guide for Presidential Nominations*, National Academy of Public Administration (2013). Congress has recently made a modest decrease in number of appointees requiring confirmation. See *Presidential Appointee Positions Requiring Senate Confirmation and Committees Handling Nominations*, Congressional Research Service, November, 2013.

13. David E. Lewis, "Testing Pendleton's Premise: Do Political Appointees Make Worse Bureaucrats?" *Journal of Politics* 69 (November 2007): 1073–1088.

14. See, for example, Paul R. Pillar, *Intelligence and U.S. Foreign Policy* (New York: Columbia University Press, 2011), pp. 331–352.

15. See Sean Gailmard and John W. Patty, *Learning While Governing* (Chicago: University of Chicago Press, 2013).

16. Daniel Carpenter, "Corrosive Capture? The Dueling Forces of Autonomy and Industry Influence in FDA Pharmaceutical Regulation," in *Reviewing Regulatory Capture*, ed. Daniel Carpenter and David A. Moss, (New York: Cambridge University Press), pp. 152–172.

17. Sabrina Tavernise, "F.D.A. Seeking Near Total Ban on Trans Fats," *New York Times*, 11 August 2013.

18. See Jack Goldsmith, *Power and Constraint* (New York: Norton, 2012).

19. U.S. Department of Transportation, "New DOT Consumer Rule Limits Airline Tarmac Delays," press release, http://www.dot.gov/affairs/ 2009/dot19909.htm; and Matthew L. Wald, "stiff Fines Are Set for Long Wait on Tarmac," *New York Times*, 22 December 2009.

20. Joel Sharkey, "Tarmac Purgatory Ends, But New Trials Appear," *New York Times*, 24 February 2014, http://www.nytimes.com/2014/02/25/business/tarmac-purgatory-ends-but-new-trials-appear.html.

21. Charles E. Lindblom, "The Science of Muddling Through," *Public Administration Review* 19 (Spring 1959): 79–88.

22. For a critical examination of determining what is a small increment, see Sarah Anderson and Laurel Harbridge, "Incrementalism in Appropriations: Small Aggregation, Big Changes," *Public Administration Review* 70 (May 2010): 464–474.

23. Bryan D. Jones and Frank R. Baumgartner, *The Politics of Attention* (Chicago: University of Chicago Press, 2005).

24. "Bureaucratic culture" is a particularly slippery concept but can be conceived of as the interplay of artifacts, values, and underlying assumptions. See Celeste Watkins-Hayes, *The New Welfare Bureaucrats* (Chicago: University of Chicago Press, 2009); Irene Lurie and Norma Riccucci, "Changing the 'Culture' of Welfare Offices," *Administration and Society* 34 (January 2003): 653–677; and Marissa Martino Golden, *What Motivates Bureaucrats?* (New York: Columbia University Press, 2000).

25. Jay P. Greene and Stuart Buck, "The Case for Special Education Vouchers," *Education Next* (Winter 2010): 36–43.

26. Panetta became Secretary of Defense in 2011.

27. Jane Mayer, "The Secret History," *New Yorker*, 22 June 2009, pp. 50–59; and Jane Mayer, *The Dark Side* (New York: Anchor Books, 2009).

28. Philip K. Howard, *The Rule of Nobody* (New York: Norton, 2014).

29. Daniel A. Mazmanian, "Los Angeles' Clean Air Saga-Spanning the Three Epochs," in *Toward Sustainable Communities,* ed. Daniel A. Mazmanian and Michael E. Kraft (Cambridge, Mass.: MIT Press, 2009), p. 107.

30. Jeffrey M. Berry with David F. Arons, *A Voice for Nonprofits* (Washington, D.C.: Brookings Institution, 2003); and Joseph J. Cordes and C.Eugene Steuerle, eds., *Nonprofits and Business* (Washington, D.C.: Urban Institute, 2009).

31. Eric M. Patashnik and Julian E. Zelizer, "The Struggle to Remake Politics: Liberal Reform and the Limits of Policy Feedback in the Contemporary American State," *Perspectives on Politics* 11 (December 2013): 1071–1087.

32. Tom Bartlett, "The Great Mom & Dad Experiment," *The Chronicle Review*, 24 January 2014, pp. B6–B9.

33. Daniel J. Fiorino, *The New Environmental Regulation* (Cambridge, Mass.: MIT Press, 2006).

34. Nancy Watzman, "Rulemaking in the Dark," Sunlight Foundation, 26 September 2013, http://sunlightfoundation.com/blog/2013/09/26/Rulemaking_in_the_dark_FDA/.

35. Benjamin Goad, "Under Perez, Labor Department Produces a Blizzard of New Rules," *The Hill*, 29 October 2013, http://thehill.com/blogs/regwatch/labor/188427-under-perez-labor-department-produces-a-blizzard-of-new-rules.

36. Eric Lipton, "With Obama, Regulations Are Back in Fashion," *New York Times*, 13 May 2010.

37. Joseph B. White, "Self-Driving Cars Spur New Guidelines," *Wall Street Journal*, 31 May 2013.

38. David Vogel, *The Politics of Precaution* (Princeton. N.J.: Princeton University Press, 2012).

39. Maximus, "Child Support," http://www.maximus.com/services/children-families/child-support.

40. Donald F. Kettl, "The Global Revolution in Public Management: Driving Themes, Missing Links," *Journal of Policy Analysis and Management* 16 (1997): 448.

41. Donald P. Moynihan and Stéphane Lavertu, "Does Involvement in Performance Management Routines Encourage Performance Information Use? Evaluating GPRA and PART," *Public Administration Review* 72 (July/August 2012): 592–602.

42. David G. Frederickson and H. George Frederickson, *Measuring the Performance of the Hollow State* (Washington, D.C.: Georgetown University Press, 2006), pp. 56–57.

43. Vassia Gueorguieva et al., "The Program Assessment Rating Tool and the Government Performance and Results Act," *The American Review of Public Administration* 39 (May 2009): 225–245.

Chapter 14

1. Philip Elman (interviewed by Normal Silber), "The Solicitor General's Office, Justice Frankfurter, and Civil Rights Litigation, 1946–1960: An Oral History," *Harvard Law Review* 100 (1987): 840.

2. David O'Brien, *Storm Center*, 2nd ed. (New York: Norton, 1990), p. 324.

3. Bernard Schwartz, *The Unpublished Opinions of the Warren Court* (New York: Oxford University Press, 1985), p. 446.

4. Ibid., pp. 445–448.

5. Felix Frankfurter and James M. Landis, *The Business of the Supreme Court* (New York: Macmillan, 1928), pp. 5–14; and Julius Goebel, Jr., *The History of the Supreme Court of the United States, vol. 1, Antecedents and Beginnings to 1801* (New York: Macmillan, 1971).

6. Maeva Marcus (ed.), *The Documentary History of the Supreme Court of the United States, 1789–1800, vol. 3, The Justices on Circuit, 1795–1800* (New York: Columbia University Press, 1990).

7. Robert G. McCloskey, *The United States Supreme Court* (Chicago: University of Chicago Press, 1960), p. 31.

8. Cliff Sloan and David McKean, *The Great Decision: Jefferson, Adams, Marshall, and the Battle for the Supreme Court* (New York: Public Affairs, 2009).

9. *Marbury* v. *Madison,* 1 Cranch 137 at 177, 178 (1803).

10. Interestingly, the term judicial review dates only to 1910; it was apparently unknown to Marshall and his contemporaries. Robert Lowry Clinton, *Marbury* v. *Madison and Judicial Review* (Lawrence: University Press of Kansas, 1989), p. 7.

11. "Acts of Congress Held Unconstitutional in Whole or in Part by the Supreme Court of the United States," http://beta.congress.gov/content/conan/pdf/GPO-CONAN-2013-11.pdf.

12. "Supreme Court Decisions Overruled by Subsequent Decision," http://www.gpo.gov/fdsys/pkg/GPO-CONAN-2013/pdf/GPO-CONAN-2013-12.pdf.

13. *Martin* v. *Hunter's Lessee,* 1 Wheat. 304 (1819).

14. Epstein et al., *The Supreme Court Compendium*, 5th ed. (Washington, D.C.: CQ Press, 2011)Table 2-16.

15. Garry Wills, *Explaining America: The Federalist* (Garden City, N.Y.: Doubleday, 1981), pp. 127–136.

16. Court Statistics Project, "Appeals by Right Dominate Intermediate Appellate Court Caseloads," http://www.courtstatistics.org/Appellate/AppellateABR1.aspx; U.S. Census Bureau, *Statistical Abstract of the United States: 2012,* "Law Enforcement, Courts, and Prisons," Table 335, p. 211, http://www.census.gov/compendia/statab/2012/tables/12s0335.pdf.; and John G. Roberts, Jr. "2013 Year-End Report on the Federal Judiciary," http://www.supremecourt.gov/publicinfo/year-end/2013year-endreport.pdf (excludes bankruptcy cases).

17. William P. Marshall, "Federalization: A Critical Overview," *DePaul Law Review* 44 (1995): 722–723.

18. Charles Alan Wright, *Handbook on the Law of Federal Courts*, 3rd ed. (St. Paul, Minn.: West, 1976), p. 7.

19. *Judicial Business of the United States Courts, 2013,* http://www.uscourts.gov/Statistics/JudicialBusiness/2013.aspx.

20. *Appointments of Magistrate Judges,* http://www.uscourts.gov/Statistics/JudicialBusiness/2013/appointments-magistrate-judges.aspx.

21. Ibid.

22. Linda Greenhouse, "Precedent for Lower Courts: Tyrant or Teacher?" *New York Times*, 29 January 1988, p. B7.

23. *Texas* v. *Johnson, 491* U.S. 397 (1989); and *United States* v. *Eichmann,* 496 U.S. 310 (1990).

24. *Regents of the University of California* v. *Bakke,* 438 U.S. 265 (1978).

25. *Grutter* v. *Bollinger,* 539 U.S. 244 (2003); and *Gratz* v. *Bollinger,* 539 U.S. 306 (2003).

26. *Schuette* v. *Coalition to Defend Affirmative Action,* 572 U.S. ___ (2014).

27. "Reading Petitions Is for Clerks Only at High Court Now," *Wall Street Journal,* 11 October 1990, p. B7.

28. H. W. Perry, Jr., *Deciding to Decide: Agenda Setting in the United States Supreme Court* (Cambridge, Mass.: Harvard University Press, 1991); and Linda Greenhouse, "Justice Delayed: Agreeing Not to Agree," *New York Times,* 17 March 1996, sec. 4, p. 1.

29. Jeffrey Rosen, "supreme Court Inc.: How the Nation's Highest Court Has Come to Side with Business," *New York Times Magazine,* 16 March 2008, pp. 38 et seq.

30. Perry, *Deciding to Decide*; and Gregory A. Caldiera and John R. Wright, "The Discuss List: Agenda Building in the Supreme Court," *Law and Society Review* 24 (1990): 807.

31. Doris M. Provine, *Case Selection in the United States Supreme Court* (Chicago: University of Chicago Press, 1980), pp. 74–102.

32. Perry, *Deciding to Decide,* p. 286.

33. Justice Anthony M. Kennedy, quoted in Adam Liptak, "No Vote-Trading Here," *New York Times: Week in Review,* 16 May 2010, p. 4.

34. Kevin T. McGuire, "Repeat Players in the Supreme Court: The Role of Experienced Lawyers in Litigation Success," *Journal of Politics* 57 (1995): 187–196.

35. Michael Kirkland, "Court Hears 'Subordinate' Speech Debate," 1 December 1993, NEWSNET News Bulletin Board. The oral argument in the case, *Waters* v. *Churchill,* can be found at http://www.oyez.org/cases/1990-1999/1993/1993_92_1450.

36. William H. Rehnquist, "Remarks of the Chief Justice: My Life in the Law Series," *Duke Law Journal* 52 (2003): 787–805.

37. "Rising Fixed Opinions," *New York Times,* 22 February 1988, p. 14. See also Linda Greenhouse, "At the Bar," *New York Times,* 28 July 1989, p. 21.

38. Jeffrey A. Segal and Harold J. Spaeth, *The Supreme Court and the Attitudinal Model* (Cambridge: Cambridge University Press, 1993).

39. Stefanie A. Lindquist and Frank B. Cross, *Measuring Judicial Activism* (New York: Oxford University Press, 2009), pp. 1–28.

40. Stuart Taylor, Jr., "Lifting of Secrecy Reveals Earthy Side of Justices," *New York Times,* 22 February 1988, p. A16.

41. Richard A. Posner, "The Courthouse Mice," *New Republic,* 12 June 2006, http://tnr.com/article/the-courthouse-mice.

42. Thomas G. Walker, Lee Epstein, and William J. Dixon, "On the Mysterious Demise of Consensual Norms in the United States Supreme Court," *Journal of Politics* 50 (1988): 361–389.

43. Linda Greenhouse, "Roberts Is at Court's Helm, but He Isn't Yet in Control," *New York Times,* 2 July 2006, sec. 1, p. 1. See also John P. Kelsh, "The Opinion Delivery Practices of the United States Supreme Court, 1790–1945," *Washington University Law Quarterly* 77 (1999): 137–181. For more on the Roberts Court, see Linda Greenhouse, "Oral Dissents Give Ginsberg New Voice," *New York Times,* 31 May 2007, p. A1; and Jeffrey Toobin, "Five to Four," *New Yorker,* 25 June 2007, pp. 35–37.

44. Stephen L. Wasby, *The Supreme Court in the Federal Judicial System,* 3rd ed. (Chicago: Nelson-Hall, 1988), p. 241.

45. Greenhouse, "At the Bar," p. 21.

46. National Center for State Courts, "survey of Judicial Salaries," Vol. 38, No. 2, 1 July 2013, http://ncsc.contentdm.oclc.org/cdm/ref/collection/judicial/id/382.

47. Nathan Koppel and Vanessa O'Connell, "Pay Gap Widens at Big Law Firms as Partners Chase Star Attorneys," *Wall Street Journal,* 8 February 2011, http://online.wsj.com/article/SB100014240527487045 70104576124232780067002.html; *US News and World Report,* "Law Jobs Will Be Harder to Come by," 25 June 2010, http://www.usnews.com/education/articles/2010/06/25/law-jobswill-be-harder-to-come-by; and Sam Favate, *Survey: Median Starting Salaries Plunge for New Law Grads,* WSJ Law Blog, 12 July 2012, http://blogs.wsj.com/law/2012/07/12/survey-median-starting-salariesplunge-for-new-law-grads/.

48. Carlyn Kolker, "summary Judgments for Feb 6," http://newsandinsight.thomsonreuters.com/Legal/News/2012/02_-_February/Summary_Judgments_for_Feb_6/.

49. Lawrence Baum, *American Courts: Process and Policy,* 3rd ed. (Boston: Houghton Mifflin, 1994), pp. 114–129.

50. *Caperton* v. *A. T. Massey Coal Co.,* 556 U.S. 868 (2009).

51. Wikipedia, "List of Federal Judges Appointed by Barack Obama," http://en.wikipedia.org/wiki/List_of_federal_judges_appointed_by_Barack_Obama.

52. Tajuana D. Massie, Thomas G. Hansford, and David R. Songer, "The Timing of Presidential Nominations to Lower Federal Courts," *Political Research Quarterly* 57 (2004): 145–154.

53. Sheldon Goldman et al., "Picking Judges in a Time of Turmoil: W. Bush's Judiciary During the 109th Congress," *Judicature* 90 (May–June 2007): 252–283.

54. Paul Barrett, "More Minorities, Women Named to U.S. Courts," *Wall Street Journal,* 23 December 1993, p. B1; and Sheldon Goldman and Elliot Slotnick, "Clinton's Second Term Judiciary: Picking Judges under Fire," *Judicature* 92 (May–June 1999): 264–284.

55. Kenneth L. Manning and Robert A. Carp, "The Decision-Making Ideology of George W. Bush's Judicial Appointees: An Update" (paper presented at the annual meeting of the American Political Science Association, Chicago, 2–5 September 2004).

56. Charlie Savage and Raymond Hernandez, "Filibuster by Senate Republicans Blocks Confirmation of Judicial Nominee," *New York Times,* 7 December 2011, p. A16, http://www.nytimes.com/2011/12/07/us/senate-gop-blocks-confirmation-of-caitlin-halligan-as-judg-e.html; and Joe Palazzolo, "With Rose Confirmation, Obama Sets a Record," The Wall Street Journal Law Blog, 11 September 2012, http://blogs.wsj.com/law/2012/09/11/with-rose-confirmation-obama-sets-a-record.

57. Wasby, *Supreme Court,* pp. 107–110.

58. Jeffrey Toobin, *The Nine: Inside the Secret World of the Supreme Court* (New York: Doubleday, 2007), p. 269.

59. State News Service, "statement of H. Thomas Wells Jr., President, American Bar Association re: American Bar Association Standing Committee on Federal Judiciary," 17 March 2009.

60. Sheldon Goldman. "Obama and the Federal Judiciary: Great Expectations but Will He Have a Dickens of a Time Living up to Them?" *The Forum* 7.1 (2010), http://works.bepress.com/sheldon_goldman/1.

61. Peter G. Fish, "John J. Parker," in *Dictionary of American Biography,* supp. 6, 1956–1980 (New York: Scribner's, 1980), p. 494.

62. Supreme Court Nominations, present–1789," http://www.senate.gov/pagelayout/reference/nominations/Nominations.htm.

63. "CRS Report for Congress: Supreme Court Nominations Not Filled," p. 7, 9 January 2008, http://www.fas.org/sgp/crs/misc/RL31171.pdf.

64. "supreme Court Nominee Sonia Sotomayor's Speech at Berkeley Law in 2001," *Berkeley La Raza Law Journal* (2002), http://law.berkeley.edu/4982.htm.

65. Elena Kagan, "Confirmation Messes: Old and New," *The University of Chicago Law Review* 62, No. 2 (Spring 1995): 919–942, http://www.scotusblog.com/wp-content/uploads/2010/03/Confirmation-Messes.pdf.

66. "Transcript: Kagan's Opening Statement," http://m.npr.org/news/front/128171860?page=3.

67. *Brown* v. *Board of Education II,* 349 U.S.294 (1955).

68. Charles A. Johnson and Bradley C. Canon, *Judicial Policies: Implementation and Impact* (Washington, D.C.: CQ Press, 1984).

69. *Webster* v. *Reproductive Health Services,* 492 U.S. 490 (1989).

70. *Planned Parenthood* v. *Casey,* 505 U.S. 833 (1992).

71. *Stenberg* v. *Carhart,* 530 U.S. 914 (2000); and *Gonzales* v. *Carhart,* 550 U.S. 124 (2007).

72. Alexander M. Bickel, *The Least Dangerous Branch* (Indianapolis, Ind.: Bobbs-Merrill, 1962); and Robert A. Dahl, "Decision-Making in a Democracy: The Supreme Court as a National Policy-Maker," *Journal of Public Law* 6 (1962): 279.

73. William Mishler and Reginald S. Sheehan, "The Supreme Court as a Countermajoritarian Institution? The Impact of Public Opinion on Supreme Court Decisions," *American Political Science Review* 87 (1993): 87–101.

74. Barry Friedman, *The Will of the People* (New York: Farrar, Straus and Giroux, 2009).

75. *Engel* v. *Vitale*, 367 U.S. 643 (1961).

76. James L. Gibson and Gregory A. Caldiera, "Knowing about Courts" (paper presented at the Second Annual Conference on Empirical Legal Studies, 20 June 2007), http://ssrn.com/abstract=956562.

77. Gallup Poll, "High Court to Start Term with Near Decade-High Approval," http://gallup.com/poll/122858/High-Court-Start-Term-Near-Decade-High-Approval.aspx?CSTS=alert.

78. Rebecca Rifkin, "Americans' Approval of the Supreme Court Remains Divided," *Gallup Politics,* 14 July 2014 http://www.gallup.com/poll/172526/americans-approval-supreme-court-remains-divided

79. *Kelo* v. *City of New London*, 545 U.S. 469 (2005).

80. William J. Brennan, Jr., "state Supreme Court Judge versus United States Supreme Court Justice: A Change in Function and Perspective," *University of Florida Law Review* 19 (1966): 225.

81. G. Alan Tarr and M. C. Porter, *State Supreme Courts in State and Nation* (New Haven, Conn.: Yale University Press, 1988), pp. 206–209.

82. John B. Wefing, "The Performance of the New Jersey Supreme Court at the Opening of the Twenty-first Century: New Cast, Same Script," *Seton Hall Law Review* 32 (2003): 769.

83. *New Jersey* v. *Hempele,* 120 N.J. 182 (1990).

84. Kermit L. Hall, "The Canon of American Constitutional History in Comparative Perspective" (keynote address to the Supreme Court Historical Society, Washington, D.C., 16 February 2001).

85. Baum, *American Courts*, pp. 319–347.

Chapter 15

1. Chris Strohm and Del Quentin Wilber, "Pentagon Says Snowden Took Most U.S. Secrets Ever," *Bloomberg News,* 9 January 2014.

2. Senator Dianne Feinstein, Press Release, "Feinstein on President's Review Group on Intelligence and Communications," 20 December 2013.

3. Dana Priest and William M. Arkin, "A Hidden World, Growing Beyond Control," *Washington Post,* 19 July 2010. http://projects.washingtonpost.com/top-secret-america/articles/a-hidden-world-growing-beyond-control/.

4. Learned Hand, *The Bill of Rights* (Boston: Atheneum, 1958), p. 1.

5. http://www.bbc.com/news/uk-politics-20757384; and Joint Committee on Human Rights, A Bill of Rights for the UK? Twenty-ninth Report of Session 2007–08 (London: Stationery Office, Ltd., 10 August 2008), http://www.publications. parliament.uk/pa/jt200708/jtselect/jtrights/165/165i.pdf

6. Richard E. Berg-Andersson, "Of Liberties, Rights and Powers (Part One): Just How Far Is Too Far–for Both Governments and Persons?" Green Papers Commentary, 27 April 2006, http://www.thegreenpapers.com/PCom/?20060427-0.

7. Leonard W. Levy, *The Establishment Clause: Religion and the First Amendment* (New York: Macmillan, 1986); Leo Pfeffer, *Church, State, and Freedom* (Boston: Beacon Press, 1953); and Leonard W. Levy, "The Original Meaning of the Establishment Clause of the First Amendment," in *Religion and the State*, ed. James E. Wood, Jr. (Waco, Tex.: Baylor University Press, 1985), pp. 43–83.

8. Gallup, "Seven in 10 Americans are Very or Moderately Religious," 4 December 2012; Pew Research Global Attitudes Project, "The American-Western European Values Gap," 29 February 2012; and

Pew Research Global Attitudes Project, "Worldwide, Many See Belief in God as Essential to Morality," 13 March 2014.

9. *Utah Highway Patrol Association* v. *American Atheists, Inc.*, 565 U.S. ___ (2011) (Thomas, J. dissenting from a denial of certiorari).

10. *Reynolds* v. *United States*, 98 U.S. 145 (1879).

11. *Everson* v. *Board of Education*, 330 U.S. 1 (1947).

12. *Board of Education* v. *Allen*, 392 U.S. 236 (1968).

13. *Lemon* v. *Kurtzman*, 403 U.S. 602 (1971).

14. *Agostini* v. *Felton*, 96 U.S. 552 (1997).

15. *Zelman* v. *Simmons-Harris*, 536 U.S. 639 (2002).

16. Alliance for School Choice, *School Choice Yearbook 2013–14* (Washington, DC: Author, 2014).

17. *Lynch* v. *Donnelly*, 465 U.S. 668 (1984).

18. *Van Orden* v. *Perry*, 545 U.S. 677 (2005).

19. *McCreary County* v. *ACLU of Kentucky*, 545 U.S. 844 (2005).

20. *Salazar* v. *Buono*, 559 U.S.___(2010).

21. *Engle* v. *Vitale*, 370 U.S. 421 (1962); David W. Moore, "Public Favors Voluntary School Prayer for Public Schools," 26 Aug 2005, http://www.gallup.com/poll/18136/Public-Favors-Voluntary-Prayer-Public-Schools.aspx; and "Public Opinion On 15 Controversial and Divisive Issues," 4 October 2011, http://www.harrisinteractive.com/News-Room/HarrisPolls/tabid/447/ctl/ReadCustom%20Default/mid/1508/ArticleId/874/Default.aspx.

22. *Abington School District* v. *Schempp*, 374 U.S. 203 (1963).

23. *Lee* v. *Weisman*, 505 U.S. 577 (1992).

24. Neela Banerjee, "School Board to Pay in Jesus Prayer Suit," *New York Times*, 28 February 2008, p. A16.

25. *Ahlquist* v. ___ 2012 U.S. Dist. LEXIS 3348 (USDC, D. RI) (Jan. 11, 2012).

26. "TOWN OF GREECE v. GALLOWAY," The Oyez Project at IIT Chicago-Kent College of Law, accessed 29 May 2014, http://www.oyez.org/cases/2010-2019/2013/2013_12_696.

27. Michael W. McConnell, "The Origins and Historical Understanding of the Free Exercise of Religion," *Harvard Law Review* 103 (1990): 1409.

28. *Sherbert* v. *Verner*, 374 U.S. 398 (1963).

29. Adam Winkler, "Fatal in Theory and Strict in Fact: An Empirical Analysis of Strict Scrutiny in the Federal Courts," *Vanderbilt Law Review* 59 (2006): 793.

30. McConnell, "Origins and Historical Understanding."

31. *Employment Division* v. *Smith*, 494 U.S. 872 (1990).

32. *Sebelius* v. *Hobby Lobby Stores*, The Oyez Project at IIT Chicago-Kent College of Law, accessed 29 April 2014, http://www.oyez.org/cases/2010-2019/2013/2013_13_354.

33. Laurence Tribe, *Treatise on American Constitutional Law*, 2nd ed. (St. Paul, Minn.: West, 1988), p. 566.

34. Zechariah Chafee, *Free Speech in the United States* (Cambridge, Mass.: Harvard University Press, 1941).

35. Leonard W. Levy, *The Emergence of a Free Press* (New York: Oxford University Press, 1985).

36. Mark Twain, *Following the Equator* (Hartford, Conn.: American Publishing, 1897).

37. *Brandenburg* v. *Ohio*, 395 U.S. 444 (1969).

38. *Schenck* v. *United States* v. *United States*, 249 U.S. 47 (1919).

39. *Abrams* v. *United States*, 250 U.S. 616 (1919).

40. *Gitlow* v. *New York*, 268 U.S. 652 (1925).

41. *Dennis* v. *United States*, 341 U.S. 494 (1951).

42. *Brandenburg* v. *Ohio*, 395 U.S. 444 (1969).

43. Anthony Lewis, *Freedom for the Thought That We Hate: A Biography of the First Amendment* (New York: Basic Books, 2008).

44. *Tinker* v. *Des Moines Independent County School District*, 393 U.S. 503, at 508 (1969).

45. Justin Jouvenal, "A Facebook Court Battle: Is 'Liking' Something Protected Free Speech?" *New York Times*, 8 August 2012; and Justin Jouvenal, "Facebook 'Liking' is Protected Free Speech, Federal Court Says," *Washington Post*, 18 September 2013.

46. *Chaplinsky* v. *New Hampshire*, 315 U.S. 568 (1942).

47. *Terminiello* v. *Chicago*, 337 U.S. 1, 37 (1949).

48. *Cohen* v. *California*, 403 U.S. 15 (1971).

49. *McCutcheon et al* v. *Federal Election Commission*. No. 12-536. Argued October 8, 2013—Decided April 2, 2014. http://www.supremecourt.gov/opinions/13pdf/12-536_e1pf.pdf.

50. Adam Liptak, "Supreme Court Strikes Down Overall Political Donation Cap," *New York Times*, 2 April 2014.

51. Kathleen M. Sullivan, "Two Concepts of Political Freedom," *Harvard Law Review* 124 (November 2010): 143–177.

52. *New York Times* v. *Sullivan*, 376 U.S. 254 (1964).

53. *Near* v. *Minnesota*, 283 U.S. 697 (1931).

54. For a detailed account of *Near*, see Fred W. Friendly, *Minnesota Rag* (New York: Random House, 1981).

55. *New York Times* v. *United States*, 403 U.S. 713 (1971).

56. *Branzburg* v. *Hayes*, 408 U.S. 665 (1972).

57. *Hazelwood School District* v. *Kuhlmeier*, 484 U.S. 260 (1988); and *Morse* v. *Frederick*, 551 U.S. 393 (2007).

58. *United States* v. *Cruikshank*, 92 U.S. 542 (1876); and *Constitution of the United States of America: Annotated and Interpreted* (Washington, D.C.: U.S. Government Printing Office, 1973), p. 1031.

59. *DeJonge* v. *Oregon*, 299 U.S. 353 (1937).

60. Liane Hansen, "Voices in the News This Week," *NPR Weekend Edition*, 28 October 2001 (NEXIS transcript).

61. Dan Eggen, "Tough Anti-Terror Campaign Pledged: Ashcroft Tells Mayors He Will Use New Law to Fullest Extent," *Washington Post*, 26 October 2001, p. A1.

62. Chris Boyette, "New York Police Department Disbands Unite that Spied on Muslims," CNN.com, 16 April 2014.

63. *United States* v. *Miller*, 307 U.S. 174 (1939).

64. *District of Columbia* v. *Heller*, 554 U.S. 290 (2008).

65. *McDonald* v. *Chicago*, 561 U.S.___(2010).

66. Robert Barnes, "Supreme Court Declines to Hear Gun Law Challenges," *Washington Post*, 24 February 2014.

67. *Barron* v. *Baltimore*, 32 U.S. (7 Pet.) 243 (1833).

68. *Lochner* v. *New York*, 198 U.S. 45 (1905).

69. *Chicago B&Q Railroad* v. *Chicago*, 166 U.S. 226 (1897).

70. *Gitlow* v. *New York*, 268 U.S. 652, 666 (1925).

71. *Palko* v. *Connecticut*, 302 U.S. 319 (1937).

72. *Duncan* v. *Louisiana*, 391 U.S. 145 (1968).

73. *McNabb* v. *United States*, 318 U.S. 332 (1943).

74. *Baldwin* v. *New York*, 399 U.S. 66 (1970).

75. Anthony Lewis, *Gideon's Trumpet* (New York: Random House, 1964).

76. *Gideon* v. *Wainwright*, 372 U.S. 335 (1963).

77. *Miranda* v. *Arizona*, 384 U.S. 436 (1966).

78. *Dickerson* v. *United States*, 530 U.S. 428 (2000).

79. *Wolf* v. *Colorado*, 338 U.S. 25 (1949).

80. *Mapp* v. *Ohio*, 367 U.S. 643 (1961).

81. *United States* v. *Leon*, 468 U.S. 897 (1984).

82. *Hudson* v. *Michigan*, 547 U.S. 586 (2006).

83. *Herring* v. *United States*, 555 U.S.___(2009).

84. RILEY v. CALIFORNIA. The Oyez Project at IIT Chicago-Kent College of Law, accessed 22 July 2014. <http://www.oyez.org/cases/2010-2019/2013/2013_13_132>

85. Paul Brest, *Processes of Constitutional Decision-Making* (Boston: Little, Brown, 1975), p. 708.

86. *Griswold* v. *Connecticut*, 381 U.S. 479 (1965).

87. *Roe* v. *Wade*, 410 U.S. 113 (1973).

88. See John Hart Ely, "The Wages of Crying Wolf: A Comment on *Roe* v. *Wade*," *Yale Law Journal* 82 (1973): 920.

89. Justice Harry Blackmun, interview by Ted Koppel and Nina Totenberg, *Nightline*, ABC, 2 December 1993.

90. *Webster* v. *Reproductive Health Services*, 492 U.S. 490 (1989).

91. *Hodgson* v. *Minnesota*, 497 U.S. 417 (1990); and *Ohio* v. *Akron Center for Reproductive Health*, 497 U.S. 502 (1990).

92. *Steinberg* v. *Carhart*, 530 U.S. 914 (2000).

93. *Gonzales* v. *Carhart*, 550 U.S. 124 (2007).

94. Stuart Taylor, "Supreme Court Hears Case on Homosexual Rights," *New York Times*, 1 April 1986, p. A24.

95. *Bowers* v. *Hardwick*, 478 U.S. 186 (1986).

96. Linda Greenhouse, "Washington Talk: When Second Thoughts Come Too Late," *New York Times*, 5 November 1990, p. A9.

97. Dahlia Lithwick, "*Lawrence v. Texas*: How Laws Against Sodomy Became Unconstitutional," *The New Yorker*, 7 Mar 2012, http://www.newyorker.com/arts/critics/books/2012/03/12/120312crbo_books_lithwick; and Dale Carpenter, *Flagrant Conduct: The Story of Lawrence v. Texas* (New York: W. W. Norton & Company, 2012).

98. *Lawrence and Garner* v. *Texas*, 539 U.S. 558 (2003).

99. Ibid.

Chapter 16

1. *Fisher* v. *University of Texas*, 645 F.Supp.2d 587 (2009); *Fisher* v. *University of Texas*, 631 F. 3d 213 (2011); and *Fisher* v. *University of Texas*, 570 U.S. ___ (2013).

2. Id. at 11.

3. Fisher v. University of Texas, No. 09-50822 (USCA5, 15 July 2014)

4. *Schuette* v. *BAMN*, 572 U.S. ___ (2014).

5. *The Slaughterhouse Cases*, 83 U.S. 36 (1873).

6. *United States* v. *Cruikshank*, 92 U.S. 542 (1876).

7. *United States* v. *Reese*, 92 U.S. 214 (1876).

8. *Civil Rights Cases*, 109 U.S. 3 (1883).

9. Mary Beth Norton et al., *A People and a Nation: A History of the United States*, 3rd ed. (Boston: Houghton Mifflin, 1990), p. 490.

10. *Plessy* v. *Ferguson*, 163 U.S. 537 (1896).

11. *Cummings* v. *County Board of Education*, 17 5 U.S. 528 (1899).

12. *Missouri ex rel. Gaines* v. *Canada*, 305 U.S. 337 (1938).

13. *Sweatt* v. *Painter*, 339 U.S. 629 (1950).

14. *Brown* v. *Board of Education*, 347 U.S. 483 (1954).

15. Ibid., 347 U.S. 483, 495 (1954).

16. Ibid., 347 U.S. 483, 494 (1954).

17. *Bolling* v. *Sharpe*, 347 U.S. 497 (1954).

18. *Brown* v. *Board of Education II*, 349 U.S. 294 (1955).

19. Jack W. Peltason, *Fifty-Eight Lonely Men*, rev. ed. (Urbana: University of Illinois Press, 1971).

20. *Alexander* v. *Holmes County Board of Education*, 396 U.S. 19 (1969).

21. *Swann* v. *Charlotte-Mecklenburg County Schools*, 402 U.S. 1 (1971).

22. *Milliken* v. *Bradley*, 418 U.S. 717 (1974).

23. Robert Caro, *The Passage of Power: The Years of Lyndon Johnson* (New York: Knopf, 2012).

24. Richard Kluger, *Simple Justice* (New York: Knopf, 1976), p. 753.

25. Taylor Branch, *Parting the Waters: America in the King Years, 1955–1963* (New York: Simon & Schuster, 1988), p. 3.

26. Ibid., p. 14.

27. Ibid., p. 271.

28. *Bell* v. *Maryland*, 378 U.S. 226 (1964).

29. Norton et al., *A People and a Nation*, p. 943.

30. Caro, *The Passage of Power*.

31. *Heart of Atlanta Motel* v. *United States*, 379 U.S. 241 (1964).

32. *Katzenbach* v. *McClung*, 379 U.S. 294 (1964).

33. *National Federation of Independent Business* v. *Sebelius*, 567 U.S. ___(2012).

34. But see Abigail M. Thernstrom, *Whose Vote Counts? Affirmative Action and Minority Voting Rights* (Cambridge, Mass.: Harvard University Press, 1987).

35. *Grove City College* v. *Bell*, 465 U.S. 555 (1984).

36. *Richmond* v. *J.A. Croson Co.*, 488 U.S. 469 (1989).

37. *Martin* v. *Wilks*, 490 U.S. 755 (1989); *Wards Cove Packing Co.* v. *Atonio*, 490 U.S. 642 (1989); *Patterson* v. *McLean Credit Union*, 491 U.S. 164 (1989); *Price Waterhouse* v. *Hopkins*, 490 U.S. 228 (1989); *Lorance* v. *AT&T Technologies*, 490 U.S. 900 (1989); and *EEOC* v. *Arabian American Oil Co.*, 499 U.S. 244 (1991).

38. Dee Brown, *Bury My Heart at Wounded Knee: An Indian History of the American West* (New York: Holt, Rinehart & Winston, 1971).

39. Francis Paul Prucha, *The Great Father: The United States Government and the American Indian*, vol. 2 (Lincoln: University of Nebraska Press, 1984).

40. *Arizona* v. *United States*, 567 U.S. ___ (2012).

41. Stephen Ceasar, "Hispanic Population Tops 50 Million in U.S.," http://articles.latimes.com/2011/mar/24/nation/la-na-census-hispanic-20110325.

42. U.S. Equal Employment Opportunity Commission, "Americans with Disabilities Act of 1990 (ADA) FY 1997-FY 2013," http://www.eeoc.gov/eeoc/statistics/enforcement/adacharges.cfm.

43. Lisa J. Stansky, "Opening Doors," *ABA Journal* 82 (1996): 66–69.

44. "Stonewall and Beyond: Lesbian and Gay Culture," Columbia University Libraries exhibition, 25 May–17 September 1994, http://www.columbia.edu/cu/libraries/events/sw25/.

45. Don't Ask Don't Tell Repeal Act of 2010, 22 December, 2010.

46. Rachel Maddow interview, 10 May 2012, Today on NBC, http://video.today.msnbc.msn.com/today/47368691#47368691.

47. Jesse McKinley, "Tart Questions at Same-Sex Marriage Trial's Closing," *New York Times*, 17 June 2010, p. A15.

48. *Hollingsworth* v. *Perry*, 570 U.S. ___ (2013).

49. *United States* v. *Windsor*, 570 U.S.12 (2013).

50. *Boy Scouts of America* v. *Dale*, 530 U.S. 610 (2000).

51. Cited in Martin Gruberg, *Women in American Politics* (Oshkosh, Wisc.: Academic Press, 1968), p. 4.

52. *Bradwell* v. *Illinois*, 83 U.S. 130 (1873).

53. *Muller* v. *Oregon*, 208 U.S. 412 (1908).

54. *International Union, United Automobile, Aerospace and Agricultural Implement Workers of America* v. *Johnson Controls*, Inc., 499 U.S. 187 (1991).

55. *Minor* v. *Happersett*, 88 U.S. 162 (1875).

56. John H. Aldrich et al., *American Government: People, Institutions, and Policies* (Boston: Houghton Mifflin, 1986), p. 618.

57. *Ledbetter* v. *Goodyear Tire and Rubber Company*, 550 U.S. (2007).

58. Sheryl Gay Stolberg, "Obama Signs Equal-Pay Legislation," *New York Times*, 30 January 2009.

59. *Reed* v. *Reed*, 404 U.S. 71 (1971).

60. *Frontiero* v. *Richardson*, 411 U.S. 677 (1973).

61. *Craig* v. *Boren*, 429 U.S. 190 (1976).

62. Paul Weiler, "The Wages of Sex: The Uses and Limits of Comparable Worth," *Harvard Law Review* 99 (1986): 1728; and Paula England, *Comparable Worth: Theories and Evidence* (New York: Aldine de Gruyter, 1992).

63. *J.E.B.* v. *Alabama ex rel.* T.B., 511 U.S. 127 (1994).

64. *United States* v. *Virginia*, slip op. 94-1941 and 94-2107 (decided 26 June 1996).

65. Mike Allen, "Defiant V.M.I. to Admit Women but Will Not Ease Rules for Them," *New York Times*, 22 September 1996, sec. 1, p. 1.

66. Jane J. Mansbridge, *Why We Lost the ERA* (Chicago: University of Chicago Press, 1986).

67. Melvin I. Urofsky, *A March of Liberty* (New York: Knopf, 1988), p. 902.

68. *Harris* v. *Forklift Systems*, 510 U.S. 17 (1993).

69. *Time*, 6 July 1987, p. 91.

70. *Facts on File* 206B2, 4 June 1965.

71. As quoted in Melvin I. Urofsky, *A Conflict of Rights: The Supreme Court and Affirmative Action* (New York: Scribner's, 1991), p. 17.

72. Ibid., p. 29.

73. Thomas Sowell, *Preferential Policies: An International Perspective* (New York: Morrow, 1990), pp. 103–105.

74. *Regents of the University of California* v. *Bakke*, 438 U.S. 265 (1978).

75. *Adarand Constructors, Inc.* v. *Pena*, 518 U.S. 200 (1995).

76. *Gratz* v. *Bollinger*, 539 U.S. 244 (2003).

77. *Grutter* v. *Bollinger*, 539 U.S. 306 (2003).

78. *Parents Involved in Community Schools* v. *Seattle School District No. 1*, 551 U.S. (2007).

79. Stephen Earl Bennett et al., *Americans' Opinions about Affirmative Action* (Cincinnati, Ohio: University of Cincinnati, Institute for Policy Research, 1995), p. 4; and Lawrence Bobo, "Race and Beliefs about Affirmative Action," in *Racialized Politics: The Debate about Racism in America*, ed. David O. Sears, Jim Sidanius, and Lawrence Bobo (Chicago: University of Chicago Press, 2000), pp. 137–164.

80. For example, see the eligibility standards of the Small Business Administration for "small disadvantaged business," http://www.sba.gov/sdb/indexa-boutsdb.html.

81. Seymour Martin Lipset, "Two Americas, Two Systems: Whites, Blacks, and the Debate over Affirmative Action," *New Democrat* (May–June 1995): 9–15, http://www.ndol.org/documents/May95TND.pdf.

Chapter 17

1. Address to the Nebraska Republican Conference, in Lincoln, Nebraska, on 16 January 1936. Herbert Hoover, *Addresses upon the American Road*, 1933–1938 (New York: Scribner's Sons, 1938), p. 105.

2. Estimates vary concerning the debt in 1936. A 1936 citation said $34.5 billion. See R. M. Boeckel, "The Deficit and the Public Debt," *Editorial Research Reports 1936*, Vol. I (Washington, D.C.: CQ Press, 1936). Data compiled recently by Christopher Chantrill put the debt higher. See http://www.usgovernmentspending.com/spending_chart_1930_2017USp_15s1li111mcn_H0f#tabbed.

3. Chantrill at http://www.usgovernmentspending.com/spending_chart_1930_2017USp_15s1li111mcn_H0f#tabbed.

4. Office of Management and Budget, *Budget of the U.S. Government, Fiscal Year 2015* (Washington, D.C.: U.S. Government Printing Office, 2014), Table S-13.

5. You won't learn basic economics in this chapter. For a quick summary of "ten principles of economics," see N. Gregory Mankiw, *Principles of Economics*, 7th ed. (Boston: Cengage Learning 2014), p. 3.

6. Dan Usher, in *Political Economy* (Malden, Mass.: Blackwell Publishing, 2003), offers this interpretation of Adam Smith's "invisible hand" metaphor: "Self-interested people are guided by market-determined prices to deploy the resources of the world to produce what people want to consume. This assertion, made commonplace by repetition, is so extraordinary and so completely counter-intuitive that it cannot be strictly and unreservedly true. A central task of economics is to show when the assertion is true, when public intervention in the economy might be helpful, and when markets are best left alone because public intervention is likely to do more harm than good" (p. xiv).

7. Two of the ten principles of economics that Mankiw cites in *Principles of Economics* are "#6: Markets are usually a good way to organize economic activity" but "#7: Governments can sometimes improve market outcomes."

8. Justin Fox, *The Myth of the Rational Market* (New York: Harper Collins, 2009), pp. xii–xiii.

9. National Bureau of Economic Research, "Business Cycle Expansions and Contractions," 1 December 2008, http://www.nber.org/cycles.html.

10. Shaun P. Hargraves Heap, "Keynesian Economics," in *Routledge Encyclopedia of International Political Economy*, vol. 2, ed. R. J. Barry Jones (London: Routledge, 2001), pp. 877–878.

11. *Wall Street Journal*, 18 January 2008, p. A12.

12. Nicholas Wapshott, the historian, writing at http://blogs.reuters.com/great-debate/2011/11/07/the-keynes-hayek-showdown/. See also https://www.youtube.com/watch?v=pZNCj2EcTCM.

13. "The crowd had started out as 47% pro Keynes, 33% pro Hayek, and 20% undecided. At the end of the debate, 52% favored Keynes, 42% favored Hayek, and 6% were undecided. So Keynes still had the edge,

but the Hayekians won over more of the undecideds." See Ira Stoll, 9 November 2011, http://www.futureofcapitalism.com/2011/11/hayek-versus-keynes.

14. For example, Peter Clarke, *Keynes: The Rise, Fall, and Return of the 20th Century's Most Influential Economist* (London: Bloomsbury Press, 2009); and Robert Skidelsky, *Keynes: The Return of the Master* (New York: Public Affairs Books, 2009). In contrast, see Friedrich A. von Hayek, *The Constitution of Liberty: The Definitive Edition*, ed. Ronald Hamowy (Chicago: University of Chicago Press, 2011).

15. Kathleen R. McNamara, "Monetarism," in Jones, *Routledge Encyclopedia of International Political Economy*, pp. 1035–1037.

16. The Federal Reserve Act (as amended over the years) cites "maximum employment, stable prices, and moderate long-term interest rates"; see http://www.federalreserve.gov/aboutthefed/section2a.htm.

17. See Allan H. Meltzer, *A History of the Federal Reserve, vol. 1, 1913–1951* (Chicago: University of Chicago Press, 2003). Meltzer writes that the leading banks in 1913 were privately owned institutions with public responsibilities. Fears were that they would place their interests above the public interest, but there was also concern about empowering government to control money. "President Woodrow Wilson offered a solution that appeared to reconcile competing public and private interests. He proposed a public-private partnership with semiautonomous, privately funded reserve banks supervised by a public board" (p. 3).

18. Luca LiLeo, "Fed Gets More Power, Responsibility," *Wall Street Journal*, 16 July 2010, p. A5.

19. The quote, attributed to William McChesney Martin, Jr., is in Martin Mayer, *The Fed* (New York: Free Press, 2001), p. 165.

20. Federal Reserve Bank of San Francisco, *Weekly Letter 96-08*, 23 February 1996.

21. Pew Research Center, "Economic Discontent Deepens as Inflation Concerns Rise," news release, 14 February 2008.

22. Fox, *The Myth of the Rational Market*, pp. xi–xii.

23. Charles Duhigg, "Depression You Say? Check Those Safety Nets," *New York Times*, 23 March 2008, sec. 4, pp. 1, 4.

24. Mankiw, *Principles of Economics*, pp. 170–171.

25. See the editorial "How to Raise Revenue," *Wall Street Journal*, 24 August 2007, p. A14; and Austan Goolsbee, "Is the New Supply Side Better Than the Old?" *New York Times*, 20 January 2008, p. BU6.

26. U.S. Department of Treasury, "The Debt to the Penny and Who Holds It," http://www.treasurydirect.gov/NP/BPDLogin?application=np.

27. One such "national debt clock" is at http://www.usdebtclock.org.

28. Binyamin Appelbaum, "A U.S. Boon in Low-Cost Borrowing," *New York Times*, 28 February 2012, p. B1.

29. For the FY 2015 federal budget, go to http://www.whitehouse.gov/omb/budget.

30. Damian Paletta, "Breakdown Is New Norm in Spending Showdowns," *New York Times*, 1 October 2013, pp. 1 and A4.

31. Ibid.

32. Ibid., p. 377; Concord Coalition, "Budget Process Reform: An Important Tool for Fiscal Discipline, but Not a Magic Bullet," *Issue Brief*, 5 February 2004.

33. Concord Coalition, "Budget Process Reform," p. 3.

34. James V. Saturno, *A Balanced Budget Constitutional Amendment: Procedural Issues and Legislative History*, Congressional Research Service Report 98-671 (5 August 1998), p. 14.

35. Peter H. Schuck, "The Balanced Budget Amendment's Fatal Flaw," *Wall Street Journal*, 22 July 2011, p. A15.

36. D. Andrew Austin, *The Debt Limit: History and Recent Increases*, CRS Report for Congress, RL31967 (29 April 2008), p. 3.

37. "The Budget for Fiscal Year 2015, Historical Tables," Table 7.3, http://www.whitehouse.gov/sites/default/files/omb/budget/fy2015/assets/hist.pdf.

38. Binyamin Appelbaum, "After Aiding Republicans, Business Groups Press Them on Debt Ceiling," *New York Times*, 27 July 2011, p. A16.

39. Amy Bingham, "Only One Democratic Country, Besides America, Has a Debt Ceiling," *ABC News*, 19 July 2011.

40. Richard A. Musgrave and Peggy B. Musgrave, *Public Finance in Theory and Practice*, 2nd ed. (New York: McGraw-Hill, 1976), p. 42.

41. If you can spare 24 megabytes of storage, you can download the complete text of the U.S. Internal Revenue Code, Title 26 of the U.S. Code, http://www.fourmilab.ch/uscode/26usc. If you print the tax code, expect more than 7,500 pages.

42. Office of Management and Budget, "Historical Tables, FY 2015 Budget," Table 2.2, http://www.whitehouse.gov/omb/budget/Historicals.

43. David Cay Johnston, "Talking Simplicity, Building a Maze," *New York Times*, 15 February 2004, Money and Business section, pp. 11, 14.

44. Over a dozen surveys from 1992 to 2013 found that 60 percent of respondents or more felt that "upper-income people" were paying too little in taxes. See http://www.pollingreport.com/budget2.htm.

45. Jill Barshay, "'Case of the Missing Revenue' Is Nation's Troubling Mystery," *CQ Weekly*, 17 January 2004, p. 144.

46. Tax Policy Center, "Historical Income Tax Rates for a Family of Four," 3 April 2013, http://taxpolicycenter.org/taxfacts/displayafact.cfm?DocK>=228aTopic2id=20aTopic3id=22.

47. Pew Research Center for the People and the Press, "Economic Inequality Seen as Rising, Boom Bypasses Poor," *Survey Report*, 21 June 2001.

48. Spending as percentage of GDP is a common way of measuring social welfare benefits, but it is not the only way. If spending is measured by dollars per capita, the United States, with a very high GDP, rates much more favorably. See Christopher Howard, "Is the American Welfare State Unusually Small?" *PS: Political Science and Politics* 36 (July 2003): 411–416.

49. Thom Shanker, "Proposed Military Spending Is Highest Since WWII," *New York Times*, 4 February 2008, p. A10.

50. National Priorities Project, "The Cost of War," http://costofwar.com/en/.

51. Ron Nixon, "Special Funds in Budget Called New Earmarks," *New York Times*, 6 February 2012, p. A13.

52. Executive Office of the President, *Budget of the United States Government, Fiscal Year 2015: Historical Tables* (Washington, D.C.: U.S. Government Printing Office, 2014), Table 8.3.

53. Pew Survey of 10 February 2011 at http://www.people-press.org/2011/02/10/section-3-the-deficit-and-government-spending/.

54. Fay Lomax Cook et al., *Convergent Perspectives on Social Welfare Policy: The Views from the General Public, Members of Congress, and AFDC Recipients* (Evanston, Ill: Center for Urban Affairs and Policy Research, Northwestern University, 1988), Table 4-1.

55. Cynthia Crossen, "Not Too Long Ago, Some People Begged for an Income Tax," *Wall Street Journal*, 4 June 2003, p. B1.

56. Arthur C. Brooks, "The Left's 'Inequality' Obsession," *Wall Street Journal*, 19 July 2007, p. A15. Federal income taxes do make income distribution slightly more equal. See David Wessel, "Fishing Out the Facts on the Wealth Gap," *Wall Street Journal*, 15 February 2007, p. A10.

57. Kyle Pomerleau, "Summary of Latest Federal Individual Income Tax Data," *Fiscal Facts* (Washington, D.C.: Tax Foundation), 18 December 2013.

58. Ibid.

59. Warren E, Buffett, "Stop Coddling the Super-Rich," *New York Times*, 16 August 2011, p. A19.

60. Tax Policy Center, "Distribution of Federal Payroll and Income Taxes by Expanded Cash Income Percentile, 2013," 9 September 2013, http://www.taxpolicycenter.org/numbers/displayatab.cfm?Docid=3997&DocTypeID=2.

61. Joseph A. Pechman, *Who Paid the Taxes, 1966–1985?* (Washington, D.C.: Brookings Institution, 1985), p. 80. See also Lawrence Mishel, Jared Bernstein, and Heather Boushey, *The State of Working America, 2002–2003* (Ithaca, N.Y.: Cornell University Press, 2003), p. 66.

62. Organization of Economic Development and Cooperation, *An Overview of Growing Income Inequalities in OECD Countries: Main Findings* (January 2012), p. 22, http://www.oecd.org/dataoecd/40/12/49170449.pdf.

63. Sylvia A. Allegretto, "The State of Working America's Wealth, 2011," Economic Policy Institute, Briefing Paper #292 (23 March 2011), p. 5.

64. U.S. Bureau of the Census, *Statistical Abstract of the United States 2012* (Washington, D.C.: U.S. Government Printing Office, 2012), Table 697.

65. Benjamin I. Page, *Who Gets What from Government?* (Berkeley: University of California Press, 1983), p. 213.

66. Frank Newport, "Majority in U.S. Want Wealth More Evenly Distributed," Gallup Poll Report, 17 April 2013.

67. Karlyn Bowman and Andrew Rugg, *Public Opinion on Taxes: 1937 to Today* (Washington, D.C.: American Enterprise Institute, 2012).

68. James Sterngold, "Muting the Lotteries' Perfect Pitch," *New York Times*, 14 July 1996, sec. 4, p. 1.

69. "Taxes: What's Fair?" *Public Perspective* 7 (April–May 1996): 40–41.

70. Robert J. Blendon et al., "Tax Uncertainty: A Divided America's Uninformed View of the Federal Tax System," *Brookings Review* 21 (Summer 2003): 28–31.

71. Jason White, "Taxes and Budget," *State of the States: 2004* (Washington, D.C.: Pew Center on the States, 2004), p. 30.

72. Shailagh Murray, "Seminary Article in Alabama Sparks Tax-Code Revolt," *Wall Street Journal*, 12 February 2003, pp. A1, A8.

Chapter 18

1. "41 percent of Americans Will Get Cancer," UPI Health News, 6 May 2010, http://www.upi.com/Health_News/2010/05/06/41-percent-of-Americans-will-get-cancer/UPI-75711273192042/.

2. Marilynn Marchione, "Cancer's Growing Burden: The High Cost of Care," *USA Today*, 27 February 2012.

3. Suleika Jaouad, "Life, Interrupted: Medical Bills, Insurance, and Uncertainty," *New York Times*, 9 August 2012.

4. Ryan Jaslow, "Cancer Patients More than Twice As Likely To Go Bankrupt, Study Shows," *CBS News*, 16 May 2013.

5. "At Risk: Pre-existing Conditions Could Affect 1 in 2 Americans," U.S. Department of Health and Human Services, 19 January 2011, http://www.healthcare.gov/law/resources/reports/preexisting.html.

6. "The Uninsured: A Primer," Kaiser Commission on Medicaid and the Uninsured, 23 October 2013, http://kff.org/uninsured/report/the-uninsured-a-primer-key-facts-about-health-insurance-on-the-eve-of-coverage-expansions/.

7. Adam Nagourney, "For Cowboy Poets, Unwelcome Spotlight in Battle Over Spending," *New York Times*, 10 April 2011; and Danielle Switalski, "Cowboy Poetry Gathering Drawn into Budget Battle," *Elko Daily Free Press*, 10 March 2011.

8. "State Tax Codes as Poverty Fighting Tools," Institute on Taxation and Economic Policy, September 2011, http://www.itepnet.org/pdf/poverty2011report.pdf; and Josh Goodman, "Kansas and Oklahoma Income Tax Won't Reach Zero," *Stateline: The Daily News Service of the Pew Charitable Trusts*, 18 May 2012.

9. Peter Katel, "Food Safety," *CQ Researcher*, 17 December 2010, www.cqresearcher.com; and U.S. Food and Drug Administration, "The New FDA Food Safety Modernization Act," http://www.fda.gov/Food/FoodSafety/FSMA/default.htm.

10. According to the FDA, it is four or fewer rodent hairs per twenty-five grams. See the FDA's "Defect Levels Handbook," http://www.fda.gov/food/guidancecomplianceregulatoryinformation/guidancedocuments/sanitation/ucm056174.htm#intro.

11. Gardiner Harris and William Neuman, "Senate Passes Sweeping Law on Food Safety," *New York Times*, 20 November 2010.

12. This typology is adapted from Theodore Lowi's classic article, "American Business, Public Policy Case Studies, and Political Theory," *World Politics* 16 (July 1964): 677–715.

13. Since not all charitable contributions are claimed as deductions on taxes, the actual tax expenditure is less than $350 billion. "Most Americans Practice Charitable Giving, Volunteerism," Gallup.com, 13 December 2013; and "Giving Statistics," Charitynavigator.org.

14. Diane Stafford, "FDA Intends to Clear the Air on E-Cigarettes," *Kansas City Star*, 8 January 2014.

15. Roger W. Cobb and Charles D. Elder, *Participation in American Politics*, 2nd ed. (Baltimore, Md.: Johns Hopkins University Press, 1983), p. 14.

16. Lawrence D. Brown and Lawrence R. Jacobs, *The Private Abuse of the Public Interest* (Chicago: University of Chicago Press, 2008).

17. Dana Lee Baker and Shannon Stokes, "Brain Politics: Aspects of Administration in the Comparative Issue Definition of Autism-Related Policy," *Public Administration Review* 67 (July–August 2007): 757–767.

18. Frank R. Baumgartner, Suzanna L. De Boef, and Amber E. Boydstun, *The Decline of the Death Penalty and the Discovery of Innocence* (New York: Cambridge University Press, 2008).

19. Frank R. Baumgartner, Jeffrey M. Berry, Marie Hojnacki, David C. Kimball, and Beth L. Leech, *Lobbying and Policy Change* (Chicago: University of Chicago Press, 2009), pp. 166–189.

20. Julian Hattam, "Obama Signs Drug Compounding Bill," *The Hill*, 27 November 2013.

21. U.S. Department of Transportation, "2004 Automotive Fuel Economy Program," http://www.nhtsa.gov/Laws+&+Regulations/ CAFE+-+Fuel+Economy/2004+Automotive+Fuel+Economy+ Program; and Juliet Eilperin, "EPA Issues New Fuel-Efficiency Standard: Autos Must Average 54.5 mpg by 2025," *Washington Post*, 29 August 2012.

22. "Claims Information," BP.com; and Clifford Krauss, "In BP Trial, the Amount of Oil Lost Is at Issue," *New York Times*, 29 September 2013.

23. Frank R. Baumgartner and Bryan D. Jones, "Positive and Negative Feedback in Politics," in *Policy Dynamics*, ed. Frank R. Baumgartner and Bryan D. Jones (Chicago: University of Chicago Press, 2002), pp. 3–28.

24. "Michael Kirkland, "The Issue: Is the U.S. Turning Its Back on Syrian Refugees?" UPI.com, 12 January 2014.

25. Eric Lipton and Gardiner Harris, "In Turnaround, Industries Seek U.S. Regulations," *New York Times*, 16 September 2007.

26. "H.R. 1664: Distracted Driving Prevention Act of 2013," Congress.gov; data on deaths and injuries from Distraction.gov, http://www.distraction.gov/content/get-the-facts/facts-and-statistics.html.

27. Lipton and Harris, "In Turnaround."

28. Jeffrey M. Berry and Clyde Wilcox, *The Interest Group Society*, 5th ed. (New York: Pearson Longman, 2009), pp. 155–176.

29. Michael T. Heaney, "Coalitions and Interest Group Influence over Health Care Policy" (paper presented at the annual meeting of the American Political Science Association, Philadelphia, August 2003), p. 16.

30. Robert Shapiro, "Public Opinion and American Democracy," *Public Opinion Quarterly* 75 (2011): 982–1017.

31. See, for example, Kim Parker, "Where the Public Stands on Government Assistance, Taxes, and the Presidential Candidates," Pew Research Social and Demographic Trends, 20 September 2012.

32. Data available from U.S. Department of Labor, Bureau of Labor Statistics, http://www.bls.gov/cps/prev_yrs.htm.

33. Charles Kenny, "50 Years After the War on Poverty, Poor People are Not Better Off," *Bloomberg Businessweek*, 13 January 2014; and Jared Bernstein, "The War on Poverty at 50," *New York Times*, 6 January 2014.

34. Information available at the website of the U.S. Social Security Administration, http://www.ssa.gov/OACT/ProgData/taxRates.html.

35. "Social Security Basic Facts," Social Security Administration, 26 July 2013, http://www.ssa.gov/pressoffice/basicfact.htm.

36. "Fast Facts about Social Security, 2013," Social Security Administration, http://www.ssa.gov/policy/docs/chartbooks/fast_facts/2013/fast_facts13.html#page35.

37. Clea Benson, "How Long Can Americans Work?" *CQ Weekly*, 5 July 2010, pp. 1616–1617.

38. Social Security Administration, "Cost of Living Adjustment Information," http://www.socialsecurity.gov/cola/.

39. CBS News Poll, iPOLL Databank, The Roper Center for Public Opinion Research, University of Connecticut, December 2011, http://www.ropercenter.uconn.edu/data_access/ipoll/ipoll.html.

40. *Retirement Security and Quality Health Care: Our Pledge to America*, n.d., GOP Platform, http://abcnews.go.com/Politics/story?-id=123296ftpage=1.

41. Jon Carson, "Will Extending the Payroll Tax Cut Affect Social Security? No," The White House Blog, 9 December 2011, http://www.whitehouse.gov/blog/2011/12/09/will-extending-payroll-taxcut-affect-social-security-no.

42. Matt Berman, "What Is Chained CPI?" *National Journal*, 31 December 2012; and Pete Kasperowicz, "Dems Reject Obama's Chained CPI Formula for Social Security," *The Hill*, 22 April 2013.

43. Although it has been the source of endless debate, today's definition of poverty retains remarkable similarity to its precursors. As early as 1795, a group of English magistrates "decided that a minimum income should be the cost of a gallon loaf of bread, multiplied by three, plus an allowance for each dependent." See Alvin L. Schorr, "Redefining Poverty Levels," *New York Times*, 9 May 1984, p. 27; and Louis Uchitelle, "How to Define Poverty? Let Us Count the Ways," *New York Times*, 26 May 2001, http://www.nytimes.com/2001/05/26/arts/how-to-define-poverty-let-us-count-the-ways.html?pagewanted=1.

44. U.S. Census Bureau, "Poverty Data," http://www.census.gov/hhes/www/poverty/data/threshold/. The poverty guideline for 2012 was slightly lower, at $23,050 (see the 2012 HHS Poverty Guidelines, http://aspe.hhs.gov/poverty/12poverty.shtml).

45. Nicholas Eberstadt, "The Mismeasure of Poverty," *Policy Review* 138 (August–September 2006): 1–21.

46. U.S. Census Bureau, *Income, Poverty, and Health Insurance Coverage in the United States: 2012* (Washington, D.C.: U.S. Government Printing Office, 2013).

47. Ibid.

48. Shawn Zeller, "Poverty Rate Is In the Details," *CQ Weekly*, 18 November 2013.

49. Juan Williams, "Reagan, the South, and Civil Rights," National Public Radio, 10 June 2004, http://www.npr.org/templates/story/story.-php?storyId=1953700.

50. Andrea Hetling, Monika McDermott, and Mingus Mapps, "Symbolism vs. Policy Learning: Public Opinion of the 1996 U.S. Welfare Reforms," *American Politics Research* 36, no. 3 (2008): 335–357.

51. Peter T. Kilborn, "With Welfare Overhaul Now Law, States Grapple with the Consequences," *New York Times*, 23 August 1996, p. A10.

52. Liz Schott, "Policy Basics: An Introduction to TANF," Center for Budget and Policy Priorities, 4 December 2012, http://www.cbpp.org/cms/index.cfm?fa=view&id=936.

53. Alan Weil and Kenneth Feingold (eds.), *Welfare Reform: The Next Act* (Washington, D.C.: Urban Institute, 2002).

54. Hetling et al., "Symbolism vs. Policy Learning"; and Joshua Dyck and Laura Hussey, "The End of Welfare As We Know It? Durable Attitudes in a Changing in Formation Environment," *Public Opinion Quarterly* 72, no. 4 (2008): 589–618.

55. Eugenie Hildebrandt and Patricia Stevens, "Impoverished Women with Children and No Welfare Benefits: The Urgency of Researching Failures of the Temporary Assistance for Needy Families Program," *American Journal of Public Health* 99, no. 5 (2009): 793–801; and Robert Wood, Quinn Moore, and Anu Rangarajan, "Two Steps Forward, One Step Back: The Uneven Economic Progress of TANF Recipients," *Social Service Review* 82, no. 1 (2008): 3–28.

56. LaDonna Pavetti and Liz Schott, "TANF's Inadequate Response to Recession Highlights Weakness of Block Grant Structure," Center for Budget and Policy Priorities, July 2011, http://www.cbpp.org/cms/index.cfm?fa=view&id=3534.

57. "Policy Basics: Introduction to the Supplemental Nutrition Assistance Program," Center on Budget and Policy Priorities, 10 January 2014, http://www.cbpp.org/cms/index.cfm?fa=view&id=2226; and Michael Shear, "In Signing Farm Bill, Obama Extols Rural Growth," *New York Times*, 7 February 2014.

58. U.S. Census Bureau, *Income, Poverty, and Health Insurance Coverage in the United States: 2012* (Washington, D.C.: U.S. Government Printing Office, 2013).

59. Jacque Wilson, "Your Health Care Is Covered, but Who's Going to Treat You?" *CNN*, 29 June 2012.

60. See National Health Expenditures, 2012 highlights, Centers for Medicare and Medicaid Service, http://www.cms.gov/Research-Statistics-Data-and-Systems/Statistics-Trends-and-Reports/NationalHealthExpendData/Downloads/highlights.pdf.

61. National Health Expenditure Projections, 2012–2022, Centers for Medicare and Medicaid Service, http://www.cms.gov/Research-Statistics-Data-and-Systems/Statistics-Trends-and-Reports/National-HealthExpendData/Downloads/Proj2012.pdf.

62. OECD Health Statistics 2013 - Frequently Requested Data, http://www.oecd.org/els/health-systems/oecdhealthdata2013-frequentlyrequesteddata.htm.

63. Martha Derthick, *Policymaking for Social Security*, (Washington, D.C.: Brookings, 1979), p. 335.

64. Paul Starr, *The Social Transformation of American Medicine* (New York: Basic Books, 1982), pp. 279–280.

65. Ibid., p. 287.

66. Theodore Marmor, *The Politics of Medicare* (Chicago: Aldine, 1973).

67. "Medicare at a Glance," Kaiser Family Foundation, November 2011, http://www.kff.org/medicare/upload/1066-14.pdf; and Centers for Medicare and Medicaid Services, "Data Compendium," http://www.cms.hhs.gov/DataCompendium/16_2008_Data_Compendium.asp# TopOfPage.

68. "Medicare at a Glance."

69. "Medicaid: A Primer," Kaiser Family Foundation, 1 March 2013, http://kff.org/medicaid/issue-brief/medicaid-a-primer/.

70. Ibid.

71. Ibid.

72. Status of State Action on the Medicaid Expansion Decision, 2014, Kaiser Family Foundation, http://kff.org/health-reform/state-indicator/state-activity-around-expanding-medicaid-under-the-affordable-care-act/.

73. National Health Expenditure Projections, 2012–2022, Centers for Medicare and Medicaid Service, http://www.cms.gov/Research-Statistics-Data-and-Systems/Statistics-Trends-and-Reports/National-HealthExpendData/Downloads/Proj2012.pdf.

74. "Health Timeline 2010–2015," *CQ Weekly*, 5 April 2010, p. 818; Robert Pear and David M. Herszenhorn, "Obama Hails Vote on Health Care as Answering 'the Call of History,'" *New York Times*, 21 March 2010, http://www.nytimes.com/2010/03/22/health/policy/22health.html?scp=1asq=obamao/o20hailso/o20voteo/o20ono/o20helatho/o20careast=cse; and "Health Care Reform, at Last," *New York Times*, 22 March 2010, http://www.nytimes.com/2010/03/22/opinion/22-mon5.html?scp=msq=healtho/o20careo/o20reform,o/o20ato/o20lastast=cse.

75. Kerry Young, "Controlling Medicare Costs," *CQ Weekly*, 5 April 2010, p. 826; "How Health Care Reform Reduces the Deficit in 5 Not-So-Easy Steps," *Newsweek*, 20 March 2010, http://www.newsweek.com/2010/03/20/how-health-care-reform-reduces-thedeficit-in-5-not-so-easy-steps.html; and Peter Grier, "Health Care Reform Bill

101: Who Will Pay for Reform?" *Christian Science Monitor*, 21 March 2010, http://www.csmonitor.com/USA/Politics/2010/0321/Health-care-reform-bill-101-Who-will-pay-for-reform.

76. U.S. Department of Education, "Federal Role in Education," http://www2.ed.gov/about/overview/fed/role.html?src=ln.

77. National Center for Education Statistics, *The Nation's Report Card* (Washington, D.C.: U.S. Department of Education, 2011), http://nces.ed.gov/nationsreportcard/pdf/main2011/2012459.pdf.

78. See relationship between educational attainment and earnings at "Employment Projections," Bureau of Labor Statistics, http://www.bls.gov/emp/ep_chart_001.htm.

79. Paul Manna, "Federalism, Agenda Setting, and the Development of Federal Education Policy, 1965–2001" (Ph.D. diss., University of Wisconsin-Madison, 2003).

80. Kenneth Jost, "Revising No Child Left Behind," *CQ Researcher*, 16 April 2010, www.cqresearcher.com.

81. Alyson Klein, "Obama Administration Aloof as Lawmakers Tangle over ESEA," *Education Week*, 8 August 2013.

82. Lyndsey Layton, "Some States Rebrand Controversial Common Core Education Standards," *Washington Post*, 31 January 2014.

83. Harold W. Stanley and Richard G. Niemi, *Vital Statistics on American Politics, 2013–2014* (Washington, D.C.: CQ Press, 2013); and "A Nation of Immigrants," Pew Research Center Hispanic Trends Project, 29 January 2013.

84. U.S. Census Bureau, *Income, Poverty, and Health Insurance Coverage in the United States: 2012* (Washington, D.C.: U.S. Government Printing Office, 2013).

85. U.S. Department of Homeland Security, "Yearbook of Immigration Statistics, 2012," http://www.dhs.gov/yearbook-immigration-statistics-2012-legal-permanent-residents.

86. Congressional Budget Office, *Immigration Policy in the United States: An Update*, December 2010.

87. Migration Policy Institute, "Public Benefits Use," http://www.migrationinformation.org/integration/publicbenefits.cfm.

88. "Yearbook of Immigration Statistics, 2012."

89. Ed O'Keefe, "Senate Approves Comprehensive Immigration Bill," *Washington Post*, 27 June 2013.

90. Andrew Dugan, "Passing New Immigration Laws Is Important to Americans," Gallup.com, 11 July 2013.

91. "Data on Individual Applications and Petitions," U.S. Citizenship and Immigration Services, http://www.uscis.gov/tools/reports-studies/immigration-forms-data/individual-applications-and-petitions/data-individual-applications-and-petitions.

92. David Harrison, "Of Boundaries and Borders: Court Case Seeks the Line," *CQ Weekly*, 22 December 2011, pp. 2646–2647.

93. Associated Press/Gfk Knowledge Networks Poll, iPOLL Databank, The Roper Center for Public Opinion Research, University of Connecticut, October 2013, http://www.ropercenter.uconn.edu.ezproxy.library.tufts.edu/data_access/ipoll/ipoll.html.

Index